DEUTERONOMY

DEUTERONOMY

A Commentary

Jack R. Lundbom

WILLIAM B. EERDMANS PUBLISHING COMPANY
GRAND RAPIDS, MICHIGAN / CAMBRIDGE, U.K.

© 2013 Wm. B. Eerdmans Publishing Co.
All rights reserved

Published 2013 by
Wm. B. Eerdmans Publishing Co.
2140 Oak Industrial Drive N.E., Grand Rapids, Michigan 49505 /
P.O. Box 163, Cambridge CB3 9PU U.K.

Printed in the United States of America

19 18 17 16 15 14 13   7 6 5 4 3 2 1

Library of Congress Cataloging-in-Publication Data

Lundbom, Jack R.
Deuteronomy: a commentary / Jack R. Lundbom.
    pages   cm
Includes bibliographical references and index.
ISBN 978-0-8028-2614-5 (pbk.: alk. paper)
1. Bible. O.T. Deuteronomy — Commentaries.
I. Title.

BS1275.53.L86 2013
223′.15077 — dc23
                                    2012043269

www.eerdmans.com

To the Memory of

David Daube

for learning, friendship, and teaching me

most about Deuteronomy

Contents

PREFACE	xvii
ABBREVIATIONS	xxii

INTRODUCTION

Name and Canonicity	1
Text and Versions	2
Qumran Scrolls	4
Paragraph Divisions	5
Deuteronomy Papyri	5
Date, Composition, and Authorship	6
The Josianic Reform	6
The Quest for Urdeuteronomium	8
Northern Provenance	10
Hezekiah's Reform	11
A New Quest for Urdeuteronomium	13
The Question of Authorship	18
Ancient Near Eastern Treaties	20
Ancient Hebrew Rhetoric	21
Rhetorical Prose	21

Contents

- *Preached Law* — 22
- *Rhetoric and Composition* — 23

The Deuteronomic Law Code — 26
- *Earlier Biblical Law* — 26
- *Later Biblical Law* — 27
- *Ancient Near Eastern Law Codes* — 27

Deuteronomy and the Prophets — 28
- *Amos* — 29
- *Hosea* — 33
- *Micah* — 35
- *Isaiah* — 35
- *Jeremiah* — 37

Deuteronomy and Wisdom — 44
- *Humane Treatment and Benevolence to the Poor and Needy* — 47
- *Teaching of Children* — 50
- *Blessing: Life, Goodness, and Longevity in the Land* — 52
- *Avoidance of Shame* — 54
- *Discerning False from True Prophets* — 58

Theological Ideas in Deuteronomy — 59
- *The Name of Yahweh* — 59
- *Yahweh the One and Only God* — 60
- *Yahweh a Holy God* — 60
- *Yahweh Is Heard but Not Seen* — 61
- *Yahweh a God of Love* — 61
- *Yahweh a God Faithful to His Promises* — 62
- *Yahweh a Righteous God* — 62
- *Yahweh an Impartial Judge* — 63
- *Israel a Holy People* — 63
- *The Election of Israel* — 63
- *The Covenant at Horeb (Sinai)* — 64
- *The Land as a Gift and Tenure in the Land* — 65
- *Holy War* — 66

Contents

Divine Blessing	68
Covenant Obligations	69
Doing the Commandments	70
Love to Yahweh and to Others	70
Fear of Yahweh	71
Walking in Yahweh's Way	71
Serving Yahweh	72
Gratitude to Yahweh	72
The Book of Deuteronomy	73
The First Edition (1-28)	73
Prologue (1–4)	74
The Covenant at Horeb (5–11)	75
The Deuteronomic Code (12–26)	77
Blessings and Curses (27–28)	86
First Supplement (29–30)	89
Second Supplement (31–34)	90
Deuteronomy and the New Testament	93
The Synoptic Gospels	93
The Gospel of John and the Johannine Epistles	94
Acts of the Apostles	94
Pauline and Deutero-Pauline Letters	95
The Epistle of James	96
The Epistle to the Hebrews	96
Revelation of Saint John	97

BIBLIOGRAPHY

Text and Reference Works	98
Commentaries	104
Books, Monographs, and Articles	105

Contents

TRANSLATION, NOTES, AND COMMENTS

I. Superscription to the Prologue and First Edition (1:1-5)	155
II. Prologue to the Deuteronomic Law (1:6–4:40)	163
A. The Land Is Set Before You (1:6-46)	163
B. Pass Peaceably through Seir (2:1-8a)	187
C. Pass Peaceably by Moab (2:8b-15)	194
D. Do Not Go near Ammon (2:16-23)	199
E. I Have Given Sihon into Your Hand (2:24-37)	204
F. I Have Also Given Og into Your Hand (3:1-11)	212
G. Apportionment of Transjordan Land (3:12-17)	216
H. The Focus Now Is Beyond the Jordan (3:18-22)	221
I. Moses Asks to Cross the Jordan (3:23-29)	224
J. Listen to the Statutes and Ordinances and Do Them (4:1-40)	229
1. Forget Not the Horeb Revelation (4:1-24)	229
2. What Will Happen If You Do Forget (4:25-40)	246
III. Refuge Cities in the Transjordan (4:41-43)	258
IV. Subscription to the Prologue (4:44-49)	260
V. The Covenant at Horeb (5–11)	264
A. Law and Covenant (5:1-33)	264
1. This Covenant Was with You! (5:1-5)	264
2. The Ten Words (5:6-21)	270
3. Moses: Mediator for Subsequent Laws (5:22-33)	298
B. Fear Yahweh and Keep the Commandment (6:1-3)	304
C. Liturgical Injunction (6:4-9)	308
D. Forget Not, Test Not (6:10-19)	316
1. Forget Not Yahweh (6:10-15)	316
2. Test Not Yahweh (6:16-19)	317
E. What Mean These Commandments? (6:20-25)	323
F. You Are a Holy People (7:1-26)	326
1. Yahweh Will Clear Away Large and Mighty Nations (7:1-6)	326
2. Yahweh Chose You Because He Loved You (7:7-11)	326

Contents

- 3. Yahweh Will Keep Covenant and Love You (7:12-16) 326
- 4. Yahweh Will Defeat the Larger Nations (7:17-26) 327
- G. Remember Yahweh and His Testing (8:1-20) 344
- H. You Are a Rebellious People (9:1-29) 357
  - 1. Yahweh Will Clear Away Larger and Mightier Nations (9:1-3) 357
  - 2. Conquest Due to Canaan's Wickedness and Oath to the Fathers (9:4-6) 357
  - 3. Remember Your Wilderness Rebellion (9:7-29) 357
    - a) Remember the Calf at Horeb and Moses' Intercession (9:7-21) 357
    - b) Remember Taberah, Massah, and Kibroth-hattaavah (9:22-24) 358
    - c) Moses' First Intercession on the Mountain (9:25-29) 358
- I. With the Covenant Renewed the Journey Can Continue (10:1-11) 380
  - 1. Moses Makes New Tablets (10:1-5) 380
  - 2. Journey to Moserah Where Aaron Died (10:6-7) 381
  - 3. Levites to Carry the Ark (10:8-9) 381
  - 4. Intercession Successful; Rise Up and Resume Your Journey (10:10-11) 381
- J. Fear, Walk Straight, Love, and Serve Yahweh (10:12–11:17) 387
  - 1. Circumcise Yourself to Yahweh (10:12-22) 387
  - 2. Consider Yahweh's Discipline (11:1-9) 398
  - 3. The Promised Land Will Have Rain from Heaven (11:10-12) 402
  - 4. But Rain Hinges on Keeping the Commandments (11:13-17) 404
- K. Liturgical Injunction (11:18-21) 407
- L. Consequences of Obedience and Disobedience (11:22-32) 408
  - 1. Be Very Careful with All This Commandment (11:22-25) 408
  - 2. The Blessing and the Curse (11:26-28) 409
  - 3. Be Careful to Do the Statutes and Ordinances (11:29-32) 409

VI. The Deuteronomic Code (12–26) 413
- A. The Central Sanctuary (12:1–13:1[12:32]) 413
  - 1. Destroy All Places of Their Gods (12:1-4) 413
  - 2. On Tithes and Offerings (12:5-14) 414

Contents

	a) Offerings at the Central Sanctuary (12:5-9)	414
	b) Once Again: Offerings at the Central Sanctuary (12:10-14)	414
	3. On the Clean and Unclean (12:15-28)	414
	a) Nonsacrificial Meat in the Towns (12:15-16)	414
	b) Offerings at the Central Sanctuary (12:17-19)	415
	c) Nonsacrificial Meat in the Towns (12:20-25)	415
	d) Holy Offerings at the Central Sanctuary (12:26-28)	415
	4. Seek Not Their Gods (12:29–13:1[12:32])	415
	Excursus 1: Centralized Worship in the Reforms of Hezekiah and Josiah	442
B.	Yahweh Testing for Faithfulness (13:2-19[1-18])	447
	1. Beware of Prophets and Dreamers (13:2-6[1-5])	447
	2. Beware of Family and Friends (13:7-12[6-11])	448
	3. Beware of Worthless Men (13:13-19[12-18])	448
C.	Israel a Holy People to Yahweh (14:1-21)	461
	1. Holiness in Lamenting (14:1-2)	461
	2. Clean and Unclean Animals (14:3-8)	461
	3. Clean and Unclean Waterfowl (14:9-10)	461
	4. Clean and Unclean Winged Creatures (14:11-20)	461
	5. Holiness in Eating and Food Preparation (14:21)	462
D.	Tithes, Remissions, and Offerings (14:22–15:23)	478
	1. Tithing Year by Year (14:22-27)	478
	2. Tithing Every Three Years (14:28-29)	478
	3. Remissions Every Seven Years (15:1-18)	478
	a) Debt Remission (15:1-11)	478
	b) Remission of Hebrew Slaves (15:12-18)	479
	4. Firstborn Gifts Year by Year (15:19-23)	479
E.	Keeping the Feasts (16:1-17)	502
	1. Feast of Passover (16:1-8)	502
	2. Feast of Weeks (16:9-12)	503
	3. Feast of Booths (16:13-17)	503
F.	Office Holders in Israel (16:18–18:22)	519
	1. The Judge and Matters of Judgment (16:18–17:13)	519

Contents

a) Appointing Judges and Officials (16:18-20)	519
b) Regarding Abominations (16:21–17:1)	526
c) Judgment for Covenant Transgressors (17:2-7)	528
d) Extraordinary Cases to the Priests and the Judge (17:8-13)	532
2. What Sort of King for Israel? (17:14-20)	537
3. Rights of the Levitical Priests (18:1-8)	543
a) The Levites' Inheritance Is Yahweh (18:1-2)	543
b) Offerings Due the Levites (18:3-5)	543
c) Altar Privileges for All Levites (18:6-8)	543
4. How May We Know the Word of Yahweh? (18:9-22)	547
a) No Practitioners of the Secret Arts (18:9-14)	547
b) Testing for the False Yahweh Prophet (18:15-22)	554
G. Judicial Procedure (19:1-21)	562
1. Cities of Refuge (19:1-13)	562
2. No Moving of Boundary Markers (19:14)	563
3. Regarding Witnesses (19:15-21)	563
H. When You Go to War (20:1-20)	577
1. Choosing Warriors (20:1-9)	577
2. Conduct of Holy War (20:10-18)	578
3. Respect Fruit Trees in a Siege! (20:19-20)	578
I. Expiation for an Unsolved Murder (21:1-9)	591
J. Marriage to a Woman War Captive (21:10-14)	596
K. Rights of the Firstborn (21:15-17)	600
L. Death for Rebellious Sons (21:18-21)	605
M. Hanged Criminals (21:22-23)	608
N. Miscellaneous Laws (22:1-8)	611
1. Restoring Lost Property (22:1-3)	611
2. Lifting Up Fallen Animals (22:4)	611
3. No Wearing the Apparel of the Opposite Sex (22:5)	612
4. Sparing Mother Birds (22:6-7)	612
5. Parapets on Roofs (22:8)	612
O. More Miscellaneous Laws (22:9-12)	621
1. No Mixing of Seeds, Yoked Animals, and Cloths (22:9-11)	621

Contents

2. The Tassel Exception (22:12)		621
P. On Chastity and Marriage (22:13–23:1[22:30])		625
1. Unchaste Brides (22:13-21)		625
2. Sex with Another Married Woman (22:22)		626
3. Sex with a Betrothed Girl in the City (22:23-24)		626
4. Sex with a Betrothed Girl in the Country (22:25-27)		626
5. Sex with an Unbetrothed Girl (22:28-29)		626
6. Sex with a Father's Wife (23:1[22:30])		627
Q. On Purity and Cleanliness (23:2-19[1-18])		642
1. Purity within Yahweh's Assembly (23:2-9[1-8])		642
a) Blemished Men Excluded (23:2-3[1-2])		642
b) Ammonites and Moabites Excluded (23:4-7[3-6])		642
c) Edomites and Egyptians Not Abominations (23:8-9[7-8])		642
2. Purity and Cleanliness in the Camp (23:10-15[9-14])		651
3. Hospitality to Runaway Slaves (23:16-17[15-16])		654
4. No Holy Prostitutes! (23:18-19[17-18])		656
R. Laws on Loans, Vows, and Theft (23:20-26[19-25])		661
1. Loans to Brothers Interest-Free (23:20-21[19-20])		661
2. Pay Your Vows Promptly! (23:22-24[21-23])		661
3. No Crop Stealing! (23:25-26[24-25])		662
S. Humane Laws (24:1–25:4)		668
1. Marriage, Divorce, and Remarriage (24:1-5)		668
a) Divorcee May Not Return to First Husband (24:1-4)		668
b) Newlywed War Deferment (24:5)		669
EXCURSUS 2: DIVORCE WITHIN JUDAISM AND EARLY CHRISTIANITY		676
2. Pledges and Scale Disease (24:6-13)		678
a) No Millstones as Pledges (24:6)		678
b) No Stealing of Persons (24:7)		678
c) Warning about Scale Disease (24:8-9)		679
d) Kindness in Exacting Pledges (24:10-11)		679
e) No Sleeping in a Poor Man's Pledge (24:12-13)		679
3. Justice and Benevolence to the Needy (24:14-22)		689

Contents

	a) Paying Hired Laborers (24:14-15)	689
	b) Each in His Own Sin Shall Die (24:16)	689
	c) No Perversion of Judgment to the Needy (24:17-18)	689
	d) The Needy to Get Gleaning Rights (24:19-22)	689
	4. A Limit on Flogging (25:1-3)	697
	5. No Muzzle on a Threshing Ox (25:4)	698
T.	Miscellaneous Laws (25:5-19)	703
	1. Levirate Marriage (25:5-10)	703
	2. Wives Interfering in a Fight (25:11-12)	703
	3. Just Weights and Measures (25:13-16)	703
	4. Wipe Out the Remembrance of Amalek! (25:17-19)	703
U.	Rituals at the Central Sanctuary (26:1-19)	719
	1. Ritual of the Firstfruits (26:1-11)	719
	2. Ritual of the Third-year Tithe (26:12-15)	720
	3. Be Careful and Do These Commands (26:16-19)	720

VII. Blessings and Curses (27–28) — 737

A.	Covenant Renewal at Shechem (27:1-26)	737
	1. Yahweh's Law on Large Stones (27:1-8)	737
	2. Today You Have Become Yahweh's People (27:9-10)	742
	3. Let the Tribes Ascend the Mountains (27:11-13)	743
	4. Let the People Say "Amen" (27:14-26)	743
B.	Blessings and Curses of the Deuteronomic Covenant (28:1-68)	751
	1. If You Obey the Covenant (28:1-14)	751
	a) The Six Blessings (28:1-6)	751
	b) Victory in Battle, Prosperity, World Respect (28:7-14)	751
	2. If You Do Not Obey the Covenant (28:15-68)	752
	a) The Six Curses (28:15-19)	752
	b) Disease, Famine, Defeat in Battle (28:20-26)	752
	c) Incurable Disease, Madness, Displacement (28:27-37)	753
	d) Crop Failure, Impoverishment, Dependent Status (28:38-46)	753
	e) Curses of the Siege (28:47-57)	754
	f) Egypt Revisited! (28:58-68)	755

Contents

VIII.	Subscription to the First Edition (28:69[29:1])	798
IX.	First Supplement (29–30)	799
	A. The Covenant Is Something You Do (29:1-8[2-9])	799
	B. Enter into the Sworn Covenant! (29:9-28[10-29])	803
	C. When the Blessings and Curses Come upon You (30:1-10)	814
	D. The Word Is Very Near You (30:11-14)	821
	E. The Two Ways: Life and Death (30:15-20)	823
X.	Second Supplement (31–34)	827
	A. Moses' Death Draws Near (31:1–32:52)	827
	1. I Cannot Cross Over This Jordan (31:1-6)	827
	2. Joshua to Head the Army, the Law Entrusted to the Levites and Elders (31:7-13)	831
	a) Joshua Receives Charge from Moses (31:7-8)	831
	b) A Public Reading of the Law Every Seven Years! (31:9-13)	831
	3. Yahweh Addresses Moses and Joshua (31:14-23)	835
	a) Joshua to Receive His Charge (31:14-15)	835
	b) Moses to Write a Song (31:16-22)	836
	c) The Charge to Joshua (31:23)	836
	4. Moses' Parting Words about the Song (31:24-30)	843
	5. The Song of Moses (32:1-43)	848
	EXCURSUS 3: HISTORY OF RESEARCH INTO THE SONG OF MOSES	852
	6. Take These Words to Heart (32:44-47)	909
	7. Ascend this Mountain (32:48-52)	910
	B. Moses' Departure (33:1–34:12)	913
	1. The Blessing of Moses (33:1-29)	913
	2. Moses' Death and Burial (34:1-12)	941
APPENDIX: Citations of Deuteronomy in the New Testament		950
AUTHOR INDEX		956
SCRIPTURE INDEX		968

Preface

In James Michener's novel *The Source* (Michener 1965), an American archaeologist in charge of excavating Tell Makor, Harvard-educated Dr. Cullinane of Chicago, is told by his Israeli colleague, Dr. Ilan Eliav, that if he really wants to understand the Jewish people, he should read Deuteronomy five times. The American Irish Catholic questions whether the book is worth five readings. Dr. Eliav answers:

> Deuteronomy is so real to me that I feel as if my immediate ancestors — say, my great-grandfather with desert dust still on his clothes — came down that valley with goats and donkeys and stumbled onto this spot.

So the American began reading — first in the Authorized King James Version, and last in the Hebrew Bible — and found that not only did he understand the Jews and Judaism better, but also the Christian faith in which he had been reared. Michener writes:

> . . . as his eyes ran down the columns they caught phrases and sentences which he had once vaguely supposed to be from the New Testament: "Man doth not live by bread only" . . . and "Thou shalt love the Lord thy God with all thine heart, and with all thy soul, and with all thy might." He discovered concepts that lay at the core of his New Testament Catholicism: "But the word is very nigh unto thee, in thy mouth, and in thy heart, that thou mayest do it." (Michener 1965, 158-59)

It is no fiction that Deuteronomy has exercised enormous influence on both Judaism and Christianity over the centuries. No fewer than two hundred of the traditional six hundred thirteen commandments of Pharasaic Judaism are said to have been based on Deuteronomy, and commentator Jeffrey Tigay (xxvii), who points this out, goes on to say that Deuteronomy's contribution to Jewish worship in the daily liturgy and on special occasions has been extensive and profound. The Shema in Deut 6:4 has been at the heart of Jewish theology and worship for centuries, and its importance for Judaism continues up to the present day. The debt owed to Deuteronomy by the Christian Church is also considerable. The Decalogue has, in fact, been an important document in the minds of many great thinkers, e.g., Philo, Luther, Calvin, Immanuel Kant, Thomas Jefferson, Friedrich Nietzsche, and others (Kuntz 2004).

Deuteronomy's celebrated rhetorical prose, although flowing and not particularly difficult Hebrew, is nevertheless a challenge to the translator, for which reason I am not always satisfied with my renderings into English. As in my Jeremiah commentary (Lundbom 1999; 2004a; 2004b), so also here, I have stayed as close as possible to the Hebrew. This will not always lend itself to readings in public worship, but since I am writing a commentary, I want the reader to get a feel for the language, grammar, and style of the original, much of which is lost when translation is done according to the "dynamic equivalent" principle, or with an aim to render Biblical Hebrew into good English prose. I want the reader to hear the repetitions, the building of phrases, the parallelisms, the many dependent clauses, the concrete idioms, the added pronouns, and the inverted word order, the latter of which make for emphasis, which pervades the original. Much of this has been entirely lost in all modern English translations since the King James Version of 1611.

I am also in sympathy with modern Jewish scholars such as Richard Friedman, William Propp, and others, who quite intentionally want to render in English, with less change than is customary, an ancient language decidedly not English, having as it often does a strangeness to the modern ear. Translation of the Hebrew in Friedman's *Commentary on the Torah* (2001) has much to recommend it, and I have used it with profit in my own translation of Deuteronomy. For a recent translation of Exodus that goes even further in preserving characteristics of the original, see Propp's Anchor Bible commentary on *Exodus* (Propp 1999, 40-41). In a commentary, characteristic features of ancient Hebrew can perhaps be allowed, and may even be preferred, in translation. My hope, then, is that the reader will be charitable in assessing the translation of the present work. I have no desire to be doggedly literal or otherwise to render ancient Hebrew into inelegant English.

I have chosen to cite in notes of the commentary a full listing of Deuteronomy's stereotyped words and phrases the first time they occur, and then refer back to the note in question when they turn up again. One may consult the exhaustive lists of characteristic words and phrases in Driver (lxxvii-lxxxiv) and Weinfeld (1972, 320-65), but I think it useful to see the distinctive language of

Deuteronomy in contexts where it occurs. Of even greater importance will be to see how language contributes to important theological concepts contained in the book. Deuteronomy is a rich book of theology, and this theology is embodied first and foremost in language and rhetoric, not in concepts derived from great philosophical thinkers ancient and modern.

Deuteronomy's influence on writers of the New Testament can hardly be overemphasized. Phrases and entire passages from the book are cited, abridged, paraphrased, or slightly altered on pages throughout the New Testament, by my count some 113 times (see Appendix). Deuteronomy's strident monotheism was also pressed into service by the church fathers, who used it as a weapon against anyone worshipping gods other than the God revealed in Holy Writ, which included Roman authorities, and Christian heretics such as the Gnostics, Marcionites, and Arians (Hilhorst 1994).

The Decalogue of Deuteronomy and key phrases from Deuteronomy turn up in Luther's Larger and Smaller Catechisms. In the Smaller Catechism, Luther begins his explanation of each commandment with the words, "We should fear and love God," embodying two important teachings of Deuteronomy. Many prominent New Testament themes — e.g., the love, righteousness, and faithfulness of God; the divine election of a holy people (Israel initially, then an expanded Israel to which Gentiles belong); the importance of love, fear, gratitude, obedience, and service on the part of covenant people towards God; a mandate for benevolent and humane treatment of sojourners, orphans, widows, poor, and the needy in general; divine judgment and exclusion from the Kingdom for human disobedience and foolishness — all these come straight out of Deuteronomy. So while the New Testament is known to draw heavily upon Isaiah and the Psalms, it is permeated as well with a host of important teachings from Deuteronomy.

One realizes in the preparation of a commentary how indebted one is to others who labored earlier in the field. In the study of Deuteronomy, the commentary of S. R. Driver in the ICC series is where everyone has to begin, filled as it is with enormous learning and sanely appropriating a century and more of German scholarship on the Pentateuch, to which is added an encyclopedic knowledge of the Hebrew language and Deuteronomy's distinctive vocabulary and style. All commentators and students of Deuteronomy have profited from Driver in the years since his work was published in 1895. Driver's mastery of Deuteronomy was recognized by Rudolph Kittel, who assigned to him the textual work of Deuteronomy for his first edition of *Biblica Hebraica* (BH^1) in 1905, and by Cyrus Adler, who edited the *Jewish Encyclopedia (JE)* published in the years 1901-1906. Driver was one of the greats — perhaps the greatest — of nineteenth-century British Old Testament scholars (Emerton 2001; 2002; John Rogerson, *TRE* 9:190-92). His mastery of Biblical Hebrew is seen in collaborat-

Preface

ing with Francis Brown and Charles Briggs to produce the *Hebrew and English Lexicon of the Old Testament* (BDB), a revision of the important lexical work of Wilhelm Gesenius (Smend 2007, 63-64). Driver also possessed a broad knowledge of ancient Hebrew religion and culture, and was not, like many scholars proficient in the ancient languages today, ignorant of Old Testament theology. Driver's *Deuteronomy* is thus the commentary with which one has to begin, and a careful reading of its contents — including discussions in small print and in footnotes — will more than repay the effort. Although dated, it is nevertheless a veritable mine of information.

I am also much indebted to work in Deuteronomy carried out by two recent Jewish scholars, Moshe Weinfeld and Jeffrey Tigay. Weinfeld's *Deuteronomy 1-11* in the Anchor Bible series (Weinfeld 1991), regrettably left unfinished, and a large number of publications on Deuteronomy and subjects relating to Deuteronomy combine to make Weinfeld the premier modern interpreter of this biblical book. The *Deuteronomy* commentary by Tigay in the JPS Torah Commentary (Tigay 1996) is also a very important work, and from him, too, I have learned much. Although written largely for a Jewish audience, it is of great value to non-Jewish readers.

German scholars of the nineteenth and twentieth centuries have made significant contributions to the study of Deuteronomy, even though no German language commentary ranks with those of Driver, Weinfeld, and Tigay. Modern critical study of Deuteronomy owes much to W. M. L. de Wette's dissertation of 1805, which anchored the book in the seventh century B.C., and to essays written in the 1930s and 1940s by Gerhard von Rad. On these two important Old Testament scholars, see Smend 2007, 43-56, 170-97. Von Rad's commentary on Deuteronomy, published in English in the OTL series, fell way short of expectation, and was replaced in the series by a new commentary written by Richard Nelson. It, too, is brief, but contains much helpful information on the text, particularly readings of Dead Sea Scroll fragments. Another major German contributor to the study of Deuteronomy has been Norbert Lohfink, whose work on rhetorical structures has been of particular value.

Other Deuteronomy commentaries can also be consulted with profit. There is considerable learning in William Moran's "Deuteronomy" in *A New Catholic Commentary on Holy Scripture* (1969), even though his treatment is brief and the work is not a full commentary like those of Driver, Weinfeld, and Tigay. Other Deuteronomy commentaries have been written over the years, and from these too insights may be gleaned in studying this important biblical book. One realizes in the preparation of a commentary, like any scholarly enterprise, how much one stands on the shoulders of those who labored earlier, to whom an enormous debt of gratitude is owed.

Ancient place names and distances between ancient sites contained in the

Preface

Onomasticon of Eusebius of Caesarea *(Onom.)* and the *Liber Locorum* of Jerome *(Sit.)* are taken from the new English translation of these works by G. Freeman-Grenville (Eusebius 2003), where the entries are listed in alphabetical order and Eusebius's distances appear in Excursus II of the volume.

The section on "Deuteronomy and Wisdom" in the Introduction is an abridged version of an essay published earlier in a *Festschrift* for Richard Nelson (Lundbom 2010c).

I wish to express thanks to the National Endowment for the Humanities for a grant in 2004-2005 enabling me to begin work on this commentary at the Albright Institute of Archaeological Research in Jerusalem. It was David Noel Freedman who invited me to write the Deuteronomy volume for a projected Eerdmans Critical Commentary Series, of which he was the general editor. He lived to edit only the completed work on chapters 12-26. As always, his many pages of single-spaced, typewritten critique were filled with learned comment and helpful suggestions. I remain greatly indebted to this extraordinary biblical scholar and teacher over a period of forty years, from the beginning of graduate study at the San Francisco Theological Seminary and Graduate Theological Union in the fall of 1967 to the summer prior to his death in April 2008. My thanks to Eerdmans for accepting the work as a self-standing volume after the commentary series was closed down, and specifically to the able and congenial Allen Myers, who guided the work through to publication.

JACK R. LUNDBOM
Garrett-Evangelical Theological Seminary

Abbreviations

AASOR	*Annual of the American Schools of Oriental Research*
AAWG	Abhandlungen der Akademie der Wissenschaften in Göttingen
AB	Anchor Bible, ed. William F. Albright and David Noel Freedman
ABD	*Anchor Bible Dictionary*, ed. David Noel Freedman. 6 vols. New York, 1992
ABRL	Anchor Bible Reference Library
AbrN	*Abr-Nahrain* (continued by *Ancient Near Eastern Studies*)
AcOr	*Acta orientalia* (Copenhagen)
AcSu	*Acta sumerologica*
AfO	*Archiv für Orientforschung*
AfOB	*Archiv für Orientforschung: Beiheft*
AGSJU	Arbeiten zur Geschichte des Spätjudentums und Urchristentums
AHw	Wolfram von Soden, *Akkadisches Handwörterbuch*. 3 vols. Wiesbaden, 1959-81.
AJBI	*Annual of the Japanese Biblical Institute*
AJP	*American Journal of Philology*
AJSL	*American Journal of Semitic Languages and Literatures*
AJSR	*Association for Jewish Studies Review*
AJT	*American Journal of Theology*
Akk	Akkadian
Al.T	Donald J. Wiseman, *The Alalakh Tablets*. London, 1953
AmT	The Bible: An American Translation, trans. J. M. Powis Smith and Edgar J. Goodspeed. Chicago, 1935
AnBib	Analecta biblica
ANE	Ancient Near East(ern)
ANEP[2]	*The Ancient Near East in Pictures,* ed. James B. Pritchard. 2nd ed. with Supplement. Princeton, 1969

Abbreviations

*ANET*³	*Ancient Near Eastern Texts Relating to the Old Testament*, ed. James B. Pritchard. 3rd ed. with Supplement. Princeton, 1969
AnOr	Analecta Orientalia
AOAT	Alter Orient und Altes Testament
AOS	American Oriental Series
APOT	*The Apocrypha and Pseudepigrapha of the Old Testament*, ed. R. H. Charles. 2 vols. Oxford, 1913
ApOTC	Apollos Old Testament Commentary
Aq	Aquila
Ar	Arabic
ArBib	The Aramaic Bible
ARM	Archives royales de Mari
ArOr	*Archiv Orientální*
AS	Assyriological Studies
ASOR	American Schools of Oriental Research
ATANT	Abhandlungen zur Theologie des Alten und Neuen Testaments
ATR	*Anglican Theological Review*
AuOr	*Aula orientalis*
AUSS	*Andrews University Seminary Studies*
AV	Authorized King James Version, 1611
b.	Babylonian Talmud
BA	*Biblical Archaeologist* (continued as *NEA*)
BAR	*Biblical Archaeology Review*
BASOR	*Bulletin of the American Schools of Oriental Research*
BASORSup	Bulletin of the American Schools of Oriental Research: Supplement Series
BBVO	Berliner Beiträge zum Vorderen Orient
BDB	*A Hebrew and English Lexicon of the Old Testament*, ed. Francis Brown, S. R. Driver, and Charles A. Briggs. Oxford, 1907
BETL	Bibliotheca ephemeridum theologicarum lovaniensium
BH	*Biblia Hebraica*
*BH*¹	*Biblia Hebraica*. 1st ed., ed. Rudolf Kittel. Stuttgart, 1905-6
*BH*³	*Biblia Hebraica*. 3rd ed., ed. Rudolf Kittel. Stuttgart, 1937
BHM	*Bulletin of the History of Medicine*
BHQ	*Biblia Hebraica Quinta*. 5th ed., ed. Adrian Schenker et al. Stuttgart, 1998-
BHS	*Biblia Hebraica Stuttgartensia*, ed. Kurt Elliger and Wilhelm Rudolph. Stuttgart, 1983. *Liber Jeremiae* prepared by Wilhelm Rudolph. Stuttgart, 1970
BHT	Beiträge zur historischen Theologie
Bib	*Biblica*
BibOr	Biblica et orientalia
BIW	The Bible in Its World

Abbreviations

BJRL	*Bulletin of the John Rylands Library*
BJS	Brown Judaic Studies
BN	*Biblische Notizen*
BRev	*Bible Review*
BRS	Biblical Resource Series
BW	*The Biblical World*
BWANT	Beiträge zur Wissenschaft vom Alten und Neuen Testament
BZ	*Biblische Zeitschrift*
BZAW	Beihefte zur Zeitschrift für die alttestamentliche Wissenschaft
CAD	*The Assyrian Dictionary of the Oriental Institute of the University of Chicago*, ed. Ignace J. Gelb et al. Chicago, 1956-
CB	Century Bible, ed. Walter F. Adeney
CBC	Cambridge Bible Commentary
CBQ	*Catholic Biblical Quarterly*
CBSC	Cambridge Bible for Schools and Colleges. OT ed. Alexander Francis Kirkpatrick
CD	Cairo Genizah copy of the *Damascus Document* (= "Zadokite" Document)
CH	Code of Hammurabi
CIS	*Corpus inscriptionum semiticarum* (Paris)
ConBOT	Coniectanea biblica: Old Testament Series
COS	*The Context of Scripture*, ed. William W. Hallo. 3 vols. Leiden, 1997-2003
CovH	*Covenant Hymnal*. Chicago, 1950
CovQ	*Covenant Quarterly*
CP	*Classical Philology*
CPSSup	Cambridge Philological Society: Supplementary Volumes
CQ	*Classical Quarterly*
CRFB	*Christian Rural Fellowship Bulletin*
CUF	Collection des Universités de France
CurTM	*Currents in Theology and Mission*
D	Deuteronomic source of the Pentateuch
DDD	*Dictionary of Deities and Demons in the Bible*, ed. Karel van der Toorn, Bob Becking, and Pieter W. van der Horst. Leiden and Grand Rapids, 1999
DH	Deuteronomic Historian
Dict Talm	*A Dictionary of the Targumim, the Talmud Babli and Yerushalmi, and the Midrashic Literature*, ed. Marcus Jastrow. 2 vols. London, 1903; Peabody, 2005
Did	*Didache*
DJD	Discoveries in the Judaean Desert
DMB	*Danish Medical Bulletin*
DMOA	Documenta et monumenta Orientis antiqui

Abbreviations

DSD	*Dead Sea Discoveries*
E	Elohist source of the Pentateuch
EA	El-Amarna tablets. According to the edition of J. A. Knudtzon, *Die el-Amarna-Tafeln.* Leipzig, 1908-15. Repr. Aalen, 1964. Continued in A. F. Rainey, *El-Amarna Tablets, 359-79.* 2nd rev. ed. Kevelaer, 1978.
EBib	*Etudes bibliques*
ECB	*Eerdmans Commentary on the Bible,* ed. James D. G. Dunn and John W. Rogerson. Grand Rapids, 2003
EDSS	*Encyclopedia of the Dead Sea Scrolls,* ed. Lawrence H. Schiffman and James C. VanderKam. 2 vols. Oxford, 2000
EncB	*Encyclopaedia Britannica*
EncIs	*Encyclopaedia of Islam.* New (2nd) ed., ed. C. E. Bosworth et al. Leiden, 1960-
EncJud	*Encyclopaedia Judaica,* ed. Cecil Roth and Geoffrey Wigoder. 18 vols. Jerusalem, 1982-92
ErIsr	*Eretz-Israel*
EstBib	*Estudios bíblicos*
ETL	*Ephemerides theologicae lovanienses*
EVV	Modern English Versions of the Bible
ExpTim	*Expository Times*
FRCS	Folklore Research Center Studies
FRLANT	Forschungen zur Religion und Literatur des Alten und Neuen Testaments
FS	Festschrift
G^B	Codex Vaticanus
Gk	Greek
GKC	*Gesenius' Hebrew Grammar,* ed. E. Kautzsch; trans. A. E. Cowley. 2nd ed. Oxford, 1963. Orig. 1910
GNB	Good News Bible (New York, 1976)
GRBS	*Greek, Roman and Byzantine Studies*
GTA	Göttinger theologische Arbeiten
H	Holiness Code in Leviticus 17-26
HAR	*Hebrew Annual Review*
HDB	*A Dictionary of the Bible,* ed. James Hastings. New York, 1902
Heb	Hebrew
Hen	*Henoch*
Hist. eccl.	Eusebius, *Ecclesiastical History*
HL	Hittite Laws
HS	*Hebrew Studies*
HSM	Harvard Semitic Monographs
HSS	Harvard Semitic Studies
HTR	*Harvard Theological Review*

Abbreviations

HUB	Hebrew University Bible
HUCA	Hebrew Union College Annual
IB	*Interpreter's Bible*, ed. George A. Buttrick. 12 vols. New York, 1951-57
ICC	International Critical Commentary, ed. S. R. Driver, Alfred Plummer, and Charles A. Briggs
IDB	*Interpreter's Dictionary of the Bible*, ed. George A. Buttrick. 4 vols. New York, 1962
IDBSup	*Interpreter's Dictionary of the Bible, Supplementary Volume*, ed. Keith Crimm. Nashville, 1976
IEJ	Israel Exploration Journal
Int	Interpretation
IOS	Israel Oriental Studies
IR	Iliff Review
J	Yahwist source of the Pentateuch
JANES	Journal of the Ancient Near Eastern Society of Columbia University
JAOS	Journal of the American Oriental Society
JB	Jerusalem Bible
JBL	Journal of Biblical Literature
JBW	Jahrbücher der biblischen Wissenschaft
JCS	Journal of Cuneiform Studies
JE	*Jewish Encyclopedia*, ed. Cyrus Adler et al. 12 vols. New York, 1901-6
JE	Combined Yahwistic and Elohistic sources of the Pentateuch
JEA	Journal of Egyptian Archaeology
JEOL	Jaarbericht van het Vooraziatisch-Egyptisch Genootschap "Ex oriente lux"
JHI	Journal of the History of Ideas
JJS	Journal of Jewish Studies
JLA	Jewish Law Annual
JNES	Journal of Near Eastern Studies
JNSL	Journal of Northwest Semitic Languages
JP	Journal of Philology
JPOS	Journal of the Palestine Oriental Society
JPS	Jewish Publication Society
JQR	Jewish Quarterly Review
JRev	Juridical Review
JSOT	Journal for the Study of the Old Testament
JSOTSup	Journal for the Study of the Old Testament: Supplement Series (Continued as LHB/OTS)
JSS	Journal of Semitic Studies
JTS	Journal of Theological Studies
Jub.	Jubilees
K	Kethib ("what is written")

Abbreviations

KAI	*Kanaanäische und aramäische Inschriften.* 2nd ed., ed. Herbert Donner and Wolfgang Röllig. 3 vols. Wiesbaden, 1962-71
KBL³	Ludwig Köhler and Walter Baumgartner, *Hebräisches und Aramäisches Lexikon zum Alten Testament.* 3rd ed. Leiden, 1967-90
KEH	Kurzgefasstes exegetisches Handbuch zum Alten Testament
KRT	*La Légende de Keret,* C. Virolleaud. Paris, 1936; H. L. Ginsberg, BASORSup 2-3, 1946
KTU	*Die keilalphabetischen Texte aus Ugarit,* ed. Manfred Dietrich, Oswald Loretz, and Joaquin Sanmartín. AOAT 24. Neukirchen, 1976
Lane	E. W. Lane, *An Arabic-English Lexicon.* London 1863-93
Lat	Latin
LCL	Loeb Classical Library
LE	Laws of Eshnunna
LHB/OTS	Library of Hebrew Bible/Old Testament Studies (continuing JSOTSup)
LI	Laws of Lipit-Ištar
Liv. Pro.	*Lives of the Prophets*
Loeb	Loeb Classical Library
LOS	London Oriental Series
LUN	Laws of Ur-Nammu
LXX	Septuagint, according to *Septuaginta II.* 8th ed., ed. Alfred Rahlfs. Stuttgart, 1965
M^A	Masoretic Text according to the Aleppo Codex (Codex A)
M^L	Masoretic Text according to the Leningrad Codex $B19^A$ (Codex L)
MAL	Middle Assyrian Laws
Mandelkern	Solomon Mandelkern, *Veteris Testamenti Concordantiae.* Tel Aviv, 1964
Mart. Isa.	*Martyrdom of Isaiah*
MS(S)	Manuscript(s)
MSU	Mitteilungen des Septuaginta-Unternehmens
MT	Masoretic Text, according to *BH³* or *BHS*
NAB	New American Bible
NCBC	New Century Bible Commentary
NEA	*Near Eastern Archaeology* (continuing *BA*)
NEAEHL	*New Encyclopedia of Archaeological Excavations in the Holy Land,* ed. Ephraim Stern. 4 vols. Jerusalem, 1993
NEB	New English Bible
NEcB	Die Neue Echter Bibel
NIV	New International Version
NJB	New Jerusalem Bible

Abbreviations

NJV	Tanakh: A New Translation of the Holy Scriptures According to the Traditional Hebrew Text. Philadelphia, 1985
NKZ	*Neue kirchliche Zeitschrift*
NRSV	New Revised Standard Version
NT	New Testament
OBO	Orbis biblicus et orientalis
OEANE	*Oxford Encyclopedia of Archaeology in the Near East,* ed. Eric M. Meyers. 5 vols. Oxford, 1997
OED	*Oxford English Dictionary.* 2nd ed. Oxford, 1989
OIP	Oriental Institute Publications. University of Chicago
OJA	*Oxford Journal of Archaeology*
Onom.	*Onomasticon* of Eusebius
Or	*Orientalia*
OrAnt	*Oriens antiquus*
OT	Old Testament
OTL	Old Testament Library
OTP	*Old Testament Pseudepigrapha,* ed. James H. Charlesworth. 2 vols. Garden City, 1983-85
OTS	Oudtestamentische Studiën
OTWSA	Die Oudtestamentiese Werkgemeenskap in Suid-Afrika
P	"Priestly" source of the Pentateuch
PEFQS	*Palestine Exploration Fund. Quarterly Statement* (continued as *Palestine Exploration Quarterly*)
PEQ	*Palestine Exploration Quarterly* (continuing *Palestine Exploration Fund. Quarterly Statement*)
PIBA	*Proceedings of the Irish Biblical Association*
POS	Pretoria Oriental Series
PRU	Le Palais Royal d'Ugarit, ed. Claude F.-A. Schaeffer
PSBA	*Proceedings of the Society of Biblical Archaeology*
Q	Qere ("what is read")
QT	Qumran *Temple Scroll*
RA	*Revue d'Assyriologie et d'Archéologie Orientale*
RB	*Revue biblique*
REB	Revised English Bible
RES	*Revue des études sémitiques*
RevQ	*Revue de Qumrân*
RGG^1	Die Religion in Geschichte und Gegenwart, 1st ed. Tübingen, 1909-13
RHA	*Revue hittite et asianique*
RIDA	*Revue internationale des droits de l'antiquité*
RLA	*Reallexikon der Assyriologie,* ed. Erich Ebeling und Bruno Meissner. Berlin, 1932-
RSV	Revised Standard Version

Abbreviations

RV	Revised Version
S	Syriac
SAA	State Archives of Assyria
Sam	Samaritan Pentateuch
SAOC	Studies in Ancient Oriental Civilization
SBAB	Stuttgarter biblische Aufsatzbände
SBL	Society of Biblical Literature
SBLABS	Society of Biblical Literature Archaeology and Biblical Studies
SBLDS	Society of Biblical Literature Dissertation Series
SBLMS	Society of Biblical Literature Monograph Series
SBLSCSS	Society of Biblical Literature Septuagint and Cognate Studies Series
SBLSymS	Society of Biblical Literature Symposium Series
SBLTT	Society of Biblical Literature Texts and Translations
SBLWAW	Society of Biblical Literature Writings from the Ancient World
SBS	Stuttgarter Bibelstudien
SBT	Studies in Biblical Theology
ScrHier	Scripta hierosolymitana
Sem	*Semitica*
SHANE	Studies in the History of the Ancient Near East
Sib. Or.	*Sibylline Oracles*
Sit.	Jerome, *De situ et nominibus locorum Hebraicorum (Liber locorum)*
SJLA	Studies in Judaism in Late Antiquity
SJOT	*Scandinavian Journal of the Old Testament*
SJT	*Scottish Journal of Theology*
SLR	*Stanford Law Review*
SRR	*Seminary Ridge Review*
STDJ	Studies on the Texts of the Desert of Judah
StPB	Studia post-biblica
Symm	Symmachus
T	Targum(s)
T^{MS}	Targum Manuscript
T^{Nf}	Targum Neofiti
T^{Onq}	Targum Onqelos
T^{PsJ}	Targum Pseudo-Jonathan
T. Levi	*Testament of Levi* (in *The Testament of the Twelve Patriarchs*)
T. Reu.	*Testament of Reuben* (in *The Testament of the Twelve Patriarchs*)
T. Sim.	*Testament of Simeon* (in *The Testament of the Twelve Patriarchs*)
TA	Tel Aviv
TAPS	*Transactions of the American Philosophical Society*
TB	Theologische Bücherei
TDOT	*Theological Dictionary of the Old Testament,* ed. G. Johannes Botterweck, Helmer Ringgren, and Heinz-Josef Fabry. 17 vols. Grand Rapids, 1974–

Abbreviations

Text	*Textus*
Theod	Theodotion
TLZ	*Theologische Literaturzeitung*
TRE	*Theologische Realenzyklopädie*
UF	*Ugarit-Forschungen*
Ug	Ugaritic
UgT	Ugaritic text
UM	Cyrus H. Gordon, *Ugaritic Manual.* AnOr 35. Rome, 1955
UT	Cyrus H. Gordon, *Ugaritic Textbook.* AnOr 38. Rome, 1965
VAT	Vorderasiatische Abteilung Tontafel. Vorderasiatisches Museum, Berlin
Vg	Vulgate
VT	*Vetus Testamentum*
VTE	D. J. Wiseman, *Vassal Treaties of Esarhaddon. Iraq* 20 (1958) 1-99; also London, 1958
VTSup	Supplements to Vetus Testamentum
War Scroll	*Scroll of the War of the Sons of Light against the Sons of Darkness* (1QM)
WHJP	*World History of the Jewish People.* 1st ser.: Ancient Times, ed. E. A. Speiser et al. Jerusalem, 1964-79
WW	*Western Watch*
YJS	Yale Judaica Series
ZA	*Zeitschrift für Assyriologie und verwandte Gebiete* (continued as *Zeitschrift für Assyriologie und vorderasiatische Archäologie*)
ZAW	*Zeitschrift für die alttestamentliche Wissenschaft*
ZDMG	*Zeitschrift der deutschen morgenländischen Gesellschaft*
ZDPV	*Zeitschrift des deutschen Palästina-Vereins*

Introduction

NAME AND CANONICITY

Deuteronomy is the fifth book of the canonical Hebrew Scriptures/Old Testament (OT). In Jewish tradition the first five books are "The Torah" (Sirach, *Prologue*), going otherwise by their Latin name, *Pentateuch*. Greek πεντάτευχος (= "five rolls") is an adaptation of the Hebrew חֲמִשָּׁה חֻמְשֵׁי הַתּוֹרָה, meaning "five-fifths of the Law" (*JE* 9:589). A Dead Sea Scroll fragment (1Q30:1 line 4) has turned up the expression [ס]פרים חומשים, which may denote either the five books of the Torah or the five books of the Psalter (Barthélemy and Milik 1955, 132-33).

It is not known when the division into five books occurred, although it is generally thought to have been long before the Second Temple/New Testament (NT) period (*EncJud* 13:232). In the Talmud (*b. B. Bat.* 14b-15a), the author of this work, except perhaps for the last eight verses of Deuteronomy, is said to have been Moses. These concluding verses report Moses' death, for which reason certain rabbis said they must have been written by Joshua. Already in 1 Kgs 2:3 and 2 Kgs 14:6 are references to a written "law of Moses" (cf. Josh 8:31; 23:6; Ezra 3:2). Mosaic authorship of Deuteronomy is affirmed by Josephus, although with the qualification that Moses left things in a scattered condition (*Ant.* 4.196-97).

The name *Deuteronomion* in the Greek Septuagint (LXX) derives from τὸ δευτερονόμιον τοῦτο in LXX 17:18, which is its rendering of אֶת־מִשְׁנֵה הַתּוֹרָה הַזֹּאת. The LXX translator(s) took the expression to mean "this second law," whereas T[Onq] translates "a copy of this law" (cf. Josh 8:32), now the generally accepted interpretation. Hebrew מִשְׁנֶה can mean "double, second, copy." Mishnah *Sanh.* 2:4 says the king was to write for himself "a scroll of the law," which it takes to mean "an additional scroll" (Blackman 1977, 4:244). The Qumran *Tem-*

ple Scroll (11QT 56:21) simply has "this law," instead of "a copy of this law," removing the ambiguity (Yadin 1983, 1:345; 2:254). In Rabbinical Hebrew Deuteronomy is called *Mishneh Torah* (תּוֹרָה מִשְׁנֵה), which means "repeated law" (Weinfeld, *EncJud* 13:232). This name and the LXX name are therefore not inappropriate, since Deuteronomy repeats earlier law from Exodus, and in 28:69(29:1) the Deuteronomic covenant is distinguished from the covenant made at Horeb (Sinai). Luther took מִשְׁנֵה תּוֹרָה to mean "second Law," but said there was no difference between this law and the law given at Horeb. Latin *Deuteronomium* of the Vulgate (Vg) comes into English as "Deuteronomy." The Hebrew name for Deuteronomy is *Debarim* (דְּבָרִים), "(the) Words," taken — as elsewhere in the Pentateuch — from the opening words of the book: "These are the words" (אֵלֶּה הַדְּבָרִים).

TEXT AND VERSIONS

The text of Deuteronomy is relatively good, only occasionally requiring correction from the ancient Versions (Driver 1895, xcv). It has none of the problems found in Samuel, Hosea, Jeremiah, and certain other OT books. Difficult or problematic readings occur mainly in the poetry of chapters 32 and 33, and even then, these are not many.

The Hebrew Masoretic Text (MT) survives in modern times in the Leningrad Codex (M^L), dated ca. A.D. 1010, and is the text on which BH^3 and *BHS* are based (Sanders and Beck 1997). It is also the text on which *Biblia Hebraica Quinta (BHQ)* and the *Oxford Hebrew Bible,* both currently in preparation, will be based. Deuteronomy in *BHQ* has been prepared by Carmel McCarthy; for a summary of her work on the text, see McCarthy 2007. M^L is the oldest complete manuscript of the Hebrew Bible in existence, housed in the Russian National Library in St. Petersburg. A fascimile was published recently by David Noel Freedman et al. (1998). The other important medieval manuscript of the Hebrew Bible is the Aleppo Codex (M^A), dated to the tenth century A.D. This codex has been published in a facsimile edition by Moshe Goshen-Gottstein (1976) and is the text being used in the *Hebrew University Bible (HUB)*. The Aleppo Codex is only 70 percent complete, however, a number of folios having been lost as a result of the Aleppo riots of 1948. Most of the Pentateuch is missing. The codex presently begins with the last word of Deut 28:17, "and your baking bowl" (וּמִשְׁאַרְתֶּךָ), after which the remainder of Deuteronomy is preserved.

The LXX of the Pentateuch, translated probably in the early or middle third century B.C. by Jews in Alexandria, is a relatively good translation of the Hebrew text (Eissfeldt 1965, 604-5, 702-4; Fohrer 1968, 508). Variants in Deuteronomy are largely the sudden and frequent changes between second singular and second plural (both "you") in the speeches of Moses (the so-called *Numeruswechsel*) and minor differences bearing little or not at all on the sense. There are cases where the LXX translator seems not to have correctly understood the Hebrew, e.g., in 28:5 he mistranslates מִשְׁאַרְתֶּךָ ("your kneading bowl") with τὰ ἐγκαταλείμματά σου ("your reserve"), and in 28:20 he translates אֶת־הַמְּאֵרָה אֶת־הַמְּהוּמָה וְאֶת־הַמִּגְעֶרֶת ("curse, panic, and rebuke") with τὴν ἔνδειαν καὶ τὴν ἐκλιμίαν καὶ τὴν ἀνάλωσιν ("poverty and famine and destruction"), which are not quite right.

The LXX appears not to manifest any anti-anthropomorphic bias in its translation, as might be expected (Wittstruck 1976). Fritsch (1943) claimed for the Greek Pentateuch numerous anti-anthropomorphisms, but this thesis has been refuted by Orlinsky (1944) and Wittstruck (1976). It finds little support in Deuteronomy, and of the examples cited by Fritsch many occur not in the law code, but in the poetry of chapters 32 and 33, where unusual coinages might be expected. The LXX text of Deuteronomy gets full and detailed discussion in Wevers 1978 and 1995.

A couple of LXX readings in Deut 32:8 and 43 (the Song of Moses) have taken on new importance in light of Dead Sea Scroll readings, which vindicate them partially or wholly against readings in MT (see below).

The Samaritan Pentateuch (Sam), dating in all likelihood from a time soon after the Pentateuch was canonized in ca. 400 B.C., contains a reported six thousand divergencies from the MT, most of which are orthographic (Eissfeldt 1965, 695; Fohrer 1968, 505; Waltke, *ABD*, 5:932). Roughly one-third agree with the LXX against MT. While some do correct or improve readings of MT, the vast majority are insignificant differences in spelling and grammar that do not affect the sense. Waltke (*ABD*, 5:938) says the Sam is therefore of little value in determining original readings. Occasionally variants are of substance. One is the substitution of "Gerizim" in Deut 27:4 for "Ebal" in MT. This could be a deliberate change giving prominence to the mountain on which the Samaritan temple was located, although Eissfeldt (1965, 216 n. 9, 695) and others think the reading is more likely an anti-Samaritan polemic in light of the schism between Samaritans and Jews in the fourth century B.C. (cf. Josephus *Ant.* 13.74-79), thus a change not in Sam, but in MT. For discussion on the Samaritan Pentateuch, see J. MacDonald in *EncJud* 13:264-68; B. Waltke in *ABD*, 5:932-40; Crawford 2005b:131-32.

The Targums, which are Aramaic paraphrases of OT books written in Palestine in the early centuries of the Christian Era, fulfill a need similar to what the LXX filled in Egypt, viz., to enable non-Hebrew-speaking Jews to understand the Hebrew Bible. They are literal renditions of the biblical text adding *halakhic* interpretation and *aggadic* embellishment. The authoritative Targum on the Torah is *Targum Onqelos* (T^{Onq}), dated in the second century A.D., but in

Introduction

Deuteronomy one can also consult readings in *Targum Neofiti* (T^Nf) and *Targum Pseudo-Jonathan* (T^PsJ).

QUMRAN SCROLLS

Numerous texts of Deuteronomy have been found at Khirbet Qumran: biblical fragments, excerpted texts, selected verses on *mezuzot* and phylacteries, and passages incorporated into sectarian and other nonbiblical documents. According to García Martínez (1994, 66), there are thirty-two extant fragments of Deuteronomy from the Judean Desert, all prior to A.D. 70. Crawford (2005a, 316) says the total is thirty-four or thirty-five, which includes one Greek Deuteronomy fragment and one Hebrew fragment each from Wadi Murabbaʿat, Naḥal Ḥever/Wadi Seiyal, and Masada. Deuteronomy is second only to the book of Psalms in numbers of copies turning up at Qumran (Crawford 2005b, 127). There is no complete manuscript to be compared with the celebrated Isaiah Scroll found in Cave 1 (1QIsa^a). The majority of Deuteronomy fragments turned up in Cave 4, a few coming from Caves 1, 2, and elsewhere. Deuteronomy is represented in nine *mezuzot** and thirty-three phylacteries,† which contain verses from the Decalogue and the *Shema* in 5:1–6:9, portions of 10:12–11:21, and in one case verses from the Song of Moses (Deuteronomy 32).

A couple of Qumran readings in the Song of Moses are of particular importance. In 4QDeut^j the reading בני אלוהים ("sons of God") occurs in 32:8 (Ulrich, Cross et al. 1995, 90), where MT and the Versions all have בְּנֵי יִשְׂרָאֵל ("sons of Israel"). The LXX supports the Qumran text with ἀγγέλων θεοῦ ("angels of God"). Also, a 4QDeut^q reading of 32:43 expands the two poetic lines of MT into three (Ulrich, Cross et al. 1995, 141). The LXX expands the verse to four poetic lines (see Note for 32:43). For a discussion of the Deuteronomy texts found in the Qumran caves and in the Judean Desert, see J. Duncan, "Deuteronomy, Book of" in *EDSS* 198-202.

The Qumran *Temple Scroll* (11QT) expounds large sections of Deuteronomy (Yadin 1977; 1983, vols. 1-2; Crawford 2005b, 137-40), although it harmonizes the Deuteronomic texts with texts from Exodus, Leviticus, and Numbers to create a unified whole. The Deuteronomic texts are largely those from chapters 12–26, 28, which can be found in 11QT 43, 48, 51-57, and 59-66. In 11QT two texts from chapter 7 are inserted into the covenant renewal passage of Exod 34:10-16. Occasionally the *Temple Scroll* makes a substantive change, e.g., in

---

*A *mezuzah* (מְזוּזָה) is a scroll affixed to doorposts (מְזוּזֹת) in a Jewish home (cf. 6:9; 11:20).
†Phylacteries (Heb תְּפִלִּין) are two black leather boxes containing Scripture passages that are bound by leather strips to the left hand and the head (cf. 6:8; 11:18).

Deut 21:22, where the biblical text reads: "and he is put to death and you hang him upon a tree," it changes the word order to read: "you shall hang him on a tree, and he shall die" (11QT 64:8; Yadin 1983, 1:81; 2:289-90). Here the author makes the cause of death the hanging, which is not what the biblical passage intends. The *Temple Scroll* also changes grammar so that God, not Moses, is speaking (Yadin 1983, 1:71-73), which brings the Deuteronomic discourse into line with the discourse of Exodus. This has the law given directly by God, not handed down through Moses. Other Qumran documents indicating the importance of Deuteronomy in the Dead Sea Community include 4Q473 on "The Two Ways" (Brooke et al. 1996, 292-94); 4QMMT (Qimron and Strugnell 1994, 58-61; Fraade 2003, 150-51); and 1Q22 on the "Words of Moses" (Barthélemy and Milik 1955, 91-96).

PARAGRAPH DIVISIONS

The MT, Samaritan Pentateuch, Qumran biblical fragments, and Qumran *Temple Scroll* all contain paragraph divisions. There are two types: the closed section, marked by a *setumah* (ס), and the open section, marked by a *petuḥah* (פ). The texts simply have blank spaces at the beginning, middle, and end of lines, or between lines; the sigla ס and פ are put in later, their first known appearance being in an edition of Isaiah and Jeremiah published at Lisbon in A.D. 1492 (Ginsburg 1885, 3:xvi). Before the Dead Sea Scrolls were found, these section markings were thought to be later. The Mishnah (ca. A.D. 200) mentions paragraphs in the Pentateuch and the Prophets, but the distinction between open and closed sections is first made in the Talmud (cf. A.D. 500). Jerome's Hebrew text shows the subdivisions plainly (Pfeiffer 1948, 81). Now that sections have turned up in Qumran texts, we realize that they are even more ancient, and that they can be very useful in delimiting discourse units.

DEUTERONOMY PAPYRI

Some important early papyri contain portions of Deuteronomy. The Nash Papyrus (S. A. Cooke 1903), a liturgical text written in Hebrew, comes from Egypt, perhaps Fayum, and is dated by Albright (1937, 149) to the second half of the second century B.C. It contains the entire Decalogue (Exod 20:2-17; Deut 5:6-21) and the Shema (Deut 6:4-5). The text of the Decalogue appears to combine Exodus and Deuteronomy. The Roberts Papyrus (P. Ryl. Gk. 458; Roberts 1936), a Greek text also from Egypt and dated to the end of the second century B.C., a mere one hundred years after the Torah was translated into Greek in Alexandria (LXX), contains four fragmented columns of a Deuteronomy scroll (23:25–24:3; 25:1-3; 26:12, 17-19; 28:31-33). These were used along with a fragment of the *Iliad* to wrap a mummy.

From the early second century A.D. comes the Chester Beatty Biblical Papyri (Kenyon 1935), another important collection of twelve Greek manuscripts of the Bible emanating from Egypt, probably having been discovered in the ruins of an early Christian church or monastery in the neighborhood of Fayum. Papyrus VI is a codex of what originally were the complete books of Numbers and Deuteronomy (216 pages, or 108 leaves). A large portion of Deuteronomy has survived (1:20-33, 35-46; 2:1–3:21; 3:23–4:49; 5:1–7:10; 7:12-13, 15-20; 9:26, 29; 10:1-2, 5-7, 11-12, 19-21; 11:12-13, 17-18, 31-32; 12:2-4, 15-17; 18:22; 19:1, 4-6, 10-11, 13-14, 16; 27:6-8, 13-15; 28:1-4, 7-10, 12-13, 16-20, 22-25, 27-30, 32-35, 38-41, 43-68; 29:1-18, 20-21, 23-27; 30:1, 4-6, 10-11, 12-13, 16-17, 19-20; 31:3-4, 8-16, 18, 21-23, 26-29; 32:3-5, 10-13, 17-19, 24-25, 27-29; 33:24-26; 34:11-12). This manuscript presents few textual problems and contains no notable new readings (Roberts 1936, 41).

DATE, COMPOSITION, AND AUTHORSHIP

The Josianic Reform

Modern research in Deuteronomy — indeed in the entire Pentateuch — builds on the thesis of W. M. L. de Wette (1830; 1843, 2:150-54), published originally in 1805, that Deuteronomy was the lawbook found in the temple during the reign of King Josiah (2 Kgs 22:8). Some early church fathers, viz., Athanasius, Chrysostom, Jerome, and Theodoret, also made the identification (Nestle 1902), but de Wette went farther in arguing that Deuteronomy had been written shortly before it was found. This appropriated earlier critical views rejecting Mosaic authorship and put Deuteronomy's composition in the seventh century. De Wette also compared Deuteronomy with Joshua to 2 Kings and found here a peculiar style and content, now called "Deuteronomic." His thesis was widely accepted, becoming the linchpin in modern critical theory of the Pentateuch (Rowley 1963b, 161; Eissfeldt 1965, 173).

By the time of Wellhausen, in 1878, Deuteronomy (Source D) had become one of the four pillars of pentateuchal theory, and it was agreed that D preceded Priestly legislation (Source P) in Numbers, Leviticus, and portions of Exodus, rather than vice versa (Wellhausen 1957). Since D was found exclusively in Deuteronomy, or nearly so, it did not have to be disentangled from other source documents. Wellhausen's views were presented convincingly to Anglo-American scholars by S. R. Driver who, in the *Introduction* to his ICC *Deuter-*

onomy (lxxvii-xciv), compiled extensive lists of vocabulary and phraseology characterizing the D source and, in the words of one scholar, "brought down to earth what had hitherto dwelt in the clouds."

A seventh-century date for Deuteronomy is now widely accepted, although some would push back the composition to the reigns of Manasseh or Hezekiah, arguing that portions of the book betray a northern provenance and may date from before or just after the fall of the northern kingdom (722). A postexilic date for P and its dependence upon D have more recently been challenged by Yehezkel Kaufmann (Greenberg 1950; Weinfeld 1972, 179-80; 2004, 3-74; *EncJud* 13:240), and there is a growing consensus — particularly among Jewish scholars — that P is older, preexilic in any case, and perhaps contemporary with D (Freedman; Weinfeld 2004, xii). Weinfeld sees the two documents as representing two theological schools: P characterized by a theocentric approach; D characterized by an anthropocentric approach (Weinfeld 1972, 179-89; 2004, 77-94).

The Josianic reform, as reported in 2 Kings 22-23, appears to owe much to Deuteronomy. The purge carried out by the young king in Jerusalem, Judah, and sites to the north (2 Kgs 23:4-20) is said to have taken place immediately following the finding of the scroll in the temple, and specific acts of the purge — the temple cleansing and destruction of vessels and other cult objects dedicated to foreign deities; the destruction of high places with their altars, pillars, and Asherim; the deposition of idolatrous priests in Jerusalem and slaying of idolatrous priests in the northern cities; the tearing down of chambers in the temple belonging to cult prostitutes; and the elimination of various other elements of foreign worship — all seem to correlate with the prohibitions in Deut 5–26, 28 — not only in content, but in vocabulary and phraseology (Driver 1895, xlv; Paton 1928, 325-26; Weiser 1961, 127-28; Nicholson 1967, 3).

According to 2 Kings 23, a covenant renewal ceremony preceded the purge, and a grand celebration of Passover took place afterwards, in Jerusalem, now the one and only legitimate sanctuary for Yahweh worship. Covenant renewal and centralization of worship are at the heart of Deuteronomy, which mandates that worship occur only at "the place that Yahweh your God will choose (out of/in all your tribes) to put his name there," or descriptions of the like (12:5, 11, 14, 18, 21, 26). Finally, since Huldah's oracle (2 Kgs 22:16-17) declares certain judgment upon Judah for covenant violation, some scholars (G. A. Smith 1918, 194; G. E. Wright 1953, 320; H. L. Ginsberg 1982, 39) have argued that the curses of Deuteronomy 28 must be included on the temple scroll.

Introduction

THE QUEST FOR *URDEUTERONOMIUM*

In the years following the placement of Deuteronomy in the context of the Josianic reform, a quest for *Urdeuteronomium* ("proto-Deuteronomy") began, since it was thought that the scroll of 622 could not possibly contain all the material now found in our present book of Deuteronomy. The quest began with Wellhausen (1889, 191-95), who believed that the newly found scroll contained only the core legislation in chapters 12–26. This core, in his view, appeared in two editions, each of which contained its own introduction: chapters 1–4 and chapters 5–11 (Wellhausen 1957, 369). DeWette had argued earlier (1843, 2:131) that 4:44 began a new collection of Mosaic law containing a sermonic admonition similar to the first admonition in 1:1–4:40. This view of two editions was adopted by J. Estlin Carpenter (1883, 254-55) and numerous other scholars.

S. R. Driver (1895, lxvi-lxxii, 135), however, pointed out soon after that so far as language and style were concerned, there was nothing in chapters 5–11 to suggest a different author from chapters 12–26, and he concluded that chapters 5-26 were the work of a single author, a view that gained broad acceptance (G. E. Wright 1953, 318; von Rad 1962a, 832). Driver also saw no reason to assign chapters 1–3(4) to a different hand than chapters 5–26 (Driver 1895, lxxii; 1913, 94; cf. Albright 1957b, 319), though he did concede the view of earlier scholars that, for some reason, the book contained two superscriptions: 1:1-5 and 4:44-49. He said (p. 79) that the summary in 4:44-49 appeared to be superfluous after 1:1-5, introducing as it does not simply chapters 1–4, but the Deuteronomic discourses generally (v. 5: "to make plain this law"). Despite this difficulty, numerous scholars have followed Driver in viewing 1:1-5 and 4:44-49 as double superscriptions surviving in the present book (G. E. Wright 1953, 314; Nicholson 1967, 18; Fohrer 1968, 171; Lohfink 1968, 7; Weinfeld, 233-34; 1972, 69), a point to which we will return shortly.

A solution to this puzzlement of two apparent introductions was offered by Martin Noth in his study of the Deuteronomic History, published in 1943 (Noth 1981). Noth believed Deuteronomy was intended as an introduction to the entire Deuteronomic History (Deuteronomy to 2 Kings) and was the work of a single author. In his view, the Deuteronomic History could not begin with Creation, since he found no signs of Deuteronomic editing in Genesis to Numbers. But he did see a linkage of Deut 31:1-13 and 34 with Joshua 1. The Introduction to this great work must therefore have been Deuteronomy 1–3(4) (Noth 1981, 12-14). Viewed in this manner, the chapters did not introduce the Deuteronomic law, as Wellhausen and Driver imagined, but rather the larger history beginning with the conquest of Canaan and ending with the collapse of the Israelite nation.

Noth believed the Deuteronomic Historian took over the Deuteronomic law consisting of Deut 4:44-30:20, which meant he was still taking 4:44-49 to be an introduction (p. 16). Since the last event recorded in 2 Kings is to be dated ca. 562, the writing of the Deuteronomic History was put shortly after. This thesis of Noth had wide appeal, although many scholars continued to believe that much of the Deuteronomic History was written before the fall of Jerusalem, some arguing that the work went through two editions (G. E. Wright 1953, 317; Freedman 1962, 716; Cross 1968; R. D. Nelson 1981). Freedman said the First Edition could be seen reaching a climax in 2 Kings 22–23, which reports the Josianic reform, and that "what follows is a melancholy epilogue." Lohfink (1976, 231), too, thinks 2 Kings 22–23 contains material probably composed in Josiah's lifetime. If this be the case, then Deuteronomy 1–4 as an introduction to the First Edition of the Deuteronomic History could be preexilic (Albright 1957b, 315). Fohrer (1968, 177) believes chapters 1–3 cannot be removed from the rest of the book and made the beginning of a Deuteronomic historical work, and agrees with Driver that these chapters are better taken as introducing the Deuteronomic law code.

Noth's theory underwent further revision in the work of David Noel Freedman (1962, 716-18), who saw continuity between the end of Numbers and the beginning of Deuteronomy (he calls Deuteronomy 1–4 a "bridge" to what has gone before). Freedman believed therefore that the document completed ca. 560 was not the Deuteronomistic History, but rather a work he calls the "Primary History," viz., Genesis to 2 Kings. Albright (1957b, 345) had earlier expressed the view that the Pentateuch existed in substantially its present form before 522. Only later was the Pentateuch separated out from the Primary History, according to Freedman, occasioned by an interest of the exilic community in the person of Moses and Israel's experience in the wilderness. A linking between Numbers and Deuteronomy was seen also by Eissfeldt (1965, 157), who said that Deuteronomy 31–34 must be a direct continuation of Numbers 27, in that here Joshua's appointment as Moses' successor is brought to conclusion; also, in chapter 34 of Deuteronomy the last words and the death of Moses are reported.

Other source-critical studies were part of the quest for an *Urdeuteronomium*. Staerk (1894, 76-93) and Steuernagel (1894), for example, attempted to show that the sudden and frequent changes between second singular and second plural forms of the verb in the speeches of Moses (the so-called *Numeruswechsel*) were an indication of sources. But these theses failed to gain acceptance (von Rad 1962a, 832; Lohfink 1963a, 240; Fohrer 1968, 171; Hillers 1964a, 32-33), even along lines later proposed by Minette de Tillesse (1962). Lohfink considers the change to be a stylistic device, which it probably is (Begg 1994). G. Ernest Wright (p. 362) says: "Hebrew writers have the disconcerting habit of completely disregarding consistency in the use of pronouns (cf. e.g., 6:4 with 6:5; 6:13 with 6:14; 6:16-17 with 6:18-19)," and he discounts attempts to find different sources in the singular and plural use of pronouns. I take the shift to be simply another facet of the celebrated Deuteronomic rhetoric: the singular "you" perhaps addressing the people as a whole, and the plural "you" addressing each person individually and emphatically (= "each and every one of you"). Shalom Paul (1991, 150) sees the shift from plural to singular in Amos 4:12 to be just the reverse, saying that with the singular in 4:12 "the impending chastisement is now addressed individually to each member of the nation." Tigay (1996, 62) says the same with regard to Deueronomy: the singular emphasizes the responsibility of each individual, and the plural is used to emphasize Israel's collective responsibility. Milgrom took this same position in responding to a paper of mine read at the Albright Institute in Jerusalem on 3 February 2005. Either way, we have support for the idea that "individual responsibility" does indeed exist in Deuteronomy and the Deuteronomic History (Albright 1957b, 326). Even Weinfeld (1992b, 174), who thinks the exchange may indicate different layers in the text, concludes by saying: "In general the interchange reflects stylistic variations introduced by the same author." Sonsino (1980, 198), too, having compared the Deuteronomic discourse with the ANE treaties, treaty curses, and royal inscriptions, remarks:

> These extra-biblical examples show that the particular grammatical inconsistencies noted in the biblical texts are really part of the normal literary style of the ancient Near East and need not be explained by recourse to a theory of editorial reworking.

No consensus has therefore emerged on what portion of the present book may confidently be assigned to *Urdeuteronomium* (Eissfeldt 1965, 173-76; Fohrer 1968, 169-72). There is simply general agreement that the 622 lawbook contained at most chapters 5–26, 28 (Freedman 1962, 715; Nicholson 1967, 22; Weinfeld, *EncJud*, 5:1574), and it may well have contained less. Von Rad (1962a, 832) stated more than forty-five years ago: "Obviously the zeal for literary analysis has flagged for a long time." The quest for *Urdeuteronomium* had reached a dead end, with nothing more known about the contents of *Urdeuteronomium* than was purportedly known at the turn of the century (Lundbom 1976, 294).

Northern Provenance

Another search into Deuteronomy's prehistory was carried out during the last century, viz., an inquiry into the book's provenance. It began largely with Adam Welch, who argued that the book of Deuteronomy came originally from North Israel (Welch 1924, 184-85, 190-91). Welch said the author of 27:4

evidently regarded the sanctuary at Ebal as being the first which was erected in Palestine, and as owing its authority to the direct command of the great lawgiver. Again we have a significant hint as to the provenance of the Deuteronomic code, for we are carried to Northern Israel and to one of its leading sanctuaries.

Welch found Deuteronomy's mandate for a single sanctuary only in chapter 12, although he argued that 12:1-7 was a later addition (1932, 205). His view of chapter 12 did not win the day, nor also his view that Deuteronomy was composed in the tenth century, but his idea about Deuteronomy having a northern provenance had considerable impact (Albright 1957b, 315; G. E. Wright, 326; von Rad 1962a, 836; 1966a, 94; Nicholson 1967, 58-82; Fohrer 1968, 175).

The view of Alt (1953b) that Deuteronomy was a restoration program in North Israel after the fall of Samaria in 722 has little to recommend it, and is best laid to rest (Nicholson 1967, 80-81). The two passages testing for inauthentic prophets, in chapters 13 and 18, seem to me to be a legacy of Northern Israel's experience with prophets during the reign of Ahab (Lundbom 1996, 309-12). Nicholson (1967, 69) sees "vital contacts between Deuteronomy and the teaching of the prophetic party in northern Israel," saying that a good case can be made for Deuteronomy owing its origin to prophetic circles in northern Israel (p. 79).

Others have argued that Deuteronomy originated largely in Judah (Lohfink; Weinfeld), perhaps even before the time of Hezekiah. The passage on judges in 16:18-20 points to the reign of Jehoshaphat (873-849), who carried out a judicial reform in Judah (2 Chr 19:4-11) and is reported by the Chronicler as having sent out princes and Levites to teach people the law (2 Chr 17:7-9). Ahab reigned in the north and Jehoshaphat in the south during the mid-ninth century, with both the Deuteronomic Historian and the Chronicler reporting good relations between the two kings (1 Kgs 22:45[44]; 2 Chr 18:1-3). Ahab is not likely to have sponsored an early Deuteronomic program, but Jehoshaphat could have (Albright 1957b, 320).

If the book of Deuteronomy or portions of it did originate in North Israel, that book was most likely brought to Jerusalem after the fall of Samaria in 722. Fohrer (1968, 175) thinks it was deposited in the temple in the time of Hezekiah. To what extent it could have played a role in Hezekiah's reform before coming to light in the time of Josiah is the question to which we now turn.

Hezekiah's Reform

De Wette's view that Deuteronomy was written shortly before its discovery in the temple has been challenged over the years, by many rejected outright,

Introduction

largely because the time span between the young Josiah's accession in 640 and the discovery of the lawbook in 622 is too brief. It is usually assumed that the newly found lawbook had been lost for some time (Driver 1895, liv-lv), for which reason many scholars have pushed back the date of Deuteronomy's composition to the reigns of Manasseh (687-642) or Hezekiah (715-687). Manasseh's reign was nearly a half-century of idolatrous worship, yet some argue that during this time a reform document could have been written for the future, if and when an opportunity came for its use (Nicholson 1967, 101-2). Still, it is a stretch to imagine a vibrant document like Deuteronomy being written during the reign of Manasseh. Pfeiffer (1948, 180) says: "During the reign of Manasseh D[euteronomy] would have been consigned to the flames, like Jeremiah's book later on (Jer. 36:23)."

A reform document such as Deuteronomy is more likely to have emanated from a reform in progress (like documents of the Reformation, or more recently Vatican II), favoring the reign of Hezekiah over the reign of Manasseh. In the Bible, a reform by Hezekiah is reported briefly in 2 Kgs 18:4, 22[= Isa 36:7], where it says that Hezekiah removed high places, altars, and other objectionable cult symbols in a move to purify Yahweh worship and centralize it in Jerusalem. In 2 Chronicles 29–31 this reform gets extended coverage. The Chronicler states that the good king began in his first year to make repairs in the temple (2 Chr 29:3), concluding his reform and other faithful acts before Sennacherib invaded Judah and encamped against its fortified cities (2 Chr 32:1).

Wellhausen (1957, 25) did not believe such a reform ever took place. He doubted the report in 2 Kings and dismissed out of hand the account of the Chronicler who, in his view, was not a credible historical source. More recently Na'aman (1995) and Fried (2002) have challenged the results of archaeological studies pointing to a reform by Hezekiah, stating that the research does not support a reform. Besides being dismissive of the biblical accounts, they both misconstrue and outrun the archaeological evidence they cite and base too much on "arguments from silence."

The Deuteronomic Historian and the Chronicler agree that Hezekiah carried out reforming activities at the beginning of his reign. There are, to be sure, chronological problems associated with Hezekiah's accession and uncertainty too about the campaign(s) of Sennacherib against Judah and Jerusalem; nevertheless, a window of opportunity for carrying out a reform is arguable between 712 and 701 (Rainey 1994, 333 says between 715 and 701). Many scholars have accepted the biblical testimony that Hezekiah did carry out a reform, one that did away with objectionable objects of worship and aimed at creating a central sanctuary in Jerusalem. This reform was short-lived (Nicholson 1967, 99: between 705 and 701), as many reforms are, but not so short-lived that Deuteronomy could not have been written while it was in progress, or else soon after. Freedman (1987d, 20-26) argued that the books of the eighth-century prophets, Amos, Hosea, Isaiah, and Micah, were assembled during the reign of Hezekiah to mark the destruction of the northern kingdom by the Assyrians in 722, the reason being that Israel failed to repent of its rebellion against Yahweh and gross violation of covenant demands, also because of Judah's deliverance from the Assyrians in 701, at which time Hezekiah repented of his rebellion and violation of covenant demands (cf. Jer 26:19). Freedman says: "Only a king of such stature and ethical sensitivity, as Hezekiah is described to be, could and would have encouraged such a work" (Freedman 1987d, 24).

Most current scholars state their views on the composition of Deuteronomy in general terms, usually content to say that the book was written in the seventh century, or between the reigns of Hezekiah and Josiah. It is difficult to be more precise when we do not know more. For a fuller discussion of Hezekiah's reform and issues related to the reform, see Excursus 1.

A New Quest for *Urdeuteronomium*

Since Wellhausen, a change has taken place in appraising the work of the Chronicler. Wellhausen believed the Chronicler was late and unreliable. Welch (1939) viewed the Chronicler more positively, but his assessment has been largely ignored. The change occurred with Albright (1957b, 273; 1963, 76-77), whose views survived in the work of his students: John Bright (1981, 229), also Frank M. Cross and David Noel Freedman (1953). Cross and Freedman pointed out that so far as the Josianic reform was concerned, the Chronicler's scheme of events correlated better with the extrabiblical records documenting Assyria's decline. Nicholson (1967, 11-12) in his overview therefore concludes that the Chronicler's report of the Josianic reform is basically reliable, which is what Albright concluded about the Chronicler's report of the reform of Hezekiah.

In an earlier work (Lundbom 1976), I proposed that the Chronicler's account of the Josianic reform be given precedence over the account of the Deuteronomic Historian (DH), which would mean putting the main purge of pagan worship in 628, rather than 622, and seeing the legal portions of Deuteronomy as being the moving force behind the reform activity in that year. Deuteronomy 5–26, 28 — or better, Deuteronomy 1–28 — was not the lost lawbook. The lawbook newly found in 622 was the much briefer Song of Moses in Deuteronomy 32.

Two lines of evidence point to one and the same conclusion. The first is this: Two stanzas of the Song of Moses (Deut 32:15-22) compare closely in content to a portion of Huldah's oracle in 2 Kgs 22:16-20. Huldah was the prophetess to whom Hilkiah went with the lawbook in order to obtain a divine oracle. She heard the scroll read, or else read it herself, and responded with a two-part oracle, the first part directed to the nation (vv. 16-17) and the second part to the king (vv. 18-20). It is the first part that draws upon the Song of Moses. The relevant texts are the following:

Deut 32:15-22

15 וַיִּשְׁמַן יְשֻׁרוּן וַיִּבְעָט שָׁמַנְתָּ עָבִיתָ כָּשִׂיתָ
וַיִּטֹּשׁ אֱלוֹהַּ עָשָׂהוּ וַיְנַבֵּל צוּר יְשֻׁעָתוֹ
16 יַקְנִאֻהוּ בְּזָרִים בְּתוֹעֵבֹת יַכְעִיסֻהוּ
17 יִזְבְּחוּ לַשֵּׁדִים לֹא אֱלֹהַּ אֱלֹהִים לֹא יְדָעוּם
חֲדָשִׁים מִקָּרֹב בָּאוּ לֹא שְׂעָרוּם אֲבֹתֵיכֶם
18 צוּר יְלָדְךָ תֶּשִׁי וַתִּשְׁכַּח אֵל מְחֹלְלֶךָ

19 וַיַּרְא יְהוָה וַיִּנְאָץ מִכַּעַס בָּנָיו וּבְנֹתָיו
20 וַיֹּאמֶר אַסְתִּירָה פָנַי מֵהֶם אֶרְאֶה מָה אַחֲרִיתָם
כִּי דוֹר תַּהְפֻּכֹת הֵמָּה בָּנִים לֹא־אֵמֻן בָּם
21 הֵם קִנְאוּנִי בְלֹא־אֵל כִּעֲסוּנִי בְּהַבְלֵיהֶם
וַאֲנִי אַקְנִיאֵם בְּלֹא־עָם בְּגוֹי נָבָל אַכְעִיסֵם
22 כִּי־אֵשׁ קָדְחָה בְאַפִּי וַתִּיקַד עַד־שְׁאוֹל תַּחְתִּית
וַתֹּאכַל אֶרֶץ וִיבֻלָהּ וַתְּלַהֵט מוֹסְדֵי הָרִים

2 Kgs 22:16-17

16 כֹּה אָמַר יְהוָה
הִנְנִי מֵבִיא רָעָה אֶל־הַמָּקוֹם הַזֶּה וְעַל־יֹשְׁבָיו
אֵת כָּל־דִּבְרֵי הַסֵּפֶר אֲשֶׁר קָרָא מֶלֶךְ יְהוּדָה
17 תַּחַת אֲשֶׁר עֲזָבוּנִי וַיְקַטְּרוּ לֵאלֹהִים אֲחֵרִים
לְמַעַן הַכְעִיסֵנִי בְּכֹל מַעֲשֵׂה יְדֵיהֶם
וְנִצְּתָה חֲמָתִי בַּמָּקוֹם הַזֶּה וְלֹא תִכְבֶּה

Deut 32:15-22

15 Yes, Jeshurun got fat and kicked;
       you got fat, you grew thick, you became gorged.
    Then he abandoned the God who made him,
       and took to be foolish the Rock of his salvation.
16 They made him jealous with strangers,
       with abominations *they provoked him.*
17 *They sacrificed* to demons, no gods,
       gods they had not known.
    New ones recently come in,
       your fathers were not awed by them.

18 *The Rock* that begot you, *you neglected,*
   and *you forgot the God* who bore you in travail.

19 So Yahweh saw and spurned
   because of *the provocation* of his sons and daughters.
20 And he said, I will hide my face from them,
   I will see what their end will be.
   For a generation of perversities they are,
   children in whom is no faithfulness.
21 They, they have made me jealous with a no-god,
   they provoked me with their nothings.
   So I, I will make them jealous with a no-people,
   with a foolish nation I will provoke them.
22 For *a fire is kindled in my anger,*
   and it will burn to the depths of Sheol.
   Yes, it will consume the earth and its yield
   and set ablaze the mountains' foundations.

2 Kgs 22:16-17

16 Thus says Yahweh:
   Behold I will bring evil upon this place and upon its inhabitants —
   all the things of the book which the king of Judah has read.
17 Because *they have forsaken me and have burned incense to other gods,* that *they might provoke me with all the work of their hands.* Therefore *my wrath will be kindled* against this place *and it will not be quenched.*

One can immediately see that while the vocabularies of the two passages are somewhat different, the substance is the same. In both we note: (1) that Israel is indicted because she has *forgotten* Yahweh and *provoked him by sacrificing to other gods;* and (2) that Yahweh's *wrath* is promised to *burn* in judgment like an *unquenchable fire.* Huldah has restated the message of the Song in the current idiom, or else the DH has stylized her speech using the current idiom (so Driver 1895, xlv). The result, in either case, is the oracle as we now have it. Since this exact combination of ideas is not to be found elsewhere in the OT in the way it appears in these two passages, we may conclude that Huldah drew the substance of her indictment against Israel from the Song of Moses.

The second bit of evidence comes from a rhetorical structure in the prose frame to the Song. In Deut 31:24-30 and 32:44-46 a keyword chiasmus makes Moses' "song" (שִׁירָה) into a "law" (תּוֹרָה), with "words" (דְּבָרִים), a good Deuteronomic term, mediating in between:

31:24	אֶת־דִּבְרֵי הַתּוֹרָה־הַזֹּאת
28	אֵת הַדְּבָרִים הָאֵלֶּה
30	אֶת־דִּבְרֵי הַשִּׁירָה הַזֹּאת
32:44	אֶת־כָּל־דִּבְרֵי הַשִּׁירָה־הַזֹּאת
45	אֶת־כָּל־הַדְּבָרִים הָאֵלֶּה
46	אֶת־כָּל־דִּבְרֵי הַתּוֹרָה הַזֹּאת

31:24	the words of *this law*
28	*these words*
30	the words of *this song*
32:44	all the words of *this song*
45	all *these words*
46	all the words of *this law*

One final piece of evidence serves to connect the Song of Moses to the lawbook of 622. The expression, סֵפֶר הַתּוֹרָה ("book of the law"), which in Deut 31:26 refers to the scroll on which the Song of Moses — not the entire Deuteronomic code — was written, occurs also in 2 Kgs 22:8, where it refers to the temple lawbook. The identification is thus complete: *Deuteronomy 32 is the lawbook Hilkiah found in the temple in 622.*

Some scholars (Kaufmann 1960, 175; Holladay 1966, 26; 2004, 73-74) have suggested that the Song of Moses be included in *Urdeuteronomium*, but if added to a document containing 5–26, 28, or 1–28, we have a scroll rather large to have been read three times in one day. It is possible, but not likely. It is better, therefore, to take only the Song of Moses as the lawbook of 622. In my view, the Song is the core of the second supplement (chs. 31–34) to the First Edition, this supplement having been added after the Song's discovery in the temple. This final expansion in our present book of Deuteronomy could have been completed in the latter years of Josiah, at the same time the First Edition of the Deuteronomic History was written.

What then are we to make of the narrative in 2 Kings 22–23, which leads us to believe that all the reform activity came about because of the lawbook's discovery in 622? The passage out of chronological order in the scheme of the DH appears to be 2 Kgs 23:4-20. The purge reported there took place six years earlier (2 Chr 34:3-7). My solution would be to take 2 Kgs 23:4-20, which describes the purge, as a separate account that the DH has incorporated into his narration of the Josianic reform. It speaks of the "book of the covenant" (2 Kgs 23:2-3, 21), which as Carpenter (1883, 277) noted years ago, was a title well-suited for the Deuteronomic Code, beginning as it does with the "covenant" of

Horeb and ending with the "covenant" of Moab (5:2; 28:69[29:1]). We can then proceed to discover another rhetorical structure for 2 Kgs 22:8–23:25, even if we remain unable to judge the DH's knowledge or lack of knowledge about how the reform activity actually played out. It is reasonable to assume that he did know the actual sequence of events, simply choosing for whatever reason to schematize his reporting of them.

The DH intends to make the purge the center and climax of his narrative. We know it is the climax because of the space he gives it: seventeen verses compared to five by the Chronicler. But it is also the center, as we can see by observing a keyword chiasmus in the prose frame to the account. This is a structure similar to the one framing the Song of Moses in Deut 31:24-30 and 32:44-46:

2 Kings 22:8–23:25

סֵפֶר הַתּוֹרָה מָצָאתִי בְּבֵית יהוה	22:8
אֶת־דִּבְרֵי סֵפֶר הַתּוֹרָה	11
אֶת־כָּל־דִּבְרֵי סֵפֶר הַבְּרִית הַנִּמְצָא בְּבֵית יהוה	23:2
אֶת־דִּבְרֵי הַבְּרִית הַזֹּאת הַכְּתֻבִים עַל־הַסֵּפֶר הַזֶּה	3
Account of the Purge	4-20
כַּכָּתוּב עַל סֵפֶר הַבְּרִית הַזֶּה	21
אֶת־דִּבְרֵי הַתּוֹרָה הַכְּתֻבִים עַל־הַסֵּפֶר אֲשֶׁר מָצָא . . . בֵּית יהוה	24
כְּכֹל תּוֹרַת מֹשֶׁה	25

22:8	I have found *the book of the law* in the house of Yahweh
11	the words of *the book of the law*
23:2	all the words of *the book of the covenant* that had been found in the house of Yahweh
3	the words of *this covenant* that were written in *this book*
4-20	Account of the Purge
21	as it is written in *this book of the covenant*
24	the words of *the law* that were written in *the book* that [Hilkiah] . . . found in the house of Yahweh
25	according to all *the law of Moses*

The account in 2 Kgs 22:8–23:25 is a conflation at two points: (1) it combines the purge of 628 with whatever reform measures took place in 622, mak-

Introduction

ing it appear that Josiah undertook a single purge of pagan worship centers after the lawbook was found; and (2) it combines a "(book of the) law" from Moses (22:3-20; 23:24-25) with a "book of the covenant" (23:1-3, 21-23), making it appear that a single temple scroll inspired Huldah's oracle, formed the basis for Josiah's covenant renewal ceremony, led to the purge of pagan worship centers, and guided the king to host the grandest Passover in Jerusalem since the days of the Judges. The "(book of the) law" was the Song of Moses (32); the "book of the covenant" was the First Edition of Deuteronomy (1–28). A conflation of the same sort occurred in Deuteronomy 31–34, where the Song of Moses was integrated into the First Edition of Deuteronomy and made a part of Moses' ever-expanding collection of "torah" (Lundbom 1990).

Some earlier scholars believed that 2 Kings 22–23 altered or schematized events in Josiah's reign in order to create the impression that Deuteronomy was Josiah's lawbook, but they did so to argue for an exilic or postexilic date of Deuteronomy (Nicholson 1967, 4-7). I agree that the events in 2 Kings 22–23 have been schematized to create the impression desired by the DH, but I do not think an exilic or postexilic date for the book is at all likely. As noted earlier, 2 Kings 22–23 is the climax to a First Edition of the Deuteronomic History, in my view a preexilic work.

The Question of Authorship

With critical theory concluding that Moses was not the author of Deuteronomy, nor of the Pentateuch as a whole, the question was then: "Who wrote Deuteronomy?" Carpenter (1883), Driver (1895, xxv-xxix), and others emphasized the prophetic character of Deuteronomy, Driver believing that the work, although legal in nature, nevertheless built on foundations laid by the prophets, mainly Hosea and Isaiah. He called Deuteronomy a "prophetic lawbook."

Along with Wellhausen and others of his time, Driver saw the prophets as moral giants in ancient Israel, individuals who "held up before the people high conceptions of life and duty." Deuteronomy was the spiritual heir of Hosea, joining him in repudiating nature worship and acknowledging Yahweh as the true giver of earth's bounty. Driver says Deuteronomy agreed with Hosea in giving prominence to the emotional side of religion — love, affection, and sympathy are all present, particularly love. This love is a moral love, limited when necessary by the demands of righteousness; thus idolatry and immorality cannot be tolerated or condoned by it.

Driver pointed to the monotheistic creed of Deuteronomy (4:35, 39; 6:4; 7:9; 10:17) as another development of prophetic teaching. Deuteronomy preaches and teaches monotheism more formally and explicitly than earlier biblical books. The single sanctuary, in his view, was the corollary to the monotheistic idea. That worship at one Jerusalem altar developed later into a false religion of security (Jer 7:1-15) did not render invalid Deuteronomy's view at an earlier stage.

At the same time, Driver (1895, xxx) says that with priestly institutions the author of Deuteronomy has greater sympathy than with prophets generally. He evinces a warm regard for the priestly tribe; he guards its privileges (18:1-8), demands obedience for its decisions (24:8; cf. 17:10-12), and commends its members to Israelite benevolence (12:18-19; 14:27, 29, etc.). This author has no desire to see ceremonial observances current at the time abolished; sacrifice, though not emphasized, is taken for granted. Offerings on which Deuteronomy lays the greatest stress are those expressive of gratitude to God as Giver of all good things in the land (14:22-27; 15:19-23; 16:10, 15, 17; 26:10). Religious feasts are to be occasions of gladness before Yahweh and a display of generous hospitality towards the destitute (12:7, 12, 18; 14:26-27; 16:11, 14; 26:11). In Deuteronomy the tribe of Levi is confirmed in its possession of priestly rights, and it alone is to supply ministers for the sanctuary (Driver 1895, xxv).

The term "Levites" in Deuteronomy refers to all priests. The expression, הַכֹּהֲנִים הַלְוִיִּם, "the priests, the Levites" (= the Levitical priests), appears in 17:9, 18; 18:1; 24:8; 27:9 and other literature earlier than Nehemiah, e.g., Josh 3:3; 8:33; Jer 33:18; Ezek 43:19; 44:15. It need not be taken, then, as an archaism by someone writing in the postexilic period. According to Levine (1993, 104-5, 449, 450), stratification of the tribe into two groups, priests and Levites, first occurs explicitly in Numbers (chs. 3–4, 8, 16-17). There is no reference to the subordination of Levites in Exodus. On the priests and Levites, see further G. E. Wright (1954) and Emerton (1962).

The question of authorship, therefore, took a different turn with von Rad (1953; 1962a, 835-37), who believed that although Deuteronomy reflected an ancient Shechemite cultic festival (11:26-32), the preachers behind its sermons were post-701 Levitical priests from the Judean countryside. Von Rad cites Neh 8:1-8, where the Levites instruct as Ezra reads people the law. The Chronicler, too, makes numerous references to the Levites as teaching priests (2 Chr 15:3; 17:7-9; 35:3). One notes that Deut 31:9 says the Deuteronomic code, after being written down by Moses, was put into the hands of the Levitical priests. In Deut 20:2-4, too, the (Levitical) priests have a prominent role in addressing people before Israel is to go to war. Von Rad's views were accepted by G. E. Wright, Muilenburg (1959, 348-350), and others, with Wolff (1956) arguing that Deuteronomy owed its origin to Levites in northern Israel who had been excluded from sanctuaries at Bethel and Dan by Jeroboam I (1 Kgs 12:31-32). Hosea, in Wolff's view, was linked to this circle of Levites.

Priestly authorship of Deuteronomy came under scrutiny with Weinfeld

(1967; 1972, 158-71; *EncJud* 5:1578-79), who argued that the authors of Deuteronomy were scribes. Weinfeld agreed that Deuteronomy contained material of northern provenance, but was not surviving oral torah from preaching Levites. What we have in Deuteronomy is rather a written document compiled by scribes of the Jerusalem court. Such a conclusion, he argues, is supported by wisdom elements in the book, e.g., the education of children and various humanistic laws, which have no counterpart in any other pentateuchal book (Weinfeld 1960a). Numerous parallels exist also between Proverbs and Deuteronomy, e.g., Deut 19:14 with Prov 22:28; Deut 23:17[16] with Prov 30:10; and Deut 25:13-16 with Prov 20:10, 23. Citing ANE treaty parallels to Deuteronomy, Weinfeld argues that scribes must have authored Deuteronomy, since only they would have been familiar with the treaty structures.

Weinfeld makes his case for scribal authorship of Deuteronomy, but his case against priestly authorship falls short of being decisive. Besides the evidence that von Rad presents for priestly authorship are biblical texts putting the torah in the hands of priests (Jer 18:18; Ezek 7:26). Also, 2 Chr 34:13 tells us that "some of the Levites were scribes," which indicates that Weinfeld may have overdrawn his separation of the two vocations. This reference in Chronicles is important, since it occurs in the context of the Josianic reform. In Nehemiah 8, Ezra is called both "Ezra the priest" and "Ezra the scribe" (Neh 8:1, 9). If these overlaps in terminology correspond to reality in preexilic times, which is not hard to imagine (Mowinckel 1955, 206; Muilenburg 1970a, 230-31), Weinfeld's argument that Deuteronomy is authored by scribes, not Levites, loses much of its force. The authors of Deuteronomy could have been both Levites and scribes. Finally, a presence of wisdom elements in Deuteronomy is not a sure pointer to scribal authorship. Amos and Jeremiah are brim full of wisdom teaching, and both are prophets, not scribes. Priests, scribes, and prophets from the eighth to sixth century, all shared a common intellectual and rhetorical tradition, fully capable of producing the discourse and teaching of Deuteronomy.

ANCIENT NEAR EASTERN TREATIES

By the mid-1950s the focus of Deuteronomy studies had shifted to the Hittite vassal treaties (1450-1200) unearthed at Boghazköy, published two decades earlier. George Mendenhall, in an important study (1955), pointed out the formal similarities between these treaties concluded between suzerains and their vassals, and the biblical covenants. Dennis McCarthy (1963, 109-40) went on to make it even more clear that the covenant form in Deuteronomy was the real beneficiary of the new comparison. Hittite treaties typically contained six elements: (1) a preamble, introducing the speaker (cf. Deut 1:1-5); (2) a historical prologue (cf. chs. 1–4); (3) the stipulations (cf. chs. 5; 12–26); (4) provisions for depositing the document in the temple and a periodic reading (31:9-13, 26); (5) a list of the gods as witnesses (no parallel in Deuteronomy); and (6) blessings and curses (cf. chs. 27–28).

In 1958 D. J. Wiseman published the Vassal Treaties of Esarhaddon, which were shown to have striking parallels to the maledictions in Deuteronomy 28. Subsequent studies have therefore focused on these treaties rather than those of the Hittites (D. J. McCarthy 1963, 68-79; Weinfeld 1991, 6-9; 1972, 59-157; 1976a; 1992b, 169-171), one reason being that they date from the same time as Deuteronomy, the seventh century. After examining these treaties, Weinfeld judged Deuteronomy to be a "loyalty oath" imposed by a suzerain (Yahweh) on his vassal (Israel) prior to a leadership change (Moses to Joshua). Similarities between the two were seen to extend even into the language, e.g., the terms for loyalty in both were "to go after" (= to follow), "to fear," and "to hearken to the voice of"; and in both the vassal was commanded "to love" the suzerain "with all the heart and all the soul" (cf. Deut 6:5). On the use of the term "love" in the ANE treaties, see Moran 1963b. It is now generally accepted that these international treaties — both Hittite and Assyrian — influenced the form of the biblical covenants, particularly Deuteronomy (Weinfeld 1991, 9). Phillips (1983, 2) argues that the treaty form entered Israelite theology only after the fall of the northern kingdom, which would bring it into the time when Deuteronomy was written.

ANCIENT HEBREW RHETORIC

Rhetorical Prose

Since the beginning of pentateuchal criticism it has been recognized that Deuteronomy has a distinctive rhetorical style, characterized by stereotyped vocabulary and phraseology (Driver 1895, lxxvii-xci; 1913, 99-102; Weinfeld 1972, 320-65). Its prose teems with *accumulatio,* i.e., nouns heaped up in twos, threes, and fours, and longer phrases balanced rhythmically in parallelism, also *asyndeton.* This prose occurs also in the Deuteronomic History, particularly Kings, and in the book of Jeremiah (Lundbom 1999, 126-27). Deuteronomy, according to Driver, is fond of the emphatic form of וּן in the second and third person plurals of the Imperfect, of לְבָב (47x) over לֵב, and of אָנֹכִי (56x) over אֲנִי. He believes these preferences are probably due to the writer's sense of what harmonized best with the oratorical rhythm of his discourse. In Deuteronomy also are the frequent changes between second singular and second plural forms, about which we spoke earlier, and these must be reckoned as another rhetorical feature of Deuteronomic discourse.

Introduction

Preached Law

Gerhard von Rad, following the lead of August Klostermann (1893), said of Deuteronomy in comparison to the Book of the Covenant:

> Deuteronomy is not divine law in codified form, but preaching about the commandments — at least, the commandments appear in a form where they are very much interspersed with parenesis. (von Rad 1953, 15; cf. 1966b, 30)

The point was made also by Breit (1933) and by Driver in his *Deuteronomy* commentary. Driver saw Deuteronomy's rhetorical discourse as aiming to inculcate religious and moral principles, being therefore of greater importance than the historical and legislative discourse in the book (Driver 1895, xix, lxxvii-lxxxviii). So far as Deuteronomy being a lawbook was concerned, Driver took it as a manual addressed to the people intended for popular use (Driver 1895, xxvi). H. Wheeler Robinson (1980, 3) said the exhortations in Deuteronomy could be compared with a sermon:

> It is a sermon so reported as to preserve the spiritual warmth of a Bernard preaching the Crusade, the flaming zeal of a Savonarola kindling the Florentine fire of vanities; whilst with this more passionate feeling against idolatry there is a noble humanitarianism, a consideration for the stranger and the helpless, an appeal to deep human sympathies, not unworthy of a Francis of Assisi.

Von Rad's desire was to advance the study of Deuteronomy from a rhetorical and homiletical standpoint. His method was form criticism, worked out with consummate skill in "The Form-Critical Problem of the Hexateuch" (1966b) and *Studies in Deuteronomy* (1953). Von Rad also initiated a search for Deuteronomy's *Sitz im Leben* ("situation in life"), paying particular attention to Deuteronomy 27 and Joshua 24. He concluded that Deuteronomy reflected a covenant renewal ceremony at Shechem, appropriating the view of Adam Welch (1924) that the book's provenance was northern Israel. But, as we have said, von Rad viewed the preachers behind Deuteronomy's sermons as post-701 Levitical priests from the Judean countryside (2 Chr 17:7-9). In any case, Deuteronomy contained all the marks of a scroll having been read aloud to a gathered assembly.

Rhetoric and Composition

Despite the consuming interest in treaty forms among Deuteronomy scholars of the past half-century, James Muilenburg felt in the 1950s that more work in this homiletical treasure needed to be done along rhetorical lines. He said:

> the large and varied terminology associated with covenantal formulations requires closer attention, the composition and rhetoric and structural forms need to be studied more carefully. (Muilenburg 1959, 348)

To some extent it was already being done. In the 1960s, Roman Catholic scholars at the Pontifical Biblical Institute in Rome were applying to the Old Testament a method of rhetorical research practiced earlier in the century by Scripture scholars such as A. Condamin (1905; 1920; 1933), A. Bea, and H. Galbiati (Lohfink 1960, 123 n. 2). Two scholars were engaged in Deuteronomic research: William L. Moran (1969), and Norbert Lohfink (1963a; 1968). On the Protestant side, foundational work on "chiasmus" had been done by University of Chicago–trained Nils W. Lund (1930; 1933; 1942), dean of North Park Theological Seminary in Chicago. The methods these scholars employed were not unlike Muilenburg's own (1953; 1956; 1969), seeking to locate in the text keyword, motif, and speaker distributions forming inclusios and chiasms (concentric inclusions).

Lohfink (1963b; 1976, 229), in discovering these structures, did not concur with von Rad that Deuteronomy betrayed a "preaching style," noting that the book's language had many ties with language of the court and wisdom language, also that the international treaties possessed a rhetorical cast and were meant to be read aloud in solemn public ceremonies. With respect to Deuteronomy's final composition, Lohfink followed Kleinert (1872, 167) in arguing that the book was an "archive," its main divisions marked by the headings in 1:1; 4:44; 28:69(29:1); and 33:1 (Lohfink 1962, 32-34; 1968, 7-9; 1976, 229; 1992). Although not giving up entirely the view that Deuteronomy preserved traditions from northern Israel, the accent for Lohfink (1963b) was now upon a written document of Jerusalem origin, not an oral document of northern provenance.

Rhetorical work in Deuteronomy continued apace in the following decades with tangible results, e.g., the work of G. Seitz (1971). The present writer, besides the work noted earlier in connection with the Song of Moses, has shown in other studies that inclusio and framing devices are the controlling structures within Deuteronomy 1–28 (Lundbom 1996) and that a framing mode of composition has been used in Deuteronomy 29–34 (Lundbom 1990). The inclusio and chiasmus, along with other framing devices, are well attested in the poetry and prose of Jeremiah (Lundbom 1975; 1999; 2004a; 2004b), which de-

Introduction

rive from the same general period. On the method of rhetorical criticism as practiced in the OT generally, and in Jeremiah in particular, see Muilenburg (1969) and Lundbom (1997).

Rhetorical criticism has advanced our understanding of Deuteronomy's composition at two important junctures. The summary statements of 4:44-49 and 28:69(29:1) are shown not to be superscriptions, as commonly supposed, but subscriptions, the function of which is to effect closure within the Deuteronomic discourse (Lundbom 1996). There has been ongoing debate whether 28:69 is a superscription or subscription (Nicholson 1967, 21 n. 6), perhaps in part because of the section markings before and after verse 69, and also because some MSS of the LXX, the Vg, and certain English Versions take verse 69 as 29:1. But it never seems to have occurred to earlier critical scholars that 4:44-49 could be a subscription. These verses continued to be viewed as a "second introduction" to the legal material in the book (Nicholson 1967, 19-20). But once it is recognized that the controlling structure in all of Deuteronomy 1-28 is the inclusio, it makes considerably more sense to take both 4:44-49 and 28:69 as forming inclusios with the superscription in 1:1-5 (Lundbom 1996, 302-4, 312-13).

Keywords showing that the summary in 4:44-49 is intended to repeat and create an inclusio with the summary in 1:1-5 are the following:

Deut 1:1-5	Deut 4:44-49
	And this is the law
Moses spoke . . . all Israel	Moses spoke . . . children of Israel
beyond the Jordan	beyond the Jordan
Arabah	
Moses . . . struck down	
Sihon king of the Amorites	Sihon king of the Amorites
who dwelt in Heshbon	who dwelt in Heshbon
	Moses . . . struck down
Og king of the Bashan	Og king of the Bashan
beyond the Jordan	beyond the Jordan
	Arabah
this law	

Chapters 1-4 are then the proper introduction to the Decalogue and Deuteronomic law, which is what Driver and others have taken them to be (*pace* Noth), but we must include all of chapter 4, not bracket out 4:44-49 as a "second introduction." Noth may still be correct in viewing chapters 1–3(4) as an Introduction to the Deuteronomic History, but if so, the chapters take on a dual function: initially introducing the Decalogue and Deuteronomic law, then later introducing the Deuteronomic History once Deuteronomy has been integrated into the Deuteronomic History. This integration will have occurred in the early exile. There is no longer any reason to follow Noth in taking Deuteronomy 1-4 as an exilic work.

In similar fashion, the summary statement in 28:69(29:1) makes another inclusio with the book's superscription in 1:1-5 (Lundbom 1996, 312-13):

> *These are the words* that *Moses* spoke to *all Israel* beyond the Jordan ... beyond the Jordan, *in the land of Moab,* Moses sought to make plain *this law:* (Deut 1:1-5)

> *These are the words of the covenant* that Yahweh commanded *Moses* to cut with *the children of Israel in the land of Moab,* besides the covenant that he cut with them in Horeb. (Deut 28:69[29:1])

The controlling structures in Deuteronomy are rhetorical, dictated by canons of Hebrew rhetoric, known and practiced in the late eighth and early seventh century. With 28:69 taken as a subscription, functioning to bring an initial work on Deuteronomic law and covenant to a conclusion, chapters 1-28 become the first identifiable book of Deuteronomy, herein called the First Edition. A written (Deuteronomic) law is referred to already in 28:58 and 61.

The process from Deuteronomy to Pentateuch can be provisionally sketched as follows:

> Deuteronomy 1-28 issued in a First Edition, perhaps in Hezekiah's reign
> Deuteronomy 29-30 added as a supplement to the First Edition sometime between the reigns of Hezekiah and Josiah, or in Josiah's reign
> Deuteronomy 31-34 added as a second supplement to the First Edition and Supplement I in Josiah's reign, after the temple lawbook (the Song of Moses) was found in 622. The Song now becomes Mosaic "law" along with the rest of Deuteronomy (31:26; 32:46)
> Deuteronomy 1-34 made the introduction to the larger Deuteronomic History (Deuteronomy to 2 Kings), completed in the early exile
> Primary History (Genesis to 2 Kings) completed ca. 560
> Pentateuch separated from the Primary History in the postexilic period, and canonized ca. 400

On the completion of the Primary History and the separation of the Pentateuch, see Freedman 1962.

Introduction

THE DEUTERONOMIC LAW CODE

The book of Deuteronomy contains the Decalogue in 5:6-21, following with its own law code in chapters 12–26, 28. In all of 5–26, 28 preaching is mixed in, with even the laws in 13–18 cast largely in homiletical form. The core of the Deuteronomic Code is casuistic law in chapters 19–25. According to 5:22, only the Decalogue was given to the people at Horeb; the Deuteronomic law was given separately to Moses (5:31), who was now presenting it to Israel in the plains of Moab (1:1-5; 4:44-49). This latter law contained the terms of the covenant made in Moab, to be distinguished from the covenant made at Horeb (28:69[29:1]; cf. 5:2-3). The Deuteronomic Code builds on earlier law in Exodus (JE), but not on Priestly law (P) contained in Exodus, Numbers, and Leviticus. It may indeed know of Priestly law, but does not build on it as systematically presented (Driver 1895, xiv). Deuteronomy also contains parallels with other ancient Near Eastern law, although the major law codes uncovered in excavations thus far are considerably older than Deuteronomy (2200 to 1300), which means one must simply be content with comparisons and contrasts, stopping short of any arguments for dependence of Deuteronomy upon older Near Eastern law.

Earlier Biblical Law

Critical theory has reached a broad consensus that the laws of Deuteronomy build on JE legislation in the book of Exodus. Exodus 20–23 is taken to be a legal collection from the early monarchy, to which the name "Covenant Code" is given. It begins with the Decalogue in Exod 20:1-17. Other important law from this earlier period is contained in Exod 13:3-16 and 34:10-26. The main parallels between the Covenant Code and the Deuteronomic Code are these:

Exod 21:1-11	Deut 15:12-18
Exod 22:15-16(22:16-17)	Deut 22:28-29
Exod 22:24-26(22:25-27)	Deut 24:10-13
Exod 23:4-5	Deut 22:1-4
Exod 23:8	Deut 16:19
Exod 23:14-19	Deut 16:1-17
Exod 23:19b	Deut 14:21b

Other overlaps exist. The Covenant Code has more laws dealing with personal injury (Exod 21:18-27) and liabilities relating to animals, personal goods, and property (Exod 21:28–22:14[22:15]) than Deuteronomy. Deuteronomy does not deal with damages or civil suits, which occupy a large part of the Covenant Code. It is concerned rather with protecting human individuals, particularly individuals who have little or no means of protecting themselves (Weinfeld 1961, 243; 1967, 261). The Deuteronomic Code contains only two laws on property: the law prohibiting removal of a landmark (19:14) and the law concerning just weights and measures (25:13-16). Both have parallels in Proverbs (Prov 11:1; 20:10, 23; 22:28; 23:10) and other wisdom literature of the ANE. For a fuller comparison between Deuteronomic law and the laws of Exodus, see Driver 1895, iii-xix; "Deuteronomy" in *JE*, 4:539; Weinfeld, *EncJud*, 5:1579-81.

Later Biblical Law

Priestly laws so-called are found in Exodus, Numbers, and Leviticus. They are concerned largely with cultic practice, which includes sacrifice, purity, and ceremonies of various description. Critical theory recognizes a separate law code in Leviticus 17–26, which has come to be called the "Holiness Code" (H). It is generally agreed that Deuteronomy is not dependent upon the Holiness Code (Driver 1895, xi-xiv; Weinfeld in *EncJud*, 5:1579; Milgrom 1991, 13-35), but whether it antedates all the Priestly legislation in Exodus, Numbers, and Leviticus is a debated question. Scholars following Wellhausen believed that Priestly law, dated to the postexilic period, was later than Deuteronomic law and dependent upon it. But Weinfeld (1972, 179-89) thinks that P and D are concurrent documents emanating from two preexilic literary schools: D from the royal court and P from the temple. Priestly law has a theocentric approach; Deuteronomy is anthropocentric, having its roots in wisdom teaching. For comparisons between Priestly law and Deuteronomy, see Driver 1895, iii-xix; "Deuteronomy" in *JE*, 4:540; Weinfeld 1972, 179-89; Milgrom 1973.

Ancient Near Eastern Law Codes

Archaeological excavations of the past century and a half have brought to light numerous law codes of the ANE, the major ones being:

> Code of Ur-Nammu (LUN), of Third Dynasty of Ur (ca. 2050; Good 1967, 2200; cf. *ANET*^{3}, 523-25; *COS* 2, 408-10)
> Code of Lipit-Ishtar (LI) of Isin (ca. 2017-1985; cf. *ANET*^{3}, 159-61; *COS* 2, 410-14)
> Laws of Eshnunna (LE), author unknown, reference to King Dadusha in the superscription (ca. 1800; *ANET*^{3}, 161-63; *COS* 2, 332-35)
> Code of Hammurabi (CH), king of Babylon (ca. 1700; *ANET*^{3}, 163-80; *COS* 2, 335-53)

Introduction

Middle Assyrian Laws (MAL) (ca. 1400; tablets from 1100; *ANET*³, 180-88; *COS* 2, 353-60)

Hittite Laws (HL) (ca. 1300; *ANET*³, 188-97; *COS* 2, 106-19)

To these major codes may be added fragmentary collections of Sumerian laws, e.g., "The Edict of Ammisaduqu" (1646-1626; *ANET*³, 526-28; *COS* 2, 362-64), and a fragmentary collection of "Neo-Babylonian Laws" (635-539; *ANET*³, 197-98; *COS* 2, 360-61). Older English works exist on (1) Laws of Eshnunna: Yaron (1969); (2) Old Babylonian and Neo-Babylonian laws: Johns (1904; 1914) and G. R. Driver and Miles (1952; 1955); (3) Assyrian laws: G. R. Driver and Miles (1935); and (4) Hittite laws: Neufeld (1951).

Study of these ancient nonbiblical law codes has brought to light two basic types of law in the OT: apodictic law and casuistic law. The important work here was done by Albrecht Alt. Alt noted that most of the Ten Commandments contain the second singular "you" together with an emphatic and unconditional "not" (לֹא), which makes them apodictic in form (Alt 1966c, 117-23). Commandments on keeping the Sabbath and honoring one's parents are positive, and also stated differently. The same obtains in the Decalogue of the Covenant Code. Other laws in Deuteronomy and the Covenant Code, also in law codes of the ANE, are stated in casuistic form: "If someone does such and such, then such and such will be the punishment" (Alt 1966c, 88-103). "The ordinances" (מִשְׁפָּטִים) of the Covenant Code (Exod 21:1) are casuistic law, beginning most often with the conjunction כִּי ("when"). Casuistic laws in Deuteronomy 24–25 occur in the midst of apodictic laws (24:14-16; 25:4, 13-14). Casuistic laws are suited for use in a court of law. Apodictic law, more absolute than law containing provisions for punishment, has no parallel in Mesopotamian law. Alt believed that apodictic law was distinctly Israelite and that casuistic law was taken over from the Canaanites after Israel's settlement in the land.

DEUTERONOMY AND THE PROPHETS

Earlier critical scholars, as we mentioned, called Deuteronomy a "prophetic law code." In the view of Wellhausen and his school it was the prophets who gave ancient Israel its high ethical and spiritual teaching. Deuteronomy was therefore thought to have originated among heirs to the great eighth-century prophets (H. W. Robinson 1907, 33-43; Pfeiffer 1948, 179-80; Nicholson 1967, xi). Pfeiffer believed that the teaching of the prophets, beginning with Amos, was too revolutionary to make an impact on the masses, so a Jerusalem priest, upon whom the prophetic teaching did make an impact, wrote a book of Moses that became the kernel of Deuteronomy. Whereas Amos talked about righteousness as a principle (Amos 5:24), Deuteronomy went on to define righteousness as "doing the commandments" (Deut 6:25). For Deuteronomy, as for Hosea, love for God is the essence of true religion (Deut 6:5), but Deuteronomy says love must be shown in keeping the commandments (7:9; 10:12-13; 11:1, 13, 22; 19:9).

So while the writer of Deuteronomy may be credited for bringing the revolutionary teaching of the eighth-century prophets to the masses, it doubtless happened that Amos and Hosea gradually achieved stature among the common people, especially after the northern kingdom fell to the Assyrians in 722. The book of Deuteronomy was therefore written with another purpose in mind, viz., to establish Moses as a "prophet" in Israel, one who predicted, among other things, that another like himself would arise in the latter days to speak words that Yahweh put into his mouth (Deut 18:15-18). When the book of Deuteronomy was brought to final completion, Moses had become prophet nonpareil, one greater than all who preceded him (34:10-12).

Scholars of this earlier period were more or less agreed that eighth-century prophetic preaching did not betray any indebtedness to Deuteronomy (Driver). Influence seemed to be in the reverse, although this doubtless owes something to the view that Deuteronomy in its written form could not be earlier than the reign of Hezekiah. Deuteronomy knows the election of Israel, about which Amos speaks, and it learned from Hosea about the love of God and Israel's obligation to reciprocate that love. The book, then, may very well owe a debt to the preaching of Amos and Hosea, confirming the view that its provenance is the northern kingdom of Israel.

Deuteronomy also contains parallels to Micah and Isaiah, prophets active in Judah in the late eighth century. But in each case influence one way or another is unclear. We must be content simply to draw parallels. With Jeremiah, influence of both the Song of Moses and core Deuteronomy is clear in the poetry and prose of this prophet, and the influence is considerable. Other seventh- and sixth-century prophets seem also to have been influenced by Deuteronomy, but parallels in diction and ideas are not what they are between Amos, Hosea, Jeremiah, and Deuteronomy. One can say, at the very least, that all the major prophets understood the conditional nature of the Horeb covenant and to this extent appropriated Deuteronomy's message that a nation in violation of the Horeb covenant would be punished by Yahweh.

AMOS

Amos was a shepherd and dresser of vines from Tekoa, a Judahite town just south of Jerusalem (Amos 1:1). In the middle of the eighth century he was found up at the northern sanctuary of Bethel (Amos 7), preaching judgment against nations of the region, especially northern Israel. Whether he preached in Israel over a longer period is not known. Judah, too, comes under indictment for rejecting Yahweh's law and not keeping his statutes (Amos 2:4), which could lie behind Deuteronomy's message that the covenant people must be sure to "keep the commandments, the statutes, and the ordinances" once they become settled in the land (Deut 4:1; 8:11, etc.).

In his preaching against northern Israel, Amos has earned the reputation of being Israel's greatest preacher of justice and righteousness, finding in this northern kingdom an appalling lack of both (Lundbom 2010a, 42-47). Among the other nations of the world, with whom Yahweh has no covenant, Amos finds inhumane and moral outrages, making them candidates, too, for punishment from Yahweh (Amos 1:3–2:3). This conception of Yahweh's "moral government of the world" may be reflected in Deut 9:4-5, where Israel is told that Yahweh will drive out the former inhabitants of Canaan because of their wickedness (H. W. Robinson 1907, 40).

The overlap of ideas between Amos and Deuteronomy is considerable. Not all parallels have the same value as evidence, but there is reason enough to support the view that Deuteronomy was written in response to the preaching of this prophet from Tekoa. Amos, in one of his most celebrated statements, says that Israel has been elected as Yahweh's own people, which is why Yahweh will punish her for all her iniquities (Amos 3:2). Israel's election as Yahweh's holy people becomes a major teaching in Deuteronomy (Deut 4:20, 34, 37; 7:6-8; 9:26, 29; 10:15; cf. 32:8-9), which states also that the nation will be punished for disobeying the commandments (7:10; 11:28; 28:15-68).

Amos knows, as we might expect, that Yahweh brought Israel out of Egypt, cared for it in the wilderness, and gave it the land of the Amorites (Amos 2:10). Deuteronomy emphasizes the same: Yahweh's deliverance of Israel from Egypt (Deut 4:20, 37; 5:6, and passim); Yahweh's care of the nation in the wilderness (8:2, 15; 29:4[29:5]; cf. 32:11-12); and Yahweh's gift of land to Israel, fulfilling a promise made to the fathers (1:8, 21, 25, and passim). Amos says that Yahweh destroyed the Amorites to give Israel its land (Amos 2:9-10). Successful battles against the Amorite kings, Sihon and Og, are reported in Deuteronomy, which also reports the giving of Amorite land to Reuben, Gad, and the half-tribe of Manasseh (Deut 2:24–3:17).

Amos censures Israel for boasting about success in war being due to its own might (Amos 6:13). Deuteronomy, perhaps in response to this, says the conquest of Canaan will not be due to its own righteousness, but rather because of the wickedness of the Canaanites, and because of the promise Yahweh made to the fathers that their descendants would be given the land (Deut 9:4-6). The conquest of Canaan will succeed because Yahweh will go before Israel as the head of the army (Deut 1:30-33). Yahweh is the one who made the Exodus deliverance possible, and the one who cared for Israel in the wilderness. The deliverance from Egypt was due not to Israel's strength, says Deuteronomy, but came about because of the great strength of Yahweh (4:37-38; 9:29). So when Israel comes to inhabit the land, it must not boast that by its own strength it gained wealth in the land; the strength will come from Yahweh (8:17-18).

Amos censures in strong terms the worship taking place at Israel's multiple sanctuaries: Bethel, Samaria, Dan, Gilgal, and Beersheba. It is displeasing to Yahweh (Amos 3:14; 4:4-5; 5:5; 8:14). In fact, Yahweh hates the feasts and solemn assemblies (Amos 5:21-23). Deuteronomy seeks to remedy this problem by saying that Yahweh has decided now upon a single sanctuary for worship (Deut 12:5-14, and passim). At festivals carried on at this central sanctuary Yahweh wants joyful celebration (Deut 12:7, 12, 18; 14:23; 16:11, 14; 26:11; 27:7). This, too, may answer Amos's censure of the music at the multiple sanctuaries, which to Yahweh is a disgusting noise (Amos 5:21-24). Amos says that Yahweh will turn the feasts into mourning, their songs into lamentations (8:10). The high places too, says Amos, will be made desolate (7:9). Deuteronomy forbids high place worship (Deut 12:2). What is happening at the multiple sanctuaries of Samaria, Dan, and Beersheba is that people are swearing by other gods (Amos 8:14), which Deuteronomy forbids. Israel must swear only by the name of Yahweh (Deut 6:13; 10:20).

Sexual adventurism also comes under attack in Amos. Fathers and sons are having sex with the same maiden (Amos 2:7). In Deuteronomy, sexual activity is regulated by law (Deut 22:22–23:1[22:30]). In the marketplace injustice is rife, with merchants using false weights and measures (Amos 8:5-6). Deuteronomy says there must be no false weights and measures in the marketplace (Deut 25:13-16). Amos says the urban rich are oppressing the poor and needy (Amos 2:6-7; 4:1; 5:11-12; 8:4-6). In response, Deuteronomy says there must be no oppression of the poor and needy; people are to show them benevolence and generosity (Deut 1:16; 15:1-11; 24:17).

At the heart of Amos's message is the charge that Israel has rejected justice and righteousness (Amos 5:7; 6:12). People are oppressing the righteous (Amos 2:6; 5:12), and justice is not being carried out in the city gate (5:10, 15). So Amos says: "Let justice roll down like waters, and righteousness like an everflowing stream" (5:24). Deuteronomy could not agree more. It tells the people: "Righteousness, righteousness you shall pursue" (Deut 16:20; cf. 6:25; 24:13). There must be no perversion of justice to orphans, widows, or sojourners (Deut 24:17; 27:19). Yahweh, Deuteronomy points out, executes justice to orphans and widows (10:18). Amos says that judges are taking bribes (Amos 2:6; 5:12). Deuteronomy responds by saying that judges are to judge with righteous judgment, and not take bribes (Deut 16:18-19; 27:25). And it points out, once again, that Yahweh is not one to take bribes (10:17).

Introduction

Israelite society is rife with corruption. People are sleeping on garments taken in pledge (Amos 2:8). The Deuteronomic Code says that the pledge of the poor cannot be slept on and must be returned to its owner at sundown (Deut 24:12-13). As for widow's garments, they must not be taken as pledges under any circumstances (24:17). Honest testimony is not being heard in the city gate, says Amos (Amos 5:10). The Deuteronomic Code repeats the commandment about not bearing false witness (Deut 5:20) and says that malicious witnesses will be punished according to the *lex talionis* (19:16-21).

Amos tells people to "seek Yahweh" and "seek the good" and they will live (Amos 5:4, 14). Deuteronomy echoes this in passing along the wisdom teaching that by obeying Yahweh and his commandments people will walk the path that leads to life (Deut 4:1; 8:1; 16:20; 30:16, 19; 32:47). Amos says that Israel should praise the name of Yahweh (Amos 4:13; 5:8; 9:6). Deuteronomy goes a step further in developing a full-blown "name" theology (Deut 12:5, 11, 21; 14:23, and passim).

Amos knows that Yahweh is the creator of heaven and earth (Amos 4:13; 5:8-9; 9:5-6). So does Deuteronomy, which says that to Yahweh belong heaven and earth and everything in it (Deut 10:14). In both Amos and Deuteronomy, Yahweh resides in the heavens (Amos 9:6; Deut 4:36; 26:15 — although see Deut 23:15[23:14]). Amos says that in the past Yahweh has withheld rain (Amos 4:7). In Deuteronomy Yahweh promises abundant rain in the good land of Canaan (Deut 11:10-12; 28:12), but this hinges on Israel doing the commandments (11:13-17). Deuteronomy knows that if Israel breaks the covenant, one of the curses will be that the heavens overhead will become hard as bronze and the rain in the land will be dust and dirt (28:23-24). Amos says that Yahweh has brought blight, mildew, and pestilence upon Israel (Amos 4:9-10). Deuteronomy includes all three among its covenant curses (Deut 28:21-22; cf. 32:24).

Yahweh raised up prophets in Israel, says Amos, but people told them not to prophesy (Amos 2:11-12). Deuteronomy knows, too, that Yahweh raised up prophets within Israel and says it will continue in the future (Deut 18:15-22), but when society as a whole becomes hopelessly corrupt and people no longer listen to prophets who seek to reform it, Amos says Yahweh will raise up against Israel a nation to punish it for unrighteousness, injustice, and hubris (Amos 6:14). Deuteronomy agrees, saying that Yahweh will raise up against Israel a nation to punish it for not joyfully serving Yahweh (Deut 28:49-57). Amos says Israel will surely go into exile for not allowing prophets to preach (Amos 7:17). Deuternomy does not use the term "exile" (גלה) but does say that Israel will be scattered among the nations for covenant disobedience (Deut 4:27; 28:64-68; 29:27[29:28]).

HOSEA

Hosea was Israel's great prophet of divine compassion (Lundbom 2010a, 48-57). Among the major Hebrew prophets, he is northern Israel's only homegrown herald of the divine word. A contemporary of Amos, Hosea preached in the mid-eighth century, during the years just prior to the fall of Samaria and the demise of northern Israel. He may have survived the fall of Samaria, and if so would have been a contemporary of Isaiah in Judah. We don't know.

It has long been maintained that Deuteronomy owes its greatest debt to Hosea (Driver 1895, xxvii; H. W. Robinson 1907, 40; H. L. Ginsberg 1982, 19-24; Weinfeld 1972, 366-70). Ginsberg shows how Deuteronomy echoes the diction of Hosea, ideas from Hosea, and adopts its legislation in response to the preaching of Hosea. Although northern Israel had Samuel, Elijah, Elisha, and the fearless Micaiah, no other prophet from the north has left us a written legacy of his preaching, only Hosea. H. W. Robinson said it was from Hosea, whose conception of Yahweh was the richest, that Deuteronomy derived its highest ideals. Jeremiah, later on, was also greatly influenced by Hosea in his early preaching, particularly in chapters 2–3 and 30-31 of his book (Lundbom 2004a, 371-75).

The recurring theme in Hosea's preaching is Israel's whoring and adultery. It exists in society at large, and the prophet uses it metaphorically to describe Israel's abandonment of Yahweh. Israel's daughters are guilty of whoring and adultery, but then so are the men, who are sacrificing with cult prostitutes (Hos 4:13-14; cf. Deut 22:21; 23:18-19[23:17-18]). Priests and lay people are both guilty (Hos 4:10, 12). Because the nation behaves like a whore and an adulteress (Hos 1:2; 2:4, 7[2:2, 5]; 4:15, 18; 5:3-4; 6:10; 7:4; 9:1; cf. Deut 31:16), Hosea marries a woman of this description to act out his message symbolically (Hos 1:2; 3:1). Language about "forgetting Yahweh" and "going after other gods" (Hos 2:7, 15[2:5, 13]; 3:1; 8:14; 13:6) is precisely what turns up in Deuteronomy (Deut 6:12; 8:11, 14, 19), having prominence also in the Song of Moses, which says this was Israel's way of showing gratitude for all of Yahweh's goodness (Deut 32:10-18). Hosea sees in Israel an unawareness that Yahweh is the one who supplied it with the grain, wine, and oil, not Baal (Hos 2:7, 10, 14[2:5, 8, 12]. Deuteronomy therefore makes it plain that Yahweh is the one who gave Israel food and drink in the wilderness and promises to bring Israel into a land that will yield abundantly. If Israel obeys the commandments, it will reap ongoing material blessing from Yahweh (Deut 6:10-15; 7:13-14; 8:3-20; 11:10-17; 28:4-5, 11-12).

The problem in eighth-century Israel is Baal worship, to a lesser extent Asherah worship (Hos 4:12; cf. Deut 7:5; 12:3; 16:21), also idols and images associated with that worship (Hos 4:17; 8:4-5; 10:5-6; 13:2; 14:9[8]; cf. Deut 4:16-18, 25-31; 5:8-10; 7:25; 12:3; 16:21-22). Deuteronomy says the people saw no form of Yahweh at Horeb, only a voice (Deut 4:12, 15, 35-36). Hosea speaks against Israel's multiple sanctuaries: Gilgal and Bethaven (= Bethel) (4:15; 9:15; 12:12[11]; cf. Deut 12:2-4 and passim); the high places (Hos 4:13; 10:8); the feasts occurring there (2:13, 15[2:11, 13]; 9:5); the sacrifices connected with the feasts (4:13, 19[MT]; 6:6; 9:4; 11:2), and the gashing taking place at the feasts (7:14; cf. Deut 14:1-2). Yahweh has no delight in any of this, and will put an end to the feasts (Hos 2:13, 15[2:11, 13]; 8:13). Hosea judges Israel's many altars (Hos 4:19[LXX]; 8:11; 10:1-2, 8; 12:11); the pillars by the altars (10:1-2); and the priests officiating at the altars (4:6; 5:1; 6:9), who he says will be punished (10:5) along with prophets preaching empty oracles (9:7-8; cf. Deut 13:2-6[13:1-5]; 18:20-22). Deuteronomy's response to this is one sanctuary for the worship of Yahweh (Deut 12:5-14 and passim; H. L. Ginsberg 1982, 21).

Hosea says that Ephraim has been "mixing with the peoples," i.e., foreigners (Hos 7:8), and as a result has become like them. Deuteronomy therefore mandates that Israel separate itself from other peoples, particularly in worship (Deut 23:4-7[23:3-6]), so they will not adopt their abominable religious practices (Deut 4:15-20; 7:1-5; 12:29-31; 17:2-7; 18:9-14). If they do, harsh punishment will follow. Hosea says Israel will now have to return to "Egypt" (Hos 9:3, 6). At the conclusion of Deuteronomy's curses, Yahweh says this is precisely what he will do, although it was a journey he promised would never happen (Deut 28:68; H. L. Ginsberg 1982, 20).

In Hosea's view, Israel is in gross violation of Yahweh's law and covenant (Hos 4:6; 8:1), particularly the Ten Commandments (4:2; 6:9). Injustice is not a major theme in this book, as it is in Amos, but it is there. Princes are like those who remove the landmark (Hos 5:10), a prohibition included in the Deuteronomic Code (Deut 19:14). The nation is said to behave like a trader with false balances (Hos 12:7), which may issue forth in another Deuteronomic law (Deut 25:13-15). Hosea, in hopes of reforming a sinful people, tells them to "sow righteousness" and "hold fast to steadfast love and justice" (Hos 10:12; 12:7[12:6]), qualities to be found in Yahweh (2:21[2:19]; cf. Deut 10:18). Deuteronomy has a good deal to say about the practice of justice and righteousness (Deut 6:25; 16:20; 24:13, 17; 27:19).

Hosea preaches that there is no God but Yahweh, which becomes defining theology in Deuteronomy (Hos 13:4; cf. Deut 4:35, 39; 6:4). Dominant themes in Hosea are the "love" (אַהֲבָה and חֶסֶד) Yahweh has bestowed upon Israel, particularly when it was a child (Hos 3:1; 11:1-4; Deut 4:37; 7:8; 23:6[23:5]), and the love Yahweh expects in return (Hos 12:7[12:6]; cf. Deut 6:5; 10:12; 11:1, 13; 30:16). The problem, says Hosea, is that Israel's love is "like a morning cloud, like the dew that goes early away" (Hos 6:4). Israel loves the wrong things: cakes of raisins (3:1); sacrificial flesh (8:13); a whore's hire on the threshing floor (9:1); and oppression resulting from deceitful practices (12:8[12:7]). At one point Yahweh says he will love Israel no more (9:15), and yet, after healing their faithlessness, he will again love them freely (2:21[2:19]; 14:5[14:4]). For a list of Deuteronomy's prototypical terminology in Hosea, see Weinfeld 1972, 364.

MICAH

Micah was a late-eighth-century prophet from a town in the Judean foothills southwest of Jerusalem, best remembered for having raised his voice against violence, injustice, and oppression in both Israel and Judah, also for preaching that Yahweh would make Samaria and Jerusalem heaps of ruins (1:2-9; 3:9-12; Jer 26:18; Lundbom 2010a, 57-62). He followed in the tradition of Amos, but parallels exist also between his preaching and the Deuteronomic Code.

Those engaged in evildoing, said Micah, were the leaders and wealthy citizens, who preyed on helpless and other unknowing folk (Mic 3:1-3, 9-11; cf. Deut 1:16; 15:1-11; 24:17). Blood was being spilled, which meant people were being murdered (Mic 3:10; 7:2; cf. Deut 5:17; 19:11-13); fields were being coveted and seized (Mic 2:2; cf. Deut 5:21), and women — probably widows — were being forced out of their houses (Mic 2:9; cf. Deut 10:18; 24:17; 27:19). Princes and judges were taking bribes (Mic 3:11; 7:3; cf. Deut 16:19; 27:25), and merchants were carrying on business in the marketplace using false scales and bogus weights (Mic 6:11; cf. Deut 25:13-16). In a memorable prophetic word, Micah says that doing justice (מִשְׁפָּט), loving faithfulness (חֶסֶד), and walking humbly with your God (וְהַצְנֵעַ לֶכֶת עִם־אֱלֹהֶיךָ) are all more important to Yahweh than burnt offerings, year-old calves, thousands of rams, and even the offering of one's firstborn son (Mic 6:6-8; cf. Deut 5:33; 10:12-19; 16:18-20; 24:17; 25:6; 27:19).

Idolatry and images were a problem for this prophet, including stone pillars and wooden posts to Lady Asherah (Mic 1:7; 5:12-13[5:13-14]; cf. Deut 5:8-10; 7:5, 25; 12:3; 16:21-22). Behind false worship lay false practitioners of religion, with Micah citing here not only diviners, sorcerers, and soothsayers (Mic 2:11; 3:7; 5:11[5:12]; cf. Deut 18:10), but (peace) prophets and priests, many of whom who were in the business mainly for money (Mic 3:5, 11; cf. Deut 18:20-22). But Micah anticipated the day when the law and Yahweh's word would go forth from Zion (Mic 4:2[= Isa 2:3]), which could find fulfillment in the appearance of the book of Deuteronomy.

ISAIAH

Isaiah was a prophet in Jerusalem during the late eighth and early seventh century, which puts him roughly a couple decades after Amos and Hosea in the north and makes him a contemporary of Micah in the south. Isaiah is remembered among other things for describing Yahweh as the "Holy One of Israel" (Isa 1:4; 5:16, 19, 24; 6:3; 8:13; 10:20; 12:6; 17:7, etc.; Lundbom 2010a, 62-78), an epithet that Deuteronomy may have known (Deut 32:51), but if so, preferred rather to express the complementary idea that Israel was Yahweh's "holy people" (Deut 7:6; 14:2, 21; 26:19; 28:9).

Yahweh, for Isaiah, is the one and only God, although people may not know this until his terrible "day" dawns (Isa 2:10-11, 17; cf. Deut 4:35, 39; 6:4). Along with the other prophets, Isaiah speaks out against the proliferation of idols (Isa 2:8), which are not tolerated by Deuteronomy (Deut 4:16-18; 5:8-10; 7:25; 12:3; 16:21-22). The reason given in Deuteronomy is that Israel saw no form of Yahweh in the revelation at Horeb (Deut 4:12, 15, 35-36). Isaiah says that idols and images will come under judgment in Yahweh's future day of visitation, at which time people will literally throw them away (Isa 2:18, 20; 10:11; 30:22; 31:7).

In his indictment of the nation, Isaiah repeats the now common charges that people have forsaken Yahweh (Isa 1:4; cf. Deut 6:12; 8:11, 14, 19; 32:10-18) and rejected his law (Isa 5:24; cf. Deut 4:1; 8:11, and passim). This manifests itself in foreign religious practices, which are flourishing, and in flagrant violations of covenant law. The land is full of soothsayers, charmers, mediums, and wizards (Isa 2:6; 8:19), all of whom are outlawed in Deuteronomy (Deut 18:10-14). People are seeking out seers and prophets who speak smooth things and illusions (Isa 30:9-11; cf. Deut 13:2-6[13:1-5]; 18:20-22). A more serious covenant violation is the shedding of blood, i.e., murder (Isa 1:15, 21; 5:7; cf. Deut 5:17; 19:11-13).

Along with Amos and Micah, Isaiah is uncompromising in his condemnation of injustice and oppression, particularly with regard to the poor and needy. Because of evil decrees, oppressive laws, and evasive tactics by those in power, the needy are turned aside from justice, the poor are robbed of their rights, widows become spoil and orphans become prey (Isa 3:14-15; 5:23; 10:1-2; 32:7; cf. Deut 1:16-17; 5:21; 10:18; 24:17; 27:19). No one will defend the cause of the orphan and the widow (Isa 1:23), the reason being that everyone wants a bribe (Isa 1:23; 5:23; cf. Deut 16:19; 27:25). Isaiah says the city once filled with justice has become a whore; righteousness is replaced by murder (Isa 1:21). The evil there is like that found rife in Sodom and Gomorrah (Isa 1:9-10; 3:9; cf. Deut 29:22[23]; 32:32). Yahweh, on a visit to his vineyard, looked for justice but found only bloodshed, for righteousness but heard only a cry (Isa 5:7). All this is intolerable to Yahweh, for he is exalted in justice, shows himself holy in righteousness, and cannot be bribed (Isa 5:16; cf. Deut 10:17-18).

Because Zion reminds Yahweh of Sodom, he could not care less about the multitude of sacrifices and holy feasts in his honor (Isa 1:11-14). Polluted altars and Asherim beside them will be thrown down and broken into pieces (Isa 27:9; cf. Deut 7:5; 12:3; 16:21). Support is present here for a single sanctuary in Jerusalem (Deut 12:5-14 and passim). Yahweh will judge the ruthless people who are obstructing justice in the city gate (Isa 29:21; cf. Deut 27:19).

Isaiah, despite all his indictments and judgments, hopes nevertheless for reform. We hear him admonishing people to seek justice, defend orphans and widows (Isa 1:17), and let Yahweh be their fear (Isa 8:13). In Deuteronomy, fearing Yahweh consists of doing the commandments (Deut 4:10; 5:29; 6:2, 24; 10:12-13, and passim), and special care for orphans and widows gets repeated mention (Deut 14:29; 16:11, 14; 24:17; 27:19). Yahweh exercises special care for them (Deut 10:18). Isaiah preaches early on the very essence of Deuteronomic theology, i.e., that if people are obedient, they will eat the good of the land, but if they refuse, the sword will devour them (Isa 1:19-20; cf. Deut 11:13-17, 26-28; 28:1-19).

Isaiah looks for a better day to come, in which evil will be replaced by the goodness Yahweh requires. The people of Zion will cast away their idols and images (Isa 30:22; 31:7), and out of Zion shall go forth the law and Yahweh's word (Isa 2:3 = Mic 4:2). There will no longer be regard for pagan altars and standing Asherim (Isa 17:8; cf. Deut 7:5; 12:3; 16:21). Zion will become the city of the appointed feasts (Isa 33:20), which may reflect Hezekiah's centralization program and laws in the Deuteronomic Code (Deut 12:5-14; 16:1-17). Judah will become a righteous nation (Isa 26:2), and Jerusalem will be a city known for holiness, justice, and righteousness, one in which the fear of Yahweh will be in evidence (Isa 1:26-27; 4:3; 28:16-17; 33:5-6, 14-15). When the Spirit is poured out from on high, justice will dwell in the wilderness and righteousness in the orchard (Isa 32:15-16). In this wonderful transformation, the meek and the needy will once again rejoice in the Holy One of Israel (Isa 29:19). A Davidic king and his princes will rule in justice and righteousness, delight in the fear of Yahweh (Isa 9:6[9:7]; 11:1-3), and judge with equity the poor and the meek (Isa 11:4-5; 32:1).

There are some puzzlements, however, in a comparison of Isaiah with Deuteronomy. How could Isaiah propose that a pillar to Yahweh will mark Egypt's future conversion (Isa 19:19) when pillars are prohibited in Deut 16:22? Driver (1895, xlix) notes, too, that although Isaiah speaks against images, he does not wage war against local sanctuaries as such (but see Isa 1:29) and hardly ever alludes to the worship of "other gods" (cf. Isa 17:10b). The term "other gods," so common in Deuteronomy and Jeremiah, does not occur in Isaiah. Maybe this is because Hezekiah removed the high places and centralized worship in Jerusalem (2 Kgs 18:4, 22; 21:3).

JEREMIAH

Jeremiah was the last major prophet residing in ancient Israel, which by the late seventh century had been reduced to the rump kingdom of Judah. He lived more than fifty years during this final period of Israelite nationhood, witnessing the reform of Josiah, its undoing by Kings Jehoiakim and Zedekiah, and the fall of Jerusalem to the Babylonians in 586. Another four years were spent in a community of remnants at Mizpah, until the Babylonian-appointed governor was murdered and a contingent of Mizpah residents fled to Egypt. Jeremiah, and his scribal companion Baruch, went with them to Egypt, where he was last heard from (Lundbom 1999, 102-20; 2010a, 88-100).

Jeremiah's earliest preaching betrays indebtedness to the Song of Moses (Deuteronomy 32), both in language and in key ideas (Lundbom 1999, 110-14). Jeremiah learned from this Song that Yahweh is a just and upright Father, the one who created Israel and gave her — along with other nations — land as an inheritance (Deut 32:4-8; Jer 2:5, 7; 3:19; 5:4-5; 9:23[9:24]; 10:12-16; 27:5; 32:17). From the Song Jeremiah learned also that Yahweh's goodness to Israel in the inhospitable wilderness (Deut 32:10-12; Jer 2:6) and his gift of land with all its bounty (Deut 32:13-14; Jer 2:7) were repaid by ingratitude: Israel became sated, forgot Yahweh, and went after gods it had not known (Deut 32:15-18; Jer 2:5-9). The idea appears in both the Song and in Jer 2:7-8 that the settlement was the time when things began to go bad.

Jeremiah learned from the Song that Yahweh becomes greatly provoked when his covenant people forget him and go after other gods (Deut 32:16, 22; Jer 4:4; 7:18; 8:19; 15:14; 17:4) and in burning anger will bring against Israel another nation as his punishing agent (Deut 32:19-25; Jer 4:5-8, 13-17; 5:10-13, 15-17). But the Song also taught him, as other traditions — in Deuteronomy and elsewhere — undoubtedly did, that Yahweh's burning anger will nevertheless stop short of completely wiping out his covenant people (Deut 32:26-33; cf. 9:6-29; Exod 32:7-14). If he were to destroy them completely, the enemy will take credit for having brought about the destruction.

The Song then turns to describe Yahweh's holy wrath against other nations, which will have a positive result in bringing deliverance to Israel (Deut 32:34-43). This elicits from Jeremiah a number of oracles against foreign nations (Jer 25:15-38; 46-51). The brief poem in Jer 2:27c-28 — the language and also the irony — derives from Deut 32:37-38, where Yahweh promises self-vindication before devotees of gods now shown to be powerless. In the Song, the grand sweep of divine history goes from salvation to salvation: Yahweh, who began a saving work among his people, will end things with another saving work: vindication of Israel and a simultaneous judgment against enemy nations. This informed Jeremiah's hope oracles for the future (Jeremiah 30-33), the most important of which was the new/eternal covenant prophecy (Jer 31:31-34; 32:38-40). The Song of Moses was the temple lawbook of 622, which, after its finding, Jeremiah consumed (Jer 15:16).

Jeremiah was also influenced by core Deuteronomy, i.e., chapters 1–28, the document that inspired young King Josiah's purge of pagan religious practices in Jerusalem and Judah, even in sanctuaries to the north, where the king extended his reform once the Assyrians had left the territory and returned home (2 Kgs 23:4-20; 2 Chr 34:3-7). Following the Chronicler, I take the purge to have occurred in 628 (Lundbom 1976). Jeremiah was influenced by the Song of Moses and core Deuteronomy, both of which were written documents in his time. Driver (1895, xlvii) says, "Jeremiah exhibits marks of [Deuteronomy] on nearly every page."

From core Deuteronomy Jeremiah came to know the "prophet like Moses" passage in Deut 18:15-18, incorporating it into his prophetic call (Jer 1:4-12; Lundbom 1999, 233-35). He learned from Deuteronomy that the Horeb covenant was conditional: If Israel keeps the covenant, which means keeping the commandments and other covenant conditions, it will continue to live long in the land; if it does not, the nation will be destroyed and the land will be lost (Deut 5:32-33; 28; Jer 7:3-15). Influence here extends even into Jeremiah's diction: Deuteronomy says if Israel keeps the statutes and the ordinances, "it will go well with you . . . and you will live long in the land" (Deut 4:40; 5:16, 33; 6:2-3, 18; 10:13, and passim; Jer 7:23; 22:15; 35:7; 38:20; 40:9; 42:6).

Other early reform preaching of the prophet echoes Deuteronomy, e.g., Jeremiah's calling for a "circumcision of the heart" (Deut 10:16; 30:6; Jer 4:4); preaching covenant obedience and the consequences of disobedience (Deut 11:13-17, 27-28; 27:10; 28:1-19; Jer 11:1-13); and calling for observance of the fourth commandment on Sabbath rest (Deut 5:12-15; Jer 17:19-27).

But Jeremiah's task was more difficult than that of the Deuteronomic preacher, for he was called by Yahweh to indict Israel for covenant violation and announce that Yahweh's punishment was forthcoming. But here again, he drew heavily upon Deuteronomy. Israel had "forgotten" or "forsaken" Yahweh (Jer 1:16; 2:13, 17, 19, 32; 3:21; 5:7, 19; 18:15, and passim), which went to the heart of the covenant relationship. Deuteronomy warned people to be careful lest they forget the extraordinary events of the wilderness (Deut 4:9); the covenant and then make for themselves an idol (Deut 4:23); and most importantly Yahweh himself, who brought the nation out of Egyptian slavery (Deut 6:12; 8:14). Forgetting Yahweh meant not keeping the commandments, and Deuteronomy warned against this repeatedly (Deut 8:11). It said if Israel forgets Yahweh and goes after other gods, it will surely perish, as the other nations did (Deut 8:19). Deuteronomy lays much stress on "remembering" — remembering Yahweh, his mighty works, his deliverance in the exodus, and how Israel provoked him in the wilderness (Deut 5:15; 7:18; 8:2, 18-19; 9:7; 15:15; 16:3, 12; 24:18, 22). Remembering the deliverance from Egypt should issue forth in doing the commandments. Jeremiah pleads with Yahweh not to break his covenant with the people (Jer 14:21), which, according to Deuteronomy, was something Yahweh said he would not do (Deut 4:31).

Introduction

Jeremiah reflects Deuteronomy's idea that forsaking Yahweh occurs when Israel goes after other gods (Jer 7:6, 9; 11:10; 13:10; 16:11; Deut 6:14; 8:19; 11:28; 13:7[13:6]), a violation of the first commandment (Deut 5:7). The expression "other gods" occurs seventeen times in Jeremiah and seventeen times in Deuteronomy. Jeremiah says that prophets have been and still are prophesying by Baal (Jer 2:8; 23:13), which is strictly forbidden in Deut 13:2-6(13:1-5) and 18:20. People have also built high places to burn their sons and daughters to other gods (Jer 2:20; 3:6; 7:31; 13:27; 19:5) and have been carried away by astral worship, both of which are forbidden in Deuteronomy (Jer 8:2; Deut 4:19; 12:2, 31; 17:2-7; 18:10).

Jeremiah knows Deuteronomy's prohibition of diviners, soothsayers, and sorcerers (Jer 27:9; 29:8; Deut 18:10, 14), finding a problem also with prophets and dreamers in Jerusalem and Babylon who are not getting the message right (Jer 5:12-13, 31; 14:14; 23:14-22, 25-32; 29:21-23; Deut 13:2-6[13:1-5]; 18:20-22). Small wonder, when false practitioners of religion proliferated under the evil Manasseh (2 Chr 33:6). Both Jeremiah and Deuteronomy are concerned about people "obeying Yahweh's voice" (Jer 3:13; 9:12[9:13]; 11:7; 42:13; Deut 4:30; 8:20; 9:23; 13:5[4]; 15:5, and passim) and "rebelling" against Yahweh (Jer 4:17; Deut 1:26-46; 9:24). Deuteronomy — except for the wilderness recollection in 1:26-46 — simply warns against disobedience and rebellion; Jeremiah in his day reports that people are guilty of both.

Jeremiah in one of his celebrated "Temple Oracles" lists six of the Ten Commandments that people have broken: no other gods; idols; swearing falsely; murder; adultery; and stealing (Jer 7:9; cf. Deut 5:7-20). Elsewhere, Jeremiah censures people for (1) setting up idols and images (Jer 7:30; 8:19; 10:1-5, 8-9, 14-15; 13:27; cf. Deut 5:8-10); (2) erecting sacred pillars and Asherim (Jer 2:27; 17:12; cf. Deut 7:5; 12:3; 16:21-22); (3) swearing falsely (Jer 5:2; cf. Deut 5:11; 6:13; 10:20); (4) murder, i.e., the shedding of innocent blood (Jer 7:6; 22:3, 17; cf. Deut 5:17; 19:10, 13; 21:8-9); (5) adultery (Jer 5:7-8; 9:1[9:2]; 13:27; 23:10, 14; 29:22-23; cf. Deut 5:18); and (6) Sabbath breaking (Jer 17:21-23; cf. Deut 5:12-15). Deuteronomy prohibits all of these. Added to "adultery" is the sin of "going whoring" (זנה), which Jeremiah probably gets from Hosea.

Jeremiah warns — more often indicts — Judah and its king for not executing justice and righteousness (Jer 7:5; 21:12; 22:3, 13-17), also for oppressing the poor, needy, sojourner, orphan, and widow (Jer 2:34; 5:26-28; 7:6; 22:3). This is a blatant violation of the Deuteronomic Code (Deut 24:14-15, 17; 27:19). Since Yahweh does justice and righteousness (Jer 5:1; 9:23[9:24]; Deut 10:18), people must do the same. Josiah practiced these cardinal virtues, but his son Jehoiakim did not (Jer 22:15-17). Jeremiah thus looked ahead to a future Davidic king who would do justice and righteousness (Jer 23:5; 33:15).

Evil in Jerusalem made it like the proverbial cities of Sodom and Gomorrah (Jer 23:14; cf. Deut 29:22[29:23]), which suffered punishment from Yahweh. In preaching punishment to come, Jeremiah draws heavily on the curse language of Deuteronomy. Deuteronomy 28 states that a multitude of curses will descend upon Israel for not obeying the voice of Yahweh or for not being careful to do Yahweh's commands (Deut 28:15). In his call for covenant obedience (Jer 11:3-7), Jeremiah uses the "cursed . . . amen" formula of Deut 27:15-26, with the one difference that he speaks the "amen" on the people's behalf. The "cursed be the man who" phrase of Deut 27:15 appears three times in Jeremiah's preaching (Jer 11:3; 17:5; 20:15). In the bulk of Jeremiah's preaching, the Deuteronomic curses are either currently being carried out or slated to come in the near future.

Jeremiah in some cases reproduces the actual wording of the Deuteronomic curses. The following curses from Deuteronomy 28 occur in one form or another in Jeremiah:

> Deut 28:18 — curse on the fruit of your body, the fruit of your ground, the increase of your cattle and young of your flock (Jer 5:17).
> Deut 28:21 — curse of pestilence (Jer 14:12; 15:2; 18:21; 21:5-6, 9-10, and passim).
> Deut 28:23-24 — curse of no rain (Jer 3:3; 23:10). Both Deuteronomy and Jeremiah recognize that Yahweh sends the rain, with Deuteronomy making it conditional on Israel's obedience of the commandments (Deut 11:11-17; Jer 5:24; 14:22).
> Deut 28:25 — curse of being a "fright" (זַעֲוָה) to other nations (Jer 15:4; 24:9; 29:18; 34:17).
> Deut 28:26 — curse that dead bodies will be food for the birds of the air and the beasts of the earth (Jer 7:33; 15:3; 16:4; 19:7; 34:20).
> Deut 28:30 — curse that one will betroth a wife and another will lie with her; one shall build a house and not live in it; one shall plant a vineyard and not eat its fruit (Jer 6:11-12; 8:10). This is reversed in Jer 29:5-6; 31:5. Deuteronomy knows what obtains in ordinary times (Deut 20:5-7).
> Deut 28:33 — curse that a nation you have not known shall eat up the fruit of your ground and all of your labors (Jer 5:15-17; cf. 3:24). See also Deut 28:49-52.
> Deut 28:37 — curse that Israel will become a "desolation" (שַׁמָּה), a "proverb" (מָשָׁל), and a "taunt" (שְׁנִינָה) among all peoples (Jer 24:9; 25:9, 11; 18, and passim).
> Deut 28:48 — curse that the enemy will put a "yoke of iron" on your neck (Jer 28:14).
> Deut 28:49-52 — curse that a nation from afar, whose language you do not know, shall eat the offspring of your cattle and the fruit of your ground (Jer 5:15-17). See also Deut 28:33.

Deut 28:49 — curse of an enemy that flies swiftly, like an eagle, coming against Israel (Jer 48:40; 49:22).

Deut 28:53 — curse that people will eat the flesh of their own sons and daughters in the siege (Jer 19:9).

Deut 28:54, 56 — curse that the most delicately-bred men and women will do indelicate things in the siege (Jer 6:2).

Deut 28:59, 61 — curse of sicknesses (מַכּוֹת), severe and lasting, coming upon the people (Jer 6:7; 10:19; 14:17; 15:18; 19:8; 30:12, 14; 49:17).

Deut 28:64 — curse that Israel will be scattered among foreign nations (Jer 9:15[9:16]; 30:11). See also Deut 4:27.

Jeremiah cites Deuteronomy's divorce and remarriage law to make the point that Israel cannot, at least for now, return to Yahweh (Jer 3:1; Deut 24:1-4). In his court trial (Jer 26:12-15), Jeremiah's testimony, "Yahweh sent me," betrays a knowledge of the authentication legislation in Deut 13:2-6(13:1-5); and in his encounter with Hananiah, initial acquiescence and eventual judgment on this Yahweh prophet (Jer 28:15-17) show an understanding of the authentication legislation in Deut 18:20-22. Jeremiah censures Zedekiah and the people (Jer 34:14) for not abiding by the seven-year law of release in Deut 15:12-18. The firstfruit legislation of Deut 16:9-12 and 26:1-11 is in Jeremiah's mind when he reports his vision of the good and bad figs (Jer 24:1-10). To a Jerusalem under siege, Jeremiah parodies "the way of life and way of death" preaching in Deut 30:15-20, telling people that surrendering to the Babylonians will lead to life, resisting them will lead to death (Jer 21:8-10; cf. 38:17-18; 42:10-22). The main difference between Deuteronomy and Jeremiah is that the former warns people not to break the covenant and tells what will happen if they do. Jeremiah argues that the covenant has been broken and people must either repent or suffer the consequences.

In judgment preaching Jeremiah speaks of Yahweh's steadfast love (חֶסֶד) toward Israel, only to say that it has been withdrawn (Jer 16:5). The problem is that Israel has other lovers: the strange gods (16:11; cf. 2:25, 33; 8:2; 14:10). Deuteronomy says that Yahweh's steadfast love depends on Israel keeping the commandments (Deut 5:10; 7:9, 12). People have also ceased to fear Yahweh (Jer 2:19; 3:8; 5:22, 24; 44:10), which Deuteronomy admonished them to do (Deut 5:29; 6:2, 13, 24; 8:6; 10:12, 20, and passim). Jeremiah knew the need for this important inner disposition (Jer 10:7), with people rising to his defense at the trial of 609 and pointing out too that the good King Hezekiah feared Yahweh, with the result that Yahweh rescinded evil planned against the nation (26:19). Jeremiah looked ahead to the day when people would fear Yahweh forever (32:39). In passages of hope, Jeremiah affirmed that Yahweh's love or steadfast love remains (31:3; 32:18; 33:11[from Pss 100:5; 106:1; 107:1; 136:1]).

Jeremiah's diction — in both poetry and prose — draws heavily on the sermonic prose of Deuteronomy (Driver 1895, xcii-xciv; Weinfeld 1972, 320-61). There are the stereotyped clichés: "and these are the words" (Deut 1:1; 28:69[29:1]; Jer 29:1; 30:4); "as at this day" (Deut 2:30; 4:20, 38; 8:18; 10:15; Jer 11:5; 25:18; 32:20); "with outstretched hand and with strong arm" (Deut 4:34; 5:15; 7:19; 11:2; 26:8; Jer 21:5[reversed]); "sojourner, orphan, and widow" (Deut 10:18; 14:29; 16:11, 14; Jer 7:6; 22:3); "the place that (Yahweh your God will choose) to make his name reside there" (Deut 12:11; 14:23; 16:2, 6, 11; Jer 7:12), carrying with it the "name" theology of Deuteronomy; and many more. Some rhetorical questions of Jeremiah also echo Deuteronomy, e.g., "Ask around . . . and see if there has been anything like this: 'Has a nation exchanged gods, even though they are no-gods?'" (Jer 2:10-11), which is like the string of questions in Deut 4:32-34:

> Indeed ask, would you, about the former days that were before you, from the day that God created human beings upon the earth, and from one end of the heaven to the other end of the heaven: Has a great thing like this happened or has anything like it been heard of? Has a people heard the voice of a god speaking from the midst of the fire as you, you have heard, and lived? Or has a god attempted to go and take for himself a nation from the midst of another nation by testings, by signs and by wonders, and by war, and by a strong hand and by an outstretched arm, and by great terrors, according to all that Yahweh your God did for you in Egypt before your eyes?

We do not hear from Jeremiah, as we do from Deuteronomy and Hosea, preaching about the love Yahweh expects in return for the love he has shown Israel. Jeremiah mentions only the love Israel showed Yahweh in the wilderness (Jer 2:2) and then does not speak about it again. Holiness is also not a major theme in Jeremiah. In Deuteronomy it is not so much Yahweh being the "Holy One of Israel" (but see Deut 32:51), as in Isaiah, but Israel being Yahweh's holy people (Deut 7:6; 14:2, 21; 26:19; 28:9), which carries over into Jeremiah. Israel is remembered as being holy to Yahweh in the wilderness (Jer 2:3), but it presumably lost that distinctive quality due to its sinful behavior. Jeremiah does say, however, that he himself was made holy at the time Yahweh called him to be a prophet (Jer 1:5).

Finally, Jeremiah's announcement of a new/eternal covenant (Jer 31:31-34; 32:38-40) is another indication that he understood himself to be "the prophet like Moses" (Lundbom 2010b, 37). Moses presented the Horeb covenant to Israel; Jeremiah presents Israel with a new covenant for the future.

Introduction

DEUTERONOMY AND WISDOM

Wisdom is commonly defined as an intellectual capacity or quality of the mind enabling one to live well in the world, to succeed, and to counsel others in the way of success (Blank 1962, 852-53). Its opposite is foolishness, usually reduced to the lack of good sense or good judgment in a person. The wise are admired; fools are held up to ridicule. "Wise women" appeared in the early monarchy in ancient Israel (2 Sam 14:2; 20:16), and by Isaiah and Jeremiah's time "wise men" were a distinct professional class in Jerusalem (Isa 29:14; Prov 25:1; Jer 8:8-9; 9:11, 22[12, 23]; 18:18; Weinfeld 1967, 262; 1972, 161-62). Wise men were prominent in neighboring nations to Israel, particularly Egypt (Gen 41:8; Exod 7:11). Jeremiah tells us that tribal wisdom resided in Teman, a northeast region of Edom (Jer 49:7; cf. Eliphaz the Temanite in Job 2:11; 4:1), and years later Paul says wisdom was highly sought after by the Greeks (1 Cor 1:22). In the Bible, Wisdom is also something infinitely above and beyond human beings, being the first of God's creation (Prov 8:22; cf. John 1:1).

That wisdom is found in other cultures, to some extent in all cultures, helps us distinguish it from belief or godly faith. Wisdom deals largely with matters of earth, i.e., it is not generally concerned with God or the things of God, which we call theology. And while wisdom can certainly come by divine revelation, it need not be so acquired. More often than not, it comes by living fully and attentively in this world. Wisdom is thus akin to humanism (Rankin 1936, 3; Weinfeld 1961, 242-43). And yet, says Daube (1969a, 28), wisdom in ancient Israel was deeply religious. Psalm 111:10 and Prov 9:10 say: "The fear of the Lord is the beginning of wisdom." Without the fear of the Lord, wisdom becomes foolishness, as the book of Job teaches.

Wisdom has three defining characteristics. It may have more, but it has at least these three: (1) wisdom builds on knowledge; (2) wisdom requires discrimination, or discernment; and (3) wisdom resides in individuals who utilize the knowledge and discernment they possess. Wisdom is something you do (Matt 7:24-27; Lundbom 2010c). Wisdom is not the same as knowledge; it is the larger and more comprehensive of the two terms. Similarly, foolishness takes in more than ignorance, even stupidity (= "slow-wittedness"). A wise person is well informed, having acquired knowledge from: (a) the teaching of others (older folk, parents, teachers); (b) practical experience both positive and negative; and (c) personal observations or reflections upon the natural order and the world in which one lives. Some identify wisdom with common sense. For persons of faith, knowledge can come because God reveals things to them. But not everyone possessing knowledge is wise. Francis Bacon, advisor to Queen Elizabeth I, was called by some "the most learned fool in the world."

The wise person recognizes similarities, but also perceives differences, and is able to discriminate among knowledge he or she possesses. The wise person knows how to "sort things out." Wisdom often teaches a doctrine of the "two ways," the way of the righteous and the way of the wicked (Psalm 1; Prov 4:10-19), the way to life and the way to death (Deut 30:15-20; Jer 6:16; 17:5-8; 21:8-9; Matt 7:13-14). The wise person makes judgments about good and bad, right and wrong, truth and falsity, and knows the difference — when there is one — between appearances and reality. The wise person observes actions, discerning whether they contradict words issuing from the mouth. King Solomon was wise because he was able to *discern* the real mother of the baby placed before him by two women, both of whom claimed it was theirs (1 Kgs 3:16-28).

To be wise you must use your knowledge to get on in the world, to avoid shame, or even more importantly, to keep yourself from suffering catastrophic loss. The wise person is a teacher and counselor. In ancient times the wise man was a counselor to the king, advising the best course of action to take in war, also when and how to make peace. Fathers passed on wisdom to their sons — warning them of hidden dangers, how to succeed in life, the virtues of a good wife, and so on (Proverbs). Mothers taught daughters how to succeed in getting a husband (cf. Ruth 3:1-5) and find success in other ways.

The wisdom element in the book of Deuteronomy is identified by its use of terms for wisdom and being wise, also by themes found in the wisdom literature of the Old Testament, i.e., Proverbs, Ecclesiastes, Job, certain Psalms, and in the Protestant Apocrypha, Wisdom of Solomon and Sirach (Ecclesiasticus), the last-named said by some to be the wisdom book *par excellence*. We also have for comparison wisdom texts and international treaties in extrabiblical literature. The latter would include the Instruction of Amen-em-opet ($ANET^3$, 421-25), the Sefire Stela (Fitzmyer 1961; 1967; D. J. McCarthy 1963), the Vassal Treaties of Esarhaddon ($ANET^3$, 534-41), and others. The Instruction of Amen-em-opet invites comparison to Prov 22:17–24:22 ($ANET^3$, 421).

We see early on in Deuteronomy a concern that Israel be a nation imbued with wisdom. Moses says regarding the statutes and ordinances he is teaching the people:

> So you shall be careful and you shall do, for that will be your wisdom and your understanding in the eyes of the peoples, who, when they hear all these statutes, will say, "Surely a wise and understanding people is this great nation!" (Deut 4:6)

The concern here is with appearances, how Israel appears to other nations. This is an appeal to shame, a wisdom theme expounded all throughout Deuteronomy (Daube 1969a, 50).

In three different passages in the Pentateuch, leaders and magistrates are appointed to aid Moses in governing the people, and in each passage the personal qualities cited are different from the others (Weinfeld 1967, 257; 1972, 244-45). In Exod 18:21, Jethro tells Moses to "choose *able men* from all the people, *such as fear God, men who are trustworthy and hate a bribe.*" In Num 11:16-30, God endows the elders aiding Moses with a *divine spirit.* But in Deut 1:13-17, Moses is to appoint from the tribes *wise, understanding, and knowledgeable men* (v. 13).

We may compare the Covenant Code (Exodus 21–23) with Deuteronomy at another point to show how, in the view of the Deuteronomic author, the judge is expected to possess wisdom. Exodus 23:8 states: "And you shall take no bribe, for a bribe blinds the officials, and subverts the cause of those who are in the right." But Deut 16:19 says: "you shall not take a bribe, for a bribe blinds the eyes of the *wise* and subverts the cause of the righteous." Weinfeld points out that the intellectual qualities of wisdom, understanding, and knowledge are traits that characterize leaders and magistrates in the wisdom literature. A personified Wisdom declares in Prov 8:15-16: "By me kings reign, and rulers decree what is just; by me princes rule, and nobles, all who govern rightly."

Deuteronomy contains laws having clear parallels in the book of Proverbs. The law on not removing the neighbor's landmark in Deut 19:14, and the curse for the same in 27:17, have parallels in Prov 22:28 and 23:10. The law in Deut 25:13-16 about merchants not using false weights and measures has parallels in Prov 11:1 and 20:10, 23. In Deut 8:5, we are also told that as a man disciplines his son, so Yahweh disciplines his people, which echoes the teaching of Prov 3:11-12. And the law in Deut 23:22-24(23:21-23) about being sure to pay a vow has parallels in Prov 20:25; Eccl 5:3-4[4-5]; Sir 18:22 (Weinfeld 1972, 279).

Deuteronomy also picks up characteristic vocabulary from Proverbs, for example, the term "abomination" (תּוֹעֵבָה), often in the expression, "abomination to Yahweh," which appears only in Deuteronomy and Proverbs. "Abomination" occurs 21 times in Proverbs (3:32; 6:16; 8:7; 11:1, 20; 12:22; 13:19; 15:8, 9, 26; 16:5, 12; 17:15; 20:10, 23; 21:27; 24:9; 26:25 (plural); 28:9; 29:27 [2x]), and 16 times in Deuteronomy (7:25, 26; 12:31; 13:15[14]; 14:3; 17:1, 4; 18:9, 12; 20:18; 22:5; 23:19[23:18]; 24:4; 25:16; 27:15; 32:16). The term appears also in the Egyptian "Instruction of Amen-em-opet" (Weinfeld 1972, 267-68).

Promient wisdom themes in Deuteronomy are the following:

Humane treatment and benevolence to the poor and needy
Teaching of children
Blessing: life, goodness, and longevity in the land
Avoidance of shame
Discerning false from true prophets

Humane Treatment and Benevolence to the Poor and Needy

Deuteronomy's concern that humanitarian treatment be accorded certain individuals in society has long been noted (Driver 1895, xxiii-xxv; E. Day 1911; Weinfeld 1961). Driver (1895, xxv) says of the Deuteronomic writer:

> The author speaks out of a warm heart himself; and he strives to kindle a warm response in the heart of everyone whom he addresses. Nowhere else in the OT do we breathe such an atmosphere of generous devotion to God, and of large-hearted benevolence towards man; nowhere else are duties and motives set forth with greater depth and tenderness of feeling, or with more winning and persuasive eloquence; and nowhere else is it shown with the same fulness of detail how high and noble principles may be applied so as to elevate and refine the entire life of the community.

Scholars of an earlier generation attributed this humanitarian outlook to the influence of Hebrew prophecy, but Kaufmann (1960, 157-66) took issue with this view, and Weinfeld (1961, 244-47; 1972, 293-97) countered with a thesis that influence came rather from Israel's school of wisdom. Daube (1969a) agreed, at least to the extent that Deuteronomy is seen to contain a strong shame-cultural element, which he attributed to wisdom influence. Daube went on to say: "In a system where how you appear to others is of enormous importance, to look on your fellow with benevolence becomes a prominent virtue, to look on him with ill-will a prominent vice, indeed danger" (1969a, 50). He thought it no accident that Deuteronomy alone in the Old Testament uses the expression "his eye is evil, grudging, toward somebody" (15:9; 28:54, 56).

Deuteronomy shows particular concern for the sojourner, orphan, and widow, also the Levite in town, who has no inheritance (= landed property) and in the seventh century is out of a job. Local sanctuaries have been closed down in the reform of Hezekiah (2 Kgs 18:22[= Isa 36:7]), which centralized worship in Jerusalem, and soon after they may well have been ruined by enemy invaders. The local Levite thus gets a share of offerings made at the central sanctuary (14:27; 18:1-5); is entitled to the third-year charity-tithe in the town where he lives (14:28-29; 26:12-13); and is invited to accompany families and their servants in the annual pilgrimages to the central sanctuary, where all are enjoined to eat and be glad (16:10-11, 14). At harvest time, the sojourner, orphan, and widow are accorded gleaning rights (24:19-21). Deuteronomy teaches that justice must not be perverted toward the sojourner, orphan, and widow (24:17; 27:19), for Yahweh loves them and treats them justly (10:17-18). Israel, for its part, would do well to reflect on its own past, remembering that it was once a band of slaves in the land of Egypt (10:19; 16:12; 24:18, 22).

We learn from Egyptian, Akkadian, and Ugaritic texts that in other societies, too, special care was taken to protect and treat justly the orphan, widow, and outcast (Fensham 1962a; Galpaz-Feller 2008). From ancient Egypt comes the Instruction for King Meri-ka-Re (twenty-second century), in which a ruler gives this advice to his son and successor: "Do justice while you endure on the earth. Quiet the weeper; do not oppress the widow" ($ANET^3$, 415). In The Protest of the Eloquent Peasant (twenty-first century), a peasant beaten and robbed of donkeys on a trip to Egypt seeks redress from the Pharaoh's chief steward, whom he addresses as "the father of the orphan, the husband of the widow, the brother of the divorcee, and the apron of him who is motherless" ($ANET^3$, 408). The Laws of Ur-Nammu (162-68) mandated protection for the orphan, widow, and the poor ($ANET^3$, 524). King Hammurabi in the epilogue to his Law Code (lines 30-90) boasts that he "promoted welfare in the land . . . in order that the strong might not oppress the weak, that justice might be dealt the orphan and the widow in Babylon" ($ANET^3$, 178). And in the Keret Legend from Ugarit, King Keret is reprimanded by his son Yaṣṣib for neglecting the orphans and the widows, and told to step down so Yaṣṣib can reign (KRT C vi 25-50; $ANET^3$, 149). Finally, in the Tale of Aqhat it is the good Daniel who judges the cause of the widow and the orphan (Aqht A v 1-10; Aqht C i 20-30; $ANET^3$, 151, 153). In the NT, justice to widows lies at the heart of Jesus' parable of the Poor Widow (Luke 18:1-8).

Many of the laws of Deuteronomy are humanistic in character. The following, which are peculiar to Deuteronomy, relate to human life and human dignity:

> Required construction of a parapet (low wall encircling a flat roof) on a new house to eliminate the danger of someone falling off the roof and being killed (22:8).
>
> The attitude to fair maidens captured in (foreign) wars and wanted by Israelite men for wives — that the maidens be allowed time to mourn and improve their appearance before the marriage is consummated. If the marriage does not work, the women are free to go wherever they want. They must not be sold as slaves, as was commonly done, or treated as slaves by the men who married them, assuming the marriage was largely to satisfy the man's lustful urges (21:10-14).
>
> The giving of asylum to slaves escaping to Israel, and not returning them to their (foreign) masters. They are to dwell in Israelite towns, and not be oppressed (23:16-17[23:15-16]).
>
> The attitude on debt remission (= cancellation) to a poor Israelite in the seventh year. The creditor shall not refuse to lend because the seventh

year is approaching. The aim is to eliminate poor in the land, but this will obtain only if people obey the commands. There is no danger that the poor will cease (or grow fat) in the land (15:1-11).

The warning against a man discriminating against an unfavored wife and her firstborn son in the liquidation of his estate, giving the younger son of the favored wife the (double) portion, and the actual firstborn son what is left. The rights of the firstborn are to be given to the firstborn, even if he is the son of the unfavored wife (21:15-17).

The attitude about not taking hand-mills or upper millstones in pledge, which would deprive the poor (women) of their only means to grind grain and prepare daily bread. This would be tantamount to taking a life in pledge (24:6).

The attitude toward collecting a pledge as security for a loan, that the creditor not enter the house and fetch it for himself, but wait outside and have it brought to him (24:10-11).

The attitude toward the poor laborer or sojourner, that he receive his wages the same day that he has worked, before the sun goes down (24:14-15).

The attitude about not taking a widow's garment in pledge under any circumstances (24:17).

Two laws in Deuteronomy deal with cruelty to animals:

The prohibition against taking the mother bird with her eggs or her young from a nest happened upon by chance; the mother must be chased away (22:6-7).
The prohibition against muzzling an ox treading grain (25:4).

Other humanitarian laws in Deuteronomy have parallels or precedents in the Covenant Code:

The attitude on giving fellow-Israelites interest-free loans, intended as relief for poor and insolvent people who might be victims of war, famine, pestilence, a death in the family (2 Kgs 4:1), or some other adversity over which they had no control (23:20-21[23:19-20]; cf. Exod 22:24[25]).
The attitude regarding a poor man from whom a garment has been taken as a pledge, that the creditor not sleep in the pledge, but restore it to the man before sundown (24:12-13; cf. Exod 22:25-26[26-27]).

The law regulating manumission of Hebrew slaves in Deut 15:12-18 is more enlightened than the corresponding law in Exod 21:1-11. In the Deuteronomic law, both male and female slaves are set free when their term is up (Deut 15:12), whereas in the Covenant Code female slaves do not go free (Exod 21:7). The freed slave in the Deuteronomic Code is also given a gift at the time of manumission (15:12-14), which is not specified in Exodus law. According to Weinfeld (1967, 261), Deuteronomy does not consider the Hebrew slave as property (cf. Exod 21:21), rather as a "brother" (15:12). And in Deuteronomic law nothing is said about a wife given to a male slave by his master and children born to that wife, that they not go out with him, which is specified in the law of the Covenant Code (Exod 21:4).

TEACHING OF CHILDREN

Teaching and learning, with a larger aim of promoting doing, are important wisdom themes. The didactic temper, according to Weinfeld (1972, 298), is present in the wisdom literature because its concern is with education. Moses is the great teacher in Deuteronomy (P. D. Miller 1987). He teaches Yahweh's commands to the people (4:1, 5, 14; 5:31; 6:1; 31:19, 22), who are then supposed to teach the same to their children (4:9-10; 6:7; 11:19). Teaching children is not something you believe in; it is something you do. The verb "teach" (למד Piel) occurs ten times in Deuteronomy (4:1, 5, 10, 14; 5:31; 6:1; 11:19; 20:18; 31:19, 22) and the verb "learn" (למד Qal), seven times (4:10; 5:1; 14:23; 17:19; 18:9; 31:12, 13). The verb "teach" appears in no other book of the Pentateuch, only in Deuteronomy (Weinfeld 1972, 303).

The related matter of discipline, which is a major theme in Proverbs (Prov 3:11-12; 5:7-14, 23; 6:23; 12:1; 13:24; 15:10; 19:18; 22:15; 23:13; 29:17), and in wisdom literature generally, finds a prominent place in Deuteronomy (Deut 4:36; 8:5; 11:2; 21:18-21; 22:18).

One of the ways in which extraordinary things of the past stay with people is by someone teaching them to the children and grandchildren. Parents are to teach children the mighty acts of God in redeeming Israel from Egyptian slavery. In Deut 6:20-25 we read:

> When your son asks you in the future: "What mean the testimonies and the statutes and the ordinances that Yahweh our God commanded you?" then you shall say to your son, "Slaves we were to Pharaoh in Egypt, and Yahweh brought us out from Egypt by a strong hand, and Yahweh gave signs and wonders, great and severe against Egypt, against Pharaoh, and against all his house, before our eyes, and us he brought out from there, in order that he bring us in to give to us the land that he swore to our fathers. And Yahweh commanded us to do all these statutes, to fear Yahweh our God, for

our own good all the days, that he might let us live, as at this day. And righteousness it will be for us when we are careful to do all this commandment before Yahweh our God, just as he commanded us."

A liturgical injunction admonishing people to hear, internalize, and teach Yahweh's commands to their children appears twice in the book (6:4-9; 11:18-20). In 6:4-9 it is preceded by the Shema ("Hear, [O Israel] . . ."):

Hear, O Israel, Yahweh our God, Yahweh is one. And you shall love Yahweh your God with all your heart and with all your soul and with all your might. And these words that I am commanding you today shall be upon your heart. And you shall impress them to your children, and you shall speak about them when you sit in your house and when you walk in the way, and when you lie down and when you rise. And you shall bind them as a sign upon your hand, and they shall be as headbands between your eyes. And you shall write them upon the doorposts of your house and within your gates.

Teaching of children is a prominent theme in Proverbs. In Prov 6:20-22 the son is told to keep the teachings of both father and mother. See also Prov 7:1-3 and 8:32-34. Most education in ancient Israel took place in the home (Crenshaw 1985; 1998).

In the verses immediately preceding the injunction of 6:4-9, Moses stresses the importance of doing his teachings in the land the people are about to inherit. Keeping the commands by them and their children will lead to fearing Yahweh (6:1-2), which, as was said earlier, is an important wisdom theme in Deuteronomy and all throughout the Bible (Weinfeld 1972, 274-81). Elsewhere in Deuteronomy, people are told to make known to the children and grandchildren the extraordinary events at Horeb and the words Yahweh spoke there (4:9-10).

In Deuteronomy, Moses calls for a public reading of the Law every seven years at the Feast of Booths. Entire families — and even sojourners — are to be present to hear the Law read aloud by the Levitical priests (31:10-13):

And Moses commanded them: "After seven years' time, at the appointed time of the year of remission, at the Feast of Booths, when all Israel comes to appear before Yahweh your God, in the place that he will choose, you shall recite this law in front of all Israel in their hearing. Assemble the people, the men and the women and the little ones, also your sojourner who is within your gates, so that they may hear and so that they may learn to fear Yahweh your God and be careful to do all the words of this law; yes their children who have not known may hear and may learn to fear Yahweh your

God all the days that you live on the soil that you are crossing over the Jordan to take possession of it."

When Moses is commanded by Yahweh to teach people a song before he passes from the scene (Deut 32:1-43), which will serve as a witness to future generations of Israel's rebelliousness in the wilderness, the writer adds parenthetically that this song "will live unforgotten in the mouths of their descendants" (31:21). Teaching of this song will thus be required. After Moses gave the song, he again told the people that they must impart this teaching to their children (32:46).

The ANE treaties have a clear didactic concern. In the Sefire Stela:

Thus we spoke (and thus we wr)ote. What I, Mati'el, have written (is) a reminder to my son (and) my grandson who come af(ter) me. Let them do the right thing. . . . (D. J. McCarthy 1963, 192)

And from the treaty of Esarhaddon (ca. 672):

(You swear that) as you stand in the place of this oath you will not swear with the words of the lips (alone), but with your whole heart, (and) you will teach the treaty to your children who live afterwards. (D. J. McCarthy 1963, 200)

BLESSING: LIFE, GOODNESS, AND LONGEVITY IN THE LAND

The Horeb covenant, being conditional in nature, stands fortified by blessings and curses. Blessing is what Israel lives for. Deuteronomy recalls Yahweh's blessing in the past and anticipates more of the same in the future. Opposite of blessing is the curse, and about the covenant curses Deuteronomy has more to say than any other book of the Pentateuch. If Israel obeys Yahweh's commands, it will be blessed; if it disobeys, a multitude of curses will descend upon the nation. Blessings and curses are therefore announced in Deut 11:26-32, where reference is to a covenant renewal festival on Mount Gerizim and Mount Ebal (cf. 27:12-13), and then are described in copious detail in chapter 28, where the curses outnumber the blessings nearly four to one. For what will happen after Israel has experienced the blessings and the curses, see 30:1-10.

Elsewhere in Deuteronomy, Israel is promised blessing (and multiplication) if it obeys Yahweh's commands (7:12-16; 8:6-10). Blessing will come when Israelites give the third-year charity-tithe to the Levite, sojourner, orphan, and widow (14:28-29); grant debt remission in the seventh year, most importantly to the fellow-Israelite who is poor (15:1-11); manumit Hebrew slaves — male and female — in the seventh year, providing them also with a departing gift (15:12-18); loan to fellow-Israelites without interest (23:20-21[23:19-20]); restore garments taken in pledge from the poor before sundown (24:12-13); and permit the sojourner, orphan, and widow to glean at harvest time (24:19-22). Deuteronomy says that Yahweh will bring abundant harvests in the good land, and these will be a blessing (2:7; 12:7, 15; 14:24; 15:14; 16:10, 15, 17). And at the presentation of the firstfruits, the worshipper is to request Yahweh's ongoing blessing on Israel (26:15).

Deuteronomy describes blessing as material reward: life, goodness, and longevity in the land (Weinfeld 1960b). Weinfeld (1967, 257) says:

> Like the wise teacher who stresses the material benefits that accrue from proper behavior, the author of Deuteronomy makes repeated references to the good fortune that will be the lot of those who observe God's commandments. The principal deuteronomic inducement to observe the Torah is, as in the wisdom literature, material retribution. In no other book of the Pentateuch does the concern for material welfare occupy so great a place as in the book of Deuteronomy. Life, good fortune, longevity, large families, affluence and satiety, the eudemonistic assurances which constitute an essential part of wisdom teaching — these constitute the primary motivation for the observance of God's laws.

One meets up often in the book with the stereotypical phrase about "living long in the land" (5:33; 11:9; 22:7; 32:47). Land tenure depends upon Israel keeping the covenant, which is doing the commands. If Israel goes after other gods, it will not live long in the land (4:26; 30:18). Doing the commands gives "life" to the covenant people (4:1; 8:1; 32:47). "Life" also comes to those who practice "justice, and only justice" (16:20; cf. Prov 21:21). Weinfeld (1972, 273) notes that Proverbs speaks often about doing justice and righteousness to preserve one's life or to keep one from death (Prov 10:2; 11:4, 19; 12:28; 16:31). He thinks this emphasis on "life" has its ultimate source in Egyptian wisdom teaching, e.g., The Instruction of Amen-em-opet.

Deuteronomy pulls all these ideas together in its "two ways" teaching in 30:15-20, which invites comparison with Prov 4:10-19. The "two ways" teaching:

> See I have set before you today the life and the good, and the death and the bad. [If you listen to the commandment of Yahweh your God] that I am commanding you today, to love Yahweh your God, to walk in his ways, and to keep his commandments and his statutes and his ordinances, then you will live and you will multiply, and Yahweh your God will bless you in the

Introduction

land into which you are entering to possess it. But if your heart turns away and you do not listen, and you are drawn away and you worship other gods and serve them, I declare to you today that you shall surely perish; your days will not be prolonged on the soil that you are crossing over the Jordan to enter to take possession of it. I call to witness against you today the heavens and earth: Life and death I have set before you, blessing and curse, so you can choose life in order that you and your descendants may live, to love Yahweh your God, to obey his voice, and to cling to him, for it is your life and the prolonging of your days to dwell on the soil that Yahweh swore to your fathers, to Abraham, to Isaac, and to Jacob, to give to them.

AVOIDANCE OF SHAME

David Daube (1969a; 1969b) argues that Deuteronomy contains a strong shame-cultural element, and as such teaches the avoidance of shame. This shame-cultural bias he attributes to wisdom influence in the book. He says:

> The principal explanation of Deuteronomy's shame-cultural bias seems . . . to lie in the affiliation with Wisdom. . . . Deuteronomy does not belong to Wisdom literature but it stands in close relation to it. . . . In so far as Wisdom governs, authority is more diffused, appeal is made to a larger number of people who are of correspondingly less overwhelming stature [than the single towering figure of a father for the culture in which guilt is more prominent] — the neighbours, peers, well-thinking citizens, and so forth; it is in these conditions that shame culture tends to come to the fore. (Daube 1969a, 27, 51-52)

Because wisdom has its eye on success in society, concern is expressed for the impression created by an act, on applause and disapproval. Yet, as we said earlier, Hebrew wisdom is deeply religious. Daube says this is so because the guilt mechanism is vigorous. Guilt is present or imputed when one has succumbed to wrongdoing — particularly against God or the commands of God. Daube finds a curious blend of guilt culture and shame culture in ancient Israel and says that guilt culture may still predominate. Yet he believes that unless attention is paid to the admixture of shame culture, our picture of Deuteronomy and conclusions drawn from it will be seriously distorted.

A shame element can be seen in a number of Deuteronomic laws:

20:8. The officer responsible for recruiting the militia concludes his speech before the assembly by saying that the fearful and weakhearted should depart and not go to battle. This appeals to a man's sense of shame, says Daube

(1969a, 29), particularly when preceded by an earlier admonition from the priest that men not be fearful and weakhearted when Yahweh will give them the victory (vv. 3-4). It is evident that disgrace awaits anyone who slips away due to fear and weakheartedness. Conversely, glory awaits those who, after being offered an opportunity to opt out, do stay to fight. Acceptance, favor, and honor are great rewards in a shame culture. Shame is contrasted to honor in Prov 3:35.

21:22-23. The body of a criminal executed and hanged must be taken down before sunset, an injunction that appears only in Deuteronomy. The reason for not allowing the body to hang all night is so the land will not be defiled. Daube (1969a, 46-47) says the look of things is important for the writer of Deuteronomy, just as when a corpse lies unburied (21:1) or the camp is left unclean (23:13-15[23:12-14]).

22:1-4. A cluster of directives warns against "hiding oneself" from awkward situations. None has a parallel outside Deuteronomy. One must not hide oneself from someone's animal that has wandered off, or when finding something a person has lost, or from someone's animal that has fallen. The law concerning a stray animal in Exod 23:4 calls simply for a return by the one who finds it; there is no mention of "hiding oneself" from it. Daube (1969a, 29-30) says this means that a person must not give in to the temptation to avoid an awkward sight and in a manner that dispenses with outright refusal. He says the injunction "do not hide yourself" introduces a shame aspect more common in the Orient than in the West. The Deuteronomic writer assumes that one will be embarrassed at an unseemly object and will try to escape without being noticed. A similar "hiding of oneself" is evident in Jesus' parable of the Good Samaritan (Luke 10:31-32).

22:13-21. This law concerning a bride charged by her husband with coming to him and not being a virgin is promulgated with shame in mind. Daube (1969a, 30) says: "The importance of what people think of you, of your name, your reputation, could not be brought out more clearly." The entire procedure is carried out in public, before the elders in the city gate. There the bedcloth of the wedding night is displayed for all to see. If the charge proves false, the groom must pay the bride's father a sum of money and he may not divorce her. Daube emphasizes the reason given: "because he has brought an evil name upon a virgin of Israel" (v. 19). If the charge is true, the bride is stoned at the door of her father's house, the house where she lived when she misbehaved. Her conduct has brought shame upon all Israel.

23:2-7(23:1-6). Here certain categories of people are not permitted entrance into the assembly of Yahweh: eunuchs, bastards, Ammonites, and Moabites. Edomites and Egyptians may enter only in the third generation. The creation of classes in which tainted individuals are deprived of full rights, says Daube, is "a mighty weapon in the shame cultural arsenal."

23:13-15(23:12-14). This legislation about relieving oneself outside the camp and covering up one's excrement is promulgated so that Yahweh, when touring the camp, will not see "an unseemly thing." The expression (עֶרְוַת דָּבָר) occurs only one other time in the OT, in the Deuteronomic law dealing with divorce (24:1), and Daube says it is a direct reference to the shame aspect.

23:19(23:18). The wages of a cult prostitute — male or female — are not to be brought into the assembly of Yahweh. They are tainted by the disgraceful way in which they were received.

24:1-4. The description of the primary divorce in this law reflects a preoccupation with shame. The wife loses favor in the eyes of her husband, which Daube (1969a, 32) says in a shame culture is a terrible misfortune. The great aim in a shame culture is to find favor in the beholder's eyes. The point is further stressed when it says the husband has found some "unseemly thing" (עֶרְוַת דָּבָר) in her. Daube compares this with the Roman concept of *repudium* (1969a, 33; 1969b).

24:8-9. This law regarding scale disease requires that one follow the instructions of the priests minutely. Remember, the Deuteronomic writer adds, what Yahweh did to Miriam when Israel came out of Egypt. Miriam (and Aaron) had questioned Moses' authority, and Miriam was smitten with the disease. Moses interceded on her behalf, but Yahweh replied: "If her father had but spit in her face, should she not be shamed seven days?" So Miriam was sent outside the camp for seven days (Num 12:14). Scale disease was seen as a mark of disfavor brought upon by Yahweh, comparable to the disgrace of a child whose father had spit in his face.

24:10-11. In this law regarding a loan where a pledge is required, the creditor is not permitted to go into the house to seize the pledge but must remain outside and wait there for the pledge to be brought to him. Daube says this is a striking instance of sensitivity to shame. If the creditor were to enter the house and seize whatever he desired for a pledge, it would be a great dishonor to the debtor and his family. Handing over outside preserves appearances.

25:1-3. Here the wrongdoer sentenced to a whipping must not be given more than forty stripes. If he were given an excessive number, says the Deuteronomic writer, the brother would "be rendered contemptible" (קלה) in the eyes of others. Daube says a man subjected to a wild, unlimited bastinado will lose his dignity and be degraded forever.

25:5-10. Here is the only law in the Pentateuch where punishment consists exclusively in public degradation. If a man refuses to carry out the duty of taking his dead brother's wife in a levirate marriage, the widow shall come up to him in the presence of city elders, pull off his sandal, spit in his face, and recite a degrading word over him (v. 9). His name shall forever be: "The house of him who had his sandal pulled off." Emphasis is laid here upon preserving "the name" of the dead man, which is of great importance in a shame culture (Daube 1969a, 35).

25:11-12. Here is the only law in ancient Israel explicitly mandating maiming. It results from a situation where a woman intervenes in a fight involving her husband and grabs hold of the opponent's "shameful parts" (מְבֻשִׁים). She is punished by having her hand cut off, bringing her permanent disfigurement and eternal shame.

27:16. In Deuteronomy's Dodecalogue, which deals with clandestine transgressions, a curse is placed on anyone who treats his father or mother "with contempt." The verb is the same as in 25:3 (קלה), which deals with a brother rendered "contemptible" in the sight of others if subjected to an unlimited bastinado. In Exodus and Leviticus the death penalty awaits anyone who "curses" or "strikes" his parents (Exod 21:15, 17; Lev 20:9), which Daube (1969a, 38-39) says is a significant difference. Cursing or striking is more serious and can usually be witnessed by others. Contempt is shown in subtle ways and may be out of public view (Weinfeld 1972, 277-78). Weinfeld says that because dishonoring one's parents is here a clandestine act, it cannot be penalized. But Proverbs says such behavior is unacceptable and will be punished (Prov 15:20; 23:22; 30:17).

The Deuteronomic Code in other ways shows itself to contain a shame-cultural element. One may note, for example, the deterrent function of punishment (Daube 1969a, 40). Four times after mandating capital punishment for an offense, the writer of Deuteronomy adds "and all Israel/all the people/those who remain shall hear and fear" (13:12[11]; 17:13; 19:20; 21:21). Public example is very important in a shame culture. Deuteronomy also speaks eleven times about the duty to "utterly remove (בער) evil/guilt of innocent blood from your midst/from Israel" (13:6[5]; 17:7, 12; 19:13, 19; 21:9, 21; 22:21, 22, 24; 24:7). Daube (1969a, 41, 48-49) says the concern in all these cases is with the look of things. On a happier note, Deuteronomy expects entire families — also servants and invited guests — to "rejoice" (שמח) at the annual pilgrim festivals (12:7, 12, 18; 14:26; 16:11, 14, 15; 26:11). Communal display of happiness on specific occasions suits a culture preoccupied with appearances. The other side of ritual merry-making is exclusion from the assembly (23:2-9[23:1-8]).

Other vocabulary in Deuteronomy supports the thesis that the book has a shame-cultural bias. There is the expression, "you/he may not do (such and such)" (לֹא־תוּכַל/יוּכַל), which is not the same as the apodictic "you/he shall not." This expression occurs seven times in the book (12:17; 16:5; 17:15; 21:16; 22:3, 19; 24:4) and means something like "you/he must not even think of doing (such-and-such)." The appeal is to one's sense of shame. Daube says the expression is similar to the modern English expression, "this is impossible behavior," where reference is to an infringement of appearances. There is also the Deuteronomic expression, "when there is found" (כִּי־יִמָּצֵא), which occurs four

Introduction

times in the book. It is used with reference to legislation concerning: (1) a man or woman who does evil and has gone and served other gods (17:2-3); (2) someone found slain in the open field, where it is not known who killed the individual (21:1); (3) a man found lying with another man's wife (22:22); and (4) someone caught kidnapping a person and enslaving or selling him to another (24:7). This expression, says Daube, which occurs also in the prohibition of 18:10 against passing a son or daughter through the fire, shifts "the emphasis from the fearfulness of the crime to the fearfulness of the resulting appearance in the eyes of the beholder — God above all" (1969a, 43-50; 1971a). It is not so much the transgression that is condemned, but its display. And when shame is felt towards God, we are approaching the realm of guilt. Daube says:

> The beholder is horrified not only by wicked acts in progress, idolatry, adultery, theft of a fellow-Israelite, but also by a corpse lying unappeased. In fact, the latter spoils the appearance of the land almost more than any of the other incidents.

In these latter passages, the legislation concludes with the phrase: "you shall utterly remove the evil/guilt of innocent blood from your midst/Israel," which as we said, has to do with the look of things.

Daube concludes his brilliant essay by saying that the most remarkable appeal to shame is the plea that God not wipe out the Israelites, however rebellious, for then their enemies will conclude that he was powerless to lead them to triumph or was ill-intentioned against them from the start (1969a, 51). While this argument occurs elsewhere in the OT (Exod 32:12; Num 14:13-19), it occasions no surprise to find it in the preaching of Deuteronomy (Deut 9:27-29) and also in the Song of Moses (32:26-27).

DISCERNING FALSE FROM TRUE PROPHETS

The Old Testament records two tests for false prophecy, and both occur in Deuteronomy. The first is found in chapter 13, which includes a law in sermonic dress admonishing people not to follow other gods. Verses 2-6(1-5), which contain the first point of a three-point sermon, focus on the prophet and "dreamer of dreams." Should one of these individuals give a sign or a wonder — even with a predictive word that comes to pass — people are not to pay heed if the individual leads them in the way of other gods. Prophets and "would-be prophets" who lead people in the way of other gods are ingenuine and must be put to death. Yahweh gives them success only so that he may test people to see whether they love him and are committed to walk in his way. People are to apply the "Yahweh only" test to see which prophets are false and which prophets are true. The true prophet speaks for Yahweh and leads people in the way of Yahweh. The false prophet leads people in the worship of other gods.

So long as it was between prophets of Yahweh and prophets of other gods the choice was simple. But what does one do when all the prophets are Yahweh prophets and there is disagreement among them? How does one tell the false prophet? Or the true prophet? For this situation a second test of true and false prophecy is given in Deut 18:20-22:

> But the prophet who presumes to speak a word in my name that I did not command him to speak, or who speaks in the name of other gods, yes, that prophet shall die. And if you say in your heart, "How shall we know the word that Yahweh has not spoken?" When the prophet speaks in the name of Yahweh, and the word does not happen, or does not come to pass, that is the word that Yahweh has not spoken. The prophet has spoken it presumptuously; you need not be afraid of him.

When Yahweh prophets speak contrary words, such as happened in 1 Kings 22, or later in Jeremiah 28, the test for true and false prophecy comes in fulfillment of the prophetic word. Words spoken by false Yahweh prophets will not be fulfilled. And for good measure, the older test of Deut 13:2-6(1-5) is incorporated into this new test by the addition of the words "or who speaks in the name of other gods" in v. 20.

With wisdom being concerned about discerning what is true from what is false, these texts on true and false prophets must be included with other passages in the book showing influence from wisdom traditions.

THEOLOGICAL IDEAS IN DEUTERONOMY

THE NAME OF YAHWEH

The name of Israel's God is Yahweh, and a glorious and awesome name it is (28:58; 32:3). This name has been put upon Israel (28:10), which implies ownership, as we know from Egyptian texts. In Deuteronomy much is said about the central sanctuary being the place where Yahweh has caused his name to dwell (12:5, 11, 21; 14:23; 16:2, 6, 11; 26:2). Von Rad therefore identified what he called a "name (שֵׁם) theology" in Deuteronomy, as opposed to a "glory (כָּבוֹד) theology" in the Priestly document (von Rad 1953, 37-44). Deuteronomy affirms that Yahweh himself is not present in the worship place; he has only put his name there. Yahweh's residence is in the heavens (4:36; 26:15; 33:26; cf. 1 Kgs 8:27-30).

Introduction

In older Yahwistic theology, Yahweh is depicted as residing on earth (Gen 3:8-13), and in other pre-Deuteronomic theology Yahweh is invisibly present on his ark, which serves as his throne (Num 10:35-36; 1 Sam 4:4). Later Priestly theology became even more anthropomorphic, seeing the tabernacle (= tent of meeting) as the place on earth where Yahweh's "glory" met with the people (Exod 29:43; Num 14:10; 16:19). And yet in older material one does find the statement that Yahweh speaks from heaven (Exod 20:22), and it has been argued recently (Hundley 2009) that Deuteronomy and the Deuteronomic History do not absent Yahweh from earth, but simply leave the exact nature and extent of Yahweh's presence on earth ambiguous (cf. Deut 4:39).

Because Yahweh's name is like no other, Israel is told in the third commandment not to lift up the name of Yahweh in emptiness, or "in vain" (5:11). When people swear oaths, however, they are to swear them in Yahweh's name (6:13; 10:20). Priests are to serve and bless the people in Yahweh's name (10:8; 18:5, 7; 21:5), and bona fide prophets speak in the name of Yahweh (18:19). Prophets must not speak in the name of other gods or speak in Yahweh's name if Yahweh has not commanded them to speak (18:20, 22).

Yahweh the One and Only God

The Shema, which has become the preeminent testimony of faith for the Jewish people, affirms the oneness of Yahweh God (6:4), some would say also his uniqueness and exclusivity. The exclusivity of Yahweh, i.e., he is God and there is no other, is clearly attested in 4:35 and 39, also in the Song of Moses (32:39), which anticipate the spirited monotheism of Second Isaiah (Isaiah 40–48). Deuteronomy says Yahweh is God of gods and Lord of lords (Deut 10:17), i.e., he is supreme God and supreme Lord. Yahweh has absolute sovereignty over any other claimants to the title. Moses tells Israel: "Yahweh your God is God" (7:9). Yahweh alone led Israel through the inhospitable wilderness (32:12), and to Yahweh belong the heavens and the earth (10:14).

Yahweh a Holy God

The idea of Yahweh being a holy God, which is celebrated by the prophet Isaiah (Isa 6:3), is not prominent in Deuteronomy, nor in Jeremiah. Moses says only in Deut 32:51 that because he and Aaron broke faith at Meribat-kadesh in not revering Yahweh as holy, they were denied entrance into the promised land. Yahweh's habitation, however, is holy (26:15). Deuteronomy's more important teaching is that Israel is a holy people.

Theological Ideas in Deuteronomy

Yahweh Is Heard but Not Seen

Deuteronomy makes it clear that Yahweh is a God who can be heard but not seen. The Ten Commandments were revealed first to the people out of the fire, on the day of assembly (4:10-13; 5:22), when they heard the divine voice but saw no form (cf. Exod 33:18-23). Hearing the divine voice was remarkable enough, and it is a wonder that the people remained alive (Deut 4:33; 5:23-26; cf. Exod 20:18-19). Because Israel saw no form at Horeb, images of Yahweh were disallowed (Deut 4:15-18, 23; 5:8). Images of the divine introduce a visual element into religion, and this was rejected in ancient Israel. The expression "face to face," when used of Israel's encounter with Yahweh (5:4), or Moses' encounter with Yahweh (34:10; cf. Exod 33:11), has no visual dimension whatever; there is only an exchange of words.

Yahweh a God of Love

Deuteronomy has more to say about "love" than any other OT book — both Yahweh's gracious love toward Israel and Israel's obligation to love Yahweh. In fact, Yahweh's love for the patriarchs and for Israel is expressed only in Deuteronomy in the Pentateuch. It occurs also in the preaching of Hosea (Hos 2:21[2:19]; 3:1; 11:1, 4; 14:5[14:4]), who speaks about the covenant as a bond of love between husband (Yahweh) and wife (Israel). This metaphor is never made explicit in Deuteronomy. In the Blessing of Moses, an old poem predating Deuteronomy, it says that Yahweh left behind thousands of holy ones in his mountain abodes to throw in his lot with "peoples," specifically the peoples of Israel. It was done because of his love for them (33:2-3). Deuteronomy elsewhere states that Yahweh became attached to the patriarchs in love (10:15), then became attached in love to Israel (7:7-8, 13). Balaam's curse was turned into blessing because of Yahweh's love for Israel (23:6[23:5]). This love was a gracious disposition on the part of Yahweh, a divine mystery admitting no further explanation.

Love in Deuteronomy is closely tied in with election (4:37; 7:7-8; 10:15) and with the covenant (5:10; 7:12). In fact, Moses says in 5:10 that Yahweh shows steadfast love to those who love him and keep his commandments (cf. Exod 34:7). The same holds for the future (7:12-13). Deuteronomy employs two words for love: the common אַהֲבָה, which is a term of emotion and embodies the idea of "breathing," and חֶסֶד, which is "covenant love." אַהֲבָה never describes the covenant in Deuteronomy. Yahweh chose Israel for two reasons: (1) because he loved Israel; and (2) because he was keeping an oath sworn to the patriarchs (7:8). Yahweh loves the sojourner too, supplying him with food and clothing

Introduction

(10:18), which shows that divine love is tied in with justice and benevolence and that it is not only for Israel, but for all who reside in the land, even foreigners.

YAHWEH A GOD FAITHFUL TO HIS PROMISES

The Song of Moses says that Yahweh is "a God of faithfulness" (32:4), which is affirmed also in 7:9, where it says that Yahweh keeps covenant and steadfast love indefinitely for those who love him and keep his commandments (cf. Exod 34:6-7). The Horeb covenant is conditional; nevertheless, Yahweh will not forget or break this covenant so long as his people remain obedient (4:31; 7:12-13). Deuteronomy affirms Yahweh's faithfulness mostly in pointing out how Yahweh is keeping the oath to the fathers to drive out the wicked Canaanites and give Israel their land (1:8; 6:10, 18, 23; 9:5; 10:11, and often). This oath is rooted in the covenant with Abraham (Gen 12:7; 13:14-15, 17; 15:18-21, etc.), which included a promise that Abraham would have a myriad of descendants (Gen 12:2; 13:16; 15:5, etc.). Israel's multiplication in the land, strength to attain wealth in the land, (prolonged) life in the land, blessing in the land, and the promise of enlarged borders are rooted in Yahweh's promises to Abraham (8:1, 18-19; 11:9, 21; 13:18-19[13:17-18]); 19:8-9; 26:14-15; 28:8-11; 30:19-20). But all depends upon Israel doing the commandments. Yahweh loved and elected Israel as his chosen people because of his oath to the fathers (7:7-8; 29:11-12[29:12-13]). Deuteronomy also knows of other oaths sworn by Yahweh, which he promised to keep and did keep, e.g., that the unfaithful generation would die in the wilderness (1:34-36; 2:14) and that Moses would not enter the promised land (4:21)

YAHWEH A RIGHTEOUS GOD

Deuteronomy is much concerned with righteous behavior, but the book proper makes no claims about Yahweh being righteous, which is heard so often in the Psalms (Pss 11:7; 116:5; 119:137; 129:4). Only the Song of Moses states explicitly that Yahweh is righteous (32:4). Yet we assume that Deuteronomy believes Yahweh to be righteous since he hates sin and wrongdoing. Worship of other gods (17:3-4), idols and idolatrous rites (7:25-26; 12:31; 13:15[13:14]; 20:18; 27:15; 32:16), magic and divination (18:12), immoral customs (22:5; 23:19[23:18]; 24:4), blemished sacrifices (17:1), and commercial injustice (25:16) are all "abominations" to him.

Yahweh an Impartial Judge

Yahweh is a God of justice and impartial in carrying out justice. Testimony to Yahweh as a God of justice is prominent in the Song of Moses, which says that all God's ways are just (32:4). Because Yahweh can be counted on to act justly, vengeance can be left to him, which gets the emphasis at the end of the Song (32:35, 41, 43). Elsewhere in Deuteronomy the emphasis is on the appointing of impartial judges in Israel (1:16-17) and requiring just practices in the marketplace (25:13-15). The reason for needing impartial judges is that the judgment they render is God's (1:17). Yahweh is impartial in judgment and will not take a bribe (10:17). Yahweh executes justice for the orphan and widow, loving also the sojourner (10:18). And as a good judge, Yahweh tempers his judgments with compassion and mercy (4:31; 13:18[13:17]). In fact, his steadfast love is said to be infinitely greater than his judgment (5:9-10; 7:9-10; cf. Exod 34:6-7).

Israel a Holy People

Israel is a people "holy" to Yahweh (7:6; 14:2, 21; 26:19; 28:9; cf. Exod 19:6), which is to say that in the economy of God Israel has been set apart for a special purpose. To Yahweh belong heaven and earth (Deut 4:39; 10:14); nevertheless, his favor rests upon a single, treasured people: Israel. This idea carries over into the New Testament, where it is given expanded application to the church (1 Pet 2:9-10).

The Election of Israel

The concept of election is tied in with the verb בחר, "to choose," which occurs often in Deuteronomy (Driver 1895, lxxx #23). Yahweh's choice surpassing every other choice was Israel as his own possession out of all the peoples on earth (4:37; 7:6; 10:15; 14:2; 26:18; cf. 32:9). The concept of election derives from Israel being a "holy (= set apart) people" (7:6; 10:15). Israel's election is given its fullest explanation in the OT in 7:6-8, where election is said to have come not because of numbers, for Israel was the smallest of peoples, even less because of righteousness, for Israel was a people given to rebellion. The divine decision, hidden forever in mystery, was an act of grace stemming from Yahweh's love for Israel and his determination to keep the oath sworn to the fathers. Yahweh's covenant with Abraham was unconditional and eternal, and thus could not be broken. Israel's election was asserted by the prophet Amos, who went on to allow no exception for it having to be punished (Amos 3:2). In his New Testament gospel, John says that followers of Jesus were chosen out of the world because of God's love for them (John 15:12, 19).

THE COVENANT AT HOREB (SINAI)

While the term "covenant" seldom occurs in older biblical material, it appears twenty times in Deuteronomy and is common from the seventh century on (Eichrodt 1966, 302). The Horeb (Sinai) covenant is unlike the other covenants made with Noah, Abraham, Phinehas, and David, in that it contains human obligations. It is a conditional covenant, given freely by Yahweh, who promises to keep it but requires obedience on the part of Israel for it to remain intact. If Israel disobeys the terms of the covenant, it is declared broken and must be renewed. In the end this covenant was broken to the point where it could not be renewed, so the nation was destroyed. Jeremiah therefore announced for Israel and Judah a new and eternal covenant (Jer 31:31-34; 32:40), unlike the Horeb covenant in that it contained no conditions and would be for all time.

Deuteronomy presents the Horeb covenant more clearly than any other Old Testament book, appropriating as it does the form of international treaties in the ancient Near East, in which the vassal king is under obligation to keep the terms set forth by his suzerain. One sees this clearly in the blessings and curses coming at the end of both the treaties and the covenant of Deuteronomy (27:13-26; 28; cf. 11:26). Deuteronomy promises blessings for covenant obedience (11:27; 27:12; 28:1-14) and a multitude of curses for covenant disobedience (11:28; 27:13-26; 28:15-68). If Israel hearkens to Yahweh's voice and does his commands, it will live, multiply, and receive blessing in the land (11:27; 30:16). If it does not hearken and do the commands, it will be overcome with incurable diseases (28:58-61), diminish in numbers (28:62-63), become subservient to other nations (28:36-57), and lose the land given to it by Yahweh (11:28; 30:17-18). Israel therefore has a choice between life and death, and the Deuteronomic preacher enjoins Israel to choose life, so it may live long in the land promised to Abraham, Isaac, and Jacob (4:40; 5:16, 32-33; 7:12-14; 30:19-20).

Since Deuteronomy affirms both the promise and unconditional covenant given to Abraham and the conditional covenant with the nation given through Moses, how are the two reconciled in the book? The conditional covenant given through Moses deals largely with nationhood and tenure in the land. If Israel breaks this covenant, the nation will be under a curse and will lose the land. Deuteronomy still holds to the covenant with Abraham, since Yahweh — even in his most far-reaching judgments — provides for a remnant that survives (1:34-39; 9:13-14; 28:62-68; 32:26-27).

The Land as a Gift and Tenure in the Land

The land looms exceedingly large in Deuteronomy. Because Yahweh swore an oath to Abraham to give his descendants the land in which he was presently journeying (Gen 12:7; 13:14-15, 17; 15:18-21, etc.), an oath repeated to Isaac and Jacob (Gen 26:3-4; 28:13; 35:12), this land came to be called the promised land. In Deuteronomy, Moses addresses Israel in the plains of Moab as it prepares to cross the Jordan and enter the land for the purpose of taking it. It is usually assumed that the promised land is only Canaan, which lies west of the Jordan. But Moses in his Moab discourse reflects also on a conquest already achieved, which took place in Transjordan as a result of successful battles against the Amorite kings Sihon and Og (2:26–3:11), and the settlement of Reuben, Gad, and the half tribe of Manasseh in their land (3:12-17). In Deuteronomy, then, land in Transjordan becomes part of the promised land. Weinfeld argues that for Deuteronomy the beginning of the conquest and the fulfillment of the promise to the fathers begins with the crossing of the Arnon in Transjordan (2:24). The promised land, however defined, is a divine gift and, like Israel's election, is an act of grace, decided aeons ago — perhaps soon after the creation of the world — by Yahweh, who keeps it a secret from the people of earth (32:7-9). This land is Israel's inheritance (4:21; 12:9-10; 15:4), and it will be enlarged if Israel keeps the commandments (19:8-9; cf. 12:20). Deuteronomy emphasizes that the land being given to Israel is a "good land" (1:25, 35; 3:25; 4:21-22; 6:18; 8:7-10, etc.) and Israel is getting this land not because of its own righteousness, but because the wickedness of Canaan's inhabitants is complete and because Yahweh is confirming the oath made to Abraham, Isaac, and Jacob (9:4-5; cf. 6:10, 18; 8:1; 10:11, and passim; cf. Jer 7:7; 11:5; 16:15; 25:5; 30:3, and passim).

Settlement in the land, what Deuteronomy calls "coming into rest" (3:20; 12:9) or Israel "attaining rest from all its enemies round about" (12:10), has both opportunities and dangers. Israel will begin to harvest crops, and because this land is a good land, it will eat and become sated. What it must do, then, is to bless Yahweh (8:10) and present the firstfruits to Yahweh in gratitude for the land's abundant yield (26:1-4). Sacrifices will also take place in the land, but these must be only at the single sanctuary of Yahweh's choosing (12:5-14). The danger of settlement, seen already in the Song of Moses, is that Israel will become sated and forget Yahweh, going after the gods of the land (31:20-21; 32:13-18; cf. Jer 2:5-9). Deuteronomy therefore warns Israel constantly to destroy all vestiges of Canaanite worship once it settles in the land and not chase after other gods or succumb to idolatry (12:1-3, 29-31; 18:9-14). When Israel crosses the Jordan, one of the first things it must do is to write the law clearly on large stones at Mount Ebal, which will be a visual reminder to Israel of the commandments it must keep (27:1-10). Tenure in the land is contingent upon Israel keeping the commandments. Keeping the commandments is what will give Israel long life in the land (4:40; 5:33; 6:2; 11:8-9, etc.). If Israel fails to keep them, the good land will be lost. It fell to Jeremiah to proclaim this message to the last remnant of the once proud Israelite nation (Jer 7:14; 24:10).

Holy War

The Israelite march to enter and possess the promised land came as a result of holy war, so called, a war in which Yahweh took the lead as "Lord of hosts" (= Lord of the army). Yahweh promised Israel the land, and Deuteronomy makes it ever so clear that taking it would be successful only if the conquest was directed and executed by Yahweh, who delivered Israel from Egypt and cared for it in the wilderness (1:30-33; 2:31-36; 3:2-4; 7:1-2; 31:3-8). But success will also be contingent on Israel keeping the commandments (11:22-25). Yahweh will put "dread" (פַּחַד) and "fear" (יִרְאָה) in the opposition, which is language of holy war (2:25; 11:25; cf. 31:6). Other holy war language in Deuteronomy is seen in commands to the soldiers for upcoming battles: "Be strong and be bold" (31:6, 7, 23). All able-bodied men are to be mustered, although Deuteronomy does make an allowance for some to opt out of the fighting (20:1-9). Newly married men get a one-year deferment to stay at home with their wives (24:5). The subject of holy war is discussed by von Rad (1953, 45-59; 1991, 115-27) and de Vaux (1965, 258-67), with both pointing out that holy war traditions have their clearest and most complete expression in Deuteronomy.

According to the rules of holy war, the camp must be ritually pure (23:13-15[23:12-14]). Once the battle has been fought and won, conquered people who survive were not to be taken as prisoners, and sometimes the spoil, too, was not to be taken as booty; all was to be devoted (= dedicated) to Yahweh. People were to be put to death. Hebrew הַחֲרֵם ("devote to destruction") is a defining term in holy war, referring to the ban (חֵרֶם) placed upon captured people and goods to be given over to Yahweh (2:34-35; 3:6; 7:1-2; 13:16-18[13:15-17]; 20:16-17). In the holy wars against Sihon and Og, men, women, and children were put under the ban, but not the animals (2:34-35; 3:6-7). In wars against the Canaanites, nothing was to be kept alive (20:16-18). But when Israel will fight wars in distant cities, only the (adult) males will need to come under the ban; women, children, cattle, and other goods can be taken as booty (20:10-15). And Deuteronomy provides for females captured in distant wars that Israelite soldiers want to marry, allowing that such marriages be permitted to take place (21:10-14).

As things turned out, every living thing in Jericho — except Rahab, who hid the spies, and her household — was devoted to destruction (Josh 6:21). Silver and gold and vessels of bronze and iron went into the treasury of Yahweh

(Josh 6:19, 24). In the second attempt to capture Ai, everything was slated to come under the ban except cattle and spoil, which could be taken as booty by the people (Josh 8:2, 27). In some wars, people failed to honor the ban and were judged with severity (Achan in Joshua 7; King Saul in 1 Samuel 15). When Canaanite peoples could not be driven out, they were subdued and put to forced labor (Josh 16:10; 17:13; Judg 1:27-35; 1 Kgs 9:20-21).

The reason given in Deuteronomy for waging holy war was that if the former inhabitants were allowed to remain in the land, they and their abominable religious practices would become a snare to Israel (7:1-5, 16; 18:12; 20:16-18; cf. Exod 23:31-33; 34:11-16). Also, Yahweh was said to be punishing these nations for their wickedness (Deut 9:4).

Holy war ideology offends modern sensibilities, particularly when one reads in Deuteronomy that holy war with the ban was commanded by Yahweh. The offense came earlier. The command of Deuteronomy was mitigated already by the rabbis in their time, and so far as the Christian church is concerned, it is no stretch to say that this ideology goes ill with New Testament teaching. Even in the church's doctrine of a just war, nations are only to go to war as a last resort. And, needless to say, the Jewish Holocaust of the twentieth century has been condemned by virtually everyone.

The holy war teaching of Deuteronomy must nevertheless be understood in the context of what obtained generally among peoples of the ancient world. Israel was not the only nation that practiced the holy war ban on other nations. The term *ḥrm* appears on the ninth-century Moabite Stone (line 17), where Mesha says he "devoted" seven thousand Israelite men, boys, women, girls, and maidservants to Ashtar-chemosh. Other parallels exist from the ancient world.

Israelite practice must also be seen in larger perspective. The חרם law, severe as it was, particularly with Israel emerging the victor and other peoples being exterminated, was carried out also by Israelites against their own people. When Achan defied the ban by taking devoted things for himself, he and everything belonging to him — sons, daughters, oxen, asses, and sheep — were destroyed (Josh 7:24-25). Deuteronomic law stated also that if an entire Israelite city falls victim to idolatry, it must be devoted to destruction (Deut 13:13-19[13:12-18]). And the day came when what remained of the Israelite nation fell under Yahweh's holy war judgment for breach of covenant — which consisted largely — but not exclusively — of going after other gods and practicing idolatry. First northern Israel and then Judah were destroyed. And here it was the same Yahweh carrying out holy war! Jeremiah uses holy war terminology in announcing Yahweh's judgment upon the nation (Jer 6:4-5; 22:7). In this holy war even beasts would be destroyed (Jer 7:20; 21:6; 36:29).

We should note also with Moran (1963a) that Deuteronomy begins by reporting how Israel undertook an "unholy war," going up to take Canaan after

Introduction

Yahweh told the people not to go up. The result was that they were roundly defeated (1:41-44).

DIVINE BLESSING

Deuteronomy puts great emphasis on blessing. Yahweh has blessed Israel in the past (1:11; 2:7; 23:6[23:5]) and promises blessing in the future (1:11; 12:7, 15; 14:24; 15:4, 6; 16:10), although the latter is said to be contingent upon charity to the poor and needy (14:29; 15:10, 14, 18; 16:17; 23:21[23:20]; 24:19) and obedience to the covenant demands (7:12-14; 11:26-32; 28:1-14; 30:1, 16, 19). The needy will bless his fellow Israelite for kindness that is shown (24:13). Yahweh's blessing is to be sought (26:15), but Israel is expected to bless Yahweh's name for the land it is to receive (8:10; 10:8; 16:15; 21:5). Israel is to receive Yahweh's blessing in the covenant renewal ceremony at Shechem (27:12), although no blessings are stated, only curses for sins done in secret (27:9-26). Deuteronomy states climactically that covenant obedience will bring blessing in the land of Canaan; disobedience will bring the opposite, viz., a host of terrible curses (ch. 28).

Deuteronomy, taken as a whole, has considerably more to say about blessing than about curses, making its preaching positive in the main. Fohrer (1968, 177) says:

> Unlike the prophetic tradition, however, which generally took quite a negative view of Israel's prospects for the future, Deuteronomic theology seeks to deliver the people as a whole from the threatened judgment of destruction, without in any way detracting from the seriousness of the situation.

Only in the Song of Moses and its attendant prose (chs. 31–32) does the upbeat message of Deuteronomy give way to ominous predictions about Israel's future. But even then, the book concludes with Moses pronouncing a blessing on the twelve tribes of Israel (ch. 33).

Divine blessing in Deuteronomy develops largely out of Genesis, where it is rooted in traditions about Abraham. It is not carried over from the Covenant Code or indeed from any other material in Exodus, where the one reference to divine blessing occurs in the explanation of the fourth commandment. There, repeating Genesis, it says that Yahweh blessed the Sabbath (Exod 20:11; cf. Gen 2:3). In Priestly material, too, the blessing theme is largely nonexistent, occurring only in the Aaronic benediction (Num 6:22-27) and in blessings spoken by the non-Israelite seer Balaam son of Beor (Numbers 22-24).

Divine blessing originates in Genesis, where it comes at creation and is then imparted to select individuals, first to Noah (Gen 9:1), then to Abraham and his descendants. At creation, God's blessing rests upon sea creatures and birds (Gen 1:22), then on humans, male and female (Gen 1:28; 5:2). To be blessed here is to be fruitful and multiply and with man and woman to subdue the earth. To the patriarchs, Abraham, Isaac, Jacob, and also Joseph, blessing means multiplication, gaining wealth, receiving a promise of land, and being a blessing to all people on earth (Gen 12:1-3; 18:18; 22:17-18; 26:3-5, 24; 28:3-4, 13-14, etc.). Genesis anticipates Deuteronomy in promising blessing to Abraham, the reason being that he obeyed Yahweh's voice and kept his commands (Gen 22:15-18; 26:5). Blessing in Genesis is otherwise a pure act of divine grace.

In Deuteronomy, divine blessing means that Israel will multiply exceedingly, rule over other nations (15:6), and reap abundant crops in the land Yahweh is giving it. Moses tells Israel that it is already a multitude and can expect more increase in the future (1:10-11). Israel was blessed on the wilderness trek (2:7), and now in Moab stands ready to possess the land promised to the fathers. Because even more wealth will obtain after settlement in the land, all of which will be a mark of Yahweh's blessing (12:7, 15; 14:24; 15:4, 13-14), the nation will owe to Yahweh a return blessing (8:10; cf. 21:5; Gen 14:18-20), be under obligation to present offerings to Yahweh (Deut 16:10, 16-17), and act graciously toward the less fortunates in society. These, above all, are the sojourner, orphan, widow, and pensioned Levite, who will be invited to share in the yearly feasts at the central sanctuary (16:13-15), who will receive their portion of the third-year tithe in the cities and towns where they live (14:28-29), and who will have the privilege of gleaning fields after the crops have been harvested (24:19). Benevolence must also be extended to others who are poor and needy. Hebrew slaves are to be released after six years (15:18); fellow-Israelites in need of interest-free loans are to be given them (23:21[23:20]), and the same is to be extended to the poor in general, who may have no chance of repayment and will not grow fat in the land (15:10). Yahweh will compensate the generous lender for any loss he might incur. All these benevolent acts prescribed in Deuteronomy are to issue forth because of the blessings Israel has received at the hand of Yahweh.

COVENANT OBLIGATIONS

Because the Horeb covenant is conditional and requires obedience on Israel's part, there are obligations Israel must fulfill. Freedman (1964) calls this covenant, which has its closest parallel in international treaties of the ANE, a covenant of "human obligation."

Introduction

Doing the Commandments

This is perhaps the most oft-repeated admonition in the book, that Israel be sure to do the commandments, where the commandments consist first and foremost of the Ten Commandments and, following them, the commandments, statutes, and ordinances of the Deuteronomic Code. Heading the list are commandments one and two of the Horeb covenant: No other gods and no idols, which get attention throughout the book but receive particular emphasis in the sermons of chapters 6–11. Interior dispositions — loving, clinging to, and fearing Yahweh — also walking in Yahweh's way, serving Yahweh, and expressing gratitude to Yahweh show themselves, according to Deuteronomy, in doing the commandments (4:10; 5:32-33; 6:1-2, 4-9; 10:12-13; 11:1, 18-20).

Love to Yahweh and to Others

Israel is to love Yahweh, which is a fitting and proper response to the love Yahweh has shown Israel (7:9). Included here is "clinging to Yahweh," which means loving him (10:20; 11:22; 13:5[13:4]; 30:20). The Shema says: "And you shall love Yahweh your God with all your heart and with all your soul and with all your might" (6:5), pointing up one of the most important features of love in Deuteronomy and throughout the Bible, i.e., that this is a love which can be commanded (10:12; 11:1). It has the same force as the love demanded of vassal kings by suzerain kings in the ANE treaties (Moran 1963b). It goes hand in hand with obeying the covenant, the terms of which lie in the commandments (7:9; 11:13, 22; 19:9; 30:16, 20; cf. John 15:10). Yahweh, in fact, tests Israel by allowing prophets and dreamers initial success when their end game is to lead people in the way of other gods, to see if they really love him (13:4[13:3]). When the curses come upon Israel for disobeying the covenant, Deuteronomy says that Yahweh will open the people's heart so they can once again love him, and live (30:6).

While the teaching to "love your neighbor as yourself," which looms so large in the NT (Matt 22:39; John 13:34-35; Gal 5:14; Rom 13:8-9, etc.), comes not from Deuteronomy but from Lev 19:18, it is still the case that Deuteronomy teaches love toward other people. Besides its benevolence program toward the poor and needy, which is certainly an expression of love towards them, Israel is told explicitly to love the sojourner. Why? Because Yahweh loves the sojourner, but also because Israel is to remember that it, too, was once a sojourner in the land of Egypt (Deut 10:19).

Fear of Yahweh

Deuteronomy contains much teaching on the "fear of Yahweh," where "fear" does not carry with it the debilitating effects so common in much of ancient religion, but denotes rather the interior dispositions of "awe" and "reverence." The verb "to fear" (ירא) in the OT does have both positive and negative meaning. It can simply mean "be afraid of," where, for example, Yahweh or his divine messenger so often tells individuals to "fear not!" (Gen 15:1; 21:17, etc.) or where in Deuteronomy Moses tells Israel not to fear the enemy (1:21, 29; 3:2, 22). The fear Yahweh puts in the opposition when carrying on holy war is also this type of fear (2:25; 11:25). But when people are told to "fear" Yahweh it means they are to "stand in reverent awe of" Yahweh, not to dread arbitrary and capricious divine action, such as people typically do in other religions ancient and modern.

In Deuteronomy fearing Yahweh goes hand in hand with loving and serving him, swearing by his name, and walking in his way (6:13; 8:6; 10:12, 20; 13:5[13:4]), all of which translates into not going after other gods (6:13-14) and doing Yahweh's commandments. Fear of Yahweh can be taught (4:10; 5:29; 6:1-2, 24; 8:6; 10:12-13; 13:5[13:4]; 14:23 [in tithing]; 28:58; 31:12-13), for which reason Deuteronomy teaches that children are to learn to fear Yahweh. They will learn this if they are instructed in the commandments. Fear of Yahweh, says Deuteronomy, should be present always, i.e., throughout life or as long as Israel lives in the land. Eating the yearly tithe at the central sanctuary is one way of Israel learning to fear Yahweh (14:23). Israel's king is to read the Deuteronomic law all his days, so he may learn to fear Yahweh and do Yahweh's commands (17:19). Even the sojourner is to hear Yahweh's law, learn to fear him, and do his commands (31:12). Moses tells the people that if they do not "fear this glorious and awesome name" of Yahweh, they will suffer great sickness and suffering (28:58-59). But in the eternal covenant announced later by Jeremiah after the curses have fallen, Yahweh promises that he will put the fear of himself in the hearts of people, so they will not turn from him (Jer 32:38-40).

Walking in Yahweh's Way

"Walking in Yahweh's way" has broad application in Deuteronomy, just as it does elsewhere in the OT, referring to the whole of life for individuals and for the Israelite nation. It includes the interior dispositions of love and fear, also one's conduct, which in Deuteronomy is measured in terms of doing the commandments (8:6; 10:12; 11:22; 13:5[13:4]; 19:9; 26:17; 28:9; 30:16). One walks in Yahweh's way so that one may live, that it may go well with one, and that one's days may be prolonged in the land. No turning aside to the right or to left (5:32-

Introduction

33), which means not walking after other gods Israel has not known (11:28; 13:6[13:5]). Going after other gods and the idols of neighboring peoples is to "walk in the stubbornness of one's heart" (29:15-18[29:16-19]). Moses admonishes people to keep the commandments ever before them, speaking about them when they sit in the house and when they walk in the way (6:7; 11:19).

Serving Yahweh

Israel is also under obligation to "serve Yahweh," where "serve" too has broad meaning but often means simply "worship" (so Targums). As commandments one and two make clear, people are not to serve/worship other gods — also the heavenly bodies — or bow down before idols (4:19; 5:8-9; 6:13-14; 8:19; 11:16; 17:3-5; 30:17; 31:20); if they do these things, they will perish. Worship of heavenly bodies has been allotted to other peoples (4:19), but not to Israel (29:25[29:26]. Some individuals will go after other gods and want to lead fellow Israelites to do the same (13:3, 7, 14[13:2, 6, 13]; 17:3-5; 29:17, 25[29:18, 26]), but these are to be wholly resisted. Such individuals must be put to death. If people do make gods of wood and stone, Yahweh says he will scatter them among nations where they can serve these lifeless wonders (4:28; 28:36, 64). People are expected to serve Yahweh with gladness and goodness of heart; if they do not, they will end up having to serve their enemies in great privation (28:47-48). Yahweh's holy war ban is carried out so that Israel will not turn to serving the Canaanite gods (7:16). Canaanite worship places are to be destroyed for the same reason (12:2). Even after these sanctuaries are destroyed, Israel is warned not to revert to serving gods that were once worshipped there (12:30). Marriages with the Canaanites are to be disallowed, for then the Israelite son or daughter may end up turning from Yahweh to serve other gods (7:3-4). Serving Yahweh, like all the other interior dispositions and covenant obligations, means keeping the commandments (10:12-13, 20; 11:13; 13:5[13:4]).

Gratitude to Yahweh

Moses calls upon Israel to show gratitude for Yahweh's liberation of the nation from Egyptian slavery, for the victory over Pharaoh's army at the Red Sea, for Yahweh's care in the wilderness (11:2-5), and for blessings received and to be received in the settlement — first in Transjordan, later in Canaan. Deuteronomy is repeatedly saying "Remember," and "Do not forget." Gratitude is an obligation, just like the other covenant obligations. The Song of Moses shows how ungrateful Israel was following the Transjordan settlement. Yahweh fed the people so they became sated, and they thanked him by turning to other gods (32:13-18). Moses expects they will do the same in the future (31:20). Curses for disobeying the covenant anticipate the same, saying that this will result in Israel having to serve its enemies amidst great want (28:47-48). Ingratitude for the wonders of Egypt was shown when Israel first refused to go up and take the land (1:26-27, 30-33).

Israel is to serve Yahweh in joy and gladness of heart for everything received at Yahweh's hand, sharing its abundance with orphans, widows, sojourners, and pensioned Levites (12:7, 12, 18; 14:27; 16:11, 14-15; 26:11; 27:7). The firstfruits to be presented at the sanctuary are to be an expression of gratitude for Yahweh's gift of the land and the abundant yield it has brought forth (26:9-10). At the three yearly feasts no male is to appear empty-handed before Yahweh (16:16-17), for that would be a sign of ingratitude. Benevolence to all who are poor and needy should proceed from the same glad and grateful heart. The person who gives grudgingly to the needy, says Deuteronomy, has evil in his heart (15:10).

THE BOOK OF DEUTERONOMY

The book of Deuteronomy is a collection of addresses by Moses to Israel in the plains of Moab, just before his death and before Israel is to cross the Jordan under Joshua and begin its conquest of Canaan. The speaker in Deuteronomy is Moses (1:1, 5; 5:1), not Yahweh, as in the Covenant Code (Exod 20:1). The first identifiable book of Deuteronomy is chapters 1–28, called here the First Edition. It specifies itself as the words of the covenant Moses brokered between Yahweh and Israel in the plains of Moab, to be distinguished from the covenant Moses brokered at Mount Horeb/Sinai (28:69[29:1]).

The First Edition was expanded at some point with two supplements: (1) chapters 29–30, which further exhorts Israel to keep the commandments and says Israel can do it; and (2) chapters 31–34, which adds two old poems, the Song of Moses (ch. 32) and the Blessing of Moses (ch. 33), and closes with a report of Moses' death and burial.

THE FIRST EDITION (CHS. 1–28)

The First Edition of Deuteronomy is held together by an inclusio made from its concluding verse and the opening superscription:

1:1-5   *These are the words* that *Moses* spoke to *all Israel* beyond the Jordan . . . beyond the Jordan *in the land of Moab*, Moses undertook to make plain *this law*. . . .

Introduction

> 28:69[29:1] *These are the words of the covenant* that Yahweh commanded Moses to cut with *the children of Israel in the land of Moab*, besides the covenant that he cut with them in Horeb.

We do not know when this first book of Deuteronomy was written or when it was made public. It contains material that appears to have a northern Israel provenance. If it were written in the north, it would then, at the very latest, have been brought south after northern Israel's fall to the Assyrians in 722. But it seems more probable that this First Edition was written in Judah. Again, one can only speculate as to when this might have been. It could be preaching of traveling princes and priests who, in a judicial reform during the reign of Jehoshaphat (873-849), went out to teach people the law (2 Chr 17:7-9). Or it could be a document associated with the reform of Hezekiah (712-701). Von Rad thought it was a post-701 document written by Levitical priests from the countryside who were put out of a job by the centralization of worship in Jerusalem. While many commentators continue to call Deuteronomy a seventh-century document, it was surely written long before the temple lawbook was found in 622 (see pp. 6-7, "The Josianic Reform").

Prologue (1–4)

The Prologue to Deuteronomy (chs. 1–4) begins with a superscription in 1:1-5, after which Israel's journey from Mount Horeb to Kadesh-barnea is recounted. The narrative does not begin with the Exodus or even with the encampment at Horeb, where the covenant was brokered and the Decalogue given. It begins with Israel's departure from Horeb (1:6-7). Recollections of the revelation at Mount Horeb do come, however, in chapter 4. From Kadesh-barnea Israel launched its first attempt to enter Canaan, which was unsuccessful (ch. 1).

The forty long years of wandering in the wilderness is not reported. The Deuteronomic writer only refers back to the wilderness experience in later sermons of chapters 8-10. After the failed attempt to enter Canaan, the narrative moves on to Israel's march northward, and the people are told not to confront Edom, Moab, and Ammon, but rather to do battle with Sihon and Og, Amorite kings residing north of the Arnon. The battles are successful, and Moses settles Reuben, Gad, and the half-tribe of Manasseh in the newly won land (chs. 2–3). Israel is now encamped at Beth-peor in Moab (3:29). In the historical survey are also a few antiquarian notes (2:20-23; 3:9, 11, 13b-14).

A sermonic discourse fills most of chapter 4, which begins with a variation of Deuteronomy's signature introduction: "And now, O Israel" (4:1). Moses, speaking now in the valley opposite Beth-peor, begins by shifting from past to present. He tells people that the law is life, also a mark of Israel's wisdom (4:1-8). The core teaching (4:9-31) goes on to impress upon Israel that it must do the commandments and refrain from idolatry, which anticipates commandments one and two of the Decalogue. It also warns what will happen if his admonition is not heeded: destruction, scattering, repentance, and eventual return. Moses, returning now to the past, reminds the people how Yahweh spoke the Decalogue to them directly out of the fire, even before the written tablets were brought down from the mountain. Moses says in conclusion that the greatness of the statutes and ordinances is proved by Yahweh alone being God, that there is no other (4:32-40).

Following this discourse, the Deuteronomic writer reports Moses' allocation of three refuge cities in the Transjordan (4:41-43). The Prologue then concludes with a subscription in 4:44-49.

The Covenant at Horeb (5–11)

Moses in Deuteronomy is presenting a new law code, but before doing so he must repeat the Decalogue to those present in the assembly (5:1-21). This defining law, which lies at the heart of the Horeb covenant, was not just for the generation who heard the "ten words" out of the midst of the fire, but for the generation now assembled in Moab (5:2-5). Deuteronomy makes it clear that after the Decalogue was given to the people Yahweh added nothing more (5:22). To Moses alone Yahweh gave other commandments, statutes, and ordinances that will now be taught to the people (5:30-31). These make up the Deuteronomic Code that Moses is delivering in the plains of Moab.

The discourse in chapters 5–11 contains three sermons: (1) 5:1–6:3; (2) 6:4–8:20; and (3) 9:1–11:32. Each begins with "Hear, O Israel" (5:1; 6:4; 9:1). The sermons are not unified compositions, rather compilations of shorter discourses, and in chapters 9–11 they include, like the discourse in chapters 2–3, antiquarian notes. The first sermon presents the Decalogue and stresses its ongoing importance to the Moab assembly.

The discourse following in chapters 6–11 stresses obedience to commandments one and two of the Decalogue: (1) no other gods besides Yahweh and (2) no idols. The second sermon (6:4–8:20) is introduced with the words of the Shema: "Hear, O Israel, Yahweh our God, Yahweh is one. And you shall love Yahweh your God with all your heart and with all your soul and with all your might" (6:4-5). A liturgical injunction follows, admonishing people to keep the commandments ever before them (6:6-9). Canaan is filled with cities Israel did not build and orchards it did not plant; therefore when Israel arrives in the land it must not forget Yahweh and go after other gods. It muat also not test Yahweh, as it did at Massah in the wilderness (6:10-19). Yahweh was gracious to Israel in the exodus and now again shows himself to be a God of grace in his gift of the land. When children later inquire about the meaning of the commandments, parents are to relate this to them (6:20-25).

In this second sermon, after Moses says that Yahweh will clear away the seven nations in Canaan and Israel wipes out all vestiges of their religion (7:1-5), an important teaching is given about Israel's election as Yahweh's holy people. The love Israel owes to Yahweh is to be a response to Yahweh's love, for Yahweh's choice of Israel as a holy people was not because Israel was larger than other peoples, because she was not. It was because Yahweh loved Israel and because Yahweh was fulfilling a promise to the fathers (7:6-8). Yahweh promises to keep his covenant and continue in this love, although much will hinge on Israel keeping the commandments (7:9-16). Once again, Yahweh promises to clear away these nations before Israel, little by little. Once the kings are subdued and their land is taken, the idols of their gods must be burned with fire (7:17-26).

This sermon continues into chapter 8, with Moses telling the people that Yahweh humbled them in the wilderness in order to test them. They must therefore keep the commandments (8:1-6). Now Yahweh is bringing Israel into a good land, so good that it will eat and become sated. For this goodness Israel must bless Yahweh (8:7-10), not forget him by disobeying the commandments. Forgetting and remembering get the emphasis, as they do elsewhere in the book. Yahweh's care in the wilderness — including the manna provided — is to be remembered (8:11-16). The bottom line is that Israel must not go after other gods and serve them; if it does, it will perish like the nations now being destroyed so Israel can possess their land (8:17-20).

The third sermon (9:1–11:32) contains another important teaching, this one about Yahweh's gift of the land. Israel is not getting the land because of its own righteousness, rather because the nations now living there are wicked. Yahweh is also fulfilling an oath made to the fathers (9:1-5). Moses then proceeds to document how rebellious Israel has been — from the day it came out of Egypt, at Horeb, and in the wilderness (9:6-24). Were it not for Moses' mediation at Horeb, Israel would have been destroyed (9:25-29). But the covenant was renewed and the Decalogue written on new tablets (10:1-5). The journey to the promised land could therefore continue (10:10-11). What now does Yahweh ask of Israel? Answer: that Israel fear him, walk in his ways, love him, and serve him heart and soul. All this translates into doing the commands (10:12-13). To Yahweh belong heaven and earth, and let Israel not forget that, for Yahweh has done great things (10:14-22).

Other sermonic discourse follows, much of it on keeping the commandments. This is what loving Yahweh is about. Israel is to consider Yahweh's discipline and greatness, in Egypt, at the Red Sea, and especially in the wilderness

(11:1-9). The promised land, unlike Egypt, will have abundant rainfall, but rain will hinge on keeping the commandments (11:10-17). The liturgical injunction on keeping the commandments then repeats (11:18-21). This third sermon closes with three brief exhortations on obedience and disobedience (11:22-32), the middle one telling of a blessing and curse ceremony to take place on Mount Gerizim and Mount Ebal (11:26-28). Israel has two choices: it can obey the covenant and be blessed or it can disobey and be cursed.

The Deuteronomic Code (12–26)

The Deuteronomic Code begins in chapter 12 and continues through to chapter 26. Chapter 12 is an introduction mandating worship at a single sanctuary, and chapter 26 contains rituals on the firstfruits and the third-year tithe. Together, chapters 12 and 26 frame the legal material in chapters 13-25. The narrative on covenant renewal at Shechem, with its curses on crimes carried out in secret (ch. 27), combines with the listing of blessings and curses relating to the Deuteronomic Code (ch. 28), which concludes the First Edition.

Chapter 12, besides mandating a single sanctuary and stating what need or need not be offered there, introduces the forthcoming laws on tithes and offerings (vv. 5-14) and ritually clean and unclean eating (vv. 15-28). The laws themselves come in chapters 14–15, but in reverse order: (1) laws on clean and unclean foods (14:1-21) and (2) laws on tithes and offerings (14:22–15:23). Chapter 12 begins and ends with a solemn word about rooting out Canaan's multiple worship sites and multiple gods (vv. 2-4, 29-31), a subject covered fully in chapter 13. So while chapter 12 quite intentionally begins the Deuteronomic Code, it introduces only the legal material in chapters 13–15.

The Deuteronomic Code builds on the Decalogue and presents its laws so they will correlate sequentially — in some cases by extension or by association — with commandments of the Decalogue:

Decalogue	Deuteronomic Code
I. No other gods before Yahweh (5:7)	Go not after other gods (13:2-19[1-18])
II. No images of Yahweh (5:8-10)	
III. No empty oaths in Yahweh's name (5:11)	
IV. Keep the Sabbath Day holy (5:12-15)	Clean and unclean foods for a holy people (14:1-21) Tithes and offerings (14:22–15:23) Keeping the annual feasts (16:1-17)

Introduction

V. Honor your father and your mother (5:16)	Judges, judgment, and miscellaneous prohibitions (16:18–17:13) Concerning the king (17:14-20) Concerning the Levitical priests (18:1-8) Concerning the prophet (18:9-22)
VI. You shall not murder (5:17)	Homicide and refuge cities (19:1-13) Regarding false witnesses (19:15-21) Rules of warfare (20:1-20) Unsolved murder (21:1-9) Regarding women war captives (21:10-14) Regarding estate liquidation (21:15-17) Death for rebellious sons (21:18-21) Corpses hung for public display (21:22-23) Restoration of lost property (22:1-3) Help for fallen animals (22:4) No transvestism (22:5) Taking eggs or young birds as food (22:6-7) Roofs require parapets (22:8) Regarding mixtures (22:9-12)
VII. You shall not commit adultery (5:18)	Unchaste brides (22:13-21) Sex with married woman (22:22) Sex with betrothed woman (22:23-27) Sex with unbetrothed woman (22:28-29) Sex with a father's wife (23:1[22:30]) On purity and cleanliness (23:2-15[1-14]) Hospitality to runaway slaves (23:16-17[15-16]) No cult prostitutes (23:18-19[17-18])
VIII. You shall not steal (5:19)	No lending at interest (23:20-21[19-20]) Prompt payment of vows (23:22-24[21-23]) No stealing of crops (23:25-26[24-25]) No return to first husband (24:1-4) Pledge prohibitions (24:6) No stealing of persons (24:7) On fetching pledges (24:10-13) Paying hired servants (24:14-15) Pledges from the needy (24:17-18) Gleanings for the needy (24:19-22)
IX. No false witness against neighbor (5:20)	Court decisions and punishment (25:1-3)
X. No coveting of neighbor's property (5:21)	Levirate marriage (25:5-10) Wives intervening in a fight (25:11-12) Just weights and measures (25:13-16)

The opening legislation of the Deuteronoic Code forbidding Israel to go after other gods is more like a three-point sermon (13:2-19[13:1-18]). Yahweh gives certain prophets and would-be prophets a brief day in the sun only to test people whether they really love Yahweh heart and soul (13:4[13:3]). The sermon does contain casuistic law, however, as it provides a sentence of death for individuals and even entire cities if they violate commandment one of the Decalogue.

Clean and unclean foods are listed in 14:1-21, the point here being that Israel is a people holy to Yahweh its God. Certain animals, waterfowl, and winged creatures may not be eaten. Various obligations are then enumerated in 14:22–15:23, those coming up each year, every three years, and every seven years. Included here are laws regarding tithes and offerings of agricultural produce and firstborns from one's flocks and herds. Israelites are to be granted debt remission and slave remission every seven years, with particular emphasis put on care for the poor and needy and benevolences to the orphan, widow, sojourner, and Levite living in one's town.

Israel's three annual feasts, Passover (Unleavened Bread), Weeks (Pentecost), and Booths, are covered in 16:1-17, where it is said that every adult male is to journey to the central sanctuary. Other family members may come also, and no one is to appear empty-handed before Yahweh. Offerings are to be brought to the feasts. Orphans, widows, sojoiurners, and resident Levites are invited to join the pilgrimages to the central sanctuary and share in the gladness of the feast.

In 16:18–18:22 are listed the four major officeholders who will govern national life once Israel is settled in the land: judges (16:18-20; 17:2-13), kings (17:14-20), priests (18:1-8), and prophets (18:9-22). Listed with the judges are subordinate officials, also priests who will assist judges in difficult cases. Preceding the legislation on the prophets is a catalog of Canaanite religious functionaries who are not to mediate between Yahweh and his covenant people (18:9-14). Three miscellaneous laws against abominable worship practices are interspersed in 16:21–17:1, which have no apparent relation to the discourse on the major officeholders.

Substantive laws and judicial matters, over which judges, city elders, and priests are to have jurisdiction, come in chapters 19–25, in which there is also less sermonizing than in chapters 13–18. Laws in chapters 19–22, with one exception, have no parallel in the Covenant Code. The exception is the first law dealing with accidental homicide (19:1-13), which is dealt with briefly in Exod 21:12-14. If someone unwittingly kills his fellow, he can escape to one of three refuge cities that will be set up in Canaan. Three cities of refuge were set up earlier in Transjordan (Deut 4:41-43). Individuals found to be actual murderers, however, will not be permitted to remain in these cities, but will be handed over to the avenger of blood, who will put them to death. Combined with this law is another stating that in all litigation — not just criminal cases — two or three witnesses are required for conviction. False witnesses are also dealt with. Punishment for them is to be carried out according to the talion principle (19:15-21).

Introduction

Interspersed between these two laws is another about not moving back the boundary marker of one's fellow (19:14).

In 20:1–21:14 are laws dealing with the institution of holy war. Deuteronomy is the only book in the Pentateuch to contain laws of this nature. The first law deals with mustering an army (20:1-9); conduct of war against enemies far and near (20:10-18); and respect for fruit trees when a city is being besieged (20:19-20). The second law deals with women war captives desired as wives (21:10-14). In between is a law on expiation for an unsolved murder (21:1-9). Priests and officials in charge of recruitment and deferrals are to give spirited speeches in mustering an army for battle. Deferrals in certain cases are permitted. When Israel is fighting a distant city it is first to offer peace, which, if accepted, will require the inhabitants of the city to submit to forced labor. If they refuse, war is to be fought. When Yahweh gives the victory, all surviving adult males of the enemy are to come under the holy war ban. Women, children, beasts, and goods can be taken as spoil. But in holy war against the Canaanites, everything is to come under the ban. The stated reason is that otherwise these people would teach Israel their abominable worship practices.

Some captive women in distant wars will be desired as wives, and the law in 21:10-14 deals with this. Taking foreign women as wives is permitted, but there are subtle indications in the law that such marriages may be ill-advised. The young and presumably beautiful woman is to be brought to the man's house, where she is to shave her head, pare her nails, discard her captive clothing, and mourn her mother and father for a month. She presumably has not been married, therefore she has no husband to mourn. At the end of a month, the Israelite man may cohabit with her. If it should happen that his war bride no longer delights him, he may send her away and she can then go wherever she wants. He may not sell her as a slave or oppress her in any other way, for he has dishonored her by marrying her and then casting her off.

In between these holy war laws is a law dealing with expiation for an unsolved murder (21:1-9). If a slain person turns up in a field outside of town and the slayer is not known, the city nearest the site must assume responsibility for the crime. A young heifer, which has not yet been worked, is to be slain near a water-filled wadi in an expiation rite presided over by the priest. Its shed blood will rid the city — and all Israel — from the bloodguilt brought about by the crime.

The law in 21:15-17 regulates liquidation of an estate when a man has two wives, one loved and one unloved, and both have borne him sons. The man may not give the double portion due the firstborn to the son of the loved wife if the son of the unloved wife is his actual firstborn. The firstborn is the firstfruits of his generative power, and the rights of the firstborn belong to him. This son gets a double portion of everything the man has.

In 21:18-21 is law dealing with a stubborn and rebellious son. If a son continually refuses to obey his mother and father and will not accept discipline, the parents are to bring him (forcibly) out to the city gate and state before the elders that he is a glutton and a drunkard. The men of the city will then stone the fellow to death, since he is a liability not only to his family but to the whole city. With his death evil will be removed from the city, and all Israel shall duly hear and fear.

When criminals are put to death, their bodies are to be hung on a tree for public display (21:22-23). But this law states that the bodies must be taken down by evening and buried. Such persons are cursed of God, and the land must not be defiled by the extended display of a corpse.

Five brief laws end the collection expanding upon the sixth commandment, "You shall not murder" (22:1-8). They aim to preserve human and animal life, promote security and well-being in the community, and prohibit role switching between the sexes. The law in 22:1-3 deals with the restoration of lost property. One must not ignore the stray ox or ass of a fellow Israelite but make every effort to see that it is returned. It matters not if the owner lives far away or is unknown to the finder. The finder is to bring the animal home for safekeeping until the owner comes looking for it. The same applies to lost asses, garments, or any item one happens to find. The law in 22:4 deals with fallen animals. One must also give help to a fellow Israelite if his ox or ass has fallen along the way, helping the owner to raise the animal to its feet.

Transvestism will not be sanctioned in the land (22:5). No article worn or carried by a man is to be found on a woman, nor is a man to wear women's clothes. Male-female role switching, found among other peoples, is an abomination in the eyes of Yahweh. People must also exercise control in taking birds as food (22:6-7). If one happens upon a mother bird with her nestlings or eggs, the nestlings and eggs may be taken, but not the mother bird; it is to be chased away. Finally, newly built houses must have parapets, i.e., low walls on all sides of the flat roof (22:8). This will prevent people from falling off, causing accidental death and bringing bloodguilt upon the house.

Miscellaneous laws on mixtures follow in 22:9-12. When a new vineyard is planted from seed, grapes may not be eaten for three years. In the fourth year they are to be consecrated to Yahweh. In the fifth year the owner can eat his grapes. He may therefore want to plant a second crop in the vineyard while waiting for the grapes to be deconsecrated, but this law prohibits him from doing so (22:9). If he did plant a second crop of wheat, barley, or other nonfruit, it would be consecrated along with the grapes, so he could not eat it until the fifth year. So two crops in a vineyard are disallowed. In vineyards five or more years old, this law will not apply.

An ox and an ass may not be yoked together for plowing (22:10). This would be harmful for both animals, the stronger ox and the weaker ass. There must also be no mixed blends of wool and linen in one's garments, which will preserve the

Introduction

distinction in dress between priests and the laity (22:11). Only priests are permitted to wear clothes of linen and wool. The one exception is with the tassels on one's garments, which may contain mixed threads of wool and linen (22:12).

In 22:13–23:1(22:30) are six laws dealing with improper commerce between the sexes, expanding upon the seventh commandment, "You shall not commit adultery." Their aim is to preserve chastity and marriage in Israel. With one exception, these laws do not appear in the Covenant Code. The exception is the law on sex with an unbetrothed girl, which appears in Exod 22:15-16(22:16-17). The law prohibiting sex with a father's wife is repeated in Lev 18:8, where it appears with other laws against incest.

The law on unchaste brides (22:13-21) deals with a woman accused by her newlywed husband of not being a virgin on the night of their marriage. He will have gone public with his charge and is thus giving the woman a bad name. The mother and father of the bride are then to bring the bloodstained sleeping garment to the elders at the city gate, repeat the husband's charge, and display the garment. Upon this evidence, the husband will be given a whipping, fined a hefty one hundred shekels of silver, and not allowed to divorce his wife in the future. If the garment cannot be produced, the woman will be presumed guilty and executed at the entrance to her father's house.

The law on sex with another married woman (22:22) is straightforward casuistic law on the seventh commandment forbidding adultery. If a man — married or single — has sex with a woman married to another man and they are found out, both are executed by stoning.

If a man — married or single — has sex with a betrothed girl in the city (22:23-24), the case is treated the same as an adultery case. A betrothed girl is one for whom the bride-price has been paid, so she is legally married, even though the ceremony has not occurred and her husband has not yet taken her. The act is presumed to be consensual, since it occurred in the city. If it had been rape, she would have cried out and someone would have heard her. Both man and woman are executed.

If a man — married or single — has sex with a betrothed girl in the country (22:25-27), the girl is given the benefit of the doubt, because had she cried for help, no one would have heard her. The act here is presumed to be rape, even though it may not have been. Only the man is put to death. The girl is not punished.

If a single man has sex with an unbetrothed girl (22:28-29), i.e., premarital sex, the man must pay a fine of fifty shekels to the girl's father and the two of them will be married. Here, again, the man will not be able to divorce his wife any time in the future.

The final law in the group forbids a man from having sex with his father's wife (23:1[22:30]). This would be a woman who is not the man's mother and the father presumed to be dead.

In 23:2-19(23:1-18) is a group of laws on purity and cleanliness. Purity must be preserved within Yahweh's assembly, with certain persons, all presumably foreigners, excluded forever or for just two generations (23:2-9[23:1-8]). Blemished men, i.e., those with bruised or crushed testicles or those who have been castrated (eunuchs), are excluded. Individuals born of illicit unions are also forbidden entrance to Yahweh's assembly, even to the tenth generation, i.e., forever (23:2-3[23:1-2]). Ammonites and Moabites are excluded forever (23:4-7[23:3-6]), the Ammonites because they refused hospitality to Israel in the wilderness and the Moabites because they hired Balaam to curse Israel. Edomites and Egyptians are excluded only for two generations (23:8-9[23:7-8]). Neither is considered an abomination, the Edomites because they are brothers to Israel and the Egyptians because Israel sojourned in Egypt in the time of Joseph. The third generation of these people may enter the assembly of Yahweh.

Purity and cleanliness must be preserved in the camp when holy war is being carried on (23:10-15[23:9-14]). If a man has a night accident, he is to go outside the camp until evening, at which time he can wash and return. There must also be a place outside the camp for relieving oneself. When going outside, each person is to carry a spike for digging a hole, and when he is finished he must not forget to cover up his excrement. Because Yahweh walks about in the camp, it must be kept holy. If Yahweh sees anything unseemly, he will turn away.

Connected by catchwords to the latter purity law are two other laws: one requiring hospitality to runaway slaves (23:16-17[23:15-16]) and another forbidding holy prostitutes in Israel (23:18-19[23:17-18]). Slaves escaping to Israel from foreign countries are to be given asylum; they are not to be surrendered to their masters. These individuals may live anywhere they choose and are to be treated like any other resident alien, not being oppressed. No female or male sacred prostitute, which was part of the Canaanite religious scene, is to be allowed in Israel. What is more, the hire of a whore or price of a dog is not to be brought into Yahweh's sanctuary in payment of a vow. Dirty money is an abomination to Yahweh.

Three laws develop from the eighth commandment, "You shall not steal" (23:20-26[23:19-25]). Loans to fellow Israelites must be given interest-free (23:20-21[23:19-20]). These can be loans of silver, food, or anything at all, which will provide temporary relief for a brother who has fallen on hard times. Interest-free loans must be made even to a brother who is solvent. To a foreigner who will be in the land as a merchant or trader, one may loan at interest. Providing interest-free loans will bring a blessing from Yahweh on all of one's undertakings.

A law on the payment of vows follows in 23:22-24(23:21-23). When vows are made to Yahweh, they are not like loans which take time to repay, but must be paid promptly. A vow is a promise to Yahweh that one will carry out a certain act if Yahweh grants the petitioner's request, which could be for the birth of a child, deliverance from sickness, enemies, or death, or some other life crisis.

Not paying a vow will be reckoned as sin. But since vows are voluntary, it is no sin to refrain from vowing. One simply has to pay a vow one has made and pay it promptly.

When Israel becomes settled in the land and has vineyards and crop-bearing fields, it will be permissible when passing by another's vineyard to pick grapes for eating or to pluck standing ears of grain from another's field for eating. But one must not carry away grapes in a basket nor put a sickle to the standing grain of one's fellow. That would be crop stealing (23:25-26[23:24-25]).

In 24:1–25:4 is a collection of laws, which, for the most part, deal with humane treatment to individuals being punished or who have a precarious position in Israelite society due to poverty or some other misfortune. One law deals with humane treatment to a threshing ox (25:4). The law in 24:1-4 states that a divorced woman may not return to her first husband if she has contracted a second marriage. The first husband has found something indecent in her — not adultery, but indecent behavior of some sort — and he divorces her. She marries another man, but he also divorces her or he dies, at which point the woman may not return to her first husband. She has been rendered unclean to her first husband, and to remarry him would be an abomination to Yahweh. It would also bring guilt upon the land. This law seeks to preserve the second marriage. Because the woman has had two husbands, there is also the possibility of intrigue, and if the woman received an inheritance at the death of her second husband, the first husband could gain financially by taking her back. This would be unjust financial gain and may explain why the law follows other laws dealing with theft.

A law providing war deferment for a newlywed man is connected by catchwords to the law on divorce and remarriage (24:5). It states that for one year a newlywed man may be free from war and war-related obligations so he can attend to his wife and enjoy her. One year together will allow the marriage to be established and will also be enough time for a child to be born.

Four laws following regulate the exacting of pledges, in between which is a warning about the danger of scale disease. In taking pledges for a loan, one may not take a hand-mill or an upper millstone, for that would amount to taking a life in pledge (24:6). There must also be no stealing of persons as pledges, with the creditor then lording it over the debtor or selling him or her to another as a slave (24:7). Anyone doing this will be put to death. Then comes the warning about scale disease (not leprosy), which has no apparent relation to the laws on pledges (24:8-9). Here one must do all that the Levitical priests say. Miriam's punishment in the wilderness is called to remembrance. The third law on pledges states that a creditor coming to collect his pledge must not enter the debtor's house to fetch it, but wait outside for the debtor to bring it to him (24:10-11). The fourth law states that under no circumstances is a creditor to sleep in a poor man's pledge (24:12-13). He must return it to the debtor at sundown so he can sleep on his garment. The poor man will then bless him, and it will be righteousness to the creditor before Yahweh.

Four more laws of a humane nature focus on justice, compassion, and benevolence to the poor and needy. The first law deals with hired laborers (24:14-15). They are to be paid their wages each day at sundown. They wait for them, and their needs are immediate. Employers failing to do this will cause the laborer to cry out to Yahweh, and it will be reckoned to the employer as sin. The second law (24:16) redefines the principle of retribution, stating that fathers shall not be put to death on account of their children and children shall not be put to death on account of their fathers. Each for his own sin shall die. The third law states that there must be no perversion of judgment to the needy, many of whom are without an advocate (24:17-18). Under no circumstances is a creditor to take the cloak of a widow in pledge. People are to remember that they were once slaves in Egypt and Yahweh ransomed them. The fourth law gives gleaning rights to sojourners, orphans, and widows (24:19-22). They are permitted to gather forgotten sheafs in the field, olives on the boughs or on the ground in the orchards, and grapes uncut in the vineyards. Yahweh will bless the owners, who again are told to remember that Israel was once a slave in Egypt.

Two more humane laws follow, one regarding a fellow who is to receive a beating, the other on an animal treading grain. If in a dispute brought to court, one man is acquitted as innocent and the other condemned as guilty and it is determined that the guilty deserves a beating commensurate with the offense committed, the man is to lie down and take his stripes in the presence of the judge. He may be given forty stripes, but no more, lest he be dishonored in the eyes of the people (25:1-3). An ox threshing grain is not to be muzzled (25:4). Working animals deserve to nibble from food that is continually before their eyes. This law appears only in Deuteronomy.

The legal portion of the Deuteronomic Code concludes with three miscellaneous laws and a closing admonition to wipe out the remembrance of Amalek. The first law deals with the custom of the levirate marriage (25:5-10). If two brothers are living together on the family estate and the one dies without leaving a son, the wife of the deceased is not to marry outside the family. Her brother-in-law is to take her as a wife and have intercourse with her in the hope of raising up a son. The first son born to the woman will keep alive the name of the deceased and will gain the deceased's share of the inheritance. The widow will also be provided for. Otherwise the surviving brother would get the entire inheritance. The levirate obligation, however, can be rejected. City elders will try to persuade the man to take his brother's wife, but if he refuses, the wife will publicly shame him, taking off his sandal and spitting in his face. The man's name will thus live on, but in infamy.

The second law deals with a woman who interferes in a fight between her husband and another man, attempting to rescue him by grabbing hold of the other man's testicles. Punishment for her is having her hand cut off, since the offense was committed with the hand (25:11-12). This is the only law in the OT explicitly calling for punishment by maiming.

The third law has to do with just weights and measures (25:13-16). Traders and merchants must not carry two weights in their bag, one great and one small. And when measuring grain, they must not have two ephahs, one great and one small. All stones must be full; all ephahs must be full. People must act honestly with one another if they want to live long in the land. Those who deal deceitfully are an abomination to Yahweh, for Yahweh loves justice and the practice of fair trade.

The legal portion of the code closes with an admonition to wipe out any remembrance of Amalek when people are settled in the land (25:17-19). On the way out of Egypt, the Amalekites showed no fear of God by cutting off stragglers at Israel's rear — people unable to defend themselves. For this treachery, Amalek's remembrance is to be wiped out.

Concluding the Deuteronomic Code are two rituals to be performed by each Israelite at the central sanctuary: (1) a ritual of the firstfruits (26:1-11) and (2) a ritual regarding the third-year charity tithe (26:12-15). Moses then closes with an admonition that Israel be sure to obey the statutes and ordinances Yahweh has commanded the people in the plains of Moab (26:16-19).

At the Feast of Weeks (Pentecost), when Israel is settled in the land, the worshipper is to bring his firstfruits in a basket, present them to the priest in office, and affirm with joy and thanksgiving that he is now settled in the land and has realized the land's bounty. The priest will take the basket and set it next to the altar. The worshipper will then say his "A wandering Aramean was my father" confession. The basket is to be left with the priest, after which the worshipper is to host a feast for his family, servants, the Levite, and the sojourner, probably also the orphan and widow who are along.

At the Feast of Booths the worshipper must attest to having distributed the third-year tithe designated for the Levite, sojourner, orphan, and widow residing in his town. The worshipper is to say before Yahweh that he has completely removed the sacred tithe from his house and given it to the recipients of charity. The worshipper then asks for a blessing from Yahweh's heavenly sanctuary.

Blessings and Curses (27–28)

The First Edition of Deuteronomy (1–28) ends with blessings and curses. Chapter 27 is an interpolation into the First Edition, breaking continuity with the conclusion to the Deuteronomic Code (ch. 26) and the blessings and curses relating to the Code (ch. 28). It is a fragmented report of a covenant renewal ceremony slated to be carried out at Shechem.

Once the people have crossed the Jordan they are to set up large stones, coat them with lime, and write on them the Deuteronomic law (27:1-8). The writing is to be legible. These stones will give Israel entitlement to the land. They are to be erected at Mount Ebal, which looks down upon the city of Shechem. People are also to build an altar there for burnt offerings and peace offerings.

Moses tells the people that on this day they have become Yahweh's people (27:9-10). He told them this before, but it bears repeating. They must therefore do the commandments Moses has taught them. This sermonizing is similar to what appears in 26:16-19 and may be an earlier tie-in between the conclusion of the Deuteronomic Code and the blessings and curses of chapter 28.

The tribes are then instructed to ascend the mountains above Shechem, Mount Gerizim on the south and Mount Ebal on the north (27:11-13). Six will bless Israel from Mount Gerizim (Simeon, Levi, Judah, Issachar, Joseph, and Benjamin), and six will speak curses from Mount Ebal (Reuben, Gad, Asher, Zebulun, Dan, and Naphtali). Nothing more is said about the ceremony, and it is unclear whether the curses following were a part of this ceremony or some other ceremony at the same location. No blessings are given, which means that the narrative as it stands is incomplete.

What remains is a litany of twelve curses, each of which is to be recited in full voice by the Levites, to which the people are to respond with a loud "Amen" (27:14-26). The curses are on people engaged in clandestine acts prohibited by Israelite law. The first sin is against Yahweh, falling on people who set up idols in secret (v. 15). This violates the second commandment. Next come four curses on people committing social sins: (1) dishonoring father or mother (v. 16); (2) moving back a fellow's boundary marker (v. 17); (3) misleading a blind person on the road (v. 18); and (4) perverting justice to the sojourner, orphan, and widow (v. 19).

Four curses follow on men secretly engaging in illicit sexual commerce: (1) a man who has sex with the wife of his father, even if she is not his mother (v. 20); (2) a man who has sex with a beast (v. 21); (3) a man who has sex with his sister or half-sister (v. 22); and (4) a man who has sex with his mother-in-law (v. 23).

Two curses return to social crimes, both of which are criminal in nature: (1) on the person who strikes down — to severely wound or kill — another person in secret (v. 24); and (2) on the person who takes a bribe to strike down (= kill) another person, which predictably will occur in secret (v. 25). A final curse is on anyone who does not perform the words of this law by doing them

(v. 26), which is a crime against Yahweh. To all of these curses the people are to give their loud "Amen."

Chapter 28 contains blessings and curses on those obeying or disobeying the Deuteronomic covenant. The collection is a compilation, containing a core of balanced and tightly knit blessings and curses, to which have been added a Blessing Supplement and five Curse Supplements. The core collection may survive from the Shechem renewal ceremony described in chapter 27, which, as we said, is incomplete as it stands (27:11-13).

Six blessings will come to people who obey the Deuteronomic covenant (28:1-6). They are general in nature, encompassing the whole of life. The six curses on those disobeying this covenant use the same words, except for the substitution of "cursed" in place of "blessed" (28:15-19). The center curses reverse the sequence of the center blessings, employing the same sort of variation found in the liturgical injunctions of 6:6-9 and 11:18-20.

The Blessing Supplement (28:7-14) expands upon the core blessings by promising Israel victory in battle, prosperity, dominance over enemies, and world respect. All will come to Israel if it keeps Yahweh's commandments and walks in his ways.

Curse Supplement I (28:20-26) expands upon the core curses by promising Israel disease, famine, crop failure, battle panic, defeat by enemies, and ultimate ruin. All will come to Israel for its evil doings and because it has forsaken Yahweh.

Curse Supplement II (28:27-37) announces incurable diseases; madness; oppression by enemies, with none to help; robbery of wives, sons and daughters, houses, vineyards, animals, and everything one owns; and for survivors, banishment to a distant place where they can serve gods of wood and stone. Yahweh will be the one leading his people away.

Curse Supplement III (28:38-46) speaks about crop failure, impoverishment, and dependent status; even the sojourner will rise above the lowliest Israelite. He will be the head; the Israelite will be the tail. The end will be Israel's destruction because it did not heed the voice of Yahweh and keep the Deuteronomic covenant. Israel's descendants will forever suffer because of this.

Curse Supplement IV (28:47-57) announces the terrible curses of the siege, where the conditional language of the previous curses gives way to language now that is absolute. Israel's disobedience of the Deuteronomic covenant is an established fact, and what we are hearing is preaching like that emanating from the prophets. Israel will serve its enemies in hunger and thirst, in nakedness and in want of everything, and the enemy will put an iron yoke upon its neck. The siege will force the most delicate of men and women to do the most indelicate of things, eating their own children and not sharing this unholy food with dear wives, dear husbands, or the last living child.

Curse Supplement V (28:58-68) speaks again about disease, only now it is the diseases of Egypt, which Moses said would never again be visited upon Israel (7:15). Moses also said that Yahweh promised never again to return Israel to Egypt (17:16), but now this may happen (the language here is conditional: the curses depend on disobedience to the Deuteronomic law and not fearing Yahweh's glorious and awesome name). Israelite men and women will offer themselves for sale as slaves, but no one will buy them. Dread and uncertainty will be unimaginable, with life hanging each day by a single thread. This supplement refers twice to Deuteronomy as a written book (28:58, 61), which must mean that the supplement is added later to the First Edition. The First Edition concludes with the subscription in 28:69(29:1).

First Supplement (chs. 29–30)

This supplement to the First Edition of Deuteronomy consists of two addresses — maybe more than two — in which Moses calls for faithfulness to the covenant demands. It is said by some to be in the nature of a peroration. Moses begins by making the point that the covenant is something you do (29:1-8[29:2-9]). Israel has been witness to Yahweh's mighty acts of the past, but they have not understood them until now. Israel must therefore be careful to do the words of the covenant, and in so doing it will prosper.

People are then bid to enter into a sworn covenant with Yahweh, one that will be binding on them and future generations (29:9-28[29:10-29]). Warnings are given about the danger of idol worship, which Israel observed ever since it left Egypt, and the curses awaiting Israel if it succumbs to this poisonous and bitter fruit. But Moses ends this discourse on a positive note. While the secret things belong to Yahweh, the revealed things belong forever to Israel and its children, so they may do all the words of this law.

The discourse in chapter 30 follows up on the covenant renewal ceremony and its warnings about blessings and curses with a word about what will happen after the curses come to pass (30:1-10). This will not be the end. Restoration is promised after exile, at which time Israel will return to Yahweh and obey his commands. There will be numerical growth and prosperity. This discourse also concludes on a positive note. The word of Yahweh is not in heaven or across the sea; it is very near people, which means obeying Yahweh's commands is something they can do (30:11-14). The nation can choose one of two ways: obedience to the sworn covenant, which is the road to life and good fortune, or disobedience to the sworn covenant, which is the road to misfortune and death (30:15-20). People are told to choose life, so they and their descendants may live.

Introduction

SECOND SUPPLEMENT (CHS. 31–34)

In a second and final supplement, the book of Deuteronomy is brought to completion. This supplement prepares for Moses' death and adds two old poems, the Song of Moses (32:1-43) and the Blessing of Moses (33:1-29). The Song of Moses is the core of the supplement, in my view the temple lawbook found during Josiah's reform in 622. The prose in this supplement reports (1) a directive to Moses to write down the Deuteronomic law and entrust it to the Levites and elders; (2) a warning to Israel about future disobedience and covenant infidelity; (3) the commissioning of Joshua as Moses' successor; and (4) Moses' death and burial.

The supplement begins by Yahweh telling Moses once again that he cannot cross the Jordan and that Joshua will succeed him as the people's leader (31:1-6). Moses is advanced in age and no longer able to conduct holy war. He has reached the full number of his days. Yahweh will be with Israel in the conquest of Canaan, doing the same to the kings there as he did to the Amorite kings, Sihon and Og, in Transjordan. The conquest will succeed. People are told to be strong and bold and not to fear the enemy. Yahweh will go with them and will not abandon them.

Moses then summons Joshua to charge him before the people, telling him to be strong and bold as he leads Israel into the promised land (31:7-13). Then Moses is said to have written down the Deuteronomic law and entrusted it to the Levites and the elders. He instructed them that the law be read publicly every seven years at the Feast of Booths, at which time all Israel — men, women, small children, and even sojourners — were to be present.

In the next segment of prose Yahweh speaks first to Moses, then to Joshua (31:14-23). Moses is first told to summon Joshua so Yahweh may commssion him at the tent of meeting. The two of them go there, and Yahweh appears in a pillar of cloud at the door (31:14-15). But before the actual commissioning takes place, Yahweh instructs Moses to write a song that will witness against Israel's disobedience and unfaithfulness after he dies (31:16-22). Then the commissioning of Joshua takes place, and a word is given him about being strong and bold in his mission (31:23).

The next segment tells how Moses, after he had written the Song, told the Levites to put it beside the ark of the covenant, over which they had jurisdiction (31:24-30). In the ark were the tablets of the Decalogue. The Levites were then told what Yahweh had said to Moses about Israel being rebellious in future days. Moses then calls for an assembly of tribal elders and officials, to which the same is announced. Evil will come upon Israel when it falls into idolatry. Then Moses recited the Song in its entirety to the assembly (v. 30).

What follows is the Song itself, a masterful poetic composition that

The Book of Deuteronomy

served as a model for all subsequent prophetic preaching (32:1-43). The poem consists of eight well-structured stanzas in four pairs, metrically balanced, with an introduction and a conclusion. It is rich in rhetorical features: climactic and ballast lines, repeated words and particles in strategic collocations, chiasms, partial chiams, inclusios, rhetorical questions, and shifts in direct address. It is poetry of a very high order.

The Introduction (vv. 1-3) begins like a wisdom poem, calling on the heavens and the earth to hear the poet proclaim the name of Yahweh and the greatness of Israel's God.

Stanza 1 (vv. 4-9) acclaims Yahweh's greatness, perfect in all his created works, just in all his ways, faithful to the covenant, and in whom no wrong can be found. Israel, by contrast, is a corrupt and perverse adversary, foolish to repay Yahweh in the way it has. In hoary antiquity, Yahweh Most High gave to the nations their inheritance, and Israel was singled out as his special portion.

Stanza 2 (vv. 10-14) recalls Yahweh's gift of salvation to Israel, finding her as he did in a desert wasteland, caring for her there, and leading her to a bountiful land having every good thing.

Stanza 3 (vv. 15-18) goes on to say how Israel repaid the favor by becoming "fat and sassy." She forsook Yahweh and stirred him to jealousy by chasing after "no gods," gods that neither she nor her fathers had known.

Stanza 4 (vv. 19-22) says that Yahweh therefore passed sentence on Israel, stirring it to jealousy with a "no people." A divine fire burned not to be quenched.

Stanza 5 (vv. 23-27) focuses on the extent of Israel's punishment. It was great; nevertheless, Yahweh stopped short of destroying Israel completely, lest her enemies — and Yahweh's too — think that the nation's ruin was their doing.

Stanza 6 (vv. 28-33) looks further at Israel's punishment in retrospect. Yahweh is the one who sold Israel into the hands of its enemy. Israel's Rock has nothing in common with their "rock."

Stanza 7 (vv. 34-38) shifts to punishment for the enemy and salvation for Israel. Vengeance belongs to Yahweh. The enemy's foot will slip, and calamity will come. Israel will be vindicated when it sees that its support is gone. The poem therefore begins and ends with salvation; judgment comes in the middle.

Stanza 8 (vv. 39-42) acclaims the infinite and incomparable power of Yahweh. Yahweh kills and Yahweh makes alive, Yahweh wounds and Yahweh heals. Yahweh will take vengeance on his adversaries, repaying all those who hate him.

The Conclusion (v. 43) calls for the heavens (or the nations) to give ringing praise to Yahweh, for he avenges the blood of his servants and makes atonement for his people and his land. The LXX expands a four-colon MT verse to eight colons, with 4QDeut^q expanding it to six colons. The longer LXX version

Introduction

makes the Conclusion comparable in length to the Introduction, which is eight colons.

The prose following the Song reports that Moses recited the poem to the people, Joshua being with him (32:44-47). He then exhorted the people to take these words to heart and to teach them to their children, so they might learn them and do Yahweh's "law." These were not empty words, but words of life, which would prolong Israel's days in the land it would soon possess.

In the next prose segment Moses is told to ascend Mount Nebo, view the land of Canaan, and die there (32:48-52). This addition appears to derive from the Priestly writer. Yahweh repeats that Moses and Aaron were unfaithful to him at the waters of Meribath-kadesh, not honoring him as holy in the midst of the people. Moses will therefore be permitted a look at the land across the Jordan, but he will not be able to enter there.

What follows is the Blessing of Moses (33:1-29), another poem of separate origin that aids in bringing closure to the book of Deuteronomy. It is particularly welcome after the Song of Moses, which contains a riveting indictment and judgment of Israel for breaking covenant with Yahweh. The Blessing brings a needed word of healing for the Israelite tribes as they prepare to cross the Jordan and enter Canaan.

The Introduction to the Blessing (vv. 2-5) tells how Yahweh came from holy mountains in the southland, where he was surrounded with brilliant radiance and myriads of holy ones, leaving all this behind because of his love for people, specifically the tribes of Israel. Yahweh became King in Israel. Blessings are then given to each of Israel's twelve tribes (vv. 6-25). Simeon is omitted, but its loss is compensated for by blessings on the two sons of Joseph: Ephraim and Manasseh. The conclusion (vv. 26-29) returns to address Israel as a whole. There is no God like the one Israel has known. He rides triumphantly through the heavens, yet comes to Israel's aid in her time of need. This God is Israel's refuge; underneath her are the everlasting arms. Israel is therefore to be happy. It is a nation like no other, knowing Yahweh's salvation and gift of a bountiful land. Yahweh will be Israel's sword and shield as she marches triumphantly against her enemies.

The supplement closes with a report of Moses' final days in Moab, how he was given a look at the promised land from the top of Mount Nebo, and then died (34:1-12). Burial was in an unmarked grave in the valley opposite Bethpeor. No one knows just where. The narrator concludes by saying that no prophet has arisen like Moses, with whom Yahweh could speak "face to face." No prophet could perform the signs and wonders Moses performed in Egypt, and no prophet could demonstrate the power Moses demonstrated before all Israel.

DEUTERONOMY AND THE NEW TESTAMENT

Deuteronomy is one of four Old Testament books that writers of the New Testament cite most frequently; the others are Genesis, Isaiah, and the Psalms (see Appendix). Citations and allusions occur in all four Gospels, Acts, the Pauline and Deutero-Pauline letters, Hebrews, James, the Johannine Epistles, and Revelation. Of all the OT books known to Matthew, the most influential seems to have been Deuteronomy — thirteen explicit quotations in his Gospel (Brodie 1992, 699). To the citations, near-citations, and allusions must be added other teachings in the NT that show a clear indebtedness to Deuteronomy, making the influence of this OT book upon writers of the NT considerably greater than a list of citations would indicate.

The Song of Moses is quoted in Acts (2:40); in Romans (10:19; 11:11; 12:19; 15:10) and other Pauline letters (1 Cor 10:20, 22; Phil 2:15); in Hebrews (10:30); and in Revelation (9:20; 15:3; 16:5; 18:20; 19:2). The expanded LXX text of 32:43 is quoted in Hebrews (1:6) and in Revelation (6:10; 18:20; 19:2).

THE SYNOPTIC GOSPELS

The Synoptics report Jesus as upholding without exception all the Ten Commandments. Commandments one and two get support by quotations of the Shema, that God is one and is to be loved heart and soul (Mark 12:29-33; Matt 22:37; Luke 10:27). Jesus reflects Deuteronomy in warning about false prophets who show signs and wonders, but who lead people astray (Mark 13:22; Matt 24:24). Commandment three about no empty swearing is affirmed in the Sermon on the Mount (Matt 5:33-37). Commandment four on keeping the Sabbath is not cited directly, but is affirmed nevertheless in Jesus' celebrated dictum: "The Sabbath was made for man, not man for the Sabbath" (Mark 2:27). Jesus' disciples are said to have rested on the Sabbath (Luke 23:56; cf. Mark 16:1). Commandments five through nine are affirmed explicitly (Mark 7:10; 10:18-19; Matt 15:4; 19:18; Luke 18:20). Commandment ten about not coveting is affirmed indirectly by Jesus' expansion of the adultery prohibition in his Sermon on the Mount (Matt 5:27-30).

Jesus has Deuteronomy in mind during his forty days in the wilderness, where all three of his answers to the devil are quotes from Deuteronomy: (1) "man shall not live by bread alone, but by every word that proceeds from the mouth of God" (Matt 4:4; Luke 4:4); (2) "you shall not tempt/test the Lord your God" (Matt 4:7; Luke 4:12); and (3) "you shall worship the Lord your God, and him only shall you serve" (Matt 4:10; Luke 4:8).

Matthew has Jesus quoting or alluding to Deuteronomy in his Sermon on the Mount. In the sermon Jesus says that one must be "blameless before the Lord" (Matt 5:48). The *lex talionis,* taught in Deuteronomy, is to be set aside in cases of insult (5:38). The law on divorce is also cited in the Sermon on the Mount (5:31), as well as elsewhere in the Gospels (Mark 10:4; Matt 19:7). Jesus and his opponents discuss the Deuteronomic law on the levirate marriage (Mark 12:19; Matt 22:24-25; Luke 20:28), and the Deuteronomic teaching about God gathering exiles from the "uttermost parts of heaven" is applied to the judgment at the end of time (Mark 13:27; Matt 24:31). Jesus' teachings about benevolence to the poor, needy, and widowed (Mark 10:21; 12:40; Matt 19:21; 25:35-46; 26:11; Luke 20:47) are rooted in Deuteronomy's laws of benevolence. Luke has a special concern for the poor (Luke 14:13, 21; 18:22; 19:8). Matthew's teaching about settling disputes in church makes use of the Deuteronomic principle of having two or three witnesses (Matt 18:16).

The Gospel of John and the Johannine Epistles

While John in his Gospel and in the Epistles does not cite Deuteronomy directly, he fully understands Deuteronomy's teaching about love: God's love, the believer's love for God, and love one for another. John knows that love is a command, that love among people should issue forth when God's love has been shown to them (John 13:34; 15:12, 17; 1 John 4:11, 19, 21), and he grasps more fully than any other NT writer, except perhaps James, the tie-in between love and doing the commandments (John 15:10; 1 John 2:3-5; 5:2-3; 2 John 6). 1 John 2:6 contains the expression "walking in [God's] way," which is Deuteronomic. John knows the teaching of Deuteronomy that the commandments are not burdensome (1 John 5:3), and he gives explicit directives concerning benevolence to the poor and needy and to strangers (John 12:8; 1 John 3:17; 3 John 5).

Acts of the Apostles

In the Acts of the Apostles, Luke includes numerous references to Deuteronomy in the speeches of Peter, Stephen, and Paul. Peter, in a Jerusalem speech after Pentecost, cites the "prophet like Moses" promise as having been fulfilled in the Christ and points out that people must heed the prophetic word or be destroyed (3:22-23). In another speech before the Jewish high priest and the council, Peter says that God raised Jesus whom they killed by hanging on a tree (5:30). In speaking later to Cornelius, the Gentile, Peter cites the death of Jesus on a tree once again (10:39) and says he now realizes that God shows no partiality (10:34), which he gets from Deuteronomy. Stephen in his impassioned speech uses language from Deuteronomy in recalling Abraham's sojourn in a land that he would not himself inherit (7:5). He also cites Deuteronomy in saying that Israel went down to Egypt a mere seventy-five persons (7:14) and that God would raise up a "prophet like Moses" (7:37).

Paul, in a speech delivered in Antioch, cites God's care of Israel in the wilderness and his clearing away the Canaanites to give Israel an inheritance (13:18-19). Preaching at Lystra, he cites God's giving of rain to past generations to show that God did not leave himself without witness, making use of another promise out of Deuteronomy (14:17). Luke himself shows concern for neglected widows (6:1), the same sort of compassion for the poor that characterizes his gospel.

PAULINE AND DEUTERO-PAULINE LETTERS

Paul is well versed in Deuteronomy. In Ephesians he quotes the fifth commandment about honoring parents, including the benefit of well-being and long life added by the Deuteronomic writer (Eph 6:2-3). Commandments six to eight are cited in Rom 13:9, where also commandment ten about not coveting is cited. The latter appears also in Rom 7:7, where Paul says that knowing the law has made him conscious of sin. Paul applies Deuteronomic teaching in telling the Corinthian church, where immorality has been reported to him, to remove the evil from its midst (1 Cor 5:13). In his Second Letter to the Corinthians, Paul reminds the fractious church that all charges must be supported by two or three witnesses (2 Cor 13:1). Paul knows the Song of Moses' teaching about God being blameless amidst a crooked generation (Deut 32:4-5), telling people they should also be blameless amidst a generation no different (Phil 2:15). He knows the Deuteronomic verse about God showing no partiality (Gal 2:6; Rom 2:11). Paul cites Deuteronomc teaching that laborers deserve their wages in arguing that preachers of the gospel deserve their living by the gospel (1 Cor 9:3-14); he cites the law about not muzzling an ox when it is treading the grain (v. 9; cf. 1 Tim 5:18).

Deuteronomy serves Paul in his doctrinal teaching. In explaining his view that Christ has redeemed people from the curse of the law by becoming himself a curse, he cites the teaching of Deuteronomy that everyone not doing the law stands cursed by the law and then adds: "Cursed be every one who hangs on a tree" (Gal 3:10-13). Israel's election as God's chosen people is cited in Titus 2:14, but in Romans, Paul explains the hardening of the Jews by quoting the Deuteronomic verse about Israel not having the mind to understand, or eyes to see, or ears to hear the wonders of Egypt (Rom 11:7-8). Paul knows the Deuteronomic teaching about "the word of God being very near you" (Rom

10:6-8). In discussing communion, Paul says one cannot drink the cup of the Lord and at the same time drink the cup of demons (pagan sacrifices), citing the Song of Moses, where it says people sacrificed to demons and provoked Yahweh in doing so (1 Cor 10:14-22). Paul also has the Song of Moses in mind when he cites the passage about God making his people jealous with a "no people," applying it to those who have not heeded the gospel (Rom 10:19; 11:11). Paul is concerned for the hungry and thirsty, even if they are one's enemies (Rom 12:20). He takes up a collection for the poor (Rom 15:26) and is concerned about generosity generally (2 Corinthians 9). In 1 Timothy special concern is shown for widows who are real widows (1 Tim 5:3-16).

THE EPISTLE OF JAMES

James, in supporting his argument that the entire law must be followed, cites commandments six and seven as examples (Jas 2:11) and, to buttress his doctrine that faith and works are essentially one, cites the Shema that God is one (Jas 2:19). Here he finds strong support from Deuteronomy's teaching that the interior dispositions of love and fear must go hand-in-hand with doing the commandments. James has concern for orphans, widows, the hungry, and ill-clad (1:27; 2:2-6, 15-16), censuring the rich for laying up treasures for themselves while they keep back wages of the poor that should be given them daily (5:4). He therefore tells people to be patient for the coming of the Lord, as the farmer waits patiently for the rain (5:7-8).

THE EPISTLE TO THE HEBREWS

The writer of Hebrews cites Deuteronomy when reflecting on sin and judgment, particularly on those who deliberately sin after receiving the truth (Heb 10:26-31). Such persons will die without supporting testimony from two or three witnesses. God has said: "Vengeance is mine, I will repay," and the writer follows with words made famous by the fiery sermon of Jonathan Edwards: "It is a fearful thing to fall into the hands of the living God." In his sermon on discipline, the writer warns about the "root bearing poison," which jeopardizes peaceful relations among people (12:15). Believers stand before God like those present at Horeb on the day of assembly, who witnessed a blazing fire and heard a voice making them draw back in fright; even Moses trembled at the sight (12:18-21). Let the wise beware: "Our God is a consuming fire" (12:29). But the writer of Hebrews finds comfort in Deuteronomy's teaching that God "will not forsake or abandon," applying it to those who show hospitality to strangers and live honorably (13:1-5).

Deuteronomy and the New Testament

REVELATION OF SAINT JOHN

The writer of Revelation cites the Song of Moses, which begins by affirming that "all the ways [of God] are justice" (Rev 15:3; 16:5; 19:2). From the Song the writer also derives support in censuring all those who have worshipped "demons" (9:20). He gives ringing praise to a God who avenges the blood of his servants (6:10; 18:20; 19:2) and applies the Deuteronomic expression, "Lord of lords," to the Lamb, i.e., Jesus (17:14; 19:16). Finally, Deuteronomy is recalled when it comes to laying down curses: a curse of sores for those worshipping an image of the beast (16:2) and a curse on anyone adding to or taking away from the book the author has written (22:18-19).

Bibliography

TEXTS AND REFERENCE WORKS

Aeschylus
1963   *Aeschylus I.* Trans. Herbert Weir Smyth. LCL. Cambridge, MA: Harvard University Press.

Allegro, John M.
1968   *Qumrân Cave 4: I (4Q158-4Q186).* DJD 5. Oxford: Clarendon. Contains *Testimonia; Florilegium.*

Apostolic Fathers
1952   *The Apostolic Fathers I.* Trans. Kirsopp Lake. LCL. Cambridge, MA: Harvard University Press. Contains the *Didache.*

Aristophanes
1967   *Aristophanes.* Vol. 1: *Acharnians, Knights, Clouds, Wasps.* Trans. Benjamin Bickley Rogers. LCL. Cambridge, MA: Harvard University Press.
1998   *Aristophanes.* Vol. 1: *Acharnians, Knights.* Trans. Jeffrey Henderson. LCL. Cambridge, MA: Harvard University Press.

Aristotle
1961   *Aristotle: Parts of Animals.* Trans. A. L. Peck. LCL. Cambridge, MA: Harvard University Press.
1967   *Aristotle: Politics.* Trans. H. Rackham. LCL. Cambridge MA: Harvard University Press.

Attridge, Harold, et al.
1994   *Qumran Cave 4: VIII, Parabiblical Texts, Part 1.* DJD 13. Oxford: Clarendon. Contains 4Q Reworked Pentateuch (4Q364-366).

Baillet, Maurice, J. T. Milik, and Roland de Vaux
1962   *Les 'Petites Grottes' de Qumrân.* Pt. 1: *Texts.* DJD 3. Oxford: Clarendon. Contains 2QDeut^a; 2QDeut^b; 2QDeut^c; phylacteries and a mezuza from Cave 8 with Deuteronomy texts.

Barthélemy, Dominique, and J. T. Milik
1955   *Qumran Cave I.* DJD 1. Oxford: Clarendon. Contains 1QDeut^a; 1QDeut^b; "Words of Moses" (1Q22); and phylacteries with Deuteronomy texts.

Bibliography

Benoit, Pierre, J. T. Milik, and Roland de Vaux
1960 *Les grottes de Murabba'ât.* Pt. 1: *Texts.* DJD 2. Oxford: Clarendon. Contains MurDeut, phylactery and mezuza (?) with Deuteronomy texts.
1961 *Les grottes de Murabba'ât.* Pt. 2: *Photos.* DJD 2A. Oxford: Clarendon.

Blackman, Philip
1977 *Mishnayoth I-VI.* 2nd ed. Gateshead: Judaica.

Brooke, George, et al.
1996 *Qumran Cave 4: XVII, Parabiblical Texts, Part 3.* DJD 22. Oxford: Clarendon. Contains "The Two Ways" (4Q473).

Brown, Francis, S. R. Driver, and Charles A. Briggs
1907 *A Hebrew and English Lexicon of the Old Testament.* Oxford: Clarendon [Based on the Lexicon of William Gesenius].

Brownlee, William Hugh
1951 *The Dead Sea Manual of Discipline.* BASORSup 10-12. New Haven: ASOR.

Charles, R. H.
1913 *The Apocrypha and Pseudepigrapha of the Old Testament.* 2 vols. Oxford: Clarendon.

Charlesworth, James H., ed.
1983 *The Old Testament Pseudepigrapha.* Vol. 1. Garden City: Doubleday.
1985 *The Old Testament Pseudepigrapha.* Vol. 2. Garden City: Doubleday.

Charlesworth, James H., et al.
2000 *Miscellaneous Texts from the Judean Desert.* DJD 38. Oxford: Clarendon. Contains XḤev/SeDeut; XḤev/Se Phylactery.

Cicero
1968a *Cicero XXI: De Officiis.* Trans. Walter Miller. LCL. Cambridge, MA: Harvard University Press.
1968b [*Cicero:*] *Rhetorica ad Herennium.* Trans. Harry Caplan. LCL. Cambridge, MA: Harvard University Press.

Clark, Ernest G.
1998 *Targum Pseudo-Jonathan: Deuteronomy.* ArBib 5B. Edinburgh: T. & T. Clark.

Coggins, R. J., and M. A. Knibb
1979 *The First and Second Books of Esdras.* CBC. Cambridge: Cambridge University Press.

Cotton, Hannah M., and Ada Yardeni
1997 *Aramaic, Hebrew and Greek Documentary Texts from Naḥal Ḥever and Other Sites.* DJD 27. Oxford: Clarendon.

Diodorus
1968 *Diodorus of Sicily.* Vol. 1: *Books 1-2:34.* Trans. C. H. Oldfather. LCL. Cambridge, MA: Harvard University Press.

Dionysius of Halicarnassus
1968 *The Roman Antiquities of Dionysius of Halicarnassus.* Vol. 1: *Books 1-2.* Trans. Earnest Cary. LCL. Cambridge, MA: Harvard University Press.

Donner, Herbert, and Wolfgang Röllig
1968 *Kanaanäische und aramäische Inschriften.* Vol. 2: *Kommentar.* 2nd ed. Wiesbaden: Harrassowitz.
1971 *Kanaanäische und aramäische Inschriften.* Vol. 1: *Texte.* 3rd ed. Wiesbaden: Harrassowitz.

Bibliography

Eisenman, Robert H., and James M. Robinson
1991 *A Facsimile Edition of the Dead Sea Scrolls*. 2 vols. Washington: Biblical Archaeological Society.

Elliger, Kurt, and Wilhelm Rudolph
1990 *Biblia Hebraica Stuttgartensia*. Stuttgart: Deutsche Bibelgesellschaft. Orig. 1967-77.

Epstein, Isidore, ed.
1935-48 *The Babylonian Talmud*. 34 vols. London: Soncino.

Eusebius
1964 *The Ecclesiastical History*. Vol. 2: *Books 6-10*. Trans. J. E. L. Oulton. LCL. Cambridge, MA: Harvard University Press.
2003 *The Onomasticon by Eusebius of Caesarea*. Trans. G. S. P. Freeman-Grenville. Jerusalem: Carta. Contains the *Onomasticon* of Eusebius and Jerome's *Liber Locorum*.

Field, Frederick
1875 *Origenis Hexaplorum*. Vol. 1. Oxford: Clarendon. Repr. Hildesheim: Olms, 1964.

Freedman, David Noel, ed.
1998 *The Leningrad Codex: A Facsimile Edition*. Grand Rapids: Eerdmans and Leiden: Brill.

Freedman, Harry, ed.
1939 *Midrash Rabbah: Genesis I*. London: Soncino.

von Gall, August Freiherrn, ed.
1918 *Der Hebräische Pentateuch der Samaritaner*. Giessen: Töpelmann.

Gaster, Theodor H.
1964 *The Dead Sea Scriptures*. 2nd ed. Garden City: Doubleday.

Ginsburg, Christian D.
1885 *The Massorah*. Vol. 3. London: Fromme. Repr. New York: Ktav, 1970.

Gordon, Cyrus H.
1955 *Ugaritic Manual*. AnOr 35. Rome: Pontifical Biblical Institute.
1965 *Ugaritic Textbook*. AnOr 38. Rome: Pontifical Biblical Institute.

Goshen-Gottstein, Moshe H., ed.
1976 *The Aleppo Codex*. Jerusalem: Hebrew University.

Grossfeld, Bernard
1988 *The Targum Onqelos to Deuteronomy*. ArBib 9. Edinburgh: T. & T. Clark.

Herodotus
1963 *Herodotus*. Vol. 2: *Books 3-4*. Trans. A. D. Godley. LCL. Cambridge, MA: Harvard University Press.
1963 *Herodotus*. Vol. 3: *Books 5-7*. Trans. A. D. Godley. LCL. Cambridge, MA: Harvard University Press.
1966 *Herodotus*. Vol. 1: *Books 1-2*. Trans. A. D. Godley. LCL. Cambridge, MA: Harvard University Press.
1969 *Herodotus*. Vol. 4: *Books 8-9*. Trans. A. D. Godley. LCL. Cambridge, MA: Harvard University Press.

Hertz, J. H., ed.
1960 *The Pentateuch and Haftorahs*. 2nd ed. London: Soncino. Orig. 1936.

Hesiod
2006 *Hesiod*. Vol. 1: *Theogony, Works and Days, Testimonies*. Trans. Glenn W. Most. LCL. Cambridge, MA: Harvard University Press.

Bibliography

Homer
1999   *Homer. The Iliad.* Vol. 2: *Books 13-24.* Trans. A. T. Murray. Rev. William F. Wyatt. LCL. Cambridge, MA: Harvard University Press.
1953   *Homer. The Odyssey.* Vol. 2: *Books 13-24.* Trans. A. T. Murray. LCL. Cambridge, MA: Harvard University Press.

Jastrow, Marcus
1903   *A Dictionary of the Targumim, the Talmud Babli and Yerushalmi, and the Midrashic Literature.*. 2 vols. London: Luzac and New York: Putnam. Repr. Peabody: Hendrickson, 2005.

Josephus
1934   *Josephus.* Vol. 5: *Jewish Antiquities: Books 5-8.* Trans. Ralph Marcus. LCL. Cambridge, MA: Harvard University Press.
1957   *Josephus.* Vol. 3: *The Jewish War: Books 4-7.* Trans. H. St. J. Thackeray. LCL. Cambridge, MA: Harvard University Press.
1967   *Josephus.* Vol. 2: *The Jewish War: Books 1-3.* Trans. H. St. J. Thackeray. LCL. Cambridge, MA: Harvard University Press.
1967   *Josephus.* Vol. 4: *Jewish Antiquities: Books 1-4.* Trans. H. St. J. Thackeray. LCL. Cambridge, MA: Harvard University Press.
1966   *Josephus.* Vol. 7: *Jewish Antiquities: Books 12-14.* Trans. Ralph Marcus. LCL. Cambridge, MA: Harvard University Press.
1969   *Josephus.* Vol. 8: *Jewish Antiquities: Books 15-17.* Trans. Ralph Marcus. LCL. Cambridge, MA: Harvard University Press.
1969   *Josephus.* Vol. 9: *Jewish Antiquities: Books 18-20.* Trans. Louis H. Feldman. LCL. Cambridge, MA: Harvard University Press.

Juvenal
2004   *Juvenal and Persius.* Trans. Susanna Morton Braund. LCL. Cambridge, MA: Harvard University Press. Contains *Satires* of Juvenal.

Kittel, Rudolph, ed.
1905   *Biblia Hebraica.* 1st ed. Leipzig: Hinrichs. Genesis through Kings.

Köhler, Ludwig, and Walter Baumgartner
1967-96   *Hebräisches und Aramäisches Lexikon zum Alten Testament.* 4 vols. + Supp. 3rd ed. Leiden: Brill [Eng: *The Hebrew and Aramaic Lexicon of the Old Testament.* 5 vols. Trans. M. Richardson. Leiden: Brill, 1994-2000].

Lane, Edward W.
1865   *An Arabic-English Lexicon.* London: Williams and Norgate.

Liddell, Henry George, and Robert Scott
1961   *A Greek-English Lexicon.* 2 vols. New ed. rev. by Henry Stuart Jones and Roderick McKenzie. Oxford: Clarendon [1 vol. with revised supp., 1996].

Lucretius
1975   *De Rerum Natura.* Trans. W. H. Rouse. LCL. Cambridge, MA: Harvard University Press.

Martínez, Florentino García, Eibert J. C. Tigchelaar, and A. S. van der Woude
1998   *Qumran Cave 11: II, 11Q2-18. 11Q20-31.* DJD 23. Oxford: Clarendon. Contains 11QDeut.

May, Herbert G., ed.
1962   *Oxford Bible Atlas.* London: Oxford University Press.

McNamara, Martin
1997   *Targum Neofiti 1: Deuteronomy.* ArBib 5A. Edinburgh: T. & T. Clark.

Bibliography

Milik, J. T.
1977   *II, Tefillin, Mezuzot et Targums (4Q128-4Q157)*. In Roland de Vaux and Milik, *Qumrân Grotte 4*. DJD 6. Oxford: Clarendon. Contains Phylactère[a-s] (4Q128-146) and Mezuzot[a-e] (4Q149-153).

Neusner, Jacob
1988   *The Mishnah: A New Translation*. New Haven: Yale University Press.

Oppian
1963   *Oppian, Colluthus, Tryphiodorus*. Trans. A. W. Mair. LCL. Cambridge, MA: Harvard University Press. Contains Oppian's *Cynegetica*.

Pausanias
1926   *Description of Greece*. Vol. 2: *Books 3-5*. Trans. W. H. S. Jones and H. A. Ormerod. LCL. New York: G. P. Putnam's Sons.

Persius
1920   *Perse: Satires,* ed. A. Cartault. CUF. Paris: Société D'Édition 'Les Belles Lettres.'

Philo
1960   *Philo*. Vol. 8. Trans. F. H. Colson. LCL. Cambridge, MA: Harvard University Press. Contains *On the Virtues*.
1968   *Philo*. Vol. 7. Trans. F. H. Colson. LCL. Cambridge, MA: Harvard University Press. Contains *On the Decalogue* and *Special Laws, Books 1-3*.

Plato
1967   *Plato*. Vol. 10: *Laws I: Books 1-6*. Trans. R. G. Bury. LCL. Cambridge, MA: Harvard University Press.
1968   *Plato*. Vol. 11: *Laws II: Books 7-12*. Trans. R. G. Bury. LCL. Cambridge, MA: Harvard University Press.

Pliny
1961   *Pliny: Natural History*. Vol. 5: *Books 17-19*. Trans. H. Rackham. LCL. Cambridge, MA: Harvard University Press.
1962   *Pliny: Natural History*. Vol. 10: *Books 36-37*. Trans. D. E. Eichholz. LCL. Cambridge, MA: Harvard University Press.
1966   *Pliny: Natural History*. Vol. 7: *Books 24-27*. Trans. W. H. Jones. LCL. Cambridge, MA: Harvard University Press.
1967   *Pliny: Natural History*. Vol. 2: *Books 3-7*. Trans. H. Rackham. LCL. Cambridge, MA: Harvard University Press.
1967   *Pliny: Natural History*. Vol. 3: *Books 8-11*. Trans. H. Rackham. LCL. Cambridge, MA: Harvard University Press.
1969   *Pliny: Letters and Panegyricus*. Vol. 1: *Letters, Books 1-7*. Trans. Betty Radice. LCL. Cambridge, MA: Harvard University Press.

Plutarch
1969   *Plutarch's Moralia*. Vol. 5. Trans. Frank Cole Babbitt. LCL. Cambridge, MA: Harvard University Press. Contains *De Iside et Osiride* (Isis and Osiris).
1972   *Plutarch's Moralia*. Vol. 4. Trans. Frank Cole Babbitt. LCL. Cambridge, MA: Harvard University Press. Contains "The Roman Questions" *(Quaestiones Romanae)*.

Polybius
1960   *The Histories*. Vol. 3: *Books 6-8*. Trans. W. R. Paton. LCL. Cambridge, MA: Harvard University Press.

Qimron, Elisha, and John Strugnell
1994   *Qumran Cave 4: V, Miqṣat Ma'aśe ha-Torah*. DJD 10. Oxford: Clarendon. Contains 4QMMT.

Bibliography

Rahlfs, Alfred, ed.
1971   *Septuaginta*. 2 vols. 9th ed. Stuttgart: Württembergische Bibelanstalt. Orig. 1935.

Reed, Stephen A., and Marilyn J. Lundberg, eds.
1993   *The Dead Sea Scrolls on Microfiche: Inventory List of Photographs*. Leiden: Brill.

Roberts, Alexander, and James Donaldson, eds.
1981   *The Ante-Nicene Fathers*. Vol. 1. Grand Rapids: Eerdmans. Contains Justin Martyr and Irenaeus.

Schiffman, Lawrence H., and James C. VanderKam
2000   *Encyclopedia of the Dead Sea Scrolls*. 2 vols. Oxford: Oxford University Press.

Skehan, Patrick W., Eugene Ulrich, and Judith E. Sanderson
1992   *Qumran Cave 4: IV, PaleoHebrew and Greek Biblical Manuscripts*. DJD 9. Oxford: Clarendon. Contains 4QpaleoDeut[r] and 4QpaleoDeut[s], also 4QLXX Deut.

Stählin, Otto, ed.
1960   *Clemens Alexandrinus*. Vol. 2: *Stromata Buch I-VI*. Berlin: Akademie.

Strabo
1930   *The Geography of Strabo*. Vol. 7: *Books 15-16*. Trans. Horace Leonard Jones. LCL. New York: G. P. Putnam's Sons.
1949   *The Geography of Strabo*. Vol. 2: *Books 3-5*. Trans. Horace Leonard Jones. LCL. Cambridge, MA: Harvard University Press.
1960   *The Geography of Strabo*. Vol. 6: *Books 13-14*. Trans. Horace Leonard Jones. LCL. Cambridge, MA: Harvard University Press.
1969   *The Geography of Strabo*. Vol. 5: *Books 10-12*. Trans. Horace Leonard Jones. LCL. Cambridge, MA: Harvard University Press.

Tacitus
1962   *Tacitus*. Vol. 2: *The Histories: Books IV-V*. Trans. Clifford H. Moore. LCL. Cambridge, MA: Harvard University Press.

Theophrastus
1990   *De Causis Plantarum: Books 3-4*. Trans. Benedict Einarson and George K. K. Link. LCL. Cambridge, MA: Harvard University Press.

Thucydides
1969   *Thucydides*. Vol. 1: *History of the Peloponnesian War, Books I-II*. Trans. Charles Forster Smith. LCL. Cambridge, MA: Harvard University Press.

Ulrich, Eugene, F. M. Cross, et al.
1995   *Qumran Cave 4: IX, Deuteronomy, Joshua, Judges, Kings*. DJD 14. Oxford: Clarendon. Contains 4QDeut[a]; 4QDeut[b]; 4QDeut[c]; 4QDeut[d]; 4QDeut[e]; 4QDeut[f]; 4QDeut[g]; 4QDeut[h]; 4QDeut[i]; 4QDeut[j]; 4QDeut[k1]; 4QDeut[k2]; 4QDeut[k3]; 4QDeut[l]; 4QDeut[m]; 4QDeut[n]; 4QDeut[o]; 4QDeut[p]; 4QDeut[q].

Van de Sandt, Huub, and David Flusser
2002   *The Didache*. Assen: Van Gorcum and Minneapolis: Fortress.

Williams, A. Lukyn
1930   *Justin Martyr: The Dialogue with Trypho*. London: SPCK.

Yadin, Yigael
1977   *The Temple Scroll*. Vol. 3. Jerusalem: Israel Exploration Society.
1983   *The Temple Scroll*. Vols. 1-2. Jerusalem: Israel Exploration Society.

Bibliography

COMMENTARIES

Basser, Herbert W., trans.
1984   *Midrashic Interpretations of the Song of Moses.* New York: Lang.

Braulik, Georg
1986   *Deuteronomium 1–16,17.* NEcB. Würzburg: Echter.
1992   *Deuteronomium 16,18–34,12.* NEcB. Würzburg: Echter.

Calvin, John
1993   *Commentaries on the Four Last Books of Moses Arranged in the Form of a Harmony.* Vols. 3-4. Trans. Charles William Bingham. Grand Rapids: Baker.

Chavel, Charles B., trans.
1976   *Ramban (Nachmanides). Commentary on the Torah: Deuteronomy.* New York: Shiloh Publishing House.

Driver, S. R.
1895   *A Critical and Exegetical Commentary on Deuteronomy.* ICC. Edinburgh: T. & T. Clark.

ibn Ezra, Abraham
2003   *The Commentary of Abraham ibn Ezra on the Pentateuch;* Vol. 1: *Deuteronomy.* Trans. Jay F. Shachter. Hoboken: Ktav.

Friedman, Richard Elliott
2001   *Commentary on the Torah.* San Francisco: HarperSanFrancisco.

Hammer, Reuven
1986   *Sifre: A Tannaitic Commentary on the Book of Deuteronomy.* YJS 24. New Haven: Yale University Press.

Knobel, August
1861   *Die Bücher Numeri, Deuteronomium und Josua.* KEH. Leipzig: Hirzel.

Lockshin, Martin I., ed.
2004   *Rashbam's Commentary on Deuteronomy.* BJS 340. Providence: Brown University.

Luther, Martin
1960   *Lectures on Deuteronomy,* ed. Jaroslav Pelikan. Luther's Works 9. St. Louis: Concordia.

McConville, J. Gordon
2002   *Deuteronomy.* ApOTC 5. Leicester: Apollos and Downers Grove: InterVarsity.

Michaelis, John David
1814   *Commentaries on the Laws of Moses.* 4 vols. Trans. Alexander Smith. London: Rivington. Orig. 1770-75.

Miller, Patrick D.
1990   *Deuteronomy.* Interpretation. Louisville: John Knox.

Moran, William L.
1969   "Deuteronomy." In *A New Catholic Commentary on Holy Scripture,* ed. Reginald C. Fuller. Rev. ed. London: Nelson, 1969, 256-76. Orig. 1953.

Nelson, Richard D.
2002   *Deuteronomy.* OTL. Louisville: Westminster John Knox.

Neusner, Jacob
1987   *Sifre to Deuteronomy.* Vols. 1-2. BJS 98-99. Atlanta: Scholars.

Bibliography

Rabinowitz, J.
1939 *Midrash Rabbah: Deuteronomy.* London: Soncino.

von Rad, Gerhard
1966 *Deuteronomy.* OTL. Philadelphia: Westminster.

Rashi
1997 *The Metsudah Chumash/Rashi.* Vol. 5: *Devarim,* ed. Avrohom Davis. 2nd ed. Hoboken: Ktav.

Robinson, H. Wheeler
1907 *Deuteronomy and Joshua.* CB. Edinburgh: Jack.

Rosenbaum, Morris, and A. M. Silbermann
1934 *Pentateuch with Targum Onkelos, Haphtaroth and Prayers for Sabbath and Rashi's Commentary: Deuteronomy.* London: Shapiro, Vallentine. Repr. without Prayers for Sabbath, New York: Hebrew, 1964.

Slotki, Judah J.
1939 *Midrash Rabbah: Numbers.* Vol. 1. London: Soncino.

Smith, George Adam
1918 *The Book of Deuteronomy.* CBSC. Cambridge: Cambridge University Press.

Tigay, Jeffrey H.
1996 *Deuteronomy.* JPS Torah Commentary. Philadelphia: Jewish Publication Society.

Weinfeld, Moshe
1991 *Deuteronomy 1–11.* AB 5. New York: Doubleday.

Wright, G. Ernest
1953 "Deuteronomy." In *IB,* 2:311-537.

BOOKS, MONOGRAPHS, AND ARTICLES

Abel, F.-M.
1933 *Géographie de la Palestine.* Vol. 1. Paris: Librairie Lecoffre.
1938 *Géographie de la Palestine.* Vol. 2. Paris: Librairie Lecoffre.

Achtemeier, Paul
1990 "*Omne verbum sonat:* The New Testament and the Oral Environment of Late Western Antiquity." *JBL* 109:3-27.

Aharoni, I.
1937 "Vues Nouvelles sur la Zoologie Biblique et Talmudique." *RES* 5:32-41.
1938 "On Some Animals Mentioned in the Bible." *Osiris* 5:461-78.

Aharoni, Yohanan
1968 "Arad: Its Inscriptions and Temple." *BA* 31:2-32.
1969 "The Israelite Sanctuary at Arad." In Freedman and Greenfield 1969, 25-39.
1974 "The Horned Altar of Beer-sheba." *BA* 37:2-6.
1975a "Tel Masos: Historical Considerations." *TA* 2:114-24.
1975b "Excavations at Tel Beer-Sheba." *TA* 2:146-68 + pls.
1976 "Nothing Early and Nothing Late: Re-Writing Israel's Conquest." *BA* 39:55-76.
1979 *The Land of the Bible.* Trans. and ed. A. F. Rainey. 2nd ed. Philadelphia: Westminster.
1981 *Arad Inscriptions.* Jerusalem: Israel Exploration Society.

Ahituv, Shmuel
1984 *Canaanite Toponyms in Ancient Egyptian Documents.* Jerusalem: Magnes, Hebrew University and Leiden: Brill.

Ahituv, Shmuel, and Baruch A. Levine, eds.
1986 *The Early Biblical Period.* Jerusalem: Israel Exploration Society.

Albertz, Rainer
1978 "Hintergrund und Bedeutung des Elterngebots im Dekalog." *ZAW* 90:348-74.

Albright, William Foxwell
1924 "The Archaeological Results of an Expedition to Moab and the Dead Sea." *BASOR* 14:2-12.
1925 "Bronze Age Mounds of Northern Palestine and the Hauran." *BASOR* 19:5-19.
1926 "The Jordan Valley in the Bronze Age." In *AASOR* 6. New Haven: ASOR, 13-74.
1928 "The Egyptian Empire in Asia in the Twenty-First Century B.C." *JPOS* 8:223-56.
1936 "The Song of Deborah in the Light of Archaeology." *BASOR* 62:26-31.
1937 "A Biblical Fragment from the Maccabaean Age: The Nash Papyrus." *JBL* 56:145-76.
1941 "Two Letters from Ugarit (Ras Shamrah)." *BASOR* 82:43-49.
1943a "Two Little Understood Amarna Letters from the Middle Jordan Valley." *BASOR* 89:7-17.
1943b "The Gezer Calendar." *BASOR* 92:16-26.
1944a "A Prince of Taanach in the Fifteenth Century B.C." *BASOR* 94:12-27.
1944b "The 'Natural Force' of Moses in the Light of Ugaritic." *BASOR* 94:32-35.
1945a "The Chronology of the Divided Monarchy of Israel." *BASOR* 100:16-22.
1945b "The Old Testament and Canaanite Language and Literature." *CBQ* 7:5-31.
1946 *Archaeology and the Religion of Israel.* Ayer Lectures of the Colgate-Rochester Divinity School, 1941. 2nd ed. Baltimore: Johns Hopkins University Press. Orig. 1942.
1949 "The Biblical Period." In *The Jews: Their History, Culture, and Religion,* ed. Louis Finkelstein. Philadelphia: Jewish Publication Society of America, 1:3-69.
1950 "The Judicial Reform of Jehoshaphat." In *Alexander Marx Jubilee Volume,* ed. Saul Lieberman. New York: Jewish Theological Seminary of America, 61-82.
1951 "The Hebrew Expression for 'Making a Covenant' in Pre-Israelite Documents." *BASOR* 121:21-22.
1953 "New Light from Egypt on the Chronology and the History of Israel and Judah." *BASOR* 130:4-11.
1955 "New Light on Early Recensions of the Hebrew Bible." *BASOR* 140:27-33.
1956 *The Archaeology of Palestine.* Baltimore: Penguin.
1957a "The High Place in Ancient Palestine." In *Volume du Congrès, Strasbourg, 1956.* VTSup 4:242-58.
1957b *From the Stone Age to Christianity.* 2nd ed. Garden City: Doubleday. Orig. 1940.
1959 "Some Remarks on the Song of Moses in Deuteronomy xxxii." *VT* 9:339-46 [= Noth 1959, 3-10].
1961 *Samuel and the Beginnings of the Prophetic Movement.* Cincinnati: Hebrew Union College Press [= Orlinsky 1969, 149-76].
1963 *The Biblical Period from Abraham to Ezra.* New York: Harper & Row [revision of Albright 1949].
1968 *Yahweh and the Gods of Canaan.* Garden City: Doubleday.

Alday, Salvador Carrillo
1967 "El Cántico de Moisés (Dt 32)." *EstBib* 26:143-85, 227-48, 327-52.

Allegro, J. M.
1956 "Further Light on the History of the Qumran Sect." *JBL* 75:89-95.

Bibliography

Alt, Albrecht
1953a "Das Verbot des Diebstahls im Dekalog." In *Kleine Schriften zur Geschichte des Volkes Israel.* Vol. 1. Munich: Beck, 333-40.
1953b "Die Heimat des Deuteronomiums." In *Kleine Schriften zur Geschichte des Volkes Israel.* Vol. 2. Munich: Beck, 250-75.
1966a *Essays on Old Testament History and Religion.* Trans. R. A. Wilson. Oxford: Blackwell.
1966b "The God of the Fathers." In Alt 1966a, 3-77. Orig. 1929.
1966c "The Origins of Israelite Law." In Alt 1966a, 79-132. Orig. 1934.

Alter, Robert
1985 *The Art of Biblical Poetry.* New York: Basic Books.

Anbar, M.
1975 "Aspect moral dans un discours 'prophétique de Mari.'" *UF* 7:517-18.

Andersen, Francis I., and David Noel Freedman
1989 *Amos.* AB 24A. New York: Doubleday.

Andersen, Johannes Gerhard
1969 "Studies in the Mediaeval Diagnosis of Leprosy in Denmark." *DMB* 16/Sup 9:1-142.

Anderson, Cheryl B.
2004 "The Eighth Commandment: A Way to King's 'Beloved Community.'" In Brown 2004, 276-89.

Arden-Close, Charles Frederick
1941 "The Rainfall of Palestine." *PEQ* 73:122-28.

Astour, Michael C.
1979 "Yahweh in Egyptian Topographic Lists." In *Festschrift Elmar Edel,* ed. Manfred Görg and Edgar Pusch. Ägypten und Altes Testament 1. Bamberg: Görg, 17-34.

Attridge, Harold W., and Robert A. Oden
1976 *The Syrian Goddess (De Dea Syria) Attributed to Lucian.* SBLTT 9. Missoula: Scholars.

Axelsson, Lars Eric
1987 *The Lord Rose Up from Seir.* ConBOT 25. Stockholm: Almqvist and Wiksell.

Baly, Denis
1957 *The Geography of the Bible.* New York: Harper.

Barkay, Gabriel
1991 "'Your Poor Brother': A Note on an Inscribed Bowl from Beth Shemesh." *IEJ* 41:239-41.

Barstad, Hans M.
1984 *The Religious Polemics of Amos.* VTSup 34. Leiden: Brill.
1994 "The Understanding of the Prophets in Deuteronomy." *SJOT* 8:236-51.

Bartlett, John R.
1969 "The Land of Seir and the Brotherhood of Edom." *JTS* N.S. 20:1-20.
1989 *Edom and the Edomites.* JSOTSup 77. Sheffield: Sheffield Academic.

Bayliss, Miranda
1973 "The Cult of Dead Kin in Assyria and Babylonia." *Iraq* 35:115-25.

Beckman, Gary
1996 *Hittite Diplomatic Texts,* ed. Harry A. Hoffner Jr. SBLWAW 7. Atlanta: Scholars.

Bibliography

Begg, Christopher T.
1982 "The Reading *šbty(km)* in Deut 29,9 and 2 Sam 7,7." *ETL* 58:87-105.
1985 "The Destruction of the Calf (Exod 32,20/Deut 9,21)." In Lohfink 1985, 208-51.
1994 "1994: A Significant Anniversary in the History of Deuteronomy Research." In García Martínez et al. 1994, 1-11.

Beit-Arieh, Itzhaq
1988 "New Light on the Edomites." *BAR* 14/2:28-41.

Ben-Ami, Issachar
1974 "Le mariage traditionnel chez les Juifs marocains." In Ben-Ami and Noy 1974, 9-103.

Ben-Ami, Issachar, and Dov Noy, eds.
1974 *Studies in Marriage Customs.* FRCS 4. Jerusalem: Magnes, Hebrew University.

Bennett, Harold V.
2002 *Injustice Made Legal: Deuteronomic Law and the Plight of Widows, Strangers, and Orphans in Ancient Israel.* BIW. Grand Rapids: Eerdmans.

Bennett, James Risdon
1887 *The Diseases of the Bible.* Oxford: Religious Tract Society.

Benoit, Pierre
1935 "Un curieux ruminant biblique: Le daman." *RB* 44:581-82 + pls.

Ben-Tor, Amnon
1979 "Tell Qiri: A Look at Village Life." *BA* 42:105-13.

Bergey, Ronald
2003-4 "The Song of Moses (Deuteronomy 32.1-43) and Isaianic Prophecies: A Case of Early Intertextuality?" *JSOT* 28:33-54.

Bernhardt, Karl-Heinz
1960 "Beobachtungen zur Identifizierung moabitischer Ortslagen." *ZDPV* 76:136-58.

Bernstein, Moshe J.
1983-84 "כי קללת אלהים טלוי (Deut 21:23): A Study in Early Jewish Exegesis." *JQR* 74:21-45.

Bertman, Stephen
1961 "Tasseled Garments in the Ancient East Mediterranean." *BA* 24:119-28.

Best, Thomas F., ed.
1984 *Hearing and Speaking the Word: Selections from the Works of James Muilenburg.* Chico: Scholars.

Bewer, Julius A.
1938 "The Significance of Land in the Old Testament." *CRFB* 35 (Oct.): 1-7.

Beyerlin, Walter
1975 *Near Eastern Religious Texts Relating to the Old Testament.* Trans. John Bowden. OTL. Philadelphia: Westminster.

Bienkowski, Piotr, and Eveline van der Steen
2001 "Tribes, Trade, and Towns: A New Framework for the Late Iron Age in Southern Jordan and the Negev." *BASOR* 323:21-47.

Biran, Avraham
1994 *Biblical Dan.* Jerusalem: Israel Exploration Society and Hebrew Union College — Jewish Institute of Religion.

Biran, Avraham, and Joseph Naveh
1993 "An Aramaic Stele Fragment from Tel Dan." *IEJ* 43:81-98.

Bibliography

Birenboim, Hanan
2008 "'The Place Which the Lord Shall Choose,' the 'Temple City' and the 'Camp' in 11QT^A." *RevQ* 23:357-69.

Blair, Edward P.
1961 "An Appeal to Remembrance: The Memory Motif in Deuteronomy." *Int* 15:41-47.

Blank, Sheldon H.
1930 "The LXX Renderings of Old Testament Terms for Law." *HUCA* 7:259-23.
1950-51 "The Curse, Blasphemy, the Spell, and the Oath." *HUCA* 23:73-95.
1962 "Wisdom." In *IDB*, 4:852-61.

Bodenheimer, F. S.
1935 *Animal Life in Palestine*. Jerusalem: Mayer.
1947 "The Manna of Sinai." *BA* 10:2-6.
1960 *Animal and Man in Bible Lands*. Leiden: Brill.
1962 "Fauna." In *IDB*, 2:246-56.

Boessneck, Joachim
1976 *Tell El-Dab'a*. Vol. 3: *Die Tierknochenfunde 1966-1969*. Vienna: Österreichischen Akademie der Wissenschaften.

Boling, Robert G.
1975 *Judges*. AB 6A. Garden City: Doubleday.
1985 "Levitical Cities: Archaeology and Texts." In *Biblical and Related Studies Presented to Samuel Iwry*, ed. Ann Kort and Scott Morschauser. Winona Lake: Eisenbrauns, 23-32.

Bordreuil, Pierre, and Dennis Pardee
1982 "Le rituel funéraire ougaritique RS. 34.126." *Syria* 59:121-28.

Borowski, Oded
1987 *Agriculture in Iron Age Israel*. Winona Lake: Eisenbrauns.
1995 "Hezekiah's Reforms and the Revolt against Assyria." *BA* 58:148-55.

Boston, James R.
1966 "The Song of Moses: Deuteronomy 32:1-43." Th.D. Thesis, Union Theological Seminary, New York.
1968 "The Wisdom Influence upon the Song of Moses." *JBL* 87:198-202.

Bowman, Raymond A.
1948 "Arameans, Aramaic, and the Bible." *JNES* 7:65-90.

Boyer, Georges
1955 "Étude Juridique." In Jean Nougayrol, *Le Palais Royal d'Ugarit*. Vol. 3: *Textes accadiens et hourrites des archives est, ouest et centrales*. PRU 3. Paris: Imprimerie Nationale.
1958 *Textes Juridiques*. ARM 8. Paris: Imprimerie Nationale.

Brandt, William J.
1970 *The Rhetoric of Argumentation*. Indianapolis: Bobbs-Merrill.

Braulik, Georg
1978 *Die Mittel Deuteronomischer Rhetorik: Erhoben aus Deuteronomium 4,1-40*. AnBib 68. Rome: Biblical Institute Press.
1993 "The Sequence of the Laws in Deuteronomy 12–26 and in the Decalogue." In Christensen 1993, 313-35.

Breasted, James Henry
1906a *Ancient Records of Egypt*. Vol. 4. Chicago: University of Chicago Press.

1906b   *A History of Egypt from the Earliest Times to the Persian Conquest.* London: Hodder & Stoughton.

Breit, Herbert
1933   *Die Predigt des Deuteronomisten.* Munich: Kaiser.

Brenner, Athalya
1982   *Colour Terms in the Old Testament.* JSOTSup 21. Sheffield: JSOT.

Brewer, David I.
1998   "Deuteronomy 24:1-4 and the Origin of the Jewish Divorce Certificate." *JJS* 49:230-43.

Brichto, Herbert C.
1963   *The Problem of "Curse" in the Hebrew Bible.* SBLMS 13. Philadelphia: SBL.

Bright, John
1981   *A History of Israel.* 3rd ed. Philadelphia: Westminster.

Brodie, Thomas
1992   "Fish, Temple Tithe, and Remission: The God-Based Generosity of Deuteronomy 14–15 as One Component of Matt 17:22–18:35." *RB* 99:697-718.

Brody, Robert
1999   "Evidence for Divorce by Jewish Women." *JJS* 50:230-34.

Brooke, George J., ed.
1994   *New Qumran Texts and Studies.* With Florentino García Martínez. STDJ 15. Leiden: Brill.

Broshi, Magen, ed.
1992   *The Damascus Document Reconsidered.* Jerusalem: Israel Exploration Society and Shrine of the Book, Israel Museum.

Brothwell, Don, and A. T. Sandison, eds.
1967   *Diseases in Antiquity: A Survey of the Diseases, Injuries and Surgery of Early Populations.* Springfield: Thomas.

Brown, William P., ed.
2004   *The Ten Commandments.* Louisville: Westminster John Knox.

Bruin, Frans
1970   "Royal Purple and the Dye Industries of the Mycenaeans and Phoenicians." In *Sociétés et compagnies de commerce en orient et dans l'Océan Indien*, ed. Michel Mollat. Actes du huitième colloque international d'histoire maritime, Beyrouth — 5-10 Septembre 1966. Paris: S.E.V.P.E.N., 73-90.

Brunner, Hellmut
1958   "Was aus dem Munde Gottes geht." *VT* 8:428-29.

Bryan, Cyril P., trans.
1930   *The Papyrus Ebers.* London: Bles [= New York: Appleton, 1931].

Budde, D. Karl
1895   "The Nomadic Ideal in the Old Testament." *The New World* 4:726-45 [= "Das nomadische Ideal im alten Testament." *Preuszische Jahrbücher* 85 (1896): 57-79].
1920   *Das Lied Mose's, Deut. 32.* Tübingen: Mohr.

Budge, E. Wallis
1898   *The Book of the Dead.* London: Paul, Trench, Trübner.

Bullard, Reuben G.
1970   "Geological Studies in Field Archaeology." *BA* 33:98-132.

Bibliography

Burckhardt, John Lewis
1992 *Travels in Syria and the Holy Land.* London: Darf [Repr. of 1822 ed.].

Burrows, Millar
1938 *The Basis of Israelite Marriage.* AOS 15. New Haven: American Oriental Society.
1940 "The Levirate Marriage in Israel." *JBL* 59:23-33.
1955 "Ancient Israel." In *The Idea of History in the Ancient Near East,* ed. Robert C. Dentan. AOS 38. New Haven: Yale University Press, 99-131.

Calvin, John
1987 *Sermons on Deuteronomy.* Oxford: University Printing House, Banner of Truth Trust. Facsimile repr. of the 1583 ed.

Canaan, T.
1933 "The Palestinian Arab House: Its Architecture and Folklore." *JPOS* 13:1-83.

Carlson, R. A.
1964 *David, the Chosen King.* Stockholm: Almqvist & Wiksell.

Carmichael, Calum M.
1967 "Deuteronomic Laws, Wisdom, and Historical Traditions." *JSS* 12:198-206.
1974 *The Laws of Deuteronomy.* Ithaca: Cornell University Press.
1980 "'Treading' in the Book of Ruth." *ZAW* 92:248-66.
2000b "The Three Laws on the Release of Slaves (Ex 21,2-11; Dtn 15,12-18; Lev 25,39-46." *ZAW* 112:509-25.

Carmichael, Calum M., ed.
1992 *Collected Works of David Daube.* Vol. 1: *Talmudic Law.* Berkeley: Robbins Collection, University of California.
2000a *Collected Works of David Daube.* Vol. 2: *New Testament and Judaism.* Berkeley: Robbins Collection, University of California.
2003 *Collected Works of David Daube.* Vol. 3: *Biblical Law and Literature.* Berkeley: Robbins Collection, University of California.

Carpenter, J. Estlin
1883 "The Book of Deuteronomy." *Modern Review* 4:252-81.

Carrillo, Salvador. See Alday, Salvador Carrillo

Cassuto, Umberto
1973a "The Song of Moses (Deuteronomy Chapter XXXII 1-43)." In Cassuto 1973-75, 41-46. Orig. 1938.
1973b "Deuteronomy Chapter XXXIII and the New Year in Ancient Israel." In Cassuto 1973-1975, 47-70. Orig. 1928.
1973-75 *Biblical and Oriental Studies.* Trans. Israel Abrahams. 2 vols. Jerusalem: Magnes.

Cazelles, Henri
1959 "Tophel (Deut I 1)." *VT* 9:412-15.

Chalmers, Aaron
2005 "'There Is No Deliverer (From My Hand)' — A Formula Analysis." *VT* 55:287-92.

Chaney, Marvin L.
2004 "'Coveting Your Neighbor's House' in Social Context." In Brown 2004, 302-17.

Childs, Brevard S.
1962 *Memory and Tradition in Israel.* SBT 37. Naperville: Allenson.
1963 "A Study of the Formula, 'Until this day.'" *JBL* 82:279-92.
1974 *The Book of Exodus.* OTL. Philadelphia: Westminster.
1993 *Biblical Theology of the Old and New Testaments.* Minneapolis: Fortress.

Bibliography

Christensen, Duane L.
1984 "Two Stanzas of a Hymn in Deuteronomy 33." *Bib* 65:382-89.

Christensen, Duane L., ed.
1993 *A Song of Power and the Power of Song: Essays on the Book of Deuteronomy.* Winona Lake: Eisenbrauns.

Clements, Ronald E.
1965 "Deuteronomy and the Jerusalem Cult Tradition." *VT* 15:300-312.

Cody, Aelred
1969 *A History of Old Testament Priesthood.* AnBib 35. Rome: Pontifical Biblical Institute.

Cogan, Morton (Mordechai)
1974 *Imperialism and Religion: Assyria, Judah and Israel in the Eighth and Seventh Centuries* B.C.E. SBLMS 19. Missoula: SBL and Scholars.

Cohen, Chayim
1973 "The 'Widowed' City." *JANES* 5:75-81.

Collon, Dominique.
1975 *The Seal Impressions from Tell Atchana/Alalakh.* AOAT 27. Neukirchen-Vluyn: Neukirchener.

Condamin, Albert
1905 "Symmetrical Repetitions in *Lamentations* Chapters I and II." *JTS* 7:137-40.
1920 *Le Livre de Jérémie.* EBib. Paris: Lecoffre.
1933 *Poèmes de la Bible.* 2nd ed. Paris: Beauchesne.

Cooke, G. A.
1903 *A Text-book of North-Semitic Inscriptions.* Oxford: Clarendon.

Cooke, Stanley A.
1903 "A Pre-Massoretic Biblical Papyrus." *PSBA* 25:34-56 + pls.

Cornill, D. Carl Heinrich
1891 *Einleitung in das Alte Testament.* Freiburg: Mohr.

Cortez, Marc
2005-6 "The Law on Violent Intervention: Deuteronomy 25:11-12 Revisited." *JSOT* 30:431-47.

Cotton, Hannah M., and Elisha Qimron
1998 "XḤev/Se ar 13 of 134 or 135 C.E.: A Wife's Renunciation of Claims." *JJS* 49:108-18.

Cowley, A. E., ed.
1923 *Aramaic Papyri of the Fifth Century* B.C. Oxford: Clarendon.

Crawford, Sidnie White
1990 "The All Souls Deuteronomy and the Decalogue." *JBL* 109:193-206.
1993 "Three Deuteronomy Manuscripts from Cave 4, Qumran." *JBL* 112:23-42.
2005a "Textual Criticism of the Book of Deuteronomy and the *Oxford Hebrew Bible* Project." In *Seeking Out the Wisdom of the Ancients* (FS Michael V. Fox), ed. Ronald L. Troxel, Kelvin G. Friebel, and Dennis R. Magary. Winona Lake: Eisenbrauns, 315-26.
2005b "Reading Deuteronomy in the Second Temple Period." In De Troyer and Lange 2005, 127-40.

Crenshaw, James L.
1971 *Prophetic Conflict.* BZAW 124. Berlin: de Gruyter.
1985 "Education in Ancient Israel." *JBL* 104:601-15.

Bibliography

1998   *Education in Ancient Israel.* ABRL. New York: Doubleday.

Crenshaw, James L., ed.
1976   *Studies in Ancient Israelite Wisdom.* New York: Ktav.

Cross, Frank M., Jr.
1949   "The Newly Discovered Scrolls in the Hebrew University Museum in Jerusalem." *BA* 12:36-46.
1952   "Ugaritic *db'at* and Hebrew Cognates." *VT* 2:162-64.
1962   "Yahweh and the God of the Patriarchs." *HTR* 55:225-59.
1965   *Scrolls from the Wilderness of the Dead Sea.* London: British Museum.
1968   "The Structure of the Deuteronomic History." In *Perspectives in Jewish Learning.* Annual of the College of Jewish Studies 3:9-24.
1973   *Canaanite Myth and Hebrew Epic: Essays in the History of the Religion of Israel.* Cambridge, MA: Harvard University Press.
1983   "The Ammonite Oppression of the Tribes of Gad and Reuben: Missing Verses from 1 Samuel 11 Found in 4QSamuel^a." In *History, Historiography and Interpretation,* ed. H. Tadmor and M. Weinfeld. Jerusalem: Magnes, Hebrew University, 148-58.
1988   "Reuben, First-Born of Jacob." *ZAWSup* 100:46-65.
1995   *The Ancient Library of Qumran.* 3rd ed. Sheffield: Sheffield Academic. Orig. 1958.

Cross, Frank M., Jr., and David Noel Freedman
1948   "The Blessing of Moses." *JBL* 67:191-210 [= *Studies in Ancient Yahwistic Poetry,* ch. 4].
1953   "Josiah's Revolt against Assyria." *JNES* 12:56-58.
1997   *Studies in Ancient Yahwistic Poetry.* BRS. Grand Rapids: Eerdmans. Orig. 1950.

Cross, Frank M., Jr., Werner E. Lemke, and Patrick D. Miller Jr., eds.
1976   *Magnalia Dei: The Mighty Acts of God* (FS G. Ernest Wright). Garden City: Doubleday.

Dahood, Mitchell
1963   *Proverbs and Northwest Semitic Philology.* Scripta Pontificii Instituti Biblici 113. Rome: Pontifical Biblical Institute.
1964   "Hebrew-Ugaritic Lexicography II." *Bib* 45:393-412.
1973   "Northwest Semitic Notes on Dt 32,20." *Bib* 54:405-6.

Daube, David
1941   "Codes and Codas in the Pentateuch." *JRev* 53:242-61.
1947   *Studies in Biblical Law.* Cambridge: Cambridge University Press.
1949   "Concerning Methods of Bible-Criticism." *ArOr* 17/1:88-99.
1950   "*Consortium* in Roman and Hebrew Law." *JRev* 62:71-91.
1961   "Direct and Indirect Causation in Biblical Law." *VT* 11:246-69.
1963   *The Exodus Pattern in the Bible.* All Souls Studies 2. London: Faber and Faber.
1964   *The Sudden in the Scriptures.* Leiden: Brill [= Carmichael 2000a, 683-743].
1969a   "The Culture of Deuteronomy." *Orita* 3:27-52.
1969b   "Repudium in Deuteronomy." In *Neotestamentica et Semitica* (FS Matthew Black), ed. E. Earle Ellis and Max Wilcox. Edinburgh: T. & T. Clark, 236-39.
1971a   "To Be Found Doing Wrong." In *Studi in Onore di Edoardo Volterra.* Milan: Giuffrè, 2:1-13.
1971b   "One from among Your Brethren Shall You Set King over You." *JBL* 90:480-81.
1978   "Biblical Landmarks in the Struggle for Women's Rights." *JRev* N.S. 23:177-97 [= Carmichael 2000a, 231-47].
1981   "The Form Is the Message." In *Ancient Jewish Law.* Leiden: Brill, 71-116 [= Carmichael 2000a, 187-229].

1982 "Ahab and Benhadad: A Municipal Directive in International Relations." *JRev* N.S. 27:62-67.

Daube, David, and Calum Carmichael
1993 *The Return of the Divorcee.* Inaugural Jewish Law Fellowship Lecture. Oxford: Oxford Centre for Postgraduate Studies [= Carmichael 2003, 937-48].

Davies, Eryl W.
1981 "Inheritance Rights and the Hebrew Levirate Marriage." *VT* 31:138-44, 257-68.
1986 "The Meaning of *pî š^{e}nayim* in Deuteronomy xxi 17." *VT* 36:341-47.

Davies, Graham I.
1979 "The Significance of Deuteronomy 1.2 for the Location of Mount Horeb." *PEQ* 111:87-101.

Davies, W. D.
1966 *Invitation to the New Testament.* Garden City: Doubleday.
1969 *The Sermon on the Mount.* Cambridge: Cambridge University Press.

Dawson, Warren R.
1967 "The Egyptian Medical Papyri." In Brothwell and Sandison 1967, 98-111. Orig. 1953.

Day, Edward
1911 "The Humanitarianism of the Deuteronomists." *BW* N.S. 38:113-25.

Day, John
1986 "Asherah in the Hebrew Bible and Northwest Semitic Literature." *JBL* 105:385-408.
2005 "Whatever Happened to the Ark of the Covenant?" In *Temple and Worship in Biblical Israel.* LHB/OTS 422. London: T. & T. Clark, 250-70.

Dearman, J. Andrew
1984 "The Location of Jahaz." *ZDPV* 100:122-25.
1989a "The Levitical Cities of Reuben and Moabite Toponymy." *BASOR* 276:55-66.
1989b "Historical Reconstruction and the Mesha' Inscription." In Dearman 1989c, 155-210.

Dearman, J. Andrew, ed.
1989c *Studies in the Mesha Inscription and Moab.* SBLABS 2. Atlanta: Scholars.

Dempster, Stephen
1984 "The Deuteronomic Formula *Kî Yimmāṣē'* in the Light of Biblical and Ancient Near Eastern Law." *RB* 91:188-211.

Derrett, J. Duncan M.
1978 "2 Cor 6,14ff. a Midrash on Dt 22,10." *Bib* 59:231-50.

Dershowitz, Idan
2010 "A Land Flowing with Fat and Honey." *VT* 60:172-76.

De Troyer, Kristin
2005 "Building the Altar and Reading the Law: The Journeys of Joshua 8:30-35." In De Troyer and Lange 2005, 141-62.

De Troyer, Kristin, and Armin Lange, eds.
2005 *Reading the Present in the Qumran Library.* SBLSymS 30. Atlanta: SBL.

Diamond, A. S.
1957 "An Eye for an Eye." *Iraq* 19:151-55.

Dion, Paul E.
1991 "Deuteronomy 13: The Suppression of Alien Religious Propaganda in Israel during the Late Monarchial Era." In *Law and Ideology in Monarchic Israel,* ed. Baruch

Halpern and Deborah W. Hobson. JSOTSup 124. Sheffield: Sheffield Academic, 147-216.

Diringer, David
1942   "The Early Hebrew Weights Found at Lachish." *PEQ* 74:82-103.

Dothan, M.
1965   "The Fortress at Kadesh-Barnea." *IEJ* 15:134-51.

Driver, G. R.
1955   "Birds in the Old Testament." *PEQ* 87:5-20, 129-40.
1956   "Two Problems in the Old Testament Examined in the Light of Assyriology." *Syria* 33:70-78.
1958   "Once Again: Birds in the Bible." *PEQ* 90:56-58.

Driver, G. R., and John C. Miles
1935   *The Assyrian Laws*. Oxford: Clarendon.
1952   *The Babylonian Laws*. Vol. 1. Oxford: Clarendon.
1955   *The Babylonian Laws*. Vol. 2. Oxford: Clarendon.

Driver, S. R.
1890   *Notes on the Hebrew Text of the Books of Samuel*. Oxford: Clarendon.
1913   *An Introduction to the Literature of the Old Testament*. 9th ed. Edinburgh: T. & T. Clark. Repr. Cleveland: World, 1967. Orig. 1891.

Drotts, Wallace D.
1973   "A Study of the Prophet Jeremiah Compared and Contrasted with Martin Luther King Jr., with Guidelines for Prophetic Ministry Today." D.Min. thesis, San Francisco Theological Seminary.

Du Buit, M.
1959   "Quelques contacts bibliques dans les archives royales de Mari." *RB* 66:576-81.

Duke, Rodney K.
1987   "The Portion of the Levite: Another Reading of Deuteronomy 18:6-8." *JBL* 106:193-201.

Duncan, Julie A.
1995   "New Readings for the 'Blessing of Moses' from Qumran." *JBL* 114:273-90.
1997-98 "Excerpted Texts of *Deuteronomy* at Qumran." *RevQ* 18:43-62.
2000   "Deuteronomy, Book of." In *EDSS*, 1:198-202.

Dwight, Sereno E., and Edward Hickman
1974   *The Works of Jonathan Edwards*. Vol. 2. Edinburgh: Banner of Truth Trust. Orig. 1834.

Edelman, Diana Vikander, ed.
1995   *You Shall Not Abhor an Edomite For He Is Your Brother: Edom and Seir in History and Tradition*. SBLABS 3. Atlanta: Scholars.

Edenburg, Cynthia
2009   "Ideology and Social Context of the Deuteronomic Women's Sex Laws (Deuteronomy 22:13-29)." *JBL* 128:43-60.

Eichrodt, Walter
1966   "Covenant and Law." Trans. Lloyd Gaston. *Int* 20:302-21.

Eissfeldt, Otto
1958   *Das Lied Moses, Deuteronomium 32, 1-43, und das Lehrgedicht Asaphs, Psalm 78, samt einer Analyse der Umgebung des Mose-Liedes*. Berlin: Akademie.

1965   *The Old Testament: An Introduction.* Trans. Peter R. Ackroyd. New York: Harper & Row.

Emerton, J. A.
1962   "Priests and Levites in Deuteronomy." *VT* 12:129-38.
2001   "Samuel Rolles Driver, 1846-1914." In *A Century of British Orientalists 1902-2001*, ed. C. Edmund Bosworth. Oxford: British Academy and Oxford University Press, 123-38.
2002   "S. R. Driver as an Exegete of the Old Testament." In *Vergegenwärtigung des Alten Testaments* (FS Rudolf Smend), ed. Christoph Bultmann, Walter Dietrich, and Christoph Levin. Göttingen: Vandenhoeck & Ruprecht, 285-95.

Emerton, J. A., ed.
1990   *Studies in the Pentateuch.* VTSup 41. Leiden: Brill.

Emery, Walter B., et al.
1979   *The Fortress of Buhen: The Archaeological Report.* London: Egypt Exploration Society. Ch. 9: "The Buhen Horse," 191-95.

Epstein, Louis M.
1942   *Marriage Laws in the Bible and the Talmud.* Harvard Seminar Series 12. Cambridge, MA: Harvard University Press.

Eslinger, Lyle
1981   "The Case of an Immodest Lady Wrestler in Deuteronomy xxv 11-12." *VT* 31:269-81.

Eslinger, Lyle, and Glen Taylor, eds.
1988   *Ascribe to the Lord* (FS Peter C. Craigie). JSOTSup 67. Sheffield: JSOT.

Ewald, Heinrich
1856   "Das große Lied im Deuteronomium, c. 32." *JBW* 8:41-65.

Faulkner, R. O.
1955   "The Installation of the Vizier." *JEA* 41:18-29.

Feldman, Louis H.
2002   "The Portrayal of Sihon and Og in Philo, Pseudo-Philo and Josephus." *JJS* 53:264-72.

Fensham, F. Charles
1962a   "Widow, Orphan, and the Poor in Ancient Near Eastern Legal and Wisdom Literature." *JNES* 21:129-39 [= Crenshaw 1976:161-71].
1962b   "Malediction and Benediction in Ancient Near Eastern Vassal-Treaties and the Old Testament." *ZAW* 74:1-9.
1966   "The Burning of the Golden Calf and Ugarit." *IEJ* 16:191-93.

Finkelstein, Israel, and Neil Asher Silberman
2005-6 "Temple and Dynasty: Hezekiah, the Remaking of Judah and the Rise of the Pan-Israelite Ideology." *JSOT* 30:259-85.

Finkelstein, J. J.
1952   "The Middle Assyrian *Šulmānu*-Texts." *JAOS* 72:77-80.
1956   "Hebrew חבר and Semitic *$\d{H}BR$." *JBL* 75:328-31.
1961   "Ammiṣaduqa's Edict and the Babylonian 'Law Codes.'" *JCS* 15:91-104.
1966   "Sex Offenses in Sumerian Laws." *JAOS* 86:355-72.

Firmage, Edwin B., Bernard G. Weiss, and John W. Welch, eds.
1990   *Religion and Law: Biblical-Judaic and Islamic Perspectives.* Winona Lake: Eisenbrauns.

Fishbane, Michael
1972   "Varia Deuteronomica." *ZAW* 84:349-52.
1985   *Biblical Interpretation in Ancient Israel.* Oxford: Clarendon.

Fitzmyer, Joseph A.
1958   "The Aramaic Suzerainty Treaty from Sefire in the Museum of Beirut." *CBQ* 20:444-76.
1961   "The Aramaic Inscriptions of Sefire I and II." *JAOS* 81:178-222.
1967   *The Aramaic Inscriptions of Sefire.* BibOr 19. Rome: Pontifical Biblical Institute.
1978   "Divorce among First-Century Palestinian Jews." In Haran 1978, 103-10.

Fitzmyer, Joseph A., and Daniel J. Harrington
1978   *A Manuel of Palestinian Aramaic Texts.* BibOr 34. Rome: Biblical Institute.

Fleishman, Joseph
2008   "The Delinquent Daughter and Legal Innovation in Deuteronomy xxii 20-21." *VT* 58:191-210.

Fleming, Daniel E.
1993   "The Etymological Origins of the Hebrew *nābî'*: The One Who Invokes God." *CBQ* 55:217-24.

Flinder, Alexander
1989   "Is This Solomon's Seaport?" *BAR* 15/4:30-43.

Flusser, David
1964   "'Do Not Commit Adultery,' 'Do Not Murder.'" *Text* 4:220-24.

Fohrer, Georg
1968   *Introduction to the Old Testament.* Trans. David E. Green. Nashville: Abingdon.

Forrer, Emil O.
1936   "The Hittites in Palestine." *PEFQS* 68:190-203.

Fox, G. George
1942   "The Matthean Misrepresentation of *Tephillîn*." *JNES* 1:373-77.

Fox, Nili Sacher
2009   "Gender Transformation and Transgression: Contextualizing the Prohibition of Cross-Dressing in Deuteronomy 22:5." In *Mishneh Todah* (FS Jeffrey H. Tigay), ed. Fox, David A. Glatt-Gilad, and Michael J. Williams. Winona Lake: Eisenbrauns, 49-71.

Fraade, Steven D.
2003   "Rhetoric and Hermeneutics in Miqṣat Ma'aśe Ha-Torah (4QMMT): The Case of the Blessings and Curses." *DSD* 10:150-61.

Frankena, R.
1965   "The Vassal-Treaties of Esarhaddon and the Dating of Deuteronomy." *OTS* 14:122-54.

Freedman, David Noel
1955   "God Compassionate and Gracious." Inaugural Lecture, Western Theological Seminary. *Western Watch* 6/1:6-24.
1962   "Pentateuch." In *IDB*, 2:711-27 [= Freedman 1997, 1:99-132; abridged in *ECB*, 25-31].
1964   "Divine Commitment and Human Obligation: The Covenant Theme." *Int* 18:419-31 [= Freedman 1997, 1:168-78].
1967   "The Song of the Sea." In *A Feeling of Celebration* (FS James Muilenburg), ed. Robert Shukraft. San Anselmo: San Francisco Theological Seminary, 1-9 [= Freedman 1980b, 179-86].

1972	"Acrostics and Metrics in Hebrew Poetry." *HTR* 65:367-92 [= Freedman 1980b, 51-76].
1974	"Strophe and Meter in Exodus 15." In *A Light unto My Path* (FS Jacob M. Myers), ed. Howard N. Bream, Ralph D. Heim, and Carey A. Moore. Philadelphia: Temple University Press, 163-203 [= Freedman 1980b, 187-227].
1976	"Divine Names and Titles in Early Hebrew Poetry." In Cross, Lemke, and Miller 1976, 55-107 [= Freedman 1980b, 77-129].
1977	"Pottery, Poetry, and Prophecy: An Essay on Biblical Poetry." *JBL* 96:5-26 [= Freedman 1980b, 1-22].
1979	"Early Israelite Poetry and Historical Reconstructions." In *Symposia Celebrating the Seventy-Fifth Anniversary of the Founding of the American Schools of Oriental Research (1900-1975)*, ed. Frank Moore Cross. Cambridge, MA: ASOR, 85-96 [= Freedman 1980b, 167-78].
1980a	"The Poetic Structure of the Framework of Deuteronomy 33." In Rendsburg et al. 1980, 25-46 [= Freedman 1997, 2:88-107].
1980b	*Pottery, Poetry, and Prophecy: Studies in Early Hebrew Poetry.* Winona Lake: Eisenbrauns.
1986	"Deliberate Deviation from an Established Pattern of Repetition in Hebrew Poetry as a Rhetorical Device." In *Proceedings of the Ninth World Congress of Jewish Studies (Jerusalem, August 4-12, 1985). Division A: The Period of the Bible.* Jerusalem: World Union of Jewish Studies, 45-52 [= Freedman 1997, 2:205-12].
1987a	"Another Look at Biblical Hebrew Poetry." In *Directions in Biblical Hebrew Poetry*, ed. Elaine R. Follis. JSOTSup 40. Sheffield: Sheffield Academic, 11-28 [= Freedman 1997, 2:213-26].
1987b	"The Structure of Isaiah 40:1-11." In *Perspectives on Language and Text* (FS Francis I. Andersen, ed. Edgar W. Conrad and Edward G. Newing. Winona Lake: Eisenbrauns, 167-93 [= Freedman 1997, 2:232-57].
1987c	"Yahweh of Samaria and His Asherah." *BA* 50:241-49 [= Freedman 1997, 1:403-8].
1987d	"Headings in the Books of the Eighth-Century Prophets." In FS Leona Glidden Running, ed. William H. Shea. *AUSS* 25:9-26 [= Freedman 1997, 1:367-82].
1992	"Patterns in Psalms 25 and 34." In *Priests, Prophets and Scribes* (FS Joseph Blenkinsopp), ed. Eugene Ulrich et al. JSOTSup 149. Sheffield: Sheffield Academic, 125-38 [= Freedman 1997, 2:258-69].
1997	*Divine Commitment and Human Obligation: Selected Writings of David Noel Freedman*, ed. John R. Huddlestun. 2 vols. Grand Rapids: Eerdmans.
2000	*The Nine Commandments.* New York: Doubleday.

Freedman, David Noel, and Jonas C. Greenfield, eds.

1969	*New Directions in Biblical Archaeology.* Garden City: Doubleday.

Freedman, David Noel, and Shawna Dolansky Overton

2002	"Omitting the Omissions: The Case for Haplography in the Transmission of the Biblical Texts." In *'Imagining' Biblical Worlds* (FS James W. Flanagan), ed. David M. Gunn and Paula M. McNutt. JSOTSup 359. Sheffield: Sheffield Academic, 99-116.

French, A.

1956	"The Economic Background to Solon's Reforms." *CQ* 6:11-25.

Fried, Lisbeth S.

2002	"The High Places *(Bāmôt)* and the Reforms of Hezekiah and Josiah: An Archaeological Investigation." *JAOS* 122:437-65.

Bibliography

Friedman, Mordechai A.
1981 "Divorce upon the Wife's Demand as Reflected in Manuscripts from the Cairo Geniza." *JLA* 4:103-26.
1996 "Babatha's *Ketubba*: Some Preliminary Observations." *IEJ* 46:55-76.

Friedman, Richard Elliott
1977 "The Biblical Expression *mastîr pānîm*." *HAR* 1:139-47.

Fritsch, Charles T.
1943 *The Anti-Anthropomorphisms of the Greek Pentateuch*. Princeton: Princeton University Press.

Frymer-Kensky, Tikva
1980 "Tit for Tat: The Principle of Equal Retribution in Near Eastern and Biblical Law." *BA* 43:230-34.
1989 "Law and Philosophy: The Case of Sex in the Bible." *Semeia* 45:89-102.
1998 "Virginity in the Bible." In Matthews, Levinson, and Frymer-Kensky 1998, 79-96.

Gaballa, G. A.
1969 "Minor War Scenes of Ramses II at Karnak." *JEA* 55:82-88 + pls.

Gadd, C. J.
1926 "Tablets from Kirkuk." *RA* 23:49-161.
1948 *Ideas of Divine Rule in the Ancient East*. Schweich Lectures, 1945. London: British Academy and Oxford University Press.
1954 "Inscribed Prisms of Sargon II from Nimrud." *Iraq* 16:173-201 + pls.

Galling, Kurt
1950 "Das Gemeindegesetz in Deuteronomium 23." In *Festschrift Alfred Bertholet*, ed. Walter Baumgartner et al. Tübingen: Mohr, 176-91.
1963 "Eschmunazar und der Herr der Könige." *ZDPV* 79:140-51.

Galpaz-Feller, Pnina
2008 "The Widow in the Bible and in Ancient Egypt." *ZAW* 120:231-53.

Gamoran, Hillel
1971 "The Biblical Law against Loans on Interest." *JNES* 30:127-34.

García Martínez, Florentino
1994 "Les manuscrits du désert Juda et le Deutéronome." In García Martínez et al. 1994, 63-82.

García Martínez, Florentino, et al., eds.
1994 *Studies in Deuteronomy* (FS C. J. Labuschagne). VTSup 53. Leiden: Brill.

Gardiner, Alan H.
1947 *Ancient Egyptian Onomastica*. 3 vols. Oxford: Oxford University Press.

Gaster, Theodor H.
1947 "An Ancient Eulogy on Israel: Deuteronomy 33:3-5, 26-29." *JBL* 66:53-62.
1969 *Myth, Legend, and Custom in the Old Testament*. New York: Harper & Row.

Gelb, Ignace J.
1944 *Hurrians and Subarians*. SAOC 22. Chicago: University of Chicago Press.

van Gennep, Arnold
1909 *Les Rites de Passage*. Paris: Nourry. English: *The Rites of Passage*. Trans. Monika B. Vizedom and Gabrielle L. Caffe. Chicago: University of Chicago Press, 1960.

Geoghegan, Jeffrey C.
2003 "'Until This Day' and the Preexilic Redaction of the Deuteronomic History." *JBL* 122:201-27.

Gevirtz, Stanley.
1980 "On Hebrew šēbeṭ = "Judge." In Rendsburg et al. 1980, 61-66.

Gilliard, Frank D.
1993 "More Silent Reading in Antiquity: *Non Omne Verbum Sonabat.*" *JBL* 112:689-94.

Ginsberg, H. Louis
1946 *The Legend of King Keret.* BASORSup 2-3. New Haven: ASOR.
1963 "'Roots Below and Fruit Above' and Related Matters." In *Hebrew and Semitic Studies Presented to Godfrey Rolles Driver,* ed. D. Winton Thomas and W. D. McHardy. Oxford: Clarendon, 72-76.
1982 *The Israelian Heritage of Judaism.* New York: Jewish Theological Seminary of America.

Ginsburg, Christian D.
1871 *The Moabite Stone: A Fac-simile of the Original Inscription.* 2nd ed. London: Reeves and Turner.

Ginzberg, Louis
1913 *The Legends of the Jews.* Vol. 1: *Bible Times and Characters from the Creation to Jacov.* Trans. Henrietta Szold. Philadelphia: Jewish Publication Society of America.

Gitin, Seymour
1995 "Tel Miqne-Ekron in the 7th Century B.C.E.: The Impact of Economic Innovation and Foreign Cultural Influences on a Neo-Assyrian Vassal City State." In *Recent Excavations in Israel: A View to the West.* Archaeological Institute of America: Colloquia and Conference Papers 1. Dubuque: Kendall/Hunt, 61-79 + pls.
1997 "The Neo-Assyrian Empire with Its Western Periphery: The Levant, with a Focus on Philistine Ekron." In *Assyria 1995,* ed. Simo Parpola and Robert M. Whiting. Helsinki: Helsinki University Press, 77-104.
2003 "Israelite and Philistine Cult and the Archaeological Record in Iron Age II: The 'Smoking Gun' Phenomenon." In *Symbiosis, Symbolism, and the Power of the Past,* ed. William G. Dever and Gitin. Proceedings of the Albright/ASOR Centennial Symposium, Jerusalem, May 29-31, 2000. Winona Lake: Eisenbrauns, 279-95.
2004 "The Philistines: Neighbors of the Canaanites, Phoenicians and Israelites." In *100 Years of American Archaeology in the Middle East: Proceedings of the American Schools of Oriental Research Centennial Celebration, Washington D.C., April, 2000,* ed. Douglas R. Clark and Victor H. Matthews. Boston: ASOR, 57-85.

Gitin, Seymour, and Amir Golani
2001 "The Tel Miqne-Ekron Silver Hoards: The Assyrian and Phoenician Connections." In *Hacksilber to Coinage: New Insights into the Monetary History of the Near East and Greece,* ed. Miriam S. Balmuth. New York: American Numismatic Society, 27-48.

Giveon, Raphael
1964 "Toponymes ouest-asiatiques à Soleb." *VT* 14:239-55.
1967 "The Shosu Egyptian Sources and the Exodus." In *Fourth World Congress of Jewish Studies, Jerusalem, 1965.* Vol. 1. Jerusalem: World Union of Jewish Studies, 193-96.
1971 *Les Bédouins Shosou des Documents Égyptiens.* DMOA 18. Leiden: Brill.

Glasson, Thomas Francis
1963 *Moses in the Fourth Gospel.* SBT 40. Naperville: Allenson.

Glueck, Nelson
1934 *Explorations in Eastern Palestine.* Vol. 1. AASOR 14. Philadelphia: ASOR, 1-113.
1935 *Explorations in Eastern Palestine.* Vol. 2. AASOR 15. New Haven: ASOR.

1936	"The Boundaries of Edom." *HUCA* 11:141-57.
1938	"The Topography and History of Ezion-Geber and Elath." *BASOR* 72:2-13.
1939	*Explorations in Eastern Palestine.* Vol. 3. AASOR 18-19. New Haven: ASOR.
1940	*The Other Side of the Jordan.* New Haven: ASOR.
1943	"Ramoth-Gilead." *BASOR* 92:10-16.
1951	*Explorations in Eastern Palestine.* Vol. 4/1. AASOR 25-28. New Haven: ASOR.
1955	"The Third Season of Explorations in the Negeb." *BASOR* 138:7-29.
1959	*Rivers in the Desert: A History of the Negev.* New York: Farrar, Straus and Cudahy.
1967	*Hesed in the Bible.* Trans. Alfred Gottschalk. Cincinnati: Hebrew Union College Press. Orig. 1927.

Goldin, Judah

1987 "The Death of Moses: An Exercise in Midrashic Transposition." In Marks and Good 1987, 219-25.

Goldingay, John

1993 "*Kayyôm hazzeh* 'On This Very Day'; *Kayyôm* 'On the Very Day'; *Kāʿēt* 'At the Very Time.'" *VT* 43:112-15.

Goldstein, Bernard R., and Alan Cooper

1990 "The Festivals of Israel and Judah and the Literary History of the Pentateuch." *JAOS* 110:19-31.

Good, Edwin M.

1967 "Capital Punishment and Its Alternatives in Ancient Near Eastern Law." *SLR* 19:947-77.

Gordis, Robert

1944 "A Wedding Song for Solomon." *JBL* 63:263-70.
1957 "The Knowledge of Good and Evil in the Old Testament and Qumran Scrolls." *JBL* 76:123-38 [= Gordis 1971, 198-216].
1971 *Poets, Prophets, and Sages: Essays in Biblical Interpretation.* Bloomington: Indiana University Press.

Gordon, Cyrus H.

1935 "A New Akkadian Parallel to Deuteronomy 25:11-12." *JPOS* 15:29-34.
1936a "An Akkadian Parallel to Deuteronomy 21:1ff." *RA* 33:1-6.
1936b "The Status of Woman Reflected in the Nuzi Tablets." *ZA* 43:146-69.
1956 "Observations on the Akkadian Tablets from Ugarit." *RA* 50:127-33.

Graesser, Carl F.

1972 "Standing Stones in Ancient Palestine." *BA* 35:34-63.

Graetz, Heinrich

1894 *Emendationes in Plerosque Sacrae Scripturae Veteris Testamenti Libros.* Vol. 3. Breslau: Schlesische Buchdrukerei.

Granqvist, Hilma

1931 *Marriage Conditions in a Palestinian Village.* Vol. 1. Societas Scientiarum Fennica. Commentationes Humanarum Litterarum 3/8. Helsingfors: Helsingfors Centraltryckeri.

Gray, John

1949 "The Rephaim." *PEQ* 81:127-39.
1967 "Ugarit." In Thomas 1967, 145-67.

Grayson, A. Kirk

1987 "Akkadian Treaties of the Seventh Century B.C." *JCS* 39:127-60.

Greenberg, Moshe

1950 "A New Approach to the History of the Israelite Priesthood." *JAOS* 70:41-47.
1959 "The Biblical Conception of Asylum." *JBL* 78:125-32.
1960 "Some Postulates of Biblical Criminal Law." In Haran 1960b, 5-28.
1971 "The Decalogue (The Ten Commandments)" in *EncJud* 5:1435-46.
1976 "On the Refinement of the Conception of Prayer in Hebrew Scriptures." *AJSR* 1:57-92.
1983a *Ezekiel 1–20.* AB 22. Garden City: Doubleday.
1983b *Biblical Prose Prayer.* Berkeley: University of California Press.
1986 "More Reflections on Biblical Criminal Law." In Japhet 1986, 1-17.
1990 "Biblical Attitudes toward Power: Ideal and Reality in Law and Prophets." In Firmage, Weiss, and Welch 1990, 101-12.
1997 *Ezekiel 21–37.* AB 22A. New York: Doubleday.

Greenfield, Jonas C.

1965-66 "Stylistic Aspects of the Sefire Treaty Inscriptions." *AcOr* 29:1-18.
1978 "Notes on the Asitawada (Karatepe) Inscription." In Haran 1978, 74-77, 125. [Hebrew (with English summary)]
1981 "Aramaic Studies and the Bible." In *Congress Volume, Vienna, 1980.* VTSup 32:110-30.
1982 "Adi balṭu — Care for the Elderly and Its Rewards." *AfOB* 19:309-16.
1987 "Smitten by Famine, Battered by Plague (Deuteronomy 32:24)." In Marks and Good 1987, 151-52.
1990 "Some Phoenician Words." *Sem* 38:155-58.
1991 "Asylum at Aleppo: A Note on Sfire III,4-7." In *Ah, Assyria . . .* (FS Hayim Tadmor), ed. Mordechai Cogan and Israel Eph'al. ScrHier 33. Jerusalem: Magnes, Hebrew University, 272-78.

Greenfield, Jonas C., and Aaron Shaffer

1985 "Notes on the Curse Formulae of the Tell Fekherye Inscription." *RB* 92:47-59.

Gross, Karl

1930 *Die literarische Verwandtschaft Jeremias mit Hosea.* Borna: Universitätsverlag. Inaugural dissertation at Friedrich-Wilhelms-Universität zu Berlin.
1931 "Hoseas Einfluss auf Jeremias Anschauungen." *NKZ* 42:241-56, 327-43.

Gruber, Mayer I.

1980 *Aspects of Nonverbal Communication in the Ancient Near East.* 2 vols. Studia Pohl 12. Rome: Biblical Institute Press.
1986 "Hebrew *Qĕdēšāh* and Her Canaanite and Akkadian Cognates." *UF* 18:133-48.
1987 "Hebrew *Da'ăbôn nepeš* 'Dryness of Throat': From Symptom to Literary Convention." *VT* 37:365-69 [= Gruber 1992: 185-92].
1992 *The Motherhood of God and Other Studies.* Atlanta: Scholars.

Gunkel, Hermann

1913 "Das Lied des Moses." In RGG[1], 4:534-35.
1998 *Introduction to Psalms: The Genres of the Religious Lyric of Israel.* Completed by Joachim Begrich. Trans. James D. Nogalski. Macon: Mercer University Press. Orig. 1933.

Gurney, O. R.

1962 *The Hittites.* Rev. ed. Baltimore: Penguin. Orig. 1952.

Habel, Norman C.

1972 "'Yahweh, Maker of Heaven and Earth': A Study in Tradition Criticism." *JBL* 91:321-37.

Bibliography

Hackett, Jo Ann
1980 *The Balaam Text from Deir 'Allā*. HSM 31. Chico: Scholars.

Hallo, William W.
1960 "From Qarqar to Carchemish: Assyria and Israel in the Light of New Discoveries." *BA* 23:34-61.
1964 "The Slandered Bride." In *Studies Presented to A. Leo Oppenheim*, ed. Robert D. Biggs and J. A. Brinkman. Chicago: Oriental Institute, University of Chicago, 95-105.
1968 "Individual Prayer in Sumerian: The Continuity of a Tradition." *JAOS* 88:71-89.
1985-86 "Biblical Abominations and Sumerian Taboos." *JQR* 76:21-40.

Haran, Menahem
1959 "The Ark and the Cherubim: Their Symbolic Significance in Biblical Ritual." *IEJ* 9:30-38, 89-94.
1960a "The Nature of the "'ohel mo'edh" in Pentateuchal Sources." *JSS* 5:50-65.
1963 "The Disappearance of the Ark." *IEJ* 13:46-58 [= *IEJ Reader* (New York: Ktav, 1981), 1:262-74].
1977 *Temples and Temple-Service in Ancient Israel*. Oxford: Clarendon.
1979 "Seething a Kid in Its Mother's Milk." *JJS* 30:23-35.
1980-81 "Scribal Workmanship in Biblical Times: The Scrolls and the Writing Implements." *Tarbiz* 50:65-87, iv. [Hebrew (with English summary)]

Haran, Menahem, ed.
1960b *Yehezkel Kaufmann Jubilee Volume*. Jerusalem: Magnes, Hebrew University.
1978 *H. L. Ginsberg Volume*. ErIsr 14. Jerusalem: Israel Exploration Society.

Hare, Ronald
1967 "The Antiquity of Diseases Caused by Bacteria and Viruses, A Review of the Problem from a Bacteriologist's Point of View." In Brothwell and Sandison 1967, 115-31.

Harland, J. Penrose
1942 "Sodom and Gomorrah: The Location of the Cities of the Plain." *BA* 5:17-32.
1943 "Sodom and Gomorrah II: The Destruction of the Cities of the Plain." *BA* 6:41-54.

Harland, Peter J.
1998-99 "Menswear and Womenswear: A Study of Deuteronomy 22:5." *ExpTim* 110:73-76.

Harris, J. Rendel
1925-26 "Irenaeus and the Song of Moses." *ExpTim* 37:333-34.

Harris, Rivkah
1974 "The Case of Three Babylonian Marriage Contracts." *JNES* 33:363-69.

Heck, Joel D.
1984 "The Missing Sanctuary of Deut 33:12." *JBL* 103:523-29.

Held, Moshe
1961 "A Faithful Lover in an Old Babylonian Dialogue." *JCS* 15:1-26.

Hempel, Johannes. and Leonhard Rost, eds.
1958 *Von Ugarit nach Qumran* (FS Otto Eissfeldt). BZAW 77. Berlin: Töpelmann.

Henrey, K. H.
1954 "Land Tenure in the Old Testament." *PEQ* 86:5-15.

Hepner, Gershon
2006 "The Samaritan Version of the Tenth Commandment." *SJOT* 20:147-52.

Bibliography

von Herder, Johann Gottfried
1833   *The Spirit of Hebrew Poetry*. Trans. James Marsh. 2 vols. Burlington: Smith. Orig. 1782-83.

Herr, Larry G.
1993   "The Search for Biblical Heshbon." *BAR* 19/6:36-37, 68.

Hertz, Joseph Herman
1960   *The Pentateuch and the Haftorahs*. Oxford: Oxford University Press. Orig. 1936.

Herzog, Ze'ev
1981   "Israelite Sanctuaries at Arad and Beer-Sheba." In *Temples and High Places in Biblical Times*, ed. Avraham Biran. Proceedings of the Colloquium in Honor of the Centennial of Hebrew Union College — Jewish Institute of Religion, Jerusalem, 14-16 March 1977. Jerusalem: Hebrew Union College — Jewish Institute of Religion, 120-22.
1997   *Arad: The Arad Fortress* Tel Aviv: Hakibbutz Hameuchad. [Hebrew (with English summary)]
2002   "The Fortress Mound at Tel Arad: An Interim Report." *TA* 29:3-109.
2006   "Beersheba Valley Archaeology and Its Implications for the Biblical Record." In *Congress Volume, Leiden, 2004*. VTSup 109:81-102.

Herzog, Ze'ev, Anson F. Rainey, and Sh. Moshkovitz
1977   "The Stratigraphy at Beer-sheba and the Location of the Sanctuary." *BASOR* 225:49-58.

Herzog, Ze'ev, et al.
1984   "The Israelite Fortress at Arad." *BASOR* 254:1-34.

Heschel, Abraham J.
1962   *The Prophets*. New York: Harper & Row.

Hilhorst, Anton.
1994   "Deuteronomy's Monotheism and the Christians: The Case of Deut 6:13 and 10:20." In F. García Martínez et al. 1994, 83-91.

Hillers, Delbert R.
1964a   *Treaty-Curses and the Old Testament Prophets*. BibOr 16. Rome: Pontifical Biblical Institute.
1964b   "A Note on Some Treaty Terminology in the Old Testament." *BASOR* 176:46-47.

Hoffman, Yair
1994   "The Conception of 'Other Gods' in Deuteronomistic Literature." *IOS* 14:103-18.
1999   "The Deuteronomistic Concept of the Herem." *ZAW* 111:196-210.

Hoffner, Harry A., Jr.
1966   "Symbols for Masculinity and Femininity: Their Use in Ancient Near Eastern Sympathetic Magic Rituals." *JBL* 85:326-34.
1967   "Second Millennium Antecedents to the Hebrew 'ŌḆ." *JBL* 86:385-401.

Hoffner, Harry A., Jr., ed.
1973   *Orient and Occident* (FS Cyrus H. Gordon). AOAT 22. Neukirchen-Vluyn: Neukirchener.

Hoftijzer, J., and G. van der Kooij, eds.
1976   *Aramaic Texts from Deir 'Alla*. DMOA 19. Leiden: Brill.

Holladay, William L.
1958   *The Root Šûbh in the Old Testament*. Leiden: Brill.

Bibliography

1964 "The Background of Jeremiah's Self-Understanding: Moses, Samuel and Psalm 22." *JBL* 83:153-64.
1966 "Jeremiah and Moses: Further Observations." *JBL* 85:17-27.
2004 "Elusive Deuteronomists, Jeremiah, and Proto-Deuteronomy." *CBQ* 66:55-77.

Holmgren, Fredrick C.
1994 "The Pharisee and the Tax Collector: Luke 18:9-14 and Deuteronomy 26:1-15." *Int* 48:252-61.

Holtz, Shalom E.
2001 "'To Go and Marry Any Man That You Please': A Study of the Formulaic Antecedents of the Rabbinic Writ of Divorce." *JNES* 60:241-58.

Homan, Michael M.
2004a "Beer, Barley, and שֵׁכָר in the Hebrew Bible." In *Le-David Maskil: A Birthday Tribute for David Noel Freedman*, ed. Richard Elliott Friedman and William H. C. Propp. Biblical and Judaic Studies for the University of California, San Diego 9. Winona Lake: Eisenbrauns, 25-38.
2004b "Beer and Its Drinkers: An Ancient Near Eastern Love Story." *NEA* 67:84-95.

Honor, Leo L.
1953 "The Role of Memory in Biblical History." In *Mordecai M. Kaplan Jubilee Volume*, ed. Moshe Davis. New York: Jewish Theological Seminary of America, 417-35.

Hopkins, David C.
1985 *The Highlands of Canaan: Agricultural Life in the Early Iron Age.* Sheffield: Almond.

Hort, Greta
1957 "The Plagues of Egypt." *ZAW* 69:84-103.

Huehnergard, John
1985 "Biblical Notes on Some New Akkadian Texts from Emar (Syria)." *CBQ* 47:428-34.

Huffmon, Herbert B.
1959 "The Covenant Lawsuit in the Prophets." *JBL* 78:285-95.
1966 "The Treaty Background of Hebrew *Yāda'*." *BASOR* 181:31-37.
1976 "The Origins of Prophecy." In Cross, Lemke, and Miller 1976, 171-86.

Hulse, E. V.
1975 "The Nature of Biblical 'Leprosy' and the Use of Alternative Medical Terms in Modern Translations of the Bible." *PEQ* 107:87-105.

Hundley, Michael
2009 "To Be or Not to Be: A Reexamination of Name Language in Deuteronomy and the Deuteronomic History." *VT* 59:533-55.

Hunger, Hermann
1968 *Babylonische und assyrische Kolophone.* AOAT 2. Neukirchen-Vluyn: Neukirchener.

Ikeda, Yutaka
1978 "Hermon, Sirion and Senir." *AJBI* 4:32-44.
1982 "Solomon's Trade in Horses and Chariots in Its International Setting." In *Studies in the Period of David and Solomon and Other Essays: Papers Read at the International Symposium for Biblical Studies, Tokyo, 5-7 December, 1979*, ed. Tomoo Ishida. Winona Lake: Eisenbrauns, 215-38.

Bibliography

Ilan, Tal
1996 "Notes and Observations on a Newly Published Divorce Bill from the Judean Desert." *HTR* 89:195-202.

Ishida, Tomoo
1979 "The Structure and Historical Implications of the Lists of Pre-Israelite Nations." *Bib* 60:461-90.

Jackson, Bernard S.
1975 *Essays in Jewish and Comparative Legal History*. SJLA 10. Leiden: Brill.

Jacobsen, Thorkild
1943 "Primitive Democracy in Ancient Mesopotamia." *JNES* 2:159-72 [= Jacobsen 1970, 157-70].
1970 *Toward the Image of Tammuz and Other Essays on Mesopotamian History and Culture*, ed. William L. Moran. Cambridge, MA: Harvard University Press.
1987 "The Graven Image." In Miller, Hanson, and McBride 1987, 15-32.

Japhet, Sara, ed.
1986 *Studies in Bible*. ScrHier 31. Jerusalem: Magnes, Hebrew University.

Jensen, Lloyd B.
1963 "Royal Purple of Tyre." *JNES* 22:104-18.

Jericke, Detlef
2008 "Der Ort des Mose nach Deuteronomium 1:1." *JNSL* 34:35-57.

Johns, Claude H. W.
1901 *An Assyrian Doomsday Book*. Assyriologische Bibliothek 17. Leipzig: Hinrichs.
1904 *Babylonian and Assyrian Laws, Contracts, and Letters*. Edinburgh: T. & T. Clark.
1914 *The Relations between the Laws of Babylonia and the Laws of the Hebrew Peoples*. Schweich Lectures, 1912. London: British Academy.

Johnson, Aubrey R.
1953 "The Primary Meaning of גאל." In *Congress Volume, Copenhagen, 1953*. VTSup 1:67-77.
1964 *The Vitality of the Individual in the Thought of Ancient Israel*. 2nd ed. Cardiff: University of Wales Press.

Jongeling, B.
1974 "L'expression *my ytn* dans l'ancien testament." *VT* 24:32-40.

Joüon, Paul
1933 "Divers emplois metaphoriques du mot *'yad'* en hébreu." *Bib* 14:452-59.

Kallai, Zecharia
1986 *Historical Geography of the Bible*. Jerusalem: Magnes, Hebrew University and Leiden: Brill.

Kamphausen, Adolf
1862 *Das Lied Moses Deut. 32,1-43*. Leipzig: Brockhaus.

Kaufman, Stephen A.
1978-79 "The Structure of the Deuteronomic Law." *Maarav* 1:105-58.

Kaufmann, Yehezkel
1960 *The Religion of Israel*. Trans. and abr. Moshe Greenberg. Chicago: University of Chicago Press.

Keel, Othmar
1974 *Wirkmächtige Siegeszeichen im Alten Testament*. OBO 5. Freiburg: Freiburg Universitätsverlag and Göttingen: Vandenhoeck & Ruprecht.

Bibliography

1977   *Jahwe-Visionen und Siegelkunst.* SBS 84/85. Stuttgart: Katholisches Bibelwerk.
1978   *The Symbolism of the Biblical World.* Trans. Timothy J. Hallett. New York: Seabury.

Keiser, Thomas A.
2005   "The Song of Moses: A Basis for Isaiah's Prophecy." *VT* 55:486-500.

Kempinski, Aharon
1979   "Hittites in the Bible — What Does Archaeology Say?" *BAR* 5/4:21-45.
1986   "Joshua's Altar — An Iron Age I Watchtower." *BAR* 12/1:42, 44-49.

Kempinski, Aharon, et al.
1981   "Excavations at Tel Masos: 1972, 1974, 1975." In *Y. Aharoni Memorial Volume,* ed. Benjamin Mazar. Er-Isr 15. Jerusalem: Israel Exploration Society, 154-80, 82. [Hebrew (with English summary)]

Kenyon, Frederic G.
1935   *The Chester Beatty Biblical Papyri: Descriptions and Texts of Twelve Manuscripts on Papyrus of the Greek Bible.* Fasc. 5: *Numbers and Deuteronomy.* London: Walker.

King, L. W.
1900   *The Letters and Inscriptions of Hammurabi, King of Babylon.* Vol 3. London: Luzac.
1912   *Babylonian Boundary-Stones and Memorial-Tablets in the British Museum.* London: British Museum.

King, Martin Luther, Jr.
1959   *The Measure of a Man.* Philadelphia: Pilgrim.

King, Philip J.
1993   *Jeremiah: An Archaeological Companion.* Louisville: Westminster John Knox.
1994   "Jeremiah's Polemic against Idols: What Archaeology Can Teach Us." *BRev* 10:22-29.

Kiple, Kenneth F., ed.
2003   *The Cambridge Historical Dictionary of Disease.* Cambridge: Cambridge University Press.

Klein, Isaac
1979   *A Guide to Jewish Religious Practice.* New York: Jewish Theological Seminary of America.

Klein, Jacob
1990   "The 'Bane' of Humanity: A Lifespan of One Hundred Twenty Years." *AcSu* 12:57-70.

Kleinert, Paul
1872   *Das Deuteronomium und Der Deuteronomiker.* Bielefeld: von Velhagen & Klasing.

Kletter, Raz
2004   "Coinage before Coins? A Response." *Levant* 36:207-10.

Klingbeil, Gerald A.
2000   "The *Finger of God* in the Old Testament." *ZAW* 112:409-15.
2010   "The Sabbath Law in the Decalogue(s): Creation and Liberation as a Paradigm for Community." *RB* 117:491-509.

Klostermann, August
1893   *Der Pentateuch.* Leipzig: Deichert (Böhme).

Knoppers, Gary N.
1996   "The Deuteronomist and the Deuteronomic Law of the King: A Re-examination of a Relationship." *ZAW* 108:329-46.

Bibliography

Knowles, Michael P.
1989 "'The Rock, His Work Is Perfect': Unusual Imagery for God in Deuteronomy XXXII." *VT* 39:307-22.

Knox, Bernard M.
1968 "Silent Reading in Antiquity." *GRBS* 9:421-35.

Köhler, Ludwig
1923 *Deuterojesaja (Jesaja 40–55) stilkritisch untersucht*. BZAW 37. Giessen: Töpelmann.
1956 *Hebrew Man*. Trans. Peter R. Ackroyd. London: SCM. Appendix on "Justice in the Gate," 149-75.

Kooij, Arie van der
1994 "The Ending of the Song of Moses: On the Pre-Masoretic Version of Deut 32:43." In García Martínez et al. 1994, 93-100.

Kopf, L.
1958 "Arabische Etymologien und Parallelen zum Bibelwörterbuch." *VT* 8:161-215.

Kreuzer, Siegfried
1997 "Die Mächtigkeitsformel im Deuteronomium — Gestaltung, Vorgeschichte und Entwicklung." *ZAW* 109:188-207.

Kruger, Paul A.
1996 "The Removal of the Sandal in Deuteronomy xxv 9: 'A Rite of Passage'?" *VT* 46:534-39.

Krumbhaar, E. B.
1937 *Pathology*. Clio Medica 19. New York: Hueber.

Kuenen, A.
1886 *An Historico-Critical Inquiry into the Origin and Composition of the Hexateuch*. Trans. Philip H. Wicksteed. London: Macmillan.

Kuntz, Paul Grimley
2004 *The Ten Commandments in History*. Ed. Thomas D'Evelyn. Grand Rapids: Eerdmans.

Lacheman, Ernest R.
1937 "Note on Ruth 4 7-8." *JBL* 56:53-56.

Lafont, Sophie
1999 *Femmes, Droit et Justice dans l'Antiquité orientale*. OBO 165. Fribourg: Universitaires Fribourg and Göttingen: Vandenhoeck & Ruprecht.

Lambdin, Thomas O.
1953 "Egyptian Loan Words in the Old Testament." *JAOS* 73:145-55.

Lambert, W. G.
1957-58 "Morals in Ancient Mesopotamia." *JEOL* 15:184-96.
1960 *Babylonian Wisdom Literature*. Oxford: Clarendon.
1962 "The Fifth Tablet of the Era Epic." *Iraq* 24:119-25 + pl.
1965 "Nebuchadnezzar King of Justice." *Iraq* 27:1-11.

Lane, Edward W.
1973 *An Account of the Manners and Customs of the Modern Egyptians*. 5th ed. Ed. Edward Stanley Poole. New York: Dover. Orig. 1836.

Langdon, Stephen
1905 *Building Inscriptions of the Neo-Babylonian Empire*. Pt. 1: *Nabopolassar and Nebuchadnezzar*. Paris: Leroux.

Bibliography

Laubscher, F. Du. T.
1980 "Notes on the Literary Structure of 1QS 2:11-18 and Its Biblical Parallel in Deut. 29." *JNSL* 8:49-55.

Lauterbach, Jacob Z.
1936 "Tashlik: A Study in Jewish Ceremonies." *HUCA* 11:207-340.

Lemche, Niels Peter
1979 "*Andurārum* and *Mīšarum*: Comments on the Problem of Social Edicts and Their Application in the Ancient Near East." *JNES* 38:11-22.

Lenchak, Timothy A.
1993 *Choose Life! A Rhetorical-Critical Investigation of Deuteronomy 28,69–30,20.* AnBib 129. Rome: Pontifical Biblical Institute.

Leuchter, Mark
2007 "Why Is the Song of Moses in the Book of Deuteronomy?" *VT* 57:295-317.

Levine, Baruch A.
1974 *In the Presence of the Lord: A Study of Cult and Some Cultic Terms in Ancient Israel.* SJLA 5. Leiden: Brill.
1993 *Numbers 1–20.* AB 4. New York: Doubleday.
2000 *Numbers 21–36.* AB 4A. New York: Doubleday.

Levinson, Bernard M.
1996 "Recovering the Lost Original Meaning of ולא תכסה עליו (Deuteronomy 13:9)." *JBL* 115:601-20.
2001a "The Reconceptualization of Kingship in Deuteronomy and the Deuteronomistic History's Transformation of Torah." *VT* 51:511-34.
2001b "Textual Criticism, Assyriology, and the History of Interpretation: Deuteronomy 13:7a as a Test Case in Method." *JBL* 120:211-43.
2005 "Deuteronomy's Conception of Law as an 'Ideal Type': A Missing Chapter in the History of Constitutional Law." *Maarav* 12:83-119.

Levy, Abraham Juda
1931 *The Song of Moses (Deuteronomy 32).* Baltimore: Johns Hopkins University. Ph.D. Diss., Johns Hopkins University, 1925. Repr. from *The Scientific Series of Oriens — The Oriental Review* 1. Paris: 1930.

Levy, Thomas E., et al.
2004 "Reassessing the Chronology of Biblical Edom: New Excavations and ^{14}C Dates from Khirbat en-Nahas (Jordan)." *Antiquity* 78:865-79.

Lewis, Naphtali, Ranon Katzoff, and Jonas C. Greenfield
1987 "*Papyrus Yadin 18.*" *IEJ* 37:229-50.

Lewis, Theodore J.
1989 *Cults of the Dead in Ancient Israel and Ugarit.* HSM 39. Atlanta: Scholars.
1998 "Divine Images and Aniconism in Ancient Israel." *JAOS* 118:36-53.

Licht, Hans
1994 *Sexual Life in Ancient Greece.* Trans. J. H. Freese. London: Constable. Orig. 1931.

Licht, Jacob
1980 "The Biblical Claim of Establishment." *Shnaton* 4:98-128, vii-viii. [Hebrew (with English summary)]

Lichtheim, Miriam
1973 *Ancient Egyptian Literature.* Vol. 1: *The Old and Middle Kingdoms.* Berkeley: University of California Press.

1976 *Ancient Egyptian Literature*. Vol. 2: *The New Kingdom*. Berkeley: University of California Press.

Lieber, Elinor
2000 "Old Testament 'Leprosy,' Contagion and Sin." In *Contagion: Perspectives from Pre-Modern Societies*, ed. Lawrence I. Conrad and Dominik Wujastyk. Aldershot: Ashgate, 99-136.

Lincicum, David
2008 "Greek Deuteronomy's 'Fever and Chills' and Their Magical Afterlife." *VT* 58:544-49.

Lindberg, Carter
2005 "Luther on Government Responsibility for the Poor." *SRR* 7/2:5-17.

Lindquist, Maria
2011 "King Og's Iron Bed." *CBQ* 73:477-92.

Linsenmaier, Walter
1972 *Insects of the World*. Trans. Leigh E. Chadwick. New York: McGraw-Hill.

Lipinski, Edward
1981 "The Wife's Right to Divorce in the Light of an Ancient Near Eastern Tradition." *JLA* 4:9-27.

Loewe, Raphael
1955 "The Earliest Biblical Allusion to Coined Money?" *PEQ* 87:141-50.

Loewenstamm, Samuel E.
1957-58 "The Death of Moses." *Tarbiz* 27:142-57, iii-v. [Hebrew (with English summary)]
1972 *From Babylon to Canaan*. Jerusalem: Magnes, Hebrew University.
1980 *Comparative Studies in Biblical and Ancient Oriental Literatures*. AOAT 204. Neukirchen-Vluyn: Neukirchener.

Lohfink, Norbert
1960 "Darstellungskunst und Theologie in Dtn 1,6–3,29." *Bib* 41:105-34 [= Lohfink 1990, 15-44].
1962 "Der Bundesschluss im Land Moab: Redaktionsgeschichtliches zu Dt. 28,69–32,47." *BZ* N.F. 6:32-56 [= Lohfink 1990, 53-82].
1963a *Das Hauptgebot: Eine Untersuchung literarischer Einleitungsfragen zu Dtn 5–11*. AnBib 20. Rome: Pontifical Biblical Institute.
1963b "Die Bundesurkunde des Königs Josias." *Bib* 44:261-88; 461-98 [= Lohfink 1990, 99-165].
1965 *Höre, Israel!: Auslegung von Texten aus dem Buch Deuteronomium*. Welt der Bibel 18. Düsseldorf: Patmos.
1968 *Lectures in Deuteronomy*. Prepared in English for students at the Pontifical Biblical Instiutute, Rome, by Sean McEvenue.
1976 "Deuteronomy." In *IDBSup*, 229-32 [= Lohfink 1991, 15-24].
1990 *Studien zum Deuteronomium und zur deuteronomistischen Literatur 1*. SBAB 8. Stuttgart: Katholisches Bibelwerk. Contains "Zur Dekalogfassung von Dt 5" (193-209), orig. *BZ* 9 (1965) 17-32.
1991 *Studien zum Deuteronomium und zur deuteronomistischen Literatur 2*. SBAB 12. Stuttgart: Katholisches Bibelwerk.
1992 "Dtn 28,69 — Überschrift oder Kolophon?" *BN* 64:40-52.
1994a *Theology of the Pentateuch: Themes of the Priestly Narrative and Deuteronomy*. Trans. Linda M. Maloney. Edinburgh: T. & T. Clark and Minneapolis: Augsburg Fortress.

Bibliography

1994b   "The Decalogue in Deuteronomy 5." In Lohfink 1994a, 248-64.

1994c   "The 'Small Credo' of Deuteronomy 26:5-9." In Lohfink 1994a, 265-89.

Lohfink, Norbert. ed.

1985   *Das Deuteronomium: Entstehung, Gestalt und Botschaft.* BETL 68. Leuven: Leuven University Press.

Lorton, David

1999   "The Theology of Cult Statues in Ancient Egypt." In *Born in Heaven, Made on Earth: The Making of the Cult Image in the Ancient Near East*, ed. Michael B. Dick. Winona Lake: Eisenbrauns, 123-210.

Luckenbill, Daniel David

1919-20   "The 'Wandering Aramaean.'" *AJSL* 36:244-45.

Lund, Nils W.

1930   "The Presence of Chiasmus in the Old Testament." *AJSL* 46:104-26.

1933   "Chiasmus in the Psalms." *AJSL* 49:281-312.

1942   *Chiasmus in the New Testament.* Chapel Hill: University of North Carolina Press. Repr. Peabody: Hendrickson, 1992.

Lundbom, Jack R.

1973   "Elijah's Chariot Ride." *JJS* 24:39-50.

1975   *Jeremiah: A Study in Ancient Hebrew Rhetoric.* SBLDS 18. Missoula: SBL [2nd ed. Winona Lake: Eisenbrauns, 1997].

1976   "The Lawbook of the Josianic Reform." *CBQ* 38:293-302.

1978a   "God's Use of the *Idem per Idem* to Terminate Debate." *HTR* 71:193-201.

1978b   "What about Divorce?" *CovQ* 36: 21-27.

1985   "The Double Curse in Jeremiah 20:14-18." *JBL* 104:589-600.

1986a   "Baruch, Seraiah, and Expanded Colophons in the Book of Jeremiah." *JSOT* 36:89-114.

1986b   "Contentious Priests and Contentious People in Hosea IV 1-10." *VT* 36:52-70.

1986c   "Psalm 23: Song of Passage." *Int* 40:5-16.

1990   "Scribal Colophons and Scribal Rhetoric in Deuteronomy 31-34." In *Haim M. I. Gevaryahu Memorial Volume*, ed. Joshua J. Adler and Ben-Zion Luria. Jerusalem: World Jewish Bible Center, 53-63.

1996   "The Inclusio and Other Framing Devices in Deuteronomy i-xxviii." *VT* 46:296-315.

1997   "Rhetorical Criticism: History, Method and Use in the Book of Jeremiah." In Lundbom 1975, 2nd ed. xix-xliii.

1998   "Parataxis, Rhetorical Structure, and the Dialogue over Sodom in Genesis 18." In *The World of Genesis*, ed. Philip R. Davies and David J. A. Clines. JSOTSup 257. Sheffield: Sheffield Academic, 136-45.

1999   *Jeremiah 1-20.* AB 21A. New York: Doubleday.

2004a   *Jeremiah 21-36.* AB 21B. New York: Doubleday.

2004b   *Jeremiah 37-52.* AB 21C. New York: Doubleday.

2007a   "The Lion Has Roared: Rhetorical Structure in Amos 1:2-3:8." In *Milk and Honey: Essays on Ancient Israel and the Bible in Appreciation of the Judaic Studies Program at the University of California, San Diego*, ed. Sarah Malena and David Miano. Winona Lake: Eisenbrauns, 65-75.

2007b   "God in Your Grace Transform the World." *CurTM* 34:278-81.

2010a   *The Hebrew Prophets: An Introduction.* Minneapolis: Fortress.

2010b   *Jeremiah Closer Up: The Prophet and the Book.* Hebrew Bible Monographs 31. Sheffield: Sheffield Phoenix.

2010c "Wisdom Influence in the Book of Deuteronomy." In *Raising Up a Faithful Exegete* (FS Richard D. Nelson), ed. K. L. Noll and Brooks Schramm. Winona Lake: Eisenbrauns, 193-209.

Lust, Johan
1995 "The Raised Hand of the Lord in Deut 32:40 according to MT, 4QDeut^Q, and LXX." *Text* 18:33-45.

Luther, Martin
1965 *A Short Explanation of Dr. Martin Luther's Small Catechism.* St. Louis: Concordia.

Luyten, Jos
1985 "Primeval and Eschatological Overtones in the Song of Moses (Dt 32,1-43)." In Lohfink 1985, 341-47.

Macalister, R. Stewart
1912 *The Excavation of Gezer 1902-1905 and 1907-1909.* Vol. 2. London: Murray.

MacDonald, Burton
1999 "Ammonite Territory and Sites." In *Ancient Ammon*, ed. MacDonald and Randall W. Younker. SHANE 17. Leiden: Brill, 30-56.

MacDonald, Nathan
2006 "The Literary Criticism and Rhetorical Logic of Deuteronomy I-IV." *VT* 56:203-24.

MacDowell, Douglas M.
1978 *The Law in Classical Athens.* Ithaca: Cornell University Press.

Machiela, Daniel
2008 "Who Is the Aramean in *Deut* 26:5 and What Is He Doing? Evidence of a Minority View from Qumran Cave 1 (*1QapGen* 19.8)." *RevQ* 23:395-402 + photos.

Macht, David I.
1953 "An Experimental Pharmacological Appreciation of Leviticus xi and Deuteronomy xiv." *BHM* 27:444-50.

MacKenzie, R. A.
1957 "The Messianism of Deuteronomy." *CBQ* 19:299-305.

MacRae, George W.
1960 "The Meaning and Evolution of the Feast of Tabernacles." *CBQ* 22:251-76.

Maisler, B. See Mazar, Benjamin.

Malamat, Abraham
1962 "Mari and the Bible: Some Patterns of Tribal Organization and Institutions." *JAOS* 82:143-50.
1970 "Northern Canaan and the Mari Texts." In *Near Eastern Archaeology in the Twentieth Century* (FS Nelson Glueck), ed. James A. Sanders. Garden City: Doubleday, 164-77.
1975 "The Twilight of Judah: In the Egyptian-Babylonian Maelstrom." In *Congress Volume, Edinburgh, 1974.* VTSup 28:123-45 [= Malamat 2001: 299-321].
1980 "A Mari Prophecy and Nathan's Dynastic Oracle." In *Prophecy* (FS Georg Fohrer), ed. J. A. Emerton. BZAW 150. Berlin: de Gruyter, 68-82.
1982 "Longevity: Biblical Concepts and Some Ancient Near Eastern Parallels." *AfO* 19:215-24.
2001 *History of Biblical Israel: Major Problems and Minor Issues.* Leiden: Brill.

Malina, Bruce J.
1968 *The Palestinian Manna Tradition.* AGSJU 7. Leiden: Brill.

Maloney, Robert P.
1974 "Usury and Restrictions on Interest-Taking in the Ancient Near East." *CBQ* 36:1-20.

Marcus, David
1981 "Juvenile Deliquency in the Bible and the Ancient Near East." *JANES* 13:31-52.

Margalit, Baruch
1990 "The Meaning and Significance of Asherah." *VT* 40:264-97.

Markl, Dominik
2004 "Ex 3f und Dtn 1,1; 34,10-12 als literarische Eckpunkte des pentateuchischen Mosebildes." In *Führe mein Volk heraus: Zur innerbiblischen Rezeption der Exodusthematik* (FS Georg Fischer), ed. Simone Paganini, Claudia Paganini, and Markl. Frankfurt: Lang, 15-23.

Marks, John H., and Robert M. Good, eds.
1987 *Love & Death in the Ancient Near East* (FS Marvin H. Pope). Guilford: Four Quarters.

Mathers, Powys
1986 *The Book of the Thousand Nights and One Night*. 4 vols. London: Routledge & Paul. Trans. from the French of J. C. Mardus.

Matthews, Victor H., Bernard Levinson, and Tikva Frymer-Kensky, eds.
1998 *Gender and Law in the Hebrew Bible and the Ancient Near East*. JSOTSup 262. Sheffield: Sheffield Academic.

Mayes, A. D. H.
1981 "Deuteronomy 4 and the Literary Criticism of Deuteronomy." *JBL* 100:23-51.

Mazar, Amihai
1982 "The 'Bull Site' — An Iron Age I Open Cult Place." *BASOR* 247:27-42.

Mazar, Benjamin
1946 "Canaan and the Canaanites." *BASOR* 102:7-12.
1961 "Geshur and Maacah." *JBL* 80:16-28.
1962 "The Aramean Empire and Its Relations with Israel." *BA* 25:98-120.
1965 "The Sanctuary of Arad and the Family of Hobab the Kenite." *JNES* 24:297-303.
1978 "They Shall Call Peoples to Their Mountain.'" In Haran 1978, 39-41, 123. [Hebrew (with Engish summary)]
1981 "Yahweh Came out of Sinai." In *Temples and High Places in Biblical Times: Proceedings of the Colloquium in Honor of the Centennial of Hebrew Union College — Jewish Institute of Religion,* ed. Avraham Biran. Jerusalem: Hebrew Union College — Jewish Institute of Religion, 5-9.
1986a "The Early Israelite Settlement in the Hill Country." In Ahituv and Levine 1986, 35-48. [Revision of *BASOR* 241 (1981) 75-85]
1986b "Geshur and Maachah." In Ahituv and Levine 1986, 113-25 [Revision of B. Mazar 1961].

McBride, S. Dean Jr.
2006 "The Essence of Orthodoxy: Deuteronomy 5:6-10 and Exodus 20:2-6." *Int* 60:133-50.

McCarthy, Carmel
2002 "Masoretic Undertones in the Song of Moses." *PIBA* 25:29-44.
2007 "What's New in *BHQ*? Reflections on *BHQ* Deuteronomy." *PIBA* 30:54-69.

McCarthy, Dennis J.
1963 *Treaty and Covenant*. AnBib 21. Rome: Pontifical Biblical Institute.

1967 "'Creation' Motifs in Ancient Hebrew Poetry." *CBQ* 29:393-406. Repr. *Creation in the Old Testament*, ed. Bernhard W. Anderson. Philadelphia: Fortress, 1984, 87-100.
1982 "Covenant 'Good' and an Egyptian Text." *BASOR* 245:63-64.

McCartney, Eugene S.
1948 "Notes on Reading and Praying Audibly." *CP* 43:184-87.

McKay, J. W.
1972 "Man's Love for God in Deuteronomy and the Father/Teacher — Son/Pupil Relationship." *VT* 22:426-35.

Meek, Theophile J.
1948 "Old Testament Notes." *JBL* 67:233-39.
1951 "Archaeology and a Point in Hebrew Syntax." *BASOR* 122:31-33.

Meier, Samuel A.
1988 *The Messenger in the Ancient Semitic World.* HSM 45. Atlanta: Scholars.

Mendelsohn, Isaac
1949 *Slavery in the Ancient Near East.* New York: Oxford University Press.
1959a "On Marriage in Alalakh." In *Essays on Jewish Life and Thought* (FS Salo Wittmayer Baron), ed. Joseph L. Blau et al. New York: Columbia University Press, 351-57.
1959b "On the Preferential Status of the Eldest Son." *BASOR* 156:38-40.

Mendenhall, George E.
1948 "God of Vengeance, Shine Forth!" *Wittenberg Bulletin* 48/12:37-42.
1955 *Law and Covenant in Israel and the Ancient Near East.* Pittsburgh: Biblical Colloquium [Repr. from two articles in *BA* 17 (1954) 26-46; 49-76].
1973 *The Tenth Generation.* Baltimore: Johns Hopkins University Press.
1975 "Samuel's 'Broken Rib': Deuteronomy 32." In *No Famine in the Land* (FS John L. McKenzie), ed. James W. Flanagan and Anita W. Robinson. Missoula: Scholars and Institute for Antiquity and Christianity, Claremont, 63-74 [= Christensen 1993, 169-80].

Mercer, Samuel A.
1915 "The Malediction in Cuneiform Inscriptions." *JAOS* 34:282-309.
1920-21 "'The Little Man of His Eye' — Deut. 32:10." *ATR* 3:151-52.

Merritt, Benjamin D.
1935 "Inscriptions of Colophons." *AJP* 56:358-97.

Meshel, Zeev
1978 *Kuntillet 'Ajrud.* Jerusalem: Israel Museum.

Meshorer, Ya'akov
1978 "Early Means of Payment and the First Coinage." *Ariel* 45-46:127-43.
1998 *Ancient Means of Exchange, Weights and Coins.* Haifa: University of Haifa.

Meyer, Rudolf
1961 "Die Bedeutung von Deuteronomium 32,8f. 43 (4Q) für die Auslegung des Moseliedes." In *Verbannung und Heimkehr* (FS Wilhelm Rudolph), ed. Arnulf Kuschke. Tübingen: Mohr (Siebeck), 197-209.

Michener, James A.
1965 *The Source.* New York: Random House.

Milgrom, Jacob
1972-73 "šôq hattĕrûmâ — A Chapter in Cultic History." *Tarbiz* 42:1-11, I. [Hebrew (with English summary)]

1973 "The Alleged 'Demythologization and Secularization' in Deuteronomy." *IEJ* 23:156-61.
1974-75 "An Akkadian Confirmation for the Meaning of *Tĕrûmâ*." *Tarbiz* 44:189, viii. [Hebrew (with English summary)]
1976a *Cult and Conscience: The Asham and the Priestly Doctrine of Repentance.* SJLA 18. Leiden: Brill.
1976b "Profane Slaughter and a Formulaic Key to the Composition of Deuteronomy." *HUCA* 47:1-17.
1981 "Sancta Contagion and Altar/City Asylum." In *Congress Volume, Vienna, 1980.* VTSup 32:278-310.
1983 "Of Hems and Tassels." *BAR* 9/3:61-65.
1985 "'You Shall Not Boil a Kid in Its Mother's Milk': An Archaeological Myth Destroyed." *BRev* 1/3:48-55.
1990a *Numbers.* JPS Torah Commentary. Philadelphia: Jewish Publication Society.
1990b "Ethics and Ritual: The Foundations of the Biblical Dietary Laws." In Firmage, Weiss, and Welch 1990, 159-91.
1991 *Leviticus 1-16.* AB 3. New York: Doubleday.
2001 *Leviticus 23-27.* AB 3B. New York: Doubleday.

Milik, J. T.
1957 "Le travail d'édition des manuscrits du Désert de Juda." In *Volume du Congrès, Strasbourg, 1956.* VTSup 4:17-26.

Millard, Alan R.
1980 "A Wandering Aramean." *JNES* 39:153-55.
1988 "King Og's Bed and Other Ancient Ironmongery." In Eslinger and Taylor 1988, 481-92.

Miller, J. Maxwell
1989 "The Israelite Journey through (around) Moab and Moabite Toponymy." *JBL* 108:577-95.
1997 "Ancient Moab: Still Largely Unknown." *BA* 60:194-204.

Miller, Patrick D., Jr.
1964 "Two Critical Notes on Psalm 68 and Deuteronomy 33." *HTR* 57:240-43.
1984 "The Most Important Word: The Yoke of the Kingdom." *IR* 41/3:17-29.
1987 "'Moses My Servant': The Deuteronomic Portrait of Moses." *Int* 41:245-55 [= Christensen 1993, 301-12].

Miller, Patrick D., Jr., Paul D. Hanson, and S. Dean McBride, eds.
1987 *Ancient Israelite Religion* (FS Frank Moore Cross). Philadelphia: Fortress.

Miller, Perry
1973 *Jonathan Edwards.* Westport: Greenwood. Orig. 1949.

Minette de Tillesse, Georges
1962 "Sections 'tu' et sections 'vous' dans le Deutéronome." *VT* 12:29-87.

Moberly, R. W. L.
1983 *At the Mountain of God: Story and Theology in Exodus 32-34.* JSOTSup 22. Sheffield: JSOT.
1990 "'Yahweh is One': The Translation of the Shema." In *Studies in the Pentateuch,* ed. J. A. Emerton. VTSup 41. Leiden: Brill, 209-15.

Moessner, David P.
1983 "Luke 9:1-50: Luke's Preview of the Journey of the Prophet like Moses of Deuteronomy." *JBL* 102:575-605.

Moldenke, Harold N., and Alma L. Moldenke
1952   *Plants of the Bible.* Waltham: Chronica Botanica.

Montet, Pierre
1958   *Everyday Life in Egypt in the Days of Ramesses the Great.* Trans. A. R. Maxwell-Hyslop and Margaret S. Drower. New York: St. Martin's.

de Moor, Johannes C.
1988   "'O Death, Where Is Thy Sting?.'" In Eslinger and Taylor 1988, 99-107.

Moran, William L.
1959   "The Scandal of the 'Great Sin' at Ugarit." *JNES* 18:280-81.
1962   "Some Remarks on the Song of Moses." *Bib* 43:317-27.
1963a "The End of the Unholy War and the Anti-Exodus." *Bib* 44:333-42 [= Christensen 1993, 147-55].
1963b "The Ancient Near Eastern Background of the Love of God in Deuteronomy." *CBQ* 25:77-87.
1963c "A Note on the Treaty Terminology of the Sefire Stelas." *JNES* 22:173-76.
1967   "The Conclusion of the Decalogue (Ex 20,17 = Dt 5,21)." *CBQ* 29:543-54.

Morgenstern, Julian
1928   "The Book of the Covenant: Part I." *HUCA* 5:1-151.
1930   "The Book of the Covenant: Part II." *HUCA* 7:19-258.

Moriarty, Frederick L.
1965   "The Chronicler's Account of Hezekiah's Reform." *CBQ* 27:399-406.

Morse, Dan
1967   "Tuberculosis." In Brothwell and Sandison 1967, 249-71.

Mowinckel, Sigmund
1923   "Zu Deuteronomium 23,2-9." *AcOr* 1:81-104.
1932   "Die Chronologie der israelitischen und jüdischen Könige." *AcOr* 10:161-277.
1955   "Psalms and Wisdom." In *Wisdom in Israel and in the Ancient Near East* (FS H. H. Rowley), ed. Martin Noth and D. Winton Thomas. VTSup 3. Leiden: Brill, 205-24.
1962   "Drive and/or Ride in O.T." *VT* 12:278-99.

Mueller, James R.
1979-80 "The Temple Scroll and the Gospel Divorce Texts." *RevQ* 10:247-56.

Muffs, Yochanan
1992   *Love & Joy: Law, Language and Religion in Ancient Israel.* New York: Jewish Theological Seminary of America.

Muhly, James D.
1982   "How Iron Technology Changed the Ancient World and Gave the Philistines a Military Edge." *BAR* 8/6:40-54.

Muilenburg, James
1952   "The Poetry of the Old Testament." In *An Introduction to the Revised Standard Version of the Old Testament,* ed. Members of the Revision Committee, Luther A. Weigle, Chairman. New York: Nelson, 62-70.
1953   "A Study in Hebrew Rhetoric: Repetition and Style." In *Congress Volume, Copenhagen, 1953.* VTSup 1:97-111 [= Best 1984, 193-207].
1956   "Isaiah." In *IB* 5, 381-773.
1959   "The Form and Structure of the Covenantal Formulations." *VT* 9:347-65 [= Best 1984, 108-26].
1961a "The Linguistic and Rhetorical Usages of the Particle כי in the Old Testament." *HUCA* 32:135-60 [= Best 1984, 208-33].

1961b   *The Way of Israel*. New York: Harper.
1963   "The Mediators of the Covenant." Unpublished Nils W. Lund Memorial Lecture, North Park Theological Seminary, Chicago, IL.
1965   "The 'Office' of the Prophet in Ancient Israel." In *The Bible in Modern Scholarship*, ed. J. Philip Hyatt. Nashville: Abingdon, 74-97 [= Best 1984, 127-50].
1966   "A Liturgy on the Triumphs of Yahweh." In *Studia Biblica et Semitica* (FS Th. C. Vriezen, ed. W. C. van Unnik and A. S. van der Woude. Wageningen: Veenman, 233-51 [= Best 1984, 151-69].
1967   "Lectures on Deuteronomy." Unpublished class lectures given at San Francisco Theological Seminary, San Anselmo, CA.
1968   "The Intercession of the Covenant Mediator (Exodus 33:1a, 12-17)." In *Words and Meanings* (FS D. Winton Thomas), ed. Peter R. Ackroyd and Barnabas Lindars. Cambridge: Cambridge University Press, 159-81.
1969   "Form Criticism and Beyond." *JBL* 88:1-18 [= Best 1984, 27-44].
1970a   "Baruch the Scribe." In *Proclamation and Presence* (FS G. Henton Davies), ed. John I. Durham and J. R. Porter. Richmond: John Knox, 215-38 [= Best 1984, 259-82].
1970b   "The Terminology of Adversity in Jeremiah." In *Translating and Understanding the Old Testament* (FS Herbert Gordon May), ed. Harry Thomas Frank and William L. Reed. Nashville: Abingdon, 42-63 [= Best 1984, 234-55].

Mukenge, André Kabasele
2010   "'Toutefois, il n'y aura pas de nécessiteux chez toi': La stratégie argumentative de Deut. 15:1-11." *VT* 60:69-86.

Muraoka, T.
1985   *Emphatic Words and Structures in Biblical Hebrew*. Jerusalem: Magnes, Hebrew University of Jerusalem and Leiden: Brill.

Musil, Alois
1928   *The Manners and Customs of the Rwala Bedouins*. New York: American Geographical Society.

Na'aman, Nadav
1974   "Sennacherib's 'Letter to God' on His Campaign to Judah." *BASOR* 214:25-39.
1986   *Borders and Districts in Biblical Historiography*. Jerusalem: Simor.
1995   "The Debated Historicity of Hezekiah's Reform in the Light of Historical and Archaeological Research." *ZAW* 107:179-95.
2002   "The Abandonment of Cult Places in the Kingdoms of Israel and Judah as Acts of Cult Reform." *UF* 34:585-602.

Naveh, Joseph
1960   "A Hebrew Letter from the Seventh Century B.C." *IEJ* 10:129-39.

Nelson, Harold Hayden
1930   *Medinet Habu*. Vol. 1: *Earlier Historical Records of Ramses III*. OIP 8. Chicago: University of Chicago Press.
1932   *Medinet Habu*. Vol. 2: *Later Historical Records of Ramses III*. OIP 9. Chicago: University of Chicago Press.

Nelson, Richard D.
1981   *The Double Redaction of the Deuteronomic History*. JSOTSup. 18. Sheffield: JSOT.

Nestle, Eberhard
1902   "Das Deuteronomium und 2 Könige 22." *ZAW* 22:170-71, 312-13.

Neufeld, Edward
1944 *Ancient Hebrew Marriage Laws.* London: Longmans, Green.
1951 *The Hittite Laws.* London: Luzac.
1953-54 "The Rate of Interest and the Text of Nehemiah 5.11." *JQR* 44:194-204.
1955 "The Prohibition against Loans at Interest in Ancient Hebrew Laws." *HUCA* 26:355-412.
1962 "Inalienability of Mobile and Immobile Pledges in the Laws of the Bible." *RIDA* 3rd ser. 9:33-44.
1980 "Insects as Warfare Agents in the Ancient Near East." *Or* 49:30-57.

Nicholson, E. W.
1967 *Deuteronomy and Tradition.* Philadelphia: Fortress.
2006 "'Do Not Dare to Set a Foreigner over You': The King in Deuteronomy and 'The Great King.'" *ZAW* 118:46-61.

Nielsen, Eduard
1955 *Shechem: A Traditio-Historical Investigation.* Copenhagen: Gad.

Nigosian, Solomon A.
1996 "The Song of Moses (Dt 32): A Structural Analysis." *ETL* 72:5-22.
1997 "Linguistic Patterns of Deuteronomy 32." *Bib* 78:206-24.

Ninow, Friedbert
2002 "In Search of the 'City Which Is in the Middle of the Valley.'" *AUSS* 40:125-29.

Noonan, John T., Jr.
1979-80 "The Muzzled Ox." *JQR* 70:172-75.

North, Christopher R.
1958 "The Essence of Idolatry." In Hempel and Rost 1958, 151-60.

North, Robert
1954 "*Yâd* in the Shemitta-Law." *VT* 4:196-99.
2000 "Medicine and Healing in the Old Testament Background." In *Medicine in the Biblical Background.* AnBib 142. Rome: Pontifical Biblical Institute, 9-68.

Noth, Martin
1966a *The Laws in the Pentateuch and Other Studies.* Trans. D. R. Ap-Thomas. Philadelphia: Fortress.
1966b *The Old Testament World.* Trans. Victor I. Gruhn. Philadelphia: Fortress.
1981 *The Deuteronomistic History.* JSOTSup 15. Sheffield: JSOT. Orig. *Überlieferungsgeschichtliche Studien I.* Halle: Niemeyer, 1943.

Noth, Martin, ed.
1959 *Essays in Honour of Millar Burrows.* Leiden: Brill [= *VT* 9].

Novick, Tzvi
2007 "Amaleq's Victims (הנחשלים) in Dtn 25,18." *ZAW* 119:611-15.

O'Brien, John Anthony
1921 *Silent Reading.* New York: Macmillan.

O'Callaghan, Roger T.
1948 *Aram Naharaim.* AnOr 26. Rome: Pontifical Biblical Institute.

O'Connell, Kevin G.
1984 "The List of Seven Peoples in Canaan: A Fresh Analysis." In *The Answers Lie Below* (FS Lawrence Edmund Toombs), ed. Henry O. Thompson. Lanham: University Press of America, 221-41.

Bibliography

O'Connell, Robert H.
1990 "Deuteronomy viii 1-20: Asymmetrical Concentricity and the Rhetoric of Providence." *VT* 40:437-52.
1992a "Deuteronomy vii 1-26: Asymmetrical Concentricity and the Rhetoric of Conquest." *VT* 42:248-65.
1992b "Deuteronomy ix 7–x 7, 10-11: Panelled Structure, Double Rehearsal and the Rhetoric of Covenant Rebuke." *VT* 42:492-509.

Oded, Bustenay
1970 "The Settlement of the Tribe of Reuben in Transjordania." In *Studies in the History of the Jewish People and the Land of Israel*, ed. A. Gilboa et al. Vol. 1: FS Zvi Avneri. Tel Aviv: University of Haifa, 11-36, v-vi. [Hebrew (with English summary)]
1979 *Mass Deportations and Deportees in the Neo-Assyrian Empire*. Wiesbaden: Reichert.

Oesch, Josef M.
1979 *Petucha und Setuma*. OBO 27. Freiburg: Universitätsverlag and Göttingen: Vandenhoeck & Ruprecht.

Olmstead, A. T.
1931 *History of Palestine and Syria to the Macedonian Conquest*. New York: Scribner's.

Oppenheim, A. Leo
1949 "The Golden Garments of the Gods." *JNES* 8:172-93.
1956 "The Interpretation of Dreams in the Ancient Near East, With a Translation of an Assyrian Dream-Book." *TAPS* N.S. 46:179-374.
1964 *Ancient Mesopotamia: Portrait of a Dead Civilization*. Chicago: University of Chicago Press.
1965 "A Note on the Scribes in Mesopotamia." In *Studies in Honor of Benno Landsberger*, ed. Hans Güterbock and Thorkild Jacobsen. AS 16. Chicago: Oriental Institute, University of Chicago, 253-56.
1967 *Letters from Mesopotamia*. Chicago: University of Chicago Press.

Orlinsky, Harry M.
1944 Review of Fritsch, *The Anti-Anthropomorphisms of the Greek Pentateuch*. *Crozer Quarterly* 21:156-60.
1965 "The Seer in Ancient Israel." *OrAnt* 4:153-74.

Orlinsky, Harry M., ed.
1969 *Interpreting the Prophetic Tradition*. Cincinnati: Hebrew Union College Press.

Ottosson, Magnus
1969 *Gilead: Tradition and History*. Trans. Jean Gray. ConBOT 3. Lund: Gleerup.
1988 "Eden and the Land of Promise." In *Congress Volume, Jerusalem, 1986*, ed. J. A. Emerton. VTSup 40:177-88.

Palmer, E. H.
1871 *The Desert of the Exodus*. 2 vols. Cambridge: Deighton, Bell.

Parpola, Simo, and Kazuko Watanabe
1988 *Neo-Assyrian Treaties and Loyalty Oaths*. SAA 2. Helsinki: Helsinki University Press.

Patai, Raphael
1939-40 "The 'Egla 'Arufa or the Expiation of the Polluted Land." *JQR* 30:59-69.

Paton, Lewis Bayles
1928 "The Case for the Post-Exilic Origin of Deuteronomy." *JBL* 47:322-57.

Bibliography

Patrick, Dale
1985 *Old Testament Law*. Atlanta: John Knox.

Paul, Shalom M.
1971 "Amos 1:3–2:3: A Concatenous Literary Pattern." *JBL* 90:397-403.
1972 "Psalm 72:5 — A Traditional Blessing for the Long Life of the King." *JNES* 31:351-55.
1990 "Biblical Analogues to Middle Assyrian Law." In Firmage, Weiss, and Welch 1990, 333-50.
1991 *Amos*. Hermeneia. Minneapolis: Fortress.

Peckham, Brian
1968 "Notes on a Fifth-Century Phoenician Inscription from Kition, Cyprus (CIS 86)." *Or* 37:304-24.

Pedersen, Johannes
1964 *Israel, Its Life and Culture I-II, III-IV*. London: Oxford University Press. Orig. 1926.

Peels, Hendrik G.
1994 "On the Wings of the Eagle (Dtn 32,11) — An Old Misunderstanding." *ZAW* 106:300-303.

Petuchowski, Jakob J.
1958 "Not by Bread Alone." *Judaism* 7:229-34.

Pfeiffer, Robert H.
1948 *Introduction to the Old Testament*. Rev. ed. New York: Harper & Brothers. Orig. 1941.
1955 "The Fear of God." *IEJ* 5:41-48.

Pflüger, Kurt
1946 "The Edict of King Haremhab." *JNES* 5:260-76.

Phillips, Anthony
1970 *Ancient Israel's Criminal Law*. Oxford: Blackwell.
1983 "The Decalogue — Ancient Israel's Criminal Law." *JJS* 34:1-20.

Phythian-Adams, William John
1923 "On the Date of the 'Blessing of Moses' (Deut. XXXIII)." *JPOS* 3:158-66.

Piattelli, Daniela
1981 "The Marriage Contract and Bill of Divorce in Ancient Hebrew Law." *JLA* 4:66-78.

Piccirillo, Michele
1987 *Mount Nebo*. Jerusalem: Custodia Terra Santa.

Piccirillo, Michele, and Eugenio Alliata
1998 *Mount Nebo: New Archaeological Excavations, 1967-1997*. Jerusalem: Studium Biblicum Franciscanum.

Pope, Marvin H.
1955 *El in the Ugaritic Texts*. VTSup 2. Leiden: Brill.
1977 "Notes on the Rephaim Texts from Ugarit." In *Essays on the Ancient Near East* (FS Jacob Joel Finkelstein), ed. Maria de Jong Ellis. Memoirs of the Connecticut Academy of Arts and Sciences 19. Hamden: Archon, 163-82.

Pope, Marvin H., and Jeffrey H. Tigay
1971 "A Description of Baal." *UF* 3:117-30.

Porten, Bezalel
1968 *Archives from Elephantine*. Berkeley: University of California Press.
1981 "The Identity of King Adon." *BA* 44:36-52.

Bibliography

Porten, Bezalel, and Ada Yardeni
1989   *Textbook of Aramaic Documents from Ancient Egypt.* Vol. 2: *Contracts.* Jerusalem: Hebrew University.

Preuss, Julius
1978   *Biblical and Talmudic Medicine.* Trans. and ed. Fred Rosner. New York: Sanhedrin.

Price, Ira Maurice
1926   "The So-called Levirate-marriage in Hittite and Assyrian Laws." In *Oriental Studies* (FS Paul Haupt), ed. Cyrus Adler and Aaron Ember. Baltimore: Johns Hopkins University Press, 268-71.

Propp, William Henry Covici
1987   *Water in the Wilderness: A Biblical Motif and Its Mythological Background.* HSM 40. Atlanta: Scholars.
1999   *Exodus 1–18.* AB 2. New York: Doubleday.
2006   *Exodus 19–40.* AB 2A. New York: Doubleday.

Puech, Émile
2001-2   "Identification de nouveaux manuscrits bibliques: *Deutéronome* et *Proverbs* dans les débris de la grotte 4." *RevQ* 20:121-27.

Rabin, Chaim
1963   "Hittite Words in Hebrew." *Or* 32:113-39.

Rabinowitz, Jacob J.
1959   "The 'Great Sin' in Ancient Egyptian Marriage Contracts." *JNES* 18:73.

von Rad, Gerhard
1929   *Das Gottesvolk im Deuteronomium.* BWANT 47. Stuttgart: Kohlhammer.
1953   *Studies in Deuteronomy.* Trans. David Stalker. SBT 9. London: SCM [German: *Deuteronomium-Studien.* Göttingen: Vandenhoeck & Ruprecht, 1947].
1962a   "Deuteronomy." In *IDB*, 1:831-38.
1962b   *Old Testament Theology.* Vol. 1: *The Theology of Israel's Historical Traditions.* Trans. D. M. G. Stalker. New York: Harper & Row.
1966a   *The Problem of the Hexateuch and Other Essays.* Trans. E. W. Trueman Dicken. New York: McGraw-Hill [German: *Das Formgeschichtliche Problem des Hexateuchs.* BWANT 26. Stuttgart: Kohlhammer, 1938].
1966b   "The Form-Critical Problem of the Hexateuch." In von Rad 1966a, 1-78; 2005, 1-58.
1966c   "There Remains Still a Rest for the People of God: An Investigation of a Biblical Conception." In von Rad 1966a, 94-102; 2005, 82-88. [German: "Es ist noch eine Ruhe vorhanden dem Volke Gottes." In von Rad, *Gesammelte Studien zum Alten Testament 1.* Munich: Kaiser, 1958, 101-8.] Orig. 1933.
1991   *Holy War in Ancient Israel.* Trans. Marva J. Dawn. Grand Rapids: Eerdmans. German orig. *Der Heilige Krieg im alten Israel.* ATANT 20. Zurich: Zwingli, 1951.
2005   *From Genesis to Chronicles.* Ed. K. C. Hanson. Minneapolis: Fortress.

Rainey, A. F.
1970   "Compulsory Labour Gangs in Ancient Israel." *IEJ* 20:191-202.
1983   "The Biblical Shephelah of Judah." *BASOR* 251:1-22.
1994   "Hezekiah's Reform and the Altars at Beersheba and Arad." In *Scripture and Other Artifacts* (FS Philip J. King), ed. Michael D. Coogan, J. Cheryl Exum, and Lawrence E. Stager. Louisville: Westminster John Knox, 333-54.

Rankin, O. S.
1936   *Israel's Wisdom Literature.* Kerr Lectures, 1933-36. Edinburgh: T. & T. Clark.

Reed, William L.
1949 *The Asherah in the Old Testament.* Fort Worth: Texas Christian University Press.

Reif, Stefan C.
1972 "Dedicated to חנך." *VT* 22:495-501.

Rendsburg, Gary, et al., eds.
1980 *The Bible World* (FS Cyrus H. Gordon). New York: Ktav and Institute of Hebrew Culture and Education, New York University.

Renkema, J.
1995 "Does Hebrew *YTWM* Really Mean 'Fatherless'?" *VT* 45:119-21.

Revell, E. J.
1997 "The Repetition of Introductions to Speech as a Feature of Biblical Hebrew." *VT* 47:91-110.

Reviv, Hanoch
1989 *The Elders in Ancient Israel.* Trans. Lucy Plitmann. Jerusalem: Magnes, Hebrew University of Jerusalem. Orig. 1983.

Ringgren, Helmer
1995 *The Faith of Qumran.* Trans. Emilie T. Sander. New York: Crossroad.

Roberts, C. H.
1936 "A Ptolemaic Papyrus of Deuteronomy." In *Two Biblical Papyri in the John Rylands Library Manchester.* Manchester: Manchester University Press, 9-46.

Roberts, J. J. M.
1971 "The Hand of Yahweh." *VT* 21:244-51.

Robertson, David A.
1972 *Linguistic Evidence in Dating Early Hebrew Poetry.* SBLDS 3. Missoula: SBL.

Robinson, Edward
1867 *Biblical Researches in Palestine and the Adjacent Regions.* 3 vols. London: Murray.

Robinson, George Livingston
1930 *The Sarcophagus of an Ancient Civilization.* New York: Macmillan.

Robinson, H. Wheeler
1936 "The Hebrew Conception of Corporate Personaity." In *Werden und Wesen des Alten Testament,* ed. Paul Volz, Friedrich Stummer, and Johannes Hempel. BZAW 66. Berlin: Töpelmann, 49-62.
1937 "The Group and the Individual in Israel." In *The Individual in East and West,* ed. E. R. Hughes. London: Oxford University Press, 153-70.
1944 "The Council of Yahweh." *JTS* old ser. 45:151-57.
1980 *Corporate Personality in Ancient Israel.* Rev. ed. Philadelphia: Fortress [Repr. of Robinson 1936 and 1937].

Rofé, Alexander
1972 "The Strata of the Law about the Centralization of Worship in Deuteronomy and the History of the Deuteronomic Movement." In *Congress Volume, Uppsala, 1971.* VTSup 22:221-26.
1985 "The Laws of Warfare in the Book of Deuteronomy: Their Origins, Intent and Positivity." *JSOT* 32:23-44.
1986 "The History of the Cities of Refuge in Biblical Law." In Japhet 1986, 205-39.
1987 "Family and Sex Laws in Deuteronomy and the Book of the Covenant." *Hen* 9:131-59.

1988a "Qumranic Paraphrases, the Greek Deuteronomy and the Late History of the Biblical נשיא." *Text* 14:163-74.
1988b "The Arrangement of the Laws in Deuteronomy." *ETL* 64:265-87.
1994 "The Editing of the Book of Joshua in the Light of 4QJosh^a." In Brooke 1994, 73-80.
2000 "The End of the Song of Moses (Deuteronomy 32:43)." In *Liebe und Gebot: Studien zum Deuteronomium* (FS Lothar Perlitt), ed. Reinhard Gregor Kratz and Hermann Spieckermann. FRLANT 190. Göttingen: Vandenhoeck & Ruprecht, 164-72.

van Rooy, H. F.
1988 "Deuteronomy 28,69 — Superscript or Subscript?" *JNSL* 14:215-22.

Rosenbaum, Jonathan
1979 "Hezekiah's Reform and the Deuteronomistic Tradition." *HTR* 72:23-43.

Roth, Ernest
1950 "Does the Torah Punish Impudence? Notes to Deuteronomy xxv 11-12." In *Études Orientales à la Mémoire de Paul Hirschler,* ed. Ottó Komlós. Budapest: Nationalized Kerfész-Press, 116-21.

Roth, Martha T.
1989 *Babylonian Marriage Agreements: 7th-3rd Centuries* B.C. AOAT 222. Neukirchen-Vluyn: Neukirchener.
1991-93 "The Neo-Babylonian Widow." *JCS* 43-45:1-26.
1995 *Law Collections from Mesopotamia and Asia Minor.* SBLWAW 6. Atlanta: Scholars.

Rowley, H. H.
1939 "Zadok and Nehushtan." *JBL* 58:113-41.
1947 "The Marriage of Ruth." *HTR* 40:77-99 [= Rowley 1952, 163-86].
1950a "The Prophet Jeremiah and the Book of Deuteronomy." In *Studies in Old Testament Prophecy* (FS Theodore H. Robinson), ed. Rowley. Edinburgh: T. & T. Clark, 157-74.
1950b *From Joseph to Joshua: Biblical Traditions in the Light of Archaeology.* Schweich Lectures, 1948. London: British Academy and Oxford University Press.
1952 *The Servant of the Lord and Other Essays.* London: Lutterworth.
1961-62 "Hezekiah's Reform and Rebellion." *BJRL* 44:395-431.
1963a *From Moses to Qumran.* London: Lutterworth.
1963b *Men of God: Studies in Old Testament History and Prophecy.* London: Nelson.

Rowling, J. Thompson
1967 "Disease of the Alimentary System in Egypt." In Brothwell and Sandison 1967, 494-97.

Salisbury, Harrison E.
2000 *The 900 Days: The Siege of Leningrad.* London: Pan. Orig. 1969.

Saller, Sylvester J., and Bellarmino Bagatti
1949 *The Town of Nebo (Khirbet El-Mekhayyat).* Jerusalem: Franciscan.

Sanders, Henry A.
1938 "The Beginnings of the Modern Book: The Codex of the Classical Era." *Michigan Alumnus Quarterly Review* 44:95-111.

Sanders, James A., and Astrid Beck
1997 "The Leningrad Codex: Rediscovering the Oldest Complete Hebrew Bible." *BRev* 13/4:32-41, 46.

Sanders, Paul
1996 *The Provenance of Deuteronomy 32.* OTS 37. Leiden: Brill.

Sanders, T. W., and J. Lansdell
1924   *Grapes: Peaches: Melons: and How to Grow Them.* London: Collingridge.

Sandison, A. T.
1967a   "Parasitic Diseases." In Brothwell and Sandison 1967, 178-83.
1967b   "Diseases of the Skin." In Brothwell and Sandison 1967, 449-56.
1967c   "Degenerative Vascular Disease." In Brothwell and Sandison 1967, 474-88.

Sarfatti, Gad B.
1990   "The Tablets of the Law as a Symbol of Judaism." In *The Ten Commandments in History and Tradition,* ed. Ben-Zion Segal and Gershon Levi. Jerusalem: Magnes, Hebrew University of Jerusalem, 383-418. Hebrew orig. 1985, ed. Segal, 353-87.

Sarna, Nahum M.
1973   "Zedekiah's Emancipation of Slaves and the Sabbatical Year." In Hoffner 1973, 143-49.
1979   "The Psalm Superscriptions and the Guilds." In *Studies in Jewish Religious and Intellectual History* (FS Alexander Altmann), ed. Siegfried Stein and Raphael Loewe. Tuscaloosa: University of Alabama Press, 281-300.
1991   *Exodus.* JPS Torah Commentary. Philadelphia: Jewish Publication Society.

Sauer, James A.
1985   "Ammon, Moab and Edom." In *Biblical Archaeology Today: Proceedings of the International Congress on Biblical Archaeology, Jerusalem, April 1984,* ed. Janet Amitai. Jerusalem: Israel Exploration Society, 206-14.
1986   "Transjordan in the Bronze and Iron Ages: A Critique of Glueck's Synthesis." *BASOR* 263:1-26.

Schaeffer, Claude F. A.
1939   *The Cuneiform Texts of Ras Shamra-Ugarit.* Schweich Lectures, 1936. London: British Academy and Oxford University Press.

Schiffman, Lawrence H.
1991-92 "The Deuteronomic Paraphrase of the *Temple Scroll.*" *RevQ* 15:543-67.

Schley, Donald G. Jr.
1985   "'Yahweh Will Cause You to Return to Egypt in Ships' (Deuteronomy xxviii 68)." *VT* 35:369-72.

Schmidt, Nathaniel
1910   "Kadesh Barnea." *JBL* 29:61-76.

Scholz, Piotr O.
2001   *Eunuchs and Castrati: A Cultural History.* Trans. John A. Broadwin and Shelley L. Frisch. Princeton: Wiener.

Schorch, Stefan
2010   "'A Young Goat in Its Mother's Milk'? Understanding an Ancient Prohibition." *VT* 60:116-30.

Schremer, Adiel
1998   "Divorce in Papyrus Ṣe'elim 13 Once Again: A Reply to Tal Ilan." *HTR* 91:193-202.

Schumacher, Gottlieb
1886   *Across the Jordan.* London: Bentley.

Scott, R. B. Y.
1959   "Weights and Measures of the Bible." *BA* 22:22-40.

Seeligmann, I. L.
1964   "A Psalm from Pre-Regal Times." *VT* 14:75-92.

Bibliography

Seely, David Rolph
1996 "The 'Circumcised Heart' in 4Q434 Barki Nafshi." *RevQ* 17:527-35.

Segal, J. B.
1963 *The Hebrew Passover, from the Earliest Times to A.D. 70.* LOS 12. London: Oxford University Press.

Seidl, Erwin
1942 "Law." In *The Legacy of Egypt*, ed. S. R. K. Glanville. Oxford: Clarendon, 198-217.

Seitz, Gottfried
1971 *Redaktionsgeschichtliche Studien zum Deuteronomium.* BWANT 93. Stuttgart: Kohlhammer.

Seux, M.-J.
1967 *Épithètes royales akkadiennes et sumériennes.* Paris: Letouzey et Ané.

Shai, Donna
1974 "Wedding Customs among Kurdish Jews in (Zakho) Kurdistan and in (Jerusalem) Israel." In Ben-Ami and Noy 1974, 253-66.

Shulman, Ahouva
1999 "The Particle נָא in Biblical Hebrew Prose." *HS* 40:57-82.

Simons, J.
1937 *Handbook for the Study of Egyptian Topographical Lists Relating to Western Asia.* Leiden: Brill.
1947 "Two Connected Problems Relating to the Israelite Settlement in Trans-Jordan." *PEQ* 79:27-39.
1959 *The Geographical and Topographical Texts of the Old Testament.* Leiden: Brill.

Singer, A. D.
1948 "Philological Notes." *JPOS* 21:104-9.

Skehan, Patrick W.
1951 "The Structure of the Song of Moses in Deuteronomy (Deut. 32:1-43)." *CBQ* 13:153-63 [= Christensen 1993, 156-68].
1954 "A Fragment of the 'Song of Moses' (Deut. 32) from Qumran." *BASOR* 136:12-15.
1955 "Exodus in the Samaritan Recension from Qumran." *JBL* 74:182-87.
1959 "Qumran and the Present State of Old Testament Text Studies: The Masoretic Text." *JBL* 78:21-25.

Smelik, Klaas A. D.
1992 *Converting the Past: Studies in Ancient Israelite and Moabite Historiography.* OtSt 28. Leiden: Brill.

Smend, Rudolf
2007 *From Astruc to Zimmerli.* Trans. Margaret Kohl. Tübingen: Mohr Siebeck.

Smith, George Adam
1912 *The Early Poetry of Israel in Its Physical and Social Origins.* Schweich Lectures, 1910. London: Frowde.

Smith, J. M. Powis
1914 "The Deuteronomic Tithe." *AJT* 18:119-26.

Smith, W. Robertson
1880 "Animal Worship and Animal Tribes among the Arabs in the Old Testament." *JP* 9:75-100.
1885 "On the Forms of Divination and Magic Enumerated in Deut. xviii.10, 11." *JP* 13:273-87.

1903   *Kinship and Marriage in Early Arabia.* London: Black. Orig. 1885.
1927   *Lectures on the Religion of the Semites.* 3rd ed. London: Black. Orig. 1889.

Snaith, Norman H.
1983   *The Distinctive Ideas of the Old Testament.* Philadelphia: Westminster. Orig. 1944.

Snell, Daniel C.
1983-84   "The Cuneiform Tablet from *El-Qiṭār.*" *AbrN* 22:159-70.

Sonsino, Rifat
1980   *Motive Clauses in Hebrew Law.* SBLDS 45. Chico: Scholars.

Soss, Neal M.
1973   "Old Testament Law and Economic Society." *JHI* 34:323-44.

Speiser, Ephraim A.
1930   "New Kirkuk Documents Relating to Family Laws." In *AASOR* 10 (1928-29). New Haven: ASOR and Yale University Press, 1-73.
1933   "Ethnic Movements in the Near East in the Second Millennium B.C." In *AASOR* 13. New Haven: ASOR, 13-54.
1940   "Of Shoes and Shekels." *BASOR* 17:15-20.
1964   *Genesis.* AB 1. Garden City: Doubleday.

Spina, Frank
1983   "Israelite as *gērîm,* 'Sojourners,' in Social and Historical Context." In *The Word of the Lord Shall Go Forth* (FS David Noel Freedman), ed. Carol L. Meyers and M. O'Connor. Winona Lake: ASOR and Eisenbrauns, 321-35.

Staerk, Willy
1894   *Das Deuteronomium: Sein Inhalt und seine literarische Form.* Leipzig: Hinrichs.

Stager, Lawrence E.
1985   "The Archaeology of the Family in Ancient Israel." *BASOR* 260:1-35.

Steiner, Richard C.
1996   "דָּת and עֵין: Two Verbs Masquerading as Nouns in Moses' Blessing (Deuteronomy 33:2, 28)." *JBL* 115:693-98.

Stern, Ephraim
1998   "Buried Treasure: The Silver Hoard from Dor." *BAR* 24/4:46-51, 62.
2001   *Archaeology and the Land of the Bible.* Vol. 2: *The Assyrian, Babylonian, and Persian Periods.* ABRL. New York: Doubleday.

Stern, Philip D.
1992   "The Origin and Significance of 'The Land Flowing with Milk and Honey.'" *VT* 42:554-57.

Steuernagel, Carl
1894   *Der Rahmen des Deuteronomiums.* Halle: Krause.

Stulman, Louis
1990   "Encroachment in Deuteronomy: An Analysis of the Social World of the D Code." *JBL* 109:613-32.

Sturtevant, Edgar H., and George Bechtel
1935   *A Hittite Chrestomathy.* Philadelphia: Linguistic Society of America, University of Pennsylvania.

Sukenik, E. L.
1940   "Arrangements for the Cult of the Dead in Ugarit and Samaria." In *Mémorial Lagrange,* ed. L.-H. Vincent. Paris: Gabalda, 59-65 + pls.

Bibliography

Sumner, W. A.
1968 "Israel's Encounters with Edom, Moab, Ammon, Sihon, and Og according to the Deuteronomist." *VT* 18:216-28.

Sussman, Max
1967 "Diseases in the Bible and the Talmud." In Brothwell and Sandison 1967, 209-21.

Tadmor, Hayim
1958 "The Campaigns of Sargon II of Assur: A Chronological-Historical Study." *JCS* 12:22-40, 77-100.
1995 "Was the Biblical *sārîs* a Eunuch?" In *Solving Riddles and Untying Knots* (FS Jonas C. Greenfield), ed. Ziony Zevit, Seymour Gitin, and Michael Sokoloff. Winona Lake: Eisenbrauns, 317-25.

Talmon, Shemaryahu
1960 "Double Readings in the Masoretic Text." *Text* 1:144-84.
1965 "The Calendar Reckoning of the Sect from the Judaean Desert." In *Aspects of the Dead Sea Scrolls.* ed. Chaim Rabin and Yigael Yadin. ScrHier 4. Jerusalem: Magnes, Hebrew University, 162-99.
1993a "Biblical רפאים and Ugaritic *RPU/I(M)*." In Talmon 1993c, 76-90.
1993b "The Presentation of Synchroneity and Simultaneity in Biblical Narrative." In Talmon 1993c, 112-33.
1993c *Literary Studies in the Hebrew Bible.* Jerusalem: Magnes, Hebrew University and Leiden: Brill.

Tawil, Hayim
1977 "A Curse Concerning Crop-Consuming Insects in the Sefire Treaty and in Akkadian: A New Interpretation." *BASOR* 225:59-62.

Tebes, Juan Manuel
2003 "A New Analysis of the Iron Age I 'Chiefdom' of Tel Masos (Beersheba Valley)." *AuOr* 21:63-78.
2007 "A Land Whose Stones Are Iron." *Davar Logos* 6:69-91.

Thiessen, Matthew
2004 "The Form and Function of the Song of Moses (Deuteronomy 32:1-43)." *JBL* 123:401-24.

Thomas, D. Winton
1939 "The Root אהב 'love' in Hebrew." *ZAW* 57:57-64.
1960 "*Kelebh* 'Dog': Its Origin and Some Usages of It in the Old Testament." *VT* 10:410-27.

Thomas, D. Winton, ed.
1967 *Archaeology and Old Testament Study.* Oxford: Clarendon.

Thompson, Christine M.
2003 "Sealed Silver in Iron Age Cisjordan and the 'Invention' of Coinage." *OJA* 22:67-107.

Tigay, Jeffrey H.
1982a *The Evolution of the Gilgamesh Epic.* Philadelphia: University of Pennsylvania Press.
1982b "On the Meaning of *t(w)tpt.*" *JBL* 101:321-31.
1985 "The Evolution of the Pentateuchal Narratives in the Light of the Evolution of the *Gilgamesh Epic.*" In *Empirical Models for Biblical Criticism,* ed. Tigay. Philadelphia: University of Pennsylvania Press, 21-52.

1986	*You Shall Have No Other Gods: Israelite Religion in the Light of Hebrew Inscriptions.* HSS 31. Atlanta: Scholars.
1987a	"Israelite Religion: The Onomastic and Epigraphic Evidence." In Miller, Hanson, and McBride 1987, 157-94. [Shorter version of Tigay 1986]
1987b	"What Is Man That You Have Been Mindful of Him? (On Psalm 8:4-5)." In Marks and Good 1987, 169-71.
1993a	"Examination of the Accused Bride in 4Q159: Forensic Medicine at Qumran." *JANES* 22:129-34.
1993b	"A Talmudic Parallel to the Petition from Yavneh-Yam." In *Minḥah le Naḥum* (FS Nahum M. Sarna), ed. Marc Brettler and Michael Fishbane. JSOTSup 154. Sheffield: Sheffield Academic, 328-33.
1995	"Some Archaeological Notes on Deuteronomy." In *Pomegranates and Golden Bells* (FS Jacob Milgrom), ed. David P. Wright, David Noel Freedman, and Avi Hurvitz. Winona Lake: Eisenbrauns, 373-80.

Tigchelaar, Eibert

2008 "A Forgotten Qumran Cave 4 *Deuteronomy* Fragment ($4Q38D = 4QDeut^u$)." *RevQ* 23:525-28 + photo.

Toorn, Karel van der

1989 "Female Prostitution in Payment of Vows in Ancient Israel." *JBL* 108:193-205.

Toorn, Karel van der, Bob Becking, and Pieter W. van der Horst, eds.

1999 *Dictionary of Deities and Demons in the Bible.* 2nd ed. Leiden: Brill and Grand Rapids: Eerdmans.

Tov, Emanuel

1991-92 "Deut. 12 and 11QTemple LII-LIII: A Contrastive Analysis." *RevQ* 15:169-73.

Tristram, H. B.

1884 *The Survey of Western Palestine: The Fauna and Flora of Palestine.* London: Committee of the Palestine Exploration Fund. Including pls.

1898 *The Natural History of the Bible.* 9th ed. London: SPCK. Orig. 1867.

Tromp, Nicholas J.

1969 *Primitive Conceptions of Death and the Nether World in the Old Testament.* BibOr 21. Rome: Pontifical Biblical Institute.

Trumbull, H. Clay

1884 *Kadesh-Barnea.* New York: Scribner's.

1896 *The Threshold Covenant.* New York: Scribner's.

Tsevat, Matitiahu

1958a "Alalakhiana." *HUCA* 29:109-34 + 2.

1958b "Marriage and Monarchical Legitimacy in Ugarit and Israel." *JSS* 3:237-43.

1994 "The Hebrew Slave according to Deuteronomy 15:12-18: His Lot and the Value of His Work, with Special Attention to the Meaning of מִשְׁנֶה." *JBL* 113:587-95.

1996 "Three Early Rabbinic Cardinal Principles: Reasons of the Commandments." *Or* 65:435-39.

Tucker, Gene M.

1965 "Covenant Forms and Contract Forms." *VT* 15:487-503.

Tufnell, Olga

1967 "Lachish." In Thomas 1967, 296-308.

Tufnell, Olga, Charles H. Inge, and G. Lankester Harding

1940 *Lachish.* Vol. 2: *The Fosse Temple.* London: Oxford University Press.

Bibliography

Ulrich, Eugene
1994 "4QJoshua^a and Joshua's First Altar in the Promised Land." In Brooke 1994, 89-104.

Urbach, Ephraim E.
1979 *The Sages: Their Concepts and Beliefs*, trans. Israel Abrahams. 2 vols. Jerusalem: Magnes, Hebrew University and Cambridge, MA: Harvard University Press.

Van Zyl, A. H.
1960 *The Moabites*. POS 3. Leiden: Brill.

de Vaux, Roland
1965 *Ancient Israel: Its Life and Institutions*. Trans. John McHugh. London: Darton, Longman & Todd. Repr. BRS. Grand Rapids: Eerdmans and Livonia: Dove, 1997.
1967 "Les Hurrites de l'histoire et les Horites de la Bible." *RB* 74:481-503.
1971a *The Bible and the Ancient Near East*. Trans. Damian McHugh. Garden City: Doubleday.
1971b "Ark of the Covenant and Tent of Reunion." In de Vaux 1971a, 136-51.
1971c "The Sacrifice of Pigs in Palestine and in the Ancient East." In de Vaux 1971a, 252-69 [= "Les sacrifices de porcs en Palestine et dans l'Ancien Orient." In Hempel and Rost 1958, 250-65].
1978 *The Early History of Israel*. Vols. 1-2. Trans. David Smith. London: Darton, Longman & Todd.

Vedeler, Harold Torger
2008 "Reconstructing Meaning in Deuteronomy 22:5: Gender, Society, and Transvestitism in Israel and the Ancient Near East." *JBL* 127:459-76.

Vermes, Geza
1959 "Pre-Mishnaic Jewish Worship and the Phylacteries from the Dead Sea." *VT* 9:65-72.

Vierya, Maurice
1961 "Les noms du 'mundus' en hittite et en assyrien et la pythonisse d'Endor." *RHA* 19:47-55.

de Waard, Jan
1971 "The Quotation from Deuteronomy in Acts 3,22.23 and the Palestinian Text: Additional Arguments." *Bib* 52:537-40.

Waldman, Nahum M.
1980-81 "The Wealth of Mountain and Sea: The Background of a Biblical Image." *JQR* 71:176-80.

von Waldow, H. Eberhard
1970 "Social Responsibility and Social Structure in Early Israel." *CBQ* 32:182-204.

Walker, Winifred
1957 *All the Plants of the Bible*. New York: Harper.

Walsh, Jerome T.
2004 "'You Shall Cut Off Her . . . Palm'? A Reexamination of Deuteronomy 25:11-12." *JSS* 49:47-58.

Washington, Harold C.
1998 "'Lest He Die in the Battle and Another Man Take Her': Violence and the Construction of Gender in the Laws of Deuteronomy 20-22." In Matthews, Levinson, and Frymer-Kensky 1998, 185-213.

Bibliography

Waterman, Leroy
1930   *Royal Correspondence of the Assyrian Empire*. Vols. 1-2. Ann Arbor: University of Michigan Press.

Weaver, Robert J.
1976   *Grape Growing*. New York: Wiley.

Weinfeld, Moshe
1960a   "The Dependence of Deuteronomy upon the Wisdom Literature." In Haran 1960b, 89-108. [Hebrew]
1960b   "The Source of the Idea of Reward in Deuteronomy." *Tarbiz* 30:8-15, I-II. [Hebrew (with English summary)]
1961   "The Origin of Humanism in Deuteronomy." *JBL* 80:241-47.
1965   "Traces of Assyrian Treaty Formulae in Deuteronomy." *Bib* 46:417-27.
1967   "Deuteronomy — The Present State of Inquiry." *JBL* 86:249-62 [= Christensen 1993, 21-35].
1970-72   "The Covenant of Grant in the Old Testament and in the Ancient Near East." *JAOS* 90:184-203; 92:468-69.
1972   *Deuteronomy and the Deuteronomic School*. Oxford: Clarendon.
1973a   "The Origin of the Apodictic Law." *VT* 23:63-75.
1973b   "Covenant Terminology in the Ancient Near East and Its Influence on the West." *JAOS* 93:190-99.
1976a   "The Loyalty Oath in the Ancient Near East." *UF* 8:379-414.
1976b   "Jeremiah and the Spiritual Metamorphosis of Israel." *ZAW* 88:17-56.
1977   "Judge and Officer in Ancient Israel and in the Ancient Near East." *IOS* 7:65-88. Hebrew: *Proceedings of the Sixth World Congress of Jewish Studies*. Vol. 1. Jerusalem: World Union of Jewish Studies, 73-89.
1978   "Pentecost as Festival of the Giving of the Law." *Immanuel* 8: 7-18.
1982a   "'Justice and Righteousness' in Ancient Israel against the Background of 'Social Reforms' in the Ancient Near East." In *Mesopotamien und Seine Nachbarn*, ed. Hans-Jörg Nissen and Johannes Renger. BBVO 1. Berlin: Reimer, 491-519.
1982b   "The King as the Servant of the People: The Source of the Idea." *JJS* 33:189-94 [= *Essays in Honour of Yigael Yadin*, ed. Geza Vermes and Jacob Neusner. Totowa: Allanheld, Osmun, 1983, 189-94].
1983a   "Zion and Jerusalem as Religious and Political Capital; Ideology and Utopia." In *The Poet and the Historian: Essays in Literary and Historical Biblical Criticism*, ed. Richard Elliott Friedman. HSM 26. Chico: Scholars, 75-115.
1983b   "The Extent of the Promised Land — the Status of Transjordan." In *Das Land Israel in biblischer Zeit: Jerusalem-Symposium 1981 der Hebräischen Universität und der Georg-August-Universität*, ed. Georg Strecker. GTA 25. Göttingen: Vandenhoeck & Ruprecht, 59-75.
1983c   "Social and Cultic Institutions in the Priestly Source against their Ancient Near Eastern Background." In *Proceedings of the Eighth World Congress of Jewish Studies (Jerusalem, August 16-21, 1981). Panel Sessions: Bible Studies and Hebrew Language*. Jerusalem: World Union of Jewish Studies, 95-129.
1985   "Freedom Proclamations in Egypt and in the Ancient Near East." In *Pharaonic Egypt: The Bible and Christianity*, ed. Sarah Israelit-Groll. Jerusalem: Magnes, Hebrew University, 317-27.
1987   "The Tribal League at Sinai." In Miller, Hanson, and McBride 1987, 303-14.
1988   "The Pattern of the Israelite Settlement in Canaan." In *Congress Volume, Jerusalem, 1986*. VTSup 40:270-83.

1990	"The Decalogue: Its Significance, Uniqueness, and Place in Israel's Tradition." In Firmage, Weiss, and Welch 1990, 3-47.
1992a	"'Justice and Righteousness' — מִשְׁפָּט וּצְדָקָה — The Expression and Its Meaning." In *Justice and Righteousness: Biblical Themes and Their Influence* (FS Benjamin Uffenheimer), ed. Henning Graf Reventlow and Yair Hoffman. JSOTSup 137. Sheffield: Sheffield Academic, 228-46.
1992b	"Deuteronomy, Book of." In *ABD*, 2:168-83.
1992c	"Grace after Meals in Qumran." *JBL* 111:427-40.
1993	"The Ban of the Canaanites in the Biblical Codes and Its Historical Development." In *History and Traditions of Early Israel* (FS Eduard Nielsen), ed. André Lemaire and Benedikt Otzen. VTSup 50. Leiden: Brill, 142-60.
2004	*The Place of the Law in the Religion of Ancient Israel*. VTSup 100. Leiden: Brill.

Weippert, Manfred

1971	*The Settlement of the Israelite Tribes in Palestine*. Trans. James D. Martin. SBT 2nd ser. 21. London: SCM.

Weise, Manfred

1961	*Kultzeiten und kultischer Bundesschluss in der 'Ordensregel' vom Toten Meer*. StPB 3. Leiden: Brill.

Weiser, Artur

1961	*The Old Testament: Its Formation and Development*. Trans. Dorothea M. Barton. New York: Association.

Welch, Adam C.

1924	*The Code of Deuteronomy: A New Theory of Its Origin*. London: Clarke.
1925	"When was the worship of Israel centralized at the temple?" *ZAW* 43:250-55.
1932	*Deuteronomy: The Framework to the Code*. Oxford: Oxford University Press.
1939	*The Work of the Chronicler, Its Purpose and Its Date*. Schweich Lectures, 1938. London: British Academy and Oxford University Press.

Wellhausen, Julius

1889	*Die Composition des Hexateuchs und der historischen Bücher des Alten Testaments*. 3rd ed. Berlin: Reimer.
1957	*Prolegomena to the History of Ancient Israel*. New York: Meridan [= *Prolegomena zur Geschichte Israels*. 2nd ed. Berlin: Reimer, 1883]. Orig. 1878.

Wells, Bruce

2008	"What Is Biblical Law? A Look at Pentateuchal Rules and Near Eastern Practice." *CBQ* 70:223-43.
2010	"The Hated Wife in Deuteronomic Law." *VT* 60:131-46.

Wenham, Gordon J.

1990-91	"The Old Testament Attitude to Homosexuality." *ExpTim* 102:259-363.

Wenham, Gordon J., and J. G. McConville

1980	"Drafting Techniques in Some Deuteronomic Laws." *VT* 30:248-52.

Wernberg-Møller, P.

1957	*The Manual of Discipline*. STDJ 1. Leiden: Brill.

Westbrook, Raymond

1977	"The Law of the Biblical Levirate." *RIDA* 3rd ser. 24:65-87.
1986	"The Prohibition on Restoration of Marriage in Deuteronomy 24:1-4." In Japhet 1986, 387-405.
1988a	*Old Babylonian Marriage Law*. AfO 23. Horn: Berger.

Bibliography

1988b   *Studies in Biblical and Cuneiform Law.* Cahiers de la Revue biblique 26. Paris: Gabalda.

1990   "Adultery in Ancient Near Eastern Law." *RB* 97:542-80.

Westcott, B. F., and F. J. A. Hort

1882   *The New Testament in the Original Greek.* New York: Harper & Bros. Repr. Peabody: Hendrickson, 1988.

Westhuizen, J. P. van der

1977   "Literary Device in Exodus 15:1-18 and Deut 32:1-43 as a Criterion for Determining Their Literary Standards." In *Studies in the Pentateuch,* ed. W. C. van Wyk. OTWSA 17-18. Pretoria: OTWSA, 57-73.

de Wette, Wilhelm Martin Leberecht

1830   "Dissertatio critica qua a prioribus deuteronomium pentateuchi libris diversum, alius cuiusdam recentioris auctoris opus esse monstratur." In *Opuscula theologica.* Berlin: Reimerum, 149-68. Orig. 1805.

1843   *A Critical and Historical Introduction to the Canonical Scriptures of the Old Testament.* Trans. and enlarged by Theodore Parker. 2 vols. Boston: Little and Brown. Orig. 1817.

Wevers, John William

1978   *Text History of the Greek Deuteronomy.* AAWG 106. MSU 13. Göttingen: Vandenhoeck & Ruprecht.

1995   *Notes on the Greek Text of Deuteronomy.* SBLSCSS 39. Atlanta: Scholars.

White, Sidnie Ann. See Crawford, Sidnie White

Whitehead, David

1977   *The Ideology of the Athenian Metic.* CPSSup 4. Cambridge: Cambridge Philological Society.

Wiener, Harold M.

1929   *The Composition of Judges II 11 to I Kings II 46.* Leipzig: Hinrichs.

Wilcox, Max

1977   "'Upon the Tree' — Deut 21:22-23 in the New Testament." *JBL* 96:85-99.

Wilkinson, John

1977   "Leprosy and Leviticus: The Problem of Description and Identification." *SJT* 30:153-69.

1978   "Leprosy and Leviticus: A Problem of Semantics and Translation." *SJT* 31:153-66.

Wilkinson, John Gardner

1883   *The Manners and Customs of the Ancient Egyptians.* 3 vols. Rev. ed. Samuel Birch. London: Murray.

1996   *The Ancient Egyptians: Their Life and Customs.* Vol. 1. London: Random House. Orig. 1853.

Wilson, Charles W.

1873   "Ebal and Gerizim, 1866." *PEFQS,* 66-71 + map.

Wilson, Ian

2008   "Central Sanctuary or Local Settlement? The Location of the Triennial Declaration (Dtn 26,13-15)." *ZAW* 120:323-40.

Wilton, Edward

1863   *The Negeb or "South Country" of Scripture.* London: Macmillan.

Winkler, A. J.

1962   *General Viticulture.* Berkeley: University of California Press.

Bibliography

Wiseman, D. J.
1953 *The Alalakh Tablets.* London: British Institute of Archaeology at Ankara.
1958 "The Vassal-Treaties of Esarhaddon." *Iraq* 20:1-99 + pls [=*The Vassal-Treaties of Esarhaddon.* London: British School of Archaeology in Iraq, 1958].
1974 "Murder in Mesopotamia." *Iraq* 36:249-60.

Wittstruck, Thorne
1976 "The So-Called Anti-Anthropomorphisms in the Greek Text of Deuteronomy." *CBQ* 38:29-34.

Wolff, Hans Walter
1956 "Hosea's geistige Heimat." *TLZ* 81:83-94 [= Wolff 1973, 232-50].
1973 *Gesammelte Studien zum Alten Testament.* 2nd ed. TB 22. Munich: Kaiser.

Woolley, C. Leonard, and T. E. Lawrence
1936 *The Wilderness of Zin.* London: Cape. Orig. 1915.

Wright, David P.
1987 "Deuteronomy 21:1-9 as a Rite of Elimination." *CBQ* 49:387-403.

Wright, G. Ernest
1938 "Troglodytes and Giants in Palestine." *JBL* 57:305-9.
1942 "The Terminology of Old Testament Religion and Its Significance." *JNES* 1:404-14.
1950 *The Old Testament Against Its Environment.* SBT 2. London: SCM.
1952 *God Who Acts: Biblical Theology as Recital.* SBT 8. London: SCM.
1954 "The Levites in Deuteronomy." *VT* 4:325-30.
1962 "The Lawsuit of God: A Form-Critical Study of Deuteronomy 32." In *Israel's Prophetic Heritage* (FS James Muilenburg), ed. Bernhard W. Anderson and Walter Harrelson. New York: Harper, 26-67.

Wright, Jacob L.
2008 "Warfare and Wanton Destruction: A Reexamination of Deuteronomy 20:19-20 in Relation to Ancient Siegecraft." *JBL* 127:423-58.

Yadin, Yigael
1962 *The Scroll of the War of the Sons of Light Against the Sons of Darkness.* Trans. Batya Rabin and Chaim Rabin. Oxford: Oxford University Press.
1963 *The Art of Warfare in Biblical Lands.* Trans. M. Pearlman. New York: McGraw-Hill and London: Weidenfeld and Nicolson.
1969 *Tefillin from Qumran (XQ Phyl 1-4).* Jerusalem: IES and Shrine of the Book. Hebrew orig. in *W. F. Albright Volume,* ed. A. Malamat. ErIsr 9. Jerusalem: IES, 1969, 60-83. [Hebrew]
1971 "Pesher Nahum (4Q pNahum) Reconsidered." *IEJ* 21:1-12.
1972 *Hazor.* Schweich Lectures, 1970. London: British Academy and Oxford University Press.
1976 "Beer-sheba: The High Place Destroyed by King Josiah." *BASOR* 222:5-17.

Yadin, Yigael, Jonas C. Greenfield, and Ada Yardeni
1994 "Babatha's *Ketubba.*" *IEJ* 44:75-101.

Yadin, Yigael, et al.
1961 *Hazor III-IV.* Jerusalem: Israel Exploration Society and Hebrew University of Jerusalem.

Yamauchi, Edwin M.
1973 "Cultic Prostitution." In Hoffner 1973, 213-22.
1980 "Two Reformers Compared: Solon of Athens and Nehemiah of Jerusalem." In Rendsburg et al. 1980, 269-92.

Bibliography

Yaron, Reuven
1957 "On Divorce in Old Testament Times." *RIDA* 3rd ser. 4:117-28.
1959 "Redemption of Persons in the Ancient Near East." *RIDA* 3rd ser. 6:155-76.
1960 *Gifts in Contemplation of Death in Jewish and Roman Law.* Oxford: Clarendon.
1961 *Introduction to the Law of the Aramaic Papyri.* Oxford: Clarendon.
1966 "The Restoration of Marriage." *JJS* 17:1-11.
1969 *The Laws of Eshnunna.* Jerusalem: Magnes, Hebrew University.
1970 "The Middle Assyrian Laws and the Bible." *Bib* 51:549-57.

Younker, Randall W.
1999 "Review of Archaeological Research in Ammon." In *Ancient Ammon,* ed. Burton MacDonald and Younker. Leiden: Brill, 1-19.

Zakovitch, Yair
1981 "The Woman's Rights in the Biblical Law of Divorce." *JLA* 4:28-46.

Zertal, Adam
1985 "Has Joshua's Altar Been Found on Mt. Ebal?" *BAR* 11/1:26-43.
1986 "How Can Kempinski Be So Wrong!" *BAR* 12/1:43, 49-53.
1991 "Israel Enters Canaan — Following the Pottery Trail." *BAR* 17/5:28-49, 75.

Zevit, Ziony
1976 "The 'Eglâ Ritual of Deuteronomy 21:1-9." *JBL* 95:377-90.

Zimmerli, Walther
1953 "Ich Bin Yahwe." In *Geschichte und Altes Testament* (FS Albrecht Alt). BHT 16. Tübingen: Mohr (Siebeck), 179-209. Eng. *I Am Yahweh.* Atlanta: John Knox, 1982, 1-28.

Zipor, Moshe A.
1996 "The Deuteronomic Account of the Golden Calf and Its Reverberation in Other Parts of the Book of Deuteronomy." *ZAW* 108:20-33.

Zohary, Michael
1982 *Plants of the Bible.* Cambridge: Cambridge University Press.

Zunz, Leopold
1873 "Bibelkritisches I: Deuteronomium." *ZDMG* 27:669-76.

Translation, Notes, and Comments

I. SUPERSCRIPTION TO THE PROLOGUE AND FIRST EDITION (1:1-5)

1 ¹*These are the words that Moses spoke to all Israel beyond the Jordan in the wilderness, in the Arabah opposite Suph, between Paran and Tophel; yes, Laban and Hazeroth and Dizahab.* ²*Eleven days it was from Horeb by the Seir Mountain road to Kadesh-barnea.* ³*And it happened in the fortieth year, in the eleventh month, on the first of the month, Moses spoke to the children of Israel according to all that Yahweh commanded him concerning them,* ⁴*after he struck down Sihon king of the Amorites, who ruled in Heshbon, and Og king of the Bashan, who ruled in Ashtaroth, in Edrei,* ⁵*beyond the Jordan in the land of Moab, Moses undertook to make plain this law, saying:*

Rhetoric and Composition

The book of Deuteronomy begins with a Prologue (1:1–4:49) consisting of the following parts: (1) a superscription and subscription, which summarize the historical survey making up the major portion of the Prologue (1:1-5; 4:44-49); (2) the historical survey, which recalls happenings between Israel's departure from Horeb and its arrival in the valley opposite Beth-peor (1:6–3:29); (3) an exhortation that Israel keep the covenant and the commandments, and a highly emotive testimony to Yahweh's greatness and Israel's relationship to its incomparable God (4:1-40); and (4) a naming of three refuge cities in the Transjordan territories (4:41-43).

The superscription is framed by a keyword inclusio (Lundbom 1996, 300-301):

Deuteronomy 1

> *These are the words*   v. 1
>   *that Moses spoke . . .*
>   *beyond the Jordan*

>   *beyond the Jordan . . .*   v. 5
>   *Moses undertook to make plain*
> *this law . . .*

The M^L has no section markings in all of ch. 1. Its first section marking is a *setumah* after 2:1. There are also no section markings to cite from M^A, since only the last six+ chapters of Deuteronomy in this codex are extant. The Sam has sections in ch. 1, but none after v. 5.

This superscription has been much discussed, particularly the relation between vv. 1-2 and vv. 3-5. Place names in vv. 1-2, assuming that "Arabah" and "opposite Suph" go together, are in the Sinai wilderness between Mount Horeb (= Mount Sinai) and Kadesh-barnea, not in the wilderness of Edom or Moab. Verses 1-2 introduce Moses' "words" to Israel in the Sinai wilderness. Place names in vv. 3-5 are in Gilead and Bashan, with the verses themselves introducing a "law" (תּוֹרָה) given forty years later by Moses in the plains of Moab, after Sihon and Og were defeated and the Israelite tribes were settled in their land. Critical scholars see the whole of vv. 1-5 as separate sources imperfectly harmonized (Driver; von Rad). Jewish tradition, however, unifies vv. 1-5 by assuming that Moses first addressed Israel in the Sinai wilderness, then repeated the address later in the plains of Moab (ibn Ezra; Ramban; Tigay).

In my view, the superscription of 1:1-5 and subscription of 4:44-49 (see Rhetoric and Composition of 4:44-49) summarize the Prologue. The superscription also introduces the sermonic and legal material in chs. 5–26, anticipating as well the blessings and curses of chs. 27–28. Verses 1-5 of the superscription form an inclusio with 28:69(29:1), delimiting the First Edition of the book of Deuteronomy (Lundbom 1975, 141 n. 155[= 1997, 28 n. 155]; 1996, 312-13):

> 1:1-5   *These are the words* that *Moses* spoke to *all Israel* beyond the Jordan . . . beyond the Jordan, *in the land of Moab,* Moses undertook to make plain *this law. . . .*

> 28:69[29:1]   *These are the words of the covenant* that Yahweh commanded Moses to cut with *the children of Israel in the land of Moab,* besides the covenant that he cut with them in Horeb.

Some scholars have suggested that the precise dating in v. 3 — perhaps also in v. 2 — have been added by the P writer, since days, months, and years are

Deuteronomy 1

not otherwise reckoned in Deuteronomy (Driver; von Rad; Moran; Weinfeld). Also, עַשְׁתֵּי־עָשָׂר ("the eleventh") in v. 3 is said to be a P expression (Exod 26:7-8; Num 7:72; 29:20). Editing by a P writer is certainly possible. But it should be noted that Deuteronomy elsewhere does specify the number of days (9:11, 18, 25; 10:10; 34:8) and years (2:7, 14; 8:2, 4; 29:4[5]; 31:2, 10; 34:7). And we must remember that these verses are a superscription, which means the scribe writing them — whether of the D or P school — could simply choose in this case to be numerically specific (cf. Amos 1:1; Jer 1:1-3; Ezek 1:1-2).

Portions of 1:1-5 are contained in 4QDeut^h; 11QDeut; and 4Q364.

Notes

1:1 The superscription begins by introducing Moses' address to Israel in the plains of Moab. Verse 2 adds specifics about the journey from Horeb to Kadesh-barnea.

These are the words. אֵלֶּה הַדְּבָרִים. This signature introduction, which is the Hebrew name for the book of Deuteronomy, occurs also in Jer 29:1 and 30:4. Rashi took "the words" to be "words of reproof," since Israel sinned in all the places mentioned (cf. T^{OnqNfPsJ}). "These words" cover addresses by Moses to Israel at Horeb and at Kadesh-barnea (see Rhetoric and Composition).

all Israel. A large mixed assembly (29:9-10[10-11]; 31:12). The expression occurs often in Deuteronomy (5:1; 13:12[11]; 21:21; 27:9; 29:1[2]; 31:1, 7, 11; 32:45; 34:12; Driver 1895, lxxxii no. 47). Assemblies in which all segments of the society were represented convened regularly and on special occasions, in Israel and throughout the ANE (see Note for 29:9-11).

beyond the Jordan. On the eastern side of the Jordan (v. 5). The AV has "on this side [of] the Jordan," which is not right. In 3:20, 25; 11:30 the term means "the west side of the Jordan," but not here, or in 1:5; 3:8; 4:41, 46, 47, 49. Von Rad (1962a, 832) says here at the very outset we learn that the writer is located in Palestine, west of the Jordan. Rashi* noted this, so also ibn Ezra† and Rashbam.‡ Because the descriptive phrase continues "in the wilderness, in the Arabah opposite Suph," the term "beyond the Jordan" must include the Sinai Peninsula. In v. 5 the term refers to the Moabite plains. This stretch in meaning may be explained as the writer wanting to speak generally of the area outside the promised land. Na'aman (1986, 250) says: "In the biblical tradition, the sojourn of the

---

*Rabbi Solomon ben Isaac (Rashi), whose dates are A.D. 1040-1105, was one of the most famous medieval Jewish commentators. He was born in Troyes, France.
†Ibn Ezra (A.D. 1089-1164) was a medieval Jewish commentator, born in Tudela, Spain.
‡Rabbi Samuel ben Meir (Rashbam) was a medieval Jewish commentator of the Hebrew Scriptures who lived in northern France ca. A.D. 1080-1160. He was a grandson of Rashi.

Israelites in the Sinai desert was regarded as an interlude outside the border of Canaan."

in the wilderness, in the Arabah opposite Suph. בַּמִּדְבָּר בָּעֲרָבָה מוֹל סוּף. This is the wilderness along the east coast of the Sinai Peninsula, bordering on the Gulf of Aqaba/Elath. "The Arabah" (הָעֲרָבָה) is used broadly in the OT to denote any portion of the Rift Valley extending from the Sea of Galilee in the north to the Gulf of Aqaba in the south (1:1; 2:8; 3:17; 4:49). This would include the Jordan Valley, through which the Jordan River flows, the Dead Sea and semi-desert areas on both sides of the Jordan, and the Wadi el-ʿArabah, which extends from the Dead Sea to the Gulf of Aqaba (2:8). Here the term apparently refers to the lowland extension into the Sinai Peninsula, along the Gulf of Aqaba. Without the definite article, עֲרָבָה simply means "desert" (Jer 2:6).

opposite Suph. מוֹל סוּף. The preposition מוֹל ("in front of, opposite") is usually מוּל; Driver suggests vowel dissimilation (GKC §27w) due to סוּף following. The Versons (LXX, T^{Onq}, Vg) take Suph as an abbreviated form of "Yam Suph" ("Sea of Reeds"), which is likely correct. Reference would then be to the eastern finger of the Red Sea (Gk: ἐρυθρᾶς [θαλάσσης]), which is the present-day Gulf of Aqaba or Gulf of Elath. This body of water is called the "Yam Suph" in 1:40; 1 Kgs 9:26; Jer 49:21. We are not talking about the "Sea of Reeds" crossed in the exodus (*pace* T^{NfPsJ}), which is further west. Nor is Suph to be identified with "Suphah" in Num 21:14, which is located in Moab and does not fit the itinerary from Horeb to Kadesh-barnea. Weinfeld thinks Suph may have been a location near the Sea, but the term makes better sense as the Sea itself.

between Paran and Tophel; yes, Laban and Hazeroth and Dizahab. Despite uncertainties of precise identification, all these sites except Tophel can be located in the Sinai Peninsula. The Paran and Tophel regions to the north, and Dizahab on the southern Sinai coast, suggest a listing from north to south, reversing a journey that actually went from south to north (v. 2).

between Paran and Tophel. Some commentators want to identify Paran with a specific site (Weinfeld; Tigay), but the term is probably an abbreviation for "Wilderness of Paran," the main desert of east-central Sinai (1 Kgs 11:17-18), which extends from Horeb (Num 10:12) to Kadesh-barnea (Num 13:3, 26), and into the Negeb (1 Sam 25:1). The area has mountains (מֵהַר פָּארָן) in Deut 33:2 and Hab 3:3 is best translated "from the mountains of Paran"; cf. Simons 1959, 256). Attempts to identify Tophel with eṭ-Ṭafileh, an oasis between Kerak and Petra in ancient Edom (E. Robinson 1867, 2:167; Driver), have not been successful. Cazelles (1959) thinks that Tophel is a territory (not a city) in the Dead Sea region, suiting the present context admirably by providing a general reference in the east to balance off the general reference to the Paran wilderness in the west.

Laban. This appears to be the Libnah ("white place") cited with the not-far-distant Hazeroth in Num 33:17-20 (Driver; B. Mazar 1981, 6), both encampments on the journey to Kadesh. In Numbers Hazeroth is cited first, which means it lies south of Libnah. Here Laban is cited first, but as we mentioned, the present listing is from north to south. This is not the Libnah in the Shephelah (Josh 15:42; 21:13; 2 Kgs 19:8), conquered by Shishak I (Olmstead 1931, 354). Nor is it the Laban cited in the annals of Sargon II (Tadmor 1958, 78; *ANET*³, 286), which lies on the (Mediterranean) coast, on the border of "the Brook of Egypt" (= Wadi el-ʿArish). This location is too far north, and the two places should be kept separate (Levine 2000, 518; *pace* Ahituv 1984, 129; Weinfeld). The Laban here has to be in the Sinai Peninsula south of Kadesh-barnea, its exact location unknown.

Hazeroth. This is doubtless the Hazeroth of Num 33:17-18, commonly identified with ʿAin el-Khadrā, an oasis 36 km northeast of the traditional Mount Sinai, on the eastern coast of the Sinai Peninsula (Burckhardt 1992, 495; E. Robinson 1867, 1:151; Driver; Simons 1959, 255; Levine 2000, 519; Jericke 2008, 48-49). Numbers 12:16 says the people set out from Hazeroth for the Wilderness of Paran.

Dizahab. The site is probably to be identified with modern Dhahab on the eastern coast of Sinai (Burckhardt 1992, 523; Driver; Jericke 2008, 49-50), which is nearly due east of the traditional Mount Sinai and on the modern road from Taba to Sharm el Sheikh. Burckhardt found it to be a pleasant oasis with date palms and the best drinking water on the coast. Driver says דִּי זָהָב suggests a place productive of gold (LXX: Καταχρύσεα). The Vg does not translate as a place name, instead attaching *ubi auri est plurimum* ("where is much gold") to Hazeroth, which Luther recognized as not being right.

2 See 1:19. Modern travelers have made it from the traditional Mount Sinai (Jebel Musa) to Kadesh-barnea in eleven days (G. Davies 1979, 95-96; Weinfeld), a distance of some 160-170 mi (Driver). The reckoning here, which is from south to north, reverses the north to south listing of v. 1.

Horeb. חֹרֵב (lit. "desert, wasteland") is the name for Mount Sinai in Deuteronomy (except 33:2), though it does occur elsewhere in the OT (Exod 3:1; 17:6; 33:6; 1 Kgs 8:9 = 2 Ch 5:10; 1 Kgs 19:8; Mal 3:22[4:4]; Ps 106:19). Jerome (*Sit.*) expressed the opinion that Horeb and Sinai were one and the same mountain. The Israelites, after their miraculous deliverance from Egypt, entered into a covenant at Horeb with Yahweh their God. At this mountain they also received the Ten Commandments. From Horeb the Israelites journeyed to the land promised to their fathers, arriving there eventually, but only after forty years of wandering in the wilderness.

The location of Mount Horeb/Sinai has been much discussed. Biblical geography and ancient tradition combine to support a location in the southern Sinai Peninsula, although sites in the northern Sinai, northwest Arabia, and elsewhere have been proposed (G. E. Wright, *IDB*, 4:377-78; G. Davies 1979, 87-89; Beit-Arieh 1988, 35-37). Cross (1988, 59) even argued that Sinai/Horeb should be located in southern Edom or northern Midian, which is a stretch. Beit-Arieh points out that the largest concentration of ancient settlements is to be found in south-central Sinai, an area with acacia and palm trees, perennial bushes, and seasonal grasses making it ecologically well-suited to sustain life. A southern Sinai location continues to be favored by most scholars, gaining also a measure of support from the travel time stated in the present verse (G. Davies 1979, 101).

In the south are three mountains over 6000 ft: Jebel Katerina (8652 ft), Jebel Musa (7486 ft), and Jebel Serbal (6791 ft), all of which have been identified with Mount Horeb. Jebel Katerina and Jebel Musa are right next to each other; Jebel Serbal is some distance to the west, by Wadi Fieran. Jewish tradition has not attempted to locate the sacred site. By the 4th cent. A.D., Christian tradition had settled upon Jebel Musa (Eusebius of Caesarea). On its northern slope is Saint Catherine's Monastery, built by Justinian in A.D. 527 on the site where Helena, mother of Constantine, built a church two centuries earlier. An early Christian center was also located at Jebel Serbal, but records of the 4th cent. already indicate that Horeb was not here, but rather 35 Roman milestones distant (G. E. Wright, *IDB*, 4:377).

by the Seir Mountain road. דֶּרֶךְ הַר־שֵׂעִיר. Or "by way of the Seir Mountains." For the expression "on the road/in the way" in Deuteronomy, see Note for 1:19. Hebrew הַר can mean "mountain" or "mountainous region" (Driver; cf. Gen 36:9). The narrator here is naming the route taken from Horeb to Kadesh-barnea, which would be the easternmost Sinai road leading to the Seir Mountains (Trumbull 1884, 76-80). On the land of Seir, see Note for 2:4.

Kadesh-barnea. An oasis in the Wilderness of Zin (32:51; Num 20:1; 27:14; 33:36; 34:4), sometimes linked with "the waters of Meriba(t)h" (1:46; cf. Num 20:13; 27:14), and sometimes referred to as just "Kadesh" (Num 13:26; 20:1, 14, 16, and passim). From here the spies left to scout out the promised land, and soon afterwards the entire Israelite company made their first attempt to penetrate that land, which was not successful (1:19-46; cf. Numbers 13-14). In the 19th cent. Kadesh-barnea was identified with ʿAin el-Weibeh (E. Robinson 1867, 2:175, 194), then later with ʿAin Qadis, which preserves the ancient name (Trumbull 1884, 241; Driver). But Schmidt (1910, 73) was more impressed with ʿAin el-Qudeirat, and so were Woolley and Lawrence (1936, 86-88) in their travels through the area. They took a broader view, however, preferring to equate Kadesh-barnea with the entire Kossaima district, which would include both ʿAin Qadis and ʿAin el-Qudeirat. ʿAin el-Qudeirat is the largest oasis in northern Sinai (Beit-Arieh 1988, 30, with a picture), its spring said to have a water flow of 40 cu m per hour (Dothan 1965, 134). In antiquity the oasis was a junction of two important roads: one going from Suez eastward to Beersheba and

Deuteronomy 1

Hebron, the other a branch of the Via Maris from el-ʿArish or Rafiaḥ, heading south to the Gulf of Aqaba.

3 We are now brought up-to-date, being introduced here to Moses' address forty years later in the plains of Moab. This is the discourse of Deuteronomy, a series of many addresses made into one long address. Some scholars take the present verse to be an addition by the Priestly writer, but the mention of years, months, and days in a superscription might be expected from any scribe (see Rhetoric and Composition).

the fortieth year. Forty years may be a round number (2:7; 8:2; Amos 2:10; 5:25; Neh 9:21). A subtle irony exists in the juxtaposition of forty years with the eleven days of v. 2 (Tigay; Friedman).

eleventh month. In the later calendar this would be the month of Shebat (January-February).

4 Moses directed the conquest of Transjordan, which is recounted in 2:24–3:11. These battles, reported also in Num 21:21-35, contrast with the earlier beating taken from the Canaanites at Hormah (1:44; Num 14:45). At the same time they anticipate the successful conquest of Canaan under Joshua. The defeats of Sihon and Og were celebrated in Israel's psalmnody (Pss 135:11; 136:19-20). After the defeat of Sihon and Og, Sihon's territory was given to Reuben and Gad, and Og's territory to the half-tribe of Manasseh (3:12-13). Here and elsewhere Sihon is called "king of the Amorites" and Og "king of the Bashan"; nevertheless, biblical tradition considers both kings to be Amorite (4:47; 31:4; Josh 2:10; 9:10; 24:12). In Josh 9:10 Sihon is called "king of Heshbon," being identified there with the city from which he ruled.

Sihon king of the Amorites. On Sihon's kingdom in southern Gilead, see Note for 2:24.

who ruled in Heshbon. אֲשֶׁר יוֹשֵׁב בְּחֶשְׁבּוֹן. The verb יָשַׁב usually means either "sit" or "dwell." Some English Versions translate "dwelt," or the like, in the present verse (AV; RSV; NAB; NJV; NJB), but the meaning may be "sat (enthroned)," i.e., "ruled" (Weinfeld; NEB; NRSV). This meaning for יָשַׁב occurs in Ps 29:10, also in Amos 1:8, where יוֹשֵׁב מֵאַשְׁדּוֹד is to be rendered "the ruler from Ashdod." But Josh 12:2 states that Sihon dwelt (יָשַׁב) in Heshbon and ruled (מָשַׁל) from Aroer. On "Heshbon," see Note for 2:24.

Og king of the Bashan. On Og's kingdom in "the Bashan" (הַבָּשָׁן), see Note for 3:1.

in Ashtaroth, in Edrei. בְּעַשְׁתָּרֹת בְּאֶדְרֶעִי. The LXX, S, and Vg add a conjunction: "in Ashtaroth *and* in Edrei" (Josh 12:4; 13:31). But 4QDeut[h] supports the reading of MT (Ulrich et al. 1995, 63-64). Ashtaroth is named as the residence of Og in Josh 9:10, with Edrei apparently being a second royal city (Josh 13:12). Edrei is where Moses battled and defeated Og (3:1; Num 21:33-35). Eusebius *(Onom.)* put Ashtaroth about 6 Roman milestones from Edrei.

Deuteronomy 1

Ashtaroth is commonly identified with Tell ʿAshterah, a site along the King's Highway in Syria, about 20 mi east of the Sea of Galilee (Schumacher 1886, 209-10; Driver; Albright 1925, 15). It is near Karnaim (Gen 14:5: Ashteroth-Karnaim), which has been identified as Tell Saʿad, 3 mi northeast of Tell ʿAshterah (Albright 1925, 14-15; *ABD*, 1:491). Ashtaroth is mentioned in Late Bronze Egyptian, Assyrian, and Ugaritic texts (Ahituv 1984, 72-73; J. Day, *ABD*, 1:491). In the Amarna Letters (EA 256), the city is called "Ashtartu" (*ANET*³, 486). Edrei is also mentioned in Ugaritic and Egyptian texts (Ahituv 1984, 90-91). This ancient site has been identified as Derʿa in modern Syria, about 30 mi east of the Jordan River, and 60 mi south of Damascus, situated on an eastern tributary of the Yarmuk (Schumacher 1886, 148; Driver; Albright 1925, 16; Tigay, 418). The site has been continuously occupied since the 3rd mill. (Albright).

5 *in the land of Moab.* Reference is to Beth-peor, in Moab's high northern plateau region, in a valley below Mount Nebo (see Note for 3:29). Tigay 1996 believes the territory is called "the land of Moab" because it belonged to Moab before Sihon took it from Moab (Num 21:26). However, by the 7th cent. it had again been Moabite for nearly two centuries (Moabite Stone, line 10). At the time of Israel's Transjordanian conquest, cities on the descent included Kiriathaim, Sibmah, and Zerethshahar (Josh 13:19), and in the Jordan Valley, Bethharam, Bethnimrah, Succoth, and Zaphon (Josh 13:27).

Moses undertook to make plain this law. הוֹאִיל מֹשֶׁה בֵּאֵר אֶת־הַתּוֹרָה הַזֹּאת. Driver says the auxiliary יאל in the H-stem means "to resolve, take upon oneself" (RSV; NEB; NJV; NRSV; NJB; cf. Gen 18:27; Hos 5:11). The verb באר in the Piel means "to make distinct, plain," and תּוֹרָה means "law" or "teaching," although here and in 4:44 it is usually taken as denoting the Deuteronomic law. Nevertheless, Deuteronomy is teaching (and preaching) about the law and other things. It teaches Israel about Yahweh, the covenant demands, and how Israel is to worship Yahweh its God. It describes life lived under blessing and curse and how Israel can choose either. It teaches about faithlessness and rebellion in Israel's first attempt to take Canaan (ch. 1), earlier rebellions in the wilderness (ch. 9), and about Israel's success in taking the Transjordan when it followed Yahweh's leading (chs. 2–3). Moses wants to make this all clear so people will hear, understand, and in the end obey.

this law. הַתּוֹרָה הַזֹּאת. A stock expression in Deuteronomy, occurring 19 times (1:5; 4:8; 17:18-19; 27:3, 8, 26; 28:58; 29:28[29], etc.; Weinfeld 1972, 339 no. 23). It means the same as "this commandment" (הַמִּצְוָה הַזֹּאת), on which see Note for 6:25.

Deuteronomy 1

Message and Audience

This superscription introduces the First Edition of Deuteronomy (1:1–28:69 [29:1]), and eventually the entire book, to audiences beginning in the late eighth or early seventh cents., telling them that they are about to hear words that Moses spoke to all Israel beyond the Jordan, in the wilderness of Sinai, after the people left Horeb on their way to the promised land. The route to Kadesh-barnea is described in summary fashion; mentioned also is the time it took to make the trip: eleven days. The audience then learns that only after forty years had passed, which makes for a striking contrast with eleven days, Moses addressed the people after the defeat of Sihon and Og and Israel had taken possession of their Transjordanian territories. This happened while the people were still beyond the Jordan, in the land of Moab. There Moses undertook to make plain the teaching now to be heard.

II. PROLOGUE TO THE DEUTERONOMIC LAW (1:6–4:40)

A. THE LAND IS SET BEFORE YOU (1:6-46)

1 *⁶Yahweh our God spoke to us at Horeb: "Long enough you have remained at this mountain; ⁷turn and take your journey, and enter the hill country of the Amorites, and into all its neighbors in the Arabah, in the hill country, and in the Shephelah, and in the Negeb, and by the seacoast, land of the Canaanites, and the Lebanon, as far as the great river, the river Euphrates. ⁸See, I have set the land before you; enter and take possession of the land that Yahweh swore to your fathers — to Abraham to Isaac and to Jacob — to give to them and to their descendants after them."*

⁹And I said to you at that time: "I am not able to bear you alone. ¹⁰Yahweh your God has multiplied you, and look you are today as the stars of the heaven in number. ¹¹Yahweh God of your fathers add to you the likes of you a thousand times, and may he bless you as he spoke to you! ¹²How can I bear the burden of you alone, and your load and your strife? ¹³Provide for yourselves wise and discerning and experienced men, according to your tribes, and I will appoint them as your heads." ¹⁴And you answered me and said, "The thing that you have said to do is good." ¹⁵So I took the heads of your tribes, men of wisdom and experience, and I made them heads over you, chiefs of thousands and chiefs of hundreds and chiefs of fifties and chiefs of tens, also officials for your tribes. ¹⁶And I commanded your judges at that time: "Hear between your brethren, and judge righteously between a person and his brother and his sojourner. ¹⁷You shall not pay regard to faces in judgment. The small like the great you shall hear. You shall not be afraid

Deuteronomy 1

of the face of a person, for the judgment — it belongs to God. And the case that is too difficult for you, you shall bring it near to me and I will hear it." ¹⁸And I commanded you at that time all the things that you should do.

¹⁹And we took our journey from Horeb, and we went through all that great and terrible wilderness that you saw on the road to the hill country of the Amorites, just as Yahweh our God commanded us, and we came as far as Kadesh-barnea. ²⁰And I said to you, "You have come up to the hill country of the Amorites that Yahweh our God is giving to us. ²¹See, Yahweh your God has set the land before you; go up, take possession, as Yahweh God of your fathers spoke to you; do not fear and do not be dismayed." ²²Then all of you came near to me and said, "Let us send men before us, and let them search out the land for us, and let them bring back word to us regarding the road on which we will go up, and the cities into which we shall enter." ²³The thing seemed good in my eyes, and I took from you twelve men, one man for each tribe. ²⁴And they turned and went up into the hill country, and they came up to Wadi Eshcol and explored it. ²⁵And they took in their hand from the fruit of the land and brought it down to us, and they brought back word to us and said, "The land is good that Yahweh our God is giving to us." ²⁶Yet you were not willing to go up, and you rebelled against the mouth of Yahweh your God. ²⁷And you grumbled in your tents, and you said, "Because Yahweh hates us he brought us out from the land of Egypt to give us into the hand of the Amorites to completely destroy us. ²⁸To where are we going up? Our brethren have made our hearts melt, saying, 'A people greater and taller than we; great cities fortified up to heaven, and even sons of the Anakim we saw there!'" ²⁹Then I said to you, "Do not tremble and do not be fearful of them. ³⁰Yahweh your God is the one going before you; he, he will fight for you according to all that he did with you in Egypt before your eyes, ³¹and in the wilderness, where you saw how Yahweh your God lifted you up as a man lifts up his son, on every road that you went until you came up to this place. ³²And in this thing you do not believe in Yahweh your God, ³³who goes before you on the road to seek out for you a place to encamp, in fire by night, to show you on what road you should go, and in cloud by day."

³⁴And Yahweh heard the sound of your words, and he was furious and swore: ³⁵"Not one of these men, this evil generation, shall see the good land that I swore to give to their fathers, ³⁶except Caleb son of Jephunneh; he, he shall see it, and to him I will give the land on which he has set foot, and to his children, because he has gone fully after Yahweh." ³⁷Even with me Yahweh was angry on account of you, saying, "Even you, you will not enter there. ³⁸Joshua son of Nun, who is standing before you, he, he will enter there. Strengthen him, for he, he will cause Israel to inherit it. ³⁹And your little ones who you said would become a prey, and your children who today do not know good from evil, they, they shall enter there, and to them I will give it, and they, they shall possess it. ⁴⁰As for you, turn and take your journey toward the wilderness on the Sea of Reeds road."

⁴¹*And you answered and said to me, "We have sinned before Yahweh; we, we will go up and we will fight according to all that Yahweh our God commanded us." And each man put on his war gear, and you thought it easy to go up into the hill country.* ⁴²*And Yahweh said to me, Say to them: "You shall not go up and you shall not fight, for I am not in your midst, and will you not be smitten before your enemies?"* ⁴³*And I spoke to you and you did not listen, and you rebelled against the mouth of Yahweh, and you were presumptuous and went up into the hill country.* ⁴⁴*And the Amorites who lived in that hill country came out to meet you, and they pursued you as bees do, and they beat you down in Seir as far as Hormah.* ⁴⁵*And you returned and wept before Yahweh, but Yahweh did not listen to your voice, and did not give you an ear.* ⁴⁶*So you remained at Kadesh many days, according to the days that you remained.*

Rhetoric and Composition

The Prologue to Deuteronomy (1:6–4:40), which some take to be Moses' first discourse (Driver; Moran; Tigay), begins by recalling events that took place between Israel's departure from Horeb and its arrival at the valley opposite Beth-peor (1:6–3:29). This historical survey is based on (JE) traditions of Exodus and Numbers (Driver; Weinfeld) but tells the story in its own way. Moses begins by reporting Yahweh's command that the people leave Horeb and take their journey to enter the land promised to them (1:6-8). But before leaving Horeb, he recalls instructions given to the people on the installation of judges (1:9-18). Then Moses relates Israel's disbelief and disobedience, showing itself first in an unwillingness to go up into the land and then repeating when the people decide to go after Yahweh says not to go. They were defeated, painfully defeated (1:19-46). Moran (1963a) calls the misadventure Israel's "unholy war and anti-Exodus."

The M^L has no section markings in this chapter. Its first *setumah* comes after 2:1. A break is better made after 1:46 (so *BHS* and RSV), which is the chapter division. The Sam has sections after 1:8, 18, 23a, 28, 33, and 41 (von Gall 1918, 361-64). There may also be a section after v. 8 in 2QDeut^a (Baillet, Milik, and de Vaux 1962, 60; Oesch 1979, 267-68), which would support the independence of vv. 9-18 on the installation of judges.

The historical survey, generally taken as a carefully constructed literary whole (Lohfink 1960; D. McCarthy 1963, 131), is tied together by an inclusio (Lohfink 1968, 15):

1:6 Long enough *you have remained* (לָכֶם שֶׁבֶת) at this mountain
3:29 So we remained (וַנֵּשֶׁב) in the valley opposite Beth-peor.

The opening portion is likewise delimited by an inclusio:

1:6   Yahweh our God spoke to us at Horeb: *Long enough you have remained* (רַב־לָכֶם שֶׁבֶת) *at this mountain.* . . .
1:46 *So you remained* (וַתֵּשְׁבוּ) at Kadesh *many* (רַבִּים) days, according to the days that *you remained* (יְשַׁבְתֶּם).

The appointment of judges (1:9-18) is tied together by this keyword inclusio:

1:9   *at that time*   בָּעֵת הַהִוא
1:18 *at that time*   בָּעֵת הַהִוא

The expression "at that time" occurs again in the middle of the unit (v. 16), which may be part of a larger rhetorical structure in the verses.

In vv. 20-31 is a speaker chiasmus (Lohfink 1960, 122; 1968, 15; Moran, 261); the report of the scouts is the turning point:

```
[Yahweh]          vv. 6-8
  Moses           vv. 20-21
    People        v. 22
      Scouts      v. 25
    People        vv. 27-28
  Moses           vv. 29-31
[Yahweh]          vv. 34-36
```

It is unclear, however, whether Yahweh's speech belongs to the structure (Lohfink 1968, 15 omits it). It is more convincingly included if vv. 9-18 are taken to be a later insertion. In any case, the two Yahweh speeches are nicely balanced: in vv. 6-8 Yahweh gives Israel the land; in vv. 34-36 he retracts the gift. For speaker chiasms of a similar nature in Jeremiah, see Lundbom 1999, 83-84.

Another chiastic structure is seen in the naming of dramatis personae in vv. 35-40 (Moran):

```
People            v. 35
  Caleb           v. 36
    Moses         v. 37
  Joshua          v. 38
People            vv. 39-40
```

Caleb and Joshua are the two scouts granted entrance into the promised land because of their good report (cf. Num 32:11-12). Moses, at the center, is denied entrance. The present generation is also denied entrance (v. 35), but the next generation (= your little ones and children not yet adults) will go in (v. 39). Verse 40 reiterates in different terms the judgment of v. 35: The faithless generation is left to wander in the wilderness.

Portions of 1:6-46 are contained in 1QDeut[a], 1QDeut[b], 2QDeut[a], 4QDeut[h], 4QpaleoDeut[r]; and 4Q364.

Notes

1:6 *Yahweh our God spoke to us at Horeb.* Language here at the start is noticeably personal in the naming of God. This will continue throughout Deuteronomy, with the expression, "Yahweh our/your God," repeating in vv. 10, 11, 19, 20, 21(2x), 25, 26, 30, 31, 32, and 41, and occurring over 300 times in Deuteronomy (Driver 1895, lxxix). Emphasis is placed on the close relationship between Israel and its God, bonded as they will be in the Horeb covenant. Horeb = (Mount) Sinai.

Long enough you have remained at this mountain. רַב־לָכֶם שֶׁבֶת בָּהָר הַזֶּה. On the idiom רַב־לָכֶם (lit. "too much for/from you"), see 2:3 and 3:26 (with לְךָ). Here, and in 2:3, it means "long enough for you." The command to leave the holy mountain appears also in Exod 33:1.

7 This is the expanded "promised land" viewed by Deuteronomy, appearing also in other OT sources (11:24; 19:8-9; cf. Gen 15:18; Exod 23:31; Josh 1:3-5). Yahweh's promise of land to the patriarchs, presented now as a (royal) gift to Israel, is central in Deuteronomic preaching. Hebrew הַר here means "(the) hill country" (cf. 3:25), perhaps playing on הָר ("mountain") in v. 6. Israel is leaving one mountainous area for another. Psalm 78:54 calls the Amorite hill country Yahweh's "holy land."

turn and take your journey. פְּנוּ וּסְעוּ לָכֶם. A fixed expression occurring again in 1:40 and 2:1 (cf. 2:24 and Num 14:25). The verb נסע (lit. "pull up tent pegs") means "break camp and move on." Israel will move from camp to camp toward their destination (Num 33:1-49).

and enter the hill country of the Amorites. The "hill country of the Amorites" is here the entire central highlands of Palestine, both north and south of Jerusalem. In this first attempt to enter the land, which failed, Amorites were living in the southern highlands settled subsequently by Judah and Simeon (1:19-20, 44). The Gibeonites, living north of Jerusalem, were also a remnant of the Amorites (2 Sam 21:2). "Amorites" is a name given in the OT to the pre-Israelite inhabitants of Canaan and Transjordan (see Note for 2:24). Sihon and Og in Transjordan were Amorite kings (3:8; 4:47; 31:4). In Mesopotamian documents of the 2nd and 3rd mill., "the land of *Amurrû*" referred to "the West" or "the Westland," designating territory west of the Euphrates all the way to the Mediterranean, i.e., Syria and Palestine (Y. Aharoni 1979, 65-66, 149-50). The term occurs also in the 18th cent. Mari Letters (Malamat 1970); the Amarna Letters of Egypt (Gardiner 1947, 1:187-88); and in Neo-Assyrian documents (*ANET*³, 275, 277, 278). The *Amurrû* are the Amorites.

and into all its neighbors in the Arabah, in the hill country, and in the Shephelah, and in the Negeb, and by the seacoast, land of the Canaanites, and the Lebanon, as far as the great river, the river Euphrates. The gift of land is a larger region, populated by peoples other than the Amorites. "Neighbors in the Arabah . . . and by the seacoast" would be the Canaanites, who are named ("land of the Canaanites" defines the preceding "by the seacoast"). The Canaanites lived mainly along the Mediterranean seacoast and in the lowlands of the Arabah, i.e., on the west side of the Jordan between Chinnereth (the Sea of Galilee) and the Dead Sea (Gen 10:19; Deut 11:30; Num 13:29; Josh 5:1; 11:3). Israel had already settled the Arabah east of the Jordan (3:17; 4:49; Josh 12:3). The name "Canaan" first appears in an 18th-cent. text from Mari, occurring frequently as *Kinaḫḫi* also in the 14th cent. Amarna Letters (e.g., EA 137; RA xix, 100; *ANET*³, 484). Reference there is primarily to the Phoenician coastal area. The term has broader usage in Egyptian texts, denoting the entire region of Egyptian rule in Palestine and Syria (Y. Aharoni 1979, 67-69). This would take in an area from about Ekron and Timnah in the south, to Tyre and Sidon in the north.

In addition to being home for the Amorites, the "hill country" contained a mixed population of Hittites, Girgashites, Jebusites, Amalekites, Canaanites, and Perizzites (7:1; cf. Num 14:45; Josh 11:3). The Shephelah (= the lowland) is the foothill area west and southwest of Jerusalem, sloping down to the coastal plain (Rainey 1983). For its Judahite cities and villages, see Josh 15:33-44. The Negeb in the OT is the arid region (Negeb = "dry land") south of the hill country, extending roughly from Beersheba to Kadesh-barnea in the Wilderness of Zin (cf. Num 13:17, 21). It is called "the south" in the AV. Cities in the Negeb are listed in Josh 15:21-32. The Negeb is not actually desert; in the Early and Middle Bronze Ages short-lived settlements existed in parts of the area (*EncJud*, 12:928). But in the Late Bronze Age there is virtually no evidence of settled occupation throughout the Negeb (Glueck 1955, 28-29; *ABD*, 4:1061-64; however, see Bartlett 1969, 19-20). This would suggest little opposition for the Israelites in their journey from Kadesh into the hill country.

In the OT, "the Lebanon" refers primarily to the two mountain ranges in modern Lebanon: the Lebanon range, running parallel to the Phoenician coast, and the Anti-Lebanon range further inland. In between is the Bekaa Valley, an extension of the northern Jordan Valley (= "valley of Lebanon"). Mount Hermon is at the southern extremity of the Anti-Lebanon. The Lebanon range, with its natural beauty (3:25; Isa 35:2; Jer 22:6), agricultural abundance (Ps 72:16), snow-covered peaks (Jer 18:14), and celebrated stands of cedar and other trees (1 Kgs 4:33; 5:22[8]; Isa 10:34; Cant 5:15), was originally envisioned as a western boundary of the promised land in the north (11:24; Josh 1:4), but it never became part of Israel (Judg 3:3). Only the very southern portion of the valley of Lebanon was penetrated by Joshua (Josh 11:17; 12:7), and Solomon is said to have had building projects in Lebanon, perhaps in this southern area (1 Kgs 9:19). On Lebanon, see further R. H. Smith in *ABD*, 4:269-70.

The eastern limit of the promised land in the north was to be the Euphrates River, which would be its northeastern segment in upper Syria (11:24; Gen 15:18; Exod 23:31; Josh 1:4). This expanded view of the promised land may have originated with the conquests of David in the 10th cent. (G. E. Wright; cf. 2 Sam 8:3). Solomon, too, according to 1 Kgs 5:1(4:21), ruled kingdoms all the way to the Euphrates. In the Bible, also in Mesopotamian documents, one commonly finds clichés such as "from river to river," "from sea to sea," "from mountain to mountain," or the like (Gen 15:18; Exod 23:31; Mic 7:12; Ps 72:8; Weinfeld 1983a, 97-99). The description here is similar: Land to be conquered is to be from "the (Mediterranean) seacoast" to "the river Euphrates." In extrabiblical texts the cliché commonly describes the extent of imperial rule. In a Neo-Assyrian inscription, Adad-Nirari III (810-783) boasts that he has conquered territories

> from the Siluna mountain of the Rising Sun . . . as far as the Great Sea of the Rising Sun (and) from the banks of the Euphrates . . . as far as the shore of the Great Sea of the Setting Sun. (*ANET*[3], 281; cf. Josh 1:4)

the great river, the River Euphrates. In the NT, see Rev 9:14 and 16:12.

8 *See, I have set the land before you.* רְאֵה נָתַתִּי לִפְנֵיכֶם אֶת־הָאָרֶץ. "(See) I have set before you" is a stereotyped expression in Deuteronomy, referring to the land, the law, the blessing and curse, and the way of life over against the way of death (1:8, 21 [Yahweh is subject]; 2:31 [Yahweh is subject]; 4:8; 11:26, 32 ; 30:1, 15, 19; cf. Driver 1895, lxxxii no. 52; Weinfeld 1972, 346 no. 7). On נתן meaning "to give over, deliver," where reference is to Yahweh delivering up foes to someone else, see Note for 2:31. Here Yahweh is giving Israel a gift of land. On the gift of land as a royal grant, see Weinfeld 1970-72. The imperative רְאֵה ("see!") is here an interjection similar to the more common הִנֵּה ("look, behold!"); it occurs in 1:21; 2:24, 31; 11:26; 30:15; Josh 6:2; 8:1, etc. Nebuzaradan, representing the Babylonian king, says to Jeremiah after releasing him from his chains: "See, the whole land is before you" (Jer 40:4): a royal land grant of sorts. Similarly, when the Hittite king gives his vassal a gift of land, he says: "See, I gave you the Zippašla mountain land, occupy it!" (Weinfeld 1972, 72). On the significance of land in the OT, see Bewer 1938.

enter and take possession of the land that Yahweh swore to your fathers — to Abraham to Isaac and to Jacob — to give to them and to their descendants after them. This was Yahweh's promise — buttressed by a covenant — to Abraham (Gen 12:7; 13:14-15; 15:12-21; 17:1-14), that (1) Abraham would receive a myriad of descendants (Gen 12:2; 13:16; 15:5; 17:2-7; 22:17a) and (2) that his descendants would be given the land in which he was presently sojourning (Gen 12:7; 13:14-15, 17; 15:18; 17:8; 22:17b). According to Gen 15:13-14, this promise would be fulfilled following a slavery of his descendants and a deliverance from that slavery. The covenant was repeated to Isaac (Gen 26:3-4, 24) and to Jacob (Gen 28:13-14). The land in question therefore became known as the "promised land," which Ottosson (1988) thinks may have been conceptualized on the basis of the garden of Eden (Genesis 2). Initial borders of this land would be enlarged (12:20; 19:8; cf. 7:22). Yahweh's gift of land is reaffirmed all throughout Deuteronomy, being mentioned no less than 20 times with specific reference to Abraham, Isaac, and Jacob, or the fathers (1:8, 35; 6:10, 18, 23; 7:13; 8:1; 9:5; 10:11; 11:9, 21; 19:8; 26:3, 15; 27:3; 28:11; 30:20; 31:7, 20; 34:4). When Israel comes into possession of the land, Yahweh's oath to the fathers will be confirmed (9:5). On Yahweh as "God of the fathers," see v. 11.

In core Deuteronomy (1–28), the unconditional covenant made with Abraham is qualified by the covenant made with Israel at Horeb, which was conditional. This latter could be gravely broken, in which case a number of frightful curses would fall upon the nation, the most serious of which would be a loss of the land. Deuteronomy makes land tenure more conditional than any other OT law code. No one understood this better than Jeremiah, who, while affirming Yahweh's gift of land to the fathers (Jer 3:18; 7:7, 14; 11:5; 16:15), preached at great cost that tenure in the land was contingent upon covenant obedience (Jer 7:5-7) or else a repentance of covenant disobedience (Jer 25:5; 35:15). In the end, the prophet concluded to his great sorrow that the land would be lost (Jer 7:12-15; 21:9-10; 24:10; 25:8-11, etc.). Jeremiah is recorded as saying that the land grant to the fathers and to Israel was to be for all time (Jer 7:7; 25:5; cf. Lundbom 1999, 464; 2004a, 244-45), which goes considerably beyond anything said in core Deuteronomy, where obedience to the covenant will simply enable Israel "to live long in the land that you shall possess" (5:33; 11:9; 32:47; cf. 4:26; 30:18). Driver claimed that the words "and to their descendants" emphasized the perpetuity of the land promise, but that is a stretch. In any case, permanent loss of land is ruled out in the enlarged Deuteronomy (ch. 30) and in Jeremiah (16:15; chs. 30–32), where it is stated that after divine punishment Israel will once again repossess the land.

and take possession of the land. וּרְשׁוּ אֶת־הָאָרֶץ. The verb ירשׁ means "*to take possession* of the land" (1:8, 21, 39; 2:24, 31; 3:12, 18, 20; 4:1, 5, etc.) and in the H-stem "*to dispossess* another nation" (2:12, 22; 4:38; 7:17; 9:3, 4, 5; 11:23; 18:12). It occurs very often in Deuteronomy (Driver 1895, lxxix no. 10; lxxx no. 22; lxxxii no. 46; Weinfeld 1972, 342 no. 2, no. 5). In the OT the verb is frequently associated with military action (Mic 1:15; Hab 1:6; Ps 44:4[3]), an association made also on the Moabite Stone (line 7; Dearman 1989c, 94). In the Covenant Code, God will drive out Canaan's inhabitants (Exod 23:29-30), but in Deuteronomy the task is left to the people (Weinfeld 1972, 47). Yet Deuteronomy by no means lacks a concept of holy war (see Note for 1:30).

that Yahweh swore to your fathers. אֲשֶׁר נִשְׁבַּע יְהוָה לַאֲבֹתֵיכֶם. See Gen 12:1. The LXX and Sam have "that I swore." In MT Yahweh refers to himself in the third person (cf. 1:36). The verb שׁבע in the N-Stem ("to swear"), with reference to the oath sworn to the patriarchs, occurs often in JE (Gen 50:24; Exod 13:5, 11; 32:13; 33:1, etc.) and even more often in Deuteronomy (1:8, 35; 4:31; 6:10, 18, 23; 7:8, 12, 13; 8:1, 18; 9:5; 10:11; 11:9, 21; 13:18[17], etc.; Driver 1895, lxxix no. 13). Yahweh's gift of the land to the fathers is a major theme in Jeremiah (Jer 3:18; 7:7, 14; 11:5; 16:15; 24:10; 25:5; 30:3; 32:22; 35:15). The promise to the patriarchs amounted to a covenant, since in the OT covenant and oath (= promise) are overlapping concepts (Gen 26:28; Weinfeld, $b^e rît$, in *TDOT*, 2:256).

to give to them and to their descendants after them. Cf. Gen 17:8. This phraseology is legal, at home in donation texts from Mesopotamia, Ugarit, and Elephantine (Weinfeld 1970-72, 199; 1972, 78). Grant formulas typically consist of the statement "I give to you and to your descendants . . ." (cf. Num 25:12-13).

9-18 A report on the appointment of chiefs and officers to help Moses govern while Israel is still at Horeb. According to Exod 18:13-27, Moses' inability to shoulder the burden alone and his appointment of subordinates, which came at the suggestion of his father-in-law Jethro, took place prior to the arrival at Mount Sinai. Levinson (2005, 93-98) thinks the Deuteronomic writer deliberately sought to revise and correct the narrative in Exodus 18, making the creation of a judicial system subsequent to the giving of the law. The account here goes well with Num 11:14-17, where Moses is said to have selected seventy elders before leaving Sinai to ease the leadership burden. The suggestion has therefore been made that vv. 9-18 combine and adapt older traditions found in Exodus and Numbers (Moran; Weinfeld). On the appointment of judges and officers once Israel becomes settled in Canaan, see Note for 16:18.

9 *And I said to you at that time.* Speaking in the plains of Moab, Moses reflects back on what he told the people as they prepared to leave Horeb. But in his audience are many who were not there. Here as elsewhere in the Bible, all generations share a common history (see Note for 5:3). With the threefold "at that time" (בָּעֵת הַהִוא) in vv. 9, 16, 18, the Deuteronomic writer makes it clear that a judiciary was organized before leaving Horeb. The phrase is a common retrospective device in Deuteronomy (2:34; 3:4, 8, 12, 18, 21, 23; 4:14; 9:20; 10:1, 8).

I am not able to bear you alone. לֹא־אוּכַל לְבַדִּי שְׂאֵת אֶתְכֶם. Moses needs help in bearing rule (Luther). Moses says the same in Num 11:14; in Exod 18:18 he was told this by Jethro.

10 Comparing Israel to "the stars of the heaven," which is repeated in 10:22 and implied in 9:14, indicates a fulfillment of the promise to Abraham (Gen 15:5; 22:17; 26:4; Exod 32:13; Heb 11:12). Israel's spectacular increase is promised in Deuteronomy if it obeys the commandments (see Note for 6:3), but a reverse no less spectacular will occur if the covenant is disobeyed, for then the curses will come to pass (28:62). The word "today" occurs frequently in Deuteronomy (1:10, 39; 2:18; 4:4, 8, 26, 39, 40; 5:1, 3; 6:6, etc.).

11 Lest the people misunderstand Moses' statement about Israel's increase causing an added burden, Moses turns quickly to bless them, saying he wants the increase to continue. For the jussive יֹסֵף used as a blessing, see Gen 30:24; 2 Sam 24:3; Ps 115:14.

a thousand times. Joab said to David: "May Yahweh your God add to the people a hundred times as many as they are" (2 Sam 24:3). Hyperbole of this sort appears commonly in extrabiblical texts. In the Assyrian royal correspondence, a letter wishes the king blessings from the gods "a thousandfold" (Waterman 1930, 1:302-3; no. 435 lines 15-20). In an Aramaic papyrus of the 5th cent., a wish for the good health of the governor of Judaea (408) and his princes is extended "one thousand times more than now" (no. 30 line 3; Cowley 1923, 113).

as he spoke to you. Or "as he promised you" (Driver; NJV), referring to the promise of blessing through Abraham and Sarah (Gen 12:2; 17:16; 22:17). Another stereotyped Deuteronomy formula (1:11, 21; 6:3, 19; 9:3; 10:9; 11:25; 12:20, etc.; Driver 1895, lxxxi no. 29).

Yahweh God of your fathers. A Deuteronomic expression (1:11, 21; 4:1; 6:3; 12:1; 26:7; 27:3; 29:24[25]; Driver 1895, lxxx no. 16), although it is earlier (Exod 3:13, 15, 16; 4:5; Lohfink 1994c, 277). On Yahweh as God of the fathers, see Exod 6:2-3, and articles by Alt (1966b) and Cross (1962).

12 Moses returns to his point in v. 9, questioning now with greater urgency and in more detail how he alone can carry the burden of leadership. On מַשָּׂא ("load, burden"), see Num 11:11, 17. Mention also of "strife" (רִיב) means that help is needed in adjudicating legal disputes. The term "How?" (אֵיכָה) is found only in Deuteronomy within the Pentateuch (1:12; 7:17; 12:30; 18:21; Driver 1895, lxxx no. 19).

13 Moses answers his own question, telling the people to select able individuals whom he will appoint to office. In Exod 18:13-26 Moses selects the individuals himself, and in Num 11:16-17 Yahweh tells Moses to select the individuals, saying he will put some of Moses' spirit upon them. Here the selected individuals are to be "wise and discerning and experienced" (חֲכָמִים וּנְבֹנִים וִידֻעִים), the third trait (lit. "knowing") being taken by Driver to mean "of proved character and ability" (Vg: *quorum conversatio sit probata*). The LXX translates this term with συνετούς ("intelligent"), which corresponds to Targum readings. In Exod 18:21 moral qualities are sought: Jethro says to choose able men who "fear God, are trustworthy, and who hate a bribe." Driver thinks the terms in Deuteronomy also imply moral qualification; nevertheless, the emphasis rests on intellectual fitness to do the job. Here as elsewhere, Deuteronomy lifts up the virtue of wisdom, an important requisite in the Bible and elsewhere for bearing rule (Prov 8:15-16; Isa 11:1-2; Weinfeld 1972, 244-54). Solomon, when worrying about judging a people too vast to number, receives from Yahweh "a wise and discerning heart" (1 Kgs 3:12). On the selection of judges and officers in Israel and the ANE, see Weinfeld 1977.

according to your tribes. I.e., one per tribe (v. 23).

and I will appoint them as your heads. וַאֲשִׂימֵם בְּרָאשֵׁיכֶם. The בְּ is a *beth essentiae*: "*as* your heads" (Driver; GKC §119i). On the verb שִׂים, meaning "to appoint," see 17:14-15.

14 *The thing that you have said to do is good.* טוֹב־הַדָּבָר אֲשֶׁר־דִּבַּרְתָּ לַעֲשׂוֹת. Cf. the expressions in 1 Kgs 2:38, 42; 18:24. The people concur with Moses' idea. In v. 23 Moses concurs with an idea originating with the people.

15 *So I took the heads of your tribes, men of wisdom and experience.* The LXX has ἔλαβον ἐξ ὑμῶν ("I took from you"), omitting "the heads of your tribes." This simplifies the reading, since the verse goes on to say, "and I set them as heads over you" (Wevers 1995, 9). Individuals have not yet been appointed as tribal heads.

and I made them heads over you, chiefs of thousands and chiefs of hundreds and chiefs of fifties and chiefs of tens, also officials for your tribes. In the OT, the respective heads (except for "chiefs of tens") are mentioned in connection with the army (1 Sam 17:18; 18:13; 22:7; 2 Kgs 1:9, 11, 13; Isa 3:3). Battle formations organized along the same lines were used by Judas Maccabeus in the battle of Emmaus (1 Macc 3:55; Josephus *Ant.* 12.301) and appear later in "The War of the Sons of Light against the Sons of Darkness" (Cross 1949, 40; Yadin 1962, 59). The titles were not limited to the military, however. A שַׂר could be in charge of cattle (Gen 47:6), oversee a work gang (Exod 1:11), or be a warden in a prison (Gen 39:21). In a 7th-cent. letter dug up at Yavneh-Yam, a שַׂר is an official to whom a laborer complains about his garment having been taken after he finished reaping in the field, and he wants it restored (Naveh 1960, 131-35; lines 1 and 12). Later a שַׂר became simply "one of the king's men," i.e., a royal or nonroyal prince holding an upper-level civil or military position (Jer 24:1; 26:10). Some of these individuals were scribes (Jer 36:12), others were military commanders, palace guards, or members of the police force (Lundbom 2004a, 229). Here the individuals have some sort of judicial function (v. 16; cf. Exod 18:25-26). For this organizational structure in Hittite, Egyptian, Mari, and other ANE texts, also in texts from Qumran, see Weinfeld 1977.

also officials for your tribes. וְשֹׁטְרִים לְשִׁבְטֵיכֶם. The LXX has τοῖς κριταῖς ὑμῶν ("for your judges"), which reads Hebrew שֹׁפְטֵיכֶם instead of שִׁבְטֵיכֶם. This has support from v. 16, where the chiefs and officials are referred to as "your judges" (שֹׁפְטֵיכֶם). "Officials," once again, are individuals whose sphere lay chiefly but not exclusively with affairs of the army. They are not military commanders, but subordinates engaged primarily in secretarial work (see Note for 16:18). The LXX calls them γραμματοεισαγωγεῖς, a term whose meaning is not precisely known, but one that points to scribe-related work. Wevers (1995, 10) thinks the term probably means some kind of interpreters of the law. Weinfeld thinks it connotes scribes and court bailiffs. Tigay cautions about שֹׁטְרִים denoting scribes in the OT, since the evidence for this meaning is primarily extrabiblical. In the OT these individuals oversee forced labor (Exod 5:6-19) and maintain military discipline (Deut 20:5, 8, 9; Josh 1:10; 3:2). In 2 Chr 34:13 they are Levites in charge of temple repairs. Yet in each of these jobs, scribal competence can be assumed. Driver concludes: "The שֹׁטְרִים ... were subordinate officials, who were employed partly in the administration of justice, partly in the maintenance of civil order and of military discipline, and whose duty it was to put in force the mandates issued by their superiors." See further Weinfeld (1977, 83-86) and Note for 16:18.

16 *And I commanded your judges at that time.* Weinfeld (1977, 80) says the verb צוה ("command") involves imposition and obligation, apparently by oath. Hittite and Egyptian parallels exist. Weinfeld notes also the adjuration of judges attested in Greek sources.

Hear between your brethren. I.e., hear cases among your fellow Israelites, listening to arguments on both sides. In the NT, see John 7:51.

and judge righteously between a person and his brother and his sojourner. Hebrew צֶדֶק must be translated here as an adverb: "righteously" (cf. LXX). Cf. the command in 16:18.

and his sojourner. I.e., the sojourner who is party to a dispute with some (Israelite) person. The "sojourner" (גֵּר) is a resident alien in Israel and in Deuteronomy is accorded special treatment because of his dependent status (see Note for 5:14). The Deuteronomic Code makes it clear that justice must not be perverted toward the sojourner (24:14, 17; 27:19). Israelites are to love the sojourner, because God loves him and because they themselves were once sojourners in Egypt (10:18-19; 23:8[7]; 26:5). In the wilderness are now sojourners who left Egypt with the Israelites (cf. the "mixed multitude" in Exod 12:38).

17 *You shall not pay regard to faces in judgment. The small like the great you shall hear.* I.e., you shall not be partial, showing favoritism in legal proceedings. Repeated in 16:19. In the Covenant Code, see Exod 23:2-3, 6-8. A vizier in Upper Egypt named Rekh-mi-re, in the reign of Thut-mose III (ca. 1490-1436), reports in his autobiography:

When I judged the petitioner, I was not partial. I did not turn my brow for the sake of reward. I was not angry [at *him who came*] as [a petitioner], nor did I *rebuff* him, (but) I tolerated him in his moment of outburst. I rescued the timid from the violent. . . . (ANET³, 213)

This vizier had received these instructions from the Pharaoh:

[The] abomination of the god is partiality. This is the instruction, and thus shall thou act: "Thou shalt look upon him whom thou knowest like him whom thou knowest not, upon him who has access to thee like him who is far away. . . ." (ANET³, 213; Weinfeld 1977, 79)

On instructions to officials in other Egyptian and Hittite documents, see the excursus in Weinfeld's commentary: "The Judiciary in the Ancient Near East" (140-41). Impartiality in judgment is a wisdom theme (Prov 24:23b; 28:21; Weinfeld 1972, 273). In the NT see Jas 2:1-9. Luther says:

This is the highest and most difficult virtue of rulers, namely justice and integrity of judgment. For it is easy to pronounce judgment on poor and common people; but to condemn the powerful, the wealthy, and the friendly, to disregard blood, honor, fear, favor, and gain, and simply to consider the issue — this is a divine virtue.

You shall not be afraid of the face of a person, for the judgment — it belongs to God. Deuteronomy recognizes that judgment is ultimately God's (cf. Exod 18:15-16; 21:6; Prov 16:33; 2 Chr 19:6). Luther says that judgment is God's just as vengeance is (Deut 32:41-43). Weinfeld (1972, 233-36) believes Deuteronomy otherwise has a more secular attitude regarding the judicial procedure, citing the law on a slave refusing manumission (15:17) and comparing it with Exod 21:6.

And the case that is too difficult for you, you shall bring it near to me and I will hear it. Similar provisions are found in Hittite instructions (Weinfeld). According to Exod 18:19, the people bring difficult matters to Moses, who then brings them to God.

the case. Hebrew הַדָּבָר.

18 Possibly the sum of commands given to the judges, but usually taken to refer to the covenant commands given to all Israel at Horeb. According to Deuteronomy, only the Decalogue was given to Israel at Horeb (5:22), whereas in Exodus it was a larger Covenant Code (Exod 20:1–24:8; 34:11-28).

19 The narrative now picks up from vv. 7-8, reporting in short compass and without incident the journey from Horeb to Kadesh-barnea, except to say that the wilderness was "great and terrible."

all that great and terrible wilderness. כָּל־הַמִּדְבָּר הַגָּדוֹל וְהַנּוֹרָא הַהוּא. Reference is to the Wilderness of Paran (Num 12:16), which leads into the Wilderness of Zin (cf. 2:7). In 8:15 this wilderness is said to have had "serpents of fire and scorpions and thirsty ground in which there was no water." Cf. wilderness portrayals in Deut 8:15; 32:10; Jer 2:6. The terms "great and terrible" are used to describe Yahweh in 7:21; 10:17.

that you saw. See again v. 31. On generations sharing a common history, see v. 9.

on the road to the hill country of the Amorites. דֶּרֶךְ הַר הָאֱמֹרִי. This was the road leading from Horeb to Kadesh-barnea, called "the Seir Mountain road" in 1:2. According to 1:2, the journey from Horeb to Kadesh-barnea took eleven days. The expression "on the road" or "in the way" occurs with great frequency in Deuteronomy (1:2, 19, 22, 31, 33, 40; 2:1; 5:33; 6:7; 8:2, 6; 9:12, 16; 10:12; 11:19, 22, 28; 13:6[5], etc.), often denoting "the road out of Egypt." "Walking in the way" has ethical implications in the OT, referring to loving, serving, fearing Yahweh and above all, to keeping Yahweh's commandments (see Note for 5:33). On the Amorites, see Notes for 1:7 and 2:24.

Kadesh-barnea. An oasis in the Wilderness of Zin (see Note for 1:2). Kadesh-barnea was to be the southern border of the promised land in Num 34:4.

20-21 The verses repeat v. 8. From Kadesh-barnea Israel was to go up and take the land.

that Yahweh our God is giving to us. This phrase, usually with reference to land or ground, is very common in Deuteronomy (1:25; 2:29; 3:20; and some 25 times). On "Yahweh our God," see Note for v. 6.

spoke to you. Or "promised to you." The verb דבר ("speak") can also mean "promise" (1:11; 9:3). Here Hebrew has the singular לָךְ ("to you"). Deuteronomic discourse shifts frequently between singular and plural pronouns, best explained as being due to its homiletical style (see *Introduction: The Quest for Urdeuteronomium*).

do not fear and do not be dismayed. אַל־תִּירָא וְאַל־תֵּחָת. The verb חתת can also be translated "be broken, be depressed," referring to a physical or psychological condition (Lundbom 1999, 244-45). This is stereotypical war language of Deuteronomy (1:21, 29; 3:2, 22; 7:18; 20:3; 31:6, 8; cf. Josh 8:1; 10:8, 25; Driver 1895, lxxxi no. 35; Weinfeld 1972, 344 no. 12), found also in Jeremiah (Jer 1:17; 23:4; 30:10 = 46:27). Weinfeld (1972, 50-51) finds a parallel expression ("fear and dread") in Neo-Assyrian inscriptions.

22 In Num 13:1-2 God commands that spies be sent out. Here the idea originates with the people. Cf. the Danites' later scoping out of Laish to find for themselves an inheritance (Judges 18).

23 Numbers 13:4-16 names the individuals. Moses here responds to a

Deuteronomy 1

good suggestion from the people. People responded favorably to Moses' suggestion about power-sharing in v. 14.

24 Glueck (1959, 87-89, 112-14) says his "Way of the Wells," i.e., a series of springs, wells, and water holes from ʿAin Qadis and ʿAin el-Qudeirat (= Kadesh-barnea), going in a northeasterly direction, would have been the shortest, easiest, and most direct road between Sinai and Canaan. "Wadi Eshcol" (נַחַל אֶשְׁכֹּל) means "wadi of the grape cluster," so named for the cluster of grapes found by the spies and brought back to the camp. This "wadi" (Arabic: "river valley") was in the Amorite hill country (vv. 7, 19), somewhere near Hebron (cf. Num 13:22-24).

25 Here the report of the group is entirely favorable. In Num 13:25-33 it is mixed: The land is good, but the cities are fortified and giants are living there. Caleb alone advises to proceed in the conquest; the other spies say No: the inhabitants are too strong and will overcome Israel. Deuteronomy assumes a good report from Caleb in v. 36.

and brought back word to us. וַיָּשִׁבוּ אֹתָנוּ דָבָר. The LXX omits, supported by the Vg. The loss could be attributed to haplography (homoeoarcton: וי ... וי).

the fruit of the land. The promised land is not only a land of milk and honey (6:3; Exod 3:8), but a land abundant in fruit: grapes, pomegranates, and figs (Num 13:23, 27). Jeremiah calls it an "orchard land" (Jer 2:7), i.e., a land of fruit trees and vineyards.

26 The people are unwilling also in Num 14:1-10, where their rebellion is described in more detail. For the theme of Israel's rebellion in the wilderness, see also Deut 32:15-30; Exodus 32; Jer 7:24-25; 11:8; Pss 81:12-14(11-13); 106:13-27.

Yet you were not willing. וְלֹא אֲבִיתֶם. The expression "to be unwilling" occurs often in Deuteronomy (1:26; 2:30; 10:10; 23:6[5]; 25:7; 29:19[20]; Driver 1895, lxxx no. 17).

and you rebelled against the mouth. וַתַּמְרוּ אֶת־פִּי. I.e., you defied the command. The people were commanded by Yahweh to go up and take the land, but they refused (1:7-8).

27 Instead of readying themselves for battle, they sat immobile in their tents. "With Yahweh hating us" coming at the beginning their plaint, the defiance is strong (cf. 9:28b). Rashi and Rashbam say the verb רגן means "to slander" (so KBL[3]; cf. Prov 16:28; 18:8; 26:20-22). In Num 14:1-3, people vent their anger not only against Yahweh, but against Moses and Aaron. The tent grumbling is recalled in Ps 106:25.

to give us into the hand of the Amorites. The expression "to give into the hand(s) of" is Deuteronomic (1:27; 2:24, 30; 3:2, 3; 7:24; 20:13; 21:10; Driver 1895, lxxxii no. 52).

to completely destroy. The verb שמד is an internal H-stem, intensifying the meaning. It occurs with great frequency in the N-stem and H-stem in Deuteronomy (1:27; 2:12, 21, 22, 23; 4:3, 26; 6:15; 7:4, 23, 24; 9:3, 8, 14, 19, 20, 25; 12:30; 28:20, 24, 45, 48, 51, 61, 63; 31:3, 4; Driver 1895, lxxxiii no. 65).

28 *To where are we going up?* That is to say, "To what place are we going, anyway?" Hebrew אָנָה is the long form of אָן, meaning "where?" (cf. Jer 15:2).

Our brethren have made our hearts melt, saying, 'A people greater and taller than we; great cities fortified up to heaven, and even sons of the Anakim we saw there!' Here it comes out that some of the spies appear to have brought back a frightful report about those inhabiting the land (cf. Num 13:28, 31-33). See again Deut 9:1-2. The expression "melt the heart" repeats in 20:8 and is found elsewhere in the Deuteronomistic literature (Josh 2:11; 5:1; 7:5; 14:8; Weinfeld 1972, 344 no. 15). This weakened condition renders Israel unable to carry on holy war (cf. Judg 7:3).

A people greater and taller than we, great cities fortified up to heaven. Hebrew "great" (גְּדֹלֹת ... גָּדוֹל) probably means "more numerous" (people) and "large" (cities), respectively, rather than "high in stature" (T^{Onq}; Tigay) since the paired term in each case carries the latter meaning. The expression "great and many and tall" (גָּדוֹל וְרַב וָרָם) occurs in 2:10 and 21. Numbers 13:28 says the cities were "very great" (גְּדֹלֹת מְאֹד), i.e., very large (cf. Jonah 3:3). On the height of the Amorite inhabitants, see also Amos 2:9.

fortified up to heaven. Hebrew בַּשָּׁמַיִם (lit. "into the heaven[s]") has superlative meaning: "to (or beyond) the maximum" (cf. Jer 51:9). The expression is hyperbole (Rashi; cf. Gen 11:4), appearing again in 9:1. In Neo-Assyrian documents Judahite fortresses are described as "reaching high to heaven," i.e., being "sky high" (Na'aman 1974, 26-27; *ANET*^{3}, 282).

sons of the Anakim. The Anakim were a remnant of the giants living among the Amorites in the southern hill country (9:2; Num 13:28). Three are named in Num 13:22: Ahiman, Sheshai, and Talmai. They are said to have descended from the Nephilim (Num 13:33), semi-divine beings who predated the flood (Gen 6:1-4). The Anakim are likened to the Emim in Deut 2:10-11, another reputed giant race of antiquity known also as the Rephaim (see Note for 2:20-21). Og, king of Bashan, whom the Israelites defeated in Transjordan, was one of the last of the Rephaim (3:11). His bedstead was reputed to be 9 cubits in length and 4 cubits in breadth (13.5 ft by 6 ft). The Anakim were reported as living mainly in the vicinity of Hebron; Joshua and Caleb are said to have wiped them out in both the southern and northern hill country. The few left in the Philistine cities of Gaza, Gath, and Ashdod (Josh 11:21-22; 14:12-15; 15:13-14) were eliminated by David and his men (2 Sam 21:15-22).

Goliath of Gath was doubtless a descendant of the Anakim (1 Samuel 17). Excavated bones have yet to show any giant races in antiquity, although Josephus (*Ant.* 5.125) reports gigantic bones from Hebron displayed in his day (1st cent. A.D.). The Egyptians were awed by the height of Canaan's inhabitants, saying: "Some of them are of four or five cubits [i.e., 7 to 9 ft tall] (from) their noses to the heel" (*ANET*³, 477). But we may be entering here the world of mythical folklore, where megalithic structures were assumed to belong to a giant people (Driver; G. E. Wright 1938, 307; Gaster 1969, 311-12). Albright (1928, 237-38) says *Yʿnq* occurring in the Tell el-Amarna tablets is related philologically to biblical עֲנָק, but he stops short of taking the term as a reference to the Anakim. All the places cited in the Egyptian texts are located in the north, whereas in the biblical tradition the Anakim reside in the southern part of Judah and Philistia.

29 *Do not tremble and do not be fearful of them.* לֹא־תַעַרְצוּן וְלֹא־תִירְאוּן מֵהֶם. More stereotyped language of Deuteronomy (20:3; 31:6; Driver 1895, lxxxii no. 54; Weinfeld 1972, 344: nos. 12-13). On "do not tremble," see also 7:21 and Josh 1:9; on "do not fear/be fearful," see Note for 1:21. Ibn Ezra says "do not tremble" means "do not panic," referring to an unnerving kind of fear. Cf. Moses' words to Israel in a crisis situation similar to the present one, after the people left Egypt and were encamped at the Sea with the Egyptians in hot pursuit (Exod 14:13-14).

30 *Yahweh your God is the one going before you.* Yahweh went before and behind the people in the exodus (Exod 14:19), also in the trek through the wilderness, where it was in a pillar of cloud by day and a pillar of fire by night (Exod 13:21-22; Deut 1:33). Yahweh will do the same in the conquest of Canaan (Deut 31:8). The language is military: the vanguard protects those who follow; the rear guard protects those marching ahead. In the later return from Babylon, Yahweh will again be the vanguard and rear guard (Isa 52:12; 58:8). The idiom appears in the Gilgamesh Epic: "[He who goes] in front protects/saves the companion" (Old Babylonian: III, vi 27; Assyrian: III i 4; *ANET*³, 80-81), and has turned up in an inscription from Tell Dan, where an Aramaean king says: "I [fought against Israel?] and Hadad went in front of me" (Biran and Naveh 1993, 87-92).

he, he will fight for you according to all that he did with you in Egypt before your eyes. The added pronoun הוּא ("he") is for emphasis: *Yahweh* will be the one fighting for you! It will be holy war, just as the exodus from Egypt was (Exod 14:14, 25), with Yahweh conducting the battle (Deut 3:22; 20:4). Yahweh was later understood as having fought for Israel in the conquest of Canaan (Josh 10:14, 42; 23:3, 10). On Deuteronomy and holy war, see von Rad 1953, 45-59; 1991, 115-27.

before your eyes. לְעֵינֵיכֶם. This expression in variation occurs often in Deuteronomy, particularly with reference to experiences associated with the exodus (1:30; 4:34; 6:22; 9:17; 25:3, 9; 28:31; 29:1[2]; 31:7; 34:12). It becomes a favorite expression of Ezekiel (Ezek 10:2b; 21:11[6]; 36:23; 37:20; 38:16). The LXX omits, but Vg has *cunctis videntibus* ("before the eyes of all"). The Versions are trying to deal with the problem of the generation to which Moses is speaking

Deuteronomy 1

not having experienced the exodus (Weinfeld). On expressions similar to the present one, see Notes for 3:21 and 4:9.

31 Yahweh protected Israel from the Amalekites (Exod 17:8-16) and also from natural dangers in the wilderness (Deut 8:15).

Yahweh your God lifted you up as a man lifts up his son. In Exod 19:4 and Deut 32:11, Yahweh's "carrying" (נשׂא) of Israel is compared to an eagle carrying its young on the wing. In Num 11:12, the comparison is with a nurse carrying a suckling in her bosom. The image of Yahweh caring for Israel like a father caring for his son is picked up in Hos 11:1-3 and Isa 1:2 (cf. Jer 31:20). The image continues in the Bible (Isa 46:3-4; 63:9; Ps 28:9; Acts 13:18). Compassion of fathers for their children was proverbial (Ps 103:13; Job 29:16; 31:18). In Ps 91:11-12, Yahweh gives the charge to his angels. The imagery of the present verse is lost in the LXX, which has "the Lord your God nourished you as when a man nourishes his son." Wevers (1995, 18) thinks the translator may have had the manna in mind.

where you saw. See v. 19.

how Yahweh your God lifted you up. אֲשֶׁר נְשָׂאֲךָ יְהוָה אֱלֹהֶיךָ. Hebrew אֲשֶׁר is here equivalent to "how" (Driver).

until you came up to this place. I.e., to Kadesh-barnea. The phrase has reference to the valley opposite Beth-peor in 9:7 and 11:5, but not here (*pace* Weinfeld). In 26:9 it refers to the promised land of Canaan and in 29:6(7) to the Transjordan.

32-33 Disbelief was the primary problem in the wilderness (Num 14:11). The participle combined with אֵין (אֵינְכֶם מַאֲמִינִם) indicates a continued state of unbelief: "you continued not believing" (Driver; cf. 9:24). The fire made the road visible at night (T^{NfPsJ}; cf. Exod 13:21). Here we note that the ark is left out (cf. Num 10:33-34). In Deuteronomy the ark does not symbolize Yahweh's presence; it is only a wooden chest containing the tables of law (10:1-5; cf. Exod 25:16), next to which the Song of Moses is later placed (31:26; see below, p. 846).

And in this thing. I.e., the matter at hand: Yahweh's command to go up and take the land.

34-36 Yahweh's anger is described in detail in Num 14:11-20, where Yahweh wanted to destroy the entire generation and start all over with Moses. Moses persuaded Yahweh not to do that. The ten disbelieving spies die by a plague, and the disbelievers twenty years and older are left to die in the wilderness, with their children left to enter after forty years of wilderness suffering (Num 14:26-38). Here the disbelieving generation is condemned to die in the wilderness, and the children are left to enter and possess the land (Deut 1:39). But the narrative agrees with Num 14:21-24 in that only Caleb is excepted from punishment and permitted entrance into the promised land. In both accounts Joshua, too, is granted exception (1:38; Num 32:11-12; cf. Heb 3:18). For the rhe-

Deuteronomy 1

torical structure supporting both Caleb and Joshua as exceptions to the curse, see Rhetoric and Composition.

the sound of your words. NJV: "your loud complaint."

and he was furious and swore. The Hebrew is in the form of an oath: "If one of these men . . ." (cf. Num 14:21-23). This oath overrides the earlier oath to give Israel the land (v. 8).

this evil generation. Omitted in the LXX (cf. the curse in Num 14:22), and perhaps a later addition. The disbelieving generation is taken to be evil (cf. Num 32:13).

the good land. This expression, with reference to Canaan, occurs often in Deuteronomy (1:35; 3:25; 4:21, 22; 6:18; 8:7 ["a good land"], 10; 9:6; 11:17; Driver 1895, lxxxi no. 42; Weinfeld 1972, 343 no. 10). Numbers 14:23 simply has "the land." Deuteronomy consistently praises the good land of Canaan (see 8:7-10).

that I swore to give to their fathers. See Note for 1:8. "To give" is omitted in Sam, LXX, and Vg, perhaps to eliminate the difficulty of the land not being actually given to the fathers, only promised to them (Weinfeld).

Caleb son of Jephunneh. Caleb was a leader in the tribe of Judah (Num 13:6). He is called "the Kenizzite" elsewhere in the OT (Num 32:12; Josh 14:6), i.e., one belonging to a foreign clan living in the Hebron region, which over time was absorbed into the tribe of Judah (Weinfeld). Caleb was said to have conquered the giants of Hebron (Josh 14:12; 15:14).

the land on which he has set foot. I.e., Hebron (Josh 14:6-14). A Deuteronomic expression (1:36; 2:5; 11:24-25; Josh 1:3 ["every place"]; 14:9; cf. Num 14:24).

because he has gone fully after Yahweh. יַעַן אֲשֶׁר מִלֵּא אַחֲרֵי יְהוָה. The expression "go in full after" means "follow loyally," having parallels in grant terminology of the OT and in Assyrian documents (Weinfeld 1972, 75-77, 337 no. 19). See also Num 14:24; 32:11-12; Josh 14:8-9, 14. On the gift of Hebron to Caleb because of his faithfulness, see Weinfeld 1970-72, 200-201.

37 According to Num 20:2-13; 27:12-14, Moses (and Aaron) were denied entrance into the promised land because of their sin at Meribah, where they did not render Yahweh as holy in the eyes of the people (cf. Deut 32:50-52). This incident happened years later (Driver: thirty-seven years). But here — as elsewhere in Deuteronomy — Moses is punished because of the people's sin (3:26; 4:21-22). Moran thinks that Moses is innocent yet made to suffer with the guilty, but he notes that both explanations leave the punishment of Moses shrouded in mystery. Brichto (1963, 158-59) notes, too, Yahweh's unusual action in penalizing Moses for the people's action, but cites Gen 3:17 as another example of "vicarious penalization" in the OT. One might add even more strikingly the "suffering servant" figure of Isaiah 53, which Christians see as having been fulfilled in the atoning death of Jesus Christ (G. E. Wright; Moran).

Even with me Yahweh was angry. גַּם־בִּי הִתְאַנַּף יְהוָה. See also 4:21. Yahweh's anger burned against the people in 9:8 and against Aaron in 9:20. The verb occurs with Yahweh as subject also in 1 Kgs 11:9; 2 Kgs 17:18, appearing also on the Moabite Stone (Driver 1895, lxxx no. 21; Weinfeld 1972, 346 no. 9).

on account of you. On the conjunction בִּגְלַל, see Note for 15:10.

38 *Joshua son of Nun, who is standing before you, he, he will enter there.* See also 3:28; 31:3, 7, 23; cf. Num 14:30. Here and following are a string of emphatic pronouns.

Strengthen him, for he, he will cause Israel to inherit it. Joshua will be the one enabling Israel to inherit the land (3:28; 31:7), and he will need strength for the arduous task of conquest. On Yahweh's gift of the land as an inheritance, see Note for 15:4.

39 The fear that the people's children will become a prey in the wilderness is expressed in Num 14:3 and in Num 14:31, where Yahweh says what he says here, that they are the ones who will be brought in. The LXX does not make a distinction between the "little ones" and the "children who today do not know good from evil," beginning simply: καὶ πᾶν παιδίον νέον, ὅστις οὐκ οἶδεν ... ("and every young child who knows not ..."). In Num 14:29, reference is to those under twenty, which according to later rabbinic tradition was the age of accountability (Weinfeld; cf. Exod 30:14). Men twenty years and older had to do military duty (Deut 2:14; Num 1:3). If "knowing good from evil" can be equated here with the age of accountability (so Weinfeld), then reference would be to "children" under twenty years of age. But Deuteronomy may have a younger age in mind, e.g., puberty (cf. Gen 2:9; 3:1-7). See also Isa 7:14-16, although here again, we do not know the age of young Immanuel. The mention of "twenty years and upward" occurs only in Numbers, where the expression "children who today do not know good from evil" does not occur.

40 Note again the added pronoun. A word of promise has just been given regarding the little ones, with the author now returning to the disobedient generation, saying: "And as for you. . . ." Tigay sees irony in the words "turn yourselves and take a journey," echoing as they do v. 7. On variations of this Deuteronomic command, see Note for 2:24. Yahweh is no longer commanding the people to go up into the land, but to return to the wilderness (cf. Num 14:25).

on the Sea of Reeds road. דֶּרֶךְ יַם־סוּף. The "Sea of Reeds" is the Gulf of Aqaba, the eastern finger of the Red Sea (see Note for 1:1). This road would have been the one leading from Kadesh-barnea to the Gulf of Aqaba, perhaps the Via Maris branch from el-ʿArish or Rafiaḥ, heading south to Aqaba (see Note for 1:2).

41 A confession and attempt to right the wrong is recorded also in Num 14:39-40. The people, however, are still in rebellion, despite the words about fighting now "according to all that Yahweh our God commanded us." Yahweh's command is to return to the wilderness. The confession can also be judged shallow in light of what is said here about the people thinking the war could be fought easily. The Sam, LXX, Vg, and S add "our God" after the first "Yahweh."

we, we will go up. Another emphatic pronoun: "we, not the next generation."

And each man put on his war gear, and you thought it easy to go up into the hill country. Now begins what Moran (1963a) calls the "anti-holy war."

his war gear. כְּלֵי מִלְחַמְתּוֹ. The expression occurs also in Jer 51:20.

and you thought it easy. וַתָּהִינוּ. The verb is הון in the H-stem, a *hapax legomenon* in the OT whose meaning is uncertain. Some scholars (Singer 1948, 106-9; Weinfeld) connect it with Arabic *hāna*, "to be light/easy." Numbers 14:44 has וַיַּעְפִּלוּ ("and they were heedless"), which Singer says is close in meaning to the Deuteronomic term. NJV: "and [you] recklessly started for the hill country."

42 *And Yahweh said to me.* This introductory phrase occurs often in Deuteronomy (1:42; 2:2, 9, 31; 3:2, 26; 4:10; 5:28; 9:12, 13; 10:1, 11; 18:17; 31:2). Yahweh speaks directly to Moses just as he later does to the prophets. We find the same introduction in Jeremiah (Jer 1:7, 9, 12, 14; 3:6 [expanded], 11; 11:6, 9, etc.).

Say to them: "You shall not go up and you shall not fight, for I am not in your midst, and will you not be smitten before your enemies?" Yahweh now rejects the plan to go up and fight, saying that he will be absent in the enterprise. In Num 14:42-44 it says the ark remained in the camp.

43 Here again "mouth" (פִּי) means "command" (cf. v. 26). Israel's rebellion is made explicit.

44 Cf. Num 14:45, which has "Amalekites and Canaanites" instead of "Amorites." The enemy pursued Israel as a swarm of wild honeybees, which are particularly ferocious (Isa 7:18; Ps 118:12).

in Seir. Seir in the OT is a territory associated with Edom/Esau (Gen 36:8-9; Judg 5:4), although Edom proper lay east of the Arabah, from the Zered River to the Gulf of Aqaba (see Note for 2:4). Here and in 2:1 Seir is situated west of the Arabah, in the present verse extending well into the eastern Negeb if Hormah, which is usually placed between Beersheba and Arad, is "in Seir." The ancient Versions reflect uncertainty in location. The LXX, S, and Vg have "from Seir to Hormah," although this is scarcely helpful, since it puts Hormah east or southeast of Seir. Numbers 14:45 has simply "Hormah." Seir, in any case, is Edomite territory west of the Arabah and northeast of the Wilderness of Paran (Gen 14:6; Josh 15:1-4; Bartlett 1969; 1989, 44). It is centered in — but not restricted to — the mountainous area of north Sinai (1:2; 2:1; Gen 14:6), below the Dead Sea, southeast of the Wilderness of Zin (Trumbull 1884, 92-102).

Seir was earlier inhabited by the Horites (Gen 14:6; 36:20-21, 30), but after being taken over by Edom (Deut 2:12, 22) it became virtually synonymous with Edom (2:5; Gen 32:4[3]; 33:14-16; Num 24:18). In Num 20:16, Kadesh-barnea is said to be a city on the Edomite border, which may mark the limit of Seir's extension westward. The Edomites had water rights north of Kadesh, if Beeroth Bene-jaakan is to be identified with Birein (see Note for 10:6). Joshua's conquest of Palestine extended to "Mount Halak that goes up to Seir" (Josh 11:17; 12:7), which was another southern boundary, with Mount Halak usually being placed southwest of the Ascent of Akrabbim (Num 34:4; Josh 15:3; Bartlett 1969, 6). The "land(s) of Seir" and "mountain of Seir" are mentioned in the Amarna Letters (EA 288; *ANET*³, 488) and Egyptian texts of Ramses II (ca. 1290-1224) and Ramses III (ca. 1183-1152), where references are to the southern Negeb and northern Sinai (Y. Aharoni 1979, 182; Bartlett 1969, 1-2; Ahituv 1984, 169). In EA 288 the king of Jerusalem, ʿAbdu-Heba, complains about hostile acts being carried out against him to the south, "as far as the lands of Seir." Now, following the Israelite defeat at Hormah, the Israelites will circle about the Seir mountains before turning north to pass into the Edomite heartland (2:1-4).

Hormah. According to the OT, the city of Hormah was located in the eastern Negeb between Arad (Num 21:1-3; Josh 12:14) and Beersheba (Josh 19:2-3; 1 Chr 4:28-30). The Canaanite name of the city was Zephath (Judg 1:17). B. Mazar (1965, 298-99) identified Hormah with Tell el-Milḥ (Tel Malḥata), but Y. Aharoni (1968, 31; 1975a; 1979, 201) said it was more likely to be Tell Masos (Khirbet el-Meshâsh), 4 mi to the west of Tell el-Milḥ, and now the preferred location. Aharoni thinks Canaanite Arad was Tell el-Milḥ, since Tel Arad, which is to the northeast and preserves the ancient name, has a more than fifteen-hundred-year gap in occupation from the Early Bronze Age (ca. 2650) until the 11th cent. (Y. Aharoni 1979, 201; *NEAEHL*, 1:85-86; *OEANE*, 1:174). Tell Masos shows a prosperous settlement in the Early Iron Age (12th cent.) and has an abundant water source (Kempinski et al. 1981). On the archaeological work at Tell Masos and its sociopolitical structure in Iron I, see Tebes 2003.

45 The LXX has: "And you sat down (καθίσαντες) and wept," reading יָשֻׁב instead of שׁוּב. People often sit when they weep (Judg 20:26; 21:2); however, the MT reading is preferable. The Israelites returned to the encampment at Kadesh (v. 19), where their misadventure began, and remained there for a time (v. 46). Their weeping did little to change things, except to give vent to their grief. They refused to listen to Yahweh (v. 43), and now Yahweh will not listen to them.

46 On the oasis at Kadesh-barnea, see Note for 1:2. The expression "many days" is indefinite (Rashbam: "for the amount of time that you know"). The people could not have remained at Kadesh long (Weinfeld and Tigay: "[not more than] a few months"), for they had just been told by Yahweh to head back into the wilderness (v. 40), which they proceeded to do (2:1). They then wandered in the wilderness for many years (Deut 2:14: "thirty-eight years"; Num 32:13: "forty years"; cf. Deut 2:7; 8:2, 4; 29:4[5]), and precisely where this journey took them is not known. Deuteronomy says that when the people began their trek, they went about Mount Seir "for many days" (2:1).

according to the days you remained. An idiom indicating an undefined period. Driver calls it an *idem per idem,* which occurs again in 9:25 and 29:15(16). The idiom functions as an argument and conveys important theological meaning in Exod 3:14 and 33:19 (Lundbom 1978a).

Message and Audience

The audience learns here the sad story of Israel's departure from Horeb and a lack of faith that led to a misadventure in its first attempt to enter Canaan. Moses commanded the people to leave Horeb, where they had entered into covenant with Yahweh and received the Ten Commandments, as they had been there long enough. Now it was time to enter and take possession of the Amorite hill country and surrounding territory from the seacoast all the way to the river Euphrates. This was the land promised to descendants of Abraham, Isaac, and Jacob, and now it lay before them.

Before leaving Horeb, however, Moses said he could not shoulder the burden of leadership alone, so numerous had the people become, and so he told the people to choose wise, discerning, and experienced men to assist him in mustering, judging, and governing them all. These he would appoint as heads over them. The people thought the idea a good one, and it was done. In his charge to the heads, Moses admonished them to judge righteously: no bending of the law for friends or persons of high standing; no neglect of fairness to the sojourner. Judgment, after all, belongs to God. If cases were too difficult, the heads were to bring them to Moses for arbitration. Moses then laid out commands the people should follow.

The journey proceeded through the dreadful wilderness to the oasis of Kadesh-barnea, where, upon arrival, Moses said, "Now you are here, go up and take the land as Yahweh said." They were not to be fearful. But they were fearful, and they requested that scouts be sent to scope out the land, looking at what roads to take, and what cities they would enter. Moses thought this a good idea, and so he selected twelve men, one from each tribe, to go up and scope out the land. The scouts came to the Wadi Eshcol, cut branches of fruit to bring back, and returned, telling Moses and the people that the land Yahweh was giving them was a good land. Well, maybe not all the scouts were this positive.

The people, in any case, were unwilling to go, rebelling against the command of Yahweh. Grumbling in their tents, they said that Yahweh hated them in bringing them to this place and did so in order to destroy them. It seems the scouts had also reported seeing a people more numerous than their own number, taller in stature than they were, and cities with walls sky high. Some of the giants from hoary antiquity were living there. Again, Moses told them not to be fearful; Yahweh would go before them and fight for them as he did against the Egyptians, something the people had seen with their own eyes. And had the people forgotten Yahweh's care in the wilderness, how he carried them as a father carries his son, until they got to the place they were now?

But the people disbelieved the God who led them in a cloud by day and a fire by night. When Yahweh heard what they had been saying, he was wroth and swore an oath overriding his earlier oath to give Israel the land. Not one of this evil generation would see the good land of Canaan, only Caleb, the one scout who had followed him heart and soul. He would be given the land on which he set foot. Yahweh's anger spilled over also unto Moses, explained here as coming because of the people's unbelief. Moses, too, would not be allowed to enter the land. Joshua, another of the scouts who was standing before the people, would be the one to lead them in, making him a second exception to Yahweh's curse. He should now be strengthened for the rigors of battle he would face. And the children, who the people said would become a prey in the wilderness, would be a third exception. They would be brought in; they would be given the land; and they would possess it.

As for the remainder of the people, Yahweh commanded them to turn around and return to the wilderness, heading in the direction of the Sea of Reeds. The people now showed contrition, saying they would go up as Yahweh commanded them. Everyone took up his weapon of war, imagining that the conquest would be easy. But it was too late. And their contrition was shallow, perhaps ingenuine. Yahweh instructed Moses to tell them not to go, for he would not be with them and they would be hard hit by the enemy. Besides, Yahweh had just now commanded them to return to the wilderness. Moses told the people what Yahweh had said, but they would not listen and went up into the hill country anyway. They were roundly defeated. The Amorites engaged them in battle and chased them back like a swarm of bees, cutting them down all the way to Hormah. The people returned to Kadesh and wept bitterly before Yahweh. But they had not listened to Yahweh, so he would not listen to them. At Kadesh they remained encamped many days.

To a late 8th- and early 7th-cent. audience this was a sober reminder of what happens when Israel shows rebellion and a lack of faith in Yahweh. Faith comes in doing Yahweh's commands. Not doing them leads to disaster, even when covered over with hollow confessions. The prophets had been telling people in both Israel and Judah to heed the demands of the covenant, and many, too many, had refused to listen. Both Israel and Judah had been chastened.

They still had better be careful! If people continue refusing to listen to Yahweh, whose word is conveyed through Yahweh's messengers, the prophets, Yahweh will not listen to them when the enemy — now the Assyrians — threaten to chase them like bees (Isa 7:18) out of the land promised to the fathers and given to them by Yahweh their God.

Failure to take the land on the first try may also have reminded some in the audience of other instances where a major step forward was preceded by a small step backward. Kingship in Israel failed with Saul, succeeding only with David who came later. David's plan to build a temple was initially rejected by Yahweh (2 Samuel 7), accepted only later in the time of Solomon. Messianic kingship failed with Zerubbabel and other claimants to the office (Acts 5:36-37), succeeding only later — for Christians — in the coming of Jesus.

B. Pass Peaceably through Seir (2:1-8a)

2 ¹And we turned and journeyed toward the wilderness on the Sea of Reeds road, as Yahweh had spoken to me, and we went around the Seir Mountains many days. ²Then Yahweh said to me: ³"You have gone around this mountainous country long enough, turn northward ⁴and command the people: You will be crossing into the territory of your brethren, the sons of Esau, who are dwelling in Seir, and they will be afraid of you, so be very careful. ⁵Do not fight with them, for I will not give to you any of their land, not even a stepping place for the sole of the foot, because I have given the Seir Mountains as a possession to Esau. ⁶Food you shall buy from them with money, so you can eat; and water also you shall barter from them with money, so you can drink." ⁷Indeed, Yahweh your God blessed you in all the work of your hand; he knew your going through this great wilderness; now forty years Yahweh your God has been with you; you have not lacked a thing. ⁸ªSo we went on away from our brethren, the sons of Esau, who were dwelling in Seir, away from the Arabah road, away from Elath and away from Ezion-geber.

Rhetoric and Composition

Here begins the report of five encounters with the Edomites, Moabites, Ammonites, and the Amorite kings Sihon and Og (2:1–3:11). The brief narrative segments taken both as a whole and individually are structured by repeated phraseology, interspersed with antiquarian notes, and having a schematic itinerary created by the writer of Deuteronomy (Sumner 1968). The pivotal point is 2:25, where Yahweh says he will now put fear on all peoples because of Israel, after which Israel will go forth to fight successfully against Sihon and Og.

Deuteronomy 2

The present verses narrating the journey past Seir-Edom are delimited at the top end by the chapter division before 2:1 and at the bottom end by a *setumah* in M^L in the middle of v. 8. The M^L and Sam have a *setumah* after 2:1, perhaps to mark the beginning of Yahweh's word to Moses in 2:2. The Sam has a section at the end of v. 7.

Portions of 2:1-8a are contained in 4QDeut^h and 4Q364.

Notes

2:1 *And we turned and journeyed toward the wilderness on the Sea of Reeds road, as Yahweh had spoken to me.* Moses now has the people obeying Yahweh's command (1:40; cf. Num 14:25). The Israelites probably took the same road on which they came to Kadesh-barnea, i.e., the branch of the Via Maris from el-ʿArish or Rafiaḥ, which passed through Kadesh on the way to the Gulf of Aqaba (= the Sea of Reeds). See Note for 1:2. They did not go all the way to the Gulf of Aqaba, but left the road to spend time in and around the Seir Mountains to the east.

And we turned and journeyed. On this stereotyped expression, see Note for 1:7.

and we went around the Seir Mountains many days. Since the Seir Mountains (הַר־שֵׂעִיר) belonged to Edom, the Israelites are not likely to have penetrated deeply into the territory, staying rather on the periphery. At least this is the view presented by Deuteronomy. The verb סבב can mean "go around" in the sense of "avoiding" (NJV: "and we skirted the hill country of Seir"). Just how long they wandered in the area is not known. If "many days" denotes a relatively short period of time, as it does in 1:46, then we are left wondering where the people spent the next thirty-eight years, after which the journey northward began (2:14). The Deuteronomic writer has no interest in reporting the sojourn in the wilderness. According to Numbers 20, the people remained at Kadesh for a time, where Miriam died (v. 1), the people had their infamous rebellion at Meribah (vv. 2-13), and then an embassy was sent to Edom requesting passage through its territory, which was refused (vv. 14-21; cf. Judg 11:17). The people then journeyed a short distance to Mount Hor, where Aaron died (Num 20:22-29; 33:33-39). In Numbers 21 the people are said to have had modest success in defeating the king of Arad (vv. 1-3; 33:40), but after leaving Mount Hor they rebelled once again against God and Moses, bringing upon them the plague of the fiery serpents (vv. 4-9).

2 *Then Yahweh said to me.* On this introductory phrase, see Note for 1:42.

3 On the idiom רַב־לָכֶם ("long enough for you"), also the larger phrase, see Note for 1:6. The people are somewhere on Edom's southern border, near Elath and Ezion-geber (v. 8a), where they will turn northeast, ascend the pass of Wadi el-Ithm (see v. 8a), and journey along Edom's eastern border in the direction of Moab (cf. Judg 11:18).

4 *You will be crossing into the territory of your brethren, the sons of Esau, who are dwelling in Seir.* The participle עֹבְרִים expresses the imminent future: "will be crossing." Hebrew גְּבוּל (normally "border") here means "territory" (Num 20:21; Exod 13:7). Deuteronomy assumes that the Israelites will traverse some portion of Edomite territory on their journey northward (v. 8a), and Yahweh says they can ask to buy food and water from the Edomites (v. 6). Edomites are said to be dwelling in Seir. Nothing is said about Edomites dwelling east of the Arabah, a territory through which the Israelites did not pass. According to Num 20:14-21, Moses requested passage through (eastern) Edom on the King's Highway, the ancient caravan route from Ezion-geber to Damascus that passes through the heartland of Edom and Moab, but this was denied (cf. Judg 11:17). Deuteronomy has a kindly attitude toward the Edomites (e.g., 23:8[7]), not reflecting Israel's later hatred toward its kindred people (Amos 1:11; Jer 49:7-22; Obad 10; Ps 137:7-9; Mal 1:2-4).

the sons of Esau. I.e., the Edomites (Gen 36:1, 8, 19).

Seir. On the land of Seir, which is Edomite territory largely if not exclusively west of the Arabah, see Note for 1:44. The land of Edom proper lay east of the Jordan Rift Valley, being the high plateau and rugged mountainous country extending from the Zered River (Wadi el-Ḥasā) to the Gulf of Aqaba. North of the Zered was Moab. Edom (= Esau) means "red" (Gen 25:25), the region (e.g., Petra) noted for its red soil and red Nubian sandstone. East of Edom was the Syrian-Arabian desert, on the fringe of which the Israelites journeyed northward after being denied entrance into the Edomite heartland. On Edom, see Glueck (1936), Bartlett (1989), and the collection of essays in Edelman (1995). Recent archeological work at Khirbat en-Nahas in the lowlands of southern Jordan, where high-precision radiocarbon dating has been used at an Iron Age copper production center, indicates that the Edomite kingdom was settled well before the 7th and 6th cents., possibly as early as the 12th-11th cent. (T. Levy et al. 2004). According to earlier surface explorations of Glueck, Edom contained a sedentary population from ca. 2200 to 1800, followed by a period where the land was peopled by (semi)nomads who left no traces of their existence. This period extended from the 18th to the 13th cents. The 13th to the 8th cents. saw a second period of sedentary occupation, during which time the population was extensively engaged in agriculture, trade, and industry.

and they will be afraid of you. Numbers 20:18-20 says that "Edom went out against them" and Israel had to turn away. Here there is no mention of a direct encounter, but from 2:28-29 we learn that the Edomites did sell food and water to Israel. Edom was a loosely-knit confederation, its people occupying sites here and there across a broad expanse of land, much of it unsettled. Passage would therefore have been possible through the larger region without antagonizing the Edomites. Edomite chieftains are mentioned in Exod 15:15. Inhabitants of the region, as we have said, were seminomadic peoples; Egyptian texts speak of the "Bedouin tribes of Edom" (*ANET*³, 259, 262). An earlier encounter between Jacob and Esau took place after their years of estrangement (Genesis 32), only then it was Jacob afraid of meeting Esau (v. 8[7]).

so be very careful. וְנִשְׁמַרְתֶּם מְאֹד. The expression is Deuteronomic (see Notes for 4:6; 4:9; 4:23), here being a warning not to provoke Edom.

5 *Do not fight with them.* Cf. phrases in vv. 9, 19, and 24. The verb גרה in the Hithpael means "to engage in strife."

for I will not give to you any of their land, not even a stepping place for the sole of the foot, because I have given the Seir Mountains as a possession to Esau. Deuteronomy takes the view that God has allotted territory to each nation, not just to Israel, and the Seir Mountains — along with other Edomite land — have been given as a possession to Edom (cf. Gen 36:43). The same is said with regard to land inhabited by the Moabites and Ammonites (2:9, 19). This view is expressed in 32:8, reflected also in the universalism of Amos 9:7. Deuteronomy even goes so far as to say that the heavenly bodies were allotted to other nations for their worship (4:19). Weinfeld (1972, 72) points out how Hittite kings, in distributing land to their vassals, tell them not to trespass on neighboring territories.

not even a stepping place for the sole of the foot. עַד מִדְרַךְ כַּף־רָגֶל. I.e., no portion of land whatever. The expression כַּף־רָגֶל may simply mean "foot," not "sole of the foot" (Friedman). Cf. 11:24; 28:35, 56, 65; Josh 1:3.

6 The verb כרה means "purchase by trade," i.e., barter. According to Num 20:14-21, the Israelites requested passage through Edom, promising not to eat food from their fields and vineyards and not to drink water from their wells, but were refused (cf. Judg 11:17). Edomites, though seminomads, were engaged in agriculture (cf. Gen 26:12).

with money. I.e., with (cut) silver (בַּכֶּסֶף). LXX: ἀργυρίου. Coinage came later (see Lundbom 2004a, 506).

7 *Indeed, Yahweh your God blessed you in all the work of your hand.* The particle כִּי is asseverative ("indeed"). The quotation ends with v. 6, and Moses is now shifting to the present, reflecting in the plains of Moab on forty full years of blessing — a somewhat romantic view of the wilderness period (cf. Deut 32:10-12; Hos 2:16-17[14-15]; Jer 2:2; Lundbom 1999, 253; 2010b, 37-41), but qualified by the testings and rebellions reported in chs. 8–9. Blessing in the OT is defined largely — though not entirely — in terms of prosperity (Gen 24:35), which is what is being lifted up here. Yahweh provided food and water in the wilderness, increased Israel numerically (1:10-11), and promised it a land of its own, some of which has already been obtained. The people therefore had no need of Edomite land. Besides, Yahweh was not giving it to them. Rashi says Moses is telling Israel: "Behave not as poor people, but as rich people."

Deuteronomy puts great emphasis on "blessing": Yahweh blessed Israel in the past (1:11; 2:7; 23:6[5]) and promises blessing in the future (1:11; 12:7, 15; 14:24; 15:4, 6; 16:10), although the latter is contingent upon charitable action to the poor and needy (14:29; 15:10, 14, 18; 16:17; 23:21[20]; 24:19) and obedience to the covenant demands (7:12-14; 11:26-32; 28:1-14; 30:1, 16, 19). The needy will bless his fellow Israelite for kindness given (24:13). Yahweh's blessing is to be sought (26:15), and Israel is expected to bless Yahweh's name, particularly for the good land it is about to receive (8:10; 10:8; 16:15; 21:5). Israel will receive Yahweh's blessing in the covenant renewal ceremony (27:12), and core Deuteronomy states that covenant obedience will bring more of the same. Disobedience will bring the opposite, viz., the terrible curses (ch. 28). Deuteronomy concludes with Moses pronouncing his blessing upon Israel (ch. 33).

in all the work of your hand. בְּכֹל מַעֲשֵׂה יָדֶךָ. A stereotyped phrase in Deuteronomy (2:7; 14:29; 15:10 ["in all your work"]; 16:15; 24:19; 28:12; 30:9), alternating with "in every undertaking of your hand," בְּכֹל מִשְׁלַח יָדְךָ/יֶדְכֶם (12:7, 18; 15:10; 23:21[20]; 28:8, 20; Driver 1895, lxxxii no. 55; lxxxiii no. 64; Weinfeld 1972, 345 no. 2a). The phrases appear in combination in 15:10. The "work/undertaking of one's hand" usually refers to the fruit of one's labor, i.e., crops gathered in the harvest. In the wilderness people were not engaged in agriculture, being sustained with food supplied by Yahweh. In the Transjordan settlement they raised crops and domestic animals (Deut 32:13-14). The expression here is used in a general sense (Driver). Elsewhere in Deuteronomy, also in Jeremiah, "the work(s) of [one's] hands" is a disparaging term for idols, the handwork of craftsmen (Deut 4:28; 27:15; 31:29; Jer 1:16; 10:3, 9; 25:6, 14; Driver 1895, lxxxii no. 55). See also Hos 8:6; 13:2; Isa 40:19-20; 41:7; Ps 115:4; Wis 14:8. The idiom has turned up in Akkadian and Ugaritic texts (Weinfeld, 160; Lundbom 1999, 244).

he knew your going through this great wilderness; now forty years Yahweh your God has been with you; you have not lacked a thing. Yahweh "gave attention to" or "watched over" Israel in the wilderness, taking care of all its needs (1:31; 8:2, 4; 29:4[5]; Neh 9:21). This meaning of ידע ("know") occurs in Pss 1:6; 31:8[7]; Prov 27:23; Hos 13:5. Rashbam says Yahweh provided this for Israel "without money and without cost" (cf. Isa 55:1).

now forty years. זֶה אַרְבָּעִים שָׁנָה. Hebrew זֶה is here an adverb modifying a number: "now, already" (GKC §136d; cf. 8:2, 4). Moses is reckoning how long it took to make the journey from Egypt to where they are presently encamped, which is in the plains of Moab.

8a It is unclear just how Israel avoided its Edomite brethren to arrive finally at the river Zered, Edom's northern border. It says here that they stayed away from the Arabah road running south to north, also from the cities of Elath and Ezion-geber, which lay at the north end of the Sea of Reeds (= Gulf of Aqaba).

In antiquity there was a road from Ezion-geber to the Dead Sea and beyond (Axelsson 1987, 45; Bartlett 1989, 39), which is probably the same route taken by 19th-cent. European travelers, and travelers today who journey on the modern road from Eilat to Jerusalem. The Israelites did not take this Arabah road and stayed away from Elath and Ezion-geber. How then did they proceed? According to Num 21:4, they left Mount Hor, where Aaron died, and took the road to the Sea of Reeds in order to go around the land of Edom. We do not know the precise location of Mount Hor, but if the route took them in the direction of the Sea of Reeds, the Israelites must have circumvented Edom on the south, passed by Elath and Ezion-geber, and headed on what is presently the Desert Highway (Darb al-Ḥajj), east of Edom. We learn from Num 20:14-21 that the Israelites were denied permission to travel the King's Highway (cf. Judg 11:17). There is a road from Aqaba to the Eastern desert that ascends the steep Wadi el-Ithm and passes through the mountains. E. Robinson (1867, 1:174) thinks the Israelites took this road to circumvent Edom. The desert to the east is bone dry for much of the year, becoming green briefly with spring rain. Glueck (1940, 34) says:

> It must have been springtime when the Israelites, refused permission to travel through Edom and Moab, were compelled to go eastward around these countries and find their way through the desert. Only at this season of the year could man and beast in large numbers have found sufficient water and grazing to survive the rigors of the way.

away from Elath and away from Ezion-geber. Some identify Elath with the modern Jordanian city of Aqaba, others with Tell el-Kheleifeh, an ancient ruin between Aqaba and the modern Israeli city of Eilat (Bartlett 1989, 46-48). Eusebius *(Onom.)* put Elath 10 Roman milestones east of Petra. E. Robinson (1867, 1:170-71) placed it just south of the northern end of the Gulf, where the road from Petra descended through Wadi el-Ithm to the shore. The Greek name for Elath was Aila (LXX: Αιλων), known as Aqaba in medieval times and up to the present. According to 1 Kgs 9:26, Elath and Ezion-geber lay close together on the shore of the Gulf of Aqaba. Glueck (1936, 146-52; 1938), however, proposed that they were but one site with two different names, which would make the names in the present verse in apposition. The older name was Ezion-geber, which became an important seaport and refinery under Solomon. It was destroyed and rebuilt by Uzziah (Azariah) as Elath, on ruins of the old city (2 Kgs 14:22), and passed finally into the hands of the Edomites in 735. The ru-

Deuteronomy 2

ins at Tell el-Kheleifeh, which are 556 m from the Gulf of Aqaba, and 4 km west of present-day Aqaba, show occupation from the 10th cent. to the end of the 7th or beginning of the 6th cent. But this site is not on the Gulf, making it unsuitable for Ezion-geber, which had a harbor for a fleet of ships (1 Kgs 9:26; 22:49[48]). Elath was not known as a harbor, making Tell el-Kheleifeh the ruins most likely for just this one city.

Ezion-geber is now thought to have been located about 7 mi south of modern Eilat on an island 900 ft off the Sinai coast, popularly known as Coral Island (Jezirat Far'un), where a harbor of unknown date resembling Phonecian harbors (e.g., Tyre) has been found (Flinder 1989; Bartlett 1989, 48; *ABD*, 2:723-26). The harbor on the island and the sea between the island and the Sinai mainland form the only natural anchorage in the northern part of the Gulf.

Message and Audience

The audience now hears of the beginning of the march that led ultimately to the promised land. Moses says the people journeyed back into the wilderness, as Yahweh commanded, and spent many days wandering around the Seir Mountains. How many days? We do not know. Nor do we know where the people spent the next thirty-eight years, because the writer has no interest in reporting it. He says only that the day came when Yahweh told Moses that they had been wandering long enough in this mountainous country and it was time to turn north. Moses should therefore inform the people that, at some point, they will be passing through Edomite country. Although the Edomites are brothers, they will nevertheless be afraid at the sight of approaching Israelites. The people must be careful not to pick a fight with them. This is an interesting reversal of the earlier meeting of Jacob and Esau, when Jacob was the fearful one. In any event, Yahweh said he would not give Israel as much as a foot length of their land, because he had given the Seir Mountains to Edom as their possession. The Israelites should only offer to buy food and water as they journey on.

Moses then reminds the assembled in Moab that Yahweh has blessed all their toil up to this point. He watched over them in the wilderness, and during the forty long years they lacked nothing. Moses then says that the people moved on from their Edomite brethren, away from the Arabah road leading to the Dead Sea, and away from Elath and Ezion-geber.

To a late 8th- and early 7th-cent. audience this will be a kindly word regarding the Edomites and a caution against continuing expansionist policies of Uzziah into southern Edom, which took him all the way to Elath.

Deuteronomy 2

C. PASS PEACEABLY BY MOAB (2:8B-15)

2⁸ᵇ*And we turned and went on the wilderness road of Moab.* ⁹*And Yahweh said to me:* "Do not be hostile to Moab, and do not fight a battle with them, for I will not give you any of its land for a possession, because to the sons of Lot I have given Ar for a possession." ¹⁰*(The Emim formerly dwelt in it, a people great and many and tall like the Anakim;* ¹¹*they are also known as the Rephaim, like the Anakim, but the Moabites call them Emim;* ¹²*and in Seir the Horites dwelt formerly, but the sons of Esau dispossessed them and completely destroyed them from before them, and they dwelt in their place, just as Israel did to the land of its possession, which Yahweh gave to them.)* ¹³"*Now, rise up and cross over the river Zered.*" *So we crossed over the river Zered.* ¹⁴*And the time that we went from Kadesh-barnea until we crossed over the river Zered was thirty-eight years, until the entire generation of the men of war were finished from the midst of the camp, just as Yahweh swore concerning them.* ¹⁵*Yes indeed, the hand of Yahweh was against them to rout them from the midst of the camp, until they were finished.*

Rhetoric and Composition

These verses reporting the journey around Moab are delimited at the top end by a *setumah* in M^L in the middle of v. 8. M^L has a *setumah* and Sam a section after v. 16, but most modern English versons (RSV; NEB; NAB; NJV; NIV; NRSV; REB; NJB) and modern commentators (Driver; Weinfeld; Tigay; Friedman; Nelson) take v. 16 not as a summary statement of what precedes, but as an opening statement of what follows. The Sam has another section at the end of v. 8.

A keyword chiasmus exists in vv. 14-15 (cf. Moran 1963a, 334):

until the entire generation of the men of war *was finished*
  from the midst of the camp
    just as *Yahweh* swore concerning them
    yes indeed, the hand of *Yahweh* was against them to rout them
  from the midst of the camp
until they were finished

Portions of 2:8b-15 are contained in 4QDeut° and 4Q364.

Notes

2:8b The Israelites are heading northeast toward a road following the present-day Desert Highway, which will put them east of the Edomite and Moabite heartlands. They will end up on the east side of Moab (Judg 11:18). They do not head north on the Arabah road (*pace* J. M. Miller 1989, 582; Tigay), since 2:8a says they stayed away from it. And passage was denied them on the King's Highway. The "wilderness of Moab" borders the Syrian-Arabian desert, which is not desert, strictly speaking, but uncultivated land in which the Israelites could pasture sheep and goats and drink water from wells that were located there (Driver). The desert further east was Moab's greatest point of vulnerability, opening the country to periodic raids by desert tribes.

9 *And Yahweh said to me.* See Note for 1:42.

Do not be hostile to Moab, and do not fight a battle with them, for I will not give you any of its land for a possession, because to the sons of Lot I have given Ar for a possession. The expression "Do not fight a battle with them" repeats from 2:5 and will occur again in 2:19. Numbers says nothing about an encounter with the Moabites, as in the case of the Edomites, perhaps because it fully reports the Balak and Balaam incident after the victories over Sihon and Og (Numbers 22-24), also Israel's romp with the daughters of Moab and Baal of Peor (Numbers 25). Numbers reports only the encampments up to Ar, on Moab's northern border (Num 21:10-15; cf. 33:41-44). Judges 11:17-18 says that Israel sent an embassy to the king of Moab requesting passage through his land, but the king refused. The people therefore did not enter Moabite territory.

because to the sons of Lot I have given Ar for a possession. According to biblical tradition, Moab was a son of Lot (Gen 19:37; Ps 83:9[8]), and Lot a nephew of Abraham (Gen 11:26-32). Ar appears to have been a city (Num 21:28; Isa 15:1) on Moab's northern border (2:18; Num 21:14-15), which was the river Arnon (see Note for 2:24). It may have been Moab's capital city. Here and in v. 29, however, Ar represents the whole of Moab. Some identify Ar with Ir-Moab (= "the city of Moab") of Num 22:36. J. M. Miller (1989, 590-95) locates Ar at Khirbet Bālūʿ, a large ruin on a southeastern tributary of the Arnon that shows Late Bronze and Early Iron occupation.

10-12 An antiquarian note naming the previous inhabitants of Moab and Seir-Edom. Other antiquarian notes appear in 2:20-23; 3:9, 11, 13b-14; 10:6-9 and possibly 11:30. While not stated, there is an implied message here about Yahweh being more than capable of overcoming giants, whose presence in the Canaanite hill country so frightened the people that they did not trust Yahweh to give them victory in their first attempt to take the land (Tigay; cf. 1:28).

10-11 The Emim were a legendary giant people, said in Gen 14:5 to have inhabited Kiriathaim, a city on Moab's northern plateau (Num 32:37; Josh 13:19; Jer 48:1, 23; Ezek 25:9). A prehistoric population living north of the Arnon, the Emim were expelled by the Moabites (Num 21:26). They were called "Emim" (אֵמִים) because of the "terror" (אֵימָה) they evoked in others (T^{OnqPsJ}; *Gen. Rab.* 26:7; Rashi). Kiriathaim is mentioned on the Moabite Stone (line 10) and is usually identified with Khirbet al-Qureiye, about 16 km west of Madaba (Abel 1938, 419; Dearman 1989b: 176-77). This corroborates the testimony of Eusebius *(Onom.)*, who put Kiriathaim 10 Roman milestones west of Medaba. The Baluʿah Stele, discovered in Moabite territory in 1930 and dated by Albright (1956, 79, 186-87) to the end of the Early Bronze Age, is thought to have been erected by the Emim. From this stele it has been inferred that the Emim came from west Palestine and settled in Moab, where they became engaged in agricultural pursuits (Van Zyl 1960, 106-8). On the "Rephaim, a remnant that included Og, king of Bashan," see Note for 2:20-21. The Anakim were another giant people from hoary antiquity (see Note for 1:28).

a people great and many and tall. עַם גָּדוֹל וְרַב וָרָם. Cf. phrases in 1:28; 2:21.

12 *and in Seir the Horites dwelt formerly, but the sons of Esau dispossessed them and completely destroyed them from before them, and they dwelt in their place.* We are back to talking about Edomite land (v. 5; cf. v. 22). The "Horites" are thought by some to be the "Hurrians," well known from nonbiblical texts (Speiser 1933, 26-31; Gelb 1944, 51, 69; von Rad; Weinfeld; cf. KBL[3] חֹרִי III). The Hurrians were a people from the mountainous region east of the Tigris, who migrated into Syria and Palestine in the 2nd mill., reaching the height of their power in the 16th and 15th cents. by forming the state of Mitanni. Their presence is archaeologically unattested in Transjordan, however, and since the personal names in Gen 36:20-30 are mostly — perhaps entirely — Semitic, not Hurrian, many scholars (Simons 1959, 44; de Vaux 1967; Tigay; E. A. Speiser in *IDB*, 2:645; E. Knauf in *ABD*, 3:288) maintain that the Horites and Hurrians should be kept separate. On the "Hurrians," and their importance in the 2nd mill., see M. Morrison in *ABD*, 3:335-38. While the Edomites are said here to have expelled the Horites from their land, they did in fact absorb some Horite clans (Weinfeld; cf. Gen 36:20-30). The Horites are thought by some to have been "cave dwellers" (Heb חֹר = "hole") who established themselves in the Seir Mountains (Gen 14:6) and were later conquered by the Edomites (Nelson). There were and even today are cave-dwellers in Petra.

and completely destroyed them from before them. וַיַּשְׁמִידוּם מִפְּנֵיהֶם. The phrase occurs again in v. 21; see also Josh 24:8 and Amos 2:9.

just as Israel did to the land of its possession, which Yahweh gave to them. Again we see the universalism of the Deuteronomic writer, who sees the Edomites as having driven out former inhabitants, just as Israel did in Transjordan and will do again in Canaan (see Note for 2:5). Driver thinks this statement must postdate the Israelite conquest of Canaan; however, the reference could be to Israel's defeat of Sihon and Og and the taking of their land, which, by the time Moses is speaking to the people in the plains of Moab, has already taken place.

13 *Now, rise up and cross over the river Zered.* Hebrew עַתָּה is an important rhetorical particle (Muilenburg 1969, 15), signaling a discourse shift from past to present (see also 4:1; 5:25; 10:12; 26:10; 31:19; Jer 2:18; 7:13). The particle appears in the Arad ostraca (1:2; 2:1; 3:1; 40:4, and elsewhere), where, after an initial greeting, the business at hand is introduced (Y. Aharoni 1981, 12). The directive here is stock Deuteronomic phraseology (see Note for 2:24).

So we crossed over the river Zered. Numbers 21:12 says that the Israelites encamped there, but makes no mention of any direct contact with the Moabites. In Deut 2:29 it says a request was made to buy food and water from the Moabites, and Moab complied.

the river Zered. Hebrew נַחַל ("river") has no adequate English equivalent. The Arabic term is "wadi," denoting a valley in mountainous or hilly country that fills up with water in the rainy season, becoming a virtual torrent, but in summer is reduced to a brook or else goes dry. The Zered is the modern Wadi el-Ḥasā, an extraordinary canyon at the base of which flows the river (Glueck 1939, 88-89; Van Zyl 1960, 46-49; Weinfeld; J. M. Miller 1997, 194-95). The Zered was Moab's southern boundary with Edom. Moab's northern border was the Arnon (modern Wadi al-Mūjib), another spectacular canyon at the base of which lies the river (see Note for 2:24). Moab previously held territory north of the Arnon, but it was lost to Sihon (Num 21:26). Moab's western boundary was the narrow plain along the Dead Sea called "the Ghôr" (= Arabah); its eastern boundary was the Syrian-Arabian Desert beyond the modern Desert Highway. The Israelites would have crossed the Zered on Moab's eastern border (Judg 11:18).

Moab was situated on a high plateau east of the Dead Sea (elev. 3000 ft; 4300 ft above the Dead Sea), which continues the Anti-Lebanon mountain range. The Bible remains our primary source for information about Moab, although some inscriptional evidence exists. There are Egyptian texts from the reign of Ramses II (ca. 1290-1224), Assyrian texts from the 8th and 7th cents., and the mid-9th cent. Moabite (Mesha) Stone (*ANET*³, 320-21). Archaeological work, although carried on primarily above the Arnon in the northern plateau region, is adding to our knowledge of this ancient land. On the history, archaeology, and geography of Moab, see further Van Zyl 1960; J. M. Miller 1989; "Moab," in *ABD*, 4:882-93; Dearman 1989b.

14 Kadesh-barnea was the oasis in North Sinai from which the ill-fated excusion into Canaan was launched (see Note for 1:2). When the people refused to go up into the land, Yahweh swore that an entire generation would die in the wilderness (1:35-36). Here the generation is said to be the "men of war"; in Num 14:29 it is men twenty years and older, which amounts to the same thing. Following the debacle the Israelites returned to Kadesh, stayed there for an undisclosed period, and then wandered off into the wilderness for thirty-eight years (see Note for 1:46).

15 The expression "hand of God" is often associated with sickness and pestilence in the OT (Exod 9:3; 1 Sam 5:9; Jer 15:17-18; 21:5-6; Pss 32:3-4; 38:3-4[2-3]), also in Egyptian, Akkadian, and Ugaritic texts (J. J. M. Roberts 1971). A Canaanite letter from Ugarit (ca. 1400), reporting ruinous blows that have come upon the writer's city, goes on to say:

And the hand of the god is here
for the pestilence is exceeding sore (Albright 1941, 47)

People are said to have died from pestilence (דֶּבֶר) and plague (מַגֵּפָה) in the wilderness (Num 14:12, 37; 17:13-15[16:48-50]; 25:8-9, 18-19[26:1]; 31:16).

Yes indeed. וְגַם. The LXX simply has καὶ.

to rout them from the midst of the camp. לְהֻמָּם מִקֶּרֶב הַמַּחֲנֶה. The verb המם means "to rout in confusion" (Driver; cf. Exod 14:24; 23:27; Deut 7:23; 1 Sam 7:10).

Message and Audience

Moses says the people now turned to travel on the wilderness road of Moab. They were not to pick a fight with the Moabites, for Yahweh was not giving Israel any of their land. He had given it earlier to the sons of Lot as their possession. As an aside, the audience is told that the Emim used to live in Moabite land, an ancient giant race as imposing, numerous, and tall as the Anakim. Known also as the Rephaim, the Moabite name for them was Emim. Regarding Seir-Edom, where the Israelites had just been, the Horites were the original dwellers. The Edomites dispossessed them, just as Israel did to the inhabitants of Transjordan and will do soon to the inhabitants of Canaan.

Moses then told the people to cross the river Zered, which they did. Nothing is said about meeting up with the Moabites. The Deuteronomic writer simply notes that it was thirty-eight years from the time the people left Kadesh to the crossing of the Zered. An entire generation of fighting men had to die, because Yahweh swore that it would happen. And it did happen. The hand of Yahweh was heavy upon this hapless generation, until all perished and were gone from the camp.

To a late 8th- and early 7th-cent. audience, which knows that Mesha, king of Moab, took the northern Moabite plateau from Israel more than a century ago, this will be a cautionary word to Judah that it not think of doing battle with the Moabites. The land between the Arnon and the Zered belongs to the descendants of Lot, and it is their possession. On another note, the people will be reminded that giants can be overcome, and for Judah the giant presently is mighty Assyria. It has conquered all of Transjordan and brought northern Israel to ruin. But if Judah has faith in Yahweh's power to deliver, which was the message of Isaiah the prophet, Yahweh will deliver it from this awesome foe. If it does not have faith, it will perish as the wilderness generation did.

D. Do Not Go Near Ammon (2:16-23)

2 ¹⁶*And it happened as all the men of war had come to an end, dying from the midst of the people,* ¹⁷*that Yahweh spoke to me:* ¹⁸*"You are crossing today the border of Moab, that is Ar,* ¹⁹*and you shall come near the sons of Ammon. Do not be hostile to them and do not fight with them, for I will not give any of the land of the sons of Ammon to you for a possession, because to the sons of Lot I have given it for a possession."* ²⁰*(It is also known as the land of the Rephaim; the Rephaim dwelt in it formerly, but the Ammonites call them Zamzummim,* ²¹*a people great and many and tall as the Anakim, but Yahweh completely destroyed them from before them, and they dispossessed them and dwelt in their place,* ²²*just as he did for the sons of Esau who are dwelling in Seir, when he completely destroyed the Horites from before them, and they dispossessed them and dwelt in their place to this day;* ²³*also the Avvim, who were dwelling in the villages as far as Gaza; the Caphtorim, who left from Caphtor, completely destroyed them and dwelt in their place.)*

Rhetoric and Composition

These verses narrating Israel's avoidance of the Ammonites are delimited at the top end by modern Versions and modern commentators who break before v. 16 (see Rhetoric and Composition for 2:8b-15). The M^L has a *setumah* and the Sam a section after v. 16. Delimitation at the bottom end has no support from section markings; it is made after v. 23 on the basis of new content and a stereotyped opening phrase beginning in v. 24. The Sam has a section after v. 25.

Notes

2:16-17 This introduction forms a transition from v. 15. The generation under the divine curse — "men of war" (twenty years and older) — is now gone. Here the revelation formula employs the verb וַיְדַבֵּר ("and he spoke"), rather than the usual וַיֹּאמֶר ("and he said"), on which see Note for 1:42. Weinfeld says דבר is more intensive, being used here because the narrative is marking a turning point: "the rebellious generation has perished, and the words of God are now addressed to the generation that is about to enter the promised land."

18 If גְּבוּל has the usual meaning of "border" and Ar a city on Moab's northern border, then Ar must be located in Moab's northeast corner near where the Israelites are traveling (Driver). But if גְּבוּל means "territory," as it does in 2:4, then Ar is in apposition and refers to the whole of Moab (see Note for 2:9). In either case, the Israelites do not first fight Sihon and then approach Ammonite country (*pace* Tigay).

19 *and you shall come near the sons of Ammon*. The Israelites would enter Ammonite territory if they went further north. Also, they have not yet crossed the Arnon, Moab's northern border (see Note for 2:24). What we have then is simply a warning not to continue north after the crossing has been made, for this would bring Israel into Ammonite territory. The Ammonites lived along the upper courses of the Jabbok and in cities of the hill country (2:37; 3:16); their capital was Rabbath-Ammon (2 Sam 12:26), which was up over the mountains about 40 km east of the Jordan. The ancient city survives in modern-day Amman, the capital of Jordan. To the west was the kingdom of Sihon, whose capital was at Heshbon (2:24; Num 21:24 MT). Ammonite geography, religion, and culture are summarized in Herr, *OEANE*, 1:103-5. On ancient Ammonite territory and sites, see B. MacDonald (1999); for archaeological work on Ammonite sites, see Sauer (1985; 1986); Younker (1999), and E. Stern (2001, 238258).

the sons of Ammon. בְּנֵי עַמּוֹן is the biblical term for the Ammonites, a Transjordanian tribal people living northeast of Moab. From the Tell Sīrān Bottle Inscription (*COS II* 139) we learn that the Ammonite king referred to himself as "king of the sons of Ammon (*bn ʿamn*)," indicating that the Ammonites were more a tribe than a nation (Bienkowski and van der Steen 2001, 38-39).

Do not be hostile to them and do not fight with them, for I will not give any of the land of the sons of Ammon to you for a possession, because to the sons of Lot I have given it for a possession. The Israelites are not to pick a fight with the Ammonites either. Yahweh is not giving Israel any of their land; it was given to the sons of Lot. Israel therefore did not approach the Ammonites (2:37). According to biblical tradition, Ammon was another son of Lot, Abraham's nephew (see Note for 2:9). Nothing is said here about any encounter with the Ammonites, e.g., no request to buy food and water; nevertheless, according to 23:5(4), the Ammonites did not offer hospitality when they should have and are censured for it. Both the Edomites and Moabites sold Israel food and water (2:29). Numbers, too, is silent about any encounter with the Ammonites. Numbers 21:24 (MT) suggests that the Israelites refrained from moving against the Ammonites "because the border of the sons of Ammon was strong" (B. MacDonald 1999, 31; Weinfeld). The LXX of this verse reads Ιαζηρ ("Jazer") for Hebrew עַז ("strong"), which some modern English versions accept (RSV; JB; NJB; NAB; cf. יַעְזֵר in Num 21:32; 32:1, 3). NJV translates the Hebrew as an otherwise unknown "Az."

20-23 Another antiquarian note, like those in 2:10-12; 3:9, 11, 13b-14; 10:6-9. Von Rad says these notes bear witness to Israel's astonishing interest in history.

20-21 This note names the former occupants of Ammon. Ammonite territory, like the territory of Moab, was once inhabited by the Rephaim (2:10-11). The verb שׁמד in vv. 21-23 is an internal H-stem having intensive meaning: "completely destroyed" (see Note for 1:27). On the phrase "completely destroyed them from before them," see Note for 2:12.

the Rephaim. A people reputedly of giant stature, who once populated the Transjordan territory of Sihon and Og, also territory west of the Jordan (Josh 17:15). The Valley of Rephaim in the vicinity of Jerusalem (Josh 15:8; 18:16) appears to have been named for these aboriginal giants. In Deut 3:13b the Rephaim are associated with the whole of Bashan. They also occupied land of the Moabites, who called them Emim (2:10-11). The Rephaim were said to be as tall as the Anakim (see Note for 1:28), with Og of Bashan being the last living remnant (3:11; Josh 13:12). His huge bed (9 cubits by 4 cubits = 13.5 ft by 6 ft) was still on display in Rabbath-Ammon. The book of *Jubilees* (29:9-10) says the height of the Rephaim was anywhere from 10 to 7 cubits (= 15 to 10.5 ft). Giant legends belong to the world of mythical folklore, on which see Note for 1:28. Biblical tradition states that a coalition of kings headed by Ched-or-laomer, king of Elam, defeated the Rephaim at Ashtaroth-Karnaim (Gen 14:5). Soon afterwards, Yahweh promised Abraham that his descendants would possess the land of the Rephaim (Gen 15:20).

This giant race appears to be associated in some fashion with other Rephaim inhabiting the underworld. These Rephaim receive frequent mention in the OT (Isa 14:9; 26:14, 19; Ps 88:11[10]; Job 26:5; Prov 2:18; 9:18; 21:16; RSV: "the shades" or "the dead") and are known also from Ugaritic texts (Gray 1949; Pope 1977; Talmon 1993a). Weinfeld calls these Rephaim the "divine ancient heroes in Sheol" (cf. Ezek 32:27). The Rephaim in Ugaritic literature are deified ancestors, considered to be a source of fertility (Pope 1977, 167). In one text, "the Hero, King Eternal" *(rpu mlk olm)* is said to dwell and rule at Ashtaroth and Edrei, the very cities from which Og king of Bashan ruled (Deut 1:4; Pope 1977, 177; Weinfeld, 162). In another text (RS. 34.126), memorial rites take place for spirits of the Rephaim (Bordreuil and Pardee 1982). Pope also cites a Phoenician tomb inscription that invokes the Mighty Og to visit the grave robber, pointing to the quasi-mythological character of Og, king of Bashan. Talmon (1993a, 83), however, notes that quasi-mythological references to Rephaim in the OT do not appear in historiographical texts, but rather in prophetic and wisdom texts, which he believes show influence from the Ugaritic epic tradition. Weinfeld cites for comparison the Greek Cyclopes, those legendary heroes having built the walls of Mycenae and Tiryns, who lived on in Greek mythology and became objects of worship.

Zamzummim. זַמְזֻמִּים. These are the "Zuzim" of Gen 14:5, mentioned there together with the Rephaim and Emim. Nothing is otherwise known of these people. The term is said to mean "whisperers, murmurers," which suits spirits of the dead more than living giants. Arabic *zamzama* is "a distant sounding or sound such as is confused and continued," and *zîzîm* is imitative of "the low or faint sound of the jinn, or geneii, that is heard by night in the deserts" (Lane 1865, 1248-49).

22 Repeating v. 12 and expanding upon v. 5. On the "Horites," see Note for 2:12.

to this day. עַד הַיּוֹם הַזֶּה. A common expression in Deuteronomy (2:22; 3:14; 10:8; 11:4; 29:3[4]; 34:6), occurring also in the Deuteronomic History (Driver 1895, 57; cf. Childs 1963; von Rad 1966b, 28; Geoghegan 2003). Childs (p. 292) says the formula seldom has an etiological function, as some maintain, but in the great majority of cases is "a formula of personal testimony added to, and confirming, a received tradition."

23 The writer of this note wants to tell us about an earlier population even in Philistia. The Avvim, otherwise unknown, were living in Philistia (Josh 13:3; LXX includes "in the south" from v. 4). The LXX of Josh 13:3-4 puts the Avvim south of the Philistine pentapolis. In the present verse we are told that the Avvim, who occupied territory in Palestine as far south as Gaza, were destroyed by incoming Philistines.

in the villages as far as Gaza. The Avvim "villages" (חֲצֵרִים) were unwalled settlements (Lev 25:31), common among nomadic and seminomadic peoples, e.g., the tent-dwelling Kedarites (Gen 25:13-16; Isa 42:11; Jer 49:28-29). Mari texts refer to tent-dwelling nomads in unwalled villages (Malamat 1962, 146-47). Settlements of this type are attested also in Simeon and southern Judah, where one finds place names such as חֲצַר־אַדָּר in Num 34:4; חֲצַר גַּדָּה and חֲצַר שׁוּעָל in Josh 15:27-28; and חֲצַר סוּסָה in Josh 19:5. The LXX (Ασηρωθ) and Vg *(Haserim)* translated as a place name (so also T^OnqPsJ), which is how the AV translated it ("Hazerim"). But the RSV and other modern English versions (NEB; JB; NAB; NIV; NJV; NRSV; REB) change to "villages" or the like (so T^Nf), which is how modern commentators read the term (Weinfeld; Tigay; Friedman; Nelson).

Gaza. Eusebius *(Onom.)* identifies Gaza as a city of the Hivites, saying that long ago it was the Canaanite boundary with Egypt. Ancient Gaza is commonly identified with Tell Kharubeh (= Tell ʿAzza), ca. 5 km inland on the coastal highway. Gaza is first named in a campaign report of Thutmosis III (ca. 1490-1436), who lists it as one of the cities he conquered (*ANET*³, 235). It is mentioned also in Taanach Tablet no. 6 (Albright 1944a, 25) and in the Amarna Letters (EA 289, 296; cf. *ANET*[3], 489), where it is an Egyptian administrative center (*NEAEHL*, 2:464; *ABD*, 2:912). After Israel's conquest of Canaan, Gaza was set apart for the tribe of Judah (Josh 15:47; Judg 1:18), but Eusebius says Judah never ruled it. If Judah did rule the city, it was for only a short time, because by the beginning of the 12th cent. Gaza had become the southernmost city of the Philistine pentapolis (Josh 13:3; 1 Sam 6:17).

the Caphtorim who left from Caphtor. The Philistines came from Caphtor (Amos 9:7; Jer 47:4), but there were other "Caphtorim" who were not Philistines (Gen 10:14 [= 1 Chr 1:12]). Caphtor ("Keftiu" in Egyptian texts; "Kaptara" in Akkadian texts) is usually identified with the island of Crete. The LXX and Targums have "Cappadocia" for Caphtor, but Weinfeld says this results from a misspelling of כפתוך for כפתר. Cappadocia is an inland country in the heart of Asia Minor (modern Turkey). The Cretans are probably the OT "Cherethites" (1 Sam 30:14; Ezek 25:16; Zeph 2:5), another people associated with the Philistines, who lived southeast of Philistia (J. Greenfield, "Cherethites and Pelethites" in *IDB*, 1:557; cf. 1 Sam 30:14: "the Negeb of the Cherethites"). See also Zeph 2:5 and Ezek 25:16.

Message and Audience

Moses now says that after the men under the curse were gone, Yahweh spoke to him about where the journey would take them once Moab's northern border had been crossed. They would be passing Ar, located on the southern rim of the Arnon river valley, and to the north of the Arnon was Ammonite country. Not much is said about the Ammonites. Moses simply instructs Israel not to pick a fight with them, for Yahweh was not giving any Ammonite land to Israel. It had been given to the sons of Lot as a possession. What follows is another note telling the audience that Ammonite land belonged earlier to the Rephaim, whom the Ammonites called Zamzummin. This was another giant race as numerous and tall as the Anakim. Yahweh destroyed the Rephaim. The Ammonites took their land and were now dwelling in it. The same was done for the Edomites in Seir, Yahweh destroying the Horites who lived there formerly. Regarding the Avvim, who lived in villages over near Gaza, the Caphtorim — known to those listening as Philistines from Crete — completely destroyed them and dwelt in their settlements.

To a late 8th- and early 7th-cent. Judahite audience that might entertain ideas about ravaging the Ammonites, as David once did (2 Samuel 10–11), Moses' words may dissuade them against such adventurism. Ammonite land belongs to the sons of Lot and is their possession. The audience is again reminded of other peoples to whom land was given, that formerly it was occupied by others. Judah, therefore, would do well to keep focused on its own land, although by 701 Sennacherib had ravaged Judah and nearly brought Jerusalem down, which would have been the end of the Israelite nation. The Judahites might also be reminded again that Yahweh can defeat giants like the Assyrians, for which reason they should put their trust ultimately in Yahweh.

E. I Have Given Sihon into Your Hand (2:24-37)

2 ²⁴*"Rise up, take your journey, and cross over the river Arnon. See, I have given into your hand Sihon king of Heshbon, the Amorite, and his land. Begin, take possession, and fight a battle with him.* ²⁵*This day I will begin to put the dread of you and the fear of you upon the faces of the people under the entire heaven, who shall hear the report of you, and shall shake and shall writhe because of you."* ²⁶*So I sent messengers from the wilderness of Kedemoth to Sihon king of Heshbon, words of peace, saying:* ²⁷*"Let me go across your land; only by the road I will go; I will not turn aside right or left.* ²⁸*You shall sell me food for money so I can eat, and you shall give me water for money so I can drink, only let me pass through on foot,* ²⁹*just as the sons of Esau who dwell in Seir and the Moabites who dwell in Ar did for me, until I pass over the Jordan to the land that Yahweh our God is giving to us."* ³⁰*But Sihon king of Heshbon was not willing to let us go across it, for Yahweh your God hardened his spirit and made his heart obstinate, in order to give him into your hand, as at this day.* ³¹*Then Yahweh said to me: "See, I have begun to give over before you Sihon and his land. Begin, take possession, so as to possess his land."*

³²*Then Sihon came out to meet us, he and all his people, to battle at Jahzah.* ³³*And Yahweh our God gave him over to us, and we struck down him and his sons and all his people.* ³⁴*And we took all his cities at that time, and we devoted to destruction every city, men and the women and the little ones; we did not leave a survivor remaining.* ³⁵*Only the beasts we took as booty for ourselves, and as spoil the cities that we had taken.* ³⁶*From Aroer, which is on the edge of the river Arnon, and the city that is in the valley, and as far as Gilead, there was not a city that was too high for us. Everything Yahweh our God gave over to us.* ³⁷*Only to the land of the sons of Ammon you did not draw near, all the bank of the river Jabbok, and the cities of the hill country, and everywhere that Yahweh our God commanded.*

Rhetoric and Composition

These verses, which describe the victory over Sihon, are delimited at the top end by new content and a stereotyped opening phrase in v. 24 and at the bottom end by the chapter division. In M^L are no sections before v. 24 or after v. 37. The M^L has a *setumah* and the Sam a section after v. 30, perhaps because Yahweh's speech begins in v. 31.

Verses 24-31 have the following balancing structure:

2:24   *See, I have given into your hand Sihon . . . and his land.*
       Begin, take possession, and fight a battle with him.

2:31   *See, I have begun to give over before you Sihon and his land.*
       Begin, take possession, so as to possess his land.

In vv. 34-37 is this balancing structure:

2:34   . . . we did not leave a survivor remaining.
2:35   *Only* (רַק) the beasts we took as booty for ourselves. . . .

2:36   Everything Yahweh our God gave over to us.
2:37   *Only* (רַק) to the land of the sons of Ammon you did not draw near. . . .

Portions of 2:24-37 are contained in 4QDeut^d, 4QDeut^h, 11QDeut, 4Q364, and 4Q365.

Notes

2:24 *Rise up, take your journey, and cross over the river Arnon.* Moses' address resumes from v. 19 after a lengthy antiquarian note. The directive now is to cross the Arnon, Moab's northern boundary, and direct attention to the kingdom of Sihon, which is to the west. This crossing anticipates the later crossing of the Jordan, but for the writer of Deuteronomy it is more than that: Here begins the conquest of the promised land (Weinfeld, 170, 173-78; 1983b, 67-70). Weinfeld says: "The crossing of the Arnon River is perceived as the beginning of the conquest and the fulfillment of the promises to the patriarchs." On the importance of "threshold crossings," of which a river crossing is one, see Trumbull (1896, 177-83); van Gennep (1909, 29); Lundbom (1986c, 7-9). The Arnon (modern Wadi al-Mūjib) is another spectacular canyon at the base of which lies the Arnon River (Num 21:13; 22:36; Judg 11:18). The sides of this rocky gorge contain high cliffs, rock fissures, and caves in which doves and rock pigeons nest. Its caves served also as places of refuge for people in time of war (Jer 48:28). The small but perennial Arnon River, mentioned often in the Bible, flows north through the central Moabite mountains, turns west south of Aroer, and then empties into the Dead Sea. The Arnon was Moab's northern boundary throughout much of its history, except when it expanded into the northern plateau region.

Rise up, take your journey, and cross over. קוּמוּ סְעוּ וְעִבְרוּ. Asyndeton, occurring again at the end of the verse. The directive is stock Deuteronomic phraseology (1:7, 40; 2:13, 24; 10:11).

See, I have given into your hand Sihon king of Heshbon, the Amorite, and his land. Begin, take possession, and fight a battle with him. A repeat of the earlier command in 1:21, only here the Israelites will heed it. The command is from Yahweh, and Yahweh will be credited with the victory (2:33; 3:3). For Deuteronomy, this begins the occupation of the promised land. The Amorites, unlike the Edomites, Moabites, and Ammonites, were not kin to the Israelites, and Yahweh had not allotted them a territory (Driver; but see Deut 32:8). On Deuteronomy's concept of holy war, see Note for 1:30.

See. For רְאֵה as an interjection, see Note for 1:8. The LXX has ἰδοὺ ("behold").

Begin, take possession, and fight. הָחֵל רָשׁ וְהִתְגָּר. More asyndeton (cf. v. 31). Jeremiah uses asyndeton to announce imminent defeat (Jer 4:5; 25:27; 46:3-4).

Sihon king of Heshbon, the Amorite. According to the OT, Sihon's kingdom was located in southern Gilead, extending from the Arnon River in the south to the Jabbok River in the north (Num 21:24; Judg 11:22). Sihon had wrested the northern plateau — from the Arnon to about Heshbon — from a previous Moabite king (Num 21:26) and established his capital at Heshbon. The Jordan River was the kingdom's western boundary, but just how much territory Sihon claimed to the east remains unclear (Num 21:24 says to the Ammonite border; Judg 11:22 "to the wilderness"). At the time of Israel's Transjordanian conquest, the Ammonites were living along the upper courses of the Jabbok — near Rabbath-Ammon and in cities of the hill country. Sihon's territory east to west, in any case, was not great. From the Jordan over the mountains to Rabbath-Ammon was 40 km.

In biblical tradition, the Amorites were one of the peoples inhabiting Canaan before the Israelite conquest (1:44; 7:1; Gen 15:16, 21; Josh 3:10; 7:7). Amos views them as a giant race (Amos 2:9). From extrabiblical sources, including Amorite personal names that survive, we know that the Amorites were a Semitic people living in north Syria from very early times. The Akkadian term for Amorite territory was *Amurru* ("the West"), denoting the geographic area northwest of Mesopotamia (see Note for 1:7). As early as the 3rd mill., Amorites were populating an area extending from the Euphrates (Mari) to the Mediterranean (Ugarit). Amorite rule in the early 2nd mill. extended into lower Mesopo-

Deuteronomy 2

tamia and westward into Palestine and Transjordan (Gen 14:7). The Jebusites in Jerusalem before David took the city (2 Sam 5:6-9) may have been Amorites (cf. Ezek 16:2-3, 45). But in the time of Sihon and Og, links to earlier Amorite culture were much weakened, i.e., the term "Amorite" no longer had ethnic meaning, and Sihon and Og were simply kings with Syrian cultural connections. Mendenhall (*ABD*, 1:201) believes that Sihon and Og were "remnants of [North Syrian] political entities that attempted to reestablish their old political regimes in another region." Final references to Amorite kings are those occurring in the Bible. See further on the Amorites, N. Gottwald in *EncJud*, 2:875-78, and G. E. Mendenhall in *ABD*, 1:199-202.

Heshbon was located by Eusebius *(Onom.)* 20 Roman milestones east of the Jordan, in the mountains opposite Jericho. The ancient city has long been identified with Tell Ḥesbân in modern Ḥisban, a mound preserving the ancient name ca. 900 m above sea level, guarding the northern edge of the Moabite plain. The site is 19 km southwest of Amman and 6 km northeast of Mount Nebo (*OEANE*, 3:19-22; *NEAEHL*, 2:626). Early sightings by Burckhardt (1992, 365) and E. Robinson (1867, 1:551) appear to be of this tell. After Sihon was defeated, Heshbon was settled by the Israelite tribe of Reuben (Num 32:33-37; Josh 13:17). Heshbon was a fertile area (Isa 16:8-9), noted particularly for its pools (Cant 7:5[4]). Excavations carried out at Tell Ḥesbân between 1968 and 1978 failed to turn up any remains prior to 1200, with only modest Iron Age remains present. Considerable doubt has therefore been cast on this being Sihon's Heshbon, although the site has its supporters (B. MacDonald 1999, 38). Excavators more recently have turned their attention to Tell Jalul, some 5 mi south of Tell Ḥesbân and 3 mi east of Madaba, where substantial Late Bronze and Iron Age remains are attested (Herr 1993; *BAR* 31/1 [2005] 26-27; cf. Glueck 1934, 5).

25 *This day I will begin to put the dread of you and the fear of you upon the faces of the people under the entire heaven.* I.e., upon people everywhere (4:19). Divine hyperbole, reduced somewhat in 11:24-25. Here it will be sufficient if Yahweh simply inflicts the fear of Israel on Sihon and neighboring peoples. The LXX has an imperative ("In this day, begin to put your trembling and your fear upon all faces . . ."), which urges the people themselves to begin causing the trembling and the fear. In MT it is Yahweh who will begin inflicting the dread (פַּחַד) and the fear (יִרְאָה). Here are clear echoes of Exod 15:14-16, where Yahweh puts panic and dread (פַּחַד) on neighboring peoples at the time of the exodus deliverance (Moran 1963a, 340). "Dread" (פַּחַד) comes in holy war, denoting the effect of scare tactics upon an enemy.

and shall writhe because of you. וְחָלוּ מִפָּנֶיךָ. The verb "writhe (in pain)" (חוּל/חִיל) is often used with reference to a woman in labor (Isa 26:17; Jer 4:31).

26-27 It is generally recognized that after Yahweh has told Moses to start a war with Sihon and promised him victory in the war, requesting peaceful passage through Sihon's territory — even though rooted in old tradition (Num 21:21-23) — is an empty gesture (Moran; Weinfeld; Tigay; Nelson). The rabbis circumvented the problem by saying that Moses' offer of peace was not commissioned by God, whereas later Jewish interpreters imagined that the request was made before God told Moses to attack. The request is doubtless a pretext aimed at provoking war (Weinfeld). The Israelites must pass through Sihon's territory in order to cross the Jordan and enter Canaan.

the wilderness of Kedemoth. A wilderness on Moab's eastern border, with a city named Kedemoth in the same general area (Josh 13:18; cf. 21:37). The precise location of the city is not known. The preferred site is Tell es-Sâliyeh, a large tell overlooking the Wadi Sâliyeh (Van Zyl 1960, 74-75; Boling 1985, 25; Dearman 1989a, 63; J. Peterson, in *ABD*, 4:10-11), which best fits the biblical description. This would put Kedemoth just north of the Arnon, on Sihon's eastern border, near the desert. Glueck (1934, 34-36; 1951, 290-95) found large quantities of Early Iron sherds and a smaller number of Late Bronze sherds on this tell. Other suggested sites are Qaṣr ez-Zaʿferân (G. E. Wright) and the lofty Khirbet er-Remeil overlooking the Wadi er-Remeil (Abel 1938, 415). Both sites are north and west of Tell es-Sâliyeh and have Early Iron remains (Kallai 1986, 441; cf. Glueck 1934, 30-31; 1939, 118-23). Kedemoth later became a Levitical city allotted to the tribe of Reuben (Josh 21:36-37; 1 Chr 6:63-64[78-79]).

words of peace. I.e., an offer of peace delivered by the messengers.

only by the road. בַּדֶּרֶךְ בַּדֶּרֶךְ. The repetition in Hebrew expresses an exceptional quality (GKC §123e): "by the road, (only) by the road" (ibn Ezra). The LXX has just one occurrence of the term. The MT reading is supported by 4QDeut^d (Crawford 1993, 31-32; Ulrich, Cross, et al. 1995, 36-37), and the repetition should not be attributed to dittography simply on the *lectio brevior* principle (*pace* Crawford). Numbers 21:22 reads: "By the king's road [highway] we will go."

I will not turn aside right or left. The expression "turn (aside) right or left" is common in Deuteronomy (5:32; 17:11, 20; 28:14; Driver 1895, lxxxii no. 53; Weinfeld 1972, 339 no. 20), occurring elsewhere in the OT (Josh 1:7; 23:6; 1 Sam 6:12; 2 Kgs 22:2; with נטה in Num 20:17; 22:26).

28-29 Here both the Edomites and Moabites are said to have sold food and water to the Israelites, but Num 20:19-21 says the Edomites refused the Israelites water. On Esau and the land of Seir, see Note for 2:4. On Ar, see Note for 2:9.

30 Yahweh's "hardening" of Sihon's spirit recalls the exodus event, where Yahweh was said to have "hardened" the heart of the pharaoh (Exod 4:21; 7:3; 9:12; 10:20, 27; cf. Rom 9:18). Cf. 1 Kgs 12:15, where divine intervention of a similar nature comes in order to fulfill earlier prophecy. Philo, Pseudo-Philo, and Josephus do not mention the hardening of Sihon's spirit, presumably because it would violate the exercise of free will (Feldman 2002).

as at this day. כַּיּוֹם הַזֶּה. A stereotyped Deuteronomic phrase (2:30; 4:20,

38; 6:24; 8:18; 10:15; 29:27[28]; Driver 1895, lxxxi no. 40; Weinfeld 1972, 350 no. 4), occurring also in the prose of Jeremiah (Jer 11:5; 25:18; 32:20; 44:6, 22, 23). It means "as is now the case" or "right now" (Driver; Weinfeld; Goldingay 1993).

31 *Then Yahweh said to me:* On this introductory phrase, see Note for 1:42.

See, I have begun to give over before you Sihon and his land. The verb נתן is used often in Deuteronomy to mean "give over foes and/or land" (2:31, 33, 36; 7:2, 23; 23:15[14]; 31:5; Driver 1895, lxxxii no. 52). For the idiom רְאֵה נָתַתִּי לְפָנֶיכֶם, "See, I have set/given over before you," see Note for 1:8.

Begin, take possession, so as to possess his land. Asyndeton along the lines of v. 24.

32 Cf. Num 21:23; Judg 11:20.

Jahzah. יָהְצָה. Spelled יַהַץ ("Jahaz") in Isa 15:4; Jer 48:34, and elsewhere; the spelling here occurs in Jer 48:21. This city is mentioned on the Moabite Stone (lines 19-21) as having been annexed by Mesha to Dibon (*ANET*[3], 320). Its precise location is unknown, although Eusebius *(Onom.)* said it lay between Medaba and Debus (= Dibon). Suggested sites include Khirbet Iskander, 6 km north of Dibon and just west of the King's Highway (Bernhardt 1960, 155-58); Khirbet Libb, 10 km north of Dibon on the King's Highway (Simons 1959, 207 no. 42; J. M. Miller 1989, 589; Smelik 1992, 74-79); and Khirbet Medeiniyeh, 10 km east and a bit south of Khirbet Libb (Dearman 1984; *ABD*, 3:612; Levine 2000, 100). The last-named is on the eastern edge of the "tableland," and is the battle site preferred by Weinfeld. After the Israelite defeat of Sihon (Num 21:23-24; Judg 11:20-21), Jahzah was assigned to Reuben as a Levitical city (Josh 13:18; 21:36; 1 Chr 6:78).

33 See Num 21:24 and Judg 11:21-22. "His sons" (plural) is a Qere reading.

34 *And we took all his cities at that time.* See Num 21:25a. On the retrospective "at that time," see Note for 1:9.

and we devoted to destruction every city, men and the women and the little ones; we did not leave a survivor remaining. Not mentioned in Numbers 21. According to the rules of holy war, a conquered people — sometimes also spoil — were not taken as booty but destroyed and devoted (= dedicated) to God (see Note for 7:2). In contexts other than holy war, the verb חרם means "devote (to God)" (Lev 27:21, 28-29). In holy war against the Canaanites, everything was to come under the ban (20:16-17), while in subsequent wars against distant cities, only (adult) males would come under the ban (חֶרֶם); women, children, cattle, and other goods could be taken as booty (20:10-15). On the expression "We did not leave a survivor remaining," which is used often by Deuteronomic writers, see also 3:3 (= Num 21:35); Josh 8:22; 10:28, 30, 33, 37, 39, 40; 11:8, etc.). Philo, Pseudo-Philo, and Josephus fail to mention the killing of women and children, with Philo speaking only of the annihilation of Sihon's army (Feldman 2002).

men. מְתָם. A rare poetic word (Rashi; Driver; Weinfeld). Misunderstood by the LXX (Wevers 1995, 47), which translated: "their (αὐτῶν) women and their (αὐτῶν) children."

35 Here the ban is not applied to cattle and other spoils (cf. Josh 8:2, 27; 11:14).

36 Sihon's entire kingdom was taken, but it included only the southern half of Gilead (3:12; Josh 12:2).

Aroer. A city mentioned frequently in the OT, also on the Moabite Stone (line 26), which is generally identified with Khirbet ʿAraʿir (Abel 1938, 250; J. M. Miller 1989, 583; Weinfeld; *NEAEHL*, 1:92), about 5 km southeast of Dibon and 4 km west of the King's Highway, on the northern slope of Wadi Mujib (= Arnon River; see Note for 2:24). The OT places it "on the edge of the river Arnon" (2:36; 3:12; 4:48; Josh 12:2; 13:9, 16), perhaps to distinguish it from the Aroer east of Rabbath-Ammon (Josh 13:25; Judg 11:33). There was another Aroer in Judah (1 Sam 30:28). At the present time, Aroer on the Arnon belongs to Sihon. Throughout its history, Aroer was primarily a fortress guarding the King's Highway on its descent to the Arnon (Jer 48:19). After Aroer was taken from Sihon, it was assigned to the Reubenites and became the southern boundary of Israel's Transjordan territory (3:12; Josh 13:15-16). According to Num 32:34, Aroer was built up by the Gadites.

and the city that is in the valley. A city in the Arnon gorge, always mentioned in connection with Aroer (Josh 13:9, 16; 2 Sam 24:5). Ninow (2002) has recently identified it with Khirbet al-Mamariyeh, which lies in the middle of the Arnon Valley. The site is unexcavated, but preliminary examination has turned up substantial fortifications and pottery from the Late Bronze and Iron Ages.

Gilead. Gilead in its widest usage is the central Transjordan highland region between the Yarmuk River in the north and probably Heshbon in the south (3:10). "Transjordan" in the OT is divided into three main regions: the tableland (between the Arnon and Heshbon); Gilead; and Bashan (*EncJud*, 7:569). Dividing Gilead in half was the Jabbok River. The southern portion from Heshbon to the Jabbok was ruled by Sihon; the northern portion from the Jabbok to the Yarmuk was ruled by Og. Gilead's western border was the Jordan and its eastern border in the north, the Syrian-Arabian desert. In the south Gilead came up against Ammonites in the east, who lived along the upper courses of the Jabbok and in cities of the hill country (see Note for 2:19). After the Israelite conquest, Sihon's territory went to Reuben and Gad and Og's territory to the half-tribe of Manasseh (3:12-13; Num 32:33-42). Gilead was famous for its high quality balm, which was used for body oils, perfumes, and as a medicine (Gen 37:25; Jer 8:22). On Gilead, see further Ottosson 1969.

Everything Yahweh our God gave over to us. The land did not come as a result of Israel's military strength; it was a gift from Yahweh (cf. 8:17-18; 9:4-5). But Philo, Pseudo-Philo, and Josephus all go to some length in emphasizing Israel's consummate skill in warfare (Feldman 2002).

37 This reiterates the command of 2:18-19. Hebrew יָד (lit. "hand, forearm") here means "bank (of a river)" (Exod 2:5; Num 13:29; Jer 46:6; cf. Joüon 1933). The upper courses of the Jabbok were inhabited by the Ammonites; the lower course to the north, turning west and flowing into the Jordan, divided the kingdoms of Sihon and Og. The Jabbok (modern Wadi Zerqa) is where Jacob wrestled with the divine messenger (Gen 32:23-31[22-30]; Hos 12:4-5a[3-4a]).

the cities of the hill country. I.e., cities in the hill country of Ammon.

Message and Audience

After the audience has heard more history about prior inhabitants of the land on both sides of the Jordan, including the legendary giant people, the narrative resumes with Moses now telling the people to cross the river Arnon. In this version of Israelite tradition, crossing the Arnon begins the conquest of the promised land. Yahweh says he has given Sihon, the Amorite king residing in Heshbon, into Israel's hand. The Israelites are therefore told to enter his land and engage him in battle. With this act, Yahweh will begin putting the fear of Israel in people everywhere.

Moses then says he sent messengers from the wilderness of Kedemoth to Sihon with an offer of peace. The Amorite king was asked to let the Israelites go across on the road, not veering to the right or left, and to sell them food and water as the Edomites and Moabites did, so they could get to the Jordan and cross into the land Yahweh God was giving them. But the audience will see this as a ruse, for Yahweh has just told Moses to attack Sihon and promised him victory. Sihon rejected the offer, which is explained as a hardening of the king's spirit by Yahweh, echoes of Pharaoh's hardening in Egypt. The command to do battle with Sihon is repeated. Israel will possess his land.

Sihon and his people came out to meet the Israelites at Jahaz, and it happened just as Yahweh said. The Israelites defeated them in battle, and put every city with its inhabitants under the ban. Everyone was killed. Only cattle and spoil were taken as booty. Moses boasts that the victory was total: No city wall was too high for them; Yahweh gave them everything. But Moses says they did not go near the Ammonites who were living on the banks of the Jabbok and in the neighboring hill country. Yahweh had commanded him not to do this.

To a late 8th- and early 7th-cent. Judahite audience, this was a vivid recollection of how Israel took its Transjordan land, a land recently seized from Israel by the Assyrians (734). Would this land ever be restored to Israel? They did not

Deuteronomy 3

know. But what they should know is that when Israel trusts Yahweh and obeys his word, any enemy can be defeated. Do Judahites now trust in Yahweh, and are they now obeying his word? These are the questions the audience must answer.

F. I Have Also Given Og into Your Hand (3:1-11)

3 ^{1}*Then we turned and went up in the direction of the Bashan, and Og king of the Bashan came out to meet us, he and all his people, to battle at Edrei.* ^{2}*And Yahweh said to me, "Do not fear him, for I have given him and all his people and his land into your hand, and you shall do to him just as you did to Sihon king of the Amorites, who dwelt in Heshbon."* ^{3}*So Yahweh our God gave Og king of the Bashan and all his people into our hand as well, and we struck him down until there was not a survivor remaining to him.* ^{4}*And we took all his cities at that time; there was not a town that we did not take from them, sixty cities, all the territory of Argob, the kingdom of Og in the Bashan.* ^{5}*All these were fortified cities with a high wall, gates and bars, besides very many open cities in the country.* ^{6}*And we devoted them to destruction just as we did to Sihon king of Heshbon, devoting to destruction every city, men, the women, and the little ones;* ^{7}*but all the beasts and the spoil of the cities we took as booty for ourselves.* ^{8}*So we took the land at that time from the hand of the two Amorite kings who were beyond the Jordan, from the river Arnon to Mount Hermon* ^{9}*(Sidonians call Hermon Sirion, and the Amorites call it Senir),* ^{10}*all the cities of the tableland, and all of the Gilead and all of the Bashan, to Salcah and Edrei, cities of the kingdom of Og in the Bashan.* ^{11}*(For only Og king of the Bashan remained of the remnant of the Rephaim; look, his bed was a bed of iron. Is it not in Rabbah of the sons of Ammon? Nine cubits was its length, and four cubits its width, according to the usual cubit.)*

Rhetoric and Composition

The present verses are delimited at the top end by the chapter division at 3:1. The Sam has a section after 3:1, not present in M^L. Delimitation at the bottom end is by a section in Sam after v. 11. The Sam has another section after v. 7.

A portion of 3:1-11 is found in 4Q364.

Notes

3:1   A near repetition of Num 21:33. Og ruled a kingdom in "the Bashan" (the name takes the article), which means "the smooth/stoneless plain." Bashan was situated in the north Transjordanian highlands, extending from Mount Hermon in the north (3:8; Josh 12:5; 13:11) to the Yarmuk River in the south. This mountainous territory (Ps 68:16[15]) was known for its rich pasture, choice cattle (32:14; Ps 22:13[12]; Amos 4:1; Mic 7:14; Nah 1:4; Jer 50:19; Ezek 39:18), and stands of oak trees (Isa 2:13; 33:9; Ezek 27:6; Zech 11:2). Og also ruled northern Gilead (3:13), the territories of Sihon and Og being contiguous (3:8-10; Josh 12:1-5). Og's kingdom did not extend as far west as the kingdom of Sihon, for the Maacathite and Geshurite tribes occupied territory immediately east of the Sea of Galilee and the Upper Jordan Valley, now the Golan Heights (see Note for 3:14). But Og's territory extended farther to the east, all the way to the Hauran (Jebel ed-Druze) mountains (Simons 1959, 12-13). Eastern Bashan was called the Argob (see v. 4). The principal cities in Bashan were Ashtaroth and Edrei (see Note for 1:4). Edrei was on Bashan's southern border and is where the battle with Israel took place. Weinfeld (p. 181) believes that Bashan has been vastly expanded in the Deuteronomic tradition, a reconstruction from the time of the united monarchy (cf. 1 Kgs 4:13).

Then we turned. וַנֵּפֶן. Stereotyped Deuteronomic language (1:7, 24, 40; 2:1, 3, 8b; 3:1).

2 *And Yahweh said to me.* See Note for 1:42.

Do not fear him. On this stereotypical war language, see Num 21:34 and Note for 1:20-21.

I have given him . . . into your hand. On the stereotypical "to give into the hand(s) of," see Num 21:34 and Note for 1:27.

Heshbon. Sihon's capital city (see Note for 2:24).

3 This war repeats the outcome of the war against Sihon (2:34-36). See Num 21:35.

4 The Argob was a region in the east of Bashan (B. Mazar 1986b, 122), made later into an administrative district by Solomon (1 Kgs 4:13). In Solomon's time it was also said to have sixty cities, which Tigay thinks may simply be a round number. From the geographical list of Thutmoses III (ca. 1490-1436) and the 14th-cent. Amarna Letters (EA 256), we know that the region was well populated in the Late Bronze Age (*EncJud*, 3:433; *ANET*^{3}, 486). Thutmoses III mentions Ashtaroth and Edrei in his list of conquered cities (*ANET*^{3}, 242). Centuries later, the Assyrian King Shalmaneser III (859-825) boasts of marching as far as the mountains of Hauran (= the Argob) on a campaign in his eighteenth year (841), "destroying, tearing down, and burning innumerable towns, carrying booty away from them which was beyond counting" (*ANET*^{3}, 280). Targum^{Onq} identifies the Argob with Trachonitis (cf. Luke 3:1), a district about 30 mi south of Damascus, and 40 mi east of the Sea of Chinnereth (= the Sea of Galilee), presently known as el-Leja. But doubt has been cast on this basalt region containing all the ancient cities of the Argob (Driver; Weinfeld).

Deuteronomy 3

at that time. On this Deuteronomic expression, which recurs in vv. 8, 12, 18, 21, and 23, see Note for 1:9.

5 "Open cities in the country" (עָרֵי הַפְּרָזִי) are unwalled towns (1 Sam 6:18; Esth 9:19). The LXX misunderstood הַפְּרָזִי, translating it "(cities of) the Perizzites."

fortified cities with a high wall. עָרִים בְּצֻרוֹת חוֹמָה גְבֹהָה. On the grammar, see GKC §128x. The LXX takes both terms as nominatives: "fortified cities, high walls."

gates and bars. דְּלָתַיִם וּבְרִיחַ. City gates consisted of double doors anchored in sockets, secured on the inside by a horizontal bar to prevent the doors from being broken open in the center (Yadin 1963, 21-22). On the pairing of "gates and bars," see 1 Sam 23:7; Jer 49:31; Ezek 38:11; 2 Chr 8:5; 14:6(7).

6-7 See 2:34-35. On the ban imposed in holy war, see Note for 7:2. The LXX again fails to translate the rare מְתִם ("men"); cf. 2:34.

8 A summary statement, concluding in v. 10.

beyond the Jordan. I.e., the Transjordan (the writer is west of the Jordan).

the river Arnon. The southern limit of Sihon's territory (see Note for 2:24).

Mount Hermon. The southernmost peak in the Anti-Lebanon range (see Note for 1:7) and the northern limit of Og's kingdom. Mount Hermon is ca. 9200 ft above sea level and has snow much of the year (T: "mountain of snow"). Water from its slopes flows into the Jordan and the rivers of eastern Bashan (the Hauran).

9 An antiquarian note like those in 2:10-12, 20-23; 3:11, 13b-14; 10:6-9. Mount Hermon is called "Sirion" in Ps 29:6 and "Sion" in Deut 4:48. In the Ugaritic Baal Epic, "Lebanon and its trees" is balanced with "Sirion its precious cedars" (*ANET*[3], 134 vi 19-20; Ikeda 1978, 32). In the Hittite texts, Šariyana refers to the Anti-Lebanon range, and in a Hurrian mountain list it appears together with Lebanon. "Senir" balances Hermon and Lebanon in Cant 4:8; Ezek 27:5; 1 Chr 5:23, and like Sirion is to be identified with the Anti-Lebanon range. The Akkadian equivalent is *Saniru*, occurring together with Lebanon in the 9th-cent. Annals of Shalmaneser III (*ANET*[3], 280; Ikeda 1978, 36).

Sidonians. The LXX has "the Phoenicians" (οἱ Φοίνικες).

10 Concluding v. 8 after the antiquarian note in v. 9.

the cities of the tableland. "The tableland" (הַמִּישֹׁר) is the plateau region from the Arnon River to Heshbon (4:43; Josh 13:9; Jer 48:21).

all of the Gilead and all of the Bashan. Here "the Gilead" takes in territory north and south of the Jabbok, from Heshbon to the Yarmuk (see Note for 2:36). On the Bashan, see Note for 3:1.

Salcah. A city identified with Ṣalkhad on the southwestern slope of Jebel Hauran in Syria (Driver; Abel 1938, 440; Baly 1957, 222, 226, with a picture of the tell). Salcah is then located at the southeast corner of Bashan (Josh 13:11; 1 Chr 5:11).

Deuteronomy 3

Edrei. Bashan's important city on its southwestern border (see Note for 1:4).

11 *(For only Og king of the Bashan remained of the remnant of the Rephaim).* The verse is another antiquarian note like those in 2:10-12, 20-23; 3:9, 13b-14; 10:6-9. Bashan was inhabited in hoary antiquity by the legendary Rephaim (3:11, 13), a giant people who populated all the Transjordanian territory belonging to Sihon and Og (see Note for 2:20-21).

look, his bed was a bed of iron. הִנֵּה עַרְשׂוֹ עֶרֶשׂ בַּרְזֶל. The term עֶרֶשׂ means "bed" or "couch," and Og, being a very large man, is said to have possessed a bed of iron. Iron was just now coming into use, and presumably an "iron" bed would have been stronger than a bed of wood. Some think reference may be to a (basalt) sarcophagus (Driver, citing J. D. Michaelis;[*] von Rad; Moran; Weinfeld; NEB; REB; GNB), but there is no evidence that Hebrew עֶרֶשׂ denotes a sarcophagus (Millard 1988, 482; Lindquist 2011, 478-79). It makes even less sense to suppose a bed simply decorated with iron (so Tigay). Muhly (1982, 51) and Millard think Og's bed was strengthened by iron fittings, which is probably the best explanation, since the "iron chariots" of Josh 17:16, 18 and Judg 4:3 are not entire chariots of iron, but chariots with iron fittings, particularly in the hubs and other parts of the wheel.

Is it not in Rabbah of the sons of Ammon? Og apparently lost an earlier battle with the Ammonites, and his bed was kept on display in Rabbath-Ammon (see Note for 2:19). Lindquist (2011) thinks it was a large trophy taken by the Israelites and its warrior God Yahweh, comparing it to Marduk's jewel-encrusted bed taken by Sennacherib and the Assyrians from Marduk's temple in Babylon in 689 B.C. But why then was it being housed and displayed at Rabbath-Ammon?

Nine cubits was its length, and four cubits its width, according to the usual cubit). The usual cubit (אַמַּת־אִישׁ) was forearm length, from the elbow to the tip of the middle finger (ca. 18 in or 0.457 m), although Rashi takes the expression to refer to the length of Og's forearm, which would have been longer. Egypt, Mesepotamia, and possibly Israel also had a royal cubit that was slightly longer (de Vaux 1965, 196-97). The length of Og's bed, according to the usual cubit, would have been 13.5 ft by 6 ft.

Message and Audience

Things are now moving quickly northward, with Moses saying that the Israelites turned and went in the direction of Bashan, where Og, king of Bashan, came out with his people to do battle at Edrei. But Yahweh said not to fear Og, for he had

---

[*]Johann David Michaelis (1717-1791), professor at Göttingen, was one of the most important biblical scholars of the 18th cent. (Smend 2007, 30-42). His *Commentaries on the Law of Moses I-IV*, which was part of a larger work on the Old Testament, appeared in 1770-75.

already determined that this giant king would be given into Israelite hands and Israel would defeat him as it did Sihon, king of Heshbon. It happened as Yahweh said. Israel defeated Og and his company, leaving not a survivor. Israel took all of Og's cities, sixty of them, including the eastern territory of the Argob. All were fortified with high walls and secure gates. Israel also took many unwalled cities. The entire population, including women and children, was put under the ban and killed. Only the cattle and spoil were taken as booty. So Israel took land belonging to both Amorite kings, from the Arnon River to Mount Hermon — all the cities of the tableland, all of Gilead, and all of Bashan, including Salcah and Edrei. Two antiquarian notes are added, telling the audience that the Sidonians call Mount Hermon "Sirion," while the Amorites call it "Senir." They are reminded too that Og was one of the last giant Rephaim. Was not his iron bed still on display in Rabbath-Ammon, a bed measuring 9 cubits by 4 cubits?

To a late 8th- and early 7th-cent. Judahite audience, this will complete the story of how Israel initially took possession of its land in the Transjordan, land since taken from northern Israel by the Assyrians (734). The message will be the same as in the report of how Israel took over Sihon's kingdom: People do not know if this land will ever again come into their possession, but they must know that if they trust Yahweh and obey his word, any enemy can be defeated.

G. APPORTIONMENT OF TRANSJORDAN LAND (3:12-17)

*3*¹²*So we took possession of this land at that time: From Aroer, which is on the river Arnon, and half the hill country of the Gilead and its cities, I gave to Reuben and to Gad,* ¹³*and the rest of the Gilead and all of the Bashan, the kingdom of Og, I gave to the half-tribe of Manasseh. (All the territory of the Argob with all that of the Bashan — it is called the land of Rephaim.* ¹⁴*Jair son of Manasseh took all the territory of Argob, that is, the Bashan, to the border of the Geshurites and the Maacathites, and he called them after his name: Havvoth-jair, to this day.)* ¹⁵*And to Machir I gave the Gilead.* ¹⁶*And to the Reubenites and to the Gadites I gave from the Gilead to the river Arnon — the middle of the valley and a border — and to the river Jabbok, the border of the sons of Ammon;* ¹⁷*and the Arabah — also the Jordan and a border — from Chinnereth to the Sea of the Arabah, the Salt Sea, under the slopes of the Pisgah to the east.*

Rhetoric and Composition

The present verses are delimited at the top end by a section in Sam before v. 12 and at the bottom end by a section in Sam after v. 17. The M^L has no sections in either place.

Deuteronomy 3

Verses 12-17 contain a keyword chiasmus, the land distribution in vv. 12-13 going from south to north and in vv. 14-17 from north to south:

a	Aoer on the *Arnon* and half of *Gilead* hill country ... to *Reuben and Gad*	v. 12
	b the rest of *Gilead* and all of *Bashan* ... to the half-tribe of *Manasseh*	v. 13a
	b' *Jair* took Argob, i.e., *the Bashan* ... to *Machir* I gave the *Gilead*	vv. 14-15
a'	to *Reubenites and Gadites* I gave from *Gilead to Arnon* ... and Arabah	vv. 16-17

A portion of 3:12-17 is contained in 4QDeut^d.

Notes

3:12 *So we took possession of this land at that time.* A summary statement of what has preceded, functioning also as an introduction to the apportionment of territory to Reuben, Gad, and the half-tribe of Manasseh. Numbers 32 gives the reason for Reuben and Gad being permitted to settle in Transjordan: Both tribes had taken great quantities of cattle from Sihon and Og (2:35; 3:7, 19), so they asked Moses if they could remain there, since it was a good place to raise cattle (Num 32:1-5). The request was granted, but only on the condition that Reuben and Gad cross the Jordan with the other tribes to help in the conquest of Canaan (Weinfeld 1983b, 60). They agreed to do so. The half-tribe of Manasseh, led by the clans of Jair and Machir, were also allowed settlement in Transjordan after helping to take the land. On the distribution of land to Reuben, Gad, and the half tribe of Manasseh, see also Josh 13:8-13.

From Aroer, which is on the river Arnon. This belongs not with the first part of the verse, but with its conclusion (Rashi). The land distribution in vv. 12-13 goes from south to north; when repeated in vv. 14-17, it goes from north to south (see Rhetoric and Composition). The Arnon River was the southern boundary of Sihon's kingdom (see Note for 2:24), now Israel's southern boundary in Transjordan. Moab lay to the south. On the city of Aroer, see Note for 2:36.

and half the hill country of the Gilead and its cities, I gave to Reuben and to Gad. The half of Gilead's hill country refers to its southern half, i.e., from about Heshbon to the river Jabbok (see Note for 2:36). To Reuben and Gad went all of Sihon's kingdom, from the Arnon to the Jabbok, also land in the Arabah Rift Valley up to the Sea of Chinnereth (v. 17). Joshua 13:15-28 delineates this even further: Reuben receives the tableland from Aroer on the Arnon to Heshbon (vv. 15-23); Gad receives Gilead to the north, from Heshbon to the Jabbok, and Arabah land all the way north to the Sea of Chinnereth (vv. 24-28).

13a *and the rest of the Gilead and all of the Bashan, the kingdom of Og, I gave to the half-tribe of Manasseh.* Further defined in vv. 14-15; cf. Num 32:39-42. "The rest of the Gilead" is Gilead's northern portion, from the Jabbok to the Yarmuk (less the Arabah strip belonging to Sihon). All this territory went to the half-tribe of Manasseh. To the other half of the Manasseh tribe went territory west of the Jordan. On Bashan and the kingdom of Og, see Note for 3:1.

to the half-tribe of Manasseh. לַחֲצִי שֵׁבֶט הַמְנַשֶּׁה. On the grammar of "the Manasseh" (with the article), which yields a genitive relationship, see GKC §125d.

13b-14 Another antiquarian note like those in 2:10-12, 20-23; 3:9, 11; 10:6-9.

13b This parenthetical remark informs the listener that the Argob and the rest of Bashan was once called the land of the giant Rephaim (see Note for 2:20-21). The Argob is territory in eastern Bashan (see Note for 3:4).

14 According to this statement, Jair son of Manasseh took (לָקַח) all the territory of the Argob (v. 4) and then named villages in the territory after himself: "Havvoth-jair" (חַוֹּת יָאִיר = "tent villages of Jair"). Hebrew חַוֹּת is rendered "tent villages" on the basis of Arabic *ḥiwāʾ*, meaning "circle of tents" (BDB; KBL³). This remembrance is repeated in Josh 13:30, where the "tent villages of Jair" and sixty cities (of the Argob) are located in Bashan. But in Num 32:39-41, Jair (and Machir) are said to have taken territory in Gilead, not Bashan. This tradition is supported in 1 Kgs 4:13, which says that in Solomon's time, when the Argob was made into an administrative district, the villages of Havvoth-jair were in Gilead and the sixty fortified cities in the Argob, which is Bashan.

Complicating the picture is a mention in Judg 10:3-5 of Jair the Gileadite, a great-grandson of Manasseh's son Machir (1 Chr 2:22-23), who judged Israel for twenty-two years. His thirty sons rode on thirty asses and had thirty cities called "Havvoth-jair." Some commentators (Driver; Weinfeld; Nelson) take the two "Jairs" to be one and the same individual, which would mean that (1) the Jair who captures the "tent villages" and names them after himself is not of the Mosaic generation, but lives four generations later; (2) the tent villages in the present verse are the same tent villages said to exist in Solomon's time, and they are rightly located in Gilead, not Bashan; and (3) that "son" in the present verse means "descendant." Weinfeld says the Deuteronomic tradition assigns to Manasseh a much larger area than earlier sources. Jair's tent villages may also have been on or near the Bashan-Gilead border, which could account for the discrepancy in locating them. Or the problem could derive from the need of the Deuteronomic writer to balance the respective territories in his rhetorical

Deuteronomy 3

structure (see Rhetoric and Composition). The structure collapses if Jair does not take the Argob in Bashan.

that is, the Bashan. אֶת־הַבָּשָׁן. An awkward interpolation, relocated in the translation (cf. Weinfeld) so the plural "them" (אֹתָם) can refer ahead to the plural Havvoth-jair. This interpolation is not the source of the Bashan-Gilead problem, since the Argob is in Bashan (v. 4).

the border of the Geshurites and the Maacathites. The Geshurites lived in the fertile land of north Transjordan, between the Samakh River in the north and the Yarmuk River in the south (*ABD*, 2:996). The Yarmuk, though not mentioned in the Bible, is taken to be the boundary between Geshur and Gilead (B. Mazar 1986b, 114 n. 2, 116-17; cf. Josh 12:5; 13:11). Both Geshur and Maacah to the north were located in what is now the Golan Heights, a territory bounded on the west by the Sea of Galilee and Upper Jordan Valley and on the east by Bashan. Neither tribal group was driven out after Moses defeated Og (Josh 13:13). By the 11th cent., both had set up independent kingdoms (B. Mazar 1981, 23; 1986b, 120), and in David's time both had their own kings (2 Sam 10:6; 13:37). Geshur had friendly relations with David (2 Sam 3:3), but Maacah did not (2 Sam 10:6; 20:14). Absalom fled to Geshur after killing his brother Amnon (2 Sam 13:37-38), which was natural enough, since his mother was daughter of a Geshurite king (1 Chr 3:2). One of the Amarna Letters (EA 256) mentions a "land of Garu" (= Golan) and six Geshurite cites (Albright 1943a, 9-15; B. Mazar 1986b, 115-18; *ANET*^{3}, 486).

The Maacathites inhabited the mountainous and heavily wooded area north of Geshur, as far as Mount Hermon. Israelite tradition reckoned Maacah to be a son of Nahor, Abraham's brother, by a concubine Reumah (Gen 22:24). B. Mazar (1986b, 118-20) thinks that Maacah and the other three sons of Reumah constituted an early territorial and ethnic unit in southern Syria, since Maacah is listed in the Egyptian Execration Texts (19th to 18th cents.) as *M'k'w*. This tribal group appears then to have been an old inhabitant in the land, like Geshur (cf. 1 Sam 27:8). Sheba, after rebelling against David, fled to "Beth-Maacah" (2 Sam 20:14), i.e., "the kingdom of Maacah" (B. Mazar 1986b, 124).

to this day. עַד הַיּוֹם הַזֶּה. On this Deuteronomic expression, see Note for 2:22. The Havvoth-jair continued to exist and retain their name in the time of the Deuteronomic writer, but they had not belonged to Israel for many years. According to 1 Chr 2:23, these tent villages were taken from Israel by Geshur and Aram, in what B. Mazar (1961, 24) thinks was probably a campaign of Ben-hadad I (ca. 886). After the rise of the Aramean kingdom of Damascus, both Geshur and Maacah were apparently incorporated into that state. They were, after all, Aramean tribes to begin with (von Rad; cf. Gen 22:24; 2 Sam 15:8; 1 Chr 19:6).

15 Machir, son of Manasseh and father of Gilead (Gen 50:23; Num 32:39;

1 Chr 2:23), headed the chief clan in the half-tribe of Manasseh. His family became the Machirites (Num 26:29). To Machir went Og's land in Gilead (Num 32:39-40), i.e., northern Gilead from the Jabbok to the Yarmuk (Simons 1947, 30; see Note for 2:36). He also received Og's Bashan territory, receiving this as bounty because he was a man of war (Josh 13:29-31; 17:1; cf. Judg 5:14). According to Weinfeld (1983b, 60), Machir's colonization of Gilead took place after the conquest of Canaan. Fighting to secure Canaan (Judg 5:14) was the condition for him and others in Reuben, Gad, and the half-tribe of Manasseh settling in Transjordan (see v. 12).

16 Vv. 16-17 repeat and expand v. 12. Gilead here is its southern part, from the Jabbok to about Heshbon. Territory south of Heshbon was "the tableland" (see Note for 2:36).

the middle of the valley and a border. תּוֹךְ הַנַּחַל וּגְבֻל. The Arnon flows in the middle of the canyon and is a border with Moab (see Note for 2:24).

and to the river Jabbok, the border of the sons of Ammon. The upper course of the Jabbok running south to north was a border with the Ammonites (Num 21:24; see Note for 2:24).

17 *and the Arabah — also the Jordan and a border — from Chinnereth to the sea of the Arabah, the Salt Sea.* The territorial limits from the Sea of Chinnereth (Num 34:11)/Lake of Gennesaret (1 Macc 11:67; Luke 5:1)/Sea of Galilee (Matt 4:18; Mark 1:16, etc.) in the north to the Sea of the Arabah (4:49; 2 Kgs 14:25)/Salt Sea (Gen 14:3; Num 34:3, 12)/Dead Sea (classical writers; e.g., Pausanias, *Description of Greece*, 5:7) in the south specify what portion of the Arabah Rift Valley is indicated (see Note for 1:1). In Josh 3:16 and 12:3 both names, Sea of the Arabah and Salt Sea, occur together, as here. Chinnereth/Gennesaret was also the name of a town (Josh 11:2; 19:35; Matt 14:34; Mark 6:53), located on the lake's northwestern shore. The Sea of Chinnereth is meant here, not the town (Tigay; *pace* Rashi; Driver; G. E. Wright). Sihon apparently controlled a stretch of land in the Arabah north of the Jabbok, up to the Sea of Chinnereth (Josh 12:3; 13:27), and Gad took possession of this land, qualifying slightly the picture given in v. 12.

under the slopes of the Pisgah to the east. תַּחַת אַשְׁדֹּת הַפִּסְגָּה מִזְרָחָה. The Sea of the Arabah/Salt Sea lay under these slopes (see Note for 4:49). "The Pisgah" is either a specific peak in the Abarim range or else the range itself, the highest peak being Mount Nebo (see Note for 34:1).

Message and Audience

Now after defeating the Amorite kings, Sihon and Og, Moses says they took possession of their Transjordan land. To the tribes of Reuben and Gad went territory from Aroer on the Arnon in the south to half of Gilead's hill country in the north. The rest of Gilead and all of Bashan went to the half-tribe of Manasseh. An antiquarian note informs the audience that the Argob, along with the rest of Bashan, had been land of the giant Rephaim.

The allocation of land is repeated with more specificity. The antiquarian note goes on to say that Jair son of Manasseh took the territory of Argob, which is in Bashan, westward to the border of the Geshurites and Maacathites. The tent villages in the Argob he named after himself: Havvoth-jair. That name continues to the present day. Moses says he gave Machir the Gilead, understood here to be its northern half. Reuben and Gad were given Gilead from the river Jabbok, which was the Ammonite border, to the river Arnon. The river Arnon flowed in the middle of the Arnon gorge and was another border. To Reuben and Gad also went land in the Arabah, also the Jordan, which was another border. It went from the Sea of Chinnereth in the north to the Sea of the Arabah, or Salt Sea, in the south. The latter body of water lay below the slopes of Pisgah, to the east.

To a late 8th- and early 7th-cent. Judahite audience, this will recount how Reuben, Gad, and the half-tribe of Manasseh gained possession of their Transjordan land. It was no longer theirs, having been taken by the Assyrians before the northern kingdom fell. The last Israelites to live there were now gone or in faraway exile. It was left to Judahites to reflect on why this land was lost, and to wonder if it would ever again be repossessed.

H. THE FOCUS NOW IS BEYOND THE JORDAN (3:18-22)

3[18]*And I commanded you at that time: "Yahweh your God has given you this land to possess it; battle-ready troops shall cross over before your brethren, the children of Israel, all warriors;* [19]*only your wives and your little ones and your livestock — I know that you have much livestock — shall dwell in your cities that I have given to you,* [20]*until Yahweh gives rest to your brethren, as to you, and they, they also, have taken possession of the land that Yahweh your God is giving to them, beyond the Jordan; then you shall return each to his possession that I have given you."* [21]*And Joshua I commanded at that time: "Your eyes are those that have seen all that Yahweh your God did to these two kings; thus Yahweh will do to all the kingdoms to which you are crossing over.* [22]*You shall not fear them, for Yahweh your God, he is the one fighting for you."*

Deuteronomy 3

Rhetoric and Composition

These verses, which direct attention to the conquest beyond the Jordan, are delimited at the top end by a section in Sam before v. 18 and at the bottom end by a *setumah* in M^L and a section in Sam after v. 22. 4QDeut^d has no sections before v. 18 or after v. 22. Two segments have similar opening phrases:

> 3:18   And I commanded you at that time
> 3:21   And Joshua I commanded at that time

The first segment in vv. 18-20 contains a chiastic structure (cf. Nelson):

a		Yahweh your God has given you this land to possess it	v. 18
	b	battle-ready troops shall cross over *before your brethren* . . .	
		c only your wives, little ones, and livestock . . . shall dwell in your cities	v. 19
	b′	until Yahweh gives rest *to your brethren* . . .	v. 20
a′		and they . . . have taken possession of the land that Yahweh your God is giving to them. . . .	

Portions of 3:18-22 are contained in 4QDeut^d, 4QDeut^m, and 4Q364.

Notes

3:18-20 According to Numbers 32, the condition for settlement in the Transjordan was that battle-capable men of Reuben, Gad, (and the half-tribe of Manasseh) cross over into Canaan with the remaining tribes and help secure the territory there. When the remaining tribes are settled in Canaan, they can return to their Transjordan territories. The wives and children can remain in Transjordan with all the cattle, and with them, no doubt, will be men not able to go to war. Joshua later repeats this command (Josh 1:12-18), and the condition was satisfied (Josh 22:1-6).

And I commanded you at that time. "You" refers (inexactly) to Reuben, Gad, and the half-tribe of Manasseh (Driver; Weinfeld; cf. Josh 1:12-13), although in Num 32:28-32 Moses addresses only Reuben and Gad. The half-tribe of Manasseh has to be included (*pace* Rashi; ibn Ezra). On the phrase "at that time," which recurs in vv. 21 and 23, see Note for 1:9.

battle-ready troops shall cross over before your brethren, the children of Israel, all warriors. Hebrew חֲלוּצִים means "battle-ready troops" (lit. "loin-girded troops"). They will go at the head of the invading army (NJV: "shock troops"; Tigay: "vanguard"; cf. Josh 6:9; Judg 18:11, 16-17).

I know that you have much livestock. Cf. Num 32:1.

until Yahweh gives rest to your brethren, as to you. According to Deuteronomy, Yahweh promises his people "rest" once they become settled in the land (see Note for 12:10).

they also. גַּם־הֵם. Added for emphasis. The remaining tribes also deserve their rest and to get possession of the land Yahweh promised to give to them.

beyond the Jordan. Here west of the Jordan (cf. v. 25). On the same expression meaning "east of the Jordan," see Note for 1:1.

21 *And Joshua I commanded at that time.* The syntax is inverted from the parallel phrase in v. 18, probably for the sake of variety (see Rhetoric and Composition).

"Your eyes are those that have seen all that Yahweh your God did to these two kings; thus Yahweh will do to all the kingdoms to which you are crossing over." Joshua is reminded of the recent victories over Sihon and Og. The "kingdoms" in Canaan refer to the petty kingdoms described in the 14th cent. Amarna Letters (*ABD*, 1:174-81; cf. *ANET*[3], 483-90). See also the "kings" in Joshua 9-12. The Deuteronomic expression "your eyes are those that have seen" (עֵינֶיךָ הָרֹאֹת) occurs also in 4:3 and 11:7 (Driver 1895, lxxxiii no. 60; Weinfeld 1972, 173, 357 no. 11a; on the grammar, see GKC §116q). For similar expressions, see Notes on 1:30 and 4:9.

22 Ottosson (1969, 104) notes that this is almost a direct quote from the exodus deliverance (Exod 14:13-14). Joshua receives the same encouragement Yahweh gave Moses before he went to war against Og (3:2). The charge is repeated at Joshua's commissioning (31:7-8; cf. 1:38). Numbers 32 does not record any encouragement to Joshua. For Deuteronomy's concept of holy war, see Note for 1:30.

Message and Audience

With Transjordan territory now conquered and parceled out to Reuben, Gad, and the half-tribe of Manasseh, the focus turns to the territory across the Jordan. Israel attempted to take it once before, but failed. Moses says he reminded a new generation that Yahweh had given Israel this land, and he commanded that battle-ready troops cross over ahead of everyone else, leaving behind in the newly acquired cities wives, little ones, and livestock, until the remaining tribes achieve their rest in Canaan. The audience will assume that old men and other men who for one reason or another were not conscripted would also remain behind. Moses says parenthetically that he knows how much cattle was taken in the wars against Sihon and Og. After land beyond the Jordan is secured, the warriors of Reuben, Gad, and Manasseh can return to their Transjordan territories.

Moses says he also reminded Joshua how he had seen with his own eyes what Yahweh did to the two Amorite kings. Yahweh will do the same to kingdoms across the Jordan. Joshua is not to fear these adversaries, for Yahweh will fight for him and for Israel.

To a late 8th- and early 7th-cent. Judahite audience, this will be a recollection of the holy war Yahweh waged on Israel's behalf to take Canaan. Just now, all of Northern Israel has been lost to the Assyrians, and in 701 Sennacherib brought most of Judah's walled cities and unprotected villages to ruin, leaving only Jerusalem to a once proud Israelite nation. This audience will see a reversal in Yahweh's holy war policy and will wonder if Yahweh is still fighting for them.

I. MOSES ASKS TO CROSS THE JORDAN (3:23-29)

3 ^{23}*And I sought Yahweh's favor at that time:* ^{24}*"O Lord Yahweh, you, you have begun to show your servant your greatness and your strong hand, for who is a god in heaven and in earth that can do as your works and as your mighty acts?* ^{25}*Do let me cross over and let me see the good land that is beyond the Jordan, this good hill country, and the Lebanon."* ^{26}*But Yahweh was cross with me on your account, and would not listen to me, and Yahweh said to me: "Enough from you; do not go on speaking to me any more about this thing.* ^{27}*Go up to the top of the Pisgah and lift up your eyes to the west and to the north and to the south and to the east, and see with your eyes; but you shall not cross over this Jordan.* ^{28}*And command Joshua, and strengthen him and embolden him, for he, he shall cross over before this people, and he, he shall cause them to inherit the land that you shall see."* ^{29}*So we remained in the valley opposite Beth-peor.*

Rhetoric and Composition

The present verses are delimited at the top end by a *setumah* in M^L and a section in Sam before v. 23. At the bottom end delimitation is by a *petuḥah* in M^L and sections in 4QDeut^d and Sam after v. 29, also the chapter division. The Sam has another section in the middle of v. 26, which may have been determined by the beginning of Yahweh's speech.

These verses conclude the initial segment of Moses' opening discourse from 1:6 to 3:29. The two verses are tied together by an inclusio (see Rhetoric and Composition for 1:6-46). "So we remained in the valley . . ." in 3:29 is a sum-

Deuteronomy 3

mary statement like "So we remained at Kadesh . . ." in 1:46. Anticipated in the present verses are Moses' death and his replacement by Joshua, reported later in a Supplement to Deuteronomy 1–28 (Noth 1981, 14; cf. 31:1-8, 14-15; 32:48-52; 34:1-12).

Portions of 3:23-29 are contained in 4QDeut^c, 4QDeut^d, 4QDeut^e, and 4Q364.

Notes

3:23 Moses cannot claim entrance into the promised land on the basis of good deeds or exemplary service in Yahweh's employ; for him, too, entrance would be a gift. On seeking divine favor/grace, which always comes as a gift, see Freedman, Lundbom, *ḥānan*, *TDOT*, 5:22-36. This is the third occurrence in a row of "at that time" (cf. vv. 18, 21), stock Deuteronomic coinage (see Note for 1:9).

24 The victories over Sihon and Og were but the beginning of Yahweh's greatness and strong hand (= power) in giving Israel the land (v. 21). Moses appears to be arguing that if Yahweh is just beginning to show him mighty acts such as these, should he not be permitted to see them continue across the Jordan? Elsewhere in Deuteronomy, e.g., 4:32-34 and 10:21–11:7, Yahweh's mighty acts are recalled in connection with the exodus and wilderness wanderings.

The twin themes of debunking other gods and affirming Yahweh's incomparability are old (Exod 15:11; Deut 32:37-39), continuing unabated in Deuteronomy and in subsequent OT literature (Ps 89:7-8[6-7]; cf. Lundbom 1999, 582). Weinfeld (1972, 37-45) says that beginning a prayer by proclaiming the uniqueness of God is characteristic of Deuteronomy and the Deuteronomic literature (2 Sam 7:22-24; 1 Kgs 8:23; 2 Kgs 19:15-19; Jer 32:17-23). It carried over into later Jewish liturgy, with the rabbis citing the present verse in support of the view that petitions should be preceded by praise to God (*b. Ber.* 32a; Greenberg 1976, 71-72). Other ANE texts make similar boasts. In the ancient Babylonian "Hymn to Šamaš," the sun-god, are these lines (45-46):

> Among all the Igigi there is none who toils but you
> None who is supreme like you in the whole pantheon of the gods
> (Lambert 1960, 128-129)

See also the Babylonian Creation Epic (7:39; *ANET*^{3}, 71); the Babylonian "Hymn to Ishtar" (*ANET*^{3}, 383); and "Hymn to the Moon-God" (*ANET*^{3}, 385-86). In the last-named text, the worshipper extols the god Sin with these words (lines 22-25):

> O Lord, decider of the destinies of heaven and earth,
>   whose word no one alters,
> Who controls water and fire, leader of living creatures,
>   what god is like thee?
> In heaven who is exalted? Thou!
>   Thou alone art exalted.
> On earth who is exalted? Thou!
>   Thou alone art exalted.

Y. Kaufmann (1960, 7-20) therefore argues that the OT does not really understand the nature of pagan religion, dismissing it simply as a crude form of idolatry.

O Lord Yahweh. אֲדֹנָי יְהוִה. A form of address typical in prayers, appearing in 9:26 and elsewhere in the OT (Gen 15:2, 8; Judg 16:28; 2 Sam 7:18-29; Amos 7:2, 5). It is embellished by the interjection "Ah!" אֲהָהּ in Josh 7:7; Judg 6:22; Jer 1:6; 4:10; 14:13; 32:17; Ezek 4:14; 9:8.

you, you have begun to show. אַתָּה הַחִלּוֹתָ לְהַרְאוֹת. The pronoun puts added emphasis on Yahweh. The use of חלל in the H-stem ("begun") is intentional, referring here as before (2:24, 25, 31) to Yahweh's triumphs over Sihon and Og and Israel's taking their land (Rashi; Rashbam).

your greatness and your strong hand. אֶת־גָּדְלְךָ וְאֶת־יָדְךָ הַחֲזָקָה. A stock phrase in Deuteronomy (3:24; 11:2; Weinfeld 1972, 329 no. 16). Yahweh's "greatness" is acclaimed elsewhere in 5:24; 7:21; 9:26; 10:17; 11:2; 32:3 (Driver 1895, lxxx no. 26). On Yahweh's "strong hand," see Note for 6:21. On "strong hand and outstretched arm," see Note for 4:34. Here and in 11:2 the LXX adds "and outstretched arm" to embellish the reading.

for who is a god in heaven and in earth . . . ? The initial אֲשֶׁר is causal: "for" (LXX: γάρ).

25 *Do let me cross over.* אֶעְבְּרָה־נָּא. The particle נָּא with the cohortative is emphatic, nevertheless expressing deference (Shulman 1999, 75).

and let me see the good land that is beyond the Jordan. I.e., Canaan, which in Deuteronomy is a "good land" (see Note for 1:34-36). "Beyond the Jordan" is west of the Jordan (cf. v. 20).

this good hill country, and the Lebanon. "This good hill country" is the central highlands of Palestine, both north and south of Jerusalem. "The Lebanon" refers to the two mountain ranges of modern Lebanon: the Lebanon range, running parallel to the Phoenician coast, and the Anti-Lebanon range further inland (see Note for 1:7). Lebanon was famous for its (fragrant) cedar trees (Isa 10:34; Ezek 31:3; Pss 92:13[12]; 104:16; Cant 5:15), fruit trees and vineyards (Hos 14:7-9[6-8]; Ps 72:16), and natural beauty (Cant 4:15; 7:5[4]).

26 Despite Yahweh's assurances of being a gracious God, even a tower-

Deuteronomy 3

ing figure such as Moses cannot expect that every request will be honored (Exod 33:12-20; cf. Freedman, Lundbom, *TDOT*, 5:31). In Deuteronomy, Yahweh is angry with Moses (at Meribah) because of the people's rebellion, whereas in the Priestly source Moses (and Aaron) are faulted for not sanctifying Yahweh before the people. Both explanations lack transparency (see Note for 1:37).

But Yahweh was cross with me on your account. וַיִּתְעַבֵּר יְהוָה בִּי לְמַעַנְכֶם. The verb יִתְעַבֵּר is strong (BDB: "become furious"; Rashi: "be filled with wrath"; cf. Ps 78:21, 59, 62; Prov 20:2). Friedman brilliantly translates the pun in Hebrew: Moses says to Yahweh: "Let me cross over" (אֶעְבְּרָה) the Jordan, but then Yahweh "becomes cross" (יִתְעַבֵּר) with Moses. This is lost in the LXX, which translates the Hebrew verb with ὑπερεῖδεν ("he overlooked, disregarded"). Yahweh here simply disregards the plea of Moses.

Enough from you. רַב־לָךְ. For the Hebrew idiom, see Note for 1:6. Yahweh later tells Jeremiah to pray no longer about a specific matter (Jer 7:16; 11:14; 14:11; and by implication 15:1).

27 Moses cannot enter the promised land but is permitted to have a look at it. Yahweh's command that he ascend a high mountain is repeated in 32:49 and carried out in 34:1. See also Num 27:12. "Pisgah" is either a peak in the Abarim mountain range or else the range itself, the peak being Mount Nebo (see Note for 34:1). From there Moses will have a spectacular view of the surrounding country. Daube (1947, 24-39) has cited in Roman law a mode of transferring ownership for buildings and land (which are not moveables and therefore cannot be handed over like other commodities) which is called *traditio*. One simply takes another to the spot and points out the property, and this counts as *traditio*. The grantee acquires control, and the transfer is effected. It is not even necessary for the grantee to set foot on the land. Daube says a comparable procedure may have existed in ancient Hebrew law and imagines in the present case a prebiblical account in which Yahweh, owner of the land, is turning it over to Moses. He cites Yahweh's grant of land to Abraham and his descendants (Gen 13:14-15; cf. 35:12) and in the NT Satan's taking Jesus to a high mountain and promising him all the kingdoms of the world if he will fall down and worship him (Matt 4:8-9; Luke 4:5-7).

and lift up your eyes to the west and to the north and to the south and to the east. Cf. Yahweh's directive to Abram, showing him the promised land (Gen 13:14).

28 *And command Joshua, and strengthen him and embolden him.* Hebrew "command" (צַו) in this case means "commission, appoint to office" (cf. 1 Sam 13:14; 25:30). The directive to give encouragement to Joshua occurred earlier (1:38). Moses issues this word of encouragement in 31:7-8, with the actual commissioning coming in 31:14-15, only there it is Yahweh appointing Joshua to his office. In Num 27:18-23, Moses lays hands upon Joshua before Eleazer the priest, and invests his successor with a measure of his authority.

strengthen him and embolden him. חַזְּקֵהוּ וְאַמְּצֵהוּ. A Deuteronomic stock expression, elsewhere formulated as a command: "Be strong and bold" (31:6, 7, 23; Driver 1895, lxxxi no. 35; Weinfeld 1972, 343 no. 11).

for he, he shall cross over before this people. The added pronoun is for emphasis: Joshua is the one who will cross over at the head of the people.

and he, he shall cause them to inherit the land that you shall see." Another added pronoun for emphasis: Joshua will be the one enabling Israel to inherit the land (1:38; 31:7). On Yahweh's gift of the land as an inheritance, see Note for 15:4.

29 A terse statement like the one in 1:46, concluding the intial segment of Moses' opening discourse beginning in 1:6 (see Rhetoric and Composition). Moses is silent after Yahweh tells him he cannot cross the Jordan, reminding one of Abraham's discourse-ending silence after bargaining with Yahweh over the fate of Sodom (Gen 18:33). There — like here — Yahweh has the last word. The present verse is also silent about Israel's infamous lapse into idolatry after settling in Transjordan, which happened while Moses was still alive. Mention of Beth-peor alludes to but says nothing about Israel's romp with the daughters of Moab. This indiscretion, however, does receive passing mention in 4:3-4. It gets more coverage in Num 25:1-9 and is recalled years later by Hosea (Hos 9:10). Rashi, ibn Ezra, and Rashbam all mention the incident in connection with the present verse, which was Israel's first experience with cultic prostitution (Beth-peor = Beth Baal-peor, "House of Baal-peor").

After the conquest of Sihon, Beth-peor was assigned to the tribe of Reuben (Josh 13:20). Its precise location is unknown. Eusebius *(Onom.)* says it lay 6 mi from Livias (Tell er Rameh) on the way to Heshbon. This would be 3 or 4 mi northwest of Mehatta on the Mushaqqar Ridge, which some take as being the site of Mount Nebo. The valley opposite Beth-peor may well be the Wadi ʿAyun Musa ("Valley of Moses' Wells"), which lies just below Siyagha, the traditional site of Mount Nebo (Simons 1959, 264; Weinfeld; G. L. Mattingly, *ABD*, 1:691). On Siyagha as the site of Mount Nebo, see Note to 34:1. Here springs of water continue even to the present day (Glueck 1940, 144), a place where people would have been well supplied with water. This valley is a ways up in the mountains, not down in the Jordan Valley (the Ghor) near the Jordan River and the Dead Sea (see Piccirillo 1987, 92-93 for a picture). Here Moses gave his final address (4:46), and here he was buried (34:6).

Deuteronomy 4

Message and Audience

After Moses has reported Yahweh's assurances to Joshua about the upcoming battles, he closes this segment of his initial discourse by telling hearers again about his failed attempt to persuade Yahweh to let him cross the Jordan and enter Canaan. He says he sought Yahweh's favor, arguing that Yahweh had just begun to show him greatness and power in the taking of Transjordan land, for what god in heaven and earth could do such mighty works? Could not Moses see more of the same, crossing the Jordan to see Canaan's good hill country and the Lebanon? And could he not see more battle victories there?

But Yahweh became cross with him, saying the denial was on account of the people. He would not listen, telling Moses to speak no more about the matter. Moses would be permitted to ascend the Pisgah and view the land, but he would not be permitted to enter it. Instead, Moses should commission Joshua for the work ahead and encourage him. Joshua would lead the people across the Jordan and cause them to inherit the land. Moses fell silent; the dialogue was over. Moses says only that the people remained in the valley opposite Beth-peor. Some of those listening, perhaps many, would recall what happened afterwards at Beth-peor.

To a late 8th- and early 7th-cent. audience, which had a consuming interest in the figure of Moses, this would be a reminder that even towering individuals such as Moses do not get everything they ask for. Yahweh's ongoing work requires that others be pressed into service, and the present generation, like Moses' generation, must have faith in successors to great leaders of the past. More important, it must have faith in Yahweh, who is the real leader of Israel and its ongoing march through history. This audience will also be indirectly warned about the dangers of ensnarement. A present-day romp with idol worshippers, like those merry-makers at Beth-peor, will just as surely bear bitter fruit as it did back then.

J. LISTEN TO THE COMMANDMENTS AND DO THEM (4:1-40)

1. Forget Not the Horeb Revelation (4:1-24)

4 ^{1}*And now, O Israel, listen to the statutes and to the ordinances that I am teaching you to do in order that you may live, and you may enter and possess the land that Yahweh God of your fathers is giving to you.* ^{2}*You shall not add to the word that I am commanding you, and you shall not subtract from it, in order to keep the commandments of Yahweh your God that I am commanding you.* ^{3}*Your eyes have seen what Yahweh did at Baal-peor; indeed, every person who went after Baal-peor, Yahweh your God completely destroyed him from your midst.* ^{4}*But you*

who clung to Yahweh your God are alive, all of you today. [5]See, I have taught you statutes and ordinances, just as Yahweh my God commanded me, to do so in the midst of the land that you are entering to take possession of it. [6]So you shall be careful and you shall do, for that will be your wisdom and your understanding in the eyes of the peoples, who, when they hear all these statutes, will say, "Surely a wise and understanding people is this great nation!" [7]For what great nation is there that has for itself gods near to it as Yahweh our God, whenever we call to him? [8]And what great nation is there that has for itself statutes and ordinances as just as all this law that I am setting before you today? [9]Only be careful for yourself and take much care for your life, lest you forget the things that your eyes have seen, and lest they depart from your heart all the days of your life. So make them known to your children and to your children's children. [10]The day that you stood before Yahweh your God at Horeb is when Yahweh said to me: "Gather to me the people that I may make them hear my words, that they may learn to fear me all the days that they are living on the soil, and their children they may teach." [11]And you drew near and you stood at the foot of the mountain, and the mountain was burning with fire up to the heart of heaven — darkness, cloud, and storm cloud. [12]And Yahweh spoke to you from the midst of the fire; the sound of words you were hearing, but a form you were not seeing, only a sound. [13]And he declared to you his covenant, which he commanded you to do, the ten words, and he wrote them upon two tablets of stone. [14]And me Yahweh commanded at that time to teach you statutes and ordinances, so you might do them in the land that you were crossing over to take possession of it. [15]So be very careful for your lives, since you did not see any form on the day Yahweh spoke to you at Horeb from the midst of the fire, [16]lest you act corruptly and you make for yourselves an idol, a form of any figure, a copy of male or female; [17]a copy of any beast that is on the earth; a copy of any winged bird that flies in the heaven; [18]a copy of anything that creeps on the ground; a copy of any fish that is in the waters under the earth; [19]and lest you lift up your eyes to the heaven, and you see the sun and the moon and the stars, all the host of heaven, and you be lured away and you worship them and serve them, which Yahweh your God has allotted to all the peoples under the entire heaven. [20]But you, Yahweh took and brought you out from the iron furnace, from Egypt, to be for himself a people, an inheritance, as at this day. [21]Yet Yahweh was angry with me on account of your words, and he swore that I should not cross over the Jordan and not enter into the good land that Yahweh your God was giving to you as an inheritance. [22]Indeed, I must die in this land; I am not able to cross over the Jordan. But you are crossing over and you will possess this good land. [23]Be careful for yourselves, lest you forget the covenant of Yahweh your God that he cut with you, and you make for yourselves an idol, a form of anything about which Yahweh your God commanded you, [24]for Yahweh your God is a consuming fire; he is a jealous God.

Deuteronomy 4

Rhetoric and Composition

In ch. 4 is a shift from events of the recent past to what is expected of Israel now and in the future, viz., obedience to the covenant and terms of the covenant in the land Israel now occupies and will occupy in the future. Chapters 1–3 narrated Israel's experiences after leaving Horeb, beginning with the calamitous defeat in trying to enter Canaan, but then concluding with the successful battles against Sihon and Og, giving Israel territory in the Transjordan. Israel now is encamped in the plains of Moab, listening to Moses explicate the terms of the covenant that will govern national life in all territories where Israel is settled.

The discourse in 4:1-40 is a hard-hitting and highly emotive sermon mandating single-minded worship of Yahweh and a rejection of idolatry. It is preaching on the first and second commandments, which Israel heard directly and from Moses at Mount Horeb, and which will be repeated in ch. 5. This preaching also anticipates more of the same in chs. 6–11. So while a basic shift occurs from the recent past to the present and future, the sermon hearkens back, as chs. 1–3 did not, to Israel's experience at Horeb. In ch. 5, people will hear again the core law of the Horeb covenant, i.e., the "Ten Words" (4:13; 5:1-21), and after that commandments, statutes, and ordinances augmenting this core law which make up the Deuteronomic Code (chs. 12–28). A similar rambling homilietical piece will precede the giving of the Deuteronomic Code (ch. 12).

Because ch. 4 shifts focus and contains different content, many scholars have argued that it has a separate origin from 1:6–3:29. Noth (1981, 33) believed that 4:1-40 was a general introduction to the law, transitional in nature, but he could not be sure whether it belonged with chs. 1–3. It could have been added later. G. E. Wright, however, maintained that 4:1-40 was the proper conclusion to the historical survey and is what gave the survey meaning. He noted in 29:1-8(2-9) a sequence the same as here: historical survey — there of the exodus and wilderness wanderings — followed by an admonition to keep the covenant. Chapters 1–4 in their present form are definitely connected, as is evidenced by the transitional "and now" (וְעַתָּה) in 4:1. More recently, it has been argued that these chapters are a unified composition containing interrelationships between themes of divine presence, human obedience, election, and the land (N. MacDonald 2006).

One can dismiss earlier arguments that a reference to "scattering" in the chapter, i.e., exile (v. 27), points to a postexilic composition. Exile did not first become a reality for Israel — and also other nations — at the beginning of the 6th cent. Exiles of conquered peoples were common throughout the Assyrian Age; already in 734-722, it was the unhappy end to which northern Israel came.

It has cogently been argued that themes in chs. 4 and 29–30 frame chs. 5–28 (Mayes 1981; Tigay). Tigay points to the following:

Historical events that Israel saw:	4:3-4, 9-15, 32-38	29:1-2[2-3]
The threat of dispersion:	4:26-28	29:27[28]
Possibile repentance in dispersion	4:29-31	30:10

Weinfeld (pp. 215-17) sees in ch. 30 the conclusion to Moses' long farewell speech that began in ch. 4, making an inclusio in the book. Noted are verbal similarities in 4:25-26 and 30:17-18: warnings against idol worship and its consequences and a summoning of heaven and earth as witnesses should a lapse into idolatry take place in the future. Also, themes of repentance and restoration appear both in 4:27-31 and 30:1-10. In the chapters are also an inversion: the sequence in ch. 4 is warning/restoration; the sequence in ch. 30 is restoration/warning.

The present chapter consists then of a sermon on doing the commands and refraining from idolatry, combined with an emotive statement on Yahweh's greatness and Israel's relationship to this incomparable God (4:1-40). After that, a supplemental passage allocates cities of refuge in the Transjordan (4:41-43). The chapter closes with a subscription to the Prologue (4:44-49). These latter verses are not an introduction, as many earlier scholars alleged, but a conclusion to what precedes and a balancing summary to 1:1-5 (see Rhetoric and Composition for 4:44-49).

This sermon is highly repetitive, full of the stereotyped language for which Deuteronomy is known. Luther, noting the repetitions, said we must nevertheless listen to them. Why? "To hear God is bliss," he says, "even if he were to sound out the same syllable all the time." Nevertheless, the sermon contains structure. Braulik (1978) over-analyzes the passage in his attempt to find structure, yet his work has influenced subsequent scholars (Lohfink 1968, 16; Mayes 1981, 25; Weinfeld; Tigay). The core discourse of vv. 9-31 appears to have an introduction (vv. 1-8) and a conclusion (vv. 32-40), and the introduction does divide in two: vv. 1-4 and vv. 5-8. The problem is with Braulik's core discourse, which is divided between vv. 22 and 23. The midpoint break should come after v. 24, as section markings in M^L and Sam indicate (so also Nelson).

The sermon in broad outline has the following structure:

(a) Introduction: The law is life and a mark of Israel's wisdom (vv. 1-8)
(b) Core teaching: Do the commands and refrain from idolatry (vv. 9-31)
(c) Conclusion: The greatness of the statutes and ordinances is proved in that Yahweh alone is God and there is no other (vv. 32-40).

Deuteronomy 4

The core teaching divides in two: (1) an exhortation on being careful to do the commands (vv. 9-24); and (2) a warning of what will happen if Israel does not do them: destruction and a scattering, but then repentance and a return (vv. 25-31). Part one has these stereotyped opening phrases:

Only be careful for yourself and take much care for your life,	
lest you forget the things....	4:9
So be very careful for your lives ... lest you act corruptly....	4:15-16
Be careful for yourselves, lest you forget the covenant....	4:23

Verse 23 does not begin a unit extending all the way to v. 31 (*pace* Braulik and others); it begins a smaller unit concluding only part of the core teaching (vv. 23-24). Muilenburg (1967) called v. 24 a "superb climax," like that of v. 31. It follows, too, that "forget" (שכח) is not a structural tie-in between 4:23 and 4:31; it is a tie-in between 4:9 and 4:23.

There is more to the structure of 4:1-40. It has been noted that these verses begin and end with admonitions to keep the commandments (Weinfeld). Actually, the whole is a large chiasmus in which the core teaching is framed not only by opening and closing admonitions, but by balancing pairs of rhetorical questions. Weinfeld notes that opening rhetorical questions (4:7, 8) attest to the uniqueness of Israel, and closing rhetorical questions (4:33, 34) attest to the uniqueness of Israel's God. The structure of 4:1-40 is then the following:

a		*Listen to the statutes and to the ordinances*	4:1
		(שְׁמַע אֶל־הַחֻקִּים וְאֶל־הַמִּשְׁפָּטִים)	
		in order that (לְמַעַן) *you may live, and you may enter and possess the land....*	
	b	*For what great nation is there that has for itself*	4:7
		(כִּי מִי־גוֹי גָּדוֹל אֲשֶׁר־לוֹ) *...?*	
		And what great nation is there that has for itself	4:8
		(וּמִי גוֹי גָּדוֹל אֲשֶׁר־לוֹ) *...?*	
		c Core Teaching on Rejecting Idol Worship	4:9-31
	b′	*... Has a people heard the voice of a god*	4:32-33
		(הֲשָׁמַע עָם קוֹל אֱלֹהִים) *...?*	
		Or has a god attempted to go and take	4:34
		(אוֹ הֲנִסָּה אֱלֹהִים) *...?*	
a′		*And you shall keep his statutes and his commandments*	4:40
		(וְשָׁמַרְתָּ אֶת־חֻקָּיו וְאֶת־מִצְוֹתָיו)	
		... and in order that (וּלְמַעַן) *you may prolong your days on the soil....*	

Deuteronomy 4

The two parts of the introduction, vv. 1-4 and 5-8, are themselves rhetorical units, each held together by a keyword inclusio (Weinfeld):

. . . in order that *you may live* (תִּחְיוּ) . . .	4:1
. . . but *you* (וְאַתֶּם) . . . *are alive* (חַיִּים). . . .	4:4
. . . *statutes and ordinances* (חֻקִּים וּמִשְׁפָּטִים) . . .	4:5
. . . *statutes and ordinances* (חֻקִּים וּמִשְׁפָּטִים) . . .	4:8

Within the core teaching are three warnings against making idols, anticipating the second commandment in 5:8:

You shall not make for yourself an idol, any form . . .	5:8
and you make for yourselves an idol, a form of any figure	4:16
and you make for yourselves an idol, a form of anything . . .	4:23
and make an idol, a form of anything . . .	4:25

The upper limit of the present unit is marked by a *petuhah* in M[L] and a section in 4QDeut[d] and Sam before v. 1, which is also the chapter division. The lower limit is marked by a *petuhah* in M[L] and a section in Sam after v. 24. The Sam also has sections after vv. 4, 8, 11, and 20.

Portions of 4:1-24 are contained in 4QDeut[c], 4QDeut[d], and 4QDeut[f].

Notes

4:1 *And now, O Israel, listen to the statutes and to the ordinances that I am teaching you to do.* Hearing and doing are recurring themes throughout Deuteronomy, being also bedrock concepts in the OT and subsequent Judeo-Christian religion. Here Israel is admonished to "hear/listen to," (אֶל) שְׁמַע, the statutes and ordinances Moses is teaching people "to do" (5:1; 6:3; 7:12; cf. Jer 11:4). "Doing the law" also gets the emphasis in Deut 27:26. On the importance of hearing and doing in the NT, see Matt 7:21-27; Rom 2:13; Jas 1:22-25. Weinfeld sees in the present verse another form of the "Hear, O Israel" didactic introduction, on which see Note for 5:1.

And now. וְעַתָּה. This particle signals a discourse transition (see Note for 2:13), shifting from past to present and drawing practical conclusions to what has just been stated (Driver). Cf. "and now" in 10:12, after the historical survey in 9:7–10:11.

listen to the statutes and to the ordinances. שְׁמַע אֶל־הַחֻקִּים וְאֶל־הַמִּשְׁפָּטִים.

Deuteronomy 4

"Statutes and ordinances" (הַחֻקִּים וְהַמִּשְׁפָּטִים) is a stock expression for the laws of the Deuteronomic Code. The pair occurs often in the book (4:1, 5, 8, 14, 45; 5:1, 31; 6:1, 20; 7:11; 8:11; 11:1, 32; 12:1; 26:16, 17; 30:16; Driver 1895, lxxxi no. 37; Weinfeld 1972, 336-37 nos. 16, 21), sometimes augmented by "commandment(s)" (מִצְוָה/ מִצְוֹת) and/or "testimonies" (עֵדֹת). Another stock pair is "statutes and commandments" (4:40; 6:2; 10:13; 27:10; 28:15, 45; 30:10; Weinfeld 1972, 337 nos. 21a-b). The terms occur also singly or in other combinations (Driver 1895, lxxxi no. 37; Weinfeld 1972, 338 nos. 21c-j). While six or seven terms for law are used without distinction in the book, they nevertheless have specific meanings. חֻקִּים ("statutes") are fixed decrees of religion, worship, and ceremony, possibly being engraved on stone, wood, or other flat surface (חקק is "to inscribe"). מִשְׁפָּטִים are civil and criminal laws, also sentences handed down by judges and rulers, with their attending procedures (Driver; Muilenburg 1967). Driver says מִשְׁפָּט is a judicial decision, made authoritatively once, thus constituting a rule or precedent, which is applicable to similar cases in the future. Alt (1966c, 92) said the מִשְׁפָּטִים in the heading to the Book of the Covenant (Exod 21:1) were the entire corpus of casuistic laws, "ordinances for the administration of justice by the local secular jurisdiction." For an extended discussion on מִשְׁפָּטִים, see Morgenstern 1930, 31-208. In the Deuteronomic Code (chs. 12–26) "laws" are never called תּוֹרֹת (a rare usage in the OT; see Exod 18:20; Lev 26:46; Isa 24:5; Neh 9:13), always חֻקִּים and מִשְׁפָּטִים. Nevertheless, תּוֹרָה (singular) is used as a blanket term for Deuteronomic law (1:5; 4:8, 44; 17:18-19; 31:26; and often in chs. 27–31). מִצְוָה ("commandment") and עֵדֹת ("testimonies") are stipulations or obligations, the sort of which one finds in a treaty (see Note for 4:45). On LXX renderings of the various terms for "law," see Blank 1930.

that I am teaching you to do. I.e., in the present discourse. The verb למד ("to learn" [Qal]; "to teach" [Piel]) occurs often in Deuteronomy (4:1, 5, 10, 14; 5:1, 31; 6:1; 11:19; 14:23; 17:19; 18:9; 20:18; 31:12-13, 19, 22) and nowhere else in the Pentateuch (Weinfeld 1972, 303). Moses' task here is to *teach* Israel the commandments. But infinitely more important than Moses' teaching of the commandments is Israel's doing them (ibn Ezra).

in order that you may live, and you may enter and possess the land that Yahweh God of your fathers is giving to you. The theme of vv. 1-4 is that doing the commandments leads to life, a theme occurring throughout Deuteronomy, the corollary to which is prolonged life for Israel in the land (4:1, 40; 5:33; 6:2, 24; 8:1, 3; 11:8-9, 18-21; 16:20; 25:15; 30:6, 16, 19-20; 32:47; cf. Lev 18:5). In 8:3 Moses tells the people: "One does not live by bread alone, but one lives by everything that goes out of the mouth of Yahweh." Obeying the commandments in 30:15-20 comes down to a life and death choice, where again it is said that obedience will be blessing for Israel, whereas disobedience will result in Israel not living long in the land. These themes turn up often in the wisdom literature

Deuteronomy 4

(Weinfeld 1972, 313-16; cf. Pss 37:11, 22, 29, 34; Prov 2:21-22; 7:2; 8:35-36, etc.). Jeremiah said, too, that keeping the Sabbath means life (Jer 17:21). On the stereotyped expression "to enter and take possession of the land," see v. 5; 6:18; 7:1; 11:10, 29; 17:14; 23:21(20) and Note for 1:8.

that Yahweh God of your fathers is giving to you. Yahweh swore an oath to the fathers to give their descendants land (see Note for 1:8). On Yahweh as "God of the fathers," see Note for 1:11.

2 *You shall not add to the word that I am commanding you, and you shall not subtract from it.* This warning occurs again in 13:1(12:32), where it appears to have a dual function, applying to the prior prohibition against following other gods and ahead to the forthcoming Deuteronomic Code (see Rhetoric and Composition for 12:1–13:1). Here reference is to the commandments in their entirety (Driver; Weinfeld; Friedman), although Tigay thinks application is to the exclusive worship of Yahweh and the caution not to countenance idols (cf. a mention of Baal-peor in vv. 3-4). We meet up with this same warning in the NT. Matthew's Sermon on the Mount warns against annulling any of the lesser commandments (Matt 5:19), and Revelation closes with a solemn warning not to add or subtract from words of prophecy contained in that book (Rev 22:18-19).

Warnings not to add or subtract words are contained in texts of the ANE and the classical world. The Code of Hammurabi contains dire warnings not to alter the law the king has promulgated (*ANET*³, 178; rev. xxv 60-70; rev. xxvi 1-10). Polybius reports a treaty between Hannibal and King Philip of Macedon, which concludes:

> If we decide to withdraw any clauses from this treaty or to add any
> we will withdraw such clauses or add them as we both may agree....
> (Polybius *Hist* vii 9:9)

The same provision applied to a treaty between Rome and Judas Maccabeus (1 Macc 8:29-30). For biblical and extrabiblical examples of this warning given to messengers and scribes, that they be sure to faithfully report a divine word or words from the king, see Note for 13:1.

in order to keep the commandments of Yahweh your God that I am commanding you. The reason for not adding or subtracting: Keeping the commandments means keeping them as they were given. The expression "that I am commanding you (today)" occurs very often in Deuteronomy (4:2[2x], 40, 6:6; 7:11; 8:1, 11; 10:13; 11:8, 13, 22, 27, 28, etc.; Weinfeld 1972, 356-57 no. 7).

3-4 Nothing was said in 3:29 about Israel's breach of covenant at Beth-peor, the most grave incident in the Transjordan settlement, where twenty-four thousand people are said to have died in a plague (Num 25:1-9). But it gets mentioned here, supporting what has been said about covenant obedience bringing

Deuteronomy 4

life. Moses reminds the people that many of those standing before him were eyewitnesses to what happened at Baal-peor. But included in his audience are some who were not there; nevertheless, throughout the chapter the present generation is taken to be one with the earlier generations. For the concept of the corporate personality in ancient Israel, see Note for 5:3.

Your eyes have seen. On this Deuteronomic expression, see Note for 3:21. Hebrew psychology generally puts the emphasis on hearing, but here seeing is stressed. Israel has not seen Yahweh (v. 12), but Yahweh's mighty acts it did see (vv. 33-36).

who went after Baal-peor. The expression "go after" (הלך + אַחֲרֵי) is judicial, occurring often in Deuteronomy with the meaning of "serve" (Lohfink 1963a, 77; Moran 1963b, 82-83 n.). See also Jer 2:2, 5, 8. On (Beth) Baal-peor, see Note for 3:29.

But you who clung to Yahweh your God are alive, all of you today. "To cling (דבק) to Yahweh" is a Deuteronomic expression for showing loyal devotion (4:4; 10:20; 11:22; 13:5[4]; 30:20; Driver 1895, lxxx-lxxxi no. 28; Weinfeld 1972, 333 no. 5). The same verb is used in Gen 2:24, where it says a man is to leave father and mother and "cling" to his wife. Here Moses tells the people that rejecting pagan worship and "clinging" to Yahweh brought them life (cf. 30:20).

5 Commentators have been troubled by the Perfect form of the verb, which normally translates as past tense. Moses received the command to teach the statutes and ordinances at Horeb (v. 14; 5:31), but only now is he doing it, according to Deuteronomy, some forty years later (v. 8). At Horeb the people received only the Ten Commandments, nothing more (5:22). According to Deuteronomy, two covenants were brokered, one at Horeb and one in the land of Moab (28:69[29:1]). The verb form here is not really a problem. Weinfeld says that in Semitic languages, when one makes a formal declaration, one uses a finite verb even though the declaration pertains to the present or future. The verb could also be rendered a present perfect (NJV: "I have imparted"), conveying the idea that Moses is in process of teaching the statutes and ordinances.

See. רָאָה. Used here as an imperative (see 1:8).

just as Yahweh my God commanded me. I.e., at Mount Horeb (v. 14; 5:31).

the land that you are entering to take possession of it. On the Deuteronomic expression "to (enter and) take possession of the land," see v. 1 and Note for 1:8.

6 Doing the statutes will demonstrate Israel's wisdom and understanding to surrounding nations. Daube (1969a, 50-51) cites this verse in support of his thesis that Deuteronomy contains a shame-cultural element, for in a shame culture how you appear to others is of enormous importance. Attention to shame shows an affinity with wisdom. Daube says: "Deuteronomy does not belong to Wisdom literature but it stands in close relation to it." On the connection between law and wisdom, see Sirach 24.

Deuteronomy 4

So you shall be careful and you shall do. וּשְׁמַרְתֶּם וַעֲשִׂיתֶם. A stereotyped expression in Deuteronomy (4:6; 7:12; 16:12; 17:19; 23:24[23]; 26:16; 28:13; 29:8[9], etc.; Driver 1895, lxxxiii no. 68b; Weinfeld 1972, 336 no. 17a). On "be careful for yourself/yourselves," see Note for 4:9; on "be careful to do," see Note for 5:1. In Deuteronomy people are continually told to "be careful," particularly when it comes to "doing" the commandments.

Surely. רק. This particle is normally restrictive, but here it has affirmative, assertive force (KBL³; Muraoka 1985, 131).

great nation. Not in terms of numbers (cf. 7:7), but in terms of name and reputation. The word "great" in 26:5 (= populous) draws on Exodus 1 (Weinfeld). The next two verses contrast Israel with other "great nations."

7 The first of two rhetorical questions augmenting the claim that Israel surpasses other great nations: It has a God who is near whenever Israel calls (1 Kgs 8:52; Pss 34:19[18]; 145:18). Other nations seek to bring their god/gods near with idols.

8 This rhetorical question argues that Israel surpasses other great nations by having statutes and ordinances that are just (צַדִּיקִם). These are its "law" (1:5; 4:44). The celebrated lawgiver of Old Babylonia, Hammurabi, called himself "the king of justice" and boasted that laws in his Code were just (Epilogue; *ANET*³, 177-78; Weinfeld 1972, 150-51). "Today" is the day Moses is teaching in the plains of Moab (v. 40; 5:1; 6:6; 7:11; 8:1, 11; 11:8, etc.).

I am setting before you. I.e., for your acceptance. A stereotyped expression in Deuteronomy (see Note for 1:8).

9 *Only be careful for yourself and take much care for your life, lest you forget the things that your eyes have seen, and lest they depart from your heart all the days of your life.* After praising Israel for its incomparable God and incomparable law, Moses cautions it not to forget the wondrous revelation at Horeb and let this defining experience depart from its memory.

Only be careful for yourself and take much care for your life. Another Deuteronomic coinage in both singular and plural (4:9, 15 [expanded], 23; 6:12; 8:11; 11:16; 12:13, 19, 30; 15:9; cf. Jer 17:21; Driver 1895, lxxix no. 11; Weinfeld 1972, 357 no. 12). For a similar expression, see Note for 4:6. Here the particle רק has its usual restrictive force, meaning "only" (LXX omits).

lest you forget. Deuteronomy speaks often about "remembering" (זכר) and "forgetting" (שכח). On the importance of remembering, see Note for 5:15. On "not forgetting" Yahweh and his covenant, warned against in v. 23, see Note for 32:18.

that your eyes have seen. אֲשֶׁר־רָאוּ עֵינֶיךָ. The people are addressed as if all were present at Mount Horeb, even though many were born later. On the concept of the "corporate personality" in ancient Israel, see Note for 5:3. This stereotyped phrase occurs also in 7:19; 10:21; 29:2[3]; Driver 1895, lxxxiii no. 59;

Weinfeld 1972, 357 no. 11). Similar expressions are discussed in Notes for 1:30 and 3:21.

and lest they depart from your heart. וּפֶן־יָסוּרוּ מִלְּבָבְךָ. In Hebrew psychology the "heart" often refers to what we would call the mind (cf. 6:5; 11:18). The concern here is that the Horeb experience might vanish from memory. The LXX has: μὴ ἀποστήτωσαν ἀπὸ τῆς καρδίας σου ("lest they should leave from your heart"), i.e., disappear from your memory (Wevers 1995, 72).

all the days of your life. I.e., as long as you live. Elsewhere in the Deuteronomic preaching Israel is charged to keep Yahweh's commands, love and fear Yahweh, and not forsake the Levite "all the days (of your life)" or "all the days/your days" it lives upon the land (4:10; 5:29; 6:2, 24; 11:1; 12:1, 19; 14:23; 19:9; 31:13). If Israel does not keep this charge, it will be under curses "all the days" (28:29, 33). On other occurrences of "all the days" and "all your days" in Deuteronomy, see 4:40; 17:19; 18:5; 22:19, 29; 23:7(6). The clichés are noted in Driver (1895, lxxxi no. 41) and Weinfeld (1972, 358 no. 16), although Weinfeld says "all the days" is too common to be called Deuteronomic. The expression occurs a number of times in Jeremiah (Jer 32:39; 33:18; 35:19).

So make them known to your children and to your children's children. One of the ways extraordinary things of the past stay with people is by them being taught to their children and grandchildren. Another important wisdom theme in Deuteronomy: Teach Yahweh's mighty words and deeds to the children and grandchildren. Here the people are being told to teach Yahweh's wondrous revelation at Horeb. Elsewhere it is the signs and wonders of Egypt and the deliverance from Egyptian slavery (6:20-24; cf. Exod 12:26-27; 13:8, 14), also Yahweh's commands, whether the Decalogue (4:10), the statutes and ordinances (6:7; 11:19), the law in its entirety (31:12-13), or in a supplement to the book, the Song of Moses (32:46). The children, like their parents, will learn to fear Yahweh by hearing Yahweh's commands and making them their own (4:10; 6:2, 24; 31:12-13). In Israel, as in other ancient societies, wisdom was passed down from father to son, mother to daughter. The teaching of scribes and other professionals was carried on in schools attached to the palace or the temple; otherwise, most education took place in the home (Crenshaw 1985; 1998). International treaties had to be taught to subsequent generations. The Vassal Treaty of Esarhaddon (ca. 672), for example, contained orders to instruct sons, grandsons, offspring, and descendants to keep the treaty; otherwise they would lose their lives, their land would be destroyed, and their people would be deported (*ANET*[3], 537 no. 25).

10 *The day that you stood before Yahweh your God at Horeb.* Reference is to the day when the people gathered together at Horeb in solemn assembly (LXX expands to τῇ ἡμέρᾳ τῆς ἐκκλησίας, "on the day of the assembly"; cf. 9:10; 10:4; 18:16). On this day, Yahweh gave to Israel the Ten Commandments (see Note for 9:10).

"Gather to me the people that I may make them hear my words, that they may learn to fear me all the days that they are living on the soil." One reason people are to hear Yahweh's words, perhaps the most important reason, is so they will learn to fear Yahweh throughout life. Another important Deuteronomic theme is that Israel must learn the fear of Yahweh (4:10; 5:29; 6:2, 13, 24; 8:6; 10:12, 20; 13:5[4]; 14:23 [in tithing]; 17:19 [the king in reciting the Deuteronomic law]; 28:58; 31:12-13; cf. Exod 20:20; Jer 10:7; 32:39). "That they learn to fear me" is a stereotyped phrase in Deuteronomy (Driver 1895, lxxxii no. 45; Weinfeld 1972, 333 nos. 3a, 3b), having parallels also in the Akkadian treaties (Zunz 1873, 670; Weinfeld 1972, 332-33). Nabopolassar (I, 1:17) and his son Nebuchadnezzar (XII, 1:4; XV, 1:70; 2:7; 8:31-32), the two great builders of the Neo-Babylonian Empire, praise Marduk on building inscriptions as the one from whom they "learned the fear of the god and goddess (in their heart)" (Langdon 1905; Weinfeld 1972, 279). Similarly, on a building inscription of Nabonidus, the king says in a prayer to the moon-god Sin: "You . . . instill reverence for your great godhead (in) the hearts of its people so that they do not sin against your great godhead" (COS, 2:314).

"To fear" (יְרֵא) in the OT has both positive and negative meaning. It can simply mean "be afraid of," and we hear Yahweh or his divine messenger continually telling individuals to "fear not!" (Gen 15:1; 21:17, etc.). But to fear Yahweh also means "to revere" (Gen 22:12) or "stand in awe of" Yahweh (AmT), not to dread arbitrary and capricious divine action, as people do who worship other gods. This sense of reverence and respect for Yahweh is what we have in Deuteronomy. Pfeiffer (1955) sees in biblical fear an element of "longing" for the deity, a wanting to serve God. Jeremiah lamented the fact that people did not have a healthy fear of Yahweh, which common sense dictated and which Yahweh's law required (Jer 2:19; 5:22-24; 44:10). On the "fear of God" in Deuteronomy and elsewhere in the OT, see Weinfeld (1972, 274-78), who finds here another wisdom theme (Ps 111:10; Prov 1:7; 3:7; 9:10; 15:33; Job 28:28). Psalm 111:10 and Prov 9:10 say that "the fear of Yahweh is the beginning of wisdom."

all the days. On this expression, see Note for 4:9.

the soil. הָאֲדָמָה. Hebrew אֲדָמָה is more concrete than אֶרֶץ ("land"), referring to the soil or the ground: Latin *terra firma* (cf. Gen 2:7; 4:2). Occurring frequently in Deuteronomy, the term is often simply a synonym for "land" (31:20; 32:43).

and their children they may teach." I.e., to fear Yahweh (6:2; 31:12-13).

11 The theophany may have come in a great storm (G. E. Wright; cf. Exod 19:17-18; 24:16-17; in the NT Heb 12:18). See 5:22.

at the foot of. Hebrew תַּחַת here means "below, at the foot of," as in 4:49 and Exod 24:4.

the heart of heaven. "Heart" is here a figurative term for "center, midst"

(Driver); cf. "heart of the sea(s)" in Exod 15:8; Ezek 27:27. The LXX does not translate the term.

darkness, cloud, and storm cloud. חֹשֶׁךְ עָנָן וַעֲרָפֶל. All signify darkness, a contrast with the fire burning heavenward. Darkness was apparently at the foot of the mountain. On nouns that describe an external state, see GKC §118q.

12 The defining mark of the Horeb revelation was that there was only sound, no visual representation of God. Yahweh spoke and the people heard. In 5:4 Israel is said to have had a "face to face" encounter with Yahweh, but again, it was only to hear Yahweh *speak*. The expression "face to face," when describing OT theophanies, always refers to speaking and hearing, never to seeing (see Note for 5:4). Because Israel saw no form at Horeb, images of God were disallowed (vv. 15-18). The second commandment put the latter into law (5:8; Exod 20:4). Images of the divine introduce a visual element into religion, and this was rejected in ancient Israel.

from the midst of the fire. A stereotyped expression in Deuteronomy (4:12, 15, 33, 36; 5:4, 22-26; 9:10; 10:4; Driver 1895, lxxxiii no. 69). Yahweh revealed himself to Moses earlier in a fire coming out of a bush (Exod 3:2). T. J. Lewis (1998, 51) has suggested that "fire," being numinous and without a definite shape, may explain why images of Yahweh were prohibited in ancient Israel. Theophanies in fire — also in clouds and smoke — do not lend themselves to physical representation.

13 The "ten words" are the Ten Commandments, also called the Decalogue (5:6-21; Exod 20:2-17), which set forth the stipulations of the Horeb (Sinai) covenant (cf. 10:4). The "covenant" (בְּרִית) and the "Ten Commandments" — like law and covenant — are closely related, but not the same. The covenant is the binding relationship, expressed typically in the words, "I will be your God, and you will be my people" (Exod 6:7; Lev 26:12; Jer 7:23; 11:4; cf. Deut 29:11-12[12-13]). The Ten Commandments are the core law governing the covenant relationship (called "tablets of the covenant" in 9:9, 11, 15). The covenant was ratified under oath, leading Weinfeld (1976a) to call it a loyalty oath (see Note for 29:11). Here it says that God wrote the ten words on the tablets (Exod 31:18; Deut 9:10: "with the finger of God"), but in Exod 34:28 Moses is said to have written the tablets replacing the earlier broken ones. For a fuller discussion of the Horeb (Sinai) covenant, see Note for 5:2.

the ten words. There are different ways of reckoning the Ten Commandments (see Rhetoric and Composition for 5:6-21); nevertheless, all traditions agree that the Commandments number ten. Freedman (2000, 6-13) notes that there are ten fingers on two hands, also that the biblical record has a "ten strikes and you're out" rule: Pharaoh is given ten chances with ten plagues (Exodus 7-12), and the wilderness generation is given ten chances to comply with Yahweh's demands (Num 14:20-23).

Deuteronomy 4

two tablets of stone. See also Exod 24:12; 31:18; 34:4; Deut 5:22; 9:9-11; 10:1-4. Stone was doubtless used to make the writing permanent. In the NT, however, these tablets are diminished in importance when compared to the "tablet of the heart" on which the New Covenant is written (2 Cor 3:3, 7; cf. Jer 31:33). The Horeb tablets have been portrayed in religious art as two rectangular stones with rounded tops. On them, the short sixth, seventh, and eighth commandments are written in full, the others only in their first two words. The tablets became a religious symbol for Christians in the Middle Ages (11th cent. A.D.); Jews earlier had not assigned them symbolic value. It was Jews in Italy who took over portrayals of the tablets from Christian artists in the 15th cent., using them at first on representations of the ark of the covenant (Sarfatti 1990).

14 The pronoun "me" is emphasized in the Hebrew, contrasting with "you" in the prior verse. According to Deuteronomy, Yahweh gave Moses the statutes and ordinances of the Deuteronomic Code at Mount Horeb, but he did not teach them to the people until they were assembled in the plains of Moab. Reference here is not to the Ten Commandments, which were given to the people at Horeb directly from Yahweh (5:28), but to other laws (Rashbam; Weinfeld; cf 6:1).

in the land that you were crossing over to take possession of it. 4QDeut^c adds "[the] Jordan" after "crossing over," bringing this expression into line with others in the book (see Note for 4:25-26).

15 Repeating what was said in v. 12 about Israel not seeing any divine form at Horeb. The prior warning (see Note for 4:9) and reminder of the Horeb revelation are to preface the warnings in vv. 16-19 about lapsing into idol worship or worshipping the host of heaven, which would violate the second commandment. In the NT, see Rom 1:23.

16 An idol (פֶּסֶל) would be an image of God carved in wood, sculptured in stone, or cast in metal (cf. 5:8). Leading the forbidden list are images of male or female deities. Hebrew תַּבְנִית means "copy" or "reproduction" (Ps 106:20; Ezek 8:10). Moses again warns the people not to "act corruptly" (שׁחת H stem) in v. 25, yet he says in 31:29 they will do just that after his death.

17-18 No representation of any beast, bird, reptile, or fish is to be crafted for purposes of worship (cf. Ezek 8:10). The golden calf of Horeb has to be in the background here, cited briefly in 9:12 and reported more fully in Exodus 32. Nonidolatrous images were apparently excluded, e.g., the bronze serpent made by Moses in the wilderness, which was placed on a pole so people bit by one of the invading "burning serpents" could look up at the image and live (Num 21:8-9). But Hezekiah in his temple reform destroyed this image, along with others, because people were burning incense to it (2 Kgs 18:4). There were also the images of cherubs (winged bulls?) made to sit atop the ark (Exod 25:18-22) and the oxen, lions, cherubs, and seraphs (winged serpents) crafted to adorn Solomon's temple (1 Kgs 7:25, 29, 36, 44; Isa 6:2-7; cf. Ezek 1:5-28; 9:3; 10:1-22; 11:22). Idol worship, nevertheless, was practiced in both Israel and Judah. In Israel were the infamous golden calves at Dan and Bethel, to which sacrifices were made (1 Kgs 12:28-29, 32; 2 Kgs 17:16); in Judah the Jerusalem temple contained horses that kings had dedicated to the sun (2 Kgs 23:11). On animal worship among Arabs and other peoples in the ancient world, see W. R. Smith 1880.

anything that creeps on the ground. The LXX has: "any creeping thing (ἑρπετοῦ) that creeps on the ground." Nelson suggests MT loss of רֶמֶשׂ by haplography (homoeoarcton: ר . . . ר).

19 *and lest you lift up your eyes to the heaven, and you see the sun and the moon and the stars, all the host of heaven, and you be lured away and you worship them and serve them.* The ancients (like many moderns) were much drawn to the heavenly bodies (Ps 8:4-5[3-4]; Job 31:26-27), but in Israel these were not to be worshipped; Israel was to worship and serve only Yahweh (see Note for 6:13). Astral worship was common in Assyria and Babylonia, becoming widespread also in Israel and Judah in the 8th and 7th cents. (2 Kgs 17:16; 23:4-5). Manasseh worshipped and built altars for the host of heaven in the Jerusalem temple (2 Kgs 21:3, 5). Astral worship was done away with in Josiah's reform (2 Kgs 23:5), but soon after, in Zedekiah's reign, twenty-five men were again worshipping the sun in the temple (Ezek 8:16). Late preexilic prophets spoke out forcefully against astral worship (Zeph 1:5; Jer 7:18; 8:2; 19:13; 44:17-19, 25; Ezek 8:16). Jeremiah, for his part, met up with unyielding devotion to the Queen of Heaven (Ashtart) (cf. Lundbom 1999, 476-77). He had a derisive word for devotees of astral worship: their bones would be exhumed and spread out before the sun, moon, and all the host of heaven that they had loved and served (Jer 8:1-2). In the Deuteronomic Code, the penalty for astral worship was death (17:2-7).

all the host of heaven. I.e., the sun, moon, and stars, to which "host of heaven" stands in apposition (cf. 17:3; Jer 8:2; 33:22). "Host of heaven" occurs nowhere in the 8th-cent. prophets.

and you be lured away. וְנִדַּחְתָּ. Idolatry is seductive (13:6, 11, 14[5, 10, 13]; 30:17).

and you worship them and serve them. The expression is stock in Deuteronomy when referring to "other gods" (4:19; 8:19; 11:16; 17:3; 29:25[26]; 30:17; Driver 1895, lxxviii no. 2; Weinfeld 1972, 321 nos. 6, 8).

which Yahweh your God has allotted to all the peoples under the entire heaven. An extraordinary concession, supported in 29:25(26). Israel is not to worship the heavenly bodies; Yahweh has allotted them as objects of worship for other peoples of the world. Here is no indication that astral worship is inherently wrong, or reprehensible, if others practice it. But any resident of an Israelite town had better not engage in this worship, for it will be a capital offense

(17:2-5; cf. *Sifre Deut* §148:6). Let sojourners beware! We have here an argument for natural religion, such as Paul makes in Rom 1:20-25, although Paul goes on to argue that such religion becomes depraved. Church fathers Justin Martyr (*Dialogue with Trypho* 55) and Clement of Alexandria (*Stromateis* vi 14, 110-11) viewed the worship of heavenly bodies as granted to the nations, but only as a means of enabling them to rise ultimately to something better. The Lord was God alone, who made all things. The OT says Yahweh created the heavenly bodies (Gen 1:14-19; Ps 74:16). The point being made here and in v. 20 is that Israel must worship Yahweh, not the heavenly bodies, because Yahweh called Israel to be his special possession (Albright 1957b, 320). Cf. Deut 32:8-9; Jer 10:12-16[= 51:15-19].

all the peoples under the entire heaven. I.e., people everywhere (cf. 2:25).

20 "But you" (וְאֶתְכֶם; LXX: ὑμᾶς δὲ) is emphatic, contrasting Israel to the other nations. Unlike these other nations, Israel has been chosen by Yahweh as his special possession (7:6).

iron furnace. A small furnace in which iron is smelted. Used in the OT as a metaphor for Israel's slavery in Egypt (1 Kgs 8:51; Jer 11:4; cf. Sir 38:28).

to be for himself a people, an inheritance. Hebrew נַחֲלָה can also be translated "heritage." The term in Deuteronomy usually denotes land (10:9; 12:12; 21:16, etc.), specifically the land of Canaan, which Yahweh is about to give Israel. This land is understood as hereditary property (4:21, 38; 12:9; 15:4; 19:10, etc.; cf. Jer 2:7; 3:19; 12:7, 14). According to Deut 32:8, other nations also received a heritage from God (cf. Jer 12:15). But "inheritance/heritage" can also refer to Israel the people (9:29; 32:9; Jer 10:16[= 51:19]; 12:8-9; 2 Kgs 21:14; Ps 78:71), which is the meaning here. Jeremiah plays on both meanings in Jer 12:7-9. In the present verse, the idea is that Israel became Yahweh's heritage by virtue of the redemption from Egypt (9:26; cf. Ps 74:2). On Israel as Yahweh's (holy) people, see Note for 7:6.

as at this day. A common expression in Deuteronomy (see Note for 2:30).

21-22 A repetition of what was said in 1:37 and 3:26 about Yahweh being angry with Moses and denying him entrance into the promised land. It is not clear why this is included here; perhaps it is to qualify Israel's "chosenness" in v. 20. Yahweh's special people, because of their grumbling at Kadesh (1:27-28), bore the responsibility for Moses not getting into the promised land. Moses says it was "on account of your words."

the good land that Yahweh your God was giving to you as an inheritance. A variant of a stock expression found throughout Deuteronomy (see Note for 15:4), where "inheritance" (נַחֲלָה) is the land about to be given Israel. In v. 20 the "inheritance" was the people Israel.

the good land. I.e., Canaan (see Note for 1:34-36). The LXX omits "good."

23 Repeating the warning about idolatry in vv. 15-18, which is a defining

Deuteronomy 4

element of the Horeb covenant. On "not forgetting" Yahweh and his covenant, see Note for 32:18; on "cutting" a covenant, see Note for 5:2.

Be careful for yourselves. On this stereotyped expression, see Note for 4:9.

24 *for Yahweh your God is a consuming fire.* A superb climax to the prior warnings, repeated in 9:3 (cf. Isa 29:6). Yahweh's resplendent glory at Sinai was said to be like a consuming fire (Exod 24:17). The NT writer of Hebrews says: "Let us offer to God acceptable worship, with reverence and awe; for our God is a consuming fire" (Heb 12:28-29).

he is a jealous God. הוּא אֵל קַנָּא. "Jealousy" is related to Yahweh's holiness, which he will not share with other gods (6:14-15; 32:16, 21-22; Exod 34:14; Josh 24:19-20). Yahweh will also not tolerate idols (5:8-9[= Exod 20:4-5]; Isa 42:8).

Message and Audience

Moses now turns from narrating the Transjordan success to sermonize on the covenant that will regulate Israel's life here and in Canaan. At the heart of this covenant are the Ten Words, added to which are statutes and ordinances now being taught to the people for the first time. People heard the defining Ten Words at Horeb. Now they must hear the statutes and ordinances. The reason is simple: Doing Yahweh's commands will give people life and possession of the land that was promised to them by the God of their fathers. They must not add to or subtract from the commands. Moses recalls what happened at Baal-peor, a subject he did not broach earlier. Those who went on this idolatrous romp with the daughters of Moab died; those who clung to Yahweh were today alive. The lesson should be clear: doing Yahweh's commands means life; not doing them means death.

Moses says again that the statutes and ordinances he is teaching must be carried out in the land Israel is about to enter. People must be careful to do them, for it will show them to be a great nation of wisdom and understanding in the eyes of others. What other great nation has gods so near as Yahweh, answering people when they call? And what other great nation has statutes and ordinances that are as just as the ones now being set before the covenant people?

Once again, people must be careful lest they forget the things their eyes have seen, not letting them depart from their heart. Yahweh's revelation must be made known to the children and grandchildren. Moses says that at Horeb Yahweh told him to gather the people together so they might hear his words. By hearing these words people would learn to fear Yahweh all their days. Fear of Yahweh must also be taught to the children. The Horeb revelation was extraordinary. The people approached Moses and stood at the foot of the mountain, which burned with fire up into the heart of heaven. Below were darkness, cloud, and storm cloud. Yahweh spoke from the fire. The people heard the words, but saw no form. Then Yahweh declared his covenant and its terms.

The "Ten Words" were written on tablets of stone. To Moses, Yahweh gave a command to teach the people other statutes and ordinances that were to be carried out in the land. The people are again warned to be exceedingly careful. They saw no form when Yahweh spoke from the fire. Therefore they must not make idols for themselves, no form of any figure — male or female, beast, winged bird, reptile or fish. Moreover, they must not look up to the heavenly bodies, the sun, moon, and stars, and be lured into worshipping and serving them. Yahweh has apportioned these to other peoples. But Israel he brought out of the iron furnace of Egypt to be his own people, his own inheritance, as Israel is in the present day.

Moses then says again how Yahweh became angry with him because of the people's words at Kadesh, swearing an oath that Moses not be permitted to enter Canaan. He must die in Moab. Only the present generation will cross the Jordan. So while Israel is Yahweh's special people, it must realize that Yahweh is not above being angry with them. The first portion of this discourse closes with another warning about being careful, this time not to forget the covenant and make idols of any kind. Be warned, Moses tells the people, that Yahweh your God is a consuming fire, a jealous God who admits no rivals.

For a late 8th- and early 7th-cent. audience, this strident discourse would surely have been a trumpet call, second only to ones coming from the prophets, to refrain from Canaanite and Assyrian idol worship, whether in the making of images or in worshipping the host of heaven. The northern kingdom in its last years was rife with idolatry, and because of this it met an inglorious end. Idol worship found its way also into Judah, and the reform of Hezekiah may have been an attempt to make the present message apply to worship in Jerusalem, indeed, to get all of Judah back on track in the worship of Yahweh. Josiah's reform later in the 7th cent. was an attempt along similar lines, using the present message to attack idol and astral worship. Josiah also carried out a covenant renewal ceremony, an indication that the people had forgotten the covenant of Yahweh their God.

2. What Will Happen If You Do Forget (4:25-40)

4^{25}When you have begotten children and children's children, and become old in the land, and you act corruptly and make an idol, a form of anything, and you do evil in the eyes of Yahweh your God to provoke him to anger, ^{26}I call to witness heaven and earth against you today, that you will utterly perish quickly from upon the land that you are crossing over the Jordan to take possession of it; you will not prolong your days upon it; indeed, you will be completely destroyed. ²⁷And Yahweh will scatter you among the peoples, and you will remain a numbered few among the nations where Yahweh will drive you. ²⁸And there you will serve gods, the work of human hands, wood and stone, which do not see and do not hear and do not eat and do not smell. ²⁹Yet from there you will seek Yahweh your God, and you will find him when you search after him with all your heart and with all your soul. ³⁰In your distress when all these things find you in the days afterward, then you will return to Yahweh your God and you will obey his voice. ³¹For Yahweh your God is a God of mercy; he will not abandon you and he will not bring you to ruin and he will not forget the covenant of your fathers that he swore to them.

³²Indeed ask, would you, about the former days that were before you, from the day that God created human beings upon the earth, and from one end of the heaven to the other end of the heaven: Has a great thing like this happened or has anything like it been heard of? ³³Has a people heard the voice of a god speaking from the midst of the fire as you, you have heard, and lived? ³⁴Or has a god attempted to go and take for himself a nation from the midst of another nation by testings, by signs and by wonders, and by war, and by a strong hand and by an outstretched arm, and by great terrors, according to all that Yahweh your God did for you in Egypt before your eyes? ³⁵You, you were shown in order to know that Yahweh he is God and there is no other besides him. ³⁶From the heaven he caused you to hear his voice in order to discipline you; and on the earth he let you see his great fire, and his words you heard from the midst of the fire. ³⁷And because he loved your fathers and chose their descendants after them, yes, he brought you out with his presence with his great strength from Egypt, ³⁸to dispossess before you nations greater and mightier than you, to bring you in, to give you their land for an inheritance, as at this day. ³⁹So you shall know today and take to your heart that Yahweh he is God in the heaven above and on the earth below; there is no other. ⁴⁰And you shall keep his statutes and his commandments that I am commanding you today, so that it may go well for you and for your children after you, and in order that you may prolong your days on the soil that Yahweh your God is giving to you, all the days.

Rhetoric and Composition

In these verses Moses' teaching on rejecting idolatry widens into the future, warning what will happen if Israel, having grown old in the land, succumbs to this evil. Yahweh will be sorely provoked, with the result that Israel will perish in the land it is now inheriting and a much-reduced people will find itself scattered among the nations. There they will worship the inert gods that have so fascinated them. Yet a remnant will seek Yahweh, and find him if they seek in earnest, and will return to Yahweh and obey his voice. Yahweh, being a God of mercy, will not abandon them because of his covenant to the fathers (4:25-31). The present sermon concludes by celebrating the incomparable Yahweh as God alone, for which reason Israel must keep his statutes and commandments all the days (4:32-40).

The sermon as a whole (4:1-40) is a remarkable compendium of God's dealings with Israel — election and grace, first to the fathers, and then to Israel in the exodus; giving Israel an incomparable revelation at Horeb: a covenant, a law, and an inheritance of land; then Israel sinking into ruinous idolatry; and finally Yahweh's mercy being available if people seek him in sincerity and return to him in their distress. Teaching of such a grand scope compares only with what we have in the Song of Moses (Deuteronomy 32) and in the prophets.

The present unit is delimited at the top end by a *petuḥah* in M^L and a section in Sam before v. 25 and at the bottom end by a *petuḥah* in M^L and a section in Sam after v. 40. The Sam also has sections after vv. 31 and 34. The core teaching on rejecting idolatry ends with v. 31. The whole of 4:1-40 gives every indication of being a unity (see Rhetoric and Composition for 4:1-24).

Portions of 4:25-40 are contained in 4QDeut[c], 4QDeut[f], 4QDeut[h], 4QDeut[m], and 4QDeut[o].

Notes

4:25-26 This warning comes just after the people are told not to make idols, and cautioned about Yahweh being a jealous God (4:23-24). It also anticipates the first and second commandments in ch. 5. In concluding this teaching on idolatry, Moses first gives the curses (vv. 25-28), then the blessings (vv. 29-31), reversing the conventional covenant form. The verses are also similar to 8:19 and 30:17-18. The Horeb covenant is conditional, which is to say Israel's tenure in the land depends on obedience to the covenant and the terms of the covenant.

and become old in the land. וְנוֹשַׁנְתֶּם בָּאָרֶץ. The idea is that Israel, once long established in the land, will have lost the "spiritual freshness" it had at the beginning of the occupation (Driver). Cf. the N-stem of ישׁן in Lev 25:22; 26:10, where reference is to old stores of produce.

an idol, a form of anything. פֶּסֶל תְּמוּנַת כֹּל. Picking up from v. 23.

and you do evil in the eyes of Yahweh your God to provoke him to anger. "To do evil in the eyes of Yahweh (your God)" is a stock phrase in Deuteronomy (4:25; 9:18; 17:2; 31:29) and the Deuteronomic literature, occurring also in Jer 7:30; 18:10; 32:30 (Driver 1895, lxxxii no. 49; Weinfeld 1972, 339 no. 1). According to Deuteronomy, Israel is "to do right (and good) in the eyes of Yahweh" (see Note for 6:18). The added word about evil "provoking Yahweh to anger" employs another common Deuteronomic phrase (4:25; 9:18; 31:29), one assuming prominence in the Song of Moses (32:16, 19-22) and used often by the compiler of Kings (1 Kgs 14:9, 15; 15:30; 16:2, 7, 13, 26, 33; 2 Kgs 17:11, 17; 21:6, 15, etc.). It also occurs frequently in Jeremiah (Jer 7:18-19; 8:19; 11:17; 25:6-7; 32:29, 30, 32; 44:3, 8; Driver 1895, 72; Weinfeld 1972, 340 no. 6). Yahweh is provoked to anger by idols. His anger also burns when Israel breaks the covenant and goes after other gods (see Note for 6:15).

I call to witness heaven and earth against you today. Apostrophe. Heaven and earth are summoned as witnesses because they are sure to be around to give testimony if Israel disobeys the covenant in the future. Heaven and earth endure for all time (cf. 11:21). See also 30:19; 31:28; 32:1; Ps 50:4; Isa 1:2.

you will utterly perish quickly from upon the land. אָבֹד תֹּאבֵדוּן מַהֵר מֵעַל הָאָרֶץ. A variant of a stock Deuteronomic phrase, in some cases referring to Yahweh's action against other nations (4:26; 6:15; 7:4; 9:3; 11:17; 28:20, 63; Weinfeld 1972, 346 no. 10; 347 no. 12).

the land that you are crossing over the Jordan to take possession of it. This expression with variations is also stereotyped in Deuteronomy (4:14, 22, 26; 6:1; 9:1; 11:8, 10, 11, 31; 30:18; 31:13; 32:47; Driver 1895, lxxx no. 22; Weinfeld 1972, 342 no. 3). See also Note for 1:8.

you will not prolong your days upon it. The negative version of a stock Deuteronomic phrase (4:26, 40; 5:16, 33; 6:2; 11:9; 17:20; 22:7; 25:15; 30:18, 20; 32:47; Driver 1895, lxxviii no. 3; Weinfeld 1972, 345 no. 1). If Israel obeys Yahweh's commands, its days will be prolonged in the land (5:16 [cf. Exod 20:12]; 6:2; 25:15); if it does not obey, its days will not be prolonged. On the longevity theme in Deuteronomy, for the individual and for the nation, see Malamat 1982.

indeed, you will be completely destroyed. Reading an asseverative כִּי. The N-stem of שׁמד is particularly strong (see Note for 1:27).

27 *And Yahweh will scatter you among the peoples.* A circumlocution for exile, which was one of the covenant curses (28:64; 30:3; cf. Jer 9:15[16]; 30:11; Weinfeld 1972, 347 no. 14). Deuteronomy does not use the Hebrew word for "exile" (גלה). Mass deportations were carried out by the Assyrians already in the 9th cent. (Oded 1979; see Note for 28:36). Northern Israel was first to be exiled when Tiglath-pileser overran Galilee and Transjordan in 734-733 and deported their inhabitants to Assyria (2 Kgs 15:29).

a numbered few. מְתֵי מִסְפָּר is lit. "men of number," i.e., a numbered few (LXX: ὀλίγοι ἀριθμῷ). The term occurs also in Gen 34:30. One of the covenant curses was that Israel's numbers would diminish dramatically in dispersion (see Note on 28:62).

28 It is as if God says, "Very well, if gods of wood and stone are what

Deuteronomy 4

you want, then these are what you will get" (cf. 28:36, 64; Jer 16:13). T^{OnqPsJ} soften to "you will serve the nations who worship idols/you will . . . serve the worshippers of idols." The second commandment forbids worshipping and serving images; Israel is to worship and serve only Yahweh (see Note for 6:13).

and there you will serve gods. LXX: "other gods."

the work of human hands. I.e., idols (see Note for 2:7).

wood and stone. A disparaging expression for the other gods in Deuteronomy (4:28; 28:36, 64; 29:16[17]) and Jeremiah (Jer 2:27; 3:9), showing them to be inert. Hosea mocks people who inquire of "a thing of wood" (Hos 4:12). Gods made from wood are also held up for ridicule in Isa 44:13-19. The Asherah, which was a feminine fertility symbol, was either a live tree or wooden pole positioned alongside altars (Deut 16:21). The masculine fertility symbol was the stone pillar. Fertility symbols of wood and stone were forbidden from early times (Exod 34:13; Deut 12:3; 16:21) but had joined other cultic furnishings at the high places. Josiah did away with them in his reform (2 Kgs 23:6-15). On the Asherah, see de Vaux 1965, 286; also "Asherah" in *ABD*, 1:483-87. For a picture of a female fertility figurine from Jerusalem, which may be this goddess, see P. J. King 1993, 110.

which do not see and do not hear and do not eat and do not smell. Driver notes the emphatic יון endings (cf. 1:17). Derisive speech about crafted idols appears only in Deuteronomy and perhaps in Lev 26:30, among the pentateuchal books (27:15; 28:36, 64; 29:16[17]; 31:29). It is common in the prophets (Hos 4:12; 8:6; 13:2; 14:4[3]; Isa 2:8; Mic 5:12[13]; Jer 10:5), especially Second Isaiah (Isa 40:19-20; 41:7; 44:9-20; 46:6-7). See also Pss 115:4-7; 135:15-17; Wis 13:18; 15:15. In the NT, see Rev 9:20.

29 A return after exile is envisioned again in 30:1-10 and anticipated also in Hosea (Hos 5:15–6:3) and Jeremiah (Jer 29:10-14). See in addition Lev 26:40-45; 1 Kgs 8:47-51. Israel's alienation from God will not be permanent. The distress of being scattered abroad (v. 30) will effect a change of heart in the nation, and if people seek Yahweh in sincerity, Yahweh will accept their repentance and once again show them favor. The verb דרש ("to seek") here means "to pray" (cf. Jer 10:21; 29:7; Isa 55:6; 65:1; Acts 17:27. Second Isaiah says:

> Seek Yahweh while he may be found,
>   call upon him while he is near;
> Let the wicked forsake his way,
>   and the unrighteous person his thoughts.
> Let him return to Yahweh, that he may have mercy upon him,
>   and to our God, for he will abundantly pardon. (Isa 55:6-7)

Felix Mendelssohn used the present verse combined with Jer 29:13 in his *Elijah* oratorio (1846), where Obadiah sings in the tenor solo:

"If with all your hearts ye truly seek me,
Ye shall ever surely find me." Thus saith our God.
Oh! that I knew where I might find Him,
That I might even come before His presence!

The chorus follows with words from Jer 29:14:

Thus saith our God, "Ye shall ever find me."
Thus saith our God. (Part I, no. 4 Air; no. 5 Chorus)

and you will find him. Adding the pronominal suffix ("him") with Sam and Vg.

with all your heart and with all your soul. A stock expression in Deuteronomy (4:29; 6:5; 10:12; 11:13; 13:4[3]; 26:16; 30:2, 6, 10; Driver 1895, lxxxii no. 51; Weinfeld 1972, 334 no. 9), appearing also in Josh 22:5; 23:14; 1 Kgs 2:4; 8:48; 2 Kgs 23:3, 25. The words appear in the mouth of Yahweh in Jer 32:41, but this is rare. Here the condition of being found by Yahweh is a heart-and-soul searching on Israel's part. No superficial or self-serving motives, only a radical change in the heart of the nation will do. In the Assyrian treaties, vassals are expected to give whole-hearted support to the Assyrian king (Frankena 1965, 140-41).

30 Israel's return will come about because of the distress of exile (cf. Hos 5:15–6:1). The verb שׁוּב means both "return" and "repent." Israel's return to Yahweh is also anticipated in 30:2. Repentance is a key theme in the prophets (Amos 4:6-12; Hos 6:1; 14:2-3[1-2]; Jer 3:1–4:2, etc.) and is picked up by the Deuteronomic Historian in relating Solomon's prayer at the dedication of the temple (1 Kgs 8:47-53).

all these things. I.e., the destruction at home and horrors abroad (vv. 26-27).

in the days afterward. בְּאַחֲרִית הַיָּמִים. Sometimes "in future days" or "at the end of days," although the phrase does not have the latter meaning here. It simply denotes a distant but undetermined future time, which is the meaning in 31:29 and elsewhere in the OT (Gen 49:1; Num 24:14; Isa 2:2; Jer 23:20; 30:24; 48:47; 49:39; Ezek 38:16). In Dan 2:28; 10:14 it becomes a technical term for the End Times (Seebass, *aḥᵃrît*, in *TDOT*, 1:210-11), a meaning it has also in line 14 of 4QMMT (Qimron and Strugnell 1994, 58-59; Fraade 2003, 151-54).

and you will obey his voice. On this important Deuteronomic theme, where obeying Yahweh's voice means doing the commandments, see Note for 13:5. The present verse is combined with 30:1-3 in 4QMMT (Fraade 2003, 150-54).

31 *For Yahweh your God is a God of mercy.* That Yahweh is a God of mercy is attested in the divine self-disclosure of Exod 34:6. Yahweh is ready to accept Israel's penitence providing it is sincere (30:2-3), but as the verse goes on to say, Yahweh's mercy stems also from a remembrance of the covenant with the fathers.

Deuteronomy 4

he will not abandon you and he will not bring you to ruin. לֹא יַרְפְּךָ וְלֹא יַשְׁחִיתֶךָ. The verb רפא in the H-stem means "let go, let drop, abandon." Rashi: "He will not let loose of you." The promise is repeated in 31:6. After Israel's great sin in the wilderness, Moses entreated Yahweh not to bring his people to ruin (9:26), and Yahweh answered the prayer (10:10).

and he will not forget the covenant of your fathers that he swore to them. The covenant with Abraham was unconditional and eternal; therefore it could not be broken (Gen 17:1-7; Exod 32:13; Freedman 1964). The Abrahamic covenant is cited also in 7:8-9, 12; 8:18; 29:12(13).

32 With the core teaching concluded, people are now asked to embark on a fact-finding mission. Has such a great thing (= revelation) ever happened or been heard of since creation, anywhere on earth, like what happened to Israel? The verse has an echo in Jer 2:10-11, where Yahweh calls for messengers to go west and east — to the Greek islands and to Kedar in Arabia — and inquire whether it has ever happened that people have exchanged gods even though they are no-gods? For other calls to undertake fact-finding missions, see Deut 32:7-9; Jer 5:1; 18:13; Amos 6:2; Job 8:8-10.

In these verses, and in 7:6-11 and 10:12–11:8, basic Deuteronomic themes are presented:

1. Yahweh's love of the fathers and of Israel, and Israel's election (v. 37; 7:7-8; 10:15)
2. Israel's redemption from Egypt (vv. 34, 37; 7:8; 11:2-4)
3. Yahweh alone is God (vv. 35, 39; 7:9; 10:17)
4. Israel is to observe Yahweh's commandments (v. 40; 7:11; 10:13; 11:1, 8)

Indeed ask, would you. כִּי שְׁאַל־נָא. Reading again an asseverative כִּי. The particle נָא with the imperative makes a forceful, but polite, request (Shulman 1999, 67).

from one end of the heaven to the other end of the heaven. לְמִקְצֵה הַשָּׁמַיִם וְעַד־קְצֵה הַשָּׁמָיִם. I.e., throughout the earth. In 13:8(7); 28:64 the expression is "from one end of the earth to the other end of the earth" (cf. Jer 12:12; 25:33; Weinfeld 1972, 358 no. 17). The "end of the heaven" is the horizon (ibn Ezra; Ps 19:7[6]). In 30:4; Isa 13:5; Neh 1:9, "the end of the heaven" is the farthest distant point on earth.

33 The first of two rhetorical questions is about the Horeb revelation, which Deuteronomy speaks of not as God's descent to the mountain (Exod 19:11, 18-20), but simply as a "voice from the midst of the fire" (see Note for 4:12). In Deuteronomic theology, Yahweh remains in the heavens (4:36; 26:15; 1 Kgs 8:27-53; but see Deut 23:15[14]). Moses earlier heard God's voice from a burning bush (Exod 3:1-6). Yahweh's holiness was believed to be so great that it

Deuteronomy 4

was a wonder people heard the voice and still remained alive (5:25; cf. Exod 3:4-6; 20:18-19). The Horeb revelation, extraordinary as it was, was completely auditory, for Yahweh did not permit himself to be seen, even by Moses (cf. Exod 33:20-23). In this revelation, the people were given the Ten Commandments directly from Yahweh (see Note for 9:10). What Moses gave the people were the tablets on which the commandments had been written.

the voice of a god. The LXX and T^{Nf} add "living" (cf. 5:26), leading some commentators and modern Versions to read "God" instead of "a god" (Weinfeld; AV; NEB; NIV; NAB; JB and NJB: "living God"). Others have "a god" (Driver; RSV; NRSV; NJV; REB), which is the better reading.

speaking from the midst of a fire. The Horeb revelation in Deuteronomy (see Note for 4:12).

you, you have heard. שָׁמַעְתָּ אַתָּה. The emphatic pronoun here follows the verb.

34 The second rhetorical question addresses the wonders of Egypt, the war with Pharaoh's army, and Yahweh's redemption of Israel in the exodus. No other god has ever attempted (נסה) to do such things. But according to the credo recited by worshippers offering their firstfruits (26:8), Yahweh has done them. Jeremiah affirms the same in a prayer following his purchase of the field at Anathoth (Jer 32:20-21).

Or has a god . . . ? Here we must read "a god" rather than "God" (Rashi; Driver; Weinfeld; and most modern English Versions; *pace* T^{OnqNfPsJ}; ibn Ezra; Friedman; AV).

testings. מַסֹּת. Mentioned again in 7:19; 29:2(3), these are the plagues of Egypt that "tested" Pharaoh and the Egyptians. Ibn Ezra calls them miracles. The Bible as a whole does not put primary emphasis on God's creative acts, rather on his redemptive acts (G. E. Wright). The OT warns people not to test God, as happened repeatedly in the wilderness (6:16; cf. Exod 17:2, 7; Num 14:22; Pss 78:18, 41, 56; 95:9; 106:14). Gideon later appears to be an exception (Judg 6:39-40). But God tests people, according to Deuteronomy, in order to humble them and know their hearts (8:2, 16; 13:4[3]; cf. Exod 15:25; 16:4; 20:20). The Psalmist prays that Yahweh will put his trust and faithfulness to the test (Ps 26:1-3).

by signs and by wonders. The "wonder" (מוֹפֵת) is an unusual or spectacular occurrence, thus a miracle; the "sign" (אוֹת) — either usual or unusual — points beyond itself to God and acts greater than the sign. In 11:3 the expression is "signs and deeds." "Signs" and "wonders" become virtual synonyms, referring to miracles on the spot or predictions that will require later fulfillment. Both were performed in public (Exod 4:30). The turning of a rod into a serpent, and miracles of like nature, took place immediately (Exod 4:2-9; 7:9-10), whereas the plagues of Egypt were both miracles of the moment and signs of a greater

Deuteronomy 4

fulfillment (Exod 7:3-5; 12:13). In Deuteronomy the "signs and wonders" are the marvels in Egypt at the time of the exodus (6:22; 7:19; 11:3; 26:8; 29:2[3]; 34:11). Ibn Ezra says the "wonders" here are the Ten Plagues (Exod 11:10). Signs and wonders are aimed at bringing about belief in the God of Israel (Exod 4:1-9; 10:1-2). Signs and wonders performed by prophets and dreamers who go on to lead people in the worship of other gods, even if they come to pass, are not to be heeded. Yahweh is simply using them to test whether people love him heart and soul (13:2-4[1-3]; cf. Jer 44:29). Signs and wonders get another twist in 28:46, where they refer to the curses awaiting fulfillment if Israel and future generations disobey the covenant. Signs assume great importance in the NT (John 2:11; 4:54; 6:30), with Paul saying that Jews require them (1 Cor 1:22; cf. Mark 8:11-12; Luke 11:29-30).

and by war. Reference is to the battle at the Red Sea (Exod 14:21-25; 15:1-12; Deut 11:4).

by a strong hand and by an outstretched arm. בְּיָד חֲזָקָה וּבִזְרוֹעַ נְטוּיָה. A stereotyped expression occurring first in Deuteronomy, referring to Yahweh's exodus deliverance (4:34; 5:15; 7:19; 11:2-3; 26:8; Driver 1895, lxxix no. 12; Weinfeld 1972, 329 no. 14). Kreuzer (1997) thinks the earliest occurrences are in Deut 5:15; 26:8. On Yahweh's "strong hand," see also Note for 6:21. An "outstretched arm" (9:29) signifies power (2 Kgs 17:36; Jer 27:5; 32:17; cf. Exod 6:6). The Amarna Letters (EA 286:12; 287:27; 288:14, 34; ANET³, 487-89) and other Egyptian texts speak of the "strong/outstretched arm" of the Egyptian king. The image is depicted also in battle scenes carved on temple walls (H. H. Nelson 1930, Plate 18; 1932, Plate 62; Gaballa 1969, 83, 87 fig. 5a; Keel 1974, 158-60). The Babylonian king, Nabopolassar, boasts of being "led by the outstretched arm of Nebo/Nabu and Marduk" (Langdon 1905, 48-49, 54-55; I, 1:14; II, 1:3-4).

and by great terrors. וּבְמוֹרָאִים גְּדֹלִים. This expression (in the singular) is found in 26:8; 34:12, where in both cases reference is to awesome manifestations of power at the time of Israel's departure from Egypt. In 26:8 this power is attributed to Yahweh and in 34:12 to Moses. The two terms appear as separate adjectives in 10:21, referring there to Yahweh's deeds in Egypt. See also Jer 32:21. Here and in 26:8 the LXX has καὶ ἐν ὁράμασιν μεγάλοις, "and by great visions," having misread the verb ירא as ראה. See similarly T^{OnqPsJ}.

before your eyes. On this Deuteronomic expression, see Note for 1:30.

35 The added pronoun at the beginning is for emphasis. This is the pre-eminent statement of monotheistic belief in Deuteronomy, which is repeated in v. 39 and affirmed also in the Song of Moses (32:39). See in addition 6:4; 7:9; 10:17; 32:12. The idea becomes full-blown in Second Isaiah (Isa 45:21). All the extraordinary wonders of Egypt were to show Israel that Yahweh alone is God and there is no other. The scribe talking to Jesus in Mark 12:32 echoes the words here.

36 According to Deuteronomic theology, Yahweh's dwelling-place is in

Deuteronomy 4

heaven, out of which the divine voice came to earth (at Horeb) "from the midst of the fire" (see Notes for 4:12 and 4:33). In Exod 20:22 Yahweh says to Moses: "I have talked with you from heaven." The purpose of the heavenly voice was to "discipline" Israel (11:2), where the verb יסר ("correct, admonish, chasten") is the sort of discipline a parent employs in the training of a child (8:5; Prov 19:18; 29:17). The LXX softens to παιδεῦσαί σε ("to instruct you"). In 4:10 Yahweh's words at Horeb are said to have been spoken so people would learn to fear him and teach their children the same.

37 *And because he loved your fathers and chose their descendants after them.* Yahweh's love for the patriarchs and for Israel are taught only in Deuteronomy among the pentateuchal books. The verb בחר ("choose") is a favorite of the Deuteronomist (see Note for 12:5). The verbs "love" and "choose" appear together also in 7:7; 10:15. Yahweh chose Israel because he loved her. On Yahweh's love and election of Israel, see Notes for 7:6-8.

And because. וְתַחַת כִּי. An unusual form of the conjunction.

and chose their descendants after them. The Hebrew has "and he chose *his* descendants after *him*" (וַיִּבְחַר בְּזַרְעוֹ אַחֲרָיו), referring to the descendants of Abraham. Plurals occur in the same phrase in 10:15.

yes, he brought you out with his presence and with his great strength from Egypt. In Exodus, after the golden calf episode, Yahweh said he would send an angel to go before the people on their journey to Canaan but would not himself go up (Exod 33:1-15). Moses and the people were deeply troubled. Then Yahweh relented, telling Moses: "My presence (פָּנַי) will go with you" (v. 14), i.e., I will myself go. The idiom stresses direct personal involvement (Moberly 1983, 74; cf. 2 Sam 17:11). In Deuteronomy, angels (= mediators) never play a role in Yahweh's acts of deliverance, as in other books of the Pentateuch (Exod 23:20, 23; Num 20:16). It says here that Yahweh brought the people out of Egypt "with his presence" (בְּפָנָיו). On Yahweh's "great strength" (כֹּחַ גָּדוֹל) seen in the exodus deliverance, see also 9:29; Exod 32:11; 2 Kgs 17:36; Neh 1:10. The expression is used in Jeremiah with reference to Yahweh's extraordinary power in creation (Jer 27:5; 32:17).

38 On Yahweh's gift of land to Israel as an inheritance, see Note for 15:4. Deuteronomy speaks often of nations "dispossessing" (הוֹרִישׁ) other nations, primarily of Israel "dispossessing" the Canaanites (see Note for 1:8). These other nations were "greater and mightier" than Israel (9:1; 11:23). In 7:1; 9:14 they are said to be "more numerous and mightier."

as at this day. On this stock Deuteronomic expression, see Note for 2:30. Reference here is to dispossession of the Transjordanian lands belonging to Sihon and Og (2:30; 4:20; 6:24), not anachronistically to dispossession of Canaanite land (*pace* Driver). Moses is speaking in Moab.

39 The thought of v. 35 repeated: Yahweh is God of all creation, and God alone. On Yahweh as God of heaven and earth, see also 10:14; Jer 23:23-24.

Deuteronomy 4

So you shall know today. וְיָדַעְתָּ הַיּוֹם. Moses' command that Israel "know (today)" occurs often in Deuteronomy (4:39; 7:9; 8:5; 9:3, 6; 11:2; Weinfeld 1972, 357 no. 9).

and take to your heart. וַהֲשֵׁבֹתָ אֶל־לְבָבֶךָ. Or "and keep in mind" (NJV). Driver says the idiom means "consider, reflect." A stereotyped Deuteronomic expression (4:39; 30:1; cf. 1 Kgs 8:47; Lam 3:21; Weinfeld 1972, 357 no. 10).

40 *And you shall keep his statutes and his commandments that I am commanding you today.* Moses' admonishment that Israel keep the statutes, commandments, and ordinances in the present day is one of the most oft-repeated in the book (4:2, 40; 6:6, 17; 7:11; 8:1, 11; 10:13; 11:8, 13, 22, 27, 28, etc.; Driver 1895, lxxix no. 9; lxxxi no. 37; Weinfeld 1972, 336 no. 16). Here the admonishment is a return to vv. 1-8. Often in Deuteronomy, admonishments about keeping the commandments function as inclusios for segments of discourse (6:6-9 and 11:18-20; 12:1 and 13:1[12:32]; 13:1 and 19[12:32 and 13:18]; cf. Lundbom 1996, 304-8).

so that it may go well for you and for your children after you. "So that it may go well for you (אֲשֶׁר יִיטַב לָךְ) is another stock phrase and important theological concept in Deuteronomy (4:40; 5:16, 29; 6:3, 18; 12:25, 28; 22:7; Driver 1895, lxxxi no. 42; Weinfeld 1972, 345-46 nos. 4-4a), sometimes in the form לְטוֹב לָךְ/וְטוֹב לָךְ (5:33; 19:13) or לְטוֹב לָנוּ/לְטוֹב לָךְ (6:24; 10:13). See also Jer 7:23; 22:15; 38:20; 40:9; 42:6. Here and elsewhere, well-being in the land extends to the children. Deuteronomy sees the fruit of blessing as material reward: well-being, health, long life, an abundance of children, joy, plenty, and long tenure in the land, themes that are prominent in the wisdom literature (Weinfeld 1960b).

in order that you may prolong your days on the soil that Yahweh your God is giving to you, all the days. Land tenure in Deuteronomy has everything to do with keeping the commandments. On the expression "prolong/not prolong your days," see Note for 4:26. On the expression "all the days," see Note for 4:9.

and in order that. וּלְמַעַן. Repeating from 4:1 (see Rhetoric and Composition for 4:1-24).

Message and Audience

Moses' sermonizing on the covenant continues by looking ahead to the future. When the people have begotten children and grandchildren, and have lost the freshness of the early days of settlement, and act corruptly by making idols, in any form whatever, Yahweh will be sorely provoked. Moses calls heaven and earth as witnesses against them, that they perish quickly on the land they are now crossing the Jordan to possess. Their days will not be prolonged; they will be completely destroyed. Yes, there will be some survivors, but their numbers will be small, and these hapless souls will be scattered among the nations. People bent on worshipping idols will now get what they want — gods of wood and stone, crafted by human hands, who cannot see, cannot hear, cannot eat, and cannot smell. These they will now have the privilege of serving.

In this hollow life in faraway places people will seek Yahweh their God, and they will find him, provided their seeking is with passion and with sincere motives. In their distress they will return to Yahweh and commit themselves to obey his voice. Yahweh, to his everlasting credit, is a God of mercy and will not abandon his people. He will not bring them to ruin and will not forget the covenant sworn to the fathers. Is Yahweh a great God? People are told to inquire into times past, back to creation itself, and query further throughout the whole wide earth if anything so great has ever been heard of. Has any people ever heard the voice of a god speaking from the midst of the fire and lived to tell the story? Or has any god ever attempted to take for itself a nation from the midst of another nation by testings, signs and wonders, war, a strong hand and outstretched arm, and great terrors, as Yahweh did for Israel in Egypt, before people's very eyes? Yahweh did all this to show Israel that he alone is God and there is no other.

The voice heard out of heaven was to discipline Israel, and on earth it was seeing the great fire from which Yahweh's words came forth. Because Yahweh loved the fathers and chose their descendants after them, he brought Israel out of Egypt with great strength, and in person. It was to give them an inheritance, to bring them into the land where they are today, to dispossess nations greater and mightier than they. Moses concludes by saying that Israel must know and take to heart that Yahweh is God of heaven and earth; there is no other. Israel must keep the commandments being taught today, so it will go well for the people and their children and that their days may be prolonged on the soil Yahweh God is giving them.

For a late 8th- and early 7th-cent. audience this warning about growing old in the land and sinking into idolatrous worship will speak directly to a Judahite audience that has seen this very thing take place among Israelite brothers and sisters to the north and knows what happened. Exile came to them in 734-733 and 722. And with the Assyrians having traversed Judah a few years later, this message will have been a chilling word to all Judahites. Their numbers have been reduced. Their cities have been brought to ruin. Some of their people are probably in exile.

But Moses' hopeful word is that in the distress of this scattering people will seek Yahweh and be found by him, if the seeking is genuine. Yes, they will return to Yahweh and obey his voice. Yahweh, being a God of mercy, will not abandon his people and bring them to final ruin. He will remember his covenant with Abraham. Moses' address is a clarion call for Judahites to remember that Yahweh is God and there is no other. The revelation at Horeb was like no other; the deliverance from Egypt like no other. Yahweh's heavenly voice was to discipline the Horeb generation, and if heard by the present generation, it will discipline them too. Let the present generation of Judahites know and take to heart that Yahweh is God of heaven and earth. There is no other. It must keep the terms of the Deuteronomic covenant. If it does, it will go well for people and their children, and instead of their days ending in the land, they will be prolonged indefinitely.

III. REFUGE CITIES IN THE TRANSJORDAN (4:41-43)

4 ^{41}*Then Moses set apart three cities beyond the Jordan to the east,* ^{42}*for a killer who killed his fellow without knowing — and he had not hated him formerly — to flee there, so he might flee to one of these cities and live:* ^{43}*Bezer in the wilderness, in the tableland, belonging to the Reubenites, and Ramoth in the Gilead, belonging to the Gadites, and Golan in the Bashan, belonging to the Manassites.*

Rhetoric and Composition

This unit is delimited at the top end by a *petuḥah* in M^L and a section in Sam before v. 41. There are no sections in M^L or Sam after v. 43, but *BHS* makes a break there. Many older scholars argued that this passage was secondary and intrusive (Wellhausen 1957, 162; Driver; von Rad), although Driver said its phraseology was thoroughly Deuteronomic. Here, and in the subscription of 4:44-49, Moses is no longer the speaker, which Rashbam viewed as an interruption before Moses resumed his discourse in ch. 5. But with a subscription concluding the Prologue at the end of ch. 4, this passage about refuge cities in Transjordan, which the writer apparently wanted to include, is in as good or better a location than anywhere else in the book.

Notes

4:41-42 The purpose of the refuge cities is explained more fully in 19:1-13, where refuge cities in Canaan are set forth. See also Numbers 35 and Joshua 20.

Then. אָז. Equivalent to Deuteronomy's more usual "at that time" (see Note for 1:9; cf. BDB). Cities of refuge could have been designated any time after the Transjordan settlement, not necessarily after Moses' address in 1:6–4:40.

beyond the Jordan. I.e., east of the Jordan (1:1, 5).

to the east. שֶׁמֶשׁ מִזְרְחָה. Lit. "toward the (place of) sunrise" (3:17, 27).

a killer who killed his fellow without knowing. רוֹצֵחַ אֲשֶׁר יִרְצַח אֶת־רֵעֵהוּ בִּבְלִי־דָעַת. The verb is רצח, which in the Decalogue (5:17) and elsewhere in the OT denotes killing with (fore)knowledge, viz., murder. "Without knowing" means unintentionally. Today we would call this accidental homicide.

and he had not hated him formerly. Hebrew מִתְּמוֹל שִׁלְשׁוֹם is lit. "from yesterday (and) the third day," where the third day is the day before yesterday. The expression means "formerly." The killing here was without malice.

these cities. הֶעָרִים הָאֵל. The rare הָאֵל ("these") occurs also in 7:22; 19:11; the pronoun is normally spelled הָאֵלֶּה (1:35; 3:21, etc.).

43 *Bezer in the wilderness, in the tableland, belonging to the Reubenites.* Bezer was a town on Sihon's tableland near the Syrian-Arabian desert (cf. Josh 20:8). It had adjacent pasturelands (Josh 21:36). The "tableland" in the OT is the plateau region from the Arnon to about Heshbon (see Note for 3:10). Bezer is listed as a former Israelite city on the Moabite Stone (line 27; $ANET^3$, 320-21), one that Mesha rebuilt. There it appears to be in the vicinity of Aroer and Dibon, which would be just north of the Arnon. But some scholars prefer a site east of Madaba. Suggested sites are Umm al-Amad, 14 km northeast of Madaba (Abel 1938, 264; Weinfeld) and Tell Jalul, 5 km east of Madaba (Dearman 1989a, 61), although the latter more recently has been proposed as the site of Sihon's Heshbon (see Note for 2:24).

belonging to the Reubenites. לָרֵאוּבֵנִי. Or "for the Reubenites" (RSV; Friedman).

and Ramoth in the Gilead, belonging to the Gadites. According to Eusebius (*Onom.*), Ramoth lay 15 Roman mi west of Philadelphia (present-day Amman). But modern scholars prefer a location north of Amman (cf. Geram [= Gerasa] in T^{Nf}). Glueck (1943; 1951, 98-104) identified Ramoth-Gilead with Tell Rāmîth, 7 km south of Ramath, and near the modern border between Syria and Jordan, on the Damascus-Amman road. This site has been widely accepted (Weinfeld; *ABD*, 5:620-21). Ramoth-Gilead was a border area in biblical times, where Israel and Syria did battle (1 Kings 22; 2 Kgs 8:28). It had adjacent pasturelands (Josh 21:38).

belonging to the Gadites. לַגָּדִי. Or "for the Gadites" (RSV; Friedman).

and Golan in the Bashan, belonging to the Manassites. Eusebius (*Onom.*) says that while "Golan" refers to a region (κώμη μεγίστη), it was also a city of refuge. In his day it was a large city called "Gaulon," including the surrounding region. The location of the city is not known, but Saḥem el-Joulan on the east bank of the el-'Allan River has been named as a possible site (*ABD*, 2:1057).

belonging to the Manassites. לַמְנַשִּׁי. Or "for the Manassites" (RSV; Friedman).

Deuteronomy 4

Message and Audience

The late 8th- and early 7th-cent. audience now hears, at the close of Moses' initial address, about the three designated refuge cities in the Transjordan: Bezer in the south, Ramoth in the center, and Golan in the north. In Transjordan, as well as in Canaan, cities were set apart as (temporary) safe havens for people who accidentally killed someone and needed protection from a hasty blood revenge. More will be heard in the Deuteronomic Code about three refuge cities in Canaan and their purpose.

IV. SUBSCRIPTION TO THE PROLOGUE (4:44-49)

4^{44}*And this is the law that Moses set before the children of Israel.* ^{45}*These are the testimonies and the statutes and the ordinances that Moses spoke to the children of Israel when they came out of Egypt,* ^{46}*beyond the Jordan in the valley opposite Beth-peor, in the land of Sihon king of the Amorites, who ruled in Heshbon, whom Moses and the children of Israel struck down when they came out of Egypt.* ^{47}*And they took possession of his land and the land of Og king of the Bashan, two kings of the Amorites, who were beyond the Jordan to the east,* ^{48}*from Aroer, which is on the edge of the river Arnon, and as far as Mount Sion (it is Hermon),* ^{49}*and all the Arabah beyond the Jordan eastward, and as far as the Sea of the Arabah, at the foot of the slopes of the Pisgah.*

Rhetoric and Composition

This historical and geographical summary is not a "second introduction" in the present book of Deuteronomy, as many scholars have taken it (de Wette; Driver; von Rad; Noth 1981, 16; G. E. Wright; Fohrer 1968, 171; Lohfink 1968, 7; Weinfeld 1972, 69; 1991, 233-34; Tigay; Nelson). It is argued that v. 44 and v. 45 are doublets (Driver; Weinfeld; Nelson), which would make two headings: v. 44 and vv. 45-49 (von Rad). Luther took v. 44 to be a conclusion, and more recently Wevers (1995, 93) suggests that v. 44 may be a subscription. What we have in this older view is a legacy of earlier source-critical ideas about the composition of Deuteronomy, which have to be given up. These verses — as most everyone recognizes — essentially repeat the content of 1:1-5 and should be taken as a balancing summary to 1:1-5, making an inclusio for Deuteronomy's Prologue (Lundbom 1975, 141 n. 155 [= 1997, 28 n. 155]; 1996, 302-4). So instead of 4:44-49 being a superscription or patchwork superscription, it is a unified subscription.

The two summaries, 1:1-5 and 4:44-49, contain significant repetitions,

Deuteronomy 4

with some of the collocations being reversed, as commonly happens in rhetorical structures of this type:

Deut 1:1-5	**Deut 4:44-49**
	And this is the law
Moses spoke . . . all Israel beyond the Jordan	Moses spoke . . . children of Israel beyond the Jordan
the Arabah	
Moses . . . struck down Sihon king of the Amorites who ruled in Heshbon	Sihon king of the Amorites who ruled in Heshbon Moses . . . struck down
Og king of the Bashan	Og king of the Bashan
beyond the Jordan	beyond the Jordan
	the Arabah
this law	

The inclusio, employed variously throughout the OT, is the preeminent closure device in Deuteronomy 1-28 (Lundbom 1996). It should not be confused with "resumptive repetition" so-called, a literary technique recognized by Wiener (1929, 2-3) and said by Tigay to be operative in the present verses. The two devices are not totally in opposition; still, they are not the same. Resumptive repetition as defined by Wiener is a device employed by ancient editors who inserted new material into their narrative and, when they resumed the narrative, aided the listener by repeating the phrase just prior to the insertion (Tigay 1985, 48; Talmon 1993b, 117; Revell 1997, 93). Tigay cites Abravanel, who said that recapitulation was necessary here because of the long digression in 1:6–4:40. The inclusio is something different. It is a device employed by a speaker, narrator, or editor to bring closure to discourse or a segment of discourse. Closure comes in a repetition that ties in the end with the beginning. There is, in any case, no need to posit multiple sources in the Prologue. As for von Rad's comment about the syntax in the present verses being "something of a monstrosity" (1996, 55), this may be due simply to the writer's attempt to make linear and inverted correlations with 1:1-5.

This subscription has no sections before v. 44 in M^L or Sam, but at the lower end is delimited by a *petuḥah* in M^L and a section in Sam after v. 49, which is also the chapter division.

Portions of 4:47-49 are contained in 1QDeut[a].

Deuteronomy 4

Notes

4:44 I.e., the law/teaching (תּוֹרָה) beginning in 5:1 (Rashi). This is the same law referred to in 1:5. A similar prefacing word in Exod 21:1 comes after the Decalogue and before the Covenant Code.

45 *the testimonies and the statutes and the ordinances.* "Testimonies" (הָעֵדֹת) are solemn declarations of God's will on moral and religious duties (Driver), the verb עוּד in the H-stem meaning "solemnly warn, admonish" (8:19; 2 Kgs 17:13; Jer 11:7). On one of the Arad ostraca (24:18-19) the verb means "to warn" (Y. Aharoni 1981). "Testimonies" can be stipulations or obligations in a treaty (KBL³). The term עֵדֹת occurs often in the Psalms (Pss 25:10; 78:56; 93:5; 99:7; 119:2, 14, 22, 24, 31, etc.). In P writings, עֵדֻת denotes the Decalogue in the expression אֲרוֹן הָעֵדֻת, "ark of the testimony" (Exod 25:22; 26:33-34; cf. 31:18). Statutes (חֻקִּים) are fixed decrees of religion, worship, and ceremony, and ordinances (מִשְׁפָּטִים) are civil and criminal laws, also sentences handed down by judges and rulers (see Note for 4:1).

when they came out of Egypt. בְּצֵאתָם מִמִּצְרָיִם. Better: "after they came out of Egypt." In Deuteronomy this expression refers to the entire period between the exodus and the encampment in Moab (4:45, 46; 23:5[4]; 24:9; 25:17). Israel's present location, as v. 46 indicates, is in the valley opposite Beth-peor, and there is where Moses gave the covenant stipulations.

46 *beyond the Jordan in the valley opposite Beth-peor.* The standpoint here is in Canaan, as in 1:1, 5 and again in 4:47. On the valley opposite Beth-peor, see 3:29.

in the land of Sihon king of the Amorites, who ruled in Heshbon, whom Moses and the children of Israel struck down when they came out of Egypt. Moses is giving his address on land formerly belonging to Sihon, whom he defeated in battle (1:4; 2:24-37). On Sihon the Amorite and his capital at Heshbon, see Note for 2:24. The verb ישׁב normally means "to sit, dwell," but here it means "to sit (enthroned)," i.e., "to rule" (see Note for 1:4).

47 *And they took possession of . . . the land of Og king of the Bashan.* A successful war was waged also against Og king of the Bashan, and Israel took possession of his land (1:4; 3:1-12). Regarding Og and his territory in Bashan, see Note for 3:1.

two kings of the Amorites. Although Og is called "king of the Bashan," he is nevertheless an Amorite king (see Note for 1:4).

who were beyond the Jordan to the east. Again the standpoint is Canaan. Targum[Onq] has "on this side of the Jordan, towards the sunrise," but T[NfPsJ] have it right: "who were beyond the Jordan toward the sunrise/east." Hebrew מִזְרַח שָׁמֶשׁ ("to the east") is lit. "toward the (place of) sunrise" (see Note for 4:41-42).

48 The entire Transjordanian land taken from Sihon and Og. The lofty city of Aroer on the Arnon, which was Sihon's southern boundary (Num 21:13), became the southern boundary of Israel's Transjordan territory (see Note for 2:36). On the river Arnon, see Note for 2:24.

Mount Sion (it is Hermon). Mount Hermon was Bashan's northern boundary (see Note for 3:1). Because the name "Sion" was apparently not well known — it appears nowhere else in the OT — the biblical writer adds parenthetically that Mount Hermon is indicated. For other names of Mount Hermon, see Note for 3:9. The term שְׂאִיאן denotes a lofty peak (cf. Job 20:6).

49 *and all the Arabah beyond the Jordan eastward.* "The Arabah" refers here to the Jordan Rift Valley, from the Sea of Chinnereth (Sea of Galilee) to the Dead Sea (see Note for 1:1).

and as far as the Sea of the Arabah. The LXX omits, which Nelson attributes to haplography (homoeoteleuton: ה . . . ה). The "Sea of the Arabah" is another name for the Salt Sea or Dead Sea (see Note for 3:17). Sihon's territory went to the river Arnon (v. 48), which empties into the Dead Sea.

at the foot of the slopes of the Pisgah. תַּחַת אַשְׁדֹּת הַפִּסְגָּה. "The Pisgah" (it takes the article) is either a specific peak in the Abarim mountain range or else the range itself, the highest peak being Mount Nebo (see Note for 34:1). Simons (1959, 75) thinks the slopes must refer to the entire edge of the Moabite plateau. The Sea of the Arabah (Salt Sea/Dead Sea) lies below the Pisgah (cf. 3:17; Josh 12:3); so does Beth-peor, though not all the way to the valley floor, where Moses gave his farewell address (Josh 13:20). The Targums (as in 34:1) translated הַפִּסְגָּה as a common noun (T[PsJ]: "beneath the slopes of the heights"; T[Onq]: "below the area of the discharge from the heights"). The LXX strayed even further from the Hebrew: ὑπὸ Ασηδωθ τὴν λαξευτήν ("under Asedoth hewn out of the rock"). Eusebius in his *Onomasticon* translates אַשְׁדֹּת הַפִּסְגָּה as a city called Asedoth Phasgo that is "rock-hewn." Jerome and Luther also took אַשְׁדֹּת to be the name of a city. The term is now generally rendered "slopes" (Akk *išdu:* "base, bottom, foundation"; cf. *CAD,* 7:235-40).

at the foot of. Hebrew תַּחַת here means "below, at the foot of," as in 4:11.

Message and Audience

With the Prologue now completed, three Transjordan refuge cities named, a late 8th- and early 7th-cent. audience is prepared to hear the law Moses set before the people of Israel. The core of this law is the Ten Commandments, spoken by Yahweh directly to the assembly at Horeb. Augmenting this law will be statutes and ordinances given to Moses at Horeb but not taught to the people until now, when they are assembled beyond the Jordan, in the valley opposite Beth-peor, on land seized from Sihon who ruled in Heshbon. The audience hears once again that Israel took land belonging to Sihon and Og, two ruling Amorite kings in Transjordan. The newly-acquired territory reached from Aroer on the river Arnon in the south to Mount Sion or Mount Hermon in the north. All of the Arabah east of the Jordan was taken, as far south as the Sea of the Arabah, which lay under the slopes of Moab's lofty Pisgah.

This summary repeats with minor differences the summary given at the beginning of the book (1:1-5), omitting only references to the journey from Horeb to Kadesh, the time it took to get to Kadesh, and the time Israelites spent in the wilderness before they came to the place where they now stand. With the Prologue concluded, Moses' teaching can begin.

V. THE COVENANT AT HOREB (5–11)

A. LAW AND COVENANT (5:1-33)

1. This Covenant Was with You! (5:1-5)

5:1*And Moses called to all Israel and said to them, Hear, O Israel, the statutes and the ordinances that I am speaking in your ears today, and you shall learn them and you shall be careful to do them.* 2*Yahweh our God cut with us a covenant at Horeb.* 3*Not with our fathers did Yahweh cut this covenant, but with us, those of us who are here today, all of us alive.* 4*Face to face Yahweh spoke with you at the mountain from the midst of the fire —* 5*I was standing between Yahweh and you at that time, to declare to you the word of Yahweh, for you were afraid because of the fire and did not go up on the mountain — saying:*

Rhetoric and Composition

Here begins Moses' main discourse on law and covenant. It does not begin at 4:44, as many earlier scholars alleged, since 4:44-49 is a subscription concluding the prologue (see Rhetoric and Composition for 4:44-49). The opening words make an inclusio with the concluding words of ch. 11, exhorting people at the beginning and exhorting them at the end to be careful to do the covenant demands (Lohfink 1968, 20; Lundbom 1996, 304-5):

> 5:1   Hear, O Israel, *the statutes and the ordinances* that I am speaking in your ears *today,* and you shall learn them and *you shall be careful to do them.*

11:32 *So you shall be careful to do all the statutes and the ordinances* that I am setting before you *today*.

According to Driver, chs. 5–26, 28 consist of two parts distinguished by content and the opening words of 12:1. The first part (chs. 5–11) is sermonizing on the general principles whereby the nation is to be governed, with particular attention given to developing the first commandment. The second part (chs. 12–26, 28) contains the laws of the Deuteronomic Code. The present verses double as an introduction to the Decalogue (5:6-21) and as an introduction to the Deuteronomic Code (5:1: "Hear, O Israel the statutes and the ordinances . . .").

A chiastic structure has been proposed for the whole of chs. 5–28 (Tigay), which requires the inclusion of ch. 27, widely taken to be a later addition:

a   *Yahweh our God cut a covenant with us in Horeb* (5:2)
  b   Ceremony at *Mounts Ebal and Gerizim* (11:26-32)
    c   *These are the statutes and the ordinances that you shall be careful to do* . . . (12:1)
      d   *The Deuteronomic law and covenant* (12:2–26:15)
    c′   *these statutes and the ordinances, and you shall be careful and do them* (26:16)
  b′   Ceremonies at *Mounts Ebal and Gerizim* (27)
a′   . . . *besides the covenant that he cut with them in Horeb* (28:69)

Within chs. 5-11 are three clearly defined sermonic discourses, all of which open with "Hear, O Israel" (cf. Carpenter 1883, 256). They are the following:

1. The Decalogue and sermonic discourse, beginning "Hear, O Israel" (5:1)
2. Sermon on loving Yahweh heart and soul, beginning "Hear, O Israel" (6:4)
3. Sermon warning about covenant disobedience, beginning "Hear, O Israel" (9:1)

In the first sermonic discourse, Deuteronomy's characteristic didactic formula makes a tie-in between beginning and end:

5:1   *Hear, O Israel* . . .   שְׁמַע יִשְׂרָאֵל

6:3   *And you shall hear, O Israel*   וְשָׁמַעְתָּ יִשְׂרָאֵל

Weinfeld, however, thinks that the conclusion of ch. 5, where Moses returns again as speaker (5:32-33), forms an inclusio with the beginning of the chapter:

Deuteronomy 5

5:1 Hear, O Israel, the statutes and the ordinances that I am speaking in your ears today, and you shall learn them and *you shall be careful to do them.*

5:32 *And you shall be careful to do* just as Yahweh your God commanded you; you shall not turn aside, right or left.

The present verses are demarcated at the top end by a *petuḥah* in M^L and a section in Sam before v. 1, which is also the chapter division. Demarcation at the bottom end is by a *setumah* in M^L and a section in Sam after v. 5. 4QDeut^j has no section after v. 5.

Portions of 5:1-5 are contained in 4QDeut^j, 4QDeut^n, and 4QDeut^o; also on phylacteries from Qumran (1Q [18?]; 4Q128, 129, 134, 135, 137, 142; 8Q3).

Notes

5:1 The verse is similar to 4:1, calling for hearing, learning, and obedience, not so much to the Ten Commandments, but to the Deuteronomic Code (chs. 12–26). In these latter chapters are the "statutes and ordinances" (12:1: "These are the statutes and the ordinances that you shall be careful to do . . ."). The Deuteronomic Code is similarly introduced in 6:1. Moses has convened an assembly to present Israel with the laws given him by Yahweh. He is not himself the lawgiver, only a mediator (v. 5). In Old Babylonia the lawgiver was the king, as the preamble to the Code of Hammurabi makes clear. In Israel, however, the lawgiver is Yahweh (see Note for 5:22).

And Moses called to all Israel. An earlier assembly convened at Horeb (5:22). Assemblies would be called in the future whenever all Israel needed to be addressed (31:10-13). On such occasions tribal leaders, elders, judges, and other officeholders would be present, perhaps others also (Josh 23:2; 24:1), On the use of "all Israel" in Deuteronomy, see Note for 1:1.

Hear, O Israel. שְׁמַע יִשְׂרָאֵל. A didactic introduction occurring often in Deuteronomy (5:1; 6:3[modified]; 6:4; 9:1; 20:3; 27:9; Driver 1895, lxxxiii no. 66; Weinfeld 1972, 355 no. 1). Cf. "Hear, my son" in Prov 1:8; 4:10; 23:19.

the statutes and the ordinances. A stock expression for the Deuteronomic laws beyond the Ten Commandments (see Note for 4:1).

and you shall learn them. I.e., study and memorize them. The verb למד (Qal: "to learn"; Piel: "to teach") occurs often in Deuteronomy but nowhere else in the Pentateuch (see Note for 4:1). By learning the statutes and ordinances one learns to fear Yahweh (see Note for 4:10).

and you shall be careful to do them. וּשְׁמַרְתֶּם לַעֲשֹׂתָם. "To keep/be careful to do (the commandments)" is a very common Deuteronomic expression (5:1, 32; 6:3, 25; 7:11; 8:1; 11:22, 32; 12:1; 13:1[12:32]; 15:5; 17:10; 19:9; 24:8; 28:1, 15, 58; 31:12; 32:46; Driver 1895, lxxxiii no. 68a; Weinfeld 1972, 336-37 nos. 17, 17a, 17b). For the similar phrase "be careful and do," see Note on 4:6. Learning Yahweh's commands is not enough; what matters more is doing them.

2 The Horeb covenant was a sacred bond between Yahweh and the nation, where Yahweh said "I will be your God" and Israel said "We will be your people" (Exod 6:7; Lev 26:12; Jer 30:22; 31:1). Terms of the covenant were statements of law, the core of which was the Ten Commandments (see Note for 4:13). This core law, presented earlier in Exod 20:2-17, is now repeated in vv. 6-21. According to Exodus, the core law was expanded with other statutes (Exodus 21-23), which we now refer to as the Covenant Code. In Deuteronomy the collection of statutes and ordinances in chs. 12–26 is called the Deuteronomic Code. This code gives specificity to the covenant made in Moab (28:69[29:1]). The third important legal collection in the OT is contained in Leviticus 17-26, called the Holiness Code, and in this code are provisions much like those appearing in the Decalogue (ch. 19; cf. Weinfeld 1990, 18-21).

The expression "cut a covenant" reflects a ceremony such as the one described in Gen 15:17-21 and Jer 34:18-20, where a calf was cut in two and people passed between the severed parts (Albright 1951; *ABD*, 6:654; see Note for 29:9-11). If one party failed to live up to the covenant, it would suffer the fate of the severed animal. The Horeb covenant was a covenant of mutual obligation (Freedman 1964). Yahweh agreed to hold up his end, and Israel had to do likewise, or the covenant would be declared broken. On covenant terminology in the Bible and the ancient world, see Weinfeld 1973b.

3 A rhetorical idiom called the "exaggerated contrast" (Lundbom 1999, 132-33, 488-89), where the first of two statements is negated only for the purpose of setting off the second, which is positive, and on which the accent is meant to fall. If the first statement were to stand alone, it would be false. Yahweh *did* cut a covenant with the fathers, but the speaker wants to emphasize that Yahweh cut this covenant also with the present generation. "This covenant" refers to the Horeb (Sinai) covenant, not the covenant cut in the plains of Moab (vv. 2-5 are now introducing only the Ten Commandments). The people whom Moses is addressing must also keep this covenant. It was not made only with the Horeb generation, most of whom died in the wilderness, but for the present generation and all subsequent generations.

our fathers. These "fathers" are not the patriarchs, as elsewhere in Deuteronomy (1:8; 4:31, 37; 7:8, 12; 8:18, etc.), but "fathers" of the Horeb generation (Weinfeld; *pace* Driver, Tigay, and most commentators). The term "fathers" in the OT has various referents, depending on the context. The "fathers" in Jer 11:7, 10 are those of the exodus generation; the "fathers" in Jer 2:5 are those of the conquest and settlement generation. The covenant with Abraham was an entirely different covenant from the covenant made with Israel at Horeb, being unconditional and eternal (Freedman 1964).

but with us, those of us who are here today, all of us alive. Cf. 4:4: "But you . . . are alive, all of you today." The present generation is to understand itself as having stood at Mount Horeb together with the Horeb generation (4:10). Similarly, the covenant now being cut in the plains of Moab is for generations to come (29:13-14[14-15]; cf. 31:12-13). Israel is conceived of as essentially one body, consisting of those who have died, those who are alive, and those not yet born. H. Wheeler Robinson, in his classic study on "corporate personality" in ancient Israel, said:

> The whole group, including its past, present, and future members might function as a single individual through any one of those members conceived as representative of it. Because it was not confined to the living, but included the dead and the unborn, the group could be conceived of as living for ever. (H. W. Robinson 1936, 49; 1980, 25)

According to 11:2-7, everyone listening to Moses in the plains of Moab was present at the exodus, experiencing the signs and deeds before Pharaoh, the parting of the Red Sea, and present in the wilderness, at which time harsh judgments took place. The idea that all subsequent generations were present at the exodus is kept alive in the Jewish Passover liturgy. Weinfeld (p. 239) says:

> On the Passover night the following proclamation is to be recited: "In every generation each one has to see himself as if he was freed from Egypt. . . . Not only our ancestors had he, the Holy one blessed be his name, released from Egypt, but he also released us with them."

Christians employ the "corporate personality" concept when they conceive of every subsequent generation as having stood at the foot of the cross when Jesus was crucified. It is expressed in the spiritual, "Were you there when they crucified my Lord?"

4 Yahweh spoke directly to the people at the foot of Mt. Horeb, from the midst of the fire (4:12-13, 15; 5:22-23; 9:10). But they heard only the sound of words; they saw no form (4:10-12). Verse 5 says that Moses had to stand between the people and Yahweh because the people were afraid of the fire. This condenses the narrative framing the Ten Commandments in Exod 19:16-25; 20:18-20. In that account, Moses — and once together with Aaron — goes to the top of the mountain; the people stay a safe distance away.

Face to face. פָּנִים בְּפָנִים. A Hebrew expression not to be taken literally, for

Deuteronomy 5

no one, not even Moses, was permitted to see the face of God (Exod 33:20-23; cf. John 1:18; 1 John 4:12). Yes, Moses had "face to face" communication with Yahweh (Exod 33:11; Deut 34:10), but it is to be noted in the present verse, and also in Exod 33:11, that Yahweh *speaks* with Moses "face to face." There is no visual dimension to the encounter. The expression doubtless means the same as "mouth to mouth," where speaking and hearing, not seeing, is indicated (Num 12:8). Ibn Ezra says that when someone's voice can be heard directly the encounter is called "face to face," even when the face cannot be seen. In Gen 32:31(30); 33:10 Jacob talks about having seen the "face" of God, but this occurs only as he has seen God's face in the face of others — first in the man who wrestled with him at the Jabbok and then in the face of his brother Esau.

from the midst of the fire. On this Deuteronomic expression, see Note for 4:12.

5 *I was standing between Yahweh and you at that time, to declare to you the word of Yahweh.* An apparent qualification of v. 4, which says that Yahweh spoke directly to the people. Here we are told that Moses acted on the occasion as mediator, declaring Yahweh's word to the people. Moses is again designated mediator in 5:31 and remains so throughout Deuteronomy (see Note for 9:14). In Exodus, Moses is said to be the mediator in giving Israel the Ten Commandments (Exod 19:16-25; 20:18-20).

the word of Yahweh. The LXX, Sam, S, T, Vg, and 4QDeut^n all have "words" plural.

for you were afraid because of the fire and did not go up on the mountain. Cf. the account in Exod 20:18-19.

saying: לֵאמֹר. This carries on from the end of v. 4 (ibn Ezra; Rashbam; Weinfeld). Verse 5, except for this word, is parenthetical.

Message and Audience

In this discourse Moses begins by telling his audience to hear the statutes and ordinances being given them today. They are to be learned by the people, and more important, the people must be careful to do them. He said it before and will say it often enough again before the statutes and ordinances are actually spelled out. Just now, however, Moses has something important to say about the covenant Yahweh cut with Israel at Horeb. It was not only with the generation who stood beneath the holy mountain that Yahweh cut this covenant, but with the generation now standing before Moses in the plains of Moab, all whom are alive in the present day. To this generation Yahweh also spoke from the terrifying fire. Yes, Moses had to stand between Yahweh and the people to declare the word of Yahweh, for the people were afraid and kept a safe distance from the mountain. The present generation should have this same holy awe of Yahweh.

To a late 8th- and early 7th-cent. audience, this account will be a reminder that the Horeb covenant is also for them. They too stood at Horeb and heard Yahweh speak from the midst of the fire. Would that they also have a holy awe of Yahweh! For them, too, Moses continues to be mediator of the covenant, which is to say they must hear him, learn the words of the covenant, and do them.

2. The Ten Words (5:6-21)

5 [6]*I am Yahweh your God who brought you out from the land of Egypt, from the house of slaves:*

[7]*You shall not have other gods besides me.*

[8]*You shall not make for yourself an idol, any form that is in the heaven above, or that is on the earth below, or that is in the waters under the earth.* [9]*You shall not bow down to them, and you shall not serve them, for I am Yahweh your God, a jealous God, visiting the iniquity of fathers upon children, and upon the third and upon the fourth generations for those who hate me,* [10]*but acting with steadfast love for thousands of those who love me and those who keep my commandments.*

[11]*You shall not lift up the name of Yahweh your God in emptiness, for Yahweh will not leave unpunished whoever lifts up his name in emptiness.*

[12]*Keep the Sabbath day to make it holy, just as Yahweh your God commanded you;* [13]*six days you shall labor and do all your work,* [14]*but the seventh day is a Sabbath to Yahweh your God; you shall not do any work — you, or your son, or your daughter, or your manservant, or your maidservant, or your ox, or your ass, or any of your beasts, or your sojourner who is within your gates, in order that your manservant and your maidservant may rest like you.* [15]*Yes, you shall remember that you were a servant in the land of Egypt, and Yahweh your God brought you out from there with a strong hand and with an outstretched arm; therefore Yahweh your God commanded you to observe the Sabbath day.*

[16]*Honor your father and your mother, just as Yahweh your God commanded you, in order that your days may be prolonged, and in order that it may go well with you on the soil that Yahweh your God is giving you.*

[17]*You shall not murder.*

[18]*And you shall not commit adultery.*

[19]*And you shall not steal.*

[20]*And you shall not testify against your fellow an empty witness.*

Deuteronomy 5

²¹*And you shall not covet the wife of your fellow. And you shall not desire the house of your fellow, his field or his manservant or his maidservant, his ox or his ass or anything belonging to your fellow.*

Rhetoric and Composition

These verses containing the Ten Commandments (Decalogue) are demarcated at the top end by a *setumah* in M^L and a section in Sam before v. 6 and at the bottom end by a *setumah* in M^L and a section in Sam at the end of v. 21 (Sam has a different verse number). 4QDeut^j has no section before v. 6. M^L has nine other *setumahs*:

after v. 10	after v. 18
after v. 11	after v. 19
after v. 15	after v. 20
after v. 16	after "the wife of your neighbor" in v. 21
after v. 17	

A lack of sections after vv. 6 and 7 may account for the different numbering of the first commandments in Jewish tradition, and a section midway in v. 21 probably accounts for "coveting" being divided into two commandments in the Roman Catholic, Anglican, and Lutheran traditions. In Exodus 20, a similar situation obtains at the opening of the Decalogue: no sections within vv. 2-6. The Sam formats the text differently and adds spacing in vv. 6-18. It has sections after vv. 11, 15, 16, 18a, and 18b. The Sam also adds at the conclusion an injunction about publishing the Decalogue on Mount Gerizim, combining portions of Deut 11:29 and 27:2-4 (Hepner 2006). There are very few sections in 4QDeut^n.

Both here and in Exod 20:2-17 are Ten Commandments ("Ten Words" in Deut 4:13; 10:4; perhaps also Exod 34:28), but Jewish and Christian traditions reckon them differently (Weinfeld, 243-45; Freedman 2000, 15-16). The chart on page 272, which uses the verse numbers of Deut 5:6-21, gives the various reckonings.

Conventional Jewish interpretation takes the opening verse, "I am Yahweh your God who brought you out from the land of Egypt, from the house of slaves" (v. 6), as the first commandment and "no other gods" (v. 7) and "no idols" (vv. 8-10) as the second commandment. But some ancient Jewish authorities (Philo *Decalogue* 50-51; Josephus *Ant.* 3.91) take the opening verse (v. 6) and "no other gods" (v. 7) as the first commandment and "no idols" (vv. 8-10) as the second commandment (M. Greenberg, "The Decalogue," in *EncJud*,

Deuteronomy 5

	J1	J2	RCAL	OR
I am Yahweh your God ... (v. 6)	1	1	Prologue	Prologue
Other gods (v. 7)	2	1	1	1
Idols (vv. 8-10)	2	2	1	2
Taking the Name in emptiness (v. 11)	3	3	2	3
Sabbath (vv. 12-15)	4	4	3	4
Honoring father and mother (v. 16)	5	5	4	5
Murder (v. 17)	6	6	5	6
Adultery (v. 18)	7	7	6	7
Stealing (v. 19)	8	8	7	8
Empty witness (v. 20)	9	9	8	9
Coveting a fellow's wife (v. 21a)	10	10	9	10
Coveting a fellow's house and everything else of his (v. 21b)			10	

J1 = Conventional Jewish interpretation
J2 = Some ancient Jewish authorities, including Philo and Josephus
RCAL = Roman Catholic, Anglican, and Lutheran churches
OR = Eastern Orthodox and Reformed churches

5:1442). There are other reckonings, e.g., ibn Ezra takes the initial v. 6, not as the first commandment, but as an introduction to all the commandments and divides "coveting" in v. 21 into two commandments. Weinfeld believes that in early Jewish tradition there was no fixed division of the Decalogue. He also sees no justification for taking the opening v. 6 as a separate commandment; it is a statement of fact, not a command (p. 286).

The Christian traditions all take v. 6 as a prologue to the Decalogue and begin counting with the commandment against other gods. But the Roman Catholic Church, which builds on Augustine, and also the Anglican and Lutheran churches combine the prohibitions against "other gods" (v. 7) and "idols" (vv. 8-10) into the first commandment. The Eastern Orthodox and Reformed churches take "other gods" as the first commandment, and "idols" as the second commandment. In vv. 11-18 the Roman Catholic, Anglican, and Lutheran churches are one less in their reckonings, but they arrive at the number ten by dividing the "coveting" command: commandment nine prohibits the coveting of a fellow's wife, and commandment ten prohibits the coveting of houses and anything else belonging to one's fellow. These traditions have the support of a section midway in v. 21.

Commandments six, seven, and eight are sequenced the same in Exodus and Deuteronomy, but other ancient texts sequence them differently. In Hos 4:2 the listing is, murder, stealing, adultery, and in Jer 7:9 it is stealing, murder, adultery. Freedman (2000, 94-97), in support of his scheme of commandment violations in the Primary History, argues that the order in Jer 7:9 may have been common in Jeremiah's day. The MT sequence of Exodus and Deuteronomy — murder, adultery, stealing — occurs in 4QDeut^n; Matt 19:18 and Mark 10:19 in the NT; Sam; Targums; and Josephus (*Ant.* 3.92). The *Didache* (2:2; 5:1) puts "murder" ahead of "adultery." This traditional sequence may also be reflected in Matthew's Sermon on the Mount (Matt 5:21-42), if commandeering a coat and begging (vv. 40, 42) are taken to be acts akin to theft. Aggressive panhandling comes close to petty theft. Frank Cross identifies this as the "Old Palestinian" sequence, reflecting a text type current in Palestine at the end of the 5th cent. B.C. (Crawford 1990, 202).

The other attested order of these three commandments is adultery, murder, stealing, which is found in LXX Deut 5:17-19 (LXX Exod 20:13-15 is different); the Nash Papyrus; Luke 18:20; Rom 13:9; Jas 2:11 (partial); and in Philo (*Decalogue*, 121). In defense of this sequence, Philo says adultery is the greatest of crimes. The readings in Nash Papyrus, Luke, Romans, James, and Philo all appear to follow the LXX, reflecting what has been called the "Egyptian order" (Crawford 1990, 202-3), since the LXX, Nash Papyrus, and Philo all have an Egyptian provenance. Flusser (1964, 220) says the Egyptian Jews probably knew only this order.

The generally accepted numbering of the Ten Commandments today is the following:

1. No other gods
2. No idols
3. No taking of Yahweh's name in emptiness
4. Observing the Sabbath
5. Honoring father and mother
6. No murder
7. No adultery
8. No stealing
9. No empty witness
10. No coveting

Despite the various reckonings, all traditions have Ten Commandments. Why the number ten? Freedman (2000, 7) suggests ten fingers on the two hands, which is reasonable. It could be a mnemonic device helping people to remember them.

D. N. Freedman, in his book *The Nine Commandments* (2000), put forth the thesis that the nine (not ten) commandments were used as a structural device for some Deuteronomic scribe in composing the Primary History (Genesis to 2 Kings). At the beginning of Genesis we meet up with a "command — violation — exile" pattern in the Adam and Eve and Cain and Abel stories; then beginning with Exodus, the book in which the covenant was ratified and the commandments given, this unknown scribe went through the Primary History book by book, including in each a showcase example of how each command was violated. In order to arrive at this scheme, Freedman combines the "no other gods" and "no idols" commandments into one and follows the sequence of "steal, murder, adultery" in Jer 7:9. The tenth commandment on coveting is not included in the scheme.

The thesis is a brilliant one, but in my view the tenth commandment belongs in the scheme. It cannot come at the end, but it can come at the beginning. The showcase example of the coveting commandment being violated is in the garden of Eden (Gen 3:6), where Eve "covets" and "desires" the forbidden fruit, to use the wording of Deut 5:21, and then eats it (see Notes). This ingenious scribe then has not eliminated the tenth commandment, but has simply found a showcase example of it being violated in the first book of the Primary History. The advantage of this revised scheme is that it includes both the tenth commandment and the book of Genesis, which Freedman left out.

According to the revised scheme, the Ten Commandments and their showcase violations in the Primary History are the following:

10. No coveting — violated in the garden of Eden story (Gen 3:6)
1-2. No other gods and no idols — violated in golden calf episode (Exod 32:7-8)
3. No empty use of the Name — violated in man's blasphemy (Lev 24:10-17)
4. Observing the Sabbath — violated by wood-gathering man (Num 15:32-36)
5. Honoring father and mother — violated by rebellious son (Deut 21:18-21)
6. No stealing (no. 6 in Jer 7:9) — violated in Achan's stealing (Josh 7:20-26)
7. No murder (no. 7 in Jer 7:9) — violated with Levite's concubine (Judg 19:22-30)
8. No adultery (no. 8 in Jer 7:9) — violated by David with Bathsheba (2 Samuel 11)
9. No empty witness — violated by testimony against Naboth (1 Kings 21)

The combining of the "no other gods" and "no idols" commandments into one finds support in there being no section after v. 7. Also, McBride (2006, 142-43) argues that vv. 6-10 form a chiasmus with divine self-asseverations at beginning and end and center injunctions alternating plural, singular, and plural objects:

a		*I am Yahweh your God . . .*	v. 6
		(אָנֹכִי יְהוָה אֱלֹהֶיךָ)	
	b	*You shall not have other gods . . .*	v. 7
		(לֹא יִהְיֶה־לְךָ אֱלֹהִים אֲחֵרִים)	
	c	*You shall not make for yourself an idol . . .*	v. 8a
		(לֹא־תַעֲשֶׂה־לְךָ פֶסֶל)	
	b′	*You shall not bow down to them . . .*	v. 9a
		(לֹא־תִשְׁתַּחֲוֶה לָהֶם)	
a′		*For I am Yahweh your God . . .*	v. 9b
		(כִּי אָנֹכִי יְהוָה אֱלֹהֶיךָ)	

Thematically, the Ten Commandments are commonly divided into two groups: (1) those dealing with conduct towards God (nos. 1 through 5); and (2) those dealing with conduct towards fellow human beings (nos. 6 through 10). Those in the first group all contain the words "Yahweh your God." The one difficulty with this division is that the fifth commandment on honoring one's parents is not directed towards God per se. Philo (*Decalogue* 106-7), while accepting the five and five division, nevertheless took the fifth commandment as a "bridge" between the two groups. He supported the traditional division by reasoning that parents copy God's nature by begetting children. Also, a five and five division would be most natural if the commandments are written on two tablets of stone. They were depicted as such when later represented in Christian and Jewish art (see Note for 4:13). It is claimed also that in each group the commandments are listed in order of descending importance: In the first group the commandment to have no other gods besides Yahweh is the most important; in the second group the most important commandment is the one not to murder.

In the NT, the Ten Commandments are summarized by two general injunctions. Jesus says to the scribe who asks him which is the first commandment:

> The first is, Hear, O Israel: The Lord our God, the Lord is one; and you shall love the Lord your God with all your heart, and with all your soul, and with all your mind, and with all your strength. The second is this, You shall love your neighbor as yourself. There is no other commandment greater than these. (Mark 12:28-31; cf. Matt 22:35-40)

The first commandment is reduced to the Shema in Deut 6:4-5 and the second to the command in Lev 19:18 that one must love one's neighbor as oneself (cf. Matt 4:10; 19:17-19; Luke 10:25-28). In the Apocrypha, the rabbinic literature, and other early Christian writings, the commandments are summed up as love for God and love for one's fellow human beings (Weinfeld, 245).

Deuteronomy 5

Portions of 5:6-21 are contained in 4QDeut^j, 4QDeut^n, and 4QDeut^o; also on phylacteries from Qumran (1Q[18?]; 4Q128, 129, 134, 137, 139, 142; 8Q3), and a Qumran *mezuzah* (4Q149). The entire Decalogue (Exod 20:2-17 and Deut 5:6-21) is contained on the Nash Papyrus (S. A. Cooke 1903), a liturgical text dated by Albright (1937, 149) to the second half of the 2nd cent. B.C.

Notes

5:6 Yahweh's redemption of Israel from Egyptian slavery is the supreme basis upon which law is imposed upon the nation. Daube (1949, 88-89; cf. 1947, 39-62) says that according to the biblical writers, the exodus was "an application, on a higher level, of the social laws concerning the redemption of slaves" (cf. Lev 25:47-55). In the ancient world, where people fell into slavery and could, under certain conditions, be redeemed by a family member or someone else, the "redemption need not lead to the immediate freedom of the person redeemed; it may involve a passing, temporary or permanent, into the power of the redemptor" (Yaron 1959, 155). On a higher and vastly more significant level, Yahweh in the exodus becomes Israel's גֹּאֵל ("redeemer"), with the result that the nation passes into his power and becomes his servant. Liberation in the OT is not an unconditional ticket to freedom; it is a "change of masters" (Daube 1963, 42-46): Pharaoh is the old master; Yahweh is the new. But servitude under the new master is a preferable kind of subjection, since it is considerably milder than under the old (30:11-14; Exod 34:6-7; cf. Matt 11:29).

Biblical theologians point out that in the OT grace precedes law, the antilaw polemics of Paul and Luther notwithstanding. This defining statement about Yahweh being the one who brought Israel out of Egyptian slavery begins the Decalogue also in Exod 20:2, serving in both places as a fitting introduction to the first commandment prohibiting the worship of other gods (cf. Judg 6:8-10; Ps 81:10-11[9-10]). Actually, the statement is an eminently suitable introduction to all the commandments (cf. Deut 5:15 on the sabbath commandment). On the basis of Yahweh's exodus deliverance rest also the Deuteronomic statutes and ordinances (6:20-25). Jewish tradition divides in taking the present verse either as the first commandment or as part of the first commandment together with the prohibition against "other gods" (v. 7). In Christian tradition, this verse is a prologue to all the commandments (see Rhetoric and Composition).

I am Yahweh your God. Here and in the first and second commandments (vv. 7-10), Yahweh speaks in the first person; in the remaining commandments (vv. 11-21), the speaker is Moses. The present words constitute a "self-presentation" formula, the sort of which occurs in ancient royal inscriptions. The Yehawmilk of Byblos Inscription begins:

I am Yehawmilk, king of Byblos, the son of *Yeharba'l*, the grandson of Urimilk, king of Byblos, whom the mistress, the Lady of Byblos, made king over Byblos. (*ANET*³, 656)

The Kilamuwu Inscription begins:

I am Kiliamuwa, the son of Hayya . . . (*ANET*³, 654)

The Moabite Stone begins:

I (am) Mesha, son of Chemosh-[. . .], king of Moab, the Dibonite . . . (*ANET*³, 320)

In the Code of Hammurabi, the "self-presentation" comes at the beginning of the Epilogue:

I, Hammurabi, the perfect king
was not careless (or) neglectful of the black-headed people . . .
(*ANET*³, 177)

In the OT the formula may begin or end a discourse segment (Exod 6:2, 6, 8, 29; 12:12). Yahweh, in his classic self-revelation in Exod 34:6, begins with a proclamation of his name: "Yahweh, Yahweh." The Holiness Code contains a number of "I am Yahweh (your God)" asseverations (Leviticus 18-19; 25:55; 26:1-2, 13, 44-45; Zimmerli 1953). See also Ps 81:11(10), where the asseveration precedes a statement about the exodus deliverance.

who brought you out. אֲשֶׁר הוֹצֵאתִיךָ. The verb יצא refers here to a freeing from slavery; one could also translate the expression "who liberated you" (Weinfeld; Propp 2006, 167).

the house of slaves. Hebrew עֲבָדִים is a numerical plural, not an abstract noun, thus "slaves" rather than "slavery." Boling (1975, 126) translates the term as "slave-barracks" in Judg 6:8. "House of slaves" is a common Deuteronomic expression (5:6; 6:12; 7:8; 8:14; 13:6, 11[5, 10]; cf. Jer 34:13; Driver 1895, lxxix no. 5; Weinfeld 1972, 326-27 no. 2), although it also occurs in Exodus (Exod 13:3, 14; 20:2).

7 The preeminent commandment comes first (cf. Exod 20:3). In Judaism and in Christianity the first commandment is the greatest and most important (Mark 12:29-30; Matt 22:36-38; Luke 10:27). Deuteronomy and the Deuteronomic literature repeatedly admonish people not to "go after other gods" or "serve (i.e., worship) other gods" (see Note for 6:14). If either has occurred, and often it has, it is censured in the strongest of terms. The expression

"other gods" occurs 17 times in Deuteronomy, also 17 times in Jeremiah. "Other gods" in early Israelite history would refer to the Canaanite Baals and the gods of Egypt, but later during the monarchy reference would include gods worshipped in countries of the east. Other ancient law codes and paralegal documents contain nothing comparable to the first commandment. In ch. 125 of the Egyptian *Book of the Dead,* a mortuary text dated between 1550 and 950 (*ANET*³, 34-35), the deceased tells a posthumous court that he has not blasphemed a god (A8; B42), stolen the property of a god (B8), or been abusive against a god (B38), but no disclaimer is made about having worshipped other gods.

You shall not have. לֹא יִהְיֶה־לְךָ. The Hebrew is lit. "there shall not be for you." This commandment and all but two of the others contain the second singular "you" together with an emphatic and unconditional לֹא ("not"), making them apodictic in form (Alt 1966c, 117-23). The commandments on keeping the Sabbath and honoring father and mother are positive and also stated a bit differently. Other legislation in Deuteronomy and the Book of the Covenant, also in known law codes of the ANE, e.g., the Laws of Ur-Nammu (*ANET*³, 523-25); the Lipit-Ishtar Code (*ANET*³ 159-161); the Laws of Eshnunna (*ANET*³ 161-163); the Code of Hammurabi (*ANET*³ 163-180); and the Middle Assyrian (*ANET*³, 180-88), Hittite (*ANET*³, 188-97), and Neo-Babylonian (*ANET*³, 197-98) codes, is stated in casuistic form: "If someone does such and such, then such and such will be the punishment" (Alt 1966c, 88-103). The "ordinances" (מִשְׁפָּטִים) of Exod 21:1 are casuistic laws. Casuistic law, says Alt, is suited for use in normal jurisdiction, i.e., in a court of law. Alt goes on to say: "The categorical prohibition lays down the law in a much more absolute fashion than the provision of the severest punishment . . . the Decalogue, more than the other lists, refrains from naming actual individual cases, but tends rather to lay down principles, without getting lost, however, in abstractions" (Alt 1966c, 122). The Ten Commandments are more direct statements of principle than anything preserved in Mesopotamian law (Lambert 1957-58, 186-87). The "you" is directed to every man and woman in society, except the tenth commandment, which is directed — at least at the beginning — only to every man. Weinfeld (1973a) finds parallels to Israelite apodictic law in the Hittite Palace Instructions (*ANET*³, 207-10) and the Esarhaddon royal correspondence (680-669), but these are not law codes.

besides me. עַל־פָּנָי is lit. "upon my face." The expression usually translates either as "before me," i.e., in my presence (LXX: πρὸ προσώπου μου; Vg: *in conspectu meo;* Rashi; Weinfeld; Friedman; AV; RSV; NRSV), or "besides me," i.e., other than me (ibn Ezra; Rashbam; Tigay; Nelson; JB; NAB; NJV; REB; NJB). The LXX in Exod 20:3 has πλὴν ἐμοῦ ("except me"), but the Vg *coram me* ("before me"). Rashbam, who translates "besides me," says that even if one believes in Yahweh, that person should not have any other form of a god in addition to Yahweh. He cites as an example the "household gods" (תְּרָפִים) of Laban in Gen 31:19, 34-35, which were used for divination. Interpretation here largely turns on how one assesses Israelite faith in the early centuries — from the Mosaic period, on through the years of Israelite nationhood, into the Babylonian exile. Was it henotheism (the belief in one god, but not claiming that he is the only god); or monolatry (the worship of one god, where other gods may be supposed to exist); or monotheism (the belief in one God, who is claimed to be the only God)? And how does this commandment compare with the claims in 4:35-39, which state that Yahweh is God and there is no other besides him? Albright (1957b, 297) and Friedman believe the first commandment is monotheistic. But Tigay says the first commandment is not so much a theological statement denying the existence of other gods, as a practical statement ruling out relationships with other beings or objects taken to be gods. Propp (2006, 167) thinks the Decalogue neither concedes nor denies the existence and efficacy of other gods.

Israel, we know, had its origins in polytheism (Josh 24:2), an affirmation made by Jews every year in the Passover liturgy (Daube 1963, 45). We know also that in the exile, Second Isaiah was preaching a full-blown monotheism (Isa 41:4; 44:24; 45:5-6, 14, 18, 21-22; 46:9). But monotheism in Israel has to be much older (Deut 32:15-22, 39), having a very early origin (Albright 1957b, 297). We know, too, that ordinary Israelites, in the wilderness, in the early years of the Transjordan settlement, and all during the monarchy — in northern Israel and in Judah — compromised the "Yahweh alone" religion taught by the nation's loftier minds (Tigay 1986, 1; Freedman 2000, 29-34), rendering moot the question of Israel's "essential" faith over the centuries. A bottom-line interpretation of the first commandment is that Yahweh alone must be worshipped. Jesus understood the commandment so (Matt 4:10; 6:24). Worship of other gods was considered to be as loathsome as adultery (Exod 34:14-16; Ezek 16:17-19).

8 *You shall not make for yourself an idol.* לֹא־תַעֲשֶׂה־לְךָ פֶסֶל. The wording of this second commandment, which takes in vv. 8-10, is nearly identical to the wording in Exod 20:4-6. Similar commands prohibiting idols and idol worship are found in Exod 20:23; 34:17; Lev 19:4; 26:1. In Deuteronomy, warnings against idols come in the homiletical discourse of 4:16-18, 23, 25 and elsewhere and receive a ceremonial curse in 27:15. An idol (פֶסֶל) could be an image in the form of a human or an earthly, heavenly, or underwater creature, made to be worshipped. Idols were crafted from wood, stone, bronze, or precious metals. Those of wood were commonly plated in silver and gold or dressed sumptuously in garments of blue or purple, colors of royalty (Oppenheim 1964, 184; Jacobsen 1987, 15; Jer 10:3-4, 9; Isa 44:9-20; 46:6). Images in human form could conceivably be of Yahweh, Baal, or some other god. The reason Deuteronomy gives for prohibiting images is that the people saw no form when Yahweh spoke to them at Horeb out of the fire (Deut 4:15-18). Another reason for images being disallowed would be that human beings — male and female — are the *imago dei* (Gen 1:27). No prohibition like the present one exists in law codes and paralegal documents of the ANE, because texts from Egypt to Babylon all attest to the centrality of idols in the worship of the gods (Freedman 2000, 34). On cult statues and cult ritual in ancient Egypt, see Lorton 1999.

This second commandment is closely tied to the first, since the OT writers — even more the prophets and psalmists — base their polemic against idols on the notion that the idol is identical to the god it represents (Oppenheim 1964, 184; M. Greenberg, *EncJud*, 5:1442). Jacobsen (1987, 16-23) agrees, but cautions that the statue mystically becomes — through ritual acts — the god it represents, which means the god *is* and at the same time *is not* the cult statue. On divine images and aniconism in ancient Israel, see T. J. Lewis 1998. The showcase example of commandments one and two being violated comes in Exodus, where people made a golden calf in the wilderness (Exod 32:7-8; cf. Deut 9:12-21; Freedman 2000, 37-45).

any form that is in the heaven above, or that is on the earth below, or that is in the waters under the earth. Idols other than those human in form are also disallowed (Deut 4:16-18).

9-10 *You shall not bow down to them, and you shall not serve them.* Repeated from the Covenant Code (Exod 23:24). The two verbs together mean "to worship," which could include the making of offerings (Tigay). In the affairs of the world, "bowing down" and "serving" denote submission (Gen 27:29; Ps 72:11). As a covenant people Israel is to worship only Yahweh, a theme stressed throughout Deuteronomy (see Note for 6:13).

for I am Yahweh your God, a jealous God. Yahweh's jealousy, or passionate zeal (קַנָּא), stems from a holiness he will not share with any other. It also stems from an intolerance of idols (see Note for 4:24).

visiting the iniquity of fathers upon children, and upon the third and upon the fourth generations for those who hate me. This OT retribution formula reverses the order of its classical expression in Exod 34:6-7. There Yahweh's grace and mercy is stated first. Reversal occurs also in Exod 20:5-6. Cf. the formulas in Deut 7:9-10; Num 14:18; Nah 1:3; Jer 32:18. Four generations (the father being the first) are equivalent to a normal life span, corresponding to the "seventy years and perhaps eighty" of Ps 90:10. Someone living to be seventy or eighty will likely see the birth, and maybe even the maturity, of the fourth generation. This is taken as a blessing in the Bible (Gen 50:23; 2 Kgs 10:30; 15:12; Job 42:16) and in other ANE literature (the "Agbar, Priest of the Moon-God" tomb inscription [7th cent.] in *ANET*[3], 661; the "Mother of Nabonidus" tomb inscription [6th cent.] in *ANET*[3], 561). "Four generations" of retribution is the curse.

Malamat (1982, 217) says: "The idea of the fourth generation as the maximum life span is the basis for the divine admonition to the sinner that he will not escape retribution even into his descendants' lifetimes." The Hittites understood this. A document of instruction to Hittite palace and temple officials says:

> If then . . . anyone arouses the anger of a god, does the god take revenge on him alone? Does he not take revenge on his wife, his children, his descendants, his kin, his slaves, and slave-girls, his cattle (and) sheep together with his crop and will utterly destroy him? Be very reverent indeed to the word of a god! ($ANET^3$, 208)

In another Hittite document (14th cent.), King Mursilis prays to the Hattian storm-god to stay a plague that has come because the people of Hatti land broke an oath made with the god. He says:

> My father sinned and transgressed against the word of the Hattian Storm-god, my lord. But I have not sinned in any respect. It is only too true, however, that the father's sin falls upon the son. So, my father's sin has fallen upon me. ($ANET^3$, 395)

Mursilis then confesses his father's sin and prays that the god will be pacified. So while the sinner's idolatry means punishment for himself and three generations of descendants, the point here is that Yahweh's anger is limited, lasting only a lifetime. His steadfast love, mentioned next, has no limit.

This retribution formula became a proverb: "Fathers have eaten sour grapes and children's teeth are set on edge" (Jer 31:29; Ezek 18:2). Jeremiah preached this retribution formula early on (Jer 2:5-9), but later both he and Ezekiel shortened the retribution range from four generations to one. Now only "the soul that sins will die" (Ezek 18:4; Jer 31:30). This reduced formula could have been derived from the law in Deut 24:16, which states that fathers shall not be put to death for the sins of their children, nor also children for the sins of their father, a law found only in Deuteronomy. For a discussion of corporate liability and punishment in the ancient world, see Note for 24:16.

but acting with steadfast love for thousands of those who love me and those who keep my commandments. The Targums read לַאֲלָפִים, "to the thousandth generation" (cf. לְאֶלֶף דּוֹר in 7:9), which is adopted by some modern Versions (NJV; NAB; NIV; NRSV). The term, in any case, should not be taken literally. The point is that Yahweh's steadfast love is boundless, far exceeding his wrath. Hebrew חֶסֶד ("steadfast love") binds Yahweh to Israel in the covenant; it is "covenant love" (7:9; Exod 34:6; 1 Kgs 8:23; Glueck 1967, 79-83; Weinfeld 1973b, 191-92). Unlike "grace/favor" (חֵן), covenant love carries with it rights and obliga-

Deuteronomy 5

tions, demanding also a favorable attitude from both parties to the relationship. A relationship built upon חֶסֶד is meant to be long term. חֶסֶד must be kept, whereas "grace/favor" is given freely and can be freely withdrawn (Freedman, Lundbom, ḥānan, in *TDOT,* 5:25). According to Jeremiah, חֶסֶד is a love Israel must also show toward Yahweh (Jer 2:2). One sees in this phrase the conditional nature of the Horeb covenant. While Yahweh's steadfast love may be boundless, it extends here only to those who love Yahweh and keep his commandments. The principle is individualized in the NT Gospel of John (John 15:1-11).

my commandments. Reading the Qere, which is supported by the LXX and perhaps 4QDeut[n] (Cross 1965, 31; Crawford 1990, 197). The K has "his commandments." The MT of Exod 20:6 has "my commandments."

11 *You shall not lift up the name of Yahweh your God in emptiness.* לֹא תִשָּׂא אֶת־שֵׁם־יְהוָה אֱלֹהֶיךָ לַשָּׁוְא. Commandments from this point on are formulated in the third person. The wording of this commandment is identical with Exod 20:7, being restated also in the Holiness Code (Lev 18:21) and in the casuistic law of Lev 5:22(6:3). This commandment forbids the use of God's name in an empty (שָׁוְא) manner, where reference could be to swearing false or frivolous oaths (Exod 22:9-10[10-11]), blasphemy, or buttressing declarations falsely (Philo, *Decalogue* 84-95; cf. 1 Kgs 17:12). Philo says some people have the evil habit of swearing incessantly and thoughtlessly about ordinary matters, where nothing is in dispute, filling up the gaps in their talk with oaths, not realizing that it would be better if they were silent altogether. He says from much swearing spring false swearing and impiety. Josephus (*Ant.* 3.91), too, says one should not swear by God on any frivolous matter. The frivolous oath is censured in an old Akkadian text (Lambert 1960, 39, line 22; *ANET*[3], 597), but reference is to someone who has sworn an oath to the god and not carried it out, which sounds more like a vow having gone unfulfilled (cf. Deut 23:22-24[21-23]). Herod uttered a frivolous oath to the daughter of Herodias, leading to the beheading of John the Baptist (Matt 14:6-9).

Deuteronomy instructs people to swear in Yahweh's name (Deut 6:13; 10:20). The typical oath was "as Yahweh (your God) lives" (Hos 4:15; 1 Kgs 17:12; Jer 4:2; 5:2; Lachish Letters nos. 3 and 6; *ANET*[3], 322). In the NT period, "heaven," "the temple," "the gold of the temple," "the temple altar," or "the gift on the altar" were substituted for God's name (Matt 23:16-22). In Old Babylonian marriage contracts, oaths were sworn in the name of the king (Westbrook 1988a, 115-16). Modern oaths are taken with a raised hand or a hand on the Bible, and a false statement under oath is perjury. People today buttress statements with "I swear on a stack of Bibles" or "I swear on my mother's grave." Oaths are conditional self-curses ("May Yahweh do such and such to me if I did/did not do such and such"). Peter denied Jesus under oath, and in his third denial he invoked a self-curse (Matt 26:72-74).

Deuteronomy 5

The showcase example in the Primary History of someone using Yahweh's name in an empty manner comes in Leviticus, where it is reported that a man with an Israelite mother whose father was Egyptian blasphemed the Name (of Yahweh) and cursed, for which he was stoned to death (Lev 24:10-17, 23; Freedman 2000, 47-55). Hosea included "swearing an oath" (אָלֹה) in his list of Decalogue violations (Hos 4:2) and said that people were making covenants by "swearing empty oaths" (אָלוֹת שָׁוְא), with the result that judgment was springing up like poisonous weeds (Hos 10:4). Jeremiah, in one of his Temple Oracles, includes "swearing falsely" (הִשָּׁבֵעַ לַשֶּׁקֶר) in a list of Decalogue violations (Jer 7:9). In another prophecy, Jeremiah cited false oaths as being rife in Jerusalem (Jer 5:2). Malachi, too, pronounced judgment on those swearing falsely (Mal 3:5).

Jeremiah would prefer that people not swear oaths at all, at least not until after they return to Yahweh and remove all "wretched things" from Yahweh's presence. Only then, he says, can they again swear "by Yahweh's life" in truth, justice, and righteousness (Jer 4:1-2). Jesus, in his Sermon on the Mount, believes the present commandment does not go far enough. He, too, said it would be better if one used no oaths at all, saying simply "Yes" or "No" (Matt 5:33-37). Philo (*Decalogue*, 84-91) said that not swearing at all was the best course of action and that swearing even truly was only the "second best voyage," the reason being that swearing an oath casts suspicion on the trustworthiness of the person. But should a person find it necessary to swear an oath, he needs to consider carefully all that an oath entails: It is an appeal to God as witness on matters in dispute, and to call God as witness to a lie is the height of profanity.

False oaths were not taken lightly in the ancient world. Diodorus of Sicily (i 1-2) says that in Egypt the penalty for perjurers was death, since the person was guilty of two great transgressions: being impious towards the gods and violating the mightiest pledge on earth. In the Egyptian *Book of the Dead*, the deceased tells a posthumous court that he has not blasphemed a god (*ANET*[3], 34-36; A8; B42). Hesiod (*Works and Days*, 283-85) says a false oath hurts both the person making it and the cause of justice. In the end, his family will suffer. Herodotus (vi 86) cited a certain Glaucus who contemplated swearing a false oath that he had not wrongfully taken money from a stranger, but after being warned in an oracle that this would put an end to his offspring, he asked the god to pardon him and gave the stranger his money back. Herodotus says that he was telling the story because to the present day there was no descendant of Glaucus. He and his house had been utterly uprooted in Sparta.

for Yahweh will not leave unpunished whoever lifts up his name in emptiness. An Egyptian man confesses in a prayer that his suffering is punishment for taking a false oath in the name of Ptah:

I am a man who has sworn wickedly by Ptah, the Lord of truth, and he has made me see darkness by day. Now I will tell of his power to the one who does not know it, and to the one who does know it, the small and the great. Beware of Ptah, the Lord of truth. He leaves no man's action unnoticed. Keep from mentioning the name of Ptah falsely. See, the one who mentions his name falsely comes to ruin. (Beyerlin 1975, 36)

In Lev 5:21-26(6:2-7), a person caught swearing falsely about having seized something from his fellow must restore it in full, add one-fifth as a penalty, and make a guilt offering. The flying scroll of the prophet Zechariah carries a curse that will descend upon anyone who swears falsely, cutting him down and consuming his house timber and stone (Zech 5:3-4).

12 *Keep the Sabbath day to make it holy.* שָׁמוֹר אֶת־יוֹם הַשַּׁבָּת לְקַדְּשׁוֹ. The fourth commandment on Sabbath observance takes in vv. 12-15. The Sabbath is the seventh day of the week. The infinitive "keep" (שָׁמוֹר) acts here as an imperative meaning "observe!" (cf. 16:1). The verb שמר occurs often in Deuteronomy, with reference to keeping the commandments (4:2, 40; 5:10, 29; 6:2, 17; 7:9, 11, etc.) and in the stock expressions, "you shall be careful (שמר) and you shall do" (see Note for 4:6); "be careful (שמר) for yourself/yourselves" (see Note for 4:9); and "be careful (שמר) to do" (see Note for 5:1). The wording in Exod 20:8 is "*Remember* the Sabbath day to make it holy," which is on the Nash Papyrus. Luther in his Catechism follows Exodus (Luther 1965). The Sabbath command is referred to elsewhere in Exod 23:12; 31:12-17; Lev 19:3; 23:3; 26:2. Here, as in the next commandment on honoring father and mother, the injunction is positive, although in the interpretation there is a negative statement about not doing any work (v. 14; cf. Exod 20:10).

The Sabbath day is holy to Yahweh (Gen 2:3), so people are to keep it holy. To keep the Sabbath holy means "to set it apart for a sacred use, to consecrate it" (cf. 15:19). The amplification interprets this as desisting from work (the verb שבת means "cease, desist, rest"; Exod 23:12; Lev 23:32). Once Israel had become settled in the land, the Sabbath became a time for visiting holy places and sanctuaries, making offerings and joining in acts of worship there (Lev 24:8-9; Num 28:9-10; Isa 1:13; Ezek 46:1-5; Isa 66:23). One might even visit a prophet on the Sabbath (2 Kgs 4:23). It was a day of joyful celebration (Hos 2:13[11]; Isa 58:13).

Jeremiah called for Sabbath observance among Judahites who were paying the commandment no heed (Jer 17:19-27). Second Isaiah said later that the man is blessed who keeps justice and keeps the Sabbath (Isa 56:2). Jesus supported the Sabbath commandment (although it is omitted in Matt 19:18-19), but the Gospels portray him rather as relaxing the strict interpretations of the Pharisees, particularly when it came to healing on the Sabbath (Matt 12:1-8, 9-14; Mark 2:23-28; 3:1-6; Luke 6:1-5, 6-11; 13:10-17; 14:1-5; John 5:9-18; 7:22-24; 9:13-

41). The commandment had become a victim of overinterpretation (*m. Šabb.* 7:2-4). Jesus countered these overinterpretations by saying such things as "the Sabbath was made for man, not man for the Sabbath" (Mark 2:27) and "the Son of man is lord of the Sabbath" (Matt 12:8; Mark 2:28; Luke 6:5). But even these statements show support of the Sabbath commandment. Jesus spent time teaching in the synagogue on the Sabbath (Mark 1:21; 6:2; Luke 4:16-22, 31-32; 13:10), and his disciples are reported to have rested on the Sabbath because of the commandment (Luke 23:56).

just as Yahweh your God commanded you. The phrase is absent in Exod 20:8. It repeats in the next commandment (v. 16), where Exodus also does not have it. Here it aids in making an inclusio for the commandment and its interpretation (cf. Lohfink 1990, 198-99; 1994b, 252-53):

Keep (שָׁמוֹר) *the Sabbath day*   v. 12
   just as Yahweh your God commanded you . . .
   therefore Yahweh your God commanded you   v. 15
to observe (לַעֲשׂוֹת) *the Sabbath day*

The expression belongs to the rhetorical prose of Deuteronomy (20:17; cf. 6:25; 24:8).

13-14 "You" refers here to both husband and wife (Weinfeld; cf. 12:12, 18; 16:11, 14). The reason for keeping the Sabbath is social: children, servants, and sojourners can rest along with every Israelite adult. Even the working animals get a rest (cf. Exod 23:12).

you shall not do any work. The prohibition is general, not specifying what is work or what is not work. After the exodus deliverance, when people began their wilderness wanderings, Moses commanded them to gather a double amount of manna on the sixth day and prepare food on that day, so they could rest on the Sabbath (Exod 16:22-30). The Covenant Code mandates that the Sabbath rest had to be kept in seasons of plowing and harvesting (Exod 34:21). Violation of the Sabbath commandment was a capital offense (Exod 31:14-15; 35:2), e.g., a man who gathered firewood in the wilderness on the Sabbath was stoned to death (Num 15:32-36). In the Primary History, this became the showcase violation of the Sabbath commandment (Freedman 2000, 65-66).

Amos in his time found that merchants were the biggest grumblers about the Sabbath rest (Amos 8:5). Things changed little in Jeremiah's time. Jeremiah said that one should not carry a load through the city gates or out of one's house on the Sabbath (Jer 17:21-22). The "load" was probably produce being brought into Jerusalem from outlying areas and goods from one's house to sell in the marketplace. Ezekiel, too, complained about the Sabbath being profaned (Ezek 22:8). In the postexilic period, Sabbath neglect was rife — people were treading grapes, harvesting grain, and bringing produce to market on the Sabbath. This brought a stern rebuke from Nehemiah, who closed the city gates on the Sabbath eve (Neh 13:15-22). The Mishnah (*Šabb.* 7:2-4) lists thirty-nine types of work disallowed on the Sabbath, e.g., sowing, ploughing, reaping, binding sheaves, threshing, winnowing, kneading, baking, shearing wool, weaving two threads, separating two threads, tying [a knot], loosening [a knot], writing two letters, erasing in order to write two letters, striking with a hammer, etc. Today Orthodox Jews in Jerusalem will not answer telephones or push elevator buttons on the Sabbath.

or your ox, or your ass, or any of your beasts. Exodus 20:10 has only "and your beasts." Hebrew בְּהֵמָה ("beast") refers here to domestic cattle, specifically draft animals. Kindness to animals is reflected in other OT laws (Exod 22:29[30]; Lev 22:27-28; Deut 22:6-7, 10; 25:4).

your sojourner. The sojourner (גֵּר) is a resident alien who does not have the same status as an Israelite, but in Deuteronomy is accorded benefits because of his dependent status. Along with other needy persons in society, he is promised justice, receives benevolences, and is included in the yearly feasts (1:16; 10:18-19; 16:11, 14; 24:14, 17; 26:11-13; 27:19; Spina 1983, 321). Here he is accorded a Sabbath rest. On justice and benevolences to the "orphan, widow, and sojourner," in Israel and in neighboring societies, see Note for 10:18. The reason for justice and benevolence to the sojourner is given in 10:19, repeated from Exod 22:20(21); 23:9: Israel was once a sojourner itself in Egypt (cf. v. 15).

within your gates. "Gates" in the OT is a synecdoche for "(walled) cities," occurring 25 times in Deuteronomy (e.g., 12:12, 15, 17, 18, 21; 14:21, 27, 28, 29; 15:7, 22; 16:5, 11, 14, 18, etc.; Driver 1895, lxxix no. 6). In Exodus the term occurs only in the fourth commandment (Exod 20:10).

in order that your manservant and your maidservant may rest like you. These words are lacking in Exod 20:10. How a Sabbath rest worked out for menservants and maidservants once Israel became settled in the land we can only imagine. Concessions had to be made. There is a modern French proverb about farmers having to work on Sunday: "The good God governs the world, but he does not do the milking" (W. D. Davies 1966, 352).

15 This is Deuteronomy's rationale for the Sabbath rest, the focus here being on the menservants and maidservants. Israel was itself a servant (i.e., a slave) in Egypt, and because Yahweh redeemed Israel from this servitude, he now makes the Sabbath commandment broad enough to include those who are currently servants. There is an emphasis here on "remember" (זכר), which is not passive recall but an active calling to mind of what happened in the past so appropriate action will be taken in the present. Deuteronomy continually calls upon Israel to "remember": its own slavery in Egypt, the hard labor there, and Yahweh's deliverance in the exodus (see Note for 8:2). The expression "Remember that you were a servant in (the land of) Egypt" is stereotyped in Deuteronomy (5:15; 15:15; 16:12; 24:18, 22; Driver 1895, lxxxi no. 33; Weinfeld 1972, 327 no. 3). This commandment is given a different rationale in Exod 20:11 (Klingbeil 2010, 499-505). There it says: "for in six days Yahweh made heaven and earth, the sea and all that is in them, and rested the seventh day; therefore Yahweh blessed the Sabbath day and hallowed it" (cf. Gen 2:2-3). If God rested on the seventh day of creation, Israel must rest on the seventh day of the week.

with a strong hand and with an outstretched arm. On this expression with reference to the exodus deliverance, see Note for 4:34.

therefore Yahweh your God commanded you. The stock expression in Deuteronomy is "therefore I am commanding you," with Moses speaking in the first person (see Note for 15:11).

16 *Honor your father and your mother.* כַּבֵּד אֶת־אָבִיךָ וְאֶת־אִמֶּךָ. The fifth commandment admonishes children not simply to honor old age, which Scripture does enjoin (Lev 19:32; 1 Tim 5:1-2), but to honor the persons who brought them into the world (Prov 23:22-25), who fed them and carried them in their arms when they could neither eat nor walk by themselves, and who reared them during the formative years of youth. Yahweh showed parental care of Israel from the time of its birth as a people (Deut 32:10-14; Hos 11:3; Ezek 16:4-14; Isa 46:3-4). Parents (and grandparents) are deemed worthy of honor all throughout life, but they need it especially in old age (Ruth 4:14-15; Sir 3:12). Honor of father and mother is also enjoined in Lev 19:3. There is a clear link between this commandment and the wisdom tradition (Daube 1969a, 39). In Proverbs, honoring parents means adhering to their teaching and showing them respect when they are old (Prov 1:8; 4:1-5; 23:22-25), both of which will bring them much gladness. One must not rob from a mother's or father's possessions (Prov 28:24). Honoring father and mother — in word and deed — is lifted up in Sir 3:1-16, where it says that glorifying and respecting them brings the same to oneself.

The Deuteronomic Code contains two laws dealing with sons and daughters who dishonor their parents (21:18-21; 22:13-21). A curse on anyone dishonoring them occurs also in 27:16. The incident of the rebellious son in 21:18-21 became the showcase example in the Primary History of this command being violated (Freedman 2000, 76-79). Insults and curses are the opposites of respect and honor, in the Bible and also in Akkadian and Ugaritic texts (Weinfeld 1990, 7). The Covenant Code says that anyone who strikes father or mother or curses them shall be put to death (Exod 21:15, 17; cf. Mark 7:10; Matt 15:4). The Holiness Code, too, enjoins the death penalty for anyone cursing father or mother (Lev 20:9; cf. Prov 20:20). In the Code of Hammurabi (CH 195), a son who strikes his father gets a hand cut off. The OT notes that there are nevertheless those who do curse their fathers and do not bless their mothers (Prov 30:11; cf. Ezek 22:7), but they do so at great peril. Proverbs 30:17 continues:

Deuteronomy 5

> The eye that mocks a father and scorns to obey a mother
> will be picked out by the ravens of the valley and eaten by vultures

Judgment on failing to honor one's father is contained in an Akkadian wisdom text, which says:

> If a man does not honor his father, he will perish quickly.
>
> (Albertz 1978, 363)

Throughout the ancient world it was expected that parents receive honor during their lifetime, and when they got old, their children were to give them special care — provide housing, food, clothing, serve them, dress them, and attend to their needs — as long as they lived and when they died, to provide them with a proper burial (Greenfield 1982). An Old Babylonian marriage contract (BE 6/2 48, lines 27-32) stipulated that sons must support their mother with 720 litres of grain, 6 mina of wool and ... litres of oil annually. Any heir not providing her with grain, oil, and wool will forfeit property belonging to the father (Westbrook 1988a, 115-16). Adopted children were required to do the same. In Nuzi texts on sale adoption, the adopted son or daughter was enjoined to revere the mother and father as long as they lived, providing them with food and clothing ($ANET^3$, 219-20). There were severe penalties in Sumerian law for anyone who says, "You are not my father" or "You are not my mother" (Daube 1947, 7). In the Old Babylonian marriage contract cited above (BE 6/2 48, lines 17-20), sons who say to their mother, "You are not our mother," forfeit their father's property. In the Code of Hammurabi if an adoptive son made such a statement, his tongue would be cut out (CH 192).

The present commandment is cited no less than six times in the NT (Matt 15:4; 19:19; Mark 7:10; 10:19; Luke 18:20; Eph 6:2-3). In Jewish tradition, honor is defined to mean that one "must give [his father] food and drink, clothe and cover him, lead him in and out" (b. Qidd. 31b). Josephus (Ant. 4.261-65) said scornful youths need to be reminded that their parents came together so they might have children to care for them in old age. If the youths accept this correction, well and good; if they do not, let them be stoned. Philo said parents are the servants of God for the task of begetting children, and one who dishonors the servant dishonors the Lord (Decalogue 119-20).

Honor and respect for parents obtained in ancient Greek culture. Plato (Laws iv 717) said that honor was to be paid to living parents for the care and pain they suffered on the children's behalf. Throughout life children must therefore be reverent in speech to their parents, for light words will bring a heavy penalty. They must even yield to their parents when they are angry, giving rein in word and deed to their own anger, and pardon them (cf. Sir 3:13).

Deuteronomy 5

And they must compensate them in old age, for that is when they need help the most.

just as Yahweh your God commanded you. A Deuteronomic addition, as in the fourth commandment (see v. 12).

in order that your days may be prolonged, and in order that it may go well with you on the soil that Yahweh your God is giving you. Characteristic language and theology of Deuteronomy. On the expression "prolong/not prolong your days," see Note for 4:25-26. On the phrase "so that it may go well with you," see Note for 4:40. Exodus 20:12 lacks "and in order that it may go well with you," but Freedman and Overton (2002, 106) argue that this could be attributed to haplography (homoeoteleuton: ך ... ך). The words occur in the LXX and in the Nash Papyrus. This is the only commandment containing a promise, which is noted in Eph 6:2-3. Sirach 3:6 says: "Whoever glorifies his father will have long life."

17 The sixth commandment both here and in Exod 20:13; in LXX Deut 5:17 it is the seventh commandment (see Rhetoric and Composition). The AV translated רצח as "kill" rather than "murder," which is retained in some modern English Versions (RSV; JB; NAB; NJB). The verb is used to refer to accidental homicide in 4:42; 19:3-4; Num 35:11, 25-26, where "kill" is the proper translation. In Num 35:30 it is used for capital punishment (Propp 2006, 179), and there it means "put to death" (RSV). Obviously, the present commandment does not prohibit accidental homicide (see 19:1-13), just as it does not prohibit killing in war or capital punishment (von Rad). The Covenant Code attempts to distinguish between intentional and accidental homicide (Exod 21:12-14). In the present commandment, רצח means "to murder" (Michaelis 1814, 3:218-19), which is how more recent English Versions translate it (NEB; NIV; NRSV; REB). Covered under this commandment would be suicide (Weinfeld), although Phillips (1970, 99) argues that suicide was not a crime in ancient Israel, since the OT legislation does not mention it. Nevertheless, it is murder, and a particularly grievous form of murder, since it allows no possibility of repentance.

The command not to murder appears also in Exod 21:12; Lev 24:17; Num 35:30-34, where the specified punishment is death. Numbers 35:30-34 states that two witnesses are required for the death penalty to be carried out, also that no ransom can be accepted, as was true in other societies, where the family of a murder victim could accept monetary settlement (Jackson 1975, 35, 47). Muhammad allowed for monetary compensation in murder cases (see Note for 19:6). Deuteronomy 27:24 speaks a curse on anyone who smites (to kill) his neighbor in secret. But the first murder in the Bible, Cain murdering Abel, brings no death sentence for Cain, only a lesser curse followed by a promise from God that Cain's evil will not be avenged (Gen 4:8-16). In Gen 9:6 the command not to murder is rooted in the idea that human beings are created in the image of God. David's arranged killing of Uriah the Hittite in an attempt to cover up his adultery with Bathsheba was murder (2 Sam 11:6-25), as was the miscarriage of justice resulting in the death of Naboth (1 Kgs 21:19). Both of these murders were committed by kings, and not surprisingly, neither was punished. The showcase example in the Primary History of this commandment being violated was the murder of the Levite's concubine reported in Judges (Judg 19:22-30; Freedman 2000: 114-18).

In the NT, the sixth commandment is upheld in Matt 5:21; 19:18; Mark 7:21; 10:19; Luke 18:20; Rom 13:9; Jas 2:11. Paul, himself a murderer, or at least in league with murderers before his conversion (Acts 8:1; 9:1), lists murder as a godless and lawless crime (Rom 1:29; 1 Tim 1:9). Murder is condemned by other NT writers; murderers are not numbered among Christian believers (1 Pet 4:15; 1 John 3:12, 15; Rev 9:21; 21:8; 22:15).

The Code of Hammurabi, the Middle Assyrian Laws, and the Hittite Laws have no statutes against murder, probably because relatives of the deceased took care of avenging the crime. In MAL A10 and B2, relatives are free to determine the murderer's fate and, if they choose, can accept damages instead of pressing for a capital sentence. In HL 1-4, 174 are no demands for the death of the murderer; instead persons from the murderer's family must be surrendered to make good the loss ($ANET^3$, 189, 195; Phillips 1970, 86). If the victim was a slave, the number of persons to be turned over is half that of a free person. In the Egyptian *Book of the Dead*, the deceased tells a posthumous court that he has not killed or given orders to a killer ($ANET^3$, 34-35, A14-15, B5).

The OT prophets were scandalized by murders occurring in their time (Hos 4:2; 6:9; Isa 1:21; Jer 2:34; 7:9; Ezek 22:9). Prophets themselves were being murdered (Jer 26:20-23; cf. Matt 23:31-35; Acts 7:52). The vicious murder of Gedaliah, the Babylonian-appointed governor of the remnant community at Mizpah, led to the break-up of the community and made necessary the remnant's flight to Egypt (Jeremiah 41). Jesus, in his Sermon on the Mount, upheld the present commandment but went a step beyond, censuring the passion that could lead to murder: provocative anger (Matt 5:21-26).

18 This is the seventh commandment both here and in Exod 20:14, although in LXX Deut 5:18 it is the sixth commandment (see Rhetoric and Composition). Adultery was committed in the ancient world when a man — married or unmarried — had sexual intercourse with a woman married (or engaged) to another man. It was the status of the woman that defined the act; the status of the man was irrelevant. If a married man had sexual relations with an unmarried woman, it was "fornication," "harlotry" (זנה)), or whatever one would like to call it (e.g., Judah with Tamar in Gen 38:13-18). But it was not adultery.

Adultery was a serious crime in antiquity, the reason being that it could bring into the woman's family a child her husband did not want. The person most offended by adultery was the *husband* of the adulterous woman (Westbrook 1990; cf. Prov 6:32-35). Adultery was interpreted more broadly in the NT, where either a married man or a married woman divorcing a spouse *in order to marry* someone else was guilty of adultery (Mark 10:10-12; Matt 5:32; 19:9; Luke 16:18; see Note for 24:1). In the *Didache* (2:2; 5:1), "you shall not fornicate" is included along with other commandments warning against "the way of death." In modern American law, although state laws vary, the marital status of both man and woman defines adultery,* where it is reasoned that either breaks marital vows if sexual intercourse occurs with someone else.

Adultery is strongly condemned in the Bible, where punishment for both parties is death by stoning (Deut 22:22-24; Lev 18:20; 20:10; John 8:3-11). Deuteronomy waives punishment for an engaged woman if a man other than her fiancé had sexual relations with her in the open country, the assumption being that had she cried for help, no one would have heard her. In this case, the man is put to death, but the woman goes free (Deut 22:25-27). If two persons are not caught *flagrante delicto*, but the woman is suspected of adultery by her husband, the woman must appear before the priest and submit to an ordeal, after which the priest will deal with her according to the outcome of the ordeal and the law (Num 5:11-31). Like the crime of murder, the OT disallows mitigation of the death sentence for adultery. In other societies, a death sentence could be waived or mitigated by the woman's husband, by a monetary settlement, by a lesser punishment such as mutilation, by royal edict, or by a combination of these (CH 129; MAL 14-16; HL 198; Greenberg 1960, 11-12; 1986, 1-4; Westbrook 1990, 543). In most cases, waiving punishment for the woman meant waiving it also for the man. On monetary settlements, see Note for 19:21.

While adultery was treated as a serious crime in the ancient world, married women also had to be careful. In the Laws of Ur-Nammu (2050), if the wife of a man, employing her charms, went after another man and he slept with her, the woman was put to death but the man went free (LUN 222-31; $ANET^3$, 524). The Laws of Eshnunna (1800) stated that if a woman was caught in the lap of another man, she was put to death (LE 28; Yaron 1969, 59; $ANET^3$, 162).

Abimelech, king of Gerar, was deeply worried when he found out that he came close to committing adultery with Abraham's wife (Genesis 20). Abimelech called it "a great sin" (Gen 20:9), precisely what it is called in a 9thcent. Egyptian marriage contract (Rabinowitz 1959). The deceased in the Egyptian *Book of the Dead* tells a posthumous court that he has not committed adultery ($ANET^3$, 35, B19). A Ugaritic text reports that the wife of Ammištamru, king of Ugarit, was found guilty of a "great sin," causing her to flee Ugarit. Moran (1959) says the "great sin" was most likely adultery. After returning

---

*I owe this information to Mr. Ted Ryan, an attorney in Waterbury, CT.

home, the wayward woman was put to death. Joseph was falsely accused of adultery with the wife of Potiphar, which landed him in prison (Gen 39:6b-20). In this case, also in the case involving Abimelech and Sarah, adultery was taken to be a sin against God (Gen 20:6; 39:9; cf. Ps 51:6[4]). Greenberg (1960, 11; 1986, 2) believes this is because in Israel God, not the king, was the supreme author of all law. But Loewenstamm (1980) points out that in Mesopotamia, too, adultery was a sin against the gods and resulted in divine punishment.

Adultery and harlotry are solemnly warned against in Proverbs (Prov 2:16-19; 5:1-23; 6:24-35; 7:5-27; 9:13-18), where the young man is told to abandon loose women and join himself rather to Lady Wisdom (4:6-9; 7:4; 8:1-36). Job says the adulterer waits for twilight, thinking no one will see him (Job 24:15). The most flagrant example of adultery in the OT, and the showcase example in the Primary History of this commandment being violated, was David's sin with Bathsheba, wife of Uriah the Hittite (2 Samuel 11; Freedman 2000, 130-35). For this crime David was severely rebuked by Nathan the prophet, but he was not put to death (2 Sam 12:1-13), just as he was not put to death for arranging Uriah's murder — two crimes for which the prescribed punishment was death, and neither is applied to David! Freedman (2000, 133) says there was probably no one in the kingdom to punish David (cf. Westbrook 1990, 545). But the child born to Bathsheba died (2 Sam 12:18).

The Hebrew prophets strongly censured those who violated this commandment, especially Hosea (Hos 4:2, 13-14; 7:4) and Jeremiah (Jer 5:7; 7:9; 9:1[2]; 13:27; 23:10), but also Ezekiel (Ezek 16:32; 23:37, 43-45) and Malachi (Mal 3:5). Jeremiah found that even prophets were committing adultery (Jer 23:14; 29:23). Hosea discovered adultery in his own wife (Hos 2:4[2]; 3:1). The present commandment is quoted in Matt 5:27; 19:18; Mark 10:19; Luke 18:20; Rom 13:9; Jas 2:11. In Matt 5:27-30, Jesus goes a step further in censuring the passion leading to adultery. And in what has to be one of the most misunderstood passages in the entire Bible, Jesus refuses to condemn a woman caught in adultery who was brought before him (John 8:1-11). The reason is that the person or persons who should have begun the stoning did not step forward. Where were the witnesses to the crime, who were to throw the first stones (Deut 17:7)? And where was the offended husband? There is certainly more to the story than what is reported; the Gospel writer says only that the scribes and Pharisees were "testing" Jesus. There had to be mitigating factors in the case, but we do not know what they were. In his answer, Jesus supports capital punishment for an adulteress but refuses to condemn her when everyone else has walked away. If others who were present failed to carry out the prescribed punishment, why should he condemn her? A very smart move! Also, we should note that Jesus does not pardon the woman; he simply does not condemn her. His parting words to her were simply a rebuke: "Go, and don't sin again" (v. 11). Adultery is strongly censured also by Paul (Rom 2:22; 7:3; 1 Cor 6:9).

19 The eighth commandment, repeating Exod 20:15, prohibits all sorts of theft, including kidnapping. The verb גנב means "to take something that does not belong to you," usually in a secretive fashion (Gen 31:19; Prov 9:17). Job says one turns to theft when it is night (Job 24:14). Hebrew has a stronger verb גזל, which means "to seize, rob, take violent possession of." While (violent) seizure of people or property would be a violation of this commandment, acts of this nature in war would doubtless be excluded. Some think the present commandment originally referred only to kidnapping (Rashi; Alt 1953a; von Rad), but that is too restrictive. The rabbis reasoned that reference was to kidnapping because this commandment followed the commandments on murder and adultery, both capital crimes. Kidnapping was a capital crime (Exod 21:16; Deut 24:7), taken as such also in the Code of Hammurabi (CH 14). The present commandment must include theft of property (Weinfeld; Tigay), which is condemned throughout the Bible. Also, the Ten Commandments are apodictic law that does not include modes of punishment, making capital sentences for murder and adultery irrelevant in determining what sort of punishment is envisioned here for stealing. Moreover, this commandment on stealing must have the same broad meaning as the commandment on coveting, to which it is related. That commandment takes in both persons and property. Cheryl Anderson (2004) agrees that the present commandment must include the theft of persons, saying this fits in with Martin Luther King's vision of a "beloved community." Theft of property is given extended treatment in the Covenant Code (Exod 21:37–22:12[22:1-13]). In the Holiness Code, stealing is simply prohibited (Lev 19:11).

The showcase example in the Primary History of this commandment being violated is Achan's theft of war booty — a beautiful mantle, 200 shekels of silver, and a bar of gold weighing 50 shekels — after the battle of Jericho, for which he was stoned to death (Josh 7:20-26; Freedman 2000, 104-8). Hosea and Jeremiah spoke out against theft (Hos 4:2; 7:1; Jer 7:9), and Zechariah's flying scroll carried a curse waiting to descend upon the thief and his house (Zech 5:3-4). In the Egyptian *Book of the Dead,* the deceased tells a posthumous court that he has neither stolen nor robbed ($ANET^3$, 35, B2, B4, B15). The present commandment is upheld four times in the NT (Matt 19:18; Mark 10:19; Luke 18:20; Rom 13:9). Jesus shows disdain for those who steal (Matt 6:19-20; 21:13; Luke 12:33; John 10:1, 10). Paul, too, speaks out against thieves and against theft (Rom 2:21; 1 Cor 5:10-11; 6:10; Eph 4:28).

20 The ninth commandment repeats Exod 20:16, only there the reading is עֵד שֶׁקֶר ("false witness"), which is the more common OT expression (Deut 19:18; Ps 27:12; Prov 6:19; 14:5; 25:18). The Nash Papyrus and 4QDeut[n] follow Deuteronomy. In Exod 23:1 an שֵׁמַע שָׁוְא ("empty report") is prohibited. The NT upholds this commandment in Matt 19:18; Mark 10:19; Luke 18:20.

The verb ענה ("to answer, respond") means "to testify" (19:16, 18; 21:7). The commandment is forbidding false testimonies, particularly in court, where the accused could be on trial for his life. In the modern courtroom false testimony would be lying under oath, i.e., perjury. Whereas the third commandment prohibited "empty" or "frivolous" oaths sworn in God's name, this commandment prohibits "empty" or "false" testimonies against other persons. What we have then is not a general prohibition against lying, as bad as lying might be, but against lying testimony regarding another person (Phillips 1970, 142), something far more serious. In the ancient world great significance was attached to the testimony of a witness (von Rad).

The penalty for false testimony is given in 19:16-21, where the guilty person is sentenced according to the talion principle: he or she receives the same punishment that would have been meted out to the person testified against. The same occurs in other law codes. In the Code of Hammurabi, a person making a false testimony in a murder case is himself put to death (CH no. 1, no. 3; *ANET*[3], 166). Diodorus of Sicily (i 4) reports, too, that among the Egyptians a person falsely accusing another has to suffer the penalty that would have been meted out to the accused had he been found guilty. The deceased in the Egyptian *Book of the Dead* tells the posthumous court that he has not told lies (*ANET*[3], 35, B9). In the much older Ur-Nammu Code (2050), punishment for false testimony is simply a fine (see Note for 19:21).

The most flagrant example of false testimony in the OT, and the showcase example in the Primary History of this commandment being violated, is Jezebel's frame-up of Naboth for not surrendering his vineyard to the king. Naboth was executed on the testimony of false witnesses (1 Kgs 21:1-16; Freedman 2000, 141-44). False witnesses were brought forth in the trial of Jesus (Matt 26:59-61; 27:12-13), and when confronted with the testimonies, Jesus remained silent.

your fellow. While רֵעַ can denote one's "neighbor" (e.g., 19:14), it has the broader meaning of "friend, companion, fellow" (Weinfeld: "anyone else"). This applies even in the well-known verse of Lev 19:18, which is usually translated "you shall love your neighbor as yourself." Tsevat (1996, 435) says the term is not limited to a person living in one's vicinity, but "includes everyone with whom one has contact ordinarily or occasionally." In the present commandment, רֵעַ refers to one's adversary (cf. 1 Sam 15:28; 2 Sam 12:11).

21 The tenth commandment is unlike the other nine in that it pertains to an interior disposition, not a concrete action, making prosecution impossible. Coveting is not a verifiable crime (*pace* Phillips 1970, 149). Since coveting another's wife is mentioned, this commandment may be directed largely, if not exclusively, to the Israelite man (Friedman). But it goes without saying that women, too, can covet houses, slaves, and property belonging to another. The verb חמד means "to covet," and the verb אוה in the Hithpael means "to desire, long for." Both verbs can have positive meaning (Pss 45:12[11]; 68:17[16]), but here the meanings are negative. Some (e.g., von Rad) have argued that since חמד may also mean "take, seize," this commandment could include the actual *taking* of someone else's wife, house, servants, etc. But that has not been the traditional interpretation; what is more, it would make a redundancy after the commandments on adultery and stealing. "Taking" someone else's wife is adultery, and "taking" someone else's house, field, servants, animals, or other possessions is stealing. The two verbs in the verse mean the same thing (Driver). The LXX uses ἐπιθυμήσεις for both; Exod 20:17 uses only one verb, חמד, and is followed by the Nash Papyrus.

We are talking here about an interior disposition, a strong and passionate disposition, that can lead to adultery, stealing, and a great deal more (cf. Josh 7:21; Mic 2:2; Mark 7:20-23), nevertheless a disposition that has not yet resulted in action (Moran 1967, 548; Jackson 1975, 211; Phillips 1983, 17-18; Weinfeld; Tigay). Tigay adds, however, that this mental state "go[es] beyond simple, or passive, desire" and that the command could be paraphrased as "do not scheme to acquire . . . do not long for." The human will is involved, which in Hebrew thought resides in the heart (A. R. Johnson 1964, 75-87). Reference is not to a fanciful notion or lighthearted wish, which would be harmless and unlikely to be censured by anyone.

The wording in Exod 20:17 is different from the wording in Deut 5:21. There the fellow's house is put first and "his field" is omitted. The commandments in the two texts read:

Exod 20:17	**Deut 5:21**
You shall not covet the house of your fellow	And you shall not covet the wife of your fellow
You shall not covet the wife of your fellow	And you shall not desire the house of your fellow
	his field
or his manservant or his maidservant	or his manservant or his maidservant
or his ox or his ass	his ox or his ass
or anything belonging to your fellow	or anything belonging to your fellow

The Nash Papyrus follows Deuteronomy, including "his field" and putting "wife" before "house." Luther in his Catechism follows Exodus. Some argue that "house" in Exodus means "household" (Gen 7:1; 35:2; Num 16:32; Deut 11:6), for which reason the wife is included. Deuteronomy is said to have a more enlightened view of women (Daube 1978, 1981, 100; Weinfeld 1972, 291; Phillips 1983, 6;

cf. 15:12-18; 21:10-14, 15-17, 18-21; 22:13-19; 24:5), putting the wife in a category by herself and taking "house" simply as meaning "dwelling." There is merit in these suggestions. A section after "And you shall not covet the wife of your fellow" in Deut 5:21a sets off these words from the rest of the verse; Exod 20:17 has no section dividing the verse (see Rhetoric and Composition). One should note also that in Deut 28:30 the curse on the wife comes before the curse on the house.

Moran (1967, 550-51) discovered in a Ugaritic text a listing virtually identical to the one in Deuteronomy, which would argue for the listing here conforming to a well-established type. In a royal grant to a certain Takḫulenu, this individual will receive, upon the death of the grantee:

his houses
his fields
his men-servants
his maidservants
his [oxen]
his asses
everything (else) belonging to him

The *Book of the Dead* shows that covetousness in ancient Egypt was regarded as a sin (*ANET*³, 35, B3). And "The Hymn to the Sun-God," an Old Babylonian text found in the library of Assurbanipal (668-627), says that a net will be spread wide to catch the man who has coveted the wife of his comrade. Coveting here is assumed to have led to wrongdoing, because the weapon of Šamaš will be turned against the man and no one will be able to save him. His father will not defend him in court, and his brothers will stand mute before the judge. The poor fellow will be "caught in a copper trap that he did not foresee" (Lambert 1960, 131, lines 87-94; *ANET*³, 388, ii).

The earliest case of "desire" and "coveting" in the Hebrew Bible, and the showcase example in the Primary History of this command being violated, is in the garden of Eden, where the woman saw the forbidden fruit as "something desirable" (תַאֲוָה), "coveted" (חמד) it, and ate it in violation of Yahweh's command. She then gave it to her husband, and he ate (Gen 3:6). Precisely what the "forbidden fruit" symbolizes has been the subject of much discussion, but a case has been made for "knowledge" in Genesis 2–3 being "sexual knowledge" (Gordis 1957). After the man and woman ate the fruit, they became aware of their nakedness (v. 7).

The prophet Micah censured people who were coveting fields and houses, then going on to seize them (Mic 2:2; Chaney 2004). His contemporary, Isaiah, uttered a woe on those who were doing the same thing (Isa 5:8). Jeremiah scored lustful desire, comparing one so enflamed to a wild ass in heat, sniffing the wind to pick up the scent of the male (Jer 2:24). Covetous desire is censured also in the Psalms (Pss 10:3; 112:10) and Proverbs (Prov 13:4; 21:25-26).

Philo (*Decalogue* 142-43, 173) says that passionate desire is the hardest to deal with, being like a flame in the forest that spreads and destroys everything. In the *Apocalypse of Moses,* a work dated no earlier than the 1st cent. A.D., lust is called "the root and beginning of every sin" (*APOT,* 2:146, xix 3). But *4 Macc* 2:1-6 says that covetous desire, though a great passion, can be controlled by reason, with Joseph cited as an example in his resisting the sexual advances of Potiphar's wife (Gen 39:6b-23).

To a fellow anxious to have his brother divide the inheritance, Jesus says: "Take heed, and beware of all covetousness, for a person's life does not consist in the abundance of his possessions" (Luke 12:13-15; cf. 1 Tim 6:6-10). And in the Sermon on the Mount, Jesus goes behind the Adultery commandment to call an evil glance at a woman "adultery" in the man's heart (Matt 5:28; cf. Mark 7:21-22; Matt 15:19; 2 Pet 2:14). Here again, it is wanting to do the act that defines the interior disposition and makes the difference. Luther said one had to possess a genuine desire to carry out an adulterous affair to be guilty of "adultery in the heart." If the will was lacking, adultery was lacking. Jesus was scarcely concerned about male fantasies, which should be evaluated for what they are: gross exaggerations of male prowess or one's irresistibility to women or one woman in particular, which harm no one, pass quickly, and leave all but the most depraved of men wishing they had not entertained such thoughts in the first place. The interior disposition Jesus is talking about, which could certainly lead to wrongful action, is likely based on this commandment against coveting. The Coveting commandment is cited and coveting is censured by Paul (Rom 1:29; 7:7-8; 13:9; Eph 5:3, 5; Col 3:5) and is the basis of an exhortation by James, who says people are killing and waging war because of a desire for what they do not have (Jas 4:2).

Message and Audience

Moses here repeats the Ten Commandments given to the Horeb assembly. Most will have heard them before, but now all are told to stand with the Horeb generation at the holy mountain and hear again this defining law given by Yahweh God. It lies at the heart of Yahweh's covenant with Israel. All but two of the commandments are strong prohibitions, those on Sabbath observance and honoring father and mother being stated positively. These latter commandments are provided with amplification, like the commandment on idols; the others are pretty much straight to the point. Clarification and fine points of interpretation occur elsewhere. Nothing is said about punishment for those who disobey, which is the nature of apodictic law. Some of the commandments were violated in the wilderness, and punishment followed. The people know this. They also know that the Ten Commandments are the law by which Israel must live.

To a late 8th- and early 7th-cent. audience, these commandments should be known; if they were forgotten, the prophets called them to remembrance. Hosea censured people in northern Israel for not obeying them. Micah and Isaiah did the same in Judah. And a century later, Jeremiah scored Judah for disobeying the Ten Commandments along with other laws of the Deuteronomic Code.

In the NT period, the Ten Commandments, along with the Shema (Deut 6:4-5), were recited daily in the temple (*m. Tamid* 5:1). According to the Gospel writers, Jesus without exception honored the Ten Commandments, in some cases expanding their interpretation to include passions leading to the acts they forbade. Jesus' disciples obeyed the commandment calling for a Sabbath rest. In Jewish tradition, the revelation at Sinai (Horeb) and the giving of the law were celebrated during the Feast of Weeks (Pentecost), at which time the Decalogue was recited.

3. Moses: Mediator for Subsequent Laws (5:22-33)

5:22 *These words Yahweh spoke to your whole assembly at the mountain from the midst of the fire, the cloud, and the storm cloud, a great voice, and he did not add. Then he wrote them on two tablets of stone, and gave them to me.* 23 *And it happened as you heard the voice from the midst of the darkness, and the mountain was burning with fire, that you came near to me, all the heads of your tribes and your elders,* 24 *and you said, "Look, Yahweh our God has shown us his glory and his greatness, and his voice we have heard from the midst of the fire; this day we have seen that God may speak to a human and he will live.* 25 *But now, why should we die? Indeed, this great fire will consume us if we go on listening to the voice of Yahweh our God any longer, then we will die!* 26 *For who of all flesh is there that has heard the voice of the living God speaking from the midst of the fire as we, and lived?* 27 *Go near, you, and hear all that Yahweh our God says; and you, you speak to us all that Yahweh our God speaks to you, and we will hear and we will do."* 28 *And Yahweh heard the sound of your words when you were speaking to me, and Yahweh said to me, "I heard the sound of the words of this people, which they spoke to you; they have done well in all that they have spoken.* 29 *Who could make it that this, their heart, would be to fear me and to keep all my commandments all the days, in order that it might go well for them and for their children forever?* 30 *Go, say to them, 'Return to your tents.'* 31 *But you, stand here next to me, and I will speak to you all the commandment, that is the statutes and the ordinances which you shall teach them, so they may do them in the land that I am giving to them to take possession of it."*

32And you shall be careful to do just as Yahweh your God commanded you; you shall not turn aside, right or left. 33In all the way that Yahweh your God commanded you, you shall walk, in order that you may live and it may be well for you, and you may prolong your days in the land that you shall possess.

Rhetoric and Composition

The present verses conclude the Decalogue, reporting that at Horeb Yahweh added nothing to the Ten Words. He simply wrote this law on two tablets of stone, presumably on the mountain, and turned them over to Moses. Yahweh then designated Moses as the recipient of the remainder of his law (5:30-31), viz., the statutes and ordinances of the Deuteronomic Code (6:1).

These verses are demarcated at the top end by a *setumah* in M^L and a section in Sam before v. 22 (Sam has different numbering). At the bottom end, the Sam (with different numbering) has a section after v. 33, which is the chapter break. The M^L has no section there. The Sam (with different numbering) has another section midway in v. 28, just prior to where Yahweh's speech begins.

The concluding verses of the chapter, where Moses returns as speaker (5:32-33), tie in with the beginning (5:1-5), where Moses is also the speaker (Weinfeld). Key verses are 5:1 and 5:32:

5:1   Hear, O Israel, the statutes and the ordinances that I am speaking in your ears today, and you shall learn them and *you shall be careful to do them.*

5:32 And *you shall be careful to do* just as Yahweh your God commanded you; you shall not turn aside, right or left.

Portions of 5:22-33 are contained in 4QDeut^j, 4QDeut^{k1}, and 4QDeut^n; also on Testimonia, phylacteries (1Q[18?]-19; 4Q128, 129, 135, 137, 139, 140), and a *mezuzah* from Qumran (4Q151).

Notes

5:22 *These words Yahweh spoke to your whole assembly at the mountain from the midst of the fire, the cloud, and the storm cloud, a great voice.* The "words" are the Ten Commandments, which were first spoken to the entire assembly (4:10-13; 5:4-5; 9:10; 10:4). The spectacular acts of the natural order accompanying the Horeb theophany — fire, cloud, and storm cloud — are reported in the same terms in 4:11. Here they become the reason why people ask Moses to mediate for them in the future (vv. 23-27). Cf. the description in Exod 20:18. On Yahweh's voice coming "from the midst of the fire," see Note for 4:12. The "cloud" (עָנָן) could have been a cloud mass or fog (Hos 6:4: "morning fog"), the "storm cloud" (עֲרָפֶל) a rain cloud accompanied by heavy darkness (Pss 18:10[9]; 97:2). The "great voice" (קוֹל גָּדוֹל) was a "loud sound," which may have been thunder (Weinfeld; cf. Exod 19:16-19). This theophany is recalled in Heb 12:18-19.

to your whole assembly. The Horeb convocation, at which time the Ten Commandments were given (9:10; 10:4).

and he did not add. וְלֹא יָסָף. The verb is יסף ("to add"). The AV and other modern English Versions translate "and he added no more," or the like (cf. וְלֹא יָסָפוּ, "and they said no more," in Num 11:25). Yahweh gave only the Decalogue to the Horeb assembly (G. E. Wright; Weinfeld; Tigay). The remainder of the law, according to Deuteronomy, was given to Moses alone, who kept it until the end of the wilderness trek and was now delivering it to the people in the plains of Moab (5:31). The Targums read a different verb, סוף, meaning "to end, cease," yielding the translation "and it did not cease" or the like (T^{OnqNf}). According to Weinfeld, this interpretation reflects the rabbinic view that the Torah has eternal validity. But the rendering could also mean that Yahweh's revelation of law did not *end* with the Ten Commandments, but continued with yet more laws. The Deuteronomic author, however, seems to be saying that *only* the Decalogue was given to the Horeb assembly; the statutes and ordinances of the Deuteronomic Code, entrusted for now only to Moses, were given to the people later on. Exodus has a somewhat different view. There Israel is said to have received the words of the Book of the Covenant at Sinai (Exod 24:3-8).

Then he wrote them on two tablets of stone, and gave them to me. Moses' stay of forty days and forty nights on the mountain, when he received the Ten Commandments written by "the finger of God," is reported in 9:9-12; cf. 4:13. The lawgiver in Israel was God, unlike other societies, where it was the king (Greenberg 1960, 9-13; Tigay). Hammurabi was the Babylonian lawgiver.

23-24 We are backtracking now to what happened before the commandments were written on stone (v. 22b), which happens every now and then in Hebrew narrative. The people were frightened by the Horeb revelation, expressing amazement that they managed to survive. Nothing quite like that had ever happened before (4:33). In fact, it was dangerous, and in vv. 25-27 the people say that it might be better if it is only Moses who goes near to Yahweh.

the heads of your tribes. In the wilderness these were said to be men of wisdom and experience, organized along military lines, who performed some sort of judicial function (see Note for 1:15). They continued in Israel as rulers and judges (see Note for 29:9-11). For discussion on the various office holders in ancient Israel, see Note on 16:18.

Deuteronomy 5

and your elders. The "elders" (זְקֵנִים) figured prominently in city life throughout Israel's history, playing an important role in deciding criminal cases (Josh 20:4; 1 Kgs 21:8, 11; Isa 3:14; Jer 26:17). As in neighboring nations, so also in Israel, elders were men of advanced age and social status (*EncJud*, 6:578). According to Deuteronomy, city elders would be called upon to assist in certain judicial matters once Israel was settled in the land (19:12; 21:2-6, 19-20; 22:15-18; 25:7-9). Here we see that they advise and give assistance to Moses (cf. 27:1; 29:9[10]; 31:9, 28), being official representatives of the people (Moran). Reviv (1989) says that although Deuteronomy looks at the wilderness period from a later perspective, the elders must nevertheless be regarded as a premonarchical institution, deeply rooted in Israel's patriarchal past. Israel's tribal character can be compared to that in Mesopotamia and Syria-Palestine in an even earlier period. On the role of the judges, see Note for 17:8.

Yahweh our God has shown us his glory and his greatness. Yahweh's "glory" (כָּבוֹד) is his radiant, shining presence (NJV: "majestic Presence"); nevertheless, it is a presence not even Moses is permitted to behold (Exod 33:18-23). Here the "glory" was seen in the fire atop Mount Horeb, which, for a time, was hidden by a cloud cover (Exod 24:16-17). Yahweh's "greatness" (גֹּדֶל) is affirmed often in Deuteronomy (see Note for 3:24), celebrated also in the Song of Moses (32:3).

25 The spectacle was so terrible that the people did not want it to continue; it could prove fatal for them (cf. 18:16; Exod 20:19).

But now. On the rhetorical particle עַתָּה, which signals a discourse shift, see Note for 2:13.

26 See 4:33. "All flesh" here means all humans (Gen 6:12-13; Isa 40:4-6), who are fragile beings in the presence of the living God.

the living God. אֱלֹהִים חַיִּים. This epithet for Yahweh occurs often in the OT (1 Sam 17:26, 36; Hos 2:1[1:10]; Jer 10:10; 23:36; Pss 42:3[2]; 84:3[2], etc.). Jeremiah calls Yahweh "the spring of living water" (Jer 2:13). On the oath "as Yahweh (your God) lives," see Note for 5:11.

27 The people decide that mediation will be best for the future: Moses should approach God, hear him, and then relay his word to them (cf. Exod 20:19). The people promise that what they hear from Moses they will do (cf. Exod 24:7).

Go near, you. קְרַב אַתָּה. The pronoun is for emphasis (Driver; cf. Exod 20:19; Judg 8:21; 1 Sam 17:56). The construction repeats in v. 31, only there the pronoun precedes the imperative.

and you, you speak to us. וְאַתְּ תְּדַבֵּר אֵלֵינוּ. This added pronoun puts emphasis on the person of Moses. The form is feminine (ibn Ezra), but used here as a masculine (BDB, 61; cf. Num 11:15; Ezek 28:14). Driver suggests it be repointed to אַתָּ, as in Ps 6:4; 1 Sam 24:19, etc.

28 Yahweh overheard the people asking Moses to be a mediator (cf.

1:34) and said their words were well spoken (18:17), meaning the request was approved.

29 The Hebrew is difficult. Yahweh hopes that the people's obedient frame of mind will continue, that they will have the heart to fear him and keep his commandments forever (cf. Jer 32:39-40).

Who could make it? מִי־יִתֵּן. On this idiom expressing a wish or longing, see Note for 28:67. A prayer in 2 Macc 1:4: "May [God] open your heart to his law and his commandments."

to fear me and to keep all my commandment all the days. The idea appears to come from Exod 20:20, but in Deuteronomy it develops into a major theme (see Note for 4:10).

in order that it might go well for them and for their children forever. A stock phrase in Deuteronomy (see Note for 4:40).

30 The assembly is concluded, and the people are to return to their tents. The LXX updates to "your houses" (τοὺς οἴκους ὑμῶν).

31 Moses will now get from Yahweh the statutes and ordinances to be taught to the people at a later time (cf. 4:14). "Doing" the commandment(s) in Deuteronomy is the concrete expression of loving Yahweh, walking in his ways, serving him, and holding fast to him (10:12-13; 11:22; 19:9; 30:16).

all the commandment, that is the statutes and the ordinances. "The commandment" singular (הַמִּצְוָה) is a general term in Deuteronomy, here standing in apposition to "the statutes and the ordinances" (cf. 6:1; 7:11, etc.). Along with "the law" (הַתּוֹרָה), reference is to the entire Deuteronomic Code (see Notes for 27:1 and 30:11).

which you shall teach them, so they may do them. Moses' job is to "teach" Israel the whole commandment, and Israel's job is to learn it and do it (see Note for 4:1).

in the land that I am giving to them to take possession of it. A variant of a stock expression in Deuteronomy (see Note for 15:4).

32 Moses is now the speaker, repeating what Yahweh has just said about doing the commandment. Verses 32-33 conclude the present discourse (see Rhetoric and Composition), although some take them as being transitional along with 6:1-3 to 6:4 (von Rad; Moran; Weinfeld; Nelson). They are not necessarily a later addition (*pace* Rofé 1985, 5-14). On the stereotyped Deuteronomic expression "you shall be careful to do," see Note for 5:1.

you shall not turn aside, right or left. On this expression, see Note for 2:26-27.

33 "Walking in the way (of Yahweh)" has ethical implications in the OT (Muilenburg 1961b), translating into loving, serving, and fearing Yahweh. In Deuteronomy it means keeping Yahweh's commandments (5:33; 6:7; 8:6; 10:12; 11:19, 22; 13:6[5]; 19:9; 26:17; 28:9; 30:16; cf. Exod 18:20). The phrase "to walk in (all) Yahweh's/his way(s)" is stock in Deuteronomy (Driver 1895, lxxxi no. 31;

Deuteronomy 5

Weinfeld 1972, 333 nos. 6-6a), occurring also in Jeremiah (Jer 5:4-5; 6:16). Christians in the early church were said to belong to "the Way" (Acts 9:2; 19:9; 24:14, 22). Walking in Yahweh's way leads to life, increase, and blessing (30:16); turning aside from it, seen most blatantly in going after other gods, leads to death (11:28). The latter happened already at Horeb, when people made a golden calf (9:12). Moses in his Song says that the same will doubtless happen after he is gone (31:29). But here the Deuteronomic preacher has a positive outlook, hoping that people will choose life, well-being, and longevity (4:1; 30:19-20). Nebuchadnezzar on a building inscription (XV, 1:29) said that after being born he "walked in the way of god" (Langdon 1905, 118-19).

in order that you may live. The LXX has: "in order that he might give you rest."

and it may be well for you. On this stock Deuteronomic phrase, see Note for 4:40.

and you may prolong your days in the land that you shall possess. On this stock phrase, see Note for 4:25-26.

Message and Audience

Moses says the "Ten Words" were spoken to the Horeb assembly amidst a grand display of natural phenomena, but once they had been given, Yahweh said no more. The Commandments were written on two tablets of stone and given to Moses. Moses then recalls how, when the divine voice was heard, leaders came to him and expressed disbelief that they had survived the experience. It was fraught with danger, and they feared that if such a thing continued they would die. This had never happened before — the living God speaking from the midst of the fire and people living to tell the story! Tribal heads and elders suggested that from now on Moses alone approach God, listen to what God says, and then relay it to the people. They promised to listen and do what Moses said.

Yahweh overhears the conversation and says the idea is a good one. Would that the people might have it in their hearts to fear Yahweh and keep his commandments forever, for then it would go well with them and their children! Yahweh then tells Moses to send the people home and remain alone with him. He will give Moses additional law, i.e., the statutes and the ordinances, and Moses can teach these to the people just before they cross over into Canaan.

Moses turns to the people and tells them again to be careful to do what Yahweh has commanded, not to turn to the right or to the left. In the way of Yahweh people must walk, so they may live, enjoy well-being, and prolong their days in the land they are about to possess.

To a late 8th- and early 7th-cent. Judahite audience this will be a reminder that obeying the Ten Commandments, important as this may be — and it is important — is not enough. They must also obey the laws in the Deuteronomic Code, which the Levitical priests, now acting the part of Moses, are teaching them. If they do this, they will not suffer the calamity that befell northern Israel and even now was threatening Judah, but will live, have well-being, and experience a prolonged life in the land Yahweh has given them.

B. FEAR YAHWEH AND KEEP THE COMMANDMENT (6:1-3)

6:1And this is the commandment, the statutes and the ordinances, which Yahweh your God commanded to teach you to do in the land into which you are crossing over to take possession of it, 2in order that you may fear Yahweh your God, to keep all his statutes and his commandments that I am commanding you, you and your children and your children's children, all the days of your life, and in order that your days be prolonged. 3And you shall hear, O Israel, and you shall be careful to do that it may go well for you and that you may multiply greatly, just as Yahweh the God of your fathers spoke to you, in a land flowing with milk and honey.

Rhetoric and Composition

With the Decalogue narrative now complete, Moses turns to the present to announce the statutes and ordinances that will regulate national life in the land they are about to enter. The introductory verse in 6:1 picks up from 5:31, indicating that the statutes and ordinances entrusted to Moses at Horeb are the ones Moses will now be giving to the people. These statutes and ordinances of the Deuteronomic Code, however, will not actually be presented until chs. 12–26. In the intervening chapters (chs. 6-11) Moses will deliver sermonic discourses, which will be largely expositions on the first and second commandments.

Chapters 5–11 contain a number of rhetorical structures in which repeated words and phrases highlight the themes being emphasized. The first of three major sermonic discourses in chs. 5–11 is delimited to 5:1–6:3 (see Rhetoric and Composition for 5:1-5). This discourse is held together by an inclusio made from Deuteronomy's didactic formula:

5:1	Hear, O Israel...	שְׁמַע יִשְׂרָאֵל
6:3	And you shall hear, O Israel	וְשָׁמַעְתָּ יִשְׂרָאֵל

While 6:1 in one sense appears to mark a new beginning in the larger discourse, there is nevertheless continuity between 6:1-3 and 5:27-32. Lohfink (1963a,

67-68) finds in these verses a chiastic structure made up of verbs on keeping the commandment, which with minor alterations consists of the following:

5:27	hear . . . we will hear and we will do	שָׁמָע . . . שָׁמַעְנוּ וְעָשִׂינוּ
5:29	to fear . . . and to keep	לְיִרְאָה . . . וְלִשְׁמֹר
5:31	you shall teach them so they may do	תְּלַמְּדֵם וְעָשׂוּ
5:32	you shall be careful to do	שְׁמַרְתֶּם לַעֲשׂוֹת
6:1	to teach . . . to do	לְלַמֵּד . . . לַעֲשׂוֹת
6:2	you may fear . . . to keep	תִּירָא . . . לִשְׁמֹר
6:3	you shall hear . . . and you shall be careful to do	שָׁמַעְתָּ . . . וְשָׁמַרְתָּ לַעֲשׂוֹת

Moses is to *teach* Israel Yahweh's commandment; Israel, for its part, is to *hear* and *be careful to do* it, for in doing Israel will learn to *fear* Yahweh its God.

A keyword inclusio also ties chs. 6–11 together. It consists of the exhortation to be careful to do Yahweh's commandment immediately preceding the liturgical injunction in 6:4-9 and the warning along similar lines immediately following the injunction when it is repeated in 11:18-20 (Lundbom 1996, 305-6):

6:3   And you shall hear, O Israel, *and you shall be careful to do* . . .

11:22   *If you will be very careful* with all this commandment that I am commanding you *to do* . . .

Chapter 6 by itself begins and ends with statements about doing the commandment. Keywords and phrases in the opening and closing verses make this inclusio:

6:1-2   *And this is the commandment, the statutes* and the ordinances, which *Yahweh your God commanded* to teach you *to do* in the land into which you are crossing over to take possession of it, *in order that you may fear Yahweh your God,* to keep all his statutes and his commandments that I am commanding you, you and your children and your children's children, *all the days of your life,* and in order that your days be prolonged.

6:24-25   And Yahweh commanded us to do all these statutes, *to fear Yahweh our God,* for our own good *all the days,* that he might let us live, as at this day. And righteousness it will be for us when we are careful to do *all this commandment before Yahweh our God, just as he commanded us.*

The present verses are delimited at the top end by a section in Sam before v. 1, which is the chapter division. M^L has no section there. Delimitation at the

305

Deuteronomy 6

bottom end is by a *petuḥah* in M^L and a section in Sam after v. 3. Framing these verses is another inclusio on *doing* the commandments in the *land*:

> 6:1 And this is the commandment . . . which *Yahweh your God* com-manded . . . *to do in the land* . . .
>
> 6:3 And you shall hear, O Israel, and you shall be careful *to do* . . . *Yahweh the God of your fathers* . . . *in a land* . . .

Portions of 6:1-3 are contained in 4QDeut^j and 4QDeut^n; also on phylacteries from Qumran (4Q128, 129, 135, 137, 140; 8Q3) and a *mezuzah* from Qumran (4Q151).

Notes

6:1 "The commandment" here is a general term, referring with "the statutes and the ordinances" to the entire Deuteronomic Code (see Note to 5:31). Reference is not back to the Decalogue (*pace* Nelson). The present introduction repeats the introduction in 5:1, occurring again in 12:1 where the Deuteronomic Code actually begins.

which Yahweh your God commanded to teach you. I.e., commanded me [Moses] to teach you (4:1, 14; 5:31).

in the land into which you are crossing over to take possession of it. A stock expression in Deuteronomy (see Note for 4:26).

2 *in order that you may fear Yahweh your God, to keep all his statutes and his commandments that I am commanding you.* Israel is to learn Yahweh's commandment so it will fear Yahweh and obey the statutes and ordinances within the commandment. Fearing Yahweh and keeping his commandments go hand in hand (see Note for 5:29). On the importance of fearing Yahweh in Deuteronomy, see Note for 4:10.

you and your children and your children's children. The LXX and Vg have a plural (cf. 4:9). If the singular is correct, then the Deuteronomic writer is shifting from the nation to the individual (Driver). Children and grandchildren must learn to fear Yahweh and obey his commandments.

all the days of your life, and in order that your days be prolonged. Fear of Yahweh should lead to obedience, and obedience will lead to one's days being prolonged. On the Deuteronomic theme of one's days being prolonged (in the land), see Note for 4:26.

3 *And you shall hear, O Israel, and you shall be careful to do.* Hearing must lead to doing (cf. Matt 7:24). In 5:27 the people said: "we will hear and do." "And you shall hear, O Israel" is a modified form of Deuteronomy's "Hear, O Israel" introduction (see Note for 5:1). For the structural importance of this expression in 5:1–6:3, see Rhetoric and Composition. The expression "you shall be careful to do" is stock in Deuteronomy (see Note for 5:1).

that it may go well for you. A second reason for doing the statutes and ordinances is that it will lead to well-being. On this stock Deuteronomic phrase, see Note for 4:40.

and that you may multiply greatly. Deuteronomy looks for Israel to multiply (1:10-11), which will come from doing the commandments (6:3; 7:13; 8:1; 13:18[17]; 28:63; 30:16).

just as Yahweh the God of your fathers spoke to you. Hebrew דִּבֶּר can also be translated "he promised" (AV and most English Versions). On Yahweh's promise of descendants and land to the patriarchs, see Note for 1:8.

in a land flowing with milk and honey. The Hebrew lacks "in" before "land" (ibn Ezra notes the omission). Lohfink (1994c, 278) says the expression is Deuteronomic (6:3; 11:9; 26:9, 15; 27:3; 31:20), although found in older pentateuchal sources (Exod 3:8, 17; 13:5; 33:3). It occurs in Jer 11:5 and 32:22. The land promised to the patriarchs was a fertile land that would yield great abundance (6:11; 7:13-14; 8:7-10; 11:9-15). In a Ugaritic text (*KTU* 1.6), the storm-god Baal, when he becomes alive again in the spring, is said to provide the land with a rain of fat/oil and honey. The relevant couplet reads:

The heavens rain fat/oil
The wadis flow with honey

The publisher of the text (P. Stern 1992) suggests that the biblical expression "a land flowing with milk and honey" may have its origin in the rivalry with Baal. More recently it has been argued that חָלָב ("milk") should be repointed to חֵלֶב ("fat"), which would give the reading "a land flowing with fat and honey" (Dershowitz 2010; cf. Gen 45:18). In any case, Yahweh, who never dies, will reliably furnish Israel with milk/fat and honey when Israel takes over Canaanite land.

Message and Audience

Moses turns now from Horeb, where the Ten Commandments were given, to prepare Israel for the statutes and ordinances it will hear in the plains of Moab. Yahweh gave Moses these statutes and ordinances at Horeb, but the people will learn of them only now. Israel must live by these statutes and ordinances when it crosses into Canaan. Learning the statutes and ordinances will make people fear Yahweh and do what Yahweh commands. This applies to the children and grandchildren as well. Obedience is to be carried on throughout life, that one's

Deuteronomy 6

days may be prolonged. Doing the commands will also bring well-being and increase, which is what Yahweh promised Abraham along with a land yielding an abundance of good things.

For a late 8th- and early 7th-cent. audience this will be a call for obedience to the Deuteronomic Code, if Judah hopes to stem the losses inflicted by a ruthless Assyrian enemy. Judah must return to the teaching of Moses; if it does, it can hope for prolonged days, well-being, multiplication — not a reduction — of the Israelite people, and ongoing life in the land flowing with milk and honey.

C. LITURGICAL INJUNCTION (6:4-9)

6 *⁴Hear, O Israel, Yahweh our God, Yahweh is one. ⁵And you shall love Yahweh your God with all your heart and with all your soul and with all your might. ⁶And these words that I am commanding you today shall be upon your heart. ⁷And you shall impress them to your children, and you shall speak about them when you sit in your house and when you walk in the way, and when you lie down and when you rise. ⁸And you shall bind them as a sign upon your hand, and they shall be as headbands between your eyes. ⁹And you shall write them upon the doorposts of your house and within your gates.*

Rhetoric and Composition

This liturgical injunction repeats in 11:18-21, framing the homilies of chs. 6–11 (Lundbom 1996, 304-6). When the two injunctions are viewed together, one notes that the center sections are reversed:

Deut 6:6-9	**Deut 11:18-20**
And these words that I am commanding you today shall be upon your heart	So you shall place these words of mine upon your heart and upon your soul
And you shall impress them to your children, and you shall speak about them when you sit in your house and when you walk in the way, and when you lie down and when you rise	and you shall bind them as a sign upon your hand, and they shall be as headbands between your eyes
And you shall bind them as a sign upon your hand, and they shall be as headbands between your eyes	And you shall teach them to your children, to speak of them when you sit in your house and when you walk in the way, and when you lie down and when you rise

Deuteronomy 6

And you shall write them upon the doorposts of your house and within your gates	And you shall write them upon the doorposts of your house and within your gates

The present verses are demarcated at the top end by a *petuḥah* in M^L and a section in Sam before v. 4, and at the bottom end by a *setumah* in M^L and a section in Sam after v. 9.

Portions of 6:4-9 are contained in 4QDeut^p; also on phylacteries from Qumran (4Q130, 135, 136[?]), 140, 142; 8Q3; XḤev/SePhyl) and Wadi Murabbaʿat (Mur4); and on *mezuzot* from Qumran (4Q150, 151, 152), and possibly Wadi Murabbaʿat (Benoit, Milik, and de Vaux 1960, 85-86; 1961, Pl. XXIV). The beginning of the Shema (6:4-5) is contained on the Nash Papyrus (S. A. Cooke 1903), a liturgical text dated by Albright (1937, 149) to the second half of the 2nd cent. B.C.

Notes

6:4 The Shema (שְׁמַע = "Hear") is the preeminent testimony of faith for the Jewish people, to be recited by the pious twice daily (*m. Ber.* 1:1-2; Josephus *Ant.* 4.212). In Hebrew Bibles the final letters of the first and last words are exaggerated so as to form the word עֵד ("witness, testimony"). The Shema, taking in at least 6:4-5, sums up and renders positively the first and second commandments, which affirm the oneness of Yahweh and deny the plurality of other gods (P. D. Miller 1984, 18). These two themes dominate the remaining sermonic material in chs. 6–11. In the Nash Papyrus (lines 22-23), and in the LXX, this verse is prefaced with: "And these are the statutes and ordinances that Moses (LXX: the Lord] commanded the children of Israel in the desert when they went forth from the land Egypt" (S. A. Cooke 1903, Pl. II). On the Shema in Jewish Liturgy, see Vermes (1959) and Tigay (Excursus 10; pp. 440-41).

Hear, O Israel. שְׁמַע יִשְׂרָאֵל. An important didactic introduction in Deuteronomy, which here is opening the second major sermonic discourse in chs. 5–11 (see Note for 5:1).

Yahweh our God, Yahweh is one. יְהוָה אֱלֹהֵינוּ יְהוָה אֶחָד. The four Hebrew words can be translated in different ways, as one can see from the Targums and modern English Versions:

The Lord is our God, the Lord is one	(T^{Onq})
The Lord is our God, one Lord	(NEB)
The Lord is our God, the Lord our one God	(REB)
The Lord our God, the Lord is one	(T^{PsJ}; NIV)

The Lord our God is one Lord	(T^Nf; AV; RSV)
The Lord is our God, the Lord alone	(NJV; NAB; NRSV)
Yahweh our God is the one Yahweh	(JB)
Yahweh our God is the one, the only Yahweh	(NJB)

It is agreed that this credo is affirming the oneness (or unity) of Yahweh God, where "one," referring to Yahweh, contrasts with "many," referring to other gods. The credo also implies, if not stating outright, that Yahweh is unique and exclusively Israel's God (ibn Ezra; Driver; G. E. Wright; Moran; Weinfeld; Tigay; Friedman; cf. 1 Chr 29:1). Exclusivity is explicit if אֶחָד ("one") means "one (alone)," which it can mean (NJV; NAB; NRSV; cf. Zech 14:9; Mark 12:32). But Weinfeld says exclusivity is not explicit in the credo, i.e., it does not say, "Yahweh is Israel's God and there is no other besides him," which is stated in Deut 4:35, 39, and elsewhere in the OT (1 Kgs 8:60; 2 Kgs 19:15, 19; Isa 44:5-6; 45:6, 14, 18, 22; 46:9). Moberly (1990, 213-15), translating "Yahweh our God, Yahweh is one," says the words confess the oneness of Yahweh, not an exclusive relationship between Yahweh and Israel; nevertheless, he concedes exclusivity since he thinks it is presupposed in "Yahweh our God." There is fairly wide agreement that the credo is monotheistic ("Yahweh is the one and only God"), but Tigay also dissents, saying monotheism is present only in 4:35 and 39.

5 Deuteronomy has more to say about the love of God and love for God than any other book of the OT. Yahweh's love for Israel is given classic expression in 7:7-8 (see Note there). Here Israel is told it must love Yahweh. The two are intertwined. Theologically, it is usual to affirm that Yahweh's love for Israel preceded the command for Israel to return that love (von Rad; Moran 1963b). Yahweh loved the fathers (4:37; 7:12 ["steadfast love"]; 10:15) and loved Israel in choosing the nation as his special possession (7:6-8; 10:15; 23:6[5]). However, 5:10 (= Exod 20:6) and 7:9 say that Yahweh shows steadfast love (חֶסֶד) to those who love (אהב) him and keep his commandments (cf. 7:12-13). So while Yahweh's love remains prior and unconditional, in Deuteronomy it is fragile within a conditional covenant, which is to say, that from Yahweh's end, Israel's disobedience of the covenant will damage the love relationship, even if it does not terminate it, and on Israel's end, loving Yahweh will bring the much-needed rain (11:13-14); will cause Yahweh to dispossess nations before Israel (11:22-23); will lead to Yahweh expanding Israel's borders (19:8-9); and most important, will lead to Israel possessing the precious gift of life (30:16, 20). If Israel fails to love Yahweh, the covenant curses will fall.

The mutuality of this divine-human love is paralleled by suzerain-vassal love in the ANE treaties (Moran 1963b; Frankena 1965), where the suzerain promises to love the vassal king and the vassal king must love the suzerain in return. In the Mari texts of the 18th and 17th cents., the term "love" is used to describe the loyalty and friendship between independent kings, suzerain and vassal, also king and subject (Moran 1963b, 78-79). Moran says "love" is stock terminology in Egyptian treaties of the Amarna period (14th cent.). In a later Vassal Treaty of Esarhaddon (7th cent.), a vassal king is told he must love the crown prince Assurbanipal, son of Esarhaddon, king of Assyria (Wiseman 1958, 49-50; iv 266-68; Frankena 1965, 144; *ANET*³, 537). In the OT generally, there is considerable overlap between אַהֲבָה ("love") and חֶסֶד ("covenant love"). The exhortation to love Yahweh is stock in Deuteronomy (6:5; 7:9; 10:12; 11:1, 13, 22; 13:4-5[3-4]; 19:9; 30:6, 16, 20; Driver 1895, lxxviii no. 1; Weinfeld 1972, 333 no. 4), where "loving" Yahweh goes hand in hand with fearing him, walking in his way, clinging to him, serving him, obeying his voice, and doing his commandments. This is a love that shows itself in action. For Israel it means, above all, obedience to Yahweh, his covenant, and his commandments.

While the international treaties give us perhaps the best background for the kind of love spoken about in Deuteronomy, love from other contexts informs Deuteronomy's covenantal theology. It is said, for example, that "love" is vocabulary from family life, denoting the bond that exists between husband and wife, or between father and son (G. E. Wright 1942; McKay 1972). Hosea seems to have been the first to use the term to express Yahweh's affection for Israel, which he compared to the love of a husband for his wife (Hos 3:1) and the love of a father for his son (Hos 11:1). Hosea does not use אַהֲבָה to speak about Israel's love for Yahweh, but does say that Israel was expected to show "steadfast love" (חֶסֶד) toward Yahweh, which it apparently did, but it was fleeting — like the morning fog that goes early away (Hos 6:4-6). Jeremiah, too, portrayed the covenant in marital terms, and said that Israel's "love" (אַהֲבָה) for Yahweh was alive only during the wilderness trek (Jer 2:2). The LXX translated the Hebrew in this verse with ἀγάπης. So while Israel's love for Yahweh doubtless has an intimate and even emotional quality — D. W. Thomas (1939, 64) said the Hebrew אהב combines "breath" and "emotion" — Deuteronomy does not transfer into its covenantal language the love existing between husband and wife or between father and son. But the obligatory love in the father-son relationship may, nevertheless, be presupposed by the Deuteronomic writer, even if it is not explicitly expressed (McKay 1972, 426-27, 433-35). In Deuteronomy, love for Yahweh goes along with fear and reverence (10:12; 13:4-5[3-4]).

What is particularly important about Deuteronomy's "love" is that it can be commanded, which, in the case of Israel's love for God, brings loyalty and obedience into the picture (Frankena 1965, 140-41; Weinfeld 1972, 333 no. 4). Love may well be a spontaneous inner passion, but it may not be, and if it is not, it must be sought after and acquired. Israel is enjoined to love the sojourner (10:19), which may or may not come naturally. Jesus understood this characteristic of love when he called the Shema the "great (and first) commandment" (Matt 22:37-38; Mark 12:29-30; Luke 10:27). In the Gospel of John he tells his disciples: "This is my commandment, that you love one another as I have loved you" (John 15:12; repeated in v. 17). And in John 15:10 Jesus says that abiding in his love means keeping his commandments.

with all your heart and with all your soul and with all your might. The expression "with all your heart and with all your soul" is stereotyped in Deuteronomy (see Note for 4:29). The "heart" in Hebrew psychology is not just the emotional center of the human person; it is also the seat of the mind and the will (A. R. Johnson 1964, 75-87). When the present verse is quoted in Mark 12:30, "and with all your mind" (καὶ ἐξ ὅλης τῆς διανοίας σου) is added. In Hebrew psychology the "soul" is the נֶפֶשׁ, the vitality of the individual (A. R. Johnson 1964, 3-22); it is often translated as "life" or with the personal pronoun "I." It is the "breath (of life)." The Ugaritic cognate means "throat, neck." When the body dies, the נֶפֶשׁ dies; there is no immortality of the soul, as in Greek thought. "With all your might" (LXX: ἐξ ὅλης τῆς δυνάμεώς σου) means "as much as you can" (ibn Ezra; Rashi's "with all your possessions" follows T). But the expression here is not to be broken into segments; it is to be taken as a totality: One is to love Yahweh with one's total being, in complete devotion. The full expression appears in 2 Kgs 23:25, which says that Josiah "turned to Yahweh with all his heart and with all his soul and with all his might, according to all the law of Moses" — an echo of the present verse. In a Vassal Treaty of Esarhaddon, the Assyrian king warns the vassal king about swearing to the treaty with his lips but not "with his whole heart" (see v. 7).

6 The LXX adds "and in your soul" (cf. 11:18). "These words" could refer just to the Shema (vv. 4-5), but more probably refer to the entire Deuteronomic law (ibn Ezra: all the commandments; Driver; Moran; Tigay; Nelson; cf. 11:18). Deuteronomy assumes that Yahweh's words will find their way into the human heart (30:14), which is bedrock OT wisdom teaching (Ps 119:10-11, 34-36; Prov 3:1-3; 4:4, 21; 6:21; 7:3; McKay 1972, 429). The same occurs in other wisdom literature. The "Instruction of Amen-em-opet," an Egyptian text (ca. 7th to 6th cent.) on attaining life and prosperity, begins:

> Give thy ears, hear what is said;
> Give thy heart to understand them.
> To put them in thy heart is worth while... (*ANET*³, 421)

Although Deuteronomy intends that Yahweh's words find their way into the human heart, it knows, as does Jeremiah, that the heart is deceitful and layered with evil (10:16; 11:16; Jer 4:4; 5:23; 17:1, 9). As it turns out, this "heart talk" in Deuteronomy is important background for and determines the articulation of

Deuteronomy 6

Jeremiah's "new covenant," which will be written on the heart (Jer 31:33; cf. 24:7; Ezek 11:19; 18:31; 36:26).

7 *And you shall impress them to your children.* וְשִׁנַּנְתָּם לְבָנֶיךָ. The importance of teaching children the commandments is so that they will come to fear Yahweh, an important Deuteronomic theme (see Note for 4:9). The verb here is שנן, "sharpen" (Deut 32:41), which means "incise, impress." In 11:19 the verb is "teach," למד (cf. 4:10). Today we might say: "drill them into your children." Since the teaching will be oral, Tigay thinks the verb means "instruct by repetition." In Syrian and Assyrian treaties it is expected that the party to the treaty will inform his children and grandchildren.

Sefire Stela:

Thus we spoke (and thus we wr)ote. What I, Mati'el, have written (is) a reminder to my son (and) my grandson who come af(ter) me. Let them do the right thing.... (D. McCarthy 1963, 192)

Vassal Treaties of Esarhaddon (no. 385):

(You swear that) as you stand in the place of this oath you will not swear with the words of the lips (alone), but with your whole heart, (and) you will teach the treaty to your children who live afterwards.... (D. McCarthy 1963, 200; *ANET*³, 538 no. 34)

See Fitzmyer (1967) on the Sefire Treaties, and Weinfeld (1976a, 391-92) on both treaties.

and you shall speak about them when you sit in your house and when you walk in the way, and when you lie down and when you rise. "Sit" and "walk," "lie down" and "rise" are merisms, like "coming in" and "going out" in 28:6 and 19 (see Note for 28:6). People are to speak (ibn Ezra: and think) about Yahweh's words wherever they are and at all times (cf. 17:19; Josh 1:8; Ps 1:2; Prov 6:22). Paul in the NT says to "pray constantly/without ceasing" (1 Thess 5:17), i.e., "pray always." "Walking in the way" means walking in Yahweh's way (see Note for 5:33).

8 Perhaps originally meant metaphorically (Moran; von Rad; Friedman), these words may have carried on from v. 7, stressing the need to keep Yahweh's words ever in mind. Similar expressions in Exod 13:9, 16, which call for ongoing remembrance of the Passover or firstborn ritual (Exod 13:9: "for a memorial [לְזִכָּרוֹן] between your eyes"), are generally taken metaphorically. The "binding" and "writing" of a father and mother's teaching on one's head, neck, fingers, and (tablet of the) heart in Prov 1:8-9; 3:1-3; 6:20-21; 7:1-3 are also metaphorical. Moran cites the advice of a Sumerian sage: "The instructions of a

Deuteronomy 6

father are precious, put them about your neck." Nevertheless, interpretation is debated. The command here (and in 11:18b) was later taken literally by the Jewish people, and some commentators (ibn Ezra; Driver; Weinfeld; Tigay) think the meaning was literal from the beginning.

And you shall bind them as a sign upon your hand. When this injunction was taken literally (*b. Menaḥ.* 43b), which was at least by the late Second Temple period (2nd cent. B.C. *Let. Aris.* §159; Josephus *Ant.* 4.213), a small leather capsule containing parchments on which scriptural passages were written was to be worn on the left arm (i.e., the hand) at specified times. Attachment was by leather straps. The scriptural passages were Deut 6:4-9; 11:13-21; Exod 13:1-10, and 11-16. This capsule, and the one worn on the forehead, are called *tefillin* (Aramaic) in the Targums; in Greek they were called φυλακτήρια, "phylacteries" (Matt 23:5), which Jews consider an ill-advised equivalent, since this term means "safeguards, amulets," something the *tefillin* were not meant to be. The Jews, of course, did make amulets or (lucky) charms (*EncJud*, 2:906-15 + photos), and sometimes *tefillin* were so employed (Fox 1942, 379), but Maimonides roundly condemned the practice. Binding Yahweh's words on the hand was to be a "sign," a reminder to the wearer of Yahweh's words and a witness to others of the God Jewish people worshipped. Jesus censured the Pharisees for "broad phylacteries" that were ostentateous (Matt 23:5).

and they shall be as headbands between your eyes. וְהָיוּ לְטֹטָפֹת בֵּין עֵינֶיךָ. Words of Yahweh were also to be affixed to the forehead. The טֹטָפֹת ("frontal bands, headbands") over time came to denote the leather capsules containing scriptural passages worn on foreheads of the pious (*b. Menaḥ.* 43b). Tigay (1982b) argues that the rare Hebrew term means "headband," pointing out that Syro-Palestinian dress from early times included a headband (for portrayals in Egyptian art and Assyrian inscriptions, see *ANEP*[2], nos. 52, 54, and 351-55, 366). If a head-*tefillah* was worn already in preexilic times, it would not have stood out from normal dress. The LXX did not translate טֹטָפֹת, probably because it was not understood (Wevers 1995, 117). Scriptural passages in the capsules were the same as those on the hand: Exod 13:1-10, 11-16; Deut 6:4-9; 11:13-21, although head-*tefillin* found at Qumran contained the Decalogue and other biblical passages (Yadin 1969, 13, 32-35; Barthélemy and Milik 1955, 72-76; Baillet, Milik, and de Vaux 1962, 149-57; Milik 1977, 33-85). The capsules had moulded compartments into which the parchments, folded and bound together by tendon thread, were placed (Yadin 1969, 9-11 + photos in Pls. XI). Women, slaves, and minors did not wear the headband (*m. Ber.* 3:3), only grown men. A young boy would begin wearing it when he reached majority, which was thirteen years of age. On the *tefillin*/phylacteries, see G. Henton Davies, "Phylacteries," in *IDB*, 3:808-09; Ruth Fagen, "Phylacteries," in *ABD*, 5:368-70; Louis Rabinowitz, "Tefillin," in *EncJud*, 15:895-904; and Tigay, Excursus 11: *Tefillin and Mezuzot*

Deuteronomy 6

(pp. 441-43). On the *tefillin* from Qumran, see Vermes (1959) and Yadin (1969). Photos of *tefillin* fragments found in Qumran Caves 4 and 8 and at Wadi Murabbaʿat, are in Yadin (1969, Pls. I-XX); *EncJud*, 14:1371; *IDB*, 3:808.

9 The term for "doorposts" is מְזוּזֹת (Exod 12:7, 22), which later came to denote the written Scripture affixed to doorposts of Jewish homes and city gates (*b. Menaḥ.* 43b). Presumably the scriptural words were intended originally to be visible, but at some point they were written on parchment and put into small cases for posting. The Scriptures were Deut 6:4-9 and 11:13-21. Placement of the *mezuzah* was to be on the upper right-hand portion of the doorpost or gate. The custom may have been Egyptian, taken over and adapted by the Israelites. Before leaving Egypt, the Israelites were commanded to sacrifice a lamb and put some of its blood on the doorposts and lintels of their houses, for then Yahweh would pass over those houses when slaying the Egyptians. This, too, was to be a rite for all time (Exod 12:21-27).

The ancient Egyptians themselves would inscribe over the doors of their houses such things as "the good house," the name of a king, or some symbol as a good omen (J. G. Wilkinson 1996, 6). A corresponding practice has carried over into modern times. Painted on the doors of present-day Egyptian houses one will see quotations from the Qur'an, such as "He (i.e., Allah) is the Great Creator, the Everlasting," or just "O Allah," reminding the resident of the house when he enters of his mortality. Merchants place over their shops a paper inscribed with the name of Allah, or the Prophet, or both, otherwise a profession of faith or verse from the Quran (Lane 1973, 6, 253). The *mezuzah* was to remind the Jew whenever he entered and departed his house that Yahweh's commands were to be obeyed. It also gave Yahweh's commands a public witness.

Earliest evidence for the fulfillment of this command comes in the Second Temple period (2nd cent. B.C. *Let. Aris.* §158; Josephus *Ant.* 4.213). A *mezuzah* parchment measuring 6.5 cm by 16 cm was found in Qumran Cave 8 (8Q4), containing writing from Deut 10:12–11:21 (Baillet, Milik, and de Vaux 1962; *EncJud*, 11:1474-77). Others were found in Qumran Cave 4 (Milik 1977, 80-85). At this time the Decalogue and other scriptural passages could be put into the *mezuzot*, but later it was only Deut 6:4-9 and 11:13-21. At various times the *mezuzot*, like the *tefillin*, were employed as amulets to protect a house or a city, but this drew the ire of Maimonides, who forbade the practice. Today the *mezuzah* is to be affixed to the entrance of every Jewish home and to the door of every living room in the house (excluding bathrooms, storage rooms, etc.). After the Six Day War (1967), *mezuzot* were affixed to the gates of the Old City of Jerusalem (*EncJud*, 11:1476). For more on the *mezuzot*, see Louis Rabinowitz, "Mezuzah," in *EncJud*, 11:1474-77; and Tigay 1996, Excursus 11: *Tefillin and Mezuzot* (pp. 443-44).

Deuteronomy 6

Message and Audience

Moses now gives the people an injunction having all the marks of a well-crafted liturgy. At the beginning is a confessional statement defining Israel's faith: "Hear, O Israel, Yahweh our God, Yahweh is one." Next, Moses tells all Israelites to love Yahweh with their total being and to do so with all the strength they can muster. This is followed by a consummate word about keeping Yahweh's commandments — the Ten Commandments, first and foremost, but also commands he has given the people in the plains of Moab. These commands must find their way into people's hearts and minds. They must be drilled into their children and must be spoken about at every turn — when they are sitting in their houses, when they are walking outside, at evening before they go to bed, and in the morning when they get up. These commands must also be a testimony to others, worn, as it were, on the hand and on the forehead. And they must be written upon the doorposts of their houses and within their city gates.

For a late 8th- and 7th-cent. audience, these words will be a reminder to everyone of what they believe, or should believe. With the rise of Assyria, and the influx of Assyrian religion into Judah, many Judahites will have followed the lead of Ahaz, and later Manasseh, in taking on Assyrian beliefs and emulating Assyrian worship. Perhaps Hezekiah took the present words to heart in carrying out his reform. Isaiah and Micah may have listened to the contemporary Moses, calling people back to obeying the covenant and the commands of the covenant. But would the ordinary citizens of Judah plant Yahweh's commands in their heart? Would they drill them into their children? Would they talk of them evening and morning and wherever they happened to be during the day? And would they give witness — on their person and in public places — to their faith, so others would know the God who gave these commands?

D. FORGET NOT, TEST NOT (6:10-19)

1. Forget Not Yahweh (6:10-15)

6[10]*And it will happen when Yahweh your God brings you into the land that he swore to your fathers, to Abraham, to Isaac, and to Jacob, to give you great and good cities that you did not build,* [11]*and houses filled with every good thing that you did not fill, and hewn cisterns that you did not hew, vineyards and olive trees that you did not plant, and you eat and become sated,* [12]*be careful for yourself, lest you forget Yahweh who brought you out from the land of Egypt, from the house of slaves.* [13]*Yahweh your God you shall fear, and him you shall serve, and in his name you shall swear.* ¹⁴*You shall not go after other gods from the gods of the peoples who surround you.* ¹⁵*For a jealous God is Yahweh your God in your midst, lest the anger of Yahweh your God burn against you, and he completely destroy you from upon the face of the earth.*

2. Test Not Yahweh (6:16-19)

6 ¹⁶*You shall not test Yahweh your God as you tested at Massah.* ¹⁷*You shall surely keep the commandments of Yahweh your God, and his testimonies and his statutes that he has commanded you.* ¹⁸*And you shall do what is right and what is good in the eyes of Yahweh, in order that it may go well with you, and you may enter and take possession of the good land that Yahweh swore to your fathers,* ¹⁹*to thrust out all your enemies from before you, just as Yahweh promised.*

Rhetoric and Composition

These verses are demarcated at the top end by a *setumah* in M^L and a section in Sam before v. 10 and at the bottom end by a *setumah* in M^L and a section in Sam after v. 19. A *setumah* after v. 15 in M^L divides the unit in two. The two homiletical themes, one on not forgetting the God who gave Israel the good land and a second on not putting God to the test as happened at Massah in the wilderness are bound together by a keyword inclusio (Nelson):

> 6:10 ... when *Yahweh your God brings you into the land that he swore to your fathers, to Abraham, to Isaac, and to Jacob,* to give you great and *good cities* that you did not build. ...
> 6:18 ... *and you may enter* and take possession of *the good land that Yahweh swore to your fathers.* ...

Portions of 6:10-19 are contained in 4QDeut^p; also on a Qumran phylactery (4Q128).

Notes

6:10-11 Moses is concerned here about what may happen when Israel enters Canaan, coming into possession of cities already built, houses filled with every good thing, cisterns hewn by others, mature vineyards and olive trees, and then becoming sated. It may lead to people forgetting Yahweh (v. 12). A similar caution is sounded in 8:7-18. Such a thing happened before, as the Song of Moses attests: Yahweh gave Israel abundant life in Transjordan, and what did it do? It became fat, ungrateful, and went on to forget Yahweh (32:13-18; cf. 31:20). Joshua, before he died, recalled Yahweh's gift of land along similar lines (Josh 24:13). See the stereotyped list in Neh 9:24-25. A summary of the present verses turned up in the Qumran *"Words of Moses"* (1Q22, lines 2-4; Barthélemy and Milik 1955, 93-94).

you did not build . . . you did not fill . . . you did not hew . . . you did not plant. Israel will come into a wealth it did nothing to create. It was created by others. But for Israel, it is to be reckoned as a gracious gift from Yahweh. On the common pairing of "building" and "planting," see 20:5-6 and 28:30; also Amos 9:14; Zeph 1:13; Jer 1:10; 18:9; 24:6; 29:5, 28; 31:4-5, etc. Deuteronomy and the prophets warn that covenant disobedience will cause this blessing to be reversed (Deut 28:30, 49-51; Amos 5:11; Mic 6:15; Zeph 1:13; Jer 5:17; 6:12; 8:10), which is what happened (Lam 5:1-9).

the land that he swore to your fathers. Yahweh promised this land to Abraham and the fathers (see Note for 1:8).

to give you great and good cities that you did not build. As it turned out, Israel conquered or took over a number of Canaanite cities (Joshua 6-8; 10:28–12:24; Judges 1). The large and strategic city of Shechem apparently acquiesced peacefully. Other large cities, e.g., Beth-shean, Megiddo, and Gezer, were not conquered at first (Judg 1:19-36), and neither was Jerusalem fully, until David took it (2 Sam 5:6-7). It is reported to have been taken early on, but the Jebusites living there were not driven out (Judg 1:8, 21).

and houses filled with every good thing that you did not fill. See Job 22:18.

and hewn cisterns that you did not hew. With rain coming in Canaan only between October/November and April/May and few cities — particularly in the Judean highlands — having natural springs, cisterns large and small had to be cut in rock to collect rainwater or store water from more distant water sources. The common cistern was bottle-shaped, with a narrow opening at the top. It was lined with a waterproof lime plaster to hold the water (cf. Jer 2:13). Cisterns with waterproof lining have been excavated at Late Bronze Hazor and Taanach, which predate Israel's entry into Canaan. Water in the cities and towns was stored in community cisterns and cisterns dug beneath private houses or in courtyards (Stager 1985, 10; cf. 2 Kgs 18:31 = Isa 36:16; Moabite Stone lines 24-25; $ANET^3$, 320). Zertal (1991, 34-36), however, believes that cisterns became common in Israel only after 1000. In his view, water in the early years of occupation was stored in large collar-rim jars, about 70 in high, holding 10 to 15 gal of water. He imagines that at this time the Israelites bought water from the Canaanites (cf. Lam 5:4), put it in jars, and transported it by donkey to their villages. King Uzziah is reported to have dug many cisterns in Jerusalem

Deuteronomy 6

(2 Chr 26:10), and into a near empty Jerusalem cistern Jeremiah was cast, where he sank in the mud (Jer 38:6).

vineyards and olive trees that you did not plant. Both are abundant even today in Israel. Grapes were eaten fresh, dried into raisins, or made into wine. Olive oil was used in eating, cooking, lighting, healing, and anointing. Tigay says grapes and olives were second in importance only to cereals (8:8; 28:51), symbolizing the abundant life (Judg 9:7-13; Ps 104:15). Vineyards and olive trees require years to develop, and Israel would enjoy their fruit without having done the planting.

and you eat and become sated. Deuteronomy says often that when Israel enters the promised land, it will eat to the point of becoming "sated" (6:11; 8:10, 12; 11:15; 14:29; 26:12; 31:20; Driver 1895, lxxxiii no. 61). This happened already in Transjordan (32:15a). Satiety can be a blessing, but it can also be a prelude to disaster or become the disaster itself (Prov 30:8-9, 22; Hos 13:6; Jer 5:7; Job 1:4-5). Moses here has the latter in mind if it leads to forgetting Yahweh (v. 12). A sated Israel should bless Yahweh (8:10).

12 Verses 12-14 develop from the first commandment and its preface (5:6-7). On the warning to "be careful," see Note for 4:9. Forgetting Yahweh following his exodus deliverance, his caring in the wilderness, and his gift of material goodness — beginning in Transjordan and anticipated in Canaan — looms large in the Song of Moses, the homilies of Deuteronomy, Hosea, and Jeremiah (see Note for 32:18).

the house of slaves. A Deuteronomic expression for the place of confinement where slaves were kept (see Note for 5:6).

13 Direct objects can precede verbs for emphasis (Driver). A slightly longer version of this directive appears in 10:20. In the present verse, the LXX adds καὶ πρὸς αὐτὸν κολληθήσῃ ("and to him you shall cleave"), which equals 10:20.

Yahweh your God you shall fear. Fear, or holy reverence (see Note for 4:10), says Driver, is "the fundamental element of the religious temper and the basis of other religious emotions, e.g., devotion and love" (cf. 6:2, 24; 10:12). "Fear" in Akkadian literature means loyally serving god and king (Weinfeld 1972, 83-84, 332 no. 3). Fear so defined ought therefore to issue in service and oaths sworn in Yahweh's name. One is not to fear other gods (Judg 6:10; 2 Kgs 17:35).

and him you shall serve. "Serving Yahweh" is another major theme in Deuteronomy (6:13; 10:12, 20; 11:13; 13:5[4]; 28:47; cf. Exod 23:25; Weinfeld 1972, 332 no. 2), where "serve" (עבד) has broad meaning, but often — particularly when referring to other gods — means "worship" (5:9; 8:19; 11:16; 17:3; cf. Jer 13:10; 22:9; 25:6; Exod 23:24; 2 Kgs 17:35). Targums in the present verse translate עבד as "worship." Psalm 100:2 says: "Serve Yahweh with gladness." One of the

Deuteronomy 6

curses of Deuteronomy is that people who do not serve Yahweh with gladness and goodness of heart will end up having to serve their enemies amidst great want (28:47-48). Serving Yahweh is a parallel concept in the OT to serving ordinary rulers (Greenberg 1976, 64; cf. 2 Kgs 18:7; Jer 27:6-7, 11; 28:14). We see this language in treaties and diplomatic letters (the Amarna Letters) of the 2nd and 1st mill. (Weinfeld 1972, 83-84, 332 no. 2). Most importantly, Israel is not to serve other gods (7:4, 16; 8:19; 11:16; 13:3, 7, 14[2, 6, 13]; 28:14; 29:17[18]; Weinfeld 1972, 320 no. 3). If it does, and Moses says this may happen after his death (31:20), Israel will lose its land and perish as a nation (8:19; 17:3-5; 28:14; 30:17-18) or else be taken to a place where it can serve other gods (4:28; 28:36, 64). The land, too, will come under a curse (29:23-27[24-28]). Also, Israel must not serve or worship heavenly bodies (4:19; 17:3) or images (5:9). It is to serve Yahweh only (6:13; 10:12, 20; 11:13; 13:5[4]; 28:47; cf. 1 Sam 7:3-4; Weinfeld 1972, 332 no. 2), where serving means devotion and loyal obedience to Yahweh (Greenberg 1976, 66). In the OT, Israel's national sin, says Greenberg, is defined as exchanging one sovereign for another. Jesus quotes the present words when tempted by Satan (Matt 4:9-10; Luke 4:7-8).

and in his name you shall swear. Oaths can be sworn in Yahweh's name (typically "As Yahweh lives"); the third commandment simply disallows swearing in an empty manner (see Note for 5:11). Implied in the present verse is that one not swear in the name of another god (cf. Josh 23:7; Amos 8:14; Zeph 1:5; Jer 5:7; 12:16). One must swear by Yahweh's name only (Matt 4:10 and Luke 4:8 add "only"). Swearing in Yahweh's name expresses loyalty to Yahweh. In an ancient Sumerian petition, the suppliant affirms loyalty by saying that he has not sworn by a foreign king (Hallo 1968, 79). In future days, the prophets say that people from all nations will swear by Yahweh's name (Isa 19:18; 45:23; Jer 12:16).

14 *You shall not go after other gods from the gods of the peoples who surround you.* A corollary to the first commandment (5:7). The expression "go after other gods" is stereotyped in both Deuteronomy and Jeremiah (Deut 6:14; 8:19; 11:28; 13:3[2]; 28:14; Jer 7:6, 9; 11:10; 13:10; 16:11; 25:6; Driver 1895, lxxviii no. 2; Weinfeld 1972, 320 nos. 1-2; Hoffman 1994), where "go after" (הלך + אַחֲרֵי) means "(loyally) serve" (8:19; 28:14). The idiom has a parallel in Akkadian *alāku arki,* which occurs in treaty contexts (Weinfeld 1972, 83-84, 332 no. 1). The preeminent act of apostasy in Transjordan was Israel "going after" Baal of Peor (4:3). Israel is to "go after" Yahweh (13:5[4]; 2 Kgs 23:3). Because Moses speaks here about "the gods of the peoples who surround you" (cf. 13:8[7]), reference would be to the Canaanite Baals and Asherahs (Judg 2:12-13). Later on, Jeremiah includes gods and goddesses of Egypt and countries to the East (Jer 7:18; 43:12-13; 44:15-25; 50:2; 51:44). "Going after other gods" was equated in rabbinic literature with following the "evil inclination," sometimes personified as Satan/Belial/the Angel of Death (Weinfeld, 355-56; cf. Matt 4:1-11; Mark 1:12-13; Luke 4:1-13). "Two Inclinations" were said to reside in the human heart, "the good inclination" (יצר הטוב) and "the evil inclination" (יצר הרע); see further Urbach 1979, 471-83.

15 *For a jealous God is Yahweh your God in your midst.* Jealousy is related to Yahweh's holiness, which he will not share with another (see Note for 4:24). On Yahweh dwelling "in the midst" of his people, see 1:42; 7:21; 31:17; Exod 17:7; 33:3, 5; Josh 3:10; Hos 11:9; Jer 14:9.

lest the anger of Yahweh your God burn against you. Yahweh's anger burns hot when Israel breaks the covenant and goes after other gods (7:4; 11:17; 13:13-18[12-17]; 29:17-27[18-28]). Yahweh is provoked also by idols (see Note for 4:25-26).

and he completely destroy you from upon the face of the earth. A stereotyped Deuteronomic phrase (see Note for 4:25-26). Cf. Exod 32:12; 1 Kgs 13:34; Amos 9:8. The idiom "(from) upon the face of the earth" occurs elsewhere in 7:6 and 14:2 and turns up often in Jeremiah (Jer 8:2; 16:4; 25:26, 33; 28:16; 35:7).

16 Turning now to the matter of "testing" Yahweh, Moses picks up from the mention in v. 11 of abundant water being provided in Canaan, warning Israel not to test Yahweh as it did at Massah. The place was also called "(waters of) Meribah" (Exod 17:7; Num 20:13) or "Meribat-kadesh" (Deut 32:51). This wilderness incident, which loomed large in Israel's collective memory, is mentioned again in 9:22 and 32:51-52, also in the Blessing of Moses (33:8), but in each case — like here — only in passing. A full account is given in Exod 17:1-7 and Num 20:1-13 (see Notes to 32:51-52 and 33:8).

The AV translated לֹא תְנַסּוּ "ye shall not tempt," which is not quite right. The verb נסה means "test" or "prove" to see if someone will act in a particular way (Exod 16:4; Judg 2:22; 3:4) or whether one's character is established (1 Kgs 10:1; Driver). Yahweh sometimes puts individuals, e.g., Abraham, and all Israel, to the test (Gen 22:1; Exod 20:20; Deut 8:2; 13:4[3]), but Israel is not to test Yahweh. Ibn Ezra says there is no need to test God. At Massah, the people "tested" Yahweh to see whether or not he was "in their midst" (Exod 17:7); here people are warned against "testing" Yahweh about keeping the commandments (v. 17; cf. Ps 78:56; Weinfeld). People must know that if the commandments are violated, Yahweh will punish. Jesus cites the first part of this verse to Satan when Satan tests him in the wilderness (Matt 4:7; Luke 4:12).

17 This exhortation that Israel be sure to keep the statutes, commandments, and ordinances is one of the most oft-repeated in the book (see Note for 4:40).

18 *And you shall do what is right and what is good in the eyes of Yahweh.* A Deuteronomic expression, sometimes without "what is good" (6:18; 12:25, 28; 13:19[18]; 21:9; cf. 1 Kgs 11:33, 38; Jer 34:15; Driver 1895, lxxxii no. 48; Weinfeld 1972, 335 no. 15). In 12:8, Moses tells the people that each person is doing "everything that is right in his own eyes" (cf. Judg 17:6; 21:25). Deuteronomy also uses the stereotypical "do what is evil in the eyes of Yahweh" (see Note for 4:25-26). In the Qumran *Temple Scroll* (11Q 55:13-14; 59:16-17), "do[ing] what is right and good (הישר והטוב) in my eyes/the eyes of Yahweh" follows admonitions about keeping the commandments (Yadin 1983, 2:248-49, 269).

in order that it may go well with you. לְמַעַן יִיטַב לָךְ. Another stereotyped phrase and key idea in Deuteronomy (see Note for 4:40). The verb יִיטַב in Hebrew ("it may go well/be good") supplements טוֹב ("good") and טוּב ("good thing"), which occur in vv. 10, 11, 18 (2x).

and you may enter and take possession of the good land that Yahweh swore to your fathers. On the Deuteronomic expression "to enter and take possession of the land," see 4:1, 5; 7:1; 11:10, 29; 17:14; 23:21(20); Note for 1:8. Deuteronomy refers consistently to Canaan as "the good land" (see Note for 1:34-36).

19 This verse appears to build on Exod 23:23-31 (Milgrom 1976b, 5), where vv. 27-30 contain the promise referred to here. The uncommon הדף ("thrust out") occurs also in 9:4.

Message and Audience

After a defining exhortation that Israel be loyal to the one God, loving him heart and soul, and keeping his commandments, Moses now warns the people what could happen after they enter the land promised to the fathers. Canaan is a good land — great cities, well-stocked houses, hewn cisterns, mature vineyards, and olive trees bearing abundantly. Israel will have done nothing to create all of this; it is a gift from Yahweh their God. The people, to no one's surprise, will eat and become sated, which could and should be a blessing, but woe to them if they forget the slave barracks of Egypt, and more importantly, woe if they forget the God who delivered them from this indignity and brought them to the goodness they now possess. Moses says Israel must fear Yahweh, serve Yahweh, and swear only in Yahweh's name. Why? Because Yahweh is a jealous God; if Israel chases after gods of the surrounding peoples, Yahweh's anger will burn, and he will destroy Israel off the face of the earth.

The people are also warned not to test Yahweh. At Massah they tested him because they lacked water; here they may be testing to see whether Yahweh will act if Israel does not keep the commandments. Israel must keep the commandments, doing what is right in the eyes of Yahweh. If it does, things will go well; Israel will succeed in possessing the land promised to the fathers and will thrust out their enemies, as Yahweh promised they would.

To a late 8th- and early 7th-cent. audience, this will be a reminder of how Israel came into the good land it now possesses. It will also be reminded of what will happen if people forget the God who delivered Israel from slavery and graciously gave it this land. Things have not gone well of late, for the process seems to have been reversed. Enemies have entered the land and thrust out the Israelites — many of them. Transjordan and the northern kingdom are gone. Things could get even worse. Will the same happen to Judah? Will those remaining in the land realize that it is foolishness to test Yahweh to see whether he will punish them for not keeping the commandments? Judah must fear Yahweh, serve Yahweh, and swear by Yahweh's name, not by the names of other gods, which many have done and are still doing. If people do not heed these words of Moses, Yahweh's anger will continue burning, and Judah, like northern Israel, will be driven off the face of the earth.

E. What Mean These Commandments? (6:20-25)

6²⁰*When your son asks you in the future: "What mean the testimonies and the statutes and the ordinances that Yahweh our God commanded you?"* ²¹*then you shall say to your son, "Slaves we were to Pharaoh in Egypt, and Yahweh brought us out from Egypt by a strong hand,* ²²*and Yahweh gave signs and wonders, great and severe against Egypt, against Pharaoh, and against all his house, before our eyes,* ²³*and us he brought out from there, in order that he bring us in to give to us the land that he swore to our fathers.* ²⁴*And Yahweh commanded us to do all these statutes, to fear Yahweh our God, for our own good all the days, that he might let us live, as at this day.* ²⁵*And righteousness it will be for us when we are careful to do all this commandment before Yahweh our God, just as he commanded us."*

Rhetoric and Composition

The present verses are delimited at the top end by a *setumah* in M^L and a section in Sam before v. 20, and at the bottom end by a *setumah* in M^L and a section in Sam after v. 25, which is also the chapter division. Verses 24-25 make an inclusio with vv. 1-2 beginning the chapter (see Rhetoric and Composition for 6:1-3).

Portions of 6:20-25 are contained on a phylactery from Qumran (4Q128).

Notes

6:20   As stated in the Shema, children are to be taught the commandments (6:7). At some point they will want to know the story behind them. The question-and-answer method of instruction is old, here assumed to take place between father and son. Children will ask about the Passover service (Exod 12:26-27), the redemption of firstborn animals (Exod 13:14-16), and stones from the Jordan that were set up at Gilgal (Josh 4:6-7, 20-24). The two questions here are to be answered with a testimony about the exodus deliverance. Verses 20-21 survive in the modern Seder meal (cf. 16:1-8). In our own day, children in Germany are asking their parents about what went on in their country during the time of Hitler and National Socialism, and answers, when they come, are not easy to give.

in the future. מָחָר (lit. "tomorrow") is sometimes used with reference to the distant future (Rashi; cf. Exod 13:14; Josh 4:6, 21; 22:24, 27-28).

What mean? The interrogative pronoun מָה, normally "what?" can be translated "why?" or "what mean(s)?" For the latter translation, which suits the present context (AV and all modern English Versions), see elsewhere Exod 12:26; 13:14; Josh 4:6.

the testimonies and the statutes and the ordinances. See Notes for 4:1 and 4:45.

21 Cf. the confession in 26:7-8. On the importance of collective memory in ancient Israel, which survives in the Seder meal, see Honor 1953, 427-28.

Slaves we were to Pharaoh in Egypt. "Slaves" occupies the emphatic position in the clause.

a strong hand. A stereotyped expression in Deuteronomy (6:21; 7:8; 9:26; 34:12; Driver 1895, lxxix no. 12; Weinfeld 1972, 329 no. 14). On "your greatness and your strong hand," see Note for 3:24. On "strong hand and outstretched arm," see Note for 4:34.

22 Reference to "signs and wonders" is found throughout Deuteronomy (see Note for 4:34).

great and severe. גְּדֹלִים וְרָעִים. Or "great and (very) bad." Describing the plagues that afflicted Pharaoh, his house, and all Egyptians (Exodus 7-12; cf. Gen 12:17).

before our eyes. On this Deuteronomic expression, which assumes a corporate personality in ancient Israel, see Note for 1:30.

23 *and us he brought out from there.* Once again, "us" occupies the emphatic position.

24 *And Yahweh commanded us to do all these statutes, to fear Yahweh our God.* Hearing the commandments and doing them will teach Israel to fear Yahweh (see 6:1-2 and Note for 4:10).

for our own good all the days. Keeping the commandments is for Israel's long-term good (10:13). On the stock expression "all the days," see Note for 4:9.

that he might let us live. Deuteronomy views keeping the commandments as nothing less than the way to life (30:15-20; see Note for 4:1).

as at this day. I.e., today (see Note for 2:30).

Deuteronomy 6

25 This usage of "righteousness" (צְדָקָה) — another word in the emphatic position — is like that found in Gen 15:6, which says that Abraham believed Yahweh and "[Yahweh] reckoned it to him as righteousness." It was to Abraham's credit that he believed Yahweh. In Deut 24:13, returning a pledge to the poor before nightfall will be reckoned as doing "righteousness" before Yahweh, i.e., it will be a meritorious deed in the eyes of Yahweh. See also Ps 106:31. In an Aramaic papyrus of the 5th cent. B.C., Yedoniah requests the governor of Judea to provide help in rebuilding the Jewish temple at Elephantine, saying: "and a credit (וצדקה) it will be to you before Ya'u the God of Heaven" (Cowley 1923, 113-14, 30 line 27; *ANET*³, 492). In all these cases, צְדָקָה means "merit" or "credit," which is the meaning here (NJV). The LXX, as in 24:13, translates with ἐλεημοσύνη ("mercy"), which is not quite right.

we are careful to do. For this stock Deuteronomic expression, see Note for 5:1.

this commandment. הַמִּצְוָה הַזֹּאת. A stock expression in Deuteronomy, meaning all the commandments (6:25; 11:22; 15:5; 19:9; 30:11; Weinfeld 1972, 338 no. 22). The term means the same as "this law" (הַתּוֹרָה הַזֹּאת), on which see Note for 1:5.

Message and Audience

With Moses having admonished Israel to teach the commandments to the children, the day will doubtless come when they will want to know what it all means. Parents are to tell them the "old, old, story" of redemption (G. E. Wright). The people of Israel were slaves to Pharaoh in Egypt, and Yahweh, with a strong hand, brought them out with signs and wonders, bringing great affliction to Pharaoh and his house, in order that he might give them the land sworn to their fathers. These are the two great events in Israel's salvation history: deliverance from Egyptian slavery and a gift of land. The children must know Yahweh's charge that Israel keep the commandments. The larger purpose is to teach Israel to fear him, for its own long-term good and to gain the coveted gift of life. It will be reckoned to Israel as righteousness if it is careful to keep the commandments.

To a late 8th- and early 7th-cent. audience, the message is essentially the same. Children must be told Israel's "old, old story" and must know that keeping the commandments has the larger aim of bringing them to fear Yahweh, for their own good and to give them the coveted gift of life.

Deuteronomy 7

F. YOU ARE A HOLY PEOPLE (7:1-26)

1. Yahweh Will Clear Away Large and Mighty Nations (7:1-6)

*7*¹*When Yahweh your God brings you into the land that you are entering to take possession of it, and he clears away large nations from before you, the Hittites and the Girgashites and the Amorites and the Canaanites and the Perizzites and the Hivites and the Jebusites — seven nations more numerous and mightier than you, ²and Yahweh your God puts them before you and you strike them down, you shall utterly devote them to destruction; you shall not cut a covenant with them and you shall not show them favor. ³Also, you shall not make marriages with them — your daughter you shall not give to his son, and his daughter you shall not take for your son, ⁴for he would turn away your son from following me, and they would serve other gods, and the anger of Yahweh would burn against you, and he would completely destroy you quickly. ⁵But thus you shall do to them: their altars you shall break down, and their pillars you shall break in pieces, and their Asherim you shall cut down, and their idols you shall burn with fire. ⁶For you are a holy people to Yahweh your God. You Yahweh your God chose to be for himself a treasured people from all the peoples who are on the face of the earth.*

2. Yahweh Chose You Because He Loved You (7:7-11)

⁷Not because you were larger than all the peoples did Yahweh become attached to you and choose you — indeed, you were the smallest of all the peoples, ⁸rather out of Yahweh's love for you and his keeping the oath that he swore to your fathers, did Yahweh bring you out with a strong hand, and ransom you from the house of slaves, from the hand of Pharaoh, king of Egypt. ⁹Know then that Yahweh your God, he is God, the faithful God, who keeps the covenant and steadfast love for those who love him and those who keep his commandments, to the thousandth generation, ¹⁰and repaying those who hate him to his face, to destroy him; he will not delay toward one who hates him to his face; he will repay him. ¹¹So you shall keep the commandment, and the statutes and the ordinances that I am commanding you today, to do them.

3. Yahweh Will Keep Covenant and Love You (7:12-16)

¹²And it will happen because you listen to these ordinances, and you are careful and do them, that Yahweh your God will keep for you the covenant and the steadfast love that he swore to your fathers. ¹³And he will love you and bless you and multiply you; yes, he will bless the fruit of your womb and the fruit of your soil, your grain and your wine and your oil, the offspring of your cattle and the young of your flock, on the soil that he swore to your fathers to give to you. ^{14}*More blessed you will be than all the peoples; there shall not be among you a barren male or a barren female, or among your beasts.* ^{15}*And Yahweh will turn away from you every sickness and every disease of Egypt, the bad ones that you knew; he will not set them upon you, but will put them upon all who hate you.* ^{16}*And you shall consume all the peoples that Yahweh your God is giving to you; your eye shall not have pity upon them. And you shall not serve their gods, for it would be a snare to you.*

4. Yahweh Will Defeat the Larger Nations (7:17-26)

^{17}*If you say in your heart, "These nations are more numerous than I; how can I dispossess them?"* ^{18}*You need not be fearful of them; you shall surely remember what Yahweh your God did to Pharaoh and to all Egypt,* ^{19}*the great testings that your eyes have seen, the signs and the wonders, and the strong hand and the outstretched arm by which Yahweh your God brought you out. So Yahweh your God will do to all the peoples before whom you are fearful.* ^{20}*Moreover, there are the hornets Yahweh your God will send against them, until those remaining and those hiding are destroyed before you.* ^{21}*Do not tremble before them, for Yahweh your God is in your midst, a great and awesome God.* ^{22}*And Yahweh your God will clear away these nations from before you little by little; you shall not make an end of them quickly, lest the wild beasts of the field multiply against you.* ^{23}*But Yahweh your God will put them before you, and he will confuse with a great panic, until they are completely destroyed.* ^{24}*And he will give their kings into your hand, and you shall make their name perish from under the heaven; one shall not stand his ground before you, until you have completely destroyed them.* ^{25}*The idols of their gods you shall burn with fire; you shall not desire silver or gold upon them and take for yourself, lest you be ensnared by it, for it is an abomination to Yahweh your God.* ^{26}*And you shall not bring an abomination into your house, that you become a banned thing like it; you shall utterly detest and utterly regard as an abomination, for it is a banned thing.*

Rhetoric and Composition

This unit is delimited at the top end by a *setumah* in M^L and a section in Sam before v. 1, which is also the chapter division. Delimitation at the bottom end is by *a petuḥah* in M^L and a section in Sam after v. 26, which is another chapter division. There are four parts to the unit, all demarcated in M^L and Sam by section markings. In M^L these consist of:

a *setumah* after v. 6
a *petuḥah* after v. 11
a *setumah* after v. 16

Chapter 7 is a coherent whole, building on the narrative in Exod 23:20-33 (Lohfink 1963a, 167-88; Weinfeld, 380-82). One main difference between the two passages is that in Exodus an "angel" is said to go before the Israelites in their conquest of the land (vv. 20-23), whereas in Deuteronomy it is God himself who will bring the people in (Deut 7:1). The Deuteronomy narrative is structured into a keyword chiasmus:

a   Yahweh will defeat the *larger nations* (גּוֹיִם־רַבִּים)   vv. 1-6
  b   *Yahweh loves you* (מֵאַהֲבַת יְהוָה אֶתְכֶם) and has
      chosen you   vv. 7-11
  b' *Yahweh will love you* (וַאֲהֵבְךָ) and keep covenant
      with you   vv. 12-16
a' Yahweh will defeat the *larger nations* (רַבִּים הַגּוֹיִם)   vv. 17-26

In a and a' the keywords are inverted. A more complex chiastic structure has been proposed by R. O'Connell 1992a.

Portions of 7:1-26 are contained in 4QDeut^c, 4QDeut^e, 4QDeut^f, 4QDeut^m, and 4paleoDeut^r; also on a phylactery from Qumran (4Q128). The Qumran *Temple Scroll* (11QT 2) inserts portions of 7:1-2, 5, and 25-26 into the covenant renewal passage of Exod 34:10-16 (Yadin 1983, 2:1-4).

Notes

7:1 Seven "nations" are said to reside in the land Israel is about to possess (cf. Acts 13:19). All except the Girgashites are mentioned in 20:17, where their omission could be due to haplography (see Note there). These peoples, and a few others, are often listed in the OT in stereotypical fashion (Gen 15:19-21; Exod 3:8; Josh 3:10; 24:11; Ishida 1979). According to Driver, the enumerations are rhetorical rather than geographical or historical, designed to present an impressive picture of the number and variety of nations dispossessed by the Israelites. Mendenhall (1973, 155) says, however: "the traditions about the seven nations do not stem merely from some legendary formula, but are based upon social and political realities of the early period before the monarchy." The peoples are called "nations" (גּוֹיִם), which sounds stranger to the modern ear than to a hearer in antiquity, where "nation" and "people" translate the same Hebrew word גּוֹי. The point here at the beginning of the present discourse is that while these peoples are more numerous and mightier than the Israelites, Yahweh will clear them away. The promise is repeated in vv. 17-24.

When Yahweh your God brings you into the land that you are entering to take possession of it. In Exod 23:23 an "angel" will go before Israel to bring it into the land, whereas Deuteronomy affirms God's direct role in salvation history. The phrase "to enter and take possession of the land" is stereotyped in Deuteronomy (4:1, 5; 6:18; 7:1; 11:10, 29; 17:14; 23:21[20]; Note for 1:8).

and he clears away. וְנָשַׁל. The verb here and in v. 22 means "dislodge," i.e., uproot from where something is attached and fixed (Rashbam; cf. 19:5; 28:40; 2 Kgs 16:6). As it turned out, these nations were not entirely expelled from the land (Judg 1:21-36; 3:5-6). Those still around in Solomon's time were made slaves (1 Kgs 9:20-21; 2 Chr 8:7-8). Canaanites, Hittites, Perizzites, Jebusites, and Amorites were still present in the postexilic period, at which time people were intermarrying with them (Ezra 9:1).

the Hittites. A people listed in the Table of Nations as the eponymous ancestor Heth, the son of Canaan, son of Ham (Gen 10:15). A considerable amount is known today about the Hittite *(ḫatti;* Heb *ḥeth)* people, who carved out a state in Anatolia (modern Turkey) during the 2nd mill. (ca. 1650 to 1200), one that rivaled Egypt as a world power. The Hittite Empire extended into northern and central Syria. Its capital, as revealed by archaeological excavations, was Boghazköy (ancient Ḫattušas), about 150 km east of present-day Ankara. The great Hittite kingdom came to a sudden end during the brief reign of Suppiluliumas II (ca. 1180), just as the "Sea Peoples" from Greece, Crete, and the islands of the Aegean migrated eastward, causing major upheaval throughout the ANE (cf. *ANET*[3], 262-63). But Hittite presence did not end in the region, as Neo-Hittite states survived in Syria for another five centuries, after which they gradually became assimilated into the Assyrian Empire.

During the patriarchal period, Hittites in Palestine appear to have been a settled population around Hebron (Gen 23; 49:29-30; 50:13) and Beersheba (Gen 26:33-34; 27:46). Abraham, the newcomer (Gen 23:4), bought a tomb from Ephron the Hittite at Hebron to bury Sarah, his wife. After the Hittite Empire collapsed, hosts of Hittite refugees and immigrants came down into Palestine, and with them came the Jebusites, Hivites, and Girgashites, who settled in the hill country (Bright 1981, 117; Mendenhall 1973, 145, 156; B. Mazar 1986a, 42-43). Records of Ramses III (ca. 1183-1152) tell us that Hittites fled along with others to Syria at this time (Gurney 1962, 39; cf. Josh 1:4). Mendenhall notes, too, that Hittite sources prior to the Amarna Age refer to people from Anatolia migrating to territory under Egyptian control, which would include Palestine.

Deuteronomy 7

At the time of the Israelite conquest, Hittites inhabit the hill country along with Amorites, Perizzites, and Jebusites (Josh 11:3; cf. Num 13:29). The man at Luz-Bethel who leaves the area and goes to "the land of the Hittites" to build another Luz (Judg 1:22-26) is possibly a Hittite (Forrer 1936, 200; B. Mazar 1986a, 40-41). Hittites may also have been living in Jerusalem. Ezekiel later says to Jerusalem: "Your father was an Amorite, and your mother a Hittite" (Ezek 16:3; cf. v. 45).

The Hittites were never completely driven out of Palestine by the Israelites (Judg 3:5-6). David found a comrade in Ahimelech the Hittite when being pursued by Saul (1 Sam 26:6) and later was well served by Uriah the Hittite, although he failed to reward this man's loyalty in one of the most shameful incidents in the king's career (2 Samuel 11-12). Solomon sold horses to Hittites (1 Kgs 10:29; 2 Chr 1:17) and married Hittite women (1 Kgs 11:1). The Hittites to whom the horses were sold would have been Neo-Hittite kings residing in Syria after the demise of the empire (Forrer 1936, 196-97; cf. 2 Kgs 7:6). On the Hittites, see further Gurney 1962; I. J. Gelb, "Hittites," in *IDB*, 2:612-15; and G. McMahon, "Hittites in the OT" in *ABD*, 3:219-25, 231-33. Archaeological finds at Boghazköy and elsewhere are summarized in Kempinski 1979.

the Girgashites. In the Table of Nations (Gen 10:15-16), these people are also descendants of Canaan, but about them the Bible tells us nothing, save that they were inhabitants of Palestine at the time of the conquest. Mendenhall (1973, 145) notes that their name has turned up in Ugaritic and Egyptian sources of the Late Bronze Age (*grgš* [*UM* 328:14] and *bn grgš*, "son of Grgs"[*UM* 145:15]; cf. *ABD*, 2:1028). Eusebius *(Onom.)* identifies Gergasei as a city in Gilead beyond the Jordan, said to be Gerasa (modern Jerash), noting also that the NT makes mention of the Gerasenes (Matt 8:28; Mark 5:1; Luke 8:26, 37). However, some NT manuscripts read "Gergesenes" or "Gadarenes." Both Gerasa and Gedara are too far distant from the site where Jesus' miracle takes place, leaving el-Koursi on the east side of the Sea of Galilee as the most reasonable site for Gergasa (*ABD*, 2:991). But this still places descendants of the Girgashites on the east side of the Jordan. Ishida (1979, 461-64) says that of the 27 enumerations in the Bible, only three contain seven nations (Deut 7:1; Josh 3:10; 24:11). These include the Girgashites, who Ishida thinks expand the more common six-name list (11 times) in order to make the nations number seven. The Girgashites apparently came from Karkiša in Hittite Anatolia, a region mentioned in Egyptian texts dating from the time of Ramesses II (Lichtheim 1976, 61-67).

the Amorites. One of two common names for the pre-Israelite population of Palestine (1:44; Gen 15:16; Josh 7:7), the other being "Canaanites." The Amorites are listed in the Table of Nations as descendants of Canaan (Gen 10:16). They lived mainly in the hill country (Josh 11:3), but also in the plain (Judg 1:34-36). From extrabiblical sources we know that the Amorites were a

Semitic people inhabiting northern Syria from the 3rd mill. (see Note for 2:24). Ezekiel says to Jerusalem: "Your father was an Amorite and your mother a Hittite" (Ezek 16:3; cf. v. 45).

the Canaanites. Canaan in the Table of Nations is the eponymous ancestor of the Canaanites and the father of the Hittites (= Ḥeth), Jebusites, Amorites, Girgashites, Hivites, and other peoples (Gen 10:15-18; cf. 1 Chr 1:13-15). Canaan in the 13th cent. was an Egyptian province embracing western Palestine, most of Phoenicia, and southern Syria (Bright 1981, 116). "Canaanite" therefore designated the predominantly Semitic population of this province settled along the Mediterranean seacoast, in the Esdraelon Plain, in the Jordan Valley, and thinly in the hill country (see Note for 1:7). "Canaan" and "Canaanites" are mentioned in Egyptian texts from the 15th to 13th cents., i.e., from the reigns of Amenhotep II ($ANET^3$, 246); Seti I ($ANET^3$, 254); Ramesses III ($ANET^3$, 261); and Merneptah ($ANET^3$, 378). See further Ahituv 1984, 83-85.

In the Bible, "Canaanite," like "Amorite," is a general term referring to the pre-Israelite population of Palestine. The Canaanites were to be expelled in the Israelite conquest (1:7; 7:1; 20:17; Josh 3:10), but many were not driven out (Judg 1:27-33). Nevertheless, the Canaanite period for all practical purposes ends with Israel's settlement in Palestine. After this, Canaanite culture survives mainly in the coastal cities of the north, i.e., Tyre, Sidon, and Gebal (*EncJud*, 5:101).

the Perizzites. Since these people are not listed in the Table of Nations as descendants of Canaan (Gen 10:15-18), it has been surmised that they were survivors of a pre-Canaanite population in Palestine. Nuzi-Hurrian personal names suggest that the Perizzites may be of Anatolian-Hurrian origin (*EncJud*, 13:288). At the time of the conquest, they were said to be living in the hill country around Bethel and Shechem (Gen 13:7; 34:30; Josh 11:3), also in wooded country north of Shechem (Josh 17:15). After Joshua's death, Judah defeated the Perizzites and Canaanites at Bezek (Judg 1:4-5). Weinfeld says they appear to be non-Semites, because they are often grouped together with the Hivites and Jebusites, who are said to have migrated from Hittite Anatolia (see below).

the Hivites. These people are mentioned often in the OT, appearing initially in the Table of Nations as descendants of Canaan (Gen 10:17). From extrabiblical sources we learn nothing about them. In the patriarchal period, Hivites are living at Shechem (Gen 34:2), and after the Israelite conquest, at Gibeon, Chephirah, Beeroth, and Kiriath-jearim (Josh 9:17). Other Hivites lived in the Lebanon Mountains, from Mount Hermon to Hamath (Josh 11:3; Judg 3:3; 2 Sam 24:7). Those living to the north were not driven out in the conquest, and those living in Gibeon and neighboring Benjaminite cities were allowed to remain in the land because they successfully deceived Joshua into making peace with them (Joshua 9; 11:19). Speiser (1933, 26-31; *IDB*, 3:615, 664-66) argued that the biblical Hivites were in fact Hurrians, about whom a good deal is known from extrabiblical sources, e.g., the Nuzi texts (*EncJud*, 8:791-92; *ABD*, 3:335-38). This thesis, while not proven, is nevertheless credible, given the fact that Hurrians are nowhere mentioned in the Bible, an omission difficult to explain. Mendenhall (1973, 154-63) prefers to connect the Hivites with people from Kue/Cilicia (1 Kgs 10:28) and see them as another migrant people entering Palestine at the end of the Late Bronze Age when the Hittite Empire collapsed. Kue is in southern Turkey, near the city of Tarsus. Another possibility is that "Hivites" may be a variant or mistaken spelling of "Horites," a population from the northern Mesopotamian kingdom of Mitanni, which existed during the second half of the 2nd mill. (G. E. Wright).

the Jebusites. These people are also listed as descendants of Canaan in the Table of Nations (Gen 10:16). About them we know next to nothing, other than that they lived in the hill country at the time of the conquest (Num 13:29; Josh 11:3) and inhabited Jebus (= Jerusalem; Josh 18:28; Judg 19:10) when David took the city (2 Sam 5:6-7; cf. Josh 15:63; Judg 1:21). Jebusites continued to live in Jerusalem, for David bought a threshing floor from Araunah the Jebusite (2 Sam 24:18-25). In the view of Rowley (1939), David's priest Zadok, whose origins are obscure, was earlier a priest of the Jebusite shrine in Jerusalem (cf. Gen 14:17-20; Ps 110:4; Heb 5:6, 10; 6:20; 7:1-28). Weinfeld (1983c) points out that the Jerusalem priestly cult has many affinities with Hittite-Hurrian rituals. In his view, the Jebusites may have migrated, like the Hivites, from Anatolia after the collapse of the Hittite Empire.

seven nations more numerous and mightier than you. Deuteronomy emphasizes that the nations to be dispossessed are "more numerous/greater and mightier" than Israel (v. 17; 4:38; 9:1; 11:23). The LXX has πολλὰ καὶ ἰσχυρότερα ὑμῶν ("numerous and stronger than you").

2 *and Yahweh your God puts them before you and you strike them down.* Yahweh will give the nations into Israel's hand, and Israel will destroy them in holy war (see Note for 1:30).

you shall utterly devote them to destruction. Hebrew הַחֲרֵם ("devote to destruction") is a term taken from holy war, referring to the ban (חֵרֶם) placed upon a captured city's inhabitants — sometimes also cattle and other spoil — for the purpose of devoting (= destroying) them as a gift to Yahweh (2:34-35; 3:5-6; 7:1-2, 26; 13:16-18[15-17]; 20:16-17; Exod 22:19[20]; Josh 6:21; 1 Sam 15:3). According to Lev 27:29, no one falling under the ban could be ransomed; he or she must be put to death. In the earlier wars against Sihon and Og, men, women, and children came under the ban, but not the animals (2:34-35; 3:6-7). In Israel's subsequent wars against distant peoples, only (adult) males need be destroyed; the women, children, cattle, and other material goods could be taken as booty (20:10-15). But in wars against the Canaanites, with the apparent exception of Ai, everything was to be devoted to destruction (20:16-18; cf. Josh

6:21). Some wars did in fact become חֵרֶם wars (Josh 10:28-40; 11:10-20), but we learn from the biblical narrative that the command to devote everything to destruction was not always carried out. Sometimes people simply disobeyed the command and were judged for their disobedience (Achan in Joshua 7; King Saul in 1 Samuel 15). When the people went up against Ai the second time, they were permitted to take cattle and spoil for themselves (Josh 8:2). It happened, too, that some of the Canaanites simply could not be driven out, in which case they were subdued and usually put to forced labor (Josh 16:10; 17:13; Judg 1:27-35; 1 Kgs 9:20-21).

Devoting conquered peoples to the gods was practiced by other ancient peoples. The term *ḥrm* appears on the 9th-cent. Moabite Stone (line 17), where Mesha says he "devoted" seven thousand Israelite men, boys, women, girls, and maidservants to Ashtar-Chemosh (C. D. Ginsburg 1871, 5-6; *ANET*[3], 320). For other parallels in the ancient world, see Lohfink, *ḥāram*, in *TDOT,* 5:180-99.

The חֵרֶם law has been viewed as unnecessarily severe on the part of Yahweh, particularly with Israel emerging the victor and other peoples being exterminated. Seeds are present for an extreme form of nationalism. Yet the Moabites did it. And the biblical witness makes it clear that people within Israel suffered a fate no less severe if they did evil, particularly in worshipping other gods. And the day came, too, when the entire nation of Israel came under holy war judgment from Yahweh, resulting in its destruction. When Achan defied the ban by taking devoted things for himself, he and everything belonging to him — sons, daughters, oxen, asses, and sheep — were destroyed (Josh 7:24-25). If an entire Israelite city fell victim to idolatry, it would be devoted to destruction (13:13-19[12-18]). Isaiah and Jeremiah tell us that Yahweh, in announcing utter destruction upon the nations, included what remained of Israel (Isa 34:1-15; Jer 25:9). Jeremiah, above all, had the unpleasant task of informing Judah and the northern Israel remnant that Yahweh had declared holy war on it for breach of covenant; no one would be exempt (Jer 5:17; 6:21; 9:20[21]; 16:3-4, and passim). Even the beasts would be destroyed (Jer 7:20; 21:6; 36:29). Judgment on such a grand scale did occur, and the complaint heard often in the book of Jeremiah is that Yahweh's destruction left the land without "human or beast" (Jer 32:43; 33:10[2x], 12).

Subsequent generations have nevertheless remained horrified at the idea of חֵרֶם wars. Uneasiness over the commands here and in 20:17 is expressed in the Talmud and by later Jewish writers (Hoffman 1999, 197), not to mention the horror of Jews and everyone else over the Holocaust of the last century. Christians, too, have had great difficulty in reconciling the present law with NT teaching. An attempt is commonly made to give qualified justification for the practice of holy war in biblical times, pointing out, for example, what the OT says about the need to destroy the Canaanites so their abominable religious practices would be wiped out (7:4; 20:18; cf. Exod 23:33; Driver; G. E. Wright). Those who do this, typically go on to affirm that in the light of Gospel teaching there is no longer a place for such a practice. Wright (1953, 458) says:

> The conception is one which a Christian has great difficulty in accepting, though the perplexing thing is that if Israel had been dominated by any less tolerant attitude she would have amalgamated with her pagan neighbors and in so doing lost all that she was to contribute to the world. The ideas behind the conception of the ban cannot be accepted as the Word of God for the modern Christian, but they may well have been so for Israel in the sense that they must be understood in the light of God's purpose and what was needed in that day and under those conditions to accomplish it.

Hoffman (1999, 198), a Jewish humanist, sees a problem with holy war ideology. His response is simply to take exception to the law in the present day. The rabbis, in fact, mitigated the holy war command already in their time. For further discussion of the holy war "ban," see Weinfeld, 382-84; and Tigay, Excursus 18. On Deuteronomy and holy war, see von Rad 1953, 45-59; 1991, 115-27.

you shall not cut a covenant with them. Israel was to make no covenants (treaties) with the inhabitants of Canaan (7:1-2; cf. Exod 23:32; 34:11-16; Judg 2:2). Such might otherwise have been brokered if the conquered people agreed to perform forced labor in exchange for their lives (Joshua 9; 1 Sam 11:1). Agreements of this type for corvée work are attested in Egypt (Weinfeld 1985). Deuteronomy allows covenants in exchange for corvée labor only if Israel is fighting a distant enemy (20:11-15). The Gibeonites tricked Israel into making a covenant (Josh 9:6), but later Ahab was chastised by an unnamed prophet for making a covenant with Ben-hadad after defeating him and the Syrians, instead of "devoting" the Syrian king to destruction (1 Kgs 20:34-43).

and you shall not show them favor. וְלֹא תְחָנֵּם. The verb is חנן ("to be gracious, show favor"). Israelites are not to show Canaanite peoples any favor, which in this case means "mercy" (Freedman, Lundbom, *ḥānan*, in *TDOT*, 5:35).

3-4 Mixed marriages were considered ill advised even in the patriarchal period (Gen 24:3; 27:46; 28:6-9), also during the time of the Judges (Judg 14:3), yet they did occur (Gen 26:34-35; Judg 14:8). The danger of intermarrying with the Canaanites was that Israel would then be led to worship other gods (Exod 34:11-16), which would break the covenant, provoke Yahweh to anger, and cause Yahweh to destroy his people. And that is precisely what happened when Israel was unable to drive out certain inhabitants of the land (Judg 3:3-6; cf. Josh 23:12-13). Mixed marriages became a great problem with Solomon (1 Kgs 11:1-13) and with Ahab (1 Kgs 16:30-33), in both cases leading to a worship of foreign gods. Weinfeld notes that in the postexilic period, when idolatry had ceased to be a threat, mixed marriages were disallowed because they would contaminate the holy race (Ezra 9:2). But why are mixed marriages being disallowed here, when the command is that Israel completely exterminate all peoples in the land? Does Moses already anticipate that the extermination will not be complete, in which case Israel is told not to intermarry with Canaanites who remain? Or perhaps he is simply giving this directive as another reason for Yahweh wanting the holy war ban applied broadly and unconditionally.

and you shall not make marriages with them. וְלֹא תִתְחַתֵּן בָּם. Literally, "you shall not make yourself a son-in-law with them" (cf. Gen 34:9; Josh 23:12; 1 Sam 18:21).

for he would turn away your son from following me. I.e., the foreigner, who gives the son or daughter in marriage. Here, as elsewhere in Deuteronomy, Moses sometimes slips into the speaking voice of Yahweh (7:4; 11:14-15; 17:3; 28:20, 68; 29:4-5[5-6]).

and they would serve other gods. Both husband and wife would end up serving other gods. On the importance in Deuteronomy of serving Yahweh and only Yahweh, see Note for 6:13. Not going after other gods is covered in the first commandment (5:7). Throughout Deuteronomy it is a constant warning (see Note for 6:14).

and the anger of Yahweh would burn against you. Yahweh's anger will burn hot if Israel breaks the covenant and goes after other gods (see Note for 6:15).

and he would completely destroy you quickly. For variations of this stock Deuteronomic phrase, see Note for 4:25-26.

5 All sacred objects of the Canaanites — altars, stone pillars, and wooden Asherim, must be destroyed (12:2-3; cf. Exod 23:24; 34:13). Upright stone pillars were masculine fertility symbols, and Asherim were feminine fertility symbols, either trees or wooden poles. Once Israel became settled in the land, people were not to erect pillars or place Asherim beside Yahweh's altar (16:21-22). An Asherah next to Yahweh's altar would make the Canaanite goddess Yahweh's consort. This indignity appears to have occurred during the monarchy. On Asherah in the OT and the extrabiblical literature, including the archaeological evidence for "Yahweh and his Asherah," see J. Day 1986 and Note for 12:3.

6 *For you are a holy people to Yahweh your God.* Israel is marked as Yahweh's (own) people, or Yahweh's "holy people" (4:20; 7:6; 9:29; 14:2, 21; 26:18-19; 27:9; 28:9; 29:12[13]; cf. Jer 2:3; Driver 1895, lxxix no. 7b; Weinfeld 1972, 328 no. 10), where "holy" (קָדוֹשׁ) has the meaning "set apart." The term does not denote superior moral character. Israel is to be a people set apart from the Canaanites, whose religious symbols have just been consigned to destruction. Israel is named Yahweh's own people in the Song of Moses (32:9) and the Blessing of Moses (33:29), two old poems incorporated into Deuteronomy, also in

Exod 19:5-6, from where Deuteronomy may have quarried the idea (Milgrom 1976b, 5). Israel's holiness gets renewed emphasis in Leviticus 17–26, a legal corpus called the "Holiness Code." There the point is made that Israel is holy because Yahweh its God is holy (Lev 19:2). Childs (1993, 421-22) says: "The most basic Old Testament term to describe God's special relationship to Israel is the expression 'people of Yahweh.'" Citing an earlier work of von Rad (1929), Childs continues: "It has long been observed that the most extensive and profound theological reflection on the subject of the people of God is found in the book of Deuteronomy." In the NT, the church is addressed as "a chosen race, a royal priesthood, a holy nation, God's own people" (1 Pet 2:9).

For. The particle כִּי functions to underscore the gravity of the prior commands (vv. 2-5) and to mark Israel as a people "set apart" from those peoples to be dispossessed in Canaan.

You Yahweh your God chose to be for himself a treasured people from all the peoples who are on the face of the earth. The pronoun "you" stands at the beginning of the Hebrew sentence for emphasis. The expression "to be to someone" (היה ל) means to attain a certain status in relation to somebody (Weinfeld). In Deuteronomy "to be a people to him (i.e., Yahweh)" is stereotyped (4:20; 7:6; 14:2; 26:18; 27:9; Weinfeld 1972, 327 no. 6). The verb "choose" (בחר) occurs often in Deuteronomy with reference to choices Yahweh has made and choices Israel must make (see Note for 12:5). Here it denotes for the first time in the book Yahweh's choice of Israel as a holy people (4:37; 7:7; 10:15; 14:2). The idea, however, occurs elsewhere in the OT, e.g., in the celebrated statement of Amos, where Yahweh says: "Only you have I known of all the families of the earth . . ." (Amos 3:2; Lundbom 2007a, 72). Election is a bedrock OT concept. Yahweh elected Abraham to bring blessing on all peoples on earth (Gen 12:1-3; G. E. Wright 1950, 50) and named Jeremiah as a prophet even before forming him in the womb, where the ideas of election and holiness combine, as they do here (Jer 1:5; Lundbom 1999, 230-32). Election of Israel becomes a full-blown concept in the Servant Songs of Second Isaiah (Isa 41:8-9; 42:1; 43:10, 20; 44:1-2; 45:4; 49:7). On Israel's election as God's chosen people, see also Num 23:19-24; 1 Kgs 3:8; Jer 33:24; Isa 65:9, 15, 22; Pss 33:12; 135:4; cf. G. E. Mendenhall, "Election," in *IDB*, 2:76-82; L. H. Silberman, "Chosen People," in *EncJud*, 5:498-502. In the NT, see Paul's discussion in Romans 11.

a treasured people. עַם סְגֻלָּה. Hebrew סְגֻלָּה, occurring also in 14:2; 26:18; Exod 19:5; Ps 135:4; Mal 3:17, denotes a special possession, something treasured and prized. Ibn Ezra says reference is to something beautiful, the likes of which can be found nowhere else (cf. Eccl 2:8; and 1 Chr 29:3, where it refers to royal wealth). Israel is therefore Yahweh's prized possession. Cf. תִּפְאֶרֶת ("glorious decoration") in Jer 13:11 and designations given the church in 1 Pet 2:9. An Akkadian text of the 2nd mill. calls the king of Alalakh "servant of the god IM, beloved of the god IM, devotee *(zi-ki-il-tum)* of the god IM" (Collon 1975, 12-13), which Weinfeld (p. 368) says offers help in understanding the Aramaic rendering "beloved" *(ḥbyb)* for סְגֻלָּה.

on the face of the earth. עַל־פְּנֵי הָאֲדָמָה. On this idiom, see Note for 6:15.

7-8 *Not because you were larger than all the peoples did Yahweh become attached to you and choose you — indeed, you were the smallest of all the peoples, rather out of Yahweh's love for you and his keeping the oath that he swore to your fathers.* Yahweh's choice of Israel had nothing to do with numbers, since she was the smallest of peoples (4:38; 9:1; 11:23). It was rather because of Yahweh's love for Israel, and a determination to keep the promise to the fathers. Both were acts of pure grace. This love remains a mystery (Moran), a divine secret (G. E. Wright), known only to Yahweh. Deuteronomy is the only book in the Pentateuch teaching God's love for and election of Israel where the two ideas often occur together (4:37; 7:7-8; 10:15; Moran 1963b). Some believe that Yahweh's love for Israel was first taught by Hosea, who was the first to use a marriage metaphor to describe the covenant bond (Hosea 1-3; 9:15; 11:1-4; 14:5[4]). That may well be the case, but in Deuteronomy this metaphor is never explicit. Other OT texts stating Yahweh's love for Israel include 1 Kgs 10:9; Zeph 3:17; Jer 31:3; Isa 43:4; 48:14; 63:9; Mal 1:2. Hebrew אהב ("to love") is a term of emotion, embodying the idea of "breathing" (D. W. Thomas 1939). In the NT, John says that God sent forth Jesus, his only son, because he "loved the world" (John 3:16).

did Yahweh become attached to you. חָשַׁק יְהוָה בָּכֶם. The verb חשק means "stick, bind to" (Exod 27:17; 38:17, 28), denoting in some cases the desire or attachment felt by a man towards a woman (Gen 34:8; Deut 21:11). Here it says Yahweh became attached to Israel in love; in 10:15 it says that Yahweh had an attachment to the fathers.

rather out of Yahweh's love for you. כִּי מֵאַהֲבַת יְהוָה אֶתְכֶם. The particle כִּי here means "rather" (Rashi).

and his keeping the oath that he swore to your fathers. I.e., to give them and their descendants the land (see Note for 1:8).

did Yahweh bring you out with a strong hand, and ransom you from the house of slaves, from the hand of Pharaoh, king of Egypt. "Yahweh brought you out with a strong hand" is a stock expression in Deuteronomy (see Note for 6:21). On the stereotypical "strong hand and outstretched arm," which is used to refer to Yahweh's deliverance in the exodus, see v. 19 and Note for 4:34.

and ransom you from the house of slaves. וַיִּפְדְּךָ מִבֵּית עֲבָדִים. The verb פדה occurs often in Deuteronomy (7:8; 9:26; 13:6[5]; 15:15; 21:8; 24:18; Driver 1895, lxxxii no. 56; Weinfeld 1972, 326 no. 1) and can be translated "ransom" or "redeem." Driver goes with "ransom," preferring "redeem" for גאל, which has a basic meaning of "reclaim" (Lev 25:25-33; Jer 32:7-8). On גאל in Deuteronomy,

Deuteronomy 7

see Note for 19:6. The LXX translates here with ἐλυτρώσατο ("he ransomed"), which together with derivatives occurs commonly in the NT (cf. Mark 10:45). When either פדה or גאל is used of God's deliverance in the exodus, there is no thought of a price being paid (G. E. Wright). "House of slaves" is the Deuteronomic term for the place of confinement where slaves were kept (see Note for 5:6).

9-10 Yahweh's act of election is followed now by a statement about his nature, similar to the self-asseveration in Exod 34:6-7. Yahweh is long on steadfast love to those who love him and keep his commandments but short with those who hate him, where hatred is expressed most pointedly in disobedience to the covenant demands (cf. Exod 20:5-6; Deut 5:9-10; Num 14:18; Jer 32:18-19). Here one is reminded of the conditional nature of the Horeb covenant. The unconditional oath made to the fathers was cited in v. 8. People may think that because of Yahweh's oath to the fathers they do not need to obey the covenant demands.

Know then that Yahweh your God, he is God. There is no other (see Note for 4:35). On the expression "so you shall know" in Deuteronomy, see Note for 4:39.

the faithful God, who keeps the covenant and steadfast love. Yahweh can be counted on to hold up his end of the covenant. He is "the faithful God" (הָאֵל הַנֶּאֱמָן), an attribute attested in the Song of Moses (Deut 32:4) and elsewhere (Ps 30:10[9]; Isa 49:7), and has shown "steadfast love" (חֶסֶד) toward Israel, which is the love of the covenant (see Note for 5:9-10). Faithfulness and steadfast love can be seen also in Yahweh keeping his promises (Gen 24:27; 1 Kgs 3:6; 8:23-25). The LXX translates θεὸς πιστός ("the God who is trustworthy/deserving belief").

for those who love him. On Deuteronomy's teaching of "love for God" and what it entails, see Note for 6:5. The Assyrian king, in response to the kindness of his servant, promises "goodness and kindness" to his descendants (Weinfeld 1973b, 195).

to the thousandth generation. לְאֶלֶף דּוֹר. I.e., indefinitely, not just for three or four generations, which is how long his wrath lasts (see Note for 5:9-10).

and repaying those who hate him to his face, to destroy him; he will not delay toward one who hates him to his face; he will repay him. There is another face of God, which is to repay blatant evil and enmity towards him (32:35, 41; Jer 32:18; 51:6; Isa 59:18). The plural suffix on מְשַׁלֵּם refers to "every one of his enemies" (ibn Ezra; Driver; Moran). Rashbam says God will punish sinners either in their own lifetime or (subsequently) up to the fourth generation (cf. Exod 20:5; 34:7; Deut 5:9; Num 14:18). In his view, there is no punishment for any sin beyond the fourth generation. But the verse may be reflecting the retribution formula in Deut 24:16, reiterated in Jeremiah and Ezekiel (Jer 31:30; Ezek 18:4),

Deuteronomy 7

which states that each person will be held accountable for his own sin. If so, the present verse is departing from the old retribution formula, which holds that the sins of the ancestors are meted out on subsequent generations (Weinfeld). But Rashbam is correct in saying that vv. 9-10 reiterate the principle that "the measure of good [i.e., reward] is greater than the measure of misfortune [i.e., punishment]." Weinfeld says that praying congregations in postexilic times preserved both the old formula expressing communal responsibility and the Deuteronomic formula expressing individual responsibility. In the NT, punishment will come to some individuals after death (Matt 13:24-30, 36-43, 47-50; Luke 16:19-31, and passim).

11 This is the bottom line, so far as Deuteronomy is concerned: Each Israelite must do Yahweh's commandments (4:40; 6:1-2). On the Deuteronmic expression "to keep/be careful to do," see Note for 5:1.

12 Looking to the future, Moses reiterates the conditional nature of the Horeb covenant: If Israel is careful to do these ordinances, Yahweh will keep the covenant and his steadfast love will continue. On the stock expression "you shall be careful and you shall do," see Note for 4:6.

13 Israel can expect three gracious outpourings for covenant obedience: love, blessing, and fecundity. Yahweh's love for Israel is longstanding (v. 8), so too his blessing upon Israel (see Note for 2:7). Continued blessing is contingent here upon Israel obeying Yahweh's commands. The Horeb covenant contains blessings and curses, and these will affect "the fruit of your body and the fruit of your soil" (28:4, 11, 18, 51, 53; cf. Exod 23:25-26).

and multiply you. See Note for 6:3.

the fruit of your womb. פְּרִי־בִטְנְךָ, an idiom (ibn Ezra: euphemism) meaning "human offspring," occurs often in Deuteronomy (7:13; 28:4, 11, 18, 53; 30:9; Weinfeld 1972, 345 no. 2b) and elsewhere in the OT (Gen 30:2; Isa 13:18; Mic 6:7; Pss 127:3; 132:11). Hebrew בֶּטֶן (lit. "belly") can also mean "womb" (*TDOT*, 2:94; cf. Jer 1:5; Job 3:11; 10:19). The LXX translates τῆς κοιλίας σου ("of your belly").

your grain and your wine and your oil. The principal crops of Canaan (8:8-9; 28:38-40). The "grain, wine, and oil" triad is found throughout Deuteronomy (7:13; 11:14; 12:17; 14:23; 18:4; 28:51; Driver 1895, lxxxi no. 30); also in Hos 2:10, 24(8, 22); Jer 31:12, and elsewhere.

the offspring of your cattle. שְׁגַר אֲלָפֶיךָ. I.e., your calves.

and the young of your flock. וְעַשְׁתְּרֹת צֹאנֶךָ. I.e., your lambs and young goats. The term for "young" (עַשְׁתְּרֹת) is related to Ashtoreth (= Astarte), goddess of fecundity.

on the soil that he swore to your fathers to give to you. On this Deuteronomic expression, see Note for 1:8.

14 Moses lapses here into hyperbole. Blessing is again measured in terms of fecundity (v. 13; Exod 23:26). "Beasts" refer to domesticated cattle.

Deuteronomy 7

15 On the diseases of Egypt, see 28:27, 35, 60-61; Exod 15:26. A Jewish tradition identifies the "sickness" (חלי) here as one arising from bile (Preuss 1978, 187).

16 Returning to the holy war theme of vv. 1-5: the destruction of Canaan's inhabitants.

your eye shall not have pity upon them. A common Deuteronomic admonition in cases where people may be inclined toward leniency (7:16; 13:9[8]; 19:13, 21; 25:12; Driver 1895, lxxxi no. 34). There are cases where Yahweh, too, shows no pity in meting out judgment (Jer 13:14; Ezek 7:4; 24:14).

And you shall not serve their gods, for it would be a snare to you. Serving other gods will prove to be a snare to Israel (v. 25; Exod 23:33; Judg 2:3; Ps 106:36), leading ultimately to loss of the land and dispersion to a place where other gods can be served (see Note for 6:13).

17 Returning to the beginning of the discourse (v. 1: "nations more numerous and mightier than you"). See also 9:1 and 11:23 ("greater and mightier than you"). The people, not surprisingly, are concerned about their weakness. On the expressions "If you say in your heart" or "Do not say in your heart," see also 8:17; 9:4; 18:21.

18 *You need not be fearful of them.* Stereotypical war language in Deuteronomy (see Note for 1:20-21).

you shall surely remember what Yahweh your God did to Pharaoh and to all Egypt. This is Moses' answer to Israel's fear about being outmanned by an enemy. In the first place, Yahweh will lead the battle and secondly, Israel must simply remember what Yahweh did against the mighty Egyptians. On the importance of "remembering" in Deuteronomy, see Note for 8:2.

19 *the great testings that your eyes have seen, the signs and the wonders.* "The testings" were the plagues that tested Pharaoh and the Egyptians; "the signs and wonders" included the plagues, but more broadly were the spectacular occurrences pointing beyond themselves to God (see Note for 4:34). On the stock expression "that your eyes have seen," see Note for 4:9.

the strong hand and the outstretched arm. On this Deuteronomic cliché, see Note for 4:34.

by which Yahweh your God brought you out. So Yahweh your God will do to all the peoples before whom you are fearful. Yahweh brought Israel out of Egypt; this time Yahweh will overcome the foes in Canaan.

20 It is unclear whether actual hornets are meant (Rashi; Driver) or whether "hornets" is a metaphor for the invading Israelites (ibn Ezra; Moran; Weinfeld; cf. 1:44; Exod 23:28; Josh 24:12; Isa 7:18-19; Ps 118:12). Ibn Ezra takes הַצִּרְעָה to be a bodily sickness (cf. Lev 13:2), and Driver sees the hornets as a plague penetrating hiding places of Canaanites who remain, forcing them out. Another suggestion has been put forth by Neufeld (1980). He points out that in-

Deuteronomy 7

sects were used as warfare agents in the ANE, so what we may have here is an early form of biological warfare.

21 *Do not tremble before them, for Yahweh your God is in your midst.* Moses told the Israelites not to "tremble" before the Canaanites when they prepared to enter the land the first time (1:29-30), and for the same reason: Yahweh would fight for them. Now he says the same thing (cf. 20:3; 31:6). On Yahweh's promise of dwelling in Israel's midst, see Note for 6:15.

a great and awesome God. אֵל גָּדוֹל וְנוֹרָא. On Yahweh's greatness, see Note for 3:24. Yahweh is "awesome" (10:17), and his name, too, is "awesome" (28:58).

22 Repeating Exod 23:29-30. Rashbam says לֹא תוּכַל is to be translated "you shall not" or the like, not "you will not be able"; the idiom is an admonition (cf. 12:17; 17:15). The idiom is also Deuteronomic (7:22; 12:17; 16:5; 17:15; 21:16; 22:3, 19, 29; 24:4; Driver 1895, lxxxii no. 44). That the conquest was not completed all at once is attested in Judg 2:20-23. The nations inhabiting Canaan were only gradually driven out.

little by little. מְעַט מְעָט. The repetition expresses a gradual process (GKC §133k).

23 Yahweh will wage a noisy and chaotic battle to confuse (וְהָמָם) the enemy (cf. Exod 23:27). The same happened when the Egyptians pursued the Israelites at the Red Sea (וַיָּהָם in Exod 14:24). Here, as there, the foe will be completely destroyed. The N-stem of שמד ("be completely destroyed") and the internal H-stem in v. 24 are both strong verbs (see Note for 1:27).

and he will confuse. The Versions have "he will confuse them."

24 *And he will give their kings into your hand.* According to the book of Joshua, this is what happened (Josh 10:22-27; 11:12; 12:7-24).

and you shall make their name perish from under the heaven. "Making perish" or "blotting out" the name (from under heaven) means that no remembrance of them will survive (25:19; Exod 17:14). A variation of a stock Deuteronomic expression, occurring also in Northwest Semitic and Assyrian inscriptions (7:24; 9:14; 25:19; 29:19[20]; Weinfeld, 410; 1972, 107-8; 347 no. 13).

one shall not stand his ground before you. לֹא־יִתְיַצֵּב אִישׁ בְּפָנֶיךָ. Another stock Deuteronomic expression (7:24; 11:25; cf. Josh 1:5; 10:8; 23:9; Weinfeld 1972, 344 no. 14).

25 *The idols of their gods you shall burn with fire.* The command to burn idols is found only in Deuteronomic law (Weinfeld; cf. 7:5). Idols were commonly made of wood with gold and silver overlay (Isa 30:22; Hab 2:19; Jer 10:4), so they could be burned. The Assyrians and Babylonians decked their gods with gold garments or gold ornament attached to garments, a mode of decoration attested in Babylonian texts from the 7th cent. (Oppenheim 1949, 180). For the fashioning of idols in silver and gold, see also Hos 13:2; Isa 40:19 (silver chains); 46:6; Pss 115:4; 135:15; Ep Jer; Wis 13:10.

you shall not desire silver or gold upon them and take for yourself, lest you be ensnared by it, for it is an abomination to Yahweh your God. Here it is not the idol itself threatening to ensnare the Israelite (v. 16), but the gold and silver that is on it.

an abomination to Yahweh. תּוֹעֲבַת יְהוָה. The terms תּוֹעֲבַת יְהוָה ("abomination to Yahweh") and תּוֹעֵבָה ("abomination") occur often in Deuteronomy (Driver 1895, lxxxiii no. 70; Weinfeld 1972, 323 nos. 1, 1a), referring to persons (23:8[7]; 25:16), practices (24:4), or things (12:31; 14:3) deemed detestable. What Yahweh finds most detestable are idols (7:25-26; 27:15; cf. Jer 16:18) and people leading others in idolatrous ways (13:13-15[12-14]; 17:2-4). The latter include diviners, soothsayers, and other practitioners of the secret arts (18:9-12). Pagan magic is an abomination to Yahweh (see Note for 18:9). Practices associated with idolatrous worship are also abominations (20:18), the most odious being child sacrifice (12:31; 18:9-10; cf. Jer 7:30-31; 32:35). Offerings to Yahweh emanating from cultic prostitutes — both men and women — are abominations as well (23:18-19[17-18]).

The earliest OT occurrence of the term "abomination" is in Deut 32:16 (Weinfeld 1972, 323), where reference is to practices associated with the worship of other gods. An abomination to Yahweh is one who weighs deceitfully on the scales (25:13-16; cf. Jer 6:15 = 8:12), eats forbidden foods (14:3), offers blemished sacrifices (17:1), and wears clothes of the opposite sex (22:5; see Note there). In the Babylonian literature, judges who pervert justice are said to be an abomination to the gods (see Note for 16:19). The term "abomination" appears often in the book of Proverbs, where deceit, hypocrisy, false pretension, and wickedness in general come in for censure (Prov 8:7; 11:20; 12:22; 15:8; 16:12; 21:27; 29:27). For the various abominations in Deuteronomy and Proverbs, with parallels in Egyptian and Babylonian literature, particularly the Egyptian Wisdom of Amenemope (*ANET*³, 423, chs. 10 and 13), see Hallo (1985-86, 35-38) and Weinfeld (1972, 267-69).

26 Precious metal from idols must not be brought into one's house; it comes under the ban and must be devoted to Yahweh (Josh 6:18-19, 24). If one does such a thing, that person will come under the ban. Achan suffered this fate because he took for himself spoil of silver and gold after the battle of Jericho, causing Israel's defeat in the follow-up battle against Ai (Joshua 7).

you shall utterly detest. שַׁקֵּץ תְּשַׁקְּצֶנּוּ. The verb is used in Leviticus with reference to prohibited foods (Lev 11:11, 13, 43; 20:25). In Deut 29:16(17), שִׁקּוּצֵיהֶם ("their detestable things") is a disparaging term, referring to the disgusting idols (Weinfeld 1972, 323 no. 3; cf. Jer 4:1; 7:30; 13:27; 16:18; 32:34).

for it is a banned thing. כִּי־חֵרֶם הוּא. The noun חֵרֶם ("ban, devoted thing") occurs one other time in 13:18(17). The LXX translates the Hebrew term with ἀνάθημα. On the ban in holy war, see Note for 7:2.

Deuteronomy 7

Message and Audience

Moses begins this discourse by listing the seven nations Israel will meet up with when it enters the land. All are more populous and stronger than Israel, but Moses says that Yahweh will clear them away before the people's eyes. When this happens and Israel has put them down, the conquered foes are to be totally destroyed and devoted to Yahweh. No covenants with them, no mercy, no marriages. Israel may be tempted to intermarry with some who are still around, but they must not do that, for the foreigners would doubtless turn away sons (and daughters) from worshipping Yahweh and in no time they would be worshipping other gods. Then the anger of Yahweh would burn hot, and he would quickly destroy Israel. What Israel must do is to break down their altars, smash the stone pillars, cut down the Asherim, and burn the idols with fire. Israel is a holy people to Yahweh, who chose the nation as a treasured possession from all peoples on the face of the earth.

How did it come about that Yahweh chose and became attached to Israel? Moses says it was not because of its size, for Israel was the fewest of all peoples. It was rather because of Yahweh's love for Israel and his determination to keep the promise sworn to Israel's fathers. Both were acts of divine grace, and any further reason for the choice is known only to Yahweh. What is known, however, is that Yahweh ransomed Israel from Egyptian slavery, the purpose of which was to make Israel know that Yahweh is God, the faithful God who keeps covenant and steadfast love to those who love him and keep his commandments. His promise is for a thousand generations, that is, indefinitely. But Israel is put on notice that the Horeb covenant remains conditional and requires obedience on Israel's part to be kept intact. Yahweh will repay all who openly hate him, and their destruction will come about quickly. Moses therefore reminds Israel to keep all the statutes and ordinances he is commanding them this day.

So far as the future is concerned, if Israel listens to these commandments and is careful to do them, Yahweh will keep his covenant and the steadfast love sworn to the fathers. He will love, bless, and multiply Israel, which is to say children will be born, the land will yield grain, wine, and oil, and the flocks and herds will bring forth young in abundance. Israel will be blessed among all nations, with no barrenness in people or animals. Health and well-being will be the norm, for Yahweh will take away all the horrible sicknesses and diseases of Egypt, which some may still remember, and put them on those who hate Israel. The nations soon to be given into Israel's hand will be consumed, and Israel is to show them no pity. Above all, Israel is not to serve their gods, for that would be a snare to them.

If they are still thinking in their heart, "These nations are larger than we are; how can we dispossess them?" Moses says they should not fear them. Let the fearful of heart remember what Yahweh did to Pharaoh and all Egypt. Let him remember the plagues, the signs and the wonders, and Yahweh's strong arm that brought Israel out of the place. Yahweh will do it again, sending hornets to flush out any still hiding in caves. All will be destroyed. So Israel should not tremble. Yahweh is in its midst, and Yahweh is a great and awesome God. He will clear away the nations, not quickly, but little by little, lest the wild beasts multiply and give them another kind of trouble.

Yahweh promises to wage a noisy battle that will throw the enemy into confusion, causing panic, routing, and final destruction. Kings will be given into Israel's hand and remembered no more. No one will be able to stand against the Yahweh-led host. Idols of all gods, as Moses just said, must be burned. And let no one think of stripping silver and gold off the idols for themselves, for even the precious metals on these inert wonders is an abomination to Yahweh. It too will be a snare. Let no one bring any abomination into their house, lest they themselves become a banned thing. Moses says the people must utterly detest any abomination; it comes under the ban and must be devoted to Yahweh.

A late 8th- and early 7th-cent. Judahite audience will be reminded here about the idolatrous religion of the nations Israel dispossessed in taking the land and how Israel was to be a people set apart as Yahweh's special possession. It will also be reminded that Yahweh chose Israel because of his unexplainable love for the people. Now, more recently, religious practices of peoples near and far have penetrated the land of promise, and people have experienced firsthand the heavy hand of divine judgment. The Assyrians cleared out Transjordan and Galilee in 734, and in 722 they destroyed Samaria, bringing the northern kingdom to an end. In 701 Judah was overrun by this same ruthless foe, and only a miracle kept Jerusalem from being destroyed. Will the people remaining realize that blessing comes from covenant obedience and curses come from covenant disobedience? This sermon put into the mouth of Moses states the matter clearly enough.

G. REMEMBER YAHWEH AND HIS TESTING (8:1-20)

8¹*All the commandment that I am commanding you today you shall be careful to do, in order that you may live and multiply and enter and possess the land that Yahweh swore to your fathers. ²And you shall remember all the way that Yahweh your God led you these forty years in the wilderness, in order that he might humble you to test you to know what was in your heart, whether you would keep his commandments or not. ³Yes, he humbled you and made you hungry, then he fed you the manna that you did not know and your fathers did not know, in order* *that he might make you know that one does not live by bread alone, but one lives by everything that goes out of the mouth of Yahweh.* ⁴*Your outer garment did not wear out upon you, and your foot did not swell these forty years.* ⁵*So you shall know with your heart that just as a man disciplines his son, Yahweh your God disciplines you.*

⁶*So you shall keep the commandments of Yahweh your God, to walk in his ways and to fear him.* ⁷*For Yahweh your God is bringing you into a good land, a land of streams of water, springs, and deep rivers, going forth in the valley and in the mountain;* ⁸*a land of wheat and barley, and vines and fig trees and pomegranates, a land of olives bearing oil and honey;* ⁹*a land in which you will not eat bread in scarcity — you will not lack anything in it; a land in which its stones are iron and from its mountains you can dig copper.* ¹⁰*And you will eat and become sated, then you shall bless Yahweh your God upon the good land that he has given you.*

¹¹*Be careful for yourself, lest you forget Yahweh your God by not keeping his commandments and his ordinances and his statutes that I am commanding you today,* ¹²*lest you eat and become sated, and good houses you build and dwell in them,* ¹³*and your herds and your flocks be multiplied, and silver and gold be multiplied for you, and all that you have be multiplied,* ¹⁴*then your heart be lifted up and you forget Yahweh your God, the one who brought you out from the land of Egypt, from the house of slaves,* ¹⁵*the one who led you in the great and awful wilderness — serpents of fire and scorpions and thirsty ground in which there was no water, the one who brought you water out of the rock of flint,* ¹⁶*the one who fed you manna in the wilderness, which your fathers did not know, in order that he might humble you and in order that he might test you, to do you good in your end,* ¹⁷*and you say in your heart, "My strength and the bones of my hand made for me this wealth,"* ¹⁸*then you shall remember Yahweh your God, for he is the one who gives you strength to make wealth, in order that he might confirm his covenant that he swore to your fathers, as at this day.* ¹⁹*And it will happen if you completely forget Yahweh your God, and you go after other gods and serve them and worship them, I call to witness against you today that you will surely perish.* ²⁰*Like the nations that Yahweh makes to perish before you, thus you will perish, because you did not obey the voice of Yahweh your God.*

Rhetoric and Composition

Chapters 8–11 recall the exodus and wilderness experience, about which little has been said thus far in Deuteronomy, save for the ill-fated attempt to take the land from Kadesh-barnea (ch. 1). We must otherwise go to Exodus and Numbers to find out what happened on the wilderness trek, how Israel sorely provoked Yahweh during the forty years spent in this inhospitable place.

Deuteronomy 8

Chapter 8 — like chapter 7 — is a self-contained discourse, delimited at the top end by a *petuḥah* in M^L and a section in Sam before v. 1, which is the chapter division. Delimitation at the bottom end is by a *petuḥah* in M^L and a section in Sam after v. 20, which is also a chapter division. M^L has another *petuḥah* after v. 18, the Sam has added sections after vv. 4 and 10. 4QDeut^f has a section after v. 6, and 4QDeut^n has sections after vv. 6, 8, 9, and 10, which may indicate an early liturgical use of vv. 5-10 in connection with the meal benediction of v. 10 (see Notes). Verses 5-10 are a separate pericope in Sam and 4QDeut^n (Cross 1965, pl. 19, p. 20; Ulrich, Cross et al. 1995, 117, 122-23; Duncan 2000, 201).

The present discourse builds on the concepts of "remembering" and "forgetting" (vv. 2, 11, 14, 18, 19), contrasting also the harsh wilderness with the good land of Canaan. It compares closely to 6:10-15. The discourse has an overall chiastic structure, first seen by Lohfink (1963a, 194-95; 1965, 76), although his general categories and selective reading make revision necessary (R. O'Connell 1990, 438). Lohfink's "parenetic frames" in v. 1 and vv. 19-20 are too general, failing also to account for the same sort of parenesis in vv. 11-13. Weinfeld's revision of the Lohfink scheme is likewise too general, although he correctly discovers promise at the beginning and threat at the end. Finally, Lohfink, and some revisers of his scheme, e.g., Moran and Tigay, leave out v. 5, which has to be included. Tigay's outline (1996, 92) is the best, and the following chiasmus modifies his structure to improve the flow of ideas and highlight repeated keywords:

a   Do the commandment and you will live (v. 1)
    b   Remember the *wilderness and the manna* (vv. 2-5)
        c   Keep the *commandments* in the good land (vv. 6-10)
        c′   Do not forget Yahweh and his *commandments* in the good land (vv. 11-14)
    b′   (Remember) the *wilderness and the manna* (vv. 15-16)
a′   Remember and do not forget Yahweh, or you will perish (vv. 17-20)

One should also note the climactic analogies in vv. 5 and 20, which other schemes fail to incorporate:

So you shall know with your heart that just as a man disciplines his son,
    Yahweh your God disciplines you. (v. 5)
Like the nations that Yahweh makes to perish before you, thus you will
    perish, because you did not obey the voice of Yahweh your God. (v. 20)

Although a later Jewish liturgy developed from vv. 5-10, in my view v. 5 originally concluded vv. 1-5; vv. 6-10 form another unit. In vv. 1-5 is this keyword chiasmus:

Deuteronomy 8

a		... the land that Yahweh swore to *your fathers*	v. 1
	b	Yahweh your God led you *these forty years* in the wilderness ...	v. 2
	b′	... your foot did not swell *these forty years*	v. 4
a′		... just as a man disciplines *his son*, Yahweh your God disciplines you.	v. 5

A keyword chiasmus occurs also in vv. 7-10 (Moran; Lundbom 1996, 299):

a	*a good land*				v. 7
	b	*a land* of streams ... in the mountain			
		c	*a land of wheat* ...		v. 8
			d	*a land* of olives bearing oil ...	
		c′	*a land* ... bread		v. 9
	b′	*a land* ... iron ... *its mountains* ... copper			
a′	*the good land*				v. 10

"The good land" in v. 10 repeats from v. 7 and is the seventh occurrence of "land" in the structure.

Portions of 8:1-20 occur in 1QDeut^a, 1QDeut^b, 4QDeut^c, 4QDeut^e, 4QDeut^f, 4QDeut^j, and 4QDeut^n; also on a phylactery from Qumran (4Q128). In 4QDeut^n, 8:5-10 precedes the Decalogue in ch. 5 (Crawford 1990; J. Duncan, *EDSS*, 201).

Notes

8:1 Moses in vv. 1-10 is reminding Israel about Yahweh's care of the covenant people in the wilderness. He begins, as he does so often in Deuteronomy, by telling Israel to be careful therefore to do the commandments. This is the key to life and fecundity in the land and the key to successfully entering and possessing the land. On the land as Yahweh's promise to the fathers, see Note for 1:8.

all the commandment. The term "commandment" (singular) in Deuteronomy refers to the whole of Deuteronomic law (see Note for 27:1).

you shall be careful to do. On this Deuteronomic expression, see Note for 5:1.

that you may live and multiply. Obeying Yahweh's commandment is the road to life (v. 3; 5:33; 30:15-20 and Note for 4:1) and will enable Israel to multiply numerically (see Note for 6:3).

and enter and possess the land. On this Deuteronomic expression, see Note for 1:8.

2 *And you shall remember all the way that Yahweh your God led you these forty years in the wilderness, in order that he might humble you to test you to know what was in your heart.* The Deuteronomic preacher presents here a major theme in his work, viz., Israel's need to "remember" Yahweh, his mighty acts, and the covenant demands (cf. Blair 1961). Remembering — particularly the good things — is not an exercise in nostalgia, where one is longing for a return to the past, but something quite different. Israel is to bring its past into active remembrance, then act upon that remembrance (Propp 2006, 175). Propp notes that when Exod 20:8 says to "remember the Sabbath day," it means Israel is to observe it and refrain from work.

From its past, Israel must remember both Yahweh's gracious acts and its own acts of rebellion (9:7-29). In regard to the latter, Moses prays fervently that Yahweh will remember the patriarchs, Abraham, Isaac, and Jacob, and not regard Israel's wilderness rebellion, which nearly led to its destruction (9:27). The corollary to remembering is not forgetting (see Note for 32:18). The key verbs here are thus "remember" (זכר) and "forget" (שׁכח). In the present verse, Moses is telling Israel to remember Yahweh's leading during the forty years in the wilderness, the purpose of which was to humble the people and test them to the quick (see v. 16; 29:4-5[5-6]; cf. Amos 2:10). The testing was the hardship Israel had to endure. Israel must remember its slavery in Egypt, which is a stereotyped admonition in Deuteronomy (5:15; 15:15; 16:12; 24:18, 22; Driver 1895, lxxxi no. 33; Weinfeld 1972, 327 no. 3). More than that, it must remember its own redemption carried out amidst great signs and wonders before Pharaoh (5:15; 7:18-19; 16:3). Remembering its past hardships should enable Israel to exercise justice toward the sojourner, orphan, and widow (24:17-18) and allow them to glean its fields (24:19-22) and to share in the gladness of harvest festivals (16:9-12). The Sabbath commandment admonishes Israel to also give its servants rest, remembering its own slavery in Egypt where the toil was hard (5:12-15). Israel must remember its former slavery when enslaving its own Hebrew men and women, releasing them in the seventh year and furnishing them liberally with food and drink upon their release (15:12-15).

The Song of Moses censures Israel for forgetting Yahweh after its settlement in Transjordan (32:15-18). The same happened later in Canaan, and it became the unwelcome task of Jeremiah to have to indict Judah for this serious neglect (Jer 2:32; 3:21; 13:25; 18:15; 23:27). A covenant people forgetting Yahweh and his gracious acts will perish (vv. 19-20), and so it happened that nationhood in Israel came to an inglorious end. And yet, it is said that Israel "never lost consciousness of a past preceding its settlement in the land" (Honor 1953, 422; cf. Childs 1962, 50-56). Honor says this consciousness was a significant factor in its development as a people, seen most dramatically in the Judahite exiles of the 6th cent., whose historic consciousness was not destroyed.

Deuteronomy 8

these forty years. The LXX omits, but the words are present in 4QDeut^c, 4QDeut^e, and 4QDeut^f. On זֶה as an enclitic before numbers (also in v. 4 and in 2:7), see GKC §136d.

in order that he might humble you. לְמַעַן עַנֹּתְךָ. The verb ענה means "to bring down, humble, or lower someone." It describes what Shechem did to Dinah (Gen 34:2; cf. Deut 21:14; 22:24, 29) and what the Egyptians did to Israelite slaves (Exod 1:11). Yahweh's intent was not to degrade, however, but to discipline and teach Israel dependence upon him (vv. 3, 16).

to test you to know what was in your heart, whether you would keep his commandments or not. Feeding people with manna (vv. 3, 16) tested their obedience and trust (Exod 16:4; cf. Num 21:5). Here it is said that Yahweh's testing was to see whether or not the people would keep his commandments. On Yahweh's probing, knowing, testing, and assessing the human heart, see Deut 13:4(3); 1 Sam 16:7; Jer 17:10; Pss 7:10(9); 17:3; 26:2; Prov 17:3; 21:2; 2 Chr 32:31; in the NT, see Acts 1:24; 15:8; 1 John 3:20. Perhaps the greatest testing in the OT was when Yahweh told Abraham to sacrifice his son (Gen 22:1), a test Abraham successfully passed (22:12).

3 *Yes, he humbled you and made you hungry.* Israel was humbled by being made hungry. Fasting thus became a self-humbling act (Ps 35:13; Isa 58:3, 5; Ezra 8:21; Dan 10:2-12).

then he fed you the manna that you did not know and your fathers did not know. Yahweh provided hungry Israelites with manna (מָן from מָן הוּא, "What is it?") in the wilderness (Exodus 16; Num 11:4-9; 21:5; 1 Cor 10:3), a strange food neither they nor their fathers had known (Exod 16:14-15). Manna was not bread (לֶחֶם can also mean "food"), but most likely (sweet) pinhead to pea-sized drops on Sinai tamarisk bushes during three-six weeks of early summer (May, June). It is now believed to have been an excretion not of the tamarisk itself, but of two types of scale insects that suck sap from the tamarisk (Bodenheimer 1947; J. Mihelic, *IDB*, 3:259-60). The tradition linking manna with the tamarisk originates with ancient monks at St. Catharine's Monastery, and the desert excretion observed in modern times corresponds remarkably well with the sweet substance reported in the Bible. Yet, this honeydew excretion could not have provided wandering Israelites with food year round — for one year, much less forty years (*pace* Exod 16:35; Josephus *Ant.* 3.32). The tradition requires more explanation. One may note that the intent of Exodus 16 is not to report the manna but to inculcate regular observance of the Sabbath (Malina 1968, 19-20, 50). On the stock expression "you have not known" in Deuteronomy, which occurs again in v. 16, see Note for 11:27-28.

in order that he might make you know that one does not live by bread alone, but one lives by everything that goes out of the mouth of Yahweh. Daily food is but one God-given gift for sustaining life. The words here, so often quoted, embody a great biblical truth, i.e., that everything proceeding from God is life-sustaining. The Deuteronomic preacher never tires of telling Israel that doing the commandments leads to life (see Note to 4:1). Jesus quoted the present verse when answering Satan in the wilderness (Matt 4:4; Luke 4:4). Satan wanted him to turn stones into loaves of bread, which was temptation enough for Jesus who was fasting forty days. The rabbis, for their part, established a relationship between bread and Torah on the basis of this verse (Petuchowski 1958, 231-32; cf. Amos 8:11). An Egyptian phrase has turned up in the Harris Papyrus (44.6), where the god Ptah is quoted as saying that "one lives from what comes out of his mouth" (Brunner 1958).

4 More evidence of Yahweh's protective care in the wilderness, although the claim may well contain a measure of exaggeration. "Your outer garment" (שִׂמְלָתְךָ) would be one's clothes. The expression "your outer garment did not wear out" is Deuteronomic (Weinfeld 1972, 358 no. 19), found also in 29:4(5). With swollen feet one could not have worn shoes (T[NfPsJ]: "you did not walk barefoot"), but Moses says their feet did not swell.

5 The wilderness privations were to discipline Israel, a comparison being made to a father disciplining his son (cf. Prov 3:11-12). Discipline of children is an important wisdom theme (Prov 4:1; 19:18; 29:17; Ps 94:12). Job 5:17 says: "Behold, happy is the man whom God reproves; so the chastening of the Almighty do not despise." In the NT see Heb 12:7. Weinfeld says the noun מוּסָר ("discipline, instruction"), which occurs in 11:2 with reference to Yahweh's discipline, means education in general (Prov 1:2, 8; 4:1). In the educational process, punishment seeks to bring about future improvement (Weinfeld 1972, 316-17). Yahweh therefore chastened Israel in the wilderness for its future benefit (v. 16).

with your heart. עִם־לְבָבֶךָ. I.e., upon thoughtful and willful reflection.
that just as a man disciplines his son. כִּי כַּאֲשֶׁר יְיַסֵּר אִישׁ אֶת־בְּנוֹ. 4QDeut[j] adds כן, and the LXX οὕτως ("so, thus"), to fill out the comparison (cf. v. 20; Jer 2:26; 5:27; 6:7; 18:6).

6 "Walking in Yahweh's way" has strong ethical implications in the OT (see Note for 5:33), and "fearing Yahweh" is another recurring Deuteronomic theme (see Note for 4:10). In Deuteronomy to walk in Yahweh's way means above all to keep the commandments (5:32-33; 6:7; 8:6; 10:12-13; 11:19, 22; 19:9; 26:16-17; 28:9; 30:16). 4QDeut[n] reads "to love" instead of "to fear," but MT is supported by LXX, 4QDeut[f], and the Versions. On "fearing Yahweh," see Notes for 4:10 and 6:13.

7-9 Deuteronomy lays stress on the promised land being a good land (1:25, 35; 3:25; 4:21, 22; 6:18; 8:7, 10; 9:6; 11:17; cf. 2 Kgs 18:32; Jer 2:7). Weinfeld takes vv. 7-10 as a long protasis, for which v. 11a: "Be careful for yourself lest you forget . . ." is the beginning of the apodosis (cf. 6:10-12). But vv. 7-10 can also be

Deuteronomy 8

read as an independent sentence. Unlike 6:10-12, the call here in v. 10 for Israel to bless Yahweh when it has eaten and become full interrupts the protasis-apodosis argument. The meaning, however, is little affected.

a good land. 4QDeut^f, 4QDeut ^{j}, 4QDeut^n, Sam, and LXX have "a good and broad land." It is possible that "and broad" could have been lost by haplography (homoeoteleuton: ה . . . ה), but Duncan thinks the term is expansionistic (Ulrich, Cross et al. 1995, 86). The rhetorical structure of vv. 7-10, where "good land" in v. 7 balances "good land" in v. 10, argues for "and broad" being an add-on (see Rhetoric and Composition). Neither argument, however, is decisive.

a land of streams of water, springs and deep rivers, going forth in the valley and in the mountain. Streams (Arabic: "wadis") are full and flow rapidly in rainy (winter) season but are dry as bone in summer. The "deep rivers" (תְהוֹם) are the subterranean waters (4:18; cf. Gen 1:2). In 11:11 the good land of Canaan is said to drink (abundantly) water from heaven. Valleys in Israel are wide, often stretching into plains. On Canaan being a land of "valleys and mountains," see 11:11.

a land of wheat and barley. The principal grains of Canaan. In the "Story of Sinuhe" from 20th-cent. Egypt, a traveler into northern Canaan or Syria reports having settled in

> a good land . . . figs were in it and grapes. It had more wine than water. Abundant was its honey, plentiful its oil. All kinds of fruit were on its trees. Barley was there and emmer, and no end of cattle of all kinds. (Lichtheim 1973, 226; *ANET*^{3}, 19).

In a partially damaged 8th-cent. Syrian inscription (KAI, 214:5-7), a certain Panamuwa I of Yaudi thanks his gods who gave him "a land of barley . . . [and] a land of wheat" (Donner and Röllig 1968, 214-15). "Grain, wine, and oil" became the principal crops in Israel and the staples in its economy (see Note for 7:13). On harvesting these crops prior to the Feast of Booths, see Note for 16:13.

and vines and fig trees and pomegranates. Grapes off the vine were eaten fresh, dried into raisins, or made into wine (see Note for 6:11). The produce of fig trees, two and sometimes three crops of fruit in a year, was eaten fresh, baked into cakes — sometimes as a medicine (2 Kgs 20:7 = Isa 38:21), or made into wine. On figs and fig trees, see P. J. King 1993, 148-49. Pomegranates, likewise abundant in Canaan, were eaten fresh or dried, and from their juice one could also make wine. Grapes, figs, and pomegranates were brought back by the spies who made the first foray into Canaan (Num 13:23). Vines and fig trees became symbols of prosperity and peace (1 Kgs 4:25; 2 Kgs 18:31 = Isa 36:16; Mic 4:4; Joel 2:22; 1 Macc 14:12); pomegranates were prized as objects of beauty and became a symbol of fertility because of their many seeds (*ABD*, 2:808). Pomegranates were also widely used as decoration in religious and secular art (Exod 28:33-34; 1 Kgs 7:18, 20, 42; Jer 52:22-23).

a land of olives bearing oil and honey. Olive trees were abundant in Canaan (6:11; 2 Kgs 18:32), said to have been cultivated there for over six thousand years (*ABD*, 2:807). The honey referred to here is not honey from bees, but from palm dates (*b. Ber.* 41b; *'Erub.* 4b). Date palms graced Jericho, which was called "the city of palms" (34:3; Judg 1:16; 3:13; 2 Chr 28:15; cf. Josephus *B.J.* 4.458). They also grew further north in the Jordan Valley and at Beth Shean and Tiberias. On Canaan as "a land flowing with milk and honey," see Note for 6:3. Large-scale oil production in the 7th cent. has been discovered in excavations of Tel Miqne-Ekron (Gitin 1995, 63-69; 1997, 84-93).

you will not eat bread in scarcity. לֹא בְמִסְכֵּנֻת תֹּאכַל־בָּהּ לֶחֶם. The noun מִסְכֵּנֻת (a *hapax legomenon* in the OT) is derived from an adjective meaning "poor" (Eccl 4:13; 9:15 [2x], 16; BDB, 587). It appears to be a loanword from Akk *muškēnūtu*, meaning "poverty" (*CAD*, 10/2:276). The sense here is that people will never eat bread (= food) in poverty.

a land in which its stones are iron and from its mountains you can dig copper. Here the Deuteronomic preacher claims a bit much for Canaan. While the Israelites would doubtless have been familiar with mining operations in the Arabah as they journeyed north, and would also have seen mining operations in (northern) Transjordan after settling there, Canaan proper would in fact yield little in the way of iron, copper, and bronze (which was 90 percent copper and 10 percent tin). The area had no abundance of mineral resources (Driver; Noth 1966b, 43; Muhly 1982, 45). True, small deposits of iron existed in Galilee (e.g., the hot springs of Tiberius contained iron), but both iron and copper ores were more plentiful in the Transjordan, north of the Jabbok in Gilead, and farther north in the Bekaa Valley, Aleppo, and Hamath. If basalt rock — which contains 20 percent iron — is to be taken into account, we could include the basalt known to exist in the Jezreel Valley. In the southern Negeb, however, about 38 km north of the Gulf of Aqaba, huge deposits of copper ore have been found at Jebel Mene'iyeh on the Palestinian side of the Arabah (Glueck 1940, 77-79). Glueck says this is the largest and richest copper mining and smelting center in the entire Arabah. Iron Age sherds have been found there from the age of Solomon and later. Seven sites were identified in the larger area, but no water was found.

Most of the copper and iron ore deposits were in the Arabah Rift Valley south of the Dead Sea, although Josephus (*B.J.* 4.454) mentions a so-called "Iron Mountain" in the region of Moab. Glueck (1940, 83) says that long before the advent of the Israelites mineral deposits in the Wadi Arabah were well known and mines were exploited there by the Kenites and Edomites. The Kenites were smiths, and Glueck suggests it was perhaps from the Kenites that

Deuteronomy 8

Moses learned to make his copper serpent (Num 21:9). Tubal-cain (a Kenite) is said to have been the first forger of copper and iron instruments (Gen 4:22).

Numerous copper mines and smelting sites have been discovered in the southern Arabah (Glueck 1940, 50-88; Bartlett 1989, 39), e.g., Khirbet Nahas, ca. 36 km south of the Dead Sea, which was the center of numerous mining and smelting sites during and after the time of Solomon, also Khirbet Gheweibeh and Khirbet Jariyeh, both just a short distance away from Khirbet Nahas (Glueck 1940, 56-63). Mines were worked in Edom in the region of Pûnon = modern Feinan (Num 33:42-43), which had an abundant water supply year around (Glueck 1940, 68-71), also at Timna (Weinfeld). Glueck (1940, 79-83) discovered an Iron Age mining and smelting site at Khirbet Mrashrash overlooking the northwest corner of the Gulf of Aqaba. There was also a large smelting operation at Ezion-geber on the Gulf (Glueck 1940, 66). Copper deposits are known to have existed in Sinai, where smelting operations were carried on by the Egyptians (Glueck 1940, 69, 81). But all these sites are outside of Canaan proper. On metals and mining in the Arabah Rift Valley and surrounding areas, see Noth 1966b, 43-45; "Mining," in *IDB*, 3:384-85; "Metals and Mining," in *EncJud*, 11:1431-33. On the development of iron technology in the ancient world, which did in fact develop at the time of the Israelite conquest (ca. 1200), beginning the so-called Iron Age, see Muhly 1982.

10 When Israel eats and becomes sated in the good land, which will surely happen (cf. v. 12 and 6:10-11), it is to bless Yahweh who gave it the land. "Bless" here can mean "thanks," e.g., "Blessed are you, O Lord" is equivalent to "Thank you, O Lord" (Tigay). The NJV translates: "Give thanks to the Lord your God." In later Judaism this verse became the basis for requiring table grace after meals, the rabbis pointing out that it was the only blessing explicitly commanded in the Torah (Petuchowski 1958, 230, 233). This table grace consisted of three benedictions: (1) a benediction for the food; (2) a benediction for the land, the Torah, and the covenant; and (3) a benediction for the city of Jerusalem (*m. Ber.* 6:8; *b. Ber.* 44a; cf. *Jub.* 22:6-7). Because 8:5-10 turned up as a separate pericope in 4QDeut[n] (see Rhetoric and Composition) and a blessing occurs in 4Q434, Weinfeld (1992c) thinks there is evidence for a table grace after meals at Qumran. Josephus (*B.J.* 2.131) says the Essenes said a table grace before and after the morning meal. A threefold benediction after meals occurs also in the *Didache* (ch. 10).

11 Once again, on the heels of a command to "remember" is a warning not to "forget" (see also v. 14). Israel above all must not forget Yahweh's commandments. On forgetting Yahweh in Deuteronomy, Hosea, and Jeremiah, see Note for 32:18. On the Deuteronomic warning to "be careful," see Note for 4:9.

12 The danger of eating and becoming sated in the land and then forgetting Yahweh gets repeated emphasis in Deuteronomy (see 6:11-12). The idea oc-

Deuteronomy 8

curs also in the Song of Moses (32:15-18). Reference here is to houses the Israelites will have built for themselves (cf. Hos 8:14); in 6:11 the Israelites are envisioned as taking over houses others have built.

13 On multiplying treasures in silver and gold, see the warning to the king in 17:17 and cf. Hos 2:10(8).

14 Israel must not forget her slavery in Egypt (cf. 6:12). On "the heart being lifted up," which means becoming unduly proud, see 17:20; Hos 13:6. "House of slaves" is a Deuteronomic expression (see Note for 5:6).

15 *the one who led you in the great and awful wilderness.* On the inhospitable wilderness, see 1:19; 32:10; Jer 2:6.

serpents of fire and scorpions and thirsty ground in which there was no water. The mention of fiery serpents in Num 21:6-9 remains obscure. These may have been fiery inflammations caused by bites of the serpents (H. G. May, *IDB*, 2:267). Herodotus (ii 75; iii 109) mentions flying serpents inhabiting the Sinai desert and South Arabia, and Isaiah (30:6) knows of flying serpents in the Negeb, but these appear to be different creatures entirely. For illustrations of winged serpents in Egypt, see Keel 1977, 77.

the one who brought you water out of the rock of flint. While ground in the wilderness may have been dry as bone, water lay hidden in rocks that were even harder (Exod 17:1-7; Num 20:1-13; Pss 78:15-16; 114:8). Ibn Ezra says "flint" (חַלָּמִישׁ) is any hard stone (32:13; Job 28:9).

16 Repeating vv. 2-3. Yahweh took delight in doing Israel good (28:63). "Your end" refers here to the settlement in Canaan. Driver says Israel is being represented as an individual whose training in early life has been severe for the purpose of fitting it better for the position it has to fill in riper years. Discipline looms large in the wisdom literature (Job 8:7; 42:12; Prov 23:14-18; Weinfeld 1972, 316-17).

17 On mistaken notions residing in the human heart, see v. 14a. Greenberg (1990, 106) says here is an instance of the Torah warning Israel against assuming economic power (חַיִל can mean "power, strength, wealth"). Yahweh is the one who gives power to get wealth (v. 18). Job knows he would have been remiss to rejoice because of his great wealth or because his hand had gotten him much, for then he would have been false to God (Job 31:25-28). Ezekiel, seeing hubris of the same sort in the prince of Tyre, says it will bring him down (Ezek 28:1-10).

18 *then you shall remember Yahweh your God, for he is the one who gives you strength to make wealth.* Upon reflection, Israel can remember what it already knows, viz., that Yahweh is the one who gives strength to make wealth.

in order that he might confirm his covenant that he swore to your fathers. Confirmation of the oath made to the fathers, Abraham, Isaac, and Jacob, is given also in Deuteronomy as a reason for Israel's election as Yahweh's special

Deuteronomy 8

people (7:8) and for Israel being successful in its conquest of the land (9:5). On the covenant sworn to the fathers, see Note for 1:8. A significant space exists at this point in 5QDeut 1 ii 11, and Milik thinks "Abraham, Isaac, and Jacob" could have been present in the text (Baillet, Milik, and de Vaux 1962, 170-71; cf. 9:5). Weinfeld says that "confirm/establish his covenant" (הָקִים אֶת־בְּרִיתוֹ) is an expression one might expect to find in the Priestly writer (Gen 6:18; 9:9, 11; 17:7, 19; Exod 6:4; Lev 26:9); in Deuteronomy the expressions are "confirming the word" (9:5), "confirm the words of this law" (27:26), "confirm you to himself as a holy people" (28:9), and "confirm you today as a people" (29:12[13]).

as at this day. A common Deuteronomic expression (see Note for 2:30). Moses says the promise to the fathers about Israel being given a land is being confirmed in the present day.

19 The conditional Horeb covenant as preached throughout Deuteronomy (11:13-17), which, like the international treaties of the ANE, is fortified with curses for noncompliance (Fensham 1962b, 6; cf. 11:26-28; 28:1-68). Forgetting Yahweh, according to the Song of Moses, led to Israel going after other gods (32:15-18). The complaint that people had forgotten Yahweh is heard often in Jeremiah (Jer 2:32; 3:21; 13:25; 18:15; 23:27). On the importance of serving Yahweh and Yahweh only, see Note for 6:13. "Going after other gods," is stock in Deuteronomy (see Note for 6:14).

I call to witness against you. The LXX adds "heaven and earth" (οὐρανὸν καὶ τὴν γῆν), which will act as the witnesses (cf. 4:26; 30:19). Milik thinks 5QDeut 1 ii 12 had a text identical to LXX (Baillet, Milik, and de Vaux 1962, 170-71).

20 A comparison to balance the one in v. 5 (see Rhetoric and Composition). If Israel fails to obey the voice of Yahweh, it stands to suffer the same fate as nations currently being thrust out of Canaan (7:1). Cf. Lev 18:24-28.

because you did not obey the voice of Yahweh your God. Obeying Yahweh's voice in Deuteronomy means doing the commandments (see Note for 13:5).

because. עֵקֶב. A conjunction meaning "following after, in the footsteps of" (Weinfeld), here introducing a consequence (cf. 7:12).

Message and Audience

The present discourse stresses once again the importance of Israel doing the commandments it has received from Moses. This will give the people life and fecundity in the land promised to the fathers, which Israel is now ready to enter and possess. Israel is told to remember Yahweh's guidance during forty years in the wilderness, an exercise meant to humble and test Israel to see whether it would keep the commandments. Israel was humbled in being fed manna, showing people that one does not live by bread alone but by everything that proceeds from Yahweh. The people's clothes did not wear out, nor did their feet swell. Yahweh disciplined Israel like a father his son.

The people are again admonished to keep Yahweh's commandments, to walk in his way, and to fear him. The land awaiting Israel is an exceedingly good land, with streams, springs, water deep in the earth — enough to more than fill hill and dale. This land will produce wheat and barley, lush vineyards, groves of fig trees, and an abundance of pomegranates, not to mention olive trees and honey coming from date palms. People will lack nothing. This land is also said to contain an abundance of minerals, iron and copper, but this appears to be a stretch. In any case, when the people eat and become sated, they are to bless Yahweh for the good land he has given them.

What follows is a sober warning about forgetting, the opposite of remembering. Israel must not forget Yahweh by failing to keep his commandments. The people may become sated, build and inhabit fine houses, witness a multiplication of herds and flocks, silver and gold, and everthing else and then become proud and arrogant, leading them to forget Yahweh their God, the one who brought them out of the house of slaves and led them in the inhospitable wilderness, inhabited by serpents and scorpions, where the ground was as hard as bone. Even there, Yahweh provided the people with water from flinty rock, which was to humble and test them, with a larger aim of doing Israel good in the future. Israel dare not think this wealth will come by its own might. If it does, it must remember that Yahweh is the one who gives power to attain wealth. He does so to make good on the covenant sworn to the fathers.

The sermon closes with a warning. If Israel forgets Yahweh and goes after other gods to worship and serve them, which has happened before, the nation will surely perish. It will become like the nations Yahweh is destroying so Israel could be given their land. Israel will pay a great price if it does not obey the voice of Yahweh God.

For a late 8th- and early 7th-cent. audience, the present sermon may well be aimed at a people thinking they can live and multiply in the land without doing Yahweh's commandments. But that is not happening: people are dying, being carried off into exile, and much land has been lost. Those surviving would do well to remember the wilderness experience, when Yahweh humbled and tested Israel to see if it would do his commandments. This audience is also given a clear description of the conditional Horeb covenant. If people do not obey Yahweh's voice and do his commands, they will perish off the face of the earth — a timely word, when Israel and now more recently Judah have suffered much at the hands of the Assyrians. There will be more of the same unless people take seriously Moses' words about obeying the commandments.

Deuteronomy 9

H. You Are a Rebellious People (9:1-29)

1. Yahweh Will Clear Away Larger and Mightier Nations (9:1-3)

9 ¹*Hear, O Israel, you are crossing today the Jordan, to enter and to take possession of nations greater and mightier than you, cities great and fortified up to heaven, ²a people great and tall, sons of the Anakim, whom you yourselves know and you yourselves have heard. Who can hold one's ground before the sons of Anak? ³So you shall know today that Yahweh your God, he is crossing before you, a consuming fire, he himself will completely destroy them, and he himself will subdue them before you, so you shall dispossess them and make them perish quickly, just as Yahweh spoke to you.*

2. Conquest Due to Canaan's Wickedness and Oath to the Fathers (9:4-6)

⁴*Do not say in your heart when Yahweh your God thrusts them out from before you: "Because of my righteousness Yahweh has brought me in to take possession of this land." No, because of the wickedness of these nations Yahweh is dispossessing them from before you. ⁵Not because of your righteousness and because of your upright heart are you entering to possess their land. Indeed, because of the wickedness of these nations Yahweh your God is dispossessing them from before you, in order that he might confirm the word that Yahweh swore to your fathers, to Abraham, to Isaac, and to Jacob. ⁶So you shall know that not because of your righteousness Yahweh your God is giving to you this good land to take possession of it, for a stiff-necked people you are.*

3. Remember Your Wilderness Rebellion (9:7-29)

a) Remember the Calf at Horeb and Moses' Intercession (9:7-21)

⁷*Remember — do not forget — that you made Yahweh your God furious in the wilderness; from the day that you came out of the land of Egypt, until you came to this place, you have been rebellious with Yahweh. ⁸Yes at Horeb you made Yahweh furious, and Yahweh was angry enough with you to completely destroy you. ⁹When I went up the mountain to receive the tablets of stone, the tablets of the covenant, which Yahweh cut with you, and I remained on the mountain forty days and forty nights, bread I did not eat and water I did not drink. ¹⁰And Yahweh gave to me the two tablets of stone, written with the finger of God, and*

upon them were according to all the words that Yahweh spoke with you on the mountain from the midst of the fire, on the day of the assembly. ¹¹And it happened at the end of forty days and forty nights, Yahweh gave to me the two tablets of stone, the tablets of the covenant.

¹²Then Yahweh said to me: "Rise up, go down quickly from here, for your people whom you brought out from Egypt have acted corruptly; they have turned aside quickly from the way that I commanded them; they have made for themselves a metal thing." ¹³And Yahweh said to me: "I have seen this people, and have a look, it is a stiff-necked people. ¹⁴Let me alone, and I will completely destroy them, and I will wipe out their name from under the heaven, and I will make of you a nation mightier and more numerous than they."

¹⁵So I turned and came down from the mountain, and the mountain was burning with fire, and the two tablets of the covenant were in my two hands. ¹⁶And I looked, and there it was! You had sinned before Yahweh your God, you made for yourselves a metal calf; you had turned aside quickly from the way that Yahweh commanded you. ¹⁷So I took hold of the two tablets, and I threw them from my two hands, and I broke them before your eyes. ¹⁸Then I fell prostrate before Yahweh as formerly, forty days and forty nights; bread I did not eat, and water I did not drink, over all your sin that you sinned, to do what was evil in the eyes of Yahweh, to provoke him to anger. ¹⁹Indeed, I was in dread because of the anger and the wrath for which Yahweh was furious toward you, to completely destroy you, but Yahweh listened to me also at that time. ²⁰And with Aaron Yahweh was very angry, so as to completely destroy him, and I prayed also on behalf of Aaron at that time. ²¹And your sin that you made, the calf, I took and I burned it in the fire, and I beat it, grinding it thoroughly until it was fine as dust, and I threw its dust into the stream, which came down from the mountain.

b) Remember Taberah, Massah, and Kibroth-hattaavah (9:22-24)

²²And in Taberah and in Massah and in Kibroth-hattaavah you were making Yahweh furious. ²³And when Yahweh sent you from Kadesh-barnea, saying, "Go up and possess the land that I have given to you," then you disobeyed the command of Yahweh your God, and you did not believe him, and you did not obey his voice. ²⁴You have been rebellious with Yahweh from the day I knew you.

c) Moses' First Intercession on the Mountain (9:25-29)

²⁵So I fell prostrate before Yahweh forty days and forty nights that I fell prostrate, because Yahweh said he would completely destroy you. ²⁶And I prayed to Yahweh and I said: "O Lord Yahweh, do not bring your people and your inheritance to ruin, whom you ransomed by your greatness, whom you brought out from Egypt

Deuteronomy 9

by a strong hand. ²⁷*Remember your servants, Abraham, Isaac, and Jacob; do not look to the stubbornness of this people, or to its wickedness, or to its sin,* ²⁸*lest the land from which you brought us out say, 'Yahweh was not able to bring them into the land that he promised them, and because he hated them he brought them out to kill them in the wilderness.'* ²⁹*Yes, they are your people, and your inheritance, whom you brought out by great strength and by an outstretched arm."*

Rhetoric and Composition

The sermon in this chapter counterbalances the sermon in ch. 7. There Moses told Israel it was a holy people and went on to state that Yahweh had elected Israel to be his special people among all the peoples of the earth. The focus was on what Yahweh had done for Israel in the past. Now Moses is telling Israel that it is a rebellious people, and includes an important lesson about the conquest soon to be undertaken. The emphasis is on what Yahweh will do in the future, but the focus is on the past, Israel's past, which has been characterized from the beginning by rebellion.

The rebellion began at Horeb, at the very time Moses was receiving the tablets from Yahweh and preparing to bring them down to the people. The sin of the golden calf dominates the present chapter (9:7-21), with Moses now calling to remembrance a defining incident about which nothing was said in the Prologue. The Deuteronomic author bases his narrative in 9:9–10:11 on Exod 24:12-18; 31:18–34:28; and Numbers 11 (see Driver 1895, 112-14).

The chapter is delimited at the top end by a *setumah* in M^L and a section in Sam before v. 1, which is also the chapter division. The opening "Hear, O Israel" (v. 1) is the same opening word as in 5:1, which there introduced the Ten Commandments. Delimitation at the bottom end is by a *petuḥah* in M^L and a section in Sam after v. 29, which is the next chapter division. The Sam has other sections after vv. 5, 8, 12, 17 and 24.

At the beginning of the chapter Yahweh promises to clear away nations larger and mightier than Israel (9:1-3), repeating essentially what was said in 7:1-6. The opening verses are tied together by a keyword inclusio with inversion (Nelson):

you are crossing/today the Jordan	v. 1a
So you shall know *today*/that *Yahweh . . . is crossing* before you	v. 3a

What follows is the great teaching of the chapter, i.e., that the conquest will meet with success because Yahweh is punishing the Canaanites for their wickedness while at the same time confirming his oath to the patriarchs (9:4-

6). Israel must not think holy war is being waged in support of its own righteousness, because it is not. In the next section (9:7-21), which is the core of the teaching on rebellion, Moses calls to remembrance Israel's sin of the golden calf and how Moses had to intercede to dissuade Yahweh from destroying the people. Within this section is a chiastic structure describing the apostasy (Nelson):

they have turned aside quickly from the way that I commanded them	v. 12b
they have made for themselves a metal thing	v. 12c
you made for yourselves a metal calf	v. 16b
you had turned aside quickly from the way that Yahweh commanded you	v. 16c

The LXX omits "quickly" in v. 16c, which is best taken as a loss attributable to haplography (homoeoarcton: מ . . . מ), not an add-on from Exod 32:8 (*pace* Nelson).

Nelson points out another chiastic structure in vv. 15-21:

I turned and came down from the mountain . . . with fire	v. 15
you had sinned . . . you made	v. 16
your sin that you had made	v. 21a
with fire . . . the stream which came down from the mountain	v. 21c

The next section, vv. 22-24, reports other instances of Israel's rebellion in the wilderness. This is a supplement to the main narrative, but the verses, together with vv. 7-8, frame the sin of the golden calf (Lohfink 1963a, 211; Zipor 1996, 24). The balancing phrases are in vv. 7 and 24:

. . . from the day that you came out of the land of Egypt	v. 7
. . . from the day I knew you	v. 24

For a larger rhetorical structure proposed for vv. 7-24, see R. O'Connell 1992b, 494-97.

The chapter concludes with a prayer by Moses, vv. 25-29, which is another supplement. It belongs chronologically after v. 14, where it fills out Moses' first intercession on the mountain (see Notes). The supplement is linked to vv. 13-14 by the verb "completely destroy":

and I will completely destroy them	וָאַשְׁמִידֵם	v. 14
Yahweh said he would completely destroy you	אָמַר יְהוָה לְהַשְׁמִיד אֶתְכֶם	v. 25

This prayer itself contains a keyword inclusio (Lohfink 1994c, 277; Zipor 1996, 26):

Deuteronomy 9

your people . . . whom you brought out from Egypt by a strong hand	v. 26
your people . . . whom you brought out by great strength and by an outstretched arm	v. 29

Portions of 9:1-29 are contained in 1QDeut^a, 1QDeut^b, 4QDeut^c, 4QDeut^f, 4QDeut^g, XḤev/SeDeut, and 4Q364; also on a phylactery from Qumran (4Q128).

Notes

9:1 *Hear, O Israel, you are crossing today the Jordan, to enter and to take possession of nations greater and mightier than you.* This sermon begins like the sermon in ch. 7, citing the inhabitants of the land as "nations more numerous and mightier than you" (see Note for 7:1). For Deuteronomy's stereotypical language about crossing the Jordan to enter and take possession of the land, see Note for 4:25-26. Deuteronomy makes much of border crossings (2:4: "You will be crossing into the territory of your brethren"; 2:18: "You are crossing today the border of Moab"), which are rites of territorial passage (Trumbull 1896; van Gennep 1909; Lundbom 1986c). On the frequent use of "today" in Deuteronomy, which should not be taken literally but refers generally to the present time, see Note for 1:10.

Hear, O Israel. An important didactic introduction in Deuteronomy, here opening the third major sermonic discourse in chs. 5–11 (see Note for 5:1).

cities great and fortified up to heaven. Hyperbole, on which see Note for 1:28.

2 The Anakim were a remnant of aboriginal giants who lived among the Amorites in the southern hill country (see Note for 1:28). In 2:10-11 they are compared to the Emim, another giant race formerly inhabiting Moab. The alternate expression, "sons of Anak," which employs the singular "Anak," means the same as "sons of the Anakim." "Who can hold one's ground before the sons of Anak?" is probably a well-known proverb (cf. Prov 27:4: "Who can stand before jealousy?" Ps 147:17: "Who can stand before [Yahweh's] cold?").

a people great and tall. The inhabitants of Canaan, who descended from the Anakim. The LXX expands to λαὸν μέγαν καὶ πολὺν καὶ εὐμήκη ("a people great and numerous and tall"), reflecting MT readings in 2:10, 21.

whom you yourselves know and you yourselves have heard. Emphatic constructions. The people heard about the Anakim from the spies (1:28; cf. Num 13:28).

3 The crossing of the Jordan, the destruction of Canaan's inhabitants, and the dispossession of Canaanite land will be led by Yahweh, who goes at the head of the army. Yahweh is Lord of Hosts and will be waging holy war (31:3). Destruction will come quickly; Yahweh has so promised. On the institution of holy war, see Note for 1:30.

So you shall know today. On this Deuteronomic expression, which repeats in v. 6, see Note for 4:39.

Yahweh your God, he is crossing before you, a consuming fire. "Consuming fire" stands in apposition to "Yahweh your God" (Weinfeld; cf. LXX; T[OnqPsJ]); it is not an adverbial accusative, i.e., "as a devouring fire" (*pace* Driver; Nelson). The difference is slight. Yahweh is said to be a "consuming fire" in 4:24, where Israel is warned about what judgment will be like if it violates the covenant. Here the metaphor describes Yahweh's judgment on the inhabitants of Canaan. The "consuming (אכל) fire" metaphor may derive from the Song of Moses (Deut 32:22). It is picked up later by Isaiah (Isa 29:6; 30:27, 30) and by Jeremiah (Jer 5:14, 17).

he himself will completely destroy them, and he himself will subdue them. The verb שׁמד, which occurs 6 times in the chapter (vv. 3, 8, 14, 19, 20, 25), is an internal H-stem with intensive meaning: "completely destroy" (see Note for 1:27). Supplemental pronouns for both verbs give added emphasis. Canaan's inhabitants — including the Philistines — were later reported as having been subdued (Judg 3:30; 4:23; 8:28; 11:33; 1 Sam 7:13; 2 Sam 8:1).

so you shall dispossess them and make them perish quickly. On this stereotypical language, see Note for 4:25-26. Hebrew מַהֵר is rightly translated "quickly," where the idea is that when the enemy is engaged, victory will come speedily (Rashbam: the people will be quickly victorious in war, not requiring a long-term effort of building mounds and siegeworks). The first battle at Jericho showed precisely this, where, after seven days of marching around the city, the shout went forth and the battle went so quickly that the city wall was said to have "fallen down flat" (Josh 6:20). The conquest as a whole, however, will be spread out over a longer period of time (7:22; cf. Exod 23:29-30). There is no contradiction between the present verse and 7:22. It is a recurring theme in Scripture that God's actions occur "suddenly" (Daube 1964). A similar problem of interpretation occurs at the close of the NT, where in Rev 22:20 ἔρχομαι ταχύ should be rendered "I come quickly," as in the AV, not "I am coming soon," as in the RSV. In the present verse two LXX MSS omit ἐν τάχει, "quickly" (Wevers 1995, 158).

so you shall dispossess them. וְהוֹרַשְׁתָּם. The LXX omits, which results from haplography (homoeoarcton: וה . . . וה).

just as Yahweh spoke to you. כַּאֲשֶׁר דִּבֶּר יְהוָה לָךְ. Or "just as Yahweh promised you"; the verb דבר can also be translated "to promise." Moses may have in mind Yahweh's promise of land to the fathers, which he now repeats to the present generation (1:21). But Deuteronomy has usually been emphasizing that Israel will succeed in taking the land (ch. 7), where earlier victories over the Egyptians (1:30) and the Transjordanian kings (4:37-38) are cited for comparison.

4 Here begins Deuteronomy's great teaching about the basis on which the conquest will rest. Success will come, first of all, because the inhabitants of Canaan are "full up" with wickedness. Abraham was told, when Yahweh made a covenant with him, that his descendants would not return to Canaan for four generations, because "the iniquity of the Amorites [was] not yet complete" (Gen 15:16). Moses wants Israel to know that it is not being given the land because of its own righteousness, which he will document in vv. 6-24. The terms צְדָקָה ("righteousness") and רִשְׁעָה ("wickedness") might also be translated "innocence" and "guilt" (Lohfink 1963a, 202-4; cf. 25:1).

Holy war is commonly conceived of as righteous nations going to battle against wicked nations (e.g., Roman Catholic doctrine of a just war, beginning with Augustine; Islamic *jihad*), but that is not the case here. Yes, the inhabitants of Canaan are wicked and are being punished for their wickedness (12:31; 18:12; 20:18; cf. 1 Kgs 14:24; 21:26; 2 Kgs 16:3, etc.), but Israel, on behalf of whom Yahweh is waging this war, is not righteous. A positive reason for Yahweh waging this holy war is given in the followng verse, viz., that Yahweh is confirming an oath made to the fathers to give the Canaanite land to their descendants (v. 5). Later on, when the tables are turned and Yahweh is declaring holy war on Israel, the prophets — particularly Isaiah and Habakkuk — have difficulty understanding how Yahweh can use a wicked nation as the rod of his anger (Isa 10:5-11; Hab 1:5-11; Lundbom 2010a, 70-71, 81). But that, alas, is what happened when Assyria and Babylon became Yahweh's punishing agents. All Yahweh would tell his prophets was that when punishment of the covenant people was complete, the punishing agents would get the same. This teaching is an old one, present already in the Song of Moses (Deut 32:19-22). The principle in all cases is the same: Yahweh punishes wicked nations with nations who are themselves wicked, the basis, perhaps, for Paul's NT teaching that "all have sinned and fall short of the glory of God" (Rom 3:23).

Do not say in your heart. On mistaken notions residing in the human heart, see also 8:14, 17.

when Yahweh your God thrusts them out. בַּהֲדֹף יְהוָה אֱלֹהֶיךָ אֹתָם. On the uncommon verb הדף ("to thrust out"), see also 6:19.

5 Moses repeats what he has just said about Israel lacking a righteous character and a righteous cause, but this time adds a positive reason for carrying out the conquest: that Yahweh may fulfill his oath made to the fathers. This reason is given also in 7:8 for Israel's election as a holy people (cf. Jer 11:5), the other reason being because of Yahweh's love. In 8:18 the oath to the fathers is the reason for Israel achieving the strength to attain wealth. On the covenant sworn to the fathers, see Note for 1:8.

Deuteronomy 9

Luther, as one might expect, rings the changes on Israel not being permitted to trust in its own righteousness. The gift of the land comes not on the merits of righteousness, he says, but is due to the grace and goodness of God. God fulfills his promise to the fathers on grace alone. According to Luther, evil comes upon the godless by merit, but we enjoy good things not because of our own righteousness, but because of divine goodness. Actually, we deserve the very opposite. Thus the verdict stands: "Not on account of our righteousness is any good thing given to us, but in order that God may fulfill the Word which he willed from eternity, lest we be puffed up and make an idol out of our righteousness."

in order that he might confirm the word. The H-stem of קוּם ("confirm, fulfill") is lit. "to make stand," as opposed to "let fall" (1 Sam 15:13; 1 Kgs 2:4; 8:20; 12:15; Jer 28:6; 29:10; 33:14; 35:16; Driver; Weinfeld 1972, 350). In the NT, see Rom 15:8. Hebrew דָּבָר ("word") can also be translated "oath" or "covenant," where parallels exist in Akkadian, Sumerian, Hittite, and Greek (Weinfeld, *bᵉrît*, in *TDOT*, 2:257). The LXX translates "covenant" (διαθήκην) in the present verse. In 8:18 the wording is "confirm his covenant that he swore to your fathers."

6 Moses' third disclaimer in succession regarding Israel's righteousness, which Friedman says is to drive the point home. Here it is added that Israel is a "stiff-necked" (קְשֵׁה־עֹרֶף) people (cf. v. 13). The image is one of an obstinate, intractable animal, sufficiently strong to resist the yoke on the back of the neck (cf. Isa 48:4). "Breaking the yoke and tearing the straps" is language used in the OT to describe Israel's breaking of the Horeb/Sinai covenant (Jer 2:20; 5:5), also any other rebellion against Yahweh (Ps 2:3). In Deut 10:16 the people are told to "stiffen the neck" no more, i.e., be no longer stubborn. But when Moses teaches the people a song to witness against them after he is gone, he cites their past "rebelliousness and stiffness of neck" and says it will only increase after he is gone (31:27). Israel's stubborn behavior was manifested preeminently at Horeb, when it fashioned the golden calf (Exod 32:9; 33:3, 5; 34:9), an incident Moses recalls in the verses following (vv. 7-21). Jeremiah calls the Judahite people "stiff-necked" (Jer 7:26; 17:23; 19:15), and the characterization occurs elsewhere in the OT (2 Kgs 17:14; Neh 9:16, 17, 29; 2 Chr 30:8; 36:13; Prov 29:1; Sir 16:11). The term appears also in the Qumran *Manual of Discipline* (1QS 4:11; 5:5, 26; 6:26). Stephen calls Israel "stiff-necked" in his NT speech before the high priest and the council (Acts 7:51) and goes on to pay the supreme price for doing so.

7 Here begins the real substance of the larger argument about what basis on which the conquest will rest. Israel has a rebellious past (vv. 7-24). Deuteronomy, up to this point, and generally throughout the book, shows a positive attitude about Israel being able to keep the commandments, but that is a hope for the future. Even in the supplement of chs. 29–30, Moses' concluding admonition to obey the commandments and choose life is upbeat: the people can do it. Only in 31:16-29, in a second supplement introducing the Song of Moses, is the future no longer promising. Now when Israel's past is assessed, the tone is overwhelmingly negative. The wilderness trek was one rebellion after another. It began at Horeb with the fashioning of a golden calf and continued at Taberah, Massah, and Kibroth-hattaavah (vv. 22-24). And what is one to say about the disobedience that led to the failed attempt to enter the land, which Deuteronomy recalls in the Prologue (1:26-46; cf. Numbers 14)? Indeed, Israel has had a rebellious temper from the day it came out of Egypt (v. 7a), or for as long as Moses (MT) has known the people (v. 24). Were it not for Moses' intercession, and Yahweh's mercy, Israel would have ceased to exist. This is a much different picture of the wilderness experience than one gets from Hosea and Jeremiah, where it is idealized (Hos 2:16-17[14-15]; Jer 2:2-3; Lundbom 1999, 253-56; 2010b, 37-41).

Remember — do not forget. Two themes recurring all throughout Deuteronomy (see Notes for 8:2; 32:18).

you made Yahweh your God furious. הִקְצַפְתָּ אֶת־יְהוָה אֱלֹהֶיךָ. See vv. 8, 19, 22; 1:34.

until you came to this place. I.e., the valley opposite Beth-peor (3:29; 4:46). Reference is to Beth-peor again in 11:5, but to Kadesh-barnea in 1:31, the land of Canaan in 26:9, and Transjordan in 29:6[7].

you have been rebellious with Yahweh. מַמְרִים הֱיִיתֶם עִם־יְהוָה. The participle with היה emphasizes an action continuing in the past (Driver; GKC §116r): Israel has been continually rebellious with Yahweh. See again v. 24: "you were (continually) making Yahweh furious."

8 Yahweh was particularly furious with Israel at Horeb. There Yahweh gave the people the Ten Commandments, and they returned the favor by crafting an idol. It would have led to Israel's extinction, except that Moses interceded on Israel's behalf (Exodus 32-33).

to completely destroy you. The verb שמד, appearing again in vv. 14, 19, 20, 25 and often in Deuteronomy, is an internal H-stem with intensive meaning (see Note for 1:27),

9 The story line develops from Exodus, with some portions being quoted verbatim. The present verse is dependent upon Exod 24:12-18 and 31:18, in between which is a long digression about the ark, the tabernacle, priestly dress, and ordination.

the tablets of stone, the tablets of the covenant. Containing the Ten Commandments (5:7-21). The Deuteronomic author adds "tablets of the covenant" to "tablets of stone" (vv. 11, 15; cf. Exod 24:12) because the Ten Commandments are the terms of the Horeb covenant (4:13; 5:2-3; cf. 1 Kgs 8:9). Yet Exod 34:28 also calls the Ten Commandments "the words of the covenant."

forty days and forty nights. See Exod 24:18b. Moses spends another forty days and forty nights in prayer to Yahweh after the covenant is broken (v. 18) and yet another forty days and forty nights on the mountain to renew the covenant (Exod 34:28; cf. Deut 10:10). Forty-day periods are stereotyped in the Bible, e.g., Gen 7:4, 17; 50:2-3; 1 Kgs 19:8; Jonah 3:4.

bread I did not eat, and water I did not drink. The objects, bread and water, come first in the clauses for emphasis. A miraculous occurrence, if the fasting was total and encompassed both day and night (so Midrashic commentators; Tigay). According to Exod 34:28, Moses fasted again during his second forty days and forty nights on the mountain. When Elijah was fleeing to Mount Horeb to escape the wrath of Jezebel, he is said to have gone forty days and forty nights on the strength of food and drink provided him in the wilderness — another extraordinary feat! Jesus fasted for forty days in the wilderness after being baptized by John (Luke 4:2).

10 It is assumed that the Ten Commandments were given directly to the people on the day of the assembly, when they heard with great fear Yahweh's voice speaking out of the fire (cf. 4:10, 12, 33; 5:22-27; 10:4; 18:16). On the voice "from the midst of the fire," see Note for 4:12. The tablets were subsequently written by Yahweh on the mountain and given to Moses, who then delivered them to the people. The written words were the same as Yahweh's spoken words. On the iconography of the two tablets of stone, which has its origins in the Christian tradition, see Note for 4:13.

according to all the words. כְּכָל־הַדְּבָרִים. I.e., "according to the exact words" (T^Onq). The Hebrew is idiomatic; the LXX, Vg, and T^Nf do not translate the preposition כְ ("like").

written with the finger of God. See Exod 31:18b; cf. 32:16. The use of "finger" is not a synecdoche for "hand," which is the common biblical term used with reference to God and the one that came to represent God in later religious art. The expression is simply to acknowledge God's presence, creative power, and involvement in human affairs (Klingbeil 2000). It has these meanings in the third plague of Egypt, where a contest was taking place between Yahweh and Pharaoh (Exod 8:15[19]). Jesus, in response to those seeking to discredit his exorcism of a demon and claiming that he accomplished it through the power of Baalzebul, said in response: "But if it is by the finger of God that I cast out demons, then the kingdom of God has come upon you" (Luke 11:20). Stephen, citing Moses' revelation in his NT speech, says it was an angel who gave him the revelation (Acts 7:38).

on the day of the assembly. בְּיוֹם הַקָּהָל. Here and elsewhere in Deuteronomy (18:16; 23:2, 3, 4, 9[1, 2, 3, 8]; 31:30) the LXX translates קָהָל with ἐκκλησία ("assembly, church"), a term occurring in Matthew (16:18; 18:17 [2x]) but in no other NT Gospel (Brodie 1992, 700).

11 A repetition of v. 10a, only with the addition that it was *at the end* (מִקֵּץ) of the forty days and forty nights that Moses received the tablets. Weinfeld says the narrator recapitulates in order to stress the fact that on the very day the tablets were given the people were already in violation of the covenant.

12 The language here, as has often been pointed out, "distances" Yahweh from the people and from Moses: "*your* people whom *you* brought out from Egypt." Weinfeld notes that this is the only place in the OT where the exodus is ascribed to Moses. Cf. the "distancing language" in the NT parable of the Prodigal Son, where the older brother says to the father: "But when *this son of yours* came, who has devoured *your living* with harlots" (Luke 15:30).

Rise up, go down quickly. In Deuteronomy, Moses is told to descend the mountain "quickly" (Weinfeld: "at once"), giving him no time for the intercession recorded in Exod 32:7-14. In Exod 32:7 Moses is simply told to go down, but before he does, he intercedes for the people and Yahweh withdraws his threat to completely destroy them.

they have turned aside quickly from the way. סָרוּ מַהֵר מִן־הַדֶּרֶךְ. The expression "turn aside from the way" is stereotyped in Deuteronomy (9:12, 16; 11:28; 31:29; Weinfeld 1972, 339 no. 2a). Moses repeats the words in v. 16. "Walking in Yahweh's way" has ethical implications in the OT and is an important theme in Deuteronomy (see Note for 5:33). In the eternal covenant (= new covenant) announced later by Jeremiah, Yahweh expresses the hope that people will fear him and not turn aside (סוּר) from him (Jer 32:40).

they have made for themselves a metal thing. עָשׂוּ לָהֶם מַסֵּכָה. According to Exodus, the calf was made from gold rings supplied by the people (Exod 32:2, 24). The gold was presumably melted down in the fire (v. 24), beaten into gold leaf (v. 4; cf. Jer 10:9), and then used as plating over a core of wood or other inferior metal (C. Dohmen, *massêkâ*, in *TDOT*, 8:434; cf. Isa 30:22; Jer 10:3-4). Since the idol was later burned, a core of wood makes sense (Propp 2006, 550, 559). Gold leaf is hammered in a similar way today in Burma (Myanmar). The wooden figure would have been carved with a knife (like Swedish Dalarna horses). Propp does not think "molten" is quite the right translation for מַסֵּכָה, since this would suggest that the calf was solid gold, which probably it was not. He renders the term "metal" (Friedman is better with "metal thing"). That the calf was meant to be an idol is clear from Exod 32:31, where Moses complains to Yahweh that the people have made "a god of gold."

A silver leaf calf from 1550 turned up in excavations at Ashkelon. According to Lawrence Stager, the excavator:

> Less than 4.5 inches long and 4 inches high, the calf . . . is a superb example of Canaanite metalwork. . . . The body is made of bronze; only 2 to 5 percent is tin, the rest copper. . . . The calf was once completely covered with a thick overleaf of pure silver. (P. J. King 1993, 183; 1994, 27)

For the fashioning of idols in silver and gold, see Hos 13:2; Hab 2:19; Jer 10:3-4, 9; Isa 30:22; 40:19; 46:6; Pss 115:4; 135:15.

Deuteronomy 9

13 Yahweh repeats what Moses said in v. 6, telling Moses to look for himself at what the people have done. Hebrew הִנֵּה needs a more vigorous rendering than "behold." The LXX inserts Λελάληκα πρὸς σὲ ἅπαξ καὶ δίς ("I have spoken to you once and again") after "And Yahweh said to me." It is unclear why the insertion is made. Exod 32:7, 9 have two "And Yahweh spoke/said to Moses" introductions. Wevers (1995, 164) thinks it is because Yahweh calls Israel "stiff-necked" twice in Exod 33:3, 5. The RSV and NRSV accommodate the LXX reading by adding "furthermore" (NJV adds "further").

14 This is the great test for Moses, which he passes successfully by refusing to accept Yahweh's offer of abandoning the covenant with Abraham and beginning over with himself. Yahweh did, of course, make a new beginning with Noah (Genesis 6–9), who was a "new Adam" of sorts (Propp 2006, 554), but to abandon the covenant with Abraham and begin again with Moses would pose a huge problem, since the covenant with Abraham was unconditional and eternal and could not by any reasonable stretch be broken (see Note for 4:31). Moses wisely rejects the idea (vv. 26-29; Exod 32:12b-13), and in the end Yahweh agrees (Exod 32:14). Moses — here as elsewhere (5:5, 31; 9:18-20, 25-29; 10:10) — is acting in the role of "covenant mediator."

When Yahweh says "Let me alone" (הֶרֶף מִמֶּנִּי, lit. "loosen [your grip] from me"; cf. Exod 32:10; Judg 11:37), he is anticipating intervention. According to Exodus, intercession was made (Exod 32:11-14), and here in Deuteronomy that intercession comes as a supplement in vv. 25-29 (see Note for 9:25). Later Jewish interpreters became uncomfortable with a bold anthropomorphism that depicts Moses as wanting to physically prevent Yahweh from carrying out his intent (*b. Ber.* 32a; T^{Onq}: "Stop your prayer from before me"; T^{Nf}: "Refrain yourself before me;" T^{PsJ}: "Desist from your prayer to me"). Exodus 32:10 has simply הַנִּיחָה לִּי ("Let me rest").

Moses, Samuel, and Jeremiah were Israel's primary "covenant mediators" (Muilenburg 1959, 360-65; 1963; 1965, 87-97; 1968; cf. Jer 15:1; Hos 12:14; Ps 99:6-8), engaged often in intercessory prayer on Israel's behalf (Lundbom 2010a, 29-31). On Moses as intercessor, see Exod 32:11-14, 30-34; 33:1-17; Num 11:2; 14:11-24; 16:20-48; on Samuel as intercessor, see 1 Sam 7:5-9; 8:6-9; 12:17-18; 15:10-11; and on Jeremiah as intercessor, see Jer 7:16-20 (unsuccessful); 11:14-17 (unsuccessful); 14:7-16 (unsuccessful); 14:20–15:4 (unsuccessful); 18:20; 21:2; 37:3; 42:1-17 (rejected by the people). Yahweh, when no longer wanting Jeremiah to intercede, says: "Do not pressure me," אַל־תִּתְפַּלֵּל (Jer 7:16; 11:14; 14:11), which is similar to the rebuff here. Later Jewish tradition remembers Jeremiah as the one who prayed much for the people and Jerusalem (2 Macc 15:14). In the NT, Paul prays constantly for the churches and admonishes the churches to do the same for each other (1 Thess 1:2-3; 5:17; Rom 1:9; 12:12). In the NT book of Hebrews, Jesus becomes "the mediator of a new covenant" (Heb 8:6; 9:15; 12:24).

Deuteronomy 9

I will completely destroy them. On the verb שׁמד, see v. 8 and Note for 1:27.

and I will wipe out their name from under the heaven. Variation of a stock Deuteronomic phrase, attested also in Northwest Semitic and Assyrian inscriptions (see Note for 7:24). "Wiping out the name" means "wiping out the remembrance" (cf. 25:19; Exod 17:14). Israel was told to wipe out the remembrance of the Canaanites and Amalakites. Weinfeld (1972, 107-8) says the curse of wiping out one's name "seems to derive from a genre of curses originally put on those who erased or mutilated words of an insription." In an Esarhaddon treaty the Assyrian king states:

> He who erases (my) written name or alters this . . . erases his name and his seed from the land. (Weinfeld 1972, 108)

Punishment of the offender would be according to the *lex talionis*, i.e., measure for measure.

and I will make of you a nation mightier and more numerous than they. "A nation mightier and more numerous" is a Deuteronomic expression (see Note for 7:1), here applied not to the nations Israel will be dispossessing, but to Israel's own strength and numbers at the present time (1:10; 10:22). The LXX adds "great" (cf. 26:5). Yahweh is proposing to replace his covenant with Abraham (Gen 15:5; 22:17; 26:4) with a new covenant made with Moses. Moses wisely rejects the proposal (9:25-29; cf. Exod 32:11-13), and Yahweh withdraws it (Exod 32:14). According to Num 14:1-24, Yahweh made the same proposal to Moses when Israel murmured after hearing the report of the spies (Num 14:12), but then he withdrew it as a result of Moses' intercession. This detail in the first attempt to enter the land goes unmentioned in Deuteronomy 1. Presently, Moses is telling Israel it can enjoy even more spectacular increase if it keeps the commandments (see Note for 6:3).

15 *So I turned and came down from the mountain.* Moses does not intercede with Yahweh before descending the mountain, as he is reported to have done in Exod 32:11-14. But Deuteronomy reports the intercession in the supplement of vv. 25-29.

and the mountain was burning with fire. "Fire" symbolizes the divine presence (4:11, 24, 36; 5:22-27).

and the two tablets of the covenant were in my two hands. The tablets of stone are called "tablets of the covenant" in v. 11. The Ten Commandments were the terms of the Horeb covenant, and according to Deuteronomy, only they came to Israel at Horeb. The remainder of the law was given to Moses alone, who is teaching it now to Israel in the plains of Moab (see Note for 5:22).

16 Moses now sees the calf for himself and calls it a "sin" because the second commandment had already been given to the people in the fiery revelation at the Horeb assembly (see v. 10). He thus tells the people they have turned aside "quickly" from the way Yahweh commanded them. Some Sam and LXX MSS omit "quickly," which should be retained (see Rhetoric and Composition).

17 Moses was angry, and his breaking of the tablets meant that the covenant was now broken (von Rad; Moran; Weinfeld; cf. Exod 32:19). Akkadian *ṭuppam hepû* means "to break a tablet," which invalidates a document (*CAD*, 6:170-73; 19:138-39). Intentionally tearing up a document — later, and even today — has the same effect (cf. *b. B. Bat.* 168b).

before your eyes. On this Deuteronomic expression, see Note for 1:30.

18 This intercession in vv. 18-20 is being compared to the earlier intercession that took place when Moses was on the mountain with the tablets ("as formerly"), namely, the one recorded in Exod 32:9-14 and truncated in vv. 13-14. In Deuteronomy this first intercession — reported as not being successful — is given in a supplement (vv. 25-29). In Exodus Moses makes two intercessions: (1) after hearing from Yahweh while still on the mountain that the people had made a calf (Exod 32:7-14); and (2) after he had gone down to see the calf, punished the sinners, and gone up the mountain a second time to make atonement for the people (Exod 32:30-34). Tigay thinks the sequence in Deuteronomy is still a problem, however, for it is unlikely, he says, that Moses would have broken the tablets, interceded for forty days and forty nights, and then destroyed the idol (vv. 17-21). A forty-day intercession is a long hiatus between the breaking of the tablets and the destroying of the idol. In Exodus, Moses broke the tablets and destroyed the idol immediately (Exod 32:19-20). But the problem is reduced and perhaps eliminated if the destruction of the idol reported in v. 21 is being viewed in retrospect, in which case the sequence of events in Exodus, where the destruction of the idol took place *before* the second intercession, remains unaffected.

Then I fell prostrate before Yahweh. To prostrate oneself before Yahweh is to fall face down on the ground, the purpose being to emphasize the urgency of the entreaty and the suppliant's dependence upon divine mercy (Gruber 1980, 131-36; cf. Ezra 10:1).

as formerly. כָּרִאשֹׁנָה. Referring to Moses' prostration when he interceded on the mountain the first time, unmentioned in vv. 13-14 (also in Exod 32:11-14) but reported in v. 25.

bread I did not eat, and water I did not drink, over all your sin that you sinned. Moses fasted when he was on the mountain receiving the tablets (v. 9), but here he fasts in response to the people's sin, also his fear of what will happen as a result (v. 19). Exodus 32:30 says this was Moses' attempt to atone for the people's sin.

to do what was evil in the eyes of Yahweh, to provoke him to anger. The expression "do evil in the eyes of Yahweh (your God)" is stock in Deuteronomy (see Note for 4:25-26).

Deuteronomy 9

19 *Indeed, I was in dread because of the anger and the wrath for which Yahweh was furious toward you, to completely destroy you.* "I was in dread" (יָגֹרְתִּי) is a rare verb (Driver; cf. 28:60; Job 3:25; 9:28; Ps 119:39).

but Yahweh listened to me also at that time. The intercession was successful like the first, which Deuteronomy does not record but which is stated in Exod 32:14 (cf. Ps 106:23). Yahweh can and does change his mind in response to mediation! On Yahweh "repenting," see "Excursus: When God Repents" in Andersen and Freedman 1989, 638-79 [= D. N. Freedman 1997, 1:409-46]. The power of intercessory prayer is an important element in biblical faith (G. E. Wright; Isa 53:12; Acts 12:5; Jas 5:16), seen particularly in the prophets (Gen 20:7; Jer 27:18; 42:1-3; Lundbom 2010a, 29-31).

20 Aaron made the golden calf (Exod 32:2-5, 21-24), but Exodus records no intercession on his behalf. Aaron lived many more years (10:6; Num 33:38-39), which means the intercession must have been successful (ibn Ezra). The verse is self-standing (Weinfeld), and here in Deuteronomy it connects with Moses' second intercession (v. 18). But in Sam the verse is added to Exod 32:10, putting it at the beginning of Moses' first intercession. A Qumran text of Exod 32:10-30 (4QEx[a]) places it in the same location (Skehan 1955, 184-86).

Tigay thinks Aaron's intention was not to make an idol, but simply a pedestal for Yahweh. Nevertheless, the people immediately began to worship it (Exod 32:4), and Moses called it "a god of gold" (Exod 32:31). Moses' language may simply be extravagant for purposes of disparagement. Sarna (1991, 204) quotes Rashbam and other medieval Jewish commentators who argued that the people "could not have been so stupid" as to believe that this freshly manufactured image was itself a deity responsible for the exodus. Needless to say, Yahweh took the calf to be an idol.

21 Destruction of the calf by Moses is viewed here in retrospect; according to Exodus it did not take place after the second intercession, but after the first, when Moses came down from the mountain, saw the calf, and broke the tablets in a fit of anger (Exod 32:20). The destruction conforms to Deuteronomic descriptions of breaking and shattering idols and idolatrous altars in the book of Kings. In the Josianic reform, for example, it says:

> And [Josiah] brought out the Asherah from the house of Yahweh outside Jerusalem, to the brook Kidron, and beat it to dust and cast the dust of it upon the graves of the common people. (2 Kgs 23:6)

Again:

> And the altars on the roof of the upper chamber of Ahaz, which the kings of Judah had made, and the altars which Manasseh had made in the two

Deuteronomy 9

courts of the house of Yahweh, the king pulled down and broke in pieces from there, and cast the dust of them into the brook Kidron. (2 Kgs 23:12)

And again:

Moreover the altar at Bethel, the high place erected by Jeroboam the son of Nebat, who made Israel to sin, that altar with the high place, [Josiah] pulled down and broke in pieces its stones, crushing them to dust; also he burned the Asherah. (2 Kgs 23:15)

In Ugaritic texts that report the destruction of Mot, the god of death, the process is similar, with some of the same verbs being used: "burn," "grind," "scatter" (Fensham 1966; Begg 1985, 211-15). In the Baal-Anath cycle is this description:

(Anath] seizes the Godly Mot —
With sword she doth cleave him.
With fan she doth winnow him —
With fire she doth burn him —
With hand-mill she grinds him —
In the field she doth sow him.
Birds eat his *remnants*
Consuming his *portions*
Flitting from remnant to remnant.

(*ANET*^{3}, 140; I AB ii, beginning at line 30)

Begg cites other parallels in Egyptian, Mesopotamian, and Hittite texts, concluding that "the OT's descriptions of Moses' actions against the calf can indeed be related to a wide range of ANE presentations dealing with the elimination of undesirable entities" (Begg 1985, 228).

I took. לָקַחְתִּי. The Hebrew verb is a perfect, which should perhaps be taken as a pluperfect: "I had taken" (GKC §106f; Weinfeld). The action was completed in the past; cf. 1 Sam 28:3: "And Saul had put (הֵסִיר) the mediums and the wizards out of the land."

I burned it in the fire. The Ugaritic texts show variation in describing Mot's destruction, for which reason some have suggested that details are not important and should not be taken literally. Begg says: "Both the Biblical and extrabiblical writers wanted above all to underscore, by their piling up a whole series of destructive acts, that the reprobate being described was, in fact, thoroughly, utterly annihilated" (Begg 1985, 214-15, 229; Weinfeld, 412). Yet the burning of the calf is credible, particularly if the core was of wood. The gold would simply melt in the fire.

and I beat it, grinding it thoroughly until it was fine as dust. This detail is also credible. Gold today is beaten thin with a hammer and then filed with a file to produce gold powder.

the stream, which came down from the mountain. In Exod 32:20 it says simply that Moses scattered the dust upon the water and made the people drink it. Begg (1985, 213-14) says this may be compared to the birds eating of Mot's remains in one version of the Ugaritic text. In another version, Mot's remains are scattered "in the sea."

22 Verses 22-24 are the first of two supplements at the end of the chapter, describing other instances of Israelite rebellion in the wilderness. The rebellion at Taberah (= "burning"), said in Num 10:33 to be a three-day journey north of Mount Horeb, is recounted in Num 11:1-3. There the people grumbled about their misfortunes, causing Yahweh's anger to "burn" in the camp. The exact location of Massah is not known, but the rebellion occurring there, which included Israel's complaint that it had no water and wished it was back in Egypt (Exod 17:1-7; Num 20:1-13), loomed large in Israel's collective memory (see Note for 33:8). Deuteronomy 6:16 recalls Massah as the place where Israel put Yahweh to the test, and Moses says that must not happen again. The rebellion at Kibroth-hattaavah, where the people cried out for a lack of meat, is recounted in Num 11:4-34. The place is mentioned in Num 33:16, but its location is not known. On all three occasions Moses interceded for Israel and was successful (Exod 17:4-6; Num 11:2, 11-18; 20:6-11).

you were making Yahweh furious. מַקְצִפִים הֱיִיתֶם אֶת־יְהוָה. The participle with היה emphasizes a continuing action in the past (GKC §116r). See earlier v. 7: "you have been (continually) rebellious with Yahweh."

23 Reference is to the rebellion recorded in 1:19-32, which resulted in a failed attempt to take the land. Kadesh-barnea is an oasis in the Wilderness of Zin (see Note for 1:2), from where Israel launched its abortive penetration.

the command of Yahweh your God. אֶת־פִּי יְהוָה אֱלֹהֵיכֶם. Lit. "the mouth/speech of Yahweh your God." The Hebrew is idiomatic, with "mouth" meaning either "word" or "command." The LXX has: τῷ ῥήματι κυρίου τοῦ θεοῦ ὑμῶν ("the word of the Lord your God").

and you did not obey his voice. "Obeying Yahweh's voice" in Deuteronomy means keeping the commandments (see Note for 13:5).

24 Repeating the indictment of v. 7. See also 31:27, where Moses anticipates that Israel's rebellion will continue in the future. This refrain of Israel's ongoing rebellion is commonly heard in Jeremiah (Jer 3:24-25; 11:7-8; 22:21; 25:4-7; 26:4-5; 29:19; 32:30; 35:14b-15). The LXX has "he [i.e., Yahweh] was known to you." Huffmon (1966, 35) says that by adopting this reading, the verb ידע takes on the more technical meaning of "know" that occurs in the international treaties of the ANE, where Moses would be saying that Israel has been rebellious from the time it entered into covenant with Yahweh. But v. 7 states that Israel has been in rebellion since it came out of Egypt.

25 This intercession in vv. 25-29 corresponds to the *first* intercession in Exod 32:11-14, but some commentators (e.g., Driver, Weinfeld, Tigay, Nelson) think it expands the intercession of v. 18, which it cannot. The intercession of v. 18 occurs when Moses is on the mountain a *second* time. The intercession in Exod 32:11-14 takes place when Moses is still on the mountain with the tablets in hand, i.e., his *first* intercession (Driver notes this). Better sense is made if the present intercession is placed after v. 14, filling out what in vv. 13-14 is a truncated report of the first intercession. We noted earlier that Yahweh's "Let me alone, and I will completely destroy them" (v. 14) anticipated intervention by Moses. Now with the supplement in vv. 25-29, we learn that Moses did, in fact, intervene. Why? Because Yahweh said he was about to completely destroy Israel (v. 25). The verb "completely destroy" links vv. 14 and 25 (see Rhetoric and Composition). This reconstruction brings the Deuteronomic account in harmony with the Exodus account, i.e., both now report an intercession by Moses when he was on the mountain the first time, before he went down to see the calf in the camp. A comparison of Exod 32:7-14 with Deut 9:12-14, 25-29 yields the following:

Exod 32:7-14	Deut 9:12-14, 25-29
⁷Then Yahweh spoke to Moses: "Go down, for your people, whom you brought up from the land of Egypt, have acted corruptly; ⁸they have turned aside quickly from the way that I commanded them; they have made for themselves a metal calf, and they have worshipped it. . . ."	¹²Then Yahweh said to me: "Rise up, go down quickly from here, for your people whom you brought out from Egypt have acted corruptly; they have turned aside quickly from the way that I commanded them; they have made for themselves a metal thing."
⁹And Yahweh said to Moses: "I have seen this people, and have a look, it is a stiff-necked people. ¹⁰Now let me rest, that my wrath burn hot against them, and I will consume them, but I will make of you a great nation."	¹³And Yahweh said to me: "I have seen this people, and have a look, it is a stiff-necked people. ¹⁴Let me alone, and I will completely destroy them, and I will wipe out their name from under the heaven, and I will make of you a nation mightier and more numerous than they."
	²⁵So I fell prostrate before Yahweh forty days and forty nights that I fell prostrate, because Yahweh said he would completely destroy you.
¹¹And Moses sought the face of Yahweh his God and he said: "Why, Yahweh,	²⁶And I prayed to Yahweh and I said: "O Lord Yahweh, do not bring your

does your wrath burn hot against your people, whom you brought out from the land of Egypt by great power and by a strong hand?

¹²Why should the Egyptians say, 'With evil intent did he bring them out, to slay them in the mountains, and to consume them from upon the face of the ground'? Turn from your fierce wrath, and repent over the evil against your people.

¹³Remember Abraham, Isaac, and Israel, your servants, to whom you swore by your own self, and spoke to them, I will multiply your descendants as the stars of the heaven, and all this land that I have promised I will give to your descendants, and they shall inherit it forever."

¹⁴And Yahweh repented over the evil that he said he would do to his people.

people and your inheritance to ruin, whom you ransomed by your greatness, whom you brought out from Egypt by a strong hand.

²⁷Remember your servants, Abraham, Isaac, and Jacob; do not look to the stubbornness of this people, or to its wickedness, or to its sin,

²⁸lest the land from which you brought us out say, 'Yahweh was not able to bring them into the land that he promised them, and because he hated them he brought them out to kill them in the wilderness.' ²⁹Yes, they are your people, and your inheritance, whom you brought out by great strength and by an outstretched arm."

Verses 25-29 are then a supplement to the narrative in vv. 13-14, what Daube (1941; 1947, 74-101) calls a "coda." It happens in the Bible, also in other ancient legal writing, that a scribe, instead of inserting material in the text where it would fit naturally and chronologically, will instead tack it on at the end. Daube finds this occurring in Roman legal texts. Another example of narrative supplement in the Bible is in Jeremiah 36, where the report of Baruch having taking Jeremiah's first scroll from dictation and then reading it on a fast day in the temple (vv. 1-8) is supplemented in vv. 9-32 with a detailed account of what happened when Baruch did read the scroll and what occurred subsequently (Lundbom 1986a, 106; 2004a, 583, 596).

So I fell prostrate before Yahweh forty days and forty nights that I fell pros-

trate. The repetition of "that I fell prostrate" after "so I fell prostrate" is a Hebrew idiom called by Driver an *idem per idem*. See v. 18: "over all your sin that you sinned." The idiom occurs also in 1:46 (see Note there) and 29:15(16). Moses' prostration is not mentioned in Exod 32:11. On the act of prostration, which is falling face down on the ground, see v. 18.

forty days and forty nights. The length of time Moses was on the mountain the first time to receive the tablets (vv. 9, 11; cf. Exod 24:18). Reference is not to Moses' second forty-day stay on the mountain, mentioned in v. 18 (*pace* Driver; Tigay; Nelson).

26 Here and in v. 29 Moses counters the alienation language of v. 12, saying to Yahweh: "These are *your* people, not mine!" (Moberly 1983, 49-50). This is the first of three arguments seeking to dissuade Yahweh from bringing Israel to ruin. Yahweh performed a great redemptive act in the exodus, bringing Israel out from the land Egypt. Israel's "inheritance/heritage" (נַחֲלָה), here and in v. 29, is the land (see Note for 15:4).

O Lord Yahweh. אֲדֹנָי יְהוִה. On this form of address used in prayers, see Note for 3:24. The LXX has Κύριε κύριε βασιλεῦ τῶν θεῶν ("O Lord, Lord, King of gods").

whom you ransomed by your greatness. On the frequent use of the verb פדה ("ransom/redeem") in Deuteronomy, see Note for 7:7-8. Reference here is to Yahweh's deliverance of Israel from Egyptian slavery. Yahweh's "greatness" is affirmed often in Deuteronomy (see Note for 3:24), declared also in the Song of Moses (32:3).

whom you brought out from Egypt by a strong hand. On Yahweh's "strong hand," which is stock Deuteronomic language, see Note for 6:21. But cf. Exod 32:11b.

27 The second argument put forward by Moses against annihilating Israel, occurring also in Exod 32:13: Yahweh should refrain from doing so out of consideration for the patriarchs, Abraham, Isaac, and Jacob, with whom Yahweh made an eternal covenant to bless all people. It was to the fathers that Yahweh promised the gift of the land (see Note for 1:8). The verbal construction זְכֹר לְ has the technical meaning of "remember to one's credit" (Childs 1974, 556 n. 13; Jer 2:2; Pss 25:7; 132:1; 136:23; 2 Chr 6:42). On the theme of "remembering" (and "not forgetting") in Deuteronomy, see Note for 8:2. After "Jacob," the LXX adds: "to whom you yourself swore" (cf. Exod 32:13).

The idea of individuals interceding by referring to their ancestors is old. In the ANE, ancestors were believed to serve as protectors of their descendants, whose wickedness might justify their destruction (Weinfeld, 415-16). The Akkadian term for intercession was "to keep fatherhood" (cf. *abbūtu*, CAD, 1/1:50-51), which occurs in a Mari letter, the Babylonian "Šamaš Hymn" (Lambert 1960, 132-33; lines 99-100), and the Vassal Treaties of Esarhaddon (Wiseman

1958, 59-60; lines 417-18). The merits of the ancestors assumed importance in later Jewish tradition, where the ancestors were invoked in Jewish prayers on fast days and the New Year (Urbach 1979, 504). The term for intercession in the rabbinic literature is "to invoke the merit of the fathers." The "merits of the saints" carried over into doctrine of the Christian church and became a key issue in sparking the Protestant Reformation.

do not look to the stubbornness of this people, or to its wickedness, or to its sin. Not mentioned in Exod 32:11-13. The noun קְשִׁי ("stubbornness") is a *hapax legomenon* in the OT, but occurs in Sam and the Dead Sea Scrolls (קְשִׁי, KBL³). The verb קשׁה, meaning "to be hard, severe, show stubbornness," is well-attested in the OT. On the idiom "stiff-necked" (קְשֵׁה־עֹרֶף), see v. 6.

28 Moses' third argument is particularly strong: Destroying Israel will injure Yahweh's name among the nations, bringing it into disrepute (Luther; cf. Greenberg 1983b, 384). This same argument has turned up in the Hittite Plague Prayer of Mursilis (14th cent.), where the suppliant says that all the surrounding countries have begin to attack Hatti land; therefore he prays: "Let it again become a matter of concern to the Sun-goddess of Arinna! O god, bring not thy name into disrepute!" (*ANET*³, 396). That God must act for the sake of his holy name is a common argument in the OT, appearing in Exod 32:12; Num 14:13-16; Josh 7:9, and often in the Prophets and the Psalms (Jer 14:7, 21; Ezek 20:14, 44; 36:22-23; 39:25; Joel 2:17; Pss 25:11; 79:9-10; 109:21; 115:1-2). It is present, too, in the Song of Moses, where Yahweh himself reflects on the punishment of Israel:

> I thought: I will strike them down,
>   I will surely make their memory cease from humankind.
> Except I feared provocation of the enemy,
>   lest his adversaries should misjudge,
>   lest they say: Our hand is raised up,
> And not Yahweh has done all this. (Deut 32:26-27)

Daube (1969a, 51) says the argument is an appeal to shame, which is a potent weapon in the ancient world. These three arguments: appeals to God's reputation; invoking the fathers' merits; and reciting the gracious qualities of God became the three pillars of Jewish prayers for forgiveness, and they continue to be so to the present day (Weinfeld).

lest the land. I.e., the people of the land (Sam: עַם הָאָרֶץ; LXX: οἱ κατοικοῦντες τὴν γῆν; Targums: "the inhabitants of the land"). The Hebrew is idiomatic (cf. Gen 41:57; 1 Sam 17:46; 2 Sam 15:23). Exodus 32:12 has "the Egyptians."

29 Cf. Exod 32:11. On the affirmation of Israel being Yahweh's (holy) people, see Note for 7:6. Israel is also Yahweh's inheritance (32:9; Jer 10:16b; 51:19b). This verse concludes Moses' first intercession, with no mention made of Yahweh acceding to Moses' request and withdrawing his threat to annihilate Israel (cf. Exod 32:14). In Deuteronomy it is only after the second intercession that Yahweh hearkens to Moses' plea (v. 19b).

by great strength and by an outstretched arm. בְּכֹחֲךָ הַגָּדֹל וּבִזְרֹעֲךָ הַנְּטוּיָה. The expression occurs with reference to the exodus deliverance in 2 Kgs 17:36; Bar 2:11 and with reference to Yahweh's awesome creation in Jer 27:5; 32:17 (cf. Weinfeld 1972, 329 no. 15). The parallel account in Exod 32:11 has "by great strength and by strong hand." The stock expression in Deuteronomy is "strong hand and outstretched arm" (see Note for 4:34).

Message and Audience

Following the sermons on Israel's election (ch. 7) and the wilderness privations that were intended to humble the people and test their obedience to Yahweh (ch. 8), Moses now focuses on the upcoming conquest, stating the basis on which its success will rest.

The sermon starts out much the same as the sermon in ch. 7, promising Israel that it will overcome peoples who are greater and mightier than they, whose cities also are great and fortified sky high. Israel knows about the mighty Anakim, having heard about them in the report of the spies. How can such a formidable foe be overcome? The first attempt to penetrate Canaan was a disaster, ending in humiliating defeat. But Moses says that Yahweh will be marching at the head of the army, a consuming fire is this God of Israel, and he will completely destroy the Canaanites. Battles will go quickly, and people will perish quickly. Yahweh told Israel this before.

But more needs to be said about the basis on which the conquest will rest, for Moses thinks Israel will likely conclude that success in battle will be due to its own righteousness. Nations going to war commonly reason this way: the enemy is wicked; we are righteous. About the wickedness of the Canaanites there can be no argument. They are wicked; in fact, their wickedness has reached the point where Yahweh is determined to rain judgment upon them. That is one reason why Yahweh is clearing these nations away to give Israel their land. The other reason is that Yahweh is making good his promise to Abraham, Isaac, and Jacob to give their descendants the land. What Israel must simply realize is that getting the land is not due to its own righteousness, for it is plainly not a righteous people. Israel is stiff-necked, as past history makes all too clear.

Moses says Israel has had a rebellious temper ever since it left Egypt. The one rebellious act eclipsing all the others occurred at Horeb, when Israel made the golden calf. Yahweh was so angry that he was ready to destroy the people. Moses recalls how he went up the mountain to receive the stone tablets, which were tablets of the covenant, and stayed there forty days and forty nights, fasting the entire time. Yahweh gave him the tablets, written by himself, which contained the same words spoken to Israel on the day of the assembly, when the voice of God was heard from the midst of the fire and the people were afraid for their lives. At the end of forty days the tablets were given to Moses. But on this very day something terribly wrong was going on below. Yahweh, knowing what has happened, told Moses to go down quickly, for the people he brought out of Egypt had turned aside from his way and made themselves an idol. They were in violation of a commandment that came in the fiery revelation, explicitly forbidding them to make idols and worship them. Yahweh would not countenance the idols of Canaan and throughout the ancient world. He called the people stiff-necked and told Moses to speak of them no more. He would destroy these rank unbelievers and begin all over again with Moses. There was a precedent of sorts with Noah.

Moses then went down from the mountain, burning as it was with fire, and carried in his two hands the two tablets of the covenant. When he arrived in the camp below, he saw for himself the thing that had enraged Yahweh and told the people that they had sinned before Yahweh, turning aside quickly from the way Yahweh commanded. In a fit of rage Moses threw the tablets to the ground, breaking them in pieces as the people looked on. Then he fell prostrate before Yahweh, praying and fasting another forty days and forty nights, knowing that Yahweh was greatly provoked by what the people had done. Moses says he was himself in dread because of Yahweh's threat to completely destroy Israel. But to Moses' great relief, Yahweh listened to him as before and the threat was withdrawn. With Aaron, too, Yahweh was wroth, for he had supervised the crafting of the idol. Moses in his second ascent up the mountain interceded for him, and the audience knew the intercession was successful, for Aaron went on to live many more years.

Moses then tells what he did with the wretched thing. He burned it in the fire, which melted the gold and consumed its wooden core, if it had one, and then he beat the gold, grinding it till it was fine as dust, and threw the dust into a mountain stream.

The audience then hears about other wilderness rebellions occurring at Taberah, Massah, and Kibroth-hattaavah, all of which made Yahweh furious. At Taberah the people grumbled about their fate in an inhospitable wasteland; at Massah they complained about a lack of water and wished they were back in Egypt; and at Kibroth-hattaavah they cried out for a lack of meat. To this might be added the rebellion at Kadesh-barnea, where Israel at first did not want to go up into the land, but then later did go up, against Yahweh's command that it not go. This sad story began the Moab discourse. Yes, Israel has rebelled against Yahweh for as long as Moses has known the people.

The audience then hears an otherwise unreported intercession when Moses was on the mountain the first time, only hinted at in the main narrative. Here we learn that Moses prostrated himself before Yahweh for forty days and forty nights, interceding for a people Yahweh had a mind to completely destroy. Moses argued that Yahweh would be ill-advised to destroy the very people he redeemed from Egypt. He asks Yahweh to remember the patriarchs. What would become of his reputation if other nations concluded that he brought Israel out of Egypt and then could not settle it in the promised land, deciding rather to kill all the people in the wilderness? Moses tells Yahweh that Israel is his — not Moses' — people, whom he brought out of Egypt with a great display of power.

To a late 8th- and early 7th-cent. audience, the giants presently in the land were the Assyrians, and the people might do well to remember that with Yahweh as their God this foe could be subdued as easily as the Canaanite foe. But the people must not trust in their own righteousness, for they are not righteous. They never have been. If Yahweh defeats the current enemy, it will be an act of grace, a confirmation of the covenant made with Abraham and conditional only on Israel obeying the commandments. Obedience in the present day must exceed the obedience in the wilderness.

So far as the golden calf is concerned, a late 8th- and early 7th-cent. audience would have been able to draw a parallel to the golden calves set up by Jeroboam I at Bethel and Dan (1 Kgs 12:28-29), idols roundly condemned by both Hosea and the scribes of Jerusalem (Hos 8:4-6; 13:2; 2 Kgs 10:29). They were said to have led to the downfall of northern Israel (2 Kgs 17:16). Weinfeld says that vv. 7-24 reflect the pessimistic view of Israel's history after the fall of Samaria. What might a later audience have thought about idolatry currently awash in Judah? Would Yahweh be any less furious about it than with the idolatry in the wilderness? Idols in Judah must be destroyed, and in Josiah's late 7th-cent. reform they were destroyed.

Later still, the church fathers (e.g., Irenaeus, Tertullian, Origen, and others) made much of the calf incident at Horeb, citing it as the reason why the Jews rejected Jesus and why God had rejected the Jews (Lundbom, "New Covenant," in *ABD*, 4:1093-94).

I. WITH THE COVENANT RENEWED THE JOURNEY CAN CONTINUE (10:1-11)

1. Moses Makes New Tablets (10:1-5)

10¹*At that time Yahweh said to me, "Shape for yourself two tablets of stone, like the first ones, and come up to me on the mountain, and make for yourself an ark* of wood, ²and I will write upon the tablets the words that were on the first tablets that you broke, and you shall put them in the ark." ³So I made an ark of acacia wood, and I shaped two tablets of stone like the first ones, and I went up the mountain, and the two tablets were in my hand. ⁴And he wrote upon the tablets as he had written the first ones, the ten words that Yahweh spoke to you on the mountain from the midst of the fire, on the day of the assembly, and Yahweh gave them to me. ⁵Then I turned and came down from the mountain, and I put the tablets in the ark that I made; and they are there, just as Yahweh commanded me.

2. Journey to Moserah Where Aaron Died (10:6-7)

10⁶And the children of Israel journeyed from Beeroth Bene-jaakan to Moserah. There Aaron died, and he was buried there, and Eleazar his son functioned as priest in his stead. ⁷From there they journeyed to Gudgodah, and from Gudgodah to Jotbathah, a land with wadis of water.

3. Levites to Carry the Ark (10:8-9)

10⁸At that time Yahweh set apart the tribe of Levi to carry the ark of the covenant of Yahweh, to stand before Yahweh, to minister to him, and to bless in his name, to this day. ⁹Therefore, there is not for Levi a portion or an inheritance with his brothers; Yahweh, he is his inheritance, just as Yahweh your God spoke to him.

4. Intercession Successful; Rise Up and Resume Your Journey (10:10-11)

10¹⁰And I, I stayed on the mountain as the first time, forty days and forty nights, and Yahweh listened to me also that time. Yahweh was not willing to bring you to ruin. ¹¹And Yahweh said to me, "Rise up for journeying before the people, that they may enter and possess the land that I have sworn to your fathers to give to them."

Rhetoric and Composition

These verses report (1) a covenant renewal, in which Moses makes a second pair of stone tablets and an ark, and Yahweh writes the Ten Commandments on the tablets (10:1-5); (2) the journey from Beeroth Bene-jaakan to Moserah, where Aaron died and was buried (10:6-7); (3) the choice of the Levites to carry the ark, minister to Yahweh, and bless people in Yahweh's name (10:8-9); and (4) Moses' successful intercession, after which comes a directive from Yahweh to get on with the journey (10:10-11). The opening narrative reporting Moses' making of a second set of tablets, which closely follows Exod 34:1-4 (Driver; Morgenstern 1928, 29-30), picks up from 9:21. The present verses are demarcated at the top end by a *petuḥah* in M^L and a section in Sam before v. 1, which is the chapter division. Demarcation at the bottom end is by a *petuḥah* in M^L and a section in Sam after v. 11. The Sam has additional sections after vv. 5 and 7.

Time indicators begin the three narrative sections (vv. 6-7 are an antiquarian note):

I	*at that time*	v. 1
II	*at that time*	v. 8
III	*as the first time . . . also that time*	v. 10

Portions of 10:1-11 are contained in 2QDeut^c, 4QDeut^c, 4QpaleoDeut^r, MurDeut, and 4Q364; also on a phylactery from Qumran (4Q128).

Notes

10:1-2 *At that time Yahweh said to me, "Shape for yourself two tablets of stone, like the first ones, and come up to me on the mountain.* The people have been forgiven and restored to Yahweh's favor, thanks to Moses' intercession (9:19b; 10:10), and the covenant will now be renewed (cf. Exod 34:1-4). Moses is therefore told to make two new tablets on which will be written the words of the first tablets, which he broke. These will be the Ten Commandments, given initially to the people in the voice out of the fire, on the day of the assembly, and then written for them on tablets of stone (see Note for 9:10). Moses is to make the tablets (cf. Exod 32:16, where the first tablets were "the work of God"). In Deuteronomy, this is Moses' second trip up the mountain (9:9); if we add another ascent after the sinners are punished (cf. Exod 32:30-31), then it is Moses' *third* trip up.

At that time. A general reference to when the calf incident took place. The narrative picks up from 9:21, which is to say that for the Deuteronomic writer the command to make new tablets occurs after the calf was destroyed and Moses' intercession had been successful (9:19b).

and make for yourself an ark of wood, and I will write upon the tablets the words that were on the first tablets that you broke, and you shall put them in the ark." In Exod 34:1-4 is no mention of the ark. In Deuteronomy the ark functions simply as a receptacle for the tablets. Yahweh will again write the ten words on the tablets (cf. 9:10; Exod 31:18b; 32:16), and Moses is to deposit them in the ark. They are there as Moses speaks in the plains of Moab (v. 5) and are still there during the monarchy (1 Kgs 8:9 [= 2 Chr 5:10]), at which time nothing else is in the ark. Later Moses will put his Song "beside the ark," but not in it (see Note for 31:26).

Elsewhere in the OT, the ark took on an expanded function, particularly in the Priestly traditions: It was a symbol of the divine presence and accompanied Israel in its various movements, especially as it went into battle (Num 10:33-36; 14:44 [contrast Deut 1:42]; Josh 3:6; 1 Sam 4:3-4, 6-7; 2 Sam 11:11). It was also a throne for the invisible Yahweh (1 Sam 4:4; 2 Sam 6:2 [= 1 Chr 13:6]; 2 Kgs 19:15 [= Isa 37:16]; Jer 3:16-17). On the ark as Yahweh's footstool, see Haran 1959. Overlaid in pure gold (Exod 25:11; 37:2), the ark (of the covenant) was the nation's most sacred object, kept later in the temple's holy of holies (1 Kgs 8:6; cf. Exod 25:10-22; 37:1-9). All of this goes unmentioned in Deuteronomy, where the ark is nothing more than a box containing the tablets. After Solomon's reign (1 Kgs 8:9) practically nothing is said of the ark, and Weinfeld thinks it was nonexistent in the time of Jeremiah (Jer 3:16). But according to 2 Chr 35:3, the ark was in its place when Josiah celebrated Passover (622). Haran (1963; 1977, 1:276-88) thought Manasseh removed the ark from the temple and replaced it with symbols for Baal and Asherah (cf. 2 Kgs 21:7; 23:4). After that it disappeared. 2 Maccabees 2:4-8 knew a tradition that Jeremiah hid the ark, the tabernacle, and other temple treasures in a cave on Mount Nebo, where they were to remain until God gathered his people in a new act of grace (b. Šeqal. 6:1-2; Yoma 53b). J. Day (2005) thinks it was probably destroyed along with the temple in 586. But the truth is we really do not know what happened to the ark.

and you shall put them in the ark. Treaties and other documents in the ancient world were stored in boxes (Weinfeld; Tigay), otherwise on shelves in temple and palace libraries (2 Kgs 22:8; Lundbom 1986a, 90).

3 Moses made the ark, two stone tablets like the first ones, and then ascended the mountain (cf. Exod 34:4). In Exodus, instructions for making the ark were given when Moses was on the mountain the first time (Exod 25:10-22). Bezalel, a talented craftsman, was chosen to supervise the construction (Exod 31:7; 37:1-9). Bezalel was also chosen to make the tabernacle and its furnishings. When Moses now takes the new tablets up the mountain, they are blank; Yahweh will again write on them the Ten Commandments.

So I made an ark of acacia wood. וָאַעַשׂ אֲרוֹן עֲצֵי שִׁטִּים. Acacia wood was highly prized in antiquity. Besides being used for the ark, it was also the wood of choice for tabernacle furnishings (Exod 25:23, 28; 26:26, 32, 37; 27:1, etc.). The acacia tree (שִׁטִּים) — the *acacia seyal* and somewhat larger *acacia tortilis* — grows in the Arabah rift valley, mainly south of the Dead Sea, the Sinai Peninsula, and in Egypt (Arabic *sunt*), being at home in desert and semidesert areas (Isa 41:19) wherever water is available (Moldenke and Moldenke 1952, 24-26; Walker 1957, 192-93; Zohary 1982, 116). The *acacia seyal* is commonly found in the Sinai Peninsula, and Moldenke says the *acacia tortilis* is conspicuous on Mount Sinai (Horeb). Acacia wood is hard, close-grained, and beautiful orange-brown in color. It is not attacked by insects. The LXX term, ξύλων ἀσήπτων, means "wood not liable to rot." In Egypt acacia wood was used to clamp shut mummy-coffins. In OT Priestly traditions the ark was said to have been overlaid and adorned variously with gold (Exod 25:11-18; 31:4; 37:2-7). About this Deuteronomy says nothing.

4 Yahweh wrote the tablets, as before (4:13; 9:10; cf. Exod 31:18; 32:16). But the text here says "he" (cf. Exod 34:28b), not "YHWH," as Weinfeld translates. The use of the pronoun for Yahweh may be intentional, like 34:6, to convey reverence and mystery about the writing. These were the exact words Yahweh spoke to the people directly out of the fire, on the day of the assembly (see Note for 9:10). On the number of commandments being ten, see Note for 4:13.

on the day of the assembly. The LXX omits.

5 The Ten Commandments deposited in the ark are still there as Moses speaks in Moab. A book of the law, viz., the Song of Moses, was later placed "beside" the ark (31:26).

6 Verses 6-7 are an antiquarian note like those in chs. 2–3 (see Note for 2:10-12). The note does not include all of vv. 6-9 (*pace* RSV; NRSV; NIV; NEB; REB; Weinfeld). It interrupts the narrative to report the death of Aaron and the succession of Eleazer, the first two Levites consecrated to the priesthood (Exod 4:14). In v. 8, where the narrative resumes, the Levites get the privilege of carrying the ark.

The children of Israel journeyed from Beeroth Bene-jaakan to Moserah. According to the P itinerary listing (Numbers 33), the journey went from Moseroth to Bene-jaakan (v. 31). Here the reference to Beeroth Bene-jaakan ("wells of the sons of Jaakan") is because of the wells belonging to this Edomite clan (1 Chr 1:42; cf. Akan in Gen 36:27). The precise location of these wells is not known; Driver thinks they would be in or near the Arabah, not far from Edom. Birein, about 15 mi north of Kadesh, and 6 mi south of el-'Auja, has been put forth as a possible site (Abel 1933, 387; 1938, 262-63; *ABD*, 1:647). This would put Edomite water rights rather far west, but the location is still possible (see Note for 2:4). The location of Moserah ("Moseroth" plural in Num 33:31) is not known. Since in Numbers (20:22-29; 33:38-39) Aaron's death and burial are placed at Mount Hor, Abel (1933, 387) suggested that Mount Hor could be part of a Moseroth mountain range, just as Mount Nebo was a part of the Abarim range (see Note for 32:49).

and Eleazar his son functioned as priest in his stead. Aaron was the founder of a hereditary priesthood. Eleazar figured prominently in the battle against the Midianites (Numbers 31).

7 Gudgodah is called Hor Haggidgad ("the hollow of Gidgad") in Num 33:32-33 (Rashi), although ibn Ezra says the two are not the same place. In his view, Gudgodah is a general name for a region that includes Zalmonah, Punon, and Oboth (Num 33:41-43). Judging from the itinerary in Num 33:32-35, these are encampments north of Ezion-geber. Jotbathah is said to be a land of water-filled wadis (streams), and Eusebius *(Onom.)* says the same about Gudgodah, which he calls Gadgada. Neither encampment is known, although a suggested site for Gudgodah is the Wadi el-Ghadhaghed, a stream that flows into the Wadi Jerafeh, and for Jotbathah, ʿAin ṭābah and eṭ-ṭābah (LXX: Ετεβαθα), a swampy depression about 11 mi southwest of Eilat on the western shore of the Gulf of Aqaba, which becomes a lake in winter (Wilton 1863, 130-31; Abel 1938, 215-16; Simons 1959, 259; *ABD*, 3:1021).

a land with wadis of water. A *wadi* (Arabic) is a riverbed without water in the dry season, but in the rainy season a torrent of fast-moving water. Jotbathah was a place with wadis having an ample supply of water.

8 The narrative resumes. "At that time" refers to the encampment at Horeb when the calf was made and the covenant was renewed (Rashi; Rashbam; G. E. Wright; Tigay), not to Aaron's death, which occurred almost forty years later (Num 33:38). According to Exod 32:25-29, the Levites rallied to Moses when he called for support after viewing the golden calf, and they showed their zeal by putting the sinners to the sword. Moses said to the Levites after the slaughter, "Today you ordain yourselves for the ministry of Yahweh, each one at the cost of his son and of his brother, that he may bestow a blessing upon you this day." The Levites, then, were not charged with sin in the calf affair.

to carry the ark of the covenant of Yahweh, to stand before Yahweh, to minister to him, and to bless in his name. The three principal functions of the tribe of Levi were: (1) to carry the ark (31:9; Josh 3:3; 6:6, 12; 8:33; 1 Kgs 8:3, 6[= 2 Chr 5:4-5, 7]; 1 Chr 15:2, 15, 26; Num 3:31, which was assigned to the family of the Kohathites); (2) to minister to Yahweh, which included presiding over sacrificial offerings, receiving oracles, and participating in other divine decisions (18:5, 7; 21:5; Jer 33:21; 1 Chr 16:4; 23:13); and (3) to bless in Yahweh's name, which was a singular privilege because it presupposed an association with Yahweh's holy name (21:5; Num 6:23, 27; 1 Chr 23:13). On the "Levitical priests" in Deuteronomy, see 18:1 and Note for 12:12. A history of the priesthood in the OT is given in Cody 1969.

the ark of the covenant of Yahweh. The ark contained the Ten Commandments, the terms of the Horeb (Sinai) covenant (4:13).

to stand before Yahweh, to minister to him. The phrases are in apposition to one another; "to stand before Yahweh" means "to be in Yahweh's ministry/

Deuteronomy 10

service" (1:38; 1 Kgs 10:8; 12:8; 17:1; 18:15; 2 Kgs 3:14; Jer 15:19; 36:21; 40:10, etc.). The priest enjoys special service as Yahweh's minister (17:12; 18:7; Judg 20:28; Ezek 44:15; 2 Chr 29:11).

to bless in his name. Aaron and his sons are to give the priestly blessing of Num 6:24-26. In bestowing a blessing one lifts up the hands (Rashi; cf. Lev 9:22).

to this day. The Levites were carrying out these duties to the present day. On this stock Deuteronomic expression, see Note for 2:22.

9 All the other tribes were given an inheritance, i.e., a share of territory in the promised land. The tribe of Levi received no such inheritance, their share being reckoned as the dues and other offerings made to Yahweh by the people (18:1-5; cf. 12:12; 14:27, 29; Josh 13:14, 33; 18:7). Because the Levitical priests received their livelihood from dues and offerings, it was said that "Yahweh was their inheritance" (Num 18:20). But the (Levitical) priests could own land (1 Kgs 2:26; Jer 32:6-9); they possessed cities and pastureland outside cities (Num 35:1-8; Lev 25:32-34).

just as Yahweh your God spoke to him. In Num 18:20 Aaron alone is told that he will have no inheritance and that Yahweh will be his portion and inheritance. The lack of an inheritance is announced more generally to the Levites in Num 18:21-24.

10 Verses 10-11 cannot continue from vv. 1-5 (Driver), where Moses goes up the mountain to receive Yahweh's writing on the second set of tablets. Moses' intercession is in the past, and the people are forgiven. Verses 10-11 must then be another supplement (like 9:25-29), filling out the truncated report of Moses' second intercession in 9:18-19, the purpose of which was to atone for the people's sin (Exod 32:30-34; see Note for 9:18). The forty days and forty nights are the same forty days and forty nights referred to in 9:18.

and Yahweh listened to me also that time. Repeated from 9:19 (Driver). The LXX omits "as the first time."

11 The people, now forgiven, are told by Yahweh to get on with their journey (Luther). The directive is reported differently in Exod 32:34, where Yahweh says only his angel will now go before the people. This had to be negotiated further, for Moses wanted Yahweh himself to accompany the people. In the end, Yahweh agreed he would do that (Exod 33:1-17).

Rise up for journeying. קוּם לֵךְ לְמַסָּע. A variant of stock Deuteronomic phraseology in chs. 2–3 (see Note for 2:24).

Message and Audience

The people are now forgiven of their great sin, and Moses says Yahweh commanded him to make two stone tablets like the first and come again up the mountain. Moses is also instructed to make an ark in which to deposit the tablets. Moses says he made an ark out of acacia wood, crafted two tablets like the first ones, and went up the mountain. Yahweh then wrote on the tablets the Ten Commandments, which the people heard out of the fire on the day of the assembly. Yahweh gave the tablets to Moses, who went down the mountain and put them in the ark. He told the people: "There they are!"

The audience is then told how people journeyed from the wells of Benejaakan to Moserah, where Aaron died and was buried. Eleazar his son became priest in his stead. From Moserah the people journeyed to Gudgodah, and from Gudgodah to Jotbathah, where there were streams of water. Reflecting back to the time at Horeb, the audience is then told that the tribe of Levi was chosen to carry the ark, to minister to Yahweh, and to give blessings in Yahweh's name. This they had been doing to the present day. The Levites were not given an inheritance in the promised land, as were the other tribes. Yahweh would be their inheritance, as Yahweh told them.

In a final supplement, Moses says he stayed on the mountain forty days and forty nights, as when he received the first tablets, and Yahweh heard his intercession, saying he would not bring Israel to ruin. The audience will presumably know that reference is to the second intercession on the mountain, when Moses made atonement for the people. At this time, Yahweh told him to get up and resume the journey into the land that Yahweh promised to the fathers.

To a late 8th- and early 7th-cent. audience, this will be a word of hope in an otherwise difficult time, when Assyria has entered the land and destroyed Samaria, Galilee, and the Transjordan and under another ambitious Assyrian king has ravaged Judah during the reign of Hezekiah. Yahweh, nevertheless, will forgive sin, renew the covenant, and give Judah hope of continued living in the land promised to the fathers. This message, along with preaching from the prophets, could have inspired Hezekiah to carry out his reform in the years prior to 701.

J. Fear, Walk Straight, Love, and Serve Yahweh (10:12–11:17)

1. Circumcise Yourself to Yahweh (10:12-22)

10 ^{12}*And now, Israel, what does Yahweh your God ask from you, except to fear Yahweh your God, to walk in all his ways, and to love him, and to serve Yahweh your God with all your heart and with all your soul;* ^{13}*to keep the commandments of Yahweh, and his statutes that I am commanding you today, for your own good?*

¹⁴Look, to Yahweh your God belong the heavens, yes the heavens of heavens, the earth and all that is in it. ¹⁵Only with your fathers did Yahweh become attached to love them, and he chose their descendants after them, you, out of all the peoples, as at this day. ¹⁶So you must circumcise the foreskin of your heart, and your neck stiffen no longer. ¹⁷For Yahweh your God, he is God of gods and Lord of lords, the great, the mighty, and the awesome God, who does not show partiality and does not take a bribe; ¹⁸the one who does justice to the orphan and the widow, and who loves the sojourner, giving to him bread and an outer garment. ¹⁹So you shall love the sojourner, for sojourners you were in the land of Egypt. ²⁰Yahweh your God you shall fear, him you shall serve, and to him you shall cling, and in his name you shall swear. ²¹He is your praise, and he is your God, who has done with you these great and awe-inspiring things, which your eyes have seen. ²²Seventy persons your fathers went down to Egypt, and now Yahweh your God has made you as the stars of the heaven for multitude.

Rhetoric and Composition

The present verses form a unit (Driver; Tigay) in which the preaching of chs. 6–10 is summed up. The unit is demarcated at the top end by a *petuḥah* in M^L and a section in Sam before 12. Delimitation at the bottom end is after v. 22, which is the chapter division. There are no sections in M^L and Sam between vv. 12-22. Sam has its next section after 11:1, which is not present in M^L.

The verses contain a structure that rhythmically alternates between commands and reasons for the commands (Moran):

10:12-13   *Command:* Fear Yahweh; walk in all his ways; love and serve him; and keep his commandments.
10:14-15   *Reason:* To Yahweh belong heaven and earth, and Yahweh it was who chose the fathers and their descendants.

10:16   *Command:* Open your heart and stiffen your neck no longer.
10:17-18   *Reason:* Yahweh is God of gods, great, mighty and awesome; a God who shows no partiality nor will he take a bribe; he does justice to the orphan and the widow and loves the sojourner.

10:19a   *Command:* You shall love the sojourner.
10:19b   *Reason:* You yourselves were sojourners in Egypt.

10:20   *Command:* Yahweh you shall fear; him you shall serve; to him you shall cling; and in his name you shall swear.

10:21-22 *Reason:* Yahweh is your praise; your God, who has done these great and awe-inspiring things; he has multiplied you from seventy persons going down to Egypt to a veritable multitude, now as the stars of the heavens.

The closing command balances the opening command:

10:12-13 *Fear Yahweh;* walk in all his ways; love and *serve him;* and keep his commandments.
10:20 *Yahweh you shall fear; him you shall serve;* to him you shall cling; and in his name you shall swear.

The unit is also tied together by the rhetorical particle וְעַתָּה ("and now"), which occurs at beginning and end, making an inclusio (vv. 12, 22).

Portions of 10:12-22 are contained in 4QDeut^l, 4QpaleoDeut^r, and 4Q364; also on phylacteries from Qumran (1Q20, 21-22; 4Q128, 138, 143; 8Q3) and *mezuzot* from Qumran (4Q150, 151; 8Q4).

Notes

10:12 A tidy summary of Deuteronomic theology, which calls for total commitment to Yahweh. These internal and external inclinations are augmented by a command to keep the commandments (v. 13). The call echoes the Shema and liturgy in 6:4-9, the latter repeated in 11:18-20. "Fearing Yahweh" (see Note for 4:10) is an interior disposition consisting of awe and reverence, showing itself in worship (Luther; cf. Rev 14:7). "Walking in Yahweh's way" has strong ethical implications in the OT (see Note for 5:33). "Loving Yahweh" in Deuteronomy is the proper response to Yahweh's love for Israel (see Note for 6:5). Another major theme in Deuteronomy is the call for Israel to "serve" Yahweh, which again includes the worship of Yahweh and only Yahweh (see Note for 6:13). The warning more often in Deuteronomy is not to "serve other gods" (see Note for 4:19), or idols, which is an express violation of the second commandment (5:9). Liberation in the OT — also in the NT — is a change of masters (Daube 1963): In Egypt Israel did hard service for Pharaoh; now Israel is to serve Yahweh joyfully and with ease (30:11-20; cf. Matt 11:28-30).

what does Yahweh your God ask from you. The prophet Micah later poses the same question. His answer: "To do justice, and *to love* steadfast love, and *to walk* humbly with your God" (Mic 6:8). Suzerain kings in the ANE demanded nothing less from vassal kings. Adad, lord of Halab, says to Zimri-Lim, king of Mari:

Am I not Adad, Lord of Halab, who raised you . . . and who made you regain the throne of your father's house? . . . This is what I demanded from you, and what I have communicated to you, you will do. You will heed my word. . . . (Malamat 1980, 73; Anbar 1975, 517)

and now. On the rhetorical particle עַתָּה, which recurs in v. 22, see Note for 2:13. Here the particle marks a transition from past history (9:7–10:11) to the present, in which some practical conclusions are to be drawn. See a similar use of this particle in 4:1.

with all your heart and with all your soul. A stock Deuteronomic phrase (see Note for 4:29).

13 The conclusion of the rhetorical question. In Deuteronomy, this is what fearing Yahweh, walking in all his ways, loving and serving him heart and soul add up to: keeping the commandments. Luther says keeping the commandments will not please God unless it emanates from a heart that fears, loves, obeys, and serves.

for your own good. More expansive statements are in 4:40; 5:32-33. See also 6:24.

14 An appeal to look to Yahweh the creator, after which Israel is to consider Yahweh's love of the patriarchs and choice of their descendants (v. 15). This is the reason for the command to commit oneself totally to Yahweh (vv. 12-13). God the creator is here extolled *before* God the savior and benefactor of Israel, which happens also in prayers of Jeremiah (Jer 32:16-22) and Ezra (Neh 9:6-15).

Look. הֵן. A variant of the emphatic particle הִנֵּה (cf. Jer 3:1; Isa 41:24).

the heavens, yes the heavens of heavens. הַשָּׁמַיִם וּשְׁמֵי הַשָּׁמָיִם. Hebrew שְׁמֵי הַשָּׁמָיִם ("the heavens of heavens") is an idiom expressing the superlative: "the highest heavens" (1 Kgs 8:27[= 2 Chr 6:18]; Ps 148:4; Neh 9:6; GKC §133i). Cf. קֹדֶשׁ הַקֳּדָשִׁים ("the holy of holies") in Exod 26:33, which means the most holy place. The cosmology of ancient Israel gives no indication of assuming multiple heavens, although the plural שָׁמַיִם, which English Bibles often translate simply as "heaven," may presuppose a more complex celestial sphere. But in Babylonian thought, where the earth was believed to be flat, three superimposed heavens were imagined. They are first attested in the Babylonian story of creation, *Enūma Eliš* (W. G. Lambert, "Himmel," in *RLA,* 4:411-12), which Lambert dates to probably the 12th cent. We hear of multiple heavens (and multiple earths) in the NT: e.g., Jesus tells his disciples that he is going to leave them to prepare a house with "many rooms" (John 14:2). Paul, too, speaks about a "third heaven" in 2 Cor 12:2, and Eph 4:10 says that Jesus decended into "the lower parts of the earth" and then ascended "far above the heavens." In Jewish *aggadah,* which are rabbinic homilies in Talmudic and Midrashic literature, seven heavens and seven earths are imagined (L. Ginzberg 1913, 9-11). Later still Dante, in the *Divine Comedy,* imagines nine circles of hell and nine spheres of heaven.

15 Now comes an appeal to reflect on Yahweh's dealings with Israel, which began with Yahweh loving the patriarchs and choosing their descendants after them (4:37). In the NT, see 1 Pet 2:9. The verb בחר ("choose") is a favorite of the Deuteronomic writer (see Note for 12:5). Israel, then, should love God because God first loved Israel (cf. 1 John 4:19). On Yahweh's election of Israel as his own people, and his attachment to Israel in love, see Notes for 7:6-8. Hebrew רַק ("only") is a sharp disjunctive and restrictive adverb, making vivid the contrast between an entire universe and a single people (G. E. Wright).

did Yahweh become attached to love them. חָשַׁק יְהוָה לְאַהֲבָה אוֹתָם. See 7:7 on Yahweh's attachment to Israel in love, which was a free act of divine grace.

as at this day. A common Deuteronomic expression (see Note for 2:30).

16 One figure censures closure in people, the other hardness; both conditions are to be eradicated in Israel. The figures occur in combination in the Qumran *Manual of Discipline* (1QS 5:5), also in Stephen's NT speech (Acts 7:51). On "stiffening the neck," which means being stubborn, see Note for 9:6. Here people are told to open and soften themselves, responding appropriately to the mighty God who shows no partiality, does justice to the orphan and widow, and loves the sojourner (vv. 17-18).

circumcise the foreskin of your heart. This bold trope occurs also in 30:6, where Yahweh says he will do the circumcising work himself. Here people are called upon to "open up" their own hearts. The "heart" (לֵב) in Hebrew thought is the preeminent metaphor for the inner being of a person, the seat of intelligence (thus often translated "mind"); the seat of emotions; and the seat of volition, i.e., the will. The present figure was called an *abusio* in the classical rhetorical handbooks (*ad Herennium* iv 33; Lundbom 1999, 129, 330; 2004b, 586), which is an implied metaphor (Brandt 1970, 139-41). The figure was picked up by Jeremiah (Jer 4:4; 9:25[26]) and occurs elsewhere in the Bible (see Note for 30:6). It has turned up also in sectarian documents among the Dead Sea Scrolls, e.g., the *Manual of Discipline* (1QS 5:5); the *Habakkuk commentary* (1QpHab 11:13); and 4Q434 *Barki Nafshi* (1 i 4; Seely 1996). In the present verse, T^{NfPsJ} use neither "circumcision" nor "foreskin." Censure of "hard heartedness" also occurs throughout the Bible (15:7; Ps 95:8; Mark 8:17; Rom 2:5; 2 Cor 3:14; Heb 3:8).

17 Here in vv. 17-18 comes the reason for the command to open hearts and soften hard necks. The verses shift into hymnic style (von Rad; Weinfeld; cf. Ps 136:2-3), with titles piling up to emphasize the incomparable Yahweh, who shows no partiality and will not be bribed.

For Yahweh your God, he is God of gods and Lord of lords. "God of gods" and "Lord of lords" are more superlatives (GKC §133i), meaning "supreme God" and "supreme Lord." While the expressions probably have their origins in polytheistic religion, their meaning in Deuteronomy is not "chief among the gods" (4:35, 39; 6:4; 32:39). For monotheism in Deuteronomy, see Note for 4:35. In the present verse, T[Onq] and T[PsJ] make substitutions (T[Onq]: "the God of judges and the Lord of kings"; T[PsJ]: "the God of judges and Master of kings"). Along with other accumulated titles, these, too, simply aim at expressing the absolute sovereignty and supremacy of Yahweh. Titles "God of gods" and "Lord of lords" for Yahweh occur in Ps 136:2-3; a foreign king confesses Daniel's God to be "God of gods and Lord of kings" (Dan 2:47). In the NT, God is "King of kings and Lord of lords" in 1 Tim 6:15, and the Lamb is "Lord of lords and King of kings" in Rev 17:14 and 19:16. The second article of the Nicene Creed confesses Jesus as "God of God, Light of Light, Very God of Very God." In later Judaism, the Holy God is called "King of kings" (*m. Sanh.* 4:5; *'Abot* 3:1; 4:22).

Kings in the ANE were given superlatives to express their greatness. Bestowed on the Assyrian kings, especially Esarhaddon (680-669) and Assurbanipal (668-627), were the titles "king of kings" (*šar šarrāni*), "lord of lords" *(bēl bēlē)*, "king of lords" *(šar bēlē)*, and "lord of kings" *(bēl šarrāni)*. Sometimes the kings applied the titles to themselves (Seux 1967, 55-56, 304, 318-19; *ANET*³, 290, 297). A certain Belibni, in letters to Assurbanipal, addressed the king as "lord of kings, my lord" (Letters nos. 280-86; nos. 520-21; no. 1136; Waterman 1930, 1:190-99, 364-65; 2:292-93). Similar titles were bestowed on the kings of Egypt. In a late 7th-cent. letter in Aramaic, Adon, king of Ekron, addresses the pharaoh as "Lord of kings" (Porten 1981, 36-39), and on a Canaanite sepulchral inscription, Eshmunʿazar, king of Sidon, calls his suzerain, "Lord of kings" (Galling 1963; Porten 1981, 39; *ANET*³, 662). Titles of a similar nature are applied in the Bible to foreign kings, e.g., Nebuchadnezzar is called "king of kings" in Ezek 26:7; Artaxerxes introduces himself as "king of kings" in Ezra 7:12; and Daniel addresses the king for whom he is interpreting a dream as "king of kings" in Dan 2:37.

the great, the mighty, and the awesome God. הָאֵל הַגָּדֹל הַגִּבֹּר וְהַנּוֹרָא. On Yahweh's "greatness," see Note for 3:24. The epithets "great" and "awesome" occur together in 7:21. In 28:58 people are exhorted to fear Yahweh's "glorious (נִכְבָּד) and awesome name." The "mighty" (גִּבֹּר) epithet suggests a God who is acting as a "warrior" (Ps 24:8; Isa 9:5[6]; 10:21; Zeph 3:17; Jer 20:11; Isa 42:13), where associations are primarily but not exclusively with the exodus deliverance (Exod 15:3). See also Ps 47:3(2); Jer 32:18; Neh 9:32. According to the Talmud, the men of the great synagogue were lauded because they restored the divine attributes (*b. Yoma* 69b); Weinfeld says they introduced them into the Jewish Amidah prayer.

who does not show partiality, and does not take a bribe. Hebrew אֲשֶׁר לֹא־יִשָּׂא פָנִים is lit. "(one) who does not lift up faces," which is an idiom meaning showing no partiality. Yahweh does not show partiality. Yahweh also cannot be bribed, which Rashi says means that he cannot be appeased with monetary gifts. One might well add sacrifices and other offerings (1 Sam 15:22; Mic 6:6-8; Jer 7:21-23; Ps 40:7[6]). According to Deuteronomy, judges in Israel must act similarly: no partiality and no bribes (1:17; 16:19; cf. Exod 23:8). In the NT, Peter applies this teaching about God showing no partiality to his acceptance of Cornelius (Acts 10:34), and Paul applies it when assessing the relative merits and failings of Jews and Greeks (Gal 2:6; Rom 2:11).

18 First mention in the book of a great Deuteronomic theme: Justice and benevolent treatment must be accorded the vulnerable and disadvantaged in Israelite society. This includes the poor (עָנִי), the needy (אֶבְיוֹן), the orphan (יָתוֹם), the widow (אַלְמָנָה), the sojourner (גֵּר), and in the 7th cent. the Levite, who resides in Israelite towns and is now deprived of income once worship had become centralized in Jerusalem. Yahweh all throughout the OT is seen to have a special concern for the poor, vulnerable, and disadvantaged (Hos 14:4[3]; Pss 10:14, 18; 68:6[5]; 146:9). If they cry out to him, which they will do if they are without an advocate, he will hear them and will bring their oppressors to judgment (Exod 22:22-23[23-24]).

Because Yahweh is proactive in seeking justice and benevolence for needy individuals, Israel must do likewise. There is thus a genuine humanitarian concern in the OT, especially in Deuteronomy (E. Day 1911; Pedersen 1964, 1-2:356-57; de Vaux 1965, 74-76; Weinfeld 1961). This shows itself in Deuteronomic laws that require lending freely to the needy (15:7-11); not sleeping in the pledge of a poor man, or keeping it overnight (24:12-13); giving the poor man his wages daily (24:14-15); and making sure the sojourner, orphan, and widow receive justice in the gate (1:16-17; 24:17), receive the third-year charity tithe (14:28-29; 26:12-13), and have a share in Israel's bountiful harvests (16:11, 14; 24:19-21). If anyone perverts justice towards the sojourner, orphan, and widow, a curse will fall, to which the people have given their ringing "Amen" (27:19). Cf. injunctions of a similar nature in the Covenant Code (Exod 22:20-21[21-22]; 23:6-9) and the Holiness Code (Lev 19:9-10, 15, 33-34). Justice for the sojourner, orphan, widow, and other needy souls was sung in temple psalms (Pss 82:3-4; 94:6) and preached with passion by the prophets, who reminded Israel without letup about this covenant obligation (Isa 1:17; Jer 7:5-7; 22:3), but discovering to their sorrow that the obligation, all too often, had not been carried out (Amos 4:1; Isa 1:23; 10:2; Jer 5:28; 22:15-16; Ezek 22:7; Zech 7:9-11; cf. Job 22:9). In the end, the nation paid a heavy price for its neglect (Lam 5:3).

Von Waldow (1970, 189) says that social responsibility for the poor and underprivileged in ancient Israelite society built on the special conditions of nomadic society, where there was a sense of responsibility for one another. People not in kinship groups were afforded protection, and the typical outsiders were the sojourners, widows, and orphans. The idea was retained, he says, even after Israel became a settled people, where it became a basic element of the covenant relationship between Yahweh and Israel. However, this benevolence program receives radical critiquing by H. V. Bennett (2002, 10-11), who thinks the Deuteronomic laws were more beneficial to those who formulated them than to the widows, sojourners, and orphans, serving to protect the interests of the power elite instead of diminishing the suffering and misery of the poor. Using a model of modern (Marxist) critical theory, he argues that the Deuteronomic laws were part of a strategy to regulate the behavior and shape the ideas of local peasant farmers regarding the distribution of goods in ancient Israel — to stave off potential uprisings by local peasant farmers in northern Israel during the Omride dynasty (9th cent.). Bennett (2002, 173) concludes his study of widows, orphans, and sojourners:

> The laws represented in the text used a category of socially weak but politically useful persons as pawns in a scheme to siphon off percentages of produce and livestock from overburdened peasant farmers and herders in the biblical communities during the Omride administration.

That there was a growing alienation between the rich and poor during the Omride dynasty in northern Israel cannot be doubted, but to suppose that these laws were created *de novo* between the 10th and 7th cents. only for the self-interest of the power elite, to stave off a potential peasant uprising, is pure speculation, a reduction of theology to politics, and assumes a rather sinister form of social and economic policy. The argument could also be made that Deuteronomy's benevolence program was to counter social policies of the Omri dynasty, just as the preaching of Amos and Hosea sought to do.

We learn from Egyptian, Akkadian, and Ugaritic texts that special care was exercised in other societies towards the orphan, widow, and outcast (Fensham 1962a; Galpaz-Feller 2008). From ancient Egypt comes the "Instruction for King Meri-ka-Re" (22nd cent.), in which a ruler gives this advice to his son and successor: "Do justice whilst thou endurest upon the earth. Quiet the weeper; do not oppress the widow" ($ANET^3$, 415). And in "The Protest of the Eloquent Peasant" (21st cent.), a peasant beaten and robbed of his donkeys on a trip to Egypt seeks redress from the pharaoh's chief steward, whom he addresses as "the father of the orphan, the husband of the widow, the brother of the divorcee, and the apron of him that is motherless" ($ANET^3$, 408). It took him a while to get the justice he sought, but in the end justice was done. The Laws of Ur-Nammu (162-168), dated ca. 2000, also mandated protection for the orphan, widow, and the poor ($ANET^3$, 524). King Hammurabi (1700), in the epilogue to his Law Code (lines 30-90), boasts that he "promoted the welfare of the land . . . in order that the strong might not oppress the weak, that justice might be dealt the orphan (and) the widow, in Babylon" (*ANET*³, 178).

In the "Keret Legend" from Ugarit, King Keret is reprimanded by his son Yaṣṣib for neglecting orphans and widows and told to step down so he himself can reign (KRT C vi 25-50; H. L. Ginsberg 1946, 32; *ANET*³, 149). In the "Tale of Aqhat," it is the good Daniel who judges the cause of the widow and the orphan (Aqht A v. 1-10; Aqht C i 20-30; *ANET*³, 151, 153). Societal justice in antiquity had everything to do with the kings (Ps 72:1-4; Prov 29:14; Isa 11:4). A text in the British Museum introduces a king devoted to justice at a time when the social order was in complete collapse. Lambert (1965), who called attention to the text, believes the unnamed king to be the much-maligned Nebuchadnezzar of Babylon. It says that before this king emerged people used to devour one another like dogs, the strong plundered the weak, the rich seized property from the poor, the regent and prince defended neither cripple nor widow before the judge. If their cases did come before the judge, he would not preside unless offered a bribe. The new king then restored justice and drew up a law code. Lambert calls him a "second Hammurabi."

In the NT, the problem of justice toward those who have no advocate is vividly portrayed in Jesus' parable of the Persistent Widow (Luke 18:1-8). On practicing justice and benevolence, see also Matt 5:42; 23:23-24; 25:31-46. Christians are required to visit orphans and widows in Jas 1:27.

the orphan and the widow . . . the sojourner. The triad is stock in Deuteronomy (10:18; 14:29; 16:11, 14; 24:17, 19, 20, 21; 26:12, 13; 27:19; Driver 1895, lxxx no. 27; Weinfeld 1972, 356 no. 6). See also Jer 7:6 and 22:3.

orphan. Probably the "fatherless" in ancient Israel (so AV; Ringgren, *yātôn*, in *TDOT*, 6:479; Lam 5:3; Ps 109:9), although Renkema (1995) believes that "orphan" properly translates יָתוֹם. In his view, the term means a child who has lost both father and mother.

widow. It has been argued, largely on the basis of parallels in Akkadian and Egyptian, that Hebrew אַלְמָנָה, which is translated "widow" in the OT, does not necessarily apply to every woman who has lost a husband, but rather to "a once married woman who has no means of financial support and who is thus in need of special legal protection" (C. Cohen 1973; M. T. Roth 1991-93, 2; H. Hoffner, '*almānâ*, in *TDOT* 1:287-91). Women whose husbands have died but who have an adult son, brother, father, or father-in-law as protector are not considered to be "widows" in this special sense. The same holds true for a woman whose husband has died, who then contracts a second marriage (levirate or otherwise), or who embraces a profession (*almattu* in *CAD*, 1/ 1:364). This view may have obtained also in ancient Israel, where some women bereft of husbands in the OT are never called "widows," e.g., Tamar, Abigail, Bathsheba, Ruth, Orpah, and others. The early church, too, singled out "widows who [were] real widows" (1 Tim 5:3-16). In ancient Egypt widows were protected by contracts providing for their care once their husband had died, but in the Bible there is no evidence of such contracts, which may go some way in explaining the benevolence program in Deuteronomy (Galpaz-Feller 2008, 251-52). For a comparison of the treatment toward widows in Egypt and in ancient Israel, and the legal protection widows received in both cultures, see Galpaz-Feller 2008. On laws relating to widows in the Neo-Babylonian period, see M. T. Roth 1991-93.

sojourner. גֵּר. A resident alien (see Note for 5:13-14). While the sojourner was afforded special protection in ancient Israel, uncircumcised sojourners were not permitted to eat the Passover meal (Exod 12:43-49). In the Deuteronomic code, they were exempted from the law against eating dead carcasses (Deut 14:21) and could be charged interest on loans (Deut 23:21[20]).

giving to him bread and an outer garment. The poor and needy require food and clothing. Deuteronomic law provides them with the third-year tithe (14:28-29), invites them to share in the yearly feasts (16:11, 14), and gives them gleaning rights (24:19-21). It also mandates giving loans to them, presumably so they can buy food and clothing (15:7-11). Deuteronomic law also precludes a creditor from taking a poor man's garment overnight (24:12-13) and a widow's garment under any circumstances (24:17). The NT, too, teaches that food and clothing are to be given to the poor and needy (Matt 5:42; 19:21; 25:35-46; Luke 12:33; 16:19-31; Jas 2:15-16; Heb 13:2).

19 This is the second reason why Israel is to love the sojourner: It was once a sojourner in Egypt (Exod 22:20[21]; 23:9; Lev 19:34; Honor 1953, 431). Deuteronomy says repeatedly that Israel should practice justice towards the sojourner and have charitable attitudes because of its own experience in Egypt (5:14-15; 15:12-15; 16:10-12; 23:8[7]; 24:17-18, 19-22).

20 A return to v. 12 and a repetition of 6:13, which here is supplied with a reason (vv. 21-22): A God great as Yahweh deserves reverence, service, love, and veneration.

and to him you shall cling. A Deuteronomic expression for loyal devotion to Yahweh (see Note for 4:3-4).

and in his name you shall swear. Oaths were typically sworn with the words "as Yahweh (your God) lives" (see Note for 5:11).

21 More acclaim of Yahweh, who is praiseworthy because of his mighty acts. Hebrew תְּהִלָּה ("praise, song of praise") is language out of the Psalms (Pss 22:26[25]; 71:6; 109:1, etc.), picked up also in Jer 17:14. Ibn Ezra translates הוּא תְהִלָּתְךָ "He is your glory," which is followed by NJV, Weinfeld, and Tigay. The LXX has καύχημα, "dignity, pride," which Wevers (1995, 185-86) finds an unusual translation. The Greek term also means "boast," but if taken positively could translate as "praise." In 1 Cor 5:6 it means boasting that is not good. But the related καύχησις in 2 Cor 7:4, which Luther cites for comparison, is a legitimate boast.

these great and awe-inspiring things. The "great things" (הַגְּדֹלֹ֖ת) are the hidden, wondrous, and miraculous works of God (4:34; 11:2-7; 26:8), among which the deliverance through the Sea ranks as the greatest (Exod 15:11; Pss 77:16-20; 106:7-12, 22).

which your eyes have seen. A stereotyped Deuteronomic expression (see Note for 4:9).

22 More reason to give Yahweh the commitment asked for in v. 20: Israel has multiplied from a mere seventy persons to a numberless multitude (1:10; 26:5; 28:62; cf. Gen 46:27; Exod 1:5-7). The promise of numberless descendants goes back to the covenant with Abraham (Gen 15:5; 22:17; 26:4; Exod 32:13).

Seventy persons. בְּשִׁבְעִים נֶ֫פֶשׁ is lit. "with seventy persons" (cf. בְּ *essentiae* in GKC §119i).

and now. וְעַתָּה. Repeating from v. 12, creating an inclusio (see Rhetoric and Composition).

Message and Audience

Having reported now that the covenant was renewed and Israel could proceed on its journey to the promised land, Moses turns to the present, asking people what Yahweh requires of them as they stand in the plains of Moab, ready to cross the Jordan into Canaan. His answer: What Yahweh wants is for people to fear him, walk in all his ways, love him, and serve him heart and soul. This translates into doing the commandments and statutes being given to them today. It will be for their own good. To Yahweh belong the entire heavens, the earth, and all that is in it. What is more, it was only with Israel's fathers that Yahweh attached himself in love, choosing their descendants after them. These descendants are the people hearing Moses today.

Moses says people must circumcise the foreskin of their hearts, i.e., open up their hearts, and also soften their stiff necks. Why? Because Yahweh is God of gods and Lord of lords, a great, mighty, and awesome God, who is not partial to anyone and cannot be bribed. He does justice to the orphan and widow and loves the sojourner, giving him food and a coat if he needs them. Israel is to show the same love toward the sojourner. Why? Because it, too, was a sojourner in Egypt.

Moses says again that Israel must fear Yahweh and serve him, clinging to him in love, and swearing oaths in his name. Why? Because Yahweh is praiseworthy, Israel's own God, who has done great and awe-inspiring things. Some of those present have seen these things with their own eyes. The promise of Abraham has been fulfilled. A mere seventy people went down to Egypt, and now Israel is a huge multitude.

For a late 8th- and early 7th-cent. audience, this message will have the same relevance as to people in any generation. If Israel is to go on being Yahweh's people, it must fear Yahweh, walk in all his ways, love him, and serve him heart and soul. And it must do the commandments given by Moses in the plains of Moab.

2. Consider Yahweh's Discipline (11:1-9)

11:1*And you shall love Yahweh your God, and you shall keep his charge, and his statutes, and his ordinances, and his commandments, all the days.* ²*And you know today — but not your children who have not known and who have not seen — the discipline of Yahweh your God, his greatness, his strong hand and his outstretched arm,* ³*and his signs and his deeds that he did in the midst of Egypt, to Pharaoh, king of Egypt, and to all his land;* ⁴*and what he did to the army of Egypt, to its horses and to its chariots, how he caused the waters of the Sea of Reeds to overflow upon them when they pursued after you, and Yahweh destroyed them, until this day;* ⁵*also what he did to you in the wilderness until you came to this place;* ⁶*and what he did to Dathan and Abiram, sons of Eliab, son of Reuben, how the earth opened its mouth and swallowed them and their households and their tents and all those living creatures who followed them, in the midst of all Israel.* ⁷*For your eyes have seen every great deed of Yahweh that he did.* ⁸*So you shall keep all the commandment that I am commanding you today, in order that you may be strong and enter and take possession of the land that you are crossing over to possess it,* ⁹*and in order that you may prolong the days on the soil that Yahweh swore to your fathers to give to them and to their descendants, a land flowing with milk and honey.*

Rhetoric and Composition

This sermon is delimited at the top end by the chapter division prior to v. 1, although some commentators put 11:1 with what precedes, beginning the present unit in v. 2. The Sam has a section after v. 1, which is not present in M^L. Delimitation at the bottom end is by a *setumah* in M^L and a section in Sam after v. 9. The sermon treats subjects already covered in chs. 6–10, developing as they do from the first and second commandments. The focus here is on Yahweh's discipline of Israel in the wilderness, which was discussed in 8:1-20. The sermon in 8:1-20 —

Deuteronomy 11

like so many sermons in Deuteronomy — emphasizes doing the commandments (see Rhetoric and Composition for 8:1-20), It also contrasts the harsh wilderness with the good land of Canaan, which happens again here. The present sermon is followed in 11:10-17 by two sermons on the good land of Canaan.

The present sermon has a chiastic structure, like the sermon in 8:1-20:

a		And you shall love Yahweh your God, and *you shall keep his charge, and his statutes, and his ordinances, and his commandments,* all the *days* . . .	v. 1
	b	. . . *your children who* have not known and have not seen	v. 2a
		c Yahweh's *discipline* of Israel [*in the wilderness*]	v. 2b
		d signs and deeds against Egypt — plagues and the drowning of the army at the Sea of Reeds	vv. 3-4
		c' [*discipline*] of rebels *in the wilderness*	vv. 5-6
	b'	for *your eyes have seen* . . .	v. 7
a'		*you shall keep all the commandment* . . . *today* . . .	v. 8

The climax is in the center (d), which is where we expect it in a chiasmus. There Yahweh's deeds against Egypt are celebrated.

Portions of 11:1-9 appear in 4QDeut^c, 4QDeut^j, 4QDeut^{k1}, MurDeut, 4Q364, and 4QLXXDeut; also on phylacteries from Qumran (1Q21-22, 23-25; 4Q128, 138, 143, 144; 8Q3) and *mezuzot* from Qumran (4Q150; 8Q4).

Notes

11:1 In Deuteronomy Israel's love for Yahweh is gauged by its keeping of the commandments (6:5-9; 7:9, 12; 10:12-13; 11:1, 13, 22; 13:4-5[3-4]; 19:9; 30:6-8, 16). More than that, Yahweh loves those who keep his commandments (5:10). For Deuteronomy's teaching on "love for God" and what it entails, see Note for 6:5. Love of God goes together with fear of God in Deuteronomy (10:12), and since the prior sermon closes by calling people to "fear Yahweh" (10:20), the present sermon now calls people to "love Yahweh."

and you shall keep his charge. וְשָׁמַרְתָּ מִשְׁמַרְתּוֹ. An expression occurring only here in Deuteronomy, referring to Yahweh's commands generally (Driver; Gen 26:5; Josh 22:3; 1 Kgs 2:3).

2 Reference is to Yahweh's discipline of Israel in the wilderness, which was discussed in 8:2-5. But a distinction is made here between those who experienced that discipline and a younger generation who did not (2:14-15; cf. Num 14:29-35).

Deuteronomy 11

And you know today. On this Deuteronomic expression, see Note for 4:39.

his greatness. Yahweh is a "great God" (see Note for 3:24). Reference may be to Yahweh's greatness in the wilderness, seen in the disciplining of Israel there (vv. 5-6), not to Yahweh's mighty acts in the exodus (*pace* ibn Ezra). Verses 3-4 recall signs and deeds in connection with the exodus.

his strong hand and his outstretched arm. On this stereotypical expression, which usually refers to the exodus deliverance, see Note for 4:34.

3 On "signs and wonders," which is the usual OT pairing, see Note for 4:34. The signs and deeds in Egypt were probably the plagues (6:22; Neh 9:10).

4 The deliverance at the Sea of Reeds (Red Sea) is recounted in Exodus 14 and celebrated supremely in the Song of the Sea (Exod 15:1-18). See also Pss 78:53; 106:8-11; 136:11-15; Neh 9:11.

until this day. Success over Egypt continues to the present day. On this Deuteronomic expression, see Note for 2:22.

5 Now we learn more about Yahweh's discipline of Israel in the wilderness (v. 2). Reference is not to the manna, which was the "humbling" experience in 8:3 (*pace* ibn Ezra), but to judgment that came upon Dathan, Abiram, and their rebellious comrades (v. 6). "This place" is the valley opposite Beth-peor (see Note for 9:7).

6 Dathan and Abiram were leaders in Korah's rebellion so-called, which is reported in Numbers 16. These individuals and their followers rose up against Moses and Aaron, and Yahweh acted decisively to destroy them, their households (i.e., wives and children [ibn Ezra]), all their possessions, and those who followed them (Num 16:31-33). Korah, who figures prominently in the Priestly account of the rebellion, is not mentioned here. The Sam, some Qumran phylacteries (4Q128; 4Q138), and one Qumran *mezuzah* (8Q4) add "and all the men that belong to Korah" (ואת כול האדם אשר לקורח).

how the earth opened its mouth and swallowed them. I.e., they were destroyed, going down into the bowels of the earth, to Sheol, the place of the dead (cf. Gen 4:11; Num 16:33). Whether this was a natural phenomenon, such as an earthquake, or simply a poetic way of describing the slaying of the rebels and their families and a destruction of their possessions is uncertain.

and all those living beings who followed them. וְאֵת כָּל־הַיְקוּם אֲשֶׁר בְּרַגְלֵיהֶם. The verb קוּם, usually "stand (up), arise" (34:10), also means "exist" in Late Hebrew (*Dict Talm* 591, 1330), leading most modern Versions and commentators to translate כָּל־הַיְקוּם as "every existing/living thing" or the like. This translation is influenced also by Gen 7:4, 23 (AV; RSV), the only other occurrences of the expression in the OT. Reference could be either to every living thing (animals?) belonging to Dathan and Abiram (T[OnqPsJ]; RSV; NEB; NAB; NJV; NIV) or to every living being joining in the rebellion (T[Nf]; NRSV; REB; NJB). The latter interpretation seems preferable: 250 men followed Korah,

Deuteronomy 11

Dathan, and Abiram (Num 16:2). Hebrew בְּרַגְלֵיהֶם (lit. "at their feet") means "(who) followed them" (cf. Exod 11:8; 1 Sam 25:27).

7 On Yahweh's "great deeds," see Josh 24:31; Judg 2:7, 10. The expression "for your eyes have seen" is stereotyped in Deuteronomy (see Note for 3:21).

8 The sermon concludes by saying that Israel will be strong if it keeps all the commandment and will thereby be able to cross the Jordan and take the land of Canaan. "The commandment" singular (הַמִּצְוָה) denotes the entire Deuteronomic Code (see Note for 5:31).

in order that you may be strong. לְמַעַן תֶּחֶזְקוּ. The people are told to "be strong" (חִזְקוּ) in facing the Canaanite opposition (31:6). Joshua, too, is exhorted to "be strong" (חֲזַק) in leading the endeavor (31:7, 23). This is the language of holy war.

the land that you are crossing over to possess it. On this stock Deuteronomic expression, see Note for 4:25-26.

9 *and in order that you may prolong the days on the soil that Yahweh swore to your fathers to give to them and to their descendants.* Israel, by doing the commandments, will live long in the land (see Note for 4:1). On the idiom "prolong/not prolong your days," which is stereotyped in Deuteronomy, see Note for 4:25-26.

a land flowing with milk and honey. On this description of the promised land, see Note for 6:3. A link is thus made to the next sermon, which speaks of the good land of Canaan (11:10-12).

Message and Audience

This sermon begins by picking up on love for Yahweh, which is equated with keeping Yahweh's charge, his statutes, his ordinances, and his commandments in the days ahead. Those listening, but not their children, know and have seen for themselves Yahweh's discipline in the wilderness. They also know and have seen Yahweh's signs and deeds before Pharaoh and what Yahweh did to Pharaoh's army at the Sea of Reeds. The waters covered his horses and chariots, and they sank "like a stone" (Exod 15:5). This success over Egypt continues even into the present.

The preacher then returns to what Yahweh did to Israel in the wilderness, citing the rebellion in which Dathan and Abiram played a leading role. Yahweh brought them to judgment: They, their wives and children, all their possessions, and those who followed them were brought down — not into the sea — but into the depths of the earth. All Israel witnessed it. The lesson in all this is that Israel must keep the commandments given now in the plains of Moab. Why? So Israel will be strong and able to enter and possess the land, also that its subsequent days will be prolonged on Canaanite soil, the land that Yahweh swore to the fathers. A good land it is, flowing with milk and honey.

To a late 8th- and early 7th-cent. audience, the point is made again that doing the commandments is everything. Yes, Yahweh disciplines a people prone to rebellion, which will have unsettling parallels to what Israel and Judah have experienced recently at the hands of the Assyrians. But now, if Judah wants to prolong its days in the land, it simply must keep Yahweh's commandments.

3. The Promised Land Will Have Rain from Heaven (11:10-12)

*11*¹⁰*For the land that you are entering to take possession of it, it is not like the land of Egypt out of which you came, where you sowed your seed and you watered it with your foot, as a vegetable garden.* ¹¹*Yes, the land that you are crossing over to possess is a land of mountains and valleys, by the rain of the heavens it drinks water,* ¹²*a land that Yahweh your God cares for continually. The eyes of Yahweh your God are upon it, from the beginning of the year to the end of the year.*

Rhetoric and Composition

This brief sermon follows naturally the sermon in 11:1-9, going well also with the next sermon in 11:13-17. It is delimited by section markings and should probably be taken as a self-standing unit. Demarcation at the top end is by a *setumah* in M^L and a section in Sam before v. 10, and at the bottom end by a *setumah* in M^L and a section in Sam after v. 12.

Portions of 11:10-12 are contained in 4QDeut^c and 4QDeut^j; also on phylacteries from Qumran (1Q23-25, 26-27; 4Q128, 138, 144), and a *mezuzah* from Qumran (8Q4).

Notes

11:10 The land of Canaan will be infinitely better than Egypt so far as the cultivation of crops is concerned. Egypt gets little rain, its only water resource being the Nile and the Delta, where artificial modes of irrigation are necessary much of the year. The headwaters of the Nile are in the Blue Nile of present-day Ethiopia, and in antiquity, when the mountain snow melted and the spring rains came, the Nile would rise dramatically, in some places as much as 50 ft (Breasted 1906a, 7-9). A vast system of canals carried water to the fields, somewhat like in the Central Valley of California, where canals dug in the early 1900s brought Sierra water to fields and orchards in the valley.

Deuteronomy 11

By the beginning of November, the Nile begins to recede, leaving the water level well below the fields. Crude machines must then be employed to raise the water, though on a relatively small scale. In modern times, the *shadûf* (a crude machine bringing up water in buckets) and the *sâkiyeh* (a vertical wheel turned by an ox, raising water in earthen pots attached to cords) are employed. The *shadûf* was used in ancient Egypt, and operating it was hard labor (Lane 1973, 327-28 + picture; E. Robinson 1867, 1:19, 581-82; G. A. Smith 1918, 147). Montet (1958, 104-5) says in the New Kingdom it seemed only to have been used for watering gardens; it is never found in scenes depicting agricultural work. The water wheel, which raises larger quantities of water to irrigate fields, is not attested in any ancient Egyptian documents.

For the land that you are entering to take possession of it. On the stereotyped Deuteronomic expression "to enter and take possession of the land," see Note for 1:8.

and you watered it with your foot, as a vegetable garden. וְהִשְׁקִיתָ בְרַגְלְךָ כְּגַן הַיָּרָק. Hebrew יָרָק means "greens, vegetables" (Prov 15:17), and גַן הַיָּרָק is thus a "vegetable garden" (T^OnqNf; Rashi, AV; RSV; cf. 1 Kgs 21:2). Afro-Americans today call vegetables "greens." What is not known is how seed was watered "with the foot" (AV; RSV; REB) or "by foot" (NEB; NIV; NRSV; NJB). None of the known machines employed in raising water are foot-operated, although the suggestion has been made that in antiquity a smaller type of water wheel could have been operated by foot, rather than by oxen (E. Robinson 1867, 1:582). Perhaps "by foot" simply means "by human labor" (NJV: "by your own labors"). Rashi says in Egypt [there were times when] you had to bring water on foot from the Nile in order to irrigate the land. The point, in any case, seems to be that in Egypt (hard) labor was necessary even in watering vegetable gardens.

11 Canaan is not flat like Egypt, but a land of mountains and valleys (8:7), drinking up quantities of rain from the heavens. For the heavens as a celestial storehouse of rain, see Note for 28:12. The contrast, nevertheless, seems a bit overdrawn (von Rad: "rather Utopian"; Weinfeld: "fanciful"). In the wilderness, at least, people remembered Egypt as a fertile land (Gen 13:10; Exod 16:3), at one point calling it "a land flowing with milk and honey" (Num 16:13). But Tigay points out how the Egyptians, too, were aware of differences in the source of irrigation in their country and in other countries. In the "Hymn to the Aton" (ca. 1380-1362; *ANET*³, 371), the worshipper addresses Aton, the sun-god:

> For thou hast set a Nile in heaven,
> That it may descend for them and make waves upon the mountains,
> Like the great green sea,
> To water their fields in their towns.

> How effective they are, thy plans, O lord of eternity!
> The Nile in heaven, it is for the foreign peoples. . . .

the land that you are crossing over to possess. On this stock Deuteronomic phrase, see Note for 4:25-26.

12 *a land that Yahweh your God cares for continually. The eyes of Yahweh your God are upon it.* Here is the main point of the sermon: The land Yahweh is giving Israel is one he watches over continually, giving it all the rain that it needs (28:12; Ps 147:8; cf. Gen 8:22). Crops grow not by arduous physical labor, but by Yahweh's constant care. The verb דרשׁ ("seek") can also mean "care for" (Jer 30:14, 17; Ps 142:5[4]). The LXX has ἐπισκοπεῖται ("watches over").

from the beginning of the year to the end of the year. With the early rains and the latter rains (v. 14; Jer 5:24), water will be available year round.

Message and Audience

Moses in this brief sermon picks up again on the good land of Canaan, saying that it is not like Egypt, where seed is sown and watered only by hard labor. Canaan is a land of mountains and valleys, which drink rain abundantly from the heavens. Yahweh cares for this land constantly, and as a result, water is available year round.

For a late 8th- and early 7th-cent. audience this will simply be a reminder of the good land Yahweh has given Israel. Sometime the rain does not come, but that will be dealt with in the next sermon.

4. But Rain Hinges on Keeping the Commandments (11:13-17)

11 [13] And it will happen if you surely listen to my commandments, which I am commanding you today, to love Yahweh your God and to serve him with all your heart and with all your soul, [14] then I will give rain for your land in its time, the early rain and the latter rain, that you may gather your grain and your wine and your oil. [15] And I will give grass in your field for your beasts. Yes, you shall eat and become sated. [16] Be careful for yourselves, lest your heart be deceived, and you turn aside and serve other gods, and you worship them. [17] Then the anger of Yahweh will burn against you, and he will shut up the heavens so there will not be rain, and the soil will not give its yield, and you will perish quickly from off the good land that Yahweh is giving to you.

Deuteronomy 11

Rhetoric and Composition

This sermon, qualifying Moses' statement about abundant rain in Canaan (11:10-12), is delimited at the top end by a *setumah* in M^L and a section in Sam before v. 13. Delimitation at the bottom end, after v. 17, is made on the basis of the liturgical injunction beginning in v. 18. The structure of the sermon is relatively simple: If people love and serve Yahweh and really heed his commandments, rain will come (vv. 13-15); if they turn to other gods, the heavens will be shut up, the soil will not produce, and people will perish in the good land Yahweh has given them (vv. 16-17).

Portions of 11:13-17 are contained in 4QDeut^c, 4QDeut^j, and 4QDeut^{k1}; also on phylacteries from Qumran (4Q128, 130, 131, 136, 144; 8Q3; XḤev/SePhyl) and Wadi Murabbaʿat (Mur3), and *mezuzot* from Qumran (4Q153; 8Q4).

Notes

11:13-14 A protasis-apodosis ("If ... then ...") argument, making conditional the fertility said to exist in Canaan. The protasis (v. 13) combines love and service with heeding Yahweh's commandments, which is bedrock Deuteronomic theology (10:12-13). The apodosis (v. 14) says that rain will then come, and Israel will have abundant harvests. Muilenburg (1959) pointed out that the protasis-apodosis construction — expressed both positively and negatively: "If ... then ... if not ... then") — is a formal element in covenant speech (11:13-14, 22-23, 27-28; 28:1-68; Exod 19:5-6; Josh 24:15, 20; 1 Sam 12:14-15, 25). For Deuteronomy's teaching on "love for God" and what it entails, see Note for 6:5. On serving Yahweh and only Yahweh, see Note for 6:13. The expression "with all your heart and with all your soul" is stock in Deuteronomy (see Note for 4:29).

if you surely listen to my commandments. Another stock Deuteronomic expression (11:13, 27, 28; 28:13; Weinfeld 1972, 337 no. 18). "To listen" means here "to heed" or "to obey" (RSV).

then I will give rain for your land in its time. Moses, here and in v. 15, assumes the voice of Yahweh, which happens occasionally in Deuteronomy (see Note for 7:4). The Sam, LXX, a Qumran phylactery (4Q128), and a Qumran *mezuzah* (8Q4) read "he will give" (cf. RSV; NRSV).

the early rain and the latter rain. Canaan has one rainy season, beginning usually in October or November and lasting until April, sometimes early May. From June to September there is no rain (Arden-Close 1941). The rainy season compares to that of California. The early rain (יוֹרֶה) starts in October or November, softening hard ground after a rainless summer for plowing and plant-

Deuteronomy 11

ing, also filling the cisterns. The latter rain (מַלְקוֹשׁ) is more gentle, coming in March and April (Hos 6:3; Jer 5:24; Joel 2:23; Zech 10:1). Farmers (and others) wait for both rains (Jas 5:7; cf. Jer 14:4).

your grain and your wine and your oil. Grain, grapes, and olives are the principal crops of Canaan (see Note for 7:13).

15 *And I will give grass in your field for your beasts.* Draft animals, too, suffer for a lack of food (Jer 14:5-6).

Yes, you shall eat and become sated. On this promise once Israel is settled in the land, see Note for 6:11.

16 The Song of Moses says the people ate and became sated and then turned to other gods (Deut 32:13-18). Hosea said that Israel forgot it was Yahweh who gave her the grain, wine, and oil, crediting these instead to Baal (Hos 2:10-15[8-13]). The expression "turn aside from [Yahweh's] way" is stereotyped in Deuteronomy (see Note for 9:12).

lest your heart be deceived. פֶּן יִפְתֶּה לְבַבְכֶם. Hebrew יִפְתֶּה is usually taken as coming from the root פתה, "to deceive, entice" (Job 31:9, 27), but Meek (1948, 235-36) thinks it derives from פתח, "to be open," which is supported by LXX's πλατυνθῇ ("become wide open"). He translates: "Take care lest your mind become so open that you turn aside and serve other gods." The complaint of Deuteronomy (and the prophets) was that people were too tolerant of alien gods.

17 Yahweh's anger will burn hot if Israel forsakes the covenant and goes after other gods (see Note for 6:15). The result will be drought in an otherwise fertile land (1 Kgs 8:35). The heavens will become brass and the earth iron (28:23; reversed in Lev 26:19). On the heavens as a celestial storehouse of rain, see Note for 28:12. Severe droughts came to Israel in the time of Elijah (1 Kings 17–18) and to Judah in the time of Jeremiah (Jer 3:3; 14:1-11, 17-22). Droughts occurred also in Egypt, as we know from the Joseph story (Gen 41:1-36). An Egyptian text from the reign of Ramses II (ca. 1280) says: "Our lord Seth is angry with us, and the skies do not give water over against us" (*ANET*[3], 257).

and you will perish quickly from off the good land that Yahweh is giving to you. Variant of a stock Deuteronomic phrase (see Note for 4:25-26). On Canaan as the "good land," see Note for 8:7-9. In Scripture, Yahweh's action often occurs "quickly" (Daube 1964; see Note on 9:3).

Message and Audience

Having just told the people that Canaan is not like Egypt, its mountains and valleys drinking up abundant rain from the heavens, Moses now qualifies this statement, saying that if this is to happen, Israel must love Yahweh and serve him heart and soul, which translates into heeding the commandments. Only then will the early and late rains come and will there be a good harvest of grain, wine, and oil. Animals, too, will have plenty of grass to eat. Yes, people will eat and become sated, but this, too, has its dangers. They must not be deceived. If they eat to the full and then turn from Yahweh to the worship of other gods, Yahweh's anger will burn hot, and he will shut up the heavens so rain does not come. The earth will not bring forth its yield, and Israel will perish off the good land Yahweh is giving it.

For a late 8th- and early 7th-cent. audience, the drought in the time of Elijah will not have dimmed in Israel's collective memory, which should be witness enough to what will happen when people turn to the Baals. More recently, northern Israel, the Transjordan, and much of Judah have perished or suffered greatly in the good land. Will people realize that what matters to Yahweh is that Israel love him, serve him, and heed his commandments?

K. LITURGICAL INJUNCTION (11:18-21)

11 ^{18}*So you shall place these words of mine upon your heart and upon your soul, and you shall bind them as a sign upon your hand, and they shall be as headbands between your eyes.* ^{19}*And you shall teach them to your children, to speak of them when you sit in your house and when you walk in the way, and when you lie down and when you rise.* ^{20}*And you shall write them upon the doorposts of your house and within your gates,* ^{21}*in order that your days and the days of your children may be multiplied on the soil that Yahweh swore to your fathers to give to them, like the days of the heavens over the earth.*

Rhetoric and Composition

This liturgical injunction repeats from 6:6-9, making an inclusio within chs. 6–11 (Lundbom 1996, 305). In its repetition here the center sections are inverted (see Rhetoric and Composition for 6:6-9). There are no sections in either M^L or Sam before v. 18. Delimitation at the bottom end is by a *setumah* in M^L and a section in Sam after v. 21.

Portions of 11:18-21 are contained in 4QDeut^c and 4QDeut^j (v. 21 conjectured); also on phylacteries from Qumran (4Q128, 130, 131, 136, 143, 144, 146; 8Q3; XḤev/SePhyl), Wadi Murabbaʿat (Mur3), and *mezuzot* from Qumran (4Q153; 8Q4).

Deuteronomy 11

Notes

11:18-20 See exegesis for 6:6-9.

18 *upon your heart and upon your soul.* "And upon your soul" is not present in 6:6.

19 *And you shall teach.* וְלִמַּדְתֶּם. In 6:7 the verb is שׁנן ("to incise, impress").

21 *in order that your days and the days of your children may be multiplied on the soil that Yahweh swore to your fathers to give to them.* This is the alternative to disobedience (v. 17), which will lead to Israel perishing off the land. In Deuteronomy the usual idiom is "that your days may be prolonged" (see Note for 4:25-26).

like the days of the heavens over the earth. כִּימֵי הַשָּׁמַיִם עַל־הָאָרֶץ. I.e., as long as the heavens remain above the earth, or in perpetuity (Driver). In the Bible, and throughout the literature of the ANE, the permanence of the heavens, moon, stars, and sometimes the sun becomes a standard for the length of days, or eternity (Jer 31:36; 33:20-21, 25-26; Pss 72:5; 89:3, 30, 37-38[2, 29, 36-37]; Job 14:12; cf. S. Paul 1972, 353-55; Porten 1981, 36-37; Tigay 1987b, 170).

Message and Audience

Israel once again hears the injunction to keep the commandments ever before it. Added is an alternative to the dire warning of v. 13: If people keep the commandments, they will live in the land as long as the heavens are above the earth. This promise has force also for Judahites in the late 8th and early 7th cents.

L. Consequences of Obedience and Disobedience (11:22-32)

1. Be Very Careful with All This Commandment (11:22-25)

11 ²²*Indeed, if you will be very careful with all this commandment that I am commanding you to do, to love Yahweh your God, to walk in all his ways, and to cling to him,* ²³*then Yahweh will dispossess all these nations from before you, yes, you will dispossess nations greater and mightier than you.* ²⁴*Every place on which the sole of your foot treads, for you it shall be, from the wilderness and the Lebanon; from the river, the River Euphrates, and to the Western Sea shall be your territory.* ²⁵*No one will hold his ground before you; the dread of you and the fear of you Yahweh your God will put upon the face of all the earth on which you tread, just as he promised you.*

2. The Blessing and the Curse (11:26-28)

11 ²⁶*See, I am setting before you today blessing and curse,* ²⁷*the blessing when you listen to the commandments of Yahweh your God, which I am commanding you today,* ²⁸*and the curse if you do not listen to the commandments of Yahweh your God, and you turn aside from the way that I am commanding you today, to walk after other gods that you have not known.*

3. Be Careful to Do the Statutes and Ordinances (11:29-32)

11 ²⁹*And it will happen when Yahweh your God brings you into the land that you are entering to take possession of it, then you shall set the blessing on Mount Gerizim and the curse on Mount Ebal.* ³⁰*Are they not beyond the Jordan — behind the west road in the land of the Canaanites, who dwell in the Arabah opposite Gilgal — beside the oaks of Moreh?* ³¹*For you are crossing over the Jordan to enter to possess the land that Yahweh your God is giving to you, and you shall possess it and you shall dwell in it.* ³²*So you shall be careful to do all the statutes and the ordinances that I am setting before you today.*

Rhetoric and Composition

This cluster of three brief sermons concludes Moses' teaching and preaching in chs. 5–11. The whole is tied together by a keyword inclusio, which restates the warning that Israel must be careful to do the covenant demands (Lohfink 1968, 20; Lundbom 1996, 304-5):

5:1	Hear, O Israel, *the statutes and the ordinances* that I am speaking in your ears *today,* and you shall learn them and *you shall be careful to do them.*
11:32	*So you shall be careful to do all the statutes and the ordinances* that I am setting before you *today.*

The unit is delimited at the top end by a *setumah* in M^L and a section in Sam before v. 22. Delimitation at the bottom end is by the chapter division after v. 32. Neither M^L nor Sam has a section after v. 32. The lack of a section after v. 32 does not mean that vv. 31-32 are an introduction to the Deuteronomic Code, as argued by Rofé (1972, 222-23) and Tigay. The Deuteronomic Code has its own introduction (see Note for 12:1). Three subunits in the cluster are marked by a *setumah* in M^L and a section in Sam after v. 25 and a *setumah* in M^L after v. 28. The Sam has another section after v. 30.

Deuteronomy 11

The rhetorical structure of the cluster is the following:

   I *Be very careful to do this commandment*   vv. 22-25
   II Blessings and curses   vv. 26-28
   III *Be careful to do the statutes and the ordinances*   vv. 29-32

An inclusio ties together the concluding sermons in vv. 26-32 (Lohfink 1963a, 233):

   See, I am setting before you today . . .   v. 26
   . . . that I am setting before you today   v. 32

Portions of 11:22-32 are contained in 1QDeut^a, 1QDeut^b, 4QpaleoDeut^r, and 4Q364.

Notes

11:22-23 A protasis-apodosis argument similar to 11:13-14, where heeding the commandments, loving and serving Yahweh were said to ensure fertility in the land. On the protasis-apodosis construction in covenant speech, see Note for 11:13-14. Here heeding the commandments will lead to a successful conquest (cf. 11:8). On the "be careful to do" command, which is stock in Deuteronomy, see Note for 5:1. The command repeats in v. 32, tying the sermon cluster together (see Rhetoric and Composition). For Deuteronomy's teaching on "love for God" and what it entails, see Note for 6:5. "Walking in Yahweh's way" has strong ethical implications in the OT and is another Deuteronomic theme (see Note for 5:33). On "clinging to Yahweh," see Note for 4:3-4.

Indeed. Translating כִּי as an asseverative.

then Yahweh will dispossess all these nations from before you, yes, you will dispossess nations greater and mightier than you. See 4:38; 7:1; 9:1-3.

24 "Every place on which the sole of your foot treads" is a Deuteronomic expression (see Note for 2:5). The "wilderness" is the Negeb and southern desert; "the Lebanon" takes in the two mountain ranges in modern Lebanon: the Lebanon range, running parallel to the Phoenician coast, and the Anti-Lebanon range further inland (LXX has Ἀντιλιβάνου). The Euphrates River is its northwestern portion in upper Syria, and the Western Sea is the Mediterranean (34:2; Zech 14:8; Joel 2:20). On these boundaries for the promised land, see Note for 1:7.

the River Euphrates. Sometimes referred to in the OT simply as "the River" (Num 22:5; Josh 24:3, 14; Jer 2:18); other times named, as here (Gen 2:14; 15:18; Jer 46:2, 6). The LXX has "the great river, the River Euphrates" (cf. 1:7).

the Western Sea. הַיָּם הָאַחֲרוֹן. Literally, "the behind sea." The Eastern Sea, called "the front sea" (הַיָּם הַקַּדְמֹנִי), is the Dead Sea (Joel 2:20; Ezek 47:18; Zech 14:8). Ancient maps were east-oriented, unlike modern maps, which are north-oriented: East is front; west is back; north is left (שְׂמֹאל); south is right (יָמִין). Quarters of the heavens were similarly defined (אַחֲרוֹן, BDB, 30).

25   Cf. 7:24. Yahweh will put the dread (פַּחַד) and fear (יִרְאָה) of Israel in the opposition (see 2:25). For "all the earth on which you tread," see 1:36.

just as he promised you. See 7:1-24; cf. Exod 23:27; Josh 2:9.

26   Verses 26-28 bring Moses' teaching and preaching in chs. 5–11 to a climax. This teaching and preaching takes in the Ten Commandments and sermons developing from commandments one and two: Israel must love and serve Yahweh, and Yahweh only, and not go after other gods. Obeying the commandments will bring blessing; disobeying them will bring a curse. Anticipated here is the more extensive list of blessings and curses in ch. 28, also the curses in 27:15-26. Israel is faced with two options and must choose (cf. 30:15-20; Josh 24:14-15). The word for "curse," here and in v. 28, is קְלָלָה, which means "harm, calamity, misfortune" (see Note for 27:12-13).

See. On רְאֵה used as an interjection, see Note for 1:8.

27-28   *the blessing when you listen to the commandments of Yahweh your God, which I am commanding you today, and the curse if you do not listen to the commandments of Yahweh your God.* The choice boils down to heeding Yahweh's commandments or not heeding them. One leads to life, the other to death (30:15-20). On the protasis-apodosis construction in covenant speech, see Note for 11:13-14.

and you turn aside from the way that I am commanding you today. The expression "to turn aside from the way" is stereotyped in Deuteronomy (see Note for 9:12).

to walk after other gods that you have not known. Hosea says: "I am Yahweh your God from the land of Egypt, you know no God but me" (Hos 13:4). The Song of Moses censured Israel for sacrificing to gods it had never known (32:17). The expression "you have not known," in association with foreign gods, a foreign nation, a foreign land, a foreign language, and foreign food (manna), occurs often in Deuteronomy, also in Jeremiah (Deut 8:3, 16; 11:28; 13:3, 7, 14[2, 6, 13]; 28:33, 36, 64; 29:25[26]; Jer 5:15; 7:9; 9:15[16]; 14:18; 15:14; 16:13; 17:4; 19:4; 22:28; 44:3; Driver 1895, lxxxi no. 39; Weinfeld 1972, 324 no. 6; 357 no. 14). Israel is not to walk after other gods (see Note for 6:14), but to walk in the way of Yahweh (see Note for 5:33).

29   On the stock expression "to enter and take possession of the land," see Note for 1:8. Joshua is said to have carried out the present directive (Josh 8:30-35). About the location of these mountains there is no doubt. They overlook the biblical city of Shechem (modern Nablus), Mount Gerizim being on

the south and Mount Ebal being on the north. Shechem is mentioned often in the OT as an important gathering place (Josh 24:1; Judges 9; 1 Kgs 12:1, 25). The bones of Joseph were buried there (Josh 24:32). Mount Gerizim is 2898 ft above sea level, Mount Ebal slightly higher at 3029 ft. Both mountains rise more than 1000 ft above the valley floor (C. W. Wilson 1873, 66). A blessing and curse ritual on the slopes of these mountains is prescribed in 27:11-13.

30 The two mountains lie across the Jordan, beside the oaks of Moreh at Shechem, an important crossroad below the mountains (Gen 12:6; 35:4; Josh 24:25-26; Judg 9:6). In what may be another antiquarian note (see Note for 2:10-12), the mountains are said to be behind the west road in the land of the Canaanites, who live in the Arabah rift valley opposite Gilgal. Canaanites resided both in the Jordan Valley (cf. Num 13:29; Josh 5:1; 11:3) and along the Mediterannean seacoast (see Note for 1:7). Gilgal is the well-known Gilgal near Jericho (Josh 4:19-20; 5:9-10).

beyond the Jordan. I.e., "on the west side of the Jordan," as in 3:8, 20, and 25. In Deuteronomy the same expression can mean "on the east side of the Jordan" (see Note for 1:1).

behind the west road. אַחֲרֵי דֶּרֶךְ מְבוֹא הַשֶּׁמֶשׁ, lit. "behind the road of the setting sun." Glacier National Park has a "Going-to-the-Sun-Road." Ancient roads, like many modern roads, are named for the cities or places where they terminate. The road here is one that led from the Jordan Valley, past Tirzah (Y. Aharoni 1979, 60), Shechem, and Samaria, to the Mediterranean.

beside the oaks of Moreh. אֵצֶל אֵלוֹנֵי מֹרֶה. An ancient cultic site associated with Abraham, where perhaps some Canaanite diviner gave oracles (Tigay). Not to be confused with the "oaks of Mamre," also in the Abraham tradition, which were at Hebron (Gen 13:18; 14:13; 18:1). Here the site is called "oaks (plural) of Morah," whereas in Gen 12:6; 35:4 it is "oak (of Moreh)." The LXX in the present verse has a singular. The place may have been a grove of trees. The oak tree (אַלּוֹן) has also been identified as a "terebinth," probably *pistacia terebinthus* or *pistacia palestina* (J. C. Trever, "Terebinth," in *IDB*, 4:574).

31 On this stereotyped language of Deuteronomy, see Note for 4:25-26.

32 The teaching and preaching in chs. 5–11 concludes with the most common of Deuteronomic injunctions: Do all the statutes and ordinances of the Deuteronomic code, now to be laid out before you in chs. 12–26. "And you shall be careful to do," which began the present sermon cluster in v. 22, is stereotyped in Deuteronomy (see Note for 5:1). "That I am setting before you" is another stock Deuteronomic expression (see Note for 1:8). Here and in v. 26 it ties together the sermons in vv. 26-32 (see Rhetoric and Composition).

Message and Audience

In readiness for the Deuteronomic Code that is to come next, Moses reiterates what he has been saying all along: Israel must be careful to do all of Yahweh's commandment. In doing so, it will show that people love Yahweh, resolve to walk in Yahweh's ways, and cling to Yahweh in total devotion. If they do so, Yahweh will dispossess all the mighty nations Israel will face when it crosses the Jordan. Every place on which their foot treads shall become a possession — from the wilderness in the south to the Lebanon in the north, from the Euphrates in the east to the Mediterranean in the west. No people will be able to hold its ground in the upcoming battle, for Yahweh will put the dread and fear of Israel before everyone, as he promised to do.

Israel has a choice, however, between blessing and curse. The nation will be blessed if it heeds the commandments of Yahweh; it will be cursed if it does not and turns aside to walk after other gods it has not known.

When Israel enters the land, it is go to Mount Gerizim and Mount Ebal for a ceremony of blessing and curse. Does Israel remember that these mountains are beside the oaks of Moreh, which figured prominently in stories about Abraham? They are beyond the Jordan, behind the west road of the Canaanites who dwell in the Arabah opposite Gilgal. Israel is now to cross the Jordan to enter the land of promise. It must therefore be careful to do all the statutes and ordinances that Moses is setting before it.

An audience of the late 8th and early 7th cents. will hear once again the voice of Moses telling it to obey commandments in the Deuteronomic code. It will also hear the blessing and curse, wondering if perhaps it has not reaped more the latter than the former at the hands of the Assyrian army.

VI. THE DEUTERONOMIC CODE (12–26)

A. THE CENTRAL SANCTUARY (12:1–13:1[12:32])

1. Destroy All Places of Their Gods (12:1-4)

*12*¹*These are the statutes and the ordinances that you shall be careful to do in the land that Yahweh the God of your fathers has given to you to possess it, all the days that you are living on the soil.* ²*You must indeed destroy all the places where the nations that you are dispossessing have served their gods, upon the high mountains and upon the hills and under every leafy tree.* ³*And you shall break down their altars and shatter their pillars, and their Asherim you shall burn with fire, and the idols of their gods you shall hew down, and you shall destroy their name from that place.* ⁴*You shall not do thus for Yahweh your God.*

2. On Tithes and Offerings (12:5-14)

a) *Offerings at the Central Sanctuary (12:5-9)*

12 ⁵But to the place that Yahweh your God will choose out of all your tribes to put his name there, to make it reside, you shall seek and each of you shall go there. ⁶And you shall bring there your burnt offerings and your sacrifices, and your tithes and the contribution of your hand, and your votive offerings and your freewill offerings, and the firstborns in your herd and your flock. ⁷And you shall eat there before Yahweh your God, and you shall be glad in every undertaking of your hand, you and your households, because Yahweh your God has blessed you. ⁸You shall not do like everything that we are doing here today, each person, everything that is right in his own eyes; ⁹for up till now you have not come to the resting place and to the inheritance that Yahweh your God is giving to you.

b) *Once Again: Offerings at the Central Sanctuary (12:10-14)*

¹⁰When you cross over the Jordan and you dwell in the land that Yahweh your God causes you to inherit, and he gives you rest from all your enemies round about, so you dwell securely, ¹¹then it shall be: the place that Yahweh your God will choose to make his name reside there — to there you shall bring everything that I am commanding you — your burnt offerings and your sacrifices, your tithes and the contribution of your hand, and all the best of your votive offerings that you vow to Yahweh. ¹²And you shall be glad before Yahweh your God, you, and your sons and your daughters, and your menservants and your maidservants, and the Levite who is within your gates, for he has no portion or inheritance with you. ¹³Take care for yourself, lest you offer up your burnt offerings in every place that you see. ¹⁴But in the place that Yahweh will choose in one of your tribes, there you shall offer up your burnt offerings, and there you shall do everything that I am commanding you.

3. On the Clean and Unclean (12:15-28)

a) *Nonsacrificial Meat in the Towns (12:15-16)*

12 ¹⁵Only with all your soul's desire you may slaughter and eat meat according to the blessing of Yahweh your God that he has given you within all your gates; the unclean and the clean may eat it, like the gazelle and like the deer. ¹⁶Only the blood you shall not eat; you shall pour it out upon the earth like water.

b) Offerings at the Central Sanctuary (12:17-19)

¹⁷ You may not eat within your gates the tithe of your grain or your wine or your oil, or the firstborns in your herd or your flock, or any of your votive offerings that you vow, or your freewill offerings or the contribution of your hand. ¹⁸ But before Yahweh your God you shall eat it, in the place that Yahweh your God will choose, you, and your son and your daughter, and your manservant and your maidservant, and the Levite who is within your gates. And you shall be glad before Yahweh your God in every undertaking of your hand. ¹⁹ Take care for yourself, lest you forsake the Levite all your days on your soil.

c) Nonsacrificial Meat in the Towns (12:20-25)

²⁰ When Yahweh your God enlarges your territory just as he promised you, and you say, "I will eat meat," because your soul desires to eat meat, with all your soul's desire you may eat meat. ²¹ When the place that Yahweh your God will choose to put his name there is far from you, then you shall slaughter from your herd and from your flock what Yahweh has given you, just as I commanded you, and you may eat within your gates with all your soul's desire. ²² But just as the gazelle and the deer are eaten, thus you shall eat it, the unclean and the clean alike may eat it. ²³ Only be firm not to eat the blood, because the blood, it is the life, and you shall not eat the life with the meat. ²⁴ You shall not eat it; you shall pour it out upon the earth like water. ²⁵ You shall not eat it in order that it may go well for you and for your children after you, when you do what is right in the eyes of Yahweh.

d) Holy Offerings at the Central Sanctuary (12:26-28)

²⁶ Only your holy things that you have and your votive offerings, you shall carry and go to the place that Yahweh will choose, ²⁷ and you shall make your burnt offerings — the meat and the blood — upon the altar of Yahweh your God, and the blood of your sacrifices shall be poured out upon the altar of Yahweh your God, but the meat you may eat. ²⁸ Be careful that you hear all these words that I am commanding you, in order that it may go well for you and for your children after you forever, when you do what is good and what is right in the eyes of Yahweh your God.

4. Seek Not Their Gods (12:29–13:1[12:32])

12 ²⁹ When Yahweh your God cuts off from before you the nations whom you have come to possess, and you have taken possession of them and you dwell in their

land, ³⁰*take care for yourself, lest you become ensnared after them, after they have been completely destroyed before you, and lest you seek their gods, saying, "How did these nations serve their gods? And I will do thus, even I." ³¹You shall not do thus for Yahweh your God, for every abomination to Yahweh that he hates they have done for their gods; indeed even their sons and their daughters they burn in the fire to their gods.* **13**¹*Every word that I am commanding you, you shall be careful to do it; you shall not add to it and you shall not subtract from it.*

Rhetoric and Composition

Chapter 12 introduces the legal core of Deuteronomy, which consists of chs. 13–25. It is a rambling homiletical piece, similar to the homiletical discourse introducing the Horeb covenant in ch. 4. For Luther, the spiritual explanation of the first commandment was now finished and the heart duly instructed. Moses therefore moves on to develop the outward worship of God in action and ceremonies. Chapter 26, with its rituals for the firstfruits and the third-year tithe, is a conclusion, making a frame with ch. 12 for the legal core. The Deuteronomic Code, then, consists of chs. 12–26, comparable in nature to the Covenant Code in Exodus 21–23.

The Deuteronomic Code builds upon the Decalogue, which is true also for the Covenant Code. In Exodus, however, the Covenant Code follows immediately the Decalogue in ch. 20, whereas in Deuteronomy the Decalogue is in ch. 5, with the Deuteronomic Code not coming until chs. 12–26, after six chapters of intervening homiletical material. But the Deuteronomic Code, particularly chs. 13–18, appears in the same homiletical dress as other preaching in the book. Some laws are well-structured units, others — particularly in chs. 19–25 — are loosely linked together by word association. Braulik (1993, 319-20) finds these keyword and associative links too "unsystematic" for his liking, yet we know Hebrew composition used associative devices, word associations in particular, however much they go against modern modes of composition.

It has also been shown that the Deuteronomic Code, in expanding the Decalogue, follows the sequence of the Decalogue, i.e., one can see a general progression from the first commandment to the tenth commandment (S. A. Kaufman 1978-79; Braulik 1993). The idea is not new. Luther in his *Lectures on Deuteronomy* (1960, 67) noted from the beginning of ch. 6 on through to the end of the book a clear exposition of the Ten Commandments. By the end of the book he meant ch. 26, where the exposition concluded. Correlations were not found at every point, but Luther pointed to them when he saw them.

One should not expect to find a rigid correlation between the Decalogue and laws of the Deuteronomic Code, particularly if material al-

Deuteronomy 12

ready having form is given a later form, which is what we seem to have in the book. Kaufman, however, is correct to see in the Deuteronomic Code an intentional expansion of the Decalogue. His correlations extend only through to the eighth commandment (stealing), but I think they go farther, all the way through to the ninth and tenth commandments. Braulik is more confident about a correlation between the Deuteronomic Code and commandments five through ten. His scheme contains a couple "transitional" sections, whereas I am inclined to take certain laws as miscellaneous add-ons, connected to other laws by catchwords.

The present outline follows with minor changes the outlines of Kaufman and Braulik. Laws in square brackets are miscellaneous in character, i.e., they may or may not correlate with the corresponding law of the Decalogue:

Decalogue	**Deuteronomic Code**
I. No other gods before Yahweh (5:7)	Introducing Yahweh worship after judging Canaanite worship (12:1–13:1[12:32])
II. No images of Yahweh (5:8-10)	
III. No empty oaths in Yahweh's name (5:11)	Do not go after other gods (13:2-19[1-18])
IV. Keep the Sabbath Day holy (5:12-15)	Clean and unclean foods; a reminder that Israel is a holy people (14:1-21)
	Tithes and offerings (14:22–15:23)
	Keeping the feasts (16:1-17)
V. Honor your father and your mother (5:16)	Judges, judgment, and miscellaneous prohibitions (16:18–17:13)
	Concerning the king (17:14-20)
	Concerning the Levitical priests (18:1-8)
	Concerning the prophet (18:9-22)
VI. You shall not murder (5:17)	Homicide and refuge cities (19:1-13)
	[No moving of landmarks (19:14)]
	Regarding false witnesses (19:15-21)
	Rules of warfare (20:1-20)
	Unsolved murder (21:1-9)
	Taking of war brides (21:10-14)
	[Rights of the firstborn (21:15-17)]
	Death for rebellious sons (21:18-21)
	Hanged criminals (21:22-23)
	[Restoring lost property (22:1-4)]
	[Transvestitism prohibited (22:5)]
	Protecting mother birds (22:6-7)
	Roofs require parapets (22:8)
VII. You shall not commit adultery (5:18)	Prohibition of mixtures (22:9-11)
	Tassels on clothing (22:12)
	Unchaste brides (22:13-21)
	Sex with married woman (22:22)

417

Deuteronomy 12

	Sex with betrothed woman (22:23-27)
	Sex with unbetrothed woman (22:28-29)
	Sex with a father's wife (23:1[22:30])
	Ritual purity (23:2-10[1-9])
	Sexual purity and cleanliness (23:11-15[10-14])
	[Harboring escaped slaves (23:16-17[15-16])]
	No cult prostitutes (23:18-19[17-18])
VIII. You shall not steal (5:19)	No lending at interest (23:20-21[19-20])
	Prompt payment of vows (23:22-24[21-23])
	No stealing of crops (23:25-26[24-25])
	No return to first husband (24:1-4)
	[Newlywed war deferment (24:5)]
	Pledge prohibitions (24:6)
	No stealing of persons (24:7)
	[Warning about scale disease (24:8-9)]
	On fetching pledges (24:10-13)
	Paying hired servants (24:14-15)
	Deferred punishment (24:16)
	Pledges from the needy (24:17-18)
	Gleanings for the needy (24:19-22)
IX. No false witness against neighbor (5:20)	Court decisions and punishment (25:1-3)
X. No coveting of neighbor's property (5:21)	[No muzzling an ox (25:4)]
	Levirate marriage (25:5-10)
	Interfering wives (25:11-12)
	Just weights and measures (25:13-16)

Chapter 12, as we mentioned, is balanced in the book by ch. 26, the two chapters serving to frame the central law code. This balance goes beyond content to include a repetition of keywords, forming an expanded chiasmus:

a		These are *the statutes and the ordinances that you shall be careful to do* . . .	12:1
	b	*the place that Yahweh your God will choose* . . . *to put his name there*	12:5
		your tithes and the contribution of your hand . . . *and the firstborns*	12:6
		and you shall be glad . . .	12:7
		the place that Yahweh your God will choose to make his name reside there . . .	12:11
		your tithes and the contribution of your hand	
		And you shall be glad . . . *and the Levite*	12:12

b′	*the first of all the fruit*	26:2
	to the place that Yahweh your God will choose	
	to make his name reside there	
	And you shall be glad . . . and the Levite	26:11
	you have finished tithing all the tithe . . . the year	26:12
	of the tithe . . . to the Levite	
a′	*these statutes and these ordinances, and you shall*	26:16
	be careful and you shall do them . . .	

The present verses are delimited at the top end by the chapter division before v. 1 and at the bottom end by a *petuḥah* in M^L and a section in Sam after 13:1. The Vg and some modern English Versions (AV; RSV; NEB) number this latter verse 12:32. We get less help from M^L and Sam in delimiting internal units. Neither M^L nor Sam has a section after v. 4. Sam has sections after vv. 7, 12, and 16, and both M^L and Sam have sections after v. 19. M^L has a *setumah* there. An introductory type clause begins v. 20: "When Yahweh your God enlarges your territory. . . ." Sam has a section after v. 25. After v. 28, M^L has a *setumah* and Sam a section marking.

Chapter 12, with its considerable repetition (Luther), is difficult to outline. But there are definite structures within the chapter. At the center is a sermon on what may and need not be offered at the central sanctuary. It contains instructions in which key elements have to do with

(1) tithes and offerings (vv. 5-14)
(2) ritually clean and unclean eating (vv. 15-28)

In chs. 14–15 these themes are reversed in actual laws on

(1) clean and unclean foods (14:1-21)
(2) tithes and offerings (14:22–15:23)

On both sides of this sermon (12:5-28), creating a frame, is a divided discourse in vv. 2-4 and vv. 29-31 on rooting out Canaan's multiple worship sites and multiple gods (cf. Rofé 1988b, 277-78), a subject developed more fully in ch. 13. At the very beginning and end of the chapter are solemn warnings about doing the commandments (12:1; 13:1[12:32], which lie ahead in the Deuteronomic Code (Lundbom 1996, 306-7).

The overall structure of the chapter is a chiasmus of keyword repetitions and pivotal sentences. All six units contain the verb עשה ("to do"), with five of the six having another key verb, שמר ("take care"). Keywords in the center units (cc′) show inversion:

Deuteronomy 12

a		These are the statutes and the ordinances that *you shall be careful to do* . . .	12:1
	b	Places of *their gods* to be destroyed	12:2-4
		You shall not do thus for Yahweh your God	12:4
		c On tithes and offerings	12:5-14
		You shall not do . . .	12:8
		When you cross over the Jordan . . .	12:10
		Take care for yourself . . .	12:13
		c′ On the ritually clean and the unclean	12:15-28
		Take care for yourself . . .	12:19
		When Yahweh . . . enlarges your territory . . .	12:20
		Be careful . . . when you do . . .	12:28
	b′	Do not seek after *their gods*	12:29-31
		take care for yourself . . .	12:30
		You shall not do thus for Yahweh your God	12:31
a′		Every word that I am commanding you, *you shall be careful to do it*	13:1[12:32]

This structure supports the Vg numbering, which closes the discourse at 12:32. In MT and LXX this verse is 13:1. Driver prefers the Hebrew (and Greek) numbering, saying that the verse is best taken as a preface to the ordinances following (cf. 4:2). But Fishbane (1972, 350) takes 13:1 as a conclusion to the cultic prescriptions in ch. 12. There is admittedly ambiguity in the text, since the verse in question also shares a key verb צוה ("command") with the closing verse of ch. 13, arguing for 13:1, 19[12:32; 13:18] making an inclusio within ch. 13:

> 13:1[12:32] Every word that *I am commanding you,* you shall be careful to do it; you shall not add to it and you shall not subtract from it.
>
> 13:19[18] . . . to keep all his commandments that *I am commanding you* today, to do what is right in the eyes of Yahweh your God.

We may need to conclude that in the present book, at least, 13:1[12:32] assumes a dual role, closing ch. 12 and beginning ch. 13, which would explain the later uncertainty in assigning chapter and verse numbers.

In vv. 1-4 is another keyword inclusio:

you shall be careful to do . . .	תִּשְׁמְרוּן לַעֲשׂוֹת	v. 1
you shall not do . . .	לֹא־תַעֲשׂוּן	v. 4

The "tithes and offerings" discourse (vv. 5-14) has a structure made up of keywords and pivotal phrases:

a	*But to the place that Yahweh your God will choose out of all your tribes to put his name there, to make it reside . . .*	v. 5
	And you shall bring there your burnt offerings and your sacrifices, and your tithes and the contribution of your hand, and your votive offerings . . .	v. 6
	and you shall be glad . . . you and your households . . .	v. 7
	You shall not do like everything that we are doing here today, each person, everything that is right in his own eyes . . .	v. 8
a′	*When you cross over the Jordan . . .*	v. 10
	then it shall be: the place that Yahweh your God will choose to make his name reside there —	v. 11
	to there you shall bring . . . your burnt offerings and your sacrifices, your tithes and the contribution of your hand, and . . . your votive offerings	
	And you shall be glad . . . you, and your sons and your daughters . . .	v. 12
	Take care for yourself, lest you offer up your burnt offerings in every place that you see.	v. 13

The "clean and the unclean" discourse (vv. 15-28) repeats essentially the same content in two parts, but with the difference that the instruction on nonsacrificial eating in the towns alternates with the instruction on sacrificial eating at the central sanctuary:

a	eating nonsacrificial meat in the towns	vv. 15-16
	eating tithes and offerings at the central sanctuary	vv. 17-19
a′	eating nonsacrificial meat in the towns	vv. 20-25
	eating holy offerings at the central sanctuary	vv. 26-28

Keywords and pivotal phrases giving structure to this discourse:

a	*Only with all your soul's desire you may . . . eat meat . . . within all your gates; the unclean and the clean may eat it, like the gazelle and like the deer.*	v. 15
	Only the blood you shall not eat; you shall pour it out upon the earth like water.	v. 16
	You may not eat within your gates the tithe of your grain or your wine or your oil, or the firstborns	v. 17

Deuteronomy 12

	in your herd or your flock, or any of your votive offerings that you vow, or your freewill offerings or the contribution of your hand	
	. . . you shall eat it, in the place that Yahweh your God will choose	v. 18
a'	*When Yahweh your God enlarges your territory . . .*	v. 20
	. . . you may eat within your gates with all your soul's desire.	v. 21
	just as the gazelle and the deer are eaten . . . the unclean and the clean . . . may eat it	v. 22
	Only be firm not to eat the blood . . . you shall pour it out upon the earth like water.	vv. 23-24
	Only your holy things that you have and your votive offerings,	v. 26
	you shall carry and go to the place that Yahweh will choose,	
	and you shall make your burnt offerings . . . but the meat you may eat	v. 27

Portions of 12:1–13:1 are contained in 1QDeut[a], 4QDeut[c], 4QpaleoDeut[r], and MurDeut.

Notes

12:1 *These are the statutes and the ordinances that you shall be careful to do in the land.* These words introduce the Deuteronomic Code (chs. 12–26), the book's major collection of laws expanding upon the Decalogue (ch. 5). The Covenant Code is similarly introduced in Exod 21:1: "Now these are the ordinances that you shall set before them." Other Deuteronomic statements of introduction and conclusion have similar wording, e.g., 4:45 (conclusion); 5:1 (introduction); and 6:1 (introduction). The Deuteronomic Code does not begin with 11:31 (*pace* Rofé 1972, 222-23; Tigay); 11:31-32 is a conclusion to chs. 5–11 (von Rad; G. E. Wright), v. 32 forming an inclusio with 5:1 (see Rhetoric and Composition for 5:1-5 and 11:22-32).

the statutes and the ordinances. הַחֻקִּים וְהַמִּשְׁפָּטִים. I.e., the specific points of law at the heart of the Deuteronomic covenant, to be spelled out in chs. 12–26. Within the Deuteronomic Code these laws are never called תּוֹרֹת, always חֻקִּים and מִשְׁפָּטִים. On the expression "statutes and ordinances" and stereotyped expressions of a similar nature in Deuteronomy, see Note for 4:1.

that you shall be careful to do. Deuteronomy is continually warning people to "be careful to do" the commandments after they settle in the land (see Note for 5:1).

Yahweh the God of your fathers. Yahweh is God of Abraham, Isaac, and Jacob (see Note for 1:11).

all the days that you are living upon the soil. Israel's obligation to carry out statutes and ordinances of the Deuteronomic Code is long-term. On the question of land tenure, Deuteronomy is clear: Israel can remain in the land only so long as it obeys the covenant demands. If it obeys, it will be blessed and live long in the land; if it disobeys, curses will fall and the God-given land will be lost (ch. 28). On the expression "all the days (of one's life)," see Note for 4:9.

2 *You must indeed destroy all the places where the nations that you are dispossessing have served their gods.* All Canaanite worship sites are to be destroyed (7:5). The Covenant Code says as much in Exod 23:24, and the Priestly writer the same in Num 33:50-52. As things turned out, after the sites were destroyed Yahweh worship was often carried out on the same location (Judg 6:26; 1 Kgs 18:23-35; de Vaux 1965, 332). Exodus 34:11-16 expressed the concern that Yahweh worship might coexist with indigenous Canaanite worship, and there is evidence aplenty, both in the Bible and from archaeological excavations, that this did, in fact, take place (Jer 17:2-3a).

all the places. The "places" are sacred places (1 Sam 7:16), open-air sanctuaries for the most part, which are called "high places" (בָּמוֹת) in the OT (1 Kgs 12:31; 13:32). But the term בָּמוֹת does not occur in Deuteronomy.

upon the high mountains and upon the hills and under every leafy tree. A poetic description of the Canaanite high places, where a debased form of Israelite worship later took place. Mention of "every leafy tree" adds a touch of irony, in that something pleasant is denigrated. There is also nice assonance in הֶהָרִים הָרָמִים ("the high mountains"). The full phrase occurs variously in the OT (1 Kgs 14:23; 2 Kgs 17:10; Jer 2:20; 3:6; 17:2-3a; Ezek 6:13; 20:28, and elsewhere). Fertility rites were carried out on hills, under spreading trees, and in ancient religion generally these rites included sex-related activities (Hos 4:13). Yahweh worship too, both early and late, occurred on mountains and hills (Gen 22:2; Exod 19:3; Deut 11:29; 27:12-13; 2 Sam 15:32; 1 Kgs 18:19), even on "high places" (1 Sam 9:13-14, 19; 10:5), and alongside trees ("the oak[s] of Moreh" in Gen 12:6-8; Deut 11:30). The prophets heaped scorn on high-place worship (Hos 4:13; Jer 3:23; 17:2-3; Ezek 6:3-4), with the result that high places were abolished in the reforms of Hezekiah and Josiah (2 Kgs 18:4, 22[= Isa 36:7]; 23:8, 13, 15). Jeremiah would later lament that the mountains are what led Israel astray (Jer 50:6). Albright (1957a) believed that "high places" were funerary shrines, situated usually — but not always — on hills or ridges (cf. de Vaux 1965, 287; P. J. King 1993, 110-11). The sites needed only to be elevated, not situated on the very top of a hill. Some sites were in cities (1 Kgs 13:32; 2 Kgs 23:5); the infamous Topheth against which Jeremiah spoke was located in the Ben Hinnom Valley (Jer 7:31; 32:35). Leafy trees were selected for their shade, but also because all throughout the ANE trees took on a sacred character (de Vaux).

An open-air cult site, dating from the Early Iron Age and thus taken to be Israelite, has been discovered in the territory of Manasseh, between Dothan and Beth-shan, a short distance south of the modern city of Jenin. It is located on the top of a remote ridge. Among the finds were a stone pillar (מַצֵּבָה) and a small bronze bull figurine (A. Mazar 1982). Other early Israelite cult sites have been discovered at Dan (Biran 1994, 159-214), Arad (Y. Aharoni 1976, 60-61; Herzog et al. 1984, 11-26), and Hazor (Yadin 1972, 132-34). At Hazor, in Stratum XI (11th cent.), numerous cult objects were found, including incense stands and a bronze figurine of a seated male divinity wearing a coned helmet (Yadin et al. 1961: Area B pls. XXXVIII nos. 1-2; CCIV no. 1; CCV no. 2; CCCXLV no. 11; CCCXLVI nos. 1-6). All these sites would be what the Bible calls "high places."

under every leafy tree. Hebrew רַעֲנָן does not mean "green," but "luxuriant, spreading" (T: "leafy, productive, beautiful"). Reference is to a tree overspreading with leaves. The LXX has δένδρου δασέος, "thick, leafy tree" (cf. Hos 4:13; Ezek 6:13; 20:28).

3 *And you shall break down their altars and shatter their pillars.* The "pillars" (מַצֵּבוֹת) were upright stones in Canaanite sanctuaries serving as male fertility symbols. These, together with Canaanite altars, had to be broken into pieces (7:5; cf. Exod 23:24; 34:13). Egypt from ancient times (early 2nd millennium) had much larger obelisks, many of which stood tall in Heliopolis. These were colossal four-sided granite monuments, some more than 100 ft in height and weighing in excess of 200 tons. They were spoken against by Jeremiah upon his arrival in Egypt (Jer 43:13; Lundbom 2004b, 148-50). According to Deuteronomy, Yahweh worship could have its altars, but not any pillars (16:22). Pillars were erected anyway (1 Kgs 14:23; 2 Kgs 17:10) and have turned up at excavated sites all over the ANE, e.g., the one found at the open-air site in Manasseh, mentioned above. On excavated standing stones in ancient Palestine, see Graesser 1972.

Once again, sacred pillars had been erected by Israel's ancestors, e.g., by Jacob after his divine revelation at Bethel (Gen 28:18-22; 31:13) and again at Bethel after he returned from Paddan-aram (Gen 35:14-15). Even Moses, according to Exod 24:4, surrounded an altar at Mount Sinai with twelve pillars. But the prophets attacked these pillars because of their association with pagan worship (Hos 3:4; 10:1-2; Mic 5:12[13]; Jer 2:27; 3:9; cf. 1 Kgs 16:33; 2 Kgs 13:6; 17:16), and certain Israelite and Judahite kings destroyed them (2 Kgs 3:1-2; 10:27; 18:4; 23:14). Josiah is said to have torn down altars (2 Kgs 23:12, 15) that previous kings had made (1 Kgs 16:32; 2 Kgs 21:3). Altars also came under attack by the prophets (Hos 10:2; Isa 27:9; Jer 17:2).

and their Asherim you shall burn with fire. The "Asherim" (אֲשֵׁרִים) were feminine fertility symbols dedicated to Asherah, the Canaanite mother goddess, who was a consort of Baal at Tyre. They were either sacred trees (Rashi) or wooden poles (T^{Onq}) and could therefore be cut down and burned. The LXX, imagining a large number of them, has τὰ ἄλση αὐτῶν ("their groves"). Felix Mendelssohn used the LXX translation in his "Elijah" oratorio, referring to "the prophets of the groves" (Part I, Recitative no. 10), and then had Ahab addressed with the words

As if it had been a light thing for thee to walk in the sins of Jeroboam
Thou hast made a grove and an altar to Baal
And served him and worshipped him. (Part II, Recitative no. 23)

The Asherim were set up near the altar and, like the sacred pillars, were forbidden by Deuteronomy for Yahweh worship (16:21). They were set up anyway (1 Kgs 14:15, 23; 16:33; 2 Kgs 17:10; 21:3, 7) and therefore came under prophetic censure (Mic 5:13[14]; Isa 27:9; Jer 2:27; 3:9; 17:2). Hezekiah and Josiah abolished them (2 Kgs 18:4, 22[= Isa 36:7]; 23:6, 14-15). On Asherah, see further W. R. Smith 1927, 187-88; Reed 1949; de Vaux 1965, 286; J. Day 1986; and "Asherah" in *ABD*, 1:483-87. For a picture of a female fertility figurine from Jerusalem, which may be this goddess, see P. J. King 1993, 110.

and the idols of their gods you shall hew down. Idols (פְּסִילִים) of any kind were forbidden by the second commandment (5:8-10) and warned against throughout Deuteronomy (4:16-18, 23). Israel was told that if it made such things, it would soon perish from the land it was about to possess (4:25-26). But it did so anyway (Isa 10:10), and so we hear the prophets crying out against these lifeless wonders in their denunciation of Israelite and Judahite worship (Hos 11:2; Mic 5:12[13]). Idols were sometimes made of metal or stone (Mic 1:7; Isa 21:9), or they could be wooden carvings overlaid with gold or silver (Isa 30:22). Those made of wood could be cut down and burned. The LXX in the present verse reads καὶ τὰ γλυπτὰ τῶν θεῶν αὐτῶν κατακαύσετε πυρί ("and the carvings of their gods you shall burn with fire"). Burning Canaanite idols is commanded in 7:5 and 25. As was mentioned, a bronze idol of a warrior god has turned up at the high place of Hazor, and others have been found at excavated sites in the ANE.

and you shall destroy their name from that place. I.e., The very names of deities venerated at Canaanite worship sites are to be destroyed and forgotten (Exod 23:13; Zeph 1:4; Zech 13:2). Rashi says this could mean giving them contemptuous nicknames, which was later done. For example, in the OT vowels of the Hebrew word for "shame" (בֹּשֶׁת) served to misvocalize Ashtart to Ashtoreth (1 Kgs 11:5, 33), Baal to Bosheth (Hos 9:10), and Melek to Molech (Jer

32:35; 2 Kgs 23:10). This anticipates v. 5, where Israel is told to seek out the place where Yahweh has put his "name."

4 You are not to destroy Yahweh's name from the place he has chosen to put it. Targum[PsJ] says: "You are not permitted to erase the writing of the Name of the Lord your God." The indictment on northern Israel in 2 Kgs 17:9-11 shows precisely what happened when people did the opposite of what they were instructed to do here.

5 "The (one) place" (הַמָּקוֹם) for Yahweh worship contrasts with "all the places" (כָּל־הַמְּקֹמוֹת) at which Canaanite worship has been carried out (v. 2). The worship of Yahweh shall not take place upon high mountains and hills and under leafy trees. There shall be one sanctuary, and Yahweh will choose it. Deuteronomy does not name the place, which is understandable, since it would create an obvious anachronism in that Jerusalem is not yet an Israelite city (Clements 1965, 312). In the Deuteronomic History, the single sanctuary is openly said to be Jerusalem (1 Kgs 11:36; 14:21) or else the temple in Jerusalem (1 Kgs 9:3; 2 Kgs 21:4, 7), which is how it was in the late 8th and early 7th cents. Earlier, "the place chosen by Yahweh" could have been Shechem (Josh 24:1; Deut 27:1-14; von Rad 1953, 41; 1962a, 837), Shiloh (Jer 7:12; Rashi), Bethel (Amos 7:13), or some other place. De Vaux (1965, 338-39) suggests Shechem or Bethel. Y. Kaufmann (1960, 173), who does not think Deuteronomy presupposes a central sanctuary, says that the reference could be to any number of Israel's early sanctuaries. The novelty of Deuteronomic law, in his view, is not the concept of a central sanctuary, since from earliest times the great sanctuaries of Shechem, Bethel, Dan, Gibeon, and Jerusalem overshadowed smaller local altars. To these sanctuaries it was the custom to make pilgrimages three times a year (1 Samuel 1; 1 Kings 8). The new feature of Deuteronomy is its emphatic prohibition of all sacrifices outside the one chosen site (12:13-14, 17, 26-27).

The OT focus on a single sanctuary, according to Welch (1925), begins when the Deuteronomic Historian announces Solomon's decision to build the temple in Jerusalem (1 Kgs 8:15-21). The Covenant Code presupposes multiple sanctuaries (Exod 20:24: "In every place where I cause my name to be remembered I will come to you and bless you"). Centralization in Jerusalem began in earnest with the reforms of Hezekiah (2 Kgs 18:4; 2 Chr 29-31) and Josiah (2 Kings 22-23; 2 Chr 34-35), which were likely royal responses to prophetic preaching against worship currently going on at regional sanctuaries (Amos 4:4-5; 5:4-5; Hos 4:11-19), where syncretistic practices were rife and where the religion of Yahweh found itself in grave danger. In the north, it happened earlier during the time of Ahab, bringing Elijah to the fore as the mighty restorer of Yahwistic faith (1 Kings 18-19). Other factors in the 8th cent. helped to bring centralization about. The political reality of the time was a much-reduced Israel. The northern kingdom had been destroyed by the Assyrians in 722 (2 Kgs

18:9-10; cf. Tadmor 1958, 36), and not long afterwards Sennacherib truncated Judah by destroying forty-six of its cities in 701, leaving little more than Jerusalem intact.

A century later, Jeremiah takes for granted a single sanctuary in Jerusalem (Jer 7:1-15; 26:1-6) and Ezekiel mocks those who want to build a high place in Babylon, saying that Yahweh's holy mountain in Jerusalem is where Yahweh desires to be worshipped (Ezekiel 20). Weinfeld says, too, that it never entered the minds of returning exiles to renew high places in Israel, indirect testimony to the effective work of Josiah in centralizing worship in Jerusalem. "The place that Yahweh your God will choose" in the Qumran *Temple Scroll* (11QT) has been argued recently to be an expanded temple and temple precinct erected on the entire area of Jerusalem, becoming in effect a "temple city" (Birenboim 2008). On the importance of a single Jewish temple in Jerusalem in the NT period, see John 4:20.

the place that Yahweh your God will choose out of all your tribes to put his name there, to make it reside. A combination of two Deuteronomic expressions stating that Yahweh "will choose a place to put/make reside his name" (12:5, 11, 14, 18, 21, 26; 14:23-25; 15:20; 16:2, 6, 11, 15, 16; 17:8, 10; 18:6; 26:2; 31:11; cf. Driver 1895, lxxxiii no. 63; Weinfeld 1972, 324-25 no. 1, no. 4). Von Rad (1953, 38-40) discerns in Deuteronomy a "name theology," which affirms that Yahweh himself is not present at the worship place, only his name he has put (**לָשׂוּם**) there or made to reside (**לְשַׁכֵּן**) there. This has been qualified recently by Hundley (2009), who says that Deuteronomy and the Deuteronomic History do not absent Yahweh from earth but simply leave the exact nature and extent of Yahweh's presence on earth ambiguous. In Jeremiah, the corresponding expression is "This house upon which my name is called," **הַבַּיִת הַזֶּה אֲשֶׁר־נִקְרָא־שְׁמִי עָלָיו** (Jer 7:10-11, 14, 30; 32:34; 34:15). To call someone or something by one's name is to claim ownership (2 Sam 12:28; Amos 9:12; Isa 43:1, 6-7; 63:19). The idiom has turned up outside the Bible in the Amarna Letters (EA no. 287 line 60; no. 288 line 5; *ANET*[3], 488), where it means "to take possession" (de Vaux 1967, 221). In The Lists of Ramses III (*ANET*[3], 261) is the expression "as the vested property of thy name," which also indicates ownership. In Deuteronomic theology, Yahweh locates his name on earth, in the temple, whereas his actual dwelling place is in the heaven (4:36; 26:15; 1 Kgs 8:27-30, 43; 9:3; Clements 1965, 302; Weinfeld 1972, 195-98; but see Deut 23:15[14]).

This theological conception contrasts with the older idea that Yahweh was invisibly present on his ark, which served as his throne (Num 10:35-36; 1 Sam 4:4-9). Priestly theology, being more anthropomorphic, saw the tabernacle (= tent of meeting, **אֹהֶל מוֹעֵד**) as the place on earth where Yahweh's "glory" (**כָּבוֹד**) met the people (Exod 16:10; 29:43; Num 14:10; 16:19; 20:6). In older material, one does find statements to the effect that Yahweh speaks (**דבר**)

Deuteronomy 12

from heaven (Exod 20:22) and resides (שׁכן) amidst his people in an earthly sanctuary (Exod 25:8-9; 29:44-46; cf. Isa 8:18), suggesting that perhaps Deuteronomy is merely clarifying and solidifying earlier ideas. But Weinfeld (1972, 193) states categorically: "There is not one example in the Deuteronomic literature of God's *dwelling* in the temple or the building of a house *for God*. The temple is always the *dwelling of his name*, and the house is always built *for his name*." In his view (p. 195), the song beginning Solomon's prayer in 1 Kgs 8:12-13 represents an older view that the Deuteronomic Historian is disputing.

Deuteronomy also makes repeated reference to "the place Yahweh will choose" (12:5, 11, 14, 18, 21, 26; 14:23-25; 15:20; 16:2, 6-7, 11, 15-16; 17:8, 10; 18:6; 26:2; 31:11), another stock phrase in the book referring to the central sanctuary. The Deuteronomic Historian, for his part, names Jerusalem as Yahweh's city of choice, on which he has put his name (1 Kgs 8:44, 48 [cf. v. 16]; 11:13, 32, 36; 14:21; 2 Kgs 21:7; 23:27). David is said to be Yahweh's chosen king (1 Kgs 8:16; 11:34; cf. Jer 33:26; Carlson 1964). Driver points out how often "choose" (בחר) appears in Deuteronomy and the Deuteronomic History (Driver 1895, lxxx no. 23; cf. Weinfeld 1972, 324-25 nos. 1, 1a, 3; 327 no. 5). In Deuteronomy, besides Yahweh's choice of a central sanctuary, we learn that Yahweh has chosen Israel (4:37; 7:6-7; 10:15; 14:2), the (Levitical) priests (18:5; 21:5), and will in the future choose an Israelite king (17:15). In 30:19-20, people are told to "choose life," that they and their descendants may live long in the land.

out of all your tribes. מִכָּל־שִׁבְטֵיכֶם. This is the one clear expression in the chapter that the place chosen by Yahweh is to be one *out of* (מִן) all Israel's tribes. In the Deuteronomic History (1 Kgs 8:16; 11:32; 14:21; 2 Kgs 21:7), this place is Jerusalem.

to make it reside. Repointing MT לְשִׁכְנוֹ to a Piel infinitive with suffix, לְשַׁכְּנוֹ, "to make it reside" (BDB, 1015). The Piel occurs elsewhere in a stereotyped Deuteronomic expression (12:11; 14:23; 16:2, 6, 11; 26:2). MT לְשִׁכְנוֹ is explained either as a Qal infinitive with suffix (GKC §61b), which would yield the same basic meaning, or else as an otherwise unattested noun שֶׁכֶן with suffix, "his residence," which requires linking it to the following verb "seek" (Rashi; AV: "unto his habitation shall ye seek"). The Masoretes opted for the latter interpretation by placing the *athnaḥ* under שָׁם. The meaning is little changed. People are told to seek the place where Yahweh will choose to put his name/make it reside.

you shall seek. The verb דרשׁ often means "seek Yahweh in worship" (4:29; Amos 5:4, 6; Zeph 1:6; Jer 29:13; 50:4; 2 Chr 1:5), which is the meaning here.

6 *And you shall bring there your burnt offerings and your sacrifices.* The Israelites are to bring their sacrifices to the central sanctuary at the time of the annual festivals (16:1-17), though presumably they could sacrifice there at other times. Elkanah and his family went each year to Shiloh to worship and sacrifice (1 Samuel 1).

Deuteronomy 12

your burnt offerings and your sacrifices. עֹלֹתֵיכֶם וְזִבְחֵיכֶם. The two most common types of animal sacrifices (Exod 10:25; 18:12; Jer 6:20; 7:21-22), "burnt offerings" being sacrifices of the whole animal on the altar (LXX: ὁλοκαυτώματα; Vg: *holocausta*). The (whole) burnt offering was the most important offering (Tigay: the gift *par exellence*), explained at the very first in Leviticus (ch. 1), because the entire victim was consumed on the altar as a gift to Yahweh. In the case of other animal sacrifices, referred to sometimes as "peace offerings," זִבְחֵי שְׁלָמִים (Exod 20:24; cf. Deut 27:7), the blood was thrown against the altar and only the fat was consumed by fire. Select portions of meat went to the priests, and the remainder was eaten by the worshippers (v. 27b; cf. Lev 3:1-17; 1 Sam 2:13-17). The Covenant Code stated that these sacrifices could be made on altars in every place where Yahweh caused his name to be remembered (Exod 20:24), but here in Deuteronomy they must be brought to the one altar at the central sanctuary. In the NT, the death of Jesus is explained in sacrificial terms (1 Cor 5:7; Eph 5:2; Heb 9:26), also the right living of every Christian (Rom 12:1-2).

your tithes. מַעְשְׂרֹתֵיכֶם. Israelites were expected to give a tithe (= 10 percent) of all crops (see Note for 14:22) and, according to Lev 27:32, a tithe of one's herds and flocks. These offerings early on supported the local sanctuaries, but when local sanctuaries were abolished the offerings went to support the central sanctuary, which in the 7th cent. was the temple in Jerusalem. The tithe — said in v. 17 to consist of grain, wine, and oil — is to be brought annually to the central sanctuary (14:22-27). Another tithe every third year was to be set aside for the needy, but that could be eaten in the villages (14:28-29; 26:12-15). The LXX omits "and your tithes" or else combines it with "and the contribution of your hand," having simply "and your firstfruits" (καὶ τὰς ἀπαρχὰς ὑμῶν). An omission would likely be due to haplography in the Hebrew *Vorlage* to the LXX (homoeoarcton: ואת ... ואת or homoeoteleuton: יכם ... יכם) or else an inner-Greek haplography (homoeoarcton: καὶ ... καὶ or homoeoteleuton: ὑμῶν ... ὑμῶν). The LXX includes "your tithes" in v. 11.

the contribution of your hand. תְּרוּמַת יֶדְכֶם. The תְּרוּמָה is not a "heave offering," which was a rabbinic name (the offering said to be subjected to a vertical motion). This interpretation was carried over into the AV. The term means what is voluntarily "set apart, dedicated, contributed" from some larger amount (G. A. Smith; Milgrom 1972-73; 1974-75; "Heave Offering" in *IDBSup*, 391-92), a meaning that has Targum support (T[Onq]: "personal contribution"; T[Nf]: "separated offering"). Whereas elsewhere in the OT תְּרוּמָה applies to a range of voluntary contributions (Exod 25:2-3; 29:27-28; 35:5-9; 36:3-7; Num 5:9), in Deuteronomy it refers to the "firstfruits" (Rashi; cf. 26:4: the priest takes the firstfruits from the worshipper's "hand"). The LXX, here and in vv. 11 and 17, has τὰς ἀπαρχὰς ("firstfruits"). The firstfruits offering — in Exod 34:22 just grain, but in Deut 18:4 grain, wine, oil, and wool from the sheep — are to be brought to the central sanctuary at the Feast of Weeks (Pentecost) or, in the case of wine, later, once the summer grapes have ripened (see Note for 26:2). Offerings of the firstfruits go to the priests (Num 18:12-13).

and your votive offerings and your freewill offerings. וְנִדְרֵיכֶם וְנִדְבֹתֵיכֶם. These are extraordinary offerings of various kinds, which earlier could have been made at local worship sites but here are designated for the central sanctuary. They would likely be made at an annual festival or on some other pilgrimage to the central sanctuary. Votive offerings fulfill a vow after a worshipper's prayer has been answered (23:22-24[21-23]; cf. Lev 27:1-29; Numbers 30). A freewill offering is one where no vow was made; the worshipper here is simply giving thanks for Yahweh's goodness (Ps 54:8[6]). Both offerings are essentially voluntary, for which reason they are usually treated together in the OT, but with the difference that votive offerings become obligatory once the prayer accompanying a vow has been answered. A votive offering might be made after the safe return from a journey (Gen 35:6-7; cf. 28:20-22) or at the birth of a son (1 Sam 1:21-28; cf. 1:11). For examples of freewill offerings, see Exod 35:21-29; 36:3-7. Deuteronomy calls for a freewill offering from each Israelite coming to the central sanctuary for the Feast of Weeks (Deut 16:10). Votive and freewill offerings could be either burnt offerings or peace offerings (Lev 22:17-24). The worst example of a votive offering in the OT was the reckless one made by Jephthah (Judg 11:30-40). Amos says unlawful behavior renders freewill and other offerings ineffectual (Amos 4:5). For a misuse of votive offerings, see also Mal 1:14; Matt 15:4-6; Mark 7:10-13; cf. *m. Ned.* 9:1. Vows considered binding and not binding in the Second Temple period are treated in Mishnah tractate *Nedarim*.

and the firstborns in your herd and your flock. Firstborn males of all domestic cattle — oxen, sheep, and goats — must be consecrated to Yahweh (15:19-23; cf. Exod 13:2, 12-13; 22:29[30]; 34:19-20). They are to be offered at the central sanctuary year by year (15:20). Firstborn male asses must be redeemed with a lamb; wild game, e.g., gazelle and deer, are not to be sacrificed. In the NT period, the poor could substitute a pigeon for the specified animal (Luke 2:22-24; John 2:14-16; Mark 11:15).

7 *And you shall eat there before Yahweh your God, and you shall be glad in every undertaking of your hand.* Pilgrimages to the central sanctuary (= "before Yahweh") are to be festive times, occasions to sing and dance and eat the sacrificial meal in celebration of Yahweh's bounteous gifts (Judg 21:19-23; Isa 30:29; Jer 31:4-6, 12-14; Ps 42:5[4]). Once the priest is given his portion, the worshipper and his household eat the meat of the sacrificed animals (except in whole burnt offerings) and the tithes of grain, wine, and oil (14:22-27; 15:20). The Levite is also to be an invited guest at the meal (14:27). The admonition to

"be glad" (שׂמח) at festival time occurs 9 times in the book (12:7, 12, 18; 14:26; 16:11, 14, 15; 26:11; 27:7) and is virtually a command. Indeed, if Israel does not serve Yahweh "with gladness" (בְּשִׂמְחָה), it will be placed under a curse (28:47-48). G. E. Wright says this joyous note is almost entirely lacking in P (occurring only in Lev 23:40; Num 10:10), "burdened as the latter is with the somber sense of the community's sin." The expression "you shall eat (there) before Yahweh" is stock in Deuteronomy (12:7, 18; 14:23, 26; 15:20; Driver 1895, lxxx no. 20). But the words "you shall eat and be glad before me" are inserted into the instructions in the Qumran *Temple Scroll* (11QT 52:15-16; Yadin 1983, 2:235). On this insertion and others from ch. 12 into the *Temple Scroll*, see Tov 1991-92.

in every undertaking of your hand. בְּכֹל מִשְׁלַח יֶדְכֶם is lit. "in every outstretching of your hand." The expression, which is common in Deuteronomy (12:7, 18; 15:10; 23:21[20]; 28:8, 20), denotes both "labor" and the "fruit of one's labor" (see Note for 2:7).

you and your households. Deuteronomy envisions entire households going to the festival and sharing in the celebration (vv. 12, 18; 16:11, 14). According to Exod 23:17, repeated in Deut 16:16, only males must appear at the three yearly feasts. Weinfeld (1972, 291-92) thinks Deuteronomy contains a humanistic attitude toward women (like Luke in the NT), including them more than in the past (29:10, 17[11, 18]; 31:12). Yet Elkanah, when he went to the yearly feast at Shiloh (1 Samuel 1), took with him his two wives Hannah and Peninnah, also Peninnah's sons and daughters.

because Yahweh your God has blessed you. Abundant herds, flocks, and agricultural crops are signs of Yahweh's blessing (16:17). Israel was told that even on the wilderness trek, Yahweh had blessed it "in all the work of your hand" (see Note for 2:7). Statements recalling Yahweh's past blessings, and calling for blessings in the future, occur often in Deuteronomy (12:7; 14:24; 15:6, 14; 16:10; 26:15; 30:16; Weinfeld 1972, 345 no. 2).

8 The expression about "each person doing what is right in his own eyes" is a familiar assessment of national life during the time of the Judges (Judg 17:6; 21:25), but the reference here is to sacrificing and celebrating sacrificial meals at any place one chooses. Perhaps Israel has been sacrificing here and there following its Transjordan settlement ("here today" = Moab). Reference cannot be to worship — at least not sacrificial worship — during the forty years in the wilderness, since Deuteronomy is otherwise silent about sacrifice in the wilderness, apparently not envisioning the practice as taking place until Israel is settled in the land (cf. Amos 5:25; Jer 7:22-23). In its view, only the Decalogue was given at Horeb (Deut 5:22); the remaining laws were not given until now, when Moses presents them in the plains of Moab, in anticipation of settlement in Canaan.

Since the command to sacrifice is not one of the Ten Commandments, Israel will not have received it at Horeb (Weinfeld 1976b, 53-54). The P writer views things differently. He states that instructions for sacrificial offerings were given at Horeb (Exod 20:24; Num 28:6) and records that sacrifices were made in the wilderness and before (Exod 3:18; 10:25; 24:5). So one may have to conclude that Deuteronomy is referring to unregulated sacrifice during the Transjordan settlement, or else that unregulated sacrifice is not being referred to at all, but instead a mindset people have about everything. Sacrificial worship, in any case, is to become centralized when Israel is securely settled in Canaan, i.e., when enemies have been subdued and people can make safe journeys to the place where Yahweh chooses to put his name (v. 9).

everything that is right. Targum[Nf] has "what is good and right," which is the wording in v. 28 and 6:18. MT, however, has simply "what is right" in v. 25; 13:19(18); 21:9.

9 This is probably the reason for unregulated worship at the present time: Israel has not yet taken possession of the land, which is Yahweh's promised "resting place" (v. 10). On Yahweh's gift of the land to Israel as an "inheritance" (נַחֲלָה), see Note for 15:4.

10 It is a recurring theme in Deuteronomy and the Deuteronomic History that Yahweh will give his people "rest" in the land they are about to inherit (3:20; 12:9-10; 25:19; Josh 1:13, 15; cf. Exod 33:14). The idea is present already in Exod 33:14, where Yahweh tells Moses: "My presence will go, and I will give you rest (וַהֲנִחֹתִי לָךְ)." This rest, says von Rad (1966c, 95), is "not peace of mind, but the altogether tangible peace granted to a nation plagued by enemies and weary of wandering." It is a gift from God, and although nearly revoked in the wilderness (Ps 95:11; cf. Heb 3:11; 4:5), it was said later to have been achieved, e.g., under Joshua (Josh 21:44; 22:4; 23:1), but especially under David (2 Sam 7:1; cf. v. 11) and Solomon (1 Kgs 5:18[4]; 8:56; cf. Ps 132:8, 14). Targum[PsJ] says rest will be achieved when the temple is built. The Chronicler adds that rest was achieved also in the reigns of Asa and Jehoshaphat (2 Chr 15:15; 20:30). For the writer of Hebrews, Christian believers have come into the Sabbath rest awaiting them (Heb 4:9).

11-12 These verses repeat the instructions about presenting sacrificial offerings at the central sanctuary and celebrating there with one's household, adding the Levite as an invited guest.

11 *the place that Yahweh your God will choose to make his name reside there.* The full form of the phrase appearing in v. 5, referring to the central sanctuary (see Note for 12:5).

to there you shall bring everything that I am commanding you. Moses, not Yahweh, is commanding the people (see again vv. 14, 21, 28; 13:1[12:32]). Rashi says that while reference in v. 6 is to Shiloh, here it is to Jerusalem. The distinction is contrived. The discourse is simply repeating a key idea (see Rhetoric and

Composition). The LXX adds "today" (σήμερον) at the end of the phrase, suggesting MT loss of היום due to haplography (homoeoteleuton: ם ... ם); cf. 11:8.

your sacrifices. Targums have "sanctified sacrifices" (cf. v. 26).

your tithes and the contribution of your hand. Here the LXX correctly renders both terms: τὰ ἐπιδέκατα ὑμῶν καὶ τὰς ἀπαρχὰς τῶν χειρῶν ὑμῶν ("your tithes and the offerings of your hands"); in v. 6 "and your tithes" was omitted. The LXX also adds καὶ τὰ δόματα ὑμῶν ("and your gifts"), which Wevers (1995, 213) thinks must represent Sam ונדבתיכם ("and your freewill offerings").

and all the best of your votive offerings. The expression of v. 6 is here embellished with מִבְחַר ("best"). Rashi says one's offerings are to be the choicest. Driver thinks that since a vow is something exceptional, sacrifices offered for its fulfillment should be of a superior kind.

12 *And you shall be glad before Yahweh your God.* A stock expression with variation in Deuteronomy (12:12, 18; 14:26; 16:11; 27:7; Weinfeld 1972, 346 no. 5).

your menservants and your maidservants. In v. 7 male and female slaves would doubtless be covered in "your households." These individuals — perhaps only as many as would be prudent to take — are to get respite from their labor and join in the celebration at the central sanctuary. Deuteronomy reflects this same spirit in the fourth commandment on keeping the Sabbath, stating that menservants and maidservants are to be given rest along with everyone else (5:14).

and the Levite who is within your gates, for he has no portion or inheritance with you. The Levites are not mentioned in v. 7, but they are to be among the invited guests at the sacred feast in vv. 18-19 and they continue to be a concern in the book of Deuteronomy from this point on (14:27, 29; 16:11, 14; 18:6-8; 26:11-13). Not only are they the only Israelites without an inheritance (10:9; 18:1-2), leaving them as virtual "sojourners" once the settlement has taken place (Judg 17:7-13; 19:1-30), but by the 7th cent., many were on welfare because the local worship sites had been destroyed by enemy invaders or else closed down due to the reforms of Hezekiah and Josiah, who centralized worship in Jerusalem (2 Kgs 18:4, 22[= Isa 36:7]; 23:8, 13, 15-20). At some point, Levites were deprived of altar duties and the offerings that went with them, even though 18:6-7 accords them full rights to minister at Yahweh's altar.

Teaching Levites were also deprived of a livelihood after the Assyrians destroyed northern Israel and truncated Judah to little more than Jerusalem in 701. Deuteronomy thus declares that Levites residing in one's town are to be invited to make the pilgrimage to the central sanctuary and join in the festivities there. The Levites are also to benefit from the third-year tithe eaten in the towns (14:28-29; 26:12-13). In one of Jeremiah's oracles, Yahweh invites (Levitical) priests from northern Israel to come to Jerusalem and be sated with food and drink (Jer 31:14). Conspicuously absent in the present verse, and throughout the chapter, is any mention of the "sojourner, orphan, and widow," who are to be invited to the Feast of Weeks (16:11), the Feast of Booths (16:14), and to share in the third-year tithe stored in the towns (14:29; 26:12-13).

The tribe of Levi was set apart to a priestly office (10:8-9; 33:10). Some Levites officiated at the altar (18:1-8; 33:10), and others had a teaching function, expounding the law and deciding judicial matters (17:9, 18; 21:5; 24:8; 27:9, 14; 31:9-13, 25-26; 33:10). G. E. Wright (1953, 414; 1954) goes so far as to argue that these two main functions are reflected even in Deuteronomic terminology: When it uses the term "Levitical priests" (17:9, 18; 18:1; 24:8; 27:9), it means altar clergy, whereas when it uses just "Levite(s)" alone (12:12, 18-19; 14:27, and passim), it means — with one or two possible exceptions (18:6; 27:14) — teaching priests with client status, i.e., those who need benevolent treatment along with the sojourner, orphan, and widow. But such a distinction is doubtful, and this view has been challenged (Emerton 1962; B. Levine 1993, 104-5, 449-50). In 18:1, for example, all Levitical priests appear to be altar clergy. Cody (1969, 132) says that according to Deuteronomy all Levites are *potentially* priests even though all are not *functioning* priests. In the Priestly writings, Levites are made subordinate to other Aaronic priests (Lev 1:5-8; Numbers 3-4, 8, 16-18; 2 Chr 34:12-13; cf. Ezek 44:9-14; *EncJud*, 13:1070), and only there is the expression "the priests *and* the Levites" (2 Chr 29:4; 34:30, and passim).

who is within your gates. I.e., a resident in your cities and towns (see Note for 5:14).

13 *Take care for yourself.* הִשָּׁמֶר לְךָ. The premier Deuteronomic warning (see Note for 4:9), here cautioning people not to worship at sites other than the central sanctuary. Driver says the temptation might be particularly strong. The same warning is issued again in vv. 19 and 30.

lest you offer up your burnt offerings in every place that you see. I.e., in every sacred place of the Canaanites (v. 2; cf. Ezek 20:28). "Burnt offerings" here may simply be representative of all types of offerings. Tigay notes that only partial offering lists are given after v. 6.

14 *Yahweh will choose.* The LXX has "The Lord your God will choose" (ἐκλέξηται κύριος ὁ θεός σου), which reflects the wording in 14:24; 16:7, 11.

in one of your tribes. בְּאַחַד שְׁבָטֶיךָ. The wording is different than v. 5, but still points to centralization. The place "(with)in" one of your tribes would later be Jerusalem, in Judah, but earlier could have been a central place in another tribe. Centralization for Hezekiah and Josiah meant a one and only sanctuary in Jerusalem (de Vaux 1965, 336). Welch (1924, 48-49) argued that the Hebrew should be translated "in any of your tribes," noting that "to one of these cities" (אֶל־אַחַת הֶעָרִים־הָאֵלֶּה) in 19:5 refers not to one city, but to any one of three. But with the entire chapter clearly promoting single-sanctuary worship (Welch singles out 12:1-7 as a later addition), this interpretation can hardly be right.

Also, with a broader interpretation of the expression in the present verse, the contrast with v. 13 is significantly weakened.

and there you shall do everything that I am commanding you. I.e., you shall make the sacrifices at the central sanctuary and celebrate with your households and invited guests, as directed in vv. 6-7 and 11-12. The LXX again adds "today" (σήμερον) at the end of the verse (cf. v. 11). The word is commonly present in expressions of this sort (4:40; 6:6; 7:11; 8:1, 11; 10:13, etc.), though not always.

15 The law on sacrificial animals has been spelled out in vv. 5-14, the final verse stating that burnt offerings (of domestic animals) are to be made at the central sanctuary. Now comes an exception, namely, the slaughtering and eating of nonsacrificial animals in one's own town. Hebrew רַק ("only") is a common Deuteronomic qualifier (20 times), introducing here — as in vv. 16 and 23 — an exception to a point of law. In the present verse, and in v. 21, the verb זבח means simply "slaughter," not "(slaughter to) sacrifice" (Driver; Milgrom 1976b, 1-3). Earlier all slaughter was sacrifice, but now the term is divested of its sacral meaning and can refer to the slaughter of any domestic animal for food (1 Sam 28:24; 1 Kgs 19:21). Rashi, however, says the directive refers not to the slaughter of animals for any ordinary meal, but to the slaughter of consecrated animals having a blemish, which, after being redeemed, may be eaten anywhere. This interpretation is found in the Qumran *Temple Scroll* (11QT 52:10-12), where vv. 15-16 (or vv. 22-23) have been inserted into a ruling about eating blemished animals in one's town (Yadin 1983, 1:312-20; 2:234; cf. 15:21-22). But the directive here appears to be broader in scope (see Targums), referring to slaughtering and eating as much meat as one desires, as Yahweh has blessed with abundant herds and flocks.

with all your soul's desire. A stock phrase in Deuteronomy (12:15, 20, 21; 18:6; Driver 1895, lxxx no. 18).

the unclean and the clean may eat it. When eating meat at home, it is not necessary to be ritually clean (vv. 21b-22; 15:22); this is necessary only when eating sacrificial meat (Lev 7:19-21). For other Priestly laws on purity and impurity, see Leviticus 11–15 and Numbers 19. The LXX adds ἐν σοί ("among you") after "the unclean," as it does again in v. 22, apparently to show that "unclean" refers not to the animals but to the people (Wevers 1995, 219).

like the gazelle and like the deer. Examples of game animals that are never sacrificed and may therefore be eaten at any time in one's own town (v. 22; 15:22). On the gazelle (צְבִי) and the deer (אַיָּל), see Note for 14:5.

16 *Only the blood you shall not eat.* The one proviso regarding eating of nonsacrificial meat, repeated emphatically in vv. 23-25 and often in the Pentateuch (15:23; Gen 9:4; Lev 3:17; 7:26-27; 17:10-14; 19:26). In the NT period, eating blood was an issue at the Jerusalem Conference (Acts 15), where a decision was reached that Gentiles should refrain from eating blood (Acts 15:20).

you shall pour it out upon the earth like water. At the central sanctuary blood is thrown against the altar (v. 27), but in ordinary killings in the towns it is to be poured out on the ground.

17-18 Repeating first in negative and then in positive terms the injunctions about presenting offerings at the central sanctuary and celebrating there with family, servants, and invited Levites. See vv. 5-7, 11-12, and one final time in vv. 26-27, without mention of the celebration.

17 *You may not eat.* לֹא־תוּכַל לֶאֱכֹל. The verbal idiom לֹא־תוּכַל ("you may not"), occurring only in Deuteronomy (7:22; 12:17; 16:5; 17:15; 21:16; 22:3, 19, 29; 24:4), is forceful but not the same as an apodictic "you shall not" (Rashi; Daube 1969a, 41-43). Rashi quotes Rabbi Joshua ben Korcha, who says the expression here does not mean literally "You cannot eat," for you could eat it, but you are not allowed to eat it. Daube says the idiom appeals to one's sense of shame, denoting the indignity of doing such and such. It is what Jacob's sons say to Hamor and Shechem after Shechem asks to marry their sister Dinah: "We would not think to do this thing!" (Gen 34:14). In the present case, there is nothing to prevent one from eating sacrificial offerings at home, but Deuteronomy, in keeping with the spirit of its code, considers such an action unthinkable and therefore not to be done.

and your freewill offerings. The LXX translates וְנִדְבֹתֶיךָ with καὶ τὰς ὁμολογίας ὑμῶν ("and your voluntary offerings"); its translation in v. 6 was καὶ τὰ ἑκούσια ὑμῶν ("and your freewill offerings") and in v. 11 probably καὶ τὰ δόματα ὑμῶν ("and your gifts"). The Gk τὰς ὁμολογίας means "agreement," which Wevers (1995, 216) says must refer to what one performs voluntarily. In LXX Jer 51:25[MT 44:25], τὰς ὁμολογίας ἡμῶν translates נְדָרֵינוּ ("our vows").

18 *And you shall be glad before Yahweh your God in every undertaking of your hand.* I.e., in the fruit of your labor (see above v. 7).

and the Levite who is within your gates. The LXX has "and the sojourner who is within your cities" (καὶ ὁ προσήλυτος ὁ ἐν ταῖς πόλεσιν ὑμῶν).

19 An added warning not to forsake the Levite, who is a landless sojourner and in the 7th cent. is without steady income. On the warning "take care for yourself," see v. 13.

all your days. On this Deuteronomic expression, which here means "as long as you live upon the land," see Note for 4:9.

20 *When Yahweh your God enlarges your territory just as he promised you.* The idea is expressed in Deuteronomy that after Israel comes into possession of the land, Yahweh will enlarge its borders (7:22; 19:8; cf. Exod 34:24). What follows is then a repetition, in greater detail, of what vv. 15-16 said about slaughtering and eating nonsacrificial animals in one's town, it now being clear that this will occur only after Israel has expanded its territory. Expansion did take place, but not to the extent envisioned (see Note for 19:8-9). In the 7th cent., the idea of territorial expansion was revived as Josiah moved into the former northern Kingdom following Assyrian withdrawal. Verses 20-21 are inserted into the *Temple Scroll* (11QT 53:1-2), although the text is damaged (Yadin 1983, 2:237). For a reconstruction of 11QT 53:2-8 and a comparison with vv. 20-25, see Tov 1991-92, 171-72.

and you say, "I will eat meat," because your soul desires to eat meat. Meat of domestic animals, i.e., oxen, sheep, and goats, was normally not eaten even by the rich, except at feasts or on other special occasions, e.g., to entertain guests (cf. Gen 18:7; 2 Sam 12:4; 1 Kgs 19:21). This was not the case with game animals, which were commonly eaten.

you may eat with all your soul's desire. Hebrew נֶפֶשׁ ("soul") refers here to the whole person, although it can mean simply "throat" or "appetite" (KBL³; cf. 14:26).

21-25 These verses repeat in greater detail the instructions of vv. 15-16 about slaughtering and eating nonsacrificial meat in one's own town, warning people to be sure not to eat the blood.

21 When Israel's territory expands, it may become impractical to journey to the central sanctuary to eat nonsacrificial meat. Slaughtering and eating will therefore be permitted in the towns. The Qumran *Temple Scroll* (11QT 52:14) specifies a location "near" the temple as being the distance of a three-day journey (Yadin 1983, 1:317; 2:235; Tov 1991-92, 171; cf. Exod 3:18). Here no distance is specified.

just as I commanded you. Moses realizes he is repeating what he said before.

22 *the unclean.* The LXX again adds ἐν σοί, "among you," (see v. 15), which is supported by Sam (בך) and by 11QT 52:11 (בכה).

23 *Only be firm not to eat the blood.* The first of three stern warnings not to eat the blood (cf. v. 16). Here people are told to "be firm" or "be strong" (חֲזַק) not to eat it, since they may want to (Rashi) and sometimes did eat it (1 Sam 14:32-35; Ezek 33:25). The LXX does not translate רַק ("only"), but gets equivalent force by rendering the Hebrew imperative with two words, πρόσεχε ἰσχυρῶς ("Pay great attention"). The reason for the repeated warnings not to eat the blood is doubtless because the slaughter will be taking place in the towns, not at the central sanctuary. At the central sanctuary the priest will oversee the slaughtering and will throw the sacrificial blood against the altar. People therefore will have no chance to eat the blood. But in the towns they will.

because the blood, it is the life. In ancient Hebrew thought the blood was thought to contain the life (נֶפֶשׁ) of both persons and animals (Gen 9:4; Lev 17:11). G. A. Smith (1918, 171) says this doubtless came from ordinary observation: "As the one ebbed, so did the other."

25 *You shall not eat it in order that it may go well for you.* A second reason for not eating the blood. On the Deuteronomic phrase "in order that it may go well for you," see Note for 4:40.

when you do what is right in the eyes of Yahweh. The LXX has "what is good and right" (τὸ καλὸν καὶ τὸ ἀρεστὸν), which occurs in v. 28. But 13:19(18) (MT) has only "what is right." Wevers (1995, 221 n. 45) notes in Kenn 1 46 the reading הטוב והישר, and T^Nf has "right and fitting." The omission of הטוב ו in MT could be due to haplography (homoeoarcton: ה . . . ה). But see v. 8 ("what is right in his own eyes"), also 13:19(18) and 21:9 for the same expression as here. The expression in Deuteronomy is stereotyped (see Note for 6:18). Israel is not "to do evil in the eyes of Yahweh" (see Note for 4:25-26).

26-27 These verses repeat and vary what was stated in vv. 5-6, 11, 17-18a regarding sacrifices to be offered at the central sanctuary. Omitted is a reminder to rejoice at the feast with members of one's household and the invited Levite.

26 *Only your holy things.* On exceptions introduced by רַק ("only"), see above v. 15. "Your holy things" (קָדָשֶׁיךָ) are the consecrated animals (T^Onq: "consecrated offerings") to be offered on Yahweh's altar at the central sanctuary (Rashi). They would be the (whole) burnt offerings and other animal sacrifices. On "holy things" that denote offerings in P, see Exod 28:38; Num 5:9-10; 18:8, 19. The Qumran *Temple Scroll* (11QT 53:9-14) joins vv. 26-27 with 23:22-24(21-23) on vows in its discussion of temple sacrifices (Yadin 1983, 2:239-40).

Yahweh will choose. The LXX expands to the full formula of v. 21: ἐκλέξηται κύριος ὁ θεός σου ἐπικληθῆναι τὸ ὄνομα αὐτοῦ ἐκεῖ ("The Lord your God will choose to have his name called there"). See also v. 11.

27 *the meat and the blood.* A clarification in light of what is said in vv. 21-25 about nonsacrificial slaughter in the towns. There the meat is eaten and the blood poured out on the ground. Here, in the case of (whole) burnt offerings, both the meat and blood are offered on Yahweh's altar. The LXX omits "and the blood," which is probably an inner-Greek haplography (homoeoteleuton: κρέα . . . αἷμα), since the omission is clearly wrong; the ritual requires the presence of both words (D. N. Freedman).

and the blood of your sacrifices shall be poured out upon the altar of Yahweh your God. The LXX is more precise: πρὸς τὴν βάσιν τοῦ θυσιαστηρίου ("toward the pedestal of the altar").

28 *Be careful that you hear all these words that I am commanding you.* Moses continues as Deuteronomy's lawgiver, telling people to be sure to listen to what he has commanded. The LXX and Sam add "so you will do" ("Be careful and hear so you will do"), which is unnecessary, since the verb "do" occurs at the end of the verse. On "all these words," Rashi reminds his reader that a light precept should be as dear to him as a heavy precept.

in order that it may go well for you and for your children after you forever. On this stock expression in Deuteronomy, see v. 25 and Note for 4:40.

Deuteronomy 12

what is good and what is right. A variation of the expression in v. 25 (see above).

29 *When Yahweh your God cuts off from before you the nations whom you have come to possess.* In Deuteronomy, the Israelite conquest is viewed as the direct work of Yahweh (19:1; cf. Josh 23:4); in the Covenant Code it is Yahweh's "angel" (מַלְאָךְ) who goes before the people and will bring them into the land (Exod 23:20-24). We return in vv. 29-31 to complete what was said at the beginning of the chapter about eliminating all traces of Canaanite religion, adding now that Israel must not worship Canaanite gods once their devotees have been destroyed.

30 *take care for yourself, lest you become ensnared after them, after they have been completely destroyed before you, and lest you seek their gods.* The idea appears earlier (Exod 23:24; 34:12), now in Deuteronomy and elsewhere (Deut 7:16, 25; Josh 23:13; Judg 2:3), that idolatry is nothing short of a trap. Yahweh views it similarly in ch. 13, where prophets and dreamers in the service of other gods are permitted a measure of success only for the purpose of testing people to see whether they love Yahweh heart and soul (13:2-4[1-3]).

and lest you seek their gods, saying, "How did these nations serve their gods? I will do thus, even I." The idea prevailed in antiquity that gods were indigenous to a country and may not be neglected with impunity (Driver; cf. 2 Kgs 17:25-28).

even I. גַּם־אָנִי. On this form of the emphatic "I," see Judg 1:3; 2 Sam 18:2b, 22; Job 13:2. Cf. also גַּם־הֵמָּה ("even them") in Jer 25:14 and גַּם־הוּא ("even he") in Jer 27:7.

31 *You shall not do thus for Yahweh your God.* I.e., you shall not do for Yahweh what the Canaanites did for their gods. Canaanite worship must not be reborn as Yahweh worship, which is the sort of thing that happened in ANE religion and classical religion generally. The names of the gods were changed, but practices remained the same. For the syncretism that developed in Samaria after the northern kingdom was destroyed and the Deuteronomic Historian's censure in light of the preaching here in Deuteronomy, see 2 Kgs 17:24-41.

for every abomination to Yahweh that he hates they have done for their gods; indeed even their sons and their daughters they burn in the fire to their gods. Every imaginable practice carried out by the Canaanites for their gods, Yahweh declares to be an "abomination" (תּוֹעֵבָה), the parade example being child sacrifice. The Deuteronomic Code forbids this practice and others, along with practitioners of Canaanite religion, in 18:9-12. Child sacrifice (to Molech) is forbidden also in Lev 18:21; 20:2-5. The prophets — particularly Jeremiah and Ezekiel — were scandalized by this dreadful practice (Jer 7:31; 19:5; 32:35; Ezek 16:20-22; 20:25-26, 31; 23:37-39). It is remembered elsewhere in the OT with horror (Ps

106:37-39). Both Ahaz and Manasseh sacrificed their sons (2 Kgs 16:3; 21:6), a practice that seems also to have flourished in northern Israel (2 Kgs 17:17). For the various "abominations to Yahweh" cited by the Deuteronomic preacher, see Note for 7:25. Child sacrifice is discussed also in Lundbom 1999, 496-97.

13:1[12:32] *Every word that I am commanding you.* In this seeming conclusion, Moses is looking ahead, as he does in 12:1, to the major code of law about to be presented in chs. 13-25, reminding people that they must be careful to obey it. Throughout this introductory discourse Moses is the one commanding the people (vv. 11, 14, 21, 28). The LXX again adds "today" (σήμερον), which appears also in Sam (cf. vv. 11 and 14).

you shall be careful to do it. A recurring Deuteronomic warning (see Note for 5:1).

you shall not add to it and you shall not subtract from it. The same admonition as in 4:2, where it applies to all the commandments given by Moses. Here it may have a dual function, applying to the preceding prohibition against worshipping other gods and to the Deuteronomic code, which follows (see Rhetoric and Composition for 12:1-13:1). Von Rad thinks the statement is simply a rhetorical means of appealing for careful obedience, whereas in 4:2 the concern is to protect the literary deposit of the book. For extrabiblical examples of this warning appearing in treaties and legal codes, see Note for 4:2. Weinfeld (200) thinks the injunction here relates only to the imitation of pagan worship. A warning not to subtract from the divine word occurs in Jer 26:2, which Weinfeld (1972, 360 no. 14) thinks betrays influence from Deuteronomy. Yahweh was concerned when Jeremiah was sent to deliver his riveting Temple Oracles, that the good prophet might be tempted to scale down the judgment (cf. Eli's words to the young Samuel in 1 Sam 3:17). A Neo-Babylonian text says regarding some spokesman of the god Era: "It was revealed to him during the night, and when he spoke it in the morning, he did not leave out a single line, nor did he add one to it" (Lambert 1962, 122-23; Weinfeld 1972, 262). In an Assyrian letter addressed to Assurbanipal, the scribe receiving the letter is told not to conceal anything from the king, which he presumably could do (Oppenheim 1965, 256; Fishbane 1972, 350). And in the ancient Egyptian text "The Instruction of the Vizier Ptah-Hotep" (ca. 2450), this advice is given:

> If thou art a man of intimacy, whom one great man sends to another, be thoroughly reliable when he sends thee. Carry out the errand for him as he has spoken. Do not be reserved about what is said to thee, and beware of (any) act of forgetfulness. Grasp hold of truth, and do not exceed it. (*ANET*³, 413; Meier 1988, 23)

From the "Satire on the Trades" (ca. 1840-1790), this advice is given to scribes:

Deuteronomy 12

If an official sends thee on an errand, say it (just) as he said it; do not take away or add to it. (*ANET*³, 434)

On the danger of deception in sending messengers, see Meier 1988, 168-79. Weinfeld thinks the warning not to add to or subtract from the spoken or written word emanates from wisdom circles. Proverbs 30:5-6 cautions against adding to God's true and tested words (cf. Eccl 3:14; Sir 18:6).

Message and Audience

Moses now comes to the point where he is ready to present to the people the major code of statutes and ordinances that they must take care to do in the land soon to be possessed. They must *do* the law all the days they are living on the land. Moses begins by commanding the destruction of Canaanite worship sites, all of them, scattered as they are on mountains and hills and under shade-bearing trees. People must break down altars, shatter stone pillars, burn Asherah poles, and cut down images of the Canaanite gods, thereby destroying the names of these gods from the sites at which they have been worshipped. None of this must carry over into the worship of Yahweh.

To a single place, which Yahweh will choose out of Israel's tribes to put his name, Israel shall go to worship Yahweh. To this place people shall bring their offerings and sacrifices, tithes and gifts of firstfruits, votive offerings, freewill offerings, and firstborn males from their flocks and herds. Here the worshippers shall eat before Yahweh, rejoicing with their households in the bounty that is a blessing from Yahweh. People must not repeat what has transpired in the past, everyone doing what is right in his own eyes. Moses says the people have not yet come into their rest, where they will be secure from all their enemies. This will be realized when they cross the Jordan and live in Canaan. Moses then repeats what he has just said about going to the central sanctuary to sacrifice and celebrate before Yahweh. Here he adds that the Levite living in one's town must be invited to come along; he is landless, and having no offering to bring, he will not be able to share in the feast unless he is an invited guest.

Moses goes on to say that people can slaughter nonsacrificially and eat meat in their towns to the extent that Yahweh has blessed them. Here both the ritually clean and ritually unclean may eat, just like when eating gazelle and deer. Only the people must not eat the blood; it shall be poured out on the ground like water. But not in the towns are tithes and offerings to be eaten, but at the central sanctuary, and there with family, servants, and invited guests. Moses reminds people again not to forsake the Levite.

The law regarding nonsacrificial slaughter is repeated, now said to apply when Israel's borders are enlarged. Then one may eat as much meat as one desires, and because the sanctuary may be too far distant, slaughtering can take place in the towns. As is the case with wild game, persons ritually clean and unclean may eat. Once again a stern warning — this time thrice-repeated — that blood must not be eaten, since it embodies the life of the animal; it is sacred. People are given another reason not to eat the blood: that it go well for them and their children when they do what is right in the eyes of Yahweh. Moses then repeats that the holy things, i.e., the sacrifices to Yahweh, are to be brought to the central sanctuary and offered there. People must be careful to do all that Moses is commanding them, for the same reason as in not eating the blood: that it will go well for them and their children when they do what is good and right in the eyes of Yahweh.

The discourse closes with a return to the beginning, completing what was said there about abolishing Canaanite religion. Moses says that when Yahweh cuts off the nations who have inhabited the land and Israel gains possession of it, Israel must take care not to be entrapped by emulating the people who have been destroyed. They must not inquire after their gods, asking how these people served them and deciding to do likewise. Moses repeats what he said earlier: "You shall not do thus for Yahweh your God." Every abomination these people have done for their gods Yahweh hates, the worst thing of all being the burning of their sons and daughters. In conclusion, Moses says that every word he has spoken the people must be careful to do; they must neither add to nor subtract from it.

Excursus 1: Centralized Worship in the Reforms of Hezekiah and Josiah

According to the Bible, major reforms aimed at purifying Yahwistic worship of residual Canaanite religious practices and imported Assyrian religion were carried out in Judah by Hezekiah (715-687) and Josiah (640-609). Both kings receive special commendation in the biblical record, where they are said to have done right in the eyes of Yahweh as David their father had done (2 Kgs 18:3; 22:2; 2 Chr 29:2; 34:2). Josiah gets yet another accolade from the Deuteronomic Historian, who says that no king before him or after him so turned to Yahweh according to all the law of Moses (2 Kgs 23:25).

Hezekiah's reform is reported only briefly in 2 Kgs 18:4, 22[= Isa 36:7], but in 2 Chronicles 29-31 it receives extended coverage. Josiah's reform gets balanced treatment in both 2 Kings 22–23 and 2 Chronicles 34–35, although the accounts differ in some important details (Lundbom 1976, 294-95). By destroying open-air "high places" (בָּמוֹת) and cult objects in Judah and in the northern territories, both kings are seen to have made a concerted effort to centralize worship in Jerusalem. Jerusalem, to be sure, was a central worship site prior to Hezekiah's time: David took the city and brought the ark there (2 Samuel 6), and Solomon built in Jerusalem the temple his father was unable to build (1 Kings 5–6; cf. 2 Samuel 7). Now, however, Jerusalem was made the one and only legitimate sanctuary for Yahweh worship; all other worship sites, in particular the high places, were closed down. The Deuteronomic Historian explains that high places continued in use because a temple had not yet been built (1 Kgs 3:2), after which he proceeds to fault a succession of Judahite kings, beginning with Solomon, for sacrificing at high places, not removing them, or building new high places (1 Kgs 3:3; 14:23; 15:14; 22:43; 2 Kgs 12:3; 14:4; 15:4, 35; 16:4). All this leads up to a predictably good appraisal of Hezekiah, who removed the high places after the reign of the wicked Ahaz (2 Kings 16). Pressure to abolish these sites probably came from various quarters, with Hezekiah no doubt being influenced by the preaching of Micah and Isaiah (Bright 1981, 278; Moriarty 1965, 402; cf. Jer 26:17-19), maybe Amos and Hosea earlier. The book of Deuteronomy, largely but not exclusively, because of its call for centralized worship in ch. 12 has been taken by scholars for over two centuries to be the program for one or both of these reforms, otherwise the surviving legacy of one or both of them.

Hezekiah's reform has evoked much discussion, partly because of problems interpreting the biblical accounts in 2 Kings 18–20 and 2 Chronicles 29–31, and partly because of difficulties correlating the two accounts with the Annals of Sennacherib, which give a firm date of 701 for the campaign said by the Assyrian king to have destroyed forty-six Judahite cities and countless small villages and left Hezekiah in Jerusalem "like a bird in a cage" ($ANET^3$, 287-88). There has also been controversy over archaeological data from Beersheba, Arad, Tell Ḥalif, and Lachish. In Stratum II (late 8th cent.) at Beersheba, excavators found an abolished sanctuary and a dismantled four-horned altar reused in a storehouse wall. An entire sanctuary turned up at Arad, where excavators found in Stratum VIII (late 8th cent.) a sacrificial altar buried under a meter of fill. These finds, and others, have been cited in support of Hezekiah's reform in outlying areas (Y. Aharoni 1974, 6; 1975b, 154-56; Herzog 1981; 1997, 294; 2006, 96-97; Herzog et al. 1977, 57-58; 1984, 19-22; Rainey 1994; Borowski 1995; I. Finkelstein and N. Silberman 2005-6), although Yadin (1976) thought the cultic site at Beersheba was destroyed in the reform of Josiah. The excavators did not agree with Yadin. At Tell Ḥalif, near Beersheba, a shrine room in a private house was discovered, filled with what appeared to be an array of cult objects. Here the excavators concluded that the structure was probably destroyed by Sennacherib in 701. Also, from Sennacherib's palace at Nineveh a relief turned up showing Assyrian soldiers carrying off large incense stands as booty from Lachish, after its destruction in 701 (see Borowski 1995, 153). These latter finds seem to suggest that worship sites, at certain places, continued in use until Sennacherib destroyed them. But one cannot be sure.

Na'aman (1995; 2002) and Fried (2002) do not think any of these archaeological data support a reform by Hezekiah. Fried, in her survey of excavated "high places," says the cult sites in Beersheba, Arad, Lachish (Level III), and Tell Ḥalif were all destroyed in the 701 invasion. But both she and Na'aman outrun the evidence in declaring that the biblical accounts cannot be historical. Herzog (2006, 97) says Na'aman misconstrued the stratigraphical data. Na'aman in a later article did admit that a lack of positive archaeological evidence does not indicate that a cult reform by Hezekiah never occurred (2002, 597). What may certainly be said is that after Sennacherib's invasion in 701, worship in Judah, for all practical purposes, could only be centralized in Jerusalem because no outlying sanctuaries were left.

Actually, there has been widespread support for the biblical accounts reporting a reform by Hezekiah, and many scholars have argued as a result that the composition of Deuteronomy has to be seen in the context of this reform (Rowley 1950a, 164; 1961-62, 427; de Vaux 1965, 339; Nicholson 1967, 101-2; Rosenbaum 1979, 42 n. 83), not the later reform by Josiah. Nicholson says that because Hezekiah's reform was short-lived, Deuteronomy cannot be the reform's program but must be its legacy. He thinks the book was composed during the subsequent reign of Manasseh, which was Rowley's view earlier. This assumes an incentive on the part of Judah's altar and teaching clergy to write up a new code of Mosaic law and a new program for reforming Yahwistic worship at a time when the mood of the nation had turned in another direction entirely, an unlikely scenario.

The Deuteronomic Historian and Chronicler are agreed that Hezekiah launched his reform at the beginning of his reign. The Deuteronomic Historian mentions Hezekiah's cleansing acts at the outset of his account (2 Kgs 18:4), with the Chronicler stating that the good king began in his first year to make repairs in the temple (2 Chr 29:3) and concluded his faithful acts before Sennacherib invaded and encamped against Judah's fortified cities (2 Chr 32:1). There is a problem, though, in deciding when the reign of Hezekiah began. The Deuteronomic Historian begins it when Hoshea is still king in Samaria, four years before the city's fall to Shalmaneser V in 722 (2 Kgs 18:1, 9). This gives us a date of 726 (the higher chronology). But most scholars date the beginning a decade later, ca. 715 (Mowinckel 1932, 215, 277; Albright 1945a, 22; 1953, 9; Hallo 1960, 55), which takes the twenty-nine-year reign of 2 Kgs 18:2 and the fourteenth year for Sennacherib's 701 invasion in 2 Kgs 18:13 as reliable reckonings, in addition to providing a necessary overlap with the Ethiopian Tirhakah mentioned in 2 Kgs 19:9. We learn from extrabiblical sources that Tirhakah (Taharqo) could not have led an Egyptian army against the Assyrians before 690 (Albright 1953, 8-9).

The resulting reconstruction supposes two campaigns by Sennacherib against Judah: one in 701 and another ca. 688 (the lower chronology). In the first, all Judah was laid waste except Jerusalem; Sennacherib forced the capitulation of Hezekiah, on whom heavy tribute was laid (2 Kgs 18:13-16; Sennacherib's Annals, in *ANET*³, 288). In the second, Hezekiah — with support from Isaiah — holds out, and the city is miraculously saved (2 Kgs 18:17–19:37; 2 Chr 32:1-23). This two-campaign theory, first advanced by George Rawlinson in 1858 and accepted early on by Albright (1953, 8), is the solution preferred by Bright (1981, 298-309). Hallo (1960, 59) says the theory is plausible, but he has his doubts. More recent support for a two-campaign theory comes from Lisbeth Fried and David Noel Freedman (Milgrom 2001, 2265-66), who argue that a Jubilee Year in 688/687 would correlate with Isaiah's prophecy to Hezekiah in 2 Kgs 19:29(= Isa 37:30) about a two-year fallow period (which would occur in a Jubilee Year; cf. Lev 25:20-21). Thus there would be a second campaign by Sennacherib against Judah in 689/688, after which the Assyrian king returned to Nineveh and was assassinated in 682/681. For a defense of the one-campaign theory building upon the higher chronology of 2 Kgs 18:1, 9, see Rowley 1961-62. The Chronicler in his internally consistent account avoids the difficulty by omitting the problematic chronology of the Deuteronomic Historian.

It remains to try to fit the reform of Hezekiah into known history of the period. Sargon II had been king of Assyria since 721 and during the first two years of his reign had rebellions to deal with in various parts of the empire, particularly in the western provinces (Tadmor 1958, 36-38). In 716 he established a military outpost on the border of Egypt, and in 712, three years after Hezekiah became king, his general led a successful campaign against Ashdod, which brought forth a judgment oracle from Isaiah against Judah's worthless allies, Egypt and Ethiopia, leading the prophet also to walk naked and barefoot for three years to drive the point home (Isaiah 20). An Assyrian text mentions this campaign (Tadmor 1958, 79-80). At this time Gath was also taken (*ANET*³, 286). Another fragmented Assyrian text, tentatively dated by Tadmor to 712, relates an Assyrian attack on ʿAzaqā (Tell Zakariya) in the Shephelah (Tadmor 1958, 81-83), which is biblical Azekah, 11 mi north of Lachish and 18 mi southwest of Jerusalem (Jer 34:7). This city, too, appears to have surrendered. If this fragment is correctly dated (Tadmor says it could reflect Sargon's campaign of 720), the Assyrian army is seen to be dangerously close to Jerusalem, rendering unlikely any bold act on the part of Hezekiah in 712 to declare religious and political independence from Assyria.

Bright thinks Hezekiah took modest steps at reform as soon as he became king, and Hallo (1960, 55) dates Hezekiah's grand Passover (2 Chronicles 30) to 715 or 714. Assyrian records tell of no further campaigns by Sargon into Palestine from 712 to 706, which Tadmor (1958, 84) says may be due to friendly rela-

Deuteronomy 12

tions between Sargon and the Nubian kings of Egypt during this period. In any case, we have a span of at least six or seven years until Sargon's death in 705 and maybe longer, for Hezekiah to have carried out the reform described in Kings and Chronicles. After the death of Sargon, Hezekiah would be free to openly renounce the Assyrian gods (Bright 1981, 282) and would still have a few more years to consolidate his gains before Sennacherib regained control of the empire and invaded Judah in 701.

Another major reform became necessary in Judah because Manasseh, Hezekiah's son and successor, completely undid his father's program by reviving pagan practices old and new, including the rebuilding of high places. Manasseh's long reign of fifty-five years (2 Kgs 21:1)* is viewed with unconcealed disdain by the Deuteronomic Historian (2 Kgs 21:2-18), who characterizes it as a time of deliberate violation of the commands set forth in the Deuteronomic Code. Manasseh's evils are repeated by the Chronicler, but he reports that Assyrian commanders brought the proud king to Babylon, where he humbled himself "before Yahweh," after which he was restored to Jerusalem (2 Chr 33:1-20). A reform, in any event, was much needed in Judah, and Amon, after carrying on his father's policies for two years, was assassinated and the people put Josiah on the throne in 640. This young king then went on to reform and centralize Yahwistic worship in Jerusalem, as Hezekiah had done.

The two biblical accounts of this reform are markedly different. The Deuteronomic Historian has the entire reform taking place in Josiah's eighteenth year, 622, representing a response of the king to the finding of a law book in the temple, said to be a law book of Moses (2 Kings 22–23). The Chronicler, on the other hand, reports a more gradual process. He states that Josiah in his eighth year (632) began to seek Yahweh and then in his twelfth year (628) began a purge of high places in Judah and Jerusalem, continuing with the same in the northern territories (2 Chr 34:1-7). Then in 2 Chr 34:8, 14, it says that *after* the purge of high places (vv. 3-7 compress events reported in 2 Kgs 23:4-20) a law book was found in Josiah's eighteenth year (622). Earlier scholars reconstructed events according to the account of the Deuteronomic Historian, assuming that the Chronicler was late and inaccurate. But that has changed, with the Chronicler's account now being taken with more seriousness, even given preference over the account of the Deuteronomic Historian in spreading the reform out over a period of years and putting the purge before the finding of the law book. The book of Deuteronomy continues to be a factor in carrying out the reform, but its influence may come in both 628 and 622, not simply in 622. In my view, a

---

*Bright (1981, 311) follows Albright in giving Manasseh a forty-five-year reign (687/6-642). Since Manasseh came to the throne as a child of twelve years, the biblical record may assume a coregency with his father, Hezekiah, due to the latter's serious illness in 701 (D. N. Freedman).

book comprising perhaps Deuteronomy 1–28 influenced Josiah's program in 628 and the temple law book influencing events of 622 was the Song of Moses in Deuteronomy 32 (Lundbom 1976; 1999, 105-6).

The reform of Josiah itself has evoked considerably less controversy than Hezekiah's reform, one reason being that scholars since de Wette have used it as the linchpin in arguments setting forth critical views of the Pentateuch (Rosenbaum 1979, 23-24). The reform of Josiah has secured a date for Deuteronomy in the 7th cent., and the centralization program occurring in this reform is seen to be a reflex of the centralization views in Deuteronomy 12.

There is also less difficulty in setting this reform in the context of world affairs, since the death of Assurbanipal in 627 (the Haran Inscription) marks the beginning of Assyrian decline. Babylon was in open revolt, and in 626 Nabopolassar defeated the Assyrian army outside the city of Babylon and declared himself king of Babylon (Bright 1981, 315). Assyria from this point was on the defensive and in fewer than twenty years would be no more. With Assyria having lost control over its western empire, Judah's subservience to Assyria was now ended, giving Josiah a free hand in asserting nationalistic aims and reforming Yahwistic worship. According to the Bible, he did both. A reform by this king is then perfectly credible from 628 to 622, which are the years during which it is said to have taken place. The reform lasted until Josiah died in 609, when it was undone by his son and successor.

Fried (2002, 457-60), in her survey of archaeological sites in the northern territories, Judah, and the Negeb, finds no evidence of a reform by Josiah prior to Judah's destruction by the Babylonians in 586. But once again, after analyzing the archaeological data, she uses the same *argumentum e silentio* employed earlier in denying a reform carried out by Hezekiah.

B. YAHWEH TESTING FOR FAITHFULNESS (13:2-19[1-18])

1. Beware of Prophets and Dreamers (13:2-6[1-5])

13²When a prophet or a dreamer of dreams rises up in your midst, and gives to you a sign or a wonder, ³and the sign or the wonder comes to pass, about which he spoke to you, saying, "Let us go after other gods that you have not known, and let us serve them," ⁴you shall not listen to the words of that prophet, or to that dreamer of dreams, because Yahweh your God is testing you, to know whether you do love Yahweh your God with all your heart and with all your soul. ⁵After Yahweh your God you shall walk, and him you shall fear, and his commandments you shall keep, and his voice you shall obey, and him you shall serve, and to him you shall cling. ⁶But that prophet or that dreamer of dreams shall be put to death, because he has spoken rebellion against Yahweh your God, the one who brought you out from the land of Egypt and the one who ransomed you from the house of slaves, to drive you from the way in which Yahweh your God commanded you to walk. So you shall utterly remove the evil from your midst.

2. Beware of Family and Friends (13:7-12[6-11])

13 *⁷When your brother, son of your mother, or your son or your daughter, or the wife of your bosom, or your friend who is as your own soul, entices you in secret, saying, "Let us go and let us serve other gods that you have not known," you or your fathers, ⁸from among the gods of the peoples who surround you, those near to you or those far from you, from one end of the earth to the other end of the earth, ⁹you shall not yield to him, and you shall not listen to him, and your eye shall not have pity upon him, and you shall not spare, and you shall not cover up for him; ¹⁰but you shall surely kill him; your hand shall be the first against him to put him to death, and afterwards the hand of all the people. ¹¹You shall stone him with stones and he shall die, because he sought to drive you away from Yahweh your God, the one who brought you out from the land of Egypt, from the house of slaves. ¹²And all Israel shall hear and fear, and they shall not again do an evil thing such as this in your midst.*

3. Beware of Worthless Men (13:13-19[12-18])

13 *¹³When you hear in one of your cities that Yahweh your God is giving to you to dwell there, saying, ¹⁴Worthless men have gone out from your midst and have driven away the inhabitants of their cities, saying, "Let us go and let us serve other gods that you have not known," ¹⁵then you shall inquire, and you shall search, and you shall ask thoroughly. And behold, it is true, the thing that has been done is established, this abomination in your midst, ¹⁶you shall surely strike down the inhabitants of that city to the mouth of the sword, devoting it to destruction and all who are in it, and its beasts, to the mouth of the sword. ¹⁷And all its spoil you shall gather into the midst of its open square, and you shall burn the city and all its spoil in fire, a whole-offering to Yahweh your God, and it shall be a tell forever; it shall not be built again. ¹⁸And let not anything from the ban stick in your hand, in order that Yahweh may turn from his burning anger and grant you mercy, yes, he will show you mercy and multiply you just as he swore to your fathers, ¹⁹when you obey the voice of Yahweh your God to keep all his commandments that I am commanding you today, to do what is right in the eyes of Yahweh your God.*

Deuteronomy 13

Rhetoric and Composition

The Deuteronomic Code appropriately begins with a sermon against "going after other gods," which is what the first commandment enjoins. The sermon has a threefold rhythm like the Elijah-Elisha sagas of 2 Kings 1–2 (Lundbom 1973), also like the muster speech of Deut 20:5-8. Discourses of this nature well illustrate the view of Klostermann and von Rad that Deuteronomy is "preached law" (von Rad 1953, 22-23); yet, the present preaching is still law, since disobedience is punishable by death.

The sermon warns against three potential enticers:

(1) a prophet or dreamers of dreams   vv. 2-6(1-5)
(2) a family member or close friend   vv. 7-12(6-11)
(3) certain worthless men   vv. 13-18(12-17)

The third segment differs from the first two in that (1) an entire city here falls victim to idolatry and (2) punishment is not simply a stoning of the enticers, but all-out holy war against the guilty city. The legislation in all three cases focuses on attempts to reestablish polytheism once it has been rooted out, and so it follows naturally the conclusion of the prior chapter (12:29-31). Mention of the "prophet" at the very beginning of this sermon makes for a tie-in with the "prophet" discussed in 18:20-22. On the structure of this subunit in 13-18, see Rhetoric and Composition for 18:15-22.

Segment I of the sermon is bound together by a keyword inclusio:

When a prophet . . . rises up *in your midst*	בְּקִרְבְּךָ	v. 2(1)
So you shall utterly remove the evil *from your midst*	מִקִּרְבֶּךָ	v. 6(5)

Segments I and II are linked by the same words, here showing inversion:

So you shall utterly remove the evil *from your midst*	מִקִּרְבֶּךָ	v. 6(5)
they shall not again do an evil thing as this *in your midst*	בְּקִרְבֶּךָ	v. 12b(11b)

Segments II and III are linked together by a keyword repetition:

And all Israel *shall hear* and fear	יִשְׁמְעוּ	v. 12a(11a)
When *you hear* in one of your cities	תִשְׁמַע	v. 13(12)

Cf. the law in 17:2-7, which is tied together by an inclusio made from "in your midst" and "from your midst" (see Rhetoric and Composition there). The final verse of the present sermon (v. 19[18]) may be a later add-on, intending to form

Deuteronomy 13

an inclusio with the similar injunction in 13:1[12:32] (see Rhetoric and Composition for 12:1–13:1[12:32]).

The verses are delimited at the top end by a *petuḥah* in M^L and 11QT, also sections in Sam and 4Q38^c (Puech 2001-2, 122), before v. 2. At the bottom end delimitation is by a *setumah* in M^L and a section in Sam after v. 19, which is also the chapter division. There also appears to be a section in 11QT after v. 19, although Yadin (1983, 2:249) does not note it. Segment I of the sermon is delimited at the bottom end by a *petuḥah* in 11QT and a section in Sam after v. 6; there is no marking here in M^L. A break after v. 6 occurs also in 1QDeut 4.9 (Barthélemy and Milik 1955, 55). Segment II of the sermon is delimited at the bottom end by a *setumah* in M^L and a section in Sam after v. 12. The entire passage is reproduced in the Qumran *Temple Scroll* (11QT 54:8–55:14), although the last word of v. 7[6] and vv. 8-12[7-11] are now missing. Yadin (1983, 2:246) says they were originally present. Concluding 11QT 55 is the related law on idolaters in 17:2-5.

Portions of 13:2-19 are contained in 1QDeut^a, 4QDeut^c, and 4QpaleoDeut^r.

Notes

13:2(1) *When a prophet or a dreamer of dreams rises up in your midst.* In this first of three casuistic formulations dealing with enticers to idolatry, the prophet and dreamer of dreams are singled out as representative figures of the religious establishment, also because in Israel they will likely be taken as genuine if their signs are fulfilled (1 Sam 28:6). But Yahwistic worship forbids diviners, soothsayers, and other practitioners of the secret arts (18:10-11).

When. The Qumran *Temple Scroll*, here and in vv. 7, 13, and 19 (11QT 54:8, 19; 55:2, 13), has אם instead of כי, which would have to be translated "if."

prophet. נָבִיא. The Targums have "false prophet," which discredits anyone going by the title "prophet" from the outset. The prophetic movement in Israel began with Samuel (Albright 1961; Huffmon 1976, 176-77; cf. Acts 3:24), although Samuel also went by the older title of "seer" (1 Sam 9:9, 11, 18-19; Orlinsky 1965). Samuel was also last of the Judges (1 Sam 7:15-17). Moses' designation as a "prophet" — in Deuteronomy he is prophet *par excellence* — is a later coinage (Deut 34:10). According to Albright (1957b, 303), the term נָבִיא means "one who is called (by God)," corresponding to Akk *nibîtu*, meaning "one called (by the gods)." But more recently it has been argued that the Akk verb *nabû* also has an active sense and that *nibîtu* can mean "one who invokes the gods" (Fleming 1993). Greek προφήτης means "one who speaks for another" (cf. Exod 7:1). The prophet, in any event, is someone possessing the power of agency, enabling him to speak in the name of God or the gods (Lundbom

Deuteronomy 13

2010a, 19). The prophet under scrutiny here could be any prophet, a Yahweh prophet, or a prophet in the service of some other god. Yahweh prophets are tested for genuineness in 18:20-22. The present text and the one in 18:15-22 are the only legal passages in the OT dealing with prophets and prophecy. They may reflect the time when false prophecy became a serious problem in northern Israel, i.e., during Ahab's reign in the mid-9th cent. (Lundbom 1996, 310-12; 1999, 261). Background for the testing of Yahweh prophets is 1 Kings 22; background for the testing of prophets generally is 1 Kings 17–19, where Baal and Asherah prophets dominate the scene prior to the celebrated performance of Elijah the Tishbite on Mount Carmel (1 Kgs 18:19-46).

a dreamer of dreams. חֹלֵם חֲלוֹם. "Dreamer of dreams" could be simply another name for a prophet (cf. Jer 23:25-28) or else a title in its own right. Dreams are generally viewed positively in the OT, as they are elsewhere in the ANE, being recognized as a bona fide medium of divine revelation. Only with Jeremiah are they brought into disrepute (Jer 23:25-32). On dreams and dreamers in the OT and the ancient world, see Oppenheim 1956 and Lundbom 2004a, 204-6.

and gives to you a sign or a wonder. This "sign" (אוֹת) or "wonder" (מוֹפֵת) is not a miracle on the spot (Exod 4:2-9; 7:9-10) but a prediction that requires fulfillment (v. 3). It is also a public act (Exod 4:30). On signs and wonders, see Note for 4:34. In the NT, false messiahs and false prophets performing great signs and wonders are promised for the end times (Matt 24:24; Mark 13:22).

3(2) *and the sign or the wonder comes to pass, about which he spoke to you.* The prophet has given a predictive word, or the dreamer has related a dream about some future happening — with perhaps an interpretation — and it has come to pass. The success may be taken as proof of divine power. The plagues upon Egypt were promised signs and wonders that came to pass (Exod 7:3; 10:1-2; Deut 11:3); Moses and Aaron performed them, and initially so did the magicians of Egypt (Exod 7:8-11, 20-22; 8:1-3[5-7]). Samuel gave Saul signs of his anointment as king over Israel, all of which came to pass (1 Sam 10:1-9). See also 1 Kgs 13:3-5; 2 Kgs 19:29-37. If the prophet or dreamer here is not in the service of Yahweh, his signs and wonders are nevertheless not to be credited to another god. Behind all such phenomena stands Yahweh; fulfillment cannot be attributed, even on a limited or temporary basis, to any other god (von Rad).

"Let us go after other gods that you have not known, and let us serve them." On whosoever's behalf the prophet or dreamer is acting, we now learn that he wants people to follow him in worshipping other gods. The Targums take "serve" (עבד) here to mean "worship" (5:9; 8:19; 11:16; 17:3). The expression "to go after other gods that you have not known" is stock in Deuteronomy (see Note for 11:27-28). Deuteronomy drives home the point that Israel is to serve Yahweh and only Yahweh (see Notes for 6:13 and 6:14).

Deuteronomy 13

The legislation here contains striking similarities to provisions in treaties and loyalty oaths in the ANE, where Weinfeld (1976a, 381) identifies three component parts: (1) loyalty, (2) uncovering rebels, and (3) curses. Israelite religion, then, has taken over fundamental ideas from the realm of ANE law and politics. For example, in Sefire Treaty III and the Assyrian Treaty of Esarhaddon, the vassal must swear loyalty to the suzerain, and anyone inciting rebellion is to be reported, delivered up to the suzerain or the authorities, and punished (Fitzmyer 1958; 1967, 94-120; Frankena 1965, 128-29, 142-43; Weinfeld 1972, 91-100; 1976a). The Esarhaddon Treaty has an entire section denouncing inciters to rebellion, and among those mentioned as possible inciters are religious functionaries (*VTE* 116-17), variously identified as prophets, ecstatics, and dreamers of dreams (Wiseman 1958, 38; Weinfeld 1972, 98; *ANET*³, 535). Hittite documents from the 14th-13th cents. contain oaths for officers swearing loyalty to the king and uncovering rebels and turning them over to the king (Weinfeld 1976a, 381). One Hittite text has this clause: "If a noble, a prince, or a relative... brings up seditious words... (saying): 'Come let us join another (king)'..." (Weinfeld 1972, 94).

4(3) Some say "You can't argue with success," but here that is precisely what you must do. Yahweh is testing people for their love toward him, a key theme in Deuteronomy (6:5; 7:9; 10:12; 11:1, 13, 22; cf. Moran 1963b), and to determine this he gives individuals not in his service temporary success. But it is a success that will not last. We recall that from the magicians of Egypt Yahweh wrung a confession of faith once their power to perform signs and wonders was gone. They said: "This is the finger of God!" (Exod 8:15[19]). In the NT, false prophets are promised who will show great signs and wonders, the purpose of which will be to lead people astray (Matt 24:24). Also, the beast of Revelation will work great signs in order to deceive people into idolatrous worship (Rev 13:13-14).

Yahweh your God is testing you. 11QT 54:12 has "I (אנוכי) am testing you."

whether you do love Yahweh your God. The particle יֵשׁ asserts existence with emphasis; Driver translates הֲיִשְׁכֶם אֹהֲבִים "whether you *do* love" (cf. BDB, 441). On Deuteronomy's teaching about Israel's love for Yahweh, see Note for 6:5.

with all your heart and with all your soul. The expression is stereotyped in Deuteronomy (see Note for 4:29).

5(4) *After Yahweh your God you shall walk.* The Sam reading תלכון ("you shall walk") is supported by 1QDeut 4.9 (Barthélemy and Milik 1955, 55), 4QDeutᶜ (Ulrich, Cross et al. 1995, 22), and 11QT 54:14 (Yadin 1983, 2:244). On the paragogic *nun*, see GKC §47m. "Walking in Yahweh's way" has ethical implications in the OT (see Note for 5:33).

and him you shall fear. Another key Deuteronomic theme (see Note for 4:10).

Deuteronomy 13

and his commandments you shall keep, and his voice you shall obey. Obeying Yahweh's voice means keeping the commandments (v. 19[18]; 9:23; 15:5; 26:14, 17; 27:10; 28:1). Israel did not obey Yahweh's voice in the wilderness (9:23; cf. Jer 22:21), but if it obeys now, blessing and life will be the result (28:1-2; 30:20); if it disobeys, curses will fall and the nation will perish (8:20; 28:15, 45, 62; cf. Jer 9:11-12[12-13]). Then, after Israel is scattered among the nations, it will return to obeying and keeping the commandments (4:30; 30:1-2, 8; cf. Jer 3:13), although this will require a commitment on Israel's part if such a happy circumstance is to occur (30:9-10).

and him you shall serve. וְאֹתוֹ תַעֲבֹדוּ. Israel must serve Yahweh and only Yahweh (see Note for 6:13). The LXX omits, which Dion (1991, 152) notes can be attributed to haplography (homoeoarcton: ו . . . ו or homoeoteleuton: ו . . . ו). 1QDeut 4.9 supports MT (Barthélemy and Milik 1955, 55).

and to him you shall cling. On this expression, see Note for 4:3-4. The demands for love, obedience, and fidelity all have parallels in the ANE treaties (Frankena 1965, 140-41; Weinfeld 1972, 96-97; 1976a, 381-87).

6(5) *But that prophet or that dreamer of dreams shall be put to death, because he has spoken rebellion against Yahweh your God.* The emphasis of v. 5 continues with: "But that prophet . . . ," which inverts normal syntax. Punishment for leading people into idolatry, the worst of all sins in Israelite religion, is death (17:5; Exod 22:19[20]; cf. 2 Pet 2:1). The prophets of Baal were put to death after the famous contest between them and Elijah on Mount Carmel (1 Kgs 18:40). Good (1967, 970-71) says the religion of Israel was unique in its intolerance of other religious practices, prescribing the death penalty for anyone worshipping a god other than Yahweh. The penalty is so severe, says Weinfeld, because religious treason is being treated here as if it were political treason. Loyalty oaths state that if one incites rebellion against a king, the crown prince, or someone else in the royal line, the penalty will be death (Weinfeld 1976a, 389). At his trial in 609, Jeremiah simply testified: "Yahweh sent me" (Jer 26:12, 15), which drew indirect support from the present legislation and was accepted by those hearing the case.

he has spoken rebellion. דִּבֶּר־סָרָה. Hebrew סָרָה is from the verb סוּר ("to turn aside"; H-stem: "cause to turn aside"; cf. 7:4). It means "rebellion, defection" (T^OnqPsJ; AV; Driver; cf. 9:12, 16; 11:16; 1 Sam 12:20). The Treaty of Esarhaddon (*VTE* 502) uses the same expression: *dabab surrāte* (Wiseman 1958, 67-68; Weinfeld 1972, 99). So does the Qumran *Damascus Document* (CD XII 2-3; Broshi 1992, 32-33), which contains an even closer parallel. It reads:

Any man over whom the spirits	כל איש אשר ימשלו בו
of Belial rule, *and who speaks rebellion,*	רוחות בליעל ודבר סרה
like the judgment of the necromancer	כמשפט האוב
or wizard he shall be judged	והידעוני ישפט

Deuteronomy 13

The verb does not mean "uttering falsehood" (*pace* Tigay), although turning people from Yahweh is certainly false prophecy. Hananiah is accused by Jeremiah of having "spoken rebellion" concerning Yahweh (Jer 28:16) and is given a sentence of death. Another prophet among the 6th-cent. Babylonian exiles, Shemaiah, is similarly accused of having "spoken rebellion" concerning Yahweh (Jer 29:32). But both are Yahweh prophets preaching a false message, which is not exactly the situation here.

the one who brought you out from the land of Egypt and the one who ransomed you from the house of slaves. Accepting a rebel prophet translates into ingratitude for Yahweh's deliverance of Israel in the exodus (cf. 8:14). "House of slaves," here and in v. 11, is a Deuteronomic expression (see Note for 5:6).

to drive you from the way in which Yahweh your God commanded you to walk. Moreover, this rebel prophet is diverting you from the path Yahweh has told you to walk (v. 5). Turning aside from Yahweh's way means going the way of idolatry (9:12, 16; 11:28; 31:29). The verb נדח, here and in vv. 11 and 14, is strong, meaning "thrust, drive (away)"; cf. 4:19; 30:17. On the stereotyped Deuteronomic phrase, "to walk in (all) Yahweh's/his way(s)," see Note for 5:33.

So you shall utterly remove the evil from your midst. The Targums have "evildoer(s)" instead of "evil," which has equivalent meaning. This phrase about "utterly removing" (בער II KBL³; Ug *b'r* "expel") evil or innocent blood from Israel occurs 11 times in Deuteronomy (13:6[5]; 17:7, 12; 19:13, 19; 21:9, 21; 22:21, 22, 24; 24:7; Driver 1895, lxxx no. 24; Weinfeld 1972, 355 no. 2), at or near concluding statements about punishment for evildoers and, except for 19:19, in reference to capital punishment. Daube (1969a, 48; 1971a, 9-10) notes that it appears in all passages beginning with the Deuteronomic idiom "when there is found" (17:2; 21:1; 22:22; 24:7). In the view of Deuteronomy, evil and (the guilt of) innocent blood must be completely eradicated from the people of Israel and from the land. Paul appears to follow the same principle when he tells the Corinthian church: "Drive out the wicked person from among you" (1 Cor 5:13).

7(6) This second of three laws on the first commandment pertains to family members and intimate friends, for whom it will be easy to make excuses should they lapse into idolatry and entice others to follow them (v. 8). The verb יסת means "to stir up, entice" (1 Sam 26:19). See also 29:17[18]. The Esarhaddon Treaty (*VTE* 115-16) states: "If you listen to or conceal any word . . . from the mouth of your brothers, your sons, your daughters . . ." (Wiseman 1958, 37-38; Weinfeld 1972, 98; *ANET*³, 535). See also lines 76-77 of the same treaty.

son of your mother. i.e., your own brother (Gen 27:29; Ps 50:20). The LXX and Sam read "son of your father or son of your mother," which is preserved in 4QDeut^c; 11QT 54:19; and T^PsJ. This would include a half-brother (cf. Lev 18:9). But S, T^OnqNf, and Vg support the shorter MT reading. Modern English Versions divide, and so do scholars, some supporting the longer reading (G. A.

Deuteronomy 13

Smith; Moran), some the shorter reading (Tigay; Levinson 2001b). The MT has likely suffered a loss due to haplography (homoeoarcton: בֶן א ... בֶן א), since this is legal material and the omitted words are logically necessary.

or your son or your daughter. 4QDeut^c omits "or your daughter" (אוֹ־בִתֶּךָ), which again is probably due to haplography (homoeoarcton: או ... או or homoeoteleuton: ךָ ... ךָ).

or the wife of your bosom. For this expression denoting intimacy, doubtless intentional, see also 28:54; Mic 7:5. Targum^{Onq}, to avoid the literalism, has "wife of your covenant."

or your friend who is as your own soul. Another expression of intimacy; recall David and Jonathan (1 Sam 18:1, 3; 20:17).

in secret. Unlike the enticement of the prophet or dreamer of dreams, which is carried out in public, this enticement is done in secret. Thus a cover-up is possible and a greater likelihood that no action will be taken against the guilty person (Tigay). The Esarhaddon Treaties contain rebellion clauses (*VTE* 73-82, 108-22, 147-61, 494-512), which say in effect: "May the gods look on if we rebel or revolt . . . if we hear (men) speaking secretly . . . unseemly acts . . . and conceal it and do not report it" (Weinfeld 1976a, 380).

"Let us go and let us serve other gods that you have not known," you or your fathers. The expression "go and serve other gods" is stock in Deuteronomy (13:7, 14[6, 13]; 29:25[26]). Here the quotation is expanded to "Let us go and let us serve other gods that you have not known," with the narrator also adding "you or your fathers" (8:3; 28:36, 64; Jer 9:15[16]; 16:13, etc.). The latter expansion accents the familial character of the injunction.

8(7) *from among the gods of the peoples who surround you, those near to you or those far from you.* Influence of other gods can come from far or near (cf. 28:64; 1 Kgs 11:5, 7). By the 8th and 7th cents., especially under Judahite kings Ahaz and Manasseh, religious influence was as much from Assyria as from the Canaanites.

from one end of the earth to the other end of the earth. The expression occurs also in 28:64 (see Note for 4:32).

9(8) *and your eye shall not have pity upon him, and you shall not spare.* If the person is family or an intimate friend, one may want to overlook the indiscretion and seek leniency. But Yahweh shows neither pity nor leniency in later judgment on Judah (Jer 13:14; 21:7). Pity is ruled out elsewhere when death or maiming is the prescribed punishment (7:16; 19:13, 21; 25:12).

and you shall not cover up for him. וְלֹא־תְכַסֶּה עָלָיו. The verb כסה ("to cover") is usually taken here in the sense of "conceal, shield," which yields the interpretation "You shall not conceal him (in a hiding place)" (T^{NfPsJ}; AV; RSV; NEB; NJV). Bernard Levinson (1996, 603-5) says this interpretation builds on the LXX reading, οὐδ' οὐ μὴ σκεπάσῃς αὐτόν ("and you shall not shelter him").

According to the LXX, the inciter is not to be concealed through silence (cf. Pss 32:5; 40:11[10]), for the next verse goes on to say: "You shall make a report concerning him." Weinfeld (1972, 94-96), in light of the emphasis placed in treaties about not concealing inciters to rebellion, but reporting them, supports the LXX reading. But Levinson says this is not the intended meaning of the Hebrew; כסה + the preposition על means "to cover over, forgive" (Jer 18:23; Neh 3:37[4:5]). In his view, the string of negative commands concludes with a climactic "You shall not condone him," with the next verse stating that the inciter to rebellion must be executed (MT). This is the meaning preserved in T^{Onq}, which has "or show mercy to him."

10(9) *but you shall surely kill him.* כִּי הָרֹג תַּהַרְגֶנּוּ. The LXX reading, ἀναγγέλλων ἀναγγελεῖς περὶ αὐτοῦ ("you shall make a report concerning him"), carries forward its interpretive conclusion of v. 9, presumably recognizing that if a capital sentence is to be carried out, it must be done according to due process (Wevers 1995, 232). Wevers says this makes the practice consistent with 17:2-7. It also makes for consistency with v. 15 of the present passage. Since this rebellion is hatched in secret, an investigation will probably be necessary. Weinfeld supports the LXX reading because, in the treaties, anyone hearing of a conspiracy is required to report it. Dion (1991, 154, 156) also goes with the LXX, but for the less compelling reason that the verb הרג does not otherwise occur in Deuteronomy. If the LXX is translating an H-stem of נגד ("to announce, report"), as *BHS* suggests, it may be misreading הרג ("to kill").

your hand shall be the first against him to put him to death, and afterwards the hand of all the people. The family member or friend who is witness to the rebellious talk must take the lead in carrying out the death sentence. In 17:7, the first stones are thrown by witnesses to the crime.

11(10) *You shall stone him with stones and he shall die.* Stoning is the most common form of capital punishment in the Bible, normally occurring outside the city gate (17:5; 22:24; Lev 24:14; Num 15:35-36; 1 Kgs 21:13). Cf. in the NT, John 8:5; Acts 7:58-60.

because he sought to drive you away from Yahweh your God. Again, the reason for such a severe punishment (see v. 6). Hebrew מֵעַל is an idiom meaning "from attachment to" (Driver; cf. Hos 9:1; Jer 2:5; 32:40; Ezek 6:9; 8:6).

the one who brought you out from the land of Egypt, from the house of slaves. Yahweh's deliverance of Israel from Egyptian slavery is the basis on which the first commandment rests (see Note for 5:6).

12(11) Capital punishment, here and in 17:13; 21:21, is believed to have a deterrent function (Stulman 1990, 620). Daube (1969a, 40), commenting on this line, says the force of public example is particularly appreciated in a shame culture. The present statement follows capital sentences 4 times in Deuteronomy (13:12[11]; 17:13; 19:20; 21:21; Weinfeld 1972, 356 no. 3). Jesus' parting words

Deuteronomy 13

to the woman caught in adultery, even though no stoning took place, were nevertheless "Go and do not sin again" (John 8:11).

and all Israel shall hear and fear. The warning "to hear and fear" is stereotyped in Deuteronomy (13:12[11]; 17:13; 19:20; 21:21; Driver 1895, lxxxiii no. 67).

and they shall not again do. וְלֹא־יוֹסִפוּ לַעֲשׂוֹת. The LXX, Sam, Vg, and many Gk MSS strengthen the verb with עוֹד or a presumed עוֹד; 4QDeut^c supports MT.

13(12) *When you hear in one of your cities.* Yahwistic religion is first envisioned as under threat by a public religious figure. It may also be endangered by family or friend in a secretly-hatched plot. Now, rumor has it, an entire city has been enticed to abandon Yahwistic religion.

14(13) *This is the rumor.* Worthless men within an Israelite city — not strangers from elsewhere (Rashi) — have managed to drive away inhabitants by calling them to the worship of other gods. Defection has already occurred.

Worthless men. בְּנֵי־בְלִיַּעַל is lit. "sons of Belial" (AV). The ancient Versions do not translate a proper name, in spite of such renderings in the Pseudepigrapha (*Jub.* 1:20; 15:33; *Mart. Isa.* 1:8-9; 2:4; 3:11; *Sib. Or.* 2:167; *Liv. Pro.* 4:6, 20; 17:2; *T. Reu.* 4:8, 11; 6:3; *T. Sim.* 5:3; *T. Levi* 3:3; 19:1, etc.; sometimes "Beliar"), the Dead Sea Scrolls (1QS 1:18, 23-24; CD 4:13, 15; 5:18; 8:2; 12:2; 19:14; 1QM 1:1, 5; 2:13; 4:2; 11:8; 13:4; etc.; 1QH 40:9), and 2 Cor 6:15, where Belial has become the Prince of Evil (= Satan). The term occurs more than 30 times in the Qumran scrolls (*OTP,* 1:349 n.). Hebrew בְּלִיַּעַל is said to be a compound of בְּלִי ("without") and יַעַל ("worth, use"); when referring to persons, it has the meaning "worthless, good-for-nothing" (Rashi; Judg 19:22; 1 Sam 1:16; 10:27; 30:22; 1 Kgs 21:10, 13). The LXX in the present verse calls these men "lawless ones" (παράνομοι); the Targums speak of individuals with bad character. It has also been suggested that the Hebrew expression may originally have meant "inhabitants of the netherworld," i.e., Sheol (Tigay; cf. 2 Sam 22:5-6), but this interpretation is rejected by B. Otzen (*b^eliyya'al,* in *TDOT,* 2:132). On "Belial," see H. Ringgren 1995, 74-76; T. H. Gaster, in *IDB,* 1:377; and T. J. Lewis, in *ABD,* 1:654-56.

and have driven away the inhabitants of their cities. For the verb נדח ("to drive away"), see v. 6. 11QT 55:3 has "have driven away all (כול) the inhabitants . . . ," making it clear that the entire city has gone the way of idolatry (11QT 55:6 has "all the inhabitants" again in v. 16). The LXX, too, reads: πάντας τοὺς κατοικοῦντας τὴν πόλιν αὐτῶν ("all the inhabitants of their city"). These readings presuppose wickedness on the scale of proverbial Sodom (and Gomorrah), wherein worthless men resided (Genesis 18-19). But probably not everyone in the Israelite city will have defected, unless the investigation (v. 15) and subsequent holy war (v. 16) are to be carried out by inhabitants of another city.

Deuteronomy 13

15(14) In this case, the charge of defection has to be investigated thoroughly to see if it is true. Cf. an almost identical statement in 17:4, and note the need to investigate for false witnesses in 19:15-18. Hebrew אֱמֶת נָכוֹן הַדָּבָר is best translated as two statements in apposition (cf. AV): "it is true, the thing is established." The *accumulatio* consists of words or expressions in two clusters of three:

then you shall inquire	וְדָרַשְׁתָּ
and you shall search	וְחָקַרְתָּ
and you shall ask thoroughly	וְשָׁאַלְתָּ הֵיטֵב

And behold, it is true	וְהִנֵּה אֱמֶת
the thing that has been done is established	נָכוֹן הַדָּבָר נֶעֶשְׂתָה
this abomination in your midst	הַתּוֹעֵבָה הַזֹּאת בְּקִרְבֶּךָ

abomination. On this strong Deuteronomic term, often used of idolatry, see Note for 7:25.

16(15) No stoning of the inciters here; the entire city to be "devoted to destruction" (חרם H-stem). Even the beasts are to be killed (cf. 1 Sam 15:3). Daube (1947, 182) cites this as a parade example in Deuteronomy of communal responsibility for a crime, a time-honored principle in antiquity (cf. Gen 18:23). The crime requires an atoning ritual when a murdered man is found in an open field (21:1-9). Sefire Treaty III (12-13) prescribes similar punishment if an entire city is won over by conspirators. It says: "If it is a city, you must strike it with a sword" (Fitzmyer 1967, 98-99; Weinfeld 1972, 99). So whereas Israel carried out holy war against the former occupants of Canaan (7:2; 20:17), it practiced the same against its own people. Capital punishment was also meted out to Achan and his family for Achan's theft of booty from Jericho, which should have gone into the sacred treasury; even his animals were destroyed (Josh 7:24-25; cf. 6:24). Later on, the entire remnant of Judah became a holy war victim when, at Yahweh's command, both people and beasts were destroyed (Jer 7:20; 21:6; 32:43; 33:10, 12). For a discussion of holy war and the holy war ban, see Note for 7:2.

the inhabitants of that city. 11QT 55:6 adds כול ("all"), as in v. 14; the LXX, too, reads πάντας τοὺς κατοικοῦντας ("all the inhabitants"), as it does in v. 14. With or without "all," the point is that the entire city must be destroyed.

to the mouth of the sword. I.e., "to the hilt" (see Note for 20:13-14).

all who are in it. I.e., all its inhabitants.

and its beasts, to the mouth of the sword. The LXX omits, which appears to be a loss due to haplography (homoeoarcton: ואת . . . ואת). 4QDeut^c has ואת בהמתה ("and its beasts").

Deuteronomy 13

17(16) *And all its spoil you shall gather into the midst of its open square, and you shall burn the city and all its spoil in fire, a whole-offering to Yahweh your God.* The city must be burned, and with it the spoil that might otherwise be taken by those punishing the offenders. When Canaanite cities were destroyed, booty was usually kept (Josh 8:2, 27; 11:14). Jericho was an exception (Josh 6:18), which is what led to Achan's sin.

open square. Hebrew רְחֹב is a broad open space in ancient eastern cities, something like the modern marketplace, where public gatherings took place and justice was administered (Isa 59:14; Ezra 10:9; 2 Chr 32:6). It was usually just inside the city gate (Job 29:7; Neh 8:1, 3). Burning the spoil in the open square would make a public spectacle of it.

a whole-offering to Yahweh your God. The entire city shall become a whole (burnt) offering (כָּלִיל) to Yahweh (cf. 33:10). In destruction, the city offers to Yahweh worship it earlier denied. See 20:10-18; Judg 20:40.

and it shall be a tell forever; it shall not be built again. A tell is a mound of abandoned city ruins (Jer 30:18); sometimes the ruins were not rebuilt (Josh 8:28; 11:13; Jer 49:2).

18(17) *And let not anything from the ban stick in your hand, in order that Yahweh may turn from his burning anger and grant you mercy, yes, he will show you mercy.* The noun חֵרֶם ("ban, devoted thing") occurs one other time in 7:26. On the rules of the ban in holy war, see Note for 7:2. Total destruction of the rebellious city will assuage Yahweh's anger, which in Deuteronomy is said to burn hot when Israel abandons the covenant and goes after other gods (see Note for 6:15). After judgment Yahweh turns from his anger (Josh 7:26), and mercy is granted. The narrator emphasizes in the repetition that mercy will indeed be shown once the punishment has been carried out.

and multiply you just as he swore to your fathers. One would think that destroying an entire city is a sure way to diminish a people, but here the reverse is affirmed: it will lead to multiplication. On the Deuteronomic theme of Israel multiplying, see 1:10-11 and Note for 6:3.

19(18) *when you obey the voice of Yahweh your God to keep all his commandments that I am commanding you today.* See above v. 5. This verse appears to be an add-on (see Rhetoric and Composition), as Segment III of the sermon might end perfectly well with v. 18.

to do what is right in the eyes of Yahweh your God. A stock Deuteronomic expression (see Note for 6:18). The Sam and LXX add "and what is good," which finds support in a reconstructed 4QpaleoDeut[r] reading (Skehan, Ulrich, and Sanderson 1992, 140). Cf. 12:25, where MT has "what is right," but LXX and other textual witnesses have "what is good and right." T[Nf] has "what is right and fitting," and 11QT 55:14 similarly הישר והטוב, which Yadin (1983, 2:249) thinks is an addition.

Message and Audience

The Deuteronomic Code now begins with Moses delivering a rhythmic and riveting sermon against anyone found in violation of the first commandment and inciting others to the same. The Horeb covenant requires absolute loyalty toward Yahweh, who delivered Israel from Egyptian slavery. Yahweh therefore will not tolerate anyone who says: "Let us go after other gods and serve them." When a prophet or dreamer of dreams rises up and gives people a sign or wonder that comes to pass and then wants to draw them away to serve gods about which Israel has no knowledge, the people must not pay heed. True, the divine wonders have enjoyed public success. Never mind. Yahweh is allowing them their day in the sun to test Israel, to see whether Israel loves Yahweh heart and soul. The covenant to which Israel signed on requires that it walk after Yahweh, fear him, keep his commandments, obey his voice, serve him, and cling to him. This prophet or dreamer of dreams must be put to death for speaking rebellion against Yahweh, who ransomed Israel from slavery. Only by carrying out the ultimate sentence can this insidious evil be removed from Israel.

Moses then envisions a family member or close friend who secretly entices people to do the same. Other gods both near and far are at issue. Though pressure here will be significantly greater, one must nevertheless not yield, not have pity, and not cover up for the offender. The person must likewise be put to death. Whoever is witness to the seditious words shall throw the first stone; then all the people will join in. The reason for a capital sentence is the same as before. Such a person has sought to drive the covenant people away from Yahweh, Israel's redeemer. This punishment is designed to put the fear of God in others, so apostasy of this sort will not happen again.

Finally, Moses envisions a more grave situation, where rumor has it that worthless men in one of Israel's cities have enticed people to go after other gods. Indeed, they have already done so. Here an investigation has to be made, either by people within the city or people from some other city. If the rumor is true, the entire city must be put to the sword. It is holy war all over again: People and animals alike are to be destroyed. Not even spoil is to be taken. It is to be collected in the open square and burned as a whole offering to Yahweh. The city is to become a tell for all time, not to be rebuilt. Shades of Sodom and Gomorrah! People are reminded once again not to have sticky fingers for any of the loot. A later audience will perhaps remember Achan and his violation of the holy war ban at Jericho. Only by a complete destruction of the apostate city will Yahweh's anger be assuaged and divine mercy return to multiply Israel as the fathers had been promised. This will happen when Israel obeys Yahweh's voice, keeps his commandments, and does what is right in the eyes of Yahweh.

This sermon presupposes the struggle between Yahwism and Baalism in

Deuteronomy 14

the mid-9th cent., during the reign of Ahab, when the battle was joined. Weinfeld (1972, 100) thinks the law preserves ancient material, but says its form cannot be earlier than the 7th cent., i.e., the time of Josiah. A Josianic date is also given to the material by Dion (1991, 204-5). A late 8th- and early 7th-cent. audience will hear in this sermon a justification for the judgment carried out by Elijah against the prophets of Baal (1 Kgs 18:40).

C. Israel a Holy People to Yahweh (14:1-21)

1. Holiness in Lamenting (14:1-2)

*14*¹*Children are you to Yahweh your God. You shall not cut yourselves, and you shall not make a bald spot between your eyes for the dead.* ²*For you are a holy people to Yahweh your God, and Yahweh chose you to be for him a people, a treasure-piece out of all the peoples who are on the face of the earth.*

2. Clean and Unclean Animals (14:3-8)

³*You shall not eat any abomination.* ⁴*These are the beasts that you may eat: ox, lamb of the sheep and kid of the goats,* ⁵*deer and gazelle and roebuck and wild goat and oryx and antelope and mountain-sheep.* ⁶*So every beast that has a hoof and cleaves the cleft into two hooves, and chews the cud, are among the beasts you may eat.* ⁷*But these you shall not eat from those who chew the cud and from those who have the cloven hoof: the camel, and the hare, and the rock badger, because they chew cud but do not have the hoof; they are unclean for you.* ⁸*And the swine, because it has the hoof but has no cud, is unclean for you; from their flesh you shall not eat, and their carcass you shall not touch.*

3. Clean and Unclean Waterfowl (14:9-10)

*14*⁹*These you may eat from everything that is in the waters: everything that has fin and scale you may eat,* ¹⁰*and everything that does not have fin and scale you shall not eat; it is unclean for you.*

4. Clean and Unclean Winged Creatures (14:11-20)

*14*¹¹*Every clean bird you may eat.* ¹²*And these are what you shall not eat from: the eagle, and the vulture, and the osprey;* ¹³*and the kite, and the falcon, and the buz-*

zard according to its kind; ¹⁴*and every raven according to its kind;* ¹⁵*and the ostrich, and the owl, and the seagull, and the hawk according to its kind;* ¹⁶*the small owl, and the great owl, and the ibis;*¹⁷*and the pelican, and the carrion-vulture, and the cormorant;* ¹⁸*and the stork, and the heron according to its kind; and the hoopoe, and the bat;* ¹⁹*and every winged swarming thing is unclean for you; they shall not be eaten.* ²⁰*Every clean winged creature you may eat.*

5. Holiness in Eating and Food Preparation (14:21)

²¹*You shall not eat any carcass; to the sojourner who is within your gates you may give it so he can eat it, or sell it to a foreigner. For you are a holy people to Yahweh your God. You shall not boil a kid in its mother's milk.*

Rhetoric and Composition

The present verses constitute a self-standing collection of laws on what makes Israel a people holy to Yahweh. In the center are foods declared to be clean and unclean according to the following categories:

(1) animals	vv. 3-8
(2) waterfowl	vv. 9-10
(3) birds and winged insects	vv. 11-20

Before and after these dietary laws, making a frame for the whole, are four miscellaneous prohibitions joined to statements affirming Israel's status as a holy people. In the opening section (vv. 1-2), two miscellaneous laws are positioned in between statements on Israel belonging to Yahweh. The second is expanded into a broader statement on election. In the closing section (v. 21), a single statement on Israel belonging to Yahweh lies in between two more miscellaneous laws. Making an inclusio for the whole is the phrase "For you are a holy people to Yahweh your God":

> 14:1-2 *Children are you to Yahweh your God*
>   You shall not cut yourselves
>   and you shall not make a bald spot between your eyes
>   for the dead
>   *For you are a holy people to Yahweh your God, and Yahweh*
>   *chose you to be for him a people, a treasure-piece out of all*
>   *the peoples who are on the face of the earth.*

| 14:21 | You shall not eat any carcass; to the sojourner who is within your gates you may give it so he can eat it, or sell it to a foreigner |

For you are a holy people to Yahweh your God
    You shall not boil a kid in its mother's milk.

The prohibition against boiling a kid in its mother's milk is usually treated separately (Daube 1947, 84 takes it as a later add-on), but we see from the framing structure that it belongs to v. 21.

The list of birds and insects is bound together by another inclusio:

| *Every clean bird you may eat* | כָּל־צִפּוֹר טְהֹרָה תֹּאכֵלוּ | v. 11 |
| *Every clean winged creature you may eat* | כָּל־עוֹף טָהוֹר תֹּאכֵלוּ | v. 20 |

If these statements are saying the same thing, which is debated, then עוֹף ("winged creature") in v. 20 means "bird" (see Notes).

The unit is delimited at the top end by a *setumah* in M^L and a section in Sam before v. 1, which is also the chapter division. Delimitation at the lower end is by a *petuḥah* in M^L and sections in Sam and 4QpaleoDeut^r after v. 21. A *setumah* in M^L and a section in 4QpaleoDeut^r after v. 2 set off the opening section of miscellaneous laws. A *setumah* in M^L and a section in Sam after v. 8 divide the sections on animals and waterfowl, and another *setumah* in M^L after v. 10 divides the section on waterfowl from the section on birds and winged insects. There are no sections in M^L and Sam after v. 20, which might be expected to set off the miscellaneous laws from the section on birds and winged insects.

This list of clean and unclean animals, waterfowl, birds, and winged insects is paralleled by a more expanded prohibition in Lev 11:1-23. The two lists are harmonized in the Qumran *Temple Scroll* (11QT 48:1-6), although where the text is damaged are only partial readings. In the *Temple Scroll* the ban on lacerations follows the dietary laws (11QT 48:7-10), reversing the sequence in Deuteronomy, where it precedes the list (Yadin 1983, 2:205-9). Most scholars take the longer discussion in Leviticus 11 to be an expansion of Deut 14:3-21, but Milgrom (1991, 698-704) is of the opinion that Deuteronomy abridges Leviticus.

Portions of 14:1-21 are contained in 1QDeut^a, 4QpaleoDeut^r, and 4Q366.

Notes

14:1 *Children are you to Yahweh your God.* Occasionally the OT refers to Israel as the son(s)/children" of Yahweh (Exod 4:22-23; Hos 11:1; Isa 1:2, 4; Jer 31:20), but here the masculine plural "you" (אַתֶּם) extends the metaphor to include individual Israelites (Driver). Verbal shifts from the second feminine singular (addressing the nation) to the second masculine plural (addressing individual Israelites) achieve the same purpose throughout the book. Here, "children" in the Hebrew sentence gets the accent.

You shall not cut yourselves, and you shall not make a bald spot between your eyes for the dead. No disfigurement is to be permitted in mourning the dead (cf. Lev 19:27-28; 21:5 [for priests only]; Jer 16:6), which would imitate Canaanite rites and those of other neighboring peoples (Isa 15:2; Jer 47:5; 48:37). As it turned out, Israelites did this anyway (Hos 7:14; Jer 41:5). In the north, self-inflicted slashing was done by prophets seeking to force the hand of Baal (1 Kgs 18:28). These laws, like those in ch. 13, appear to reflect northern Israel in the 9th to 7th cents., when rites imitating indigenous religious practices had become widespread. Shaving oneself bald as a sign of mourning was widely practiced in antiquity (Gaster 1969, 590-602). Herodotus (iii 8) says the Arabs cut their hair round the head and shave it from their temples as a religious rite (cf. Jer 9:25[26]; 25:23). "Between your eyes" is usually taken to mean "on the forehead" (T^{Nf}, RSV; NJB; cf. Deut 6:8), but reference is doubtless to forelocks (NEB; NRSV) or hair above the forehead (NJV; NAB; NIV). This injunction against disfigurement may reflect the same concern as the injunctions in Lev 21:16-23, which disqualify a priest having a physical blemish from officiating at Yahweh's altar and blemished animals from being sacrificed to Yahweh (G. E. Wright; Milgrom 1990b, 180-81; Tigay). In the NT, Paul warns the Corinthians not to defile the body, which he calls "a temple of the Holy Spirit within you" (1 Cor 6:19).

2 Israel's view of itself as a holy people is rooted in the idea that Yahweh "set it apart" (= "made it holy") from all peoples on the face of the earth (v. 21; Exod 19:4-6; see Note for 7:6). According to Lev 20:26, Israel is made holy because Yahweh himself is holy. Israel's holiness translates into rejecting certain customs and not eating certain foods (I. Klein 1979, 303; Milgrom 1990b, 182; cf. Lev 20:24b-26). The present verse is given reinterpretation for the church in Titus 2:14.

and Yahweh chose you. וּבְךָ בָּחַר יְהוָה. The verb בחר ("to choose") is important and occurs often in Deuteronomy (see Note for 12:5). On Israel's election, which is rooted in Yahweh's promise to Abraham, see also 4:37; 7:6-8; 10:15.

a treasure-piece. סְגֻלָּה. A term of endearment, used here and elsewhere with reference to Israel's election (see Note for 7:6).

3 *You shall not eat any abomination.* "Abomination" (תּוֹעֵבָה) is a strong word (see Note for 7:25), referring here to the forbidden foods through v. 21. Animals, waterfowl, birds, and winged insects are not abominations in themselves; eating them is the abomination (Rashi).

4 *These are the beasts that you may eat.* Clean beasts are not named in Lev 11:2-3.

ox, lamb of the sheep and kid of the goats. The "ox" (שׁוֹר) was a working animal, whereas sheep and goats were raised largely for their milk, the sheep also for wool. Ordinary people ate meat only on special occasions, e.g., the arrival of a guest, a festal occasion, or when spoil was taken in war (Gen 18:7; 1 Sam 14:32; 16:20; 25:18; 28:24; 2 Sam 12:4). Kings, needless to say, ate meat every day (1 Kgs 5:2-3[4:22-23]), and by the 8th cent. the rich too, according to Amos, were feasting regularly on lambs and calves (Amos 6:4).

5 *deer.* Hebrew אַיָּל appears to be a general term for "deer," though it may also apply to a particular species (Tristram 1898, 99; Bodenheimer 1962, 251). Ugaritic *'yl* means "deer" (*UT* 356 no. 148). LXX ἔλαφον is a deer, male or female. This animal was common in antiquity. Bodenheimer (1960, 49) says there were three main types in Palestine and Mesopotamia: the red deer, the fallow deer, and the roe deer, all of which can still be found in localities of the Middle East.

gazelle. צְבִי. The identification of this graceful, swift, and beautiful animal is not in doubt (Rashi; Bodenheimer 1962, 247; Ug *ẓby, UT* 407 no. 1045), although צְבִי may also be a general term covering several species of gazelle and antelope. The LXX translates with δορκάς, an antelope or gazelle, so called because of its large bright eyes. G. A. Smith identifies the species as the *gazella dorcas,* a horned animal about the size of a roebuck, but more graceful, numerous in Syria and Arabia. Tristram (1884, 6; 1898, 127-31) says the צְבִי is a roe deer (= gazelle), comparable to the *ghazal* of the Arabs. He says small herds can be found in every part of Palestine. Graceful gazelles are common (with lions) in hunting scenes depicted on reliefs, seals, and paintings from Syria, Assyria, and Egypt (Bodenheimer 1960, 49-50). The Arab poets, too, compare objects of their admiration to black-eyed gazelles. Dorcas of Joppa is mentioned in the NT (Acts 9:36). In Deuteronomy, the deer and gazelle are representative of clean edible game (12:15, 22; 15:22).

roebuck. יַחְמוּר. A male roe deer, so translated in most recent English Versions since the RSV. Some Versions (NAB; NIV) opt for the more inclusive "roe deer," which was preferred by G. A. Smith. Arabic *yaḥmur* is a "roe, roebuck," which Driver a century ago said could still be found in the thickets of Mount Carmel. Others prefer "fallow deer" (Rashi; Bodenheimer 1962, 251; cf. AV), which is similar. Early on Tristram (1898, 83-85) doubted the fallow deer because of its rarity in Palestine, preferring a species of antelope, perhaps the bubale (LXX: βούβαλον; Vg: *bubalum*), but later he went with the roebuck *(cervus capreolus),* which he had seen on the southern edge of Lebanon (Tristram 1884, 4). King Solomon had deer, gazelle, and roebuck on his table (1 Kgs 5:3[4:23]).

wild goat. אַקּוֹ. The usual identification of this animal rests largely on its translation in the LXX (τραγέλαφον, "goat-stag"), which gets additional support from Rashi, Tristram (1898, 97), I. Aharoni (1938, 464: *capra aegagros*), and all English Versions since the AV (JB and NAB: "ibex"). The Targums translate with יָעֵל ("mountain goat"). The wild goat, or ibex, is common in Palestine. But Bodenheimer (1960, 170; 1962, 251) does not think wild goats existed in Israel or Egypt in earlier times, and so he says the animal's identity is unknown.

oryx. דִּישֹׁן. Some modern Versions (RSV; NAB; NJV) identify this animal as the "ibex" (an old-world wild goat with curved horns), which could be the same animal as Akk *daššu*, the buck of a gazelle or goat (*CAD*, 3:120). Although the identity of the animal remains less than certain (Rashi transliterates with *dyshon*), it is now generally thought to be a type of antelope (JB). The LXX has πύγαργον, a white-rumped antelope common to North Africa. The Vg followed with *pygargon*, and the AV too with "pygarg" (NEB: "white-rumped deer"). Tristram (1884, 5; 1898, 97, 126-27) opts for the white addax, a large antelope well known to the bedouin and inhabiting the Arabah south of the Dead Sea. Bodenheimer (1960, 50; 1962, 251) prefers the Arabian oryx *(oryx leucoryx)*, a straight-horned antelope, also white, inhabiting the deserts and steppes of Syria, Arabia, and Mesopotamia.

antelope. תְּאוֹ. Modern English Versions identify this as another antelope, but according to Bodenheimer (1962, 251), its true identity is unknown. The LXX has ὄρυγα (the ὄρυξ is a type of gazelle or antelope in Egypt and Libya, with pointed horns). Tristram (1884, 5; 1898, 56-58) suggests a larger antelope, either the oryx with long curved horns (so JB and NAB) or the bubale (= African hartebeest), which is the "wild cow" known to the Arabs, found in the area around the Dead Sea. For an ancient description of the bubale, see Oppian *Cynegetica* ii 300-314.

mountain-sheep. זֶמֶר. The identity of this animal has long been a problem, Bodenheimer (1962, 251) concluding that we do not know what it is. LXX's καμηλοπάρδαλιν ("camel leopard, giraffe") and Vg *camelopardalum* are improbable, since this animal is native only to Africa. Rashi's chamois, a small goatlike antelope, is adopted by the AV. But this identification is rejected by Tristram (1898, 73) and most everyone else, since the chamois is the antelope of Central Europe and unknown in Palestine. Tristram said the זֶמֶר was possibly a "wild mountain-sheep," which is the translation adopted in most recent English Versions (NEB: "rock-goat").

6 Beasts that meet both conditions may be eaten (cf. Lev 11:3). Hooves must be completely divided into two nails (Rashi).

that has a hoof. מַפְרֶסֶת פַּרְסָה. The H-stem of פרס is a denominative, making the proper translation here and in Lev 11:3 "has a hoof" (BDB; Milgrom 1991, 646). The term does not mean "divide."

and chews the cud. I.e., regurgitates food from the stomach to the mouth and back again.

7 In Lev 11:4-6 these same animals are reckoned unclean, therefore not edible. Why only a few animals are so specified is unclear. Perhaps they were meant to be representative of a larger number. Tristram (1884, viii) in the 19th cent. said there were 348 known species of fauna in Palestine. But Milgrom (1991, 647), citing the Talmud (*Ḥul.* 59a), says the reason for only four prohibited animals is that there are no others. An even greater puzzlement is the criteria used to distinguish clean from unclean animals: the fully divided hoof and chewing the cud. There is broad agreement that we actually do not know why such criteria were selected. Yet, distinguishing clean from unclean animals is doubtless very old (Gen 7:2, 8; 8:20; Tigay). In some cases, meat from prohibited animals posed a clear danger to health, noted already by Maimonides (I. Klein 1979, 302). The most obvious case is the pig, which is a known carrier of trichinosis and other diseases (Milgrom 1990b, 175). Pliny (*Nat.* viii 206) in antiquity said the pig was particularly liable to disease, especially quinsy (throat disease) and scrofula (tuberculosis). More recently it has been shown in controlled experiments that meat from three of the quadrupeds prohibited here, the camel, the hare, and the pig, is very toxic, whereas meat from the ox, calf, sheep, goat, and deer, is not (Macht 1953). Yet all the prohibited animals — even the pig and wild boar — are eaten by other peoples. In the NT, the distinction between clean and unclean foods is set aside, with all meats considered edible (Acts 10:15; 1 Cor 10:25; 1 Tim 4:4; cf. Matt 15:11). Only if eating certain foods in another's presence might have a harmful effect on that person must one refrain from eating those foods (Rom 14:20-21).

camel. גָּמָל. This "ship of the desert" is the one-humped species common to Syria, Moab, and southern Judah and cannot be eaten. It chews the cud, but has no hoof, simply hardened skin on the foot, divided into two toes (Milgrom 1991, 648). Yet camel meat is eaten routinely by Arabs.

hare. אַרְנֶבֶת. There is no doubt about this animal being the common hare of Palestine (Rashi; Bodenheimer 1962, 251). Akkadian *arnabu* (*CAD*, 1/2:294) and Arabic *'arnab* are both hares. The LXX has δασύποδα (lit. "hairy foot"), which is a hare or rabbit. There are no actual rabbits in Syria or Palestine (*pace* NIV). Tristram (1884, 8; 1898, 98) says the hare here is the *lepus syriacus*, the only Palestinian variety inhabiting wooded and cultivated districts, found also in wooded areas of North Syria and on the Lebanon-Philistine coast. The hare does not have a hoof, and contrary to what is stated here and in Lev 11:6, it does not chew the cud. It only seems to chew the cud because of its habit of constantly grinding the teeth and moving the jaw. The hare is commonly eaten in Arabia.

rock badger. שָׁפָן. There has been a problem naming this animal in English because of the AV translation "coney," the term used for שָׁפָן by Wyclif and the Coverdale Bible of 1535 (*OED*, 3:885). "Coney" is an old English word for rabbit, which this animal is not. Rabbits burrow holes in the ground, whereas this animal lives in rocks (Ps 104:18; Prov 30:26). The preferred name has therefore become "rock badger" (RSV; NEB; NAB; cf. German *Klippdachs*). This animal, in any case, is widely agreed to be the *hyrax syriacus* (Tristram (1884, viii, 1; picture on title overleaf; 1898, 75-77; Bodenheimer 1960, 49; 1962, 247), which is found in North Galilee, gorges around the Dead Sea, and in Arabia. Other names include the hyrax (JB) and the daman (NJV; cf. Benoit 1935 with a picture). The rock badger, like the hare, has no hooves, nor does it chew the cud, though it seems to because of its lip movement. This animal is eaten routinely by all nomads in the Middle East.

8 The swine is disallowed because it is the only animal with cloven hooves that does not chew the cud (*b. Ḥul.* 59a). Milgrom (1991, 649) therefore thinks that cud-chewing was added as a second criterion for the sole purpose of eliminating the pig. Also, this prohibition extends even to touching the animal's carcass (cf. Lev 11:7-8). Rashi says the rabbis taught that one must not touch the carcass of a swine only during festival time, when every male must be in a state of ritual cleanliness. It is unthinkable, he says, that the ordinary Israelite (i.e., a nonpriest) be prohibited from touching a carcass all during the year (cf. Lev 21:1).

swine. חֲזִיר. Covered by this term are both the wild boar and the pig (LXX: ὗν, where Gk ὗς is a pig or boar). The pig was domesticated early in Mesopotamia, where it was bred and eaten (de Vaux 1971c, 256). The wild boar of Mesopotamia is known from lively hunting scenes that have survived (Bodenheimer 1960, 51). Tristram (1884, 3; 1898, 54-55) says that while the animal prohibited here could be the wild boar, which is abundant in marshes and thickets throughout the country, all biblical references except Ps 80:14[13] are to the domesticated pig. The more recent English Versions (NEB; JB; NAB; NIV; NRSV) translate חֲזִיר as "pig." Both wild boars and pigs can be found near the Sea of Galilee (cf. Matt 8:30-32), below Mount Tabor, Mount Carmel, and in the Plain of Sharon. Tristram says they are also abundant in the valleys of Moab and Gilead, in the streams of the Arnon, the Jabbok, and along the Jordan and the Dead Sea. While both animals were eaten by the Babylonians, others besides Jews — Phoenicians, Cypriots, Syrians, and nonnomadic Arabs — considered their meat taboo and did not eat them (G. A. Smith; de Vaux 1971c, 266). In the case of the Syrians, it is unclear whether the animal became sacrosanct because it was holy or unclean (W. R. Smith 1927, 153, 290-91; cf. *Dea Syria* 54; Attridge and Oden 1976, 57).

Evidence of secret rites involving the eating of swine meat appears in Isa 65:4-5; 66:3, 17. W. R. Smith (1927, 621) says the pig was a sacred animal of Ninurta and Gula in Babylonia, and there is evidence also for pigs having been sacrificed in Palestine in the pre-Israelite period (de Vaux 1971c). Pliny (*Nat.*

viii 205-12) says both the pig and the wild boar were eaten, the latter being considered a luxury. At the same time, the pig was derided in antiquity, just as in modern times. An Assyrian text from the sixth year of Sargon II (716) contains popular anecdotes about the pig, saying it has no sense, is unseemly in eating its food and dirtying its backside; it also makes streets smell and pollutes houses. Therefore it is not permitted to walk on pavements, being an abomination to the gods and unfit for the temple (VAT 8807 rev. III, 5-16; Lambert 1960, 215). And as was noted above, this animal is liable to the transmission of disease. Milgrom (1991, 649) notes that besides other dirty habits, it eats carrion.

9 Cf. Lev 11:9-12, which elaborates slightly. No species of fish is named in the entire OT, although names appear later in the Mishnah and Talmud (Bodenheimer 1960, 200). Tristram (1898, 284) notes that the Greek language by contrast has more than four hundred names for various fishes. There was doubtless a fish market in Jerusalem, since the city had a Fish Gate (Zeph 1:10; Neh 3:3; 12:39). Milgrom (1991, 661) cites a study showing that before the opening of the Suez Canal in 1869, which brought into the Mediterranean marine life from the Red Sea, the eastern Mediterranean was impoverished in terms of marine life. He goes on to say:

> The Israelites were unacquainted with fish not because they had no contact with the sea but, to the contrary, the sea with which they had contact was virtually devoid of fish. The fish brought to Jerusalem by Tyrians (Neh 13:16) came from fishing fleets that plied the far-off waters of the Aegean but were beyond the reach of the Israelites. Hence, it is this piscatorial dearth in the immediate vicinity of ancient Israel that accounts for the fact that denominations for the fish are lacking.

But there were fish in the Sea of Galilee and in rivers emptying into the Jordan and Dead Sea. For scale fish populating these inland waters in the 19th and early 20th cents., see Tristram 1884, 164-77 and Bodenheimer 1935, 422-33.

10 This would rule out eels, tuna, dolphins, sharks, porpoises, and all shellfish from the Mediterranean. Dolphins are clearly depicted with tuna and sharks on ancient Palestinian pottery (Bodenheimer 1960, 175). Macht's study (1953) showed that waterfowl without scales and fins also had very high toxic levels, while fish with scales and fins had low toxic levels.

11 Both here and in Leviticus 11 clean birds are not listed. These would include game birds (quail, partridge, pheasant), passerine birds (sparrow, swift, pigeon, swallow), ducks, chickens, geese, and certain other species (Tristram 1898, 158; cf. Exod 16:13; Lev 5:7; Num 11:31-32). Later Jewish practice permitted the eating of chicken, turkey, duck, goose, pigeon, and, according to some authorities, pheasant (I. Klein 1979, 305). Ancient Israel was home to a great vari-

Deuteronomy 14

ety of birds, many of them edible and doubtless taken as clean. The Talmud states that the species of clean birds is innumerable (*b. Ḥul.* 63b). Tristram (1898, 165-68) collected 322 species of birds and said another thirty could easily be added to the list. Species do not vary that much from known species in Northern Europe and Great Britain. Tristram found only twenty-six species peculiar to Palestine. The OT makes no mention of domestic poultry (in the NT, see Matt 23:37; 26:34), although such existed. King Solomon had "fattened fowl" (בַּרְבֻּרִים אֲבוּסִים) on his table (1 Kgs 5:3[4:23]), which G. R. Driver (1955, 133-34) thinks were young chickens, noting that Arabic *birbir* means "young chickens." Other birds caught with the aid of blinds, snares, and clap-nets (Ps 124:7; Prov 7:23; Amos 3:5; Jer 5:26-27) were for eating. Even today in cities and towns of the Near East, one will see young boys along the road offering strings of small birds for sale.

12 *And these are what you shall not eat from.* Most — but not all — of the following are raptorial birds (birds of prey), or scavengers. The Mishnah (*Ḥul.* 3:6) says the ruling of the sages was that "any fowl that seizes is unclean." G. R. Driver (1955, 7) thinks the true reason is ritual uncleanness, consisting of (1) eating blood and (2) having contact with a corpse. The list of twenty birds in Lev 11:13-19 is virtually the same as the list of twenty-one here, with רָאָה in v. 13 most likely a misspelling of דָּאָה (see below). Hebrew עַיִט is a collective meaning raptorial birds (Tristram 1898, 168-69; cf. Gen 15:11). Tristram found forty-three raptorial species in Palestine, noting also that Hebrew and Arabic have a particularly rich vocabulary for such birds: fifteen distinct names in Hebrew, and in Arabic three species of vultures, five names for falcons, three for eagles, and two for kites. Distinguished also in Arabic are four different types of owls. But in the present list is also the ostrich, which is not a raptorial bird. Macht (1953) showed that birds of prey have very toxic levels of flesh, whereas the chicken, duck, goose, turkey, pigeon, and quail have very low toxic levels. On the face of it, one can hardly escape the conclusion that birds eating carrion (dead flesh) will infect others with impurities and that this must have figured somehow in the prohibition (G. R. Driver 1955, 7). Other birds, like the hoopoe, are simply unpleasant to eat. Tristram (1898, 158) says the rules about what birds to eat and not to eat follow generally the instincts of civilized people in all ages, noting also that tribal peoples of Syria and Arabia eat birds repugnant to our tastes and that mountain people of Lebanon eat eagle without scruple. I ate hawk served by missionaries in central Africa, with no adverse effect.

eagle. נֶשֶׁר. This bird, whose characteristics and habits are cited often in the OT, is the eagle (LXX: ἀετός) or griffon-vulture. Tristram's (1884, 95-96; 1898, 172-80) identification with the griffon-vulture (*gyps fulvus*), which he says is the only species satisfying the "baldness" described in Mic 1:16, is now accepted by many scholars. But G. R. Driver (1958, 56-57), who adopted this view early on, changed his mind and said he now believed the נֶשֶׁר was the golden eagle (cf. 32:11). The griffon-vulture is not really bald; the white patch on its head simply gives an appearance of baldness. The "bald eagle," also not bald, is found only in North America (Tigay). Both the eagle and griffon-vulture ascend to great heights (Isa 40:31; Prov 23:5), have great powers of sight (Job 39:29), descend swiftly to their prey — the golden eagle flies 3 to 4 mi in ten minutes (Deut 28:49; Hab 1:8; Jer 4:13; Lam 4:19), and feed on carrion (Prov 30:17; Job 39:30; Matt 24:28). These birds also have a great wingspan — some 8 to 10 ft across (Ezek 17:3; cf. Exod 19:4; Deut 32:11). Eagles build their nests in trees or in cliffs, vultures almost always in lofty cliffs (Jer 49:16; Job 39:28).

vulture. The פֶּרֶס (lit. "the breaker") is the ossifrage (AV), "lamb vulture" *(Lämmergeier),* or "bearded vulture" *(gypaetus barbatus),* so-called because it habitually ascends to great heights with its prey and then drops it on a rock or other hard surface to break the bones (cf. Akk *parāsu,* "to break [bones]"). The process is repeated sometimes eight or ten times until the bones are completely shattered. This huge bird is another carrion feeder but also eats bone marrow, tortoises, and snakes. It is also known to push lambs, kids, or hares over cliffs and then devour them. Tradition has it that the poet Aeschylus met his death in Gela (456) when a tortoise was dropped on his bald head by one of these birds *(EncB* 11th ed., 1:272; *Aeschylus I:* xxiii). Tristram says this "prince of the vultures" can be found in most of the mountainous regions of Palestine, but only singly or in pairs. Other vultures congregate in large numbers. These birds inhabit the gorges opening into the Jordan Valley and the Dead Sea and have been observed in the Jabbok and Arnon Gorges of Moab.

osprey. עָזְנִיָּה. The traditional identification of this bird is the osprey (LXX: ἁλιαίετος), a fish-eating eagle known to inhabit Palestine in small numbers (AV; RSV; JB; NAB). Tristram in his study of Holy Land birds named it as the osprey (1884, 98-99, 107; 1898, 182-86) but said the Hebrew term was probably generic, taking in a number of other eagles, e.g., the short-toed eagle *(circaetus gallicus),* the imperial eagle *(aquila mogilnik),* and the "golden eagle" *(aquila chrysaetus).* The short-toed eagle is the most common in Palestine, eating reptiles in summer and coastal frogs in winter. The golden eagle is found throughout the country in winter, but in summer only in the mountain ranges of Lebanon and Hermon. The osprey has been seen in the Jabbok Gorge, Mount Hermon area, and lagoons north of the River Kishon. All eat carrion, but unlike vultures will kill if necessary for food. Others scholars and translations, however, take this bird to be a type of vulture (I. Aharoni 1938, 471-72; G. R. Driver 1955, 10; NEB; NJV; NIV).

13 *kite.* Hebrew רָאָה may be a scribal error for דָּאָה, the spelling of the first bird in Lev 11:14 (Driver 1895, 162 n. 13: "The text of Deuteronomy is certainly corrupt"). The latter noun is a *hapax legomenon* in the OT, but the verb

Deuteronomy 14

דאה ("to fly swiftly") is well-attested, referring commonly to eagles in flight (Deut 28:49; Jer 48:40; 49:22). Leviticus 11:14 lists only two birds in the verse, which is what the LXX has there and in the present verse: καὶ τὸν γύπα ("vulture") καὶ ἰκτῖνα ("kite"). The present verse in MT has three birds (RSV; NEB; JB; and NAB delete one), which further complicates things in that the third bird, דַּיָּה, is perhaps a variant spelling of דָּאָה (see below). The Talmud (b. Ḥul. 63b) recognizes the problem, quoting one authority as saying that the two names, רָאָה and דָּאָה, are one and the same. The דָּאָה, in any case, is a bird of prey, most likely a hawk or a kite (G. R. Driver 1955, 10; cf. BDB; KBL³).

falcon. אַיָּה. This bird has been variously identified as a "kite" (AV; NEB; JB; NAB; NIV), "buzzard" (RSV), or "falcon" (NJV). Tristram (1884, 102; 1898, 187-89) thought it was probably the kite or red kite, but G. R. Driver (1955, 11) takes the term to be generic for the larger falcon (RSV translates אַיָּה as "falcon" in Job 28:7). Job 28:7 says the bird in question is keen-sighted, but that applies to all birds of prey. The true identity then of this bird is not known.

buzzard. דַּיָּה. Another bird of prey whose identity is unknown. It is not listed in Lev 11:14, and in the present verse the LXX and Sam omit. The term occurs only one other time in Isa 34:15, where reference is to a bird that inhabits ruins. Hebrew דַּיָּה may actually be a variant spelling of דָּאָה, which occurs in Lev 11:14 but not here. Tristram (1884, 98, 102) suggests for this bird the common buzzard *(buteo vulgaris)*, a migrant plentiful on coasts and in the plains during summer, or else the black kite *(milvus migrans)*, which is absent in winter but returns to Palestine from the south in vast numbers about the beginning of March. It feeds on village garbage and makes raids on poultry. G. R. Driver (1955, 10) rules out the black kite, saying it does not inhabit ruins.

according to its kind. לְמִינוֹ. An indication that more birds of a similar kind are covered than appear listed by name. This is the same phrase that occurs in Genesis 1.

14 *raven.* עֹרֵב. Lit. "the black one" (Cant 5:11), first mentioned in the Bible in the story of the flood (Gen 8:7). Tristram (1884, 77; 1898, 109) says the Hebrew term includes the entire crow family: crows, rooks, jackdaws, etc., which one may conclude by the following "according to its kind." These birds feed on carrion but will also attack sick, weakened, and newly born animals. They are known by their habit of first picking out the eyes of their prey (Prov 30:17; cf. Aristophanes, *Ach.* 92). Ravens lives in trees, ravines, and deep gorges throughout the country.

15 *the ostrich.* Hebrew בַּת הַיַּעֲנָה is lit. "daughter of the desert" (BDB, 419), which all the Targums, the LXX (στρουθός), and the Vg *(strutio)* take to be the ostrich. Aristophanes (*Ach.* 1105), too, used the shortened form στρουθός to mean "ostrich." Tristram (1898, 192, 233) went along with this identification, but noted that the OT employs other terms for "ostrich," e.g., רְנָנִים in Job 39:13, which seems well supported by the context. The bird appearing here and in Lev 11:16 is said elsewhere to dwell in the desert (Isa 43:20) or among ruins (Isa 13:20-21; 34:13; Jer 50:39), which causes somewhat of a problem in that the ostrich is known to inhabit open country and desert, but typically not ruins. Translators of the AV may have sensed this problem, since in Lam 4:3 they rendered כַּיְעֵנִים בַּמִּדְבָּר (Q) as "ostriches in the wilderness" but here translated בַּת הַיַּעֲנָה as "owl." Some of the more recent English Versions (Moffatt, RSV; JB; NAB; NJV) have returned to "ostrich," but I. Aharoni (1937, 38-39; 1938, 469-70) says this is a desert owl (NEB: "desert-owl"; NIV: "horned owl"). G. R. Driver (1955, 12-13) suggests the "eagle owl," since this bird inhabits ruins. Identification thus remains in doubt, but "ostrich" has the support of the ancient Versions.

owl. תַּחְמָס. The identification of this bird as an "owl" by LXX (γλαύξ) and Vg *(noctua)* has been generally accepted, although no agreement has been reached on just what kind of owl it might be. The AV took it to be the "night hawk" (T^Onq), which has been retained by the RSV and NJV. Tristram (1898, 191-92) says this may be the common barn owl *(strix flammea),* also called the "screech-owl" (JB; NIV), which is well known in Palestine and found generally in caves and around ruins.

seagull. שַׁחַף. The LXX (λάρος), Targums, and Vg *(larus)* all identify this bird as the "seagull," which has been retained by most modern English Versions. "Cuckoo" of the AV has been abandoned. Tristram (1884, 135) suggests the common "tern," a marine bird like the gull, known to be plentiful on the coast. G. R. Driver (1955, 13) follows I. Aharoni (1938, 470) in wanting another owl in the sequence, suggesting here the long-eared owl (NEB; REB), which is plentiful in the wooded districts of northern Palestine.

hawk. נֵץ. The ancient Versions (LXX, T, Vg) identify this bird as a hawk. Tristram (1884, 101, 106; 1898, 189-91) says נֵץ covers all smaller birds of prey, e.g., various species of hawks and falcons. The sparrow hawk *(accipiter nisus)* is very common about olive groves and clumps of woods in the south during winter, also in oases and shrubby places about the Dead Sea and Jordan Valley. In April it disappears from the lower country, remaining only in the hills of Galilee, in Lebanon, and in Hermon. The kestrel *(falco tinnunculus)* is common everywhere, especially in the desolate gorges of the Dead Sea, where it is known to share caves with eagles and griffon-vultures.

16 *the small owl . . . the great owl.* הַכּוֹס . . . הַיַּנְשׁוּף. The AV and majority of recent English Versions follow T^Onq in translating these birds as "the little owl and the big owl." Targum^Nf has "the owl" and "the ibis." Both birds are doubtless owls, but just what kind of owl we do not know. Tristram (1884, 93; 1898, 192-95) goes with "little owl" for כּוֹס and the Egyptian "eagle owl" for יַנְשׁוּף. G. R. Driver (1955, 140) thinks both are onomatopoeic, suggesting for כּוֹס the "tawny owl" and for יַנְשׁוּף the "screech owl."

ibis. תִּנְשֶׁמֶת. Another owl according to the Targums (not a "swan," *pace* AV), the precise species we do not know. Tristram (1884, 113; 1898, 249-51), following the LXX (ἴβις) and other ancient Versions, says this is probably the Egyptian ibis or else the "purple gallinule." G. R. Driver (1955, 15) thinks it may be the "little owl," one of the most common owls in Palestine.

17 *pelican.* קָאָת. The ancient Versions (LXX, T, Vg) all identify this bird with the pelican, whose Hebrew name is alleged to be "vomiter" (from קיא). In storing quantities of fish in its pouch, the pelican "disgorges" them to feed its young. Elsewhere in the OT this bird is said to inhabit ruins and wilderness areas (Isa 34:11; Zeph 2:14; Ps 102:7[6]). Tristram (1884, 108; 1898, 251) thinks both characteristics can describe the pelican, which, although a fish-feeder, does resort to open, uncultivated areas after feeding. The roseate pelican frequents the Sea of Galilee area; other species are found along the Syrian coast. The AV translated קָאָת as "pelican," and this has been retained by the RSV, JB, and NJV. But G. R. Driver (1955, 16) thinks the bird has to be another owl and suggests the "scops-owl." Milgrom (1991, 663) and Tigay also take the bird to be an owl (cf. NEB and REB: "horned owl"; NAB; NIV; NRSV: "desert owl").

carrion-vulture. רָחָמָה. This bird appears to be another vulture, perhaps the "(white) carrion-vulture" (RSV; NRSV; the AV following T has "gier eagle"; cf. Ar *raḥm*). Tristram (1884, 96; 1898, 179-80) identified it with the "Egyptian vulture" or "Pharaoh's hen" *(neophron percnopterus)*, which feeds on filth and exists over the entire country in summer, but is never seen in winter. Found in pairs, this bird nests in the lower parts of cliffs. G. A. Smith says its flesh is forbidden meat in Arabia, yet mothers give it to their children to expel worms. G. R. Driver (1955, 16-17) thinks this bird is the fish-eating osprey. The bird has turned up in the Deir ʿAlla inscription (Hackett 1980, 25 line 8), where it is paired with the נשר (eagle; griffon vulture) and followed by the יענה (ostrich; eagle-owl?) and the ח[סד] (stork).

cormorant. שָׁלָךְ. Another fish-eating bird whose name means "plunging" or "hurling (from above)." Rashi says it derives its name because it "draws up" (שלך = שלה) fishes out of the sea. It is commonly identified with the cormorant *(phalacrocorax carbo)*, found on the coast and in all inland waters of Palestine (Tristram 1884, 107; 1898, 252-53). This bird, which is similar to the pelican, watches for fish at the mouth of the Jordan.

18 *stork.* The חֲסִידָה in all probability is the "stork," otherwise the "heron." The term could refer to both birds (G. R. Driver 1955, 17). Tristram (1884, 111-12; 1898, 244-49) identified it with the white stork *(ciconia alba)*, a garbage-eater that is a passing migrant in Palestine (Jer 8:7).

heron. אֲנָפָה. The precise identification of this bird is not known, although it is generally thought to be another fish-eating wader (G. R. Driver 1955, 17-18). Milgrom (1991, 664) on the basis of Targum translations thinks it may be a type of hawk. Tristram (1884, 109; 1898, 241) suggests the common heron *(ardea cinerea),* which is scattered throughout the country, especially about the marshes of Lake Huleh, the Sea of Galilee, the Jordan, the Kishon, and along the coast.

hoopoe. דּוּכִיפַת. This bird is clearly identified in all the ancient Versions as the "hoopoe" *(upupa epops),* a migrant that leaves Syria and Palestine in winter for Egypt and oases of the Sahara and then returns at the beginning of March (Tristram 1884, 89; 1898, 208-10; Bodenheimer 1935, 165). The hoopoe inhabits desert wadis, woods, gardens, and villages, living in foul nests and known to be a filthy eater, hunting out insects in dunghills. This bird turns up in James Michener's novel, *The Source,* where the smart little engineer building the 10th-cent. walls of Makor and constructing an underground water tunnel to defend the city against the Phoenicians is given the bird's name (Michener 1965, 199-273).

bat. עֲטַלֵּף. A mammal, actually, not a bird. Aristotle *(Part an.* iv 13. 8-10) saw this creature as an anomaly, having feet unlike birds and yet unlike other quadrupeds, also not having a quadruped's tail because it is a flier, nor a bird's tail because it is a land animal. On bats in modern Palestine, see Bodenheimer 1935, 91-94.

19 *winged swarming thing.* שֶׁרֶץ הָעוֹף. I.e., winged insects. Leviticus 11:20-23 adds: "that go upon all fours," providing certain exceptions. Hebrew שֶׁרֶץ is a collective meaning "swarming thing(s)," which inhabit waters (Gen 1:20) and also move upon land (Lev 11:29; cf. Gen 7:21). The latter go unmentioned in Deuteronomy, but Lev 11:29-30 reckons as unclean the weasel, mouse, various lizards, etc. Flying insects, particularly flies and mosquitos, are known carriers of disease (malaria-bearing mosquitos continue to be a big problem in Africa and India).

20 *Every clean winged creature you may eat.* כָּל־עוֹף טָהוֹר תֹּאכֵלוּ. It is unclear here whether עוֹף ("winged creature") means birds, insects, or both. The AV (following Rashi) took the term to mean birds, which meant a repetition of the statement in v. 11. But Driver and others (G. A. Smith; Milgrom 1991, 698-99; Tigay), to avoid a repetition, take עוֹף to mean "winged insect(s)" (NEB: "You may eat every clean insect"). This latter view assumes the present verse to be an abbreviation of Lev 11:21-22, where certain clean insects (leaping locusts, crickets, grasshoppers) are specified. But it is not at all clear that the present verse is abridging Leviticus, as Milgrom (like Driver before him) maintains. Leviticus 11:20-23 is concerned only about four-legged insects, making it narrower in focus than v. 19 here, which covers all winged insects. The present verse may simply be a repetition in different words of v. 11, in which case the unit in vv. 11-20 is tied together by an inclusio (see Rhetoric and Composition). It is better to translate עוֹף as "winged creature(s)" or the like, as most modern

English Versions do (RSV; JB; NAB; NJV; NIV; NRSV; REB). The Qumran *Temple Scroll* (11QT 48:3-4) follows Leviticus in listing four winged insects that may be eaten: locust, bald locust, cricket, and grasshopper (Yadin 1983, 2:205, 207). The Mishnah (*Ḥul.* 3:7) reckons as clean locusts those that have (1) four legs, (2) four wings, (3) pointed legs, or (4) wings covering the greater part of the body. Insects are eaten by people in many parts of the world. G. A. Smith says that Arabs and other eastern peoples treat locusts as a delicacy, frying them or making them into cakes.

21 *You shall not eat any carcass; to the sojourner who is within your gates you may give it so he can eat it, or sell it to a foreigner.* Hebrew נְבֵלָה is a "carcass," referring here to an animal that has died a natural death or been torn by beasts. The latter is prohibited in Exod 22:30(31), where it is prefaced by the words: "You shall be holy men to me." There it is specified that such flesh be thrown to the dogs. Driver thinks that animals killed in either manner would be unwholesome as food, also not thoroughly drained of blood (cf. 12:16). The law undergoes modification in Lev 17:15-16, where anyone — Israelite or sojourner — eating an animal that dies of itself or is torn by beasts must simply carry out a cleansing ritual. Priests, however, must not eat such flesh (Lev 22:8; Ezek 44:31).

the sojourner. גֵּר. The resident alien in Israel, who has dependent status in the country (see Note for 5:13-14). 11QT 48:6 omits "to the sojourner who is within your gates you may give it so he can eat it" (Yadin 1983, 2:205), reflecting the law in Leviticus, where this provision does not exist.

a foreigner. נָכְרִי. Someone not permanently settled in Israel, either trading in the country or just passing through. Such individuals were economically better off than sojourners and could support themselves (cf. 15:3).

For you are a holy people to Yahweh your God. Repeating the affirmation of v. 2. Since Israel is a holy people, it must not eat anything unclean.

You shall not boil a kid in its mother's milk. This law occurs also in Exod 23:19b; 34:26. It is a miscellaneous law (see Rhetoric and Composition), therefore not a dietary prohibition strictly speaking (*pace* Milgrom 1985, 55; 1991, 703). Although definitely a legal prescription, it may also have had a proverbial function, in which case the prohibition would apply equally to the boiling of lambs and calves. Since the prohibition is against boiling a kid in the milk of its own mother, and not just any milk, there may be prima facie indignity in such an action (*b. Ḥul.* 113b-14a, citing the law in Lev 22:28). Cf. the laws in Exod 22:29(30); Lev 22:27; Deut 22:6-7, which are similarly based on humane considerations. In Arabia, sheep and goats are cooked in milk to improve the flavor, and the same may have been true in ancient Israel (Haran 1979, 28-30). Haran notes that Abraham served his guests butter and milk together with meat, where the butter and milk were apparently side dishes intended to enhance the taste of the meat and diminish thirst (Gen 18:7-8). This prohibition becomes the basis for the later rabbinic law requiring separation of dairy and meat dishes (*m. Ḥul.* 8:1; *b. Ḥul.* 113a-16a). But it has been argued more recently that גְּדִי בַּחֲלֵב אִמּוֹ means "suckling kid," which would give the reading: "You shall not boil a kid (still) at its mother's milk" (Schorch 2010).

Message and Audience

Moses has finished telling the people who they are not. Now he must tell them who they are. Israel is sons and daughters to Yahweh its God. People must not cut themselves and shave their heads for the dead, as the Canaanites do. They are a set-apart people to Yahweh. Yahweh chose Israel to be his very own, wanting it as a treasure-piece among all peoples on the face of the earth.

What follows then are dietary laws, the observance of which will set Israel apart as a holy people. Certain beasts can be eaten, both domestic animals and game, distinguishing marks being whether they have a fully-divided hoof and chew the cud. The four exceptions are camel, hare, rock badger, and swine, both wild and domesticated. In the case of swine, people are also not to touch their carcasses. How absolute this last prohibition was to be left even some Jewish sages wondering.

People may eat any fish that has a fin and scales. Lacking these, they are unclean and must not be eaten. No specific fish is named. People can eat clean birds, and here again they are expected to know what these are. Listed only are the birds not to be eaten, which are typically birds of prey that eat carrion or have other filthy habits. Winged insects also must not be eaten.

In conclusion, two more miscellaneous laws relating to living as a set-apart people are given. People are not to eat any dead carcass, whether it has died a natural death or been torn by beasts. Such can be given to the sojourner for food, or sold to a foreigner, but Israel as Yahweh's holy people may not eat it. It is also incumbent upon any Israelite not to boil a kid in its mother's milk.

Nothing in this sermon by the great lawgiver presupposes Israelite life in the 7th cent.; by then dietary laws as well as the miscellaneous prohibitions will have been well established. Dietary laws were set aside in the early church, with Peter being told in a vision not to refrain from eating animals, reptiles, and birds considered by Jews to be unclean (Acts 10:9-16). Paul, too, said that no foods were unclean in and of themselves; one should simply refrain from certain foods if eating them became a stumbling block to someone else (Rom 14:13-23; cf. 1 Tim 4:3-4).

D. Tithes, Remissions, and Offerings (14:22–15:23)

1. Tithing Year by Year (14:22-27)

14 ^{22}You shall surely tithe all the yield of your seed, and what comes forth from the field, year by year. ^{23}And you shall eat before Yahweh your God in the place that he will choose to make his name reside there, the tithe of your grain, your wine, and your oil, and the firstborns in your herd and your flock, in order that you may learn to fear Yahweh your God all the days. ^{24}And if the road is too long for you, that you are not able to carry it because the place that Yahweh your God will choose to put his name there is too far from you, when Yahweh your God will bless you, ^{25}then you shall turn it into silver, and you shall bind the silver in your hand, and you shall go to the place that Yahweh your God will choose with it. ^{26}And you shall turn the silver into anything that your soul desires, into one of the herd or into one of the flock, or into wine or into beer, yes, into anything that your soul asks you for; and you shall eat there before Yahweh your God, and you shall be glad, you and your house. ^{27}And you shall not forsake the Levite who is within your gates, for he has no portion or inheritance with you.

2. Tithing Every Three Years (14:28-29)

14 ^{28}At the end of three years you shall bring forth all the tithe of your yield in that year, and you shall deposit it within your gates; ^{29}and the Levite shall come, for he has no portion or inheritance with you, and the sojourner, and the orphan, and the widow who is within your gates, and they shall eat and become sated, in order that Yahweh your God may bless you in all the work of your hand that you do.

3. Remissions Every Seven Years (15:1-18)

a) Debt Remission (15:1-11)

15 ^{1}After seven years' time you shall make a remission. ^{2}And this is the manner of the remission: every owner of a loan in his hand is to remit what he has loaned to his fellow; he shall not press his fellow or his brother, because a remission to Yahweh has been proclaimed. ^{3}With the foreigner you may press, but whatever of yours is with your brother, let your hand remit. ^{4}However, there should not be a needy person among you, for Yahweh will surely bless you in the land that Yahweh your God is giving to you for an inheritance to possess it, ^{5}if only you surely obey the voice of Yahweh your God, to be careful to do all this commandment that I am *commanding you today.* ⁶*For Yahweh your God is blessing you, just as he promised you, and you will lend to many nations, but you, you will not borrow; and you will rule over many nations, but they will not rule over you.* ⁷*When there is a needy person among you, from one of your brethren within one of your gates in your land that Yahweh your God is giving to you, you shall not harden your heart, and you shall not close your hand from your needy brother;* ⁸*but you shall surely open your hand to him and you shall surely lend him enough for his need, whatever his need may be.* ⁹*Be careful for yourself, lest there be a good-for-nothing thought in your heart: "The seventh year, the year of remission, is near," and your eye be evil against your needy brother, and you do not give to him, and he cry out to Yahweh against you, and it be a sin in you.* ¹⁰*You shall surely give to him, and your heart shall not be evil when you give to him, for on account of this thing Yahweh your God will bless you in all your work and in every undertaking of your hand.* ¹¹*For the needy person will not cease from the midst of the land. Therefore I am commanding you: You shall surely open your hand to your brother, to your poor, and to your needy in your land.*

b) *Remission of Hebrew Slaves (15:12-18)*

15¹²*When your brother, a Hebrew or a Hebrewess, is sold to you and he serves you six years, then in the seventh year you shall send him away free from you.* ¹³*And when you send him away free from you, you shall not send him away empty-handed;* ¹⁴*you shall be sure to make a necklace for him from your flock and from your threshing-floor and from your winepress; as Yahweh your God has blessed you, you shall give to him.* ¹⁵*Yes, you shall remember that you were a slave in the land of Egypt, and Yahweh your God ransomed you; therefore I am commanding you this thing today.* ¹⁶*And it will be if he says to you, "I will not go out from you," because he loves you and your house, because it is good for him with you,* ¹⁷*then you shall take an awl and put it in his ear and in the door, and he shall be for you a manservant forever; furthermore, to your maidservant you shall do the same.* ¹⁸*It shall not be too difficult in your eyes when you send him away free from you, for double the wages of a hired laborer he served you six years, and Yahweh your God will bless you in all that you do.*

4. Firstborn Gifts Year by Year (15:19-23)

15¹⁹*Every firstborn that is brought forth in your herd and in your flock, which is male, you shall consecrate to Yahweh your God; you shall not work with the firstborn of your ox, and you shall not shear the firstborn of your sheep.* ²⁰*Before Yahweh your God you shall eat it year by year in the place that Yahweh will* *choose, you and your house.* ²¹*But if it has a blemish, it is lame or blind, any bad blemish, you shall not sacrifice it to Yahweh your God.* ²²*Within your gates you shall eat it — the unclean and the clean together, like a gazelle and like a deer.* ²³*Only its blood you shall not eat; you shall pour it out upon the ground like water.*

Rhetoric and Composition

These verses contain four cultic obligations to be performed at various times: (1) tithing year by year; (2) tithing every third year; (3) remissions every seventh year; and (4) gifts of firstborn animals year by year. The discourse has a rhetorical structure, placing at beginning and the end obligations to be performed "year by year" (Lohfink 1968, 26; Lundbom 1996, 309):

Tithing *year by year*	14:22-27
Tithing every third year	14:28-29
Remissions every seventh year	15:1-18
Gift of firstborns *year by year*	15:19-23

The third-year tithe and the two remission laws in the seventh year — the remission of debts (15:1-11) and the remission of Hebrew slaves (15:12-18) — acknowledge Yahweh's blessing that accrues when one acts to aid the poor and needy. The yearly tithe and yearly gift of the firstborns honor Yahweh with festive meals for the worshipper, his family, and the Levite as an invited guest.

This rhetorical structure, in which obligations coming up "year by year" are put at beginning and end, explains why the tithe law mentions the presentation of firstborns in 14:23 ("and the firstborns in your herd and your flock"), which is not itself part of the tithe. This is an innerbiblical harmonizing technique, similar to one in ch. 18, where the criterion for false prophecy in 13:2-6(1-5) is added in a context where it does not otherwise belong (18:20: "or who speaks in the name of other gods").

In 15:4-6, where the Deuteronomic preacher digresses briefly from legal pronouncement to express the view that Israel ought have no needy souls in the future, is a repetition of Yahweh's promised blessing, giving the digression an inclusio:

. . . *for Yahweh will surely bless you* . . .	v. 4
For Yahweh your God is blessing you, just as he promised you	v. 6

The unit is demarcated at the top end by a *petuḥah* in M^L and sections in Sam and 4QpaleoDeut^r before 14:22 and at the bottom end by a *petuḥah* in M^L

Deuteronomy 14–15

and a section in Sam after 15:23, which is also a chapter division. A *setumah* in M^L and sections in Sam and 4QpaleoDeut^r after 14:27 end the tithing obligation that comes up year by year. A *setumah* in M^L and sections in Sam and 4QDeut^c after 14:29, which is also a chapter division, end the tithing obligations that come up every third year. A *petuhah* in M^L and a section in Sam after 15:18 end the obligation on remissions that comes up every seventh year, and the unit is further divided in M^L by a *setumah* and in Sam by a section after 15:6 and another *setumah* in M^L and a section in Sam after 15:11. These divisions delineate further subject matter within the unit: 15:1-6 deals generally with remission of loans; 15:7-11 deals specifically with loan remissions to the poor; and 15:12-18 deals with remission of Hebrew slaves. It has been argued that all the loan remissions (15:1-11) form a coherent whole (Mukenge 2010).

Portions of 14:22–15:23 are contained in 1QDeut^a, 1QDeut^b, 4QDeut^c, 4QpaleoDeut^r, MurDeut, and 4Q364. The tithe commandment in 14:22-27 is developed in the *Temple Scroll* (11QT 43).

Notes

14:22 A tithe (= 10 percent) is to be surrendered from all of one's agricultural produce, i.e., grain, wine, and oil (v. 23), also from any other produce whose "growth is from the soil" (*m. Ma'aś.* 1:1; T^{Onq}: "all the produce of your sowing"; cf. 2 Chr 31:5). Since the Covenant Code says nothing about tithing, many view the provisions in Deuteronomy as being the oldest of their kind in legal material of the OT (14:22-29; cf. 12:6, 11, 17-18; 26:12-15). Other tithing legislation occurs in Num 18:21-32 and Lev 27:30-33 (both P material), but opinion is divided whether these passages predate Deuteronomy or come later. Critical scholars following Wellhausen date P to the postexilic period, but many recent scholars follow Kaufmann in dating P prior to or contemporary with Deuteronomy. For a discussion of the two views relative to the tithe, see Greenberg 1950, 42-44.

In P legislation, tithes go to the Levites and priests (they are "holy to Yahweh"), with Lev 27:32 calling additionally for a tithe of one's herds and flocks (cf. 2 Chr 31:6). In Deuteronomy, the tithe consists only of agricultural produce (cf. Tob 5:13; Jdt 11:13), and it is eaten by the worshipper and his household or in the third year is given to the poor and needy. In all years the Levite is an indirect recipient of the tithe, being an invited guest to the feast at the central sanctuary (14:27) or sharing in the third-year tithe eaten in the village (14:29). Because of differences in the Priestly and Deuteronomic legislation, some (G. E. Wright; H. Guthrie, in *IDB,* 4:654) have suggested that Deuteronomy reflects cultic practice in northern Israel while the P material reflects cultic practice in Judah at the Jerusalem temple. A different explanation is given by J. M. P. Smith

(1914, 126), who says that Deuteronomy is not a law book but a collection of sermonic addresses, and "we go to preachers not for legislation but for inspiration." In any case, the obvious differences between the Deuteronomic and Priestly legislation required harmonization in later Judaism, which is what happened. The tithe now came to consist of both agricultural products and firstborn animals. A "first tithe" based on Num 18:21-26 became the tithe given to the Levites, and a "second tithe" based on Deut 14:22-27 became the tithe brought to Jerusalem and eaten by the worshipper, his household, and invited guests (Tob 1:6-8; Josephus *Ant.* 4.68, 205, 240-43; Rashi, following T^{NfPsJ}; *m. Ma'aśerot* and *Ma'aśer Šeni*). The result was not altogether satisfactory. Two tithes meant an annual tax of 20 percent on one's yield, which was too high, making implementation of tithe laws nigh unto impossible (*EncJud*, 15:1161-62).

Most everyone agrees that tithing predates Deuteronomy and was likely an ancient Israelite practice (J. M. P. Smith 1914, 119). Abraham gave a full tithe of war booty to Melchizedek, priest-king of Salem (= Jerusalem), after achieving success in battle (Gen 14:20). Jacob promised a tithe of everything after his dream at Bethel if Yahweh would return him safely to his father's house after a sojourn in Paddan-aram (Gen 28:20-22). While these etiological stories cannot be said to reflect custom or established practice in the patriarchal period, they serve, nevertheless, to link the tithe to Jerusalem in the south and Bethel in the north, cities that later became royal sanctuaries (cf. Amos 7:13). That tithes were presented in northern Israel at Bethel and Gilgal before the Deuteronomic Reformation, in the mid-8th cent., is clear from Amos 4:4.

The tithe, perhaps originally a voluntary gift made at a local sanctuary acknowledging divine ownership of the land and Yahweh's right to the yield (Gen 28:22; Amos 4:4), became under the monarchy a tax supporting temple and state, which it was in Ugarit, Neo-Babylonia, and elsewhere (Johns 1904, 204-7; *EncJud*, 15:1156-57). Samuel warned the Israelites about this when they asked for a king. He told them that kings

> will take the best of your fields and vineyards and olive orchards and give them to his servants. He will take the tenth of your grain and of your vineyards and give it to his officers and to his servants. He will take your menservants and maidservants, and the best of your cattle* and your asses, and put them to his work. He will take the tenth of your flocks, and you shall be his slaves. (1 Sam 8:14-17 RSV)

In Deuteronomy the tithe is obligatory, whereas in Amos 4:4 and Lev 27:30-33 it occurs contextually among voluntary-type gifts and therefore may

---

*So LXX (βουκόλια ὑμῶν); MT has "your young men" (בַּחוּרֵיכֶם).

not be obligatory (Tigay; *EncJud*, 15:1158). In later Judaism, tithes for the support of temple and clergy were obligatory (Neh 10:38-40[37-39]; 13:10-12), although this commitment was not always faithfully carried out (cf. Mal 3:6-12).

Tithing was common in the ancient world. It was known already at Ugarit in the 14th cent. (de Vaux 1965, 140-41; *EncJud*, 15:1156-57) and was practiced among the Neo-Babylonians, Persians, Greeks, and other ancient peoples (Driver; Johns 1904, 206-7; J. M. P. Smith 1914, 119). It may also have been practiced in Egypt, as evidenced by the Harris Papyrus (Breasted 1906a, 178, no. 354 lines 11-13; cf. Gen 41:34). At Tel Miqne-Ekron, a storage jar found in a temple complex bore a sign suggesting that its contents were to be set aside as a tithe (Gitin 2003, 289; 2004, 68).

It is not known precisely what relation, if any, tithes had to the presentation of firstfruits. The two are associated in 26:1-15 and elsewhere (Tob 1:6); nevertheless, they may have been separate offerings. It has been suggested that the tithe was the fixed amount of the yearly crop to be surrendered, with the firstfruits being simply a token gift presented earlier (Wellhausen 1957, 157-58; G. E. Wright). But the firstfruits went to the priest (18:4), whereas in Deuteronomy the tithe did not. Also, the Covenant Code calls for a gift of the firstfruits (Exod 22:28[29]) but says nothing about tithes. On the tithe in later Judaism, see *m. Ma'aserot* and *Ma'aser Šeni* ("Second Tithe").

year by year. In a seven-year cycle this will be the first, second, fourth, and fifth years. In the third and sixth years the tithe goes to the poor and needy (vv. 28-29). In the seventh year the land lies fallow, so there is no planting and no harvesting (Exod 23:10-11; Lev 25:2-7). J. M. Powis Smith (1914, 121) suggested that perhaps crop rotation was practiced, in which case a farmer's entire field would not lie fallow in the seventh year. He noted that crop rotation appears to have been practiced in Assyria (cf. Johns 1901, 19-20). Smith also compared the present law with the release of Hebrew slaves every seventh year (15:12-18; Exod 21:2-6). Here the release takes place not in a set year, but whenever the six-year period is up. Short-term fallowing and crop rotation in Early Iron Age Palestine has been advanced more recently by D. C. Hopkins (1985, 194-95).

23 *And you shall eat before Yahweh your God in the place that he will choose to make his name reside there, the tithe of your grain, your wine, and your oil, and the firstborns in your herd and your flock.* The tithe of produce shall be brought to the central sanctuary and there consumed by the offerer, his family, and invited guests (cf. 12:5-7). Firstborns of the herds and flocks are not part of the tithe (see Rhetoric and Composition), but are to be brought at the same time, consecrated to Yahweh (15:19-23), and eaten along with the tithe. As was mentioned earlier, in northern Israel the tithe originally went to some local sanctuary (Amos 4:4), but in the 7th cent. its destination was the central sanctuary in Jerusalem. Here in Deuteronomy it is the offerer himself and his family

Deuteronomy 14–15

who eat the tithe; the Levites are simply invited guests (v. 27). In Lev 27:30-33 the tithe goes to the priests and in Num 18:21 to the Levites.

We do not know precisely when the Israelite farmer brought his tithe to the central sanctuary. It could have been at the Feast of Weeks (Pentecost) when the firstfruits were presented (16:9-12; Exod 23:16) or else at the Feast of Booths (16:13-15; Exod 23:16), which is perhaps more likely, since this was the ingathering festival at year's end (Wellhausen 1957, 91). Tigay believes it could have been on any occasion when the farmer made a pilgrimage to the central sanctuary.

The worshipper, his family, and the invited guests could not possibly eat all the tithe brought to the sanctuary. Maimonides said: "Inasmuch as the man and his household would not be likely to consume the whole of the tithe, he would be compelled to give part away in charity" (Hertz 1960, 810). More likely, some was put into storage facilities, as was true in Mesopotamian society, where it went into the temple treasuries (*EncJud*, 15:1158). From there it could be distributed as needed to people whenever they made pilgrimages to the central sanctuary. The stored food could also have been drawn upon in the third year when the charity tithe remained in the villages, as well as in the seventh year when there was no harvest (cf. Lev 25:20-22). Grain could easily be stored (Gen 41:47-57); the same with wine, which was being stored in a temple chamber when Jeremiah brought the Rechabites there to give Judah an object lesson on faithfulness (Jer 35:2). The temple in Jerusalem had chambers for precisely this purpose (Neh 10:38-40[37-39]; 12:44; 13:4-9, 12-13; 1 Chr 28:12; 2 Chr 31:11-12). Surrounding the holy place and holy of holies was an outer structure of side chambers (**לְשָׁכוֹת**; **צְלָעוֹת**), built in three levels (1 Kgs 6:5-6), over which the Levitical priests had jurisdiction (1 Chr 23:27-28). Some of these chambers were storage facilities for temple vessels, frankincense, cereal offerings, and incoming tithes. In the postexilic period, the prophet Malachi admonishes the people, saying: "Bring the full tithes into the storehouse, that there may be food in my house" (Mal 3:10).

your grain, your wine, and your oil. Representative agricultural produce, not the whole of it. In Mesopotamia the tithe consisted of agricultural produce, cattle and sheep, slaves, donkeys, wool, cloth, wood, metal products, silver and gold (*EncJud*, 15:1158).

in order that you may learn to fear Yahweh your God all the days. Tithing will teach one to fear Yahweh throughout life. On "fearing Yahweh" in Deuteronomy, see Note for 4:10.

24-26 If people live too far from the central sanctuary, which in the 7th cent. would be Jerusalem, they need not bring their tithe or firstborns with them, which would be an extraordinary burden. Instead they may convert their value into silver for the purchase of food and sacrificial offerings at the central sanctuary. According to Lev 27:31, when tithes were converted into money the worshipper had to give one-fifth more. In Mesopotamia, tithes could also be converted into money (*EncJud*, 15:1158).

24 *when Yahweh your God will bless you.* A passing reminder, repeated in v. 29, that all yield from the land will be a mark of Yahweh's blessing upon the Israelite farmer. On the "blessing" motif in Deuteronomy, see Note for 2:7.

25 *then you shall turn it into silver.* וְנָתַתָּה בַּכָּסֶף. By the 7th cent. silver was being used as money, although coinage came later (see Note for 22:19).

and you shall bind the silver in your hand. וְצַרְתָּ הַכֶּסֶף בְּיָדְךָ. The silver is to be put in a moneybag of some sort — perhaps a kerchief tied in a knot or a sealed pouch made from skin — and attached to the hand (Prov 7:20: "and the pouch of silver he took in his hand"). The root צרר means "to tie up." Silver pieces found in a pile on the floor at Tel Miqne-Ekron contained traces of textile impressions, suggesting that they may have been wrapped in a cloth bag (Gitin and Golani 2001, 31; Kletter 2004, 208). On moneybags, see also Gen 42:35; 2 Kgs 5:23; 12:10; Sir 18:33.

26 *And you shall turn the silver into anything that your soul desires, into one of the herd or into one of the flock, or into wine or into beer, yes, into anything that your soul asks you for.* The tithe and firstborns can both be converted into money. With such a liberal provision as the present one, we can infer that the tithe must have consisted of more than just grain, wine, and oil.

that your soul desires . . . that your soul asks you for. Hebrew נֶפֶשׁ ("soul") in the first instance refers to the whole person (NRSV), whereas in the circumlocution that follows it becomes nearly synonymous with "appetite" (RSV; cf. 12:20; 23:25[24]; Prov 23:2).

wine . . . beer. Hebrew שֵׁכָר (AV: "strong drink") is "beer" made from barley (Homan 2004a; 2004b; KBL³), thus a potentially intoxicating beverage. For the two drinks the Targums have "wine new or old."

and you shall eat there before Yahweh your God, and you shall be glad, you and your house. On the admonition in Deuteronomy to "be glad" at festival time, see Note for 12:7.

27 The LXX omits "you shall not forsake him," simply adding the Levite to the "house(hold)" as another glad participant at the communal feast. The Levites, in either case, are resident in Israelite cities (12:12) and are invited to join the families in celebrating at the central sanctuary. They have no agricultural yield from which to give a tithe and in the 7th cent. are largely unemployed, dependent on charity due to closure of the local sanctuaries. This has deprived them of income they received formerly. Milgrom (2001, 2433) goes so far as to say: "The Levites are invited to the meal not as a matter of Deuteronomy's well-attested charity, but as a consequence of Deuteronomy's guilt for having deprived the Levites of their prior rights to the tithe." Nevertheless, according to Deuteronomy the Levites still receive portions of all sacrificial animals as well

Deuteronomy 15

as the firstfruits of grain, wine, oil, and wool (18:1-4). Some Levites owned property, real estate or personal, which could be sold if necessary (18:8; cf. J. M. P. Smith 1914, 123).

28 This third-year tithe, which is called "the year of the tithe" in 26:12, receives no mention in the other OT law codes. In the third and sixth years of a seven-year cycle this tithe is to remain in the town, where it is to be used to benefit the poor and needy. It is not brought to the central sanctuary. Here, again, the tithes were doubtless placed in storage facilities and doled out as needed (J. M. P. Smith 1914, 123). As Tigay remarks, it is unlikely that the poor were fed only two years out of seven.

all the tithe. NJV: "the full tithe." Cf. v. 22: "*all the yield of your seed.*" In the liturgy of 26:13-15, the worshipper states that *all* the tithe was paid, also that no portion was defiled or put to another use. See also Mal 3:10 on giving the "full tithe." Rabbi Gamaliel I (The Elder), grandson of Hillel and teacher of the Apostle Paul (Acts 22:3), cautioned people: "Accustom not thyself to tithe by conjecture" (*m. 'Abot* 1:16), i.e., there must be no guesswork in tithing.

deposit it within your gates. Targums^{OnqPsJ}: "store it in your cities."

29 *and the Levite shall come . . . and the sojourner, and the orphan, and the widow who is within your gates, and they shall eat and become sated.* Here the sojourner, orphan, and widow, who are accorded special treatment in Deuteronomy (see Note for 10:18), join the Levite as recipients of the third-year tithe. Israelites are told to care particularly for the sojourner, orphan, and widow because Yahweh does (10:18-19; in the NT, see Jas 1:27). On Yahweh's promise that Israel will eat and become sated in the promised land, see Note for 6:11.

in order that Yahweh your God may bless you in all the work of your hand that you do. On this expression, see Note for 2:7. Giving a tithe to the needy will not lead to economic hardship; rather, it will bring greater prosperity because Yahweh's blessing will rest upon the worshipper. Deuteronomy stresses the point that Yahweh's future blessing will come from charitable acts in the present (15:10; 23:21[20]; 24:19).

15:1 *After seven years' time you shall make a remission.* This opening statement pertains only to debt remission (von Rad; cf. T^{OnqPsJ}), which is dealt with in vv. 1-11. The Targums take קץ to mean "end," but here and in 31:10 the term is better rendered "(period of) time," which is its meaning in Jer 34:14 (Lundbom 2004a, 563). If קץ is translated "end," the remission will not occur until the end of seven years (Maimonides: "at sunset on the last day of the seventh year"; cf. Tigay 1996, 370 n. 8). But if it means "period of time," then the remission will occur as soon as the seventh year has arrived (Driver), which would be at the end of six years. The LXX's Δι' ἑπτὰ ἐτῶν ("Every seven years") supports the latter interpretation. Hebrew slaves go free at the end of six years

(v. 12; Jer 34:14). In this year of remission, called "the seventh year" in v. 9, the law is to be read publicly before the people (31:10-11), which will serve to remind them of this obligation.

remission. Hebrew שְׁמִטָּה is lit. "a letting go, a release." The verb שׁמט occurs in Exod 23:11, suggesting to some (Driver; von Rad) that the present law about remitting debts has developed from an older law in Exod 23:10-11 about leaving the land in remission (= uncultivated) during the seventh year. Leviticus 25:1-7 (H) contains yet another law about giving the land a Sabbath rest. Neither the Covenant Code nor the Holiness Code says anything about debt remission, the subject being omitted also in the Qumran *Temple Scroll* (Yadin 1983, 2:246). Deuteronomy, for its part, is silent about the land lying fallow in the seventh year. Whether the present law has developed from Exod 23:10-11 is impossible to determine. About all one can say is that both laws reflect the same ideology: the land and indebted Israelites are both entitled to a remission in the seventh year.

The Priestly law in Lev 25:1-7 differs in important respects from the laws in Exod 23:10-11 and here, particularly in that it provides for debt-remission only in the Jubilee Year. Tigay believes, therefore, that "the laws of Leviticus 25 are not based on those of Exodus 21-23, and in important respects are incompatible with them" (1996, 467). Weinfeld (1972, 224), in comparing the law in Lev 25:1-7 with the present law, says the two are not mutually exclusive, and he believes both were likely observed. It is simply that "The Priestly author is interested only in the sacral aspect of the seventh year, while the author of Deuteronomy is interested solely in its social aspect and completely ignores the sacral side." In Neh 10:32(31) the laws of land and debt remission are mentioned together. Both act to benefit the poor. Some have questioned whether the debt remission was to be a cancellation or simply a one-year suspension of the power to call the debt in. But it is now widely agreed, particularly in light of v. 9, that the remission was to be a permanent cancellation. Philo (*Virt.* 122) took it to be a cancellation, and this is the view expressed in the Mishnah (*Šeb.* 10:1).

2 This law states that creditors, in the seventh year, must cancel all debts of fellow Israelites; they must not press for repayment, which under normal circumstances they would do. Creditors will also be obliged to return any pledges taken as security (see Note for 24:6). In the postexilic period, after a covenant was made to walk in God's law, people agreed to remit loans in the seventh year as the law here required (Neh 10:32[31]). More than a century earlier, across the Aegean (594), the reforming archon of Athens, Solon, alleviated a crisis by cancelling debts of the poor who could not pay them back (French 1956, 21; Yamauchi 1980, 276-77). On one of the Aramaic ostraca from Arad (4th cent.) is this inscription (no. 41): "Who demands the money [which he had lent]," which could be a demand for payment of a debt or a decree proclaiming debt-remission (Y. Aharoni 1981, 168; Weinfeld 1982a, 498). Problems of indebtedness were compounded in antiquity by creditors charging exorbitant interest rates (Mendelsohn 1949, 23). For this reason, and in keeping with its overall aim to assert God's sovereignty over the created order and make possible a more egalitarian society (Greenberg 1990, 107), Deuteronomy also disallowed the charging of interest to fellow Israelites (23:20-21[19-20]). The interest-free loans anticipated here were not to be for business purposes or other commercial ventures, but for the relief of poor and insolvent people who might be victims of poverty due to war, famine, pestilence, a death in the family (2 Kgs 4:1), or some other adversity over which they had no control (Exod 22:24[25]; Lev 25:35-37). An old Babylonian text (1646-1626), entitled "The Edict of Ammisaduqa," records a king's cancellation of debts and obligations at the beginning of his reign. He did this by means of a *mīšarum* (= justice) act, which contained other charitable provisions (*ANET*³, 526-28; J. Finkelstein 1961, 101; Lemche 1979, 11-15). His cancellation, however, did not apply to business debts (*ANET*³, 527 §8).

And this is the manner of the remission. וְזֶה דְּבַר הַשְּׁמִטָּה. Translating here with the AV and RSV (T^Onq: "the nature of the remission"). A similar phrase occurs in *m. Šeb.* 10:8: וזה דבר השמטה, "And this is the manner of the release" (Blackman 1977, 1:286-87). The LXX translates דָּבָר with πρόσταγμα ("command"), as it does in 19:4, giving דָּבָר more the sense of "law." S. R. Driver (1890, xv-xvi) found the same idiom as here in the Siloam Tunnel Inscription: וזה היה דבר הנקבה ("And this was the manner of the piercing through").

every owner of a loan in his hand. I.e., "every holder of a loan" (Friedman). R. North (1954, 199) takes יָד ("hand") to denote power, translating יָדוֹ "(at) his disposition." The LXX, perhaps to avoid the Hebrew idiom, translates: πᾶν χρέος ἴδιον ("every private debt"), but 4QDeut^c joins Sam, T, and S in reading MT's כָּל־בַּעַל ("every owner").

his fellow or his brother. אֶת־רֵעֵהוּ וְאֶת־אָחִיו. "Brother" often has broader meaning in the OT than blood brother, sometimes meaning "fellow-Israelite." Here the terms "fellow" and "brother" appear to be synonymous or nearly so (Driver), for which reason doubts have arisen about the reading. Talmon (1960, 168) thinks we have a doublet resulting from conflation. The LXX omits "his fellow or," but this can be due to haplography (homoeoarcton: את . . . את). Both terms should probably be retained, since "fellow" (רֵעַ) is used earlier in the verse and "brother/brethren" (אָח, אַחִים) are used subsequently in vv. 3-11 (5 times). The two terms could also be read in apposition: "his fellow, that is, his brother" (cf. Tigay).

because a remission to Yahweh has been proclaimed. The proclamation is to be formal and public (Lev 25:9-10; Jer 34:8; 36:9; Isa 61:1-2). Targum^PsJ has: "when the Court has announced a remission before the Lord." In the Edict of Ammisaduqa cited above, it was the Babylonian king who issued the *mīšarum*

Deuteronomy 15

proclamation. Similarly, in Jesus' parable of the Unmerciful Servant, it is a king who remits the first debt owed by a servant (Matt 18:23-27). But here the proclamation is issued "to Yahweh," i.e., in Yahweh's honor (Driver; cf. Exod 12:11, 14, 42; Lev 25:2), and by implication it is also issued under his divine authority.

3 *With the foreigner you may press.* Remission of debts does not apply to "the foreigner" (הַנָּכְרִי), from whom one may press for repayment. Foreigners will enter the country for purposes of trade (Driver; G. E. Wright; Tigay), for which reason they do not benefit also from the law disallowing loaning at interest (23:21[20]). King Ammisaduqa cancelled debts only of Akkadians and Amorites living in Babylon (*ANET*³, 526-28).

let your hand remit. Reading תַּשְׁמֵט as an H-stem jussive (Driver).

4 Reading with T^{Onq}: "There *should* be no poor among you." The reason is that Yahweh promises to bless Israel, i.e., give it prosperity and dominance in the world (v. 6). The Deuteronomic preacher thus pauses to express a qualified hope for the future. He cannot say for certain that needy souls will never exist in the land, because they will (v. 11). Also, the hope expressed is conditional: It will be realized only if Israel is careful to do Yahweh's commandments (v. 5). So in projecting himself back into the presettlement era, the Deuteronomic preacher is not given to a utopian idea (*pace* Driver), one conflicting with the realism expressed in vv. 7-11. But he is making a very positive statement, much like the one in 30:11-14 about people being fully able to do the commands. The early church realized the same hope for a time; Acts 4:34 says "there was not a needy person among them."

However. אֶפֶס כִּי. This construction qualifies what has been stated in vv. 1-3 (cf. Num 13:28; Judg 4:9; Amos 9:8). After presenting a law giving debt-relief to the poor, Moses now tells the people that there should be no need for such a law, since Yahweh promises to bless Israel with abundant harvests and economic success if it obeys Yahweh's commands.

for Yahweh will surely bless you. I.e., with prosperity and dominance over other nations (v. 6). The promise is emphatic. "Blessing" permeates this entire passage on "seven-year" remissions (vv. 4, 6, 10, 14, 18) and is a key theme throughout Deuteronomy (see Note for 2:7).

in the land that Yahweh your God is giving to you for an inheritance to possess it. A variant of the stereotyped expression appearing throughout Deuteronomy (4:21, 38; 12:9-10; 15:4; 19:3, 10, 14; 20:16; 21:23; 24:4; 25:19; 26:1; Driver 1895, lxxviii-lxxix no. 4; Weinfeld 1972, 341 no. 1). The "inheritance/heritage" (נַחֲלָה) Yahweh will give Israel is the promised land, and through Joshua its possession will be secured (1:38; 3:28; 31:7). Jeremiah says later that it was a beautiful gift (Jer 2:7; 3:19). Background for Israel's gift of land is contained in the Song of Moses (32:8-9), where it says that a decision regarding land distribution to the nations was made soon after the creation of the world. The term "inheritance/

Deuteronomy 15

heritage" can also refer to the people Israel (2 Kgs 21:14; Jer 12:7-9; Ps 74:2). The usages appear together in Deut 4:20-21. The covenant relationship is one of reciprocity: Yahweh is Israel's portion; Israel is Yahweh's tribal heritage (Jer 10:16; 51:19). In Jer 2:7 the (promised) land is called Yahweh's "inheritance/heritage."

5 Here is the condition for eliminating poverty. In Deuteronomy, "obeying Yahweh's voice" means doing the commandments (see Note for 13:5). On the stock expression "be careful to do," see Note for 5:1.

if only. רַק אִם. Another emphatic construction (cf. 1 Kgs 8:25; 2 Kgs 21:8).

6 *For Yahweh your God is blessing you, just as he promised you.* The verb for "blessing" is a perfect, which should perhaps be translated present (T^{PsJ}). In v. 4, blessing is promised for the future; here it is a present reality. The Deuteronomic preacher knows, however, that Yahweh promised Israel blessing ages ago; cf. Exod 23:25, and the promise of blessing to Abraham (Gen 12:2-3; 18:18; 22:17, and passim) and to Sarah (Gen 17:16). Rashi cites in the present connection the promise of blessing for covenant obedience in 28:3-12.

and you will lend to many nations, but you, you will not borrow. Lending indicates wealth and well-being; borrowing indicates poverty. See again the promised blessing of 28:12. But if Israel does not keep the commandments, 28:43-44 reverses this blessing into a curse: "The sojourner . . . shall lend to you, but you, you shall not lend to him; he, he shall be the head, and you, you shall be the tail."

and you will lend. וְהַעֲבַטְתָּ. The H-stem here and in v. 8 means "lend on pledge to" (Rashi; Driver; Moran). On pledges taken as security for loans, see Note for 24:6.

and you will rule over many nations, but they will not rule over you. The ability to lend goes hand in hand with dominant status (Prov 22:7: "The rich rules over the poor, and the borrower is the slave of the lender"). Yahweh promised Abraham that he would become a mighty nation and would dominate other nations (Gen 18:18; 22:17). The same promise was repeated to Israel (Deut 28:1). Josephus (*Ant.* 14.115) quoted Strabo as having said about the Jews even in dispersion: "This people has already made its way into every city, and it is not easy to find any place in the habitable world which has not received this nation and in which it has not made its power felt" (Loeb).

7-8 The Deuteronomic preacher returns to the realism underlying the promulgation of this law (vv. 1-3), warning potential creditors not to refuse a loan to the needy because the debt may be remitted in the seventh year. The call here is for an open heart and an open hand. Israelites are to be generous and lend to needy persons in their towns, whatever their need may be.

a needy person. The "needy (person)" (אֶבְיוֹן) is usually someone poor in material goods (15:7-9, 11; 24:14), although he can also be one who is oppressed and powerless (Amos 2:6-7; 5:12; Jer 20:13). The Psalms speak often about the

Deuteronomy 15

plight of the poor (עָנִי) and needy and the help they should receive (Pss 9:19[18]; 12:6[5]; 35:10; 37:14; 40:18[17], and passim).

you shall not harden your heart. לֹא תְאַמֵּץ אֶת־לְבָבְךָ. The verb אמץ is used with God as subject in 2:30 and with Zedekiah as subject in 2 Chr 36:13. In the NT, see 1 John 3:17: "But if any one has the world's goods, and sees his brother in need, yet closes his heart against him, how does God's love abide in him?"

and you shall not close your hand from your needy brother. The image changes to one of a tight fist (T^{Onq}). Barkay (1991, 241) reexamined a bowl from an Iron Age cemetery in Beth Shemesh containing a roughly-chiseled inscription, "your brother" (אחך), and speculated that the bowl may have been used at a worship site to collect offerings for the "needy brother," which would then have been distributed by priests to the needy.

whatever his need may be. But Rashi says one is not commanded to make him rich.

9 *Be careful for yourself, lest there be a good-for-nothing thought within your heart: "The seventh year, the year of remission, is near," and your eye be evil against your needy brother, and you do not give to him.* A warning not to refuse a loan to the needy brother because the year of remission approaches. Such a hesitancy to loan would doubtless develop and did, in fact, in later Judaism (1st cent. B.C. to 1st cent. A.D.), where a means to circumvent debt-remission was devised. Before making a loan, a creditor could present a declaration to the court, signed by witnesses, that his loan not be subject to cancellation in the seventh year. This declaration, established by Hillel the Elder (*m. Šeb.* 10:3), was called a *prozbul*. Hillel devised the *prozbul* because people were refusing to loan at the approach of the seventh year. Nevertheless, the Psalms praise righteous souls who are liberal in giving and ever willing to lend (Pss 37:25-26; 112:5). Such people are known for their sense of justice, will not suffer want themselves, and their children will become a blessing.

Be careful for yourself. The premier warning in Deuteronomy (see Note for 4:6).

a good-for-nothing thought. דָּבָר ... בְלִיַּעַל. Or "a worthless thought." Cf. "worthless men" (בְּנֵי־בְלִיַּעַל) in 13:14(13).

and your eye be evil. וְרָעָה עֵינְךָ. This expression is unique to Deuteronomy (15:9; 28:54, 56) among the books of the Pentateuch (Daube 1969a, 51) and means being envious or grudging towards someone (Driver; cf. Prov 23:6; 28:22; Tob 4:6; Sir 14:3-10). One of Jesus' parables highlights a grudging attitude toward a generous owner who overpaid hired laborers (Matt 20:15).

and he cry out to Yahweh against you, and it be a sin in you. The brother refused a loan will have only Yahweh to cry to, and when he does so, the refusal will be reckoned in you as a sin. The same will happen if you afflict the widow or the orphan (Exod 22:21-22[22-23]), if you fail to restore the pledge of a poor

Deuteronomy 15

man before sundown (Exod 22:25-26[26-27]), or if you fail to pay the poor man his wages on the day he earns it (Deut 24:15). Why are all of these a sin? Because Yahweh hears the cry of the poor, and unlike the hard-hearted and tight-fisted person, he is gracious.

and he cry out. The verb קרא means "call in a loud voice, proclaim, shout" (KBL³).

and it be a sin in you. וְהָיָה בְךָ חֵטְא. Or "and you incur guilt" (T^Onq), where "guilt" = "the guilt resulting from sin." The expression occurs also in 23:22, 23[21, 22] (with "not"); and in 24:15 (Driver 1895, lxxxi no. 36; Weinfeld 1972, 356 no. 5).

10 *You shall surely give to him.* The construction is emphatic. But how many times must one do this? Rashi says "even a hundred times" (cf. Matt 18:21-22). The LXX adds from v. 8: "and surely lend him enough for his need, whatever his need may be," which Wevers (1995, 259) thinks may be to avoid the possible idea that the loan is an outright handout. But the addition could be due to dittography, since the word immediately preceding the phrase — here and in v. 8 — is αὐτῷ ("to him"). The Sam, T, S, Vg, and 4QpaleoDeut^r do not have the added words.

and your heart shall not be evil when you give to him. What is more, you shall not give when your heart is not in it (heart = will). Hebrew לֹא־יֵרַע לְבָבְךָ requires a more vigorous translation than "your heart shall not be sad" (so Driver, who cites 1 Sam 1:8 and Prov 25:20; cf. T^Onq: "and do not feel bad"). Note the balancing of "evil heart" with "evil eye" in v. 9. In v. 7, the "hard heart" was balanced with the "tight fist." But Driver rightly points out that רָע ("evil") is a correlative of טוֹב ("good"), which, when referring to the heart, implies cheerfulness (28:47; 1 Kgs 8:66). One is then to loan willingly and cheerfully. Paul says that God loves a cheerful giver (2 Cor 9:7).

for on account of this thing Yahweh your God will bless you in all your work and in every undertaking of your hand. Two stock Deuteronomic expressions in combination (see Notes for 2:7 and 12:7). The point being made here is that Yahweh will compensate the generous lender for any loss he might incur (cf. Lev 25:20-21). On the Deuteronomic theme that blessing will come as a result of charitable action, see also 14:29; 23:21(20); 24:19.

for on account of. כִּי בִּגְלַל. This uncommon conjunction, בִּגְלַל ("on account of"), occurs also in 1:37; 18:12; 1 Kgs 14:16; Jer 11:17; 15:4.

11 *For the needy person will not cease from the midst of the land.* כִּי לֹא־יֶחְדַּל אֶבְיוֹן מִקֶּרֶב הָאָרֶץ. Translators ancient and modern have taken the verb חדל to mean "cease," which gives a proverbial statement that the needy (or poor) will never cease in the land (T^Onq; Mark 14:7; Matt 26:11; John 12:8). Yet, as was noted earlier, this seems to contradict the optimism of v. 4, even if we translate there: "There should not be a needy person among you." The tension is apparent in two Targum readings, T^Nf and T^PsJ, where, in different ways, the statement about needy persons never ceasing to exist in the land is preceded by a conditional word about Israel keeping the law. Targum^Nf reads: "For if the children of Israel keep the instruction of the law and do the commandments there will not be any poor among them" (McNamara 1997, 85). Targum^PsJ reads: "For because the house of Israel does not rest in the commandments of the Law, the needy are not ceasing from the midst of the land" (Clark 1998, 46). The traditional reading may in fact be the correct one, but excellent sense can be made of the Hebrew if we read חדל II, meaning "to grow fat" (KBL³). Employing this verb, the statement would be: "The needy will never grow fat in the midst of the land" (Freedman, Lundbom, ḥādal, in *TDOT*, 4:221), where one would also have to read the prefixed מ on מִקֶּרֶב הָאָרֶץ as "in," not "from," a meaning attested in Ugaritic. It improves the translation of מֵרָחֶם ("in the womb") in Jer 20:17 (Lundbom 1999, 872). The idea will then be that loans made to those standing to benefit from the seventh-year remission will not contribute to the needy becoming wealthy. Such a thing will never happen, which oddly enough, brings us back to the traditional rendering about the needy never ceasing from the land. Since the Hebrew verb can carry both meanings, we could also have from the Deuteronomic preacher a deliberate *double entendre*.

Therefore I am commanding you: You shall surely open your hand to your brother, to your poor, and to your needy in your land. Moses' argument aimed at moving Israelites to charity is now complete. He can thus command people to open hands to their poor and needy brethren. "Your brother" here becomes synonymous with "your poor" and "your needy." The two terms, עָנִי and אֶבְיוֹן, occur together again in 24:14. On the expression "Therefore I am commanding you (to do this thing today)," see also 5:15 (in the third person, referring to Yahweh); 15:15; 19:7; 24:18, 22 (Driver 1895, lxxxiii no. 57; Weinfeld 1972, 357 no. 8).

your land. I.e., the land you are about to possess.

12 Hebrew men and women, after being enslaved to one of their own for six years, are to be given their freedom in the seventh year. This release will not be general, nor will it occur on a date predetermined by the calendar. The release of slaves in the Jubilee (Lev 25:39-46) has both of these characteristics (see Zedekiah's release in Jer 34:8-10), likewise general slave-releases known to have been carried out elsewhere in the ANE (Lundbom 2004a, 558-59). Here the Hebrew slave goes free whenever his or her six years is up. The present law has a parallel in the Code of Hammurabi (CH 117), which states that a citizen's wife, son, or daughter sold into slavery because of an unpaid debt is required to serve only three years. In the fourth year he or she must go free (*ANET*³, 170-71). Mendelsohn (1949, 75) says the reason for this law is that three years' service in the house of the creditor was deemed sufficient to work off any debt. The suggestion has been made by Carmichael (2000b, 520) that the biblical law is influenced by the story of Jacob and Laban, where Jacob agrees to serve (עבד) Laban six years for each of his two wives (Gen 29:18, 30).

The present law aims at limiting the servitude of Israelites reduced to this indignity by hunger, indebtedness, or other misfortune, casting them headlong into the ranks of the poor (Mendelsohn 1949, 23; *IDB*, 4:385). Failure to repay a loan, if it occurred before the year of remission, could result in the debtor being forced to serve his creditor or be sold as a slave to someone else. His wife and children could be sold, or all of them could be sold together. In Nehemiah's time, a major crisis developed first because of a famine, then when people had to mortgage property and borrow money at (high) interest from fellow-Israelites, and then when some debtors could not repay the loans and had to sell their sons and daughters into slavery (Neh 5:1-13).

The present law reworks an earlier law in Exod 21:2-11, embellishing its legal provisions with the homiletical rhetoric of the Deuteronomic preacher, but also making substantive changes, e.g., in putting the Hebrew woman on an equal footing with the Hebrew man. In Exodus 21, the wife of the Hebrew slave goes free only if she came in with her husband. If the slave came in single and the master gave him a wife, that wife would have to remain with the master after her husband went free. Also, under the old law, if a man sold his daughter into slavery, she would not go free as male slaves do (Exod 21:7). But here in Deuteronomy, both the Hebrew man and Hebrew woman — without qualification — go free in the seventh year. Von Rad thinks that in the meantime the woman has become capable of owning property (2 Kgs 8:3) and can therefore sell herself into slavery if that becomes necessary. On the advanced status of woman as reflected in the book of Deuteronomy, see Daube 1978; 1981, 100. But Tigay is not so sure that the "Hebrewess" in the present verse is the "daughter" of Exod 21:7-11. He says the two laws could well refer to different cases.

By the mid-8th cent. the poor in northern Israel were faring badly at the hands of the rich (Amos 2:6; 8:6). The prophet Amos is outraged because the righteous is sold for silver and the needy for a pair of shoes. These individuals seized by the rich and made slaves were poor folk unable to pay their debts (Mendelsohn 1949, 32-33; Sarna 1973, 148). In Judah, problems of another sort surfaced in the time of Jeremiah. There the present law mandating the release of Hebrew slaves after six years had not been enforced, apparently for some time (Jer 34:14). That this law was difficult to enforce may be inferred also from the parallel law in Lev 25:39-46, where there is no release at all after six years, only a general release in the Jubilee. The omission of the present law in the Qumran *Temple Scroll* (Yadin 1983, 2:246) may be in deference to P legislation. On slavery in the ANE and the OT, see Mendelsohn 1949; "Slavery in the OT," in *IDB*, 4:383-91; de Vaux 1965, 82-83; and M. Dandamayev, "Slavery (ANE and Old Testament)," in *ABD*, 4:58-65.

a Hebrew or a Hebrewess. הָעִבְרִי אוֹ הָעִבְרִיָּה. These terms are unusual, although in Jer 34:9 they appear in a context similar to the present one. When "Hebrew" occurs elsewhere in the OT, it usually retains its older association with slavery and is spoken chiefly by foreigners or else by an Israelite identifying himself to a foreigner (Gen 39:14, 17; 40:15; 1 Sam 4:6; 14:21; cf. de Vaux 1965, 83). Von Rad thinks that in Deuteronomy the term "Hebrew" no longer retains its older (lower) class meaning (cf. Akk: *'apiru*) and is on its way to naming one's nationality (Gen 14:13; Jonah 1:9). But one cannot be so sure, since the present law deals with an Israelite again being reduced to slavery. "Hebrew" and "Hebrewess" may have been deliberately chosen by the Deuteronomic preacher because they retained overtones of their ancient meaning. The two terms, in any case, broaden "brother" to include both males and females. Driver thinks "Hebrewess" would not have been added here unless the present legislation in some way modified the law of Exodus 21.

is sold to you. יִמָּכֵר לְךָ. The N-stem of מכר can mean either "be sold" or "sell oneself" (BDB; KBL[3]). Rashi thinks the person here will have been sold to a fellow-Israelite by someone else; he will not have sold himself into slavery, a circumstance dealt with in the legislation of Lev 25:47-55. But Rashi goes on to argue that the person in question will have been enslaved because of theft, which interprets the law too narrowly. Von Rad says: "Here [the law in its earlier form] no longer has to do with the purchase of a man who is not free, or in any case of one who is not of the same blood, but of an Israelite who once was free and has sold himself into slavery" (1966, 107). On the basis of vv. 16-17, where the Hebrew slave may decide to remain with his master after his six years are up, it is argued by Mendelsohn (1949, 16-19) that "self-sale" or "voluntary slavery" did exist in ancient Israel, only in this case the slavery becomes permanent, as it becomes at Nuzi. In the present situation a person is enslaved because of indebtedness, rendering him powerless to avoid being sold and, for all practical purposes, making his slavery enforced rather than voluntary.

you shall send him away free from you. תְּשַׁלְּחֶנּוּ חָפְשִׁי מֵעִמָּךְ. The verb שלח + חָפְשִׁי(ם) means "send away free" (Jer 34:9; Isa 58:6).

13 The release of the Hebrew slave shall be like Yahweh's release of Israel from slavery, when he saw to it that people received gifts from the Egyptians upon their departure (Exod 3:21-22; 11:2-3; 12:35-36; Ps 105:37). There may also be an allusion to the Jacob and Laban story, where there is a question as to whether Jacob will receive departing gifts — here consisting of wives, children, herds, and flocks — after completing service to Laban (Gen 31:17-54). Jacob leaves without telling Laban, later accusing his uncle of intending to send him away empty-handed (Daube 1963, 66-72; Carmichael 2000b, 521-22). The law in Exod 21:2-11 says nothing about lavishing gifts upon the freed slave.

14 The Israelites departing Egypt were given gold and silver jewelry, also clothing. The verb ענק in the H-stem means "to make a necklace," with the Infinitive-Imperfect construction reminding the slaveowner to be sure to perform this act of kindness. Rashi says the cognate noun (עֲנָק) denotes an ornament worn high up on the body, where it will be conspicuous. In this way, the goodness of the one freeing his slave will be seen by all. Necklaces were typically made of silver, gold, and jewels (Judg 8:26; Cant 4:9). Here the verb is used metaphorically to mean "equip liberally." The one freeing his slave is to lavish gifts of sheep or goats, grain, and wine upon the freed slave. These gifts were later taken to be simply representative, with comparable items also being acceptable (Rashi; cf. *b. Qidd.* 17a). Tigay compares this practice of giving gifts to the departing slave with the modern custom of giving severance pay to a person at the termination of his employment.

from your threshing floor and from your winepress. "Threshing floor" and "winepress" are a common OT pair (16:13; 2 Kgs 6:27; Hos 9:2). The modern equivalent would be "food and drink."

as Yahweh your God has blessed you, you shall give to him. Here the Deuteronomic preacher makes the point that one is under obligation to give because Yahweh has blessed him in times past. Elsewhere the emphasis is on reaping future blessing because of charitable action in the present (see v. 10). On the divine name, 1QDeut² has אדני for MT's יהוה (Barthélemy and Milik 1955, 58).

15 A second reason for this command to release Hebrew slaves after six years of servitude: Israel was herself a slave in Egypt, and Yahweh ransomed her (see Note for 8:2). People are to emulate the kindness and generosity of Yahweh. Let Israel never forget Yahweh's most gracious act, upon which the entire law is based. The same reminder is given in 24:18, where the Israelite is told not to pervert justice to the sojourner, orphan, and widow.

therefore I am commanding you this thing today. On this recurring directive, see Note for 15:11. The term "today" appears frequently in Deuteronomy (see Note for 1:10).

16-17 Hebrew slaves, if they wish to remain with their master after their six-year term is up, can do so, in which case they will become indentured for life. The old law in Exodus 21 anticipates that the male slave may want to remain permanently with his master because the wife given to him in slavery cannot go free with him. Also, any children born to the two are likewise unable to go free. That may still obtain under the present law if the man completes six years before his wife does. Yet once the wife has completed six years of servitude, she too can go free. Because the slave here may decide to remain with his master because he loves both him and his household, and because it has been good for him in the master's service, we may be able to infer that slavery for a Hebrew or Hebrewess in ancient Israel was not that harsh (Driver; Tigay; cf.

5:14b; 12:12, 18; 16:11, 14). This finds indirect support in the Leviticus law, where the master is told to treat his fellow Hebrew not as a slave, but as a hired servant or sojourner (Lev 25:39-40). In Exod 21:6 the rite for making a slave permanent has a sacral character: The master is to bring him "to God," which must mean going to the local sanctuary. Hebrew הָאֱלֹהִים is not to be translated "(the) gods" in this verse, as argued by Carmichael (2000b, 521). Carmichael thinks the Exodus law alludes to the "household gods" belonging to Laban (Gen 31:19, 30-35) and that the law has the slave brought to the master's house and the household gods residing there. The "to God" reference is omitted here in v. 17, indicating that the Deuteronomic law has lost its sacral character. Also, in the 7th cent. there are no more local sanctuaries.

then you shall take an awl and put it in his ear and in the door. I.e., to pierce his ear (Rashi). Driver thinks the ear-piercing in Exod 21:6 would have been done on a door of the sanctuary, but here in Deuteronomy it is done at the master's house. Earlier the ceremony was official and public; now it is purely a domestic affair. Piercing the slave at the master's house makes for a symbolic act: the slave is now permanently attached to his master and his house. In other ANE law codes, slaves are punished by having their ears pierced (MAL A 44; *ANET*³, 184) or completely cut off (CH 282; *ANET*³, 177).

In antiquity, slaves were "marked" in the same way animals were (Mendelsohn 1949, 42-50). Fugitive slaves in Old Babylonia were branded, probably with a hot iron, and if the "slave mark" was to be removed later, the skill of a surgeon would be required (CH 226-27; *ANET*³, 176). In the Neo-Babylonian period, branding was done on temple slaves and on animals. The practice survives today in marking ownership of range cattle. In Neo-Babylonian texts are also numerous references to tattooing the name of the owner on a slave's hand or wrist, a practice that carried over into the Persian period and later. Also, there are references in Old Babylonian texts to slave marks being "broken" at the time of the slave's release, suggesting that the mark may have been a small tablet of clay or metal hung on a chain around the slave's neck, wrist, or ankles. We have evidence of slave tags from Nuzi. Clay tags on cords, tied around the necks or horns of animals, were also widely used in ancient Babylonia. In our own day, identification tags are attached to the ears of domestic cattle. Mendelsohn suggests that the ear-piercing here, which was probably a small nearly invisible hole, was for pushing through a ring or cord on which was fastened a tag made of clay or metal. But he does not exclude the possibility of a tattooing mark, since elsewhere in the Bible tattoos signify possession (Gen 4:15; Ezek 9:4; Isa 44:5; 49:16).

forever. Rashi says עֹלָם does not mean for all time, but only until the Jubilee Year when the slave shall return to his family (Lev 25:10). But the talmudic sages were in doubt whether the law of the Jubilee was ever enforced, since it was not observed at all during the Second Temple period (Mendelsohn 1949, 90; EncJud, 14:578-82).

to your maidservant you shall do the same. Rashi says the woman will not have her ear pierced. But the plain meaning of the present words is that the rite for her will be the same as for the man. In the Code of Hammurabi (CH 146; ANET³, 172), female slaves receive a "slave mark."

18 The owner releasing his Hebrew slave after six years of labor is told in conclusion that the release should not appear too difficult a thing to do. He has received a handsome return. What is more, any incurred loss will be more than compensated for by Yahweh's blessing on future endeavors. This homiletical word is not given in Exod 21:2-6. The main question here is what does "double the wages" mean. It has been suggested that reference may be to the custom of employing a hired man for three years. Perhaps the owner is being told that he has received double the return he would have received from a hired man for three years, thus adequate compensation (Moran; cf. Isa 16:14). Moran also cites the Sumerian Lipit-Ishtar Code (LI 14; ANET³, 160), which seems to provide for the release of a slave after he has given in service the equivalent of double his debt. And in the Code of Hammurabi (CH 117; ANET³, 170-71), a debtor-slave and all his family members go free after three years. But Tsevat (1958a, 125-26; 1994) argues that "double" (מִשְׁנֶה) here simply means "equivalent payment." This is the meaning it has when referring to Yahweh's just punishment in Jer 16:18 and Isa 40:2 (Lundbom 1999, 771).

19 *Every firstborn that is brought forth in your herd and in your flock, which is male, you shall consecrate to Yahweh your God.* The farmer brings his firstfruits to Yahweh; the herdsman brings to Yahweh firstborn males from his herds and flocks (cf. Gen 4:2-4). The latter offering is rooted in the exodus event, when the firstborns of the Egyptians were slain and the firstborns of the Israelites were spared (Exod 13:14-15). Because of this gracious divine act, all firstborns were deemed holy to Yahweh (Exod 34:19: "All that opens the womb is mine, all your male cattle, the firstborns of ox and sheep"; cf. Exod 13:2, 12; Num 18:15; Lev 27:26). The command to sacrifice male firstborns from one's flocks and herds is found in the Covenant Code (Exod 22:28b-29(29b-30) and is even projected back into the Primeval History, where Abel is said to have offered firstborns of his flock to Yahweh (Gen 4:4).

The law here in Deuteronomy is only partial, e.g., nothing is said about the redemption of firstborn sons or the redemption of male animals unfit for sacrifice (cf. Exod 13:13; 34:20; Num 18:15-18). Unclean beasts, e.g., asses, camels, and horses, could be redeemed for money (Num 18:15-16; Lev 27:27) or else a sheep or goat could be offered in their stead. If the owner did not choose to redeem an animal, he was obliged to break its neck (Exod 13:13). Leviticus 27:27 states that redemption is to be at the animal's valuation plus one-fifth. The pres-

Deuteronomy 15

ent law is cited in the Qumran *Temple Scroll* (11QT 52:7-12a) in connection with restrictions on slaughtering animals in and around the temple (Yadin 1983, 1:314-15; 2:233-34).

you shall consecrate. תַּקְדִּישׁ. I.e., you shall treat the animal as holy, not putting it to ordinary use. On "keeping (something) holy," see Note for 5:12.

you shall not work with the firstborn of your ox, and you shall not shear the firstborn of your sheep. The young ox must not be put to work and the young lamb must not be sheared before their consecration to Yahweh. According to Deuteronomic law, a year might pass before the owner takes his animal to the central sanctuary. Under the older law, the consecration would have taken place at a local sanctuary on the eighth day after birth (Exod 22:29[30]; Lev 22:27). So now the owner must be reminded not to derive any economic benefit from an animal waiting to be consecrated (Tigay). One should also note that first shearings of other sheep go to Yahweh along with the firstfruits (18:4).

work with. The verb עבד + בְּ means "work with (an animal)."

20 Here in Deuteronomy firstborn males of all domestic cattle are to be taken to the central sanctuary, consecrated to Yahweh, and eaten there by the owner, his household, and the invited Levite (12:6-7, 17-18). If the distance to the central sanctuary is too far, the animals may be converted into money and the money spent to purchase oxen and sheep upon arrival at the sanctuary (14:23-27). According to the Priestly law in Num 18:17-19, the firstborns of oxen, sheep, and goats become the exclusive property of the (Aaronite) priests. Subsequent Jewish interpretation harmonized the two traditions, taking the present verses as being addressed to the priests (Rashi; cf. Neh 10:37[36]). However, they are not addressed to the priests. It is now generally agreed that the two laws regulated practice in two different periods of history (Driver), but a question remains as to which law is older. Scholars following Wellhausen date Deuteronomy before the Priestly writings, but those following Y. Kaufmann date P legislation before Deuteronomy. For a discussion of the dates of D and P, see Note for 14:22. What is clear is that the centralized worship assumed in Deuteronomy precludes any support for local sanctuaries and their clergy. The Mishnah tractate *Bekorot* ("Firstlings") discusses further the consecration of firstborns.

year by year. It is not known when the firstborns were taken to the central sanctuary. Some commentators (Driver; G. A. Smith; G. E. Wright; Tigay) think it was probably at one of the yearly festivals, perhaps Passover or the Feast of Weeks (Pentecost). The argument for Passover is supported by the juxtaposition of instructions for both the Feast of Unleavened Bread and the offering of firstborns in Exod 13:1-16. Moran believes that since the consecration did not need to take place eight days after birth (so Exod 22:29[30]; Lev 22:27), it could have been any time during the year. In his view, the likely time would have been when the tithes were brought (14:23).

21 Any ox or sheep having a blemish or other defect must not be sacrificed; this would be an abomination to Yahweh (17:1; Lev 22:17-25). Such sacrifices dishonor Yahweh, says the prophet Malachi, who asks people if the governor would like such a gift (Mal 1:6-8).

22-23 Blemished animals, like wild game, can be eaten at home as ordinary food (12:15-16, 22-25), the only proviso being that one must not eat the blood. Since the owner will be doing the slaughtering, he must pour out the blood upon the ground like water (see Note for 12:16).

the unclean and the clean together. I.e., people ritually clean and unclean (12:15, 22).

Message and Audience

In this discourse on yearly obligations, Moses first tells the people that every year they must set aside a tithe of all produce harvested from their orchards and fields. It is to be brought to the central sanctuary along with firstborn animals to be dedicated to Yahweh and eaten there by the worshipper and those with him. In this way, the worshipper will learn to fear Yahweh all his days. If the worshipper lives too far from the central sanctuary and it is impractical to bring his tithe and animals with him, he may convert all of it into silver and take the silver to the sanctuary to buy whatever he desires there. At the feast he and his household are to rejoice over Yahweh's goodness. The Levite from the worshipper's town is not to be forgotten. Since he has nothing to tithe, he is simply to join the pilgrimage and be welcomed to the feast as an invited guest.

Every third year, however, the tithe is to remain in the town or village, where it is to be deposited in storage facilities. Here again, the Levite is to be invited to sit at table with the householder and his family and share the bounty that has been brought in. To this feast the sojourners, orphans, and widows in the town are also to be invited. All are to eat and be satisfied, so that Yahweh will continue to bless the farmer in all of his subsequent labor.

After seven years' time, people are told they must remit all outstanding loans to needy Israelite brethren. Creditors shall not press for repayment because in the seventh year a remission will be proclaimed. To the foreigner the law does not apply. Such persons enter the country for commercial reasons, and they can be pressed for repayment. But any loan to an Israelite brother must be remitted. Moses then digresses briefly to tell the people that there should be no needy persons among them, for Yahweh will give them abundant harvests and other material blessings in the land they are about to possess. Yet there is a condition: people must obey Yahweh's voice and do all the commands Moses is laying before them this day. As it is, Yahweh is already blessing the people as he

Deuteronomy 15

promised he would, to the end that they are destined to become a lender not a borrower, a ruler of nations and not a nation to be ruled over.

Moses says that when a needy person does arise, one of the brethren living in their town, they must not harden their hearts nor close their hand to the needy brother. Rather, they must open the hand and lend the brother whatever he needs. Another warning: People must take care not to harbor base thoughts as the seventh year approaches, knowing it is the year of remission. Nor must they cast an evil eye on the needy brother and refuse him a loan. Admittedly, the loan may end up being cancelled. But the brother will be faced with an even greater crisis as the seventh year approaches. He will be strapped for cash at a time of no planting and harvesting. He will therefore have no one but Yahweh to turn to. When he does cry out to Yahweh, Yahweh will hear him, and it will be a sin for the one refusing the loan. Again, people are told they must be sure to give to persons in need. What is more, their heart must be in it. Yahweh will bless cheerful givers in all the work they undertake. Yes, needy persons will not cease to exist in the land; neither will they grow fat on loans not called in. For this reason, Moses says he is commanding the people to be sure to open their hand to their brother, their poor and needy brother, in the land soon to be theirs.

There is another kindness to the Hebrew brother — here man and woman — in the seventh year. When a Hebrew or Hebrewess is sold to one of their own and serves him for six years, in the seventh year he or she shall go free. When they are released, owners shall not send them away empty-handed. Rather they shall make a necklace of good things — sheep or goats from the flock, grain from the threshing floor, and wine from the winepress. As Yahweh has blessed them, so are they to give to the one being released. People are told to remember Egypt, how Israel was a slave there, how Yahweh ransomed it, and not incidentally, how Yahweh commanded the Egyptians to lavish silver, gold, and clothing on people as they hurried to leave. Moses says this is why he is commanding the people to act kindly and liberally to manumitted slaves when Israel settles in the land. If it should happen that the slave does not wish to go free, because he loves his master and it has gone well for him in his master's house, then the owner shall take an awl and bore a hole in the slave's ear against the door of the master's house. The slave shall then be indentured permanently. For the female slave the owner shall do the same. The owner shall not see this release as a difficult thing to do. The slave has given him adequate compensation for six years. What is more, Yahweh promises to bless the owner in all future endeavors.

Concluding his discourse on yearly obligations, Moses returns to an obligation that people have year by year, which is to set apart all male firstborns from their flocks and herds and consecrate them to Yahweh at the central sanctuary. No longer do these need to be presented on the eighth day after birth, only when the owner goes to the central sanctuary on one of the yearly pilgrimages. The young ox must not be worked before consecration, nor must the lamb be sheared. The owner must not derive any economic benefit from animals set apart to Yahweh. Let the people remember the exodus, when the firstborns of Egypt were slain and Israel's firstborns were spared. The animals now brought for consecration will afterwards be slaughtered and eaten by the owner, his household, and the invited Levite. If the animal has any sort of blemish, it cannot be sacrificed to Yahweh, who wants only the best. Blemished animals, like wild game, can be eaten by the ritually clean and unclean at home. Only one must remember when slaughtering animals at home not to eat the blood. It must be poured out on the ground like water.

The tithing law reflects the late 8th and early 7th cents., when gifts of agricultural produce were being brought to the central sanctuary in Jerusalem and the Levites had become charity recipients along with the sojourner, orphan, and widow. The same holds on laws of remission. The law providing debt-remission for fellow-Israelites reflects a time when indebtedness had become an acute social problem, and Moses could only be imagined as foreseeing an egalitarian Israelite society without any needy or poor. The law on manumitting Hebrew slaves reflects the 8th and 7th cents. in that both male and female slaves are to be released. Gone is the Covenant Code proviso about wives given to the slave by his master and daughters born in slavery having to remain with the master after the man goes free. This law also reflects a time when the poor were suffering at the hands of the rich and Israelites were selling their own into slavery. This was the mid-8th cent., when Amos was preaching social justice in northern Israel, and a century or more later in Judah, when this law was not being enforced. The law on male firstborns also reflects the 7th cent., when animals were no longer brought to some nearby altar on the eighth day after birth, but were taken or converted into money and brought to the central sanctuary in Jerusalem at one of the annual feasts.

E. Keeping the Feasts (16:1-17)

1. Feast of Passover (16:1-8)

16¹Keep the month of Abib, and you shall hold a Passover to Yahweh your God, for in the month of Abib Yahweh your God brought you out from Egypt by night. ²And you shall sacrifice a Passover to Yahweh your God, one of the flock or the herd, in the place that Yahweh will choose to make his name reside there. ³You shall not eat leavened bread with it; seven days you shall eat unleavened bread, the bread of affliction, with it (for in haste you came out from the land of Egypt), in order that you will remember the day you came out from the land of Egypt all the days of your life. ⁴*So leaven shall not be seen by you in all your territory seven days, and from the meat that you sacrifice in the evening of the first day none shall remain until morning.* ⁵*You may not sacrifice the Passover within one of your gates that Yahweh your God is giving to you,* ⁶*but at the place that Yahweh your God will choose to make his name reside there; you shall sacrifice the Passover in the evening as the sun goes down, the time of day you came out from Egypt.* ⁷*And you shall cook and you shall eat in the place that Yahweh your God will choose for it; then you shall turn in the morning and go to your tents.* ⁸*Six days you shall eat unleavened bread, and on the seventh day shall be an assembly to Yahweh your God; you shall not do work.*

2. Feast of Weeks (16:9-12)

16⁹*Seven weeks you shall count for yourself; when the sickle is first put to the standing grain you shall begin to count seven weeks.* ¹⁰*Then you shall hold a Feast of Weeks to Yahweh your God, the measure of freewill offering in your hand that you shall give being according to that with which Yahweh your God shall bless you.* ¹¹*And you shall be glad before Yahweh your God, you, and your son and your daughter, and your manservant and your maidservant, and the Levite who is within your gates; and the sojourner, and the orphan, and the widow who are in your midst, in the place that Yahweh your God will choose to make his name reside there.* ¹²*So you shall remember that you were a slave in Egypt, and you shall be careful and you shall do these statutes.*

3. Feast of Booths (16:13-17)

16¹³*The Feast of Booths you shall hold for yourself seven days, when you gather in from your threshing floor and from your winepress.* ¹⁴*And you shall be glad in your feast, you, and your son and your daughter, and your manservant and your maidservant, and the Levite, and the sojourner, and the orphan, and the widow who are within your gates.* ¹⁵*Seven days you shall celebrate a pilgrim feast before Yahweh your God in the place that Yahweh will choose, because Yahweh your God will bless you in all your yield and in all the work of your hands, so you will be only glad.*
    ¹⁶*Three times in the year every one of your males shall appear in the presence of Yahweh your God in the place that he will choose: in the Feast of Unleavened Bread, and in the Feast of Weeks, and in the Feast of Booths, and he shall not appear in the presence of Yahweh empty-handed.* ¹⁷*Each man the gift of his hand corresponding to the blessing of Yahweh your God that he gives you.*

Deuteronomy 16

Rhetoric and Composition

The present verses give instructions for keeping three annual feasts: Passover (vv. 1-8), the Feast of Weeks (vv. 9-12), and the Feast of Booths (vv. 13-15). These feasts are repeated in summary fashion at the end of the discourse, where Passover is called the Feast of Unleavened Bread (vv. 16-17). This concluding summary gives the discourse a structure not otherwise found in Deuteronomy (Lundbom 1996, 306). Closure in Deuteronomy 1–28 is usually brought about by the inclusio.

The unit is demarcated at the top end by a *petuḥah* in M^L and a section in Sam before v. 1, which is also the chapter division. In 11QT 17:5 an open section appears prior to the Passover instructions. In the *Temple Scroll* these instructions derive from multiple biblical sources and the book of *Jubilees* (Yadin 1983, 1:96; 2:73). At the bottom end demarcation is by a *setumah* in M^L and a section in Sam at the end of v. 17. A *setumah* in M^L and sections in Sam and 4QDeut^c at the end of v. 8 conclude the Passover instructions, and a *petuḥah* in M^L and a section in Sam at the end of v. 12 conclude the instructions on the Feast of Weeks. In 11QT 17:9-10 a section separates the Passover instructions from instructions on the Feast of Unleavened Bread (Yadin 1983, 1:98; 2:74), and in 11QT 18:10 a closed section precedes the instructions on the Feast of Weeks (Yadin 1983, 1:99; 2:78). The beginning and end of the Feast of Booth instructions in the *Temple Scroll* are not extant. Finally, 1QDeut 4:13 has an interval after v. 4 (Barthélemy and Milik 1955, 56), but this does not appear to be a section marking. The editor questions whether it might be a side margin.

Portions of 16:1-17 are contained in 1QDeut^a, 4QDeut^c, and 4Q366.

Notes

16:1 The instructions here are very simple, containing a minimum of detail and an abundance of theological overlay. Israel is to keep a Passover in the month of Abib, remembering in the rite Yahweh's deliverance of the people from Egyptian slavery. "Israel does not remember festivals," says Brevard Childs (1962, 55), "but observes them in order to remember." Passover is the first and most important of Israel's three yearly feasts, the others being the Feast of Weeks (Gk: Pentecost) and the Feast of Booths (v. 16). The same three feasts are enjoined upon the people in Exod 23:14-18 (Covenant Code) and repeated in Exod 34:18, 22-25. A Jewish calendar found in Qumran Cave 4, dated ca. A.D. 68, mentions the three feasts along with other holy days. It names priests in a rota for sacred service (Milik 1957, 24-25; Segal 1963, 39-41; Talmon 1965, 170; cf. 1 Chr 24:7-18). Passover, or the Feast of Unleavened Bread, with which it is here combined, is discussed elsewhere in Exod 12:1-20, 43-49; 13:3-10; 34:18; Lev 23:5-8; Num 9:1-14; 28:16-25. The dramatic events in Egypt providing background for the rite are recounted in Exod 12:21-39. Passover instructions in the Qumran *Temple Scroll* (11QT 17:6-9) draw upon all the biblical codes, but have their greatest affinity with the book of *Jubilees,* ch. 49 (Yadin 1983, 1:50, 84-85, 96-99; 2:73-74). The Mishnah discusses Passover in tractate *Pesaḥim.* Passover, or the Feast of Unleavened Bread, looms large in the NT Gospels (Matt 26:1-30; Mark 14:1-26; Luke 2:41-50; 22:1-38; John 2:13-25; 6:4; 11:55–13:30; 18:1–19:16), where also in the Synoptics Jesus' Last Supper with his disciples is generally regarded as having been a Passover meal. In the early church, the Passover became transformed in light of the death and resurrection of Jesus. For Christians, Jesus becomes the paschal (Passover) lamb that was sacrificed (John 1:29: "Behold, the Lamb of God, who takes away the sin of the world"; 1 Cor 5:7: "For Christ, our paschal lamb, has been sacrificed"). See also 1 Pet 1:19 and Rev 5:6.

Keep the month of Abib. שָׁמוֹר אֶת־חֹדֶשׁ הָאָבִיב. The same basic wording that appears in Deuteronomy's commandment on the Sabbath (5:12). Hebrew חֹדֶשׁ ("month") is lit. "new moon." Abib (= "young ears of grain"; Exod 9:31; Lev 2:14) is the first month, March/April, in the ancient Israelite calendar, later called Nisan (Neh 2:1; Esth 3:7). A different calendar is presupposed in Exod 23:16, where the old year ends and the new year begins at the Feast of Ingathering (Booths), which is in the fall. Elsewhere in the OT Abib is the first month (Exod 12:2, 18; Lev 23:5; Num 9:5; 28:16), and months are always counted beginning in the spring (Tadmor, *WHJP,* 4/1:50). In the Qumran calendar, Passover comes at the beginning of the year (Talmon 1965, 172; cf. *m. Roš Haš.* 1:1: the first of Nisan is the New Year for kings and for festivals).

We are told in other OT law codes that Passover begins the evening of the 14th of Abib, followed on the 15th by the Feast of Unleavened Bread (Lev 23:5-6; Num 28:16-17). On the second day of Unleavened Bread a sheaf of new barley is brought to the temple, the first of the firstfruits (Lev 23:9-14). This marks the beginning of the harvest season, which goes on continuously to the Feast of Weeks (Wellhausen 1957, 87; Haran 1977, 295; cf. 2 Sam 21:9-10; Jer 5:24; Ruth 2). In Deuteronomy the days of Passover are not specified, nor is any distinction made between Passover and the Feast of Unleavened Bread (see v. 3). For all practical purposes, it is a single feast held in the month of Abib.

and you shall hold a Passover to Yahweh your God. "To hold a Passover" means "to hold a Passover sacrifice" (Haran 1977, 317). Passover (Heb פֶּסַח; Gk πάσχα) commemorates the night when Yahweh "passed over" the Israelite houses in carrying out his final plague against the Egyptians, which was the slaying of their firstborn sons and animals (Exod 12:11-13, 21-27). The verb פסח means "to protect, spare" (Isa 31:5), and Israel's firstborns were spared on this fateful night, when the people killed a "passover lamb" and daubed the blood on their lintels and doorposts (Exod 12:21-28). The Bible records a Passover celebrated later at Sinai (Num 9:1-5) and another at Gilgal after Israel crossed the Jordan (Josh 5:10-12). King Solomon is also on record as having celebrated Passover along with the other yearly feasts during his reign (1 Kgs 9:25; 2 Chr 8:12-13).

The first Passover to which a specific date can be assigned is the one celebrated by King Josiah in 622 (2 Kgs 23:21-23; 2 Chr 35:1-19). The Chronicler says that those present in Jerusalem kept this Passover and Feast of Unleavened Bread for seven consecutive days, and a grand affair it must have been, for no Passover like it had been kept in the last four hundred years (2 Kgs 23:22: "since the days of the judges"; 2 Chr 35:18: "since the days of Samuel"). The Chronicler also reports a Passover celebration in the time of Hezekiah, after a long period in which the rite had been neglected (2 Chronicles 30). This is not recorded in 2 Kings. After the Babylonian exile, another Passover is reported to have been celebrated by returnees to the land (Ezra 6:19-22). Two ostraca and one papyrus from Elephantine tell us that Passover was celebrated in this Jewish colony of Egypt during the 5th cent. (Segal 1963, 8-10; "The Passover Papyrus" in *ANET*³, 491). That the Passover was kept throughout the Second Temple period (*EncJud,* 13:163-64) is corroborated by numerous references to the feast in the NT. Passover celebration continues into the modern day, although the offering of the paschal lamb ended with the destruction of the temple in A.D. 70.

for in the month of Abib Yahweh your God brought you out from Egypt by night. The basic wording may derive from Exod 34:18, although here is added that the departure from Egypt was "at night" (v. 6; cf. T^{PsJ}). In other pentateuchal sources, only the dramatic events prior to the exodus are said to have taken place at night (Exod 12:12, 30-31, 42; cf. 1 Cor 11:23); the exodus itself occurred in broad daylight (Num 33:3: "in the sight of all the Egyptians"; cf. H. L. Ginsberg 1982, 57). Targum^{Onq} avoids a night departure by translating: "the Lord your God brought you out of Egypt and performed miracles for you at night"; but T^{Nf} turns this around, translating: "the Lord your God brought you out redeemed from the land of Egypt by night and worked signs and mighty deeds for you during the daytime." The Passover meal, in any case, became an evening celebration (Josh 5:10; Matt 26:20; Mark 14:17; cf. Exod 12:8, 42). Haran (1977, 320) notes that Passover is the only sacrificial meal to be eaten at night and says this is quite extraordinary. He thinks that Passover has nomadic origins, noting that nomads typically eat at night.

2 Exodus 12:3-5 says a lamb or kid (שֶׂה) shall be sacrificed, a male one year old "from the sheep or from the goats." It also states that if a lamb or kid is too much for one household, neighbors should be invited to share the meat. In the present verse cattle are added as acceptable offerings, which would certainly require sharing the meat with other households. The Chronicler, in reporting Josiah's grand Passover, says that the king made a contribution of thirty thousand lambs and kids and three thousand bulls, with his princes and temple officers contributing smaller but nevertheless generous quantities of the same (2 Chr 35:7-9).

Here in Deuteronomy the Passover is not to be celebrated in homes, as appears to have been the case at an earlier time (Exod 12:7, 46), but at the central sanctuary. To get to Jerusalem in the 7th cent. people would have to undertake a חַג, i.e., a "pilgrimage." Driver compares it to the Muslim *ḥajj*, the annual pilgrimage to Mecca, which is one of the five "pillars" of Islam (*EncIs*, 3:31-38). This pilgrimage to Jerusalem, like all the others, is to be a joyful occasion of feasting, music, and dancing (see Note for 12:7). All adult males are expected to go (16:16; cf. Exod 23:17; 34:23), but here in Deuteronomy entire households are invited to the feast (12:7, 12, 18; 16:11, 14; 31:11-12; Haran 1977, 293-94). In the NT, too, women are present in Jerusalem with the men for Passover (Luke 2:41; Matt 27:55; Mark 15:40-41; Luke 23:49, 55). Haran points out, however, that the entire country will not be emptied as a result of everyone going to the feast. Many for one reason or another will remain home, which may explain in part why the Deuteronomic preacher stresses in v. 5 that Passover sacrifices are not to be carried out in the towns. Haran says that these pilgrimages "were mainly regarded as praiseworthy manifestations of piety and fear of God." Something similar holds true for the pilgrimage to Mecca, where it is the duty of every Muslim man or woman to make the *ḥajj* once in a lifetime, provided the individual has the means to do so.

3 *You shall not eat leavened bread with it; seven days you shall eat unleavened bread, the bread of affliction, with it (for in haste you came out from the land of Egypt).* Leaven (yeast) causes fermentation in the dough, for which reason it became a symbol of corruption in antiquity (see v. 4). During the seven days of Passover "leavened" bread (חָמֵץ) may not be eaten (Exod 12:20; 13:3, 7; 23:18; 34:25). If one did eat it — whether an Israelite or a sojourner — that person would be cut off (Heb הִכָּרֵת) from Israel (Exod 12:15, 19). Unleavened bread, or "matzot" (מַצּוֹת, plural of מַצָּה), was flat bread made of unleavened barley dough. It was baked quickly and probably resembled today's pita bread found in Jerusalem and elsewhere in the Near East. Unleavened bread was eaten at ordinary meals, though usually when food had to be prepared at short notice (Gen 19:3; Judg 6:19; 1 Sam 28:24). It became the main symbol for Passover, eaten as a remembrance of the hurried departure out of Egypt when bread was not given time to rise (Exod 12:33-39). This may be a later explanation, however, reflecting the time when the festival developed historical associations (Wellhausen 1957, 88, 91-92; *JE*, 9:553).

In Christianity, Passover underwent further historicization, replaced as it was by Easter that celebrated the sacrificial death and resurrection of Jesus. The blood daubed on lintels and doorposts prior to the exodus never became a Passover symbol (Segal 1963, 57; cf. Exod 12:7, 21-28), not even in the four cups of wine introduced later into the Passover meal. Here in Deuteronomy it is the words of the Deuteronomic covenant that are to be written on the doorposts of one's house (6:9; 11:20). The Christian Eucharist contains two symbols derived from the Last Supper (Passover) celebrated by Jesus with his disciples: bread and wine, the wine being a substitute for the sacrificial blood of Jesus (Mark 14:22-24; Matt 26:26-28; Luke 22:19-20).

Wellhausen believed that the Passover originally had independent standing and only later became connected with the Feast of Unleavened Bread. His views survive in Driver, von Rad, Tigay, and others who take the two feasts as being originally distinct. It is pointed out, for example, that Lev 23:5-6 and Num 28:16-17 seem to distinguish between Passover, which is set for the 14th of Nisan, and the Feast of Unleavened Bread, which is set for the 15th of Nisan. Passover is also believed to originally have been a nomadic or pastoral feast (Wellhausen 1957, 92-93) and Unleavened Bread originally a spring agricultural feast taken over from the Canaanites (*JE*, 9:553-54; *EncJud*, 13:163, 171). More recently, Goldstein and Cooper (1990) have argued that the Feast of Unleavened Bread was originally a festival in northern Israel and the Passover a festival in southern Judah, a view expressed earlier by G. Beer and D. C. Steuernagle (Segal 1963, 79-81). But in Deuteronomy the two feasts are treated as one. The present verses speak of Passover, while in the summary the same is called the Feast of Unleavened Bread (v. 16). According to Haran (1977, 342), the uniting of Passover with the Feast of Unleavened Bread cannot be a Deuteronomic innovation, since in his view all the biblical sources recognize a connection between the two feasts. In the Synoptic Gospels the names are used interchangeably (Mark 14:1; Matt 26:17; Luke 22:1, 7; Acts 12:3-4). Only in John is the feast always called Passover, never the Feast of Unleavened Bread, perhaps because for this Gospel writer Jesus himself is the "true bread from heaven" (John 6:32).

the bread of affliction. לֶחֶם עֹנִי. The "affliction" is presumably Israel's prior affliction in Egypt, which the unleavened bread calls to mind (Rashi; cf. Exod 3:7, 17; 4:31; cf. 1:11-14). In the other law codes this bread is to be eaten with "bitter herbs" (Exod 12:8; Num 9:11).

(for in haste you came out from the land of Egypt). A parenthetical remark explaining why unleavened bread is to be eaten for seven days (Exod 12:11, 33-39). Driver says that חִפָּזוֹן denotes more than "haste"; it is hurry mingled with alarm. The verb חפז has this meaning in 20:3; 1 Sam 23:26; 2 Sam 4:4; 2 Kgs 7:15; Ps 48:6(5). In the new exodus anticipated from Babylon, the prophet of the exile tells people that they shall not go out "in haste" (Isa 52:12).

with it. עָלָיו. Lit. "upon it," but here an idiomatic use of עַל together with the verb אכל, "eat" (Exod 12:8; Lev 19:26; 1 Sam 14:32).

in order that you will remember the day you came out from the land of Egypt all the days of your life. On the call for Israel to remember its slavery in

Deuteronomy 16

Egypt and Yahweh's deliverance of the nation from that slavery, see again v. 12 and Note for 8:2.

all the days of your life. On this Deuteronomic expression, see Note for 4:9.

4 *So leaven shall not be seen by you in all your territory seven days.* Not only must people refrain from eating leavened bread during the seven days of the feast, leaven (שְׂאֹר) itself must not even be seen in Israelite territory. Hebrew לְךָ used here with a passive verb probably means "by you" (Driver; cf. לָכֶם in Exod 12:16), although לְ could also express "belonging" (KBL³), which would give the translation "belonging to you" (Tigay: "of yours"). The expression "(there) shall not be seen" is said by Daube (1969a, 49; 1971a, 12) to be a variation of the oft-used Deuteronomic expression "there shall not be found" (see Note for 17:2), which condemns not the blemish but its display. The present injunction aims at shaming anyone who would think to retain (old) leaven during Passover. Later rabbinic law mandated that houses be cleansed of all leaven on the night before the 14th of Nisan, which made necessary an inspection of all nooks and corners by household members (*JE*, 9:550).

Leaven had both positive and negative meaning in the ancient world. A negative meaning seems to be attached to the verb in Hos 7:4, where the prophet disparages adulterers in Ephraim. In the NT, negative meanings for leaven become explicit. Jesus uses leaven to describe the "puffed up" teachings of Pharisees and Sadducees that one must take care to avoid (Matt 16:6-12; Mark 8:15). For Paul, too, leaven is the false teachings of others (Gal 5:9), also boasting of Christians themselves from which they must be cleansed, to be replaced by the unleavened bread of sincerity and truth (1 Cor 5:6-8). Jesus gives leaven positive meaning when it is used to describe the growth expected in the kingdom (Matt 13:33; Luke 13:21). In the Talmud (*b. Ber.* 17a), "yeast in the dough" refers to the evil impulse within a person (*JE*, 7:655; cf. *Midr. Gen. Rab.* 34:10). In the classical tradition, too, leaven symbolized moral laxity. Plutarch (*Quaest. rom.* 109) says: "Yeast is itself also the product of corruption, and produces corruption in the dough with which it is mixed . . . and altogether the process of leavening seems to be one of putrefaction" (Loeb). The Roman satirist Persius used *fermentum* (yeast) in a similar manner (*Sat.* 1.24-25).

and from the meat that you sacrifice in the evening of the first day none shall remain until morning. The meat of Passover must be consumed during the night of the first day, which is the 14th of Nisan (Rashi). None of it may remain until morning; if any does remain, it must be burned (Exod 12:10). This is to imitate the Passover sacrifice in Egypt (Exod 12:8-10; 23:18; 34:25). Elsewhere is added that not a bone of the sacrificial offering shall be broken (Exod 12:46; Num 9:12; *Jub.* 49:13-14), which the Gospel writer John applies to the sacrifice of Jesus on the cross (John 19:36).

Deuteronomy 16

5-6 *You may not sacrifice the Passover within one of your gates that Yahweh your God is giving to you, but at the place that Yahweh your God will choose to make his name reside there.* In Deuteronomy the Passover sacrifice may not be carried out in one's town, but must be done at the central sanctuary. In Egypt, the Passover lamb was killed at home and the blood daubed on the lintel and doorposts of the house (Exod 12:21-28). But where was the Passover sacrifice carried out in the pre-Deuteronomic period? Was it at a nearby high place, at a solitary altar in one's town or village, or at home? Some believe that Deuteronomy moved the Passover sacrifice from the home to the central sanctuary (Driver; von Rad; H. L. Ginsberg 1982, 56), while others think that Passover, like other communal feasts, was celebrated early on at a local shrine (Segal 1963, 133). Haran (1977, 348) says the present injunction can only be directed against offering the Passover sacrifice at a worship site other than the central sanctuary. In the Second Temple period, the lamb was killed in the temple courtyard, after which the meat was taken home to be roasted and eaten (*JE*, 9:553). When Jesus celebrated the Passover with his disciples, they would have slaughtered their lamb at the temple and then found an "upper room" in the city where they could prepare the meat and eat the meal together (Mark 14:12-16; Matt 26:17-19; Luke 22:7-13).

You may not. On this form denoting the indignity of doing something, see Note for 12:17.

6 *you shall sacrifice the Passover in the evening as the sun goes down, the time of day you came out from Egypt.* The evening rite is to imitate the Passover meal in Egypt. The celebration as a whole lasts seven days, from sunset on the 14th of Nisan to sunset on the 21st of Nisan (*JE*, 9:548). Hebrew מוֹעֵד means "fixed time" (Exod 9:5; 1 Sam 9:24; 13:8), here "(fixed) time of day" (Driver).

7 *And you shall cook.* וּבִשַּׁלְתָּ. The translation of בשׁל has been problematic, since the verb means "boil" in the parallel text of Exod 12:9. There it is stated that the Passover sacrifice shall *not* be boiled (בשׁל) in water. The rabbinic solution to this apparent contradiction was to interpret בשׁל here in Deuteronomy as "cook" (Driver; Segal 1963, 205; H. L. Ginsberg 1982, 57-58; cf. NJV; NRSV; NJB), which is one of its meanings (BDB; KBL³; Akk *bašālu* can also mean "boil, roast, bake, cook a meal"; cf. *CAD*, 2:135-37), and assume that the Passover sacrifice was not to be boiled but roasted (Rashi; Rashbam; T^PsJ: "you shall roast"; cf. AV; NIV). This would explain why Exod 12:9 specifies that the sacrifice not be boiled in water. Eli the priest was accustomed to boil (בשׁל) sacrificial meat in large kettles at the Shiloh sanctuary (1 Sam 2:13-15). The Chronicler, reporting Josiah's Passover, says "they cooked the passover sacrifice with fire" (יְבַשְּׁלוּ הַפֶּסַח בָּאֵשׁ), i.e., they roasted it, and "they cooked" (בִּשְּׁלוּ) the other holy offerings in kettles and pots, i.e., they boiled them (2 Chr 35:13). The LXX in the present verse came up with a conflated reading:

Deuteronomy 16

καὶ ἐψήσεις καὶ ὀπτήσεις ("And you shall boil and you shall roast"), which does not make sense.

then you shall turn in the morning and go to your tents. וּפָנִיתָ בַבֹּקֶר וְהָלַכְתָּ לְאֹהָלֶיךָ. The expression "turn and go to your tents" is an archaism surviving from nomadic life, taken here to mean "go home" (Driver; Haran 1977, 296; H. L. Ginsberg 1982, 55; Tigay; T^(OnqPsJ): "and go to your city"). In 5:30 the same expression occurs with שׁוּב ("return"), but in Josh 22:4 the verb is פנה ("turn"), the same as here. The plain meaning of the directive is that the worshipper and those with him, on the day after Passover, are to return home and not remain at the central sanctuary to celebrate the Feast of Unleavened Bread. Von Rad thinks this directive survives from the time when Passover and the Feast of Unleavened Bread were independent festivals, but as we noted above, the two feast names are used interchangeably in the present chapter and appear to be one. Still, the worshipper could return home to celebrate the six days of Unleavened Bread in his own town, in which case Unleavened Bread would not be a חַג ("pilgrimage") per se (so Haran). The assembly on the seventh day would also have to take place in the local town, since it is unlikely that people would make another pilgrimage back to the central sanctuary at the end of the week. Segal (1963, 211) thinks the seventh day is to be celebrated at some (local) shrine. Driver says the worshipper on the morning after Passover is now at liberty to return home, which means he could remain at the central sanctuary or else return home. Another possible interpretation of this directive would be to take the expression "turn and go to your tents" as meaning "return to your tents in Jerusalem," where "tents" would be the worshippers' temporary dwellings while they were at the feast (G. A. Smith). If this is what "turn and go to your tents" means, then the pilgrims will actually be spending the entire week in Jerusalem, returning home only after the convocation takes place and all the festivities are concluded. The Qumran *Temple Scroll* (11QT 17:11-12) states that sacrifices are to be offered by people all seven days of the Feast of Unleavened Bread (Yadin 1983, 2:74-75), which seems to assume a week-long stay in Jerusalem.

8 Here in Deuteronomy, as in Exod 13:6, an assembly is slated only for the seventh day. This reflects the weekly rhythm of six days labor and rest on the seventh (5:12-14; Exod 20:10-11; 31:14-15). But in Exod 12:16; Lev 23:7-8; Num 28:18, 25, assemblies are slated for both the first and last days of the week-long festivities. On neither day may work be done, except what is necessary in preparing the food.

an assembly. עֲצֶרֶת. The Sam has חַג, "(pilgrim) feast" (cf. Exod 13:6), which is not quite right (Haran 1977, 296). The Targums (T^(Nf): "there shall be a congregation of rejoicing"; T^(PsJ): "you shall gather in praise") envision a joyous gathering rather than a "solemn assembly" (so AV; RSV; NJV; NAB; NRSV), but in reality it could be both.

Deuteronomy 16

9-10 This second yearly feast is announced with the same brevity and lack of specificity characterizing Deuteronomy's announcement of Passover. Seven weeks after the first standing grain (= barley) is cut, a Feast of Weeks is to be held, at which time an appropriate and freely-given offering is to be made to Yahweh. This festival later went by the name of Pentecost ("fiftieth") among Greek-speaking Jews (Tob 2:1; 2 Macc 12:32; Acts 2:1; 20:16; 1 Cor 16:8), occurring as it did fifty days after the barley "sheaf" (Heb עֹמֶר) was presented at the Feast of Unleavened Bread (Lev 23:15-16). The Targums thus add the barley sheaf presentation in their paraphrase of v. 9. For the Feast of Weeks two loaves of bread baked from new grain were to be brought to the temple, which marked the completion of the wheat harvest (Lev 23:17). In the Covenant Code (Exod 23:16) the Feast of Weeks is called the "Feast of Harvest," in Exod 34:22 "the firstfruits of wheat harvest" (cf. Num 28:26). The seven weeks were then the joyful weeks of the grain harvest (Isa 9:2[3]; Jer 5:24), the barley harvest commencing at Passover, and the wheat harvest ending at Pentecost.

Here in Deuteronomy, as is the case also in the Covenant Code, the Feast of Weeks is not assigned a fixed date. This is probably because the harvest did not begin each year at the same time (Moran; Tigay). Later attempts to fix a date began with the Sabbath reference in Lev 23:10-11, 15-16, counting from the day after the Sabbath when the barley sheaf was presented. (In P material the first day of the Feast of Unleavened Bread was a day of holy convocation, thus a day of Sabbath rest; see Note for 16:8). As things turned out, this day after the Sabbath became the 16th of Nisan (Rashi), putting the Feast of Weeks fifty days later on the 6th of Sivan (Sivan = May/June). The Qumran *Temple Scroll* (11QT 18:10-13) follows Lev 23:15-16, counting from the Sunday when the barley sheaf was presented, "seven full Sabbaths" to the Sunday after the seventh Sabbath, a total of fifty days (Yadin 1983, 1:103-4; 2:78-79). The Feast of Weeks was just a one-day observance (Haran 1977, 297; Num 28:26; Lev 23:21), not a weeklong celebration like Passover–Unleavened Bread and the Feast of Booths (16:3-4, 8, 13-15).

Seven weeks. The months of harvesting barley and wheat are cited on the 10th-cent. Gezer Calendar (Albright 1943b; Borowski 1987, 36-38; *ABD*, 1:817). In Albright's view (1943b, 25), the line reading "his month is harvest and festivity" (Borowski: "a month of harvesting [wheat] and measuring [grain]") is a direct reference to Pentecost.

sickle. חֶרְמֵשׁ. The term appears again in 23:26(25). Another tool, מַגָּל, was of a similar nature (Jer 50:16; Joel 4:13[3:13]). Flint sickles (flint pieces attached to handles of wood or bone) were used along with metal sickles in ancient Israel. Archaeological excavations have turned up both types in quantity, e.g., the very fine collection of iron sickles from Hazor (Borowski 1987, 61-62). A surviving painting of an Egyptian harvest (15th cent.) shows two men cutting grain with sickles (for a picture, see *ANEP²*, 27 no. 91). On reaping in ancient Israel, see Borowski 1987, 57-62; also "Harvests, Harvesting" in *ABD*, 3:63-64.

standing grain. קָמָה is standing grain or grain still on the stalk (BDB; KBL³; NIV). Reference here is to ripe, unharvested barley. The AV translated "corn," which then had broader meaning in English than it does today. We are not, in any case, talking about modern (American) corn (= maize), which this cereal is not. The translation "standing corn" of NEB is thus misleading.

Feast of Weeks. חַג שָׁבֻעוֹת. Hebrew חַג is a "pilgrim feast." Haran (1977, 297) notes that nowhere in P and H is this holy day called a חַג. In Num 28:26; Lev 23:16-21 it is simply "(the day of) firstfruits," suggesting that a pilgrimage to the temple may not have been required. Haran notes further that this yearly feast is omitted from Ezekiel's list in Ezek 45:21-25. But Josephus (*B.J.* 1.253; 2.43; *Ant.* 14.337; 17.254) reports huge crowds gathering in Jerusalem for the Feast of Weeks, which is corroborated by the Pentecost account in Acts 2:5-11.

the measure of freewill offering in your hand that you shall give being according to that with which Yahweh your God shall bless you. The Hebrew is difficult, with מִסַּת נִדְבַת יָדְךָ being a triple construct chain and the OT *hapax legomenon* מִסַּת best translated "measure." Rashi (1997, 196): "The fullness (דֵּי) of the gift of your hand, wholly commensurate with the blessing." The idea is expressed again in v. 17, also in 15:14, that certain gifts should be determined by the individuals themselves on the basis of blessings received from Yahweh. Loaves made of new grain were offered as firstfruits of the grain harvest, but other gifts were also brought on this feast day (18:4; Num 18:12-13). These would include tithes, firstborns, and other offerings obligatory and freewill (12:5-6; 14:22-27; 15:19-20; cf. Num 28:26-31; Lev 23:15-20). The figs sitting before the temple in Jeremiah's vision, which would have ripened in late May or early June, were probably brought for this feast (Jer 24:1; cf. Lundbom 2004a, 228). The firstfruits ceremony of 26:1-11 is thought to be connected with the Feast of Weeks, although nothing is stated in the text to that effect (H. L. Ginsberg 1982, 59). There was doubtless a connection, however (Exod 34:22; Num 28:26), although the later rabbinic view was that firstfruits and other gifts could be brought to the temple any time between the Feast of Weeks and the Feast of Booths (*m. Bik.* 1:10). For further discussion, see Note on 26:2.

11 *And you shall be glad before Yahweh your God.* The seven weeks of grain harvest was a season of gladness (Isa 9:2[3]), which was true of harvests generally (Ps 126:5-6; Ruth 2-3). Deuteronomy stresses that feasts are to be joyful celebrations (see vv. 14-15 and Note for 12:7). The Feast of Weeks was a holy convocation day on which no work was permitted (Lev 23:21; Num 28:26).

you, and your son and your daughter, and your manservant and your maidservant. According to Deuteronomy, entire households are invited to attend the feast at the central sanctuary (see v. 14 and Note for 12:7), even though

Deuteronomy 16

it is stated in v. 16 (similarly in Exod 23:17; 34:23) that only the adult males are obliged to make the pilgrimage.

and the Levite who is within your gates; and the sojourner, and the orphan, and the widow who are in your midst. On charity to be extended toward the sojourner, orphan, and widow that resides in one's town, see Note for 10:18. The dependent Levite in one's town was also to be an invited guest at the feast (see v. 14 and Note for 12:12).

in the place that Yahweh your God will choose to make his name reside there. I.e., the central sanctuary, which in the 7th cent. is the Jerusalem temple (see Note for 12:5).

12 This connection with Israel's prior slavery seems contrived and is therefore judged secondary by some (G. A. Smith; de Vaux 1965, 494; H. L. Ginsberg 1982, 56), particularly since the Deuteronomic preacher does not connect the Feast of Booths following with any event in Israel's salvation history, such as we have, for example, in Lev 23:43 (von Rad). But the call to remember Israel's prior slavery may simply be to follow up the directive to be sure to include the sojourner, orphan, and widow in the feast (G. E. Wright; see Notes for 8:2 and 24:18). It is widely believed that both the Feast of Weeks and the Feast of Booths were originally agricultural celebrations, very likely Canaanite in origin, their observances commencing with Israel's settlement in the land (Wellhausen 1957, 91; Driver; von Rad; de Vaux 1965, 494; Haran 1977, 318 n.). By the 2nd cent. A.D. the Feast of Weeks in Judaism had come to celebrate the giving of the Law on Mount Sinai (*b. Pesah.* 68b; de Vaux 1965, 494-95; Weinfeld, 267-75; 1978). Weinfeld, however, thinks the covenantal roots of the Feast may be more ancient. In any case, Israel's arrival at Sinai as reported in Exod 19:1-2 was later calculated to be fifty days after the Exodus (T[PsJ] on Exod 19:1, 16 dates it to the 6th day of the third month [Sivan]). Pentecost thus became the "birthday of the Torah" (*JE*, 9:593). This historicizing tendency went in a different direction in nascent Christianity, where Pentecost came to celebrate the coming of the Holy Spirit, making it the "birthday of the church" (Acts 2).

And you shall be careful and you shall do these statutes. A stereotyped expression in Deuteronomy, on which see Note for 4:6.

13 Deuteronomy describes this third yearly feast once again with more brevity and lack of specificity than do other OT law codes. The Feast of Booths (חַג הַסֻּכֹּת), or Feast of Tabernacles (Vg: [*festum*] *tabernaculorum* = "[Feast] of Tents"), celebrates the end of the harvest season when all the grain cut earlier has been threshed, winnowed, and stored away for winter, when all the summer fruit has been harvested from the orchards and vineyards, and when all the grapes have been pressed, made into wine, and sealed in receptacles for the winter and beyond. Processing of grain lasts throughout the summer. The grape harvest begins in late June or July, with grapes being pressed and made into wine on through to the end of summer. The olive harvest peaks in October but may go on longer. As I write, olives are being harvested in Jerusalem during the first weeks of November. Harvested grains would be barley, wheat, and other cereals; summer fruits would most commonly be grapes, olives, figs, pomegranates, dates, and mulberries.

Deuteronomy gives no date for this festival, stating only that it shall be celebrated after the ingathering "from your threshing floor and from your winepress." Elsewhere (Lev 23:39; 1 Kgs 8:2; Ezek 45:25) the feast is assigned a date beginning on the 15th of the 7th month (Tishri = September/October), which is roughly four months after the wheat harvest ends on Pentecost (the 6th of Sivan = May/June). The Feast of Booths is called the Feast of Ingathering in Exod 23:16; 34:22, but the more common name in the OT, particularly in later texts, is the Feast of Booths (Deut 31:10; Lev 23:34; Zech 14:16, 18-19; Ezra 3:4; 2 Chr 8:13). Numbers 29:12-39 prescribes a large number of offerings — obligatory and freewill — for days of the feast, which here and in Lev 23:39-43 are eight instead of seven (see v. 15). A holy convocation is to be held on the first and last days, at which time no work may be done.

The Feast of Booths is prominent in the calendar in certain OT texts, where it is called "*the* pilgrimage feast," הֶחָג (1 Kgs 8:2, 65 (= 2 Chr 5:3; 7:8); 12:32; Neh 8:14). But, as von Rad points out, there is no hint of prominence in Deuteronomy. Haran (1977, 298) says the prominence is due to the large number of sacrifices prescribed in Num 29:12-34, far more than for the Feast of Unleavened Bread and the Feast of Weeks. In Neh 8:17 it says that since the days of Joshua people had neither made nor dwelt in booths as they were doing now, but this does not necessarily mean that the feast suffered a decline during the time of the monarchy, as some have suggested (*JE*, 11:659-60). If Solomon's dedication of the temple coincided with the Feast of Booths (1 Kings 8), as Josephus indicates (*Ant.* 8.99-129), the feast appears to have been very much alive during the monarchy. On that occasion the feast was extended to fourteen days (1 Kgs 8:65 MT). Also, if the Deuteronomic law was to be read every seven years at the feast, as 31:10-11 states, many people would doubtless be there to hear it (Tigay). Some have suggested that the yearly feast at Shiloh reported in Judg 21:19-23, where Benjaminite men took wives from the dancing girls of Shiloh, was a fall harvest festival, thus a Feast of Booths (G. A. Smith; MacRae 1960, 252; Haran 1977, 299). If so, it would be the one OT report of a Feast of Booths celebration prior to the time it was transferred to the central sanctuary in Jerusalem. In the NT, the Feast of Booths is mentioned once in John 7:1-10, where Jesus is said to have been urged by his disciples to go to Jerusalem to attend the feast. At first he refused, but later he changed his mind and went up secretly. For the celebration of the Feast of Booths during the Second Temple period, see Mishnah tractate *Sukkah*. The Feast of Booths is cited or discussed in four places in the Qumran *Temple*

Scroll (11QT 11:13; 27:10–29:12; 42:10-17; 44:6-7), although some columns have missing lines (Yadin 1983, 1:134-36; 2:46, 120-27, 176-80, 186). Discussion here centers on the sacrifices to be offered at the feast (Numbers 29) and the erection of booths for elders and leaders of the congregation on the third-story roof of the temple's outer court, neither of which concern the Deuteronomic preacher.

Feast of Booths. סֻכֹּת means "booths," referring elsewhere in the OT to temporary dwellings of branches and foilage used by soldiers in the field (1 Kgs 20:12, 16), shepherds and herdsman protecting flocks and cattle (Gen 33:17), watchmen guarding fruit trees (Job 27:18), and individuals residing in vineyards during the grape harvest (Isa 1:8). See also Jonah 4:5; Pss 27:5; 31:21(20). It has therefore been suggested that the feast derived its name from the vineyard booths in which farmers resided while they were harvesting grapes (G. A. Smith) and as such was originally an agricultural feast like the Feast of Weeks, of probable Canaanite origin (MacRae 1960, 251-52). It began with Israel's settlement in the land (see Note for 16:12). The Feast of Booths has no tie-in here with Israel's salvation history, but in Lev 23:39-43 a connection is made to Israel's wandering in the desert, where instructions are given for people to reside in booths during the seven days of the feast. During the desert wandering Israelites resided in tents, which the booths presumably symbolize (Driver; Tigay citing Rashbam). The point seems to be that the Israelites had to leave more permanent homes in Egypt for a tent existence in the desert.

threshing floor . . . winepress. A common OT pairing (see Note for 15:14).

14 A repeat of what has been prescribed for celebrating the Feast of Weeks (16:11). See further Note for 12:7. Israel's anticipated gladness approaches hyperbole when mentioned again in v. 15b. Jewish tradition calls for the singing of certain psalms at the Feast of Booths, e.g., Pss 29, 42-43, 76, 81, 113-118 (the Hallel), and 132 (MacRae 1960, 263-64). In 31:10-13 it is stressed that a broad audience of men, women, children, and the sojourner are to be present so they can hear the reading of the Deuteronomic law every seventh year.

15 *Seven days you shall celebrate a pilgrim feast before Yahweh your God in the place that Yahweh will choose.* The verb חָגַג means "celebrate a pilgrim feast" (KBL³; Haran 1977, 356). Priestly legislation concurs in designating this a seven-day feast, nevertheless it adds an eighth day for the concluding convocation (Num 29:12, 35; Lev 23:36, 39). For an eight-day feast, see also 2 Macc 10:6 and *m. Sukkah* 4:1. The concluding day is called "the great day" in John 7:37.

in the place that Yahweh will choose. The LXX expands to "in the place that Yahweh your God will choose."

because Yahweh your God will bless you in all your yield and in all the work of your hands. A variant of a common Deuteronomic expression, where "work of your hands" means "the fruit of your labor" (see Note for 2:7). The Deuteronomic preacher is anticipating Yahweh's blessing as it comes in an abundant harvest.

16 *Three times in the year every one of your males shall appear in the presence of Yahweh your God in the place that he will choose.* See also Exod 23:17; 34:23. The Talmud says "your males," excluding women; nevertheless, women did take part in the pilgrimages, if they were able (Haran 1977, 293-94; Tigay). According to Deuteronomy, entire households are invited to feasts at the central sanctuary (see Note for 12:7), which must mean that only adult men are under obligation to go. Even so, it was impossible for this pilgrimage — like any other — to be fully observed (see Note for 16:2). Tigay says the duty to appear before Yahweh three times a year has to do with Yahweh's sovereignty (Zech 14:16). Yahweh is like the ANE suzerain who requires vassels to appear before him regularly at his residence, to bear him greetings, inquire about his well-being, but most important to bear him tribute (Haran 1977, 290). Cf. the Message from Prince Piḫawalwi to Ibirānu, king of Ugarit (Oppenheim 1967, 137); the treaty between the Hittite king Mursilis II and Niqmepa of Ugarit (D. J. McCarthy 1963, 181-82); and Assurbanipal's "Campaign against the Arabs" (*ANET*³, 297). Neo-Assyrian texts also report violations of this obligation (Cogan 1974, 124, table 2 no. 5). Zedekiah was obliged to appear before Nebuchadrezzar in Babylon to affirm loyalty and perhaps also to bear tribute (Jer 51:59; cf. Bright 1981, 329; Lundbom 2004b, 506).

appear in the presence of. According to Driver, a stock OT phrase for visiting the sanctuary as a worshipper, especially at the great pilgrimages (Exod 34:23-24; Deut 31:11; 1 Sam 1:22; cf. Isa 1:12).

the Feast of Unleavened Bread. Here used in place of Passover as the name for the first yearly feast, indicating that for the Deuteronomic preacher the two feasts are one (see Note for 16:3).

and he shall not appear in the presence of Yahweh empty-handed. See also Exod 23:15b; 34:20b. To appear before Yahweh empty-handed would be a sign of ingratitude.

17 Cf. Ezek 46:5, 11: מַתַּת יָדוֹ ("as much as he can give"). A typical Deuteronomic admonition, that the amount of the gift be left for the worshipper to decide but should be assessed over against the blessing received from Yahweh. Essentially the same thing is said regarding the offerings to be brought for the Feast of Weeks (v. 10). Rashi says those who have large households (lit. many eaters) and great possessions are to bring many burnt offerings and many peace (= other animal) offerings.

Message and Audience

Moses now turns his attention to the yearly feasts, telling people first to be sure to keep Passover in the month of Abib, for in Abib Yahweh brought Israel out of

Egypt by night. For this festival each Israelite is to sacrifice an animal from the flock or the herd, a sacrifice that must be carried out at the central sanctuary. With the meat, no leavened bread may be eaten. For seven days the worshipper must eat only unleavened bread, here called the "bread of affliction," in remembrance of the affliction experienced daily in Egypt. Moses also reminds the worshipper parenthetically of something he or she undoubtedly knows, namely, that the departure from Egypt took place in great haste. Eating this bread will aid the worshipper in remembering this day of days for the rest of his life.

Leaven must not be seen anywhere in the land for seven days. So far as the sacrificial meat is concerned, it must be consumed that night in its entirety. None is to remain until morning. Moses stresses once again that the Passover animal may not be sacrificed in the town where one resides, which repeats the command about making the sacrifice at the place where Yahweh has made his name reside. It may also be a warning to people not making the pilgrimage, that they not sacrifice their Passover animal at home. Again it is stated that the sacrifice shall be carried out in the evening, at sunset, since the exodus is remembered as a night departure. The Passover animal shall be cooked and eaten at the central sanctuary. Then, in the morning, people are to go to their tents. Does this mean go home or go to their temporary dwellings in Jerusalem? Whichever place, the worshipper is to eat unleavened bread for the remaining six days, and on the seventh day attend a holy convocation to Yahweh. On this day no work may be done.

The people are next told to hold a Feast of Weeks to Yahweh, which is to take place seven weeks after the sickle is first put to the standing grain. The grain referred to is barley, and people presumably know about the presentation of the first sheaf of barley during the Feast of Unleavened Bread. For this feast, which lasts only one day, the offering is to be commensurate with Yahweh's blessing to them. One's entire household is invited to make the pilgrimage, and to the feast shall be invited also the Levite, sojourner, orphan, and widow residing in one's town. There, at the central sanctuary, all shall joyfully celebrate the goodness of Yahweh. In showing charity toward the Levite, sojourner, orphan, and widow, people will remember that they, too, were once slaves in Egypt, for which reason they must carry out statutes such as the present one.

Finally, the people are told to hold a seven-day Feast of Booths after they have gathered in all the harvested grain and completed the harvest of the summer fruit, with grapes now being crushed, made into wine, and sealed in jars for storage. Presumably they will know when this feast will take place, for a date is not given. The Deuteronomic preacher tells them once again that they and their entire households are to be glad in this feast, reminding them again that the Levite, the sojourner, orphan, and widow of their towns must be invited to join in. The seven days of celebration are to be at the central sanctuary, and because Yahweh's blessing is sure, people will be glad.

In summary, people hear once again the Covenant Code dictum that all adult males are to appear before Yahweh at the central sanctuary three times a year, at the Feast of Unleavened Bread, or Passover, at the Feast of Weeks, and at the Feast of Booths. No one is to show up empty-handed. As was stated with reference to the Feast of Weeks, each worshipper must bring a gift commensurate with the blessing received from Yahweh.

The audience hearing this call for the celebration of three yearly feasts will be one that has been long settled in the land, far removed from the Canaanite harvest festivals that served as prototypes for the feasts, particularly the Feast of Weeks and the Feast of Booths.

F. Office Holders in Israel (16:18–18:22)

1. The Judge and Matters of Judgment (16:18–17:13)

a) Appointing Judges and Officials (16:18-20)

16 ^{18}*Judges and officials you shall put for yourself within all your gates that Yahweh your God is giving to you for your tribes, and they shall judge the people with righteous judgment.* ^{19}*You shall not pervert judgment, you shall not pay regard to faces, and you shall not take a bribe, because the bribe will blind the eyes of the wise and pervert matters of righteousness.* ^{20}*Righteousness, righteousness you shall pursue, in order that you may live, and you may possess the land that Yahweh your God is giving to you.*

Rhetoric and Composition

The larger discourse beginning with these verses sets forth regulations concerning the four major officeholders in Israelite society: (1) the judge (16:18-20; 17:2-13); (2) the king (17:14-20); (3) the priest (18:1-8), and (4) the prophet (18:9-22). The priest also figures into the section on judges, since he assists in difficult legal cases (17:9, 12). In the section on the prophet, other practitioners not permitted to mediate between Yahweh and his people are named first (18:9-14). The three laws against abominable worship practices in 16:21–17:1 have no apparent connection to the present discourse and must be judged intrusive (Driver).

The present law is delimited at the top end by a *setumah* in M^L and a section in Sam before v. 18 and at the bottom end by a *setumah* in M^L after v. 20. The corresponding section in the Qumran *Temple Scroll* (11QT 51:11-18), which embellishes the law and supplements it with a command that one perverting judgment be put to death, begins after a *petuḥah* and ends with a *petuḥah* (Yadin 1983, 2:227-29). On the use of this passage in the *Temple Scroll*, see Schiffman 1991-92, 562-66.

The law regarding judges has an inclusio made from stereotyped phraseology:

> ... within all your gates *that Yahweh your God is giving to you*   v. 18
> ... the land *that Yahweh your God is giving to you*   v. 20

Notes

16:18 *Judges and officials you shall put for yourself within all your gates that Yahweh your God is giving to you.* Again a broad principle set forth, with no attempt to regulate details of a judicial system (Driver). The present law follows the account in 1:9-18, where Moses appoints judges and officials in the wilderness to assist him in administering justice (cf. Exod 18:13-26). Following settlement in the land, judges and assisting officials are to be appointed in every city, implying that the judicial system set up in the wilderness will not continue or at least will require reconstitution in light of the new reality in Canaan. These judges will be professionals, able to interpret legal principles and decide disputes (25:1). Judges in the wilderness doubled as military commanders (שָׂרִים; Exod 18:21-22; Deut 1:15-16). According to Weinfeld (1977, 73-75), even during the monarchy royal appointees acted in accordance with their military rank, as was true in the Hittite state and at Mari.

Judges are to be distinguished from city elders who decide local matters of a family and community nature, the consequences of which are clear beforehand (Moran; Weinfeld 1977, 81; *EncJud*, 6:578). In a patriarchal society, the natural guardians of justice are men of judgment and experience within the tribe, i.e., heads of families or "elders" (Driver). City elders play a major adjudicating role in five Deuteronomic laws (see Notes for 5:23-24 and 19:12). In one of these, the law regarding the unknown murderer (21:1-9), elders and judges work together to expiate the crime. In particularly difficult cases, judges work together with the priests (17:8-12; 19:15-19). Von Rad believed that originally justice in Israel was carried out not by professional judges, but by city elders. But Weinfeld (1977, 87-88) says it is useless to look for any development within ancient Israel's judicial institution, since its basic judicial procedures were common to all peoples of the ANE. In the premonarchal period Samuel acted as judge in Ramah, making also yearly visits to Bethel, Gilgal, and Mizpah to judge there (1 Sam 7:15-17). Weinfeld notes that Hittite commanders also traveled to towns under their guard to settle disputes among the population. The same was true with provincial supervisors at Mari and district judges in Greece, both of whom went on a circuit to settle disputes. Samuel appointed his sons as judges, but because they took bribes and perverted justice (1 Sam 8:1-3) people rejected them and demanded rule by a king.

The "officials" (שֹׁטְרִים) were individuals whose sphere lay chiefly with the affairs of the army. During the monarchy they were drawn from the military (Weinfeld 1977, 68). They were not military commanders, rather subordinate officials engaged primarily — but not exclusively — in scribal work (1:15; 20:9; see Note for 20:5). Akkadian *šaṭāru* means "to write" (*CAD*, 17/2:225-41). As assistants to the judges, they perhaps functioned like modern court clerks (Driver; Weinfeld, 138; 1977, 83-86). For an Egyptian relief depicting a seated scribe recording judicial evidence, see *ANEP*^{2}, 73 no. 231. Rashi took these officials to be bailiffs. In late rabbinic literature (*Sifre Deut.* §15), the שֹׁטְרִים were those "who administered the lashing" (Hammer 1986, 39). The term "officials" is doubtless comprehensive, referring to all subordinate personnel in the employ of the judges.

It has often been noted (Driver; Albright 1950, 74-82; von Rad; Weinfeld 1977, 65-67) that the procedure here has striking similarities to the judicial reform of King Jehoshaphat (873-849), reported by the Chronicler (2 Chr 19:4-11). Jehoshaphat appointed judges in all Judah's fortified cities, and in Jerusalem set up a high court of leaders and priests to decide disputed cases. Here in Deuteronomy, a high court for settling difficult cases is provided for in 17:8-13. Albright points out also that the reform of Jehoshaphat has a striking parallel in the reform of the Egyptian judiciary under Harmais (Ḥaremḥab; ca. 1350-1319), in which both priests and lay officials were appointed as judges. The same is attested in Hittite documents (Weinfeld 1977, 76).

within all your gates. I.e., in all your cities. On this usage in Deuteronomy, see Note for 5:13-14. In ancient Israel judgment also took place in the city gate (Köhler 1956, 149-75).

that Yahweh your God is giving to you for your tribes. Judges must be appointed separately for each tribe (Rashi; cf. 1:13, 15). The Qumran *Temple Scroll* (11QT 51:11) omits these words, which Schiffman (1991-92, 562-63) thinks may be due to its author sensing a tension between setting up tribal courts and courts in the cities.

and they shall judge the people with righteous judgment. See 1:16. True justice is rooted in "righteous judgment" (מִשְׁפַּט־צֶדֶק), i.e., correct (Weinfeld 1992a, 236) or fair (KBL^3) judgment (cf. Lev 19:15). The OT also says a great deal about "justice and righteousness," with the prophets in particular decrying its absence in kings and the society at large (Gen 18:19; 1 Kgs 10:9; Amos 5:7; Isa

1:21; Jer 22:3, 15; Ps 72:1-2). Weinfeld points out that this latter hendiadys denotes the concept of social justice. Judges, kings, and indeed all others are to practice righteous judgment because Yahweh loves it and practices it (Pss 33:5; 89:15[14]; Job 8:3; 37:23). The tenth benediction in the Eighteen Benedictions of Jewish daily prayer is: "Blessed are you, O Lord, the king who loves justice and righteousness" (Weinfeld 1992a, 231). Yahweh, because of his love of justice, established justice and righteousness in Israel (Ps 99:4; cf. Isa 9:6[7]). According to Snaith (1983, 72-73), both the masculine צֶדֶק and the feminine צְדָקָה originally meant "straightness," for which reason the terms came to be used "for what is or ought to be firmly established, successful, and enduring in human affairs." In general, צֶדֶק refers to the abstract principle of righteousness, whereas צְדָקָה refers to the concrete act (Weinfeld 1992a, 236). Isaiah 56:1 exhorts people to עֲשׂוּ צְדָקָה ("do righteousness!"); גּוֹי אֲשֶׁר־צְדָקָה עָשָׂה in Isa 58:2 means "a nation that did righteousness," i.e., acted righteously. On justice and righteousness in the OT and elsewhere in nations of the ANE, see Weinfeld 1982a; 1992a; also Lundbom 2004a, 111-14, 119-20 on Jer 21:11-12 and 22:3.

19 These instructions are addressed to the people as a whole, who can then repeat them to judicial appointees at the time of their installation. As in the Hittite and Egyptian texts following, judges are forewarned about (1) perverting justice; (2) showing partiality; and (3) taking bribes. Cf. in the Covenant Code Exod 23:2-3, 6-8; see also 2 Chr 19:7, which reports Jehoshaphat's instructions to judges newly appointed at the time of his reform. An Old Babylonian proverb states:

> A judge who perverts justice
> a curse which falls on the righteous party . . .
> these are abominations of Ninurta

Another proverb from Ur states:

> A judge who perverts justice
> a judgment which favors the wicked party
> it is an abomination of Utu (Hallo 1985-86, 23-24)

In the "Military Instructions of the Hittite King Tudhaliya," judges receive these instructions at their installation:

> The lawsuits of the country which you judge, judge them properly, let nobody apply it (the judgment) to his house, his brother, his wife, relative . . . or to his friend for gain of bread and beer; do not make a just case unjust and do not make the unjust case just. (Weinfeld 1977, 76-77)

The Code of Hammurabi spells out harsh treatment for corrupt judges (CH 5; ANET³, 166). If they alter a previously (sealed) judgment, they must pay twelvefold the claim of the case, after which they are expelled from the bench, and may never be reinstated. The sons of Samuel, as was mentioned above, were discredited for taking bribes and perverting justice.

You shall not pervert judgment. לֹא־תַטֶּה מִשְׁפָּט. Here the H-stem of נטה means "to bend, turn aside, pervert" (Friedman: "You shall not bend judgment"). In Exod 23:6 these words are applied specifically to the needy, in Deut 24:17; 27:19 to the sojourner, orphan, and widow. Yahweh does justice (מִשְׁפָּט) for the orphan and the widow and loves the sojourner (Deut 10:18). Amos censures those who turn aside (הִטּוּ) the needy in the gate (Amos 5:12).

you shall not pay regard to faces. לֹא תַכִּיר פָּנִים. Moses gave the same charge to judges appointed in the wilderness, going on to say that they must hear the small and the great alike (1:17). Throughout the OT it is expected that judges will administer justice equitably and impartially (Exod 21:22; 23:1-3, 6-8; Lev 19:15, 35; cf. Ps 82:2; Prov 18:5; Mal 2:9; 2 Chr 19:7). Showing partiality is censured repeatedly in both judicial and wisdom material. The idiom "to pay regard to the face (in judgment)" occurs only in Deuteronomy (1:17; 16:19) and Proverbs (24:23; 28:21), although it has turned up in an Egyptian text (Weinfeld 1972, 245; 1977, 79; 1991, 138, 141). "The Installation of the Vizier" contains these instructions from Thut-mose III (ca. 1490-1436) to his newly appointed vizier, Rekh-mi-Re:

> . . . he is one who does not turn his face towards magistrates or councils, and who does not make for himself [a partisan] of anyone. . . . Do not judge (?) [unfairly (?)], for God abhors partiality. This is a teaching; act accordingly. Regard him whom you know like him whom you do not know, him who is near you like him who is far [from you]. (Faulkner 1955, 22)

See ANET³, 213; A 37-38; B 12-13. It is a problem in every age that people of wealth and power get lenient treatment before the law, while poor folk receive harsh treatment or else no hearing at all. Jeremiah complained about cases of the orphans and the needy not even being heard by the judges (Jer 5:28). Cf. in the NT Jesus' parable about the persistent widow (Luke 18:1-5). Once again, judges are admonished not to show partiality because Yahweh does not (Deut 10:17).

and you shall not take a bribe, because the bribe will blind the eyes of the wise and pervert matters of righteousness. Yahweh takes no bribe (10:17). Bribes are solicited and unsolicited gifts given with improper motives. Here they are payoffs to influence judges, thus perverting the cause of righteousness (Mic 3:11; 7:3; Prov 17:23). They are typically given to acquit the guilty (Isa 5:23) or condemn the innocent (Deut 27:25; Ezek 22:12; Ps 15:5). An aged Samuel said in addressing the people that he had never accepted bribes, and the people gave ringing confirmation of his integrity (1 Sam 12:1-4). Years later Isaiah lashed out at Jerusalem's princes who loved the bribe and ran after gifts, for which reason they would not defend the orphan or take up the widow's cause (Isa 1:23).

The problem is well nigh universal. King Hammurabi in a letter (VIII) reports hearing about a case of bribery in one of his cities, which he passes along to an official with instructions to investigate the matter, confiscate the money, and send the guilty parties to Babylon for punishment (L. W. King 1900, xxxix, 20-22). The Old Babylonian "Hymn to the Sun God" (lines 97-100) calls for the punishment of unscrupulous judges who accept gifts and then allow justice to miscarry, contrasting them with laudable judges who decline gifts but nevertheless "take the part of the weak" (Lambert 1960, 133; *ANET*³, 388 ii). The Assyrian "Šulmānu Texts" refer to the practice of paying *šulmānu* ("a gratuity") in order to have a lawsuit taken up by the judge, a practice that prevailed also at Nuzi (J. Finkelstein 1952, 77-80). The Mishnah (*Bek.* 4:6) states that if a judge takes payment for rendering a legal decision or to give evidence, his judgment is void. The "Stele of King Horemheb" from Egypt (ca. 1349-1319) contains this report of a pharaoh seeking out good judges, appointing them, and charging them at their installation not to take a bribe:

> I toured the country . . . and surveyed it entirely. . . . I sought out persons of integrity, good in character, knowing how to judge thought, hearkening to the words of the palace and the ordinances of the court: I appointed them to judge the Two Lands . . . every one with his stipend. I have led them in the way of life (by) guiding them to justice. . . . I have instructed them, saying: Do not associate intimately with other people, do not take a bribe from another. (Weinfeld 1977, 78; 1991, 141; cf. Pflüger 1946, 265)

Jehoshaphat in his reform that took him throughout the country instructed all newly appointed judges not to take bribes (2 Chr 19:7).

the bribe will blind the eyes of the wise. In contrast to the wording in the Covenant Code (Exod 23:8), the judge here is expected to be "wise," an important concept in Deuteronomy (Weinfeld 1972, 245). Judges who accept bribes are not wise.

matters of righteousness. דִּבְרֵי צַדִּיקִם. I.e., matters dealing with righteousness. But other interpretations are possible. The AV had "words of the righteous," the idea being that bribed judges inevitably twist the words of righteous individuals, presumably litigants or witnesses in the case (so T^Onq; NAB; NJV; NIV; Friedman). But T^NfPsJ assume that bribed judges will be twisting their own words. Other modern Versions (RSV; NRSV; NJB) follow Driver who translated דִּבְרֵי (lit. "words") as "cause." He said that reference here was to statements, arguments, pleas, which in the aggregate made up a man's "case" or "cause" (cf. דְּבָרִים in Exod 24:14; Josh 20:4; 2 Sam 15:3).

20 A grand principle for individuals and societies to embrace. The repetition, צֶדֶק צֶדֶק ("righteousness, righteousness"), is for emphasis. For judges righteousness is everything. Here it is said to be the key to life and possession of the land, two important themes in Deuteronomy (see Note for 4:1). The prophets, too, saw justice and righteousness as necessary for Israel's survival (Isa 1:27; 9:6[7]; 16:5; Hos 2:21[19]; Jer 23:5; 33:15). In the "Hymn to the Sun God," cited above, the judge who takes up the cause of the weak without accepting gifts is said to please the god Šamaš, who "will prolong his life" (Lambert 1960, 133, line 100). The Qumran *Temple Scroll* (11QT 51:16-18), citing this passage, adds at the end that judges taking bribes will get the death sentence, which may be an application of the penalty for the false prophet in 13:6(5) and especially 18:20 (Schiffman 1991-92, 566).

Message and Audience

Moses turns now to discuss leadership once Israel becomes settled in the land. He begins by telling the people to appoint judges and officials in all their cities, just as he himself appointed judges and officials in the wilderness. These shall exist in all of Israel's tribes and shall judge the people with righteous judgment. Instructions for carrying out righteous judgment are given to the whole assembly, who can pass them on to those chosen for office. Speaking to the people directly, Moses says that judges must not pervert judgment, show partiality, or take a bribe. Bribes blind the eyes of the wise, and judges are expected to be men of intellectual and practical wisdom. Bribes also pervert matters in which righteousness stands as a guiding and lofty principle. The point bears repeating. Righteousness only must the judges pursue. Why? To the end that people may live and possess the land Yahweh is giving them.

This homiletical piece on the appointment of judges and subordinates can fit any period of Israel's history, as the principles advocated are found in all countries of the ANE. But it nicely anticipates the mid-9th-cent. reform of King Jehoshaphat, which will be remembered by a late 8th- and early 7th-cent. audience. This audience may also know censures from prophets like Amos, Isaiah, and Micah for judicial abuses in Israel and Judah. And for those living in the time of Jeremiah, Moses' words will come down hard on a nation rife with injustice and plunging headlong into ruin.

Deuteronomy 16

b) Regarding Abominations (16:21–17:1)

16 ^{21} You shall not plant for yourself an Asherah, any piece of wood, beside the altar of Yahweh your God, which you shall make for yourself. ^{22} And you shall not set up for yourself a pillar, which Yahweh your God hates. 17 ^{1} You shall not sacrifice to Yahweh your God an ox or one of the flock that has a blemish, anything bad, for it is an abomination to Yahweh your God.

Rhetoric and Composition

These three miscellaneous laws are widely taken to be an interpolation, having nothing to do with subject matter before or after (Driver). The grouping is delimited at the top end in M^L by a *setumah* before 16:21 and at the bottom end by a *setumah* in M^L and a section in Sam after 17:1. The prohibition against planting an Asherah is separated from the prohibition against erecting pillars by a *setumah* in M^L after 16:21. The prohibition against erecting pillars is separated from the prohibition against sacrificing blemished animals by a *setumah* in M^L after v. 22, which is also the chapter division.

In the Qumran *Temple Scroll* is a brief prohibition (11QT 51:19-21) against worshipping as other nations do, i.e., sacrificing, planting Asheroth, and erecting pillars; the final line is taken from Lev 26:1. It follows the law on appointing judges and officers (11QT 51:11-18), corresponding to the sequence here in Deuteronomy. This prohibition has only an open section at the top end (Yadin 1983, 2:229-31). Then in 11QT 52:1-5 all three of the prohibitions here in Deuteronomy appear as a unit, where again a section occurs only at the top end (Yadin 1983, 2:232-33).

Portions of 16:21–17:1 are contained in 4QDeut^c.

Notes

16:21 The Asherah was either a wooden pole or live tree representing the Canaanite mother-goddess Asherah (see Note for 12:3). Here a live tree seems to be indicated, since the command states that people not "plant" (נטע) such. Earlier Moses directed the people to cut down and burn the Canaanite Asherim after settlement in the land (7:5; 12:3; cf. Exod 34:13); now they are told not to plant such symbols for the worship of Yahweh.

beside the altar of Yahweh your God. An Asherah next to Yahweh's altar would make the Canaanite goddess Yahweh's consort. Yahweh would be replacing Baal, thus assimilating Yahwistic worship into old Canaanite worship. Nevertheless, this very thing seems to have happened during the monarchy. An in-

Deuteronomy 17

scription turned up at Quntillet ʿAjrud in the southern Negeb (dated ca. 800) makes reference to "Yahweh of Samaria and his Asherah" (J. Day 1986, 391-93; Freedman 1987c). Freedman believes that ca. 800, when Jehoahaz and son Jehu ruled in the northern kingdom, an official cult in Samaria may have sponsored the worship of Yahweh and his consort Asherah. Margalit (1990, 279-86) goes on to suggest that the imagery of Israel as Yahweh's wife, which appears in Hosea a half-century later (Hos 2:4-22[2-20]) and survives in Jeremiah (Jer 2:2; 3:1, 20) and in Ezekiel (Ezekiel 16; 23), could be an implied polemical response to this feature of Canaanite religion.

which you shall make for yourself. Before worship was centralized in Jerusalem, numerous legitimate altars (here "the altar of Yahweh") were in existence at the local sanctuaries. In the late 8th and early 7th cents. there was but one altar in the Jerusalem temple. At this later time, reference would be to an altar such as the one made by Urijah the priest during the reign of Ahaz, which was modeled on an altar in Damascus (2 Kgs 16:10-11).

22 The sacred pillar (מַצֵּבָה), an acceptable cultic symbol in the patriarchal age, existing in the wilderness when Moses surrounded an altar with twelve pillars at Sinai (Exod 24:4), and appearing again after the settlement when Joshua erected a pillar in the sanctuary at Shechem (Josh 24:26), was later condemned as a Canaanite male fertility symbol (see Note for 12:3). Deuteronomy thus mandates that Canaanite pillars be broken up after settlement in the land (7:5; 12:3; cf. Exod 23:24; 34:13), adding here that new pillars must not be erected for the worship of Yahweh (cf. Lev 26:1). On standing stones in ancient Palestine, see Graesser 1972.

17:1 This repeats the proviso in the law about sacrifice of firstborns (15:21; cf. Lev 22:17-25). Offering blemished animals became a problem in postexilic times (Mal 1:8) and was doubtless a problem in every age. The principle stated in Lev 1:3, 10 is that animals offered for sacrifice must be "perfect" (תָּמִים), i.e., unblemished. In the Qumran *Temple Scroll* (11QT 52:3-4) this law introduces a discussion on restricting slaughtering in and around the temple (Yadin 1983, 1:312; 2:232).

for it is an abomination to Yahweh your God. On the term "abomination to Yahweh" in Deuteronomy, see Note for 7:25. Moran thinks the three prohibitions in the present cluster have been grouped together because all are regarded as abominations to Yahweh.

Message and Audience

In this interlude, Moses turns aside briefly from judges and judicial matters to cite three cultic acts deemed inadmissible in Yahweh worship: the planting of an Asherah beside Yahweh's altar, the erection of a stone pillar at presumably the same location, and the sacrificing of blemished animals. Yahweh hates all three, for which reason they must not be done.

c) Judgment for Covenant Transgressors (17:2-7)

17 ²*When there is found in your midst, within one of your gates that Yahweh your God is giving to you, a man or a woman who does what is evil in the eyes of Yahweh your God, to transgress his covenant,* ³*and goes and serves other gods and worships them, and the sun or the moon or all the host of heaven, which I have not commanded,* ⁴*and it is told to you and you hear it, and you inquire thoroughly, and behold, it is true, the thing that has been done is established, this abomination in Israel,* ⁵*then you shall bring out that man or that woman who has done this evil thing to your gates — the man or the woman — and you shall stone them with stones, and they shall die.* ⁶*On the testimony of two witnesses or three witnesses the one to die shall be put to death; he shall not be put to death on the testimony of one witness.* ⁷*The hand of the witnesses shall be the first against him to put him to death, and the hand of all the people afterward. So you shall utterly remove the evil from your midst.*

Rhetoric and Composition

This law on justice for Israelites who go after other gods is delimited at the top end by a *setumah* in M^L and a section in Sam before v. 2 and at the bottom end by a *petuḥah* in M^L and sections in Sam and 4QDeut^c after v. 7. In the Qumran *Temple Scroll*, this law is separated from what precedes by a section (11QT 55:15), and a reconstructed text (11QT 56:4) allows for a *petuḥah* at the end (Yadin 1983, 2:250). 11QT 55:15-21 corresponds to vv. 2-5 of the present text; the reconstructed 11QT 56:1-4 corresponds to vv. 6-7. The proviso requiring multiple witnesses is also integrated into the law on the rebellious son (Deut 21:18-23) in 11QT 64:2-13 (Yadin 1983, 1:379-82; 2:288-91).

This law contains a keyword repetition making an inclusio:

When there is found *in your midst* . . .   בְּקִרְבְּךָ   v. 2
. . . remove the evil *from your midst*.   מִקִּרְבֶּךָ   v. 7

The same keyword inclusio occurs in the first segment of the sermon in 13:2-19(1-18) and links the first segment with the second segment (see Rhetoric and Composition there).

Portions of 17:2-7 are contained in 4QDeut^c.

Notes

17:2 *When there is found in your midst.* This indirect form of expression, כִּי־יִמָּצֵא, "when/if there is found," occurs only in Deuteronomy (17:2; 21:1; 22:22; 24:7) and is said by Daube to be a reflection of the shame-cultural element in the work: "By using [this expression] the lawgiver shifts the emphasis from the fearfulness of the crime to the fearfulness of the resulting appearance in the eyes of the beholder — God, above all" (Daube 1969a, 46; 1971a, 7). This interpretation has been challenged by Dempster (1984), who argues that "to be found" (מצא N-stem) is simply a technical term for the discovery of evidence of a crime, whether eyewitness or otherwise, and that the verb denotes this elsewhere in the OT (Gen 44:9, 10, 17; Exod 21:16; 22:1, 3, 6, 7[2, 4, 7, 8]; Jer 2:26; 48:27). Dempster cites Akkadian parallels, although these do not employ the cognate verb *maṣûm* ("to be equal to, to suffice"), but another verb, *ṣabātum* ("to seize, catch, arrest"), which appears in contexts involving theft, adultery, and murder. The extrabiblical evidence, then, is not decisive. Even though מצא in the N-stem may otherwise denote the discovery of a crime in the OT, it could still reflect the shame-cultural element Daube finds in Deuteronomy. The word בְּקִרְבְּךָ ("in your midst") is lacking in G^B, but this can be attributed to haplography (homoeoarcton: ב ... ב). Other major textual witnesses all contain the word, including 4QDeut^c (Ulrich, Cross et al. 1995, 26-27).

within one of your gates. I.e., within one of your cities (T; see Note for 5:14).

a man or a woman who does what is evil in the eyes of Yahweh your God, to transgress his covenant. The covenant transgression is worship of other gods, including astral deities (v. 3; 4:19; cf. Josh 23:16). In 4:13 the "covenant" is said to consist of doing the Ten Commandments (cf. 26:13). In 4:23-25, "forgetting the covenant" and "doing what is evil in the eyes of Yahweh your God" means breaking the second commandment, which prohibits the making of idols (5:8-10). In Josh 7:11, 15, "transgressing the covenant" means violating the holy war ban. On Deuteronomy's stock expression, "to do evil in the eyes of Yahweh (your God)," see Note for 4:25-26.

3 Violations of the first and second commandments (5:7, 9). The Covenant Code, in addition to these two commandments, contains a law prohibiting the "sacrificing to any god" (Exod 22:19[20]). It says nothing about Assyrian astral worship, which flourished later during Manasseh's reign (2 Kgs 21:3-5) and was rooted out in Josiah's reform (2 Kgs 23:5, 11). But soon after it was resumed. Jeremiah censures it in a burlesque prophecy on disinterment (Jer 8:2), and in Zedekiah's reign Ezekiel reports of twenty-five men who are again worshipping the sun in the temple (Ezek 8:16). According to Deuteronomy, heavenly bodies are not to be served and worshipped because Israel saw no divine form at Horeb (4:19).

and goes and serves other gods. For this Deuteronomic expression, see Note for 13:7.

the host of heaven. The term occurs elsewhere in 2 Kgs 17:16; 21:3, 5; 23:4-5; Zeph 1:5; Jer 19:13 and 33:22 (in a good sense), but nowhere in the 8th-cent. prophets. Astarte worship was alternately called "host of heaven" worship (Lundbom 1999, 476-77). Yahweh's allotment of sun, moon, star, and host of heaven worship to people of other nations in 4:19 is taken in Jewish tradition as having no bearing on the present passage (*Sifre Deut.* §148:6).

which I have not commanded. The expression occurs in Jer 7:22, 31; 19:5; 32:35. The first person is unusual, since Yahweh is not the usual speaking voice in Deuteronomy (see Note for 7:4). But perhaps Moses is saying that he issued the command.

4 *and it is told to you and you hear it, and you inquire thoroughly.* A rumor of the same transgression in 13:13-15(12-14), which has occurred city-wide, requires investigation. Investigations in Deuteronomy are normally conducted by the city elders (19:18; 21:2-4; 22:15-21; 25:7-10). The LXX lacks "and you hear (it)," which could be an omission due to haplography (homoeoarcton: ו ... ו). Cf. 13:15[14].

and you inquire thoroughly. וְדָרַשְׁתָּ הֵיטֵב. Another possible reading is "then you shall inquire thoroughly" (cf. RSV; NJV; NIV), which interrupts the protasis (Wevers 1995, 280). The LXX, as Wevers points out, translates with a future verb: καὶ ἐκζητήσεις σφόδρα ("and you shall search out diligently"). The Targums interpret similarly. But the MT, continuing with a perfect form of the verb, argues against this interpretation (cf. AV).

and behold, it is true, the thing that has been done is established. For the translation of this phrase, which takes אֱמֶת and נָכוֹן in apposition to one another, see Note for 13:15.

this abomination in Israel. On the term תּוֹעֵבָה ("abomination"), see Note for 7:25.

5 *then you shall bring out that man or that woman who has done this evil thing to your gates — the man or the woman.* After a lengthy protasis in vv. 2-4, we now begin the apodosis. "Your gates" means the gates of the city (22:24), where justice is carried out (Köhler 1956, 149-75). The words "who has done this evil thing to your gates" are lacking in G^B, which may be attributed to haplography (homoeoarcton: א ... א). They are present in Sam, T, and 4QDeut^c.

the man or the woman. Omitted in the LXX and Vg, but present in T. Wevers (1995, 281) takes this omission along with the prior one as intentional simplification by the LXX translator.

and you shall stone them with stones, and they shall die. The punishment specified also in 13:11(10). Stonings occur outside the city (Lev 24:14; Num 15:36; Acts 7:58; Heb 13:12).

6 This being a capital offense, it is necessary that more than one witness testify against the accused (Num 35:30; Heb 10:28). But in 19:15, two or three witnesses are required for the conviction of "any sin or any iniquity." This stipulation aims at bringing objectivity to bear; otherwise it will be one person's word against another (cf. Matt 18:15-16; John 8:17). It also seeks to prevent a blatantly false witness, which would violate the ninth commandment (5:20). It is perfectly possible, of course, that two or three witnesses — or even more — may conspire to bring false testimony (cf. Exod 23:1), as happened in the case of Naboth, who fell victim to a contrived miscarriage of justice (1 Kgs 21:8-13), and happened centuries later when Jesus was put on trial (Matt 26:59-61). In most cases multiple witnesses will be a deterrent against false testimony.

Although there is no clear parallel to this law in known laws of the ANE, Yaron (1970, 552-53) points out that in Middle Assyrian Laws (MAL A 12, 17, 40) the consistent use of "witnesses" (plural) would mean two witnesses minimum. Also, in the Hittite Laws (HL 37; $ANET^3$, 190) is a reference to "two or three" men chasing after an eloper, which could refer to two or three witnesses to a crime. Witnesses (plural) are referred to in the Code of Hammurabi (CH 13; $ANET^3$, 166). In the NT, two or three witnesses are specified for deciding charges of wrongful behavior in the church (Matt 18:16; 1 Tim 5:19). Josephus (*Ant.* 4.219) adds a proviso to the present law, saying that testimonies from women or slaves are not to be accepted.

two witnesses or three witnesses. Michaelis (1814, 4:325) says this is not simply indefinite language but a requirement of three witnesses instead of two in cases where one witness is at the same time an accuser or an informer.

7 *The hand of the witnesses shall be the first against him to put him to death, and the hand of all the people afterward.* Another deterrent for false witness. A witness presenting false evidence in a capital case exposes himself to the possibility of blood revenge (von Rad). In the NT, see John 8:7; Acts 7:58.

So you shall utterly remove the evil from your midst. On this Deuteronomic phrase, which occurs slightly altered in v. 12, see Note for 13:6.

Message and Audience

The audience is told in the present law that if a man or woman in one of their cities is found to be transgressing the covenant, i.e., going after other gods and worshipping heavenly deities, which Yahweh, needless to say, never commanded, the report of such a thing having occurred must be investigated thoroughly, presumably by the city elders. If it is true and the facts are established, the accused man or woman is to be brought to the city gate for judgment, then taken outside the city and stoned. The audience is told that capital sentences such as this can be carried out only on the testimony of two or three witnesses; one witness is not enough. The witnesses testifying in the case shall throw the first stone, with people of the city then joining in the stoning until the person dies. In this way evil will be removed from the midst of Israel.

In the late 8th and early 7th cents. this law could have had application to Assyrian astral worship entering Israel in its last days (2 Kgs 17:16) and Judah during Manasseh's reign (2 Kgs 21:3-5)

d) Extraordinary Cases to the Priests and the Judge (17:8-13)

17 [8] *When the matter for judgment is extraordinary for you, between blood and blood, between claim and claim, or between injury and injury — matters of disputes within your gates, then you shall rise and go up to the place that Yahweh your God will choose.* [9] *And you shall come to the Levitical priests and to the judge who will be in those days, and you shall inquire, and they shall declare to you the word of judgment.* [10] *Then you shall do in accordance with the word that they declare to you from that place where Yahweh will choose, and you shall be careful to do according to all that they instruct you.* [11] *In accordance with the instruction that they instruct you, and according to the judgment that they speak to you, you shall do; you shall not turn aside from the word that they declare to you, right or left.* [12] *And the person who acts with presumption, not listening to the priest who stands to minister there before Yahweh your God, or to the judge, then that person shall die. So you shall utterly remove the evil from Israel.* [13] *And all the people shall hear and fear, and they shall not act presumptuously again.*

Rhetoric and Composition

This law dealing with cases to be decided by Israel's high court is delimited at the top end by a *petuḥah* in M^L and a section in Sam before v. 8 and at the bottom end by a *setumah* in M^L and a section in Sam after v. 13. 2QDeut² also has a section after v. 13 (Baillet, Milik, and de Vaux 1962, 61). These verses are partially reconstructed in the Qumran *Temple Scroll* in 11QT 56:05-07, 1-11 (Yadin 1983, 2:250-52), where they follow, as here, the law on justice in the city gates. Yadin says an open section exists prior to the beginning of the law (before 11QT 56:05), but no section is present at the bottom end (after 11QT 56:11).

Portions of 17:8-13 are contained in 2QDeut[b].

Notes

17:8 *When the matter for judgment is extraordinary for you.* The verb here is פלא, "to be extraordinary, too difficult," which occurs again in 30:11. The matter is extraordinary in that it is beyond the power of local officials to handle (Driver). In the wilderness, provisions were made for routine cases to be decided by appointed officials, with difficult cases coming before Moses (1:13-18; cf. Exod 18:13-26). Now, in anticipation of settlement in the land, a lower court in the cities is to handle routine matters, and a higher court of priests and a judge is to adjudicate difficult cases at the central sanctuary. Weinfeld (1977, 81) believes that only cases where legal principles are involved will be referred to the higher court. In the cities, elders will play a role in adjudicating certain civil and criminal cases (see Notes for 5:23-24 and 19:12). In local matters, e.g., family affairs, levirate marriage, blood redemption, and defamation of virgins, elders can act without consulting other officials. They act independently when no national or royal interests are at stake, which is what obtained in Hittite society.

The present law follows the appointment of judges and officers in 16:18-20. Both passages are to be compared with 2 Chr 19:5-11, which reports Jehoshaphat's appointment of judges in the cities of Judah and the establishment of a high court consisting of priests and national leaders in Jerusalem (Albright 1950, 74-82; Weinfeld 1977, 65-67). This high court became the prototype of the Great Sanhedrin in the Second Temple (NT) period. It met in Jerusalem and was comprised of seventy or seventy-one members, depending on whether the presiding high priest was included or omitted from the list (*m. Sanh.* 1:5-6; *Šebu.* 2:2; cf. Num 11:16, 24-25: Moses plus seventy elders). The Great Sanhedrin consisted of chief priests, elders, scribes, and other leading citizens (cf. Mark 15:1).

between blood and blood. The Targums and Rashi associate this with menstruation (T^{Nf}: "between the blood of virginity and the blood of murder"; T^{PsJ}: "between impure blood and pure blood"), but this cannot be right (Tigay). Reference is to homicide cases (Rashbam; Luther), i.e., whether they are manslaughter or (premeditated) murder (19:4-13; Exod 21:12-14; Num 35:9-34).

between claim and claim. Hebrew דין is a general term meaning "legal claim" (Jer 5:28; 22:16; 30:13; KBL^3), but some (Driver; G. E. Wright) think reference here is only to cases involving property, e.g., cases cited in Exod 22:6-14(7-15). The Targums say "between civil and capital/criminal cases" (cf. *b. Sanh.* 87a). Luther gives a broad interpretation, saying these would be cases of theft, robbery, quarrel, and slander.

or between injury and injury. Hebrew נֶגַע can mean "disease, plague" (Gen 12:17; Exod 11:1; 1 Kgs 8:37) or "stroke, injury" (21:5; 2 Sam 7:14; see Note for 24:8). The Targums took the term here to mean "plague," one example of which was leprosy (= scale disease; 24:8-9; Leviticus 13–14). But "injury" or "assault" is better (Tigay; Friedman), as the reference is doubtless to cases involving physical injury (Exod 21:18-27; 22:1-2[2-3]; Lev 24:19-20). The LXX adds a fourth case: "between controversy and controversy" (ἀνὰ μέσον ἀντιλογία ἀντιλογίας), which seems redundant after "between claim and claim," unless these claims have specific reference.

matters of disputes within your gates. I.e., within your cities. Hebrew רִיב means "dispute" or "lawsuit" (19:17; 25:1). This is a summary statement of the matters requiring judgment.

then you shall rise and go up to the place that Yahweh your God will choose. I.e., to the central sanctuary (12:5), where the case will be brought before Levitical priests and the judge in office (v. 9). Local judges and officers (16:18) will make the referral. Deuteronomy contains one case calling for referral to the central sanctuary, viz., that of the false witness (19:16-18). By the 7th cent. the high court will be convening in Jerusalem, but in the premonarchic period it will have been at one of Israel's other sanctuaries. Deborah judged people under a palm between Ramah and Bethel (Judg 4:4-5), and Samuel is said to have made yearly visits to regional sanctuaries, judging people at Bethel, Gilgal, Mizpah, and at his home in Ramah (1 Sam 7:6, 15-17). Samuel's sons judged at Beersheba, but without distinction, leading to Israel's clamor for a king (1 Sam 8:1-4).

With the establishment of the monarchy, the king with assisting officers became the supreme judicial authority and final court of appeals (2 Sam 12:1-6; 15:2-4; Jer 38:7-10). This carried on the wilderness tradition, where Moses functioned as a one-man high court (Exod 18:22; 26; Deut 1:17). Hittite texts contain instructions about "big cases" being sent to the king (Weinfeld 1977, 75). The Chronicler tells us that David appointed six thousand Levites as judges and officers (1 Chr 23:4), which could include some sitting on a high court. We do not know whether a high court existed in the time of Solomon, but one must have been established. G. E. Wright thinks it inconceivable that Solomon would have tried all cases personally, as he did the celebrated one about a baby's true identity (1 Kgs 3:16-28). A Jerusalem high court was established by Jehoshaphat, who appointed over it two heads: a chief priest over "every matter of Yahweh" and a prince (נָגִיד) over "every matter of the king" (2 Chr 19:11). How justice was administered in northern Israel during the divided monarchy is not known.

The Covenant Code speaks about bringing cases "to God" (Exod 21:6; 22:7-8[8-9]), which presumably would be before a priest at one of the sanctuaries, once again carrying on a tradition established in the wilderness (Exod 18:19). In two of the cases, Exod 18:19 and 21:6, the detail about the case being brought "to God" is omitted in Deuteronomy (Deut 1:17; 15:17), which has a more secular attitude toward judicial procedure (Weinfeld 1972, 233).

Deuteronomy 17

9 *the Levitical priests and to.* Lacking in the LXX, which is probably due to haplography (homoeoarcton: ה . . . ה, or homoeoteleuton: אל . . . אל).

the Levitical priests. The expression הַכֹּהֲנִים הַלְוִיִּם ("the priests, the Levites"), occurring in Deuteronomy (17:9, 18; 18:1; 24:8; 27:9), Jeremiah (Jer 33:18), and elsewhere (Josh 3:3; 8:33; Ezek 43:19; 44:15), means "the Levitical priests" (Driver 1895, lxxxii no. 50). In Deuteronomy all Levites are priests having rights to minister at Yahweh's altar (Deut 18:1; Driver 1895, xxv; Emerton 1962; Levine 1993, 104-5, 449-50). In P material (Numbers and Leviticus) and later in the postexilic period, the Levites are made subordinate to priests descending from Aaron (Lev 1:5-9; 2 Chr 29:4; 34:30: "the priests *and* the Levites"). See further Note for 12:12.

With the high court being located at one of the main sanctuaries and later at Jerusalem, we might expect priests to be involved. Driver says priests would possess a hereditary knowledge of civil and criminal law, giving them an advantage over local elders or lay judges. Priests were entrusted with teaching and interpreting the law (33:10; Jer 18:18; Ezek 7:26; Hag 2:10-14; 2 Chr 15:3) and took part in the administration of justice (21:5; Isa 28:7; Ezek 44:24). But Milgrom (1973, 159) says that priests sitting on the high court ranks as one of Deuteronomy's far-reaching innovations, for now priestly authority extends beyond the sacred realm. In P material, priests become involved in judicial matters only when insoluable cases must be referred to God, at which time they administer oaths, employ the Urim and Thummim, and oversee ritual ordeals (Exod 22:6-9[7-10]; 28:29-30; Num 5:11-31). But their direct involvement in judicial matters should occasion no surprise, since such is attested elsewhere in the ANE. In the Egyptian court under Harmais (Ḥaremḥab; ca. 1350-1319), priests and judges sit together in judgment (see Note for 16:18). Milgrom (1973, 158-59) therefore challenges Weinfeld's view that the (Levitical) priests had no hand in the writing of Deuteronomy and that Deuteronomy, containing as it does wisdom influence, is a "secular" document written by scribes. Milgrom says Deuteronomy grants priests more powers — not fewer — than any other biblical law code.

the judge who will be in those days. I.e., who will be currently in office. Hebrew שֹׁפֵט is singular, and virtually all Versions ancient and modern translate it "judge" (T^{Nf} has "judges"). Verse 12 again has "judge" singular, but 19:17, a reference similar to the present one, has "judges." The law here may have in mind a head judge (Tigay), which could be indicated also in 25:2. The expression "who will be in those days" is Deuteronomic (17:9; 19:17; 26:3; Driver 1895, lxxxi no. 32).

and you shall inquire. וְדָרַשְׁתָּ. The LXX and Sam have "and they shall inquire," assuming that it is the priests and/or judge who must investigate before a decision is reached. This reading may be correct (Driver; cf. 19:18). The MT reading makes sense, but in 13:15(14); 17:4; 19:18, the verb דרשׁ carries more the meaning of "investigate."

535

Deuteronomy 17

and they shall declare to you the word of judgment. The "word of judgment" (2 Chr 19:6) is the sentence of judgment (AV).

10 *Then you shall do in accordance with the word that they declare to you.* Here and in v. 11 Heb עַל־פִּי (lit. "according to the mouth of") means "in accordance with." Once the judgment sentence has been announced, it must be carried out as prescribed.

and you shall be careful to do. A stock Deuteronomic expression (see Note for 5:1).

according to all that they instruct you. כְּכֹל אֲשֶׁר יוֹרוּךָ. From ירה ("instruct") comes תּוֹרָה ("torah, instruction, law"). The noun and verb appear together in the following verse.

11 The Deuteronomic preacher repeats his point that decisions from the priests and judge are final and must be carried out without deviation. The LXX and Vg lack "that they instruct you."

you shall not turn aside . . . right or left. On this expression, see Note for 2:26-27.

12 *And the person who acts with presumption, not listening to the priest who stands to minister there before Yahweh your God, or to the judge, then that person shall die.* Hebrew זָדוֹן means "insolence, presumption, arrogance" (18:22; Jer 49:16; Ezek 7:10; Prov 13:10), where often in the OT an accompanying prediction is that the person with such an interior disposition is headed for a fall. The verb זדן describes Israel's ill-fated attempt to enter the promised land (1:43).

to the priest . . . or to the judge. The verdict will sometimes be given by the priest, sometimes by the judge, depending on the nature of the case (Driver).

the priest who stands to minister there before Yahweh your God. To "stand before someone" is to be in one's service (1 Kgs 10:8; 12:8; Jer 36:21; 40:10). Priests are in the service of Yahweh (Deut 10:8; 18:7), as are prophets (1 Kgs 17:1; Jer 15:19) and more ordinary worshippers (Jer 7:10).

then that person shall die. A capital sentence awaits the person who refuses to accept the decision of the court. Tigay says "the person" probably refers to one of the parties to the case, but Patrick (1985, 118) and Stuhlman (1990, 624) think the persons liable would be members of the lower court, who are obliged to abide by the higher court's ruling. Defiance of a high court decision by anyone in Hittite law (HL 173) is considered a capital offense:

> If anyone rejects the judgment of the king, his house. . . . If anyone rejects the judgment of a "major" (LÚ DUGUD), they shall cut off his head (Weinfeld 1977, 76).

So you shall utterly remove the evil from Israel. See 17:7 and Note for 13:6.

13 Here and in 13:12(11); 21:21 capital punishment is believed to be a deterrent to crime.

Message and Audience

In following up an earlier directive about appointing judges and officers in the cities, Moses now turns to the question of deciding extraordinary cases of homicide, civil matters, and personal injury, saying that these must be referred to the central sanctuary. At the central sanctuary a high court consisting of Levitical priests and a sitting judge will be consulted, and they will render a decision. Once a decision has been announced, all concerned must abide by it. There can be no deviation from court instructions one way or the other. Any person acting presumptuously, that is, not listening to the priest or judge's decision, shall die. In this way will evil be purged from Israel, and those observing this harsh penalty will be put on notice not to act presumptuously in the future.

This law seems aimed at premonarchic Israel, when difficult cases were referred to priests and a single judge at one of the main sanctuaries. In the late 8th and early 7th cents., when the king will be the supreme judge holding court in Jerusalem, the law will have in mind the 9th-cent. reform carried out by Jehoshaphat, as well as any subsequent judicial reform about which we have no knowledge.

2. What Sort of King for Israel? (17:14-20)

17 *¹⁴When you enter into the land that Yahweh your God is giving to you, and you take possession of it and dwell in it, and you say, "I will set over myself a king like all the nations that surround me," ¹⁵you may indeed set over yourself a king whom Yahweh your God will choose. From the midst of your brethren you may set over yourself a king; you may not put over yourself a foreigner who is not one of your brethren. ¹⁶Only he shall not multiply for himself horses, and he shall not cause the people to return to Egypt in order to multiply the horse, since Yahweh said to you, "You shall not return on this road ever again." ¹⁷And he shall not multiply for himself wives, and he shall not turn aside his heart; also silver and gold he shall not greatly multiply for himself. ¹⁸And it will be when he is seated upon the throne of his kingdom, that he shall write for himself a copy of this law upon a scroll from the Levitical priests. ¹⁹And it shall be with him, and he shall recite it all the days of his life, in order that he learn to fear Yahweh his God, to keep all the words of this law and these statutes, to do them, ²⁰that his heart not be lifted up among his brethren, and that he not turn aside from the commandment, right or left, in or-*

Deuteronomy 17

der that he will prolong the days over his kingdom — he and his sons — in the midst of Israel.

Rhetoric and Composition

These verses setting up guidelines for choosing a king are delimited at the top end by a *setumah* in M^L and a section in Sam before v. 14 and at the bottom end by a *setumah* in M^L and a section in Sam after v. 20, which is also the chapter division. Verses 14-17 appear in the Qumran *Temple Scroll* (11QT 56:12-19), after which is a closed section (Yadin 1983, 2:252-55). Verses 19-20 are missing from the top of 11QT 57, but Yadin's reconstruction (11QT 57:01-07) allows for a longer text.

Portions of 17:14-20 are contained in 1QDeut^b, 2QDeut^b, 4QDeut^c, and 4QDeut^f.

Notes

17:14-15 *When you enter into the land . . . and you take possession of it and dwell in it, and you say, "I will set over myself a king like all the nations that surround me," you may indeed set over yourself a king whom Yahweh your God will choose.* The Deuteronomic preacher anticipates in Israel precisely what occurred later: people will want a king like the other nations. Moses therefore grants permission, just as Samuel finally did, with the proviso that the king be chosen by Yahweh. Von Rad says the monarchy is a concession to later reality, which may also be indicated by many provisos and warnings of what kingship is not to be and only one positive directive, viz., that the king be sure to keep the law and its statutes. Other scholars see Deuteronomy as a whole, and this law in particular, as sharply delimiting the power of the king, particularly when a comparison is made to kingship elsewhere in the ANE (Greenberg 1990, 105-6; Knoppers 1996, 329; Levinson 2001a). Knoppers says:

> The powers of the monarchy, so dominant in the civilizations of the ancient Near East, are greatly circumscribed in Dtn 17,14-20. The belief in sacral kingship, prevalent at Ugarit, Egypt, and Mesopotamia, that a king mediates between the divine and human spheres, is absent from Deuteronomy. In Deuteronomy the relationship between God and people is primary.

Weinfeld (1985, 95-97), however, thinks that Deuteronomy has a positive attitude toward kingship, the whole of the Deuteronomic code, which in his view is

Deuteronomy 17

a manual for the king and the people. He points out that the present verses are the only <u>ones in pentateuchal law to deal with a king</u>.

This passage reflects the struggle between Samuel and the people over kingship, where the people clamor for a king and Samuel resists (1 Samuel 8). In Israel, Yahweh is King (Judg 8:23; 1 Sam 8:7; cf. Deut 33:5; Num 23:21; Isa 6:1-5; Pss 5:3[2]; 10:16; 24:7-10; 29:10). Samuel, however, concedes nothing about the corruptness of his own sons as judges (1 Sam 8:3-5). The OT suggests elsewhere that a military threat contributed to Israel's need for a king (1 Samuel 11; 12:12; cf. 8:20).

When you enter into the land . . . and you take possession of it. On the stock expression "to enter and take possession of the land," see also 4:1, 5; 6:18; 7:1; 11:10, 29; 23:21(20) and Note for 1:8.

like all the nations. See 1 Sam 8:5, 20. <u>Kingship is understood here</u> as being foreign in origin, which goes some way in explaining why Deuteronomy accepts it <u>with reserve</u>. Deuteronomy does not want Israel to be "like all the nations."

you may indeed set over yourself a king. שׂוֹם תָּשִׂים עָלֶיךָ מֶלֶךְ. The verb שִׂים ("set") here means "appoint" (cf. 1:13). The construction is emphatic, yet only to anticipate the provisos and warnings to follow, which are also emphatic (note the apodictic commands in vv. 16-17).

whom Yahweh your God will choose. This first proviso was later carried out with respect to Saul and David, also after the kingdom became divided (1 Sam 9:16-17; 10:20-24; 16:1-13; 2 Sam 6:21; 1 Kgs 11:29-39; 2 Kgs 9:1-13).

From the midst of your brethren you may set over yourself a king; you may not put over yourself a foreigner who is not one of your brethren. When David was approached about reigning as king over all Israel, those supporting him strengthened their case by saying, "Look, we are your bone and your flesh" (2 Sam 5:1). Later still Jeremiah, anticipating a rebuilt Jerusalem, envisioned a ruler who would be one of the people's own (Jer 30:21). A Hittite treaty between Suppiluliumas I of Hatti (ca. 1350) and Kurtiwaza (= Shattiwaza) of Mitanni concludes with a blessing calling for the longevity of the Hurrians' royal line, provided the vassal remain faithful to the treaty:

> If . . . you, Kurtiwaza, the prince, and (you), the Hurrians, fulfill this treaty and (this) oath, may these gods protect you. . . . May the Mitanni country return to the place which it occupied before, may it thrive and expand. May you, Kurtiwaza, your sons, and your sons' sons (descended) from the daughter of the Great King of the Hatti land, and (you), the Hurrians exercise kingship forever. May the throne of your father persist, may the Mitanni country persist. (*ANET*[3], 206; cf. Beckman 1996, 44, 48)

Still, this prohibition against a foreign king is puzzling, since so far as we know Israel was never ruled by an outsider. Moran and Daube (1971b) wonder if there might be an allusion here to Abimelech, whose half-Shechemite origin led to a revolt (Judges 9). Much later, Herod Agrippa I (10 B.C. to A.D. 44) is said to have been reading the Torah, and when he came to this passage, his eyes filled up with tears because he was not of pure Jewish origin (*m. Soṭah* 7:8; *EncJud*, 2:416-17). The Constitution of the United States (Article II Section 1) specifies that "No person except a natural born citizen . . . shall be eligible to the office of President." But Nicholson (2006) thinks the prohibition is best understood against the Neo-Assyrian hegemony over Israel and Judah, and that "foreigner" in the text has in mind "The Great King," the king of Assyria.

you may not put over yourself a foreigner. אִישׁ נָכְרִי is lit. "a foreign man." On the verbal form "you may not," which denotes the indignity of doing such and such, see Note for 12:17.

16 *Only he shall not multiply for himself horses.* Warnings about what this king is not to be, which qualify the statement acceding to kingship, begin with a restrictive רַק ("only"). The warnings are three: not to multiply horses, wives, or wealth, precisely what Solomon went on to do. Solomon had a large number of horses (1 Kgs 4:26), and since he did not wage war, these horses (and chariots) appear to have been mainly for show, i.e., to enhance his prestige in processions and ceremonies. Ikeda (1982, 223) says the writer of 1 Kgs 10:26-27 wants to depict King Solomon as "the very wealthy, extravagant 'collector,' more than a mere builder of strong military forces." Both Absalom and Adonijah augmented their claims to the throne by a public show of horses and chariots (2 Sam 15:1; 1 Kgs 1:5), but in each case without success.

and he shall not cause the people to return to Egypt in order to multiply the horse, since Yahweh said to you, "You shall not return on this road ever again." This prohibition aims at keeping people from going to Egypt for the purpose of buying horses, since upon leaving Egypt in the exodus Israel was never supposed to return. The source of this quotation is not known (but see Exod 14:13); nevertheless, Deuteronomy repeats it again in 28:68. Solomon imported horses from Egypt and Kue, and his traders exported them to kings of the Hittites and Syria (1 Kgs 10:28-29). Egypt was famous for its breed of horses (as Arabia is today), which were imported from Asia during Egypt's Second Intermediate Period (ca. 1650-1570), the period of Hyksos rule (Breasted 1906b, 222; Boessneck 1976, 25; *ABD*, 3:346). Remains of a horse have turned up at the Buhen fortress, which was destroyed ca. 1675 (Emery et al. 1979, 191-95). On the horse after its introduction into Egypt and the excellent breeds that developed there, see Ikeda 1982, 227-31.

17 *And he shall not multiply for himself wives, and he shall not turn aside his heart.* This second warning is actually a double warning: that the king not multiply wives for himself and that he not turn aside his heart (from Yahweh).

The two become related in the case of Solomon. The Qumran *Temple Scroll* makes this clearer than MT. It reads (11QT 56:18-19): "that they [the wives] not turn aside his heart from me" (Yadin 1983, 2:253; Mueller 1979-80, 250). Solomon did indeed take many foreign women — seven hundred wives, princesses, and three hundred concubines — and they turned his heart away from Yahweh in the direction of other gods (1 Kgs 11:1-8). Knoppers (1996, 345) claims that the view here does not represent the Deuteronomic Historian's stance on kingship. The issue in the present law and for the Deuteronomic Historian is *many foreign wives*.

also silver and gold he shall not greatly multiply for himself. At the beginning of his reign Solomon was promised great wealth, even though he did not seek it (1 Kgs 3:10-14). That wealth came (1 Kgs 10:14-26): in one year 666 talents of gold, besides what was gained in trading (vv. 14-15). The Deuteronomic Historian says he made "silver as common in Jerusalem as stone" (v. 27).

18 The Qumran *Temple Scroll* (11QT 56:20-21) has another hand writing up the scroll for the king, which is more likely. It reads: "And when he sits on the throne of his kingdom they shall write for him this law in a book from that which is in the charge of the priests" (Yadin 1983, 1:83; 2:254). Weinfeld (1985, 97) cites a letter written to the Assyrian king Esarhaddon, where the colophon says on behalf of the king: "I wrote it in tablets . . . and put it in my palace to my constant reading." This colophon appears also in Hunger 1968, no. 319. The later Assyrian king Assurbanipal (668-627) boasts that he is able to read and write (Hunger 1968, 98 no. 319 lines 4-8; *ABD*, 4:746-47). Noteworthy here is that Israel's king is made subject to divine law. He must learn and obey the law just like any other Israelite. In other ANE societies the king is the lawgiver; in Israel the lawgiver is Yahweh.

when he is seated upon the throne of his kingdom. Presumably when he ascends the throne.

a copy of this law. מִשְׁנֵה הַתּוֹרָה הַזֹּאת. The LXX translates as τὸ δευτερονόμιον τοῦτο ("this second law"), which is the rendering that led to the LXX name for the book: *Deuteronomion*. But Heb מִשְׁנֶה means "repetition" in the sense of "copy" or "duplicate," so the expression is better translated "a copy of this law" (T^Onq; Driver 1895, i; von Rad, in *IDB*, 1:831). Driver notes the same misrendering of מִשְׁנֶה in LXX Josh 9:5 (= MT 8:32). The Qumran *Temple Scroll* (11QT 56:20-21) has "they shall write for him this law upon a scroll" (Yadin 1983, 2:254), omitting מִשְׁנֶה ("copy"). On the names for Deuteronomy, see *Introduction: Name and Canonicity*.

from the Levitical priests. The king will get the Deuteronomic law from the Levitical priests, who will have custody of it (31:9).

19 The king must learn the Deuteronomic law by reciting it throughout his kingship (cf. 6:7; 11:19). The same basic charge is given to Joshua when he assumes leadership in Israel (Josh 1:8). By reciting the law the king will learn to "fear Yahweh," which is expected of every Israelite (see Note for 4:10). Here, as elsewhere, fearing Yahweh will result in doing the commandments.

and he shall recite it. The verb קרא here means "recite, read aloud" (31:11). Even if the king will be reading the law to himself, he will most likely read it aloud. Silent reading is attested in antiquity (Knox 1968), but it was not usual. Ancient people commonly read aloud (O'Brien 1921; McCartney 1948; Achtemeier 1990, 15-19; Gilliard 1993, 694; cf. Acts 8:30).

all the words of this law. כָּל־דִּבְרֵי הַתּוֹרָה הַזֹּאת. This phrase, together with "this law" of v. 18, occurs elsewhere only in the Prologue (1:5; 4:8, 44), in ch. 27 (27:3, 8, 26), in the final curses (28:58, 61), and in the Supplements to the First Edition of Deuteronomy (29:20, 28[21, 29]; 30:10; 31:9, 11, 24, 26; 32:46). Otherwise, provisions of the Deuteronomic covenant are called "commandment(s), statutes, ordinances, and testimonies."

20 *that his heart not be lifted up among his brethren.* Once again, the king must not be unduly exalted among his people, as in other societies. The king must be a servant of the people (1 Kgs 12:7; Weinfeld 1982b). Doubtless, due to this limitation and others put upon Israelite kings, prophets were able to address them with as much candor as they did (2 Sam 12:1-15; 1 Kgs 17:1; 18:17-19; Isa 7:3-17; 39:1-8; Jer 21:1-7; 37:6-10, 17-21; 38:14-26). On the expression of "the heart being lifted up," i.e., becoming unduly proud, see also 8:14.

and that he not turn aside from the commandment, right or left. On the expression "not turn aside . . . right or left," see 17:11 and Note for 2:26-27.

in order that he will prolong the days over his kingdom — he and his sons — in the midst of Israel. Another variation on the Deuteronomic theme that doing the commandments will prolong one's days in the land (Malamat 1982, 219; cf. Note for 4:25-26).

Message and Audience

Moses now anticipates the people requesting a king once they are settled in the land. Other nations have kings. He says that the people may indeed install a king whom Yahweh will choose. But it must be an Israelite, not a foreigner, and this king must not multiply horses, wives, or wealth. Foreign kings amass all of these, but Israel's king is not to be like kings of other nations. Many wives will turn his heart in the wrong direction. When the king ascends the throne, he is to make for himself a copy of the law that can be had from the Levitical priests. It shall be continually with him, and he shall read it all the days of his life. By so doing, he will learn to fear Yahweh and thus do Yahweh's commands. The law will also keep him from exalting himself among his brethren and will caution

Deuteronomy 18

him about deviating from the statutes of the law. The fruit of obedience will be longevity of his kingdom in Israel.

To a late 8th- and early 7th-cent. audience this law will be heard as a veiled criticism of Solomon, who multiplied horses, wives, and wealth. People may also perceive a censure of Solomon for not adhering to the covenant and its precepts at the end of his days. He began well, with approval given him by Yahweh, but the end of his kingship displeased both Yahweh and the nation.

3. Rights of the Levitical Priests (18:1-8)

a) The Levites' Inheritance Is Yahweh (18:1-2)

18 ¹There shall not be for the Levitical priests, all the tribe of Levi, a portion or an inheritance with Israel; offerings by fire to Yahweh, which is his inheritance, they shall eat. ²So an inheritance there shall not be for him in the midst of his brethren. Yahweh — he is his inheritance, just as he promised him.

b) Offerings Due the Levites (18:3-5)

18 ³And this shall be the due of the priests from the people, from those sacrificing the sacrifice, whether an ox, whether a sheep: Yes, he shall give to the priest the shoulder and the two cheeks and the stomach. ⁴The first of your grain, your wine, and your oil, and the first of the fleece of your sheep you shall give to him. ⁵For Yahweh your God has chosen him out of all your tribes, to stand to minister in the name of Yahweh, he and his sons all the days.

c) Altar Privileges for All Levites (18:6-8)

18 ⁶And when the Levite comes from one of your gates, out of all Israel where he sojourns — and he may come whenever his soul desires to the place that Yahweh will choose — ⁷then he may minister in the name of Yahweh his God like all his brethren, the Levites, who are standing there before Yahweh. ⁸Portion for portion they shall eat, besides his valuation with regard to the fathers.

Rhetoric and Composition

The present law specifies rights of the Levitical priests and is divided into three parts: (1) a statement that Levitical priests have been given no landed property; instead they receive support from offerings made to Yahweh (vv. 1-2); (2) a list

Deuteronomy 18

of sacrificial portions and first-harvested fruits and wool to which the priests are entitled (vv. 3-5); and (3) a granting of rights to any Levite to officiate at the central sanctuary when he visits there (vv. 6-8). These divisions are supported by a *setumah* in M^L after v. 2 and a *setumah* in M^L after v. 5. The unit as a whole is delimited at the top end by a *setumah* in M^L and a section in Sam before v. 1, which is also the chapter division. Delimitation at the bottom end is by a *setumah* in M^L and a section in Sam after v. 8. The Qumran *Temple Scroll* reproduces 18:3 together with P material in 11QT 20:14-16 and 22:8-11; 18:4 in 11QT 60:6-7; 18:5 in 11QT 60:10-11; and 18:6-8 in 11QT 60:12-15 (Yadin 1983, 2:273-74).

Portions of 18:1-8 are contained in 4QDeut^c and 4QDeut^f.

Notes

18:1 *There shall not be for the Levitical priests, all the tribe of Levi, a portion or an inheritance with Israel.* Hebrew נַחֲלָה ("inheritance") carries here the usual Deuteronomic meaning of inherited property. All Israel is getting land from Yahweh, and each tribe an allotment, except the tribe of Levi (10:9; 12:12; 14:27, 29). Its inheritance, as Moses goes on to say, consists of offerings presented to Yahweh, a share of which goes to them.

the Levitical priests, all the tribe of Levi. The terms are in apposition (LXX), meaning "Levitical priests" (lit. "the priests, the Levites"). This takes in all members of the tribe of Levi (Emerton 1962, 133-34; cf. RSV). For a discussion of the Levites, their priestly office, and their subordination in P and in the postexilic period to priests who were "sons of Aaron," see Note for 12:12.

offerings by fire to Yahweh, which is his inheritance, they shall eat. Hebrew אִשִּׁים ("offerings by fire") is a P term (62 times), occurring elsewhere only here and in Josh 13:14; 1 Sam 2:28 (Driver). Reference is to offerings of which a portion is burnt on the altar and a portion goes to the priests. Included would be cereal offerings, peace offerings, and guilt offerings (Lev 2:3; 7:1-10; Num 18:9-10). Burnt offerings are also "offerings by fire" (Lev 1:9), but are not included because in them the entire animal is consumed on the altar. On Paul's use of this verse to apply to those who labor in proclaiming the gospel, see 1 Cor 9:13-14.

which is his inheritance. וְנַחֲלָה. The LXX has ὁ κλῆρος αὐτῶν ("their allotment"). This parenthetical term specifies that offerings to Yahweh, which the Levite eats, will be his inheritance.

2 *Yahweh — he is his inheritance, just as he promised him.* The priestly inheritance is here stated another way: it is Yahweh himself (10:9; Num 18:20; Josh 13:33; 18:7; Ezek 44:28). Tigay thinks Yahweh's promise is recorded in Num 18:20.

3 *And this shall be the due of the priests from the people, from those sacri-*

ficing the sacrifice, whether an ox, whether a sheep. Sacrificial portions are the priests' rightful due (מִשְׁפַּט), and people are required to give them to the priests when sacrificing their ox or sheep.

Yes, he shall give to the priest the shoulder and the two cheeks and the stomach. The זְרֹעַ ("shoulder") is the foreleg from the knee-joint to the shoulder blade, and the לְחָיַיִם ("two cheeks") include the tongue (*m. Ḥul.* 10:4; Rashi). The קֵבָה is the "fourth stomach" of ruminants (LXX: τὸ ἔνυστρον). From Aristophanes (*Knights* 356; 1179) we learn that this stomach and others were favored dishes at Athens. According to P material, the priest gets the breast and the right thigh (Exod 29:22; Lev 7:32-33; Num 18:18), where the "right thigh" (שׁוֹק הַיָּמִין) is not from the foreleg, but the hind leg (Milgrom 1991, 431-32). In the fosse temple excavated at Lachish (12th cent.), which was Canaanite, a bin of animal bones beside an altar yielded metacarpals of the right foreleg of sheep and goats (Tufnell et al. 1940, 25, 93-94; Tufnell 1967, 300-301). Also, a 12th-cent. house excavated at Tell Qiri, which continued in use into the 11th cent., contained a room with cultic vessels and bones of the right forelegs of goats (Ben-Tor 1979, 111-13). In early Israel, the priest's portion was apparently not fixed, as we learn from the abuses reported at Shiloh among the sons of Eli (1 Sam 2:13-17). The Qumran *Temple Scroll* (11QT 20:14-16) specified that all five portions — shoulder, two cheeks, stomach, breast, and thigh — were to be waved in the peace offering (Yadin 1983, 1:151-53; 2:90).

those sacrificing the sacrifice. זֹבְחֵי הַזֶּבַח. The זֶבַח ("sacrifice") indicated here is the so-called "peace offering" (Exod 20:24), of which the priest receives a share. The other common animal sacrifice was the "burnt offering," where the whole animal was consumed on the altar (see Note for 12:6). On the "peace offering" see also Leviticus 3.

4 *These are the firstfruit offerings,* which also go to the priest (Num 18:12-13). Added to them are the first shearings of sheep, not mentioned in P material. The wool will doubtless be woven into clothing. Deuteronomy contains a ritual for the presentation of the firstfruits in 26:1-11. Hebrew רֵאשִׁית means both "first" in sequence and "first" in quality (Levine 1993, 394). Later laws regulating the offering of the firstfruits are contained in Mishnah tractate *Bikkurim*.

5 *For Yahweh your God has chosen him out of all your tribes, to stand to minister in the name of Yahweh.* On Yahweh's choice of the Levites for sacred ministry, see also 21:5. The verb בחר ("to choose") occurs frequently in Deuteronomy (see Note for 12:5).

he and his sons all the days. The priesthood is hereditary and ongoing.

6-7 The apodosis begins with v. 7 (T^{OnqNf}; AV; RSV; NAB; NJV; NIV; NRSV; NJB; *pace* Driver; Duke 1987, 196; NEB). Reference is to any Levite, not just dependent Levites engaged primarily in teaching (Emerton 1962, 136). The

Deuteronomy 18

closing of sanctuaries and restriction of worship to a central sanctuary (ch. 12) left many Levitical priests without a job. But here it states that any Levite wanting to serve as altar clergy when visiting the central sanctuary shall be permitted to do so. During Josiah's reform, some priests from outlying areas did not avail themselves of the opportunity to come to Jerusalem, but stayed home among their brethren (2 Kgs 23:9). They did so presumably by choice.

from one of your gates. I.e., from one of your cities.

out of all Israel where he sojourns. In Deuteronomy, Levites are reported as living in any Israelite city, where their client status makes them *de facto* "sojourners" (see Note for 12:12). In P material, they are said to reside in Levitical cities (Num 35:1-8; Joshua 21). Deuteronomy says nothing about Levitical cities.

who are standing there before Yahweh. I.e., who are serving at Yahweh's altar.

8 *Portion for portion they shall eat.* Levites visiting the central sanctuary are to get the same portions as resident priests serving there.

besides his valuation with regard to the fathers. לְבַד מִמְכָּרָיו עַל־הָאָבוֹת. The phrase is difficult, but the general sense is not in doubt. The noun מֶכֶר means "saleable item(s)" in Neh 13:16, which appears to be its meaning here. The LXX translates τῆς πράσεως τῆς κατὰ πατριάν ("the sale of that which concerns the paternal inheritance"), which Wevers (1995, 297) simplifies to "the sale of goods inherited from one's father." Priests could possess inherited goods or property, which, if necessary, could be sold for money. Jeremiah, who belonged to a priestly family in the priestly village of Anathoth, bought a field from his cousin during the siege of Jerusalem. If this cousin was a priest, which is a reasonable assumption, the transaction would involve a priest selling his portion of the family estate to one next-of-kin (Jer 32:6-15; 37:12). The point being made here is that visiting Levites possessing private sources of income are not thereby precluded from receiving equal portions at Yahweh's altar (G. R. Driver 1956). An 8th- or 7th-cent. Jerusalem priest might argue, for example, that because a visiting priest officiating at the altar possessed a family inheritance, he should not be given portions equal to the ones resident priests were receiving.

Message and Audience

Attention now turns to the Levitical priests and what rights they have among the Israelite people. Moses informs his audience that the Levitical priests, meaning all members of Levi, do not possess a land inheritance like the other tribes. Their inheritance consists of offerings burned on Yahweh's altar, of which they receive a portion to eat. So on the one hand Levites do not have an inheritance, but on the other hand they do. Put another way, Yahweh is their portion.

Moses then specifies what is rightfully due the priests from people sacrificing their ox or sheep. The worshipper shall give them the shoulder, the two cheeks, and the stomach, all choice portions. The firstfruits of grain, wine, and oil, along with first shearings from the sheep, also go to the priest. People are told that Yahweh has chosen the priests from among his people to minister in his name, and this privilege extends to their sons in perpetuity. Moses concludes by saying that any Levite sojourning in one of Israel's cities may come to the central sanctuary and serve there at Yahweh's altar. He is to get the same portions as resident priests, over and above any valuation which he might have received from his fathers.

This law presupposes a situation in which certain Levitical priests are officiating at the central sanctuary, and other Levites, who have client status in the cities, are in danger of being cut off from altar service. With centralization and the closing of local sanctuaries in the 8th and 7th cents., large numbers of Levites are out of work. But Deuteronomy invites them to Jerusalem for the annual festivals, and when they come, they are not to be denied altar service by resident clergy who are there. Resident clergy are also not to reduce their portions of the sacrificial offerings just because they possess other income derived from their ancestral families.

4. How May We Know the Word of Yahweh? (18:9-22)

a) No Practitioners of the Secret Arts (18:9-14)

18⁹When you enter into the land that Yahweh your God is giving to you, you shall not learn to do according to the abominations of those nations. ¹⁰There shall not be found in you one who passes his son or his daughter into the fire, one who divines divinations, a soothsayer or an augur or a sorcerer; ¹¹or one who casts a spell, or one who consults a ghost, or a wizard, or one who inquires of the dead. ¹²For an abomination to Yahweh is anyone who does these things; and on account of these abominations Yahweh your God is dispossessing them from before you. ¹³Blameless you shall be towards Yahweh your God. ¹⁴For these nations whom you are possessing listen to soothsayers and to diviners, but you, Yahweh your God has not given thus to you.

Rhetoric and Composition

The present verses banning an array of religious practitioners are delimited at the top end by a *setumah* in M^L, a *petuḥah* in 11QT, and a section in Sam before v. 9.

Deuteronomy 18

The M^L and 11QT both have a *setumah* after v. 13, although the unit seems rather to end at v. 14 (RSV; NAB; NJV). The Sam has no section after either v. 13 or v. 14. Verse 14 ends the discussion on soothsayers and diviners, telling people: "Yahweh your God has not given thus to you." This statement is similar to the concluding statement, "You shall not do thus for Yahweh your God," in 12:4. With a delimitation of vv. 9-14, the unit is seen to contain an inverted keyword inclusio:

. . . the land that *Yahweh your God*	יְהוָה אֱלֹהֶיךָ	v. 9
is giving to you . . .	נֹתֵן לָךְ	
. . . *he has not given thus to you,*	לֹא כֵן נָתַן לְךָ	v. 14
Yahweh your God	יְהוָה אֱלֹהֶיךָ	

The unit begins and ends with כִּי and the emphatic pronoun "you":

When you (כִּי אַתָּה) enter into the land . . . v. 9

For (כִּי) these nations whom *you* (אַתָּה) are possessing . . . v. 14
but you (וְאַתָּה), Yahweh your God has not given thus to you.

The LXX omits the personal pronoun in v. 9 and the second occurrence of the pronoun in v. 14, but does reproduce the first pronoun of v. 14 with σὺ. A final rhetorical flourish is the repetition of "soothsayers and diviners" in v. 14, which, as W. R. Smith (1885, 275) noted long ago, reverses "diviners and soothsayers" in v. 10.

The present verses are reproduced in 11QT 60:16-21 (Yadin 1983, 2:274-75). Column 60 ends with the first four words of v. 14 ("For these nations that"). Verse 14 presumably continued in column 61, but the first lines of this column are not extant. Portions of 18:9-14 are also contained in 4QDeut^f.

Notes

18:9 The "abominations" (see v. 12) are magic and superstition in other religions, from which biblical religion stands apart:

> Pagan magic is an abomination to God. His will cannot be learned, forced, or coerced by it. He cannot be tricked into revelation. He will make himself known when and by the means that he himself chooses, i.e., by his herald, the prophet, whose word shall be clearly spoken and clearly understood in contrast to the devious and mysterious world of the occult. (G. E. Wright 1953, 447)

Deuteronomy 18

10 *There shall not be found in you.* On this construction, which Daube says reflects a shame culture, see Note for 17:2.

one who passes his son or his daughter into the fire. The verb is עבר in the H-stem ("let pass through"), for which reason some commentators are not sure whether the children are being put through an ordeal by fire, where they could survive, or are being sacrificed. The LXX translates with περικαθαίρω ("to purify completely"), indicating a cleansing, not a sacrificial burning (Wevers 1995, 298). The Talmud takes this to be an ordeal in Molech (= Molek) worship (*b. Sanh.* 64b; cf. T^{Onq}). Rashi, following T^{Onq} and the Talmud, says that in Molech worship they would build a fire on either side (of a passageway) and pass the child in between. Others (Driver; G. E. Wright) have thus concluded that the children would be made to endure an ordeal by fire.

But some scholars (W. R. Smith 1885, 275; Moran), together with certain modern Versions (RSV; NAB; NIV; NJB), think the verse refers to child sacrifice, which is known to have been carried out to the god Molech. In 12:31 this is prohibited as a Canaanite practice not to be revived and is forbidden also in Lev 18:21; 20:2-5. Child sacrifice is said to have contributed to the downfall of the northern kingdom (2 Kgs 17:17), yet both Ahaz and Manasseh fell victim to this loathsome practice in Judah (2 Kgs 16:3; 21:6). Jeremiah and Ezekiel roundly condemned it (Jer 7:31-32; 19:1-13; 32:35; Ezek 16:20-21; 20:25-26, 31; 23:37, 39). In Jeremiah's time, child sacrifice was being carried on at the Topheth in the Ben Hinnom Valley, even though Topheth was earlier dismantled by Josiah as part of his reform (2 Kgs 23:10).

It is worth noting that in other OT passages referring to child sacrifice, either שׂרף ("to burn") or עבר in the H-stem ("to make pass through") is used: In Deut 12:31; Jer 7:31; 19:5 it is שׂרף; in Lev 18:21; 2 Kgs 16:3; 17:17; 21:6; Jer 32:35; Ezek 20:31 it is עבר in the H-stem. Thus עבר in the H-stem should not produce ambiguity in the present verse. It can and probably does refer to child sacrifice, particularly when the same is prohibited in Deut 12:31. For more discussion on child sacrifice in Judah and in the ancient world, see Lundbom 1999, 495-97.

one who divines divinations. קֹסֵם קְסָמִים. These are general terms for the diviner and his divining arts (W. R. Smith 1885, 275-77), the latter performed to predict future events or determine future courses of action. But Smith says קֹסֵם is perhaps not being used here in its broadest sense, since v. 14 speaks of "diviners and soothsayers." He thinks these may be the two main types of divination. Nevertheless, LXX's μαντεύομαι is the general classical term for "divine" (Wevers 1995, 298). Rashi says the קֹסֵם is one who grasps the divining rod and asks, "Shall I go or not?" (cf. Hos 4:12). According to Ezek 21:26(21), religious practitioners of this description shake (marked) arrows (in a quiver), consult the teraphim (figurine idols), and examine animal livers (hepatoscopy). See

549

further Greenberg 1997, 428-29. The Arabs practice similar forms of divination (W. R. Smith 1885, 279-80).

Balaam, who is called a "diviner" in Josh 13:22, performed divinations for a fee (Num 22:7). Diviners were indigenous to Babylonian (Ezek 21:26-27[21-22]), Canaanite (1 Sam 28:7-8), and Philistine (1 Sam 6:2) culture, and while the current law may be aimed at expelling foreign practices in response to prophetic criticisms of the 8th and 7th cents., the point in Deuteronomy is that these practices were derived from Canaanite baalism and unworthy of Yahweh worship. Smith observes that in early Israel divination was not always deemed objectionable. For example, Prov 16:10 speaks of "inspired decisions" (קֶסֶם) on the lips of a king (RSV), which presumably have equivalent value to a divine oracle. But diviners posed a threat to Yahweh worship in the minds of Micah (Mic 3:7), Isaiah (Isa 3:2), Jeremiah (Jer 27:9; 29:8), and Ezekiel (Ezek 12:24), all of whom condemned them and their practices outright. Jeremiah and Ezekiel knew of prophets who were practicing divination in Jerusalem (Jer 14:14; Ezek 13:3-23).

a soothsayer. Hebrew מְעוֹנֵן is a Polel participle of the verb עָנַן, whose meaning is uncertain. KBL³ gives as a definition for the root "to interpret signs." Arabic *'anna* means "to appear suddenly, show oneself, to intervene as a hindrance" (Kopf 1958, 190). A Ugaritic cognate *'nn* is also attested, but all that can be said is that it appears in contexts concerning deities (*UT,* 458 no. 1885). The secret art possessed by soothsaying men and women (Isa 57:3: "sons of a soothsaying woman") may have consisted of telling fortunes based on observations of natural phenomena (עָנָן means "clouds"), but this is unconfirmed. We know that astrology was well developed in Egypt and Babylonia. Babylonian cuneiform texts contain lists of omens — both good and bad — deriving from the flight of birds, screaming hens, when a house begins to look old, the casting of arrows, dreams, and signs on earth and in the heavens (e.g., planets, sun and moon, stars with coronas and tails). On ancient Babylonian astrology, see discussion in Lundbom 1999, 583-84.

The Talmud (*b. Sanh.* 65b) cites Rabbi Akiba, who said that soothsayers were individuals who calculated the times and hours, declaring when it was propitious to begin a particular activity. This interpretation survives in Rashi and Luther. The LXX translates with κληδονιζόμενος ("giving or receiving an omen"). Soothsayers are also prohibited in Lev 19:26, but they existed anyway. Isaiah said the land was full of them, as in Philistia (Isa 2:6). Micah predicted their end in a coming day of Yahweh (Mic 5:11[12]), but soothsaying was later legalized under Manasseh (2 Kgs 21:6; 2 Chr 33:6). Soothsayers were also active in the time of Jeremiah (Jer 27:9). In the NT, Paul exorcised the spirit of divination in a Philippian slave girl who brought her owners substantial gain by "soothsaying" (μαντευομένη; Acts 16:16). But once again, W. R. Smith (1885,

276) points out that in early Israel there seems to be nothing objectionable in the reference to the "Soothsayers' Oak" (אֵלוֹן מְעוֹנְנִים) in Judg 9:37.

an augur. מְנַחֵשׁ. This individual is similar to the soothsayer, in that his ability to divine the future consists of observing signs and omens. The term is a Piel participle of נחשׁ, which means "to practice divination, observe signs or omens" (BDB, 638). A cognate noun נָחָשׁ means "serpent," and it has been suggested that the belief was widespread in antiquity that powers of divination, or of understanding the prophetic speech of birds, were obtained by the aid of serpents (Driver). The LXX has in the present verse οἰωνιζόμενος, "(one) taking omens from the flight and cries of birds." Luther agrees that the augur watches the flight of birds, but he thinks such an individual makes other observations as well. The Talmud (*b. Sanh.* 65b) says the מְנַחֵשׁ is one who says: so and so's bread or staff has fallen out of his hand; his son called after him; a raven screamed after him; a deer crossed his path; or a serpent came at his right hand or a fox at his left.

From Gen 44:5 we learn that Joseph's silver cup, which was planted in his brothers' sack and therefore reckoned as stolen goods, had been used by him for augury (cf. Gen 44:15). Known as hydromancy, this type of augury consisted of watching the play of light in a cup of liquid (Driver). It was an old practice, particularly common in Egypt, and said once again by W. R. Smith (1885, 276) as not registered objectionable in the Joseph story. Neither is Laban censured for being an augur (Gen 30:27), nor also the men seeking an omen that Ahab might spare Ben-hadad (1 Kgs 20:33). Balaam recognized that there was no augury (נַחַשׁ) against Israel, for which reason he did not look for omens (נְחָשִׁים), as was his custom (Num 23:23; 24:1). Augury is forbidden also in Lev 19:26, but the practice was carried on in the northern kingdom, and is said by the Deuteronomic Historian to have aided in its downfall (2 Kgs 17:17). In Judah, Manasseh legalized augury along with other forbidden practices, effectively undoing the reform of Hezekiah (2 Kgs 21:6; 2 Chr 33:6).

a sorcerer. מְכַשֵּׁף. We move now from practitioners of divination to practitioners of magic and sorcery. Hebrew מְכַשֵּׁף is not in doubt, being the Piel participle of an attested verb meaning "to practice sorcery" (BDB; KBL³). Akkadian *kašāpu* (*CAD*, 8:284; AHw, 1:461) is close in meaning: "to bewitch, cast an evil spell." Akkadian *kaššāpu* means "sorcerer" (*CAD*, 8:292; AHw, 1:463). The LXX translates here with φάρμακος (accent corrected), meaning "sorcerer, poisoner, magician." Prior to the exodus, sorcerers joined with Egypt's wise men and magicians to counter Aaron's miracle of the rod (Exod 7:11).

The Covenant Code speaks out against sorcery, saying that a sorceress (מְכַשֵּׁפָה) must be put to death (Exod 22:17[18]). But sorcery was legalized in the north by Jezebel (2 Kgs 9:22) and in the south by Manasseh (2 Chr 33:6). Both Micah (Mic 5:11[12]) and Jeremiah (Jer 27:9) speak out against the practice. According to the prophet Nahum, a "mistress of sorcery" (בַּעֲלַת כְּשָׁפִים) will be blamed for all the dead bodies in Nineveh (Nah 3:3-4). In the postexilic period sorcerers are again active, and Malachi predicts for them swift condemnation and judgment (Mal 3:5). Sorcerers are associated with Babylon in Isa 47:9, 12; Dan 2:2. We may conclude as much from the ancient Code of Hammurabi, which begins with a law concerning the false charge of sorcery (CH 2; *ANET*[3], 166). An ordeal by water is prescribed for anyone so charged.

11 *one who casts a spell.* חֹבֵר חָבֶר. The verb חבר means "to charm, bewitch," and the noun חֶבֶר "charm, spell, enchantment" (KBL[3]). The basic meaning of the root may derive from Akk *ḫbr*, "to make an oral sound, be noisy" (*CAD*, 6:7); therefore חֹבֵר חָבֶר in the present verse would be "one who mutters sounds" (J. Finkelstein 1956). The LXX translates the Hebrew expression as ἐπαείδων ἐπαοιδήν, "one who charms a spell or charm" (Wevers 1995, 299). From Ps 58:5-6(4-5) we learn that these individuals were comparable to if not equivalent with snake charmers, the expression appearing in parallelism there with "whisperers" (מְלַחֲשִׁים), i.e., snake charmers.

one who consults a ghost. We move now from sorcerers and magicians to individuals who practice necromancy. Hebrew שֹׁאֵל אוֹב is "one who consults a spirit of the dead, or a ghost (BDB; KBL[3]). Isaiah disparages necromancers and wizards who "chirp and mutter" (Isa 8:19), referring elsewhere to the אוֹב as a ghost speaking from underground (Isa 29:4; cf. 1 Sam 28:8). Necromancy in the ancient world made use of holes in the ground, and Rabin (1963, 115) connects Heb אוֹב with Hittite *a-a-pi*, meaning "sacrificial pit." LXX ἐγγαστρίμυθος means "one who prophesies from the belly," i.e., an individual producing ghostly sounds by ventriloquism (Driver; Wevers 1995, 299). The Mishnah (*Sanh.* 7:7) states that the voice emanates from the armpit.

Saul, after ridding the land of necromancers and wizards (1 Sam 28:3), nevertheless sought out in desperation the Witch of Endor, who was a necromancer (1 Sam 28:5-19; 1 Chr 10:13). Tigay makes the point that this communication with Samuel's ghost, just like the early magic performed by Egypt's magicians prior to the exodus, is not reported in the Bible as being ineffective. Quite the contrary. In both of these cases it seems to have worked! Yet people are told in no uncertain terms not to seek out necromancers (Lev 19:31), the punishment for necromancers being death (Lev 20:6, 27). Nevertheless, Manasseh legalized them (2 Kgs 21:6; 2 Chr 33:6), with Josiah putting them away again (2 Kgs 23:24). Necromancers and wizards were said by Isaiah to be active in Egypt, where he predicted Yahweh's judgment upon them (Isa 19:3).

a wizard. יִדְּעֹנִי. A practitioner often mentioned in connection with the necromancer, but whose activity remains unclear. Etymologically, one might assume that such a person claimed access to a spirit possessing superior knowledge (Driver; Heb ידע = "to know"). The Mishnah (*Sanh.* 7:7) says the wizard

Deuteronomy 18

speaks from his mouth, unlike the necromancer who speaks from his armpit. Driver says the difference is that the אוֹב claims to call up any ghost; the יִדְּעֹנִי consults only a spirit that is "familiar." The Talmud (*Sanh.* 65b) says that wizards place the bone of an animal in their mouth and the bone speaks of itself. The LXX translates here with τερατοσκόπος ("an observer of marvels"). Persons of this description, in any event, were not to be sought out, according to Lev 19:31, and when found were to be put to death (Lev 20:6, 27). Saul put wizards out of the land (1 Sam 28:3, 9), but they were active in the time of Isaiah, who chided people being encouraged to consult them (Isa 8:19). Manasseh legalized them (2 Kgs 21:6; 2 Chr 33:6), and Josiah put them away again in his reform (2 Kgs 23:24).

one who inquires of the dead. דֹּרֵשׁ אֶל־הַמֵּתִים. A comprehensive term for anyone who does the same superstition as those already mentioned (Driver). Rashi says this is an individual who conjures up the dead into his male organ or communicates with a skull.

12 *and on account of these abominations Yahweh your God is dispossessing them from before you.* If Yahweh is clearing out the prior population because of the above-mentioned religious practitioners, he surely does not want his own people trafficking with them (12:29-31). On the term "abomination" in Deuteronomy, see Note for 7:25.

on account of. On this uncommon conjunction, בִּגְלַל, see Note for 15:10.

13 Hebrew עִם, normally "with," here means "in dealing with," almost "towards" (Driver; Ps 18:24[23]). The LXX has "before (ἐναντίον) the Lord your God," which conveys the proper sense. The term תָּמִים means "perfect, complete, blameless" (32:4; Gen 6:9; Exod 12:5). The LXX uses the adjective τέλειος, which is the same word appearing in Matt 5:48: "You therefore must be perfect (τέλειοι) as your heavenly Father is perfect (τέλειός)." Noah was said to be "blameless" in his generation (Gen 6:9), and God called Abraham to "walk before him and be blameless" (Gen 17:1). Job was "blameless," a man who feared God (Job 1:1). Joshua in his covenant renewal at Shechem tells all Israel to serve Yahweh "in blamelessness and in faithfulness," בְּתָמִים וּבֶאֱמֶת (Josh 24:14). We are not talking here about moral perfection, but about undivided commitment to Yahweh (von Rad).

14 See earlier 12:29-31. This verse is a set-up for vv. 15-22, which state what Yahweh will give to Israel: the prophet (Rashi; *pace* Barstad 1994, 244).

Message and Audience

Moses is now coming to the end of his legislation regarding major officeholders in Israel. He has discussed the judge, the king, and the priest, and it remains

553

only to name the prophet and tests on his communication of the divine word. But before doing so, he must discredit nine religious practitioners who are precluded from mediating the covenant between Yahweh and his people.

When people enter the land Yahweh is giving them, they must not adopt the abominable practices of those who lived there before. Not to be found in Israel is anyone who offers his son or daughter as a sacrifice. This practice for all purposes ended long ago with Abraham and his son Isaac on Mount Moriah. Within Israel must be no diviners, soothsayers, augurers, or sorcerers, no one who casts a spell, no necromancer, no wizard, and no one who seeks by any means whatever to communicate with the dead. Moses repeats that these are abominations in the eyes of Yahweh, and the people are reminded again that their displacement of the Canaanites is in order that they be rid forever of these rank superstitions.

Von Rad says the statements here are to be dated at the earliest in the period of the monarchy. The Covenant Code on this subject says only that a sorceress must be put to death. Preaching by the 8th-cent. prophets must also have helped galvanize public opinion against the religious practitioners mentioned here. A late 8th- and early 7th-cent. audience will hear in all this a censure of foreign practitioners, particularly of Assyrian origin, who gained entrance into Judah through two idolatrous kings: Ahaz and Manasseh. Israel, says Moses, is to be a blameless people before Yahweh. The nations driven out of the land listened to soothsayers and diviners, but Yahweh has not given these to Israel.

b) Testing for the False Yahweh Prophet (18:15-22)

18^{15}A prophet from your midst, from your brethren, like me, Yahweh your God will raise up for you; to him you shall listen, ^{16}according to all that you asked from Yahweh your God at Horeb on the day of the assembly, saying, "I can no more listen to the voice of Yahweh my God, and this great fire I can no longer see, or I will surely die." ^{17}And Yahweh said to me, "They do well in what they have spoken. ^{18}A prophet I will raise up for them, from the midst of their brethren, like you, and I will put my words in his mouth, and he will speak to them all that I command him. ^{19}And it will happen that the person who will not listen to my words that he will speak in my name, I, I shall require it from him. ^{20}But the prophet who presumes to speak a word in my name that I did not command him to speak, or who speaks in the name of other gods, yes, that prophet shall die." ^{21}And if you say in your heart, "How shall we know the word that Yahweh has not spoken?" ^{22}When the prophet speaks in the name of Yahweh, and the word does not happen, or does not come to pass, that is the word that Yahweh has not spoken. The prophet has spoken it presumptuously; you need not be afraid of him.

Deuteronomy 18

Rhetoric and Composition

The present verses containing the "prophet-like-Moses" promise and a test for identifying inauthentic Yahweh prophets are delimited at the top end by the concluding phrase in v. 14 (see Rhetoric and Composition for 18:9-14). Delimitation at the lower end is by a *setumah* in M^L, a *petuḥah* in 11QT, and a section in Sam after v. 22, which is also the chapter division. The Sam also has a section after v. 16. Most of vv. 20-22 is reproduced in 11QT 61:1-5; vv. 15-19 are not extant, as the beginning of column 61 is missing (Yadin 1983, 2:275-77). Verses 18-19 have also turned up in 4QTest (lines 5-8) and contain mainly orthographic differences from MT (Allegro 1968, 57-60; de Waard 1971, 537).

The list of Israel's major officeholders concludes here with the "prophet," which forms a tie-in with the beginning of ch. 13, where the "prophet" heads the list of those who might lead people in the direction of other gods. Mention of the prophet at the beginning and end of a subunit in the book makes an inclusio for chs. 13–18. The outer frame of this subunit treats these topics:

prophets and dreamers who lead people astray	13:2-6(1-5)
family and friends who lead people astray	13:7-12(6-11)
worthless men who lead people astray	13:13-18(12-17)
regulations regarding judges	16:18-20; 17:2-13
regulations regarding kings	17:14-20
regulations regarding priests	18:1-8
regulations regarding mantics and *prophets*	18:9-22

There may also be an intentional 3 + 4 pattern in this rhetorical structure (Lundbom 1996, 310).

In vv. 20-22 is a test for false prophets that complements the test in 13:2-4(1-3). The two passages presuppose different realities and offer different tests for authenticity (Lundbom 1996, 310). The two passages:

Deut 13:2-4(1-3)	Deut 18:20-22
Assumed Reality:	
Prophets (of various description) are giving signs and wonders that *have come to pass*	Yahweh prophets are speaking words that contradict one another
Question:	
How does one know the false prophet?	
Answer:	
It is the prophet who leads people in the way of gods *other than Yahweh*	It is the prophet whose word *does not come to pass*

Barstad (1994, 244-46), seeking a redaction in the text and driven by "ideology," argues that the present verses are a compilation of segments having no basic relation to one another. The segment on false prophecy (vv. 20-22) is unrelated to the "prophet-like-Moses" segment (vv. 15-19), and vv. 21-22 are a later attachment to v. 20. Barstad also claims that the verses on the prophet have no logical connection to the preceding verses on other religious practitioners (vv. 9-14). The distinctions are all contrived, put forth largely to support his thesis that the "prophet like Moses" is Joshua, which cannot be sustained (see Notes). The verses on other religious practitioners, who are false, function in the text as a foil for introducing the true religious practitioner, who is the prophet. And vv. 15-22 show themselves to be a perfectly coherent unit, first naming the prophet as Yahweh's chosen mediator and second, providing a test whereby one may recognize prophets who are false.

Portions of 18:15-22 are contained in 4QDeut^f and in Testimonia from Qumran.

Notes

18:15 "Prophet" comes at the head of the Hebrew sentence in order to emphasize the contrast with the diviners, magicians, and necromancers. Von Rad (1966, 123) says:

> It is now possible to sweep aside, as with a wave of the hand, the motley arsenal of mantic and occult practices, all the attempts to obtain a share of the divine powers or of divine knowledge. A quite different possibility has been disclosed to Israel, namely the Word of its prophet.

Barstad (1994, 244) is therefore not correct in saying that there is no logical connection between vv. 9-14 and vv. 15-19. Together they discuss the role of the prophet — the fourth major officeholder — in ancient Israel, the false practitioners of vv. 9-14 serving as a foil for the writer's preferred subject. This is the only passage in any of the OT law codes to discuss the prophet.

There has been much discussion over whether one is to see here a succession of prophets who will continue the work of Moses or a single prophet who will be Moses' successor. The use of "prophet" singular cannot decide the issue, as the term may be taken individually or collectively. Driver says a line of prophets will arise as the occasion demands, much like the rise of judges occurring earlier (Judg 2:16, 18). A line of prophets is assumed in the Deuteronomic History (2 Kgs 17:13), and particularly in Jeremiah (Jer 7:25; 25:4; 26:4-5; 28:8-9; 29:19, and passim). Barstad (1994, 243), citing ibn Ezra, thinks that vv. 15-19 re-

Deuteronomy 18

fer to Joshua, who will be Moses' successor. That Joshua is Moses' designated successor in Deuteronomy is clear enough (3:28; 31:14-15, 23), but to say that the 7th-cent. Deuteronomic writer aims to present Joshua as Moses' *prophetic* successor is a stretch. Nowhere in Deuteronomy, in the book of Joshua, or in the entire Bible is Joshua ever presented as a "prophet." What Barstad has done is to fuse the "successor" idea with the "prophet-like-Moses" promise, casting Joshua into a role he was never meant to assume and never did assume.

We must also rule out any inherent messianism in the present verse, even though Jesus was later seen in the early church as being the "prophet like Moses" (Acts 3:18-24). No fewer than three of the Gospels, Matthew, Luke, and John, present Jesus in one way or another as the "new Moses." In John, more than in the other Gospels, Jesus is confessed by people to be "the prophet" (John 1:45; 6:14; 7:40). R. A. MacKenzie (1957, 304) and Glasson (1963) have argued that this Gospel writer means to present Jesus as the "new Moses" of Deuteronomy 18. W. D. Davies (1969, 10-32) put forth the thesis that Matthew seeks to depict Jesus as the "new Moses" leading a "new exodus," the Sermon on the Mount being Jesus' "new Torah." More recently, it has been argued by Moessner (1983) that Luke, in his "journey to Jerusalem" narrative (Luke 9:1–19:44), portrays Jesus as "the prophet like Moses" leading a "new exodus." At the beginning is the mountain-top revelation bringing in Moses and Elijah (9:28-36).

Much closer in time to Deuteronomy is Jeremiah, who quite clearly understands himself to be the "prophet like Moses" of Deuteronomy 18 (Jer 1:9; cf. Muilenburg 1963; Holladay 1964; 1966). It is also Jeremiah who announces the "new covenant," a further indication that he is indeed the "new Moses" (Lundbom 2004a, 465). So we cannot preclude individualistic interpretations per se. At various times select individuals are understood to have fulfilled the "prophet-like-Moses" prophecy. Yet the term "prophet" must still be taken here in a collective sense, i.e., referring to a line of prophets. The "king" of 17:14-20 is likewise a collective noun, i.e., referring to a line of kings. In the NT, the present verse is quoted in Acts 3:22; 7:37.

A prophet. The prophetic movement in Israel began with Samuel (see Note for 13:2). In Deuteronomy the prophet *par excellence* is Moses (Deut 34:10), but this is an anachronism, having its origins perhaps in the preaching of Hosea (Hos 12:13). See also Num 12:6-8.

from your midst, from your brethren. I.e., not a foreigner, like the religious practitioners of "the nations" in vv. 9-14 (cf. Num 22:5-6; Isa 2:6). Israel's king must also not be a foreigner (17:15). The LXX omits "from your midst" (מִקִּרְבְּךָ), which Wevers (1995, 301) thinks is a simplification of the Hebrew by the translator. But the omission could be due to haplography (homoeoarcton מ . . . מ). Wevers also suggests that the parent reading for LXX could be Sam מקרב אחיך, "from the midst of your brethren" (cf. v. 18 and 17:15).

Deuteronomy 18

like me. I.e., like Moses, the speaker.

to him you shall listen. The prophet is a messenger of the divine "word" (v. 18), which means he must be listened to. Hearing — not seeing — is all-important in Israelite religion, and hearing the divine word must be followed up by obedience (13:5, 19[4, 18]); 15:5; 26:17; 27:10; 28:1-2; 30:20; Gen 22:18; 26:5; Jer 26:13; 38:20). Those choosing to disobey the divine word do so at great cost (8:20; 28:15, 45, 62; 1 Sam 15:22-23; Jer 9:11-12[12-13]; 32:23; 40:2-3, and elsewhere).

16 Reference is to the assembly at Mount Horeb, when the Ten Commandments were given and the people responded to the voice of Yahweh and the burning mountain with a fearful cry that if both continued, they would surely die (5:22-27; 9:10; 10:4). So they requested a mediator, and Moses was appointed by Yahweh to assume that role (5:22-31; cf. Exod 20:18-22).

or I will surely die. וְלֹא אָמוּת. Or "and I will not die." It is better here to read the לֹא as an asseverative. The LXX has a negative result clause: οὐδὲ μὴ ἀποθάνωμεν, "so that we might not die" (Wevers 1995, 302).

17 *And Yahweh said to me.* On this introductory phrase, see Note for 1:42. In Jer 1:7, 9 the phrase introduces portions of the "prophet-like-Moses" promise to come (v. 18).

"They do well in what they have spoken. הֵיטִיבוּ אֲשֶׁר דִּבֵּרוּ. The same idiom occurs in 5:28. The LXX translates הֵיטִיבוּ ("They do well") with ὀρθῶς ("correctly, rightly"), which is reflected also in two Targum readings (T^Nf: "all that they have spoken is right and proper"; T^PsJ: "What they have spoken is proper"). Cf. translations of RSV, NEB, and NRSV, which preserve the basic sense of the Hebrew.

18 *A prophet I will raise up for them, from the midst of their brethren, like you.* Yahweh's direct word, which Moses communicated to the people in v. 15.

and I will put my words in his mouth, and he will speak to them all that I command him. The distinguishing feature of the prophet is that he speaks the divine word — here "words" plural (Lundbom 2010a, 17-20; cf. Jer 23:28-29). Yahweh puts words into the prophet's mouth (Jer 1:7; cf. 2 Sam 14:3, 19, where David is king and the process works in reverse), and the prophet delivers those words with an introductory "Thus said Yahweh" (Jer 2:1, 5), the formula of the royal messenger (Köhler 1923, 102-42). Isaiah is a royal messenger in the employ of the King (Isa 6:8), and so is Jeremiah, who appropriates the present promise in his call (Jer 1:7, 9). The religious wonders of vv. 10-11 are not messengers of the divine word, nor are the prophets and dreamers of ch. 13, who perform signs and wonders.

my words. דְּבָרַי. The Masoretes have pointed this a plural, but the LXX has the singular ῥῆμά μου ("my word"). Wevers (1995, 303) thinks this is because it is God's spoken word.

Deuteronomy 18

and he will speak to them all that I command him. Moses himself was required to speak what Yahweh had commanded him (1:3; 4:5; 5:31; cf. Exod 7:2).

19 It falls to Jeremiah to inform people that what is threatened here has now come to pass (Jer 29:18-19; 35:17). In the NT, see John 12:48; Acts 3:23.

And it will happen. וְהָיָה. The LXX has only καί ("and"), omitting the verb. Wevers (1995, 303) says this is unusual (in 6:10 the LXX has καὶ ἔσται for וְהָיָה). The loss, however, could be attributed to haplography (homoeoarcton ה . . . ה).

to my words. אֶל־דְּבָרַי. The LXX omits, which could be more haplography (homoeoarcton א . . . א). Wevers (1995, 303-4) thinks the LXX has followed דבריו ("his words") of Sam.

I, I shall require it from him. אָנֹכִי אֶדְרֹשׁ מֵעִמּוֹ. The "I" pronoun is for emphasis; cf. the emphatic "you" in 18:9, 14. The verb דרשׁ in Deuteronomy often means "inquire, investigate" (13:15[14]; 17:4, 9; 19:18), but here, as in 23:22[21], it means "require" in the sense of exacting punishment (T[NfPsJ]; Driver; de Waard 1971, 539-40; cf. Gen 9:5; Ezek 33:6; 34:10). The Vg has *ego ultor existam* ("I am the avenger"). Punishment is explicit in Acts 3:23.

20 Now we deal with the problem of false prophecy, which must be addressed since the prophet has been named as Yahweh's chosen mediator. True and false prophecy was at issue in 13:2-6(1-5), but there the assumptions were different and the test for authenticity was different (see Rhetoric and Composition). Here in vv. 20-22 we are concerned primarily with prophets who speak in Yahweh's name, i.e., individuals who put themselves forward as prophets of Yahweh. The phrase "or who speaks in the name of other gods" has been added for the sake of inclusiveness, either as an addition or else as a parenthetical remark meant to cover prophets cited in 13:2-6(1-5). Harmonizing of a similar nature occurs in the supplementary "and the firstborns in your herd and your flock" in 14:23 (see Rhetoric and Composition for 14:22–15:23).

Here, as in 13:2-6[1-5], false prophecy is a capital offense and the false prophet must die. We do not know if the four hundred (false) prophets opposing Micaiah during the reign of Ahab, who were Yahweh prophets, were put to death (1 Kings 22). It is a good bet that Micaiah, also a Yahweh prophet, would have been put to death if his prophecy had not come true (vv. 26-27). The problem of distinguishing true Yahweh prophets from false Yahweh prophets became critical in the time of Jeremiah. Jeremiah himself was accused of being a false Yahweh prophet, someone therefore who should be put to death (Jer 11:21; 26:8-9). Another classic confrontation of two prophets giving contradictory words from Yahweh is recorded in Jeremiah 28, where Jeremiah meets Hananiah of Gibeon. It ended with Hananiah's death, not because anyone put him to death, but because he fell victim to the prophetic word spoken by Jeremiah (Jer 28:15-17). The LXX of Jer 35:1[= MT 28:1] calls Hananiah a "false prophet" (ψευδοπροφήτης), a term that does not appear in MT. Malamat (1975,

139-40) connects Ezek 14:9 with the death of Hananiah. A certain Shemaiah among the Babylonian exiles, presumably a Yahweh prophet, was also dealt a punishing word by Jeremiah for prophesying when Yahweh had not sent him (Jer 29:30-32). For other references in the book of Jeremiah to Yahweh prophets whom Yahweh had not sent, and who therefore were under a sentence of death, see Jer 14:14-15; 23:16-22, 25-32; 27:14-15; 29:8-9, 21-23.

Barstad (1994, 245), in separating the present verse from vv. 21-22, is led to the mistaken conclusion that Deuteronomy has a negative view of prophets. But it has long been recognized that Deuteronomy owes an enormous debt to the prophets, particularly the 8th-cent. prophets, and that it views the prophets and prophecy in a generally positive light (see *Introduction: Deuteronomy and the Prophets*). That false prophets should be identified and put to death in no way vitiates that view. The other OT legal codes contain nothing comparable to vv. 15-22, and Moses, who is the central figure in Deuteronomy, is said in 34:10-12 to be *the prophet* without peer.

But the prophet who presumes to speak a word in my name. "To act with presumption" (זִיד) is to be overconfident, thus inauthentic. See again v. 22. On presumptuous action elsewhere in Deuteronomy, see 1:43; 17:12-13.

21 The question is put in the negative, since the aim is to identify the false Yahweh prophet. The answer is similarly phrased (v. 22). The idiom "If you say in your heart" means "if you say to yourself" (8:17).

22 *When the prophet speaks in the name of Yahweh, and the word does not happen, or does not come to pass, that is the word that Yahweh has not spoken.* Time must pass before it becomes clear what is truly the word of Yahweh, who in fact has preached it, and which of two opposing words will stand. How much time is not indicated. In some cases it will be a very small amount of time; in other cases more time will be required. But this test cannot be workable for prophecies into the distant future, only for those in which fulfillment can be expected in a reasonable amount of time. Besides, who will be much concerned about judgments announced for the distant future? King Hezekiah certainly was not (2 Kgs 20:16-19 = Isa 39:5-8). And Josiah, too, may not have been (2 Kgs 22:20). Micaiah said to King Ahab as he was being led away to prison: "If you indeed return in peace, Yahweh has not spoken by me" (1 Kgs 22:28). Jeremiah, for a time, was forced to endure taunts because his prophecy went unfulfilled. People said: "Where is the word of Yahweh? Let it come!" (Jer 17:15). In his defense before the court, Jeremiah modified the present test. He said: "The prophet who prophesies peace, when the word of the prophet comes to be, the prophet whom Yahweh has truly sent will be known" (Jer 28:9). Later in Egypt, Jeremiah said to stubborn exiles unwilling to listen to his prophecy: "Then all the remnant of Judah who came to the land of Egypt to sojourn shall know whose word will be confirmed — mine or theirs" (Jer 44:28). To Ezekiel,

Yahweh spoke directly about a people who listened to the prophet but did not heed his word: "And when it comes, yes, it is coming, then they will know that a prophet has been in their midst" (Ezek 33:33).

But this test requiring fulfillment of the prophetic word, even when combined with the credential test of 13:2-6(1-5), falls short of being a complete measurement of false (and true) prophecy (Driver; Crenshaw 1971). Isaiah, for example, knew errant prophets who were drunkards (Isa 28:7-8); Jeremiah knew false prophets who were immoral, who lied, and who lacked integrity generally (Jer 23:14, 30; 29:21-23). And then there are those situations where a prophet prophesied judgment and people responded by turning from their wickedness, leading Yahweh to rescind his judgment (Jer 26:19; Jonah 3:9-10; Joel 2:13-14, 18-19; cf. Exod 32:9-14; Amos 7:1-6; Jer 18:7-10). The early church had additional tests for the false prophet, one of which was a gospel messenger who remained as a guest three days (*Did.* xi 5). On measures of authenticity in assessing the ancient Hebrew prophets, see Lundbom 2010a, 138-56.

When. Translating Heb אֲשֶׁר (so Driver; cf. Josh 4:21).

The prophet has spoken it presumptuously. בְּזָדוֹן דִּבְּרוֹ הַנָּבִיא. The LXX translates בְּזָדוֹן ("in presumption") with a stronger ἐν ἀσεβείᾳ ("in impiety").

you need not be afraid of him. לֹא תָגוּר מִמֶּנּוּ. This concluding remark tells us that the test here aims at identifying inauthentic judgment prophecies (Crenshaw 1971, 53). Otherwise, why would anyone be afraid? It is Jeremiah who expands the test to cover prophecies of peace (Jer 28:9). The LXX translates with οὐκ ἀφέξεσθε αὐτοῦ ("you shall not hold yourselves away from him"), which Wevers (1995, 306) says means that you shall not refrain from inflicting the death penalty upon him. Rashi says that one is not to refrain from finding the individual guilty. A death sentence for this prophet has been specified already in v. 20.

Message and Audience

Having just ruled out for mediation an array of religious practitioners indigenous to Canaanite culture, or who have been imported more recently from abroad, Moses now names the one figure who qualifies as a mediator between Yahweh and Israel: the prophet. Unlike popular workers of signs and wonders and magicians who dazzle people with their secret arts, the prophet speaks the divine word. Moses says Yahweh will raise up from among their number a prophet like himself, and to him people shall listen. He refers not to a single prophet, but to a succession of prophets. It was the people, after all, who asked for a mediator at Horeb when they were so frightened by the sound of Yahweh's voice and the burning mountain that they thought they would die. Yahweh agreed that their request was legitimate, and so he told Moses that he would raise up for them, in future days, a prophet like himself into whose mouth he would put his words and that prophet would speak all that Yahweh commanded him. If anyone refused to heed him, Yahweh would reckon with that person.

So far as the prophet who might speak in Yahweh's name a word he was not commanded to speak, or who might speak in the name of other gods, that same prophet shall die. If people say to themselves, "How shall we know the word that Yahweh has not spoken?" the test shall be this: when the prophet speaks in Yahweh's name and the prophecy goes unfulfilled, it is a word Yahweh has not spoken. The prophet has shown himself presumptuous, and one need not be afraid of him.

These verses, presupposing as they do prophecy as a well-established institution, must be post-Samuel (G. E. Wright). Guidelines for testing false (and true) Yahweh prophets reflect the end of Ahab's reign (mid-9th cent.), when the Yahweh prophet Micaiah contradicted four hundred other Yahweh prophets speaking in one voice (1 Kings 22). A late 8th- or early 7th-cent. date would best explain the "prophet-like-Moses" promise, also the posthumous portrayal of Moses as prophet *par excellence*. The preacher here wants to elevate Moses above the great prophets of the 8th cent. and earlier: Samuel, Elijah, Elisha, Amos, Hosea, and others. The passage also supports the view that Deuteronomy has a northern provenance, since the prophets of name in this early period are all northern figures. Even the Micaiah prophecy takes place in northern Israel (1 Kgs 22:2).

G. Judicial Procedure (19:1-21)

1. Cities of Refuge (19:1-13)

19 ¹*When Yahweh your God cuts off the nations whose land Yahweh your God is giving you, and you dispossess them and dwell in their cities and in their houses, ²three cities you shall set apart for yourself in the midst of your land that Yahweh your God is giving to you to take possession of it. ³You shall prepare for yourself the road, and you shall divide into three parts the territory of your land that Yahweh your God will cause you to inherit, and it shall be for any killer to flee there. ⁴And this is the word regarding the killer who flees there, and lives: One who strikes down his fellow without knowing, and he had not hated him formerly; ⁵or one who goes with his fellow into the forest to cut wood, and his hand is swinging with the axe to cut the wood, and the axe slips from the wood and finds his fellow, and he dies. As for him, he shall flee to one of these cities and live, ⁶lest the avenger of blood pursue after the killer when his heart is inflamed, and overtake* him because the road is long, and strike him mortally, though for him there was no sentence of death because he had not hated him formerly. ⁷Therefore I am commanding you: Three cities you shall set apart for yourself.

⁸And if Yahweh your God will enlarge your territory as he swore to your fathers, and give you all the land that he promised to give to your fathers — ⁹if you will keep this whole commandment to do it, which I am commanding you today, to love Yahweh your God and to walk in his ways all the days — then you shall add for yourself three more cities to these three, ¹⁰so innocent blood will not shed in the midst of your land that Yahweh your God is giving you as an inheritance, and bloodguilt be upon you.

¹¹But when there shall be a man who hates his fellow, and he lies in wait for him and rises up against him and strikes him mortally so he dies, and he flees to one of these cities, ¹²then the elders of his city shall send and take him from there, and give him into the hand of the avenger of blood so he may die. ¹³Your eye shall not have pity upon him, but you shall utterly remove the innocent blood from Israel, that it may be well for you.

2. No Moving of Boundary Markers (19:14)

19 ¹⁴You shall not move back the boundary marker of your fellow, which the first ones set as a boundary in your inheritance that you will inherit in the land that Yahweh your God is giving you to take possession of it.

3. Regarding Witnesses (19:15-21)

19¹⁵One witness shall not stand up against a man for any iniquity or for any sin — in any sin that one will commit; on the testimony of two witnesses or on the testimony of three witnesses a word shall stand up. ¹⁶When an unjust witness shall stand up against a man to testify a falsehood against him, ¹⁷then the two men who have the dispute shall stand before Yahweh, before the priests and the judges who will be present in those days; ¹⁸and the judges shall inquire thoroughly, then behold! the witness is a false witness, falsely he testified against his brother, ¹⁹then you shall do to him as he schemed to do to his brother, and you shall utterly remove the evil from your midst. ²⁰And the rest will hear and fear, and they will not again do such an evil thing as this in your midst. ²¹And your eye shall not have pity: life for life, eye for eye, tooth for tooth, hand for hand, foot for foot.

Deuteronomy 19

Rhetoric and Composition

This main legal corpus of Deuteronomy (chs. 19–25) begins with judicial matters over which judges, city elders, and priests have jurisdiction. The prior section dealt with the four major officeholders in ancient Israel (chs. 13–18), one of which was the judges, who were assisted by officials and, in certain cases, by priests (16:18–17:13). Laws in chs. 19–22, with one exception, have no parallel in the Covenant Code. The exception is the law on homicide and cities of refuge (19:1-13), which exists in an earlier version in Exod 21:12-14. The criminal laws in chs. 19-21 develop for the most part from the sixth commandment, "You shall not murder" (S. A. Kaufman 1978-79).

Here in ch. 19 the laws focus upon (1) homicide and cities of refuge (19:1-13); (2) moving boundary markers (19:14); and (3) the problem of false witnesses (19:15-21). The law about not moving boundary markers appears to interrupt an otherwise unified discourse, since the law dealing with false witnesses, though intended for broader application, applies to homicide cases discussed at the beginning. Homicide and false witnesses are treated together in Num 35:9-34. In Deuteronomy we often see that miscellaneous laws — usually brief and related tangentially or not at all to major law(s) under discussion — are inserted at the beginning, middle, and end of the discourse unit. This appears to be quite intentional, explaining in part, if not entirely, why the laws in Deuteronomy are perceived to be arranged in less orderly fashion (von Rad 1962a, 831; G. E. Wright). For example, miscellaneous laws are inserted at both beginning and end of the discourse on clean and unclean foods (14:1-2, 21), while in the discourse on judges (and priests) in 16:18–17:13 laws of an entirely unrelated nature are inserted in the middle (16:21-22; 17:1). Miscellaneous laws are added also at the end of the expansion on the sixth commandment (22:1-8) and at the beginning of the expansion on the seventh commandment (22:9-12).

Here, at the beginning of Deuteronomy's main legal corpus, we seem to have another miscellaneous law prohibiting the moving of boundary markers (19:14), inserted in the middle of a discourse dealing with homicide and the problem of false witnesses (19:1-13, 15-21). Carmichael (1967, 199; 1974: 113) and Rofé (1988b, 271), however, both argue that the law on boundary markers has been joined to the law on homicide and refuge cities by the catchword גְּבוּל ("border"), which in vv. 3 and 8 carries the broader meaning of "territory" but in v. 14 requires the translation "boundary marker." There may also be a link without catchwords between the law on boundary markers and the law on false witnesses, for in the Egyptian "Instruction of Amen-em-opet," both subjects are addressed (see Notes). This would help explain why the law on false witnesses states emphatically its broad applicability (v. 15: "for any iniquity or for any sin — in any sin that one will commit") and bears silent testimony to the unhappy circumstance in which a boundary dispute leads to criminal behavior (S. A. Kaufman 1978-79, 137), also to witnesses being called upon to testify. In one of the most famous land disputes during the monarchy, though not over a boundary marker, testimony by two false witnesses against Naboth resulted in a state-supported murder (1 Kgs 21:1-14).

Section markings and rhetorical features corroborate divisions indicated by content. On von Rad's comments about 19:1-13 being a parade example of sermonlike utterances in Deuteronomy, see Rhetoric and Composition for 13:2-19(1-18). The M^L has a *setumah* and the Sam a section before v. 1, which is also the chapter division. Delimiting the lower limit is a *setumah* in M^L and 11QT, and a section in Sam after v. 21, which is another chapter division. The latter section is present also in 4QDeut^f. The Sam has other sections after vv. 7 and 13.

Conclusions to segments of the primary legislation in the unit have similar admonitions on treatment of the guilty person:

    I *Your eye shall not have pity upon him* . . .   v. 13
   III *And your eye shall not have pity* . . .   v. 21

The M^L delimits three major divisions in the chapter, containing a *setumah* after v. 13 and another *setumah* after v. 14. 11QT, which does not contain vv. 1-14, marks the latter division with a *petuḥah* before v. 15. This sets off the law on not moving boundary markers. The law on homicide and cities of refuge is further divided by a *setumah* after v. 7 and another *setumah* after v. 10. The first of these distinguishes the command to set apart three initial cities (vv. 1-7), from the command to set apart three more cities once Israel's territory becomes larger (vv. 8-10). The directive about setting up the first cities of refuge in v. 2 repeats in v. 7, making an inclusio for this unit of discourse:

    three cities you shall set apart for yourself . . .   v. 2
    . . . *Three cities you shall set apart for yourself*   v. 7

The *setumah* after v. 10 sets off the provision for legitimate refuge seekers from the provision concerning refuge seekers guilty of deliberate homicide (vv. 11-13).

Portions of 19:1-21 are contained in 4QDeut^f, 4QDeut^h(?), 4QDeut^{k2}, 4QpaleoDeut^r, and 4Q365.

Notes

19:1 Cf. the introductory phrase in 12:29. The directive on setting up cities of refuge, which follows, will be carried out only after Yahweh clears the land of its former inhabitants and Israel dwells in their cities and houses. In this settled existence, refuge seekers can escape to a city where their case can be decided by elders, judges, and priests residing there.

2 *three cities you shall set apart for yourself in the midst of your land.* These are called "cities of refuge" (עָרֵי מִקְלָט) in Num 35:11, to be located "in the midst of" Canaan. Three cities of refuge were set up in Transjordan following Israel's settlement there: Bezer, Ramoth, and Golan (4:41-43). The writer makes no reference to these, but that does not mean he is unaware of them (some argue that 4:41-43 is a later addition). We learn from elsewhere that the cities chosen in Canaan were Kadesh in Galilee, Shechem in Ephraim, and Kiriath-arba (= Hebron) in Judah (Josh 20:7). These and the Transjordan cities were all Levitical cities (Num 35:6; cf. Josh 21:13, 27), but precisely when they were established has been the subject of debate. According to Joshua 20, all six cities date from the time of Joshua, after Canaan had been conquered and divided up among the tribes. But some argue (Albright 1946, 124-25; Greenberg 1959, 130-31) that the cities of refuge came into being only in the time of the monarchy. Milgrom (1981, 304-7) says Levitical cities could only have been established in Solomon's time, when altar asylums were abolished (1 Kgs 2:28-34; cf. Exod 21:13-14), but he thinks the author of Deuteronomy has not invented cities of refuge, simply inherited a tradition from older sources. They did not exist at the time of the Josianic Reform (*pace* Morgenstern 1930, 61; Rofé 1986; cf. Wellhausen 1957, 162), at which time local worship sites with their altars were abolished.

3 *You shall prepare for yourself the road.* תָּכִין לְךָ הַדֶּרֶךְ. There must be road-access to the cities from all parts of the territory. The northern hill country at the time of the conquest was still largely forested, which would require felling trees and making roads where there were none. The LXX, changing to an imperative, has στόχασαί σοι τὴν ὁδόν ("estimate for yourself the way"), which views the preparation as an estimate of distances in each territory to the refuge cities.

and you shall divide into three parts the territory of your land. The division will make the cities centrally located. Hebrew גְּבוּל can also mean "boundary" (v. 14), but here and in v. 8 the meaning is "territory" (cf. 2 Kgs 15:16; Jer 15:13).

and it shall be for any killer to flee there. The purpose of these cities is to provide temporary asylum for individuals who have unwittingly committed homicide. Since an avenger will be in hot pursuit and will kill the individual if he catches him (v. 6), that person must succeed in getting to the refuge city, making the procedure similar to an ordeal (Tigay: "leaves the killer's safety to chance"). The fleeing killer is likely to have one or more individuals accompanying him, so one would imagine that he could also defend himself if overtaken by the "avenger of blood."

any killer. כָּל־רֹצֵחַ. The verb רצח is used in the sixth commandment, although there it means "murder" (see Note for 5:17). Here and in 4:42 the participle is to be rendered "killer" or "manslayer," i.e., one who has committed homicide but whose case has not yet been adjudicated, so one does not know whether he is innocent or guilty of a crime.

4 *And this is the word regarding the killer who flees there, and lives.* Hebrew דָּבָר ("word") carries here the sense of "law" (LXX: πρόσταγμα, "command"; cf. 15:2). The writer now specifies the sort of person for whom the city of refuge is created, and why it is created.

One who strikes down his fellow without knowing. The verb נכה is strong, meaning "strike down violently" or "strike to kill." The blow is one that resulted in death. Hebrew בִּבְלִי־דַעַת (lit. "without knowing") means "unintentionally" (RSV) or "unwittingly" (NJV). See also 4:42. The LXX has ἀκουσίως ("unwillingly"), stressing lack of intent (Wevers 1995: 309).

his fellow. On רֵעַ meaning "fellow" rather than "neighbor," see Note for 5:20.

and he had not hated him formerly. Friedman translates the idiom מִתְּמֹל שִׁלְשֹׁם, "from the day before yesterday." It is recognized that some killings are without motive (cf. Num 35:23).

5 *or one who goes with his fellow into the forest to cut wood, and his hand is swinging with the axe to cut the wood, and the axe slips from the wood and finds his fellow, and he dies.* An example of accidental homicide. The NJV and NRSV translate this clause as if it is to provide an example of the unpremeditated homicide described in v. 4b, but it could be another case entirely, this one a killing that was purely accidental. If so, the text is distinguishing between unpremeditated killing and accidental killing, giving an example of each (cf. 17:8). Cf. also Num 35:22-23, which in a different way describes killings both unpremeditated and accidental. Driver thinks the verse does not mean to present a fresh case, but he facilitates his interpretation by emending the initial וַאֲשֶׁר ("and/or who") to כַּאֲשֶׁר ("as when"), which has no textual warrant.

his hand is swinging with the axe . . . and the axe slips from the wood and finds his fellow, and he dies. The verb נִדְּחָה is an N-stem passive, "is swinging," denoting indirect action. The active form נֹדֵחַ ("wielding") occurs in 20:19. The head of the axe could have come loose from the handle and struck the other man, or it could have been jarred loose from the swinging, hit the tree, and then bounced off to hit the man. It doesn't matter; the result is the same, and the action on the part of the axe-swinger is unintentional. Indirect causation in the present law is noted by Daube (1961, 254-55), who calls this a less profound way of stating the case than in the briefer version in Exod 21:12-14. There it says: "God let him [the victim] fall into his [the killer's] hand." In both cases, however, is an absence of human intent. Indirect causation is further indicated by the verb מָצָא ("finds"), where Daube notes a similarity to the law about fire that *finds* (מָצְאָה) its way into a neighbor's field (Exod 22:5[6]).

Deuteronomy 19

As for him, he shall flee to one of these cities and live. According to Josh 20:4, the one who kills unwittingly is to appear at the city of refuge and state his case before the elders, who will then let him enter the city. The law says neither this nor how long the refugee will remain in the city. From Josh 20:6; Num 35:22-28 we learn that an assembly will judge the case. If the homicide was judged to be unintentional, the refugee will be allowed to remain in the city until the death of the high priest, after which he can return home. While there he must not venture outside the borders of the city; if he does, and the avenger catches him, the avenger can kill him without incurring bloodguilt (Num 35:26-27).

6 *lest the avenger of blood pursue after the killer when his heart is inflamed, and overtake him because the road is long, and strike him mortally.* In ancient tribal societies the obligation of blood revenge is laid upon the next of kin to the person who was slain. After a homicide has occurred, this avenger will pursue the killer in the heat of passion, not being sufficiently calm to consider whether it might have been an accident, and will take the killer's life. The present law providing for cities of refuge served then to control blood revenge by giving someone innocent of murder a chance to survive. But the killer could still be struck down on his way to the city of refuge or be killed with impunity if he ventured outside the protected city. Moran says, "the demands of vengeance, though controlled, are still honored."

the avenger of blood. גֹּאֵל הַדָּם. Lit. "the redeemer of blood." A גֹּאֵל is the next of kin responsible for healing or restoring balance within the kin-group. He may be obligated to perpetuate the line of a deceased kinsman (levirate marriage), redeem a kinsman's forfeited property, or redeem a kinsman who has fallen into slavery (25:5-10; Lev 25:25, 47-55; Ruth 4:1-6; Jer 32:6-15). Here he must also avenge the murder of a kinsman, for whom redemption was not possibile (A. R. Johnson 1953; Dentan, "Redeem, Redeemer, Redemption," in *IDB*, 4:21). Blood pollutes the land and is expiated only by shed blood of the one who did the killing (Num 35:33; cf. Gen 9:5-6). In cases of accidental homicide, where the killer remained in exile, later talmudic law explained that the death of the high priest provided the expiation (Greenberg 1959, 129; cf. Num 35:28). In homicide cases no form of compensation was allowed (Num 35:31-32; although Rofé 1986, 235 thinks otherwise). This did not obtain elsewhere in the ANE, where the families could accept compensation. According to Hittite law, a murderer was either required to pay for his misdeed by his own life, or forced to make restitution, which was decided by the victim's heir. The Hittite "Proclamation of Telipinus" (§49) states:

> And a case of murder is as follows. Whoever commits murder, whatever the heir himself of the murdered man says; if he says: "Let him die," he shall die; but if he says: "Let him make restitution," he shall make restitution. At such

a time, however, let no (plea be made) to the king. (Sturtevant and Bechtel 1935, 193)

In the OT the only capital offenses for which monetary compensation was allowed were in the case of a negligent owner being responsible for his ox killing another person (Exod 21:30-31) or the case of a man engaged in a fight with a woman, where the death of an unborn child was the result (Exod 21:22). In the latter case, the husband of the woman suffering the miscarriage determined the fine, subject to approval by the judges. If the fight caused harm to the woman, the *lex talionis* was applied: If she died, the one causing her death had to pay with his own life (Exod 21:23; cf. Lev 24:17-21). Michaelis (1814, 4:236-37) faults Muhammad for allowing and even recommending monetary compensation in cases of murder. Bedouin law allows for the same (Rofé 1986, 205-6), and there are numerous attestations of this practice in the classical world (Driver 1895, 234).

and strike him mortally. וְהִכָּהוּ נֶפֶשׁ, lit. "and strike him down a life." See Gen 37:21; Jer 40:14-15.

though for him there was no sentence of death because he had not hated him formerly. The expression "for him there was no sentence of death" (לוֹ אֵין מִשְׁפַּט־מָוֶת) means "he did not deserve to die" (RSV; cf. Jer 26:16). If he reached the city safely, he would be granted asylum.

7 *Therefore I am commanding you.* For Moses' recurring injunction, see Note for 15:11.

8-9 Yahweh's promise to the fathers was a land that included Philistia, Lebanon, and Aram (Syria), extending as far east as the Euphrates River (1:7-8; 11:22-24; cf. Gen 15:18; Exod 23:31; 34:24). But as v. 9 makes clear, enlargement hinges on Israel keeping the commandments (cf. 11:22-25). This expansion never occurred, so additional cities were never designated. A revised assessment of Yahweh's land grant to the fathers is contained in Judg 2:20–3:4, where it says that Yahweh became angry with Israel for covenant disobedience and therefore left inhabitants of these lands where they were in order to test Israel, to see whether Israel would obey the commandments. As a result, Num 35:6; Josh 20:7-8 mention only six cities, three in Transjordan (cf. 4:41-43) and three in Canaan. Had enlargement taken place, there would have been nine refuge cities.

And if Yahweh your God will enlarge your territory. See the phrase in 12:20, where the initial כִּי may not be a conditional "if," but rather "when."

if you will keep this whole commandment to do it, which I am commanding you today, to love Yahweh your God and to walk in his ways all the days. Keeping the whole of the commandments amounts to fearing Yahweh (see Note for 4:10), loving Yahweh (see Note for 6:5), walking in Yahweh's ways (see Note for

5:33), and serving Yahweh heart and soul (see Note for 6:13). See also 8:6 and 10:12-13. This is the condition for Israel's territory being enlarged, which, as it turned out, did not happen. On the stock expression "keep/be careful to do," see Note for 5:1.

10 The primary motive behind the law on refuge cities. If an avenger kills a man not guilty of murder, he sheds innocent blood, even though he was well within his rights to exact vengeance. Innocent blood defiles the land and its inhabitants (Gen 4:10-12; Num 35:33; Jer 26:15), bringing guilt upon the entire community (v. 13; 21:8-9). One of the curses in ch. 27 is on anyone who takes a bribe to kill an innocent person (27:25). Jeremiah accused both people and king of shedding innocent blood (Jer 2:34; 22:17; cf. Matt 23:35), warning that this was cause enough to jeopardize Judah's tenure in the land (Jer 7:5-7; 22:3-5).

your land that Yahweh your God is giving to you as an inheritance. On this Deuteronomic phrase, which appears slightly altered in v. 14, see Note for 15:4.

bloodguilt. דָּמִים. The LXX has αἵματι ἔνοχος, "liable for blood."

11 *But when there shall be a man who hates his fellow . . .* The law now turns to address premeditated killing, which is murder and in violation of the sixth commandment. For persons charged with this crime the city of refuge offers no protection.

and rises up against him and strikes him mortally so he dies. As Cain did to his brother Abel (Gen 4:8).

12 *then the elders of his city shall send and take him from there, and give him into the hand of the avenger of blood so he may die.* The elders of the city where the killer lived will know him, and also the man whom he killed. These will then fetch him from the city of refuge and hand him over to the avenger of blood, who will put him to death (Num 35:19-21). City elders figure prominently in deciding criminal cases throughout Israelite history (see Note for 5:23-24). They played a key role in acquitting Jeremiah when he was on trial for his life (Jer 26:17-19). Elsewhere in the Deuteronomic Code they are to be involved in expiating an unknown murder (21:1-9), adjudicating the case of a rebellious son (21:18-21), adjudicating the case of a defamed virgin (22:13-21), and adjudicating the case of one who refuses a levirate marriage (25:5-10).

so he may die. וָמֵת. Sam has והומת, "so he may be put to death."

13 *Your eye shall not have pity upon him.* See also 7:16; 13:9(8); 19:21; 25:12. Allowing criminals to escape punishment, for which advocates can always be found, is a miscarriage of justice. Yahweh similarly is without pity in cases of covenant violation (Jer 13:14).

but you shall utterly remove the innocent blood from Israel. The verb is בער, which means "remove utterly" (KBL³, בער II). Friedman has "burn away" (בער I), carrying the same force but not quite the right image. The RSV conveys the right idea with "purge." Here "innocent blood" refers to the blood of the one murdered. According to Deuteronomy, innocent blood, like any other evil, must be completely eradicated from both the people and the land; see again v. 19; 21:9 and Note for 13:6. Innocent blood left unavenged is a stain upon the land, and only by the death of the murderer is that stain removed (see Note on v. 6 above). The LXX sees the death of the murderer as purifying Israel, translating בִעַרְתָּ not with the usual ἐξαρεῖς, "you shall remove" (21:9, 21; 22:21), but with καθαριεῖς, "you shall cleanse, purify" (Wevers 1995, 313-14).

that it may be well for you. Another recurring phrase and theme in Deuteronomy is that the nation is to enjoy well-being (see Note for 4:40). Removing innocent blood by putting to death the person who spilled it will achieve this.

14 *You shall not move back the boundary marker of your fellow.* This prohibition occurs in Proverbs (22:28; 23:10) and in other sapiental literature of the ANE, suggesting an affinity between this law and traditional wisdom in the ancient world (Carmichael 1967, 198; Weinfeld 1967, 257; 1972, 265-67). There are parallels also in ANE law. One might see the moving of a boundary marker as violating the tenth commandment, which prohibits coveting of a fellow's house or field. But since coveting is an inner disposition, and therefore not a punishable offense (Freedman 2000, 155), the more serious violation would be of the eighth commandment prohibiting theft. People guilty of moving boundary markers stand under a curse, to which people have said a loud "Amen" (27:17). In the Egyptian "Instruction of Amen-em-opet" (7th to 6th cents.) this word of advice:

> Do not carry off the landmark at the boundaries of the arable land,
> Nor disturb the position of the measuring-cord;
> Be not greedy after a cubit of land,
> Nor encroach upon the boundaries of a widow . . .
> Guard against encroaching upon the boundaries of the fields,
> Lest a terror carry thee off.
> One satisfies god with the will of the Lord,
> Who determines the boundaries of the arable land. . . .
>
> (Ch. 6; *ANET*[3], 422)

Here it is noted that widows are particularly vulnerable to encroachers upon boundaries, also that the god determined boundaries in the beginning (cf. Deut 32:8). Proverbs 22:28 inveighs against displacing ancient boundaries that the "fathers" have set. The OT recognizes, too, that this act of stealth is a way for the wealthy and the strong to defraud the poor (Hos 5:10; Job 24:2; Prov 23:10; cf. Isa 5:8).

Amen-em-opet goes on to say:

> Be not greedy for the property of a poor man,
> Nor hunger for his bread.
> As for the property of a poor man, it (is) a blocking to the throat,
> It makes a vomiting to the gullet.
> If he has obtained it by false oaths,
> His heart is perverted by his belly. . . . (Ch. 11; $ANET^3$, 423)

Here a connection is made between boundary encroachment and false oaths, supporting a connection between the present verse and vv. 15-21 on false witnesses. In the Egyptian *Book of the Dead* (Ch. 125 Intro: 13) is this disclaimer by the deceased before the court: "I have not encroached upon the fields [of others]" (Budge 1898, 191).

Among the Hittite Laws (ca. 1300) is this law:

> If anyone violates the boundary of a field and takes 1 furrow off (the neighbor's field), the owner of the field gets the violator's field. The violator shall also give 1 sheep, 10 loaves, (and) 1 jug of strong beer and resanctify the field. (HL 168; $ANET^3$, 195)

Several sections of the Middle Assyrian Laws deal with encroachment on a neighbor's property, including the removal of landmarks. In one case, if an encroacher is convicted, he must return not only the land wrongfully seized, but a third more; in addition he will lose one finger, receive one hundred stripes, and do forced labor for a month (Driver and Miles 1935, 302). The finger is severed because he defaced or removed (with his hand) the boundary, which is deemed sacred.

Ancient Babylonian boundary stones dating from 1450 to 550, called kudurru-inscriptions, are in the British Museum (L. W. King 1902). These conical blocks or boulders were erected on estates to define the limits and ownership of those estates. They did not themselves mark boundaries. The inscriptions also warned of a curse or punishment on anyone by the god — including descendants — who might alter, hide, or destroy the stones. The prohibition against moving boundary markers is also well attested in classical sources (Driver 1895, 234-35), where among the Romans land was held to be sacred (Michaelis 1814, 3:373).

which the first ones set as a boundary in your inheritance. The "first ones" (רִאשֹׁנִים) are the ancestors (Prov 22:28: "fathers") who mapped out family allotments at the time of the conquest (Josh 18:1-10). Naboth calls his land "the inheritance of my fathers" (1 Kgs 21:3). Here we see that the Deuteronomic writer is living at a considerably later time. "Your inheritance" (נַחֲלָתְךָ), as the verse goes on to state, is the promised land Yahweh is giving to Israel (see Note for 15:4).

15 This law as framed applies not only to capital offenses (17:6; Num 35:30), but to "any iniquity or . . . any sin." Such wrongdoings must be of a serious nature. Michaelis (1814, 4:325) surmises that there were less important cases brought before the judges where one witness was sufficient. The case of someone moving back a fellow's boundary marker, particularly if things turned ugly and harm came to one of the disputants, would likely require multiple witnesses for resolution. Michaelis thinks two or three witnesses were required only in capital cases, such as homicide cases referred to in vv. 1-13 or the apostasy case in 17:2-7. But this is unlikely, in view of the emphatic "for any iniquity or for any sin — in any sin that one will commit," which doubtless means "any (serious) iniquity or any (serious) sin." The wording is the same in 11QT 61:6-7 (Yadin 1983, 2:277-78). Cases of bodily injury would be covered under this provision, since the *lex talionis* as stated in v. 21 allows for offenses and punishments short of death. The present rule on witnesses is cited in Matt 18:16; 2 Cor 13:1; 1 Tim 5:19. On the minimum of two or three witnesses to decide capital cases, see also Note for 17:6.

16 *When an unjust witness shall stand up against a man to testify a falsehood against him.* Hebrew עֵד־חָמָס is lit. "a witness of injustice," where חָמָס does not necessarily mean "violence," as it is usually translated. Speiser (1964, 51, 117) gave as meanings "lawlessness" and "injustice" in Gen 6:11; 16:5, citing for comparison Akk *ḫabalum*, meaning "to deprive someone of his legal rights" (cf. *CAD*, 6:3-6). Akkadian *ḫabaltu* means "lawlessness, violence, damage caused by illegal action," and *ḫabālu* "lawlessness, injustice" (*CAD*, 6:3). In the present verse the LXX translates μάρτυς ἄδικος ("an unjust witness"). See also Exod 23:1; Ps 35:11. False witness violates the ninth commandment (5:20) and is what led to the death of Naboth and the seizure of his vineyard (1 Kgs 21:8-13). We get this admonition in "The Instruction of Amen-em-opet":

Do not bear witness with false words,
Nor support another person (thus) with thy tongue.
(Ch. 13; *ANET*³, 423)

to testify. For other uses of ענה with this meaning in Deuteronomy, see Note for 5:20.

falsehood. Hebrew סָרָה is usually a word of "rebellion" against Yahweh (13:6[5]; Jer 28:16; 29:32), but here it refers more generally to a false word (cf. Isa 59:13).

17 The disputants may have to swear an oath in Yahweh's name, although "standing before Yahweh" probably means standing before priests and judges who will decide the case at the central sanctuary (17:9; 25:1). On Deuteronomy's establishment of a high court for difficult cases, see 17:8-13. In Exod

22:7(8) the owner of a house from which goods were stolen "comes near to God" to show whether or not he was the thief, probably for the purpose of swearing an oath that he is innocent. Swearing falsely under oath is a crime (Lev 19:12). Moran thinks that in the sanctuary one falsely accused would likely appeal for an ordeal to establish his innocence, and that the ordeal would be an imprecatory oath. He points out that cuneiform texts document the refusal of persons to swear an oath before the divinity, which was a truly terrifying experience. Refusal led to a forfeiture of the case. In the Laws of Ur-Nammu (ca. 2200), for example, is one law dealing with a man who refused to take an oath (LUN 26′: B §35; *ANET*³, 525).

before the priests and the judges. 11QT 61:8-9 has "before the priests and the Levites and before the judges" (Yadin 1983, 2:278). In 17:9 "judge" is singular, indicating only one lay judge at the central sanctuary. "Judge" singular occurs again in 25:2.

18 *and the judges shall inquire thoroughly.* See 13:15(14); 17:4, 9. Cases need to be brought before judges when legal principles are involved (Weinfeld 1977, 81).

the witness is a false witness. עֵד־שֶׁקֶר הָעֵד. LXX ἐμαρτύρησεν ("he testified") reads הָעֵד as an H-stem perfect verb written defectively (cf. Gen 43:3), which finds confirmation in the reading העיד in 11QT 61:9-10 (Rofé 1988a, 164-65). But Rofé judges the Qumran (and LXX) reading to be secondary, reflecting later Hebrew usage.

19 *then you shall do to him as he schemed to do to his brother.* The one bearing false witness is to be punished by the court or the people ("you [plural] shall do") with the same penalty that his testimony, if true, would have brought upon the accused. The *talion* principle for false witness, elaborated in v. 21, is well attested in other ANE law codes, although in some cases these codes allow monetary compensation, which the Bible does not. The parade example in the Bible of a person suffering the punishment planned for another is Haman being hanged on the gallows prepared for Mordecai in the book of Esther (Esth 7:9-10).

and you shall utterly remove the evil from your midst. On Deuteronomy's insistence that evil be eradicated within Israel, see v. 13 above.

20 This repeats 13:12(11) and is similar to other like statements in Deuteronomy (17:13; 21:21), all of which aver that punishment for wrongdoing and shaming the criminal in public will have a positive effect on the community (see Note for 13:12).

21 *And your eye shall not have pity.* See earlier v. 13.

life for life, eye for eye, tooth for tooth, hand for hand, foot for foot. This law of retaliation appears two other times in the OT, in Exod 21:23-25 (expanded); Lev 24:18-20, in both instances cited in connection with cases involving injury or death. The principle is well attested in ANE law and must be seen both there and in the OT as a limitation on tribal vengeance, where a much greater price was exacted (Gen 4:23-24). Daube (1947, 102), however, says the principle of compensation is old, going back to the earliest period of legal history open to inquiry. Here it is simply stated that punishment shall befit the crime.

The Code of Hammurabi prescribed twenty-seven capital sentences for a variety of wrongs, including adultery, theft, and false testimony (Diamond 1957, 151; Good 1967, 968; Moran). If the false testimony alleged a lesser offense, punishment was meted out on the *talion* principle, otherwise on a graduated scale of monetary compensation depending on the class of the injured party. For example, if a seignior (= lord) came forward with a false testimony in a case and the case involved a life, he was put to death (CH 1, 3; $ANET^3$, 166). If a seignior destroyed the eye or knocked out the tooth of someone his own rank, his eye would be destroyed or his tooth knocked out (CH 196, 200; $ANET^3$, 175). But if a seignior destroyed the eye, broke the bone, or knocked out the tooth of a commoner, he had only to pay one mina of silver in compensation (CH 198, 201; $ANET^3$, 175). Injuries to slaves were assessed at one half the slave's value (CH 199; $ANET^3$, 175).

Hittite laws specified monetary compensation where an eye, tooth, or ear was lost, and here too a graduated scale of compensation was assessed depending on the class of the injured party (HL 7, 8, 15, 16; $ANET^3$, 189). The same was true in the Laws of Eshnunna (LE 42-48; Diamond 1957, 151; Yaron 1969, 42-45; M. T. Roth 1995, 65-66; $ANET^3$, 163). In the Lipit Ishtar Code (LI 33), a false accusation regarding sexual conduct resulted in a mere 10-shekel fine, which is surprising, since the accusation, if proved true, would have meant death for the woman (J. J. Finkelstein 1966, 367). In the Ur-Nammu Code (LUN 25': B §34; $ANET^3$, 525), which contains the oldest known laws from the Sumerian city of Ur (ca. 2200), perjury was punished by a fine:

> If a man appeared as a witness (in a lawsuit), and was shown to be a perjurer, he must pay 15 shekels of silver.

According to Frymer-Kensky (1980), equal retribution became standard operating procedure in the Old Babylonian period (Lipit-Ishtar Code and the Code of Hammurabi; 19th and 18th cents.), over a millennium before we meet up with this retribution formula in biblical law. For more on "talionic" sanctions in the ANE, see Diamond 1957.

According to later rabbinic exegesis, the retaliation specified in the present verse was not to be taken literally, and monetary compensations were prescribed (Rashi; Daube 1947, 106-10). Daube thinks the same was probably true in early times, except perhaps in the case of murder or attempted murder (Num

Deuteronomy 19

35:31). In the NT, Jesus tells people not to use the *lex talionis* principle (Matt 5:38-41), but he is referring simply to insult and other minor indignities.

life for life. נֶפֶשׁ בְּנֶפֶשׁ. Daube (1947, 129-30) notes that תַּחַת, meaning "in place of," is not used in each *lex talionis* example as it is in Exod 21:23-24, where literal compensation can be assumed. Instead we have בְּ. He believes that בְּ, having as it does a wide range of meanings, could imply compensation, but it may mean simply "to atone for" ("life to atone for life, eye to atone for eye," etc.). The false witness cited here does not succeed (the judges find him to be false), therefore strict compensation may not be required, as no damage was done. To the false witness would simply be done "as he schemed to do to his brother."

Message and Audience

Moses tells the Moab assembly that when Yahweh clears the land of its former inhabitants and Israel is established in cities and houses, three cities must be set apart in the new territory for individuals who unwittingly killed someone to go to for refuge. A road must be prepared. The rule for legitimate refuge-seekers is the following: the cities are there for anyone who kills a person unintentionally or accidentally, such as when men are cutting wood in the forest and the axe slips from the handle and causes the death of another. The one who killed his fellow is then given a chance to flee to the refuge city, lest the dead man's kinsman pursue him and take his life, since in the heat of passion he will not realize that the killing was innocent. Because the avenger is within his rights to pursue the killer and put him to death, these refuge cities will offer asylum to killers not deserving of death. Moses therefore commands the people to set apart three refuge cities.

Moses then says that if Yahweh enlarges Israel's territory to the dimensions promised to the fathers, which would take in Philistia, Lebanon, Aram (Syria) and land all the way eastward to the Euphrates, and just as importantly if people are sure to do Yahweh's commandment now being set before them, which is to love Yahweh and walk in his way, then another three refuge cities will be allocated. Nothing is said about the three refuge cities allocated in Transjordan. But for a late 8th- and early 7th-cent. audience who have heard Deuteronomy read from the beginning, these cities will be known. The reason for three additional cities in the enlarged territory will be the same as for the three cities in Canaan: that innocent blood not be shed in the God-given land, which will be a stain upon the people and the land. It could happen that the avenger will catch and kill the one who killed his kinsman, which will be more shedding of innocent blood.

What follows is the case of a fellow who actually does commit murder and then flees to a refuge city. Here the elders of the city from which he fled are to extradite him and turn him over to the avenging kinsman, who will put him to death. The murderer is not to be pitied. He must be put to death so that the innocent blood he shed be removed from Israel, and Israel return to well-being.

The audience then hears a command not to move back a fellow's boundary marker set by ancestors in the land. If the ancestors are the first Israelite inhabitants of Canaan, then the law is speaking directly to an audience later than the one who heard Moses in the plains of Moab. It is assumed here that the boundaries set by the first Israelite inhabitants are to be respected and left unchanged by subsequent generations.

A follow-up to the law about homicides and cities of refuge is one regarding witnesses. It deals with an aspect of the asylum procedure not dealt with above. Once refugees arrive at the city, their innocence or guilt must be determined. Witnesses may have accompanied the killer to the refuge city, and a court there will have to make a judgment on the killer's story and any testimony from accompanying witnesses. The law on witnesses may also follow intentionally the law about not removing boundary markers, for here, too, a dispute among owners could break out and judges would have to decide the case and witnesses would have to testify.

This law on witnesses has broad application, for it pertains to individuals accused of "any iniquity or any sin." It states that a conviction based on the testimony of only one witness cannot stand. Testimony from two or three witnesses is required. If one witness is suspected of giving false testimony, then he and the accused must stand before Yahweh, that is, before the priests and judges then in office. Both litigants may have to swear oaths. Judges will examine the case thoroughly, and if a witness is judged to have given false testimony, the court or community is to carry out the judgment upon him that his false witness would have brought upon the accused. This will remove the evil from within Israel. Punishment is believed to be a deterrent to crime, for others will hear and fear and not do an evil thing like the one done. Violators of the ninth commandment are not to be pitied. The *lex talionis* applies: life for a false witness testifying in a life case, commensurate injury for a false witness testifying in an injury case.

H. WHEN YOU GO TO WAR (20:1-20)

1. Choosing Warriors (20:1-9)

20 ¹*When you go forth to the battle against your enemies, and you see horse and chariot, a people more numerous than you, you shall not be fearful of them for Yahweh your God is with you, the one who brought you up from the land of Egypt.* ²*And it will be when you draw near to the battle, the priest shall then come for-*

ward and speak to the people. ³And he shall say to them, "Hear, O Israel, you are drawing near today to the battle against your enemies, let not your heart be weak; do not fear, and do not hurriedly flee, and do not tremble before them, ⁴for Yahweh your God is the one going with you to fight for you with your enemies, to save you." ⁵Then the officials shall speak to the people, saying, "Who is the man who has built a new house and has not occupied it? Let him go and return to his house, lest he die in the battle and another man occupy it. ⁶And who is the man who has planted a vineyard and has not eaten its fruit? Let him go and return to his house, lest he die in the battle and another man eat its fruit. ⁷And who is the man who has betrothed a wife and has not taken her? Let him go and return to his house, lest he die in the battle and another man take her." ⁸And the officials shall continue speaking to the people and say, "Who is the man who fears and is weak of heart? Let him go and return to his house, so the heart of his brother not melt as his heart." ⁹And it will be as the officials finish speaking to the people, then they shall appoint commanders of the armies at the head of the people.

2. Conduct of Holy War (20:10-18)

20¹⁰When you draw near to a city to fight against it, then you shall proclaim peace to it. ¹¹And it will be if it answers peace to you and opens up to you, then it will be that all the people who are found in it shall become forced labor for you, and they shall serve you. ¹²But if it does not make peace with you, but does battle with you, then you shall lay siege to it. ¹³And Yahweh your God will give it into your hand, and you shall strike down all its males into the mouth of the sword; ¹⁴only the women, and the little ones, and the beasts, and everything that is in the city, all its spoil, you shall take as booty for yourself, and you shall eat the spoil of your enemies that Yahweh your God has given you. ¹⁵Thus you shall do to all the cities that are very distant from you, which are not among the cities of these nations here. ¹⁶Only among the cities of these peoples that Yahweh your God is giving to you as an inheritance you shall not let any breathing thing live, ¹⁷but you shall utterly devote them to destruction — the Hittites and the Amorites, the Canaanites and the Perizzites, the Hivites and the Jebusites, as Yahweh your God commanded you, ¹⁸in order that they not teach you to do according to all their abominations that they have done for their gods, that you sin against Yahweh your God.

3. Respect Fruit Trees in a Siege! (20:19-20)

¹⁹When you lay siege to a city many days, to fight against it to capture it, you shall not destroy its trees by wielding an axe against it, for from it you shall eat; so you

shall not cut it down, for is the man the tree of the field coming before you in the siege? ²⁰Only a tree which you know indeed that is not a tree for food, it you may destroy and cut down and build a siegework against the city that is doing battle with you, until it falls.

Rhetoric and Composition

The present chapter belongs to a larger unit extending all the way to 21:14. One finds here another framing structure whereby a law providing for the expiation of an unsolved murder has been placed in the midst of laws relating to warfare and the conduct of war:

a   Choosing warriors and the conduct of war (20:1-20)
    b   Expiation for an unsolved murder (21:1-9)
a′   Women taken captive in war (21:10-14)

Opening and closing sections of the larger unit have similar beginnings:

When you go forth to the battle against your enemies . . .   20:1
When you go forth to the battle against your enemies . . .   21:10

Rofé (1985, 26-27; 1988b, 271) notes, too, that the expiation rite for an unsolved murder appears in the midst of laws dealing with warfare, but in his earlier publication calls this "an editorial mishap," which it is not (see Rhetoric and Composition for 19:1-21). In his later publication he decides the expiation rite has been joined to the prior warfare law by catchwords of sound and meaning.

for is the man the tree of *the field*   כִּי הָאָדָם . . . הַשָּׂדֶה   20:19
    coming before you . . . ?
When someone slain is found *on the*   כִּי . . . בָּאֲדָמָה . . . בַּשָּׂדֶה   21:1
    ground . . . fallen *in the field* . . .

A desire to link these passages may explain why בָּאֲדָמָה ("on the ground") is used instead of בָּאָרֶץ ("in the land"), the more usual term in Deuteronomy (4:14, 17, 22, 25; 5:31, 33, and passim). We find בָּאֲדָמָה only one other time in the book, in 4:18. Deuteronomy is the only book of the Pentateuch having laws about war (von Rad 1953, 49), containing also three laws where war is combined with other subjects: the law on cleanliness in the camp (23:10-15[9-14]); the deferment law for the newly married (24:5); and the law concerning the Amalekites (25:17-19).

The present chapter divides into three parts: (1) choosing warriors for battle (vv. 1-9); (2) conduct of war against enemies far and near (vv. 10-18); and (3) the preservation of fruit trees when a city is put under siege (vv. 19-20). These divisions are supported by the section markings. Before v. 1 is a *setumah* in M^L and 11QT and a section in Sam, which is also a chapter division. Another *setumah* in M^L and 11QT and a section in Sam are present after v. 9, and the third *setumah* in M^L and a section in Sam are present after v. 18. A section after v. 9 exists also in 4QDeut^{k2} (reconstructed), but not in 4QDeut^i (Ulrich, Cross et al. 1995, 72, 101). After v. 18 are possibly a section (reconstructed) in 4QDeut^{k2} (Ulrich, Cross et al. 1995, 102) and a *setumah* (reconstructed) in 11QT (Yadin 1983, 2:283). A *petuḥah* in M^L, a reconstructed section in 11QT (Yadin 1983, 2:283), and a section in Sam after v. 20 mark the end of the unit, which is also the chapter division.

Verses 1, 10, and 19 all begin with כִּי + an imperfect verb (McConville), further supporting these three divisions:

When you go forth . . .	. . . כִּי־תֵצֵא	v. 1
When you draw near . . .	. . . כִּי־תִקְרַב	v. 10
When you lay siege . . .	. . . כִּי־תָצוּר	v. 19

That the present verses embody not so much law as preached law is clear from the repetition in the officials' speech, which preserves the rhythm and rhetorical flourish of oral discourse (2 Kings 1–2; Lundbom 1973). It is similar also to the preached law in ch. 13:

> 20:5 *Who is the man who* has built a new house and has not occupied it?
> *Let him go and return to his house,* lest he die in the battle and *another man* occupy it.
>
> v. 6 *And who is the man who* has planted a vineyard and has not eaten its fruit?
> *Let him go and return to his house,* lest he die in the battle and *another man* eat its fruit.
>
> v. 7 *And who is the man who* has betrothed a wife and has not taken her?
> *Let him go and return to his house,* lest he die in the battle and *another man* take her.
>
> v. 8 *Who is the man who* fears and is weak of heart?
> *Let him go and return to his house,* so the heart of his brother not melt as his heart.

The concluding line is altered slightly: "lest he die in the battle" is omitted, and "his brother" replaces "another man." On deliberate deviations from established patterns of repetition, see Freedman 1986.

The first segment on the choosing of warriors may be linked to the second segment on the conduct of war by words having similarity in sound:

| so (it) not melt | וְלֹא יִמַּס | v. 8 |
| (for) forced labor | לָמַס | v. 11 |

The officials' final call for the "fearful" and "weak of heart" to return home brings us back to the beginning exhortation by the priest, containing also inversion as inclusio structures tend to do:

| let not your heart be weak/do not fear . . . | v. 3 |
| Who is the man who fears/and is weak of heart? | v. 8 |

Portions of 20:1-20 are contained in 4QDeut^f, 4QDeut^i, 4QDeut^{k2}, and 4Q365.

Notes

20:1 *When you go forth to the battle against your enemies.* Moses is envisioning battles Israel will face once it crosses the Jordan and enters Canaan. Here at the beginning of the discourse are no clear signs of later warfare being projected back into an earlier age; nevertheless, correlations between the anticipated warfare and biblical narratives reporting the wars of the conquest, the period of the judges, and the later monarchy are not wanting. Later in the chapter we see certain limitations being placed on the conduct of holy war, which von Rad (1991, 31) thought reflected subsequent prophetic criticism of the royal court. Driver, too, said that the present laws were not so much to regulate the conduct of war as to check the barbarity and cruelty with which war was waged, especially later by the Assyrians (cf. Amos 1:3, 13; Hos 14:1[13:16]; 2 Kgs 8:12).

and you see horse and chariot, a people more numerous than you, you shall not be fearful of them for Yahweh your God is with you, the one who brought you up from the land of Egypt. This exhortation to faith, which downplays strength and numbers of the enemy and admonishes people not to fear because Yahweh is with them, appeals climactically to Yahweh's deliverance of Israel from Egypt and is like many others in the book (1:21, 29-31; 7:17-21; 9:1-3; 31:6). It was an honorable tradition in Israel that, with Yahweh leading the hosts and a people believing in Yahweh, a foe vastly larger and stronger could easily be routed. One

Deuteronomy 20

has only to recall the battle of Gideon (Judg 7:1-23) and other subsequent battles (1 Kgs 20:27-30; 2 Chr 32:7-8). The same happened in the later wars of Judas Maccabeus against the Seleucid Greeks (1 Macc 3:16-19; 4:8-11). Yahweh's "I am/ I will be with you" is the preeminent promise in the Bible (Gen 26:3; 28:15; Exod 3:12; Deut 2:7; 20:1, 4; 31:6, 8, 23; Josh 1:5, 9; Judg 6:12, 16; Jer 1:8, 19; 15:20; 30:11; Isa 41:10; 43:5, and passim; cf. the risen Jesus' words in Matt 28:20).

horse and chariot. The LXX has ἵππον καὶ ἀναβάτην, "horse and horseman," which reads רכב as a participle. The Vg has "chariot" *(currus)*, which is the better reading. Horse-drawn chariots go back to the beginning of recorded history, where they were used not for transport but for waging war. Chariots were mobile firing platforms that gave fighters a tactical advantage on level ground, at the same time having considerable shock value against an enemy. They were in use among the Sumerians as early as the first half of the 3rd mill. By the 16th and 15th cents., a lighter version equipped with spoked wheels was being employed in Canaan and Egypt. The chariot is believed to have entered Egypt from Canaan.

Israel was pursued by Egyptian chariots in the exodus, but with Yahweh in control of the chase Israel came out the victor (Exod 14; 15:1-10). Israel, when entering Canaan, saw many horses and chariots (Josh 11:4; Judg 4:3), but its settlement in the hill country offset Canaanite technical superiority, since chariots could not be used in hilly, heavily wooded areas (Josh 17:18). This changed when Israel had designs on Canaanite cities in the plain (Josh 17:16; Judg 1:19). Only much later is Ahab reported as having success against Aram (Syria) in level terrain (1 Kgs 20:1-30). For the prophets, trust in chariots translated into a lack of faith (Isa 30:15-17; 31:1-3; Hos 14:4[3]). See also Ps 20:8[7]; Prov 21:31. On chariots and chariot warfare in the ANE, also for pictures of chariots and horsemen on wall paintings, vases, reliefs, and excavated remains, see Yadin 1963, 4-5, 36-40, 86-90, 128-39, 218-19, 240-43.

2 *the priest shall then come forward and speak to the people.* Priests played a prominent role in military operations. In narratives reporting wars that took place in the time of Moses, Saul, and David, priests are seen to be accompanying the army; carrying sacred utensils, trumpets, and the ark; and consulting Yahweh by Urim and Thummim (Num 31:6; 1 Sam 4:4; 14:3, 18, 36-42; 2 Chr 13:12-14). Here they only give encouragement before the battle. Tigay thinks vv. 3-4 are simply a précis of a longer speech, which they may be, but there is no reason to conclude as he does that the priest's speech actually followed the deferral speech of the officials. The speech offering deferrals, particularly the last deferral for the fearful and weak of heart, makes better sense if it follows the priestly exhortation calling on everyone not to be fearful or weak-hearted.

In "The War of the Sons of Light against the Sons of Darkness" *(War Scroll)*, a Qumran scroll dating from the late 1st cent. B.C. or early 1st cent. A.D., holy war ideology has again come to the fore with a future battle envisioned between the entire congregation and an enemy led by the Kittim (= Seleucid Greeks). Once again the priest plays a prominent role, addressing the congregation before battle, offering prayers before, during, and after the battle; giving words of encouragement; and directing troop movements by blowing the trumpet (Yadin 1962, 208-17 and texts; cf. Cross 1949, 40-43). On holy war speeches before battles, see also Weinfeld 1972, 45-51.

and speak to the people. "The people" being the addressee points to a volunteer militia, mobilized as the need arises and put under civilian and military leadership, who are appointed for the occasion. Deuteronomy does not envision Israel as having a standing army.

3 *"Hear, O Israel.* The priest begins with Moses' words of 5:1; 6:4 (Shema); 9:1. On this didactic introduction in Deuteronomy, and its importance in 5-11, see Note for 5:1.

let not your heart be weak; do not fear. Being "weak of heart" means being fainthearted (cf. Isa 7:4; Jer 51:46). Anyone fearful or fainthearted about entering battle is offered a deferral (v. 8).

and do not hurriedly flee. וְאַל־תַּחְפְּזוּ. I.e., do not flee from the battle in panic. The verb occurs one other time, in 16:3, where it refers to Israel's hurried flight from Egypt.

and do not tremble before them. On this Deuteronomic expression, see Note for 1:29.

4 Yahweh will lead Israel in its holy war against the Canaanites, just as he did against Sihon and Og in Transjordan (2:24-3:8). On holy war in Deuteronomy, see Note for 1:30.

5 *Then the officials shall speak to the people.* The assembled now hear a speech by certain "officials" (שֹׁטְרִים), who are nonmilitary personnel probably responsible for recruiting the militia (von Rad 1953, 51 n. 5). Michaelis (1814, 3:30-31) calls them "scribes" (LXX: γραμματεῖς), whose job it was to keep genealogical tables, select the warriors, and oversee the muster (cf. 1 Macc 5:42). These officials elsewhere are seen to be assisting judges in legal matters (16:18). The text of 11QT 62:2 [reconstructed] and 4 actually has השופטים, "the judges" (Yadin 1983, 2:280-81). These individuals, in any case, are to be distinguished from the militia commanders in v. 9 (cf. 1:15). Here they are in charge of deferrals, somewhat like the former U.S. Selective Service.

Who is the man who has built a new house and has not occupied it? Let him go and return to his house, lest he die in the battle and another man occupy it. A volunteer army, such as this is, will be comprised of men who offer themselves willingly (Judg 5:2). Some will not want to go, and some perhaps should not go, so deferrals are offered: (1) to those who have built a new house, but not yet lived in it; (2) to those who have planted a vineyard, but not yet eaten any of its fruit; (3) to those who have betrothed a wife, but have not yet taken her in marriage; and (4) to those who are fearful and weak of heart (cf. 1 Macc 3:56). This first basis for deferral, and the two following, allow a young man to fulfill legitimate obligations (Jer 29:5-6; cf. Deut 28:30) and, if taken, will not be a reproach of character (Michaelis 1814, 3:34). But according to *m. Soṭah* 8:2, those granted these deferrals were required, once they returned home, to "provide water and food and repair the roads." Driver views the deferrals as evidence of an enlightened and sympathetic recruitment policy advanced by the writer of Deuteronomy, which they may be. Under a monarchy, and where the king is dealing with subordinates, things could be different. One of the Mari Letters (no. 35) reports a king issuing a reprimand to northern subjects, saying that if a king goes out on an expedition, everyone down to the youngsters must assemble; no one is to be left behind (Oppenheim 1967, 96-97).

In the ancient Sumerian epic, "Gilgamesh and the Land of the Living," Gilgamesh before he dies wants to undertake a journey to a distant land in order to make a name for himself. He therefore puts out a call for fifty unattached men who have neither house nor mother to accompany him. The call has similarities to the call here. Gilgamesh says:

Who has a house, to his house! Who has a mother, to his mother!
Let single males who would do as I (do), fifty, stand at my side. (lines 50-51; *ANET*³, 48)

and has not occupied it? וְלֹא חֲנָכוֹ. Many modern Versions translate the verb חנך as "dedicate" (AV; RSV; JB; NEB; NJV), which appears to be influenced by the LXX's καὶ οὐκ ἐνεκαίνισεν αὐτήν. But חנך, according to Reif (1972), does not mean "dedicate," rather "initiating the use of." Reif points out — as Driver did earlier — that no dedication of a private house is attested anywhere in the Hebrew Bible, nor, says Reif, is such a thing known in subsequent Jewish religious custom. Reif suggests as a more suitable translation: "Whoever has built a house and not started to live in it." Here he is anticipated by Rashi, also by Michaelis (1814, 3:34), who translated: "Whoever had built a house and had not yet occupied it." It is possible, however, that חנך could mean "dedicate" in 1 Kgs 8:63, where a ceremony marks the completion and first use of the temple (Tigay). But in the present verse חנך probably means "to make first use of" or "to occupy."

6 *And who is the man who has planted a vineyard and has not eaten its fruit?* וְלֹא חִלְּלוֹ is lit. "and has not treated it as common," where reference is to the eating of fruit after it has been set aside as holy. According to Levitical law, fruit of newly-planted trees and vines cannot be eaten until the fifth year (Lev 19:23-25). During the first three years the fruit is not eaten at all; in the fourth year it is set aside as a praise offering to Yahweh; and in the fifth year the planter may eat it. Envisioned here is a situation where a man has planted a vineyard but has not yet enjoyed the fruit. What we could have then is a five-year deferral, and again for a perfectly legitimate reason, since the wish of every young man is to be able to eat the grapes and drink the wine from a vineyard he has planted (Jer 31:5; 1 Cor 9:7).

lest he die in the battle and another man eat its fruit. The eating by another of fruit one has planted is a covenant curse (Deut 28:30; cf. Amos 5:11; Jer 5:17).

7 Newly-married men were excused from battle for one year (24:5). Here the man has paid the bride-price (= "betrothal"; cf. 22:23, 25; Gen 34:12; 1 Sam 18:25, 27; 2 Sam 3:14) but has not come to his wedding day, after which he may take his wife home. He, too, may be granted a deferral from battle. Things do not go this well in the Legend of King Keret, where mobilization is total and the newlywed groom must leave his wife to a stranger (iii 101-3; iv 189-91; *ANET*³, 143-44). The situation here may have been unusual (Tigay); however, in later Jewish law the man who had betrothed a wife did not get a deferral if the war was a so-called "War of Duty" (*m. Soṭah* 8:7; Yadin 1962, 67-68).

8 *Who is the man who fears and is weak of heart? Let him go and return to his house.* The officials at the end of their speech call for the fearful and weakhearted to depart, which is heard in other speeches prior to battle (Judg 7:3; 1 Macc 3:56). In "The War of the Sons of Light against the Sons of Darkness," officials similarly turn back the fainthearted in their speech (Yadin 1962, 67). But in the War of Duty as defined later by the rabbis, even the fainthearted had to go into battle (*m. Soṭah* 8:7; Yadin 1962, 68). This deferral, unlike the others, is not so honorable (Calvin; Michaelis 1814, 3:37). Daube (1969a, 29) says the question put to the assembly is designed to appeal to a man's sense of shame, particularly when the priest has just finished exhorting everyone not to show cowardice (v. 3).

so the heart of his brother not melt as his heart. I.e., like what happened in the wilderness, when the people, after hearing the report of the spies, would not go up into the land (1:28). The concern here is for morale, what impact a fearful combatant will have on the fighting force as a whole. Fainthearted men will demoralize the others. The LXX, Vg, and other ancient Versions presuppose an H-stem of the verb (cf. 1:28), which simply involves a repointing from יִמַּס to יָמֵס. This gives the translation: "So he will not melt the heart of his brother as his heart." Either rendering is possible; the H-stem pointing makes the demoralizing effect of the fainthearted more explicit.

9 *then they shall appoint commanders of the armies at the head of the people.* "They" is indefinite, meaning those whose business it is to appoint (Driver). Officials will not necessarily appoint the commanders. The commanders will be in charge of thousands, hundreds, fifties, and tens (1:15; Num 31:14, 48; 1 Macc 3:55), the same battle formations prescribed in "The War of the Sons of Light against the Sons of Darkness" (see Note for 1:15).

armies. צְבָאוֹת. The LXX has the singular τῆς στρατιᾶς, "of the army."

10-11 It will not become apparent until v. 15, but the conduct here pertains only to wars in cities "very far away," not the cities of Canaan. And Israel will not be sending embassies to distant cities, but will have an army at the cities, ready to attack if need be. The warfare envisioned is like what occurred under David, when battles were fought outside Canaan proper (2 Sam 10:19), or what could have occurred if the conquest had taken in all the land originally promised, i.e., Philistia, Lebanon, and Aram (Syria) east to the Euphrates (see Note for 19:8-9). The "peace" (שָׁלוֹם) offered to these cities will be an invitation to surrender, which, if accepted, will bring its population under forced labor. The Gibeonites deceived Joshua into making a covenant with them by pretending they were sojourners from a far country, but they were put under forced labor (Josh 9:3-27). In Deuteronomy the people under Moses spoke words of peace to Sihon, king of Heshbon (2:26), where the stated objective was to gain permission to pass through Sihon's territory. But the genuineness of this offer has to be in doubt, since war with Sihon was a foregone conclusion (2:24).

forced labor. מַס. This would be task-work in agriculture and construction projects, such as David required of the Ammonites (2 Sam 12:31) and Solomon required of Canaanites who had not been expelled from the land (1 Kgs 9:15-21; cf. Judg 1:27-35). The Gibeonites became hewers of wood and drawers of water (Josh 9:21-27). The indignity would not have been like the barbaric proposal of the Ammonites to the men of Jabesh-gilead, where a peace treaty would have led to the men of Jabesh-gilead having their right eyes gouged out (1 Sam 11:1-2). But this was a known form of slavery in the ANE, where only one eye was destroyed so the slave could perform work. On forced labor in Israel and elsewhere the ANE, see Rainey 1970.

12 Von Rad (1991, 117) thought this betrayed a later age since Israel, in the days of conquest, did not possess the means to wage siege warfare. But Israel could certainly have envisioned siege warfare against Canaanite cities. The techniques were well known. Thutmose III (1490-1436) besieged Megiddo for seven months until it surrendered ($ANET^3$, 234-38). While it is true that Thutmose III had horses and chariots and Megiddo was protected by a moat and freshly-cut timbers, sieges even on a smaller scale could have been carried out successfully.

13-14 *And Yahweh your God will give it into your hand.* On this Deuteronomic coinage, see Note for 1:27.

and you shall strike down all its males into the mouth of the sword; only the women, and the little ones, and the beasts, and everything that is in the city, all its spoil, you shall take as booty for yourself. A punishment more severe will be inflicted if the enemy does not surrender. All adult males will be killed, with only women, children, and beasts being spared and taken with whatever else is captured as booty. Killing all the adult males is an extreme measure, as even Calvin admits, although we do not know to what extent this mandate was carried out. Driver says the measure still falls short of the barbarities commonly practiced in antiquity, where the most violent deaths came to women and children. The OT gives us some lurid examples (Amos 1:3, 13; Hos 14:1[13:16]; 2 Kgs 8:12). We learn also about impalings and other tortures from Assyrian texts that have come to light. It is generally agreed that Israelite warfare disallowed torture. Captured women from a distant city could be taken by Israelite men as wives (21:10-14).

into the mouth of the sword. I.e., up to the hilt. לְפִי־חָרֶב. This holy war expression (Josh 6:21; 8:24; 10:28) has traditionally been rendered "with the edge of the sword" (Vg: *in ore gladii*), where it is thought that "mouth" referred to the sword's sharp edge. Akkadian has a comparable expression, *pî patrim* (AHw, 2:874, *pû[m]* I, F). Meek (1951), however, points out that one smites the enemy quite literally "into the mouth of the sword," where the blade is represented as a tongue sticking out of an open-mouthed lion or dragon carved into the hilt (see p. 32 for drawings). Swords (and axes) of this type have been excavated in Syria, Mesopotamia, and Iran. Some have two devouring animals, explaining the "double-mouthed" swords of Judg 3:16; Prov 5:4; Ps 149:6. The "double-mouthed" sword thrust into Eglon, king of Moab, went in hilt and all (Judg 3:22).

15 "Thus you shall do" delimits the law's application (Rofé 1985, 29), which means the measures described pertain to distant cities not taken in the initial conquest, but cities to be taken later. In the verses following are measures pertaining to Canaanite cities.

these nations here. The writer of Deuteronomy is situated not in Transjordan, but in Canaan.

16 When Israel goes to war against a Canaanite city and takes it, no living thing is to survive. Even the beasts are to be killed (1 Sam 15:3). This severity in judgment — on Yahweh's part as well as on Israel's — follows the dictates of חֵרֶם war, whereby enemy populations and all they possess come under a sacred ban (v. 17). This policy was not always carried out, however, e.g., in the second battle to take Ai (see Note for 7:2). On the land as Yahweh's "inheritance" given to Israel, see Note for 15:4.

17 *but you shall utterly devote them to destruction.* Hebrew הַחֲרֵם תַּחֲרִימֵם derives from the institution of holy war, referring to the ban (חֵרֶם) placed upon the inhabitants — sometimes also animals and other spoil — of a captured city in order to devote (= destroy) them as a gift to Yahweh. On this institution, how it was carried out, and the problem posed for subsequent generations, see Note for 7:2. One should keep in mind in connection with this violent principle that Israel was also commanded to devote one of its own cities to destruction if it fell victim to idolatry (13:13-19[12-18]). The חֵרֶם injunction is unique to Deuteronomy

Deuteronomy 20

(Milgrom 1976b, 6). Milgrom points out that only Exod 23:20-33 comes close by demanding total expulsion of an indigenous people. But, he says, expulsion is not extermination.

the Hittites and the Amorites, the Canaanites and the Perizzites, the Hivites and the Jebusites. On these nations of Canaan, see Note for 7:1. The LXX adds "and the Girgashites" (καὶ Γεργεσαῖον = וְהַגִּרְגָּשִׁי), which is present in 7:1 and probably should be included (K. G. O'Connell 1984, 223-28; Freedman and Overton 2002, 109). Its omission in MT could be due to haplography (homoeoteleuton: י ... י); nevertheless, cf. Exod 23:23; Josh 11:3. In 11QT 62:14-15, where the order of nations is slightly different, the Girgashites are included (Yadin 1983, 2:282).

as Yahweh your God commanded you. Milgrom (1976b, 7) points out that nowhere in the Bible is such a command given, but he assumes that the חֵרֶם law must have a source somewhere.

18 Here is the reason for totally destroying the inhabitants of Canaan: that they not teach Israel all the abominable things they do for their gods (7:4; 12:29-31; 13; 18:12; cf. Exod 23:33; 34:11-16). The danger of Israel going after other gods and lapsing into idolatry is a main concern of Deuteronomy, perhaps its main concern. Idolatry is remembered elsewhere as the great sin in the wilderness (Exodus 32; Num 25:1-3).

all their abominations. כֹּל תּוֹעֲבֹתָם. The term "abomination" in Deuteronomy refers to a range of persons, practices, and things that Yahweh judges to be detestable (see Note for 7:25). Reference here is to practices associated with the worship of other gods, the most outrageous being child sacrifice (12:31; 18:9-10; cf. Jer 32:35).

19 *When you lay siege to a city many days, to fight against it to capture it, you shall not destroy its trees by wielding an axe against it, for from it you shall eat; so you shall not cut it down.* It was common in antiquity for armies to cut down trees and destroy fields of the enemy. The Egyptians did it, and so did the Assyrians. See "The Asiatic Campaigns under Pepi" (ca. 2375-2350), line 25 (*ANET*[3], 228); "The Campaign of Thutmose III" (1490-1436), in his fifth, sixth, and final campaigns (*ANET*[3], 239, 241), and the annals of Shalmaneser III (858-824), which reports a cutting down of the royal gardens of Hazael and Hadadezer in Damascus (*ANET*[3], 280-81). In 2 Esd 15:62, a late 3rd-cent. A.D. prophecy against the Asiatics (= Roman empire in the east), it is predicted that the anticipated enemy will burn all their "forests and fruit-trees" (Coggins and Knibb 1979, 292). In modern times, the Iraqi Criminal Tribunal charged Saddam Hussein with destroying 250,000 acres of fruit trees in Dujail (J. L. Wright 2008, 425). Israel in the 9th cent., responding to an oracle by the prophet Elisha, cut down trees and threw stones onto the grain fields of Moab (2 Kgs 3:19, 25). Here the command not to cut down fruit trees is largely for self-interest. If Israel is going to take possession of the land, it will scarcely be in its own interest to cut down fruit-bearing trees, which take time to mature and will be a ready source of food once cities have been captured (Rashbam; J. L. Wright 2008, 453). For discussion of wanton destruction in antiquity, including pictures, see J. L. Wright 2008.

for is the man the tree of the field coming before you in the siege? The Hebrew is difficult (T^{OnqNfPsJ} convert to a negative statement), but the LXX with its initial μή correctly translates the phrase as a rhetorical question, to which a negative answer is expected. Calvin and Michaelis (1814, 1:337) did similarly. Michaelis translated: "Are the trees men, that thou shouldest war against them, or besiege them?" The simple solution is to repoint the *qameṣ* under the ה to a *seghol*, which gives a question (Driver). The point is that trees can be left standing since they do not pose the threat that oncoming warriors do.

20 *Only a tree which you know indeed that it is not a tree for food, it you may destroy and cut down and build a siegework against the city.* Hebrew מָצוֹר means "bulwark" or "siegework," not "siege" (Calvin). There are, to be sure, legitimate reasons for cutting down trees of the enemy. One may need to make siege ramps, which consist of logs and tamped dirt (Jer 6:6). Nonfruit trees can be cut and used for this purpose.

Message and Audience

Moses is now heard telling the assembly that when it goes into battle in future days and sees horse and chariot amidst a much larger host, people are not to fear, because Yahweh will be with them. Those hearing these words at a later time will know the promise well, for they know not only the exodus from Egypt, but the story of Gideon defeating the Midianites and other stories of deliverance. When the battle is about to commence, the priest is to come forward and exhort the assembly not to be fainthearted, fearful, panic-stricken, or a jangle of nerves. Yahweh will fight the battle, and will deliver them. In Josiah's day, this exhortation will have aroused passionate Judahites to expand shrunken borders to more distant locations.

Next to step forward are the officials in charge of recruitment and deferrals. Is there anyone present who has built a new house but not yet occupied it, or anyone who has planted a vineyard but not yet eaten its fruit, or anyone who has betrothed a wife but not yet taken her? All such persons may return home without reproach, lest they die in battle and be deprived of pleasures to which they now look forward. Death in battle is seen by many as a curse, and it would be doubly so for them. Did the 7th-cent. kings of Israel have so enlightened a policy? The officials close the address by asking if there is anyone present who is fearful and weak of heart. Such persons should also return home, whatever shame this might bring them. If they remain, the morale of others will be affected. Those in a later audience who are acquainted with the wilderness tradition and have heard the beginning of Deuteronomy will know that faintheartedness is what brought Israel to ruin in its first attempt to take the land. After the officers have concluded their speech, commanders of the armies are to be appointed.

Moses speaks on about Israel's conduct in upcoming wars. When the people approach a distant city, they are first to offer it peace, which will be a call to surrender. If this is accepted, the city's inhabitants will be put to forced labor. If the call is not accepted, Israel is to besiege the city, and Moses says Yahweh will give it into their hand. Once victory is theirs, the people are to kill all adult males; the women, children, beasts, and everything else can be taken as spoil. Food of the enemy may be eaten. People are then told that this rule of war applies only to distant cities, not cities in Canaan. Moses retains a vision of a conquest that will take in Philistia, Lebanon, and Aram (Syria) as far east as the Euphrates. But those hearing this later will ask why the original promise was not realized. Why were not the three additional cities of refuge ever built?

So far as Canaanite cities are concerned, Yahweh will give them over to Israel, after which the entire populations are to be devoted to Yahweh. This means killing everything that breathes. These will be Hittites, Amorites, Canaanites, Perizzites, Hivites, and Jebusites. The reason for the holocaust is so these peoples will not teach Israel the abominable practices associated with the gods they worship. Should Israel adopt these practices, it will be a sin in Yahweh's eyes.

But what has happened more recently? Prophets have told Israel and Judah at great risk that the land is rife with idolatry. By the late 8th cent. the Assyrians have taken Transjordan and brought the northern kingdom down. Not long after, Sennacherib destroyed forty-six Judahite cities while Hezekiah was king. What sort of holy war is this? Just who is the enemy? And what about the Assyrian impalings, the threshing of Gilead by Aram, and the ripping open of women by the Ammonites? Moses' policy was a more enlightened one, but then Yahweh was waging a war unlike every war in recent memory!

The discourse concludes with Moses telling the assembled that when Israel besieges a city, it is not to destroy the fruit trees, which are for eating. The people are asked if trees pose the threat that oncoming warriors do. Only trees that are not fruit-bearing are to be cut down and used for siegeworks, and then only until the city falls. Israel, let it be said again, is to inhabit the land. Again the audiences — both early and late — are bound to see this as an enlightened policy; those later will recall with what abandon the Assyrians cut down trees first in Samaria, then in Jerusalem.

Deuteronomy 21

I. EXPIATION FOR AN UNSOLVED MURDER (21:1-9)

21 ¹*When someone slain is found on the ground that Yahweh your God is giving to you to take possession of it, someone fallen in the field, and it is not known who struck him down,* ²*then your elders and your judges shall go out and measure to the cities that are round about the slain.* ³*And it will be, the city nearest to the slain, the elders of that city shall then take a heifer that has not been worked, that has not pulled in a yoke,* ⁴*and the elders of that city shall take the heifer down to an ever-flowing wadi that has not been tilled and has not been sown, and they shall break the neck of the heifer there in the wadi.* ⁵*And the priests, sons of Levi, shall come forward, for Yahweh your God has chosen them to minister to him and to bless in the name of Yahweh, and every dispute and every assault shall be according to their declaration.* ⁶*And all the elders of that city nearest to the slain shall wash their hands over the heifer whose neck was broken in the wadi,* ⁷*and they shall testify and say, "Our hands did not shed this blood and our eyes did not see.* ⁸*Atone for your people Israel, whom you have ransomed, O Yahweh, and do not set innocent blood in the midst of your people Israel, but let the blood be atoned for them."* ⁹*So you, you shall utterly remove the innocent blood from your midst; for you shall do what is right in the eyes of Yahweh.*

Rhetoric and Composition

The present law deals with an unsolved murder, prescribing a rite of expiation to rid the people and the land of the bloodguilt brought about by this crime. The law has no parallel in the Covenant Code or anywhere else in the Pentateuch. Some think the law belongs with the homicide law of 19:1-13, but its location here appears to derive from catchwords — both sound and meaning — that link it to the warfare laws immediately preceding (Rofé 1988b, 271):

for is the man the tree of *the field* coming before you . . . ?	כִּי הָאָדָם . . . הַשָּׂדֶה	20:19
When someone slain is found *on the* ground . . . someone fallen *in the field* . . .	כִּי . . . בָּאֲדָמָה . . . בַּשָּׂדֶה	21:1

The priestly prayer in v. 8 is tied together by an inclusio:

Atone (כַּפֵּר) for your people Israel . . .
. . . but let the blood *be atoned* (נִכַּפֵּר) for them.

Deuteronomy 21

The unit is delimited at the top end by a *petuḥah* in M^L and a section in Sam before v. 1, which is also the chapter division. Delimitation at the bottom end is by a *setumah* in M^L, a *petuḥah* in 11QT, and a section in Sam after v. 9. There are also sections after v. 9 in 1QDeut^b and 4QDeut^f.

Portions of 21:1-9 are contained in 1QDeut^b and 4QDeut^f.

Notes

21:1 *When someone slain is found on the ground*. Hebrew חָלָל in this case is "someone stabbed to death" (Gen 34:25-27; Num 19:16). The indirect manner of speaking ("is found") occurs elsewhere in Deuteronomy, highlighting the shame such a crime will bring upon Israel (see Note for 17:2). Daube (1971a, 8) says the corpse will horrify the beholder, spoiling the appearance of the land more than uncovered excrement in the camp (23:13-15[12-14]).

someone fallen in the field, and it is not known who struck him down. Two conditions for carrying out the following rite: (1) the body is found outside of town; and (2) the murderer is unknown. A murder within town could presumably be solved after some investigation.

2 Judges and elders are from the surrounding cities, and they will measure the distance from the corpse to each of the cities to determine which is nearest. That city will then be held liable for the crime. Community responsibility for crimes is well attested in the ANE (Wiseman 1974, 259; Wells 2008, 236-38). In the Ugaritic "Tale of Aqhat," Daniel charges three cities for the murder of his son Aqhat (Aqht C iv 150-69; *ANET*^3, 154-55). In the Code of Hammurabi (CH 24), community liability is discharged by giving monetary compensation to heirs of the deceased (*ANET*^3, 167). In the Hittite Laws (HL 6), if an individual dies in another town, the person in whose field he or she dies must set aside a plot in his field so the deceased gets a burial (Neufeld 1951, 2-3; *ANET*^3, 189). Nuzi tablets state that in theft crimes, where the robber is not known, the one sustaining the loss can sue the townspeople for burglary and larceny. If men of the town swear they are innocent, the plaintiff must undergo a river ordeal to settle the matter (C. H. Gordon 1936a). But as Daube (1947, 184) points out, community responsibility is abolished in the present law by a ritual atoning for the crime. The whole town is not destroyed, which is what happens when a town turns to idolatry (13:13-17[12-16]).

your elders and your judges. Moses appointed judges in the wilderness (1:16), and after settlement in the land judges are to be appointed in all the cities of Canaan (16:18). Assisting them in deciding the case will be the city elders, who also gave Moses assistance in the wilderness (see Notes for 5:23-24 and 19:12). Weinfeld (*EncJud*, 6:578-79; 1977, 81-82) points out that among other

Deuteronomy 21

peoples of the ANE, state representatives joined with local authorities (i.e., the elders) to settle disputes. In Mesopotamia, city elders cooperated with the mayor, and in the Hittite state elders worked together with the commander of the border guards.

3-4 *the elders of that city shall then take a heifer that has not been worked, that has not pulled in a yoke, and the elders of that city shall take the heifer down to an ever-flowing wadi that has not been tilled and has not been sown, and they shall break the neck of the heifer there in the wadi.* Innocent blood cries out to Yahweh from the ground (Gen 4:10), so in lieu of a known murderer whose blood would otherwise be shed (19:12; Num 35:33), an expiation rite is to be performed with a young heifer. Yahweh requires a heifer that has not been worked or put to the yoke (cf. 15:19; Num 19:2); otherwise people might kill an old beast that had outlived its usefulness. This heifer (עֶגְלָה) will likely be a young cow about a year old (Lev 9:3; Mic 6:6; Rashi), although it could be a more mature cow (Gen 15:9; Isa 7:21; Zevit 1976, 385).

ever-flowing wadi. נַחַל אֵיתָן. The term "wadi" is Arabic for a swift moving stream in winter, but a dry waterbed in summer. The meaning of this expression has been in doubt from earliest times. Rashi rendered אֵיתָן as "hard," which has the support of Targum readings (T^{OnqNf} "untilled valley"; T^{PsJ} "uncultivated field"). The LXX translated φάραγγα τραχεῖαν ("a rugged wadi"), and the Vg *vallem asperam atque saxosam* ("rough and rocky valley"). But Aquila (χείμαρρος στερεός, "unrelenting torrent of water") and also Maimonides ("a river that flows with might") anticipate more recent scholars who compare with the Arabic *watana* ("to be constant, unfailing"), giving אֵיתָן the now widely-accepted meaning of "enduring, perennial" (Lauterbach 1936, 218-19; Driver 1895, 241-42 n.). Elsewhere in the OT the term describes rocks (Num 24:21), mountains (Mic 6:2), pastures (Jer 49:19 = 50:44), rivers (Ps 74:15), and streams (Amos 5:24). The rite needs to be carried out where running water is available, although this could pose a problem in Israel, where many wadis have water only in the rainy season and are dry as bone in summer.

that has not been tilled and has not been sown. Land along a wadi — even today — is untilled and strewn with rocks, but why this restriction for the slaughter? Perhaps so that the blood will not pollute land under cultivation (D. P. Wright 1987, 394-95) or cause land to be made sterile for future cultivation (Patai 1939-40, 66). Mishnah *Soṭah* 9:5 says sowing and tilling will henceforth be disallowed on the site, but it can be used for combing flax and quarrying stones. Von Rad says the rite is so unlike a sacrifice: the animal is killed not at a worship site, but at a waste plot.

and they shall break the neck of the heifer there in the wadi. Killing an animal by breaking the neck does not occur in a sacrifice; it happens only when a firstborn ass is not being redeemed by a lamb (Exod 13:13; 34:20; Zevit 1976, 384).

Von Rad says the rite as originally conceived might be compared to the sending off of the scapegoat into the wilderness (Lev 16:10, 22), but with the priestly prayer and the expiation of bloodguilt, it becomes in the end an offering. Driver, too, says that while this is not a sin offering proper it has to some extent the character of a sin offering (cf. Num 19:1-10). Tigay thinks it is neither a sacrifice nor a ritual transferring of guilt to the heifer, but more likely a reenactment of the murder, since it is carried out in a wasteland. For more discussion of this ritual, see Tigay 1996, "The Ceremony of the Broken-Necked Heifer," 472-76.

5 The priests will direct the proceedings, and it is quite mistaken to say with some, e.g., von Rad and Moran, that their inclusion is secondary because they do nothing at all. Levitical priests in Deuteronomy are altar clergy (18:1-8), who also have teaching and judicial functions (17:8-13). They speak the words of expiation in v. 8. On Yahweh's choice of the priests, see also 18:5. The verb בחר ("choose") is a favorite of the Deuteronomist (see Note for 12:5).

the priests, sons of Levi. This expression is Deuteronomic (31:9), although usually it occurs in the form הַכֹּהֲנִים הַלְוִיִּם, "the priests, the Levites" (17:9, 18; 18:1; 24:8; 27:9). See 18:1 and Note for 12:12.

to minister to him. לְשָׁרְתוֹ. Ministering to Yahweh is one of the Levitical functions (10:8). Wevers (1995, 336) points out that the LXX uses the verb παρεστηκέναι ("to stand by"), rather than the usual λειτουργεῖν ("to officiate [as priest]"), suggesting that it views the rite as priestly, but not cultic. The present act is thus precluded from being a bona fide sacrifice.

6-7 While the elders did not themselves shed the blood (Rashi; *m. Soṭah* 9:6), they could have witnessed it or could know the identity of the murderer. A woman at Nippur who refused to make any statement about the killing of her husband, a priest, was sentenced to death along with the murderers. The court in a split decision ruled that the woman's guilt was greater than the three murderers, the reason being that she could have passed on information to the judges, but did not (Wiseman 1974, 258-59). Here the hand-washing and disclaimer absolve the city elders of any knowledge regarding the crime. They will be saying that they do not know who the murderer is, are not protecting him, and were not witnesses to the crime. On hand-washing as a symbol of innocence, see Pss 26:6; 73:13. Elders in the present case may also be required to swear an oath to establish their innocence, which would contain a conditional self-curse (G. E. Wright; Tucker 1965, 491; cf. Exod 22:9-10[10-11]; Num 5:19-22; 1 Kgs 8:31-32).

Two disclaimers by the deceased before an otherworldly court in the Egyptian *Book of the Dead* (Ch. 125 Intro: 10-11) are these:

I have done no murder.
I have not given the order for murder to be done for me.
(Budge 1898, 191; A 14-15 *ANET*[3], 34)

Deuteronomy 21

In the NT, cf. Pilate's washing of his hands and his words claiming innocence in condemning Jesus to death (Matt 27:24).

over the heifer. The LXX has "over the head of the heifer," a reading occurring also in 11QT 63:5. Wevers (1995, 337) suggests that the priests may have placed their hands on the animal before it was slaughtered, as in the consecration rite of Exod 29:10-11, where guilt was symbolically transferred to the animal. There the animal was still alive. Wevers notes that in the LXX the animal is also not dead, simply hamstrung (v. 4: νευροκοπήσουσιν).

8 *Atone for your people Israel. . .but let the blood be atoned for them.* The Targums insert at the beginning of the verse: "The priests shall say," or the like, which has them — not the city elders — offering the prayer for forgiveness (cf. *m. Soṭah* 9:6; *Sifre Deut.* §210:2). If the repetition makes an inclusio for the prayer (see Rhetoric and Composition), then the words "but let the blood be atoned for them" must be included in the quotation (*pace* NJV; NRSV; Friedman). But if the elders continue speaking in v. 8, then we have a formal confession concluding with a prayer to God, which is what occurs in the rite of the firstfruits in 26:5-10, and the rite of the third-year tithe in 26:13-15 (Sarna 1979, 282). The NJV translates the end of v. 8: "And they will be absolved of bloodguilt," which has the narrator stating that the rite will bring about the desired result. The verb כפר in the Piel has the meaning of "cover over, wipe clean." When used with reference to sin and the alienation from God that sin brings, the term means "atone for, expiate." Here forgiveness of the offense is the end result. Sin is forgiven in the present rite, where the shed blood of the animal suffices for the shed blood of the one who committed the crime. Since not only the nearest city but all Israel bears responsibility for the shedding of innocent blood, atonement must be made between Yahweh and the entire nation.

9 *So you, you shall utterly remove the innocent blood from your midst.* The added pronoun is for emphasis. On this stereotyped Deuteronomic phrase, which repeats in v. 21, see Note for 13:6. Mishnah *Soṭah* 9:7 deals with what happens if the murderer is found. If he is found before the neck of the heifer is broken, then the animal is sent out to pasture. If he is found after the neck of the heifer is broken, then the animal is buried. In either case, the murderer is then put to death.

for you shall do what is right in the eyes of Yahweh. A stock expression in Deuteronomy (see Note for 6:18). 11QT (63:8) expands to "what is right and what is good before Yahweh your God" (Yadin 1983, 2:285). The LXX, too, has τὸ καλὸν καὶ τὸ ἀρεστὸν, "what is good and what is pleasing." Deuteronomy elsewhere attests to both readings, sometimes only "what is right" (12:25; 13:19[18]; 21:9), other times "what is right and what is good" (6:18; 12:28 [reversed]). It is right in Yahweh's eyes that the ground Yahweh is giving Israel

(v. 1) be cleansed from any innocent blood shed upon it. The present rite will effect such a cleansing.

Message and Audience

Moses tells the assembly in the present injunction what to do if a slain person turns up on the ground Yahweh is giving to Israel. Envisaged is a body lying in a field outside of town, where the slayer is not known. Elders and judges of the neighboring cities are to be summoned to measure the distance from the corpse to each city. The city found to be nearest the crime site must assume responsibility for what has happened, as the murderer could be one of its citizens. It must then carry out a rite of expiation to rid the city — and all Israel — of bloodguilt. To do this a young heifer is to be taken down to a wadi flowing with water, and its neck is to be broken there on ground not used for cultivation. Priests are to preside over the rite, with those assembled being reminded that priests are the ones designated to direct proceedings such as the present one. The elders from the nearest city will wash their hands over the heifer and declare their innocence regarding the crime. The priests will then offer up a prayer that all Israel be forgiven of this crime committed by one of Yahweh's redeemed people. Moses concludes with the oft-repeated admonishment that innocent blood must be utterly removed from Israel's midst, and Israel must do what is right in the eyes of Yahweh.

For later audiences this injunction will amount to a strong censure of both Israel and Judah for unsolved murders in their territories, even more for not carrying out a rite expressly given to rid people and the land from bloodguilt. Prophets know of bodies found on the road to Shechem (Hos 6:9) and of people who claim innocence even though bloodstains of the innocent poor are on their skirts (Jer 2:34-35). How often has such bloodguilt been removed from their midst? And who much cares anymore about doing what is right in the eyes of Yahweh?

J. Marriage to a Woman War Captive (21:10-14)

21 *10When you go forth to the battle against your enemies, and Yahweh your God gives it into your hand and you take captive its captives, 11and you see among the captives a woman beautiful in form, and you desire her and would take her to yourself for a wife, 12then you shall bring her into your house, and she shall shave her head and do her nails, 13and she shall put off her captive's garment from on her. And she shall dwell in your house and shall lament her father and her mother*

a period of a month of days. And after that you may come to her and be her husband, and she will be your wife. ¹⁴*And it will be if you have no delight in her, then you shall send her away according to her desire, but you must surely not sell her for silver; you shall not lord it over her, inasmuch as you have humbled her.*

Rhetoric and Composition

The present law regulates marriage of an Israelite man to a woman war captive. Since it begins the same as 20:1, "When you go forth to the battle," the law is thought by some to belong with laws regulating warfare in ch. 20 (von Rad). But a framing structure for all of 20:1–21:14 precludes rearrangement of the material (see Rhetoric and Composition for 20:1-20). The upper limit of the present unit is marked by a *setumah* in M^L, a *petuḥah* in 11QT, and a section in Sam before v. 10. The lower limit is marked by a *setumah* in M^L and a section in Sam after v. 14.

Catchwords connect this law with the next law on inheritances if one has multiple wives:

and she will be your *wife*	אִשָּׁה ...	v. 13
When a man shall have two *wives* . . .	נָשִׁים ...	v. 15

Rashi follows another logic in explaining the juxtaposition of this law with the two laws following. Building on the rabbinic view that marriage to foreign women is to be discouraged and that one who marries a foreign woman, particularly for her beauty, will come to hate her and will divorce her, Rashi sees the present law leading naturally to the next law dealing with a man who has two wives, one loved and one hated, and then to the third law where the man begets a rebellious son.

Portions of 21:10-14 are contained in 4QDeut^f.

Notes

21:10 This must be a battle with a distant enemy, not one of the Canaanite peoples. The חֵרֶם law applies to wars with the Canaanites (7:2; 20:12-16), and even if women in some Canaanite cities survive, Israelites are forbidden under any circumstances to intermarry with them (7:3). But Israelite men took foreign wives throughout their history. Joseph married the daughter of an Egyptian priest, who bore him Ephraim and Manasseh (Gen 41:50-52); Moses married the daughter of a Midianite priest (Exod 2:16-22; cf. Num 12:1); and Solomon

Deuteronomy 21

married women from everywhere, his Ammonite wife bearing him Rehoboam (1 Kgs 14:21). But Solomon violated Mosaic law by marrying a Sidonian, who was a Canaanite. This did not pass unnoticed by the Deuteronomic Historian (1 Kgs 11:1-2), who also did not look kindly on Ahab's marriage to the Sidonian Jezebel (1 Kgs 16:30-31). In Deuteronomy it simply states that kings must not multiply wives (17:17), not refrain from marrying foreign wives.

and you take captive its captives. On this idiom, see Judg 5:12; Ps 68:19(18).

11 *and you see among the captives a woman beautiful in form.* In wartime, particularly if defeat was imminent, women would dress up in their finery to make themselves attractive to enemy soldiers. But the woman envisaged here is possessed of natural beauty and therefore has a better than average chance of escaping the indignities commonly suffered by women in wartime. The Israelite man, for his part, simply wants the beautiful captive for a wife.

and you desire her. On the verb חשק, which is used in the OT of both God and human beings, see Gen 34:8; Deut 7:7; 10:15.

12-13 *then you shall bring her into your house, and she shall shave her head and do her nails, and she shall put off her captive's garment from on her.* The woman shall live with the man and his family in their house before the two are formally married. Upon arrival, the woman will shave her head, do her nails, and remove her garments of captivity. In the LXX and 11QT (63:12-13), the Israelite man does all of these for the woman. While the acts may not all have the same symbolic value, in the aggregate they mark a separation from the woman's former life and prisoner status to the beginning of a new life with her captor. Shaving the head in antiquity was commonly a sign of mourning (Gaster 1969, 590-602; cf. Lundbom 1999, 490). In the NT, Paul reflects the traditional Jewish view that a woman having short hair or a bald head is disgraceful (1 Cor 11:5-6). The prophet Isaiah, in his description of what lies in store for Judahite women when they are taken captive, says that along with a loss of other finery, baldness will replace well-set hair and a sackcloth will be worn in place of a lovely robe (Isa 3:24). The Mari texts speak of removing "jewelry of the head" (= hair) and clothes of female captives (Du Buit 1959, 576-77).

and do her nails. The verb is עשה ("do"), which probably refers here to "shaping" or "dressing" the nails (T^{NfPsJ}). This is doubtless to improve her appearance. In 2 Sam 19:25(24) it is said of Mephibosheth that while David was exiled from Jerusalem, he "neither did (עָשָׂה) his feet nor did (עָשָׂה) his beard," which the RSV translates: "he had neither dressed his feet, nor trimmed his beard." Targum^{Onq}, however, has "and let her nails grow." A debate over the length of her nails is said to have taken place between Rabbi Akiba and Rabbi Eliezer. R. Eliezer said she should cut them, arguing that both hair and nails should be cut. But R. Akiba reasoned that cutting the hair and letting the nails grow would make the woman ugly, which is what was intended (*Sifre Deut.*

Deuteronomy 21

§212:1). Rashi sided with R. Akiba and the T^Onq. But this interpretation is fanciful, reflecting the dim view taken generally by the rabbis of marriages to foreign women. The text says she will actually "do" something to her nails; letting them grow would be to do nothing.

and shall lament her father and her mother a period of a month of days. The woman will be unmarried, otherwise she would be lamenting the separation from her husband or his death in the war. After a month of mourning, the woman can be married to her captor. On יֶרַח יָמִים ("a month of days"), see also 2 Kgs 15:13.

you may come to her. I.e., you may have sexual relations with her. 11QT 63:14-15 adds at the end of v. 13: "But she shall not touch your pure stuff (טהרה) for seven years, and she shall not eat a sacrifice of peace offering until seven years pass; only then she may eat" (Yadin 1983, 2:286).

14 *And it will be if you have no delight in her, then you shall send her away according to her desire.* I.e., she shall be free to go anywhere she wants. It is not stated whether she will get a bill of divorce (24:1); presumably she will. On the translation of נֶפֶשׁ as "desire," see Jer 22:27; 34:16.

but you must surely not sell her for silver. Once again Deuteronomic law is seen to have a humane quality (but see Washington 1998, 206-7), although the Covenant Code disallows selling a Hebrew slave woman (to a foreigner) when she fails to please her master and is being redeemed (Exod 21:8). The woman here may not be sold as a slave (Josephus *Ant.* 4.259), which is what commonly happened to captured women in antiquity. Among the Arabs, in the time of the Prophet Muhammad, if a woman became pregnant by her captor, it was not considered proper to sell her in the market or allow her to be ransomed by her people for money. Her offspring would be freeborn and legitimate (W. R. Smith 1903, 89).

you shall not lord it over her. לֹא־תִתְעַמֵּר. The verb עמר in the Hithpael occurs only one other time in the OT, in 24:7, where, as here, the meaning is uncertain. In both places the verb is coupled with מכר, "to sell (into slavery)," which seems to have influenced translation in the ancient Versions. The LXX reads: οὐκ ἀθετήσεις ("you shall not cast aside"), and the Vg: *nec opprimere per potentiam* ("you shall not subdue by force"). The Targums have slavery in view (T^Onq: "you may not use her as merchandise"; T^NfPsJ: "you shall not trade her"), and they are followed by Rashi and accepted by Hertz (1960, 263) and Friedman. Driver thinks the meaning is probably "deal despotically, play the master" (LXX of 24:7: καταδυναστεύσας, "having overcome"), which comes close to the Vg rendering and may be the best one can do, since interpretation here depends largely on renderings of the ancient Versions.

inasmuch as. For the conjunctive expression תַּחַת אֲשֶׁר, see also 22:29; 28:47; Num 25:13; 2 Kgs 22:17; Jer 29:19; 50:7.

you have humbled her. The idiom used for having had sexual relations with a woman that brought the woman dishonor (22:24, 29; Gen 34:2; 2 Sam 13:12). Washington (1998, 208) says עִנָּה ("he humbled") denotes "sexual violence" or "misuse of a woman," which may be going too far. But the Israelite man will have married the captive woman and then cast her off, using her largely to satisfy his own lustful urges.

Message and Audience

Moses is now heard giving another law relating to war, this one about marrying women captives. Women of the Canaanites were not to be spared, but there will be other opportunities to take women captives in war, and should a beautiful woman be among them, someone no doubt will desire her for a wife. This law then regulates marriages to foreign women, specifying also what is to be done should the Israelite man come to find out that the woman he saw as being so beautiful does not delight him after all and he decides to send her away.

A captive woman wanted for a wife is to be brought into one's house. There she will shave her head, pare her nails, and discard her captive clothing. For one month she shall mourn her mother and father, whom she will never see again, and after the time is up the Israelite man may cohabit with her and make her his wife. If it happens that he no longer desires her, he is to send her away, and she may go wherever she wants. Under no circumstances is he to sell her as a slave or oppress her in any way, for he has brought dishonor upon her by marrying her and then casting her off.

Later rabbis found much in the present law to support their view that marriages to foreign women were likely to turn out badly. It must be admitted that the law does anticipate that such marriages are likely to end up in divorce, and later audiences will therefore be put on notice to exercise due caution in marrying foreign women, captives or otherwise. Paul in the NT gives similar advice to Christians, telling them they ought not be "joined together with unbelievers" (2 Cor 6:14).

K. Rights of the Firstborn (21:15-17)

21[15]*When a man shall have two wives, the one loved and the other hated, and they have borne him sons — the loved and the hated — and the firstborn son comes to the one hated,* [16]*then it will be on the day when he gives his sons the inheritance, what belongs to him, he may not make as firstborn the son of the one loved in preference to the son of the one hated, who is the firstborn,* [17]*but the first-*

born, the son of the one hated, he shall acknowledge to give him two portions of everything that is found to be his, because he was the beginning of his generative power. The right of the firstborn belongs to him.

Rhetoric and Composition

This law regulates the liquidation of an estate when a man has two wives and both have borne him sons. It is delimited at the upper end by a *setumah* in M^L and a section in Sam before v. 15 and at the lower end by a *setumah* in M^L and a section in Sam after v. 17.

This law is linked to the next two laws by similar openings (Rofé 1988b, 272):

When a man shall have two wives . . .	. . . כִּי־תִהְיֶיןָ לְאִישׁ	21:15
When a man shall have a stubborn and rebellious son . . .	. . . כִּי־יִהְיֶה לְאִישׁ	21:18
And when there shall be in a man a sin . . .	. . . וְכִי־יִהְיֶה בְאִישׁ	21:22

A fragment of 21:16 may appear in 4QDeut^{k2}.

Notes

21:15 "The one loved" and "the other hated" is a Hebraism resulting from a lack of relative particles in the Hebrew language (cf. Rachel and Leah in Gen 29:30-31). The man will simply prefer one wife over the other, as Jacob did in the case of Rachel over Leah. Polygamy was practiced in Israel, as in other ancient cultures, and was always potentially troublesome. Wives became jealous of one another, e.g., if one could not bear and another does (1 Sam 1:4-5) or over which son among many was to receive preferential treatment. Jacob had four wives — Leah and Rachel and maidservants of each — and children by them all. As it turned out, Jacob rejected Reuben, his firstborn (son of Leah), and seems to have given the birthright to Joseph (son of Rachel). Later the birthright was said to have been given to Joseph's sons, Ephraim and Manasseh (1 Chr 5:1; *b. B. Bat.* 123a). But it has been argued that the "hated wife" in the present case is a wife who has been demoted to a lower status in the household, and because this is taken as an arbitrary action on the husband's part, he forfeits the right he has to elevate a younger son and give him the birthright (Wells 2010). Wells says that fondness of one wife over another does not fit the present context and that "hate" is being used here in a legal sense, making his explanation more likely.

16-17 Another law peculiar to Deuteronomy, this one preventing a man from circumventing the rule of primogeniture (= rights of the firstborn) by passing on his estate to the firstborn of a favored wife instead of to the son who is his actual firstborn (which is what Jacob did). Firstborn sons receive a double portion. The rule is this: the father's estate is divided according to the number of sons plus one. The firstborn gets the portion set aside for the firstborn (רֵאשִׁית), then another portion from the remainder of the estate. Here there are only two sons, so the firstborn gets his initial portion, which may be better than the others, then half of what remains. The younger son gets the other half. The firstborn ends up with a double portion, the younger son with a single portion (*b. B. Bat.* 122b-23a). Cf. Jesus' parable of the Lost (Prodigal) Son in Luke 15:11-32.

A look at the patriarchal history shows that birthrights went consistently to sons other than the father's firstborn. In the way the present law is formulated — one wife loved and one wife hated — one would imagine that fathers were responsible for disregarding the rule of primogeniture. But Yaron (1960, 9-10) thinks maternal influence may have been the reason why the law of the firstborn was set aside. Firstborn sons of Abraham, Isaac, and Jacob, who were Ishmael, Esau, and Reuben, all lost their birthrights (Gen 21:10; 25:29-34; 1 Chr 5:1-2; cf. Gen 49:3-4), and in two cases wives played a key role: Sarah favored her son Isaac (Gen 21:8-10) and Rebekah favored her son Jacob (Gen 25:28; 27). But it was Jacob who favored Rachel's son Joseph (Gen 33:2; 37:3) and later favored Ephraim over Manasseh (Gen 48:13-20). Yaron says that maternal influence is evident when Bathsheba prevails on the aged David to have her son Solomon made king (1 Kings 1). So in his view the rules favoring the rights of the firstborn needed strengthening, which is what the present law does.

The Code of Hammurabi (CH 167; *ANET*³, 173) states that if a man has had two wives, the dowries of the two women are to be given to their respective children, but the paternal estate is to be divided equally between the children of both wives. The same is true in the Lipit-Ishtar Code (LI 24; *ANET*³, 160). But in the Code of Hammurabi things turn out differently if a man has children by a first-ranking wife and a slave woman (CH 170, 171; *ANET*³, 173). In that case, after the father's death, the first-ranking wife and her children get preference in the inheritance over a slave woman and her children, even if the father preferred the slave woman over the first-ranking wife. The children of both wives divide the estate equally, with the son of the first-ranking wife getting first choice. If the father did not express a preference for the slave woman while he was still alive, then the children of the slave woman get nothing (*ANET*³, 173).

In the Alalakh Tablets (Al.T 92), the son of the first of two wives gets preferential treatment in the inheritance, not the son who is actually the firstborn (Wiseman 1953, 54-55; Mendelsohn 1959a, 356-57; 1959b, 38-39). Here the father is allowed to disregard the rule of primogeniture and appoint a younger son as "firstborn." Something similar happens in the Keret Legend of Ugarit (KRT B iii 16; *ANET*³, 146), where El sets aside the law of primogeniture and says he will award the birthright to the youngest (of the sons or daughters). The law of primogeniture is set aside also in a Nuzi text containing a marriage settlement, where, if a man takes a wife and she bears him one or more sons and then he takes a second wife who also bears him one or more sons, at his death the sons of the first wife get all his land, houses, and other possessions; the sons of the second wife do not become joint heirs (no. 12; Gadd 1926, 58, 97-98).

In a Middle Assyrian legal document from Emar (modern Meskeneh), an elder son and another son and wife, who may have been adopted, are called upon by the head of the family to share the inheritance with each other like brothers (Snell 1983-84). So there are numerous examples in texts from the ANE where the law of primogeniture is put aside and the father is seen to reserve the right to select a "first-born" (Weinfeld 1970-72, 193). According to Wells, the husband has this right also in Israel in the time of the monarchy, but in Deuteronomy that right is forfeited because he arbitrarily demoted his "hated wife" to a lower status in the household.

A double portion for the eldest son is attested throughout the ANE, although as we have just seen, the practice was not always followed. In a Mari text dealing with adoption, the eldest son gets a double portion and the younger sons divide equally what remains (no. 1 21-27; Boyer 1958, 3-4; Mendelsohn 1959b, 38). In the Nuzi texts (no. 2, no. 8, no. 19, no. 21; Speiser 1930, 31-32, 38-39, 49-50, 53-54) and also in the Middle Assyrian Laws (MAL B 1; O 4; *ANET*³ 185, 188, 220), the eldest son gets a double portion.

In later Jewish law one is not entitled to disinherit his heir (*m. B. Bat.* 8:5), which strictly follows the present verses (Yaron 1960, 37). But a father can give gifts to any of his sons before he dies (cf. Gen 25:5-6). The Code of Hammurabi (CH 168, 169), too, places limitations upon anyone wanting to disinherit his heir. Such a one has to appear before the judges and announce the disinheritance, and if the son is found not to have committed any grave offense, the father cannot disinherit. If the son is guilty of a grave offense, he is pardoned the first time, and only after a second offense is the father allowed by the judges to disinherit (*ANET*³, 123).

he may not. לֹא יוּכַל. On this verbal form occurring only in Deuteronomy, which is not an apodictic "you shall not" but rather an appeal to one's sense of shame, see Note for 12:17.

in preference to. Hebrew עַל־פְּנֵי is lit. "in front of," but here takes the meaning "in preference to." The phrase may have this same meaning in the first commandment of Exod 20:3, although that would allow for a recognition of lesser divine beings in the heavenly court. If the first commandment is restricting Israel to the worship and service of one God only, then עַל־פְּנֵי has to mean "besides": "You shall have no other gods besides me" (RSV note; cf. עַל in Gen 31:50).

two portions. Hebrew פִּי שְׁנַיִם is lit. "a mouth of two" (2 Kgs 2:9). Here and in 2 Kgs 2:9 the term means "twice as much" or "double (portion)." In Zech 13:8, because the term complements a stated fraction, it means "two-thirds" (E. W. Davies 1986). The LXX has διπλᾶ ("double") here and in 2 Kgs 2:9, and τὰ δύο μέρη ("the two parts") in Zech 13:8.

the beginning of his generative power. I.e., the firstfruits of his virile power (Gen 49:3; Pss 78:51; 105:36).

Message and Audience

The audience hears Moses speak in this law about inheritance and how a man's estate is to be apportioned if he has had two wives and both have borne him sons. The law recognizes that one wife can be favored over the other, which can affect how the inheritance is parceled out. If the man's firstborn is borne by his less-favored wife, when it comes time to give the sons their inheritance the man may not treat as firstborn the son of his favored wife, placing him over a son of his other wife, who is his firstborn. He shall regard as firstborn the son of the less-favored wife and give him a double portion of everything he has. The reason given is that this son was the firstfruits of his generative power and the right of the firstborn belongs to him.

The audience will doubtless recall that the patriarchs — in some cases with help from their wives — did not honor the right of primogeniture, and was not God directing this march of events, in which the younger was consistently chosen over the older? And was not Solomon Bathsheba's choice as David's successor and in the end the choice of David himself? He was not David's firstborn. Nevertheless, the audience is being told that when a man has two wives and both have borne him sons, his firstborn must get the double portion, not another son to whom he or the favored wife would like to give it. Why was such a law promulgated? Perhaps simply to put an end to all the scheming that had gone on in the past. The law may also seek to preserve a man's first marriage, discouraging him from taking another wife if he is no longer delighted with his first wife or with the firstborn son of his first wife. If so, the law somewhat parallels the preceding law about taking war brides, where it is imagined that the man may lose interest in such a woman and send her away. That law had built-in safeguards for a foreign woman taken by an Israelite man in marriage. This law has built-in safeguards for a man's first wife and the eldest son of his first wife.

L. DEATH FOR REBELLIOUS SONS (21:18-21)

21 ^{18}*When a man shall have a stubborn and rebellious son who will not obey the voice of his father or the voice of his mother, and they will discipline him but he will not listen to them,* ^{19}*then his father and his mother shall take hold of him and bring him out to the elders of his city and to the gate of his place.* ^{20}*And they shall say to the elders of his city, "This son of ours is stubborn and rebellious who will not obey our voice, a glutton and a drunkard."* ^{21}*Then all the men of his city shall pelt him with stones so he dies. So you shall utterly remove the evil from your midst, and all Israel shall hear and fear.*

Rhetoric and Composition

This law dealing with a stubborn and rebellious son has a stereotyped beginning, "When a man shall have . . . ," and a stereotyped conclusion, "So you shall utterly remove the evil from your midst, and all Israel shall hear and fear." The unit is demarcated by a *setumah* in M^L and a section in Sam before v. 18 and a *setumah* in M^L and a section in Sam after v. 21. The small space in 11QT (64:6) after v. 21 is also likely a *setumah* section marking. For the similar openings that link this law to laws both before and after, see Rhetoric and Composition for 21:15-17.

Notes

21:18 Another law peculiar to Deuteronomy, commonly seen as a violation of the fifth commandment regarding honoring one's parents (G. E. Wright; Moran; 5:16; cf. 27:16). The case is made most strongly by Freedman (2000, 76-79), who sees this law as supporting his thesis that in Exodus to Kings showcase violations of the Ten Commandments appear one by one. The present law is the showcase violation of the fifth commandment in Deuteronomy.

In the Covenant Code, and elsewhere, it is stated that anyone striking one's parents or cursing them will be put to death (Exod 21:15, 17; Lev 20:9). But Michaelis (1814, 4:303-4) says the son here is to be punished not because of any crime committed against his parents, but because he is a drunkard who quarrels, disturbs the peace, and endangers the lives of others. He is a problem to the whole community, for which reason the community will, in the end, carry out the punishment against him. Rashi's interpretation is similar. He says this is a case where things can only get worse: after the fellow has squandered his father's property, he will be out robbing people at the crossroads. Later Jewish tradition took the son to be mentally deranged (Preuss 1978, 318).

stubborn and rebellious. סוֹרֵר וּמוֹרֶה. A hendiadys (cf. Jer 5:23; Ps 78:8).

his father or ... his mother. Failing to obey his parents puts the son in violation of the fifth commandment. He also stands under the curse of 27:16, to which the people give their "Amen."

and they will discipline him but he will not listen to them. This discipline can be either teaching or corporal punishment or both. Deuteronomy has many occurrences of the verb יסר, "to discipline," and the noun מוּסָר, "discipline" (4:36; 8:5; 11:2; 21:18; 22:18). Deuteronomy also employs למד, "to learn, teach," which occurs nowhere else in the Pentateuch (see Note for 4:1). Nothing is said here about the effectiveness of the discipline or if the parents are themselves given to sensual living. The law only states that the parents will try to correct their son's behavior, but will not succeed. The OT contains numerous proverbs about the need to discipline one's son (Prov 19:18; 22:15; 23:13-14; 29:17), which is not a sign of hatred, but of love (Prov 13:24). Similarly, Yahweh must discipline Israel (Deut 8:5). Sometimes, however, discipline does no good. Amos and Jeremiah both complained later that God's prior discipline of the covenant people had been to no good effect (Amos 4:6-11; Jer 5:3).

19 *then his father and his mother shall take hold of him and bring him out to the elders of his city.* Both father and mother are to bring the son before the town elders, not just the father (cf. 22:15). As in the prior law upholding the rights of the firstborn, here too there can be no maneuvering of a son and one parent over against the other parent. Freedman (2000, 79) says:

> This [law] seems to assure that the accusation is not simply a personal dispute between a child and one of the parents, but something both parents have experienced and believe to be a significant enough threat to the well-being of their home and/or community to require severe action.

In discipline, the two parents must act as one, which could be a warning to parents about how to go about disciplining their children before it gets to this stage.

and bring him out. Presumably out of the house.

the gate of his place. Justice will take place in the city gate (Köhler 1956, 149-75), where the elders will sit assembled (22:15; 25:7; Ruth 4:1-2). See also Amos 5:10, 12, 15; Isa 29:21; Job 31:21; Ps 127:5. Cases were normally decided in the morning, when people passed through the gate and witnesses could readily be summoned (Ruth 3:13; 4:11; Jer 21:12). Excavations show city gates with chambers that have seats along the sides.

20 *And they shall say to the elders of his city.* The parents are to present their case to the elders, since this is now a problem for the larger community. Also, the parents are not to have the power of life and death over their son (Driver; Daube 1978, 180), although at an earlier time they did. Abraham had

Deuteronomy 21

this power over Isaac in the near-sacrifice of his son (Genesis 22), and Judah was able to order the execution of his daughter-in-law for harlotry (Gen 38:24). The LXX has "men" instead of "elders," which follows v. 21. On the role of elders in deciding criminal cases, see Note for 5:23-24. Reviv (1989, 64) says this passage with its reference to elders does not show signs of a later time; it implies the adaptation of Israel's ancient (patriarchal) heritage and is therefore premonarchal.

"*This son of ours is . . . a glutton and a drunkard.*" Hebrew זוֹלֵל is lit. "a worthless one," here someone given to gluttony and drunkenness (T; LXX: συμβολοκοπῶν οἰνοφλυγεῖ, "given to feasting and is a drunkard"). The combination "glutton and drunkard" appears in Prov 23:20-21. Proverbs 28:7 states that a wise son observes the law, but the companion of gluttons (זוֹלְלִים) shames his father. Detractors of Jesus called him a "glutton and a drunkard," wanting to contrast him with the ascetic John the Baptist (Matt 11:18-19).

21 *Then all the men of his city shall pelt him with stones so he dies.* If an investigation into the truth of the parents' allegations is to occur, no mention is made of it (Driver). Tigay assumes that an investigation will have to take place. All the men in the city will take part in the stoning, since the judgment rendered is a community judgment; see also 13:10(9); 17:5. The parents are not said to participate (cf. 17:7), which would be understandable. Actually, parents do not have the legal authority to execute their children, which is seen also in the case of the slandered bride whose parents are unable to produce a bloodstained wedding garment (22:21; Frymer-Kensky 1998, 95). Josephus (*Ant.* 4.264), who connects this law to the one following, says that after the son is stoned (in the morning), his corpse is exposed to general view for the remainder of the day, then buried at night. Michaelis (1814, 4:307) notes this punishment as being particularly severe, but says it should be remembered that the ancients had no prisons such as we have in modern times, where incorrigible sons such as the present one could be kept out of society. Imprisonment in antiquity was not a means of punishment per se; it was for detaining individuals until a decision could be made on what to do with them, whether to free them or put them to death (Lundbom 2004b, 59).

Ancient Sumerian law allowed for a rebellious son to be disinherited and sold into slavery:

> If (a son) has said to his father and to his mother: 'You are not my father; you are not my mother,' he forfeits (his heir's rights to) house, field, orchard, slaves, and (any other) property, and they may sell him (into slavery) for money at full value. (Sumerian Laws 4, *ANET*³, 526; Marcus 1981, 39)

In the Code of Hammurabi (CH 195; *ANET*³, 175), if a son strikes his father they cut off the son's hand. In the Covenant Code one striking his mother or father is put to death (Exod 21:15). On juvenile delinquency in the Bible and the ANE, with comparisons to the problem in modern times and how states seek to deal with it, see Marcus 1981.

So you shall utterly remove the evil from your midst. On this phrase, see Note for 13:6.

and all Israel shall hear and fear. On this phrase, which assumes that capital puniushment will have a deterrent function, see Note for 13:12.

Message and Audience

Moses in the present law envisions a stubborn and rebellious son who continually disobeys his father and his mother; when they discipline him, he again refuses to listen. In such a case the parents are to take the son bodily out of the house and bring him before the elders at the city gate. There the mother and father will state the charge that their son is stubbornly rebellious and refuses to obey them. Before the townspeople he will be called a glutton and a drunkard. The people will doubtless know that already. On the morning of reckoning, the son may be hung over from food or drink and will have to be pulled from bed and dragged the distance. Once a decision is rendered, all the men of the city will stone the fellow to death. Moses repeats his demand that the people must utterly remove evil from their midst, and all Israel will then hear and fear.

It is widely thought that this law was probably never put into effect, serving only to shore up parental authority and deter children from disobeying their parents (Tigay). If it was put into effect, it would be a control over parents who, in the heat of passion, wanted to put their children to death. This would be disallowed, with capital punishment entrusted to the whole community. It may also serve as a reminder to parents of the need to discipline their children, and discipline them effectively, so their behavior might be corrected before things get to the point where there is no remedy left.

M. HANGED CRIMINALS (21:22-23)

21 ^{22}*And when there shall be in a man a sin requiring a sentence of death, and he is put to death and you hang him upon a tree,* ^{23}*his dead body shall not remain all night upon the tree, but you must surely bury him on that day, because cursed of God is one who is hanged. And you shall not defile your soil that Yahweh your God is giving to you as an inheritance.*

Deuteronomy 21

Rhetoric and Composition

The present law regulating the display of executed criminals follows naturally the law calling for stoning incorrigible sons, since persons stoned to death are often — but not always — hung on a tree for public viewing. Similar opening phrases link this law with the two prior laws (see Rhetoric and Composition for 21:15-17), which means this law should not grouped with the miscellaneous laws following (*pace* NRSV; NJB). The unit is demarcated at the top end by a *setumah* in M^L, a section in Sam, and a small space in 11QT (likely a *setumah*) before v. 22. Demarcation at the bottom end is by a *setumah* in M^L and a small space in 11QT (likely a *setumah*) after v. 23, which is also the chapter division.

Portions of 21:22-23 are contained in 4QDeut^i.

Notes

21:22 *a sin requiring a sentence of death.* I.e., a proved capital charge (Driver; cf. 19:6). Driver takes the two terms חֵטְא מִשְׁפַּט־מָוֶת as in apposition, with "sentence of death" defining the sin (cf. חֵטְא מָוֶת in 22:26).

and he is put to death and you hang him upon a tree. Death will come not by hanging, but by another means, usually stoning (Josephus *Ant.* 4.202; the sons of Rimmon were probably stabbed to death; 2 Sam 4:12). The corpse will then be hung upon a tree or impaled on a stake (T) for public display (*m. B. Bat,* 6:4; Rashi). Later rabbinic literature recognized only four methods of capital punishment: stoning, burning, strangulation, and killing by the sword. Hanging the corpse brings added infamy to the executed (Josh 8:29; 10:26-27), but as Morgenstern (1930, 192-93) points out, it also fits in with the Deuteronomic warning, "All Israel shall see and fear. . . ." The Egyptians practiced hanging (Gen 40:19, 22; 41:13), and so did the Babylonians. In the Code of Hammurabi (CH 21), if a man is found breaking into a house, they are to execute him and hang him in front of the very breach (*ANET*³, 167; cf. Deut 22:21). The Philistines bestowed this indignity upon Saul and Jonathan, impaling their bodies on the wall of Beth-shan (1 Sam 31:10). David, too, practiced hanging (2 Sam 4:12) or gave people to others who had them hanged (2 Sam 21:8-9).

In the *Temple Scroll* (11QT 64:8-9), the word order of this verse is changed so that the cause of death comes from the hanging itself: "You shall hang him on the tree, and he shall die" (Yadin 1983, 1:81; 2:289-90). And in 4QpNah 7-8, a Qumran commentary on Nah 2:12, it is said of the "Lion of Wrath" (= Alexander Janneus) that he "hangs men alive" (Yadin 1971, 12; Wilcox 1977, 88; cf. Allegro 1956, 91). Both could be references to crucifixion, which the Romans introduced into Palestine. The NT makes reference to the present verse in connection with the crucifixion of Jesus (Acts 5:30; 10:39). Yadin says there may have been a precedent for this later cruelty in ancient Israel, arguing that the king of Ai was hanged alive (by implication) in Josh 8:23-29. But this interpretation is open to question, since the mode of execution is not made explicit. The same lack of specificity applies to the seven sons of Saul who were given over by David to the Gibeonites, a non-Israelite people, and hanged on the mountain in 2 Sam 21:8-9. These individuals may have been executed by other means, after which their corpses were hung up for public display.

23 *his dead body shall not remain all night upon the tree, but you must surely bury him on that day.* With execution occurring in the morning, hanging up the corpse for public display is allowed during the day, but it must be taken down and buried before night. Josephus (*Ant.* 4.265) says burial on the same day should be given even to Israel's enemies, which was practiced in the biblical period (Josh 8:29; 10:26-27). Prolonged exposure of corpses to the elements was allowed by the Egyptians (Gen 40:19), and one can only wonder how long the impaled residents of Lachish were left to hang by Sennacherib after he took the city in 701. The Philistines appear to have allowed the corpses of Saul and Jonathan to hang for more than a day, although here the brave men of Jabesh-gilead, when they heard of the indignity, traveled all night to Mount Gilboa to take the bodies down (1 Sam 31:10-13). In the NT, we read that the body of Jesus was taken down from the cross in the evening, and then buried (Matt 27:57-60; Mark 15:42-46; Luke 23:50-54; John 19:31-42).

shall not remain all night. The verb תָלִין is usually read as a Qal imperfect third feminine singular (so BDB; Mandelkern; AV; RSV; REB; NJB; Yadin 1983, 2:291 on 11QT 64:11), but T^Onq has a second person, "you must not leave overnight," which is followed by NJV and Friedman. The LXX has οὐκ ἐπικοιμηθήσεται, "it shall not be left the night," and T^NfPsJ also a third-person reading. For an injunction in the second person followed by another injunction using תָלִין in the third person, see Lev 19:13.

because cursed of God is one who is hanged. Hebrew קִלְלַת אֱלֹהִים, being a construct chain, should normally be translated "curse of God," but the ambiguity of such an expression has given rise over time to various interpretations. Driver says the expression means "accursed of God," which has support from the LXX (κεκατηραμένος ὑπὸ θεοῦ, "being cursed by God"). 11QT 64:12 expands to "accursed by God and men" (Yadin 1983, 2:291). But the rabbis took אֱלֹהִים as an objective genitive, giving the translation: "a curse [= insult] to(ward) God." They taught that someone hanged brought insult to God, since humans were made in God's image (Rashi; Friedman; Tigay; NJV). In the NT, Paul gives the expression yet another twist when citing the crucifixion of Jesus, saying that Jesus' death redeemed people from the curse of the law (Gal 3:13).

For the exegesis of the present phrase in the early period, see Driver (1895, 248-249 n.) and Bernstein 1983-84.

And you shall not defile your soil that Yahweh your God is giving to you as an inheritance. A very Deuteronomic admonition about Yahweh's inheritance given to Israel (see Note for 15:4), where the concern is about defiling the soil and the shame such an indignity will bring upon the nation. An exposed corpse defiles the land; burial cleanses it. One must also remember that a corpse hung for long will bring birds to eat the flesh (Gen 40:19; Jer 7:33; 16:4), not to mention the unpleasant stench it will make after a day in the sun. On a corpse spoiling the appearance of the land more than excrement in the war camp, see Note for 21:1 and cf. Jer 9:21(22).

Message and Audience

In the present law, Moses tells the assembled that when a man is sentenced to death, then executed, and is made to suffer the further indignity by having his body hanged upon a tree, the body must not remain there during the night but be buried by evening. One who is hanged is accursed by God, and the ground given to Israel as an inheritance cannot be defiled by extended public display of a corpse.

N. MISCELLANEOUS LAWS (22:1-8)

1. Restoring Lost Property (22:1-3)

22 ¹*You shall not see your brother's ox or his sheep driven away, and hide yourself from them. You must certainly return them to your brother.* ²*And if your brother is not near to you, or you do not know him, then you shall bring it into your house, and it shall be with you until your brother comes looking for it; then you shall return it to him.* ³*And thus you shall do for his ass, and thus you shall do for his garment, and thus you shall do for any lost thing of your brother's that becomes lost by him, and you find it; you may not hide yourself.*

2. Lifting Up Fallen Animals (22:4)

22 ⁴*You shall not see your brother's ass or his ox fallen in the road, and hide yourself from them; you shall surely raise it up with him.*

3. No Wearing the Apparel of the Opposite Sex (22:5)

22⁵*An article of a man shall not be on a woman, and a man shall not wear a garment of a woman, for everyone who does these things is an abomination to Yahweh your God.*

4. Sparing Mother Birds (22:6-7)

22⁶*When a bird's nest happens to appear before you in the road, in any tree or on the ground, young ones or eggs, and the mother is brooding over the young ones or over the eggs, you shall not take the mother with the offspring.* ⁷*You must surely send the mother away, but the offspring you may take for yourself, in order that it may go well for you and you may prolong your days.*

5. Parapets on Roofs (22:8)

22⁸*When you build a new house, you shall make a parapet for your roof, that you not bring bloodguilt against your house when someone falls from it.*

Rhetoric and Composition

Here are five miscellaneous laws that bring to an end the collection of laws expanding upon the sixth ccmmandment, "You shall not murder" (see Rhetoric and Composition for 12:1-4). They are (1) a law requiring the return of lost property (22:1-3); (2) a law mandating giving help for fallen animals (22:4); (3) a law prohibiting transvestism (22:5); (4) a law protecting mother birds (22:6-7); and (5) a law requiring parapets on house roofs (22:8). The last two laws connect generally to the sixth commandment: mother birds must not be killed when their nestlings or eggs are taken; and roofs without a parapet can cause accidental death, bringing bloodguilt upon the house. The other three laws have no apparent connection with this commandment, connecting with the two others simply by catchwords.

A major break must be made after v. 8, since this is the last law connected with "killing" (Braulik 1993, 322). Also, the keyword "bloodguilt" makes an inclusio for the entire collection that expands upon the sixth commandment (19:1–22:8):

. . . and *bloodguilt* be upon you	דָּמִים	19:10
. . . that you not bring *bloodguilt* against your house . . .	דָּמִים	22:8

Deuteronomy 22

The present unit then is 22:1-8, delimited at the top end by a *setumah* in M^L before v. 1, which is also the chapter division. 11QT has a small space there, probably a *setumah*. Delimitation at the bottom end is by a *setumah* in M^L after v. 8. Law I on returning lost property is delimited at the bottom end by a *setumah* in M^L after v. 3, and Law II at the bottom end by a *setumah* in M^L after v. 4. There are also sections after vv. 3 and 4 in 4QpaleoDeut^r. Laws I and II should probably be taken as a pair: they contain related subject matter; the two together have keyword links to the remaining laws; and the two are themselves bound together by a keyword inclusio:

You shall not see your brother's ox . . . and hide yourself from them   v. 1
You shall not see your brother's ass . . . and hide yourself from them . . .   v. 4

Law III prohibiting transvestism is delimited at the bottom end by a *petuḥah* in M^L and a section in Sam after v. 5; Law IV on sparing mother birds is delimited at the bottom end by a *setumah* in M^L after v. 7; and Law V requiring a parapet on the house roof is delimited at the bottom end by a *setumah* in M^L after v. 8. 11QT has a *petuḥah* after v. 5 and a *setumah* after v. 7.

The unrelated laws at the beginning of the cluster are nevertheless integrated into the overall structure, as we find happening elsewhere in Deuteronomy (14:1-2); therefore, they should not be taken as misplaced. Laws II and III are linked by keywords to Law I, and Laws IV and V are linked by keywords to Law II. In the first instance, Law II on raising fallen animals is linked to Law I on restoring lost property by the keywords "ass" and "ox," where the repetition contains an inversion of the terms:

I	*ox . . . his ass*	שׁוֹר . . . חֲמֹרוֹ	vv. 1, 3
II	*ass . . . his ox*	חֲמוֹר . . . שׁוֹרוֹ	v. 4

Law III against transvestism is linked to Law I by the term "garment" (Rofé 1988b, 272):

I	*for his garment*	לְשִׂמְלָתוֹ	v. 3
III	*a garment*	שִׂמְלַת	v. 5

Law IV on sparing mother birds is linked to Law II on the raising of fallen animals by the keyword "in the road":

II	*in the road*	בַּדֶּרֶךְ	v. 4
IV	*in the road*	בַדֶּרֶךְ	v. 6

Deuteronomy 22

Law V, mandating a parapet on the roof, is linked to Law II by the keyword "fall(en)."

| I fallen | נֹפְלִים | v. 4 |
| IV someone falls | יִפֹּל הַנֹּפֵל | v. 8 |

Portions of 22:1-8 are contained in 4QDeut[i] and 4QpaleoDeut[r].

Notes

22:1 *You shall not see your brother's ox or his sheep driven away, and hide yourself from them.* The negative לֹא covers both verbs, which means the person also cannot hide himself from the stray animal he has seen. This is precisely what is censured in the NT parable of the Good Samaritan, only there it is a person left half dead (Luke 10:29-37). Calvin says the present law shows that it is not enough simply to abstain from evil; to be guiltless before God one must also strive to do good.

your brother. In the Covenant Code, where this law appears among others dealing with legal disputes (Exod 23:4-5), "your enemy" instead of "your brother" is used. Here "brother" is expanded to mean "fellow-Israelite" (NJV: "your fellow"; cf. 1:16; 15:2), which will include a person with whom one has a legal dispute. Deuteronomy has broadened the scope of the law so it applies to everyone in the community (Driver; von Rad).

his sheep. Hebrew שֶׂה means "one of a flock," which could be either a sheep or a goat. The animals here are representative, just like ox and ass are in v. 4. 11QT 64:13-14 expands to "his sheep or his ass," picking up the latter from vv. 3 and 4. The Sam adds או את כל בהמתו, "or any of his cattle," which could be an MT loss attributable to haplography (homoeoteleuton: ו . . . ו). Cf. the listing of animals in 5:14.

driven away. נִדָּחִים. The N-stem of נדח can mean either "gone astray" or "driven away" (Mic 4:6; Zeph 3:19; Ezek 34:4, 16), the same meanings present in LXX πλανώμενα. Whether the animals have been separated from the herd or have simply wandered off, they are lost. In a society where many people owned domestic animals, strays were common; cf. the lost asses of Saul in 1 Sam 9:3-4, 20. The LXX adds ἐν τῇ ὁδῷ, "in the way" (cf. v. 4).

and hide yourself from them. I.e., completely ignore them. Hebrew וְהִתְעַלַּמְתָּ. The moral obligation not to hide oneself from someone or something is a Deuteronomic idea (cf. Isa 58:7). Rashi says this law is speaking about "one [who] closes his eyes tight as though [he] does not see it." The injunction has a shame element; Daube (1969a, 29-30) says not hiding oneself from an-

Deuteronomy 22

other's problems is something people in the Orient understand much better than people in the West.

2 This expands the Covenant Code version, adding that if the owner lives some distance away or is unknown, one is to bring the lost animals home for safekeeping; then when the owner comes looking for them, they are to be returned to him. Hittite Law required that one bring the lost animals to the authorities, i.e., to the royal gate, or if they were found in the country, to the town elders (HL 71; Neufeld 1951, 23, 161-62; $ANET^3$, 192). The finder is allowed to harness the animals until the owner comes to claim them, this being compensation for food and other maintenance he has provided. But the lost animals must first be brought to the town officials; if the finder neglects to do this, he is counted as a thief. Later Jewish law required that lost property be publicized (Tigay). If the Hittite finder of the stray animals knew their owner, he was permitted to yoke the oxen for one day, until the stars came out, after which he must drive them back to their owner. His right to yoke the oxen until evening was again to compensate for the animals' upkeep (HL 79; Neufeld 1951, 25, 171; $ANET^3$, 192-93). Middle Assyrian Laws (MAL C + G no. 6; $ANET^3$, 187) had statutes dealing with individuals who sold property they had found. Here cases were to be decided by judges, with witnesses being present to give testimony. In the Code of Hammurabi, lost property is dealt with among laws pertaining to theft, where again decisions must be rendered by judges and witnesses must be present to give testimony (CH 9, 10, 11; $ANET^3$, 166).

then you shall bring it into your house. Ancient Palestinian houses had two levels: an upper level where the family lived and a stable on ground level where the animals were kept. Thus an animal could be brought into one's house (1 Sam 28:24). Houses of modern Arab peasants are built similarly: three-quarters of the inner space raised for the living area and a lower level where animals are stabled (Canaan 1933, 35).

then you shall return it to him. From laws dealing with goods entrusted to others for safekeeping, both in the Bible and in other ANE law codes, we learn that people often failed to return goods in custody to their owners (Exod 22:7[8]; Lev 5:20-26[6:1-7]; MAL C + G; $ANET^3$, 187).

3 *And thus you shall do for his ass, and thus you shall do for his garment, and thus you shall do for any lost thing of your brother's that becomes lost by him, and you find it.* More expansion of the Covenant Code version, extending application to any lost item one happens to find. The assumption here, since the application follows directly upon what is stated in v. 2, is that the owner will likely come looking for his lost property, and one should therefore keep it in anticipation of returning it to him. The law seeks to prevent an overhasty "finder's keeper's" attitude in regard to the lost property of another.

you may not hide yourself. On the "you/he may not" verbal form, which

Deuteronomy 22

denotes the indignity of doing a certain thing, see Note for 12:17. The form occurs again in vv. 19 and 29.

4 *ass . . . his ox*. The two most common beasts of burden, and in the case of the ox, the most commonly used animal for plowing. Later Jewish interpretation applied this law to any animal (*m. B. Qam.* 5:7). Cf. Jesus' remarks about a sheep fallen into a pit, which, according to Pharisaic teaching, may be raised even on the Sabbath (Matt 12:11-12).

you shall surely raise it up with him. Two individuals, at least, are needed to raise a fallen ass without undoing its pack or a fallen pair of oxen without removing the yoke. Even then, it could be hard work. It could take even more than two persons. Deuteronomic law is here concerned for the owner of the animals, who needs help, and for the animals themselves, who need relief from their suffering by being set on their feet.

5 *An article of a man shall not be upon a woman, and a man shall not wear a garment of a woman*. Another law peculiar to Deuteronomy, prohibiting women from wearing accoutrements of men and men from wearing women's apparel (transvestitism). Josephus (*Ant.* 4.301) connects this law with war, saying that women in battle should not put on the gear of a warrior, nor should men dress as women. One recalls the later words of the Roman satirist Juvenal (*Sat.* vi 252-53):

> What modesty can you expect in a woman who wears a helmet, abjures her own sex, and delights in feats of strength? (Loeb)

Hebrew כְּלִי is a general term referring to any article, usually worn or carried, such as "clothing" (Lev 13:49); "jewelry" (Gen 24:53); in the plural, "baggage, cargo" (1 Sam 17:22; Jonah 1:5); "weapons" (Gen 27:3); or simply "stuff" (BDB, 479). It has the same wide range of meanings in postbiblical Hebrew (*Dict Talm*, 641). LXX σκεύη is likewise a broad term, referring to anything worn by a man: apparel, arms, or other accoutrements. Hoffner (1966, 332-33) thinks reference here must be to a weapon, since a weapon — usually the bow — is the common symbol of masculinity. The term here for "man," גֶּבֶר, can be translated "strong man" or "warrior," making the sexual distinction more pronounced and supporting the translation of כְּלִי as "weapon."

It has been suggested that this law was promulgated to prohibit homosexual acts (Carmichael 1974, 147), sexual stimulation, or homosexual role-playing (Tigay), all of which were well attested in Canaanite (Astarte) and Mesopotamian (Ishtar, Inanna) cultic rites (Hallo 1985-86, 37). Hoffner (1966, 334) thinks the law sought to prohibit the ritualistic magic in Canaanite and Hittite religion, where symbols of masculinity and femininity were utilized "to maintain, restore, or eradicate the sexual potency of oneself or one's enemy." Lambert

(1960, 226 i 1-7; 230) cites a Babylonian proverb from the Middle Assyrian period that appears to reflect transvestite practices. He translates:

> ... An Amorite speaks [to] his wife, 'You be the man, [I] will be the woman. [Since . . .] . . . I became a man [. . .]. female [. . .]. male'

Moran speculates that Amorites may have been notorious for this perversion, as were the men of Sodom and Corinth and the women of Lesbos. Classical authors reported women dressed as men and men dressed as women parading in the towns and villages of Syria, Cyprus, Asia Minor, and elsewhere (Driver; Licht 1994, 124-29, 500; Gaster 1969, 316-17). One thinks in particular of *Concerning the Syrian Goddess (De Dea Syria),* ascribed to Lucian, which describes the religion of Syrian Hierapolis (ancient Mabbûg), in which the mythology associated with the goddess Rhea is permeated with castration imagery and transvestitism, and Galli priests, in devotion to Rhea, perform self-castration, abandon a male lifestyle, and wear women's clothing (Attridge and Oden 1976, 23, 37, 39, 55). Gaster cites survivals of cultic transvestitism in the modern world. In ANE religion, gods and goddesses liberally switched their roles (Daube 1978, 181), e.g., a Neo-Babylonian prayer to Ishtar calls her first a lioness, then a fierce lion (lines 31, 51; $ANET^3$, 384); a Hittite official requesting relief from his suffering says to his deity, "You, my god, are father and mother to me" ($ANET^3$, 401). One might therefore expect that worshippers of these deities would find it natural to switch male and female roles. All of this was rejected in Israelite religion, nowhere more decisively than in Deuteronomy (Hallo 1985-86, 37; Vedeler 2008, 468). Homosexuality blurs the distinction between male and female, and this is not tolerated in the OT (Frymer-Kensky 1989, 96-97). Rashi says women who dress like men want to consort with men, and this can only be for the purpose of leading them into adultery/unchastity. Rashbam the same.

The prohibition has been given a more positive interpretation, viz., that it sought to preserve the distinction between male and female set forth at creation, particularly as described in Genesis 1–2 (P. J. Harland 1998-99, 76). The same point has been made regarding laws condemning homosexuality, viz., Lev 18:22; 20:13, that this perversion violates the procreative intent of Genesis 1, also the thrust of Genesis 2, where God creates for Adam not a second Adam, but rather Eve (Wenham 1990-91, 362-63). Such a view has merit, although it assumes that the present law belongs with those prohibiting mixtures (vv. 9-11), which does not seem to be the case (see Rhetoric and Composition). For additional discussion on this prohibition against cross-dressing, see N. S. Fox 2009.

for everyone who does these things is an abomination to Yahweh your God. The expression "abomination to Yahweh" (תּוֹעֲבַת יְהוָה) is stock in Deuteronomy (see Note on 7:25), being reserved for those acts particularly distasteful to Yahweh. According to von Rad, the reason is thus a weighty one, pointing to some cultic offense (cf. Gaster 1969, 316). Homosexuality is considered an "abomination" (תּוֹעֵבָה) in Lev 18:22. An interesting parallel has turned up on Old Babylonian school tablets from Nippur, where at the conclusion of a group of proverbial sayings is an end-formula similar to the one here (Hallo 1985-86). The end-formula is climactic, Hallo calling it a "punch-line." One of the groups of sayings reads:

> A judge who perverts justice,
> a curse which falls on the righteous party,
> a (first-born) heir who drives the younger (son)
>   out of the patrimony —
> these are abominations of Ninurta.

Other sayings in this collection and collections of a similar nature conclude with: "It is an abomination of Utu"; "These are abominations of Suen"; "[This] is an abomination to Marduk," and the like. In the Egyptian "Instruction of Amen-em-opet," certain proverbs conclude with the words "the abomination of the god" (chs. 10, 13; *ANET*³ 423; Hallo 1985-86, 34). This points again to wisdom influence in Deuteronomy. In the biblical book of Proverbs are these words:

> There are six things that Yahweh hates,
>   seven that are an abomination to him:
> haughty eyes, a lying tongue,
>   and hands that shed innocent blood,
> a heart that devises wicked plans,
>   feet that make haste to run to evil,
> a false witness who breathes out lies,
>   and one who sows discord among brothers. (Prov 6:16-19)

6 Another law only in Deuteronomy, this one pertaining to a nest one comes upon along the road, where a mother is brooding on either nestlings or eggs. The mother in such a case may not be taken. This is a purely chance meeting (Rashi), indicated by the N-stem of the verb קרא (see also 2 Sam 18:9).

the ground. Hebrew הָאָרֶץ, which is a better translation here than "the earth."

7 *You must surely send the mother away, but the offspring you may take for yourself.* The verb שׁלח in the Piel means "send away," prompting some to speculate that the mother should be driven away so as not to see her nestlings or eggs being taken. Michaelis (1814, 2:427-28) thinks this directive is not a law per se, but more like "a rule, the breach of which is punished by the transgressor being no longer considered a true sportsman, but a poacher, and a disgrace to the fraternity of *Jägers* (hunters)." People taking birds along the path will do so unobserved, making this a rule hard to enforce. It will have to work largely on the honor system, like present-day hunting and fishing. Hunters will not kill young deer, and fishermen will throw back undersized fish. Michaelis does agree that judges could still have punished transgressors of this rule (just as modern-day game wardens can fine violating hunters or fishermen), also that a transgressor might later want to make a guilt offering when his conscience begins to bother him. One must also recognize a humanitarian concern in this law (Driver; von Rad), seen elsewhere in the injunction not to boil a calf in its mother's milk (14:21) and in the Levitical law not to slaughter a cow or ewe with its young on the same day (Lev 22:28). The laws here and in Lev 22:28 are both cited in the Qumran *Temple Scroll* (11QT 52:6-7) in connection with the ban against sacrificing pregnant animals (Yadin 1983, 1:312-14; 2:233)

in order that it may go well for you and you may prolong your days. Two stock phrases in Deuteronomy, on which see Notes for 4:25-26 and 4:40. The sequence is reversed in 5:16. Well-being in the land will depend upon people being careful not to extirpate indigenous birds. Michaelis (1814, 2:419-22), like Calvin and others, thought this law was promulgated in order to protect the species, to keep it from extinction or near-extinction. He says the Swedish botanist Carl Linnaeus would understand it better than theological commentators. Extirpation of a species can upset the balance of nature. Linnaeus, in 1767, noted how in the Virginia Colony of America the decision was made to wipe out a certain crow frequenting the fields. But later it was discovered that damage to the crops was really being done by beetles and these beetles, without crows to eat them, soon multiplied out of control, so that few crops remained.

8 Another law peculiar to Deuteronomy, similar in nature to the law in Exod 21:33-34 requiring that one not leave an open pit into which animals might fall. Ancient Palestinian houses, like modern Arab peasant houses, had flat roofs used as living and work areas (Josh 2:6; 1 Sam 9:25; 2 Sam 11:2; 16:22; Jer 19:13). This roof required a protective barrier so people would not fall off. Hebrew מַעֲקֶה ("parapet"), an OT *hapax legomenon,* is a low wall on all sides of the roof (Rashi). The LXX has στεφάνην ("border"). In the Laws of Eshnunna (LE 58), it states that if a wall is threatening to fall, and the owner does nothing about it after being told about the danger, and then it collapses, killing a man, it becomes a capital case subject to decree by the king (Yaron 1969, 79; $ANET^3$, 163).

that you not bring bloodguilt against your house. The Hebrew דָּמִים is best translated "bloodguilt" (cf. 19:10), since any bloodshed resulting from an accident will bring guilt upon the house. The LXX translates with φόνον ("murder, homicide"). Tigay thinks that because a human life could be involved, failure to build a parapet on one's roof would constitute criminal negligence, tantamount to homicide. But Daube (1961, 251) says that if someone falls the guilt will be upon the house, not the owner of the house, and he doubts whether vengeance would be legitimate or whether judges would pass sentence on an owner if such an accident occurred. Still, it would be a case of negligence, and some form of compensation would be required.

Message and Audience

The audience now hears at the end of laws expanding upon the sixth commandment five miscellaneous laws that aim to preserve human and animal life, promote well-being of individuals and the community, and prohibit the practice of role switching between the sexes. Moses states first that one must not ignore the stray ox or sheep of a fellow Israelite, but make every effort to see that it is returned to him. It matters not if the owner lives far away or is unknown to the finder. In such cases it must be brought home for safekeeping until the owner comes looking for it. The same goes for an ass, a garment, or any lost item one happens to find. The finder is told not to ignore it. Help must also be given if an ox or ass belonging to a fellow-Israelite has fallen along the way. This law states that one must help the owner raise his beast or beasts to their feet.

The third law states that no article worn or carried by a man is to be found on a woman, nor is a man to wear the clothes of a woman. This practice will be encountered in Canaan, and like other Canaanite practices, it must be rejected. Male-female role switching is an abomination in the eyes of Yahweh, which the audience will understand as a strong censure.

In the fourth law Moses enjoins new inhabitants of Canaan to exercise control in taking indigenous birds for food. If one happens to come upon a nest along the road, the young or the eggs may be taken, but not the mother bird with them. If people take such care of the birds — also other species of animals and fowl — things will go well and they will live long in the land.

The fifth law requires that when one comes to build a house, a parapet must be put on the roof to keep people from falling off and to prevent bloodguilt from coming against the house.

All these laws anticipate the settled life in Canaan, but could have been set before a late 8th- or early 7th-cent. audience in Judah.

Deuteronomy 22

O. More Miscellaneous Laws (22:9-12)

1. No Mixing of Seeds, Yoked Animals, and Cloths (22:9-11)

22 ⁹You shall not sow your vineyard with two kinds, lest the whole of the seed that you sow and the yield of the vineyard become consecrated.
¹⁰You shall not plow with an ox and with an ass together.
¹¹You shall not wear mixed blends, wool and linen together.

2. The Tassel Exception (22:12)

22¹²Tassels you shall make for yourself on the four corners of your garment with which you cover yourself.*

Rhetoric and Composition

Preceding a collection of laws expanding upon the seventh commandment, "You shall not commit adultery," are four miscellaneous laws on mixtures, all of which associate in some fashion with the commandment (see Rhetoric and Composition for 12:1-4). We have noted in Deuteronomy that miscellaneous laws are placed at the beginning, middle, or end of compilations (see Rhetoric and Composition for 19:1-21). In the prior collection expanding upon the sixth commandment, these came at the end (22:1-8); here they come at the beginning. The present laws consist of: (1) a prohibition on sowing two kinds of seed (v. 9); (2) a prohibition on yoking an ox and ass together for plowing (v. 10); (3) a prohibition on wearing garments of mixed blends (v. 11); and (4) an allowance for tassels on one's garments (v. 12). These laws are omitted in 11QT, where one would expect them (Yadin 1983, 2:292, 294), although Yadin says some may have existed in a portion of col. 65, which is not extant. He says v. 12 dealing with tassels was probably not included.

The first three laws are distinguished by an apodictic לֹא ("not").

    I   *You shall not* (לֹא) *sow . . .*   v. 9
   II *You shall not* (לֹא) *plow . . .*   v. 10
  III *You shall not* (לֹא) *wear . . .*   v. 11

Law IV on the wearing of tassels is stated positively. It is added because tassels contain mixed threads (see Notes), making it an exception to Law III (Rofé

---

*Reading with S and T a Hithpael, תִּתְכַּסֶּה, for MT's Piel form, תְּכַסֶּה (see Notes).

1988b, 273; Tigay). The unit as a whole is delimited at the top end by a *setumah* in M^L before v. 9 and at the bottom end by a *setumah* in M^L and a section in Sam after v. 12. Individual laws are delimited further by *setumahs* after vv. 9, 10, and 11.

S. A. Kaufman (1978-79, 136) has argued that these miscellaneous laws beginning a new collection, when juxtaposed to the miscellaneous laws concluding the prior collection, form a chiasmus of repeated and correlative ideas. A rhetorical structure does seem to be present, since the clusters begin and end with laws pertaining to dress, and these are linked by the keyword לבש ("to wear"):

I	Law regarding dress	v. 5
	Law regarding birds	vv. 6-7
	Law for a house	v. 8
II	Law for a vineyard	v. 9
	Law regarding animals	v. 10
	Law regarding dress	vv. 11-12

Portions of 22:9-12 are contained in 4QDeut^f and 4QDeut^i.

Notes

22:9 This law minus the forfeiture clause recurs in Lev 19:19, where the term "field" (שָׂדֶה) is used instead of "vineyard" (כֶּרֶם). Aside from a general recognition that certain types of mixtures are prohibited by OT law, the interpretation of this law continues to be a matter of speculation. Josephus (*Ant.* 4.228) envisions two kinds of seed being put into the ground, seeds for grapevines and seeds for another crop. Another interpretation is that two kinds of seeds are being sown in addition to seeds for the grapevines (Rashi). What is clear is that grapevines are being sown here from seed (sexual), not propagated from stem cuttings or by grafting (asexual). In modern grape growing (viticulture), seeds are not used for propagation except to develop new varieties (Winkler 1962, 151, 186-87; Weaver 1976, 13, 104). New vines grown from seeds differ greatly from the parent vine and from each other; also the quality of fruit grown from seedlings varies considerably. Soss (1973, 336-37) says mixing seeds will produce hybrid strains that will in turn bring greater yield, and Old Testament law, here as elsewhere, intends to place a restraint on capital gains that in modern society we take to be progress.

two kinds. I.e., two kinds of seed. Hebrew כִּלְאָיִם.

lest the whole of the seed that you sow and the yield of the vineyard become consecrated. What is meant by a statement that the total yield of a vineyard sown with mixed seeds will "become consecrated/holy" (תִּקְדָּשׁ)? The assumption must be that one of the crops, presumably the grapes, is subject to a ban, similar to the ban existing for fruit trees, to which passing reference is made in 20:6. According to Lev 19:23-25, fruit from newly-planted trees may not be eaten by its owner until the fifth year. During the first three years the fruit may not be eaten at all; in the fourth year it is to be set aside as an offering to Yahweh; and in the fifth year the owner is free to eat it. Here in the vineyard, if vines are planted from seeds, fruit can be expected when the vine is three or more years old (Sanders and Lansdell 1924, 28). So if grapes fall under the same ban as fruit coming from fruit trees, what is produced in the first three years may not be eaten and what grapes there are in the fourth year must be set aside as an offering to Yahweh. But why then does a second crop in the vineyard, which may be wheat, barley, or some other nonfruit, come under the ban? Milgrom (1981, 285) says the reason is that it is contiguous to the first crop, with the one seed transmitting its holiness to the total yield. As a result, both crops must be discarded in the first three years, given as an offering to Yahweh in the fourth year, and only in the fifth year may the owner eat them. The owner might therefore think that even though his new plantation of grapes will not give him any yield until the fifth year, he might at least get something from his land in the interval by sowing a second crop. But this law prohibits him from doing so. If this interpretation is correct, then the present law disallows the planting of a second crop only in newly-planted vineyards. In vineyards five or more years old, the law will not apply. Modern English Versions betray an uncertainty about what happens to the entire yield. Some assume it is forfeited to the sanctuary (RSV; NEB), whereas others follow T and Jewish tradition and assume that it is forfeited outright, i.e., not used or destroyed (AV; NJV; NIV; NRSV; REB; NJB).

Michaelis (1814, 3:340-59), discounting the rabbinic interpretations, imagined that the two seeds were of different quality, one good and one bad. But he seems to have been overly influenced by the NT parable of the Two Seeds (Matt 13:24-30), and his interpretation gives no help in explaining how the total yield ends up being holy. There is a Hittite law (HL 166; Neufeld 1951, 45, 180; *ANET*[3], 195) against "sowing seeds upon seeds," which Neufeld thinks refers to sowing one kind of seed upon another and may be traced to an ancient taboo against incest. The consequences of noncompliance in this case are grave, with violators put to a torturous death.

10 This law is to prevent yoke-mates of unequal strength, which can impose a hardship on either or both of the animals — the ox because it is left to do most of the pulling or the ass because it is forced to work harder than it is able.

Deuteronomy 22

In later Jewish tradition, this law justified the separation of the clean from the unclean. The Qumran *Temple Scroll* (11QT 52:13) inserts it prior to the prohibition on slaughtering clean animals in the towns (Yadin 1983, 1:315-16; 2:234-35). The Mishnah (*Kil.* 8:2) notes that the ox is a clean animal used for temple sacrifice, whereas the ass is an unclean animal. The rabbis went on to teach that a just man should therefore not enter into a partnership with a rascal (cf. Sir 13:17). The Mishnah (*Kil.* 8:3) states in addition that one caught leading a pair of unequal animals will get forty lashes. Paul warns Christians not to be "unevenly yoked" (ἑτεροζυγοῦντες) with unbelievers (2 Cor 6:14), which Derrett (1978) calls a midrash on the present verse. Leviticus 19:19 replaces this law with one stating that cattle must not be allowed to breed with a different kind of animal.

11 This law prohibiting "mixed blends" (שַׁעַטְנֵז) appears also in Lev 19:19. The reason for the prohibition is given in Josephus (*Ant.* 4.208; cf. *m. Kil.* 9:1): mixed blends are reserved for priests alone (Exod 28:6, 15; 39:29; cf. Milgrom 1991, 548-49). Ezekiel, however, disallows garments of mixed blends for the Levitical priests because wool causes sweat (Ezek 44:17-18).

12 Hebrew גְּדִלִים, the term used here, is lit. "twisted threads/cord," whereas in Num 15:38 the term is צִיצָת, which Driver says is a cord ending in a (flowerlike) "tassel." Tassels — singly or as part of a fringe — were typically placed on the lower border of one's outer garment, and from 2nd-mill. paintings and stone reliefs they are seen on robes, kilts, and other garments worn all throughout the ANE (Bertman 1961, with drawings; also *ANEP*², pls. 6; 433; 449; 476). In the OT their attachment to clothing is dealt with more fully in Num 15:37-41, where it is said that tassels are to aid people in remembering the commandments and to keep them from straying into wanton behavior. Bertman thinks that since in nonbiblical portrayals tassels appear on gods, kings, other rulers, and warriors, they were originally a status symbol. But the present law appears to prescribe them for everyone — men and women, royalty and common folk. The tassels were to be placed on the four corners (lit. "four wings") of one's garment, which finds a close parallel in Syrian dress as Egyptian art portrays it (Bertman 1961, 122-23). Tassels occur there at quarterway and halfway points on the garment, though not at every quarter-point. It is further specified in Num 15:38 that certain threads are to be blue in color. In Egyptian paintings the tassels are red and blue. According to later Jewish tradition, the blue threads were wool, whereas the others were linen. This is confirmed archaeologically by tassels found in the Dead Sea caves that date from the Bar Kokhba period (ca. A.D. 135; cf. Milgrom 1983, 65). If this was true also in the biblical period, then the present law constitutes an exception to the prior law disallowing clothing of mixed blends (Tigay).

your garment with which you cover yourself. Hebrew כְּסוּת is an outer garment (Exod 22:25-26[26-27]). A Hithpael תְּכַסֶּה is needed here rather than

MT's Piel form, תְּכַסֶּה, in order to get the reflexive: "you cover yourself" (so S and T; cf. *BHS*). A similar problem exists in Gen 38:14. D. N. Freedman suggests that a ת could have been lost by haplography.

Message and Audience

Here as an introduction to unholy alliances that will lead to far more serious consequences are three laws disallowing a mixing of seeds, yoked animals, wool and linen cloths and a fourth law prescribing tassels for outer garments. The first law is directed at those planting new vineyards from seed and who might want yield from another crop before the grapes are deconsecrated and free to be eaten. They are told that a second crop may not be sown in a new vineyard. If it is sown, the yield will become consecrated with the grapes by virtue of its growth in proximity to them. The second law forbidding the yoking of an ox with an ass is compassionate legislation meant to benefit both animals — the stronger ox and the weaker ass. The third law forbidding mixed blends is to preserve a distinction in dress between the laity and the priesthood, since only the latter is permitted to wear cloths of linen and wool. The fourth law allowing tassels on one's garment is an exception to the third law, since tassels mix woolen and linen threads.

The first two laws pertaining to the cultivation of crops will have applicability only when people are settled in the land, and the last two laws regulating dress of clergy and laity will also not be in force until then. After that time, all four laws will have applicability indefinitely.

P. On Chastity and Marriage (22:13–23:1[22:30])

1. Unchaste Brides (22:13-21)

22 [13] *When a man takes a wife and goes in to her, then he hates her* [14] *and attributes to her wanton acts and brings out against her a bad name, and says, "This wife I took, and I came near to her and did not find for her marks of virginity,"* [15] *then the father of the girl and her mother shall take and bring out the girl's marks of virginity to the elders of the city at the gate.* [16] *And the father of the girl shall say to the elders, "My daughter I gave to this man for a wife and he has hated her,* [17] *and behold, he attributes wanton acts, saying, 'I did not find for your daughter marks of virginity'; but these are my daughter's marks of virginity." And they shall spread out the garment before the elders of the city.* [18] *And the elders of that city shall take the man and discipline him,* [19] *and they shall fine him 100*

(shekels) of silver, and give it to the father of the girl because he brought out a bad name against one virgin of Israel. And for him she shall be a wife; he may not send her away all his days. ²⁰But if this thing was true — they did not find marks of virginity for the girl — ²¹then they shall bring out the girl to the entrance of her father's house, and the men of her city shall stone her with stones, so she dies, because she did a foolish thing in Israel, to go whoring in her father's house. So you shall utterly remove the evil from your midst.

2. Sex with Another Married Woman (22:22)

22²²When a man shall be found lying with a woman married to a husband, then they shall die, yes, the two of them — the man who was lying with the woman, and the woman. So you shall utterly remove the evil from Israel.

3. Sex with a Betrothed Girl in the City (22:23-24)

22²³When there shall be a virgin girl betrothed to a man, and a man finds her in the city and lies with her, ²⁴then you shall bring out the two of them to the gate of that city, and you shall stone them with stones, so they die — the girl on account of the fact that she did not cry out in the city, and the man on account of the fact that he humbled the wife of his fellow. So you shall utterly remove the evil from your midst.

4. Sex with a Betrothed Girl in the Country (22:25-27)

22²⁵But if in the field the man finds the betrothed girl, and the man grabs hold of her and lies with her, then the man alone who lay with her shall die, ²⁶but to the girl you shall not do a thing; the girl has not committed a sin deserving death, for just as when a man rises up against his fellow and takes his life, so also this case, ²⁷because he found her in the field; the betrothed girl cried, and there was no one to save her.

5. Sex with an Unbetrothed Girl (22:28-29)

22²⁸When a man shall find a virgin girl who is not betrothed, and he takes hold of her and lies with her, and they are found, ²⁹then the man who lay with her shall give to the father of the girl 50 (shekels) of silver, and for him she shall be a wife, inasmuch as he humbled her; he may not send her away all his days.

6. Sex with a Father's Wife (23:1[22:30])

23:1 *A man shall not take the wife of his father, and not remove the garment of his father.*

Rhetoric and Composition

The present collection of laws is concerned with improper commerce between the sexes, aiming to preserve chastity and marriage among the people of Israel. With one exception, these laws do not occur in the Book of the Covenant, where the concern is primarily with pecuniary matters. The concern in Deuteronomy is with family morality (Weinfeld 1972, 284). The one exception is the law dealing with the seduction of an unbetrothed girl (22:28-29), which occurs with variation in Exod 22:15-16(16-17). The law prohibiting a man from marrying his father's wife (23:1[22:30]) is repeated in the laws of Leviticus (18:8), where it occurs with other incest laws. It has been suggested that this latter law lies outside a tightly knit collection dealing only with regulations of women's sexuality, i.e., 22:13-29 (Edenburg 2009, 44-48).

The present laws deal with (1) the charge of an unchaste bride by her newlywed husband (vv. 13-21); (2) sex by a man — single or married — with a woman married to another, i.e., adultery (v. 22); (3) sex by a man — single or married — with a betrothed girl occurring in the city (vv. 23-24); (4) sex by a man — single or married — with a betrothed girl occurring in the country, i.e., presumed rape (vv. 25-27); (5) sex by a (single) man with an unbetrothed girl, i.e., premarital sex (vv. 28-29); and (6) sex by a man with the wife of one's father (23:1[22:30]). Von Rad (1953, 20) thought the law in 23:1[22:30], because of its apodictic style, opened a new series, although he acknowledged that so far as theme was concerned, it was rather out of line with the verses following. Thematically it goes with the laws preceding and is therefore 22:30 in the Vg and most of the modern English Versions (AV; RSV; NIV; NRSV; REB).

The unit as a whole is delimited at the top end by a *setumah* in M^L and 11QT and a section in Sam before v. 13. Delimitation at the bottom end is by a *setumah* in M^L after 23:1[22:30]. The first law concerning an unchaste bride concludes at v. 21, where M^L has a *setumah*. The M^L also has a *setumah* after v. 19, further dividing the law into an application where the allegations are false and an application where they are true. The law concerning adultery is separated from the law on the unchaste bride by a *setumah* in M^L between vv. 21 and 22. Concluding the law is a *setumah* in M^L and a section in Sam after v. 22. The next law dealing with sex by a man with a betrothed girl in the city has, for the same reason, only a *setumah* in M^L marking its lower limit after v. 24. The law dealing with sex by a man with an unbetrothed girl in the country is delimited at both ends in M^L, by a *setumah* before v. 25 and a *setumah* after v. 27. 11QT does not have a section before v. 25 but has a small space after v. 27, which appears to be a *setumah*. The Sam also has a section after v. 27. The law dealing with sex by a man with an unbetrothed girl is likewise delimited at both ends in M^L, by a *setumah* before v. 28, and by a *setumah* after v. 29. The Sam, as was just indicated, has a section before v. 28. 11QT and Sam have no sections after v. 29. Finally, the law prohibiting sex by a man with a wife of his father is delimited at both ends in M^L, by a *setumah* before and after 23:1[22:30]. The Sam has no sections in either place.

These laws, which are bound together thematically, are also linked by similar opening phrases, making a large chiasmus:

a	*When a man takes a wife . . .*		22:13
	כִּי־יִקַּח אִישׁ אִשָּׁה . . .		
	b	*When a man shall be found . . .*	22:22
		כִּי־יִמָּצֵא אִישׁ . . .	
		c *When there shall be a virgin girl*	22:23
		כִּי יִהְיֶה נַעֲרָה בְתוּלָה . . . (Q)	
		betrothed . . . and a man finds her . . .	
		מְאֹרָשָׂה . . . וּמְצָאָהּ אִישׁ . . .	
		c' *But if . . . the man finds*	22:25
		וְאִם . . . יִמְצָא הָאִישׁ	
		the betrothed girl . . .	
		אֶת־הַנַּעֲרָה הַמְאֹרָשָׂה . . . (Q)	
	b'	*When a man shall find . . .*	22:28
		כִּי־יִמְצָא אִישׁ . . .	
a'	*A man shall not take the wife . . .*		23:1[22:30]
	לֹא־יִקַּח אִישׁ אֶת־אֵשֶׁת . . .		

The wording in the first law balances the wording in the last law, with the one difference that the latter is in apodictic style. The two laws at the center deal with betrothed girls who are deflowered by another man, one act occurring in the city, the other in the country. The first three laws also have stock phrases at the conclusion, the middle one providing slight variation:

So you shall utterly remove the evil from your midst	v. 21
So you shall utterly remove the evil from Israel	v. 22
So you shall utterly remove the evil from your midst	v. 24

A chiastic structure has also been identified in punishments meted out to the guilty in the first five chastity laws (Wenham and McConville 1980, 250):

Deuteronomy 22

a		Accused bride: guilty *man fined 100 shekels of silver*	22:13-21
		Accused bride: guilty *woman executed*	
	b	Sex with married woman: *man and woman executed*	22:22
	b′	Sex with betrothed woman in the city: *man and woman executed*	22:23-24
a′		Sex with betrothed woman in the country: *man executed*	22:25-27
		Sex with unmarried virgin: guilty *man fined 50 shekels of silver*	22:28-29

This structure may indicate that the sixth law prohibiting a man from marrying the wife of his father (23:1[22:30]), while integrated with the others in the present text, was nevertheless taken from another group of laws dealing with incest. It is grouped with incest laws in Lev 18:6-18 and a smaller number of incest laws in 11QT 66:12-17 (see Notes).

Law I, dealing with misconduct charges against a new bride, contains a play on words, highlighting the charge and countercharge:

When a man ... *brings out* against her a bad name ...	וְהוֹצִיא	v. 14
then the father ... shall ... *bring out* the girl's marks of virginity ...	וְהוֹצִיאוּ	v. 15

Whereas the man has gone public with his charges, the father (and mother) now present in public evidence that will vindicate their daughter. But if the charges turn out to be true, another repetition of this key verb introduces the punishment against the girl, which will also be carried out in public:

then they shall *bring out* the girl to the entrance of her father's house ...	וְהוֹצִיאוּ	v. 21

Portions of 22:13–23:1 are contained in 4QDeut^f.

Notes

22:13-14 This law from start to finish envisions an ill-advised marriage, one certainly not made in heaven and one that probably should not have been made also on earth. The man wants out soon after it has taken place, hoping perhaps to get back the bride-price paid to the father. If he divorced her without cause, he would likely forfeit the bride-price (Tigay). On the man's sudden burst of hatred toward the woman, one recalls Amnon's later hatred of Tamar after his lust

Deuteronomy 22

was satisfied (2 Sam 13:15). One should also compare this law with the law concerning war brides in 21:10-14, where terms for a divorce at the end suggest that marriages of this kind are not likely to last.

and attributes to her wanton acts and brings out against her a bad name. To "bring out against her a bad name" (הוֹצִיא עָלֶיהָ שֵׁם רָע) means that the husband has gone public with his charges. Among modern Arab peasants *(fellahin)*, the marriage at this point could simply be dissolved and the bride-price returned, but the groom must agree to remain silent. If he makes his grievance public, then a judgment of innocence and guilt will have to be rendered, with the guilty party punished (G. A. Smith 1918, 263; Hallo 1964, 100-101).

wanton acts. Hebrew עֲלִילֹת דְּבָרִים is uncertain, one of the difficulties being whether דְּבָרִים should be translated "words" or "acts/deeds/things." The phrase could denote a "wantonness of words," i.e., baseless charges, which were put to the woman by the man (LXX; T; AV; NJV; NIV; NRSV; REB; Friedman), or it could be attributing to the woman "wantonness of acts," i.e., misconduct, by the man (RSV; NJB; Tigay). Although the former interpretation has more support in the Versions ancient and modern (see Driver), it makes for a lame redundancy with "and brings out against her a bad name." But this may explain why the Versions have opted for this translation. On עֲלִילֹת meaning "(evil) deeds," see Zeph 3:11; Ezek 14:22, 23; 36:19. The construct chain of plural nouns suggests that the man is accusing her of sexual escapades before their marriage, perhaps many of them. She is being branded as "community property."

and I came near to her and did not find for her marks of virginity. The expression "and I came near to her" (וָאֶקְרַב אֵלֶיהָ) is a euphemism for his having had sexual intercourse with her. The "marks of virginity" (בְּתוּלִים) are the bloodstains on the sleeping garment resulting from the girl's hymen having been broken on her first intercourse. When such are not present, it can be assumed that she has had prior intercourse with one or more men. For a study of virginity in the Bible and the ancient Near East, see Frymer-Kensky 1998.

15 The parents of the bride will have kept the wedding garment for just such an eventuality, although for them it is also a symbol of family pride. In other cultures, the groom or his parents take possession of the bloodstained garment (Frymer-Kensky 1998, 95). The custom of verifying wedding-night virginity survives among modern Arabs and Jews, among whom there is more openness about such things than in Western culture. Among the Moroccan Jews much is made of the girl's virginity being confirmed at the first intercourse. The bridal couple enters the chamber after the wedding ceremony, and not long after, one hears at the entrance "the cry of joy . . . confirming the virginity of the young girl" (Ben-Ami 1974, 54). The same is true among Kurdish Jews (Shai 1974, 260, 262). Here the groom's mother and sister-in-law wait outside the entrance to the bridal chamber to receive the bloodstained garment, af-

Deuteronomy 22

ter which the groom's mother displays it for all to see before turning it over to the bride's mother, who also calls in neighbors to inspect it. Driver, a century earlier, cited among Arabs of Egypt, Syria, and Palestine the custom of parents publicly displaying a wedding garment to relatives and friends.

the elders of the city at the gate. The gate is the ancient court of justice (see Note for 21:19), and there the case will be decided by the city elders. Daube (1978, 179-80) thinks that early cases of this sort fell within domestic jurisdiction (Judah and Tamar), which could still put this practice in the early settlement period. On the role of the elders in deciding criminal matters, see Note for 5:23-24. Both the father and mother speak in the girl's defense, just as in 21:19, where both mother and father bring the charges against their rebellious son. Family honor is at stake.

16-17 The father makes the defense to the elders, repeating what the husband has said publicly about his daughter. He negotiated the marriage with the husband, and the bride-price was paid to him.

"*. . . but these are my daughter's marks of virginity.*" *And they shall spread out the garment before the elders of the city.* The bloodstained garment is now spread out in the city gate for the elders to see. This is the extent of the evidence, and is apparently sufficient to decide the case in favor of the bride and her family. No witnesses are necessary, although in later talmudic sources it was realized that bloodstains were not a sufficient proof and that various measures sometimes had to be taken on the wedding night to make sure that things went as they were supposed to (Tigay 1993a, 129-30).

the garment. הַשִּׂמְלָה. This could be what the bride was wearing, otherwise the garment on which the two were lying (24:13). The term has a more general meaning in 21:13; 22:3, 5.

18 Hebrew יִסְּרוּ ("they will discipline") probably indicates corporal punishment (Josephus *Ant.* 4.248; Calvin; Rashi; Yadin on 11QT 65:14; RSV: "whip"), although Daube (1969a, 31 n. 3) says it could simply refer to the fine. Josephus says he gets the legal forty lashes less one (cf. 25:3). For use of the verb יסר in Deuteronomy, where it occurs often, see Note for 21:18. The elders in this case see to it that the prescribed punishment is carried out (cf. 19:12). Fathers no longer have life-and-death control over unfaithful daughters, as was the case with Judah and Tamar (Gen 38:24); judgment is rendered by the city elders, who are charged with upholding the social order (Frymer-Kensky 1989, 94; 1998, 93).

19 *and they shall fine him 100 (shekels) of silver, and give it to the father of the girl.* In addition to the beating, the man must pay 100 shekels of silver, which is a fixed fine (cf. Amos 2:8), not the bride-price (מֹהַר) negotiated before the marriage. This is a very heavy fine, double the amount assessed the seducer of an unbetrothed virgin (v. 29); its purpose is to compensate the father for the slander against his daughter. But one should remember that in Deuteronomy false witness is otherwise adjudicated according to the talion principle, which would mean that since this is a capital charge (the woman, if guilty, will be stoned), he could get the death penalty (19:18-21). A false accusation regarding sexual conduct in the Lipit Ishtar Code (LI 33) results in only a 10-shekel fine (see Note for 19:21). In the Code of Hammurabi (CH 127), the man guilty of this offense is dragged before the judges and half of his (hair) is cut off ($ANET^3$, 171). But in the Middle Assyrian Laws (MAL A 18), slander regarding sexual misconduct by someone other than the husband is punished by forty blows with the rod, one month's labor for the king, and a "cutting off" of some kind (Driver and Miles 1935, 391; cf. p. 70; $ANET^3$, 181), which could be either castration, or some form of social ostracism. Among the modern Rwala bedouins, one accusing a female — whether a girl or a woman — of unchastity and who cannot prove it forfeits his hand. The kinsman of the accused cuts it off (Musil 1928, 239). For false accusations against women in the ANE, see Lafont (1999, 237-88) and Edenburg (2009, 49-51).

100 (shekels) of silver. The term "shekel" does not appear in the Hebrew, similarly in v. 29 and elsewhere in Deuteronomy, but it can be assumed. The LXX has ἑκατὸν σίκλους, "a hundred shekels." "Shekel" is a measurement of weight, so we are talking about a hundred shekels of cut silver *(Hacksilber)* or silver ingots; coinage was not in use in preexilic Israel. Foreign coins began circulating in Jerusalem and the coastal cities of Tyre, Sidon, and Gaza in the mid-5th cent. and perhaps earlier (Loewe 1955, 150). Silver hoards have turned up at a number of ANE sites, some of the more spectacular being the late 11th- or early 10th-cent. hoard found at Dor and the late 7th-cent. hoard found at Tell Miqne-Ekron (E. Stern 1998; Gitin 2004; Gitin and Golani 2001, 38-40; Kletter 2004). Ingots or *Hacksilber* of standard weight and verified purity were sometimes bundled in cloth and sealed with bullae, becoming therefore a precursor to later coinage (Thompson 2003, 87, 96). For a picture of early Greek coins (6th cent.) found at Ras Shamra, see Schaeffer 1939, pl. xxii fig. 1. On coinage in the ancient world, see Loewe 1955; Meshorer 1978; 1998; Thompson 2003; Lundbom 2004a, 506.

because he brought out a bad name against one virgin of Israel. The essence of this crime is that the man will have brought shame upon a virgin of Israel (cf. 2 Sam 13:12). Deuteronomy is concerned to protect a woman's honor, as one can see also in the war bride legislation of 21:14.

And for him she shall be a wife; he may not send her away all his days. In Hebrew "his" is emphasized (cf. v. 29). Despite efforts of the man to get rid of her, the woman shall be *his*. What is more, divorce in the future is out of the question. This added stipulation is indirect evidence that he was simply trying to be rid of her by bringing the accusation. The "no divorce" stipulation may also be seen as a deterrent to actions such as the man has taken (Frymer-

Kensky 1998, 94). G. A. Smith adds: "But for her it is rough justice. A woman could not divorce a man." Frymer-Kensky says that the law ignores the girl's wishes and the possibility of a more congenial marriage. On the verbal form "you/he may not," which denotes the indignity of doing such and such, see Note for 12:17. Since this form is not apodictic, it could mean that the man must not even think of divorce.

20 I.e., the bloodstained garment was not produced by the mother and father. Again no mention of witnesses, in this case to corroborate the man's charge, although in later Jewish tradition witnesses were required for a conviction (cf. 17:6; 19:15). Rashi assumes there had to be witnesses for proof. Other texts dealing with cases similar to the present one — one Old Babylonian (Hallo 1964, 100) and another from Qumran (Tigay 1993a, 131) — report (trustworthy) women being called in to inspect the bride and hopefully to settle the matter. A similar procedure is attested among the Arabs (Tigay 1993a, 132). The whole procedure is admittedly primitive and could easily bring unjust verdicts, since women do not always emit blood on their first intercourse, hymens could have been broken for other reasons, and so on. Michaelis (1814, 1:498) says Roman law knows nothing of *signa virginitatis*. Nevertheless, the custom has survived among both Arabs and Jews into modern times.

The "blood test" could also have been circumvented to the girl's advantage, although this would have meant remaining permanently with a husband who did not want her. But she would face an equally bad or worse fate if the charge against her was upheld by lack of evidence. The parents, in order to vindicate their honor and shame the bridegroom, could always falsify the evidence by spreading animal blood on the wedding garment before the city elders examined it (Frymer-Kensky 1998, 95). An interesting passage occurs in the Arabic classic *The Thousand Nights and One Night* (212), where a royal daughter, Hayyat al-Nufus, after sleeping with her lover, Budur, had not produced the "blood of her virginity." The king and queen were much displeased, and the girl was given a second night with her lover. Budur, as it turned out, was a woman disguised as a man, so it became necessary to come up with a ruse to deceive the king and queen. The story proceeds:

> When the hour approached for a visit from the King and Queen, Hayyat al-Nufus said to Budur: 'My sister, what shall I say to my mother when she wishes to see the blood of my virginity?' 'That is easy,' smiled Budur, and going out secretly, she returned with a fowl. She cut its throat and bathed the girl's thighs and dipped the napkins in blood, saying, 'You need only show her these, for happily custom does not allow any further examination.' As soon as the supposed King had departed to his hall of justice, the King and Queen entered to their daughter, ready to give rein to violent anger if

the marriage had not been consummated. But when they saw the blood and reddened thighs, their happiness knew no bounds and they ran to set open all the doors of the apartments. The women of the palace trooped in with cries of joy and triumph, and the proud Queen placed the ensanguined napkins on a velvet cushion, and bore them in procession round all the women's quarters. (Mathers 1986, 1:49-50)

The king celebrated his happiness by throwing a grand feast.

21 *then they shall bring out the girl to the entrance of her father's house, and the men of her city shall stone her with stones, so she dies.* The unchaste daughter gets the same punishment as the rebellious son, with men of the city doing the stoning (21:21). Fleishman (2008, 191-92) says that she, like the rebellious son, has brought dishonor upon her parents; it is as if she had cursed her father and mother. Josephus (*Ant.* 4.248) adds that if she is the daughter of a priest, she is to be burnt alive, which has no authority in biblical law. The woman is executed at her father's house because, as the verse goes on to say, this is where the sin occurred. In the Code of Hammurabi (CH 21), a thief caught breaking into a house is to be punished by executing and hanging him at the breach he made (*ANET*³, 167). The present execution occurs at the father's house also in order that the entire community may know of the shame that her sin has brought upon this house (Daube 1969a, 31; Weinfeld 1972, 243; Westbrook 1990, 575-76). The punishment may also be a censuring of the parents. Westbrook says shame is brought especially on the father because he failed in his responsibility to safeguard the daughter's honor until her marriage. He cites Old Babylonian marriage contracts where a guardian is appointed over the bride and that person is then responsible for any sin the bride might commit. And this is to say nothing of the possibility that there has been collusion on the part of the father, who tried to marry off a supposed virgin (Edenburg 2009, 50). In the last century, a man reported having witnessed at the Church of the Nativity in Bethlehem the death of a girl accused of having lost her virginity (Granqvist 1931, 138).

a foolish thing. נְבָלָה. The term refers here as elsewhere to immoral and wanton behavior (Gen 34:7; Judg 19:23-24; 20:6, 10; 2 Sam 13:12; Jer 29:23).

to go whoring in her father's house. The verb is זָנוֹת ("go whoring"), which may indicate — but does not require — that her sexual misconduct took place before her engagement.

So you shall utterly remove the evil from your midst. After a lengthy narration of law in the third person, the discourse now shifts to the second person, making the admonition more direct. For this stock phrase, which occurs again in v. 22 (modified) and in v. 24, see Note on 13:6[5].

22 *When a man shall be found lying with a woman married to a husband, then they shall die, yes, the two of them — the man who was lying with the* *woman, and the woman*. This is a case of adultery, explicitly forbidden in the seventh commandment (5:18), and in ancient Israelite law said to be committed when a man — married or single — has sexual intercourse with the wife of another man. The status of the man makes no difference, only the status of the woman matters: she must be married. Adultery is a serious crime because the husband considers it his right to protect the paternity of his children. If his wife becomes pregnant by another man, this will bring an unwanted child into his family, so the crime is ultimately against him. Michaelis (1814, 4:123) calls it a "heinous theft," which is appropriate, since the issue has to do basically with property rights. However distasteful this may be to the modern mind, the woman belongs to the husband because he paid money to her father to get her. Adultery is forbidden elsewhere in the OT (Lev 18:20), and punishment for the crime is death to both parties by stoning (Lev 20:10; John 8:5). In other ANE law codes, adultery is a capital offense (LUN 7739 §1; LE 27/28; CH 129; MAL A 13-16, 23; HL 197-198), although in certain cases only the woman is put to death. In LUN 7739 §1 the man goes free if the woman chased after him (J. J. Finkelstein 1966, 369), and in MAL A 16 the same obtains if the woman seduced him by "her (crafty) words" (Driver and Miles 1935, 389; cf. *ANET*^{3}, 181). Also in LE 27/28 only one offender is put to death, but it is not certain which one it is (Yaron 1969, 33, 56). In other cases, only the man is punished. If, for example, a man is caught raping a married woman or charged by witnesses to have done the same, as in MAL A 12, where the woman does not consent and strenuously defends herself, the man is put to death, but the woman goes free. The OT has no comparable law relating to the rape of a married woman.

In the present case no provision for a reduced sentence is made, as in some other ANE law codes where the husband (or the king) can impose a lesser sentence, although Prov 6:35 is cited as indirect evidence that such was theoretically possible. Later Jewish law expressly excluded it, with the reason sometimes given that adultery was not just a sin against the husband, but also against God (cf. Gen 20:6; 39:9; Ps 51:6[4]; Hos 4:2; 7:4; Jer 5:7-8; 7:9; Greenberg 1960, 12). Adultery, after all, is expressly prohibited by the seventh commandment. Elsewhere in the ANE adultery is a sin against both the husband and the gods (Westbrook 1990, 566-69; Tigay). In Middle Assyrian Laws, where the offended husband determines the punishment, the guilty wife and her lover must be treated equally:

> If the woman's husband puts his wife to death, then he shall put the man to death; (but) if he has cut off his wife's nose, he shall make the man a eunuch and the whole of his face shall be mutilated. Or, if he has allowed his wife to go free, the man shall be allowed to go free (MAL A 15; Driver and Miles 1935, 389; cf. *ANET*^{3}, 181).

Deuteronomy 22

A reduced penalty for the adulterous wife must also be matched with a reduced penalty for the adulterer in HL 198 (Neufeld 1951, 57; *ANET*³, 196). In the Code of Hammurabi, if the woman's husband wishes to spare his wife, then the king may in turn spare "his subject" (CH 129; *ANET*³, 171). Yaron (1969, 188-89) says that equal treatment for both parties was to prevent a conspiracy of husband and wife against an "innocent" male.

Equal treatment to both parties is attested also in classical sources. Pliny (*Ep.* vi 31) tells of a case in which a woman married to a military tribune committed adultery with a centurion and the husband reported it to the governor, who in turn informed the emperor. The emperor, after sifting the evidence, dismissed the centurion from service and then banished him. The husband, out of affection for his wife, continued to keep her in his house and held back from punishing her, for which he was censured for having condoned her conduct. She was then found guilty and sentenced under Julian law, which required that she forfeit half of her dowry and a third of her property, after which she was banished to an island. Among modern Arabs, a sheikh has been known to intervene in adultery cases to save the woman's life (Granqvist 1931, 142). For discussion of adultery as treated in ANE law, see Westbrook (1990), Lafont (1999, 29-91), and Edenburg (2009, 51-53).

When a man shall be found lying with a woman married to a husband. On the form "to be found" in Deuteronomy, see Note for 17:2. Here it also means that the man and woman were caught in the act (Moran; cf. John 8:4). In cases where the husband merely suspects his wife of adultery but has no proof, the woman must undergo an ordeal before the priest (Num 5:11-31).

married to a husband. This expression בְּעֻלַת־בַּעַל is unusual, occurring only here and in the story of Abimelech and Sarah in Gen 20:3.

yes, the two of them. Hebrew גַּם is an emphatic "yes" (Daube 1978, 179). Daube says the legislator is calling attention to a breakthrough in ancient Israelite society, namely, that the woman, too, is answerable to the state for wrongdoing. Paradoxically, it is evidence of an advance of the woman's position in the society. This is the first law in Hebrew legal history to demand the death of both the adulterer and the adulteress; prior to this, adultery was dealt with by the woman's husband or in some cases, her father (Daube 1971a, 10). In the story of Abimelech and Sarah, Abimelech comes under divine judgment, but not a word is said about Sarah (Genesis 20). The same is true in the case of David's adultery with Bathsheba: David is charged with a grievous sin, but not Bathsheba (2 Samuel 11-12). The law against homosexuality in Lev 20:13 states also that both parties shall die, putting homosexuality on a par with adultery (Wenham 1990-91, 362). On the subject of law and justice for women in the ANE, see Lafont 1999.

Deuteronomy 22

So you shall utterly remove the evil from Israel. A variant of the injunction in vv. 21 and 24.

23-24 *When there shall be a virgin girl betrothed to a man, and a man finds her in the city and lies with her, then you shall bring out the two of them to the gate of that city, and you shall stone them with stones, so they die.* No evidence of force here, as in the following example, which means the woman is likely a consenting partner (Driver; Rofé 1987, 137; Frymer-Kensky 1989, 93). But Washington (1998, 208-11) is not so sure, for he says the law fails to recognize that rape can take place in town. Granted. The case, in any event, is treated just like a case of adultery, with both parties being executed at the city gate (cf. 17:5). The betrothed girl is here called a "wife," אִשָּׁה (cf. Gen 29:21; CH 130, 161; *ANET*[3], 171, 173), the reason being that the bride-price has been paid and she is considered legally married, even though the marriage ceremony has not yet occurred and the husband has not taken possession of her (20:7). In the Code of Hammurabi (CH 143), a betrothed woman found to be unchaste, running around, and dishonoring her husband is executed by being thrown into the river (*ANET*[3], 172; cf. Westbrook 1990, 572-73). According to Westbrook, her offenses occurred in the past, but need not all have been during her betrothal.

the girl on account of the fact that she did not cry out in the city, and the man on account of the fact that he humbled the wife of his fellow. It is taken for granted that the woman, had she cried out for help, would have been heard and rescued. The man is convicted because he "humbled the wife of his fellow," a reason that would apply just as well to the previous case of adultery and is applied to the deflowered virgin case in vv. 28-29. This idiom is used to describe sexual relations that have brought a woman dishonor (see Note for 21:14). For the conjunction עַל־דְּבַר אֲשֶׁר, "on account of the fact," see GKC §130c note. The LXX translates with a simple ὅτι ("because").

So you shall utterly remove the evil from your midst. See above v. 21.

25-26 *But if in the field the man finds the betrothed girl, and the man grabs hold of her and lies with her, then the man alone who lay with her shall die, but to the girl you shall not do a thing; the girl has not committed a sin deserving death.* Here the man is said to use force (הֶחֱזִיק־בָּהּ, "[he] grabs hold of her"), so it is rape (Weinfeld 1972, 286; Frymer-Kensky 1998, 92). The LXX has βιασάμενος κοιμηθῇ μετ' αὐτῆς ("forcibly lies with her"). In such a case, the man is to be put to death, but the woman goes free. In CH 130, too, if a man rapes a betrothed woman, he is executed and she goes free (*ANET*[3], 171). In the Hittite Laws (HL 197; Neufeld 1951, 56; *ANET*[3], 196) a distinction is made as to whether the man seizes the woman in the mountains, in which case he is killed, or whether he seizes her in her house, in which case she is killed. If her husband finds them, he may kill them without incurring punishment. No such distinction occurs in the Laws of Eshnunna (LE 26), where it says:

If a man gives bride-money for a(nother) man's daughter, but another man seizes her forcibly without asking the permission of her father and her mother and deprives her of her virginity, it is a capital offense and he shall die. (Yaron 1969, 32-33; M. T. Roth 1995, 63; *ANET*[3], 162)

Among the modern Rwala bedouins, the relatives of a raped girl will kill both the rapist and the child of the girl, demanding also a blood price from the violator's kin for the child. The child is not allowed to live (Musil 1928, 240). On the rape of women in the ANE, see Lafont (1999, 133-71) and Edenburg (2009, 53-56).

in the field. בַּשָּׂדֶה. The term is usually taken to mean "in the open country."

but to the girl you shall not do a thing; the girl has not committed a sin deserving death. On Heb חֵטְא מָוֶת ("a sin deserving death"), see Note for 21:22. Weinfeld (1972, 292 n. 2) points out that similarities here to Middle Assyrian Laws extend even to language; in MAL A 23: "nothing shall be done (to the adulterer or the procuress)"; in MAL A 12: "there is no sin (for the woman)"; in MAL A 16: "there is no sin (for the man)."

for just as when a man rises up against his fellow and takes his life, so also this case. I.e., because she is the victim and he the violent attacker (Rashi).

27 *because he found her in the field; the betrothed girl cried, and there was no one to save her.* The girl gets the benefit of the doubt, although she could have consented to sex in the field.

28 This law is concerned with an unmarried or unbetrothed virgin whom a man has deflowered. It is assumed that the man is unmarried. The verb is וּתְפָשָׂהּ ("takes hold of her"), which need not imply force (Frymer-Kensky 1998, 92). Weinfeld (1972, 286) thinks both parties commit the act willingly. In Exod 22:15(16) the verb is פתה, "seduce," which carries more the sense of enticement or persuasion.

and they are found. I.e., they are caught in the act.

29 This case is different from the others in that sexual intercourse outside of marriage is not here a capital offense. Whether it is seduction or rape, punishment is largely a monetary issue: the girl's father must receive compensation for his loss of the bride-price (Rofé 1987, 139). A monetary settlement is even more the issue in Exod 22:15-16(16-17). But in the present law, unlike the version in the Covenant Code, it is stated that the man may not divorce the woman at any time in the future. In the Middle Assyrian Laws (MAL A 55; Driver and Miles 1935, 423; *ANET*[3], 185), if a man meets a virgin and rapes her, in the open country or in the city, at night or at the festival, the wife of the rapist, should he happen to be married, is given by the father to another man to be raped *(lex talionis)*. The father may then give his daughter to the rapist to be married, and he may not divorce her. If the rapist has no wife, he must pay a monetary fine to the father of the girl and marry her without the possibility of divorce. But the father can also accept a fine from the rapist and give his daughter to whomever he wishes (Driver and Miles 1935, 423; *ANET*³, 185). In the Covenant Code version of this law, if the father refuses to give his daughter to the man, the man must pay him the bride-price for virgins (Exod 22:16[17]), an option not given in the present law. Moran thinks there would have been the obvious difficulty of marrying off such a daughter, so the consideration was no longer practical. Young girls among the modern Rwala bedouins suffer an even harsher fate. It often happens that they get pregnant before the wedding, in which case relatives will try to help her abort. The girl will also press her lover to marry her as soon as possible. If he refuses, she will frequently commit suicide or her father or brother will kill her secretly. If she manages to escape from her tribe, she can save her life and live elsewhere, but she can never return to her tribe (Musil 1928, 240).

50 (shekels) of silver. The term "shekel" again does not appear in the Hebrew (cf. v. 19), but can be assumed. This amount is too high to be a bride-price (de Vaux 1965, 26; Moran; cf. Lev 27:4-5) and must be a fine. The 100-shekel fine in v. 19 is double this amount.

and for him she shall be a wife. For the emphasis on "him" in the expression, see v. 19.

inasmuch as he humbled her. I.e., he had sexual relations with her, bringing her dishonor. On this idiom, see v. 24. For the conjunctive expression תַּחַת אֲשֶׁר, see Note for 21:14.

he may not send her away all his days. I.e., he should not even think of divorcing her, which is the penalty laid upon the man found guilty of slandering his bride (v. 19).

23:1(22:30) *A man shall not take the wife of his father.* I.e., he shall not marry her. The verb לקח means "take (in marriage)," just as in 22:13. Reference is to a wife of one's father other than one's mother, i.e., one's stepmother. It can probably be assumed that the father has died, since a marriage of this sort would be out of the question if the father was living. But Tigay says the prohibition could also apply to a woman divorced by a father still living. The prohibition is repeated with only slight change in Lev 18:8, where it follows another prohibition against sex or marriage with one's mother (Lev 18:7; cf. CH 157). In Lev 18:6-18 is a larger list of prohibited sexual relations (and marriages) with one's "next of kin," some of these prohibitions being joined to the present law in 11QT 66:11-17 (Yadin 1983, 2:299-300). All such unions are incestuous in nature (Mueller 1979-80, 251-52). See further Good 1967, 959-60 and Lafont 1999, 173-236 on incest in the ANE. First-cousin marriages were common in ancient Israel (Isaac and Rebekah; Jacob with Rachel and Leah), but marriages with closer relatives were forbidden (de Vaux 1965, 31-32). Reuben lost his birthright for taking his father Jacob's concubine, Bilhah (1 Chr 5:1; cf. Gen 35:22; 49:3-4). But Middle Assyrian Laws (MAL A 46; Driver and Miles 1935, 414-15; *ANET*[3], 184) permitted marriage with the wife of one's father after the father's death. In Hittite law (HL 190) there is no punishment if a man violates his stepmother, so long as the father is not alive. If the father is alive, it is a capital crime (Neufeld 1951, 54; Good 1967, 959; *ANET*[3], 196).

Von Rad thinks these are very old laws regarding the extended family, predating an Israelite state. The present law is the only one of its kind in Deuteronomy, although in ch. 27 a man having sex with the wife of his father (v. 20), his sister (v. 22), or his mother-in-law (v. 23) is cursed. In Lev 20:11, too, the death penalty is specified for any man who has sex with his father's wife, and she is put to death with him. Violating these family taboos constitutes a moral lapse, and on a large scale it threatens the existence of the entire nation. Ezekiel finds Jerusalem morally bankrupt because this crime along with others like it were rife in the city (Ezek 22:10). Paul, too, considers a man in the Corinthian church living with his father's wife to be engaged in an immorality not found even among pagans (1 Cor 5:1). But another reason for the present law seems to be that it was promulgated to keep a son from inheriting his father's wives along with the rest of his property (Moran), something that happened later with Israelite kings (2 Sam 16:21-22; 1 Kgs 2:22-25). Driver points out that in ancient Arabia a man's wives passed along with his other property to his heir; thus a son could claim his father's wives (except his mother) as part of his inheritance.

and not remove the garment of his father. I.e., he shall not remove the garment of a woman belonging to his father (cf. Lev 18:8), which more or less repeats the prohibition against "taking" her in marriage. Hebrew כָּנָף (lit. "wing") refers to one of the four "corners" of an outer garment (see Note for 22:12). Exposing nudity is a euphemism for having sexual intercourse (27:20; Lev 18:6-19) or, as in the case of Ruth with Boaz, for requesting the same (Ruth 3:7). A man covering a woman with his garment means taking her as his wife (Ruth 3:9; cf. Ezek 16:8).

Message and Audience

The audience is now introduced to legislation on chastity and marriage. Hearing it from Moses will revive memories of Israel's wilderness romp with the daughters of Moab at Shittim (Num 25:1-5), a time when sexual adventurism and the worship of Baal-peor had disastrous results. Law I deals with the case of a bride charged by her husband with premarital unchastity. He is giving her a bad name in public by accusing her of wanton deeds, saying also that he did not find in her evidence of virginity when they came together in the bridal chamber. In such a case, her mother and father are to bring the bloodstained sleeping garment to the gate, repeat there the husband's charges to the city elders, and show them the garment. Upon this evidence, the elders shall punish the man for bringing a bad name upon a virgin of Israel. He will get a whipping, a heavy fine of 100 shekels of silver, to be given to the father, and he will not be able to divorce his wife any time in the future.

If, however, the husband's charges turn out to be true, that is, the garment is not produced and witnesses perhaps come forth to substantiate his claim, the woman is to be stoned at the entrance to her father's house. That is where the sin took place, and that is where she will die. She did a foolish thing by playing the whore in her father's house, and now her own shame becomes the shame also of her father and mother. Those listening are told by Moses that they must carry out such punishments in order to remove evil from their midst. This audience — and also later audiences — will therefore be warned to exalt premarital chastity. At the same time, young men will be put on notice not to marry and then seek a false pretext for divorce; young women will be put on notice not to have premarital sex; and finally, as Calvin points out, parents will be put on notice to keep a close watch on their sons and daughters, so that eventualities such as those envisioned here will not occur.

Law II is a straightforward prohibition of adultery, which the audience knows is forbidden in the seventh commandment. Everyone knows it is a wretched evil among all peoples. It carries the death penalty for both parties. Yes, the woman too is to get stoned with the man, and once again people are told that only by carrying out these punishments can the evil be removed from Israel.

Law III deals with a related case of a man finding a betrothed woman and having sex with her in the city. The bride-price has been paid, so the woman is legally married. The penalty here is the same as for adultery: both are to be brought out to the city gate and stoned to death. The woman gets the same treatment as the man, in this case because she did not cry for help. It is assumed that if she had cried out, someone in the city would have heard her. The man dies because he has brought dishonor to the wife of his fellow. People are now told for the third time that only in this manner can the evil be removed from their midst.

Law IV is similar to Law III, the one difference being that the betrothed girl in this case has had sex with another man out in the country. How much force was used is irrelevant. Here, only the man is to be put to death. The woman is given the benefit of the doubt because, if she did cry for help, no one would have heard her. Just as in a murder case: one party judged a victim, the other party judged an aggressor.

Law V deals with premarital sex between a man and a virgin girl not betrothed. The man in this case must pay the girl's father a fine of 50 shekels of silver, inasmuch as he dishonored her. He, too, may not even think of divorcing her any time in the future.

Law VI prohibits a man from marrying a woman who was the wife of his father, whatever the circumstances. It is an unseemly thing for him to remove the garment of a woman belonging to his father. The audience will know that such things did occur earlier, with unfortunate results, and later audiences will know that this law was violated by at least two individuals in the royal family. What then must a Jerusalem audience in the time of Jeremiah and Ezekiel have thought of this law when it was being violated right and left, and the nation tottered on the verge of ruin?

Q. ON PURITY AND CLEANLINESS (23:2-19[1-18])

1. Purity within Yahweh's Assembly (23:2-9[1-8])

a) Blemished Men Excluded (23:2-3[1-2])

23^2*One bruised by crushing or whose male member is cut off shall not enter into the assembly of Yahweh.* ^{3}*A mamzer shall not enter into the assembly of Yahweh; even to the tenth generation, one of his shall not enter into the assembly of Yahweh.*

b) Ammonites and Moabites Excluded (23:4-7[3-6])

^{4}*An Ammonite or Moabite shall not enter into the assembly of Yahweh; even to the tenth generation, one of theirs shall not enter into the assembly of Yahweh forever,* ^{5}*on account of the fact that they did not come to meet you with food and with water on the road when you came forth from Egypt, and because he hired against you Balaam son of Beor, from Pethor in Aram-Naharaim, to curse you.* ^{6}*But Yahweh your God was not willing to listen to Balaam, and Yahweh your God turned for you the curse into a blessing, because Yahweh your God loved you.* ^{7}*You shall not seek their peace or their friendship all your days, forever.*

c) Edomites and Egyptians Not Abominations (23:8-9[7-8])

^{8}*You shall not regard an Edomite as an abomination, because he is your brother. You shall not regard an Egyptian as an abomination, because you were a sojourner in his land.* ^{9}*Children who will be born to them in the third generation, one of theirs may enter into the assembly of Yahweh.*

Deuteronomy 23

Rhetoric and Composition

The present laws name those persons — probably all foreigners — who may not be admitted into Yahweh's assembly, some forever, some for only two generations. Those persons and their descendants who are excluded forever are mutilated and castrated men (vv. 2-3) and Ammonites and Moabites (vv. 4-7). Those persons and their descendants who are excluded for two generations, but allowed entrance in the third generation, are Edomites and Egyptians (vv. 8-9). The listing of the four nations — Ammonites, Moabites, Edomites, and Egyptians — reverses the order in which Israel encountered them on the trek from Egypt to the settlement in Transjordan (McConville).

The unit is delimited at the top end by a *setumah* in M^L prior to v. 2 and at the bottom end by a *setumah* in M^L and a section in Sam after v. 9. Law I on mutilated and castrated men is delimited at the bottom end by a *setumah* in M^L after v. 3. This law is broken into two parts by a *setumah* in M^L after v. 2. Law II is delimited from Law III by a *setumah* in M^L after v. 7. Law III in M^L is broken in two parts by a *setumah* at midpoint v. 8, separating the Edomites and the Egyptians.

Law II, thought by some to contain later expansion in vv. 5-7 (Mowinckel 1923; Galling 1950; von Rad 1953, 20), in its present form has a repetition at beginning and end:

```
....forever   עַד־עוֹלָם ...   v. 4[3]
....forever   לְעוֹלָם ...      v. 7[6]
```

That the repetition is intentional seems evident when v. 4 is compared to v. 3. In v. 3 "tenth generation" means "forever," even though that meaning is not made explicit; in v. 4, however, "forever" is made explicit.

The English numbering of verses in ch. 22 follows the Vg, being one less than that of the Hebrew. Portions of 23:2-9 are contained in 4QDeut^i and 4QpaleoDeut^r.

Notes

23:2(1) Two body mutilations will keep adult males from entering Yahweh's assembly, both of which prevent them from begetting children. The "one bruised by crushing" (פְּצוּעַ־דַּכָּא) has testicles that are bruised or crushed (Rashi), and the "one whose male member is cut off" (כְּרוּת שָׁפְכָה) has been castrated, i.e., the (scrotum and) testicles have been cut off (T^{OnqPsJ}), the penis cut off (NRSV), or both. Rashi says the penis has a cut so it no longer forcibly ejects sperm. Hebrew שָׁפְכָה is a *hapax legomenon* in the OT, but since it comes from the root שׁפך, meaning "to pour (out)," one would imagine that the term denotes the penis rather than the testicles (BDB: "fluid-duct"). Castration in antiquity usually consisted of cutting off the testicles, otherwise both the testicles and the penis (Scholz 2001, 15-16). Although Israel did practice circumcision, in fact, requiring it as a sign of the covenant, other bodily mutilations were strictly forbidden (14:1; Lev 19:28; 21:5), associated as they were with Canaanite religion (1 Kgs 18:28). It is not known whether castration was performed on Israelite citizens. An Israelite priest with crushed testicles could not approach Yahweh's altar (Lev 21:20). Animals, too, with crushed or castrated testicles were unacceptable on Yahweh's altar (Lev 22:24). This prohibition against emasculation may then be tied in ultimately with Yahweh's demand for holiness (Tigay).

Castration was also a mode of punishment in the ANE. For example, in the Middle Assyrian Laws it was carried out on a man caught having same-sex intercourse with his neighbor (MAL A 20; Driver and Miles 1935, 391; cf. 71; *ANET*^{3}, 181). Diodorus of Sicily (i 78:4) reported that the Egyptians, too, would punish a man who violated a free married woman by emasculating him. In the "Story of Two Brothers" (*ANET*^{3}, 25) the younger brother punishes himself by self-castration to vindicate himself from a false charge that he committed adultery with his older brother's wife. Another sort of punishment is related by Herodotus, who tells the story of a certain Panionius who gained a livelihood by purchasing young boys, having them castrated, and selling them at Sardis and Ephesus for huge sums, but then at a later time falling into the hands of a certain Hermotimus, who repaid his evil deeds by forcing Panionius to castrate his own sons, after which they were compelled to castrate him (Herodotus *Hist.* viii 105; Scholz 2001, 28-29).

Eunuchs, nevertheless, were found throughout the ancient world and exist in the modern era in India *(hijras),* China (Ming dynasty [1368-1644] and Qing dynasty [1644-1911]), the Arab countries (guards at holy sites in Medina and Mecca as recently as 1990), and countries in the West (choir boys and *operatic castrati*). For discussion, see Scholz 2001. In antiquity they were employed as palace and temple servants, particularly as keepers of the harem, but they also held high positions in royal courts. They could be of any class or status, from slave to king. Assyrian reliefs depict them as beardless males. Emasculation in ANE myth and ritual was closely tied in with sacral kingship and its related ideas of androgyny, asexuality, transvestitism, homosexuality, and the like. Pharaoh Akhenaton of Egypt is depicted in one artwork as emasculated (Scholz 2001, 68-69), and from the OT we learn that the Egyptian Potiphar was a סָרִיס, "eunuch" (Gen 39:1).

The Attis cult of ancient Syria had its Galli priests, who practiced self-castration. Dating from the 7th cent., this religion is known chiefly from a Hellenistic work, *The Syrian Goddess,* ascribed to Lucian, from where we get the following report describing its religious festivals:

> On appointed days, the crowd assembles at the sanctuary while many Galli and the holy men whom I have mentioned perform the rites. They cut their arms and beat one another on the back. Many stand about them playing flutes, while many others beat drums. Still others sing inspired and sacred songs. This ceremony takes place outside the temple and none of those who performs it enters the temple.
>
> On these days, too, men become Galli. For while the rest are playing flutes and performing the rites, frenzy comes upon many, and many who have come simply to watch subsequently perform this act. I will describe what they do. The youth for whom these things lie in store throws off his clothes, rushes to the center with a great shout and takes up a sword, which, I believe, has stood there for this purpose for many years. He grabs it and immediately castrates himself. Then he rushes through the city holding in his hands the parts he has cut off. He takes female clothing and women's adornment from whatever house he throws these parts into. That is what they do at the Castration. (Attridge and Oden 1976, 55)

The Attis cult traveled to Greece and Rome where it gained adherents (Scholz 2001, 60-61, 93-123).

Eunuchs were palace servants and holders of high office in the courts of Joram in Israel (2 Kgs 9:32) and both Jehoiakim and Zedekiah in Judah (Jer 29:2; 34:19; 41:16; 52:25). Ebed-melech, the Ethiopian, was a palace eunuch in Zedekiah's employ (Jer 38:7). Tadmor (1995) argues that all these individuals were actual eunuchs, i.e., castrated males. They may also have been foreigners, like Ebed-melech; we do not know. But in the postexilic period, the exclusion of eunuchs in Yahweh's assembly was completely reversed. Yahweh says in an oracle from Second Isaiah:

> For thus said Yahweh:
> To the eunuchs who keep my sabbaths,
>   and who choose in what delights me
>   and hold fast in my covenant,
> I will give to them in my house and within my walls,
>   a monument and a name
>   better than sons and daughters;
> An everlasting name I will give them
>   which shall not be cut off. (Isa 56:4-5)

In the NT, Jesus seems unconcerned about eunuchs and does not condemn them (Matt 19:12). In the early church nothing prevents Philip from baptizing an Ethiopian eunuch (Acts 8:26-39). Later on, we hear that the great church father Origen (ca. 185-255) castrated himself while a youth in obedience to Matt 19:12 (Eusebius *Hist. eccl.* vi 8:1-5; Scholz 2001, 20-21).

shall not enter into. לֹא־יָבֹא. The form here and in all the exclusion laws is apodictic, making the prohibitions strong.

assembly of Yahweh. קְהַל יְהוָה. The term denotes an assembly of all free adult males in Israel, convening when necessary to hear Yahweh's word (Deut 5:22; 9:10), decide and fight wars (Judg 20:2; 1 Sam 17:47), choose a king (1 Kgs 12:3), distribute land (Mic 2:5), and participate in feasts, fasts, and worship (Lam 1:10; Joel 2:15-16; Ps 107:32; 1 Kgs 8:65; 2 Chr 30:13, 25). The "assembly of Yahweh" appears to be synonymous with "assembly of the people of God" (Judg 20:2), "assembly of Israel" (31:30; Josh 8:35), or simply "all Israel" (1 Chr 28:8). Some think קָהָל has the same meaning as עֵדָה, "congregation" (Tigay; Num 16:1-4; 20:1-4), but Weinfeld (*EncJud*, 5:893-96) argues that קָהָל is a broader term taking in the entire population — men, women, children, and sojourners (Gen 28:3; 48:4; cf. Deut 31:12), whereas עֵדָה denotes the indigenous, mostly arms-bearing population, which would exclude sojourners. In either case, the individuals cited here cannot be included in an organized body of Israelites. In early Israel this assembly was organized along democratic lines, with Moses at the head (Num 16:1-3), and after that with individuals such as Joshua and the charismatic judges assuming a leadership role until a monarchy was established. A "primitive democracy" existed also in Mesopotamia among the preliterate Sumerians, before autocratic kingship emerged in the early 3rd mill. (Jacobsen 1943). For the status of resident aliens *(metics)* in ancient Greece, who had certain rights and obligations but were not citizens in the full sense, see Whitehead (1977, 6-7, 69-72) and MacDowell (1978, 76-78).

3(2) *A mamzer shall not enter into the assembly of Yahweh.* Here and in Zech 9:6 MT preserves the term מַמְזֵר, which, although cited in the Mishnah (*Yebam.* 4:13) and much discussed in later Jewish tradition in connection with prohibited marriages (*EncJud*, 11:840-42), is of uncertain meaning (von Rad). Michaelis said the accepted meaning was a mere guess. The LXX translated the Hebrew with ἐκ πόρνης, "one (born) of a harlot." In Jewish tradition, the term is said to refer to a person born from a forbidden sexual relationship (Rashi: adultery or incest), the point being made that such a person may not marry an Israelite woman (cf. Neh 13:23). Older English Versions translated the term as "bastard" (AV; RSV), but more recent scholars say that reference is not to one born out of wedlock, but one born of a forbidden sexual relationship (Tigay; Friedman). The NJV renders the term "misbegotten," with other English Versions translating similarly (NIV: "one born of a forbidden marriage"; NRSV: "those born of an illicit union"; REB: "descendant of an irregular union").

Michaelis (1814, 2:236-37) suggested we redivide the consonants, repoint, and read מָם זָר, where מָם has been written defectively. This would give the rendering "blemish/defect of a stranger," where the expression could then be a synecdoche for "stranger having a blemish." The blemishes in question could be any of those listed in Lev 21:16-24, which states that Israelite priests with a blemish (מוּם) — one being crushed testicles — cannot approach Yahweh's altar. Elsewhere we learn that animals with a blemish (מוּם) — including mutilation or castration — could not be sacrificed on Yahweh's altar (Lev 22:17-25; cf. Deut 15:21; 17:1). If this original reading be accepted, then the verse would be stating that blemished males from outside Israel could not be admitted into Yahweh's assembly. Reference cannot be restricted to the eunuchs just mentioned, since the law extends the prohibition to descendants, and eunuchs do not procreate. The expression, then, must have broader reference, including as it does in Leviticus 21 to persons with birth defects (limbs too long, hunchbacks, dwarfs), bringing us back to the traditional interpretation about offspring of incestuous unions. Persons begotten of incestuous unions — not all, but surely some — would have birth defects, and these are the ones now being denied entrance into Yahweh's assembly. So interpreted, the verse would build on and broaden the scope of the prior prohibition in v. 2, encompassing persons with a range of physical defects, while at the same time serving to introduce the exclusion of Ammonites and Moabites in vv. 4-7, both of whom are foreign peoples and, according to tradition, both begotten of incestuous unions (Gen 19:36-37).

even to the tenth generation, one of his shall not enter into the assembly of Yahweh. The "tenth generation" means "never" (cf. v. 4). The LXX omits the phrase, which Wevers (1995, 364) says may be due to homoeoteleuton (three words in the Greek: εἰς ἐκκλησίαν κυρίου . . . εἰς ἐκκλησίαν κυρίου; or two words in the Hebrew: בקהל יהוה . . . בקהל יהוה). The repetition in MT lays particular stress on the exclusion of these individuals.

one of his shall not enter. Hebrew לוֹ ("of his") contains a ל of reference (Driver); cf. לָכֶם in Gen 17:10; 34:15 and לָךְ in Lam 1:10.

4(3) Ammonites and Moabites are excluded from Yahweh's assembly for all time. Envisioned here are persons from these nations living in Israel as sojourners (גֵּרִים), i.e., resident aliens. The entire verse is cited in Neh 13:1-2, where it is the basis for excluding all peoples of foreign descent (v. 3). One might think that Ammon and Moab would have been excluded because of their incestuous origin, but other reasons are given here. On the Ammonites, see Note for 2:19; on the Moabites, see Note for 2:8b.

5(4) *on account of the fact that they did not come to meet you with food and with water on the road when you came forth from Egypt*. I.e., the Ammon-

Deuteronomy 23

ites failed to offer hospitality on the journey out of Egypt. This first reason in the verse applies to the Ammonites, the second reason in the verse applies to the Moabites. According to 2:29, Edom and Moab are said to have sold Israel food and drink. Since no mention is made of Ammonite hospitality, we can assume it was denied. For a different account of Edom's reception of Israel, see Num 20:14-21.

on account of the fact. עַל־דְּבַר אֲשֶׁר. On this conjunction, see Note for 22:23-24.

on the road. בַּדֶּרֶךְ. One of the very common expressions in the book of Deuteronomy, on which see Note for 1:19. For other reminders in the legal material of what happened when Israel was "on the road (out of Egypt)," see 24:9; 25:17-18.

and because he hired against you Balaam son of Beor, from Pethor in Aram-Naharaim, to curse you. The Hebrew is שָׂכַר, "he hired," which refers to Balak, king of Moab (Numbers 22). The LXX (ἐμισθώσαντο) and Vg *(conduxerunt)* have "they hired," perhaps taking Ammonites as the subject. The English Versions also adopt this reading. The subject cannot, in any case, be both the Ammonites and the Moabites because, as was mentioned, the reason here in the second half of the verse applies only to the Moabites. The biblical account of Balaam's prophecy concerning Israel appears in Numbers 22-24. An early 8th-cent. Aramaic text from Deir ʿAlla in Jordan has come to light in which mention is made of this same Balaam (Hoftijzer and Van der Kooij 1976, 179-282), showing that Balaam was a seer of some reputation.

from Pethor in Aram-Naharaim. In an Assyrian inscription of Shalmaneser III (858-824), Pethor appears as Pitru ($ANET^3$, 278). The city was located on the west bank of the Euphrates, 60 mi northeast of Aleppo, where the Euphrates meets the river Sagur (*ABD*, 5:288). This is the region of Haran and Nahor where Abraham settled after leaving Ur (Gen 11:27-32; 24:10). It is also near the ancient Syrian city of Hierapolis (modern Mambij), where the Attis cult described in *The Syrian Goddess* was active and had a shrine (see above v. 2). The LXX omits "Pethor," which could be due to homoeoteleuton (in the Hebrew: ור ... ור; in the Greek: ρ ... ρ). In Num 22:5, the LXX transliterates Pethor with Φαθουρα. The LXX also translates Aram-Naharaim (MT points it a dual: "Two Rivers of Aram") as "Mesopotamia," which is followed in the AV and older English Versions. The region in question is northern Syria (= Aram in OT), from Carchemish and Aleppo in the west to the River Khabur in the east (O'Callaghan 1948, 131-44). The two rivers would then be the Euphrates and the Khabur. The OT also refers to this region as Paddan-Aram (Gen 28:2, 5-7).

6(5) *But Yahweh ... turned for you the curse into a blessing.* See Num 23:11; 24:10. Even on the human level, a curse can be neutralized by a blessing administered as an antidote (Judg 17:2; Blank 1950-51, 94-95; Brichto 1963, 10,

102). In ancient Babylonia, curses could be removed by prayers of the one accursed, exorcism formulas spoken by the priest, or more elaborate ceremonies aimed at destroying the evil spirit or putting the sorcerer under the ban (Mercer 1915, 304-9).

because Yahweh your God loved you. See 4:37; 7:7-8; 10:15.

7(6) *You shall not seek their peace or their friendship all your days, forever.* I.e., to form alliances (Michaelis 1814, 1:322). This interpretation of Michaelis is now supported by language turning up in treaties, letters, and other documents from the ANE, where "peace" (שָׁלוֹם) and "friendship" (טוֹבָה) refer to formal alliances and good relations generally — between kings and between nations (Moran 1963c; Hillers 1964b). Also, from the Egyptian story of Sinuhe (ca. 1900) we learn that "good/friendship" comes about as a result of shared food (*ANET*³, 19; D. J. McCarthy 1982), making the response here precisely what one would expect, since the Ammonites refused Israel food and water. Israel is not being told to hate the Ammonites and the Moabites (Driver), simply to refrain from seeking alliances of "peace and friendship" with them. Feelings on the other side appear to have been mutual (Zeph 2:8). Bad blood between Judah and Ammon was evident at the fall of Jerusalem (Ezek 25:1-6), and it continued after the fall when Ishmael ben Nethaniah, a Judahite of royal descent, made a pact with King Baalis of Ammon to kill Gedaliah and take control of the remnant Judahite community (Jer 40:13–41:15). Israelite control over Moab's northern plateau ended in the mid-9th cent. (Moabite Stone line 10; cf. 2 Kgs 3:26-27), and Moab subsequently became a vassal to the Assyrians and the Babylonians. In the latter capacity, Moab is said to have aided Nebuchadnezzar in his offensive against Judah (2 Kgs 24:2). In the postexilic period, we see the present admonition being quoted and given even broader application (Ezra 9:12).

all your days. This Deuteronomic expression (see Note for 4:9) here means "forever."

8(7) *You shall not regard an Edomite as an abomination, because he is your brother.* Edom = Esau, the brother of Israel = Jacob (Gen 25:24-30). On the basis of brotherliness, Edomites are to be treated differently than the Ammonites or Moabites. Esau, after all, did graciously accept Jacob when the two met and were reconciled (Gen 33:4-11). The verb תעב ("regard as an abomination, abhor") is strong, taken by some in the present context to mean "treat as (ritually) unclean" (von Rad; Moran;·cf. Deut 7:26). But the cognate noun תּוֹעֵבָה, "abomination," has much broader meaning in Deuteronomy (see Note for 7:25), which would seem to indicate that Edomites are not to be treated as ritually impure, but simply grouped with those permanently excluded from Yahweh's assembly (v. 9b[8b]). The attitude expressed here toward Edom is early (von Rad: before Israel was a state). Edom was brought under Israelite control by David (2 Sam 8:13-14), but this ended in the reign of J(eh)oram (ca. 849-842), king of Judah (2 Kgs 8:20-22). Before — and especially after — the fall of Jerusalem, Edom seized land on Israel's southern border, and because Edom aided in the destruction of Jerusalem, Israel developed a deep hatred towards its people (Ps 137:7; Ezek 25:12-14; Obadiah). On the history and geography of Edom, see Note for 2:4.

You shall not regard an Egyptian as an abomination, because you were a sojourner in his land. The Egyptians are given preferential treatment because they were hosts to Israel when Joseph came down to Egypt (Rashi). Another very early attitude, one overlooking the subsequent slavery Israel endured under Egyptian rule, and one not reflecting the later disillusionment Israel had about Egyptian help that did not come (Isa 30:3-5, 7; 31:1-3). Deuteronomy has a particular concern for the welfare of the "sojourner" (גֵּר), who has dependent status in Israel (see Note for 5:13-14). Israel is to love the sojourner because Yahweh loves the sojourner, also because Israel itself was once a sojourner in Egypt (10:18-19).

9(8) Third generation offspring of both peoples may be admitted to Yahweh's assembly. In Isa 56:3-8, foreigners are permitted temple access if they keep the Sabbath and hold fast to the covenant. Later Jewish tradition specified that other peoples could be admitted at once if they acknowledged the tenets of Judaism (Rashi).

Message and Audience

The audience is here told that certain individuals cannot be admitted into the assembly of Yahweh. Males with bruised testicles or who have been castrated are excluded forever. In fact, no foreigner having a blemish can ever enter the assembly, which the audience may perceive as referring to individuals born from incestuous unions. Moreover, no Ammonite or Moabite can ever be a full part of Israel. The Ammonites are excluded because they refused time-honored hospitality to Israel in the wilderness, and Balak, king of Moab, because he hired Balaam from afar to come and curse Israel. The latter came to nothing, however, since Yahweh turned Balaam's curse into a blessing. Israel is told finally that it must not seek alliances of peace and friendship with either people, now or in the future.

As for the Edomites and the Egyptians, they must also be excluded from Yahweh's assembly, but only for two generations. Children of the third generation may come in. People are told not to treat Edom with abhorrence, because of long-standing brotherly ties. The same restraint is to be exercised toward Egypt, because it hosted Israel as a sojourner in the time of Joseph. Moses wants to implant in Israel a benevolent attitude based on brotherhood and benevolence to Israel in times past. The audience must know that sojourners from Edom and Egypt are not to be excluded forever, remembering that Edom is a brother and Egypt was a kind host in years past.

2. Purity and Cleanliness in the Camp (23:10-15[9-14])

23 ¹⁰*When you go out as a camp against your enemies, then you shall keep yourself from any bad thing.* ¹¹*When there is among you a man who is not clean from a night accident, then he shall go outside the camp; he shall not enter into the midst of the camp.* ¹²*And it shall be at the turn of evening he shall wash himself with water, and when the sun goes down he may come into the midst of the camp.* ¹³*And a place you shall have for yourself outside the camp, and you shall go there outside;* ¹⁴*and a spike you shall have for yourself among your gear, and it shall be when you sit down outside, then you shall dig a hole with it and you shall turn back and cover up what has come out of you,* ¹⁵*for Yahweh your God walks about in the midst of your camp, to deliver you and to set your enemies before you, so your camp shall be holy, that he not see among you an indecent thing and turn away from you.*

Rhetoric and Composition

The laws in vv. 10-19 are miscellaneous in nature, following the collection brought together around the sixth commandment, "You shall not commit adultery" (see Rhetoric and Composition for 12:1-4). The first law on maintaining cleanliness in the camp reflects Israel's early holy wars (von Rad) and in this respect has something in common with the laws of 20:1-9 and 21:10-14. The present unit is delimited at the top end by a *setumah* in M^L and a section in Sam before v. 10 and at the bottom end by a *setumah* in M^L and a section in Sam after v. 15.

The law on cleanliness in the camp is linked to the exclusion laws immediately preceding: the key expressions are "he shall (not)/may (not) enter into" (Rofé 1988b, 273):

he shall not enter into . . .	לֹא־יָבֹא	v. 2[1]
he shall not enter into . . .	לֹא־יָבֹא	v. 3[2]
he shall not enter into . . .	לֹא־יָבֹא	
he shall not enter into . . .	לֹא־יָבֹא	v. 4[3]
he shall not enter into . . .	לֹא־יָבֹא	
he may enter into . . .	יָבֹא	v. 9[8]
he shall not enter into . . .	לֹא יָבֹא	v. 11[10]
he may enter into . . .	יָבֹא	v. 12[11]

Deuteronomy 23

This law also has keyword linkage to the next law regarding fugitive slaves. One of the repeated verbs is יָשַׁב, "to sit, dwell" (G. A. Smith; Rofé 1988b, 273), the other is נצל, "to deliver" (Braulik 1992, 172):

when you sit down outside ...	בְּשִׁבְתְּךָ חוּץ	v. 14[13]
to deliver you ...	לְהַצִּילְךָ	v. 15[14]
... who will deliver himself	אֲשֶׁר־יִנָּצֵל	v. 16[15]
he shall dwell in your midst ...	יֵשֵׁב בְּקִרְבְּךָ	v. 17[16]

This law has further links by association to the final miscellaneous law in the group on sacred prostitution, with the idea of "holiness" in v. 15 being picked up by the two terms for "holy prostitute" in v. 18 (cf. Rofé 1988b, 273-74):

so your camp shall be holy ...	וְהָיָה מַחֲנֶיךָ קָדוֹשׁ	v. 15[14]
there shall not be a female holy prostitute ...	לֹא־תִהְיֶה קְדֵשָׁה	v. 18[17]
and there shall not be a male holy prostitute ...	וְלֹא־יִהְיֶה קָדֵשׁ	

Portions of 23:10-15 are contained in 4QDeut[i] and 4QpaleoDeut[r].

Notes

23:10(9) *When you go out as a camp against your enemies.* I.e., when you go out in holy war (20:1; 21:10). Hebrew מַחֲנֶה, meaning "a host of people encamped," is an accusative defining how the going forth will take place (Driver; cf. GKC §118q).

then you shall keep yourself from any bad thing. In 17:1 the "bad thing" (דָּבָר רָע) is a physical defect rendering an animal unacceptable for sacrifice, but here the blemish relates to camp uncleanliness, of which two examples are given. These are probably only representative (Tigay), since the people are told to keep themselves from "any bad thing." For other conditions rendering a person unclean, and requiring an exit from camp, see Num 5:1-4.

11(10) *from a night accident.* מִקְּרֵה־לָיְלָה. An emission of semen; a "wet dream" (cf. Lev 15:16-17).

12(11) *at the turn of evening.* I.e., at dusk, when the new day begins (Gen 1:5).

he shall wash himself with water. See also Lev 15:16. Sexual intercourse also required a subsequent washing with water (Lev 15:18).

13(12) *a place.* Hebrew יָד is here a (designated) place for relieving oneself (Rashi).

Deuteronomy 23

14(13) *a spike.* Hebrew יָתֵד is a tent peg (Judg 4:21), which, having a pointed end, can do double-duty for digging a hole in the ground; afterwards it is to be used to cover up one's excrement.

your gear. Hebrew אָזֵן is a *hapax legomenon* in the OT, perhaps referring more specifically to the weapons one is carrying.

15(14) Another indication that the present law is promulgated against a holy war background. Here is a very anthropomorphic view of Yahweh God, in which he is perceived as touring the camp and not wanting to look upon anything indecent. Nowhere else in Deuteronomy is Yahweh so portrayed. The D source generally has Yahweh's dwelling place in heaven (von Rad 1991, 117). Anthropomorphisms such as the present one are common in the J source (Gen 3:8-24; 18:20-33), although they do occur elsewhere (2 Sam 7:6-7; Num 5:3). Here, in his walk through the camp, Yahweh must not see anything indecent, the reason being that his presence "is irreconcilable with uncleanliness" (Daube 1969a, 47; 1971a, 8).

to deliver you and to set your enemies before you. See 20:4. Another example of Hebrew rhetoric reversing logical progression. Yahweh will first set the enemies before Israel, then carry out his deliverance. Cf. "gird up your loins, get up" (Jer 1:17); "they shall fall . . . they shall stumble" (Jer 6:15); "a people comes . . . a great nation is roused" (Jer 6:22), and elsewhere.

so your camp shall be holy. "Holiness" means being set apart from anything unclean (G. A. Smith; Muilenburg, *IDB*, 2:619). An Israel engaged in holy war must be ritually pure (1 Sam 21:6[5]; 2 Sam 11:11), and its camp must also be holy (von Rad; Moran).

that he not see among you an indecent thing and turn away from you. In holy war, it is nothing short of disaster if Yahweh should turn away (1:42). Later, through the prophet Jeremiah, Yahweh promises that his eternal covenant will be one "in which I will not turn away from them" (Jer 32:40). In times past, Yahweh followed behind his covenant people and saw detestable sights, e.g., disgusting idols, and turned away from them. But in the future this will not happen.

an indecent thing. Hebrew עֶרְוַת דָּבָר is lit. "nakedness of a thing." The expression recurs in 24:1. Daube (1969a, 31-32, 50) says this is a reference to shame, a shame approaching guilt.

Message and Audience

The audience is instructed in this law about the importance of cleanliness in the camp. When Israel goes forth in holy war, the army and the camp both must be in a state of purity. For example, if a man becomes unclean due to a night accident, he must go outside the camp and stay there until evening, at which time

Deuteronomy 23

he is to wash himself and then return. There must also be a designated place outside the camp for relieving oneself. Personal matters of such a nature cannot be done in the camp. When going outside, each person must carry along a spike for digging a hole; then when finished, he must not forget to cover up his excrement. Yahweh God walks about in the midst of the camp, and the camp must be holy. If Yahweh sees anything unseemly, he will turn away.

This law reflects the time when Israel was fighting its early holy wars, moving from place to place. But the law could also have relevance after settlement in the land, when militias were called up to engage an enemy in some open battlefield.

3. Hospitality to Runaway Slaves (23:16-17[15-16])

23¹⁶*You shall not give up a slave to his master, who will deliver himself to you from his master;* ¹⁷*with you he shall dwell in your midst, in the place that he shall choose within one of your gates, in what seems good to him. You shall not oppress him.*

Rhetoric and Composition

This law providing for asylum to slaves escaping to Israel is delimited at the top end by a *setumah* in M^L and a section in Sam before v. 16 and at the bottom end by a *setumah* in M^L after v. 17. It is linked to the prior law on camp cleanliness by keywords, one of which is the verb יָשַׁב, "to sit, dwell" (G. A. Smith; Rofé 1988b, 273), the other being the verb נָצַל, "to deliver" (Braulik 1992, 172):

... who will deliver himself	אֲשֶׁר־יִנָּצֵל	v. 16[15]
he shall dwell in your midst ...	יֵשֵׁב בְּקִרְבְּךָ	v. 17[16]
when you sit down outside ...	בְּשִׁבְתְּךָ חוּץ	v. 14[13]
to deliver you ...	לְהַצִּילְךָ	v. 15[14]

Portions of 23:16-17 are contained in 4QDeut^i.

Notes

23:16(15) Since v. 17 makes it clear that the fugitive is to dwell in Israel ("in your midst ... within one of your gates"), we can assume that the law pertains to a slave who has entered Israel from a foreign country (T), perhaps to escape harsh treatment from his master. But Moran says the law could also apply to a native Israelite who was sold to a foreign master but somehow managed to escape back to Israel. The law, in any case, is remarkable, having no equivalent in slave legislation of the ANE (Mendelsohn 1949, 63-64). Mendelsohn, however, does note a possible parallel in the Code of Hammurabi (CH 280), where a native Babylonian slave who was sold into a foreign country and had fled from there was, upon his return home, set free. Runaway slaves were common in the ancient world, as we learn both from the Bible (Gen 16:6; 1 Sam 25:10; 1 Kgs 2:39-40; Philemon) and surviving Babylonian documents (Driver and Miles 1952, 105-6). The Code of Hammurabi contains a set of laws pertaining to fugitive slaves (CH 15-20; $ANET^3$, 166-67), where anyone caught aiding their flight or harboring them becomes guilty of a capital offense. Both are counted as theft. Those returning slaves to their owners get a reward.

Things were little different in earlier law codes (LI 12; $ANET^3$, 160; LE 49, 50; $ANET^3$, 163), where harboring runaway slaves for a specified number of days is counted as theft and restitution is required. But all are escapees within the country, for which the OT has no comparable laws. The Ur-Nammu Code (LUN 14; $ANET^3$, 524) and later Hittite Laws (HL 22-24; Neufeld 1951, 6-7; $ANET^3$, 190) are concerned mainly with specifying rewards for those returning runaway slaves. If slaves should escape out of the country, extradition clauses in international treaties facilitate their return. For example, among the Alalakh texts is a treaty calling for the return of a fugitive slave — male or female — to its owner (no. 5 in $ANET^3$, 531; no. 3 in Wiseman 1953, 29). When the present law was promulgated Israel presumably had no treaties with other nations. During the monarchy, David gave kind treatment to the Egyptian slave of an Amalekite. It was in the national interest to do so, therefore he promised not to return the slave to his master (1 Sam 30:11-15). Weinfeld (1972, 272-73) argues that the humanistic character of this law reflects a distinctly wisdom attitude, comparing it to the warning not to slander a servant to his master in Prov 30:10.

17(16) *with you he shall dwell in your midst.* The Hebrew puts the emphasis on "with you." What the status of this runaway will be in Israel is unclear. Tigay thinks he will become a resident alien. An Aramaic treaty (Sefire III: 4-7; $ANET^3$, 660; Greenfield 1991) that has turned up instructs a vassal not to give any food or housing to a runaway upon arrival in Aleppo, which he might otherwise do. He is to hold the fugitive till the suzerain comes to fetch him. Greenfield says such a clause is otherwise unknown in treaties of the ANE.

in the place that he shall choose. The verb בחר ("choose") is a favorite of the writer of Deuteronomy, having elsewhere in the book important theological implications (see Note for 12:5).

within one of your gates. בְּאַחַד שְׁעָרֶיךָ. Omitted in the LXX, probably attributable to haplography (homoeoarcton: ב . . . ב). On this common expression in Deuteronomy, where "gates" = "cities," see Note for 5:13-14.

You shall not oppress him. Israel's own oppression in Egypt is remembered; such must not be repeated on individuals seeking refuge in Israel (cf. Exod 22:20[21]; Lev 19:33-34).

Message and Audience

The audience here is told not to give up an escaped slave to his master. Presumably they will know that the law pertains only to foreigners who have come to Israel seeking asylum. Such individuals are to be allowed residence within Israel, to live wherever they choose. And because they remain foreigners, they are to be treated like any other resident alien and not to be oppressed.

4. No Holy Prostitutes! (23:18-19[17-18])

23 ¹⁸*There shall not be a female holy prostitute from the daughters of Israel, and there shall not be a male holy prostitute from the sons of Israel.* ¹⁹*You shall not bring the hire of a whore or the price of a dog into the house of Yahweh your God for any vow, because the two of them are an abomination to Yahweh your God.*

Rhetoric and Composition

The present law prohibits holy prostitutes among the sons and daughters of Israel, stating also that money paid to such individuals may not be used to pay vows at Yahweh's sanctuary. The unit is delimited at the top end in M^L by a *setumah* before v. 18. There is no section in M^L or Sam after v. 19, but a break there is nevertheless required *(BHS)*.

This law is linked by association to the first law in the group on cleanliness in the camp, the two terms for "holy prostitute" picking up on "holy" in v. 15 (cf. Rofé 1988b, 273-74):

so your camp shall be holy . . .	וְהָיָה מַחֲנֶיךָ קָדוֹשׁ	v. 15[14]
there shall not be a female holy prostitute . . .	לֹא־תִהְיֶה קְדֵשָׁה	v. 18[17]
and there shall not be a male holy prostitute . . .	וְלֹא־יִהְיֶה קָדֵשׁ	

The law is also linked by association to the next group dealing with theft (23:20-26[19-25]), where the keywords are "vow/make a vow" (G. A. Smith; Rofé 1988b, 274, who cites ibn Ezra):

Deuteronomy 23

v. 19[18]	לְכָל־נֶדֶר	for any vow
v. 22[21]	כִּי־תִדֹּר נֶדֶר . . .	When you make a vow . . .
v. 23[22]	וְכִי תֶחְדַּל לִנְדֹּר	But when you refrain from vowing
v. 24[23]	כַּאֲשֶׁר נָדַרְתָּ	. . . according to what you have vowed . . .

Portions of 23:18-19 are contained in 4QDeut^g.

Notes

23:18(17) Hebrew קְדֵשָׁה and קָדֵשׁ denote a woman and man respectively who are associated with sacred worship (Heb קדשׁ = "to be holy, sacred, set apart") and generally taken to be prostitutes, since the law goes on to state that "the hire of a whore or the price of a dog" shall not be brought to Yahweh's house in payment of a vow (v. 19). From other OT texts (Gen 38:21-22; 1 Kgs 14:23-24; 2 Kgs 23:7; Hos 4:14) we learn that such individuals were associated with harlotry or Canaanite fertility practices, which according to later reform standards were judged incompatible with Yahweh worship. Asa and Jehoshaphat did away with the male prostitutes (1 Kgs 15:12; 22:47[46] NRSV; REB), and Josiah tore down the temple quarters of female prostitutes devoted to Asherah (2 Kgs 23:7). The present law states that such individuals are not to be found among Israel's sons and daughters.

The T has a completely different reading of v. 18, which directly or indirectly has influenced later interpretation. It says: "An Israelite woman may not marry a male slave, and an Israelite male may not marry a female slave." Then in v. 19 it reproduces the prostitution language of the biblical text in a straightforward manner, with the result that v. 19 is disassociated from v. 18. Barstad (1984, 27-28) attempts to do the same more recently, but the two verses must be taken as a unit. Rashi connects them, although he takes קְדֵשָׁה and קָדֵשׁ to be just ordinary prostitutes, men and women ever ready for illicit intercourse. He is followed here by Ramban* (Chavel 1976, 288-91) and many modern Jewish interpreters. But there is also support for this interpretation in the reading of the LXX, which translates the terms of v. 18 as πόρνη and πορνεύων, both meaning "prostitute." The Vg terms *meretrix* and *scortator* have similar meanings. It has thus been argued that since זוֹנָה and קְדֵשָׁה occur together in the Bible, e.g., in Gen 38:15, 21-22; Hos 4:14, both terms must mean "prostitute" (Gruber 1986, 135; Tigay). Yet neither text proves that the terms are synonymous, for which reason it is argued by others that the קְדֵשָׁה is no ordinary fe-

---

*Ramban is short for Nachmanides, a rabbi in Spanish Jewry who lived in A.D. 1195-1270 and published a commentary on the Torah.

male prostitute, but rather a sacred female prostitute (Driver; G. E. Wright; Moran; Yamauchi 1973; Friedman). Friedman thinks that in the Judah and Tamar story of Genesis 38 is a play on the two terms, which there may be. In Hos 4:14 the two terms simply appear in parallelism.

The LXX expands the present verse with these words:

οὐκ ἔσται τελεσφόρος	there shall not be a sorceress
ἀπὸ θυγατέρων Ισραηλ	among the daughters of Israel
καὶ οὐκ ἔσται τελισκόμενος	there shall not be a temple initiate
ἀπὸ υἱῶν Ισραηλ.	among the sons of Israel.

Gruber (1986, 135-36 n. 8) argues that the LXX is preserving a doublet because the translator is unable to decide which of two manuscript readings is original (cf. Talmon 1960, 151), but a better explanation is that MT omits due to haplography (homoeoteleuton: מבני ישראל . . . מבני ישראל). In a reconstructed 4QDeut^g the added words of LXX cannot be made to fit (White Crawford 1993, 38; Ulrich, Cross et al. 1995, 56).

There shall not be a female holy prostitute from the daughters of Israel. There has been considerable discussion in recent years over the term קְדֵשָׁה ("female holy prostitute"), whether this woman is indeed a sacred prostitute, and more generally whether cultic prostitution as an institution existed at all in neighboring cultures, from where it was imported into Israel. "Cultic prostitution" is usually taken to mean an institution in which prostitutes — mostly female, but occasionally male — exist as part of the temple staff or work to benefit temple worship by dedicating their earnings to the deity. A related assumption is that the sponsoring religion is one in which fertility — both divine and human — plays a major role. Cultic prostitution is widely believed to have flourished in the ancient world, being particularly indigenous to Canaanite and Phoenician cults and the Ishtar-Astart cult in the ANE (Driver; G. A. Smith; von Rad; Lambert 1957-58, 195; 1960, 102-3; Moran; Yamauchi 1973, 215, 218-19; Friedman; cf. Amos 2:8). The Babylonian "Counsels of Wisdom" give this advice to men in search of wives:

> Do not marry a harlot whose husbands are six thousand.
> An Ishtar-woman [*ištarîtu*] vowed to a god,
> A sacred prostitute whose favors are unlimited,
> Will not lift you out of your trouble:
> In your quarrel she will slander you. (*ANET*³, 427)

Lambert translates *ištarîtu* as "temple harlot," but says regarding cultic prostitution: "No one doubts its prevalence, especially with the cult of ISHTAR, but little is known of its functioning."

References to cultic prostitution in the ancient world are not lacking in classical authors, e.g., Herodotus (*Hist.* i 199) and Strabo (*Geogr.* xii 3:36). Herodotus reports on the custom in Babylonia — also in Cyprus — that every woman once in her life must sit in the temple of Aphrodite (= Ishtar) and have intercourse with the first stranger to approach her. The money she receives is then considered sacred. Strabo reports on a festival in Comana (Armenia) where a woman gives her body (σώματος) for gain in dedication to the goddess. While some are ready to dismiss the testimony of Herodotus, others (Lambert 1957-58, 196; Barstad 1984; van der Toorn 1989) are hesitant to do so, particularly when it is corroborated by the testimony of Strabo. Also, the Letter of Jeremiah (= Baruch) 6:43 could be referring to the same practice reported by Herodotus. Yamauchi (1973, 220) points out, too, that many of the church fathers attest to cultic prostitution in Aphrodite worship on Cyprus and notes that the practice exists also in modern times in West Africa and India (p. 213, citing J. G. Frazer).

At the same time, hard evidence for cultic prostitution in Egyptian, Assyrian, Neo-Babylonian, and Ugaritic texts is either ambiguous or lacking altogether. It is argued that Akk *qadištu* may simply mean "woman of special status," i.e., one who plays a role in fertility and childbirth, can herself marry and have children, and is sometimes a wet nurse, but is not a prostitute (*CAD*, 13:48-50). Evidence of prostitution is also negative with respect to usages of the Ug *qdšm*, who seem to be nonpriestly temple personnel dedicated to a deity and who are free to marry and have children (van der Toorn 1989, 203). But Kornfeld (*qdš*, in *TDOT*, 12:524) says that Akk *qadištu* did at an earlier time mean "cult prostitute." In the Neo-Babylonian period the status of these women was diminished so that they were considered to be simply street prostitutes. From the Middle Assyrian Laws (no. 40) we learn that a married *qadiltum* must be veiled, whereas an unmarried *qadiltum* must be unveiled (*ANET*³, 183). This would seem to indicate that the unveiled *qadiltum* is a prostitute, since the law goes on to say that a harlot on the streets must also go unveiled. Rules regarding veiled and unveiled women were strictly enforced in antiquity (cf. Lambert 1957-58, 194). So while the Akkadian and Ugaritic terms do not attest acts of prostitution for individuals so named, it is still possible that among the temple-related tasks of these individuals prostitution could have been one of them. The same is true with respect to the Hebrew terms appearing here and elsewhere in the OT. Van der Toorn (1989, 203) says with regard to Israelite קְדֵשִׁים:

> Their functions need not be narrowed down to those of prostitutes; they may have performed a variety of menial tasks in the sanctuary as well. It cannot be denied, though, that during some periods they did also function as prostitutes in the service of the Temple. According to 2 Kgs 23:7 they had

special rooms in the Jerusalem Temple, a state of affairs intolerable to the zealous reformers, yet apparently accepted by the clergy in earlier times. Prostitutes operating, as it were, in the shadow of the Temple, then, existed in ancient Israel.

Van der Toorn (1989; *ABD*, 5:511-12) goes on to suggest that the קְדֵשָׁה was a woman led to prostitute herself in order to keep a solemn vow — a perfectly ordinary vow — when there was no other way to get the needed money. Her husband could be away, ignorant of, or otherwise unwilling to support her pious act. Here the important biblical text is Proverbs 7, particularly v. 14, although in v. 10 it says that the woman disguises herself as a זוֹנָה ("prostitute, harlot") in order to capture her man. Van der Toorn (1989, 204-5) says: "This prostitution may be called 'sacred' insofar as its revenues were spent in the payment of vows and were thus turned over to the Temple." This explanation is worthy of consideration, although it is also possible that the woman of Proverbs 7 may simply be using the payment of a vow as a pretext for seducing a man into an illicit affair.

there shall not be a male holy prostitute from the sons of Israel. The קָדֵשׁ ("male holy prostitute") is probably a sodomite (*Sifre Deut* §260; Calvin; so AV), i.e., a practicing homosexual associated directly or indirectly with temple worship. Tigay says he may be a male prostitute, either heterosexual or homosexual. Male prostitutes associated with Canaanite worship in the time of Rehoboam (1 Kgs 14:23-24) were severely censured by the Deuteronomic Historian, who commended Asa for doing away with them (1 Kgs 15:12) and Jehoshaphat the same for exterminating those who remained (1 Kgs 22:47[46]). Homosexuality is explicitly forbidden in Lev 18:22; 20:13, and perhaps indirectly in Deut 22:5; 23:2[1]. It is also roundly condemned in the NT, where it says that those engaging in this perversion cannot expect to inherit the kingdom of God (Rom 1:27; 1 Cor 6:9; Phil 3:2; Rev 22:15).

19(18) *You shall not bring the hire of a whore or the price of a dog into the house of Yahweh your God for any vow.* Hebrew אֶתְנַן זוֹנָה ("hire of a whore") is "dirty money" that Yahweh will not accept in payment for a vow. For other uses of "hire," meaning "hire of a whore," see Mic 1:7; Isa 23:17-18; Ezek 16:34. Payment could be made with a lamb (Gen 38:16-17), which Rashi says may not then be brought for a sacrifice. The same is true with respect to the "price of a dog" (מְחִיר כֶּלֶב), which is payment made to a male prostitute (Moran; cf. the Phoenician Inscription from Larnaca, *CIS* 86 A 15, B 10; G. A. Cooke 1903, 66-68). For another interpretation of the term "dog" in the Larnaca Inscription, see Peckham 1968. Some think the prostitute here is a homosexual (Wenham 1990-91, 362), where it has been suggested that he performs using the stance of a dog. In the Lachish Letters and other extrabiblical texts, "dog" is a self-abasing term, i.e., a humble reference to oneself as the (faithful) servant of his master, the (loyal) subject of the king, and so on (von Rad; D. W. Thomas 1960). But that is not its meaning here (*pace* Thomas), where it is a term of degradation. In the NT, see Phil 3:2; Rev 22:15.

vow. נֶדֶר. Here a "votive offering."

because the two of them are an abomination to Yahweh your God. I.e., the two payments are. On this phrase, see Hallo 1985-86; on "abomination," see Note for 7:25. The practices of male holy prostitutes and their Canaanite predecessors are considered abominations in 1 Kgs 14:24.

Message and Audience

The audience hears Moses instruct his people now on the holy prostitutes — male and female — who are part of the religious scene among the Canaanites, saying that such individuals have no place among the daughters and sons of Israel. What is more, hire paid to such individuals cannot be brought into the house of Yahweh in payment of a vow. Dirty money from whores and dogs is an abomination to Yahweh. This law as promulgated may date from the time of the temple ("house of Yahweh"), but otherwise it could be as early as the others warning Israel not to adopt practices of the Canaanites, who currently inhabit the land.

R. Laws on Loans, Vows, and Theft (23:20-26[19-25])

1. Loans to Brothers Interest-Free (23:20-21[19-20])

23²⁰*You shall not lend at interest to your brother — interest on silver, interest on food, interest on anything on which one pays interest.* ²¹*To a foreigner you may lend at interest, but to your brother you shall not lend at interest, in order that Yahweh your God will bless you in every undertaking of your hand upon the land that you are entering to take possession of it.*

2. Pay Your Vows Promptly! (23:22-24[21-23])

23²²*When you make a vow to Yahweh your God, you shall not delay to make good on it, for Yahweh your God will surely require it from you, and it will be a sin in you.* ²³*But when you refrain from vowing, it will not be a sin in you.* ²⁴*That which comes out of your lips you shall be careful and do according to what you have vowed voluntarily to Yahweh your God, what you promised with your mouth.*

3. No Crop Stealing! (23:25-26[24-25])

23²⁵ *When you enter into the vineyard of your fellow, then you may eat grapes according to your desire, your fill, but you shall not put any into your vessel.* ²⁶ *When you enter into the standing grain of your fellow, then you may pluck ears with your hand, but you shall not wield a sickle upon the standing grain of your fellow.*

Rhetoric and Composition

Here begins a new collection of laws expanding upon the eighth commandment, "You shall not steal" (see Rhetoric and Composition for 12:1-4). The three laws beginning the collection have to do with (1) lending practices (vv. 20-21); (2) payment of vows (vv. 22-24); and (3) eating from a fellow's vineyard (vv. 25-26). The LXX reverses the two commands in vv. 25-26, placing the one about plucking grain before the one about picking grapes.

There is no section before v. 20 in M^L or Sam, but *BHS* makes a break there. Delimitation at the bottom end is marked by a *setumah* in M^L and sections in 4QDeut^a, 4QDeut^i, and Sam after v. 26, which is also the chapter division. Law I on lending at interest is separated from Law II on the payment of vows by a *setumah* in M^L and sections in Sam and 4QDeut^f after v. 21. Law II is separated from Law III on eating from a fellow's vineyard by a *setumah* in M^L and a section in 4QDeut^i after v. 24. 4QDeut^{k2} upon reconstruction has no section after v. 24, nor does Sam.

Law II links up with the law regarding holy prostitutes concluding the prior collection (vv. 18-19) by the keywords "vow"/"make a vow" (G. A. Smith; Rofé 1988b, 274):

When you make a vow . . .	כִּי־תִדֹּר נֶדֶר . . .	v. 22[21]
But when you refrain from vowing	וְכִי תֶחְדַּל לִנְדֹּר	v. 23[22]
. . . according to what you vowed . . .	כַּאֲשֶׁר נָדַרְתָּ	v. 24[23]
for any vow	לְכָל־נֶדֶר	v. 19[18]

Portions of 23:20-26 are contained in 4QDeut^a, 4QDeut^f, 4QDeut^g, 4QDeut^i, and 4QDeut^{k2}. The Roberts Papyrus (P. Ryl. Gk. 458), an early Greek text dated to the end of the 2nd cent. B.C. (C. H. Roberts 1936, 37), contains portions of 23:25-26.

Notes

23:20(19) There are two other laws prohibiting usury (lending at interest) in the Pentateuch, one in the Covenant Code (Exod 22:24[25]) and another in the Holiness Code (Lev 25:35-37). Both give as a reason for not lending at interest the obligation to provide relief for a fellow Israelite who has become poor or needy. Poverty is a precarious state, from which it may become impossible to recover. The present law may also have the poor in view; nevertheless, it says nothing about the economic status of the borrower. One must not lend at interest to any Israelite, which would include even someone who is solvent. But Deuteronomy and the OT generally are much concerned over the plight of the poor and about reducing the gulf between rich and poor. We see this in the law of sabbatical debt release (Deut 15:1-11) and in the law of sabbatical slave release (Deut 15:12-18; cf. Exod 21:2-11) and may assume it to be a consideration here too. The Jubilee Year release of Lev 25:39-46 had a similar egalitarian aim in ancient Israel.

Such a law is rare in the ancient world, where lending at interest was widely practiced but still looked upon with great disfavor, being compared to bribery, theft, and other forms of avarice. Yet we have ancient texts censuring usury. The Code of Hammurabi deals with merchants who charge too much interest or trade in other unscrupulous ways (CH 90-96; *ANET*³, 169-70). In the Egyptian *Book of the Dead*, a mortuary text dated between 1550 and 950, the deceased tells the posthumous court that he has not practiced usury (*ANET*³, 35, B14). And in the "Hymn to the Sun God," an Old Babylonian text that turned up in the library of Assurbanipal (668-627), it says:

> What is he benefited who invests money in unscrupulous trading missions?
> He is disappointed in the matter of profit and loses his capital.
> As for him who invests money in distant trading missions and pays one shekel per . . .
> It is pleasing to Šamaš, and he will prolong his life.
> (Lambert 1960, 133, lines 103-6; *ANET*³, 388, ii)

The present law may also be compared with pre-Islamic and Islamic law among the Arabs, where in the case of the latter, a prohibition against usurious loans exists in the Koran (Neufeld 1955, 408-9). The OT looks upon lending at interest with disdain (Ps 15:5; Prov 28:8), although lending itself is highly praised, being equated with generosity and raised to the level of moral obligation for any who wish to conduct their affairs with justice (Pss 37:25-26; 112:5). This same view is expressed by the prophet Ezekiel (Ezek 18:8, 13, 17; 22:12) and repeated later by Josephus (*Ant.* 4.266). For Ezekiel it is lawful and right not to lend at interest, this being one practice among many that distinguishes the righteous from the unrighteous. Jeremiah, answering his critics, says: "I have not loaned, and they have not loaned to me, (yet) all of them curse me" (Jer 15:10).

Classical authors took a dim view of lending practices. Plato (*Leg.* v. 742) spoke out against lending at interest, and Aristotle (*Pol.* i 3:23) said usury was not in accord with nature but involved a person's taking things from another, for which reason it is most reasonably hated. Its gain comes from the money itself and not from that for which money was invented. Cicero (*Off.* ii 25) could do no better than cite a famous quote of Cato*:

> When he [Cato] was asked what was the most profitable feature of an estate, he replied: 'Raising cattle successfully.' What next to that? 'Raising cattle with fair success.' And next? 'Raising cattle with but slight success.' And fourth? 'Raising crops.' And when his questioner said, 'How about money-lending?' Cato replied: 'How about murder?'

Lending at interest is regulated in the Laws of Eshnunna (LE 18A, 19-21; *ANET*^{3}, 162) and the Code of Hammurabi (CH 48-51, 66, 88-95, 99-100; *ANET*^{3}, 168-70; Maloney 1974, 1-11). But a Ugaritic text from Ras Shamra (*ANET*^{3}, 629) contains a request for an interest-free loan, where appeal is made to the fact that the contract is drawn up between gentlemen (= free-men). Why then is lending at interest practiced in neighboring societies but prohibited within Israel's indigenous population? It is said that Israel, even in the time of Deuteronomy, was a nation almost exclusively of peasants (von Rad), one with a simple agrarian economy and without a money market of any significance (Gamoran 1971, 127-28; Tigay). This made it unlike neighboring economies, and even more unlike modern economies where commercial ventures and developing industry require increased capital and increased income (Driver), and where lending practices are highly regulated.

In Israel, loans were made largely for relieving those who had fallen on hard times (cf. Deut 15:1-6). But Neufeld (1955, 371-74, 400) warns against overstating the primitiveness of the ancient Hebrew economy, for even the Covenant Code reflects an advanced agricultural economy well acquainted with commercial transactions. Comparisons with other agricultural and cattle-breeding societies show a similar sophistication. At a later time, however, Jews did lend to other Jews at interest. It happened in postexilic Judah (Neh 5:1-13), although there the practice is roundly condemned by Nehemiah and thus discontinued. Also, from the Elephantine Papyri (456-455) we learn that Jews liv-

*Marcus Cato (234-149).

ing in Egypt loaned money at interest (nos. 10, 11, 29, 35; Cowley 1923, 29-35, 106-8, 129-31; Neufeld 1955, 411; Yaron 1961, 94; Porten 1968, 77), although other papyri from Egypt in the 2nd cent. contain loan contracts not requiring interest or else interest to be paid only if the loan became overdue. Interest on overdue loans was also called for in earlier Babylonian and Assyrian contracts (Neufeld 1953-54, 196-97; 1955, 411).

In the NT, lending at interest is not censured at all; in fact, it is commended by Jesus in one of his parables (Matt 25:27; Luke 19:23). Luther wrote a good deal on usury and profiteering, his "Short Sermon on Usury" of 1519 going through three editions together with other writings on the subject during 1520-25. In his tract "To the Christian Nobility of the German Nation" (1520), he said that taking interest was the work of the devil and the greatest misfortune of the German nation. At the end of his life, in 1540, Luther wrote an explosive tract exhorting pastors to excommunicate usurers (Lindberg 2005, 6).

interest. Hebrew נֶשֶׁךְ is lit. "something bitten off," usually explained as money or its equivalent deducted in advance from the principal (NJV: "You shall not deduct interest from loans to your countrymen"). Interest rates charged on loans in antiquity were outrageously high, ranging anywhere from 20 to 50 percent and sometimes higher (Driver and Miles 1952, 173-86; Neufeld 1953-54, 194-95; Porten 1968, 77-80; Yamauchi 1980, 270-72). Interest rates in Babylonia and Assyria were generally 20-25 percent for loans of money and up to 33-1/3 percent for loans of grain (Maloney 1974, 11-18). In the so-called "King of Justice" text housed in the British Museum (see Note for 10:18), this Neo-Babylonian king attributes the collapse of the prior social order in part to usury. He says: "The silver which you have loaned on interest you have multiplied five times. You have broken up houses, you have seized land and arable land" (Lambert 1965, 8).

your brother. I.e., your fellow Israelite. This law, like others in Deuteronomy, assumes a familial relationship (Moran) or a "theocratic brotherhood" of all Israelites (Neufeld 1955, 401-10).

21(20) *To a foreigner you may lend at interest*. Loans at interest are allowed to foreigners, who are probably merchants and traders entering the country to make a profit. This provision is not contained in the laws of Exodus and Leviticus and may well be a Deuteronomic innovation. Deuteronomy also exempted foreigners from the sabbatical debt-remission provision granted to Israelites (15:3).

in order that Yahweh your God will bless you in every undertaking of your hand. A stock expression in Deuteronomy, on which see Note for 2:7. Deuteronomy makes the point that Yahweh's future blessing will come as a result of charitable action (14:29; 15:10; 24:19).

upon the land that you are entering to take possession of it. On the stock expression "to enter and take possession of the land," see also 4:1, 5; 6:18; 7:1; 11:10, 29; 17:14 and Note for 1:8.

22(21) *When you make a vow to Yahweh your God, you shall not delay to make good on it.* A vow is a promise to God that one will carry out a certain act if God grants the petitioner's request. This could be a request for the birth of a child (1 Sam 1:11; Prov 31:2), for deliverance from enemies (Num 21:2; Judg 11:30-31), for recovery from affliction, danger, or death (Ps 22:26-27[25-26]; Jonah 1:16; 2:10[9]), or for care and protection during the course of one's life (Gen 28:20-22; 2 Sam 15:7-8). The vow has its roots in primitive religion, where people seek by various means to manipulate the deity for their own ends. It survived in Israelite religion, but without the manipulative element, becoming there simply an urgent prayer with an accompanying promise to honor God if one's prayer was answered. Vows, then, were very much like prayers, particularly prayers for deliverance. In Ps 61:6(5), "my vows" (נְדָרָי) is used as a substitute for "my prayers" (Greenberg 1976, 81). In the OT, vows are discussed together with oaths (Num 30:3-17[2-16]), being different from oaths mainly in that they are conditional in nature (Milgrom 1990a, 488). Performance is required only if God grants what is asked for.

The point here in the present law — if indeed one chooses to call it a law — is that vows must be fulfilled promptly. Unlike loans, which may take some time to pay off, vows come due as soon as the request has been granted. This point is reiterated in Num 30:3(2) and Eccl 5:3(4), the latter text demonstrating a clear link between vowing and Israelite wisdom tradition (von Rad; Weinfeld 1967, 257; 1972, 270-71). See also Prov 20:25; Sir 18:22. Milgrom points out that all vows are dedications to the sanctuary, many of them being "votive offerings" (Ps 66:13). In earlier times a sacrifice could be offered at any sanctuary, e.g., Shiloh, Hebron, or some other place, but in the 7th cent. it will have been offered on Yahweh's altar in Jerusalem (12:5-6, 11, 18, 26), usually at one of the yearly festivals. The present law occurs only in Deuteronomy.

for Yahweh your God will surely require it from you, and it will be a sin in you. Failure to fulfill a vow is a sin, sure to kindle the divine wrath (Eccl 5:3[4]: "[God] has no pleasure in fools"). Van der Toorn (1989, 196) cites a Mesopotamian medical text stating that infant diseases have been caused by unpaid vows made by the parents prior to the child's birth. Proverbs 20:25 warns, too, against making hasty vows and regretting them later. Surely the most ill conceived vow in the Bible is the one made by Jephthah, which led to the sacrifice of his daughter (Judg 11:30-40). The general rule is that men who make vows must carry them out; the same goes for women, except in cases where fathers void the vows of unmarried daughters and husbands void vows made by their wives (Num 30:3-17[2-16]). For the elaborate procedure devised later by the rabbis to annul vows, see *m. Nedarim*. The Qumran *Temple Scroll* (11QT 53:19-

21) allows a father to annul a daughter's vow if he hears her make it and expresses disapproval (Yadin 1983, 2:241). It goes without saying that vows made and performed to other gods, e.g., the vows by exiled Jews in Egypt to the Queen of Heaven (Jer 44:25-27), provoke Yahweh more than vows made to him that go unfulfilled. The Qumran *Temple Scroll* (11QT 53:9-14) combines vv. 22-24(21-23) with 12:26-27 on holy sacrifices in its discussion on Temple sacrifices (Yadin 1983, 2:239-40).

for Yahweh your God will surely require it from you. On the meaning of "require" for the verb דרש, which carries the idea of punishment, see also 18:19.

and it will be a sin in you. וְהָיָה בְךָ חֵטְא. On this expression, see Note for 15:9.

23(22) Vowing is a purely voluntary act (v. 24), so there is nothing wrong in not making vows. In the NT, see Acts 5:4.

24(23) *That which comes out of your lips.* An idiom for what one has promised (Num 30:13[12]; Ps 89:35[34]).

You shall be careful and do. A stock expression in Deuteronomy (see Note for 4:6).

25(24) Another law found only in Deuteronomy. The Covenant Code forbids only grazing — intentional or otherwise — in a vineyard or field by a neighbor's animal, and if this happens, restitution must be made (Exod 22:4[5]). In antiquity people commonly passed through the fields and vineyards of others, and this was not considered a trespass (Norway today has a similar law with respect to privately-owned property). In passing through one is given here the right to pick grapes from the vine and eat them, as many as one wishes. After harvest, one's vineyard or field is opened to gleaning by the sojourner, orphan, and widow (24:19-22). But in passing through an unharvested vineyard, one is not permitted to take any grapes away with him, for doing so would amount to theft. The law then allows for hospitality but at the same time protects the owner from abuse of the privilege. Rashi, following the Targum, gives the verse a narrower interpretation. He says the unrestricted picking of grapes applies only to one who is laboring in the vineyard; it does not apply to someone doing other work there, or to someone entering a vineyard who has no intention of working. Plato (*Leg.* viii 845 a-d), too, allows for a foreigner — with one attendant — to eat choice fruit from a field when passing by but not to take any away with him. Allowing passersby to eat is called a "gift of hospitality."

according to your desire. כְּנַפְשְׁךָ. Rashi: "as much as you like."

your vessel. כֶּלְיְךָ. I.e., your bag or other container you may have with you.

26(25) The same principle applies to fields of standing grain. It is permissible for passersby to pluck ears of grain as they walk through the field (Matt 12:1-8; Mark 2:23-28; Luke 6:1-5), but harvesting a neighbor's crop, with a sickle no less, amounts to theft.

Message and Audience

Moses tells the people in Law I that they are not to lend anything — silver, food, grain, or any other commodity — to a fellow Israelite at interest. To a foreigner entering the land from abroad they may lend at interest. The reason for this act of benevolence to one's fellow is so that Yahweh will bless the people in the land they are now about to possess. The law is probably ancient, but in its form here is well suited for any age and any place.

In Law II Moses reminds the people that when they make a vow to Yahweh, they must be prompt in fulfilling it, as Yahweh requires that vows be kept. If they are not prompt, Yahweh will count it as a sin. However, it will not be a sin if people refrain from vowing, as vows are strictly voluntary. Implicit, then, is a warning not to make vows rashly or with the intention of not keeping them. This law is also no doubt ancient and could have been promulgated at any time in Israel's early history.

In Law III Moses tells the people that when they possess vineyards after settlement in the land, passersby may enter and eat as many grapes as they wish, but they are not to carry any away with them. The same applies when entering their fellow's field of standing grain. They may pluck ears of grain as they walk, but not have with them a sickle to harvest their fellow's crop. This law too may be ancient, but does anticipate a time when Israelites will be raising crops in their own land.

S. HUMANE LAWS (24:1–25:4)

1. Marriage, Divorce, and Remarriage (24:1-5)

a) *Divorcee May Not Return to First Husband (24:1-4)*

*24*¹*When a man takes a wife and marries her, then it shall be if she does not find favor in his eyes because he has found in her an indecent thing, and he writes for her a bill of divorce and puts it in her hand and sends her from his house,* ²*and she goes out from his house and goes to belong to another man,* ³*and the latter man hates her and writes for her a bill of divorce and puts it in her hand and sends her from his house, or if the latter man who took her to be his wife dies,* ⁴*her former husband who sent her away may not return to take her to be his wife after she has been rendered unclean, because that would be an abomination before Yahweh, and you shall not make the land guilty that Yahweh your God is giving to you as an inheritance.*

b) Newlywed War Deferment (24:5)

24⁵ *When a man takes a new wife, he shall not go out with the army and not campaign with it for any matter; he shall be free at his house one year, and he shall be very glad with his wife whom he has taken.*

Rhetoric and Composition

The present collection of laws, with only a couple exceptions, mandates humane treatment to individuals being punished or who, for various reasons, have a precarious position in Israelite society due to poverty or some other misfortune (24:1–25:3). In one final case, humane treatment is to be granted an ox that is treading grain (25:4). In the present verses are two laws having to do with marriage, divorce, and remarriage: (1) a law precluding a man's remarriage to a divorced wife if she had contracted a second marriage (vv. 1-4); and (2) a law exempting a newly married man from war obligation for one year after his marriage (v. 5). The main law may be to keep a man from receiving unjust financial gain in taking back a former wife (see Notes), which would explain why it appears here after other laws dealing with theft (see Rhetoric and Composition for 12:1-4). Law II is linked to Law I by verbal association, in this case by similar opening phrases (G. A. Smith; Rofé 1988b, 274):

I	*When a man takes a wife* . . .	. . . כִּי־יִקַּח אִישׁ אִשָּׁה	v. 1
	and she goes out . . .	. . . וְיָצְאָה	v. 2
II	*When a man takes a new wife*	כִּי־יִקַּח אִישׁ אִשָּׁה חֲדָשָׁה	v. 5
	he shall not go out . . .	. . . לֹא יֵצֵא	

Law I is demarcated at the top end by a *setumah* in M^L and sections in 4QDeut^a, 4QDeut^i, and Sam before v. 1, which is also the chapter division. Demarcation at the bottom end is by a *setumah* in M^L and a section in 4QDeut^a after v. 4. The latter section delimits Law II at the top end; delimitation at the bottom end is by a *setumah* in M^L after v. 5. 4QDeut^a and Sam have no sections after v. 5. Sam has a section at the end of v. 6.

Portions of 24:1-5 are contained in 4QDeut^a, 4QDeut^f, 4QDeut^i, and 4QDeut^k2. The Roberts Papyrus (P. Ryl. Gk. 458), an early Greek text dated to the end of the 2nd cent. B.C. (C. H. Roberts 1936, 37), contains portions of 24:1-3.

Notes

24:1 The AV, presumably following the Targum (T^{OnqPsJ}), translates this verse as a self-standing statement with both a protasis and an apodosis: "When a man hath taken a wife . . . *then* let him write her a bill of divorcement. . . ." So interpreted, the verse is a separate injunction permitting divorce. But the consensus now is that all of vv. 1-3 is the protasis of a single law, with v. 4 being the apodosis. According to this reading, which is preserved in T^{Nf}, a divorced woman, after contracting a second marriage, cannot return to remarry her first husband. Calvin read the verses in this manner and so did Michaelis (1814, 2:128-29), who rejected translations of Luther and others that had both a protasis and apodosis in v. 1. Michaelis said such a rendering could not be right, and subsequent commentators have agreed (*pace* Brewer 1998, 230). An abridged version of this law in Jer 3:1 similarly precludes the return of a wife to her first husband after contracting a second marriage, where an unsettling comparison is made to Yahweh's broken relationship with Israel (Lundbom 1999, 300-302).

This law has no parallel in the ancient world (Yaron 1966, 4; Daube and Carmichael 1993, 1), and later it is turned on its head in the Koran (Sura ii 230), where it states that if a man divorces his wife it is not lawful to remarry her unless she marries a second husband and he divorces her; then the first husband may take her back. The law here in Deuteronomy presupposes a divorce law that Moses presumably gave to the people (Mark 10:2-5; Matt 5:31; 19:7), but this is not the law itself. The OT has no law on divorce, just as it has no law on marriage, although here again Tob 7:13 states that marriage had to be carried out according to the law of Moses. It could well be that marriage and divorce in ancient Israel were regulated largely by custom. The OT elsewhere assumes the existence of divorce (Lev 21:7, 14; 22:13; Num 30:10[9]), and Jewish tradition, with few exceptions, has always allowed it (see Excursus 2). Later rules concerning divorce appear in the Mishnah and the Talmud (*Giṭṭin*).

if she does not find favor in his eyes. A common OT idiom, where "favor" (חֵן) — and also its absence — is found in the eyes of another. In modern culture it is commonly looked for in the smile on another's face. Whereas the marriage vow builds on faithfulness and must therefore be kept, favor is under no such constraint; it is freely given and may be freely withdrawn at any time, unilaterally and without a reason (Freedman, Lundbom, *ḥānan*, in *TDOT*, 5:22-36). Rabbi Akiba cited the present phrase to argue that a man could therefore divorce his wife simply because he found someone else prettier than she (*m. Giṭ.* 9:10). But since the verse goes on to give a weightier reason, an interpretation that trivializes the man's action has to be precluded (*pace* Tigay), unless, of course, the charges are "trumped up."

he has found in her an indecent thing. Here again is the uniquely Deuteronomic form "to be found," which Daube (1969a, 32-33; 1971a, 8-9) says is an appeal to shame. The husband — after the manner of Yahweh in 23:15[14] — is concerned about how things look. An "indecent thing" (עֶרְוַת דָּבָר) is lit. "a naked thing," which in 23:15[14] refers to uncovered human excrement. The LXX translates with ἄσχημον πρᾶγμα, "a shameful thing." The indecency could be something sexual, although not adultery, since that would result in the woman receiving the death penalty. The Mishnah (Giṭ. 9:10) records the famous debate between the School of Shammai and the School of Hillel over the meaning of עֶרְוַת דָּבָר, which set forth the grounds for divorce for each school. The School of Shammai said the "indecent thing" had to be adultery, whereas the more liberal School of Hillel said it could be "spoiling her husband's dish (of food)." Josephus appears to align himself with the view of Hillel (*Ant.* 4.253). Neither view is of much help here, particularly the view of Shammai, since the woman is legally divorced and legally remarried. She is not stoned. As for the view of Hillel, the wife's spoiling of her husband's food would trivialize the law, the same as the husband's finding another woman more beautiful. It is thus agreed that while the indecency must be something less than adultery, it has to be something improper or indecent. Because the expression means "a naked thing," immodest exposure or immodest behavior has been suggested. Sirach 25:25-26 recommends the divorce of an evil wife who speaks boldly and is disobedient (cf. *m. Ketub.* 7:6). We really do not know what sort of indecency is envisioned. Rashi simply concludes that the woman is wicked.

The Code of Hammurabi (CH 141; *ANET*[3], 172) permits the divorce of one's wife if she pursues business interests outside the home and as a result neglects her house and humiliates her husband. In such a case, the husband may divorce her without a monetary settlement (cf. *m. Ketub.* 7:6) or, if he chooses, retain her in the house as a slave and marry someone else. In the NT, the Pharisees ask Jesus if one may divorce his wife for any cause, and in Matt 19:3-9 Jesus comes out on the side of Shammai, saying that only for unchastity can a man divorce his wife and marry another (cf. Matt 5:31-32). Mark 10:2-12 records the same debate, but with the difference that the disciples are told afterwards that a man who divorces his wife in order to marry another commits adultery and that a woman who divorces her husband in order to marry another commits adultery. But here too, as in Luke 16:18, Jesus may simply have a particular situation in mind (see Excursus 2).

and he writes for her a bill of divorce and puts it in her hand and sends her from his house. According to later Jewish tradition, two actions were required to effect a divorce: (1) the husband must give his wife a bill of divorce; and (2) he must send her out of his house (cf. Hos 9:15; Isa 50:1). Both actions are stated here. Already by the time of Deuteronomy, i.e., the 7th cent., a bill of divorce had to be written up (Yaron 1957, 117, 124-26; Daube 1969b, 238; Piattelli 1981, 77;

cf. b. Giṭ. 85ab), although earlier it was probably unnecessary. The husband could simply say to his wife, "You are not my wife," and send her away. Having the divorce statement in writing was for the woman's protection. Should she remarry, she would need proof that her former marriage was terminated, otherwise she could be charged with adultery. Here, and elsewhere in the OT (Jer 3:8; Isa 50:1), the "bill of divorce" is called a סֵפֶר כְּרִיתֻת ("document of separation"); later it was called a גֵט פִּטּוּרִין (Aramaic: "bill of dismissal") or simply a גֵט (*Dict Talm*, 233). It may only have contained the words "She is not my wife and I am not her husband" (Neufeld 1944, 180; Hos 2:4[2]), although according to the Mishnah (*Giṭ.* 9:3), the basic formula was "You are hereby permitted to (marry) anyone." Rabbi Judah is reported to have said, "Let this be to you from me a writ of divorce and letter of dismissal and deed of liberation, that you may go and marry any man you please" (Holtz 2001, 253). On a recently discovered bill of divorce (*P. Mur.* 19), dated ca. A.D. 111, these words appear:

> I dismiss and divorce of my own free will, today. I Yosef son of Naqsan, you, Miriam (daughter of) Yehonatan [fr]om [Ha]nablata, living at Masada, who was my wife previously. You are free unto yourself to go and marry any Jewish man that you please. Let this be to you from me a writ of divorce and letter of dismissal . . . (Holtz 2001, 253-54; cf. Benoit, Milik, and de Vaux 1960, 105-6)

In Old Babylonian contracts divorce was effected by the man saying to/regarding the woman, "You are not my wife" or "She is not my wife" (R. Harris 1974; Lipinski 1981, 15-19; Westbrook 1988a, 69). Sometimes the wife received a monetary settlement or was permitted to retain her dowry; other times she left the marriage penniless. In some Old Babylonian contracts the wife could also initiate the divorce by declaring, "You are not my husband," "He is not my husband," or "You may not have me" (CH 142). In CH 142 ($ANET^3$, 172), the wife's claim would be investigated, and if she was found to be blameless, she could take back her dowry and return to her father's house. But more often than not the woman repudiated the marriage at considerable cost to herself. She could end up paying her husband a monetary settlement or forfeiting house, field, and property, or worse yet, she could be defenestrated or thrown bound into the river (CH 143; $ANET^3$, 172; R. Harris 1974: Lipinski 1981, 14-16; Westbrook 1988a, 79-83). Westbrook points out that in some Old Babylonian contracts penalties are the same for whoever initiates the divorce, husband or wife. Things remained little changed in Neo-Babylonian marriage contracts, where divorce was at the husband's initiative and only rarely at the initiative of the wife (Lipinski 1981, 25; M. T. Roth 1989, 12-14, 110). Roth finds only one Neo-Babylonian contract (no. 34 lines 31-35) that considers the wife's right to divorce.

2 According to *BHS*, the LXX lacks "from his house and goes" (מִבֵּיתוֹ וְהָלְכָה), which could be due to haplography (homoeoteleuton: ה ... ה). But Wevers (1995, 378) thinks the omission is rather "and she goes out from his house" (וְיָצְאָה מִבֵּיתוֹ), which could also be a loss due to haplography (whole word: מביתו ... מביתו).

to belong to another man. I.e., she becomes another man's wife. The expression וְהָיְתָה לְ means "come to belong to, become the property of" (Driver) and is the standard expression for "be married to" (Judg 14:20; 15:2). The idiom "to belong to another" occurs in the 8th cent. Sefire treaties (3:24; cf. Greenfield 1965-66, 3).

3 *and the latter man hates her and writes for her a bill of divorce and puts it in her hand and sends her from his house.* Yaron (1957, 117-18) says the verb "hate" (שנא) can have the technical meaning of "divorce," which it has in the Elephantine papyri, and may have also in Judg 15:2; Sir. 42:9. But here, as in 21:15, a nontechnical meaning is more likely, since the phrase goes on to state the two actions effecting the divorce: writing the bill of divorce and sending the woman out of his house. Westbrook (1986) thinks this hatred on the part of the second husband makes his divorce one without justification, i.e., he has not charged the woman with misconduct as her first husband did, and because of this she will get a financial settlement. This, in turn, could explain why the first husband wants her back. Because he accused her of wrongdoing she was sent away penniless, but now that the woman has money from her second husband, the first husband decides he wants her back. This could explain the reason for the law being promulgated, viz., to prevent self-serving men from disposing of and then repossessing wives simply to make a financial gain. Westbrook (1986, 404) points out that in modern law this is called "estoppel," which is "a rule whereby a person who has profited by asserting a particular set of facts cannot profit a second time by conceding that the facts were otherwise."

or if the latter man who took her to be his wife dies. The words "latter who took her to be his wife" are not present in the Vg. If Jerome's Greek manuscript lacked the words ὁ ἔσχατος, ὃς ἔλαβεν αὐτὴν ἑαυτῷ γυναῖκα, the loss could be the result of haplography (homoeoarcton: ὁ ... ὁ). If the second husband dies the woman will get an inheritance, which again could explain why the first husband wants her back. There is also the possibility that the first husband, wanting his wife back with or without inheritance money, might conspire with the wife, someone else, or both individuals to bring about the second husband's death (Michaelis 1814, 2:137; Driver; Yaron 1966, 8). Or else the woman, having compared her two husbands and decided that the first husband was better than the second, might want to return to her first husband (cf. Hos 2:9[7]). Michaelis points out that lovers or married couples who have quarreled are easily reconciled and may desire to renew their ancient intimacy. If the first husband had it

Deuteronomy 24

within his power to get his wife back upon the death of the second husband, the latter, says Michaelis, would have an insecure existence and might end up becoming a "sacrifice" to bring about their reconciliation. Or the first husband could bribe the second husband into giving the woman a divorce. In all such cases, decency and honesty would be sacrificed. This law, then, could have been enacted to prevent such intrigues.

4 *her former husband who sent her away may not return to take her to be his wife.* The Mishnah in some cases permits remarriage to a wife the man has divorced (*Giṭ.* 4:7-8), but not after she has contracted a second marriage. Yaron (1966, 8) thinks this law is designed to preserve the second marriage, which it may be. Philo (*Spec. Laws* iii 30-31) condemns both woman and man for wanting a reconciliation of this sort, saying that a proper punishment for both would be death.

may not return. לֹא־יוּכַל ... לָשׁוּב. On the "you may not" verbal form, which denotes the indignity of doing such a thing, see Note for 12:17. The point in the present law may be that while such a remarriage may be possible, it is unthinkable. No punishment is specified in the law for those who violate its provisions.

after she has been rendered unclean. אַחֲרֵי אֲשֶׁר הֻטַּמָּאָה. Driver renders אַחֲרֵי אֲשֶׁר as a conjunction meaning "after that" (cf. BDB, 29-30; AV; RSV; and NRSV simply have "after"). The woman's defilement is taken for granted, and although this defilement figures in her not being able to return to her first husband, it is not a reason for promulgating the law. The main reason is given in the כִּי clause following: "because that would be an abomination before Yahweh." Another reason is spoken directly to the people: "And you shall not make the land guilty. . . ." "Uncleanness" commonly refers to sexual defilement (Gen 34:5, 13, 27; Lev 18:20; Num 5:13-14, 20; Ezek 18:6), and it appears that the woman will become unclean to her former husband by virtue of her sexual union with the latter (G. A. Smith). Smith says, "It cannot be a matter of indifference to him that she had been another's, as (presumably) the popular humour took it. Such easy passage of a woman from one man to another did defile her" (1918, 279). It seems, then, that such a remarriage is in fact being likened to adultery (Driver; Zakovitch 1981, 32; Tigay).

because that would be an abomination before Yahweh. On the term "abomination" as used in Deuteronomy, see Note for 7:25. Weinfeld (1972, 269) thinks the action envisioned here is an "abomination" because it shows "a lack of integrity and a hypocritical attitude toward the institution of marriage." And if Westbrook is right in arguing that such a divorce and remarriage might be carried out by the husband largely for financial gain, this would surely show a lack of integrity on the man's part, and Yahweh would find such to be an abomination.

and you shall not make the land guilty that Yahweh your God is giving to you as an inheritance. Here a shift to direct first-person speech makes the final implication of the prohibited action more immediate. Not only is the woman rendered unclean by easy passage from one husband to another, but guilt will also descend upon the land. "Guilt" here refers to the consequences of sin. Jeremiah asked rhetorically if the land "would not be greatly polluted" (הֲלוֹא חָנוֹף תֶּחֱנַף) should a wife return to her first husband, and then answered his own question by saying that "whorings and wickedness" do indeed pollute (Jer 3:1-2). On the land in Deuteronomy as Israel's inheritance from Yahweh, see Note for 15:4.

5 Another law peculiar to Deuteronomy, complementing the exemption in 20:7 offering a newly-betrothed man exception from war duty. Here a one-year deferment from war duties for the man to enjoy his new wife will have the obvious benefit of bonding them together in marriage. Calvin says it will awaken mutual love between them, for otherwise the woman, in the husband's absence, may fall in love with someone else and he too, while away, will be tempted to love or lust after other women, as happens in all wars. One year will also allow time for a child to be born, which in wartime, with its loss of life and scarcity of marriages, will help populate the next generation (Luther; Michaelis 1814, 3:35).

and he shall be very glad with his wife. Hebrew וְשִׂמַּח אֶת־אִשְׁתּוֹ. Reading וְשִׂמַּח as an internal Piel: "and he shall be very glad." The Piel might otherwise be translated "and he shall make his wife glad." The verb here is not a Qal (*pace* S and RSV).

Message and Audience

In this first law Moses is heard telling the people that if a man marries a wife, and then she ceases to find favor in his eyes because he has found something indecent in her, and he divorces her and she goes to marry another man, and then her second husband writes her a bill of divorce and sends her away, or else her second husband dies, the first husband may not remarry her. She has been rendered unclean to him, and it would be an abomination before Yahweh. What is more, such an action would bring guilt upon the land that Yahweh is giving to the people for an inheritance. Those hearing this law will likely know other reasons for such a law being given. Intrigues could develop, and perhaps the audience is being told that in cases of divorce and remarriage it is the better part of wisdom to ensure that the second marriage be preserved. There should be no easy passage from one spouse to another.

Law II is a humane gesture to newly-married husbands and wives, allowing the husbands a one-year deferment from war and war-related obligations. During this time he can attend to his house and enjoy the wife that he has taken. One year together before the husband leaves home will allow time for the marriage to be established and for a child to be born.

Excursus 2: Divorce within Judaism and Early Christianity

Judaism from earliest times has permitted marriages to be terminated by divorce, although in Deuteronomy are two exceptions to the rule. A man may not divorce his wife: (1) if his charge of premarital unchastity against her cannot be substantiated (22:19); and (2) if the marriage was forced upon him because he had sexual intercourse with her while she was still an unbetrothed virgin (22:29). In the Qumran *Temple Scroll* (11QT 57:17-19) we learn that divorce (and also polygamy) are forbidden to the king. There it states that the king may only take a second wife if his first wife has died (Yadin 1983 2: 258; cf. Fitzmyer 1978, 103-4). This appears to build on Deut 17:17, which states that kings are not to multiply wives (as Solomon did). Fitzmyer concludes from this text, and from a less clear reading in the Damascus Document (CD 2:12b-5:11), that the NT teaching against divorce may not then be such a radical break from Judaism as has previously been thought.

Documents discovered over the past fifty years in the Judaean Desert have given us new insight into marriage and divorce practices as they were carried out in the early centuries of the Christian era. A number of marriage contracts have turned up, some from the Caves of Murabbaʿat and others from the Cave of Letters at Naḥal Ḥever. From Murabbaʿat have come two marriage contracts written in Aramaic (*P. Mur.* 20, 21), the first dated A.D. 117, the second possibly earlier, before the First Jewish Revolt (Benoit, Milik, and de Vaux 1960, 109-17; Fitzmyer and Harrington 1978, 140-44), and two fragments written in Greek (*P. Mur.* 115, 116), dated A.D. 124 (Benoit, Milik, and de Vaux 1960, 243-56). From Naḥal Ḥever has come "Babatha's *Ketubba*"* (*P. Yadin* 10), which solemnized a marriage that took place by at least A.D. 125 (Yadin, Greenfield, and Yardeni 1994; M. Friedman 1996). Fragments of other marriage contracts written in Greek have also turned up at Naḥal Ḥever. One dated A.D. 131 is from the archive of Salome Komaïse (Cotton and Yardeni 1997, 57-59, 224-37), and another (*P. Yadin* 18), dated A.D. 128, solemnizes the marriage between one Judah son of Hanania and a Shelamzion daughter of Judah. This Judah was a second husband to the Babatha of *Papyrus Yadin* 10 (N. Lewis, Katzoff, and Greenfield 1987). Lewis says the marriages and remarriages were occurring between two rich Jewish families living at the time. The documents are the earliest marriage deeds known to us, containing the specifics of who is being married, where they come from, and

---

*A *ketubba* (*kĕtûbâ*) is Late Hebrew, meaning "writ, deed" (*Dict Talm*, 680) and referring particularly to a marriage contract.

Deuteronomy 24

what sort of settlement the wife will receive should her husband die or should the marriage end in divorce. An actual divorce document, called a *geṭ*, was also found at Murabbaʿat (*P. Mur.* 19) and is dated A.D. 111. It was written in Aramaic at Masada and is the first of its kind to have come down to us (Benoit, Milik, and de Vaux 1960, 104-9; Fitzmyer and Harrington 1978, 138-41).

Two teachings from Jesus in Mark 10:2-12 and Luke 16:18 disallow divorce and remarriage, putting them in a class with adultery. Jesus concedes that Moses gave a law of divorce to the people, but says that from the beginning divorce was not meant to be (cf. Gen 1:27; 5:2). His words survive in ceremonies of marriage to the present day: "What therefore God has joined together, let not man put asunder" (Mark 10:9). In 1 Cor 7:10-11 is another strong word against divorce from Paul, although the apostle says that if a woman does separate from her husband, she should either remain single or be reconciled to her husband. These words in Mark and Luke contrast with Matt 5:31-32; 19:3-9, where Jesus again comes out strongly against divorce but admits an exception if the woman is guilty of adultery. The statements in Mark 10:11-12; Luke 16:18, however, may not be as absolute as they first appear. In Mark 10:10-12 the disciples are given a private explanation, which may be saying that a man who divorces his wife *in order to* marry another commits adultery and that a woman who divorces her husband *in order to* marry another commits adultery. This teaching could presuppose a situation in which a "love triangle" has developed and the husband or wife is divorcing his or her marriage partner for someone else in waiting (Lundbom 1978b, 23). That, says Jesus, is adultery.

In the ancient period and on through the Tannaitic period (50 B.C. to A.D. 200), also beyond into the Middle Ages, divorce with few exceptions was the sole right of the husband, who had the power to initiate it and carry it out. In the Mishnah (*Yebam.* 14:1) it is stated: "The man who divorces his wife is not equivalent to a woman who receives a divorce. For a woman goes forth willingly or unwillingly. But a man puts his wife away only willingly" (Neusner 1988, 370). Divorce remained so until the 12th cent. A.D., at which time the consent of the wife became a necessary condition (Yaron 1966, 1). We know that in the Tannaitic period the woman could sue for divorce, and if the court ruled in her favor, the husband would be required to give her a bill of divorce. Mishnah *Ketub.* 7:1-10 lists the various cases, e.g., in 7:10 that a man could be forced to divorce his wife if he had a physical ailment, collected [dog excrement], was a coppersmith, or was a tanner (cf. *b. Ketub.* 77ab). In the biblical period we do not know if divorce cases required any court action. G. A. Smith notes that nothing is said here in 24:1-4 about a council of elders, as is mentioned in 22:13-21.

There has been much discussion of late, particularly in view of the new documents that have come to light, over whether a Jewish woman could go beyond compelling her husband to divorce her (for adequate cause) and begin the process on her own. In the Aramaic papyri discovered at the Jewish military colony at Elephantine (ca. 450-420) it appears that Jewish women in Egypt could initiate a divorce from their husbands (Porten and Yardeni 1989, 30-33, 60-63, 78-83; Cowley 1923, 45-46, no. 15; *ANET*³, 222-23; Yaron 1961, 54), but whether the clauses in these contracts give the wife the right or power to divorce has been challenged (N. Lewis, Katzoff, and Greenfield 1987, 245-46). It is also debated whether the Elephantine marriage contracts reflect accepted Jewish practice or constitute an exception. From the NT is the statement in Mark 10:12 that women could divorce their husbands, but this may reflect Roman rather than Jewish law, the former being more liberal on the divorce question. And then there are the celebrated — some would say infamous — cases of Herodias, who is reported by Josephus to have divorced Herod (Philip?), son of Herod the Great, to marry his brother Herod Antipas, tetrarch of Galilee, and Salome, who divorced her husband Costobarus to remarry. Josephus viewed both actions as contrary to Jewish law (*Ant.* 15.259-60; 18.136), and in the case of Herodias, John the Baptist agreed (Matt 14:3-4; Mark 6:17-18; Luke 3:18-19).

Other documents from the early Christian centuries are also said to give the wife the right to divorce her husband. In a much-discussed "waiver of claims" that turned up at Naḥal Ṣe'elim, just south of Naḥal Ḥever (XḤer/Se ar 13), and dated ca. A.D. 134 or 135, a wife from En Gedi is said to have divorced the husband (Cotton and Yardeni 1997, 65-70; Cotton and Qimron 1998, 115; Ilan 1996), but just who divorced whom remains contested. Some think it was the husband who divorced the wife (Schremer 1998; Brody 1999, 233-34). Later 10th- and 11th-cent. A.D. documents from the Cairo Geniza are said to recognize the wife's right to terminate her partnership with her husband (M. Friedman 1981). But this too has been challenged (N. Lewis, Katzoff, and Greenfield 1987, 245-46). For articles on the wife's right to divorce, see *The Jewish Law Annual* 4 (1981).

2. Pledges and Scale Disease (24:6-13)

a) *No Millstones as Pledges (24:6)*

24⁶*One shall not take in pledge a hand-mill or an upper millstone, for he would be taking a person in pledge.*

b) *No Stealing of Persons (24:7)*

24⁷*When a man shall be found stealing a person from his brethren, from the children of Israel, and he lords it over him and sells him, then that thief shall die. So you shall utterly remove the evil from your midst.*

Deuteronomy 24

c) Warning about Scale Disease (24:8-9)

24 ⁸Be careful with a touch of the scale disease, to be very careful and to do according to all that the Levitical priests direct you. Just as I commanded them, you shall be careful to do. ⁹Remember what Yahweh your God did to Miriam on the road in your going out from Egypt.

d) Kindness in Exacting Pledges (24:10-11)

24 ¹⁰When you make a loan of any kind to your fellow, you shall not go into his house to fetch his pledge. ¹¹You shall stand outside, and the man to whom you are lending shall bring the pledge to you outside.

e) No Sleeping in a Poor Man's Pledge (24:12-13)

24 ¹²And if he is a poor man, you shall not sleep in his pledge. ¹³You must surely return to him the pledge as the sun goes down, that he may sleep in his garment and bless you, and it shall be righteousness to you before Yahweh your God.

Rhetoric and Composition

Here are four laws dealing directly or indirectly with pledges, in the midst of which comes a warning about the danger of scale disease. It is unclear how the scale disease warning fits in with the surrounding material; it could have been added later (Rofé 1988b, 275). Law I forbids the taking of a hand-mill or upper millstone in pledge (v. 6); Law II forbids the seizure of persons (as pledges) and selling them into slavery (v. 7); then comes the warning about scale disease (vv. 8-9); Law III forbids a creditor from entering the debtor's house to collect his pledge (vv. 10-11); and Law IV forbids the creditor from keeping a poor man's pledge overnight (vv. 12-13). The whole is structured in such a way that the pledge laws frame the warning about scale disease:

I	No taking of millstones as *pledges*	v. 6
II	No stealing of persons [*as pledges*]	v. 7
	Warning about scale disease	vv. 8-9
III	No entering of houses to collect *pledges*	vv. 10-11
IV	No keeping *pledges* of the poor overnight	vv. 12-13

The terms for "pledge" in I are different from the terms in III and IV. Law I uses the verb חבל ("to take in pledge"), Laws III and IV the verb עבט ("to get a pledge") and the noun עֲבוֹט ("pledge").

Deuteronomy 24

Laws I and II are joined by keyword repetitions (Rofé 1988b, 275):

I *for* he would be taking *a person* in pledge . . .	כִּי־נֶפֶשׁ	v. 6
II *When* a man shall be found stealing *a person* . . .	כִּי . . . נֶפֶשׁ	v. 7

Law I is demarcated at the top end by a *setumah* in M^L before v. 6 and at the bottom end by a *setumah* in M^L and sections in Sam and 4QDeut^a after v. 6. Law II is demarcated at the top end by a *setumah* in M^L and sections in Sam and 4QDeut^a before v. 7. The M^L and Sam have no sections after v. 7, but *BHS* makes a break there. The warning at the center has no section in M^L before v. 8 but is demarcated at the bottom end by a *setumah* after v. 9. Sam also has a section after v. 9. M^L has another *setumah* after v. 8, dividing the warning about scale disease from a call to remember Miriam's outbreak of the disease in the wilderness. Laws III and IV are combined, M^L having a *setumah* and Sam a section at the top end before v. 10 and M^L a *setumah* and Sam a section at the bottom end after v. 13.

Portions of 24:6-13 are contained in 1QDeut^b, 4QDeut^a, and 4QDeut^f.

Notes

24:6 Another law aimed at protecting the poor that is without parallel in other OT law codes. While Deuteronomy disallows charging interest to a fellow Israelite (23:20[19]), it permits the taking of pledges so debtors will quicken their repayments of money, grain, seed for grain, or other borrowed items. The OT is silent on the duration of loans, except for remissions required in the seventh year (15:1-11). Neufeld (1962, 37) says that in ancient Israel, as in the whole of the ANE, grain or money for grain was commonly borrowed in the autumn in the hopes that repayment could be made when the harvest came in. Laws in the Code of Hammurabi (CH 113-115; *ANET*^{3}, 170) speak of "[a debt of] grain or money"; cf. Neh 5:10-11). Pledges could consist of almost any of the debtor's property, although here hand-mills and upper millstones are made unqualified exceptions. The prohibition is apodictic: "One shall not. . . ." The law states the reason: taking a hand-mill or upper millstone would be tantamount to taking one's "life" (נֶפֶשׁ), since a working mill is necessary for grinding flour and making daily bread (T^{OnqPsJ}). These excepted items are perhaps only examples, since the Mishnah (*B. Meṣi'a* 9:13; *'Arak.* 6:3) later expands the prohibition to include any item essential to the preparation of food or needed to sustain life — pots, an oven, a sieve, working animals, farming tools, and craftsmen's tools. Calvin expands the law in a similar fashion.

The concern, as was mentioned, is for the poor who have few possessions and thus little to offer as pledges. For them it could even come down to having children or infants snatched away. In Job, censure comes upon those who drive away the ass of the orphan and take the widow's ox in pledge (Job 24:3) or worse yet, who snatch away the fatherless child from its mother's breast and take in pledge the infant of the poor (Job 24:9). See also 2 Kgs 4:1; Job 22:6. In the Laws of Eshnunna (LE 22-24) are penalties for creditors practicing unlawful distress, i.e., seizing a debtor's dependents — free or unfree — as well as certain other property (Yaron 1969, 30-33, 163). The Code of Hammurabi (CH 113; 241; *ANET*³, 170, 176) forbids the distraint of oxen and grain; if someone forcibly seizes an ox as a pledge, he must pay a fine of one-third mina of silver. Other laws in the Code of Hammurabi (CH 115, 116; *ANET*³, 170) deal with treatment of a debtor's dependent or slave who has been forcibly taken (Driver and Miles 1952, 208).

One shall not take. לֹא־יַחֲבֹל. The LXX, S, Vg, and T^MS have a second-person form, "You shall not take."

hand-mill . . . upper millstone. Hebrew רֵחַיִם is a dual, denoting a pair of stones that made up a smaller type of mill found in most every household. The upper stone was used to rub grain over the surface of the lower (nether) stone. רֵחַיִם is not just the lower millstone, as both the Vg (*inferiorem et superiorem molam*) and Rashi assume, but the two stones together (*Dict Talm*, 1466). The second term, רֶכֶב, is just the upper millstone, in Judg 9:53 called a "rider stone" (פֶּלַח רֶכֶב) since it "rides" on the lower millstone. The phrase here is properly interpreted in the T^Onq, which says: "Do not take (whole) millstones, not even the upper one." Millstones of the period were commonly made of basalt, found in great abundance in Galilee and the Bashan in Transjordan. Its rough surface was well suited for grinding grain into flour, though not a particularly fine flour, and the stone itself was very hard (Job 41:16[24]). Some upper millstones were made of granite, sandstone, or other stone. Milling was generally done by women. Their grinding was a familiar early morning sound in the village, where the baking of bread was a daily task (Job 31:10; Jer 25:10; Rev 18:22-23; cf. Homer, *Od.* xx 105-9). Milling might also be done by slaves or men taken prisoner (Judg 16:21; Lam 5:13).

One of the common mills of antiquity was the "saddle-quern," which consisted of a large slightly concave lower stone, rectangular in shape, used together with a smaller loaf-shaped upper stone. A saddle-quern 30 in long was found at Megiddo ("Mill, Millstone," in *IDB*, 3:380-81), and a number of these turned up at Gezer (Macalister 1912, 35-37; Bullard 1970, 131). At Ebla, sixteen saddle-querns were found in the western palace (van der Toorn, "Mill, Millstone," in *ABD*, 4:831-32). This type of mill was very ancient. For a picture of a servant in the Old Kingdom of Egypt (2700-2200) grinding grain on a saddle-quern, see *ANEP*², 46 no. 149. A type of rotary quern also turned up at Gezer, although Macalister said it should not be confused with the rotary hand-quern seen in modern Palestine, which came into use much later (van der Toorn: in the Hellenistic period). Macalister (1912, 36-37) says of the Gezer rotary quern:

> It consists of two stones with plane faces, which lie in contact; the face of the nether stone has often a raised collar inside of which the upper stone fits. A conical tenon in the middle of the face of the lower stone fits into a similarly-shaped mortice in the upper: round this tenon the upper stone is rotated. These stones are almost always of small size, and are made of smoother stone than the saddle-querns. They were probably rotated in half-circles, backwards and forwards, by being grasped in the hands and turned with backward and forward motion of the wrist.

A photograph is provided (Fig. 228). The lower stones of these querns, particularly the saddle-quern, besides being bulky could also be quite heavy. The creditor might therefore want to take away only an upper stone, which was easily carried. Also, without an upper stone the mill was rendered useless. Tigay (1995, 375-76) weighed some millstones from Beth Shemesh housed in the Museum of the University of Pennsylvania and found that the lower stones weighed 90, 20.5, and 10.75 lbs, respectively. Another lower stone, unable to be moved, was estimated to be roughly the same weight as the 90-lb stone. The museum also had an 80-lb lower stone from Egypt (ca. 1550-1080). Two upper stones from Beth Shemesh were found to weigh just over 4 lbs each. So one can see how a creditor might choose to carry away an upper stone weighing 4 or 5 lbs instead of a pair of stones weighing 85 or 95 lbs. It was an upper millstone that the woman of Thebez threw from a tower to crush the head of Abimelech (Judg 9:53; 2 Sam 11:21).

for he would be taking a person in pledge. כִּי־נֶפֶשׁ הוּא חֹבֵל. The pronoun "he" (הוּא), which some modern Versions (NJV; NRSV) render with a weak "that," is for emphasis (Driver). The verb חבל ("take in pledge") is rendered "distrain" in modern legal terminology (Milgrom 1976a, 95). It refers to the seizure of property — in antiquity even persons — to force repayment of a loan. Another modern legal expression meaning the same as "distrain" is "levy a distress upon." The item seized is then called the "distress." The creditor who takes a pledge is not looking for something equal in value to the loan, much less something of greater value, as, for example, what the modern lender requires in the way of security or collateral. It could be something of little value to the creditor, e.g., a single upper millstone, as is disallowed here. The pledge is taken simply to exert pressure on the debtor to "pay up" (Daube 1982, 62; cf. Yaron 1961, 35; 1969, 163-64).

7 *When a man shall be found stealing a person from his brethren.* This law

expands upon the eighth commandment, "you shall not steal," the verb גָּנַב ("stealing") putting the kidnapping of a fellow-Israelite squarely in the category of theft (Good 1967, 953). The law appears also in the Covenant Code (Exod 21:16), although there it is not specified that the kidnapped person is a fellow Israelite. It could be assumed, however. In Hittite law the nationality of the victim makes a difference: if he is a Hittite, the penalty is greater (see below). Persons sold into slavery commonly go to a foreign land, which is what happened to Joseph (Gen 37:28), and what has occurred all throughout history, even up into modern times. In Second Isaiah, Yahweh declares metaphorically that he has not done such a thing by sending Israel into exile (Isa 50:1). In the Covenant Code, this law refers simply to kidnapping and selling a person into slavery, but here in Deuteronomy it must refer to the distraint of persons to satisfy a debt, which is what v. 6 speaks against. As was just said, persons in antiquity could be and sometimes were seized by demanding creditors (Job 24:9; cf. Matt 18:24-25).

and he lords it over him and sells him. Hebrew וְהִתְעַמֶּר־בּוֹ וּמְכָרוֹ. For the collocation of these verbs and the meaning of עמר in the Hithpael, see Note for 21:14. In the present verse, the LXX renders וְהִתְעַמֶּר־בּוֹ as καταδυναστεύσας αὐτόν ("having overcome him"). The kidnapper is now "playing the master," to use Driver's expression, wanting to sell the person whom he has seized. He does so in order to recover some or all of the money the debtor has not repaid. But in ancient Israel the pledge was always redeemable, and therefore could not be sold. It was kept in the house of the creditor as long as the debt remained unpaid; it could not be assigned or sold to anyone else (Driver and Miles 1952, 221). Neufeld (1962, 33-34) explains the ancient practice:

> There are two basic differences between the modern and the ancient notion of pledge and security. According to the modern conception, a right of pledge is extinguished only when the debt is settled. If it is not settled by the debtor himself or by some other person on his behalf, the creditor is at liberty as a rule to realize its value by sale for the purpose of satisfying his claim. Having carried out the sale, the creditor pays himself out of the proceeds and if the amount realized is in excess of his claim, he must restore the surplus to the debtor. The creditor's right to obtain satisfaction through the act of selling the thing pledged is a right of pledge.
>
> However, this was not always the case in ancient Israel, nor was it entirely so in the ancient Middle East, or even in Rome. There is evidence to show that in ancient Israel the pledge remained always redeemable and, therefore, the creditor could never acquire ownership over it. The debtor was always sure of recovering the property he had parted with as security for his debt. The creditor had no real right in the thing, and could not, therefore, alienate it, give it away, sell it or exchange it.

In certain situations the same obtained in Old Babylonia, where the creditor could work a person taken in pledge until the debt was satisfied, but that person continued to be the property of the debtor (Driver and Miles 1952, 210-21). In other cases, e.g., if a slave had been surrendered to a moneylender in order to pay an overdue debt, the slave could be redeemed for an agreed period, but after that he or she could be sold (CH 118). The ancient creditor was not like the modern pawnbroker, who has the right of disposal over an item taken in pawn. The present law supports the view that a pledge in ancient Israel may not be sold.

then that thief shall die. Rashi says the thief becomes liable to the death penalty only if the kidnapped victim is subjected to slavery. The Code of Hammurabi (CH 14; *ANET*[3], 166) states that anyone caught stealing the young son of another shall be put to death. In Hittite Law (HL 19, 20, 21), stealing a man or woman from one country and bringing him or her to another country could result in estate forfeiture, i.e., the surrender of one's entire family into slavery, a repayment of six persons, a fine of 12 shekels, or no compensation at all, depending on where the offense was committed and the citizenship of the offender and the victim (Neufeld 1951, 5-6, 138-39; *ANET*[3], 190). The severest penalty applies if the victim is a Hittite (HL 19). Daube (1971a, 10-11) also points out the shame coming upon one caught in theft (cf. Jer 2:26; 48:27).

So you shall utterly remove the evil from your midst. The phrase is stock in Deuteronomy (see Note for 13:6). The Targums substitute "evildoer" for "evil," presumably because the thief is put to death.

8 *Be careful with a touch of the scale disease.* Here the lawgiver digresses momentarily from prescriptive to homiletical discourse. Hebrew נֶגַע means "stroke, plague" (17:8; 21:5; Gen 12:17; Lev 13:2, 3, 9; 1 Kgs 8:37), reflecting the ancient belief that disease is the work of malevolent forces. The LXX translates the term with ἁφῇ, "touch, lighting, kindling." Von Rad takes the term to mean "act of God," saying it was evidently an ancient priestly technical term. Milgrom (1991, 776) points out, too, that in the Bible God is always the author of נֶגַע.

the scale disease. הַצָּרַעַת. The LXX translates צָרַעַת with the Greek word λέπρας ("scaly, scabby, rough"), which has led to a subsequent confusion between this ancient malady and leprosy (= Hansen's disease). What is referred to in the Bible as "leprosy" is not true leprosy but a variety of skin diseases, none of which is known for certain. That leprosy in the ancient world was a different phenomenon entirely was recognized already by Jean Astruc in the 18th cent. (Smend 2007, 5). These ancient diseases produced scales on the skin, giving the skin a look of "whiteness." Hulse (1975, 92-93) suggests a comparison between loosened scales from the affected area and snowflakes. These diseases appear to be most like psoriasis, favus (Hulse), or bejel (Lieber 2000, 123-31), and while certain varieties of scale disease could be any one of these, no one of them — nor any other disease known to modern medicine — fits all the characteristics

Deuteronomy 24

given in Leviticus 13-14, which, it should be added, is not a medical but a ritual text concerned with purity and impurity (Hulse 1975, 95-99; Milgrom 1991, 817-18). Scale disease is also said in the OT to show itself in clothing and on the walls of buildings, which sounds like a mildew or fungus. Michaelis (1814, 3:263) recognized already that the ancient authors (e.g., Celsus, Pliny, Galenos, Aretaios) referred to true leprosy as ἐλεφαντίασις, not λέπρα, and it is generally — but not universally — believed that ἐλεφαντίασις was nonexistent in ancient Israel, having been brought into the Near East from India in the 4th cent. by the armies of Alexander the Great (J. G. Andersen 1969, 45). Recently this view has been challenged, with some experts now saying again that true leprosy was present in Mesopotamia and Egypt from early times (Lieber 2000, 103-4). The first known author to use the term λέπρα for the disease we now call leprosy seems to have been John of Damascus (A.D. 777-857), which has resulted in the confusion between the two diseases persisting down into modern times (J. G. Andersen 1969, 47-48; Hulse 1975, 89). On צָרַעַת as "scale disease" and its differentiation from true leprosy, see J. G. Andersen (1969, 15-16); Hulse (1975); J. Wilkinson (1977; 1978), Milgrom (1991, 816-26), and Lieber (2000).

to be very careful and to do according to all that the Levitical priests direct you. The verb ירה in the H-stem refers to authoritative "direction" given by the Levitical priests (17:9-11). On the term "Levitical priests" in Deuteronomy, see Note for 17:9. On the stock expression "be careful to do," see Note for 5:1.

Just as I commanded them, you shall be careful to do. Moses is here the speaking voice, as is usual in Deuteronomy (1:18; 3:18; 4:2, 40); it is not Yahweh (*pace* Driver; von Rad). Presumably Moses gave the Levitical priests instructions about scale disease in the wilderness, which is perhaps what later becomes codified in Leviticus 13-14. In Leviticus we observe the priests functioning as a kind of "health department" within ancient Israel, being responsible for the diagnosis of scale disease and declaring a person cleansed from it.

9 The account of Miriam breaking out in scale disease is recorded in Num 12:9-15. The point made in the narrative there, and what the people are told to remember here, is that Miriam was stricken because of Yahweh's anger. She, along with Aaron, had slandered Moses on account of his Cushite wife, but their greater misdeed was to challenge Moses' authority as Yahweh's spokesman, wanting for themselves a share in that authority. As a result, Miriam was stricken immediately with scale disease and had to be put outside the camp for seven days. The divine disfavor she incurred was comparable to the disgrace suffered by a child whose father had spit in his face. Later King Uzziah was stricken with scale disease, which in his case stayed with him the rest of his life. He incurred divine disfavor for burning incense on the temple altar, which only the priests were permitted to do (2 Chr 26:16-21). On the call to "remember" in Deuteronomy, see Note for 8:2.

on the road. בַּדֶּרֶךְ. For other asides in the legal material reminding people of what happened when Israel was "on the road" out of Egypt, see 23:5(4); 25:17-18. This expression occurs very often in Deuteronomy (see Note for 1:19).

10-11 Here, in another pledge law found only in Deuteronomy, is a restraint placed upon creditors in collecting their pledges, limiting their right of seizure and forcing them to behave in a respectful manner. Creditors and debtors were by any measure unequals; typically, it was the rich lending to the poor, and one might therefore see this law as being like the one following in vv. 12-13, which aims at protecting the poor from undue hardship at having his garment seized. But since nothing is said here about the poor, we may assume that the protection offered is to anyone from whom a pledge is taken. One reason, surely, for not allowing the creditor to enter the house of the debtor is that this would further humiliate someone who already feels a sense of humiliation. Daube (1969a, 34) says: "To have the creditor inside the home, for the purpose of collecting his security, would be the most down-putting, dishonouring experience for the debtor and his family. The handing over outside preserves appearances . . . (and) formal disgrace is avoided."

Another reason for requiring the creditor to remain outside while collecting his pledge is that if he is allowed to enter the house, he might lay hands on whatever he sees. With him not present in the house, the debtor can choose what to give him (Calvin; Michaelis 1814, 2:317-18). Michaelis noted that at his own university the pawnbrokers, who lent money to students, would come into their apartments to choose their pledges, enabling them to take the very best article they laid their eyes upon. The two reasons come together in an international incident between Ahab of Israel and Ben-hadad of Aram (1 Kgs 20:1-9), where the Aramaean king wants to go through Ahab's palace to pick out persons and objects to be seized as pledges. These will ensure the latter's compliance to terms of his vassal status. When Ahab says, "I cannot do this," he means he cannot do what is demanded of him and yet retain his self-respect (Daube 1982, 62-63).

At what point does the creditor take his pledge from the debtor? It is generally agreed that in ancient Israel the pledge was commonly surrendered when the loan became due and the debtor had defaulted (Neufeld 1962, 34-35; Milgrom 1976a, 95-98; Tigay; cf. 2 Kgs 4:1-7; Neh 5:3-5), although it could happen that a pledge was taken when the debt was established. This latter procedure became usual from talmudic times onward, but in biblical times the creditor simply had a lien on the debtor's property at the time the debt was established (*EncJud*, 3:636-38). Something similar is attested in the Code of Hammurabi, also in Nuzi and other Middle Assyrian mortgage documents, viz., that pledges were normally distrained or given to the creditor after default. Only if a debtor was so impoverished that the creditor might have nothing to seize should the debt remain unpaid would he insist upon receiving the pledge up front. But for the most part, it was not like in the modern pawnshop where the pawn is handed over at the time the loan is taken out.

a loan of any kind. I.e., any type of indebtedness, as in 23:20(19).

12-13 *And if he is a poor man, you shall not sleep in his pledge. You must surely return to him the pledge as the sun goes down, that he may sleep in his garment and bless you.* This law reproduces with little change the law in Exod 22:25-26(26-27). Since the outer garment (שַׂלְמָה) was commonly used for sleeping, the poor man, having nothing else to cover himself, needed it to keep him from the night cold. Taking a widow's garment in pledge was forbidden altogether (v. 17). The concern, once again, was to keep creditors from depriving the poor of something essential to life, even though they had every right to expect repayment of their loan (cf. v. 6). The creditor must therefore not sleep in a poor man's garment overnight, or even keep it overnight, but return it to the man each night at sundown. During the day the poor man could get along without it, but not at night. One's only garment, like one's only mill, may once again be simply an example — the most obvious example — of a limited number of items not to be distrained from the poor. The Mishnah (*B. Meṣiʿa* 9:13) expands the present ruling to forbid holding a pillow overnight and a plow during the day. Garments were commonly given as pledges (Prov 20:16; 27:13), and those who callously seized them from the poor came in for strong censure (Amos 2:8; Job 22:6). Ezekiel considered the restoring of a pledge, together with other righteous acts, to be life-and-death issues for the creditor (Ezek 18:7, 12; 33:15). Tigay (1993b, 330-31) says regarding pledges on loans to the poor:

> The aim of the Torah's laws about distraint is to ensure that in such circumstances, the creditor's legitimate right to force repayment is subordinated to the survival and dignity of the debtor. Accordingly, the creditor may not take a handmill, which is necessary for making food (Deut 24:6), he may not take a widow's garment (v. 17), if he takes a poor man's night-cover he must return it every evening (vv. 12-13).... These restrictions considerably reduce the creditor's leverage in securing repayment, but they are consistent with the Bible's position that loans to the poor are acts of charity that may well turn into outright gifts.

In a Hebrew letter written in the 7th cent., the writer complains to an official that his garment seized by a creditor while he was harvesting had not been returned (Naveh 1960; *ANET*[3], 568; for a picture, see F. I. Andersen and Freedman 1989, no. 5 after p. 470). He was resting at the time, finished with what he thought was his assigned work. It is unclear whether the garment was seized for defaulting on his quota, for nonpayment of a debt, or for some other reason.

Tigay (1993b) thinks the superior distrained the garment because the laborer's negligent performance caused the superior financial loss, and he cites parallels in the Talmud where much the same thing happened.

and bless you. I.e., bless you before Yahweh (2 Sam 2:5; Ruth 2:20; 3:10). On this formula in biblical narrative, see Greenberg 1983b, 33-37.

and it shall be righteousness to you before Yahweh your God. In Deuteronomy, doing the commandments makes one righteous before Yahweh (6:25). But here Hebrew "righteousness" (צְדָקָה)) has more the meaning of "merit" or "credit" (see Note for 6:25). In Exod 22:26(27), Yahweh concludes this law by saying that if a poor man left without a garment at night cries to him, he will hear, for he is gracious (חַנּוּן). In the OT חַנּוּן, "gracious," occurs often with רַחוּם, "merciful" (Freedman, Lundbom, ḥānan, in *TDOT*, 5:25), which may explain why the LXX in the present verse has "mercy" (ἐλεημοσύνη) instead of "righteousness" (so also 6:25).

Message and Audience

Moses in the present laws is heard telling people that they must exercise due restraint in taking pledges, particularly with respect to the poor. They must not take in pledge a hand-mill or an upper millstone, for to do so would amount to taking one's life. They must also not steal a person among their brethren as a pledge, lording it over the debtor or selling him or her as a slave to another. Anyone doing this will be put to death, which is the only way such an evil can be removed from Israel. This latter law may already be known to the people, but here they see it applied to the distraint of persons — wives, children, and slaves — and then selling them.

Digressing briefly from legal prescriptions to homiletical instruction, Moses tells the people to be careful with a touch of scale disease and to follow the directions of the Levitical priests, who alone have jurisdiction over impurity and the cleansing of impurity. Moses commanded the priests about these matters, and people are to follow the commandments he has given. They are reminded about what happened to Miriam in the wilderness, how she broke out in scale disease after challenging Moses' authority and had to be put out of the camp for seven days.

Speaking again about pledges, Moses tells the people that when they make any loans, they are not to enter the debtor's house to seize a pledge. They must stand outside and let the person bring the pledge out to them. If the man is poor and has only his garment to surrender, the creditor must not keep it overnight and sleep in it. He must return it to the man each night at sundown, so the man who needs it may sleep in it. Because of this kindness, the debtor instead of cursing the creditor will bless him. What is more, the creditor will be reckoned as righteous before Yahweh.

These laws reflect simple village life where people live in houses, have a millstone and perhaps one outer garment, and must borrow from others on occasion to get food or seed for planting a crop. As such, they must surrender pledges, either when their loans are taken out or when they come due and repayment has not yet been made. Nothing is said about cases being decided by the city elders, much less in court where the king or royal appointees exercise judgment. Reference to Miriam's outbreak of scale disease gives the impression that the wilderness trek is in the recent past.

3. Justice and Benevolence to the Needy (24:14-22)

a) Paying Hired Laborers (24:14-15)

24 ^{14}*You shall not oppress a poor and needy hired laborer from your brethren or from your sojourner who is in your land, within your gates.* ^{15}*You shall give his wages in his day, and not when the sun has gone down upon it, for he is poor and he is setting his desire upon it, and that he not call to Yahweh against you, and it be a sin in you.*

b) Each in His Own Sin Shall Die (24:16)

24 ^{16}*Fathers shall not be put to death on account of children, and children shall not be put to death on account of fathers; each person in his sin, they shall be put to death.*

c) No Perversion of Judgment to the Needy (24:17-18)

24 ^{17}*You shall not pervert judgment to the sojourner, the orphan, and you shall not take in pledge the cloak of a widow.* ^{18}*So you shall remember that you were a slave in Egypt, and Yahweh your God ransomed you from there; therefore I am commanding you to do this thing.*

d) The Needy to Get Gleaning Rights (24:19-22)

24 ^{19}*When you shall reap your harvest in your field, and you have forgotten a sheaf in the field, you shall not return to take it; for the sojourner, for the orphan, and for the widow it shall be, in order that Yahweh your God may bless you in all the work of your hands.* ^{20}*When you shall beat your olive trees, you shall not go*

over the boughs after yourself; for the sojourner, for the orphan, and for the widow it shall be. ²¹When you shall make cuttings in your vineyard, you shall not glean after yourself; for the sojourner, for the orphan, and for the widow it shall be. ²²So you shall remember that you were a slave in the land of Egypt; therefore I am commanding you to do this thing.

Rhetoric and Composition

In the present verses are four more laws of a humane nature, three explicitly mandating justice and a benevolent spirit toward society's poor and needy. As happens all throughout Deuteronomy, the sojourner, orphan, and widow are singled out as objects of special concern. Law II, which forbids putting fathers or children to death for sins committed by the other, appears also to be protecting lives of the unprotected. The four laws mandate: (1) that day laborers be paid on the day of their work (vv. 14-15); (2) that fathers and children be put to death only for their own sins (v. 16); (3) that judgment not be perverted to the sojourner, orphan, and widow (vv. 17-18); and (4) that sojourners, orphans, and widows be allowed to glean in fields, orchards, and vineyards (vv. 19-22).

Law I is linked to Law IV in the prior cluster by keywords (Rofé 1988b: 275):

IV	And if he is a *poor* man	עָנִי	v. 12
	... as the sun goes down	כְּבֹא הַשֶּׁמֶשׁ ...	v. 13
I	a *poor* and needy hired laborer	עָנִי	v. 14
	... when the sun has gone down	תָבוֹא ... הַשֶּׁמֶשׁ	v. 15

Laws I and II in the present cluster are linked together by the keyword "sin" (Rofé):

I	and it be *a sin* in you	חֵטְא	v. 15
II	each person *in his sin*	בְּחֶטְאוֹ	v. 16

Laws I and III, which contain related subject matter (von Rad), begin similarly:

I	*You shall not oppress a poor and needy hired laborer* ...	v. 14
III	*You shall not pervert judgment to the sojourner, the orphan* ...	v. 17

Laws II and III connect naturally in that both have to do with the practice of justice.

Deuteronomy 24

Laws III and IV are linked together by entire phrases:

III	*the sojourner, the orphan, and . . . a widow*	v. 17
	So you shall remember that you were a slave in Egypt	v. 18
IV	*for the sojourner, for the orphan, and for the widow*	v. 19
	So you shall remember that you were a slave in the land of Egypt	v. 22

Laws in the cluster are demarcated by the following sections:

Law I has a *setumah* in M^L and a section in Sam before v. 14 and a *setumah* in M^L after v. 15.
Law II has a *setumah* in M^L before v. 16 and a *setumah* after v. 16.
Law III has a *setumah* in M^L before v. 17 and a *setumah* after v. 18. Sam also has a section after v. 18. 4QDeut^g upon reconstruction has no section either before v. 17 or after v. 18.
Law IV has a *setumah* in M^L before v. 19 and a *setumah* after v. 22, the latter of which is also the chapter division. Sam also has sections before v. 19 and after v. 22. 4QDeut^g upon reconstruction has no section before v. 19 but does have a section after v. 19, where *BHS* makes a break and 4Q38b may also have a section. M^L has no section after v. 19. A break after v. 19 separates gleaning in the fields from gleaning in the olive orchard. M^L has a *setumah* and 4QDeut^g and 4Q38d a section after v. 20, separating gleaning in the olive orchard from gleaning in the vineyard.

Portions of 24:14-22 are contained in 1QDeut^b, 4QDeut^g, and 4Q38d = 4QDeut^u (Tigchelaar 2008).

Notes

24:14 A law forbidding oppression of a day laborer who is poor and needy, whether an Israelite or a sojourner. A specific form of oppression is cited in the verse following. The LXX appears to anticipate the application in translating, "You shall not wrongfully withhold wages (Οὐκ ἀπαδικήσεις μισθὸν) of the poor and needy," but a Kennicott Heb MS and the Vg *(mercedem)* have "wages," which is supported additionally by שכר in 1QDeut^b instead of MT's שָׂכִיר ("hired laborer"). A version of this same law appears in Lev 19:13, where it says that one is not to oppress one's neighbor or rob him. Hebrew עשׁק can mean

Deuteronomy 24

both "oppress" and "rob" (Lev 5:21[6:2]; Hos 12:8[7], and in the OT the verb commonly occurs with גזל, "to rob" (28:29; Lev 19:13; Jer 21:12; 22:3; Ezek 18:18; 22:29; Ps 62:11[10]; Milgrom 1976a, 99). The Leviticus law does not mention the sojourner, nor is the concern there for the poor and needy made explicit. The prophets speak out in no uncertain terms against oppressing the poor and needy (Amos 4:1; Mic 2:2; Jer 7:6; Ezek 22:29), with Jeremiah making this a condition for Judahites remaining in the land. See also Prov 14:31; 22:16. The "poor" (עָנִי) and "needy" (אֶבְיוֹן) are those having few worldly goods (15:7-11; 24:12), and because of this they are often oppressed and powerless. On the "poor and needy," see also Note for 15:11.

hired laborer. I.e., someone hired for the day or for a particular job. Hebrew שָׂכִיר. In the NT, cf. Jesus' parable of the Laborers in the Vineyard in Matt 20:1-16.

your sojourner. The sojourner (גֵר) in Deuteronomy is to receive the same treatment as fellow Israelites, particularly Israelites who are in need (see Note for 5:13-14).

in your land. בְּאַרְצֶךָ. Two Heb MSS, the LXX, and S omit, which, as Wevers (1995, 384) points out, is probably a loss attributable to haplography (homoeoarcton: ב . . . ב).

within your gates. In Deuteronomy "gates" = "cities" (see Note for 5:14).

15 *You shall give his wages in his day, and not when the sun has gone down upon it.* The day laborer is to get his wages on the day he works (Lev 19:13; Tob 4:14; Matt 20:8-10). Job 14:6 says that he may enjoy what remains of the day. Anyone not paying him daily oppresses him and is liable to judgment (Mal 3:5; Jas 5:4-5). The Code of Hammurabi (CH 273, 274; $ANET^3$, 177) fixes the wages of laborers and craftsmen by the day, even though they are employed as seasonal workers (Driver and Miles 1952, 470-73).

You shall give his wages. The Hebrew idiom omits the indirect object, which in this case would be "to him." See also Exod 2:9; Zech 11:12.

for he is poor and he is setting his desire upon it. The poor laborer not only looks forward to receiving his wages at the end of the day (cf. Job 7:2); he needs them (T^{Onq}: "he is desperately counting on you"; T^{PsJ}: "and because of it he hopes to maintain his life"). Hebrew נֶפֶשׁ here means "desire" (cf. Hos 4:8; Jer 22:27; 34:16; 44:14; Ezek 24:25; Ps 24:4).

and that he not call to Yahweh against you, and it be a sin in you. See 15:9 and with respect to tardy payment of vows, 23:22(21). Without an earthly advocate, the poor must cry to Yahweh, who will hear his cry, just as he does the cry of the afflicted sojourner, orphan, and widow (Exod 22:22, 26[23, 27]). Greenberg (1960, 11) says that because God is the author of biblical law, failure to comply with its demands becomes a sin. Conversely, if one is kind to the poor, that person will bless him before Yahweh and he will be reckoned as righteous (24:13).

16 Another law of general principle found only in Deuteronomy, although the prophecies of Jer 31:29-30 and Ezekiel 18 argue a similar point. The oracle in Jer 31:29-30 speaks of a future day when children will not reap the bad fruit of their father's sins and each person will die for his own sin. Ezekiel tells the exilic community to change its way of thinking: "the soul that sins shall die" (Ezek 18:20). According to this prophet, the righteous man executes "true justice" (מִשְׁפַּט אֱמֶת), refrains from "oppression" (עֹשֶׁק), and does not "maltreat" (יֹנֶה) the poor and needy (18:8, 12, 18). These are all concerns of other laws here in Deuteronomy, which may explain why the present law is grouped with them.

Earlier scholars took the present law as placing a limit on corporate liability and punishment. In the ancient world a person was not an isolated entity, but was someone bound up inextricably with his family, tribe, city, and land (Y. Kaufmann 1960, 329-30). Driver therefore saw the present law as prohibiting corporate responsibility for criminal behavior, i.e., family members were not to suffer *together with* the one committing the crime. In his commentary (1895, 277 n.), Driver rendered the preposition עַל as "together with," although in BDB (754 II b) it is said to mean "on account of." Examples of corporate punishment in the ancient world are well attested. We see it in Hittite laws ($ANET^3$, 207 no. 2), and there are cases also in the Persian age (Esth 9:13-14; Dan 6:24; Herodotus *Hist.* iii 119). Driver says Achan's חֵרֶם violation in Josh 7:24-25 and Saul's sin against the Gibeonites in 2 Sam 21:1-9 were of an exceptional nature. The weakness in this interpretation is that no examples are given of fathers being put to death for the sins of their children, which the present law legislates against. Greenberg (1983a, 332-33) says none exist in the Bible, where it is never an issue. No examples are known in the extrabiblical literature. Ezekiel 18:20 makes a reverse attribution of guilt, but Greenberg says this is simply a rhetorical device for emphasizing the disassociation of generations from each other's guilt.

More recently the law has been understood as a prohibition of "vicarious punishment," which was practiced elsewhere in the ANE but not in Israel. Vicarious punishment occurs when someone other than the guilty party is surrendered to the victim's family for punishment (Greenberg 1960, 20-24). Vicarious punishment is called for in the Code of Hammurabi (CH 116, 210, 230; $ANET^3$, 170, 175-76) and in the Middle Assyrian Laws (MAL A 50, 55; $ANET^3$, 184-85; cf. Driver and Miles 1935, 347). In the former, if a man strikes the pregnant daughter of another and she miscarries and dies, that man's own daughter must be put to death (CH 210). And if a house, because of faulty construction, collapses and kills the householder's son, the builder's son must be put to death (CH 230). Greenberg says the present law means to exclude vicarious punishment and that nowhere in the Bible are secular offenses punished vicariously.

Earlier scholars also assumed an evolution in ancient Israel from corporate to individual responsibility, but that assessment is now regarded as incorrect (von Rad; Y. Kaufmann 1960, 329-30; Greenberg 1960, 22-27; Moran; Tigay). The two principles of retribution existed side by side, both in Israel and in surrounding cultures. The Covenant Code knows nothing of corporate liability for the family (von Rad). Daube (1949, 96) thinks that individual retribution existed in very early times, being expressed already in the Joseph story, which, he says, "is permeated with legal thought" (Gen 44:17). Individual responsibility is attested in the Middle Assyrian Laws, e.g., in MAL A 2, where it states that a woman — whether the wife or daughter of a seignior — heard uttering blasphemy shall bear her penalty, but her husband, sons, or daughters may not be touched ($ANET^3$, 180; cf. Driver and Miles 1935, 20-21, 347). Yaron (1970, 551) thinks this law means only to preclude vicarious liability for the blasphemous woman. In any case, Driver and Miles point out that the law constitutes an exception to other Middle Assyrian laws in which family members are punished for crimes of an individual. Herodotus, as we mentioned earlier, cited a case from the Persian age where corporate punishment was carried out, yet elsewhere (*Hist.* ix 88) he reports how Pausanias of the Greeks spared the sons of Attaginus after forcing the surrender of Thebes. Some maintain, nevertheless, that the law here in Deuteronomy is a true innovation (Yaron 1970, 551; Tigay), which it may be. It is singled out in the Deuteronomic History as the basis on which Amaziah refrained from killing the sons of those who murdered his father (2 Kgs 14:5-6).

Finally, it is generally agreed that God's punishment of children for the sins of their fathers is a different matter altogether (Driver; Greenberg; Tigay), for which reason the present law poses no conflict with passages such as Deut 5:9; Exod 20:5; 34:7; Jer 2:5-9, where the sins of the fathers are said to be visited upon the children to the third and fourth generations. Yahweh maintains a "divine prerogative" to punish others besides the person committing a crime, just as we find happening with the gods of Hittite religion ($ANET^3$, 208 no. 3; Gurney 1962, 70-71). The OT does attest to cases of collective and vicarious punishment, the most obvious being the punishment carried out by Yahweh for accumulated sin over the generations, which led to the nation's demise and large numbers of people paying the price with their lives. Greenberg (1960, 23) includes in this category the case of Achan's sons and daughters being put to death in Joshua 7 and Saul's sons being put to death in 2 Sam 21, both of which in his view are offenses that "touch the realm of the deity directly." At the time of Korah's wilderness rebellion, Moses and Aaron cried in desperation to Yahweh: "O God, God of the spirits of all flesh, shall one man sin and you be angry against all the congregation?" (Num 16:22). In this case, however, the sons of Korah did not die (Num 26:11). A distinction, nevertheless, has to be made between punishment meted out by God on the one hand and punishment by human judges on the other. God can and does carry out corporate and vicarious punishment, but human courts in Israel may not do likewise. The present law seeks then to limit the scope of punishment permissible in Israelite law courts: only the one who sins shall die.

17 The verb נטה in the H-stem ("pervert") means lit. "to bend, turn aside." Here Israelites are told that they must not pervert judgment with regard to those for whom Deuteronomy has a special concern: the sojourner, the orphan, and the widow. Judahites are told the same in Jer 22:3. The Covenant Code issues a similar warning concerning the poor (Exod 23:6). In Deut 16:19 people are told they must not pervert judgment to anyone. But to the sojourner, orphan, and widow they must be particularly vigilant in executing justice and practicing benevolence, since these are the people in society typically without an advocate. For this reason Yahweh shows them special concern (see Note for 10:18). A curse falls on anyone who fails to act in accord with the present law (27:19). Jeremiah, in his time, complained that this law was being disregarded. The wicked in Judah would not even prosecute cases of the orphan to win them (Jer 5:28). From Egyptian, Akkadian, and Ugaritic texts we learn that care was taken in other societies to look after the needs of the orphan, widow, and outcast (Fensham 1962a). In the present verse the LXX adds "and the widow" (καὶ χήρας) after "the orphan," which fills out the stereotyped triad. The Targums do not have the added term. If it was present, the loss in MT could easily be due to haplography (homoeoarcton: ו . . . ו, or possibly even ואל . . . ולא).

and you shall not take in pledge the cloak of a widow. An example of the general principle. Garments taken from the poor as pledges had to be returned at night, but a widow's garment may not be taken under any circumstances. The Mishnah (*B. Meṣiʿa* 9:13) says this applies to a widow rich or poor. Job 24:3 says calloused individuals were known to have taken a widow's ox in pledge, which was scarcely better than taking her cloak, since this too was tantamount to taking her life.

18 This motive for showing kindness to the sojourner, orphan, and widow, reasonable as it appears, nevertheless makes the injunction unique. On Deuteronomy's continual call for Israel to remember its former slavery in Egypt, which recurs in v. 22, see Note for 8:2. Here the purpose is to ensure that people not pervert right judgment due the sojourner, orphan, and widow. Cf. similar reminders in the Covenant Code (Exod 22:20[21]; 23:9) and the Holiness Code (Lev 19:34). Honor (1953, 431) says regarding this admonition to Israel to remember its experience of slavery:

> History is replete with instances of oppressed groups or individuals who struggled valiantly against their oppressors and finally succeeded in liberating themselves and who, when in the course of time they had achieved power, became oppressors and did unto others what had been done to

Deuteronomy 24

them.... In accordance with the tradition as recorded in the Pentateuch, Moses the liberator... must have sensed this correlation intuitively. He is pictured as having appreciated that as long as Israel will remember their suffering as slaves, as long as there will be a vivid recollection of the cries of anguish which they uttered when they were being oppressed, it will not be possible for his people to do unto others as had been done unto them.

therefore I am commanding you to do this thing. Moses is the speaker of these words. For this recurring directive in Deuteronomy, see again v. 22 and Note for 15:11.

19 *When you shall reap your harvest in your field, and you have forgotten a sheaf in the field, you shall not return to take it; for the sojourner, for the orphan, and for the widow it shall be.* The sojourner, orphan, and widow, being landless people, are here given the privilege of gleaning in the fields after the grain had been harvested (cf. Lev 19:9-10; 23:22). Leviticus 19:9 states that one must not harvest the corners of one's field, which, because of rounded sickles was more difficult (Soss 1973, 334), but leave these for the gleaners. One must not glean one's own field. Gleaning was a constructive way of dealing with poverty. Soss (333-34) calls it a "make-work scheme," but sees it as another important mechanism in OT law bearing upon the distribution of wealth. Ruth, as both a widow and a sojourner, was able to glean in the fields of Boaz (Ruth 2). The practice existed also in Egypt (Montet 1958, 116). "The Instruction of Amen-em-ope(t)" (ch. 28) contains a reference to someone coming upon a poor widow gleaning in the field (*ANET*³, 424).

in order that Yahweh your God may bless you in all the work of your hands. Yahweh will bless one's work if the sojourner, orphan, and widow are invited to share in the harvest tithe every three years (14:28-29). For Yahweh's blessing coming as a result of charitable action, see 23:21(20) and Note for 15:10. On the present stereotyped expression in Deuteronomy, see Note for 2:7.

20 Israel's landless minorities are also given a share in the olive harvest. Olives were beaten down with long poles; otherwise, someone would climb the tree to shake its branches, much in the way olives and nuts are harvested today. See Isa 17:6; 24:13; 27:12.

you shall not go over the boughs. לֹא תְפָאֵר. The verb is a *hapax legomenon* in the OT, but its meaning is not in doubt.

21 The "cuttings" will be of grapes (Judg 9:27). This third gleaning privilege granted to the landless means they will get a representative, if not a full, share in Israel's bounty of "grain, wine, and oil" (see Note for 7:13).

22 See v. 18. Here the call for Israel to remember its former slavery is to ensure that people treat in a benevolent manner the sojourner, orphan, and widow.

Deuteronomy 25

Message and Audience

Moses is heard telling the people in these laws and solemn warnings that they must act with compassion toward those in Israel who are poor or ever near to being poor. Those hired by the day must be given their wages at day's end. Not only do they wait expectantly for them, their needs are also immediate. This applies to the sojourner as well, for whom Israel shows more concern than do its neighbors. Since these and the poor will not likely have an advocate against oppressors, they will cry out to Yahweh, and failure to help them will end up being reckoned as a sin.

Speaking of sin, Moses adds that neither corporate nor vicarious punishment is to be carried out in Israel. Fathers may not be put to death for the sins of their children, and children may not be put to death for the sins of their fathers. Each person for his own sin shall die. Judgment must also not be perverted toward the sojourner, orphan, or widow, with the seizure of a widow's cloak as a pledge absolutely forbidden. Moses reminds the people that they were once slaves in Egypt, and because Yahweh ransomed them from this miserable condition, he now commands that they be just and benevolent toward those in the land who will know the pain and shame of subsistence living.

The sojourner, orphan, and widow shall be permitted to glean in Israel's fields, orchards, and vineyards, thus sharing in the nation's bounty of grain, wine, and oil. They may follow the reapers in the field, gathering sheaves of grain left behind; they may walk in the orchards and take what olives remain on the trees; and they may go into the vineyards and collect grapes still on the vine or left on the ground. Owners are not to glean their own fields, orchards, and vineyards. In leaving whatever remains for the sojourner, orphan, and widow, the owners will receive blessing from Yahweh for the work they have done. And once again, people are told to remember that they were once slaves in Egypt, and kind treatment now to those less fortunate than they will be the proper response to the kind treatment they received from Yahweh, who redeemed them from their miserable slavery.

These laws and warnings to practice justice and benevolence toward the needy will have applicability to any period within Israel's history, when people are deciding cases in the gates of their cities and towns and cultivating the land graciously given them by Yahweh.

4. A Limit on Flogging (25:1-3)

25 *¹When there will be a dispute between men and they draw near to the place of judgment, and they judge them, and acquit the righteous and condemn the*

wicked, ²and it will be if the wicked is worthy of a beating, then the judge shall make him lie down and have him beaten in his presence, according to the extent of his wickedness in number. ³Forty times he may beat him; he shall not add, lest he add to beat him many blows over these, and your brother be dishonored before your eyes.

5. No Muzzle on a Threshing Ox (25:4)

25⁴ *You shall not muzzle an ox in its treading of grain.*

Rhetoric and Composition

The present verses contain two laws concluding the group of humane laws in 24:1–25:4. The first limits the amount of flogging one may do of a criminal (vv. 1-3). The second prohibits muzzling an ox while it is threshing (v. 4). The unit is delimited at the top end by a *setumah* in M^L and a section in Sam before v. 1, which is also the chapter division. At the bottom end delimitation is by a *setumah* in M^L and a section in Sam after v. 4. M^L has another *setumah* after v. 3, setting apart the law on not muzzling an ox.

Portions of 25:1-4 are contained in 4QDeut^f and 4QDeut^g. The Roberts Papyrus (P. Ryl. Gk. 458), an early Greek text dated to the end of the 2nd cent. B.C. (C. H. Roberts 1936, 37), contains portions of 25:1-3.

Notes

25:1 *When there will be a dispute between men and they draw near to the place of judgment, and they judge them.* Hebrew הַמִּשְׁפָּט is here "the (place of) judgment," which will be the city gate. G^B omits "and they judge them," which can be due to haplography (homoeoarcton: ו . . . ו). More than one person will hear the case and render a judgment (1:16; 17:8). In the Middle Assyrian Laws, judges are always mentioned in the plural (Driver and Miles 1935, 338).

and acquit the righteous and condemn the wicked. וְהִצְדִּיקוּ אֶת־הַצַּדִּיק וְהִרְשִׁיעוּ אֶת־הָרָשָׁע is lit. "and they shall declare innocent the innocent and declare guilty the guilty." The righteous person is declared innocent and the wicked person declared guilty. For צדק and רשע with these meanings in the H-stem, see Exod 22:8(9); 23:7; Isa 5:23; Ps 94:21.

2 *and it will be if the wicked is worthy of a beating.* This clause is still part of the protasis; the apodosis begins in v. 2b: "Then the judge shall make him lie down...." The LXX with its subjunctive verbs in v. 1 begins the legal decision in v. 2a (Wevers 1995, 389; cf. RSV). In either case, the law is not declaring that judges decide between the innocent and the guilty (*pace* AV). Innocence and guilt has already been determined. The law is stating what will happen to the guilty person if he merits a flogging. Not every guilty man deserves a flogging (Rashi). One who brings false charges against his bride will get a flogging (22:18). The present law is concerned with a dispute between two men. The Hammurabi Code (CH 202; *ANET*[3], 175) specifies that one who strikes the cheek of a superior will get sixty lashes with an oxtail whip. In the Middle Assyrian Laws, beatings are done with rods. A man who slanders another man's wife and cannot substantiate his claim will get forty blows with rods, in addition to other punishments (MAL A 18; *ANET*[3], 181); one who encroaches a boundary will get one hundred blows with rods, in addition to other punishments (MAL B 8; *ANET*[3], 186). The Bible reports beatings with rods on the person's back (Exod 21:20; Prov 10:13; 19:29; 26:3; Isa 50:6; Acts 16:22). Whips were also used, sometimes even more vicious instruments (1 Kgs 12:11, 14; cf. Judg 8:7, 16), but we do not know if any were used in judicial punishments. The Mishnah (*Mak.* 3:10-14) allows for lashes with a strap of oxhide and specifies that one-third of the lashes are to be on the front of the body, two-thirds on the back.

worthy of a beating. Hebrew בֶּן הַכּוֹת, lit. "son of a beating." The verb נכה is strong, used in the OT often in the sense of "strike to kill."

then the judge shall make him lie down and have him beaten in his presence. The LXX has "and you shall make him lie down in the presence of the judges" (καὶ καθιεῖς αὐτὸν ἔναντι τῶν κριτῶν), shifting also to the second person with μαστιγῶσαι ("you whip") in the middle of v. 3. In MT the shift to the second person does not come until the end of v. 3: "and *your* brother be degraded in *your* eyes." The MT reading is supported by the Targums. The head judge will preside over the punishment to make sure the criminal does not suffer unduly. If beatings were left to subordinates, the number of blows could exceed what the law required. In Egypt, courts of law consisted of local dignitaries under the chairmanship of a single official, who presided over the trial (Seidl 1942, 204). In the Code of Hammurabi (CH 202; *ANET*[3], 175), a beating was to take place "in the assembly," i.e., before a court. The Middle Assyrian Laws (MAL A 57; *ANET*[3], 185) specified that beatings be carried out before judges. The person to be beaten is made to lie down before the judge. Egyptian artwork shows naked men lying prostrate on the ground, with someone holding the feet and another holding both arms over the head. The beating was administered on the back. Women also received their blows on the back, but were made to sit rather than lie down (J. G. Wilkinson 1883, 1:305 for drawings). The Mishnah (*Mak.* 3:12-13) specified that the two hands of the criminal be tied on either side of a pillar, his clothes torn and his chest bared. Blows were to be administered with the victim bending low, one-third on the chest, the remaining two-thirds on the back. The flogger was to stand on a stone above the victim, hitting him with a cowhide strap with all his might.

according to the extent of his wickedness in number. Some beatings were to be light, others heavy (cf. Luke 12:47-48). Someone was on hand to count the number of strokes. The LXX omits "according to the extent of his wickedness" (כְּדֵי רִשְׁעָתוֹ), which is probably to be attributed to haplography (homoeoteleuton: ו . . . ו).

3 *Forty times he may beat him; he shall not add.* Only the number forty (אַרְבָּעִים) occurs in the Hebrew, which has a parallel in Middle Assyrian Law A 7, where the number twenty similarly means "twenty blows" (Yaron 1970, 552). The Mishnah (*Mak.* 3:10) reduces the number to forty less one, stating also that an estimate must be made on the man's capacity to withstand the blows (*Mak.* 3:11). If it is determined that he will be unable to take the full number, a lesser number will be prescribed. In 2 Cor 11:24-25, Paul says that five times he received forty lashings less one, and that three times he was beaten with rods. The Code of Hammurabi in one law (CH 202; $ANET^3$, 175) prescribes sixty lashes. In the Middle Assyrian Laws one could receive, along with other punishments, five (MAL B 7; $ANET^3$, 186), twenty (MAL A 7; $ANET^3$, 181), thirty (MAL B 10; $ANET^3$, 186), forty (MAL A 18; $ANET^3$, 181), fifty (MAL A 19, A 21, A 40; B 9, B 14; $ANET^3$, 181, 183, 186), or as many as one hundred blows with a rod (MAL B 8; $ANET^3$, 186). In one Egyptian text a bastinado of one thousand blows is called for on a man guilty of adultery (J. G. Wilkinson 1883, 1:304), from which he could hardly survive.

lest he add to beat him many blows over these, and your brother be dishonored before your eyes. Here again is a concern in Deuteronomy to avoid shame, which would result from excessive punishment (Daube 1969a, 34-35). There is a limit on how much dishonor is permissible even toward a criminal. Rashi is nevertheless surprised to hear the wicked man now being called a "brother"! In the levirate law of vv. 5-10, things are reversed: there shame is the punishment for the man failing to perform his brotherly duty (Rofé 1988b, 276). One notes that here, as elsewhere in Deuteronomy, a shift to direct address comes at the close of the law (G. A. Smith). This same rhetoric occurs frequently in the preaching of Jeremiah (Jer 2:9; 4:30; 5:7-8, 25, 31; 8:17; 11:13; 12:13b; 16:8-9; 20:18; cf. Lundbom 1999, 658). On the Deuteronomic expression "before your eyes," see again v. 9 and Note for 1:30.

4 Another law in Deuteronomy only, although Egyptian paintings portray threshing animals without muzzles. Not muzzling oxen while they are threshing has been an ongoing practice in the Near East down into modern times. Both the Covenant Code and Deuteronomy mandate a Sabbath rest for working animals (5:14; Exod 20:10). Threshing on a small scale was done with sticks (Judg 6:11; Ruth 2:17), whereas in large harvests animals did the work. Once the ripened barley or wheat had been cropped below the ears and brought to the threshing floor, which was a well-tamped and well-swept circular area near to both field and granary ("gates" = "cities" in Jer 15:7), sheaves were thrown on the floor and trodden by the hoofs of animals. Homer (*Il.* xx 495) speaks of barley being threshed on a threshing floor beneath the feet of loud-bellowing bulls. Threshing was typically done with oxen, less often with asses (CH 268-269; *ANET*³, 177; J. G. Wilkinson 1883, 2:421; cf. Isa 30:24), where as many as four or five animals were yoked together to tread the grain evenly. The Code of Hammurabi mentions a third animal hired for threshing (CH 270), which T. J. Meek translated "goat" in *ANET*, but which Driver and Miles (1952, 469) say is probably a different animal. In Egypt and Israel threshing sleds pulled by animals were also used in the work of separation (2 Sam 24:22; Amos 1:3; on חָרוּץ, "threshing sled," see *TDOT*, 5:217). In Israel, a wheel-thresher may have been used (Borowski 1987, 65; cf. Isa 28:27-28).

Although in some biblical passages young heifers are portrayed as happy threshers (Hos 10:11; Jer 50:11), in the Egyptian paintings a driver follows behind the oxen with a stick. More and more sheaves were thrown onto the threshing floor until the entire pile was consumed. Someone also stood by with a pitchfork, continually turning over the trodden stalks (Montet 1958, 117). While threshing, the animals would want to nibble grain, and the present law forbidding them to be muzzled allows them to do this. Once the sheaves were trodden and winnowed with shovels, the clean grain was transported to the granary (cf. Matt 3:12). For more on harvesting and threshing in Egypt and Israel, see J. G. Wilkinson 1883, 2:418-21; Driver 1895, 280; Borowski 1987, 57-69. An Egyptian bas-relief from the Old Kingdom (2700-2200), found at Sakkarah, shows asses being driven over a threshing floor with one bending down to get a nibble of grain (for a picture, see *ANEP*²⋅ 26 no. 89). Another painting depicting fieldwork and agricultural activities from the Middle Kingdom (1971-1928) has survived from the Tomb of Amen-em-het. It shows oxen threshing with a driver behind prodding them with a whip (see *ANEP*², 37 no. 122, register 6; Borowski 1987, 60). The oxen in this painting are not muzzled.

The Mishnah (*B. Qam.* 5:7) applies what is stated here about the ox to other animals. The purpose of the law is clear: it allows a working animal to eat food continually before its eyes. Michaelis (1814, 2:188) says it would be an act of cruelty not to make such an allowance (cf. Prov 12:10; Job 24:10-11), and he compares this to a person working in similar circumstances. Luther says that by practicing kindness to beasts, people become more benevolent toward other people. In the Talmud (*b. B. Meṣiʿa* 88b-89a; cf. *m.* 7:2-5) the present law is discussed with another concerning laborers in a field, who are permitted to eat food they are harvesting (cf. 23:25-26[24-25]). In the Qumran *Temple Scroll*

(11QT 52:12-13), this law and the one in 22:10 about not yoking an ox with an ass are inserted into a discussion on the slaughter of clean animals (Yadin 1983, 1:315-16; 2:234). Paul cites the present law in 1 Cor 9:9 to argue that he and others laboring to proclaim the gospel have the right to food and drink. See also 1 Tim 5:17-18.

Carmichael (1974, 238-40; 1980, 250-52) thinks the present law ought not be taken literally, but rather given symbolic meaning of not denying an Israelite his portion of land (Israelite = ox). So understood, it has thus been juxtaposed to the law on levirate marriage in vv. 5-10, which seeks to remedy a family situation where a man dies childless and has no son to inherit his portion of the estate. Carmichael also notes that "treading" by a man can symbolize sexual intercourse with a woman. Noonan (1979-80, 174) cites this novel idea with approval, but thinks that the statement "Do not muzzle the threshing ox" means that "an Israelite should not prevent conception." In his view, the Deuteronomic author is alluding to Onan's refusal to perform the levirate duty to Tamar, his sister-in-law (Gen 38:8-9). Both ideas, while they seek to fit an otherwise miscellaneous law into its present context, remain highly speculative. Even if there is some hidden symbolism in the image of a threshing ox not being muzzled, Carmichael's case is not made by denying the plain sense of the law, which is self-evident. The same may be said for the interpretation given to the law by Noonan.

Message and Audience

Moses in the first law is heard to be telling the people how corporal punishment is to be administered should the situation call for it. If two men engaged in a dispute come to the place of judgment, which will be the city gate, and receive a verdict acquitting the righteous and condemning the wicked, and if it is determined that the guilty person deserves a beating, the presiding judge shall make the man lie down for a beating to be carried out in his presence. The number of blows will correspond to the offense committed. The fellow may be beaten forty times, but no more, so as not to be dishonored in people's eyes. Moses reminds the people that this fellow, although guilty of wrongdoing, is still a brother. A second law prohibiting the muzzling of a threshing ox is also given. Humane treatment is once again extended even to animals.

Both laws envision settlement in the land, where cases are being tried in the city gate and animals are employed in harvesting the bounty of the land.

Deuteronomy 25

T. Miscellaneous Laws (25:5-19)

1. Levirate Marriage (25:5-10)

25 ⁵*When brothers will dwell together, and one of them dies and has no son, the wife of the dead shall not go outside to a strange man. Her brother-in-law shall go in to her and take her to himself for a wife, and do to her the duty of a brother-in-law.* ⁶*And it shall be that the firstborn whom she will bear shall succeed to the name of his brother who died, so his name not be wiped out from Israel.* ⁷*And if the man does not want to take his sister-in-law, then his sister-in-law shall go up to the gate, to the elders, and say, "My brother-in-law refuses to raise up for his brother a name in Israel; he was not willing to do the brother-in-law's duty to me."* ⁸*Then the elders of his city shall summon him and speak to him, but if he stands firm and says, "I do not want to take her,"* ⁹*then his sister-in-law shall come to him, before the eyes of the elders, and pull off his sandal from his foot, and spit in his face, and she shall respond and say, "Thus it shall be done to the man who does not build up the house of his brother."* ¹⁰*And his name shall be called in Israel, "House of the one whose sandal was pulled off."*

2. Wives Interfering in a Fight (25:11-12)

25 ¹¹*When men will fight together, a man and his brother, and the wife of the one draws near to rescue her husband from the hand of the one striking him, and she puts forth her hand and grabs hold of his shameful parts,* ¹²*then you shall cut off her palm; your eye shall not pity.*

3. Just Weights and Measures (25:13-16)

25 ¹³*There shall not be for you, in your bag, one stone and another stone, great and small.* ¹⁴*There shall not be for you, in your house, one ephah and another ephah, great and small.* ¹⁵*A full and right stone there shall be for you; a full and right ephah there shall be for you, in order that your days may be prolonged on the soil that Yahweh your God is giving to you.* ¹⁶*For anyone who does these things, anyone who does wrong, is an abomination to Yahweh your God.*

4. Wipe Out the Remembrance of Amalek! (25:17-19)

25 ¹⁷*Remember what Amalek did to you on the road when you came out from Egypt,* ¹⁸*how he chanced to meet you on the road and cut off your tail, all the battered ones*

Deuteronomy 25

behind you, when you were faint and weary, and he did not fear God. ¹⁹*So it will be, when Yahweh your God gives you rest from all your enemies round about in the land that Yahweh your God is giving to you as an inheritance to possess it, you shall wipe out the remembrance of Amalek from under heaven; you shall not forget.*

Rhetoric and Composition

The Deuteronomic Code draws to a conclusion with three laws: (1) a law regulating the custom of levirate marriage (vv. 5-10); (2) a law prohibiting the unlawful interfering of wives in fights of their husbands (vv. 11-12); and (3) a law mandating the use of just weights and measures (vv. 13-16). At the end of the unit is an admonition for the people to remember Amalek's treachery on the road out of Egypt (vv. 17-19).

The unit is demarcated at the top end by a *setumah* in M^L and a section in Sam before v. 5 and at the bottom end by a *petuḥah* in M^L and a section in Sam after v. 19, which is also the chapter division. Law I is separated from Law II by a *setumah* in M^L and a section in Sam after v. 10. Law II is separated from Law III by a *setumah* in M^L after v. 12. Law III is separated from the final admonition by a *petuḥah* in M^L and a section in 4QDeut^g after v. 16. Law III has another *setumah* after v. 13, separating the directives on weights and measures.

The law on the levirate marriage links up to the following law on interfering wives and to the final admonition to remember Amalek. Linkage to the law on interfering wives is by similar opening phrases (Rofé 1988b, 276; Tigay, 459):

I	*When brothers* will dwell *together . . . the wife . . .*	v. 5
	כִּי־יֵשְׁבוּ אַחִים יַחְדָּו . . . אֵשֶׁת . . .	
II	*When* men will fight *together,* a man and *his brother . . . the wife*	v. 11
	כִּי־יִנָּצוּ אֲנָשִׁים יַחְדָּו אִישׁ וְאָחִיו . . . אֵשֶׁת . . .	

G. A. Smith earlier had taken "brother" in v. 9 and v. 11 to be a catchword. The two laws have a common theme, in that both deal with a man's ability to carry on the family line.

Linkage to the admonition regarding Amalek is by contrasting phrases (Tigay, 458):

I	*so his name not be wiped out from Israel*	v. 6
	וְלֹא־יִמָּחֶה שְׁמוֹ מִיִּשְׂרָאֵל	
IV	*you shall wipe out the remembrance of Amalek from under heaven*	v. 19
	תִּמְחֶה אֶת־זֵכֶר עֲמָלֵק מִתַּחַת הַשָּׁמָיִם	

The admonition regarding Amalek has a keyword inclusio:

IV *Remember* what Amalek did to you . . .   זָכוֹר   v. 17
    . . . you shall wipe out the *remembrance* of Amalek . . .   זֵכֶר   v. 19

Portions of 25:5-19 are contained in 1QDeut^b, 4QDeut^f, 4QDeut^g, and 4QDeut^k2.

Notes

25:5 To "do the duty of a brother-in-law" (יבם) is a circumlocution for having intercourse with the widow of one's brother in hopes of raising up a son that will perpetuate the "name" of the deceased. This son will inherit the share of the estate belonging to the deceased, and the widow will be provided for. There is no evidence of such a law in Egypt (Galpaz-Feller 2008, 251). In Israel, unlike other ancient societies, widows were unable to inherit property (E. W. Davies 1981, 138-39). This institution is called the "levirate marriage," *levir* being the Latin word for "husband's brother." The law exists only in Deuteronomy, which limits and mitigates an old custom described in Genesis 38 (the widowhood of Tamar) and restricts the custom as described in the book of Ruth (Boaz and Ruth). In Genesis 38 the duty of the brother-in-law is mandatory (de Vaux 1965, 37), as it is in Hittite law (HL 193; Neufeld 1951, 55, 192; *ANET*³, 196), although in the end it is carried out unwittingly by the father-in-law, which, according to Assyrian law, was allowable (MAL A 33; *ANET*³, 182; Driver and Miles 1935, 242-43).

In Deuteronomy the levirate duty can be refused, although not without cost. In the case of Ruth and Boaz, the duty to raise up a son for the deceased falls upon the next-of-kin, and in order to take the widow, one must also purchase land belonging to the deceased. Here the levir acts as a "redeemer" (גאל), whose obligations in Israelite society were many and varied (see Note for 19:6). Deuteronomy prescribes the levirate duty only for the brother-in-law, with the added stipulation that he must have been living together with the deceased on the family estate, presumably after the father had died. Since the book of Ruth is written later than the time it describes, some think that the transaction concerning Ruth and Boaz *extends* the custom of the levirate from the brother to the kinsman (Driver and Miles 1935, 245; de Vaux 1965, 38). But Neufeld (1944, 34) is of the opinion that the cases referred to in Genesis 38 and in the book of Ruth show no historical development, but are simply records of the practice in different circumstances and at different times. In the NT, all three Synoptic Gospels record a discussion between Jesus and the Sadducees on the levirate marriage and life in the resurrection (Matt 22:23-33; Mark 12:18-27; Luke 20:27-40).

Deuteronomy 25

There are no known parallels to the levirate institution in Babylonian law, but practices of a similar nature do appear in Assyrian law (MAL A 30, 33; 43; *ANET*³, 182, 184; Price 1926 [with enumerations of +1]; Neufeld 1944, 51-52), although Driver and Miles (1935, 240-50) emphasize their differences from the biblical custom, noting also that other Assyrian laws may not support the existence of a levirate marriage. In their view, both the Babylonians and the Assyrians attained the same end by legitimating children of slave-wives and concubines, and by adoption; therefore they had no need of a levirate marriage. Better parallels to the Hebrew levirate exist in Hittite law (HL 193; *ANET*³, 196; Price 1926; Neufeld 1944, 52-53; 1951, 55; Gurney 1962, 101-2), at Nuzi (C. H. Gordon 1936b; cf. Neufeld 1944, 53-54), and at Ugarit (UgT 16144), where the practice is anticipated in the royal family (Boyer 1955, 300-301; C. H. Gordon 1956; Tsevat 1958b). It has been argued by some that the levirate marriage was taken over from the Canaanites (Michaelis 1814, 2:22-25; Alt 1966c; Burrows 1940), which, however, has no support other than the fact that Judah was married to a Canaanite woman (Gen 38:2). In modern times, a form of levirate marriage is attested among the Arabs and the Bedouin (Neufeld 1944, 31-32), also among the Asian Mongols (Michaelis 1814, 2:25), Hindus in India, and the peoples of Madagascar and Brazil (Driver 1895, 282).

When brothers will dwell together. A typical casuistic law (Alt 1966c, 88-89; Burrows 1940, 25), beginning with כִּי ("when"). The levirate obligation as set forth here applies only when two brothers have been living together as joint heirs on the family estate (Driver; von Rad; Neufeld 1944, 40-41; *pace* Rashi). The father is dead (Daube 1950, 71-77; Westbrook 1977, 75-76; *pace* L. M. Epstein 1942, 86), yet the estate remains undivided. Daube says a father living at the time would take charge of the situation and either constrain or attempt to persuade the remaining son to do his bidding, i.e., to take the widow in a levirate marriage. This is what happened when Judah's son Er died (Gen 38:8-11).

Daube (1950, 74) cites for comparison an example of undivided ownership in Roman law, called *consortium*, "where on the death of a *paterfamilias* two or more of his heirs, instead of partitioning the estate and breaking up into separate families, remain together to enjoy the inheritance in common." Undivided ownership existed also in earlier Assyrian law, where in MAL B 2 and 3 reference is to "brothers who have not divided [the inheritance]" (Neufeld 1944, 41; Westbrook 1977, 75 adds MAL A 25). The OT speaks precisely to this situation in Ps 133:1: "Behold how good and how pleasant it is, brothers dwelling, yes, together." If the brothers have separated after their father's death and each has established his own family at some distance from the other, the present law will not apply. It will also not apply to brothers whose father is still alive. Extension of the law to deal with such cases occurred later (Daube 1950, 90). Later Jewish law also stated that if there were two or more surviving brothers in a family where one brother had died, the eldest had the duty to take the widow in a levirate marriage (*m. Yebam.* 2:18).

brothers. אַחִים. Calvin wants to broaden the term to include cousins and other kinsmen, but this is largely to harmonize the law with what transpires in the book of Ruth, where the widow is married to the next-of-kin. But the term should be given its literal meaning of "brothers" (Michaelis 1814, 2:32).

and one of them dies and has no son. The Heb "son" (בֵן) is changed to "seed" (σπέρμα) in the LXX. This expanded meaning of "child" — male or female — is preserved in Josephus (*Ant.* iv.254), the Talmud (*b. Yebamot* and elsewhere), the NT (Matt 22:24; Mark 12:19; Luke 20:28), and also in the Vg *(liberis)* and the AV. Rashi has "descendants of any kind." But most modern English Versions follow T^OnqNf and translate "son," which was doubtless the meaning intended here (Neufeld 1944, 45). The more inclusive "child" could have been influenced by Priestly law permitting daughters to inherit (Num 27:8; cf. *m. B. Bat.* 8:2-4; *b. B. Bat.* 109a). It also derives support from Gen 38:8, where Judah tells Onan, "Go in to the wife of your brother and do the duty of a brother-in-law to her, and raise up seed (זֶרַע) for your brother." Here, as one would expect, the LXX translates זֶרַע with σπέρμα.

the wife of the dead shall not go outside. לֹא־תִהְיֶה אֵשֶׁת־הַמֵּת הַחוּצָה. I.e., she shall not marry outside the family or clan, which she may want to do after returning to her father's house (cf. Lev 22:13). The concern is to keep her and her deceased husband's inheritance within the family (Henrey 1954, 6). Also, her husband's family has rights over her, having paid the bride-price when she was married to their son (L. M. Epstein 1942, 77; Neufeld 1944, 46). Judah still had rights over Tamar after Er died, even though she has returned to her family home (Gen 38:11-26). Huehnergard (1985, 431-32) cites an Akkadian text stating that the widow of a testator may marry an outsider only on the condition that she leave her first husband's house naked. This was to renounce symbolically any claim to her first husband's estate. In Israel widows did not inherit estates of their dead husbands. The Priestly legislation of Num 27:8-11 states that if a widow had children of her own, the estate would pass to them, first to the sons, and if she had no sons, then to the daughters. If the widow had no sons or daughters, the estate would pass to brothers of the deceased, and in the absence of brothers, to the next-of-kin.

to a strange man. לְאִישׁ זָר. The LXX has ἀνδρὶ μὴ ἐγγίζοντι ("to a man who is not next of kin"). The same expression occurs in Lev 22:12. Hosea 5:7 speaks metaphorically about Ephraim having borne "strange children" (בָּנִים זָרִים), but reference here is to unfaithful dealings with Yahweh.

Her brother-in-law shall go in to her and take her to himself for a wife, and do to her the duty of a brother-in-law. Much discussion has centered on the relation of this duty to Priestly laws in Lev 18:16; 20:21, which prohibit sexual intercourse with a brother's wife. The usual view is that the Levitical laws are general prohibitions, applicable while one's brother is living, with the present law being an exception, applying after one's brother has died (Michaelis 1814, 2:114-15). This distinction finds support in the Hittite law code, where, just after the levirate law (no. 193), another law (no. 195) states that if a man sleeps with the wife of his brother and his brother is alive, it is an abomination (Neufeld 1951, 56; ANET³, 196).

brother-in-law. יְבָם. The husband's brother; Latin: *levir*.

and take her to himself for a wife. It is generally agreed that this is no temporary sexual union, as in Hindu practice, but an actual marriage intended to be permanent (Westbrook 1977, 82; Tigay; *pace* Rowley 1947, 91). Of the two extant versions of Hittite law no. 193, neither employs an idiomatic expression denoting sexual relations, but speaks directly of taking the widow in marriage (Neufeld 1951, 192). The case of Judah and Tamar — where Judah had no more sexual relations with Tamar and did not take her as a wife — cannot be taken as representative, since union and conception were achieved by trickery. Levirate marriage in the biblical period lacked the formalities of a normal marriage, the most obvious being payment of a bride-price (Burrows 1938, 36). Burrows points out that among modern-day Yemenite Jews no second bridal-price is required; the levirate marriage is regarded as a continuation and fulfillment of the first union. In the Mishnah (*Qidd.* 1:1), the levirate marriage is specifically designated a marriage "through intercourse," to be distinguished from a marriage "through writ" or "through money." However, at this later time certain formalities were introduced. The levirate betrothal became like any other betrothal, where the widow, in the presence of witnesses, was given a ring or other object of value and perhaps presented with a writ of betrothal. In the post-talmudic period, a benediction over a cup of wine, the *huppah*, and seven benedictions over a second cup of wine were added (L. M. Epstein 1942, 117).

6 *the firstborn.* הַבְּכוֹר. The meaning here is "firstborn son" (T), who will inherit the portion of the estate belonging to the deceased. The LXX has τὸ παιδίον ("the child"), which is consistent with its more inclusive σπέρμα ("seed") in v. 5. If the brother-in-law was not previously married, the first son will be both his son and the son of the deceased. Rowley (1947, 98-99) thinks that Boaz probably had no son when he married Ruth, which would explain why in the genealogy of Ruth 4:21 (also Matt 1:5) Obed is reckoned as his son. In his view, Obed would have been son of Mahlon by virtue of a (less than full) levirate marriage and son of Boaz by virtue of a full marriage to Ruth.

shall succeed to the name of his brother who died. Hebrew יָקוּם is best translated "succeed" (NRSV). "To succeed to the name" means to gain the deceased's portion of the family inheritance (*b. Yebam.* 24a, where "name" = "inheritance"; Josephus *Ant.* iv.254; Rashi; Driver; cf. Gen 48:6; Ruth 4:5, 10). The object of the levirate custom was "not only to provide a son for the deceased, but also to ensure his succession to the deceased's share in the ancestral property" (Driver and Miles 1935, 243; cf. E. W. Davies 1981, 142). While inheritance is a key issue in the book of Ruth, nothing is said about that here in Deuteronomy. Rowley (1947, 89) offers this explanation:

> So far as the raising of children is concerned, there is no reference to property in the law of levirate marriage in Deuteronomy. But that is because the law did not contemplate the complication of a widowed mother-in-law as well. Where a man left property and a widow, the brother-in-law would not need to buy the property and marry the widow. He would marry the widow and the property would support her, until her child in due course became its heir, as the legal son of the deceased man.

so his name not be wiped out from Israel. If the name of the deceased is not wiped out in the family, it will not be wiped out from Israel. For the expression, "to wipe out (מחה) the name," see also 9:14; Pss 9:6(5); 109:13.

7 *And if the man does not want to take his sister-in-law.* In Genesis 38 the levirate duty is compulsory, even though Onan managed to avoid it, but here the brother-in-law can refuse it. He is still under obligation to marry his brother's widow and raise up a son, but cannot be forced to do it. The most likely reason for his refusal would be that a son born for his deceased brother would gain the brother's share of the family estate, whereas by not begetting a son the share of the estate belonging to the deceased will be added to his share and after his death his own son will inherit everything. The brother's widow will also be left without anything. This law, then, besides preserving the deceased brother's share of the inheritance, is looking out for the welfare of the widow, whose financial status is now in desperate straits after her husband's death.

to take. לָקַחַת. I.e., "take in marriage" (T^{OnqPsJ}).

then his sister-in-law shall go up to the gate, to the elders, and say. The widow here lacks an advocate in the father-in-law, because he too has died (Daube 1950, 72-77; Westbrook 1977, 76). Therefore she must go to the city gate and put her case before the elders, who will render a decision. On judgment in the city gate, see Note for 21:19.

"My brother-in-law refuses to raise up for his brother a name in Israel." The verb קוּם is an H-stem, meaning "to raise up." Tigay points out that "name" as used here is virtually synonymous with "offspring" (cf. Gen 38:8), adding that in Akk "name" sometimes means "heir."

8 *Then the elders of his city shall summon him and speak to him.* The brother-in-law must be summoned, for he did not come voluntarily to the city

gate. In the story of Ruth and Boaz, it is Boaz who goes to the gate in the morning and summons the next-of-kin as he passes through, so his case can be presented to the city elders and decided by them (Ruth 4:1-2). Here the elders will talk to the brother-in-law and try to persuade him to marry the widow.

but if he stands firm and says, "I do not want to take her." וְעָמַד וְאָמַר לֹא חָפַצְתִּי לְקַחְתָּהּ. The verb עמד here means "stand firm" or "stand one's ground." Persuasion will be used, but the man can still refuse to fulfill his obligation.

9 The penalty for refusal is a public shaming, which is no mean punishment. Daube (1950, 77-78; 1971a, 7-8) notes this as being the only pentateuchal law in which punishment consists in public degradation, but says it is serious enough and should not be underestimated. Roman law knew of punishment by infamy when ordinary criminal law was inapplicable. When Onan evaded his responsibility to Tamar, which was reckoned as a sin, Yahweh slew him (Gen 38:10). But no shame accrued to the next-of-kin who refused to marry Ruth. He simply passed up his right and gave it to Boaz (Ruth 4:6).

then . . . (she) shall come to him. I.e., approach him (T). Hebrew וְנִגְּשָׁה. The LXX lacks "to him," although Wevers (1995, 394) notes that a majority of witnesses add πρός αὐτόν. But he thinks the shorter text, supported by G^B and 848, is original. It is more likely, however, that Hebrew אֵלָיו has been lost due to haplography (homoeoteleuton: ו . . . ו).

before the eyes of the elders. On the Deuteronomic expression "before the eyes," see 25:3 and Note for 1:30.

and pull off his sandal from his foot. The LXX has ὑπολύσει ("will loosen"), i.e., untie the straps (cf. v. 10). Josephus (*Ant.* iv.256) uses the same verb. Either way, the action is invasive and humiliating. The LXX also has τὸ ἕν, "the one (sandal)," making it clear that just one sandal is to be loosened or pulled off. In Judaism this ceremony was called the חֲלִיצָה, *ḥaliṣah* = "what is stripped off" (*m. Yebam.* 12; *b. Yebam.* 26b, 101b-4a). Here pulling off the sandal (נַעַל) will dramatize the failure to perform a duty, whereas in the transaction to acquire Ruth it represents the concession of a right (Westbrook 1977, 81). The meanings are quite different, even though both actions contain symbolism relating to the release of property. Also, in Ruth 4:7-8 it is the one refusing the widow who draws off his own sandal and gives it to the next-of-kin. No shame is attached to the act; it simply attests to a transfer of property, giving it legal validity (Driver). A Nuzi adoption document has turned up with the phrase "And now I have just lifted my foot (from my property)," and a mortgage document from Nuzi has similar wording: "My foot from my fields and houses I have lifted up, and the foot of Urhi-Sharri I have placed." In the former, the meaning is that the adopter will never go and put his foot in his former property, which is a disclaimer similar to the one in the book of Ruth, where property is being renounced (Ruth 4:7-8). "Sale adoptions" in the Nuzi collection have similar expressions (Lacheman 1937, 53-54). See also Speiser (1940, 15-18) on the ceremonial transfer of shoes and the LXX reading of 1 Sam 12:3, which expands MT by reading ἐξίλασμα καὶ ὑπόδημα, "ransom and sandal" (cf. Sir 46:19). In Pss 60:10(8); 108:10(9) "casting the sandal on Edom" is a boast about treading Edom's land, i.e., taking possession of it.

and spit in his face. וְיָרְקָה בְּפָנָיו. Hebrew בִּפְנֵי means "in the face of," as in Num 12:14 (Driver). This rendering is supported by the LXX (καὶ ἐμπτύσεται εἰς τὸ πρόσωπον αὐτοῦ, "and she will spit in his face"), Josephus (*Ant.* iv.256), and the NJV. Later Jewish tradition softened this to "spit in front of him" (T; Rashi; Friedman), which has the woman spitting before the man, but on the ground. Luther followed this interpretation. Yet if she were spitting "before him," the Hebrew should read לְפָנָיו (cf. 25:2). In any case, Talmudic scholars deemed it sufficient if the elders saw her spitting (*EncJud*, 11:126).

and she shall respond and say, "Thus it shall be done to the man who does not build up the house of his brother." The verb וְעָנְתָה ("and she shall respond") is used because the brother-in-law has just spoken his refusal ("I do not desire to take her"), and now the widow responds with words to accompany her action. They come close to being a curse, and perhaps are a curse. The verb ענה also means "to testify" (see Note for 26:5). After releasing the brother-in-law from his duty with contemptuous gestures, the widow is free to marry whomever she desires (E. W. Davies 1981, 262; Kruger 1996).

10 Daube (1969a, 36) says: "His own name may live on, but it will perpetuate his infamy." One should note that the reputation of an entire family will now be blackened, for his name will be "House (בֵּית) of the one. . . ." Contrast the blessing on Naomi after Ruth bore Boaz a son (Ruth 4:14).

11-12 *When men will fight together, a man and his brother, and the wife of the one draws near to rescue her husband from the hand of the one striking him, and she puts forth her hand and grabs hold of his shameful parts, then you shall cut off her palm.* A law similar to the one in Exod 21:22-25, which deals with two men fighting and the pregnant wife of one suffering harm. That wife, who may or may not be party to the fray, sustains a blow or falls, resulting in a miscarriage. If no other harm comes upon her, the man responsible for her loss must pay a fine. If she herself is harmed, the man is punished according to the *lex talionis*, i.e., he must suffer the same harm as he inflicted on the woman. The law has a parallel in MAL A 21 (Driver and Miles 1935, 393; *ANET*[3], 181). In the present case, a wife watching another man getting the better of her husband intervenes to rescue him. The assumption has to be that the fight is intense and the nearly beaten man's life is in danger. Cortez (2005-6, 432) points out that the three verbs, "fight, rescue, strike" (נצה נצל נכה), appear together in only one other place, 2 Sam 14:6, where a quarrel in the field ends in one man's death. Here, with her husband pinned against a wall or down on the ground, the woman approaches the attacker from behind and grabs hold of his "shameful parts" (מְבֻשָׁיו), i.e., his genitals. The term is a *hapax legomenon* in the OT, but its meaning is not in doubt. Though her action is understandable, she is punished by having her hand cut off. The punishment is thought by some to be for her impudence, but more likely it is for injuring or possibly injuring the man's testicles, which could end his reproductive capacity (E. Roth 1950, 120-21).

This law has parallels in the Assyrian Code (MAL A 7-8; Driver and Miles 1935, 385; Paul 1990, 335-39; *ANET*[3], 181), where maiming and mutilation are common punishments. In MAL A 8, if a woman crushes a man's testicle in a brawl, one of her fingers is cut off. If the other testicle is crushed or simply becomes infected, they tear out two of some bodily organ. The text is damaged, and it is uncertain what is "torn off" or "torn out." Some think it must be the "eyes" (*ANET*[3]; Daube 1969a, 37); others presume it is the "breasts" (Paul 1990, 337) or "nipples of the breast" (Driver and Miles 1935, 30-31; Yaron 1970, 552). Yaron says that tearing out her nipples would be an example of "mirroring punishment." This would be true also of severed breasts. Cf. the punishment of the deceitful wet nurse in CH 194, who has her breasts cut off (*ANET*[3], 175). In the Assyrian code, the law immediately preceding (MAL A 7) states that if a woman has simply laid hands on a man, perhaps an immodest grasping of his genitals but not harming them, she is punished by a fine and a beating. The Nuzi tablets have produced an actual law case where the wife of a slave interfered in a street fight between two men and put her hand on one man's loin, drawing blood. In litigation she refused to permit eyewitnesses to swear an oath by the gods, so the judges imposed on her a fine of livestock, after which she was given over to the slave owner, who declared: "(As for) Imshennaya, the wife of my slave, since (her) finger seized (him), cut (it) off!" (Gordon 1935, 32).

a man and his brother. This could mean a man and his blood brother, as in v. 5, but more likely a man and his fellow Israelite (see Note on 22:1 for the use of "brother" in Deuteronomy). "Brother" is a keyword linking this law to the prior law (see Rhetoric and Composition).

rescue . . . from the hand. For this idiom, see Gen 32:12(11); 37:21-22; Exod 3:8; 18:9-10; Num 35:25; Deut 32:39; Jer 15:21.

then you shall cut off her palm. וְקַצֹּתָה אֶת־כַּפָּהּ The severing does not occur while she is clutching the man's testicles, assuming she will not let go and drastic measures must be taken to break her hold, but rather later as a punishment (E. Roth 1950, 119; Eslinger 1981, 272-73). Eslinger thinks the different word for "hand" used for the punishment, כַּף, lit. "hollow (usually of the hand or foot)," is a euphemism for the woman's genitals. The term refers to male or female genitals elsewhere in the OT (Gen 32:26, 33[25, 32]; Cant 5:5), but since talionic punishment for damage to the testicles is impossible for a woman,

Eslinger suggests a type of female circumcision. Walsh (2004) has a similar interpretation, but less severe. He agrees that כַּף refers to the concave curves of the woman's pelvic region, but thinks the verb קצץ ("cut off") in the Qal means "shave" rather than "amputate" and that the punishment consists of a public genital humiliation. It would still be talionic, assuming her indiscretion did not result in permanent damage to the man's testicles. Walsh translates: "You shall shave [the hair of] her groin." This interpretation is certainly possible, particularly since an amputation of the "palm" leaves something to be desired. But talmudic and medieval Jewish exegetes say the woman's hand is to be amputated. And other law codes prescribe a cutting off of hands and fingers for prohibited assaults (in CH 195, a son striking his father gets his hand cut off; *ANET*[3], 175), so it may be better to assume an amputation of the hand as most everyone does. The term כַּף could also have double meaning, in which case the law would be prescribing a cutting off of the hand in lieu of an associated mutilation, considerably worse.

Assuming that the traditional interpretation is correct, it is often pointed out that this is the only OT law specifically calling for punishment by maiming, which is true, but one should not conclude that maiming otherwise was not practiced in Israel. Quite the contrary. If the *talion* principle was applied (19:21; Exod 21:23-25), a whole range of maimings would have been carried out. It was a general rule in antiquity that the part of the body committing the offense was the one to be punished (Prov 30:17; cf. Matt 5:29-30), which is what happens here. The woman commits her indiscretion with the (palm of her) hand; therefore the palm of her hand gets severed. Jewish law later did away with maiming, and the woman was simply required to give monetary compensation (*b. B. Qam.* 28a; Rashi; Daube 1947, 108).

your eye shall not pity. A Deuteronomic admonition in cases where people are likely to be lenient, not wanting to carry out severe corporal punishments (see Note for 7:16).

13 One must not have in his possession different weights of the same denomination, one to purchase and one to sell (Rashi; Michaelis 1814, 3:397). In preexilic Israel, traders and merchants carried with them a pair of scales suspended from a bar (Zeph 1:11). They also had a bag of weights (cf. the Old Babylonian "Hymn to the Sun God"; *ANET*[3], 387-89, ii 48, 53; iii 28). On one scale were placed stone weights shaped like round loaves of bread, on the other the goods to be bought or sold. Weights were inscribed with numbers and a symbol for the shekel or just numbers and terms indicating a fraction of a shekel, e.g., two-sixths shekel, one-third shekel (שָׁלִשׁ, Isa 40:12), one-half shekel (בֶּקַע, Exod 38:26), one shekel, two shekels, four shekels, and eight shekels (Diringer 1942, 85, 89-91; Meshorer 1978, 131-33 — both with pictures). Weights commonly came in sets, so fine differences could be weighed out.

Fraudulent use of two standards of weights was common in the ancient world. In the Egyptian "Instruction of Amen-em-ope(t)" (7th to 6th cents.) is this word of advice:

Do not lean on the scales nor falsify the weights,
Nor damage the fractions of the measure . . .
Make not for thyself weights which are deficient;
They abound in grief through the will of god. (Chapter 16; $ANET^3$, 423)

The Egyptian *Book of the Dead* (Chapter 125, Intro: 13) contains these disclaimers by the deceased before the posthumous court:

I have not added to the weight of the scales [to cheat the seller]
I have not mis-read the position of the scale [to cheat the buyer]
(Budge 1898, 191; A 25-26 $ANET^3$, 34)

In the Old Babylonian "Hymn to the Sun God," judgment awaits the merchant who handles his scales in falsehood, who deliberately changes the weights and lowers weight on the stones. The honest merchant, by contrast, will reap a good reward ($ANET^3$, 388, ii; Lambert 1960, 133, lines 107-11). Diringer (1942) discusses the weights found at Lachish (late 7th to early 6th cents.). For pictures of ancient scales and weights, see $ANEP^2$, 33 no. 111; 36 nos. 117-21; 40 no. 133; 119 no. 350; Diringer 1942, pls. xii, xiii; Scott 1959, 33. For a picture of a pair of scales with a set of weights from Ras Shamra (15th to 14th cents.), see Schaeffer 1939, pl. xx fig. 1; O. R. Sellers, "Balances," in *IDB*, 1:343.

14 What pertains to weights pertains also to dry measures: quantities must be accurate. An "ephah" is a dry measure equal to three-fifths of a bushel (Scott 1959, 31). Grain was commonly measured by the ephah. The corresponding liquid measure was the "bath" (Isa 5:10; Ezek 45:11). Fraudulent measuring practices were also widely practiced in antiquity. In the *Book of the Dead* is an assertion by the deceased that he has neither increased nor diminished, nor has he damaged, the grain measure ($ANET^3$, 34-35, A 22, B 6). And the Old Babylonian "Hymn to the Sun God" says the following about merchants who deal either falsely or generously in measuring out grain:

The merchant who practices trickery as he holds the corn measure,
Who weighs out loans (of corn) by the minimum standard, but requires
  a large quantity in repayment,
The curse of the people will overtake him before his time.
If he demanded repayment before the agreed date, there will be guilt
  upon him.

His heir will not assume control of his property,
Nor will his brother take over his estate.
The honest merchant who weighs out loans (of corn) by the maximum standard, thus multiplies kindness.
It is pleasing to Šamaš, and he will prolong his life.

(Lambert 1960, 133 lines 112-19)

Prophets in Israel and Judah cried out loudly against merchants in the marketplace who dealt falsely with weights and measures (Amos 8:5; Hos 12:8[7]; Mic 6:11). Deceitful measuring of grain could also take place in the house (Mic 6:10). In the book of Proverbs, says Hallo (1985-86, 36), the most frequent condemnation of dishonesty is in matters of weights and measures (Prov 11:1; 20:10, 23). See also the emphasis on just weights and measures in Lev 19:35-36; Ezek 45:10-12.

15 *A full and right stone there shall be for you; a full and right ephah there shall be for you.* Some metal weights have turned up in excavations, but most of the early Hebrew weights discovered thus far are of polished stone. Some are dome-shaped, like a ball with a flattened base (Diringer 1942, 83). A full or whole stone (אֶבֶן שְׁלֵמָה) is one of proper weight; a full ephah (אֵיפָה שְׁלֵמָה) is one of the right quantity. Proverbs 11:1 states: "False scales are an abomination to Yahweh, but a full stone is his delight."

in order that your days may be prolonged on the soil that Yahweh your God is giving to you. Trading in right weights and measures, like other actions in obedience to the covenant, will give Israel long life in the land. On the present phrase, see Note for 4:40. Proverbs 28:16 says: "But he who hates unjust gain will prolong his days." In the "Hymn to the Sun God," as was noted above, the honest merchant will have his days prolonged by the god Šamaš.

16 On persons, practices, and things that are an "abomination" to Yahweh, see Note for 7:25.

17 Much stress is laid upon "remembering" (זכר) in Deuteronomy — remembering Yahweh, his mighty acts, his gracious leading in the wilderness, Israel's slavery, Israel's sin, and the covenant demands laid upon Israel by Yahweh (see Note for 8:2). To be remembered here is the battle of Rephidim, in which Joshua defeated Amalek (Exod 17:8-15).

Amalek. The OT lists Amalek as one of the grandsons of Esau, a son of Eliphaz by his concubine Timna (Gen 36:12; 1 Chr 1:36). The seminomadic clan of Amalekites is thus associated with Edom (= Esau), also the territory Edom occupied north of Ezion-geber (Mount Seir). But from early times, i.e., the 2nd mill., the Amalekites were active also in the Negeb and Sinai (Gen 14:7; Num 13:29; 1 Sam 30:1-2). At one point they are said to have penetrated Palestine as far north as Ephraim (Judg 12:15). The OT knows nothing but continual warfare between Amalek and Israel, fulfilling the prediction of Exod 17:16. The Amalekites fought Israel in the wilderness (Exod 17:8-15; Judg 10:12; 1 Sam 15:2; cf. Num 24:20) and teamed up with the Canaanites to repel Israel on its first attempt to enter the promised land (Num 14:43-45), a painful remembrance reported at the beginning of Deuteronomy (Deut 1:41-46).

During the period of the judges, the Amalekites continually harassed Israel, despite Gideon's limited success in fighting them (Judg 6:3, 33; 7:12). Only with the rise of Saul did Israel defeat them decisively (1 Sam 14:48; 15:7), but Israel's first king made a fatal mistake by relaxing the holy war ban and sparing Agag, king of the Amalekites, for which he received a severe reprimand from Samuel and with it loss of the kingship (1 Samuel 15; 28:18). David later raided the Amalekites from Gath (1 Sam 27:8-9) and Ziklag (1 Samuel 30; 2 Sam 1:1) and, after becoming king, subdued them along with everyone else in the region (2 Sam 8:12). The band of four hundred Amalekites who managed to escape after the battle of Ziklag (1 Sam 30:17) may have been the ones plotting against Israel in the Assyrian period (Ps 83:5-9[4-8]), but in Hezekiah's time that remnant was destroyed by the Simeonites (1 Chr 4:41-43; cf. 1 Sam 30:17). The Amalekites then disappear from history, as the OT mentions them no more. Extrabiblical records and archaeological work have yet to cast any light on their existence. For discussion, see G. Landes, "Amalek," in *IDB*, 1:101-2.

on the road. בַּדֶּרֶךְ. On this common expression in Deuteronomy, see Note for 1:19.

when you came out from Egypt. בְּצֵאתְכֶם מִמִּצְרָיִם. The LXX has a second singular construction (ἐκπορευομένου σου ἐξ Αἰγύπτου), as does the Vg (*quando egrediebaris ex Aegypto*), but MT is supported by 4QDeut^g and by plural readings in 23:5(4); 24:9. The *Vorlage* to the LXX may have lost a מ by haplography (three מ consonants in succession).

18 *how he chanced to meet you on the road and cut off your tail, all the battered ones behind you, when you were faint and weary.* The verb קרה means "happen upon by chance, meet without prearrangement," and זנב is a denominative verb meaning "cut off the tail," i.e., attack in the rear (Josh 10:19). The "battered ones" (הַנֶּחֱשָׁלִים) were the sick, wounded, and weary who lagged behind, unable to keep up with the others (T^{Onq}: "the stragglers"). Novick (2007) gets the same basic meaning by arguing that the verb in question was originally שחל ("to draw, trail"), altered by metathesis to חשל. These stragglers were easy targets for a marauding band. Lions hunt in similar fashion on the African savannah, isolating zebras and wildebeests that are old, lame, and cannot keep up with the herd, making them easy prey. After destroying Ziklag, the Amalekites left behind a servant who happened to fall sick, and he aided David in defeating them and recovering wives who had been captured (1 Sam 30:13). In Exod 17:8-16 the present indignity goes unreported. Weinfeld (1972, 275) says the Deuteronomic author, who had a highly developed national conscience, added it in order to supply a reason for blotting out the remembrance of Amalek.

all the battered ones. The LXX and Vg lack "all," but כֹל is present in 4QDeut^g.

when you were faint and weary. I.e., from lack of food and water. Hebrew עָיֵף often means "faint from hunger or thirst" (Gen 25:29-30; Judg 8:4-5; Isa 29:8; Job 22:7), which is probably the meaning here (Tigay). Hebrew יָגֵעַ means "weary" or "tired" (2 Sam 17:2).

and he did not fear God. וְלֹא יָרֵא אֱלֹהִים. I.e., in cutting down weak and helpless people. Amalek lacked a basic moral sense that might reasonably be expected from anyone (Driver; Weinfeld 1972, 274-75; cf. Luke 18:1-8). The Amalekites are referred to as "the sinners" (הַחַטָּאִים) in 1 Sam 15:18. The use of אֱלֹהִים is intentional, since the Amalekites were not worshippers of Yahweh (Tigay). This violation of common decency can be compared with the inhumanity displayed by nations in Amos 1-2, where innocent people were brutally killed in unimaginable ways and on an unimaginable scale. Yahweh is swift to punish such evil. Abimelech, king of Gerar, showed a "fear of God" (Genesis 20), leaving Abraham much surprised, as he thought such a thing was not possible in his country (v. 11). Gerar was located in the Negeb, in precisely the area where the Amalekites were said to be active in the 2nd mill. (Gen 14:7). On the "fear of God" as a recurring wisdom theme in Deuteronomy, see Note for 4:10.

19 *So it will be, when Yahweh your God gives you rest from all your enemies round about in the land that Yahweh your God is giving to you as an inheritance to possess it.* In Deuteronomy, and also in the Deuteronomic History, Yahweh promises to give his people rest in the land they are about to inherit, a rest that was achieved finally in the time of David and Solomon (1 Kgs 8:56; see Note for 12:9-10). On the stock Deuteronomic phrase "in the land that Yahweh your God is giving to you as an inheritance to possess it," see Note for 15:4.

you shall wipe out the remembrance of Amalek from under heaven. The LXX has ἐξαλείψεις τὸ ὄνομα ("you shall wipe out the name"), employing the wording of 9:14 in MT. There Yahweh threatened to "wipe out [Israel's] name" after the golden calf episode. Yahweh promised to wipe out Amalek's remembrance after Joshua defeated him and his company in the wilderness (Exod 17:14). Now a command to do the same is being laid upon all Israel. Nothing more is heard about the Amalakites after Hezekiah's time (see v. 17).

you shall not forget. Reinforces the "remember" command at the beginning in v. 17 (cf. 9:7).

Deuteronomy 25

Message and Audience

Moses begins this final discourse of law and admonition by instructing people in the custom of the levirate marriage. It is not a comprehensive directive, but like so many laws in Deuteronomy, it is a case meant to be representative. If two brothers happen to be living together on the family estate and one of them dies without leaving a son, the wife of the deceased is advised not to be married to an outsider. Rather, her brother-in-law shall take her as his wife and do the brother-in-law obligation, namely, have intercourse with her in hopes of raising up a son for the dead brother. The first son born to this woman will then keep alive the name of the deceased, in the family and in Israel, and will gain the deceased's share of the inheritance once the estate is divided. The widow will also be provided for, instead of being left with nothing. Later audiences will know the story of Judah and Tamar and will understand the levirate custom as practiced once Israel was settled in the land. They may also know the customs practiced in neighboring cultures.

People will likely understand that this is a solemn obligation laid upon the brother of the deceased; nevertheless, Moses informs them that it can be refused. Those knowing the later story of Judah and Tamar will know how Onan avoided his obligation and what happened as a result. The present law is not so severe; nevertheless, one refusing the levirate duty will do so at substantial cost. Moses tells the people that if the man does not want to marry his sister-in-law, the woman shall report this to the elders at the city gate, the father-in-law not being there because he too is dead, and the elders shall try to dissuade him from refusing. If he stands his ground, then the woman, with the elders looking on, shall publicly shame him, pulling off one of his sandals, spitting in his face, and uttering words close to being a curse: "Thus it shall be done to the man who does not build up the house of his brother." The name of this man and his family will indeed live on, but in infamy, for people henceforth will call him "House of the one who had his sandal pulled off."

Law II deals with two men in a fight, a man and his fellow Israelite, where the wife of one attempts to rescue her husband by grabbing hold of the other man's testicles. The punishment is to cut off the woman's hand. Some of those present will not want so severe a punishment, but Moses says that the woman is not to be pitied. The punishment must be carried out. Those hearing this law after the prior law will see that punishments shaming men are balanced off in the Deuteronomic Code with punishments that shame women.

Moses in the third and final law tells the people that traders and merchants must not carry two weights in their bag, one great and one small. Also, when measuring out grain in their houses, they must not have two ephahs, one great and one small. All stones must be full; all ephahs must be full. If people act justly with each other, and presumably also with strangers, they will live long in the land that Yahweh is now giving them. As for those doing wrong, they are put on notice that they are an abomination to Yahweh, for Yahweh loves justice and the practice of fair trade.

A concluding admonition remembers Amalek and what his clan did to Israel on the road out of Egypt. Moses gives a reason for this admonition, which people in the plains of Moab will know or will have heard about. The Amalekites came upon Israel in the wilderness and, in a cowardly act, cut off stragglers at Israel's rear — weary, battered, and helpless souls unable to defend themselves. Amalek showed no fear of God. Therefore, when Israel is given its promised rest in the land, it is to wipe out any remembrance of Amalek. For audiences hearing this admonition in the 7th cent., they will know that Amalek was indeed wiped out in Hezekiah's time.

U. RITUALS AT THE CENTRAL SANCTUARY (26:1-19)

1. Ritual of the Firstfruits (26:1-11)

26[1]*And it will happen when you enter into the land that Yahweh your God is giving to you as an inheritance, and you take possession of it and dwell in it,* [2]*then you shall take from the first of all the fruit of the soil that you bring in from your land that Yahweh your God is giving to you, and you shall put it in a basket and go to the place that Yahweh your God will choose to make his name reside there.* [3]*And you shall come to the priest who will be present in those days, and you shall say to him,*

> *"I declare today to Yahweh your God that I have entered into the land that Yahweh swore to our fathers to give to us."*

[4]*Then the priest shall take the basket from your hand and set it down before the altar of Yahweh your God.* [5]*And you shall respond and you shall say before Yahweh your God:*

> *"A wandering Aramaean was my father, and he went down to Egypt and sojourned there, a few males, and there he became a great nation, mighty and many.* [6]*And the Egyptians dealt wickedly with us, and afflicted us, and put upon us harsh labor.* [7]*And we cried out to Yahweh the God of our fathers, and Yahweh heard our voice, and saw our affliction and our misery and our distress;* [8]*and Yahweh brought us out from Egypt by a strong hand and by an outstretched arm, and by great terror and by signs and by wonders,* [9]*and he brought us into this place, and he gave to us this land, a land flowing with milk and honey.* [10]*And now, here it is! I have brought the first of the fruit of the soil that you have given to me, Yahweh."*

> *So you shall set it down before Yahweh your God, and you shall worship before Yahweh your God,* ¹¹*and you shall be glad in all the good that Yahweh your God has given to you and to your house, you, and the Levite, and the sojourner who is among you.*

2. Ritual of the Third-year Tithe (26:12-15)

¹²*When you have finished tithing all the tithe of your yield in the third year, the year of the tithe, and you have given to the Levite, to the sojourner, to the orphan, and to the widow, that they may eat within your gates and become sated,*¹³*then you shall say before Yahweh your God:*

> "*I have utterly removed what is holy from the house, and moreover, I have given to the Levite and to the sojourner, to the orphan, and to the widow, according to all your commandment that you commanded me; I have not transgressed any of your commandments, and I have not forgotten;* ¹⁴*I have not eaten any of it in my mourning; and I have not utterly removed any of it when unclean; and I have not taken any of it to the dead; I have obeyed the voice of Yahweh my God; I have done according to all that you have commanded me.* ¹⁵*Look down from your holy abode, from the heavens, and bless your people Israel, and the soil that you have given to us, just as you swore to our fathers, a land flowing with milk and honey.*"

3. Be Careful and Do These Commands (26:16-19)

¹⁶*This day Yahweh your God is commanding you to do these statutes and the ordinances, and you shall be careful and you shall do them with all your heart and with all your soul.* ¹⁷*Yahweh you solemnly proclaimed today to be God to you, and to walk in his ways, and to keep his statutes and his commandments and his ordinances, and to obey his voice.* ¹⁸*And Yahweh solemnly proclaimed you today to be a people to him, a treasure-piece, as he promised you, so to keep all his commandments,* ¹⁹*so to put you high above all the nations that he has made, for a praise and for a name and for a glorious decoration, and for you to be a holy people to Yahweh your God just as he promised.*

Rhetoric and Composition

The present chapter contains (1) a ritual for the presentation of firstfruits (vv. 1-11); (2) a ritual attesting to the distribution of the third-year tithe (vv. 12-15); and (3) an admonition reminding people to obey the covenant as presented to them in the plains of Moab (vv. 16-19). This delineation is supported at the top end by a *petuḥah* in M^L and a section in Sam before v. 1, which is also the chapter division. At the bottom end the unit is marked by a *setumah* in M^L and sections in Sam and 4QDeut^c after v. 19, which is also a chapter division. A *setumah* in M^L and a section in Sam after v. 11 and another *setumah* in M^L and sections in Sam and 4QpaleoDeut^s after v. 15 mark the internal divisions. The fragment 4QpaleoDeut^s, consisting of Deut 26:14-15, has dots functioning as word-dividers (Skehan, Ulrich, and Sanderson 1992, 154).

The creed of vv. 5-10 is not poetry, but it does appear to be rhythmic prose. Lohfink (1994c, 269-73) finds fourteen clauses containing a rhythm of threes, where also a single clause at the beginning balances a single clause at the end. But one need not conclude with Lohfink (1994c, 282-83) that the opening and closing clauses were at one time an early prayer of offering later filled out by the Deuteronomic author. This conclusion simply outruns the evidence produced from his analysis. The structure of the creed, using our translation and refining the Lohfink interpretation, is the following:

1 ^{5b}*A wandering Aramaean was my father*

Unifying factors: first person "my"; three words beginning with א

2 *and he went down to Egypt*
3 *and sojourned there, a few males*
4 *and there he became a great nation, mighty and many*

Unifying theme: the "wandering father" went to Egypt and became numerous

5 ^{6}*And the Egyptians dealt wickedly with us*
6 *and afflicted us*
7 *and put upon us harsh labor*

Unifying theme: the Egyptians made slaves of us

8 ^{7}*And we cried out to Yahweh the God of our fathers*
9 *and Yahweh heard our voice*
10 *and saw our affliction and our misery and our distress*

Unifying theme: we cried to Yahweh; Yahweh heard and saw

11 ^{8}*and Yahweh brought us out from Egypt by a strong hand and by an outstretched arm, and by great terror and by signs and by wonders*
12 ^{9}*and he brought us into this place*
13 *and he gave to us this land, a land flowing with milk and honey*

Unifying theme: Yahweh delivered us and gave us this good land

14 ¹⁰*And now, here it is! I have brought the first of the fruit of the soil that you have given me, Yahweh.*

Unifying factor: return to first person "I" and "me"

In the clusters 5-7, 8-10, and 11-13, the middle clause is the shortest, adding to the rhythm of the whole. The concluding clause (14) does not have a rhythm of three, which follows the ancient rule of deviation at the end of an established pattern (Freedman 1986).

This firstfruits ritual also contains an inclusio, made from keyword repetitions in the upper frame and creed opening, and lower frame:

	the priest . . . *shall set it down* (וְהִנִּיחוֹ) *before* . . . *Yahweh your God*	v. 4
a	*and you shall say before Yahweh your God*	v. 5a
	. . . *and he went down to Egypt and sojourned* (וַיָּגָר)	v. 5b
	So you shall set it down (וְהִנַּחְתּוֹ) *before Yahweh your God*	v. 10b
a′	*and you shall worship before Yahweh your God*	
	and you shall be glad . . . *and the sojourner* (וְהַגֵּר) . . .	v. 11

The link between "(he) sojourned" (v. 5b) and "the sojourner" (v. 11) is noted by Tigay.

The firstfruits and tithe rituals are balanced by introductory phrases (Rofé 1988b, 276):

I	. . . *and you shall say before Yahweh your God*	v. 5
	וְאָמַרְתָּ לִפְנֵי יְהוָה אֱלֹהֶיךָ	
II	. . . *then you shall say before Yahweh your God*	v. 13
	וְאָמַרְתָּ לִפְנֵי יְהוָה אֱלֹהֶיךָ	

The final admonition in 26:16 returns to the opening words of 12:1, making an inclusio for chs. 12–26 (Lundbom 1996, 304 n. 36; cf. Rofé 1986, 212). Other keyword repetitions in chs. 12 and 26 — with inversion — support the view that chs. 12–26 form a distinct unit within the book:

a		These are *the statutes and the ordinances that you shall be careful to do* . . .	12:1
	b	*the place that Yahweh your God will choose* . . . *to put his name there*	12:5
		your tithes and the contribution of your hand . . . *and the firstborns*	12:6
		and you shall be glad . . .	12:7

	the place that Yahweh your God will choose to make his name reside there	12:11
	your tithes and the contribution of your hand	
	And you shall be glad . . . and the Levite	12:12
b′	the first of all the fruit . . .	26:2
	to the place that Yahweh your God will choose to make his name reside there	
	and you shall be glad . . . and the Levite	26:11
	you have finished tithing all the tithe . . . the year of the tithe . . .	26:12
	to the Levite . . .	
a′	these statutes and the ordinances, and you shall be careful and you shall do them	26:16

The "contribution of your hand" in 12:6 and 11 refers to the firstfruits (see Notes there).

Portions of 26:1-19 are present in 4QDeut^c, 4QDeut^f, 4QDeut^g, 4QDeut^{k2}, and 4QpaleoDeut^s. The Roberts Papyrus (P. Ryl. Gk. 458), an early Greek text dated to the end of the 2nd cent. B.C. (C. H. Roberts 1936, 37), contains portions of 26:12, 17-19. The Qumran *Temple Scroll* (11QT 43) develops the tithe passage in 26:12-15 (Yadin 1983, 2:181-84).

Notes

26:1 See 17:14. On the Deuteronomic theme of Yahweh giving Israel the land as an inheritance, see Note for 15:4.

2 When the people enter the land and begin to grow crops and raise animals, they are to offer the firstfruits of crops and firstborns of animals to Yahweh. According to Deuteronomy, the firstfruits from garden and field would consist of grain, wine, oil, and wool from sheep (18:4; cf. Num 18:12-13). The Priestly Code adds bread baked from new flour (Num 15:19-21; Lev 23:17). According to the Chronicler, firstfruits brought in during Hezekiah's reign consisted of grain, wine, oil, honey, and all the produce of the field (2 Chr 31:5). Rashi mentions olive oil and honey (from dates).

The Mishnah (*Bik.* 1:3, 10) specifies seven kinds of firstfruits: wheat, barley, grapes, figs, pomegranates, olives used for oil, and dates used for honey (cf. Deut 8:8). But not all of these will be ready for the Feast of Weeks (Pentecost), which is when the firstfruits are to be presented (von Rad 1966b, 43; cf. Exod 23:16; 34:22). Grapes, for example, will not ripen until later in the summer. It seems that originally only grain was offered as a firstfruit at the Feast of Weeks (Exod 34:22; cf.

Deut 16:9-12). The Mishnah (*Bik.* 1:10), to accommodate an offering of seven different kinds of firstfruits, allows for greater latitude by stating that the firstfruits can be offered between the Feast of Weeks and the Feast of Tabernacles (Booths). The firstfruits offering, in any case, is to be presented at the central sanctuary, which in the 7th cent. would be the Jerusalem temple. An offering of firstfruits is enjoined in the Covenant Code (Exod 23:16, 19; 34:22, 26). This is simply a token offering, enough to fill a basket (T; Rashi; Milgrom 2001, 2403; cf. Lev 23:10, 17). After presentation, the fruits go to the priests (Num 18:12-13). The whole idea behind this offering is that before one proceeds to enjoy the bounty of the land, an offering must be made to Yahweh, the source of the bounty.

from the first of all the fruit of the soil. The Sam and LXX omit כָּל ("all").

that you bring in from your land. אֲשֶׁר תָּבִיא מֵאַרְצֶךָ. The LXX omits, which can be due to haplography (whole word: אֲשֶׁר ... אֲשֶׁר). Origen has the clause in his Hexapla, and it is translated in Aq, Theod, and Symm (Wevers 1995, 402).

a basket. טֶנֶא. The Hebrew term could be a loanword from Egyptian, meaning "a basket" for fruit, grain, and the like (Lambdin 1953, 151). In late Hebrew, טְנִי is a large metal vessel (BDB, 380). The LXX has κάρταλλον ("basket with a pointed bottom").

go to the place that Yahweh your God will choose to make his name reside there. I.e., to the central sanctuary. On Deuteronomy's "name theology" with reference to the central place of worship, see Note for 12:5. Presentation of firstfruits in the Second Temple period is discussed in *m. Bik.* 3:3-6.

3 *And you shall come to the priest who will be present in those days.* I.e., the priest currently in office (cf. 17:9; 19:17). Albright (1946, 108) thinks "the priest" (הַכֹּהֵן) could mean "the high priest," pointing out that Egypt had high priests of Amun at Thebes from the 14th cent. and that Ugarit too had a high priest. But the term is more likely a collective, referring to any priest on duty at the central sanctuary (G. A. Smith).

"I declare today to Yahweh your God that I have entered into the land that Yahweh swore to our fathers to give to us." Standing before the priest with firstfruits in hand, the worshipper begins his recitation by stating that he, today, is the beneficiary of Yahweh's promise to Israel's fathers to give them land (see Note for 1:8). The worshipper is addressing the priest: "to Yahweh *your* God." The LXX, however, makes the declaration more personal: κυρίῳ τῷ θεῷ μου ("to the Lord my God"). The MT reading could be due to a dittography of the כ (so *BHS*), or else the *Vorlage* of the LXX could have lost a כ due to haplography (double כ in succession). If the MT reading is correct, then first person language does not begin until v. 5, where it continues on to v. 10.

to Yahweh. ליהוה. 4QDeut^{k2} has לפני יהוה ("before Yahweh"); cf. v. 4.

4 The firstfruits are not presented upon the altar, simply set in front of

Deuteronomy 26

it. A few MSS and the LXX have "your hands." Either reading is acceptable; two hands were doubtless used to give the basket to the priest.

5-10 These verses contain a tightly-knit creed summarizing Israel's salvation history (von Rad 1953, 23; 1962b, 121-22; 1966b, 3-8, 55-56; G. E. Wright 1952, 70-72; Burrows 1955, 111-12). Inserted into Deuteronomic law and preaching, it is given to the worshipper to be recited when presenting his offering of the firstfruits. The creed states Israel's faith in a nutshell: the nation's ancestors sojourned in Egypt only to end up in a miserable slavery, but Yahweh, by great power and wondrous deeds, delivered it and brought it into the good land it now possesses. The creed shows signs of being old, beginning as it does by calling Israel's ancestor "a wandering Aramaean." An Israelite may willingly concede Aramaean ancestry up until the time of David, but he would be less eager to do so by the 9th cent., when Israel and Aram were engaged in protracted wars. Lohfink (1994c, 267-69) believes that while the creed in its present form is probably no earlier than the time of Hezekiah, he agrees that vv. 5-10 could be very old or at least could embody ancient elements. Von Rad says this creed should be compared on the one hand with the creedal statement in 6:20-25, which focuses on the exodus deliverance and Yahweh's gift of the land, and on the other hand with Joshua's more detailed recital of Yahweh's saving history at the Shechem covenant renewal ceremony (Josh 24:2-13). One should also look at Yahweh's saving history as recounted in Psalm 105, juxtaposed as it is to Israel's sinful history in Psalm 106.

5 *And you shall respond and you shall say.* וְעָנִיתָ וְאָמַרְתָּ. In Deuteronomy the verb ענה frequently means "to testify" (5:20; 19:16, 18; 21:7), which may be its meaning here (cf. 25:9). What follows will be a testimonial by the worshipper. Welch (1924, 27-28) thinks that in an age when prayer books were unavailable, the priest would supply the correct form of the confession and the illiterate peasant would repeat it after him (clergy do this even today for bride and groom saying their wedding vows).

before Yahweh your God. I.e., before Yahweh at the central sanctuary (12:7, 12, 18; 14:23, 25-26; 15:20; 16:11, 16). See again vv. 10 and 13.

"A wandering Aramaean was my father." אֲרַמִּי אֹבֵד אָבִי. These opening words contain alliteration (Lohfink 1994c, 271). The oft-discussed אֹבֵד is best rendered "wandering" (RSV; JB; NAB; NIV; NRSV; NJB), with the nomadic lifestyle of the patriarchs in Genesis being reflected (cf. Heb 11:8-10). Other translations have been proposed and are possible. In the Qal, אבד usually means "become lost, (about to) perish" (BDB; KBL³; cf. Isa 27:13; Prov 31:6; Job 29:13); when used of animals, it can mean "straying, lost" (1 Sam 9:3, 20; Ps 119:176; Jer 50:6; Ezek 34:4, 16). Driver thinks "lost by straying" would apply to Jacob, the main candidate for the patriarch in question, because of his many wanderings; however, while Genesis does report Jacob's seminomadic lifestyle

(Genesis 28-35; 46:1-7), it never portrays him as being "lost." The AV translated the phrase, "A Syrian ready to perish was my father," which, as Tigay points out, makes sense only if reference is to the famine that forced Jacob and his family to migrate to Egypt. The LXX has "my father abandoned Syria" (Συρίαν ἀπέβαλεν ὁ πατήρ μου), which Wevers (1995, 404) thinks is contextually derived: the next clause speaks about the father going down to Egypt. But more likely the LXX is reflecting a later tendency to dissociate Israel from its ancient bond with the Aramaeans = Syrians (Bowman 1948, 68 n. 12). Rashi's "a Syrian destroyed my father" appears to follow the Targums (T^{OnqNf}). He says that Laban in his pursuit of Jacob wished to exterminate an entire nation, an interpretation Tigay dismisses as fanciful. The Vg may also follow the Targums in its rendering: *Syrus persequebatur patrem meum*, "A Syrian persecuted my father." Genesis does record Laban's pursuit of Jacob; nevertheless, these readings do not suit the present context. The "wandering Aramaean" is being contrasted with the worshipper, who, along with fellow Israelites, is now settled in a land where fruits are being harvested in great abundance.

Extrabiblical texts describe the Aramaeans as "fugitives" or "plunderers," and some have therefore sought to interpret אֹבֵד in this light. Albright (1957b, 238) translated the term "a fugitive Aramaean," which carries over into the NJV ("My father was a fugitive Aramaean"). On a prism of Sargon II from Nimrud (col 7, 57-60, 69-71), the Aramaeans are called "a plundering race" (Gadd 1954, 192-93), and on the Taylor Cylinder of Sennacherib (col 5, 11) we find the expression, "the fugitive Aramaean, the runaway, the murderer, and the plunderer" (Luckenbill 1919-20). Luckenbill notes also that *ḫabbiri* (SA-GAZ) in the Amarna Letters means "plunderer." Jacob was indeed a fugitive after fleeing his brother Esau (Gen 27:43-45; 28:5; Hos 12:13[12]) and again a fugitive briefly after leaving Laban unannounced (Gen 31:17-55). Because of the latter departure, Millard (1980) has suggested that אֹבֵד be translated "refugee." But rendering אֹבֵד as "(one) plundering" is problematic, in that "destroy," or the like, is otherwise attested only for the Piel form of the verb.

Aramaean. I.e., Syrian (LXX). The term well suits Jacob, whose mother came from Aram-Naharaim (Gen 24:10), where he himself labored long (Genesis 29-31) in the service of Laban, "the Aramaean" (Gen 25:20; 28:5; 31:20, 24). Laban's two daughters, whom Jacob married, were Aramaeans. But the argument has been advanced recently, based upon a new reading of the *Genesis Apocryphon* (1QapGen 19.8), that the wandering Aramaean was Abraham (Machiela 2008). Another possibility is that the expression "A wandering Aramaean was my father" may be a collective reference to all three of Israel's ancestors, Abraham, Isaac, and Jacob (Num 20:15; Ps 105:12-13). "Aram" has turned up in extrabiblical texts as early as the 3rd mill., with "Aramaeans" mentioned explicitly only in Assyrian texts from the time of Tiglath-pileser I (ca. 1100). At this time they are a numerous Semitic people populating the Middle Euphrates region as far west as Syria (Bowman 1948, 66; B. Mazar 1962, 101). Aram was a major player in the region until the 9th cent., at which time its empire was reduced to Damascus. A century later, Tiglath-pileser III (745-727) conquered Damascus (Bright 1981, 270-75; B. Mazar 1962, 109; cf. 2 Kgs 16:9). On the Aramaeans and their relations with Israel, see B. Mazar 1962.

and he went down to Egypt and sojourned there, a few males, and there he became a great nation, mighty and many. On Jacob's migration to Egypt, see Gen 46:1-7. "To sojourn" (גּוּר) means to reside temporarily as an alien, which was the Israelite status in Egypt (10:19; 23:8[7]). In 10:22 it states that the ancestors went down to Egypt seventy persons (cf. Gen 46:27). See also Gen 34:30; Ps 105:12. That the people multiplied in Egypt and became strong is recorded in Exod 1:7-20, echoing the divine word at creation: "Be fruitful and multiply" (Gen 1:28). Cf. the curse of Deut 28:62 and what happened to Israel after the fall of Jerusalem (Jer 42:2). But that reduction will also one day be reversed (Hos 1:10; Jer 3:16; 23:3; 30:19; Ezek 36:9-11; Isa 54:1-3).

a great nation, mighty and many. לְגוֹי גָּדוֹל עָצוּם וָרָב. The LXX expands into a chiastic construction: ἔθνος μέγα καὶ πλῆθος πολὺ καὶ μέγα, "a nation great and numerous, many and great" (Wevers 1995, 404).

6 *And the Egyptians dealt wickedly with us, and afflicted us.* See Exod 1:11-12; Num 20:15.

and put upon us harsh labor. See Exod 1:14; 6:9. The same happened in exile (Isa 14:3).

7 *And we cried out to Yahweh the God of our fathers.* I.e., the God of Abraham, Isaac, and Jacob (Exod 3:15-16). On the phrase "Yahweh the God of our/your fathers," see Note for 1:11. On Israel's cry for release from its bondage, see Exod 2:23; Num 20:16. The verb צעק denotes a cry in pain or distress (22:24, 27; Gen 27:34; Pss 34:18[17]; 107:28; Isa 65:14).

and Yahweh heard our voice, and saw our affliction and our misery and our distress. See Exod 2:24-25; 3:7-9; 4:31; Num 20:16; Neh 9:9. Hebrew עָמָל is best translated "misery" (NJV; cf. Judg 10:16) or "trouble" (BDB; KBL³), not "labour" (AV) or "toil" (RSV; NRSV).

8 *and Yahweh brought us out from Egypt by a strong hand and by an outstretched arm.* The central event in Israel's salvation history, to which everything else is subordinate (4:34; 6:21; 8:14; Exod 3:8; 13:9, 14; 15:1-12; Num 20:16; Jer 2:6; 32:21; Ps 136:11-15; Neh 9:11). Deuteronomy puts much emphasis upon Israel remembering Egypt and Yahweh's deliverance from the slavery there (see Note for 8:2). Honor (1953, 429) says about Israel's collective memory:

> There can be little doubt that the intent of the recital of history so little directly related to the offering of the first fruit of the soil was to reinforce the

memory that the land which they occupied had not always been theirs, that it was given to them by the Lord as part of the covenant relationship and to help perpetuate the memories of the experiences anteceding the giving of the land.

by a strong hand and by an outstretched arm. A stereotyped phrase in Deuteronomy (see Note for 4:34). The LXX has an emphatic "even he" (αὐτὸς) beginning the phrase.

and by great terror. וּבְמֹרָא גָּדֹל. Another stereotyped phrase in Deuteronomy (see Note for 4:34). The LXX here and in 4:34 has καὶ ἐν ὁράμασιν μεγάλοις, "and by great visions," misreading the verb ירא as ראה.

by signs and by wonders. On this expression, see Note for 4:34.

9 *and he brought us into this place.* Yahweh delivered Israel out of Egypt with the aim of bringing it into the land promised to the fathers (4:37-38; 6:23; Exod 3:8; Jer 2:7; 32:22-23). "This place" (הַמָּקוֹם הַזֶּה) refers to the promised land, which in Deuteronomy includes the Transjordan north of the Arnon (see Note for 2:24). In 1:31 "this place" refers to Kadesh-barnea; in 9:7 and 11:5 to the valley opposite Beth-peor; and in 29:6(7) to the Transjordan. When Israel crosses the Jordan, "this place" will refer to the land of Canaan.

a land flowing with milk and honey. On this cliché in Deuteronomy, see Note for 6:3.

10 Here at the end of his recitation the worshipper shifts to direct speech. Gratefulness is expressed to Yahweh for his gift of the land, from which the firstfruits have come. This concluding gratitude is cast in the form of a prayer, following a pattern occurring elsewhere in Deuteronomy (Sarna 1979, 282). In the ritual of vv. 13-15, the formal confession ends with a prayer of gratitude to Yahweh. And in the ritual of the unsolved murder in 21:7-8, the confession of innocence ends with a prayer to Yahweh for absolution. The LXX adds at the end of the recitation: γῆν ῥέουσαν γάλα καὶ μέλι, "a land flowing with milk and honey," which repeats from the preceding verse and should probably be omitted as accidental dittography.

And now. On the rhetorical particle עַתָּה, see Note for 2:13.

here it is! Hebrew הִנֵּה requires something more than "behold" or "look." The worshipper has in his hands visible evidence of Yahweh's promise having been fulfilled: a basket of fruit from this "land flowing with milk and honey." Lohfink (1994c, 275) notes an exclamatory use of הִנֵּה also in Num 20:16: וְהִנֵּה אֲנַחְנוּ בְקָדֵשׁ ("and here we are in Kadesh!").

the first. רֵאשִׁית. Both "first" in sequence and "first" in quality (Levine 1993, 394).

So you shall set it down before Yahweh your God. This repeats the action stated in v. 4, restoring focus for the listener after the words of recitation and sum-

Deuteronomy 26

mary of the celebration as a whole. According to *m. Bik.* 3:6, after the worshipper finishes reciting the creed and the basket is placed beside the altar, he bows down and departs. The firstfruits are not burned on the altar, simply set there (Levine 1993, 391), after which they are taken and eaten by the priests (18:4).

and you shall worship. וְהִשְׁתַּחֲוִיתָ. Lit. "and you shall prostrate yourself."

11 The worshipper is told to enjoy to the full the festivities — at the Feast of Weeks, or whenever he makes his pilgrimage — with family, servants, and invited guests (12:6-7, 11-12, 17-18; 16:9-12). For this feast other food will have been brought from home or purchased at the central sanctuary. Only the Levite and sojourner are mentioned here as invited guests, but the orphan and widow will no doubt also be included (16:11).

and you shall be glad. וְשָׂמַחְתָּ. A Deuteronomic call to be joyful (see Note for 12:7).

the good. הַטּוֹב. I.e., all the prosperity; cf. 30:15.

12 The protasis for the command regarding the charity tithe, with the apodosis coming in v. 13a. According to Deuteronomy, a tithe (= one-tenth) of one's agricultural produce is to be brought each year to the central sanctuary (14:22-27), except in the third year, when it becomes a charity tithe for the Levite, sojourner, orphan, and widow in one's town of residence (14:28-29). This charity tithe is enjoined only in Deuteronomy. In the patriarchal period, tithes appear to have been offered voluntarily (Gen 14:20; 28:22), but after settlement in the land, and particularly after Israel had chosen a king (1 Sam 8:14-17), tithes became compulsory and were imposed on the entire population. It was the same also in Mesopotamian society. Deuteronomy assumes that most everyone in Israel will be either a farmer or a herdsman. But as Israelite society became more diversified, tithes became more diversified, as obtained also in Mesopotamian society. On the rendering of tithes in Israel and throughout the ANE, with documentation in Ugaritic (14th cent.) and Neo-Babylonian (6th cent.) texts, see *EncJud*, 15:1156-62 and Note for 14:22.

all the tithe of your yield. According to Deuteronomy, this was to consist of the yearly tithe of grain, wine, and oil (14:22-23). In Lev 27:30-32 cattle and sheep are also tithed, and the list of acceptable things was doubtless even longer (see Note for 14:23). In the NT, scribes and Pharisees are said to be tithing mint, dill, and cummin (Matt 23:23). Conceivably, tithes could come from a range of one's possessions, e.g., produce, animals, slaves, wool, cloth, wood, metals, silver and gold, which was the case in Mesopotamian society (*EncJud*, 15:1158; cf. Gen 14:20; 28:22, where Abraham and Jacob give tithes of everything; also 2 Chr 31:5-6). But according to Deuteronomy, the yearly and charity tithes were to consist simply of produce. These would have been set aside in their season, deposited in storage facilities, and distributed as needed. After giving his tithe, the Israelite peasant would then make his attestation at the central sanctuary.

in the third year, the year of the tithe. The two phrases are in apposition, i.e., "the year of the tithe" is the third-year charity tithe. Cf. "the Sabbath year, the year of remission" in 15:9.

the year of the tithe, and you have given to the Levite. The LXX reading, τὸ δεύτερον ἐπιδέκατον δώσεις τῷ Λευίτῃ, "the second tithe you shall give to the Levite," probably misreads שְׁנַת ("year") as "second" (Wevers 1995, 408). However, in later Judaism a "first tithe" (Num 18:21-32) and "second tithe" (Deut 14:22-27) constituted an attempt by the rabbis to harmonize the contradiction in the two legislations (*EncJud*, 15:1161-62; Rashi).

and you have given to the Levite, to the sojourner, to the orphan, and to the widow, that they may eat within your gates and become sated. This tithe is for the Levite who has no inheritance (= landed property), and in the 7th cent. is unemployed due to closure of the local sanctuaries, and to the sojourner, orphan, and widow. All will eat the tithe in their respective towns (14:29). On special care accorded to the "sojourner, orphan, and widow" in Deuteronomy, see Note for 10:18. On the promise that Israel will eat and become sated in the promised land, see Note for 6:11.

13a. *then you shall say before Yahweh your God.* In Deuteronomy, "before Yahweh your God" refers to the central sanctuary (see Note for v. 5), which is where the declaration will be made (I. Wilson 2008, 324). Having distributed in his own town the third-year tithe to the Levite, sojourner, orphan, and widow, the Israelite peasant must now appear at the central sanctuary and declare before Yahweh that he has done what was required. In the early days, his recitation would have been at the tabernacle, later at the Jerusalem temple. The likely festival for this recitation would have been the year-end Feast of Booths, probably in the year that the distribution took place. Rashi says it would be on Passover eve in the fourth year.

13b-15. These verses contain another tight-knit creed to be recited by the worshipper at the central sanctuary (von Rad 1966b, 3). Whereas the earlier liturgy focused on Yahweh's saving history toward Israel, this liturgy focuses on what the worshipper has done to fulfill his sacred obligation. It, too, may well antedate the 7th cent.

13b-14. These disclaimers and concluding affirmations are a declaration before Yahweh that the tithe was not desecrated, nor did the giver disobey any other of Yahweh's commandments regarding it. The confession sounds very much like the "I have . . . I have not" prayer uttered by the Pharisee in Jesus' parable (Luke 18:9-14), but it was not meant, surely, as a self-righteous boast (Driver; G. E. Wright; Holmgren 1994).

I have utterly removed what is holy from the house. I.e., the consecrated tithe is completely out of his house, where it was stored (14:28), and nothing has been kept back for himself. The LXX (ἐκ τῆς οἰκίας μου) and Vg *(de domo mea)* both have "out of my house." A Hittite text, "Instructions for Temple Officials" (*ANET*³, 210 no. 18; Milgrom 2001, 2405), contains this statement by a herdsman regarding his cattle offerings:

> If we have given this young animal to ourselves first, or have given it to our superiors, or to our wives, our children or to anyone else, we have offended the gods' feelings.

I have utterly removed. The verb here and in v. 14 is בער, which in Deuteronomy commonly means "utterly remove" (בער II, KBL³; see Note for 13:6).

what is holy. I.e., the sacred portion. הַקֹּדֶשׁ. Even though this tithe was distributed in the worshipper's own town, it is a "sacred portion" consecrated to Yahweh, just like the tithe brought to the central sanctuary and presented at Yahweh's altar (12:26; cf. Lev 27:30).

and moreover, I have given to the Levite and to the sojourner, to the orphan, and to the widow, according to all your commandment that you commanded me. See 14:28-29.

I have not transgressed. Tigay says לֹא־עָבַרְתִּי ("I have not transgressed") echoes בִּעַרְתִּי ("I have utterly removed") earlier in the verse.

any of your commandments. The LXX reads τὴν ἐντολήν σου, which omits the prepositional מ ("any"), and has "commandment" singular. Wevers (1995, 409) points out that the former could be due to haplography (double מ in succession).

I have not eaten any of it in my mourning. In the next three disclaimers the worshipper reiterates his claim that he has not taken any of the tithe for himself, citing special circumstances where he might have needed to eat from it (cf. 1 Sam 21:4-7[3-6]; Matt 12:1-4). Here he states that he did not eat from the tithe while in mourning, i.e., after touching a corpse, or having been in the same tent with a corpse (Num 19:11-16; Lev 22:4-6), which would have defiled not only what he ate, but the remainder of the tithe.

in my mourning. בְאֹנִי. Hebrew אֹן is no longer taken to be the noun אָוֶן, "sorrow" (BDB, 20), but rather a noun from the verb אנה ("to mourn"), thus "mourning" (KBL³; Ug *un*; T. J. Lewis 1989, 103; cf. Hos 9:4).

and I have not utterly removed any of it when unclean. Here the worshipper states that when he completely removed (בער) the tithe from his house he was not himself unclean (NJV: "I have not cleared out any of it while I was unclean"). Had he been unclean, he would have rendered the tithe unclean (Num 19:22). The LXX goes a different way with οὐκ ἐκάρπωσα ἀπ' αὐτῶν εἰς ἀκάθαρτον, "I have not enjoyed any of them for an unclean end."

and I have not taken any of it to the dead. The preposition לְ on לְמֵת makes for ambiguity in the disclaimer. If לְמֵת means "*for* the dead," the wor-

Deuteronomy 26

shipper may simply be saying that he has not contributed to mourning feasts, i.e., not given any of the tithe to friends mourning their dead (2 Sam 3:35; Jer 16:7; Ezek 24:17, 22), or that he has not placed any of it in a tomb of the deceased at the time of burial (Tob 4:17; cf. Sir 7:33). Both practices were common and not in violation of Israelite law, yet they would have put the worshipper in proximity with the dead and thus defiled him.

But the worshipper could be making a weightier claim, viz., that he has not used any of the tithe as an offering "*to* the dead" (RSV; NEB; JB; NAB; NJV; NIV). Although many have said that offerings to spirits of the dead were not made in Israel (G. E. Wright; de Vaux 1965, 60-61), the practice is held up for ridicule and considered idolatrous in Isa 8:19; Ps 106:28; Sir 30:18-19; Bar 6:27. Others argue that a cult of the dead did exist in Israel, similar to cults that existed elsewhere in the ANE. Even Driver conceded that giving food to the dead, commonly practiced in Egypt but not otherwise attested in the OT, might nevertheless have prevailed among superstitious Israelites for whom prohibitions such as those in 18:10-11 became necessary. Ridicule of such practices by the prophets, e.g., in Isa 8:19, point indirectly to their existence in Israel (Sukenik 1940, 62). Also, the OT records Saul's visit to the Witch of Endor (1 Samuel 28), an embarrassing account of someone (a king, no less) calling up a spirit of the dead, which is said to have succeeded. Although foods are not mentioned, necromancy elsewhere combined sacrificial offerings with invoking the dead (Gadd 1948, 88-89; Hoffner 1967). In 1 Sam 28:7, the witch is given the title בַּעֲלַת־אוֹב, which can be translated "mistress of the (bottle-shaped) pit," with אוֹב now known to mean "(ritual) pit" (Gadd 1948, 89; Vierya 1961, 51-53; Hoffner 1967, 401; cf. Ug *ib*; Akk *apu*; CAD, 1/2:201). The present disclaimer is thus taken by some to mean that the worshipper did not use any of the tithe as an offering to the dead, which would have been in direct violation of Israelite law and religion (T. J. Lewis 1989, 99, 104; Levine 1993, 477-78; Tigay). Lewis says that although normative Yahwism did not allow a cult of the dead, there is evidence enough that from time to time one did exist.

A well-developed cult of the dead existed at Ugarit (Schaeffer 1939, 46-56; Gray 1967, 149-50; Hoffner 1967, 393-94; T. J. Lewis 1989, 97). Archaeologists at Ras Shamra (Ugarit) uncovered Late Bronze (14th to 13th cents.) tombs with holes bored in the stone, clay pipes, and gutters for depositing food or pouring libations to the dead. Pits beside some of the tombs received libations from above. Pipes similar to the ones at Ugarit were a standard feature in the funerary monuments of the Egyptian pharaohs (Hoffner), and ideas about the dead being hungry and thirsty in their underworld journeys existed also among the Mycenaean Greeks (Schaeffer), where funerary rites of a similar nature to those at Ugarit appear to have been performed. Some tombs at Ugarit had windows so the dead could have access to water set aside for them in large jars. One jar contained a cup inside so the dead could imbibe its contents; others had holes in the bottom for pouring liquids into the tomb (for photos, see Schaeffer 1939, pl. xxviii fig. 1; pl. xxix figs. 2 and 3; pl. xxx). Israelite tombs with bored holes and a generous amount of pottery jars were found in Samaria (Sukenik 1940 + pictures), supporting the view that a cult of the dead flourished there. These tombs had pits in connection with them. Excavated tombs at Megiddo, Hazor, Gezer, Beth Shemesh, and Dothan also contained holes cut in the ceiling or storage jars placed directly over the heads of corpses (Friedman). Friedman thinks that offering food and drink to the dead was practiced in both Israel and Judah, being cut back in Judah only during Hezekiah's reign (ca. 700). Cults of the dead existed also among the Hittites, Assyrians, Babylonians, Cypriots, and Cretans (Gadd 1948, 88-89; Hoffner 1967; Gray 1967, 149; Bayliss 1973).

I have obeyed the voice of Yahweh my God; I have done according to all that you have commanded me. Obeying Yahweh's voice in Deuteronomy means doing the commandments (see again v. 17 and Note for 13:5).

15 *Look down from your holy abode, from the heavens, and bless your people Israel, and the soil that you have given to us.* Now after the worshipper has stated his obedience to Yahweh's commands, he asks for Yahweh's blessing upon Israel and the soil it occupies. See Note on v. 10 for the pattern in Deuteronomy of formal confessions concluding with a prayer. Daube (1969a, 49) says the present statement is a confident one, inviting divine inspection. Yahweh's sanctuary is in the heavens, which is a Deuteronomic conception (4:36; Weinfeld 1972, 198). In Zion theology, Yahweh is said to dwell on Mount Zion in a temple (Isa 8:18), the prototype of which is a sanctuary set apart (= holy) in the heavens (Ps 11:4; 1 Kgs 8:27-30; Jer 17:12; 25:30; Isa 66:1; Ps 68:6[5]; Zech 2:17[13]; 2 Chr 30:27). From this lofty abode Yahweh looks down upon the children of earth (Pss 14:2; 102:20[19]; Isa 63:15).

and bless your people Israel. Israel is Yahweh's people (v. 18), but in need of Yahweh's continual blessing.

and the soil that you have given to us. The use of הָאֲדָמָה ("the soil") in this phrase is unusual, although it occurs again in 28:11. Usually the term is הָאָרֶץ ("the land").

just as you swore to our fathers. The LXX adds δοῦναι ἡμῖν, "to give to us." On the land as a gift promised to the fathers, see Note for 1:8.

a land flowing with milk and honey." On this expression, see Note for 6:3.

16 Following the two rituals is now the familiar Deuteronomic admonition that Israel be careful to do what Yahweh has commanded (cf. 12:1; 13:1[12:32]). From the covenant language in vv. 17-18 we may conclude that this is nothing less than a call for renewed commitment to the Mosaic covenant (von Rad 1962a, 832; cf. 2 Kgs 23:3), to which the people must give wholehearted acceptance (Exod 19:5-6, 8; 24:3, 7).

This day. I.e., the day on which Moses is speaking in Moab, also every

Deuteronomy 26

subsequent day when the Deuteronomic law is read aloud to the people (see Note for 2:22).

these statutes and the ordinances. Since vv. 16-19 form a conclusion to chs. 12-26, "these statutes and the ordinances" must refer to all the law in chs. 12-26 (Driver). The LXX has "all (πάντα) these statutes and ordinances."

you shall be careful and you shall do. A stock Deuteronomic expression (see Note for 4:6).

with all your heart and with all your soul. This expression is stereotyped in Deuteronomy (see Note for 4:29).

17 *Yahweh you solemnly proclaimed today to be God to you.* Reading הֶאֱמַרְתָּ as an internal H-stem: "you solemnly proclaimed"; it is intensive, not causative (GKC §53d; NJV: "you have affirmed"). The verb occurs with the same meaning in v. 18. The LXX's εἵλου ("you chose") is not right. On the repeated use of "today" (הַיּוֹם) in Deuteronomy, see Note for 1:10.

to be God to you. From the covenant formula, completed with "to be a people to him" in v. 18. See also 29:12(13); 2 Sam 7:24; Jer 7:23; 11:4; 30:22; 31:33.

to walk in his ways, and to keep his statutes and his commandments and his ordinances, and to obey his voice. This is Israel's part of the covenant; cf. 4:5-6, 40; 7:12; 8:6; 12:1, and elsewhere. To "walk in Yahweh's way" is a major theme in Deuteronomy (see Note for 5:33), having strong ethical implications in the OT (Muilenburg 1961b). Israel's trek out of Egypt, wandering through the wilderness, and entry into the promised land came to define its history. In an oracle to Judah spoken by Jeremiah, Yahweh said:

> Stand by the ways and look,
>   and ask for the ancient paths.
> Where is it — the good way?
>   Then walk in it!
> and find rest for yourselves.
>   But they said, 'We will not walk!' (Jer 6:16)

In the present verse, the Sam and LXX omit "and his ordinances," which should probably be taken with Wevers (1995, 413) as a loss due to haplography (homoeoteleuton: יו . . . יו). See 8:11.

18 *And Yahweh solemnly proclaimed you today.* Reading הֶאֱמִירְךָ as another internal H-stem: "(he) solemnly proclaimed you." Repeated use of this verb and the covenant formula in vv. 17-18 point to Moses acting as mediator of the covenant (Driver; von Rad; Moran; Tigay). The LXX again had difficulty rendering the Hebrew, translating εἵλατό σε ("he chose you").

to be a people to him. The other part of the covenant formula. On Israel as Yahweh's (holy) people, and Yahweh's election of Israel, see Note for 7:6.

a treasure-piece. סְגֻלָּה. On this election term, see Note for 7:6.

as he promised you, so. One MS and some LXX witnesses (G^B and Papyrus 957) omit "you, so," which can be attributed to haplography (homoeoarcton: ל . . . ל). The expression is repeated at the end of v. 19 without "you."

so to keep all his commandments. This phrase seems out of place in the present verse, unless it means to put a necessary condition on the covenant. But the LXX and Vg have the phrase.

19 *so to put you high above all the nations that he has made.* See also 28:1, where Israel's place high above the nations is conditional upon obedience to the commandments (cf. 15:4b-6).

for a praise and for a name and for a glorious decoration. לִתְהִלָּה וּלְשֵׁם וּלְתִפְאָרֶת. The triad is repeated in Jer 13:11; 33:9. Hebrew תִּפְאָרֶת can be decorations on clothing (Exod 28:40) or other beautification items, such as those listed in Isa 3:18-23. According to Isa 62:3, Israel will once again be a decoration for Yahweh after her exile.

and for you to be a holy people to Yahweh your God just as he promised. On Israel as a holy people (עַם־קָדֹשׁ), see Note for 7:6. 4QDeut^c has "as he promised you," adding לָךְ at the end of the verse (cf. v. 18; 12:20). This addition is present in some LXX MSS and the S, but is absent in LXX, T, and Vg (Ulrich, Cross et al. 1995, 28).

Message and Audience

Moses at the close of his discourse on the Deuteronomic Code now lays before the people two confessions they are to make before Yahweh once they become settled in the land. They are to take the firstfruits of the land Yahweh has given them, put them in a basket, and bring them to the central sanctuary where Yahweh's name resides. There they are to present them to one of the priests in office, affirming with joy that they are now resident in the land Yahweh swore to the fathers. The priest will then take the basket of fruit and set it down before Yahweh's altar, at which point the worshipper is to recite his confession of faith. In this confession the worshipper states that a wandering Aramaean was his father, and after sojourning in Egypt, few in number, he multiplied and became a great company. But the Egyptians treated them badly, making them slaves. They cried out to Yahweh, who heard their cries and saw their distress, and he acted decisively to deliver the people out of Egypt with power, terror, and an array of wonderful deeds. He brought them finally to the abundant land in which the worshipper now stands, and so the worshipper has in his hands the firstfruits, offering them to Yahweh who gave him the good land. The Israelite pilgrim is then to leave his firstfruits at the altar, worship Yahweh, and rejoice in

Yahweh's goodness by hosting a feast for family, servants, the Levite, and the sojourner, and though they are not mentioned, in all probability the widow and orphan in their midst. After this recitation has been made to the priest, another worshipper will step forward with his basket of fruit, set it down at the altar, and recite the same words of confession. This will in most cases take place at the yearly Feast of Weeks, or Pentecost.

The second recitation will take place at the yearly Feast of Booths, or Tabernacles, after the worshipper has given the third-year tithe to the Levite, sojourner, orphan, and widow residing in his town. The recitation will occur at the central sanctuary. On this occasion, the worshipper is instructed to affirm before Yahweh and the priest that he has completely removed the sacred tithe from his house and given it to the Levite, sojourner, orphan, and widow as Yahweh commanded. Moreover, he has not transgressed any of Yahweh's commandments, nor has he forgotten them. He has not eaten any of the sacred tithe while in mourning; he has not removed any from his house while unclean; and he has not offered any of it to the dead. He has thus obeyed Yahweh and done what Yahweh commanded. The worshipper will then ask Yahweh to look down from his heavenly sanctuary and bless Israel, also the good and productive land that Yahweh has given Israel in fulfillment of his promise to the fathers.

Moses then repeats what he has said many times to the people. On this day, and every day when the worshipper gathers in sacred assembly, Yahweh is commanding the worshipper and all Israel to perform the statutes and ordinances given them in the plains of Moab. They are to respond to this heart and soul. Speaking as the covenant mediator, Moses says that this day the people have solemnly proclaimed Yahweh to be their God and they have agreed to walk in his way, to keep his commands, and to obey his voice. On this day also Yahweh has solemnly proclaimed Israel to be his people, a treasured possession, and said it will remain so if it keeps the commandments. Moreover, it is Yahweh's desire to elevate Israel high above all the other nations, to make it a praise, a name, and a glorious decoration, that Israel be to him the holy people Yahweh promised it to be.

When these two confessions are heard in sequence, the "Yahweh has done" recitation from the giver of the firstfruits will balance off the strident "I have . . . I have not" recitation from the giver of the tithe, preventing the latter from degenerating into a form of self-praise.

Deuteronomy 27

VII. BLESSINGS AND CURSES (27–28)

A. COVENANT RENEWAL AT SHECHEM (27:1-26)

1. Yahweh's Law on Large Stones (27:1-8)

27 ¹*Then Moses and the elders of Israel commanded the people: Keep all the commandment that I am commanding you today.* ²*And it will happen on the day that you cross over the Jordan into the land that Yahweh your God is giving to you, that you shall set up for yourself large stones, and you shall whitewash them with lime.* ³*And you shall write upon them all the words of this law when you cross over, in order that you may enter into the land that Yahweh your God is giving to you, a land flowing with milk and honey, as Yahweh God of your fathers promised to you.* ⁴*And it will happen when you cross over the Jordan, you shall set up these stones that I am commanding you today, on Mount Ebal, and you shall whitewash them with lime.* ⁵*And you shall build there an altar to Yahweh your God, an altar of stones; you shall not wield an iron tool upon them.* ⁶*Of whole stones you shall build the altar of Yahweh your God, and you shall offer upon it burnt offerings to Yahweh your God.* ⁷*And you shall sacrifice peace offerings, and you shall eat there and you shall be glad before Yahweh your God.* ⁸*And you shall write upon the stones all the words of this law very clearly.*

Rhetoric and Composition

Chapter 27 is widely taken to be an interpolation into the book of Deuteronomy. It breaks the continuity between the conclusion of the Deuteronomic Code in ch. 26 and the blessings and curses in ch. 28, although the latter explains the interpolation. 27:11-13 announce a ceremony of blessings and curses, after which vv. 14-26 report a curse liturgy directed by the Levites. In reporting a ceremony occurring at Mount Gerizim and Mount Ebal, the chapter introduces an old tradition associated with Shechem, with which there is otherwise no association in the book and which goes ill with Deuteronomy's consistent silence about Yahweh's chosen place of worship. But Welch (1924, 184-85) argued that a Mount Ebal sanctuary gives "a significant hint as to the provenance of the Deuteronomic code, for we are carried to northern Israel and to one of its leading sanctuaries."

The chapter also bears evidence of being a compilation, and one not terribly well executed. Repetitions in vv. 2 and 4 and vv. 3 and 8 make for redundancies above and beyond what is usual in rhetorical prose of this sort, and the command to build the altar in vv. 5-7, which may well be an interpolation (De

Troyer 2005, 150-52), creates confusion in interpreting v. 8 (see Notes). There is also the problem of reading vv. 1-3 with v. 4, the former speaking of erecting large stones on the day of the Jordan crossing and the latter of erecting these stones on Mount Ebal, a site too far distant for a ceremony on this historic day (Tigay: 30 mi and 4000 ft uphill). When the ceremony on Mount Ebal is reported as having been fulfilled in Josh 8:30-35, the battles against Jericho and Ai have already been fought. Also, ch. 27 announces a ceremony containing both blessings and curses (vv. 12-13), but only the curses are given (vv. 14-26). We expect also the blessings. And in v. 12 the tribe of Levi is stationed on Mount Gerizim to bless, but in v. 14 the Levites are leading a curse recitation by the entire assembly. The chapter, then, with its redundancies, inconsistencies, conflation, harmonization, and seeming omissions has caused difficulties for interpreters ancient and modern. Von Rad thinks vv. 1-8 and 11-26 are pre-Deuteronomic, possibly originating very early in Shechem. Verses 9-10 relate to the covenant in Moab and may be the original tie-in between chs. 26 and 28 ("today/this day" repeats in 26:16-19; 27:9-10; 28:1).

The chapter as presently constituted consists of three parts: (1) vv. 1-8; (2) vv. 9-10; and (3) vv. 11-26. These divisions are supported by section markings and by opening statements referring to Moses in the third person:

Then Moses and the elders *commanded the people:* v. 1
Then Moses and the Levitical priests spoke to all Israel: v. 9
Then Moses *commanded the people* on that day: v. 11

The first and third statements have balancing keywords, and the first two statements differ from the third — and all others in Deuteronomy — by joining another speaking voice with that of Moses (see Notes).

The present verses are delimited at the top by a *setumah* in M^L and sections in Sam and 4QDeut^c before v. 1, which is also the chapter division. At the bottom, delimitation is by a *setumah* in M^L and a section in Sam after v. 8.

Portions of 27:1-8 are contained in 4QDeut^c, 4QDeut^f, and 4QDeut^{k2}(?).

Notes

27:1 *Then Moses and the elders of Israel commanded the people: Keep all the commandment that I am commanding you today.* This introduction is similar to v. 9 in that other leaders join Moses in addressing the people. In v. 11 — and elsewhere in Deuteronomy — Moses alone addresses the people (1:1, 3, 5; 4:45; 5:1; 29:1[2]; 31:1, 30; 32:44). The elders do on other occasions render assistance to Moses (see Note for 5:23-24). This directive to keep all Yahweh's commandment, i.e., the entire Deuteronomic law, recurs throughout the book (4:1-2, 5-6; 6:17; 7:11; 8:1; 11:22, and passim). The LXX omits "the people," but ἐντολὰς ταύτας ("these commands") with the demonstrative pronoun is supported by הזאת המצוה ("this commandment") in 4QDeut[c] (Ulrich, Cross et al. 1995, 28). The Targums support MT.

2-3 *And it will happen on the day that you cross over the Jordan into the land that Yahweh your God is giving to you, that you shall set up for yourself large stones, and you shall whitewash them with lime. And you shall write upon them all the words of this law.* Moses is now the speaker. This directive to set up large (free-standing) stones, coat them with lime, and write the law on them when Israel crosses the Jordan seems not to have been carried out as commanded. On the day of the crossing, people picked stones from the Jordan and set them up at Gilgal, opposite Jericho (Josh 4:19-20), but these stones being neither large nor suitable for writing were not a fulfillment of the present command (*pace* Rashi; Moran). Also, Moses says in v. 4 that the ceremony he envisions is to be carried out on Mount Ebal, which is at Shechem, some distance from Gilgal. The book of Joshua records the Ebal ceremony as having occurred sometime later (Josh 8:30-35). A Joshua manuscript from Qumran (4QJosh[a]) appears to have recognized the problem of conflicting commands and relocated MT Josh 8:30-35 to a position near the end of Joshua 4, with the result that the ceremony was recorded as having taken place right after the Jordan crossing (Ulrich 1994; Rofé 1994; Ulrich, Cross et al. 1995, 143-46). Josephus, too, records an altar being built with the stones from the Jordan on the day of crossing and sacrifices having been made upon it (*Ant.* v.20). Then, after the conquest is completed, he records the full ceremony as having taken place at Shechem (*Ant* v. 68-70; cf. Rofé 1994, 78-79). As we have said, Mount Ebal could not have been reached on the day of the crossing, which is how most scholars interpret the phrase, בַּיּוֹם אֲשֶׁר תַּעַבְרוּ אֶת־הַיַּרְדֵּן, "on the day that you cross over the Jordan" (Driver; G. A. Smith; von Rad; Tigay; cf. בַּיּוֹם אֲשֶׁר in 2 Sam 19:20[19]; Est 9:1). Tigay (1996, 486) says that if vv. 2-3 are read in the context of v. 4, this temporal clause of v. 2 must be taken more loosely to mean "once you have crossed," i.e., not necessarily on the same day. Ulrich (1994, 95; Ulrich, Cross et al. 1995, 146) does not want to take this clause literally, suspecting that the mention of a specific place in v. 4 is a secondary insertion. For later Jewish attempts at harmonizing conflicting traditions about Moses calling for raised stones on which to write the law and a stone altar for sacrifice upon Israel's entry into the promised land, see Rofé 1994, 79-80.

Comparisons have been made here with settlement ceremonies held among the Greeks and Romans when they founded cities or new colonies (Driver; Merritt 1935; J. Licht 1980; Weinfeld 1988, 274-75, 280-83). The first settlers of a Greek colony erected stone pillars and monuments upon entering the new land (Strabo *Geogr.* iii 5:5; Herodotus *Hist.* ii 103). Sacred laws on a stela at Cyrene opened with words from Apollo, saying that these were the laws to be fulfilled in the new settlement of Libya. The laws regulated sacrifice, purity and impurity regarding sexual conduct, tithing, refuge for murderers, and other matters occurring in the Deuteronomic Code and other biblical law codes.

and you shall whitewash them with lime. וְשַׂדְתָּ אֹתָם בַּשִּׂיד. The stones were to be coated with lime, which would create a plastered surface on which one could write legibly. Lime was produced by the burning of bones (Amos 2:1). The practice of plastering and painting on stone was Egyptian, where the custom was to coat porous stones with a chalky composition before the paint was applied. Painting was done in black or some other color. The black pigment used in Egypt consisted of ivory or bone-black, and figures inscribed by this method became permanent in a dry climate (J. G. Wilkinson 1883, 2:286-88; Driver). How long an inscription made in this manner would last in damp Palestine is anyone's guess. Luther says the inscription was only for a one-time ceremony. Writing on plaster is documented in texts from Deir 'Alla and Quntillet 'Ajrud (Hoftijzer and van der Kooij 1976, 23-28; Meshel 1978; *ABD*, 4:103-9; Cross 1988, 50-51).

all the words of this law. Even if "this law" means the Deuteronomic Code (chs. 5-26) less all the sermonizing, the pillars would still have contained a great deal of writing. Von Rad thinks that originally a much shorter text was presupposed (cf. Exod 24:4; Josh 24:26). But Tigay argues that two stones of the size on which Hammurabi's laws were written could easily have contained more than the book of Deuteronomy. Still, we do not know what "all the words of this law" consisted of.

in order that you may enter into the land that Yahweh your God is giving to you. Setting up stones gives Israel its warrant to occupy the land. In the modern day, we raise the flag.

a land flowing with milk and honey. On this expression, see Note for 6:3.

as Yahweh God of your fathers promised to you. Here the verb דבר must be translated "promised." Yahweh's covenant with Abraham included a promise that his descendants would possess the land in which he was currently sojourning (see Note on 1:8). On Yahweh as "God of the fathers," see Note on 1:11.

4 Here it is clear that the stones are to be set up on Mount Ebal, suggesting editorial conflation with vv. 2-3.

Mount Ebal. One of two mountains rising above Shechem, situated north of the pass; the mountain south of the pass is Mount Gerizim. In vv. 12-13 Gerizim is designated the mountain of blessing and Ebal the mountain of curse (see Note for 11:29). From Mount Ebal will be spoken the curses of vv. 15-26. The Sam has "Gerizim" instead of "Ebal," which has generated considerable discussion in light of the schism later developing between the Samaritans and the

Deuteronomy 27

Jews (Josephus *Ant.* xiii.74-79; cf. John 4:20). Driver thinks "Gerizim" was an arbitrary alteration on the part of the Samaritan Pentateuch. Eissfeldt (1965, 216, 695) says that while this is possible, it is more probable that "Ebal" here and in Josh 8:30 represents an anti-Samaritan polemic on the part of Jews and that in both places the text originally read "Mount Gerizim."

5 The altar is to be erected at the same location. Erection of altars was part of the foundation ceremonies among the Greeks (Weinfeld 1988, 281). An altar of unhewn stones is specified in the Covenant Code (Exod 20:25). One such altar, over 7 ft square and 4.5 ft high, has turned up in an 8th-cent. Israelite temple at Arad (Y. Aharoni 1968, 19-25; 1969, 35-38; *NEAEHL*, 1: 83; Herzog 2002, 52-62). The present altar is said to be located on Ebal's northeastern slope by Zertal (1985; 1986), but its identification is still debated (Kempinski 1986).

6 *whole stones.* אֲבָנִים שְׁלֵמוֹת. I.e., unhewn stones.

and you shall offer upon it burnt offerings to Yahweh your God. "Burnt offerings" are those in which the entire animal is consumed on the altar (see Note for 12:6). According to Deuteronomy, sacrifice will begin when Israel is settled in the land (see Note for 12:8).

7 The command to sacrifice and eat in gladness before Yahweh is given in 12:6-7, 11-12, 18, where both are to occur at the single sanctuary (see Note for 12:7). Envisioned here is a covenant ceremony such as the one that took place at Horeb (Exod 24:3-8). "Peace offerings" (שְׁלָמִים) are accompanied by a sacrificial meal for the worshippers; elsewhere in Deuteronomy these offerings are simply called "sacrifices" (see Note for 12:6).

8 Repeating v. 3, which here is a concluding reminder that the words written on the large stones must be legible. One assumes that in the assembly were people who could read. Because this verse follows the command to erect a stone altar, one might conclude that the writing was to be upon the altar (cf. Josh 8:30-32). Fishbane (1985, 162) says v. 8 was later read with vv. 5-7. See *m. Soṭah* 7:5.

Message and Audience

In this interpolated narrative Moses and the elders give a repeated admonition that the people keep all the teaching Moses has given them this day. Moses says that on the day Israel crosses the Jordan into the new land people are to set up large stones, coat them with lime, and write on them the Deuteronomic law. These stones will give Israel entitlement to the good land Yahweh promised to the fathers. The command to erect these stones is repeated, and the people are told this is to take place on Mount Ebal. There the people are also to build a stone altar without aid of an iron chisel. The stones are to be whole stones, and on this altar they are to offer burnt offerings and peace offerings. In eating their portion of the peace offering, people are to be glad before Yahweh. One last reminder: the words of the Deuteronomic law must be written legibly so people can read them.

2. Today You Have Become Yahweh's People (27:9-10)

27 ⁹*Then Moses and the Levitical priests spoke to all Israel: Be silent and hear, O Israel, this day you have become a people to Yahweh your God.* ¹⁰*And you shall obey the voice of Yahweh your God and you shall do his commandments and his statutes that I am commanding you today.*

Rhetoric and Composition

This brief discourse is delimited at the top end by a *setumah* in M^L and a section in Sam before v. 9 and at the bottom end by a *setumah* in M^L after v. 10. The verses are generally agreed to be separate from vv. 1-8 and 11-26, which are later interpolations into the book. Verses 9-10 have an affinity to 26:16-19 and may have been an earlier tie-in between chs. 26 and 28. The discourse shifts back from anticipated covenant ceremonies to Moses' address in the plains of Moab. Also, with ch. 28 having no introduction, these verses may earlier have been its introduction (Nelson).

Portions of 27:9-10 are contained in 4QDeut^f.

Notes

27:9 *Then Moses and the Levitical priests spoke to all Israel.* Moses once again is joined by Israelite leaders in addressing the people (see Rhetoric and Composition for 27:1-8). On the "Levitical priests," see Note for 17:9. Discussion on the Levites, their priestly office, and their subordination to "sons of Aaron" in P material and in the postexilic period appears in Note for 12:12.

Be silent and hear, O Israel, this day you have become a people to Yahweh your God. The Sam and one Gk MS add "holy" after "people" (cf. 28:9). On Israel as Yahweh's holy people, see Note for 7:6. According to this verse, also 26:18 and 29:12(13), Israel becomes Yahweh's people on the present day in the plains of Moab. But Exod 6:6-7 seems to anticipate Israel becoming Yahweh's people in the exodus (cf. Deut 4:20, 34). Or perhaps it was at Horeb, when the covenant was made and the law given (Exod 19:3-6). It could have occurred earlier. Childs

(1993, 422) states: "Exodus 1 marks the transition from the sons of Jacob to the people of Israel," going on to say that throughout the struggle preceding the exodus the "people of Yahweh" are set in opposition to the "people of Pharaoh" (Exod 12:31). Rashi takes "this day" to mean "every day": Every day it should appear to Israel that it has entered on that very day into covenant with Yahweh.

Be silent and hear, O Israel. הַסְכֵּת וּשְׁמַע יִשְׂרָאֵל. A modified form of the "Hear, O Israel" didactic introduction in Deuteronomy, on which see Note for 5:1. The verb סכת is a *hapax legomenon* in the OT, but Akk *sakātu* and Ar *sakata* both mean "be silent" (KBL³). See also Sir 13:23. One must be silent before Yahweh in order to hear his voice (1 Kgs 19:11-12; Ps 46:11[10]; Zeph 1:7; Zech 2:17[13]).

10 The recurring theme of Deuteronomy: obeying Yahweh's voice means doing the commandments (see Note for 13:5).

Message and Audience

The audience hears that a solemn word was spoken to all Israel by Moses and the Levitical priests. The people are told to be silent and listen, for on this very day they have become a people to Yahweh their God. This repeats an admonition heard throughout the book, i.e., that Israel must obey the voice of Yahweh and do the commandments it has heard on this day.

3. Let the Tribes Ascend the Mountains (27:11-13)

27 ¹¹*Then Moses commanded the people on that day:* ¹²*These shall stand to bless the people upon Mount Gerizim when you cross over the Jordan: Simeon and Levi and Judah and Issachar and Joseph and Benjamin.* ¹³*And these shall stand for the curse on Mount Ebal: Reuben, Gad and Asher and Zebulun, Dan and Naphtali.*

4. Let the People Say "Amen" (27:14-26)

27 ¹⁴*And the Levites shall answer and say to every man of Israel in a raised voice:* ¹⁵*"Cursed be the man who makes an idol or cast image, an abomination to Yahweh, a work of the hands of a craftsman, and sets it up in secret." And all the people shall answer and say, "Amen."*

¹⁶*"Cursed be one who treats his father or his mother with contempt." And all the people shall say, "Amen."*

¹⁷*"Cursed be one who moves back the boundary marker of his neighbor." And all the people shall say, "Amen."*

¹⁸"Cursed be one who misleads a blind person on the way." And all the people shall say, "Amen."
¹⁹"Cursed be one who perverts justice to the sojourner, orphan, and widow." And all the people shall say, "Amen."
²⁰"Cursed be one who lies with the wife of his father, because he uncovers the skirt of his father." And all the people shall say, "Amen."
²¹"Cursed be one who lies with any beast." And all the people shall say, "Amen."
²²"Cursed be one who lies with his sister — the daughter of his father or the daughter of his mother." And all the people shall say, "Amen."
²³"Cursed be one who lies with his mother-in-law." And all the people shall say, "Amen."
²⁴"Cursed be one who strikes down his neighbor in secret." And all the people shall say, "Amen."
²⁵"Cursed be one who takes a bribe to strike down a person — innocent blood." And all the people shall say, "Amen."
²⁶"Cursed be one who does not confirm the words of this law to do them." And all the people shall say, "Amen."

Rhetoric and Composition

These verses are delimited at the top end by a *setumah* in M^L before v. 11 and at the bottom end by a *petuḥah* in M^L and sections in Sam and 4QDeut^c after v. 26, which is also the chapter division. The M^L also has a *setumah* after v. 14, which does not support those wanting to separate vv. 11-13 from vv. 14-26 (Driver; G. A. Smith; Tigay). If the introductory v. 14 is to go with vv. 11-13 (so von Rad and G. E. Wright), then something after v. 14 has probably been lost, since vv. 11-13 anticipate a litany of *both* blessings and curses and the blessings are not present. As the text now stands, v. 14 introduces only the curse litany in vv. 15-26, which could be part of an earlier litany of both blessings and curses or a different curse litany entirely. In vv. 15-26, M^L has a *setumah* after every curse.

The curses appear to be grouped into a chiastic structure, where the sexual crimes are given emphasis at the center (Nielsen 1955, 81-82; Tigay):

Sin against God (v. 15)
   Social sins (vv. 16-19)
      Sexual crimes (vv. 20-23)
   Social sins (vv. 24-25)
Sin against God (v. 26)

Deuteronomy 27

The last curse on anyone not performing the law is, according to Deuteronomy, a sin against God.

Portions of 27:11-26 are contained in 4QDeut^c.

Notes

27:11 This introduction, like those in vv. 1 and 9, incorporates the blessing and curse litany on Mount Gerizim and Mount Ebal (vv. 12-13), and the curse litany that follows (vv. 14-26), into Moses' address in the plains of Moab. A blessing and curse ceremony was announced earlier in 11:26-32.

12-13 A covenant renewal ceremony at Shechem is envisioned, with the Israelite tribes divided in half, six standing on the slopes of Mount Gerizim to bless and six standing on the slopes of Mount Ebal to curse (see Note for 11:29). Joshua 8:33, in describing the ceremony that eventually took place, states that the Levites carrying the ark were positioned in between the two groups. In the present verses, nothing more of the anticipated ceremony is reported, for the curses of vv. 15-26 are not the calamities in store for those disobeying the entire Deuteronomic law, such as occur in ch. 28, but maledictions (= spoken curses) on those who secretly carry out a selected number of sinful acts (Weinfeld 1972, 147-48, 276-79). Of blessings there are none.

Attempts have been made to solve this problem, but none are particularly convincing. Rashi, echoing the supplemental v. 26 in T^{PsJ} and *m. Soṭah* 7:5, assumes that a corresponding set of blessings was proffered upon those who *did not* do each prohibited act. For example, the Levites would turn toward Mount Gerizim and begin with the blessing: "Blessed be the man who does not make an idol or cast image . . . ," and the people would answer, "Amen!" Then, turning toward Mount Ebal, the Levites would speak the curse: "Cursed be the man who makes an idol or cast image . . . ," and the people would answer, "Amen!" The litany would continue in this fashion to the end.

The tribes chosen to bless are all sons of Jacob's wives, Leah and Rachel, who Luther said were more important than the others. The tribes chosen to curse are, with two exceptions, sons of Jacob's concubines, Zilpah and Bilhah. The two exceptions are Reuben, Leah's eldest, who forfeited his birthright due to an incestuous act with Bilhah (Gen 35:22; 49:4), and Zebulun, who was Leah's youngest. It has also been suggested that the tribes are divided on the basis of geography (Tigay), which is less convincing, because then Judah and the southern tribes would be favored on the mount of blessing, a circumstance unlikely in a book (and chapter) said to have a northern provenance.

The annual covenant renewal ceremony at Qumran, at which time new members entered the community and existing members underwent evaluation,

Deuteronomy 27

appears to have drawn inspiration from the ceremony described here. The dualistic and deterministic worldview pervading the sectarian literature of this community serves only to sharpen the contrast between the blessed and the cursed. Blessings and curses are present in various Qumran documents, e.g., the *War Scroll* (1QM 13:1-6), the *Temple Scroll* (11QT 59), *Berakhot* (4Q286-290), the *Miqṣat Ma'aśe ha-Torah* = 4QMMT (4Q397: 14-21; 4Q398: 11-13, 14-17), and the *Curse Scroll* (5Q141), but the main text for the covenant renewal ceremony appears in the *Rule of the Community* (1QS 1:16–2:18), which bases its blessings on Num 6:24-26 and its curses on Deut 29:17-20(18-21). Some of the Qumran documents contain only blessings, others only curses. On blessings and curses in the literature of the Judean Desert, see B. Nitzan, "Blessings and Curses," in *EDSS*, 95-100; Fraade 2003.

And these shall stand for the curse. Luther notes that "the people" is left out, which Tigay explains as a circumlocution to avoid saying that the tribes will be cursing the people. But the term here for "curse" is קְלָלָה, which does not have quite the force of an imprecation, but means something more like "harm, calamity, misfortune" (Brichto 1963, 184-86). The preceding עַל takes the meaning of "for," which is rare (Driver; cf. Exod 12:4).

14 In v. 12 the tribe of Levi is stationed on the slopes of Mount Gerizim for the blessing. If the present verse is to carry on from vv. 11-13, then we must imagine only a select number of Levites directing the litany at the center (Driver). They could be the Levites carrying the ark (Josh 8:33). But if vv. 14-26 were originally self-standing, then an infelicity has been allowed to remain after the texts were joined. The Levites, in any case, are here reciting the curse, and the people are saying the "Amen!" The verb ענה, normally "answer, reply," as when predicating "the people" in vv. 15-26, here means merely "proclaim," or the like (T^PsJ; AV and other EVV). Driver says it means "begin to speak."

in a raised voice. Travelers visiting Shechem in the 19th cent. A.D. found the setting to be a natural amphitheater, where voices could be heard from one mountain to the other (C. W. Wilson 1873).

15 Here begins the so-called "Dodecalogue" (δώδεκα = twelve) of Shechem (von Rad), with the curses appearing in the uniquely Israelite apodictic form (Alt 1966c, 114-16, 125-28). The present "Cursed be the man who . . . Amen" form is picked up by Jeremiah, who says the "Amen" on the people's behalf (Jer 11:3). Without the "Amen," see Jer 17:5; 20:15. The present curse is for a violation of the second commandment (5:8-10; Exod 20:4-6), appropriately heading the list.

Cursed be the man. אָרוּר הָאִישׁ. Hebrew אָרוּר, "curse(d)," can denote either the imprecation that misfortune be visited upon someone or something or else the misfortune that comes in response to an imprecation (Brichto 1963, 1-2). Although curses come ultimately from God, the Bible does not invoke the name of the deity in a curse, as Mesopotamian curses do (Blank 1950-51, 77-78; Fensham 1962b, 3). The power of the curse derives from the power of the words expressing it. Thus, a curse once spoken becomes self-fulfilling. All the curses in the present litany inveigh against actions forbidden in the Pentateuch, although not in one and the same code (Driver 1895, 199). Adultery is not included among the sexual sins, but three cases of incest are present, all presumably chosen because they go beyond related sins that are more obvious. The list is not comprehensive, but representative. Weinfeld (1972, 147-48) notes that the present curses are similar in form and content to Covenant Code laws in Exod 21:12-17; 22:17-19(18-20). As imprecations, they are also more similar to the Decalogue and so-called "Ritual Decalogue" in Exod 34:17-26 than they are to the curses of ch. 28. For content, cf. the twelve prohibitions of sexual intercourse in the Holiness Code (Lev 18:7-18), Ezekiel's indictment of Jerusalem's sins in Ezekiel 22, and Psalm 15.

an abomination to Yahweh. What Yahweh finds most detestable are idols and people leading others in the way of idolatry (see Note for 7:25).

a work of the hands of a craftsman. On the expression, "work of your/a craftsman's hands," which occurs often in Deuteronomy and Jeremiah with reference to idols, see Note for 2:7.

in secret. All sinful acts in the litany are clandestine, but here acting in secret is made explicit in order to make it clear that not just public idolatry is disallowed, where potential damage is great because others may be influenced to do the same. The secret idolater is also liable to judgment (13:7-12[6-11]; 29:18-19[19-20]; Job 31:26-28).

> There is something splendid about the way in which Israel on a solemn occasion acknowledges Yahweh's will expressed as laws for all spheres of life, particularly his will as binding on those occasions when a man believes he is alone by himself. Israel makes itself the agent for carrying out this divine will, by introducing it even into all the secret ramifications of life. (von Rad 1966, 168-69)

Weinfeld (1972, 276-77) notes a recurring censure of secret sins in the Wisdom literature, pointing out that there they are accompanied by exhortations to fear God.

Amen. Hebrew אָמֵן is strong assent, meaning "so be it!" (1 Kgs 1:36; Jer 28:6 [ironically]; Neh 5:13). It affirms what others have said, and blessings upon Yahweh in the Psalter sometime receive a double "Amen and Amen!" (Pss 41:14[13]; 72:19; 89:53[52]; 106:48[= 1 Chr 16:36]). Modern church liturgies make frequent use of the congregational "Amen." The woman suspected of adultery must say "Amen" to the curse upon her if she is guilty as charged (Num 5:22). In a Hittite text from the 2nd mill. (*ANET*³, 353), soldiers' loyalty oaths are confirmed by men declaring: "So be it!" Jesus turned the "amen" around, weighting his important teachings with an ἀμὴν at the beginning (Matt 5:26; 6:2, and passim). Here it is commonly translated "truly" (RSV).

16 "*Cursed be one who treats his father or his mother with contempt.*" A violation of the fifth commandment on honoring one's parents (5:16; Exod 20:12), often occurring out of public view. In the Covenant Code it is stated that anyone striking parents or cursing them shall be put to death (Exod 21:15, 17; cf. Lev 20:9; Mark 7:10). Here in the Deuteronomic Code the rebellious son is given over to the community for capital punishment after the parents say they can do nothing with him (21:18-21). The verb קלל in the H-stem means "to treat with contempt" (BDB; KBL³). It is the exact opposite of "honor" (Driver).

17 "*Cursed be one who moves back the boundary marker of his neighbor.*" This repeats a law in the Deuteronomic Code (19:14), also a warning in Prov 23:10. In addition, it violates the eighth commandment, "You shall not steal." One carrying out such a deed will obviously do it covertly. An inscription on one of the Babylonian boundary stones in the British Museum contains a curse from the gods upon anyone who moves or destroys that stone (III 2-4; IV 4-14). The boundary stone dates from the time of Meli-shipak, a 14th-cent. Kassite king reigning after the great Kurigalzu (L. W. King 1902, 22-23). Other curses apply if stones are moved by descendants. Prohibitions against moving boundary markers are well attested in classical sources (see Note for 19:14).

18 "*Cursed be one who misleads a blind person on the way.*" Another clandestine act, and a vicious one, since it exploits the disadvantaged. It is also cowardly, because the blind person cannot identify the one who has misled them (Tigay). See Lev 19:14; Prov 28:10.

19 "*Cursed be one who perverts justice to the sojourner, orphan, and widow.*" Justice for the "sojourner, orphan, and widow" is bedrock law and teaching in the Covenant Code (Exod 22:20-23[21-24]; 23:3, 6) and the Deuteronomic Code (24:17). These individuals have dependent status in Israel (see Note for 10:18).

20 "*Cursed be one who lies with the wife of his father, because he uncovers the skirt of his father.*" I.e., he uncovers the private parts of a wife belonging to his father (T^Psʲ: "for he uncovers the skirt that his father has uncovered"). Reference is presumably to a wife not the person's mother, which would be an obvious sin. Exposing nudity is a euphemism for having sexual intercourse. Hebrew כָּנָף means "extremity," which here is the corner of a garment or a skirt (BDB, 489). This private act is prohibited in the Deuteronomic Code (23:1[22:30]) and the Holiness Code (Lev 18:8). For discussion on this sexual prohibition, see Note for 23:1.

21 "*Cursed be one who lies with any beast.*" Bestiality, a perversity found

Deuteronomy 27

often in rural areas, is a capital offense in the Covenant Code (Exod 22:18[19]) and the Holiness Code (Lev 18:23; 20:15-16). Male intercourse with a cow, sheep, pig, or dog is a capital offense in the Hittite Code, where no appeal to the king is permitted (HL 187, 188, 199; $ANET^3$, 196-97). But there is no punishment for intercourse with a horse or a mule (HL 200A; $ANET^3$, 197). Ugaritic texts make reference to Baal's intercourse with a heifer ($ANET^3$, 139 v), but from this we cannot conclude that Canaanite worship included bestiality (Good 1967, 961).

22 *"Cursed be one who lies with his sister — the daughter of his father or the daughter of his mother."* Sexual relations with one's half-sister, by either parent, is forbidden in the Holiness Code (Lev 18:9; 20:17) and carried over into the Qumran *Temple Scroll* (11QT 66:14).

23 *"Cursed be one who lies with his mother-in-law."* Prohibited in Lev 18:17, where the mother-in-law is like another wife of one's father: the woman is not one's mother; nevertheless, sexual relations with her are disallowed.

24 *"Cursed be one who strikes down his neighbor in secret."* To "strike down" (נכה) can mean to severely wound or kill. This curse could be upon anyone who secretly inflicts serious bodily injury on another. It would certainly be upon anyone who kills (= murders) another in secret, since murder is forbidden in the sixth commandment (5:17; Exod 20:13). Deuteronomy has a law on expiation for an unsolved murder (21:1-9). See also Exod 21:12 in the Covenant Code and Lev 24:17 in the Holiness Code. Rashi says this curse even applies to the slanderer.

25 *"Cursed be one who takes a bribe to strike down a person — innocent blood."* Here נכה can only mean "murder," since innocent blood has been shed. Bribes are offered and taken in secret, and a bribe to murder another falls under the laws forbidding bribery in Exod 23:8; Deut 16:19. Such acts are roundly condemned by Ezekiel (Ezek 22:12).

26 *"Cursed be one who does not confirm the words of this law to do them."* A summary curse like 28:45, echoing the Deuteronomic teaching that the covenant is something you do (4:1, 13-14; 5:1; 6:1, 3; 7:11-12; cf. Jer 11:4). Cf. summary curses in the Epilogue of the Hammurabi Code (rev. xxv-xxviii), also at the end of the 8th-cent. Sefire Treaties (I C: 17-25; II C: 1-17), where the concern is expressed that someone might alter words of the text ($ANET^3$, 178-80, 660). Summary curses appear also in the Hittite and Assyrian treaties, where the suzerain is keen to warn his vassal about the consequences of rebellion (Weinfeld 1972, 106-9). In the present verse the verb קוּם in the H-stem means "cause to stand up, confirm, perform" (1 Sam 15:11, 13; 2 Kgs 23:3, 24; Jer 35:14; cf. Rom 3:31: νόμον ἱστάνομεν, "the law we uphold"). If "the words of this law/teaching" originally referred only to the prior eleven curses, in the present context they take in the entire Deuteronomic law (Driver). Paul, quoting this verse in Gal 3:10, expands its meaning even further to include the entire OT Law (Luther).

Message and Audience

Moses says here that when the people of Israel cross the Jordan and come to Shechem, the tribes are to divide on the mountains of Gerizim and Ebal for a ceremony of covenant renewal. Simeon, Levi, Judah, Issachar, Joseph, and Benjamin are to ascend Gerizim to bless the people, and across on Ebal, Reuben, Gad, Asher, Zebulun, Dan, and Naphtali are to station themselves for the curses. About the ceremony nothing more is reported. The audience, however, will likely know that the ceremony did take place after the battles for Jericho and Ai had been fought.

Attached to this command for a blessing and curse ceremony on the two mountains is an ancient litany probably carried on at this same site. Perhaps it was part of the blessing and curse ceremony. What the audience hears now, however, is simply a litany of twelve curses on people who have engaged in clandestine acts prohibited by Israelite law. In a loud voice, the Levites are to recite each curse, and the people are to answer with an equally loud "Amen!" The first curse is on anyone who makes or has a craftsman make for him an idol or cast image, the purpose of which is to set it up in secret and worship it in secret. Idols are an abomination to Yahweh, nothing more than works of a craftsman. The people know this to be a violation of the second commandment, and to the curse they add their "Amen!"

The next four curses are upon individuals guilty of social sins. One treating one's mother or father with contempt violates the fifth commandment on honoring one's parents, and this curse is supported by other Israelite laws, including one in the Deuteronomic Code about the rebellious son. Anyone moving back the boundary marker of his neighbor disregards another Deuteronomic law and is a thief, making him in violation of the eighth commandment prohibiting stealing. The one who misleads a blind person on the path or the road is a despicable soul, disregarding neighborliness and exploiting someone unable to correct the wrongdoing and identify the one who committed it. The fourth curse is on anyone perverting justice to the sojourner, orphan, and widow, again gross exploitation of disadvantaged persons and a violation of laws in the Covenant Code and the Deuteronomic Code. To all of these the people say their "Amen!"

The next four curses are upon those engaging in illicit sexual commerce. One must not have sexual relations with the wife of his father, even a wife who is not the person's mother. To do such a thing is to uncover the nakedness of a woman belonging to one's father, a sin the audience will perhaps remember was committed by Reuben. A curse also rests on one having sex with a beast, which is a perversion. A curse also falls on one having sexual relations with his sister, even if she is a half-sister. One must also not have sexual relations with a mother-in-law, a woman as much off-limits to a man as his own mother. All these acts are forbidden in Israelite law, and to the curses upon people who do them the people will shout their loud "Amen!"

The next two curses are criminal in nature. Both deal with violent action carried out against another person. One is cursed if he strikes down another person in secret, whether it results in serious injury or death. If it results in death, it will be a clear violation of the sixth commandment. A curse rests also upon one who takes a bribe to strike down another person, where the intent to murder is made clear by a reference to shedding "innocent blood." To these curses the people also say their "Amen!"

The final curse is on anyone who does not perform the words of this law by doing them, a major theme throughout Deuteronomy and a sin against Yahweh. In the early Shechem liturgy, "this law" may simply have meant the prior eleven prohibitions, but for a 7th-cent. audience it will have referred to the entire Deuteronomic Code. The people, in any case, are to respond with their "Amen!"

B. Blessings and Curses of the Deuteronomic Covenant (28:1-68)

1. If You Obey the Covenant (28:1-14)

a) *The Six Blessings (28:1-6)*

28 ¹*And it will happen if you surely obey the voice of Yahweh your God, to be careful to do all his commandments that I am commanding you today, that Yahweh your God will set you high over all the nations of the earth.* ²*And all these blessings shall come upon you and overtake you, because you will obey the voice of Yahweh your God:*

³*Blessed shall you be in the city and blessed shall you be in the country.*

⁴*Blessed be the fruit of your womb, and the fruit of your soil, and the fruit of your beasts, the offspring of your cattle and the young of your flock.*

⁵*Blessed be your basket and your bread bowl.*

⁶*Blessed shall you be in your coming in and blessed shall you be in your going out.*

b) *Victory in Battle, Prosperity, World Respect (28:7-14)*

⁷*And Yahweh will make your enemies who rise up against you smitten ones before you; on one road they shall come out to you, and on seven roads they shall flee be-*

fore you. ⁸Yahweh command the blessing to go with you in your granaries and in every undertaking of your hand, and bless you in the land that Yahweh your God is giving to you. ⁹Yahweh will confirm you to himself as a holy people, as he swore to you, because you will keep the commandments of Yahweh your God and walk in his ways. ¹⁰And all the peoples of the earth will see that the name of Yahweh is called upon you, and they shall be afraid of you. ¹¹And Yahweh will give you more than enough for good, in the fruit of your womb and in the fruit of your beasts and in the fruit of your soil, on the soil that Yahweh swore to your fathers to give to you. ¹²Yahweh will open to you his good storehouse, the heavens, to give the rain of your land in its time, and to bless all the work of your hand; and you shall lend to many nations, but you, you shall not borrow. ¹³And Yahweh will make you the head, and not the tail, and you shall only be on the top, and you shall not be on the bottom, because you will listen to the commandments of Yahweh your God that I am commanding you today, to be careful and to do, ¹⁴and you will not turn aside from all the words that I am commanding you today, right or left, to go after other gods to serve them.

2. If You Do Not Obey the Covenant (28:15-68)

a) The Six Curses (28:15-19)

28¹⁵And it will happen if you do not obey the voice of Yahweh your God, to be careful to do all his commandments and his statutes that I am commanding you today, then all these curses shall come upon you and overtake you:
    ¹⁶Cursed shall you be in the city and cursed shall you be in the country.
    ¹⁷Cursed be your basket and your bread bowl.
    ¹⁸Cursed be the fruit of your womb, and the fruit of your soil, the offspring of your cattle and the young of your flock.
    ¹⁹Cursed shall you be in your coming in and cursed shall you be in your going out.

b) Disease, Famine, Defeat in Battle (28:20-26)

²⁰Yahweh will send against you the curse, the panic, and the rebuke in every undertaking of your hand that you do, until you are completely destroyed and until you perish quickly, on account of your evil doings, because you have forsaken me. ²¹Yahweh make the pestilence stick to you, until it finishes you from on the soil that you are entering to possess. ²²Yahweh will strike you down with consumption and with fever, and with inflammation and with fiery heat, and with sword, and with blight and with mildew, and they shall pursue you until you perish.

²³ And your heavens that are over your head will become bronze, and the earth that is under you iron. ²⁴ Yahweh will make the rain of your land dust, and dirt from the heavens shall come down upon you, until it completely destroys you. ²⁵ Yahweh will make you smitten before your enemies; on one road you shall go out to him, and on seven roads you shall flee before him, and you shall be a fright to all the kingdoms of the earth. ²⁶ And your dead body shall become food for all the birds of the heavens and for the beasts of the earth, and there will be none to scare them off.

c) Incurable Disease, Madness, Displacement (28:27-37)

²⁷ Yahweh will strike you down with the boils of Egypt, and with hemorrhoids and with the scabies and with the itch, of which you cannot be healed. ²⁸ Yahweh will strike you down with madness and with blindness and with bewilderment of mind; ²⁹ and you shall become as one who gropes at noonday, just as the blind grope in thick darkness, and you shall not make prosperous your ways, and you shall become only oppressed and robbed all the days, and there will be none to deliver. ³⁰ A wife you shall betroth and another man shall violate her; a house you shall build and you shall not dwell in it; a vineyard you shall plant and you shall not eat its fruit. ³¹ Your ox shall be slaughtered before your eyes, but you will not eat from it; your ass shall be snatched away from before you and it shall not be restored to you; your sheep shall be given to your enemies, and there will be none to deliver for you; ³² your sons and your daughters given to another people, and your eyes will see and cry themselves out for them, all the day, and there will be no power in your hand; ³³ the fruit of your soil and all your toil a people whom you do not know will eat, and you shall become only oppressed and crushed all the days. ³⁴ And you shall be driven mad from the sight of what your eyes shall see. ³⁵ Yahweh will strike you down with bad boils upon the knees and upon the legs, of which you cannot be healed, from the sole of your foot to the crown of your head.

³⁶ Yahweh bring you and your king whom you will set up over you to a nation that you do not know, you or your fathers, and there you will serve other gods of wood and stone. ³⁷ And you shall become a desolation, a proverb, and a taunt among all the peoples to whom Yahweh will lead you.

d) Crop Failure, Impoverishment, Dependent Status (28:38-46)

³⁸ Much seed you shall take out to the field, and little you shall gather, because the locust will finish it off. ³⁹ Vineyards you shall plant and shall tend, but the wine you shall not drink, nor shall you gather, because the worm shall eat it. ⁴⁰ Olive trees there shall be for you in all your territory, but with oil you shall not anoint yourself, because your olives shall drop off. ⁴¹ Sons and daughters you shall beget,

but they shall not be yours, because they shall go into captivity. ⁴²*All your trees and the fruit of your soil the buzzing locust shall possess.* ⁴³*The sojourner who is in your midst shall rise above you higher and higher, and you, you shall go down lower and lower;* ⁴⁴*he, he shall lend to you, but you, you shall not lend to him; he, he shall be the head, and you, you shall be the tail.*

⁴⁵*And all these curses shall come upon you, and they shall pursue you and overtake you until you are completely destroyed, because you did not obey the voice of Yahweh your God, to keep his commandments and his statutes that he commanded you.* ⁴⁶*And they shall be with you and with your descendants, for a sign and for a wonder, forever.*

e) Curses of the Siege (28:47-57)

⁴⁷*Inasmuch as you did not serve Yahweh your God with gladness and with goodness of heart from the abundance of everything,* ⁴⁸*so you shall serve your enemies whom Yahweh will send against you, in hunger and in thirst, and in nakedness and in want of everything, and he will put a yoke of iron upon your neck until he has completely destroyed you.*

⁴⁹*Yahweh will lift up against you a nation from afar, from the end of the earth, just as the eagle flies, a nation whose language you do not understand,* ⁵⁰*a stern-faced nation that will not raise the face to the old, and to the young will not show favor,* ⁵¹*and it shall eat the fruit of your beasts and the fruit of your soil until you are completely destroyed, who shall not leave a remnant for you of grain, wine, or oil, the offspring of your cattle or the young of your flock, until it has caused you to perish;* ⁵²*and it shall cause you distress within all your gates until your high and fortified walls come down, in which you are trusting, in all your land; and it shall cause you distress within all your gates, in all your land that Yahweh your God has given to you.* ⁵³*And you shall eat the fruit of your womb, the flesh of your sons and your daughters that Yahweh your God has given to you, in siege and in hardship that your enemy shall press upon you.* ⁵⁴*The tender man among you, yes the most delicate, his eye will be evil against his brother and against the wife of his bosom and against the last of his children whom he has spared,* ⁵⁵*not giving to any of them the flesh of his children that he is eating, there being nothing else remaining to him, in siege and in hardship that your enemy shall press upon you within all your gates.* ⁵⁶*The tender and delicate woman among you, who would not venture to set the sole of her foot upon the ground because she is delicate and tender, her eye will be evil against the husband of her bosom and against her son and against her daughter,* ⁵⁷*yes, against her afterbirth that comes out from between her feet, and against her children whom she bears, because she will eat them in want of everything in secret, in siege and in hardship that your enemy shall press upon you within your gates.*

f) Egypt Revisited! (28:58-68)

⁵⁸*If you are not careful to do all the words of this law that are written in this book, to fear this glorious and awesome name, Yahweh your God,* ⁵⁹*then Yahweh will make extraordinary your blows and the blows of your descendants, great and lasting blows, also bad and lasting sicknesses.* ⁶⁰*And he will bring against you every disease of Egypt of which you were in dread, and they will stick to you.* ⁶¹*Moreover, every sickness and every blow that is not written in this book of the law, Yahweh will bring them upon you until you are completely destroyed.* ⁶²*You shall remain a few males instead of your being as numerous as the stars of the heavens, because you did not obey the voice of Yahweh your God.* ⁶³*And it will happen as Yahweh rejoiced over you to do you good and to multiply you, so Yahweh will rejoice over you to make you perish and to completely destroy you, and you shall be torn from off the soil that you are entering to possess.* ⁶⁴*And Yahweh will scatter you among all the peoples, from one end of the earth to the other end of the earth, and there you will serve other gods that you have not known, you or your fathers, of wood and stone.* ⁶⁵*And among these nations you will not rest, yes, there will not be a resting place for the sole of your foot, and Yahweh will give you there a quivering heart and cried-out eyes and dryness of throat.* ⁶⁶*And your life shall be hanging uncertain in front of you, and you shall be in dread night and day, and you shall have no faith in your life.* ⁶⁷*In the morning you will say, "Who can bring evening?" and in the evening you will say, "Who can bring morning?" from the dread of what your heart shall dread and from the sight of what your eyes shall see.* ⁶⁸*And Yahweh will bring you back to Egypt in ships, on the way that I said to you, "You shall not see it ever again," and there you shall sell yourselves to your enemies as male slaves and female slaves, but there will be none to buy.*

Rhetoric and Composition

This large collection of blessings and curses, anticipated already in 11:26-32, is demarcated at the top end by a *petuḥah* in M^L and sections in Sam and 4QDeut^c before v. 1, which is also the chapter division. Demarcation at the bottom end is by a *setumah* in M^L and a *petuḥah* in M^A after v. 68. The Sam has a section after v. 11. The blessings are separated from the curses by a *setumah* in M^L and a section in Sam after v. 14. Following v. 14, M^L has no other sections in vv. 1-68. The same holds true in M^A, which begins after a loss of folios with 28:17. The Sam has sections after vv. 21, 26, 35, 48, 53, 55, 57, and 63. Any other divisions must be made on different criteria, which is possible in the chapter, since repeated words and phrases seem to indicate where supplementary collections begin and end.

It is generally agreed that the chapter is a composite, but to what extent primary and secondary material may be identified is debated. Noth (1966a, 121-22) believed the blessings of vv. 7-14 were probably secondary because of "Deuteronomic expressions" in vv. 8b, 9, 10, 11b, 13b, and 14. He continued: "No one can now maintain that everything which now stands in the curse section of vv. 20-46 belongs to the original form," for which reason he regarded vv. 20b, 21b, 29, 34, 36, 37, and vv. 38-41 as later additions. Weinfeld (1972, 128-29), however, agrees with Hillers (1964a, 30-42) that the present chapter, like the Vassal Treaties of Esarhaddon, is a composite, not because of redactional activity but because scribes combined a variety of traditional curses currently available. The same would hold true for the collected curses in Leviticus 26. Cf. also Exod 23:20-33.

One notes in this collection a preponderance of curses over blessings (von Rad: the curses are almost four times longer than the blessings), which is paralleled in the Syrian and Assyrian treaties, but not in the Hittite treaties (D. J. McCarthy 1963, 122). The Hittite treaties ($ANET^3$, 201, 205) keep the blessings and curses in balance. But in the epilogue to the Code of Hammurabi, the blessing is brief and the curse lengthy. The Vassal Treaties of Esarhaddon (680-669) have very many curses, but no blessings ($ANET^3$, 538-41). It has therefore been argued by some scholars (D. J. McCarthy 1963, 123; Frankena 1965, 146) that the curses in Deuteronomy 28 reflect the canonical curses of Mesopotamia. Elsewhere in the biblical material, the curses in Leviticus 26 substantially outnumber the blessings, and in Ps 109:8-19 are only curses, no blessings. In the Qumran *Temple Scroll* (11QT 59), blessings and curses will come to both king and people if the king does or does not observe Yahweh's commands (Yadin 1983, 2:265-70; cf. Fraade 2003, 154). Blessings and curses occur also in the *War Scroll*, 4Q473 on "The Two Ways" (Brooke et al. 1996, 289-94), and 4QMMT (Fraade 2003, 154-59). In 4QMMT, see documents 4Q397: 14-21, 22; 4Q398: 11-13, 14-17 (Qimron and Strugnell 1994, 58-61). In the NT, the blessings beginning the Sermon on the Mount (Matt 5:3-12) are balanced by woes coming later in the Gospel (Matthew 23), but with the difference that there the blessings are conferred on one audience and the woes on another.

The present chapter is built around a core of six blessings (vv. 3-6) and six curses (vv. 16-19), which may originally have been independent (G. E. Wright; D. J. McCarthy 1963, 123). Now they are framed by warnings of what will happen if people obey or disobey Yahweh's commands (vv. 1-2, 15). The core could have been recited at the Shechem covenant renewal ceremony reported in 27:11-13, as this ceremony calls for six tribes to recite blessings from Mount Gerizim and six tribes to recite curses from Mount Ebal.

The remaining blessings and curses, which are more homiletical and which are anticipated in 7:12-16; 8:11-20; 11:13-17, come in six supplements:

Deuteronomy 28

Blessing Supplement   (vv. 7-14)
Curse Supplement I   (vv. 20-26)
Curse Supplement II   (vv. 27-37)
Curse Supplement III   (vv. 38-46)
Curse Supplement IV   (vv. 47-57)
Curse Supplement V   (vv. 58-68)

(1) The Core. A symmetrical composition, brief and compact with representative simplicity, covers the whole of community life. The first blessing balances the last, and the center blessings balance one another. Similarly, the first curse balances the last, and the center curses balance one another. But the center curses reverse the sequence of the center blessings, just as the centers of the injunctions in 6:6-9 and 11:18-20 are reversed (see Rhetoric and Composition for 11:18-21):

a		Blessed **shall you be** in the city and blessed **shall you be** in the country.	v. 3
	b	Blessed **be** *the fruit of your womb, and the fruit of your soil . . . the offspring of your cattle and the young of your flock.*	v. 4
	b′	Blessed **be** *your basket and your bread bowl.*	v. 5
a′		Blessed **shall you be** in your coming in and blessed **shall you be** in your going out.	v. 6

a		Cursed **shall you be** in the city and cursed **shall you be** in the country.	v. 16
	b′	Cursed **be** *your basket and your bread bowl.*	v. 17
	b	Cursed **be** *the fruit of your womb, and the fruit of your soil, the offspring of your cattle and the young of your flock.*	v. 18
a′		Cursed **shall you be** in your coming in and cursed **shall you be** in your going out.	v. 19

(2) Blessing Supplement (vv. 7-14) and Curse Supplement I (vv. 20-26). The conclusion of Curse Supplement I inverts keywords and phrases from the beginning of the Blessing Supplement:

And Yahweh will make your enemies who rise up against you   v. 7
   smitten ones before you; on one road they shall come out to
   you, and on seven roads they shall flee before you.

> *Yahweh will make you smitten before your enemies; on one*   v. 25
> *road you shall go out to him, and on seven roads you*
> *shall flee before him.*

(3) Core Blessings (vv. 3-6) and Blessing Supplement (vv. 7-14). The Blessing Supplement reverses themes of the Core Blessings; it also interprets and expands key terms of the Core, e.g., "city" and "country" of v. 3 are interpreted to mean commercial and agricultural prosperity in vv. 12-13a; and "coming in" and "going out" of v. 6 are interpreted to mean military expeditions in v. 7 (Tigay 1996, 490, citing Rofé). The chiastic structure incorporating the interpretations:

```
a      commercial ("city") and agricultural ("country") prosperity       v. 3
  b      fruit of the womb, soil, beasts, herds, and flocks              v. 4
    c      food ("basket . . . bread bowl")                              v. 5
      d      military expeditions ("coming in . . . going out")          v. 6
      d′     military expeditions ("enemies . . . smitten ones")         v. 7
    c′     food ("granaries . . . undertaking of your hand")             v. 8
  b′     fruit of the womb, beasts, and soil                             v. 11
a′     agricultural ("rain") and commercial prosperity                   vv. 12-13a
       ("lending . . . the head . . . on the top")
```

Since this correlation does not include the affirmation of Israel as Yahweh's holy people in vv. 9-10, one may speculate that the affirmation was to be the climactic word of the Supplement, coming as it does in the center. This same "holy people" affirmation functions as an inclusio in 14:1-21 (see Rhetoric and Composition for 14:1-21).

(4) The Entire Blessing Collection (vv. 1-14). The entire blessing collection contains a thematic and keyword tie-in between beginning and end (Tigay; Nelson), another inclusio:

vv. 1-2   . . . if you surely obey (שָׁמוֹעַ תִּשְׁמַע בְּ) the voice of Yahweh your God, to be careful to do all his commandments that I am commanding you today . . . because (כִּי) you will obey (תִשְׁמַע בְּ) the voice of Yahweh your God.

vv. 13b-14 . . . because (כִּי) you will listen (תִשְׁמַע) to the commandments of Yahweh your God that I am commanding you today, to be careful and to do, and you will not turn aside from all the words that I am commanding you today. . . .

(5) Core Curses (vv. 15-19) and Curse Supplement III (vv. 38-46). Curse Supplement III ends by repeating hortatory words introducing the Core Curses (Welch 1932, 131; Tigay), where the key phrases are inverted, forming a chiasmus:

a	*And it will happen if you do not obey the voice of Yahweh your God, to be careful to do all his commandments and his statutes that I am commanding you today*	v. 15
b	*then all these curses shall come upon you and overtake you*	
b′	*And all these curses shall come upon you, and they shall pursue you and overtake you until you are completely destroyed*	v. 45
a′	*because you did not obey the voice of Yahweh your God, to keep his commandments and his statutes that he commanded you.*	

(6) Curse Supplement II (vv. 27-37). This supplement, prior to its prediction of displacement (vv. 36-37), begins and ends with curses of "boils" and "madness," its key terms being inverted:

a	*Yahweh will strike you down with the* boils *of Egypt . . . of which you cannot be healed*	v. 27
b	*Yahweh will strike you down with* madness *and with blindness . . .*	v. 28
b′	*And you shall be driven* mad *from the sight of what your eyes shall see*	v. 34
a′	*Yahweh will strike you down with bad* boils *upon the knees and upon the legs, of which you cannot be healed*	v. 35

(7) Blessing Supplement (vv. 7-14) and Curse Supplement III (vv. 38-46). Curse Supplement III, before its sermonic wrap-up in vv. 45-46, concludes in a way similar to the Blessing Supplement:

and *you shall lend* to many nations, *but you, you shall not borrow*	v. 12
and Yahweh will make you *the head,* and not *the tail*	v. 13

he, he shall lend to you, but you, you shall not lend to him	v. 44
he, he shall be the head, and you, you shall be *the tail*	

(8) Curse Supplement IV (vv. 47-57). Keyword repetitions give this supplement its own internal balance:

until he has completely destroyed you   v. 48
until you are completely destroyed   v. 51

in siege and in hardship that your enemy shall press upon you within all your gates   v. 55
in siege and in hardship that your enemy shall press upon you within your gates   v. 57

(9) Curse Supplement III (vv. 38-46) and Curse Supplement V (vv. 58-68). Curse Supplement V begins with a summary statement reversing the ending summary statement of Curse Supplement III:

And *all these curses* shall come upon you . . . *because you did not obey the voice of Yahweh your God, to keep his commandments and his statutes that he commanded you*   v. 45

If *you are not careful to do all the words of this law* that are written in this book . . . then Yahweh will *make extraordinary your blows* . . .   vv. 58-59

(10) Curse Supplement II (vv. 27-37) and Curse Supplement V (vv. 58-68). Curse Supplement V, with its ending "Egypt" reference, echoes the "Egypt" reference beginning Curse Supplement II:

Yahweh will strike you down with the boils of *Egypt* . . .   v. 27

And *Yahweh* will bring you back to *Egypt* in ships . . .   v. 68

Weinfeld (1965, 423; 1972, 122) finds a chiastic structure in vv. 27-35, supporting his view that these verses, as an independent literary unit, balanced a series of curses in the Esarhaddon Treaties (*VTE* 419-30). But his scheme is entirely conceptual and thus too subjective. Rhetorical structures need at least some repeated vocabulary and phraseology to become verifiable.

The wrap-up here in ch. 28 can be compared to other wrap-ups in the Covenant Code (Exod 23:20-33) and Holiness Code (Lev 26:3-45). Blessing and curse language distinguish the Deuteronomic writer (the Covenant Code speaks of "blessing" only once [Exod 23:25], and in the Holiness Code, "blessing" and "curse" are not used), although it has been suggested that this could derive from a liturgy used at the Shechem renewal ceremony (G. E. Wright). The laconic style and uniform wording of the core blessings and curses seem to facilitate oral recitation (Tigay 1996, 258).

Deuteronomy 28

Portions of 28:1-68 are contained in 1QDeut[b], 4QDeut[c], 4QDeut[g], 4QDeut[l], 4QDeut[o], and 4QpaleoDeut[r]. The Roberts Papyrus (P. Ryl. Gk. 458), an early Greek text dated to the end of the 2nd cent. B.C. (C. H. Roberts 1936, 37), contains portions of 28:31-33.

Notes

28:1 *And it will happen if you surely obey the voice of Yahweh your God, to be careful to do all his commandments that I am commanding you today.* Moses is seen here to be resuming his discourse after the "Shechem" interpolation of ch. 27. Verse 1a is the protasis, vv. 1b-2 the apodosis. The protasis-apodosis form is at home in legal discourse (v. 15; 11:13-15, 22-23; Exod 23:22), but occurs often in preaching, particularly the preaching of Jeremiah (Jer 4:1-2; 12:16-17; 31:36-37; 33:20-21, 25-26). On the protasis-apodosis construction in covenant speech, see Note for 11:13-14. Obeying Yahweh's voice means doing Yahweh's commands, the essence of covenant compliance (see Note for 13:5). This will bring material blessing (vv. 2-6). Jesus in his Sermon on the Mount teaches that material blessings will accrue to those who obey God's commands: "Seek first [God's] kingdom and his righteousness, and all these things shall be yours as well" (Matt 6:33).

to be careful to do. On this stock Deuteronomic expression, which recurs in vv. 15, 58, see Note for 5:1.

today. On the day of the assembly in Moab.

that Yahweh your God will set you high over all the nations of the earth. Repeating the promise of 26:19, perhaps needed after the interpolation of ch. 27.

2 Blessings accrue from obeying Yahweh's voice, or doing his commands, a promise made earlier in Deuteronomy (7:12-16; 11:13-15; 15:4-6). The particle כִּי should be translated "for" or "because," since the blessings are said to result from covenant obedience. The conditional nature of the Horeb covenant is clarified in v. 1, which has the conditional particle אִם. Linking blessing to covenant obedience has a parallel in international treaty language (D. J. McCarthy 1963, 120). Blessings — and similarly curses (vv. 15, 45) — "are almost personified," says Driver, "represented as pursuing their objects like living agents" (see Note for 28:15). On נשׂג in the H-stem with the meaning of "overtake," see 19:6; Gen 31:25; Ps 40:13(12); Job 27:20. Yahweh, however, stands behind these "living agents," holding them back or releasing them at will (Tigay).

3 I.e., blessing shall follow you everywhere. "City" and "country" (שָׂדֶה) can mean "open country"; 1 Kgs 14:11), when used in combination, take in the whole of a specified territory (Gen 34:28; 1 Kgs 14:11; Jer 14:18). "Blessing," too, is to be interpreted here in the broadest sense possible. It does not translate simply into agricultural and commercial prosperity, as in vv. 12-13a, but will encompass the whole of life. All six of the blessings strive after totality, a defining characteristic of Hebrew rhetoric (Muilenburg 1953, 99). Blessings 1 and 4 are both merism; Blessing 2 is *accumulatio;* and Blessing 3 is metonymy (basket and bread bowl = harvest and daily food).

4 Blessing will mean fertility for you, the land, and animals in your possession, i.e., abundance of children, orchards, vineyards, fields of grain, young calves, sheep, and goats (7:13; cf. Exod 23:26). Since the phrase "and the fruit of your beasts" is not present in the primary MSS of the LXX, nor also in v. 18 in both MT and LXX, some commentators (G. A. Smith; G. E. Wright; Tigay) argue that the phrase was not part of the original formula. Smith thinks it is a gloss from v. 11. But others (Wevers 1995, 428; Nelson) say the LXX omission can be haplography (homoeoarcton: ופרי . . . ופרי or homoeoteleuton: מתך . . . מתך).

fruit of your womb. On this idiom, which means "offspring," see Note for 7:13.

the offspring of your cattle and the young of your flock. Primarily your calves, lambs, and young goats (cf. 7:13).

5 Fruits will be gathered in abundance and bread bowls will be full. There will be plenty to eat. Since firstfruits are brought to the sanctuary in baskets (26:2, 4), "basket" (טֶנֶא) is taken here by T^{NfPsJ} to be one containing firstfruits. The firstfruits are representative of the entire fruit harvest; likewise, the basket here represents many baskets filled with fruit. The מִשְׁאֶרֶת is a bowl used for unleavened dough (Exod 12:34), essential for the preparation of daily bread. Also called a "kneading-trough" (T^{OnqPsJ}; Driver; KBL^3). The LXX translates both terms: αἱ ἀποθῆκαί σου καὶ τὰ ἐγκαταλείμματά σου, "your storehouses and your reserve," which is not quite right. Ibn Ezra takes the (full) basket to symbolize plentiful stores, but "your reserve" of the LXX (from שׁאר, "to be left over") is not correct (Wevers 1995, 428).

6 Another all-inclusive blessing, like the first one. Reference is to all coming and going (a merism), which would include walks to and from home, walks in and out of the city, pilgrimages, journeys, expeditions of war, and other movements of entering and exiting, beginning and completion. The usual sequence is here reversed. Psalm 121:8 says:

> The Lord will keep your going out and your coming in
>   from this time forth and for evermore.

And "going out" precedes "coming in" in Deut 31:2; Num 27:17, 21; Josh 14:11; 1 Sam 18:13, 16; 1 Kgs 3:7; 2 Kgs 11:8; Isa 37:28; Zech 8:10, and elsewhere. In the Mari Letters it says: "one hundred fifty go out and one hundred fifty come in" (*ANET*^{3}, 482 b). The Merneptah Stela (line 25) similarly describes peace and well-being as a time when "one goes and comes with singing" (*ANET*³, 378). But in Jer 37:4 "going in and out" means moving about freely.

7 Here in the supplementary blessings, called by some promises because the word "blessing" is not used, Yahweh emerges as the moving force behind every good coming to Israel. The LXX in vv. 7-36 uses the optative mood wherever God is subject of the blessing or the curse (Wevers 1995, 427, 429). The LXX translates: παραδῷ κύριος ὁ θεός σου τοὺς ἐχθρούς σου, "May the Lord your God deliver up your enemies. . . ." In MT, success against the enemy will be assured (cf. Jer 2:3b). The enemy will come united on one road, but once defeated will flee on many roads (1 Sam 11:11). "Seven" as used here denotes any large number (ibn Ezra; cf. 1 Sam 2:5; Isa 4:1; 11:15; Prov 24:16). The Covenant Code and Holiness Code also promise decisive action against the enemy if Israel obeys Yahweh's voice and does what Yahweh commands (Exod 23:22, 27; Lev 26:3, 7-8).

8 *Yahweh command the blessing to go with you in your granaries and in every undertaking of your hand.* Variant of a stock Deuteronomic expression (see Note for 2:7).

Yahweh command the blessing to go with you. I.e., in all your labors. Driver says the jussive (יְצַו) here and in the verses following should be retained. The Sam has the long form יצוה. On Yahweh "commanding" the blessing, an unusual coinage, see also Lev 25:21; Ps 133:3.

your granaries. אֲסָמֶיךָ. A rare term in the OT, found only here and in Prov 3:10. Ibn Ezra says it must mean "storehouses" or something similar. The term has now turned up in a proper name, Ḥaṣar-asam (= "Village of the Granary"), in a 7th-cent. letter found at Yavneh-Yam (Naveh 1960, 132, 134; cf. *ANET*³, 568).

and in every undertaking of your hand. On this Deuteronomic expression, see Note for 12:7.

and bless you. וּבֵרַכְךָ. Lacking in the LXX, which could be attributed to haplography (homoeoteleuton: ךָ . . . ךָ).

9 *Yahweh will confirm you to himself as a holy people, as he swore to you.* Another theme carrying over from 26:18-19. On Israel's election as Yahweh's holy people, see Note for 7:6. Here it is stated that "holy people" status will be confirmed after settlement in the land. The verb קוּם in the H-stem can mean either "confirm" or "establish."

as he swore to you. In 7:6-8 Israel's designation as a holy people is a result of Yahweh's oath to the fathers.

because you will keep the commandments of Yahweh your God and walk in his ways. The problem is how to interpret the initial כִּי, whether as a conditional "if" or as "because," which is how it is translated in vv. 2 and 13. It is usual to give the particle conditional meaning (T; AV; RSV; JB; NJV, and most commentators), which would make "holy people" status dependent upon Israel keeping the commandments. That is the idea in Exod 19:5-6, which begins with an unambiguous אִם. Driver renders the present כִּי as "(seeing) that," which gives the phrase more positive meaning: it assumes that Israel will indeed be keeping Yahweh's commandments after settlement in the land. See also 30:10, which assumes obedience to the commands. Here the difference may not be that great, for Driver takes all of vv. 2-14 as an apodosis dependent upon the "if" (אִם) of v. 1, making vv. 1-9 a longer version of Exod 19:5-6. What is clear is that Israel's status as a holy people has been conferred as an act of divine grace, and because of this high honor, it is expected that Israel will keep the commandments.

Yahweh your God. On this expression, occurring often in Deuteronomy, see Note for 1:6.

and walk in his ways. "Walking in Yahweh's way" has strong ethical implications in the OT; in Deuteronomy it is a stock phrase and means keeping Yahweh's commandments (see Note for 5:33). Ibn Ezra says one "keeps" in thought and "walks" in deed.

10 Israel's status as a holy (= "set apart") people will impact all peoples of the earth. Yahweh's deliverance at the Red Sea functioned similarly (Josh 4:23-24). Other peoples will know that Israel has been blessed by Yahweh and the nation remains under his care. According to the P writer, this conclusion was reached finally by the prophet Balaam (Numbers 23-24).

the name of Yahweh is called upon you. In having Yahweh's name called upon the nation, Israel will enjoy Yahweh's protection. According to the Song of Moses, this protection was shown particularly in the wilderness (32:10-12). To call someone or something by one's name is to claim ownership (2 Sam 12:28; Isa 4:1; Amos 9:12; Isa 43:1, 6-7; Ezra 2:61). The Amarna Letters express ownership with the same idiom:

> Behold the king has set his name in the land of Jerusalem forever; so I cannot abandon the land of Jerusalem. (EA 287 line 60; $ANET^3$, 488)

> Behold the king my lord has set his name at the rising of the sun, and at the setting of the sun. (EA 288 line 5; $ANET^3$, 488)

In Deuteronomy the central sanctuary is said to have Yahweh's name called upon it, giving rise to the so-called "name theology" in Deuteronomy and the Deuteronomic writings (see Note for 12:5). This theology carried over into Jeremiah, where the nation (Jer 14:9), the city of Jerusalem (25:29), the temple (7:10-11, 14, 30; 32:34; 34:15), and the prophet himself (15:16) are all said to have Yahweh's name called upon them. This "name theology" is retained in Dan 9:19.

and they shall be afraid of you. I.e., because of Yahweh's protection (2:25; 11:25).

Deuteronomy 28

11 *And Yahweh will give you more than enough for good.* וְהוֹתִרְךָ יְהוָה לְטוֹבָה. The verb יתר in the H-stem means "give more than enough/a surplus" (cf. 2 Kgs 4:43, 44; Ruth 2:14). The idea repeats in 30:9. "For good" (לְטוֹבָה) means "to a good outcome" (Mic 1:12; Jer 15:11; Ps 119:122). Ibn Ezra translates: "God will grant you overabundance in prosperity" (cf. NJV). The verse goes on to specify that this surplus will show itself in an overabundance of offspring, young of the cattle, and produce from the soil.

in the fruit of your soil, on the soil that Yahweh swore to your fathers to give to you. Most modern translations shift terminology here from "soil/ground" to "land," even though Hebrew uses only one word: אֲדָמָה ("soil/ground"). The LXX remains constant with two occurrences of τῆς γῆς ("of the earth/land"). The stock phrase about Yahweh giving Israel land sworn to the fathers usually has הָאָרֶץ, "the land" (see Note for 1:8). But in 26:2-3, 15, where variations of the stock phrase occur, terminology shifts from אֲדָמָה ("soil") to אֶרֶץ ("land").

12 *Yahweh will open to you his good storehouse, the heavens.* The LXX has an optative: "May the Lord open (ἀνοίξαι) his good treasury, the heaven." Yahweh's heavenly storehouses are sealed and must be opened.

his good storehouse. אוֹצָרוֹ הַטּוֹב. The OT speaks — usually in poetry — about Yahweh's heavenly storehouses, in which are kept the rain, snow, hail, wind, and thunder (Job 37:9; 38:22; Ps 135:7; Jer 10:13 = 51:16). Rain comes from "waters above the firmament" (Gen 1:7), descending when the windows of heaven are opened and restrained when the same remain closed (Gen 7:11; 8:2; Deut 11:17). These sealed storehouses, also others containing the sun, moon, and stars, were seen by Enoch in his vision of the upper regions (*1 En.* 41:4; 60:11-22). In a Ugaritic text (RŠ 24.245 line 3), Baal is said to have eight storehouses of thunder, where Ug *iṣr* appears to mean the same as Heb אוֹצָר (Pope and Tigay 1971, 118, 123-24). Dahood (1964) says הַטּוֹב ("the good") here denotes "the rain," as it does in Jer 5:25; 17:6; Ps 85:13(12). This meaning is now attested in Ugaritic (*ṭbn* in 1 Aqht 1:46). "His good storehouse" is Yahweh's "storehouse of rain," as the verse goes on to clarify. Looking to the prior verse, we see also a link in terminology between לְטוֹבָה ("for good") and הַטּוֹב ("the good"). In v. 11 the "good" is fertility of people, animals, and land; here in v. 12 "the good" is rain in its season.

to give the rain of your land in its time. See 11:11, 14, 17; also Lev 26:4.

to bless all the work of your hand. A stock Deuteronomic expression (see Note for 2:7).

and you shall lend to many nations, but you, you shall not borrow. Economic independence will result from the prosperity described in v. 11. The same promise is made in 15:5. Psalm 37:25-26 speaks of economic independence coming to the righteous and his children.

13 *And Yahweh will make you the head, and not the tail.* Israel will enjoy a place of honor at the head of the nations. "Head and tail" imagery occurs also in Isa 9:13-14(14-15); 19:15.

and you shall only be on the top, and you shall not be on the bottom. Reiterating the same theme (cf. v. 1). In 26:19, Yahweh promises to put Israel "high above all the nations that he has made, for a praise and for a name and for a glorious decoration." Yahweh's curse, however, will bring about the exact reverse (28:43-44).

because you will listen to the commandments of Yahweh your God that I am commanding you today, to be careful and to do. The כִּי once again is best translated "because," as in vv. 2 and 9, not as a conditional "if" (*pace* AV; RSV; JB; NJV). The expression "to be careful and to do" is a recurring phrase in Deuteronomy (see Note for 5:1).

14 *and you will not turn aside from all the words that I am commanding you today, right or left, to go after other gods to serve them.* The apodosis concludes with this verse (Driver), the conditional nature of the Deuteronomic covenant being formulated as positively as possible. The Deuteronomic preacher genuinely hopes that Israel will not turn aside from Yahweh's commands. But this concluding word of blessing is already anticipating disobedience and the curses that follow. Israel must not turn aside from the commands and serve any god other than Yahweh (see Note for 6:13). In the Vassal Treaties of Esarhaddon (*VTE* 632-36) is this curse:

> (You swear) that you will not loose yourselves from Esarhaddon, king of Assyria, and Ashurbanipal, the crown prince, you will not go to the right or to the left. May scorpions devour him who would go to the right, may scorpions devour him who would go to the left. (Wiseman 1958, 77-78; *ANET*³, 540)

turn aside . . . right or left. On this expression, see Note for 2:26-27.

to go after other gods to serve them. On this Deuteronomic expression, see Note for 6:14.

15 Another protasis-apodosis construction (see Note for 11:13-14), clarifying the conditional nature of the Horeb covenant (cf. vv. 1-2). Curses of misfortune and disaster will come as a result of covenant disobedience. A warning about curses for not obeying Yahweh's voice and doing his commands repeats in vv. 45 and 62. Jeremiah had the unhappy task of informing people that they had not obeyed Yahweh's voice (Jer 3:13; 9:12[13]; 22:21), which for him meant not listening to the voice of prophets Yahweh had sent. Yet, in Jer 3:25 the people are heard confessing this neglect. Lines from the present verse and vv. 20-24 were used by Mendelssohn in his "Elijah Oratorio," Part I Chorus (no. 5):

Deuteronomy 28

> Yet doth the Lord see it not; He mocketh at us;
> His curse hath fallen down upon us;
> His wrath will pursue us, till He destroy us!
> For He, the Lord our God, He is a jealous God.

to be careful to do. On this stock expression in Deuteronomy, occurring also in vv. 1 and 58, see Note for 5:1.

then all these curses shall come upon you and overtake you. Curses, like blessings, have a quasi-independent power in pursuing their objects (28:45). At the same time, they remain subject to Yahweh's command (v. 2; 29:19[20]). Hittite curses contain the formula: "And the curses shall pursue you relentlessly" (Weinfeld 1972, 108-9). Similarly, in the Code of Hammurabi: "May they (the curses) quickly overtake him." Tawil (1977, 61) says the Sefire and Esarhaddon curses refer to the gods "letting loose" pestilence, plague, lions, snakes, beasts of prey, and swarms of insects, and he believes this same meaning is conveyed in the Hebrew verb שלח, "send" (Deut 7:20; Lev 26:25; Jer 8:17; Ezek 5:17; Ps 78:45). The OT contains many examples of personified curses: the agent of the tenth plague in Egypt is called "the Destroyer" (Exod 12:23), and "Death" very often takes on human or angelic form (Hos 13:14; Hab 2:5; Jer 9:20[21]; Job 18:13; 28:22; Ps 49:15[14]). In Jer 9:20[21], Death, like a thief, enters through house windows. Cf. in the NT, 1 Cor 15:26, 54; Rev 6:8; 20:13-14.

16 The same broad meaning should be assumed here as in the blessing (v. 3). Jeremiah saw this curse being actualized in a grim scenario of death and disease (Jer 14:18).

17 *Cursed be your basket and your bread bowl.* In the Vassal Treaties of Esarhaddon (*VTE* 443-45, 447-48) is this curse:

> May there be no mill or oven in your houses; may no grain be poured out for grinding . . . may the dough be lacking from your kneading troughs. (Wiseman 1958, 61-62; *ANET*^{3}, 538)

18 Jeremiah announced the coming of this curse (Jer 5:17; 29:32) and in one troubled moment applied it even to himself (Jer 20:14, 18). The phrase "and the fruit of your beasts," which occurs in the parallel blessing (v. 4) and is absent here in both MT and LXX, may have been lost due to haplography (homoeoarcton: ופרי . . . ופרי, or homoeoteleuton: מתך . . . מתך). The present curse is repeated in vv. 33, 42, 51, 53, where an enemy will carry it out.

19 This curse, like the blessing in v. 6, requires a broad interpretation of all coming and going.

20 *Yahweh will send against you the curse, the panic, and the rebuke in* *every undertaking of your hand that you do, until you are completely destroyed and until you perish quickly.* A general statement about curse, panic, and rebuke begins Curse Supplement I (vv. 20-26). The LXX uses optatives once again in vv. 20-36 whenever God is subject: "May Yahweh send you . . ." (Wevers 1995, 434). The NJV translates the verb שׁלח ("send") as "let loose," giving the curse quasi-independent power (see v. 15).

curse, panic, rebuke. The Hebrew has alliteration in . . . מְאֵרָה . . . מְהוּמָה מִגְעֶרֶת (Tigay). Brichto (1963, 112-13) thinks this is a hendiadys with "curse" (מְאֵרָה) being the primary term: "a curse sent to chastise and confound."

curse. מְאֵרָה. A less frequently used word meaning "curse," although it derives from the same root as the common אָרוּר of vv. 16-19 (ארר). It occurs elsewhere in Mal 2:2; 3:9; Prov 3:33; 28:27. This is not a curse in words, but a curse operative on someone or something. The LXX translates with ἔνδειαν ("want, poverty"), which narrows the meaning considerably.

panic מְהוּמָה. Panic here is confusion in war, e.g., when each person's weapon turns against his fellow (1 Sam 14:20). The term does not mean "faint from hunger" (LXX: ἐκλιμίαν). Yahweh threatened to send panic in 7:23, but this was against Israel's enemies. Jeremiah said Yahweh would now turn back the weapons of Jerusalem's defenders upon those who were wielding them (Jer 21:4), bringing great confusion. The ANE treaties contain a number of curses calling upon the gods to break and turn around the treaty-breaker's weapon, which is usually the bow (cf. Hos 1:5; Jer 49:35; Ezek 39:3). From a treaty of Esarhaddon (no. 543; Hillers 1964a, 60):

> May they break your bow . . .
> May they reverse the direction of the bow in your hand.

An Esarhaddon treaty (nos. 573-75; Wiseman 1958, 71-72; *ANET*³, 540) contains this curse:

> May they shatter your bow and cause you to sit beneath your enemy,
> May they cause the bow to come away from your hand,
> May they cause your chariots to be turned upside down.

The Code of Hammurabi contains a curse stating that the goddess Inanna will bring about confusion and defeat to the fighting warriors (*ANET*³, 179, rev. xxviii):

> May she [i.e., Inanna] shatter his weapons on the field of battle
>   and conflict;
> May she create confusion (and) revolt for him!

May she strike down his warriors, (and) water the earth with
 their blood!

rebuke. מִגְעֶרֶת. This term is a *hapax legomenon* in the OT but comes from an attested root, גער, meaning "to rebuke, restrain." Reference could be to loud, censorious cries in the heat of battle, although Tigay thinks the term refers to drought and crop failure (cf. Mal 3:11).

in every undertaking of your hand that you do. A stereotyped Deuteronomic phrase, on which see Note for 2:7. The words אֲשֶׁר תַּעֲשֶׂה ("that you do") are lacking in the G^B, but are present in other LXX MSS. Since they do not appear in the corresponding blessing of v. 8, they may be added.

you are completely destroyed. הִשָּׁמֶדְךָ. The N-stem and H-stem of שמד occur very often in Deuteronomy, particularly in curses (vv. 20, 24, 45, 48, 51, 61, 63) and are particularly strong (see Note for 1:27). The verb means "made totally useless" when referring to property (Hos 10:8) and "exterminated" when referring to persons and nations (Jer 48:42; Ezek 32:12). The nation will be completely destroyed, yet there will be survivors.

and until you perish quickly. וְעַד־אֲבָדְךָ מַהֵר. On this expression, see Note for 4:26.

on account of your evil doings. מִפְּנֵי רֹעַ מַעֲלָלֶיךָ. A reason for the curse. The present expression occurs only here in the Pentateuch (Wevers 1995, 435) but is frequent elsewhere in the OT, particularly in Jeremiah (Hos 9:15; Jer 4:4; 21:12; 26:3; 44:22; cf. Isa 1:16; Ps 28:4).

because you have forsaken me. אֲשֶׁר עֲזַבְתָּנִי. Moses here assumes the speaking voice of Yahweh (cf. 28:68 and Note for 7:3-4). A second and more important reason for the curse, anticipated in 31:16 because it takes on importance in the Song of Moses (32:15-18). "Forsaking Yahweh" becomes a constant refrain in the preaching of Jeremiah (Jer 1:16; 2:13, 17, 19; 5:7, 19; 9:12[13]; 16:11; 17:13; 19:4). Huldah's oracle of 622, based on the law book found in the temple, gave this as the reason for Yahweh's coming judgment upon Judah (2 Kgs 22:17).

21 The verb is another jussive: יַדְבֵּק, "may he make stick" (cf. v. 8). This curse was promised for the Egyptians at the time of the exodus (Exod 9:3; cf. Amos 4:10), but already in the wilderness Yahweh threatened to bring it upon Israel (Num 14:12). In the Song of Moses, Yahweh promises famine, pestilence (קֶטֶב), sword, and other calamities as a response to Israel's idolatry (Deut 32:24-25), and eventually they came. Amos knew about visitations of pestilence and sword in Israel (Amos 4:10), and Jeremiah preached without letup about the pestilence soon to come in Judah, coining the triad "sword, famine, and pestilence" (Jer 14:12; 18:21; 21:7, 9; 24:10; 27:8, 13; 29:18, and passim). Pestilence preceded Judah's defeat by the Babylonians (Jer 32:24, 36). Here we have a possible reference to "sword" in the next verse (so MT). "Sword and pestilence" are promised in Lev 26:25, having a parallel in a curse from the Esarhaddon Treaties (*VTE* 455-56):

> May Nergal, hero of [the gods], extinguish your life with his merciless dagger; may he send slaughter and pestilence among you. (Wiseman 1958, 63-64; *ANET*³, 538)

The expression "pestilence and famine" (λοιμὸν καὶ λιμὸν) occurs also in Plutarch (*Is. Os.* 47).

until it finishes you from on the soil. Pestilence (דֶּבֶר) is an infectious disease of epidemic proportions, such as the plague, usually resulting in death (Hos 13:14; Jer 21:6, 9). The LXX translates with θάνατον ("death"). Thucydides (*Hist.* ii 47-50) graphically describes a plague rampant in Athens during the Peloponnesian War (425), which may have been bubonic (Krumbhaar 1937, 158). On famine, disease, and death in the siege of Leningrad during World War II, see Salisbury 2000, 376-78, 492, 506-18.

22 Seven more plagues that will affect both people and crops, like the plagues of Egypt.

with consumption and with fever. בַּשַּׁחֶפֶת וּבַקַּדַּחַת. These diseases are cited together in the Holiness Code, where they are said to waste the eyes and cause life to pine away (Lev 26:16). שַׁחֶפֶת appears to be consumption (= tuberculosis). Arabic *suḥāf* means "consumption." The Greek term for pulmonary tuberculosis is φθίσις, but here the LXX renders שַׁחֶפֶת with ἀπορίᾳ ("distress, discomfort"), a general term applying to illness. Tuberculosis is commonly taken to be a lung disease, but actually it can affect any tissue or organ of the body. It is a chronic infection with inflammation, which can linger for months and even years, but in the end is fatal (Kiple 2003, 336-37). The disease is ancient. It has been identified in Egyptian mummies from the 2nd and 3rd mill. Mesopotamian texts from the 7th cent. prescribe treatments for pulmonary tuberculosis and scrofula, which is a lymph infection (Dawson 1967, 111; Hare 1967, 126; Morse 1967, 259-60, 263-68; Kiple 2003, 338-39).

קַדַּחַת is a disease with a high fever (Rashi; Preuss 1978, 160, 268), the term coming from the root קדח, which means "be kindled, kindle" (Deut 32:22; Jer 15:14; 17:4; Isa 50:11; 64:1[2]). The LXX translates with πυρετῷ ("fever"). We do not know precisely what disease is indicated. Some have suggested malaria, another very old disease that brings on chills and bouts of fever (Kiple 2003, 203-5). In Medieval Hebrew קַדַּחַת denoted malaria (Tigay). The NT reports diseases accompanied by a (high) fever (Luke 4:38; John 4:52).

and with inflamation and with fiery heat. וּבַדַּלֶּקֶת וּבַחַרְחֻר. Two other types of fever, or diseases accompanied by fevers. Ancient people took "fevers" to be illnesses in and of themselves, not just symptoms of illness (Preuss 1978,

160). דַּלֶּקֶת is a *hapax legomenon* in the OT, but derived from a known verb meaning "to burn." It is commonly rendered "inflammation" (T^OnqNf; AV; RSV; JB; NJV), although ibn Ezra says it is "delirium," an intense fever that occurs every three or four days. Rashi says it is a fever even hotter than קַדַּחַת. The LXX translates with ῥίγει ("shivering from cold, shuddering"). We do not know what disease this was; it, too, could be malaria (J. R. Bennett 1887, 70). We are also in the dark about חַרְחֻר, except to say that this must be another disease causing high fever (Preuss 1978, 160) or else one causing some other "burning" sensation in the body. The term is a *hapax legomenon* in the OT, usually associated etymologically with חרר, meaning "to be hot, burn, scorch." Job's bones "burned" (חָרָה) with heat (Job 30:30; cf. Ps 102:4[3]), and Isaiah speaks of a curse that leaves the inhabitants of earth "burning" (Isa 24:6). An Arabic cognate means "to thirst" (BDB, 359), which may have informed Rashi's interpretation of חַרְחֻר. He says this is a disease that makes one burning hot inside the body, so one is constantly thirsting for water. On the Greek terms πυρετῷ καὶ ῥίγει ("fever and chills"), which turn up on a curse epitaph of the 2nd cent. A.D. and in Greek magical texts, see Lincicum 2008.

and with sword. וּבַחֶרֶב. The Masoretes took the term to be "sword," pointing it חֶרֶב, but the same Hebrew pointed חֹרֶב means "drought," which is how some ancient and modern Versions have taken it (T^Onq; Sam; RSV; JB; NJV). Drought, also a terrible curse (Jer 50:38; cf. 23:10; Hag 1:11; Zech 11:17 [emended]; Rev 16:12), seems to fit the context better, since "blight" (wind damage) follows immediately and vv. 23-24 presuppose drought conditions. Dryness could also conceivably be within the human body (ibn Ezra: "dehydration"). But there is still support for the rendering "sword." The LXX has φόνῳ ("slaughter, murder"), the word it uses to translate "sword" in Exod 5:3. Targum^Nf omits the term in the text, but adds "sword" in the margin. Rashi stays with "sword." "Sword" also goes with the "pestilence" of v. 21.

and with blight and with mildew. וּבַשִּׁדָּפוֹן וּבַיֵּרָקוֹן. These sonorous terms occur together in Amos 4:9, where they refer to crop and plant damage (gardens, vineyards, fig trees, olive trees). See also 1 Kgs 8:37; Hag 2:17. Although it has been suggested that these curses, too, pertain to human illness (Tigay; Nelson), it is more likely that field crop and plant affliction are meant. The next two verses promise a ruinous drought. Rashi says these are diseases that afflict grain yet in the field (cf. 2 Kgs 19:26). שִׁדָּפוֹן is doubtless "blight," i.e., arrested growth or destruction of plants and crops by strong gusts of wind (LXX: ἀνεμοφθορίᾳ). The hot "east wind" (sirocco; ḥamsin), known even today to enter Palestine and Egypt off the desert, comes immediately to mind. It brings blight (Gen 41:6, 23, 27; Hos 13:15). In Pharaoh's dream interpreted by Joseph, seven ears of blighted grain represent seven years of famine (Gen 41:27). יֵרָקוֹן is probably "mildew" i.e., a destructive growth of minute fungi on plants, leaving a white or pale yellow coating. The LXX translates with ὤχρα ("pale-yellow"). יְרָקוֹן can also denote yellow-green paleness of the face ("jaundice"), resulting from illness or fright (Jer 30:6; cf. Akk *amurriqānu*, "jaundice"; *CAD*, 1/2:91-92). But this does not seem to be indicated here. On יְרָקוֹן see further Preuss 1978, 164-67 and Brenner 1982, 100-102.

and they shall pursue you until you perish. On quasi-independent power of curses, see v. 15.

23 A vivid image, with "bronze" and iron" turning up also as a fixed pair in Jeremiah (Jer 1:18; 6:28; 15:12). Rainless sky and rock-solid earth spell drought, thus no crops and eventually famine. Lack of rain is the cause for the curses in v. 22b, which turns around the blessing of v. 12. In Lev 26:19 the images are reversed: the heavens will be iron and the earth bronze. According to Deuteronomy, abundant rain depends upon Israel keeping the commandments (Deut 11:8-17). Jeremiah, knowing that Yahweh's commands have been broken, witnesses this curse as having come to pass (Jer 3:2-3; 5:24-25; 12:4; 14:1-6; 23:10). For a connection elsewhere in the OT between sin and a lack of rain, see 1 Kgs 8:35-36; 17:1; 18:18; Amos 4:6-8. In the Esarhaddon Vassal Treaties (*VTE* 528-32) is this curse:

> May they make your ground (hard) like iron so that [none] of you may f[lourish]. Just as rain does not fall from a brazen heaven, so may rain and dew not come upon your fields and your meadows. (Wiseman 1958, 69-70; Weinfeld 1965, 417; *ANET*³, 539)

And in the Code of Hammurabi (xxvii 61-70):

> May Adad, the lord of abundance, the irrigator of heaven and earth, my helper, deprive him of the rains from heaven (and) the floodwaters from the springs! (*ANET*³, 179; D. J. McCarthy 1963, 122)

Another drought curse comes in the Mati'ilu Treaty IV 13-14 (*ANET*³, 533; D. J. McCarthy 1963, 122).

Mendelssohn in his "Elijah" oratorio used this verse in Part I, Recitative with Chorus (no. 19):

> Elijah: Go up now, child, and look toward the sea.
> Hath my prayer been heard by the Lord?
> The Youth: There is nothing. The heavens are brass, they are brass
>   above me.
> . . . .
> Elijah: Go up again, and still look toward the sea.
> The Youth: There is nothing. The earth is as iron under me.

24 Breaking in the first clause after "dust," which takes the athnach in the verse as wrongly placed (Hillers 1964a, 38; NJV; cf. LXX). The "rain" Yahweh sends will be dust, and from the heavens (only) dirt will come down. The east wind contains fine sand, and a lack of rain will cause existing soil to be blown around. Ruinous drought conditions.

25 Israel will experience military defeat at the hands of her enemies (Lev 26:17), reversing the blessing of v. 7. The number seven is conventional, both in biblical curses (Lev 26:18, 21, 24, 28; Amos 1:3, 6, 9, etc.) and in the ANE treaty curses (Sefire I A: 21-24, 27; II A: 1-3, 5; Weinfeld 1972, 125).

and you shall be a fright to all the kingdoms of the earth. Being a "fright" (זַעֲוָה) to other nations means that Israelites will be such a horrible spectacle that those looking on will tremble. The verb זוּעַ means "to tremble" (Eccl 12:3; Esth 5:9). The expression "fright to all the kingdoms of the earth" occurs often in Jeremiah (Jer 15:4; 24:9; 29:18; 34:17), where reference is to Judah's coming exile. The LXX took the present verse as a reference to exile: "and you will become a dispersion (διασπορᾷ) among the kingdoms of the earth."

26 A common curse in the ancient world (Gen 40:19; 1 Kgs 14:11; 16:4; Isa 18:6; Ezek 39:17-20; Ps 79:2), spoken by Goliath and David (1 Sam 17:44-46) and announced for Judah by Jeremiah (Jer 7:33; 15:3; 16:4; 19:7; 34:20). Lack of a proper burial was a great indignity in antiquity, for which reason the men of Jabesh-gilead came to take the bodies of Saul and his sons off the wall of Beth-shan and bury the bones (1 Sam 31:11-13). Hillers (1964a, 68-69) points out that the present curse typically contains three elements: (1) the body will lie unburied; (2) it will be food for the birds and the beasts; and (3) it will be like refuse on the face of the earth. The Vassal Treaties of Esarhaddon (*VTE* 425-27, 483-84) contain the following curses:

> May Ninurta, chief of the gods, fell you with his swift arrow; may he fill the plain with your corpses; may he feed your flesh to the eagle (and) jackal. (Wiseman 1958, 61-62; Weinfeld 1965, 419; *ANET*^{3}, 538)

> May the earth not receive your corpses (in burial); may you be food in the belly of a dog or pig. (Wiseman 1958, 65-66; *ANET*^{3}, 539)

In the Epic of Gilgamesh (xii 152-154; *ANET*^{3}, 99), Enkidu is questioned after his descent into the netherworld:

> "Him whose corpse was cast out upon the steppe hast thou seen?"
> "I have seen:
> His spirit finds no rest in the nether world."

Deuteronomy 28

and there will be none to scare them off. No Rizpah to scare away birds and beasts (2 Sam 21:10). Rizpah stayed by the bodies of her children for months to protect them from scavengers.

27 Beginning Curse Supplement II is another series of seven diseases (vv. 27-28). The first four affect the skin (boils; hemorrhoids; scabies; itch); the last three are mental disorders (madness; blindness; bewilderment). The itch, at least, will be incurable, and so may be some of the other skin diseases. The prophets saw these curses being actualized, recognizing that Yahweh had brought them upon the covenant people because of their iniquity and rebellion (Isa 1:4-6; Jer 30:12-15; cf. Lundbom 2004a, 395-98). K. Gross (1930, 10, 16; 1931, 246-47) found considerable language of sickness (and healing) in Hosea and Jeremiah (Hos 5:13; 6:1; 7:1; 11:3; 14:5[4]; Jer 4:19; 6:7, 24; 8:18, 21, 22; 10:19; 14:17, 19; 15:18; 17:14; 30:12-17; 33:6). On the terminology of sickness in Jeremiah, see Muilenburg 1970b, 45-48.

with the boils of Egypt. בִּשְׁחִין מִצְרַיִם. This disease came as the sixth plague of Egypt, affecting the Egyptians and their cattle (Exod 9:1-10). Hebrew שְׁחִין (a collective noun) has traditionally been taken to be "boils" (AV: "botch"), although NJV renders the term as "inflammation" (cf. Rashi). Boils are accompanied by inflammation (Arabic and Aramaic cognates to Heb שׁחן mean "be hot, inflamed"; BDB, 1006). Preuss (1978, 343) says שְׁחִין is probably a "rash of blisters." We do not know precisely what this disease is, only that it affected the skin (Lev 13:18). It appears to have been a cutaneous disease particularly prevalent in Egypt. Some think that because cattle were affected, it could be a disease analogous to *anthrax* (Lat *carbuncle*), an infectious disease known to affect sheep and cattle (J. R. Bennett 1887, 67; Hort 1957, 101-3). In the plague of Egypt cattle died, but no mention is made of the disease being fatal to the Egyptian people. According to Lev 13:18-23, שְׁחִין is a disease from which one can be healed. King Hezekiah had boils that Isaiah treated successfully with a cake of figs (2 Kgs 20:7 = Isa 38:21). Job was afflicted with "bad boils" (רָע שְׁחִין), which became a rash from head to foot, but his bothersome sores seem to have crusted since he was scraping them with a potsherd (Job 2:7-8). Sandison (1967a, 181) says Job's affliction was myiasis, a parasitic disease like scabies. "Boils" are threatened again in v. 35, where they are said to break out on the legs and knees. This could be elephantiasis (see v. 35). Threatening Israel with the "boils of Egypt" makes this curse particularly harsh, for what Yahweh spared the Israelites in Egypt is now what he will bring upon them. The curses close in v. 68 with an even more horrific return to Egypt. Deuteronomy anticipated that when Israel was settled in the land, Yahweh would take away the evil diseases of Egypt (7:14-15).

and with hemorrhoids. וּבָעֳפָלִים. The Q is וּבַטְּחֹרִים, which substitutes for the Kt reading also in the account of the plague Yahweh sent among the Philistines (1 Sam 5:6, 9, 12, and passim). טְחֹרִים are hemorrhoidal tumors, and according to Jewish tradition so are עֳפָלִים, an indecent term somewhat like the English "piles" (Tigay). Arabic *'afal* denotes swellings and other symptoms in the anal area. The Targums all have hemorrhoids. The LXX reading, ἐν ἕλκει Αἰγυπτίῳ ἐν ταῖς ἕδραις ("with an Egyptian boil in the seats"), combines the first two terms into one: hemorrhoids (Wevers 1995, 438). Hemorrhoids were well known in antiquity, often treated with dates (Sussman 1967, 213). They were particularly common in Egypt (Rowling 1967, 497), receiving mention in the Papyrus Ebers from ca. 1500 (Bryan 1930, 11; Sandison 1967c, 477). The anal tumors of the Philistines, although spreading widely and causing great panic in Ashdod and Ekron, did not prove fatal to those affected (1 Sam 5:6-12). These tumors are thought to be bubonic plague (A. Macalister, *HDB*, 3:325; R. North 2000, 16).

and with the scabies and with the itch. וּבַגָּרָב וּבֶחָרֶס. Two more skin diseases, although again evading precise identification. גָּרָב is said to afflict both humans and animals in Lev 21:20; 22:22, taken there as a blemish sufficient to keep either away from Yahweh's altar. It is most often identified with scabies (Vg: *scabie*), a contagious itch caused by mites living as parasites under the skin. The LXX translates with ψώρᾳ ἀγρίᾳ ("a severe itch"). The disease had to be more virulent than modern-day psoriasis, which is not contagious and not a dangerous disease (J. R. Bennett 1887, 20-21). Arabic *jarab* is a contagious eruption consisting of pustules, the mange, or scab, and ibn Ezra says it means the same as גָּרָב. The Ebers Papyrus gives remedies for scabies, the itch, and other skin diseases (Bryan 1930, 12, 88-93). Assyrian texts from the library of Assurbanipal (ca. 650) refer also to scabies and other skin diseases (Krumbhaar 1937, 6, 157; Sandison 1967b, 449). חֶרֶס is a *hapax legomenon* in the OT, but generally taken to be another scab disease (T[PsJ]) or related skin disease causing severe itching (T[OnqNf]; ibn Ezra). The LXX translates with κνήφῃ ("itch"). חֶרֶס is a serious disease, said here to be incurable.

of which you cannot be healed. The curse of an incurable wound was common in antiquity (Hillers 1964a, 64-66). In the Code of Hammurabi (xxviii 49-64) is this curse:

> May Ninkarrak, the daughter of Anum, my advocate in Ekur, inflict upon him in his body a grevious malady, an evil disease, a serious injury which never heals, whose nature no physician knows, which he cannot allay with bandages, which like a deadly bite cannot be rooted out, and may he continue to lament (the loss of) his vigor until his life comes to an end! (*ANET*[3], 180; Hillers 1964a, 64)

The Treaty of Esarhaddon with Baal of Tyre (rev. iv 3-4) contains this curse:

May Gula the great physician [put illness and weariness in] your [hearts], an unhealing sore in your body (*ANET*³, 534; Hillers 1964a, 64)

This curse also appears in the Vassal Treaties of Esarhaddon (*VTE* 461-62; *ANET*³, 538-39).

28 The three terms, בְּשִׁגָּעוֹן וּבְעִוָּרוֹן וּבְתִמְהוֹן, are sonorous. All are diseases of the mind (ibn Ezra), recurring in Zech 12:4 (without לְבָב, "of mind"), where they refer to "a panic seizing horses and horsemen ... rendering them helpless in the fray" (Driver; cf. Jer 8:6). The curses have striking parallels in the Vassal Treaties of Esarhaddon, also in the preaching of the prophets, particularly Jeremiah.

with madness. בְּשִׁגָּעוֹן. An insanity promised again in v. 34. Cf. David's feigned madness in 1 Sam 21:13-16(12-15), also Jehu's mad chariot driving in 2 Kgs 9:20. Prophets, on occasion, were accused of acting like madmen (2 Kgs 9:11; Hos 9:7; Jer 29:26). See Preuss 1978, 313-14.

and with blindness. וּבְעִוָּרוֹן. Reference is not to physical blindness, but to insensibility or disorientation, particularly when faced with unexpected disaster (Isa 29:9-10, 18; Zeph 1:17; Lam 4:14). Targum^PsJ has "blindness and stupefaction." Metaphorical blindness is well attested in extrabiblical texts. The Babylonian Creation Story, in describing events leading up to the slaying of Tiamat, says of Tiamat's consort that "his will is distracted and his doings are confused"; when the gods saw him, "blurred became their vision" (*ANET*³, 66; iv 65-70). Held (1961, 7, 15) cites another Old Babylonian text in which a woman utters a curse of blindness on a rival woman. She says:

The one who does not love you, may Ishtar [strike] with blindness *(mi-ši-tam)*. May she, like me, be afflicted with sleeplessness. May she doze off [may she (sleeplessly) toss around] the whole night. (II 6-9)

Held says that while the curse could be calling for physical blindness, the blindness could also be metaphorical, i.e., a blindness toward reality, a lack of reasoning power. Akkadian *mišītum* comes from the verb *ešû*, meaning "to confuse or become confused; to be or become blurred, or dark" (*CAD,* 4:378-80). In the Vassal Treaties of Esarhaddon (*VTE* 422-24) is this curse:

May Shamash, the light of the heavens and earth, not judge you justly (saying): 'May it be dark in your eyes, walk in darkness.' (Wiseman 1958, 59-60; Weinfeld 1965, 418-19; *ANET*³, 538)

An Assyrian treaty imposed by Assurbanipal upon the Babylonians (rev. 8-10) contains this curse:

May the Divine Judge of heaven and the underworld [. . .] decree a violent judgment [upon us . . .]. May he remove our eyesight. (Grayson 1987, 145; Parpola and Watanabe 1988, 67)

and with bewilderment of mind. וּבְתִמְהוֹן לֵבָב. Here the oft-used Deuteronomic לֵבָב (lit. "heart") means "mind." Reference is to another mental disorder. Jeremiah 4:9 describes the coming day of Yahweh as one in which "the mind (לֵב) of the king will fail, also the mind (לֵב) of the princes; horrified will be the priests and the prophets will be bewildered (יִתְמָהוּ)." Bewilderment here will come from unfulfilled prophecies, leading to disillusionment (Lundbom 1999, 338-39).

29 *and you shall become as one who gropes at noonday, just as the blind grope in thick darkness.* The analogy is a good one, for persons physically blind experience thick darkness even when the sun is high in the sky. In crises, people stricken with metaphorical blindness become as helpless as those without eyesight (Isa 59:9-10), and others must take their arm and lead them about. The verb "to grope" (מׁשׁשׁ) also means "to feel" (cf. Gen 27:12), which again describes what blind people must do. The ninth plague of Egypt was a plague of darkness, and Exod 10:21 says it would cover the land so "one may feel (the) darkness" (יָמֵשׁ חֹשֶׁךְ).

thick darkness. אֲפֵלָה. Another term describing the ninth plague of Egypt (Exod 10:22). Jeremiah says "thick darkness" (אֲפֵלָה) lies in store for the unholy prophets and priests, which again is mental incapacitation, a slippery slope that will bring about their fall (Jer 23:12). On "darkness" as a biblical metaphor for calamity and judgment, see also Mic 3:6; Isa 8:22; Jer 4:28; 13:16; 15:9; Job 5:14; Mark 13:24-25; Matt 22:13.

and you shall not make prosperous your ways. Your actions will not succeed. This is what Jeremiah told King Zedekiah when the latter was resisting the Babylonians (Jer 32:5).

and you shall become only oppressed and robbed all the days, and there will be none to deliver. To be "oppressed and robbed all the days" (עָשׁוּק וְגָזוּל כָּל־הַיָּמִים) is to be continually denied one's legal due and divested of one's property or other possessions, here by an enemy (ibn Ezra; cf. vv. 30-33). גָּזוּל means "robbed, subjected to violent seizure." Oppression and robbery are closely linked in the OT (Lev 19:13; Jer 21:12; Ezek 18:18; Ps 62:11[10]), where "oppression" (עֹשֶׁק) may also mean "extortion." Deuteronomic law forbids oppression of the poor (24:14), but now Israel in her impoverishment will be oppressed continually, which did happen (Jer 50:33). Greenfield (1990, 156) cites a Phoenician curse upon anyone who "seizes" (גזל) a vineyard or field and takes it as his own, and he says the Phoenician verb fits the use of the Hebrew verb (cf. Mic 2:2). On biblical terminology of theft and robbery, see Westbrook 1988b, 15-38.

and there will be none to deliver. וְאֵין מוֹשִׁיעַ. The phrase recurs in v. 31. It is bad enough to be oppressed and robbed, but when there is no one to help, it is infinitely worse. When Yahweh's blessings are operative and life proceeds more or less normally, one has resource to kin, townspeople, judges, officials, military leaders, the king, and above all Yahweh (20:4; 22:27; Exod 2:17; Judg 3:9, 15; 6:36; 1 Sam 9:16; 2 Sam 14:4; 2 Kgs 6:26; Ps 72:4; Jer 14:8-9; 15:20; Zeph 3:17), but under Yahweh's curse, with an enemy in the land and a breakdown of the social order, none will be there to help the robbed and oppressed. Judahites later lamented that this is precisely what happened (Lam 1:7).

30 *A wife you shall betroth and another man shall violate her.* Representative examples of robbery and oppression now come in vv. 30-33. Curses calling for the gods to turn over wives, houses, and vineyards to the enemy are stereotypical in the ancient international treaties. In the present curses, Yahweh will deliver wives, houses, and vineyards to Israel's enemies, not letting people enjoy them as they would like (Zeph 1:13; Jer 6:11-12; 8:10). This expands the core curses of vv. 16-19 and reverses the core and supplementary blessings of vv. 3-6, 11-12, except that reference earlier was to good or bad crops. Here crops will have grown to maturity and another will come and eat them. But after Israel's judgment, these curses will be replaced by blessings over the same (Amos 9:14; Jer 29:5-6, 28; 31:5; Isa 62:8-9; 65:21-22).

This first curse is particularly vicious, but wives — which are deemed personal property in the tenth commandment (5:21; Exod 20:17) — were lost to the enemy and violated in the ancient world. In the Esarhaddon Treaties (*VTE* 428-29) is this curse:

> May Venus, the brightest of the stars, make your wives lie in the lap of your enemy before your eyes. (Wiseman 1958, 61-62; Weinfeld 1965, 419; *ANET*[3], 538)

Nathan's oracle to David, after his secret sin against Uriah the Hittite, stated that Yahweh would take David's wives and give them to another, who would proceed to lie with them in broad daylight (2 Sam 12:11). It happened (2 Sam 16:20-22). Job uttered a self-curse of the same should he be guilty of a similar wrongdoing (Job 31:10). The present curse was laid upon the nation by Jeremiah, who said Judah's wives would be seized by the Babylonians (Jer 6:11-12; 8:10).

and another man shall violate her. וְאִישׁ אַחֵר יִשְׁגָּלֶנָּה. The Q יִשְׁכָּבֶנָּה ("he will lie/sleep with her") avoids an indecent term for sexual intercourse (ibn Ezra; cf. "f . . . k"). The same verb occurs in Isa 13:16; Jer 3:3; Zech 14:2, where again the Masoretes provide Q substitutes. Rashi says יִשְׁגָּלֶנָּה is connected to

שֵׁגֵל, a noun meaning "concubine." The LXX tones down the phrase: "A wife you will take, and another man will have her." People lamented after the destruction of Jerusalem: "Women are ravished in Zion, virgins in the town of Judah" (Lam 5:11).

a house you shall build and you shall not dwell in it. In the Esarhaddon Vassal Treaties (*VTE* 429-30) the seizure of wives is followed by a seizure of house and goods:

> May your sons [not possess your house]; may a foreign enemy divide your goods (Wiseman 1958, 61-62; Weinfeld 1965, 419; *ANET*³, 538)

Amos utters this curse on those oppressing the poor: "You have built houses of hewn stone, but you shall not dwell in them" (Amos 5:11). See also Jer 6:12. When the Babylonians came, Israelite houses were turned over to aliens (Lam 5:2).

a vineyard you shall plant and you shall not eat its fruit. See again v. 39. Deuteronomic law allowed a war deferment for someone who has planted a vineyard and not yet enjoyed its fruit (20:6). But the prophets came with another message when the covenant had been broken. Amos follows his curse about house seizure with another on the seizure of vineyards:

> You have planted pleasant vineyards,
>   but you shall not drink their wine. (Amos 5:11)

Micah speaks similarly to people of Judah:

> You shall sow, but not reap;
>   you shall tread olives, but not anoint yourselves with oil;
>   you shall tread grapes, but not drink wine. (Mic 6:15; cf. Lev 26:16b)

Jeremiah says of the enemy about to descend upon Judah:

> It shall consume your harvest and your food;
>   they shall consume your sons and your daughters;
>   it shall consume your flocks and your herds;
> It shall consume your vines and your fig trees. (Jer 5:17)

This oracle is similar in content to the curses in Deut 28:49-51. On Judah's fields being given over to conquerors, see also Jer 6:12; 8:10.

and you shall not eat its fruit. וְלֹא תְחַלְּלֶנּוּ (lit. "and you shall not profane it") means "you shall not eat the fruit as common food." According to Levitical law, fruit of newly-planted trees and vines could not be eaten until the fifth year

(Lev 19:23-25). In the first three years the fruit must not be eaten at all. In the fourth year, it is set aside as a praise offering to Yahweh. Then in the fifth year it becomes "profane" (חלל), which means the one who planted it is free to eat it (cf. Lev 22:9).

31 Here we are told that enemies will rob the Israelites of their animals, and once again no one will be there to help them. The ox will be slaughtered in the owner's presence, but the owner will not eat of it. Asses and sheep will simply be snatched away and not restored. The extortion of another's ox or ass is a proverbial example of oppression (Job 24:3), with both Moses and Samuel denying that they had ever done such a thing (Num 16:15; 1 Sam 12:3). A Canaanite ruler makes the same disclaimer in the Amarna Letters (EA 280; *ANET*³, 487). From the Assyrian Annals we learn that Assyrian kings took horses, cattle, sheep, and other animals from the conquered people (*ANET*³, 280, 283). When Ashurnasirpal II (883-859) and Shalmaneser III (859-825) sacrificed sheep to their gods after conquering cities on the Phoenician coast (*ANET*³, 276; 278), one can well imagine where those sheep came from. Sennacherib (704-681), when he made his devastating campaign into Israel in the time of Hezekiah, boasted of the booty taken from the forty-six fortified Judahite cities he destroyed:

> I drove out (of them) 200,150 people, young and old, male and female, horses, mules, donkeys, camels, big and small cattle beyond counting, and considered (them) booty. (*ANET*³, 288)

before your eyes. לְעֵינֶיךָ. I.e., while you are looking on. On this common Deuteronomic expression, see Note for 1:30.

and there will be none to deliver for you. See v. 29.

32 Worse than losing animals to the enemy will be watching your children being carted off, some of whom will be sold as slaves. You will hope against hope to see them again, watching for them day and night, but they will not return, and you will be powerless to do anything about it. Jeremiah expressed the grief of all Judah when young King Jehoahaz was carried away to Egypt (Jer 22:10). He said:

> Weep not for the dead,
>   and condole not for him;
>   weep continually for him who goes away,
> Because he will not return again
>   and not see the land of his birth.

Jeremiah envisioned a great number of women and children being led out to the Babylonians after Jerusalem was taken and destroyed (Jer 38:23). It happened amidst great weeping (Lam 1:5, 16, 18). Women and children appear among exile-bound prisoners, in procession, on reliefs of Shalmaneser III (*ANEP*², 124, no. 358 lower register; 127, no. 365 lower register). Another Assyrian relief shows women and children being taken away in oxcarts (*ANEP*², 128, no. 367). Josephus (*B.J.* vii.385) asks rhetorically when describing Jewish resistance to the Romans in the 1st cent. A.D.:

> Is a man to see his wife led off to violation, to hear the voice of his child crying 'Father!' when his own hands are bound?

and your eyes will see and cry themselves out for them. וְעֵינֶיךָ רֹאוֹת וְכָלוֹת אֲלֵיהֶם. The Hebrew idiom כלו עינים, lit. "the eyes are emptied (of tears)," means something like the English "cry one's eyes out" (Gruber 1980, 390-400). Gruber notes a similar idiom in Ugaritic. The idiom occurs again in v. 65, also in Lev 26:16. Rashi says it is an expression for any desire that does not come to fulfillment (Pss 69:4[3]; 119:123; Lam 4:17). Intense crying is what followed the destruction of Jerusalem (Lam 2:11). For the same general idea with reference to Jeremiah, see Jer 8:23(9:1).

and there will be no power in your hand. וְאֵין לְאֵל יָדֶךָ. Or "and there will be no God at your hand" (Friedman; cf. T^Nf). Hebrew אֵל, more often "God," can also mean "strength, power" (BDB, 43). The idiom conveys the same idea as "and there will be none to deliver (for you)" in vv. 29 and 31. It occurs again in Neh 5:5 and is formulated positively in Gen 31:29; Mic 2:1; Prov 3:27. The present curse states that people will be powerless to bring their children back.

33 A repetition of the maledictions in vv. 29-30, which reverse the blessing of Ps 128:1-2:

> Happy is everyone who fears Yahweh,
>   who walks in his ways.
> The toil of your hands, indeed you shall eat;
>   you shall be happy, and it shall go well for you.

Jeremiah, in his time, led people in this confession about the wasted toil of generations:

> The Shame has consumed what our fathers worked for, from our youth — their flocks and their herds, their sons and their daughters. Let us lie down in our shame and let our dishonor cover us, for against Yahweh our God we have sinned — we and our fathers, from our youth unto this day. We have not obeyed the voice of Yahweh our God. (Jer 3:24-25; Lundbom 1999, 319)

Deuteronomy 28

whom you do not know. An expression occurring often in Deuteronomy and Jeremiah in association with gods, people, and other things foreign (see Note for 11:27-28).

and you shall become only oppressed and crushed. וְהָיִיתָ רַק עָשׁוּק וְרָצוּץ. To become "crushed" (רָצוּץ) means to become "oppressed" (1 Sam 12:3-4; Amos 4:1, where the verbs רצץ and עשׁק appear together). In 1 Sam 12:3-4; Jer 22:17 "crushing" means "to defraud."

34 A state of deep outrage, perhaps insanity (Preuss 1978, 313), said also in vv. 28-29 to be the result of ongoing oppression. Witnessing the loss of family, houses, animals, vineyards, and all one's other possessions would be enough to drive anyone mad.

35 Another mention of boils, here said to be "bad boils" breaking out on the knees and legs. This condition, affecting the whole body ("from the sole of your foot to the crown of your head"), is presumably a later stage of the disease. Job was afflicted with "bad boils from the sole of his foot to the crown of his head" (Job 2:7), but the boils here will be more severe than Job's boils or the "boils of Egypt" (v. 27), both of which were curable. These boils cannot be healed ("strike you down" means "strike you fatally"). Because they are said to break out on the knees and legs, some have suggested that the disease is elephantiasis, well known in antiquity. Classical writers said elephantiasis was native to Egypt (Pliny, *Nat.* xxvi 5; Lucretius, *De Rerum Natura* vi 1114-15), Lucretius adding that it was found nowhere else. Driver suggests a species known as *anaesthetic elephantiasis,* also called "joint leprosy." This disease affects joints of the fingers and toes, then later joints of the larger limbs, which drop off bone by bone. Still, we do not know precisely what disease is here indicated. There are echoes of the present verse in Rev 16:2.

36 Exile alluded to in the loss of sons and daughters to the enemy (v. 32) is now indicated more clearly, capping the disasters of vv. 28-34 and, for Deuteronomy, Israel's loss of the land. The Assyrians deported men together with their families, transporting and resettling them in groups (Oded 1979, 23-25). Reliefs show men, women, and children leaving home as deportees (*ANEP*[2], nos. 10, 358, 359, 373).

Reference to exile (although Deuteronomy never uses the term גלה) in no way requires a post-586 date for these verses (G. A. Smith; D. J. McCarthy 1963, 124). Jerusalem's destruction and the 586 exile were indeed a defining event in the life of the nation; nevertheless, forced exile was a common practice in antiquity, especially by the Assyrians (Oded 1979) and the Babylonians. Amos censures Gaza and Tyre for delivering up entire populations to Edom (Amos 1:6, 9). Tiglath-pileser III (745-727) exiled the population of Damascus to Kir (2 Kgs 16:9; Bright 1981, 275) and, according to his Annals, others to various places (*ANET*[3], 283). Sargon II (721-705) exiled peoples to Assyria (*ANET*[3],

284), and both the Bible and the Assyrian Annals tell us about Assurbanipal's exile of the population of Thebes (Nah 3:10; *ANET*³, 295 ii). The OT records yet other exiles of families and populations (1 Chr 8:6-7; Joel 4:6-8[3:6-8]). We know, too, that when Jehoiachin was later imprisoned in Babylon, other exiled kings were there (2 Kgs 25:28; Jer 52:32). The "Court of Nebuchadnezzar" document (*ANET*³, 308, v) mentions the king of Tyre, the king of Gaza, the king of Sidon, the king of Arvad, the king of Ashdod, and other kings.

Israel and Judah experienced no less than five exiles before 586, possibly six. Tiglath-pileser III exiled the Israelite populations of Galilee and Transjordan in 733 (2 Kgs 15:29; 1 Chr 5:6, 22, 26; Bright 1981, 274; *ANET*³, 284), and the remaining population of the northern kingdom — perhaps also King Hoshea three years earlier — was exiled to Assyrian and Median cities in 722 (2 Kgs 17:3-6; *ANET*³, 284-85). Sennacherib (704-681) turned over people from the forty-six Judahite cities he conquered in 701 to the kings of Ashdod, Ekron, and Gaza (*ANET*³, 288). In 609 it was the Egyptians who exiled King Jehoahaz to Egypt (2 Kgs 23:34; Jer 22:10-12), and others may have gone with him. In 597, the Babylonians, after forcing the surrender of Jerusalem, took Jehoiachin, the queen mother, and Jerusalem's leading citizens into exile (2 Kgs 24:14-16; Jer 22:24-30; 52:28). The Israelite people were all too familiar with exile and its horrors, and so were those writing the curses in ch. 28. This had been going on for 150 years or more.

Yahweh bring you. יוֹלֵךְ יְהוָה. The verb is pointed by the Masoretes as a jussive. The LXX translates with an optative: "May the Lord bring you."

and your king whom you will set up over you. Possibly an indirect criticism of the monarchy (Tigay), although Deuteronomy gives kingship qualified support in 17:14-20. The LXX has "your leaders" instead of "your king." For an 8th-cent. criticism of kingship, see Hos 8:4; 13:10-11.

that you do not know, you or your fathers. On this expression, see v. 33 and Note for 11:27-28.

and there you will serve other gods of wood and stone. Irony. The pair "wood and stone" occurs again in v. 64 and is common in both Deuteronomy and Jeremiah (see Note for 4:28).

37 Those who see the survivors in foreign places will be astonished at the sight of them and will deride them. This happened even before people went into exile: Israel's enemies derided them and a ruined Jerusalem (Lam 2:15-16; 3:14, 46, 61-63). The curse words "desolation" (שַׁמָּה), "proverb" (מָשָׁל), "taunt" (שְׁנִינָה) turn up with others in strings such as the present one in Jeremiah (Lundbom 2004a, 234-35).

a desolation. לְשַׁמָּה. See Jer 18:16; 19:8; 25:9, 11, 18, and elsewhere.

a proverb, and a taunt. לְמָשָׁל וְלִשְׁנִינָה. See 1 Kgs 9:7; Jer 24:9.

among all the peoples to whom Yahweh will lead you. See 4:27. As it

Deuteronomy 28

turned out, Yahweh dispersed the Israelites not simply to Assyria and Babylonia, but to every neighboring country and others farther away: Ammon, Moab, Edom, Syria, Media, Asia Minor and the Greek Islands, Upper and Lower Egypt, Elam, Persia, and elsewhere (2 Kgs 17:6; 24:15-16; Isa 11:11; Jer 40:11; 41:15; 44:1; Esth 3:8).

38 We are back now in Israel's own land, with the curse heading off Supplement III (vv. 38-46) speaking clearly of famine (ibn Ezra). The shift from dispersion abroad to bad conditions at home reflects the situation in 597, when Nebuchadnezzar took Judahites into exile but left behind a remnant to face war, famine, and disease, until the nation was completely destroyed (Jer 24:10; cf. Deut 28:45). Seed "taken out" to the field will be sown (T^{Nf} adds "and sow"), but little grain will be harvested (vv. 16-18, 22-24; Lev 26:16; Mic 6:15). Reflecting the present curse is one on the Neo-Assyrian Tell Fekherye Statue, where the Akkadian text on the front (lines 30-32) reads:

> May he sow but let him not reap; may he sow a thousand but get one *sūtu* in return. (Greenfield and Shaffer 1985, 53)

The Aramaic text on the back reads the same. In the present curse, what small yield there is will be eaten by locusts (cf. v. 42), another unwelcome reminder of the plagues of Egypt (Exod 10:3-20).

The Vassal Treaties of Esarhaddon (*VTE* 442-43) contain this curse: "May the locust who diminishes the land devour your harvest" (Wiseman 1958, 61-62; *ANET*³, 538). And in the 8th-cent. Sefire Treaties (1A 27) is this curse upon Mati'el if he violates the treaty:

> For seven years may the locust [ארבה] devour (Arpad), and for seven years may the worm [תולעה] eat (Fitzmyer 1961, 185; 1967, 14-15; *ANET*³, 659-60)

A locust plague is devastating. Linsenmaier (1972, 79) gives this description:

> The weight of a big swarm has been estimated at 15,000 tons, and its daily food consumption as equivalent to that of 1.5 million people. For days at a time, even for a week, locusts may darken the sky in a given region, coming to earth when the temperature drops in the evening and covering everything with a crawling layer. Where they settle almost nothing remains, not even the bark of trees less than two years old. And the eggs they leave behind are the seeds of new invasions.
>
> After a locust invasion, many animals starve to death or die from eating the poisonous plants spurned by the locusts. Famine and destitution descend on the people.

For descriptions of locust plagues in Palestine during the 19th cent., one particularly bad occurring in 1864-65, see Tristram 1898, 314-18.

the locust. הָאַרְבֶּה. One of nine Hebrew words denoting different species or various growth stages of locusts (Tristram 1898, 306). The אַרְבֶּה is the commonest word for "locust" in the OT, an adult winged insect able to fly. It is migratory, arriving and departing in swarms, as it did in the eighth plague of Egypt (Exod 10:4-19; cf. Ps 78:46). In 1 Kgs 8:37 this locust is associated with disease and famine, but since it is a "leaping" insect, Lev 11:22 says it is permissible for food.

will finish it off. יְחַסְּלֶנּוּ. The verb is a *hapax legomenon* in the OT, but an Aramaic cognate means "bring to an end." The noun חָסִיל denotes another type of locust (Isa 33:4), probably in the larva or pupa stage (Tristram 1898, 313). Joel 1:4 envisions a locust parade consuming the land.

39 Expanding the curse of v. 30.

and shall tend. וְעָבַדְתָּ. The verb עבד, which means "to labor, do work" (5:13; Exod 20:9; 34:21), refers here to tilling the soil (T^{Onq}; cf. Gen 2:5) and dressing the vines (RSV). It is the work Adam does in the garden of Eden story (Gen 2:15).

nor shall you gather. וְלֹא תֶאֱגֹר. I.e., the grapes, which are unexpressed. This uncommon verb may also mean "gather into stores" (Driver; cf. Prov 6:8; 10:5). Note here that the drinking of wine comes before the gathering of grapes, a common sequence reversal in Hebrew rhetoric, seen often in Jeremiah (Lundbom 1999, 243 on Jer 1:15).

because the worm shall eat it. כִּי תֹאכְלֶנּוּ הַתֹּלָעַת. I.e. the "grapes" (the noun is a collective; cf. "your olive[s]" in v. 40). This worm or grub (= legless larva of certain insects) could be the ἴψ (= ἴξ) of Theophrastus (*Caus. plant.* iii 22.5) and Strabo (*Geogr.* xiii 1.64), or the *convolvolus* (leaf-rolling caterpillar) of Pliny (*Nat.* xvii 47), which attack and destroy vines. The vines breed them, and then the worms turn and eat what brought them forth (cf. Jonah 4:7). This particular worm is mentioned in Sefire 1A 27 (see v. 38), where it is in parallelism with the locust.

40 Olive trees with unripe olives dropping off completes the curse on "grain, wine, and oil," the principal crops in Palestine and the staples of the Israelite economy (see Note for 7:13). Micah pronounces this curse on Israel in Mic 6:15.

but with oil you shall not anoint yourself. Olive oil is used as body lotion (2 Sam 12:20; 14:2; Ruth 3:3; 2 Chr 28:15; cf. Amos 6:6).

41 Repeating the curse of v. 32. Once again, the fruit of one's own body is taken together with the fruit of the soil, as in the blessings of vv. 4 and 11 and the curses of vv. 18 and 30-33. See also 7:13; Jer 5:17. The blessings of Ps 128:3-4 will be reversed:

> Your wife will be like a fruitful vine
>   within your house;
> Your children will be like olive shoots
>   around your table.
> Indeed, thus shall the man be blessed
>   who fears Yahweh.

but they shall not be yours. I.e., they shall not remain with you; they shall go into captivity.

42 Here we meet up with another species of locust (Tristram 1898, 313), one destructive to trees and crops. Most commentators take צְלָצַל to be the "cricket," although the word occurring only here gave the ancient Versions difficulty. Ibn Ezra says its meaning must be taken from the context. The root from which the term is derived, צלל, means "to tingle, quiver," suggesting a name that is onomatopoeic: the wings making a tingling sound (Tristram 1898, 313). A land in Upper Egypt was known for "noisy-winged" insects, צִלְצַל כְּנָפָיִם (Isa 18:1). The common Deuteronomic verb ירשׁ ("possess, dispossess") in this case means simply "take over" (T^{Onq}): the locusts will take over the trees and strip them bare.

43-44 The added personal pronouns are for emphasis. The "sojourner" (גֵר) is a resident alien, accorded certain benefits in Deuteronomy along with the orphan and the widow because of his dependent status (see Notes for 5:13-14 and 10:18). Sojourners were more often borrowers than lenders (Spina 1983, 323), a reality presupposed in the blessings of vv. 12-13a. But now the fortunes of the sojourner and the Israelite will be reversed. Crop failure will force the Israelite to borrow from the sojourner, who is not dependent for his livelihood upon the soil, with the result that the sojourner will rise higher and higher and the impoverished Israelite will sink lower and lower. The "rise" of the sojourner means that he will become more prosperous (cf. Lev 25:47) and more powerful (T^{Onq}: "he will be strong but you will be weak"). See Prov 22:7.

he, he shall be the head, and you, you shall be the tail. To be "head (over)" means "to rule" (Judg 11:11; Jer 13:21). After Jerusalem's destruction the enemy became "the head" (Lam 1:5). Jeremiah could only look ahead to the day when Israel would be "Head of the Nations" (Jer 31:7).

45 This verse coming at the close of Curse Supplement III returns to the beginning of Curse Supplement I (v. 15), giving a reason for Yahweh's curses being visited upon Israel. Curses will fall and the nation will be destroyed because it has not obeyed Yahweh's voice and not kept his commandments and his statutes.

and they shall pursue you and overtake you. On the quasi-independent nature of curses in pursuing their object, see v. 15.

46 A new twist on the "sign and wonder" language of the exodus, where signs and wonders were proofs to both the Israelites and the Egyptians that Yahweh had sent Moses (and Aaron) to deliver Israel from a miserable slavery and proofs dramatically displayed in the ten plagues against Pharaoh and the Egyptian people (Exod 3:12; 4:8-9, 17, 21, 28-30; 7:3, 9; 11:9-10; 12:13; Deut 4:34; 6:22; 34:11). Now the "sign" (אוֹת) and the "wonder" (מוֹפֵת) will be Yahweh's witness against Israel and its descendants, a judgment of great magnitude, but one not further specified. What is clear is that Israel will once again know the wonders of Egypt, only this time in reverse, because of its sin. The sign could be a reminder to Israel of past rebellion (ibn Ezra), or a warning to future generations — also foreigners — of what will happen when Israel does not listen to Yahweh and keep his commandments (29:21-27[22-28]), or both. On "signs and wonders," see Note for 4:34.

47-48 Here begins Curse Supplement IV (vv. 47-57), with vv. 47-48 reiterating — in reverse order — the summary ideas of vv. 45-46. But a more substantive change occurs: misfortunes are no longer conditional on Israel's disobedience to Yahweh and his commands; they are predicted absolutely, since disobedience is now an established fact (G. A. Smith). The Supplement begins: "Inasmuch as *you did not serve* Yahweh your God . . ." (the Hebrew has an apodictic לֹא and a Perfect tense of the verb). This is preaching such as one hears from the great prophets, e.g., Isa 5:26-30; Jer 5:15-17 (von Rad).

Inasmuch as you did not serve Yahweh your God with gladness and with goodness of heart from the abundance of everything. Deuteronomy's otherwise upbeat message is that Israel is to serve Yahweh with a glad, grateful, and generous heart. The reason given here, as elsewhere, is that Yahweh has blessed Israel with an abundance of everything. One having "goodness of heart" (טוּב לֵבָב) rejoices in the goodness of Yahweh (1 Kgs 8:66) and can be heard singing (Isa 65:14). The person "evil in heart" gives grudgingly to the needy (Deut 15:10). Deuteronomy's admonition to "be glad" (שׂמח) occurs with particular reference to festival time (12:7, 12, 18; 14:26; 16:11, 14, 15; 26:11; 27:7). Psalm 100:2 says: "serve Yahweh in gladness," where "serve" means "worship" (see Note for 6:13). Targum[Onq] substitutes "worship" for "serve" in the present verse. The other side of the same theology is that Israel must not serve or worship other gods (see Note for 6:13), stated explicitly in the second commandment (5:9) and warned against at the conclusion of the Blessing Supplement (v. 14).

Inasmuch as. Or "because." On the conjunctive expression, תַּחַת אֲשֶׁר, see Note for 21:14.

from the abundance of everything. מֵרֹב כֹּל. I.e., all the good Yahweh has lavished upon Israel. The Song of Moses describes this goodness, going on to note how Israel grew fat and forgot the Giver (Deut 32:13:18; cf. Hos 2:10[8]). Deuteronomy warns about the perils of prosperity in 6:10-15; 8:11-20.

Deuteronomy 28

so you shall serve your enemies whom Yahweh will send against you, in hunger and in thirst, and in nakedness and in want of everything, and he will put a yoke of iron upon your neck until he has completely destroyed you. A play on "serve": since Israel has not "served" Yahweh amidst great abundance, it will now "serve" enemies amidst great privation. This Supplement focuses in its remaining verses on submission to an enemy and the privation this will bring about.

in hunger and in thirst. בְּרָעָב וּבְצָמָא. Hunger and thirst are curses of war and the aftermath of war (2 Chr 32:11). Jeremiah addresses a personified Moabite city high above the River Arnon: "Come down from glory and sit in thirst, sitting daughter of Dibon" (Jer 48:18). In an oracle of the prophet Hosea, Yahweh threatens to slay Israel with thirst (Hos 2:5[3]). Hunger and thirst followed the fall of Jerusalem in 586, especially grievous for the very young (Lam 4:4).

and in nakedness. וּבְעֵירֹם. "Nakedness" here probably means being bereft of one's possessions (Job 1:21; Eccl 5:14[15]), which accompanies servitude (Isa 58:6-7).

and in want of everything. וּבְחֹסֶר כֹּל. The phrase recurs in v. 57. In the present verse it balances "in the abundance of everything."

and he will put a yoke of iron upon your neck until he has completely destroyed you. The "yoke" in the ancient world symbolized servitude to gods and kings. In the Amarna Letters: "the yoke of the king my lord is upon my neck and I carry it" (EA 296:38), and again: "my neck is placed in the yoke which I carry" (EA 257:15). The Bible assesses yoke-servitude both positively and negatively, more often negatively (Gen 27:40; 1 Kgs 12:9-11). Leviticus 26:13 used the metaphor to describe Israel's slavery in Egypt, but Hosea turned the yoke into a positive image, describing the covenant bond between Yahweh and Israel (Hos 11:4). The reason was that Israel's servitude to Yahweh was of a more benevolent sort (Daube 1963). But Israel broke Yahweh's yoke (Jer 2:20; 5:5), leading Jeremiah to announce that Israel's last remnant would be yoked to an enemy (Jeremiah 27-28). Jeremiah's "yoke of iron" (Jer 28:13-14) denoted a Babylonian servitude long and hard, which it turned out to be (Isa 47:6). But the covenant people were not completely destroyed, as promised here (see v. 20). Jesus' yoke of the new covenant promised once again an easy servitude (Matt 11:29-30). Cf. the rabbinic teaching about "taking on the yoke of the Kingdom of Heaven" (*m. Ber.* 2:2), which meant submitting to the sovereignty of God.

49-52 These verses call against Israel a nation from afar, whose language the people do not know, who will eat the offspring of cattle and the crops in the field, and who will destroy the high city walls in which people have put their trust. As a whole, the verses are very similar to Jeremiah's oracle in Jer 5:15-17; however, the opening phrase follows more closely Isa 5:26.

49 *Yahweh will lift up against you a nation from afar, from the end of the earth.* The verb נשׂא ("lift up") is not used in Jer 5:15, rather מֵבִיא ("bringing").

The LXX has ἐπάξει ("shall bring"). The phrase appears to be a borrowing from Isaiah, who predicts that "(Yahweh) will lift up (נָשָׂא) a signal for a nation from afar and whistle for it from the end of the earth" (Isa 5:26). But other considerations may have dictated the choice of the verb here. In the next verse, נשׂא occurs in the idiom "lift up the face" (= pay regard). Also, there could be an intentional play on נשׂא as used in Deut 32:11, where Yahweh on the wilderness trek was likened to a protective eagle who "lift(ed) (Israel) upon his pinion." Now in the curse, Yahweh will "lift up" another nation, which, like a swift-flying eagle, will come to destroy Israel.

a nation from afar, from the end of the earth. In Isa 5:26 the distant nation is Assyria; in Jer 5:15 it is Babylonia.

just as the eagle flies. כַּאֲשֶׁר יִדְאֶה הַנָּשֶׁר. This bird, cited often in the OT, is either an eagle or a griffon-vulture (see Note for 14:12). It ascends to great heights (Isa 40:31; Prov 23:5), sees prey from afar (Job 39:27-29), and swoops swiftly upon it (Job 9:26). The verb דאה refers to a manner of flying, either swiftly (T^NfPsJ) or in a swooping motion (T^Onq; ibn Ezra). Rashi cites the suddenness and swiftness of the approaching enemy. Good armies get there ahead of time. On the "suddenness" of divine action, see Daube 1964. The Assyrian army is likened to this swift bird in flight (Hos 8:1), so also the army of the Babylonians (Hab 1:8; Jer 48:40; 49:22). Ezekiel's "two-eagle" allegory (Ezekiel 17) describes the successive Babylonian armies coming to invade Judah.

a nation whose language you do not understand. Said of the Babylonians (Jer 5:15), earlier of the Assyrians (Isa 28:11; 33:19).

50 A syntactic chiasmus and wordplay on פָּנִים, meaning "face(s)." The enemy will be stern-looking (T^Onq: "ruthless"; LXX: ἀναιδὲς προσώπῳ, "ruthless in appearance"), showing no respect for old or young. The OT knows this severe look, עַז פָּנִים, behind which lurk wickedness, shamelessness, and impudence (Prov 7:13; 21:29; Eccl 8:1; Dan 8:23). In postexilic Hebrew עז means "anger" in Eccl 8:1; Ezra 8:22, comparable to Akk *ezzu* (Muffs 1992, 103-5). The point being made here is that the enemy will show total disregard for all survivors, which the prophets warned about (Isa 13:18; Jer 6:11; 51:20-23) and which was stated also in the Song of Moses (Deut 32:25). When the Babylonians came in 586, this is what happened (Lam 4:16; 5:11-13; Isa 47:6). Josephus, in reporting the Jewish war against Rome (*B.J.* v.433), said the Romans showed "no compassion for hoary hairs or infancy" (Loeb).

51 The destruction of young cattle, field crops, and vineyards repeats the curses of v. 18 and vv. 30-31, echoed later in Jer 5:17. The LXX omits "until you are completely destroyed," which could be due to haplography (homeoteleuton: ךָ ... ךָ). The verb שׁמד is very common in Deuteronomy (see Note for 1:27), occurring often in the curses (see 28:20).

grain, wine, or oil. See v. 40 and Note for 7:13.

the offspring of your cattle or the young of your flock. On the enemy's seizure of herds and flocks, see v. 31. Here the focus is on the young of the animals (v. 18), reversing the blessing of v. 4. See also 7:13. Jeremiah laments that the sounds of cattle on the hills and in the fields can no longer be heard (Jer 9:9[10]). "The fruit of your womb," which occurs in the blessing of v. 4 and in 7:13, is omitted here, but Tigay says this may be because v. 53 speaks of human offspring being eaten by the Israelites themselves.

until you are completely destroyed . . . until it has caused you to perish. Complete destruction will be of the nation, not of every individual (see v. 20). Targum^{Onq}: "until it ruins you."

52 The enemy will besiege Israel's fortified cities (T^{Onq}: "he will lay siege to you in all your cities"). The repetition of "it shall cause you distress in all your gates" may be accidental dittography (cf. Tigay). Wevers (1995, 450) notes that the LXX avoids the notion of siege altogether. The ruin of cities is a standard curse in the ancient world. From the Treaty of Ashurnirari V (v. 6):

> May Ashur, father of the gods, who grants kingship, turn your land into wasteland, your people into . . . , your cities into ruin mounds, your house into ruins. (*ANET*^{3}, 533; D. J. McCarthy 1963, 122)

The Sefire Treaty (I A: 32-33) contains this curse:

> And may Arpad become a mound to [house the desert animal]: the gazelle and the fox and the hare and the wild-cat and the owl and the [ ] and the magpie! (Fitzmyer 1961, 181, 185; 1967, 14-15; *ANET*^{3}, 660)

Jeremiah speaks the same curse against Jerusalem and other Judahite cities (4:26; 5:17; 9:10[11]; 26:6), and Micah earlier speaks it against Samaria and Jerusalem (Mic 1:6; 3:12).

and it shall cause you distress. The verb צרר in the H-stem means "make narrow, cause distress." Reference is to a siege (NJV: "it shall shut you up").

within all your gates. I.e., within all your cities (see Note for 5:13-14).

in which you are trusting. Deuteronomy does not otherwise address misplaced trust, but Jeremiah had a considerable amount to say on the subject, speaking not only about misplaced trust in high city walls (Jer 5:17), but about the same with reference to Baal worship (= "The Lie" in Jer 13:25), foreign alliances (Jer 2:37), brothers who are cheats (Jer 9:3[4]), all of humanity (Jer 17:5), deceptive preaching (Jer 7:4, 8; 28:15; 29:31), and the Jerusalem temple (Jer 7:14). Trust is a precious commodity, and putting one's trust in deceptions of any kind brings bitter consequences. It is trust in Yahweh that brings blessing and salvation (Jer 17:7; 39:18; cf. Prov 3:5).

Deuteronomy 28

in all your land. I.e., throughout the country. The LXX omits this second occurrence of the phrase, which Wevers (1995, 450) says could be due to haplography (homoeoteleuton: ך . . . ך).

53 The siege will brutalize some people to do the unspeakable: resort to cannibalism. A number of references to this desperate act occur in texts of the ANE, both in myth and in the royal annals. In the Atrahasis Myth, before the flood, when people turned ugly toward one another, it says that:

> When the sixth year arrived,
> They prepared [the daughter] for a meal,
> The child they prepared for food.
> Filled were [. . .]
> One house de[voured] the other. (*ANET*³, 105)

Assurbanipal in his Annals reported following a campaign against the Arabs that:

> The remainders who succeeded to enter Babylon ate (there) each other's flesh in their ravenous hunger. (*ANET*³, 298)

Again in a campaign of the Assyrian king against the Arabs:

> Famine broke out among them and they ate the flesh of their children against their hunger. (*ANET*³, 300)

Being driven to eat the flesh of one's sons and daughters was a standard curse in antiquity (Hillers 1964a, 62-63). The Ashurnirari V Treaty (iv 10-11) contains this curse:

> May they eat the flesh of their sons (and) their daughters and may it taste as good to them as the flesh of a ram or sheep. (Hillers 1964a, 62; *ANET*³, 533)

And in the Esarhaddon Vassal Treaties (*VTE* 448-50):

> May a pregnant mother (and) her daughter eat the flesh of your sons; in your extremity may you eat the flesh of your sons [. . .] (In) hunger may one man eat the flesh of another. (Wiseman 1958, 61-62; Weinfeld 1965, 425; *ANET*³, 538)

Again in the Esarhaddon Vassal Treaties (*VTE* 547-50; 568-69):

> Just as the starving ewe puts
> [the flesh of her young] in her mouth, even so

Deuteronomy 28

> may he feed you in your hunger
> with the flesh of your brothers, your sons (and) your daughters.
> (Wiseman 1958, 69-70; *ANET*³, 539)

> Just as honey is sweet, so may the blood of your women,
> your sons and your daughters be sweet in your mouth. (Wiseman 1958, 71-72; *ANET*³, 540)

Cannibalism is a curse for disobedience in Lev 26:29. In Israel it happened during Ben-hadad's siege of Samaria (2 Kgs 6:26-29) and apparently elsewhere in the north (Isa 9:18-20[19-21]). A curse on the same was put upon Judah by Jeremiah (Jer 19:9) and Ezekiel (Ezek 5:10), which came to pass in the final siege of Jerusalem by the Babylonian army (Lam 2:20; 4:10; Bar 2:3). In a later siege of Jerusalem by the Romans in A.D. 70, Josephus (*B.J.* vi.201-13) reports with horror that a certain Mary of Bethezuba took her son from her breast, killed him, and roasted him for food.

in siege and in hardship that your enemy shall press upon you. The phrase recurs as a refrain in vv. 55 and 57. See also Jer 19:9. The Hebrew has alliteration in בְּמָצוֹר וּבְמָצוֹק ... יָצִיק ("in siege and in hardship ... [it] shall press").

54-55 The most tender and delicate man will be driven in a siege to do very indelicate things. He will turn mean against his brother, his dear wife, and his last living child, and not share with them flesh of other children he is eating to satisfy his hunger. A bitter irony, because one is turning hostile against those dearest to him, cursing those he may once have regarded as blessings. Cf. Jeremiah's pathos-filled curses in Jer 20:17-18. Josephus (*B.J.* v.429-30) describes the horrors of famine in the war against Rome, how wives snatched food from husbands, children from their fathers, and mothers from the mouths of infants (cf. Isa 9:19[20]).

tender ... most delicate. Hebrew רַךְ means "tender, soft, delicate," used of flesh (Gen 18:7) or to describe weak, undeveloped character (2 Sam 3:39). The man "weak of heart" (רַךְ [הַ]לֵּבָב) fears going to war (Deut 20:8). עָנֹג is "dainty," probably "pampered" (Tigay; T^Nf: "most treated with dainties").

his eye will be evil. תֵּרַע עֵינוֹ. This expression, which occurs again in v. 56 and in 15:9, means "begrudge" or "act meanly" (T^Onq).

the wife of his bosom. A term of endearment: his dear wife (T^Onq: "the wife of his covenant"). The expression occurs also in 13:7(6).

and against the last of his children whom he has spared. Ibn Ezra says the one sparing this last child could be the enemy or someone hiding the child from the enemy. But in a siege, the enemy is not yet in the city. The man himself has probably spared the child up until now.

56-57 In siege conditions, the tender and delicate woman will turn mean against her dear husband and her own son and daughter — yes, even toward her afterbirth and infants of hers, because she will eat the afterbirth, the newborn, and the infant children in secret to satisfy her hunger. More irony, with delicate women driven to do the most indelicate of things. This horror was committed during the final siege of Jerusalem in 586 (Lam 4:3-10).

The tender and delicate woman among you, who would not venture to set the sole of her foot upon the ground because she is delicate and tender. This woman of genteel upbringing may be pampered and undeveloped in character, but what is emphasized here is the tenderness of her feet. Jeremiah predicted destruction for a personified Jerusalem, calling her הַנָּוָה וְהַמְעֻנָּגָה, "the lovely one, and the delicate one" (Jer 6:2). Second Isaiah saw the same regarding a personified Babylon, one who would no longer be called רַכָּה וַעֲנֻגָּה, "tender and delicate" (Isa 47:1).

who would not venture to set the sole of her foot upon the ground. Ladies of gentility were accustomed to being carried, e.g., foreign princesses were brought across the desert on a litter (מִטָּה) or palanquin (אַפִּרְיוֹן) to be married to King Solomon (Cant 3:6-11; Gordis 1944).

the husband of her bosom. I.e., her dear husband (T^Onq: "the husband of her covenant").

against her son and against her daughter. Older children (Rashi), who along with her husband will be denied the human flesh.

yes, against her afterbirth that comes out from between her feet, and against her children whom she bears, because she will eat them in want of everything in secret. The "afterbirth" (שִׁלְיָה) is the placenta (ibn Ezra; Preuss 1978, 398). Children eaten with the afterbirth will be the newborn and others very young (T^Onq: "the youngest of her children that emerges from her"). The fact that she will do this in secret means her husband and older children will be denied the ghastly food. She will also, needless to say, be ashamed of what she is doing.

from between her feet. מִבֵּין רַגְלֶיהָ. A euphemism (ibn Ezra: "from between her legs").

58 Curse Supplement V opens with a warning about not keeping Yahweh's covenant, the provisions of which are here specified as "all the words of this law" (כָּל־דִּבְרֵי הַתּוֹרָה הַזֹּאת). On this phrase, see Note for 17:19. After the absolute predictions of Curse Supplement IV (vv. 47-57), we are back to conditional language, the present verse being the protasis and vv. 59-60 the apodosis. On the protasis-apodosis construction in covenant speech, see Note for 11:13-14. Curses will come if Israel does not keep the teaching of this book, which in Deuteronomy is tantamount to fearing Yahweh's name (see Note for 4:10). On the expression "be careful to do," which occurred earlier in vv. 1 and 15, see Note for 5:1.

written in this book. This verse and v. 61 assume a written Deuteronomy (see Note for v. 61).

to fear this glorious and awesome name, Yahweh your God. The name of Yahweh, though shrouded in mystery (Exod 3:14; 33:19-23; Lundbom 1978a), is Yahweh himself (cf. Lev 24:15-16). This name is "glorious," נִכְבָּד (Ps 72:19; Neh 9:5), and "awesome," נוֹרָא (Pss 99:3; 111:9; Mal 1:14), and is to be treated with honor and respect (Deut 5:11; Exod 20:7). In Deut 7:21; 10:17 Yahweh is called a "great and awesome God." In 5:24 the people confess to having been shown Yahweh's "glory and greatness," which was heard, but not seen. On the fear of Yahweh in the OT and in Deuteronomy, see Note for 4:10.

59 These "blows" (מַכּוֹת) and "sicknesses" (חֳלָיִם), said here to be severe and lasting (ibn Ezra: chronic), came upon Judah in its last years and were internalized by the prophet Jeremiah (Jer 6:7; 10:19; 14:17; 15:18; 19:8; 30:12, 14).

60 Yahweh promised to exempt his people from these curses, but that hinged on obedience to the covenant (7:12, 15; Exod 15:26). Now these diseases will come (v. 27). The verb "to dread" (יגר) is rare (see Note for 9:19).

and they will stick to you. Said of the pestilence in v. 21.

61 Even sicknesses and blows not named in this book will come upon Israel, until the nation is destroyed. The destruction will be complete (vv. 20, 24, 45, 51), but not absolute.

in this book of the law. בְּסֵפֶר הַתּוֹרָה הַזֹּאת. The expression (but with הַזֶּה) occurs three other times in the book (29:20[21]; 30:10; 31:26) and nowhere else in the Pentateuch. 4QDeut[b] has the feminine הזאת in 31:26 (see Note there). See also 28:58; 29:19, 26, 28[20, 27, 29]; 31:9, which assume a written Deuteronomic law. Weinfeld (*EncJud*, 13:232) says that in Deuteronomy the "law" always refers to Deuteronomy itself, and only after the other four books of the Pentateuch are added to Deuteronomy does it acquire broader application and become a title of the Pentateuch. The occurrence in 31:26, however, appears to refer to the temple law book found during Josiah's reform (see Note for 31:26).

62 *You shall remain a few males instead of your being as numerous as the stars of the heavens.* Here it becomes clear that the "complete destruction" of v. 61 will not be absolute. There will be survivors. Cf. the modern use of "Holocaust" to describe the Jewish pogrom of World War II. But the curse is nevertheless far-reaching, with the promise of numberless descendants to the patriarchs (Gen 13:16; 15:5; 26:4; 28:14), a reality now as Moses is addressing Israel (1:10; 10:22; 26:5), being completely reversed. This reversal was anticipated in 4:27.

because you did not obey the voice of Yahweh your God. See vv. 15 and 45.

63 *And it will happen as Yahweh rejoiced over you to do you good and to multiply you, so Yahweh will rejoice over you to make you perish and to completely destroy you.* Deuteronomy and Jeremiah affirm that Yahweh rejoices in doing Israel good (8:16; 30:9; Jer 32:41). Deuteronomy is also positive about Israel multiplying in numbers (see Note for 6:3). So to say now that Yahweh re-

Deuteronomy 28

joices in bringing death and destruction to Israel and tearing Israel from off the land is harsh. Rashi avoids the indelicacy by having God cause the enemies to rejoice, but the curse remains unmitigated by ibn Ezra, who says: "Do not think that anything can harm God, or that he suffers." Heschel (1962, 46-52, 79-85, 107-15), however, finds in the preaching of Hosea (Hos 5:15–6:3; 6:4-5; 11:8-9), Isaiah (Isa 1:2-4, 11-15, 24-27; 5:1-7; 10:25; 26:20; 27:2-5; 30:18), and Jeremiah (Jer 2:1-3, 5, 31-32; 3:19; 12:7-8; 31:2-3, 20) great sorrow in the heart of God over Israel's disobedience and his need to punish Israel. According to him there are love and deep sorrow in the divine anger.

to make you perish. On this strong verb, see Note for 4:25-26.

and you shall be torn from off the soil which you are entering to possess. The verb נִסַּחְתֶּם is the N-stem of נסח, "to be pulled, torn away." Reference is to Israel's removal from the land (ibn Ezra), about which Israel was forewarned (4:26; 6:15). Akkadian nasāḫu carries the meanings "drive out, deport (people); depopulate (a region), be deported" (*CAD*, 11:1-15). Both northern Israel and Judah were exiled from the land (2 Kgs 17:23; 25:21). In Jeremiah's first "temple oracle" (Jer 7:3-7), tenure in the land is still conditional upon people making good their ways and their doings. But exile later became a certainty (Jer 7:15; 24:8-10).

64 *And Yahweh will scatter you among all the peoples.* The curse that Israel will be scattered among the nations occurred earlier (4:27; cf. Lev 26:33) and is repeated by Jeremiah (Jer 9:15[16]; 13:24) and Ezekiel (Ezek 22:15).

from one end of the earth to the other end of the earth. The expression occurs also in 13:8(7). See Note for 4:32.

and there you will serve other gods that you have not known, you or your fathers, of wood and stone. More irony (v. 36; 4:28; 13:3, 7, 14[2, 6, 13]; 29:25[26]; cf. Jer 7:9; 19:4; 44:3). Censure for worshipping gods people have not known occurs in the Song of Moses (32:17).

wood and stone. I.e., idols; see v. 36 and Note for 4:28.

65 *And among these nations you will not rest, yes, there will not be a resting place for the sole of your foot.* The verb רגע is an internal H-stem meaning "to (find) rest." Yahweh's promised "rest" in Deuteronomy and the Deuteronomic History is settlement in the land and safety from enemies round about (see Note for 12:10). Scattered now in distant lands, Israel will have no resting place.

a resting place for the sole of your foot. See Gen 8:9. For מָנוֹחַ ("resting place") the LXX has στάσις ("place in which one stands"). The "sole of your foot" may echo v. 56.

and Yahweh will give you there a quivering heart and cried-out eyes and dryness of throat. A "quivering heart" (לֵב רַגָּז) could be fear (T^PsJ; Rashi; cf. 2:25; Exod 15:14), but appears here to result from intense grief (2 Sam 19:1[18:33]). "Cried-out eyes" (כִּלְיוֹן עֵינַיִם) are eyes exhausted from weeping (see v. 32). The expression דְּאֲבוֹן נָפֶשׁ was translated "sorrow of mind" in the AV and "a languishing soul" in the RSV (T^Onq: "a despondent spirit"), where it was thought to denote a wasting away of life due to anxiety or some other cause (Driver; LXX: τηκομένην ψυχήν, "a life wasting away"). דְּאֲבוֹן is a *hapax legomenon* in the OT, derived from the root דאב, meaning "to languish, become faint" (Jer 31:25). But the idiom is now said to mean "dryness of throat" (Gruber 1987, 367), a physical symptom of depression. נֶפֶשׁ can mean "neck" or "throat," and דָּאֲבָה means "is dried-up" in Ps 88:10(9).

66 A vivid image, where life is imagined as suspended precariously in front of oneself, "upon a thread," says Driver, "which threatens every moment to break." The verb תְּלֻאִים means "be hung up, be suspended," well translated by LXX's κρεμαμένη (Job 26:7: "[God] hangs the earth upon nothing"). The idea here is that one will live amidst great and prolonged insecurity (ibn Ezra; Rashi; T^Onq: "you will live in constant suspense and be in a state of anxiety by night and by day, never sure of your life"). Cf. the sick man in Job 24:22, who has "no faith in his life," i.e., no hope of recovery.

67 *In the morning you will say, "Who can bring evening?" and in the evening you will say, "Who can bring morning?"* The image is expanded. The idiom, מִי־יִתֵּן (lit. "who can make?"), expresses a wish or longing, meaning "Would that . . . !" (Jongeling 1974; cf. 5:29; Jer 8:23[9:1]; 9:1[2]; Ps 55:7[6]). LXX πῶς ἄν means the same. The distressed will wish in the morning for evening and in the evening for morning (Job 7:4). Sick persons in the hospital often feel this way. A chiasmus is formed with terms in the prior verse: night/day//morning/evening.

from the dread of what your heart shall dread and from the sight of what your eyes shall see. The reasons for wanting time to pass: dread of heart (v. 66) and maddening sights before the eyes (v. 34). The one is anxiety about the future; the other a present-day horror. The Hebrew term פַּחַד ("terror, dread") derives from holy war (2:25; 11:25; Exod 15:16; 1 Sam 11:7).

68 This final verse contains the ultimate indignity, reversing Yahweh's promise that Israel would never again see Egypt (17:16; Exod 14:13). But a return to Egypt is anticipated by Hosea (Hos 8:13; 9:3, 6). Survivors will be brought there not as slaves, but simply as pitiful, destitute people prepared to offer themselves for sale on the Egyptian slave market, but no one will buy them. Moran says this is "surely one of the saddest lines of the Bible."

in ships. בָּאֳנִיּוֹת. These cannot be "slave galleys" (*pace* Driver; Moran; Nelson), because the survivors will not be brought to the country as slaves; they will offer themselves as slaves once they arrive. But someone will be transporting them to Egypt in ships. Schley (1985) cites a reference from the Annals of Assurbanipal in which the Assyrian king, who at the time controlled sea traffic in the eastern Mediterranean, compelled twenty-two kings and their armies, by sea and by land, to "take the road to Egypt" (*ANET*^{3}, 294). Schley thinks the

Deuteronomy 28

present verse is best understood in the context of Assyria's dominance of the Syro-Palestinian mainland, the eastern Mediterranean seaboard, and the islands of the sea during the first half of the 7th cent. Judah then was an Assyrian vassal, and Judahites could have been brought to Egypt in ships by Assyrians at their good pleasure.

on the way that I said to you, "You shall not see it ever again." Moses again assumes the speaking voice of Yahweh (see v. 20 and Note for 7:4), but in 17:16 this promise is said to have been made by Yahweh. בַּדֶּרֶךְ ("on the way/road") is a very common expression in Deuteronomy, often referring to the journey out of Egypt (see Note for 1:19).

Message and Audience

The earliest audience hearing blessings and curses for covenant obedience and disobedience may have heard only the core collection in vv. 1-6 and vv. 15-19. This could have been an assembly present at the Shechem renewal ceremony reported in 27:11-13, where six Israelite tribes recited blessings from Mount Gerizim and six Israelite tribes recited curses from Mount Ebal (cf. 11:29). The core was brief and compact, comprehensive enough to cover the whole of community life.

Subsequent audiences heard the core collection with one or more of its supplements. The earliest expanded recitation would have included the Blessing Supplement (vv. 7-14) and Curse Supplement I (vv. 20-26), since these supplements are tied together with an inclusio. The entire blessing collection (vv. 1-14) has an inclusio of its own (vv. 1-2, 13b-14), with the Blessing Supplement expanding and reversing themes of the core blessings. A later recitation would have added Curse Supplements II (vv. 27-37) and III (vv. 38-46), ending with the summary admonition in vv. 45-46. Curse Supplement II has its own internal structure. This recitation would have included the Blessing Supplement, since its conclusion balances Curse Supplement III (vv. 12-13, 44). All the curses compiled thus far are tied together with yet another inclusio (vv. 15, 45).

The curses now substantially outnumber the blessings, reflecting many of the international treaties of the ANE. The supplemental blessings and curses give specificity to blessings and curses of the core, which are more general. They specify prosperity or impoverishment, world respect or dependency status; they name diseases both troublesome and incurable, physical and mental; they speak of famine and other causes of crop failure; they specify victory or defeat at the hands of an enemy and predict exile for those surviving the ruin of the nation. All these blessings and curses would speak to Judahite life during the 7th cent., when Assyria was at its zenith as a world power and Israelites

Deuteronomy 28

from north Israel and Transjordan had already suffered defeat and exile at the hands of Tiglath-pileser III and Sargon II.

Curse Supplements IV (vv. 47-57) and V (vv. 58-68) have their greatest affinity to preaching of the prophets, mainly Hosea, Isaiah, and Jeremiah, with Curse Supplement IV having its own rhetorical structure, sounding itself like prophetic preaching (von Rad). The opening summary of Curse Supplement V (vv. 58-59) reverses the concluding summary of Curse Supplement III (v. 45), and the end of Curse Supplement V (v. 68) with its "Egypt" reference returns to the "boils of Egypt" beginning Curse Supplement II (v. 27).

When Curse Supplements IV and V were added one cannot say. Curse Supplement V makes reference to a written Deuteronomy (vv. 58, 61), which must mean it was later added to the First Edition. But nothing in either IV or V precludes a preexilic date, including their predictions of exile, which was a practice commonly employed by the Assyrians, Babylonians, and other peoples of the time (Driver; G. A. Smith; Nelson). These supplements could even be additions from the time of Jeremiah, although Welch (1932, 137) thought that Curse Supplement IV, containing the siege curses, was best understood as referring to the capture of Samaria by Sargon in 722.

VIII. SUBSCRIPTION TO THE FIRST EDITION (28:69[29:1])

28⁶⁹*These are the words of the covenant that Yahweh commanded Moses to cut with the children of Israel in the land of Moab, besides the covenant that he cut with them in Horeb.*

Rhetoric and Composition

This subscription is delimited at the top end by a *setumah* in M^L and a *petuḥah* in M^A before v. 69 and at the bottom end by a *petuḥah* in M^L and M^A and a section in Sam after v. 69, which is also the chapter division (MT; LXX Rahlfs). Some MSS of the LXX and Vg, also some English Versions (RSV; NRSV; NEB; REB; NIV), take v. 69 as 29:1. The JB, NJB, NAB, and NJV follow the numbering in the Hebrew Bible.

There is thus uncertainty about whether this verse is to be taken as a subscription to what precedes or a superscription to what follows. Some scholars take it to be a superscription (Kleinert 1872, 167; Lohfink 1962, 32-34; 1976, 229; 1992; von Rad; Moran), arguing that "words of the covenant" point ahead to the "covenant" references in 29:8, 11, 13, 18, 20, 24(9, 12, 14, 19, 21, 25). But others take it to be a subscription (Driver; H. W. Robinson; Lundbom 1975, 141

n. 155[= 1997, 28 n. 155]; 1996, 312-13; van Rooy 1988, 221; Wevers 1995, 461; Tigay), which it seems to be. The NEB and REB, although they follow the LXX and Vg renumbering of 28:69 to 29:1, nevertheless break after the present verse, presumably recognizing it to be a subscription. Cf. concluding statements in Num 36:13; Lev 27:34. Lenchak (1993, 172-73) and Nelson think the verse has a dual function, which in the present book it may have. But since the verse forms an inclusio with 1:1-5, its original function was doubtless to conclude chs. 1–28, which I have called the First Edition of Deuteronomy. The inclusio with its keywords consists of the following:

1:1-5 *These are the words* that *Moses* spoke to *all Israel* beyond the Jordan . . . beyond the Jordan, *in the land of Moab*, Moses sought to make plain *this law* . . .

28:69[29:1] *These are the words of the covenant* that Yahweh commanded *Moses* to cut with *the children of Israel in the land of Moab*, besides the covenant that he cut with them in Horeb.

Notes

28:69 See 1:5; 5:2-3; 29:11(12). This covenant, containing the Deuteronomic Code in chs. 12–26, is distinguished from the Horeb (Sinai) covenant, which consisted only of the Decalogue (4:13; 5:22).

Message and Audience

The audience hearing all or the majority of chs. 1–28 would be a late 8th- or early 7th-cent. audience, living during or in the aftermath of King Hezekiah's reform (see *Introduction*). This subscription reminds that audience that Moses made a covenant with Israel in the plains of Moab, besides the covenant made earlier at Mount Horeb. Both covenants, and the laws that accompany them, Israel is under obligation to keep.

IX. FIRST SUPPLEMENT (CHS. 29–30)

A. THE COVENANT IS SOMETHING YOU DO (29:1-8[2-9])

29 ¹*And Moses called to all Israel and said to them, You, you have seen all that Yahweh did before your eyes in the land of Egypt, to Pharaoh and to all his ser-*

vants and to all his land, ²the great testings that your eyes have seen, the signs and those great wonders. ³But Yahweh did not give you a mind to understand, or eyes to see, or ears to hear, to this day. ⁴Yes, I led you forty years in the wilderness; your clothes on your back did not wear out, and your sandals did not wear out on your feet; ⁵bread you did not eat, and wine or beer you did not drink, so you might know that I am Yahweh your God. ⁶And you came to this place, and Sihon king of Heshbon and Og king of the Bashan came out to meet us in battle, and we struck them down, ⁷and we took their land and gave it for an inheritance to the Reubenites, and to the Gadites, and to the half-tribe of Manasseh. ⁸So you shall be careful with the words of this covenant, and you shall do them, so you may have success in all that you do.

Rhetoric and Composition

Chapters 29–30 contain the first of what appear to be two supplements to the First Edition of Deuteronomy: (1) chs. 29-30; and (2) chs. 31-34 (Driver 1895, lxxiii-lxxvii; Nicholson 1967, 21-22). The introductory "And Moses called to all Israel and said to them," in 29:1(2) is the same as in 5:1. The discourse in chs. 29-30 presupposes all that has gone before: a summary of Israel's journey from Mount Horeb to the Transjordan settlement; a restating of the Ten Commandments and presentation of the Deuteronomic Code, the blessings and the curses. Moses begins by calling on Israel to remain faithful to Yahweh and to keep the terms of the covenant (29:1-8[2-9]) and ends on an uplifting note that faithfulness and obedience on Israel's part are indeed possible (30:11-14). Indeed, it is Israel's only option; it is the road to life (30:15-20).

It is possible that behind chs. 29–30 lay a covenant renewal ceremony (G. E. Wright; Nicholson 1967, 21-22). What is clear is that 29:9-14[10-15] calls all men, women, children, servants, and sojourners to enter into Yahweh's sworn covenant. Later reference to dispersion and restoration does not mean that this supplement is exilic or postexilic in date (i.e., post 586). As Wright points out, these themes emerge already in the 8th-cent. prophets. They appear also in 4:25-31 and were widely understood in the ancient world, particularly during the Assyrian age. Already in Isaiah's time Transjordan and northern Israel had been overrun by a succession of Assyrian kings and survivors taken into faraway exile.

The present verses are delimited at the top end by a *petuḥah* in M^L and M^A and a section in Sam prior to v. 1, which is also the chapter division. Concluding the unit in v. 8 is a *petuḥah* in M^L and M^A and a section in Sam. Some MSS of the LXX and the Vg number Heb 28:69 as 29:1, there evidently being uncertainty early on as to whether this verse is a subscription or a superscription. Some modern English Versions adopt the higher numbering, i.e., +1. In my view, 28:69 is a subscription (see Rhetoric and Composition for 28:69), which supports the numbering of MT.

Portions of 29:1-8 are contained in 4QDeut¹.

Notes

29:1-2[2-3] This address begins by recalling God's mighty acts in the exodus and wilderness wanderings (cf. Exod 19:4; Deut 32:10-14; Josh 24:2-13). The Prologue to Deuteronomy (chs. 1–4) began at Horeb, recalling Israel's first attempt to take the promised land, which failed, and then the victories over Sihon and Og, whose Transjordan territories were given to Reuben, Gad, and the half-tribe of Manasseh. The present recital concludes with the victories over Sihon and Og (vv. 6-7).

And Moses called to all Israel and said to them. The same introductory words as in 5:1, supporting the view that the present verse begins the supplement, not 28:69. Moses may have dismissed the people after his prior discourse and then called them to reassemble. Otherwise, this is simply a way for the author to begin his supplemental work.

You, you have seen. The added pronoun is for emphasis. In the audience are presumably some who witnessed the wonders of Egypt (1:30-31; 4:34; 7:18-19; 11:2-7). Caleb and Joshua, now present, were there, and undoubtedly there were others, despite the attrition of an entire generation (1:34-40; cf. Num 14:20-35). Luther points out that while the younger generation did not see the wonders of Egypt (cf. 11:2), they did witness Yahweh's mighty acts in the wilderness, also the victories over Sihon and Og. Deuteronomic speech also merges the generations, as happens again in v. 15 (see Note for 5:3). Cf. Joshua's words when he is about to die (Josh 23:3).

before your eyes. On this Deuteronomic expression, see Note for 1:30.

in the land of Egypt. The reference to Egypt picks up from 28:68, tying the supplement in with what precedes.

the great testings that your eyes have seen. These were the "testings" (מַסּוֹת) performed before Pharaoh in Egypt, who also witnessed "signs and wonders" (see Note for 4:34). On the expression "that your eyes have seen," see Note for 4:9.

3[4] Moses is telling the assembly — young and old — that they did not have the capability to understand Yahweh's mighty acts until now (Friedman). Moses will go on to tell them the meaning of these and other wonders in v. 5. Reference is not to Israel's perverseness (*pace* Driver; cf. 9:7, 24; Isa 6:10; Jer 5:21; Ezek 12:2-3), although there was evidence aplenty of this in the wilderness

Deuteronomy 29

(1:26-43; 9:7-8, 22-24; Num 14:22, and passim). Paul may be quoting this verse in Rom 11:7-8.

a mind to understand. לֵב לָדַעַת. Lit. "a heart to understand." The heart was the organ of understanding (see Note for 6:5).

to this day. On this Deuteronomic expression, see Note for 2:22.

4[5] *Yes, I led you forty years in the wilderness.* Here and in v. 5 Moses assumes the voice of Yahweh (see Note for 7:4). The LXX and Vg change to "he led." Yahweh led Israel in the wilderness (8:2; cf. Amos 2:10).

your clothes on your back did not wear out, and your sandals did not wear out on your feet. See earlier 8:4.

5[6] *In the wilderness it was manna and water.* Moses tells the people in 8:3:

> Yes, he humbled you and made you hungry, then he fed you the manna that you did not know and your fathers did not know, in order that he might make you know that one does not live by bread alone, but one lives by everything that goes out of the mouth of Yahweh. (cf. Matt 4:4)

Word order here emphasizes the bread, wine, and beer. "And you/they shall know that I am Yahweh" is a P phrase (Exod 6:7; 7:5; 14:4, 8; 16:12; 29:46) and occurs 50+ times in Ezekiel (Driver). The wording in Exod 8:18(22); Isa 45:3 is closer to the wording here. This is the "understanding" to which people have now come (v. 3). The LXX again changes "I" to "he" in order to retain Moses as the speaking voice.

6[7] These battles are recalled in 2:26–3:8. On Sihon, king of Heshbon, see Note for 2:24. On Og, king of the Bashan, see Note for 3:1.

to this place. I.e., to the Transjordan, but probably not the place where Moses is now speaking. For the various locations to which this expression refers, see Note for 9:7.

7[8] For the allotment of land to these tribes, see 3:12-17.

8[9] *So you shall be careful with the words of this covenant, and you shall do them.* On the stereotyped phrase "So you shall be careful and you shall do (the statutes and the ordinances)," see Note for 4:6. Cf. also Jer 11:6. This verse serves much the same function as ch. 4 does in the First Edition, following a historical survey with an admonition to keep the covenant (G. E. Wright).

the words of this covenant. I.e., the covenant brokered in the plains of Moab (28:69). Hence, another verbal tie-in between the Supplement and the First Edition.

so you may have success in all that you do. לְמַעַן תַּשְׂכִּילוּ אֵת כָּל־אֲשֶׁר תַּעֲשׂוּן. The H-stem of שׂכל means "have success, prosper" (ibn Ezra; Josh 1:7-8; 1 Sam 18:5; 1 Kgs 2:3). Israel will prosper if it obeys the terms of this covenant.

Deuteronomy 29

Message and Audience

Moses begins this supplemental discourse by reminding the assembled that they have been witness to Yahweh's mighty acts in days past. There were the signs and wonders in Egypt, forty years of guidance through a barren wilderness, during which time their clothes did not fall off their backs and their sandals did not wear out on their feet. True, they had no bread, wine, or beer, but this privation was to make them know that Yahweh was their God. They did not understand this great truth then, but they do now. What is more, there were the victories over the Amorite kings, Sihon and Og, whose land was taken and given to the Reubenites, Gadites, and half-tribe of Manasseh. Moses thus admonishes the assembly to be careful to do the words of this covenant brokered in the plains of Moab. If they follow his admonition, they will have success in all that they do.

In the late 8th or early 7th cents. this discourse would be addressing an Israel greatly reduced in size due to foreign invasion, with a remnant in exile, to remain faithful to Yahweh and to keep the terms of the covenant. If it does that, no matter how bad things have been or currently are, the people will succeed in all that they do.

B. ENTER INTO THE SWORN COVENANT! (29:9-28[10-29])

29 *⁹You are standing today, all of you, before Yahweh your God, your heads of your tribes, your elders, and your officials, every man of Israel; ¹⁰your little ones, your wives, and your sojourner who is in the midst of your camp, from the one who cuts your wood to the one who draws your water, ¹¹for your entry into the covenant of Yahweh your God and its oath that Yahweh your God is cutting with you today, ¹²in order that he may confirm you today for a people to him, and he, he will be God to you, as he spoke to you and as he swore to your fathers, to Abraham, to Isaac, and to Jacob. ¹³Not with you alone am I cutting this covenant and this oath, ¹⁴but with him who is standing here with us today, before Yahweh our God, and with him who is not here with us today. ¹⁵Indeed you, you know how we dwelt in the land of Egypt and how we crossed over in the midst of the nations that you crossed, ¹⁶and you have seen their detestable things, their blocks of wood and stone, silver and gold, that were with them. ¹⁷Perhaps there be among you a man or a woman or a family or a tribe whose heart turns away today from Yahweh our God to go and serve the gods of those nations. Perhaps there be among you a root bearing poison or wormwood, ¹⁸so it will happen when he hears the words of this oath that he blesses himself in his heart, saying, "It shall be well-being for me even though I walk in the stubbornness of my heart," resulting in the sweeping away of* the well-watered with the thirsty. ¹⁹*Yahweh would not be willing to pardon him, for then the anger of Yahweh and his jealousy would smoke against that man, and every curse written in this book would be lying in wait against him, and Yahweh would wipe out his name from under the heavens.* ²⁰*And Yahweh would single him out for evil from all the tribes of Israel, according to all the curses of the covenant written in this book of the law.* ²¹*And the generation after, your children who will rise up after you, and the stranger who will come from a distant land, will say when they see the beatings of that land and the diseases with which Yahweh made it sick —* ²²*sulphur and salt, all its land burned-out, not sown and not growing, nor any grass coming up in it, like the overthrow of Sodom and Gomorrah, Admah and Zeboiim, which Yahweh overthrew in his anger and in his wrath —* ²³*yes, all the nations will say, "Why has Yahweh done thus to this land? What is this great burning anger?"* ²⁴*And they will say, "Because they forsook the covenant of Yahweh, the God of their fathers, which he cut with them when he brought them out from the land of Egypt,* ²⁵*and they went and served other gods, and they worshipped them, gods that they had not known, and he had not allotted to them."* ²⁶*So the anger of Yahweh burned against that land, to bring upon it every curse written in this book.* ²⁷*And Yahweh uprooted them from on their soil in anger and in wrath and in great fury, and he cast them into another land, as at this day.* ²⁸*The hidden things belong to Yahweh our God, but the revealed things belong to us and to our children forever, to do all the words of this law.*

Rhetoric and Composition

In the present verses Moses addresses the assembly to enter into the sworn covenant now presented to it. This covenant will bind Israel to Yahweh through the Deuteronomic Code, referred to as "this (book of the) law" in 29:20, 28(21, 29); 30:10; 31:9-12. The discourse breaks down thematically as follows: (1) the invitation to all present to enter a sworn covenant Yahweh is cutting today with Israel (vv. 9-12); (2) the binding of this covenant on future generations (vv. 13-14); (3) a warning about the dangers of idolatry (vv. 15-16); (4) the curse for idol worship as it applies to individuals, families, and tribes (vv. 17-20); (5) the question posed by future generations and strangers about the curse having fallen upon entire cities or clusters of cities and its answer (vv. 21-27); and (6) a word about things hidden and revealed (v. 28). This final word in v. 28 may be a later add-on.

The unit is delimited at the top end by a *petuḥah* in M^L and M^A and a section in Sam before v. 9 and at the bottom end by a *setumah* in M^L and M^A and a section in Sam after v. 28, which is also the chapter division. The Sam also has sections after vv. 12 and 20. Verse numbers are +1 in the LXX, Vg, and some modern English Versions (see Rhetoric and Composition for 29:1-8).

A keyword chiasmus in vv. 9-14 begins the discourse, in which the covenant formula appears climactically at the center (Lohfink 1962, 39):

a	*You are standing today,* all of you, *before Yahweh your God* . . .	(vv. 9-10[10-11])
b	for your entry into *the covenant* . . . *and its oath that Yahweh your God is cutting with you* . . .	(v. 11[12])
c	in order that he may confirm you today *as a people to him, and he, he will be God to you* . . .	(v. 12[13])
b'	Not *with you alone am I cutting this covenant and this oath,*	(v. 13[14])
a'	but with *him who is standing here* with us *today* before Yahweh our God and with him who is not here with us today	(v. 14[15])

Portions of 29:9-28 are contained in 1QDeut^b, 4QDeut^b, 4QDeut^c and 4QDeut^o.

Notes

29:9-11[10-12] A solemn declaration to all Israel that it is about to enter a covenant made on this day of assembly. The ceremony may have included a ritual such as the one described in Gen 15:9-21 and Jer 34:18-20, where a calf was cut in two and people passed between its severed parts. As they passed through, they would have sworn an oath consenting to like treatment if they violated the terms of the covenant (see Note for 4:13). A treaty brokered between Ashurnirari V of Assyria (753-746) and Mati'ilu of Arpad was ratified by a lamb sacrifice. The self-imprecation uttered on that day of ratification began:

> If Mati'ilu sins against (this) treaty made under oath by the gods, then, just as this spring lamb, brought from its fold, will not return to its fold. . . . Mati'ilu, together with his sons, daughters, officials, and people of his land . . . will not return to his country . . . This head is not the head of a lamb, it is the head of Mati'ilu, it is the head of his sons, his officials, and the people of his land. (*ANET*^{3}, 532)

For other examples of treaties and oaths similar to the present one, both from the ANE and the classical world, see Lundbom 2004a, 565-66.

Hittite, Assyrian, and Babylonian treaties were ratified in large public assemblies consisting of men, women, and children, young and old, and all classes of society. Assemblies of a similar nature are attested also from the Greek and Roman worlds (Weinfeld 1972, 87, 101; 1976a, 392-93). Throughout Israelite history, large assemblies representing the entire population gathered for public readings of the law and covenant ratification (Exod 24:3-11; Josh 8:30-35; 24:1-28; 2 Kgs 23:2-3; Neh 8:1-3; 10:29-30[28-29]; 2 Chr 15:12-15). A public reading of the Deuteronomic law every seven years at the Feast of Booths is called for in Deut 31:10-13, and there, too, everyone is required to be there.

You are standing today. אַתֶּם נִצָּבִים הַיּוֹם. The verb נצב is more formal than עמד ("to stand"), meaning "you are presenting yourself (for a purpose)" (Driver; cf. Josh 24:1; 1 Sam 10:19). There is an emphasis on "today," in that vv. 1-8 focused on events occurring in the past. But as von Rad (1966b, 29) points out, a synchronism nevertheless existed in ancient Israel whereby later Israel could identify itself with the Israel standing at Horeb (cf. 5:2).

your heads of your tribes. רָאשֵׁיכֶם שִׁבְטֵיכֶם. The Hebrew is lit. "your heads, your tribes," an unusual construction. Numerous translations have been proposed. The LXX has οἱ ἀρχίφυλοι ὑμῶν ("your tribal chiefs"), the rendering also of Rashi, ibn Ezra, and others (cf. 1:15; 5:23). Nelson thinks שִׁבְטֵיכֶם may be an old term for "leaders" (2 Sam 7:7; Deut 33:5), a view expressed earlier by Gevirtz (1980, 61-62), who thought שְׁבָטִים here must be something like "rulers" or "judges." Gevirtz took the two terms to be in apposition to one another: "your heads, your judges." There is no need to emend MT to read "your judges" (Begg 1982; *pace* KBL³), even though the LXX adds "your judges" (οἱ κριταὶ ὑμῶν) between "your tribal chiefs" and "your elders." This may simply misread פ for ב in "your tribes," although it has been argued that a phonetic interchange between ב and פ in Ugaritic existed also in Hebrew (Dahood 1963, 10). The LXX may also have intentionally added "your judges" (see Note for 31:28). For a discussion of the various office-holders in ancient Israel, see Note for 16:18.

your elders. On the role of elders in Israel from earliest times, see Note for 5:23-24.

your officials. Army personnel engaged primarily in secretarial work (see Note for 16:18).

and your sojourner who is in the midst of your camp. The "sojourner" (גֵּר) was a resident alien in ancient Israel (see Note for 5:13-14). He, too, was invited to enter into this covenant (31:12; cf. Josh 8:35). He was, after all, protected by its laws (1:16; 24:14, 17; 27:19), granted a Sabbath rest like everyone else (5:14), and a recipient of Deuteronomy's mandated benevolences (10:18-19; 14:29; 16:11, 14; 24:19-20; 26:11-13). The "camp" survives from the wilderness period (2:14-15; 23:15[14]). Here it is a large tented area where Israel now resides in the plains of Moab.

from the one who cuts your wood to the one who draws your water. Another group of aliens resident in Israel who are required to perform menial tasks. After Israel was settled in Canaan, the Gibeonites were condemned to cut (fire)wood and draw water after deceiving Joshua in a ruse to make peace (Josh 9:21-27). The "from ... to" formula indicates that aliens performing a variety of menial tasks will reside in Israel, just as in other societies. The Legend of King Keret adds "straw-picking ones" to "wood-cutting (wives)" and "women that drew (water)" (*ANET*³, 144-45; KRT A, iii 112-13; iv 214-v. 1). There were other alien laborers (Tigay: washermen and gardeners).

for your entry into the covenant. לְעָבְרְךָ בִּבְרִית. Hebrew is lit. "for your passing over into the covenant," where reference is probably to people passing between the severed parts of the animal (ibn Ezra; Rashi; cf. Jer 34:18). Covenant-making is a rite of passage.

and its oath. וּבְאָלָתוֹ. Or "and its curse" (Neh 10:30[29]). The oath taken in the ceremony, as mentioned, is a self-curse if terms of the covenant are violated. On the close tie-in between oath and covenant — in the OT (Gen 26:28; Ezek 17:13) and in extrabiblical documents — see Tucker 1965, 488-90. Weinfeld (1976a) sees the covenant as basically a loyalty oath.

12[13] *in order that he may confirm you today for a people to him, and he, he will be God to you, as he spoke to you.* At the heart of the covenant ceremony is the covenant formula (Childs 1993, 421), lying also at the center of a rhetorical structure (see Rhetoric and Composition): Israel will be a people to Yahweh, and Yahweh will be God to Israel (cf. Exod 6:7; Lev 26:12; Hos 2:25[23]; Jer 7:23; 24:7; 30:22; 31:1). According to Deut 26:16-19, this covenant — which renews the Horeb (Sinai) covenant — contains mutual obligations, making it unlike the other OT covenants made with Noah, Abraham, Phinehas, and David, which were covenants of divine commitment (Freedman 1964). The LXX omits "today," perhaps because it already occurred twice in vv. 9-11.

and he, he will be God to you. The repeated pronoun is again for emphasis.

and as he swore to your fathers, to Abraham, to Isaac, and to Jacob. Added here is the covenant made with Abraham and his descendants (Gen 17:1-7; Deut 4:31; 7:8-9, 12; 8:18).

13-14[14-15] The present is merged with the future. Today's covenant is not only with the present generation, but with generations to come (see Note for 5:3). In this way the divine-human relationship is kept alive and contemporary (31:20-21). The ANE treaties similarly binded future generations to their terms (Weinfeld 1972, 104-5; 1976a, 391-92). In the Vassal-Treaties of Esarhaddon, the king states at the outset that sons and grandsons of the subordinate king are required to keep the terms of the treaty (*ANET*³, 534, 539). The same is true in the Sefire Treaties (Sefire 1Λ; *ANET*³, 659; Fitzmyer 1967, 12-13).

am I cutting this covenant and this oath. Moses is now assuming the speaking voice of Yahweh. See above vv. 4-5.

with him who is standing here with us today. The LXX and 1QDeut[b] omit "standing."

15-16[16-17] Moses now turns to idolatry, which constitutes the most serious threat to covenant loyalty. Some present will remember the calves of Egypt (ibn Ezra; cf. Ezek 20:7). For those too young to remember, the "we" indicates a shared history among the generations (see above v. 1). Many more saw the idols worshipped by peoples whom the Israelites encountered on their way to where they are now — in Midian, Edom, Moab, and perhaps Ammon. The Israelites even got entangled in idol worship. It was with the daughters of Moab that they had their infamous romp with Baal of Peor (4:3; Num 25:1-3).

Indeed you, you know. Another added pronoun for emphasis, with the כִּי best translated as an asseverative: "Indeed."

and how we crossed over in the midst of the nations that you crossed. The repeated verb is an idiom called an *idem per idem* by Driver, occurring also in 1:46; 9:25 (see Note for 1:46).

their detestable things. שִׁקּוּצֵיהֶם. A disparaging term for the disgusting idols, occurring often in the prophets and in the Deuteronomic History (Hos 9:10; Nah 3:6; Jer 7:30; 13:27; 16:18; 32:34; Ezek 5:11; 7:20; 1 Kgs 11:5; 2 Kgs 23:13, 24, etc.). The more common Deuteronomic term is "abomination" (תּוֹעֵבָה), on which see Note for 7:25. In 7:26 Moses tells the people: "You shall utterly detest" (שַׁקֵּץ תְּשַׁקְּצֶנּוּ) these things.

their blocks of wood and stone. Hebrew גִּלֻּלֵיהֶם ("their blocks") is a derisive term in the OT for foreign gods and their idols (Lev 26:30; Jer 50:2; Ezek 16:36, etc.), meaning "dung pellets" (Rashi; C. R. North 1958, 154-55). It was a favorite of Ezekiel (occurring 41 times). Calling idols "wood and stone" implies that they are inert (see Note for 4:28).

silver and gold. Precious metals in antiquity, cited to further mock the idols. Craftsmen overlayed idols in silver and gold (Deut 7:25; Hos 13:2; Isa 30:22; 40:19; 46:6; Hab 2:19; Jer 10:4; Pss 115:4; 135:15).

17[18] *Perhaps there be among you a man or a woman or a family or a tribe whose heart turns away today from Yahweh our God to go and serve the gods of those nations.* This warning builds on the sermon in ch. 13. See also 17:2-7. On the importance placed in Deuteronomy on worshipping Yahweh and Yahweh only, see Note for 6:13. In the Qumran *Manual of Discipline* (1QS 1:16–2:18), the blessings of the annual covenant renewal ceremony are based on Num 6:24-26 and the curses are based on vv. 17-20 here. The LXX omits "today," but it is present in 1QDeut[b].

whose heart turns away. אֲשֶׁר לְבָבוֹ פֹנֶה. The expression recurs in 30:17; cf. 8:14; 11:16. Yahweh will be the first to know, for he probes, tests, and assesses the human heart (8:2; 1 Sam 16:7; Jer 17:10; Pss 17:3; 26:2; Prov 17:3; 21:2; 1 John 3:20).

Perhaps there be among you a root bearing poison or wormwood. Hebrew שֹׁרֶשׁ ("root") can also mean "stock" (H. L. Ginsberg 1963, 74-75; Tigay; NJV), referring to the part of a tree, vine, or plant from which new branches can grow after a cutting down (cf. Isa 11:1; Job 14:7-9). Idolatry may be cut off, but it can grow again and bear its poisonous and bitter fruit. On the alien stock of Israel's enemies, see Deut 32:32-33. רֹאשׁ is a poisonous plant of some kind (Hos 10:4), identified commonly with hemlock (ibn Ezra) or gall. Bitter wormwood (לַעֲנָה) is another metaphor for suffering and death in the OT (Amos 6:12; Lam 3:19). Jeremiah speaks of "poisonous water" and "wormwood" (Jer 8:14; 9:14[15]; 23:15). In the NT, see Acts 8:23; Heb 12:15.

18[19] The problem is with people who hear the curse but continue thinking they are blessed despite idolatrous behavior (cf. Jer 7:8-10). Such individuals can infect the whole, and if they are not dealt with, the good will end up being swept away with the bad (Deut 13:2-19[1-18]). In the *Manual of Discipline*, vv. 18-20 became a curse on one who entered the Qumran community insincerely (Wernberg-Møller 1957, 23-24, 54-55; Weise 1961, 103-10; Laubscher 1980, 50; Rofé 1988a, 167-69; B. Nitzan, *EDSS*, 1:97), although there it is made clear that only the guilty person will be judged; there is no threat — explicit or implicit — to the entire community (line 14). Laubscher translates 1QS 2:11-18:

(11) Further the priests and the Levites say:
(11) Cursed because of the idols of his heart which he worships be he who enters into this covenant
(12) and sets up before himself his iniquitous stumbling-block so that he backslides through it.
(12) When he hears the words of this covenant, he blesses himself, thinking:
(13) Peace be with me, even though I walk in the stubbornness of my heart.
(14) May his spirit be destroyed, thirst as well as saturation, without pardon.
(15) May God's wrath and his zeal for his precepts consume him in everlasting destruction.
(15) May all the curses of this covenant cling to him.
(16) May God set him apart for evil.
(16) May he be cut off from all the sons of light because he has turned aside from God through his idols.
(17) May his iniquitous stumbling-block apportion his lot among those accursed for ever.
(18) And all those entering the covenant shall respond and say after them:
(19) Amen, amen.

the words of this oath. The oath, as mentioned in v. 11, was a self-curse for noncompliance. The term here comes close to meaning "covenant" (von Rad), with which it appears side by side in vv. 11 and 13. The RSV translated "sworn covenant," but the NRSV changed to "oath."

he blesses himself in his heart. Precisely the opposite of what he should be doing.

well-being. שָׁלוֹם. RSV and NRSV translate "safe" (cf. Job 5:24).

even though I walk in the stubbornness of my heart. A person will not likely speak thus about himself, particularly with שְׁרִרוּת ("stubbornness") being an irksome type of self-reliance. This is a judgment of the Deuteronomic writer, not the imagined speaker (Driver). The expression "(walk in the) stubbornness of his/their (evil) heart" is picked up in Jeremiah (Jer 3:17; 7:24; 9:13[14]; 11:8; 13:10; 16:12; 18:12; 23:17). See also Ps 81:13(12).

resulting in. Hebrew לְמַעַן expresses the result as intent (BDB; KBL[3] מַעַן). BDB (p. 775) calls the usage rhetorical, where "a line of action, though really undesigned, is represented . . . ironically as if it were designed." See elsewhere Hos 8:4; Jer 7:19; 25:7; 27:10, 15; Isa 44:9.

the sweeping away of the well-watered with the thirsty. A proverb meaning "everyone" or "everything," here taking in the innocent with the guilty or the good with the bad. Plant metaphors are retained. The verb "sweep away" (ספה) occurs four times in the Sodom and Gomorrah story (Gen 18:23-24; 19:15, 17). See also Jer 12:4, where beasts and birds are swept away with wicked people in the land. The Arabic cognate to this verb is used of wind carrying away dust.

19[20] *Yahweh would not be willing to pardon him, for then the anger of Yahweh and his jealousy would smoke against that man.* Yahweh is gracious and merciful, but will not clear the guilty (Exod 34:6-7; cf. Deut 5:8-10). The idolater will take the full measure of the divine anger (see Notes for 4:25 and 6:15). In the command against idols, Yahweh says: "For I, Yahweh your God, am a jealous (קַנָּא) God" (5:9).

would smoke. יֶעְשַׁן. An uncommon verb, but used of divine anger also in Pss 74:1; 80:5(4). The usual word for "anger" is "nose" (אַף), with the anthropomorphism here being smoke and fire issuing forth from Yahweh's nose (cf. 2 Sam 22:9 = Ps 18:9[8]; Isa 65:5).

and every curse written in this book would be lying in wait against him. The curses of ch. 28 are assumed, perhaps also the curses of ch. 27. On curses having quasi-independent power in pursuing their objects while at the same time remaining subject to Yahweh's command, see Note for 28:15. The verb רָבְצָה ("lying in wait") is lit. "lying stretched out," like a crouching animal (Gen 49:9, 14, 25). Curses wait in readiness to attack the idolater. See the same verb in Deut 33:13. Here in the present verse, the LXX (κολληθήσονται), 4QDeut[c]

Deuteronomy 29

(וְדָבַקְתָּ), and T^OnqNf read "(and) cling." Chapters 28-31 contain nine references to a written Deuteronomic law (see Note for 28:61).

and Yahweh would wipe out his name from under the heavens. Moses promised this for the idol-worshipping Canaanites (7:24-25). Yahweh threatened the same for the generation worshipping the golden calf in the wilderness, but was persuaded by Moses not to carry it out (9:14).

20[21] Again Yahweh promises judgment on the guilty person, who must not imagine he will escape if the rest of the community is innocent. If the guilty one is unknown, the process of separating him out first by tribe, then by family, then by household, and then by individual will likely be carried out by lot, as appears to have been used later in identifying Achan as the culprit who violated the holy war ban (Joshua 7).

all the curses of the covenant. I.e., the curses in 28:15-68.

this book of the law. The written First Edition of Deuteronomy, i.e., chs. 1-28 (see Note for 28:61).

21-23[22-24] The worst is imagined. An abrupt shift occurs from the judgment of a single offender, or multiple offenders, to judgment of an entire community. The lapse into idolatry is envisioned as a poison (v. 17[18]) so widespread now that an entire city or cluster of cities must be punished. This was the worst scenario envisioned in the sermon of ch. 13, where worthless men are imagined to have driven all the inhabitants of the city to the worship of other gods, with the result that the entire city must be devoted to destruction (vv. 13-19[12-18]). After the land has become a ruin, future generations — including children of the stricken generation, strangers passing by, and neighboring nations — will ask why such a thing happened. All will assume that since Yahweh was God of this people and this land, he must have brought the destruction about.

And the generation after, your children who will rise up after you. In modern times, children in Germany have asked their parents and others of the older generation why their country came to ruin as a result of World War II.

the diseases with which Yahweh made it sick. Yahweh promises curses of disease in 28:21-22, 27-28, 35, 59-61. Disease will also result from famine and the unburied dead (Jer 14:18; 16:4).

sulphur and salt, all its land burned-out, not sown and not growing, nor any grass coming up in it. A salty wasteland revives memories of Sodom and Gomorrah, cities upon which Yahweh rained "sulphur" or "brimstone" (גָּפְרִית) and "fire" (אֵשׁ) for their wickedness (Gen 19:24-26). On "sulphur and fire," see J. P. Harland 1943. In antiquity, cities were burned and then sown with salt (Judg 9:45), which prevented vegetation from growing (Ps 107:34). On "burned-out" (שְׂרֵפָה) land as a result of war and destruction, see Jer 51:25.

Sodom and Gomorrah, Admah and Zeboiim. These "Cities of the Plain"

(עָרֵי הַכִּכָּר) so-called (Gen 13:12; 19:29), were attacked and defeated by a coalition of eastern kings led by Ched-or-laomer, king of Elam, in the Valley of Siddim near the Dead Sea (Gen 14:1-12). Later they were destroyed in a conflagration widely known in antiquity, being cited in the Bible, in classical sources, and in the Koran. The biblical story appears in Genesis 18-19, where it says that Yahweh punished these cities for their wickedness despite Abraham's special pleading for Sodom (cf. Lundbom 1998). Jewish tradition records five "Cities of the Plain" (Gen 14:2, 8; Wis 10:6: "Pentapolis"; cf. *Gen. Rab.* 51:4): the four cited here and Zoar, which escaped destruction (34:3; cf. Gen 19:20-23). The Koran adds Aad and Samoud (Suras 25:38; 29:38). The memory of these cities being destroyed is reported also in Strabo (*Geogr.* xvi 44) and Tacitus (*Hist.* v. 7). Strabo says Sodom was the metropolis amidst thirteen originally-inhabited cities.

In the Bible, Sodom and Gomorrah are the proverbial cities of wickedness, their overthrow being cited directly and indirectly throughout the OT, particularly in the Prophets (Amos 4:11; Hos 11:8; Isa 1:9-10; 3:9; 13:19; Zeph 2:9; Jer 5:1-8; 20:16; 23:14; 49:18; 50:40; Ezek 16:46-52), where it is tantamount to a curse (Hillers 1964a, 74-76). In the NT, see Matt 10:15; 11:23-24; 2 Pet 2:6; Jude 7; Rev 11:8. The location of these cities is not known. They appear to have been situated at the southern end of the Dead Sea, their ruins now submerged in water less than 4 m deep (Albright 1924, 8-9; 1926, 54-58; J. P. Harland 1942; 1943; *IDB*, 4:396).

yes, all the nations will say, 'Why has Yahweh done thus to this land? What is this great burning anger?' The concern here is about how others — particularly foreign nations — will view the ruin of Israel's city, temple, and land. Daube (1969a, 51 n. 5) says this is an appeal to shame, which runs all through Deuteronomy. He ties it in with what is said in Exod 32:12; Num 14:13-16; and the Song of Moses (Deut 32:26-27), about what would happen if Yahweh had completely wiped out Israel, viz., "their antagonists would conclude that he was powerless to lead them to triumph or even that he was ill-intentioned against them from the outset."

24-25[25-26] The onlookers will answer their own question (*pace* NJV: "they will be told"). This question-and-answer form appears in 1 Kgs 9:8-9 and in Jeremiah (Jer 5:19; 9:11-13[12-14]; 16:10-13; 22:8-9). On the close parallel between vv. 23-25 and Jer 22:8-9, see Lundbom 2004a, 125-26. An excellent parallel is found in the Annals of Assurbanipal (Rassam Cylinder IX, 68-74):

> Whenever the inhabitants of Arabia asked each other: "On account of what have these calamities befallen Arabia?" (they answered themselves:) "Because we did not keep the solemn oaths (sworn by) Ashur, because we offended the friendliness of Ashurbanipal, the king beloved by Enlil!" (*ANET*³, 300)

Deuteronomy 29

Because they forsook the covenant of Yahweh, the God of their fathers. Reference is to the Horeb covenant, renewed and expanded in the Deuteronomic covenant promulgated in the plains of Moab. In Deuteronomic theology is a particularly close relation between covenant obedience and tenure in the land (11:8-9, 13-17, 26-32). Elijah later spoke of Israel having "forsaken the covenant" (1 Kgs 19:10, 14). See also Jer 22:9 and later Dan 11:30.

Because. עַל אֲשֶׁר. This construction occurs also in Jer 22:9.

and they went and served other gods, and they worshipped them, gods that they had not known. On serving Yahweh, not other gods, see Note for 6:13. The Song of Moses indicts Israel for sacrificing to gods Israel had never known (32:17). See also Note for 11:27-28.

and he had not allotted to them. I.e., as Yahweh allotted to other nations (4:19).

26[27] The question and answer is completed, with the writer of Deuteronomy now adding his own explanation for the ruined land. This statement balances the statement in v. 20 on the individual covenant violater or violaters. This term for "curse" (קְלָלָה) does not quite have the force of an imprecation, meaning basically "misfortune" (Brichto 1963, 187; see Note for 27:12-13). On references to a written book of Deuteronomy in chs. 28–31, see Note for 28:61.

27[28] Punishment for a disobedient Israel will be expulsion from the land and exile (1 Kgs 14:15; 2 Chr 7:20). Israelites are in exile at the time of writing, assuming a date after 734 when Tiglath-pileser III destroyed Galilee and Transjordan and exiled remaining inhabitants (2 Kgs 15:29; 1 Chr 5:26). Later rabbis took this to refer to the exile of the ten northern tribes (734-722) and debated over whether they would ever return. Rabbi Akiba said they would not return; Rabbi Eliezer said they would (*m. Sanh.* 10:3).

in anger and in wrath and in great fury. A triad appearing also in Jer 21:5; 32:37.

as at this day. A common Deuteronomic expression (see Note for 2:30).

28[29] A concluding aphorism, perhaps added later, which puts mysteries in the hands of Yahweh and counsels hearers to concentrate rather on what has been revealed, which is the Deuteronomic law. It will be enough if they take this law to heart and do it.

the hidden things. הַנִּסְתָּרֹת. Or "secret things" (AV; RSV; NRSV).

the revealed things. הַנִּגְלֹת. A possible play on "exile" (גּוֹלָה), which is described in the previous verse. Deuteronomy does not use Hebrew גלה meaning "exile."

all the words of this law. The Deuteronomic law (see Note for 28:61).

Deuteronomy 30

Message and Audience

After an introductory word recalling Yahweh's mighty works in days past, his guidance on the wilderness journey, and Israel's success in taking Transjordan land, concluding with a reminder to keep the covenant so Israel may prosper in all that it does (vv. 1-8[2-9]), the people are now bid to enter into this sworn covenant, which will be binding on them and future generations. They are forcefully reminded about what will happen if this covenant is disobeyed. The preeminent danger is other gods and their idols. The people saw the idols of Egypt, and they were in evidence in all places where they have been since. One bitter entanglement came in the romp with daughters of Moab at Beth-peor. A single covenant violater — man or woman — is enough to poison the whole community, and such a one must not think he can bless himself while persisting in idolatrous worship, for this would result in a sweeping away of the good with the bad. The same goes for single families or single tribes. Yahweh will not pardon the offenders, and the curses written in the present book wait to fall upon them, with dire consequences. The worst scenario would be if the larger community does not act to rid itself of the culprit or culprits, in which case whole cities or clusters of cities will come to ruin. The fate of Sodom, Gomorrah, Admah, and Zeboiim is recalled. Subsequent generations, including children of the stricken generation, strangers passing by, and other nations will ask how such a ruin came about. Knowing that this was Yahweh's land inhabited by Yahweh's people, they will be able to answer their own question. The people forsook Yahweh's covenant and went after other gods — gods Yahweh had not allotted to them. The writer repeats what Yahweh will have done in his anger — cursing the land, as stated in this book, and exiling its people to faraway places. Some languish there at the present time. A concluding aphorism, written for a later audience, states that hidden mysteries remain in the mind of Yahweh; only what has been revealed is possessed by those hearing these words and their children, on which basis they are to do all the words of this law.

Those hearing this sermon at the end of the 8th or early in the 7th cent. have been sobered by invasions of Tiglath-pileser III and subsequent Assyrian kings into northern Israel and Transjordan, bringing down the northern kingdom and exiling its remaining population. Let them be duly warned, lest it happen also to them.

C. WHEN THE BLESSINGS AND CURSES COME UPON YOU (30:1-10)

30¹*And it will happen when all these words come upon you, the blessing and the curse that I have set before you, and you take them to your heart in all the nations* where Yahweh your God has dispersed you, ²and you return to Yahweh your God and you obey his voice according to all that I am commanding you today, you and your children, with all your heart and with all your soul, ³then Yahweh your God will restore your fortunes, and he will have compassion on you, and will again gather you together from all the peoples among whom Yahweh your God scattered you. ⁴If your dispersed one is at the end of the heavens, from there Yahweh your God will gather you and from there he will fetch you. ⁵And Yahweh your God will bring you into the land that your fathers possessed, that you may possess it, and he will do you more good and make you more numerous than your fathers. ⁶And Yahweh your God will circumcise your heart and the heart of your offspring, to love Yahweh your God with all your heart and with all your soul, in order that you may live. ⁷And Yahweh your God will put all these curses upon your enemies, and upon those hating you who pursue you. ⁸And you, you shall return and you shall obey the voice of Yahweh and you shall do all his commandments that I am commanding you today. ⁹And Yahweh your God will give you more than enough in all the work of your hand — in the fruit of your womb and in the fruit of your beasts and in the fruit of your soil, for good — because Yahweh will again rejoice over you for good, as he rejoiced over your fathers. ¹⁰For you will obey the voice of Yahweh your God to keep his commandments and his statutes that are written in this book of the law, for you will return to Yahweh your God with all your heart and with all your soul.

Rhetoric and Composition

Chapter 30 follows up the covenant renewal ceremony and its warning about blessings and curses with a word about what Israel can expect after the curses have come to pass. It falls into three sections: (1) a promise of restoration after exile, when Israel returns to Yahweh and obeys his commands, which will lead to numerical growth and prosperity for Israel (vv. 1-10); (2) an assurance that obeying Yahweh's command is something Israel can do (vv. 11-14); and (3) the presentation of a "Two Ways" teaching, that doing Yahweh's commands is walking the road to life and not doing them is walking the road to death (vv. 15-20).

The present verses are demarcated at the top end by a *setumah* in M^L and M^A and a section in Sam before v. 1, which is also the chapter division. Demarcation at the bottom end is by a *petuḥah* in M^L and M^A and a section in Sam after v. 10.

The chapter teems with repeated vocabulary and phraseology, but some repeated keywords and phrases in vv. 11-20 appear to create a rhetorical tie-in with keywords and phrases in vv. 1-10:

Deuteronomy 30

a	*the blessing and the curse that I have set before you*	v. 1
	and you obey his voice	v. 2
	according to all that I am commanding you today	
	at the end of the heavens	v. 4
	to love Yahweh your God	v. 6
	in order that you may live	
	and you shall obey the voice of Yahweh and you shall do all	v. 8
	his commandments that I am commanding you today	
a′	*Indeed this commandment that I am commanding you today*	v. 11
	It is not in the heavens. . . . Who will go up for us to the heavens . . .	v. 12
	. . . that I am commanding you today	v. 16
	to love Yahweh your God	
	. . . I have set before you, blessing and curse	v. 19
	in order that you and your descendants may live	
	to love Yahweh your God, to obey his voice	v. 20

The present verses (vv. 1-10) are structured by a keyword chiasmus (cf. Nelson):

a		*return . . . obey . . . heart and soul*	v. 2
	b	*the land . . . do you more good . . . your fathers*	v. 5
		c *circumcise your heart . . . that you may live*	v. 6
	b′	*your soil . . . for good . . . for good . . . your fathers*	v. 9
a′		*obey . . . return . . . heart and soul*	v. 10

These verses also ring the changes on the verb שׁוּב ("turn, return, repent, restore, again"), but the occurrences do not make another chiasmus (*pace* Tigay and Nelson).

Portions of 30:1-10 are contained in 4QDeut[b] and 4QMMT.

Notes

30:1-3 A broad theological statement building on 29:27(28), which envisions an Israel in exile.

After 734 exile was not simply a possibility, but a harsh reality for northern Israel, including its Transjordan population. What will the future hold? Will exile be the end? Answer: No! Israel's remnant will take the blessings and curses to heart, return to Yahweh, and commit itself to obeying his commandments.

Then Yahweh will gather it from all the places to which it has been scattered. Moran says: "Curse can never be the final word on God's people; exile can only be a means God uses to effect a conversion of the heart." Verses 1-2 are the protasis; v. 3 is the apodosis (*pace* Nelson, who turns them around!). G. E. Wright thinks responsibility for repentance is placed upon the people, but notes that in v. 6 the stress is placed upon God making a change of heart possible. The statement, in any case, is a wholly positive one: Israel at some point in the future will repent and become obedient, and restoration will occur.

Verses 1-3 are paraphrased in a Qumran document (4QMMT 13-16), where, following a legal section, a hortatory epilogue states:

'And it shall come to pass, when all these things [be]fall you', at the end of days, the blessings and the curses, ['then you will take] it to hea[rt] and you will return unto Him with all your heart and with all your soul', at the end [of time, so that you may live . . .]. (Qimron and Strugnell 1994, 58-61; cf. Fraade 2003, 150-54)

In Strugnell's view, the exhortation is to obey previously mentioned laws, making it a parallel to the present verses in Deuteronomy (Qimron and Strugnell 1994, 205).

the blessing and the curse. הַבְּרָכָה וְהַקְּלָלָה. I.e., what is spelled out in ch. 28. The Hebrew term for "curse" means "harm, misfortune" (see 29:26[27] and Note for 27:12-13).

that I have set before you. A stereotyped Deuteronomic expression (see again vv. 15 and 19, also Note for 1:8).

and you take them to your heart. Another stereotyped Deuteronomic expression (see Note for 4:39). Israel must do some soul-searching in exile, and will.

where Yahweh your God has dispersed you. "Yahweh your God" repeats 12 times in the present verses, and the LXX in 4 of these omits "your God" (v. 1, twice in v. 3, v. 6). But twice (vv. 4, 8) it reads "the Lord your God" where the MT simply has "Yahweh" or the pronoun "he." The verb נדח in the H-stem means "disperse, scatter from one another." In Jeremiah it occurs frequently with Yahweh as the subject, and in Jer 23:3, 8; 29:14; 32:37, the same point is made as here, viz., that Yahweh will gather his people from all the nations where he dispersed them.

and you return to Yahweh your God and you obey his voice according to all that I am commanding you today. Returning to Yahweh translates into obeying Yahweh's commands (vv. 8-10; cf. 4:30). The verb שׁוּב ("turn, return, repent, restore, again") occurs often in the present verses, even more often in Jeremiah (Holladay 1958). That Israel will return to Yahweh after exile is anticipated in Jer 24:7 (see Lundbom 2004a, 231-32).

Deuteronomy 30

you and your children. The LXX omits. Deuteronomy places great emphasis on teaching Yahweh's commands to the children (see Note for 4:9). "Returning" will apply to them also.

with all your heart and with all your soul. This expression, repeating in vv. 6 and 10, is stereotyped in Deuteronomy (see Note for 4:29).

then Yahweh your God will restore your fortunes. A sonorous expression of שׁוּב with a cognate accusative (שְׁבוּת), picked up by Jeremiah (Jer 29:14 and often; cf. Lundbom 2004a, 355). See also Ezek 29:14. When Israel *returns* (שׁוּב) to Yahweh and obeys his commands, then Yahweh will *restore* (שׁוּב) her *fortunes* (שְׁבוּת). שְׁבוּת does not mean "captives" or "captivity," which is how the term was translated by earlier scholars. The expression has been clarified by an 8th-cent. Sefire Treaty (Sefire III 24; *ANET*[3], 661), which says: "the gods have brought about the return *(hšbw 'lhn šybt)* of my father's house" (Greenfield 1965-66, 4; 1981, 110-12).

and he will have compassion on you. וְרִחֲמֶךָ. Yahweh is a God of "compassion/mercy" (4:31; 13:18[17]; Exod 34:6; cf. Freedman 1955). Jeremiah states, too, that Yahweh will have compassion on Israel and restore its fortunes after its punishment is over (Jer 12:15; 31:20; 33:26).

and will again gather you together from all the peoples among whom Yahweh your God scattered you. The God who scatters is the God who gathers (Jer 23:3; 29:14; 31:8; Ezek 11:17-18).

4 The "end of the heavens" (קְצֵה הַשָּׁמָיִם) is the farthest region of earth, where the solid vault of heaven (= sky) was believed to rest upon the earth (Ps 19:7[6]; Isa 13:5; Neh 1:9; cf. Matt 24:31; Mark 13:27). The expression occurs also in Deut 4:32. In the present verse, the LXX has ἀπ' ἄκρου τοῦ οὐρανοῦ ἕως ἄκρου τοῦ οὐρανοῦ ("from the end of the heaven to the end of the heaven"). No matter how far distant the dispersed one is, Yahweh will fetch that person and bring him/her back to the land of Israel. The LXX expands v. 4b to "from there the Lord your God will take you," which Wevers (1995, 480) thinks is unoriginal. 4QDeut[b] supports MT.

5 Yahweh did Israel good and multiplied her numbers in the past (7:13; 8:16; 13:18[17]; 28:63), but the future will be even better, when Israel will outnumber her ancestors (T[OnqNfPsJ]).

6 Here it states that Yahweh will effect a change of heart in people and their descendants so they will love him completely and in so doing choose life (vv. 15-20). The verse is echoed in *Jub.* 1:23-24 (cf. Seely 1996, 531). In 10:16 people are told to bring about a change of heart themselves (see Note for 10:16). In the Bible God also "hardens the heart" of certain people when it suits his purposes (Exod 4:21; 7:3; 9:12; 10:1; 11:10; Josh 11:20; Rom 9:18; 11:7-8; cf. Isa 6:9-10).

Hebrew males were circumcised as a sign of the Abrahamic covenant (Gen 17:9-14), which here becomes a forceful image in driving home the point about covenant fidelity. "Circumcision of the heart" is a harsh trope, an implied metaphor called an *abusio* by classical writers (*ad Herennium* iv 33; Lundbom 1999, 129, 330; 2004b, 586; Brandt 1970, 139-41). The expression is picked up in Jeremiah (Jer 4:4; 9:25[26]), but its first use is here in Deuteronomy. *Targum Jonathan* to Jer 4:4 interprets the expression to mean "Return to the worship of the Lord," where "foreskin" is taken to be wickedness in need of removal (cf. Ezek 44:7, 9; Lev 26:41). In the present verse, T^{OnqPsJ} take foreskin to be "obduracy, stubborn impenitence" (cf. 10:16). The LXX views the circumcised heart as a cleansed heart, translating with περικαθαριεῖ, a verb meaning "to purify, cleanse, purge away" (cf. Ezek 36:26-29). NJV translates "open up your heart," which is better, since circumcision is an act of "opening up." "Uncircumcised ears" need to be opened up for hearing to take place (Jer 6:10). When Israel pledged obedience to the Ten Commandments, Yahweh told Moses that he wished this right heart — to fear him and keep his commandments — would continue always (5:29). Presumably it did not, for in 10:16 Moses is heard telling the people: "So you must circumcise the foreskin of your heart, and your neck stiffen [i.e., be stubborn] no longer." Jeremiah told Judahites the same thing (Jer 4:4), noting that the covenant people in his day were uncircumcised in heart (Jer 9:25[26]). Talk of a new or changed heart looms large in Jeremiah's and Ezekiel's preaching (Jer 24:7; 31:33; 32:39-40; Ezek 11:19-20; 18:31; 36:26-28), becoming for Jeremiah the centerpiece of his "new/eternal covenant" prophecy (Lundbom 2004a, 464-71). In Jeremiah (Jer 31:33; 32:39) and Ezekiel (Ezek 36:26-28), as also here, Yahweh must bring about the change; the people cannot do it themselves. Later rabbis were keen to make this point. In the NT, Paul has his own interpretation of circumcision and circumcision of the heart in Rom 2:25-29 (cf. Col 2:11).

and the heart of your offspring. Children, too, male and female, will need a "circumcision of the heart" (cf. Jer 32:39).

to love Yahweh your God. An important Deuteronomic theme (see Note for 6:5).

in order that you may live. The theme of vv. 15-20 (see Note for 4:1).

7 The curses of 28:15-68, cited in 29:19-20, 26(20-21, 27), will now fall upon Israel's enemies. These enemies were Yahweh's agents in punishing Israel, but now they must be punished. This working of divine justice is set forth in the Song of Moses (Deut 32:23-42), and it was clearly understood by Isaiah (Isa 10:5-19) and Jeremiah (Jer 25:28-29).

8 Repeating v. 2. The added pronoun beginning the verse is to heighten the contrast between Yahweh's judgment on the enemies and Israel's return to Yahweh (Driver). The LXX expands to "the Lord your God."

9 One blessing accruing from covenant obedience (28:11). The curse of 28:63 is reversed. Jeremiah repeats the idea that Yahweh will rejoice in doing his

people good after their punishment is over (Jer 32:41). The terms "womb, beasts, and soil" appear in a different order in the LXX and in 4QDeut^b (Ulrich, Cross et al. 1995, 10-11), but with no appreciable change of meaning (cf. 28:4, 18).

in all the work of your hand. On this Deuteronomic expression, see Note for 2:7.

the fruit of your womb. I.e., your offspring (see Note for 7:13).

10 The כִּי ... כִּי construction should be translated "for ... for," "when ... when," or "because ... because," not "if ... if," since the statement is wholly positive, not conditional (NEB; NJV; NRSV; REB; *pace* LXX, which has ἐὰν ... ἐὰν; RSV; JB; NAB; NIV; NJB). See Note for 28:9. The writer is expressing confidence that divine joy will accompany or result from people's obedience (v. 8). They will be capable of doing Yahweh's law (vv. 11-14).

his commandments and his statutes. LXX adds "and his judgments" (καὶ τὰς κρίσεις αὐτοῦ). 4QDeut^b and other ancient Versions support MT.

this book of the law. The written Deuteronomic law (see Note for 28:61).

Message and Audience

The audience has heard Moses allude to exile, which in the late 8th and early 7th cents. was a deeply troubling reality for all Israelites, north and south. The blessings and the curses, particularly the latter, have come to pass for Israelites living in the north and in Transjordan, and the question is, "What next?" Moses thus turns to look beyond exile and finds there a picture considerably brighter. Exile will not be the end. God's people will have a future. In the distant places to where they have been dispersed, they — and their children — will take the blessings and curses to heart, return to Yahweh their God, and commit themselves to obeying Yahweh's commands. Their return will be heart and soul. Then Yahweh will restore their fortunes and, more important, will have compassion on them, gathering them from all the places to where they have been dispersed. No matter where they have gone, Yahweh will fetch them and return them to the land promised to the fathers, the land of Israel. There they will possess it as before, and there Yahweh will do them more good and make them more numerous than ever. Yahweh will actively bring about this new day, circumcising the hearts of people and their children so they will love him and in so doing find life. Their curses will be transferred to the enemy, who hates them and has been persecuting them. Moses repeats that the people will return, i.e., repent, and will do the commandments Moses has given them. Yes, in the future Yahweh will give them more than enough — more children, more sheep, goats, and cattle, and more crops — rejoicing over them as he did with their ancestors. For Israel will obey Yahweh's voice, do the commands written in this law book, and repent heart and soul.

This is a positive word to Judahites who now realize that the Deuteronomic curses were no empty threat. They saw them fall on their brothers and sisters in northern Israel and wonder what will become of those exiled to faraway places. The answer given here is that Yahweh will be gracious to the dispersed remnant after their punishment is over.

D. THE WORD IS VERY NEAR YOU (30:11-14)

30 **11**Indeed this commandment that I am commanding you today, it is not too wonderful for you, and it is not far off. **12**It is not in the heavens that one should say, "Who will go up for us to the heavens and get it for us, that we may hear it and do it?" **13**And it is not from across the sea that one should say, "Who will cross over for us to the other side of the sea and get it for us, that we may hear it and do it?" **14**Indeed the word is very near you, in your mouth and in your heart, to do it.

Rhetoric and Composition

These extraordinary verses on doing the covenant demands are some of the most inspiring in the OT. Positioned climactically at the center of the chapter, the verses are demarcated at the top end by a *petuḥah* in M^L and M^A and a section in Sam before v. 11 and at the bottom end by a *setumah* in M^L and M^A and a section in Sam after v. 14.

The verses are tied together by an inclusio containing an asseverative כִּי ("Indeed"):

| Indeed this commandment . . . | כִּי הַמִּצְוָה הַזֹּאת | v. 11 |
| Indeed the word . . . | כִּי הַדָּבָר . . . | v. 14 |

Portions of 30:11-14 are contained in 4QDeut[b].

Notes

30:11 *Indeed this commandment that I am commanding you today.* "This commandment" — here being synonymous with "the word" in v. 14 — refers to the written "book of the law" mentioned in v. 10, which is the Deuteronomic law code. "The/this commandment" and "the/this law" take on inclusive meaning all throughout Deuteronomy (1:5; 4:8, 44; 5:31; 6:1; 7:11; 11:22; 19:9; 27:1, 3, 8, 26; 28:58; 31:9, 11-12, etc.).

it is not too wonderful for you. לֹא־נִפְלֵאת הִוא מִמְּךָ. The verb פלא in the N-stem means "be (too) wonderful, extraordinary, too difficult," occurring in 17:8 with reference to legal cases too difficult for local officials to decide. A better text for comparison is Job 42:3, where Yahweh's questions out of the whirlwind are said by Job to be "things too wonderful (נִפְלָאוֹת) for me, which I did not know." From here we get the idea that the term denotes things beyond one's grasp or comprehension (Prov 30:18-19), which, first and foremost, are the works of God (Pss 131:1-3; 139:6, 13-18; Sir 11:4). The latter are mysterious (ibn Ezra) or hidden (T[NfPsJ]; Rashi), making the present statement close to the one in 29:28(29). Weinfeld (1972, 258-60) cites a parallel on the inaccessibility of divine knowledge in "The Babylonian Theodicy" (ca. 1000), where the friend of one who is suffering says to the sufferer: "The divine mind is as remote as the inner part of heaven, knowledge of it is difficult, humans do not know it" (Stanza XXIV; cf. Stanza VIII; Lambert 1960, 77-78, 86-87; *ANET*[3], 603-4). The point made in the present verse is that Yahweh's commandment is not beyond human grasp.

and it is not far off. The same idea, only shifting from the vertical to the horizontal. The command of Yahweh is not out of reach (NJV). In the OT, (true) wisdom, like divine knowledge, is far off (Eccl 7:23-24), for which reason the OT says "the fear of Yahweh is (the beginning of) wisdom" (Job 28:12-28; Ps 111:10; Prov 9:10).

12 Yahweh's command is not in the heavens, where divine knowledge and wisdom reside. The question nevertheless is rhetorical, since no one can ascend to the heavens. A rhetorical question along the same lines occurs in Prov 30:4 and has turned up in an old Sumerian hymn entitled "A Pessimistic Dialogue between Master and Servant," where the master says to his servant: "Who is tall enough to ascend to heaven?" (*ANET*[3], 483). Paul quotes this passage in Rom 10:5-9 in support of his faith-righteousness doctrine, leading Luther to dislike Moses' teaching. He thinks it supports works-righteousness, for which reason Paul omitted "that we may hear it and do it" here and in v. 13.

13 Not as impossible as ascending into the heavens; nevertheless, the question is still rhetorical. The sea would doubtless be the Mediterranean (ibn Ezra).

14 This is the teaching to which all the foregoing leads up. Yahweh's command — like Yahweh himself (4:7) — is very near, residing in the mouth and in the heart, which means people can carry it out. Being "in the mouth" means it can and should be memorized (31:19), and being "in the heart" means people can and should have the will to do it (heart = will). They are to talk about Yahweh's command and keep it continually before them (6:6-9; 11:18-20; cf. Josh 1:8). This teaching is a thoroughly positive one: it assumes that people can do Yahweh's law (cf. Psalm 119). But Jeremiah discovered to his sorrow that this was not happening, for which reason he announced a "new covenant" to be written on the heart (Jer 31:33). Matthew, at the close of his Sermon on the Mount, makes the point, too, that Jesus' teaching is something people can and must do (Matt 7:21-27). Jesus' yoke is easy (Matt 11:30). Luther, alas, completely misses this point.

Message and Audience

Moses now shifts back to the present, saying that the commandment he is giving the people is neither too lofty nor too far off, neither in the heavens, where someone must ascend to get it, nor across the sea, where someone must go and fetch it. It is very near, a word that can be committed to memory and one people will want to do. What is more, it is a word people can do. This word is for the Judahites in the late 8th and early 7th cents. Despite the covenant disobedience and subsequent ruin that came upon brothers and sisters up north, Yahweh's commands remain doable, and Judahites must commit themselves to carrying them out.

E. THE TWO WAYS: LIFE AND DEATH (30:15-20)

30^{15}*See I have set before you today the life and the good, and the death and the bad.* ^{16}*[If you listen to the command of Yahweh your God] that I am commanding you today, to love Yahweh your God, to walk in his ways, and to keep his commandments and his statutes and his ordinances, then you will live and you will multiply, and Yahweh your God will bless you in the land into which you are entering to possess it.* ^{17}*But if your heart turns away and you do not listen, and you are drawn away and you worship other gods and serve them,* ^{18}*I declare to you today that you shall surely perish; your days shall not be prolonged on the soil that you are crossing over the Jordan to enter to take possession of it.* ^{19}*I call to witness against you today the heavens and the earth: Life and death I have set before you, blessing and curse, so you can choose life in order that you and your descendants may live,* ^{20}*to love Yahweh your God, to obey his voice, and to cling to him, for it is your life and the prolonging of your days to dwell on the soil that Yahweh swore to your fathers, to Abraham, to Isaac, and to Jacob, to give to them.*

Rhetoric and Composition

Moses' discourse inviting Israel to enter a sworn covenant with Yahweh concludes with an exhortation on "the two ways." The verses are delimited at the

Deuteronomy 30

top end by a *setumah* in M^L and M^A and a section in Sam before v. 15 and at the bottom end by a *petuḥah* in M^L and M^A and a section in Sam after v. 20, which is also the chapter division. 1QDeut^b also has a section after v. 20 (Barthélemy and Milik 1955, 59).

The unit is tied together by a keyword inclusio:

I have set before you today	נָתַתִּי לְפָנֶיךָ הַיּוֹם	v. 15
today . . . I have set before you	הַיּוֹם נָתַתִּי לְפָנֶיךָ	v. 19

The expression "I have set before you" also began 30:1.

Portions of 30:15-20 are contained in 1QDeut^b and 4QDeut,^{k3} also in a Qumran document entitled "The Two Ways" (4Q473).

Notes

30:15 There are "two ways" Israel can go: one leading to life, the other to death. The way to life is obeying the commandments; the way to death is disobeying them. "The good" (הַטּוֹב) refers here to prosperity (26:11; cf. Pss 25:13; 34:11, 13[10, 12]; 103:5; Job 21:13; 22:18), the cognate verb occurring frequently in Deuteronomy in the expression "that it may go well (יִיטַב) with you" (see Note for 4:40). "The bad" (הָרָע), or "the evil," refers here to "misfortune" (cf. Jer 7:6; 25:7; Ps 10:6; Prov 13:17). Ibn Ezra says "good" refers to prosperity, health, and honor and "evil" to the reverse of these (NJV: "prosperity . . . adversity"). The promise of reward and threat of punishment, so prominent in Wisdom literature, is a motif running all through Deuteronomy (Weinfeld 1960b). It carries over into the later preaching of Jeremiah, who may have recast the present words in his "two ways" sermon of Jer 21:8-10, where the way to life was surrendering to the Babylonians and the way to death was holding out in Jerusalem. This and other "two ways" teachings appear in Jer 6:16; 26:3-6; 38:2, 17-18; 42:7-22. In Jer 6:16 the prophet says he called Judahites to walk in the "good way" (דֶּרֶךְ הַטּוֹב), but they refused. Other prophets preached about seeking good and not evil (Amos 5:14-15; Isa 1:16-17; Mic 3:2). The "two ways" theme appears also in Josh 24:14-15; 1 Kgs 18:21; Psalms 1; 119; Prov 2:12-15, and elsewhere. In the NT, see Matt 7:13-14.

A Qumran text has turned up (4Q473) that imitates the present discourse. The relevant lines:

> . . . He sets [before you life and death(?) . . . before you are] t[wo] ways, one goo[d and one evil. If you walk in the good way He will guard you(?)] and bless you. But, if you walk in the [evil] way, [He will curse you and revile

Deuteronomy 30

you(?), and evil] He will br[ing] upon you and destroy you [. . .], and blight, snow, ice, and hai[l . . .] with all the angel[s of destruction(?) . . .] (Brooke et al. 1996, 292-94)

The editor notes that the style resembles "Words of Moses" (1Q22), another Qumran document in which Moses recalls Yahweh's deeds in the exodus, then exhorts and warns Israel to obey the commands and ordinances before it enters the land (Barthélemy and Milik 1955, 91-96).

See I have set before you. On this stereotyped Deuteronomic expression, see Note for 1:8.

16 The LXX begins the verse with ἐὰν εἰσακούσῃς τὰς ἐντολὰς κυρίου τοῦ θεοῦ σου ("If you listen to the commandment of the Lord your God"), which appears to have been lost in MT (cf. RSV; NEB; JB; NAB; NRSV; REB; NJB). Assuming an initial אם ("If") in the Hebrew clause (cf. v. 17), the loss can be due to haplography (homoeoarcton: א . . . א).

to love Yahweh your God. On the command that Israel love Yahweh, a major Deuteronomic theme, see Note for 6:5.

to walk in his ways, and to keep his commandments and his statutes and his ordinances. Deuteronomy continually admonishes people to walk in the way(s) of Yahweh (see Note for 5:33), where the term "way" (דֶּרֶךְ) carries strong ethical implications (Muilenburg 1961b). Loving Yahweh and walking in his ways means keeping the commandments. The LXX has a different order: decrees, commandments, ordinances.

then you will live and you will multiply. Keeping the commandments is the way to life (vv. 6, 19-20 and Note for 4:1). Yahweh wants Israel to multiply (see Note for 6:3).

and Yahweh your God will bless you in the land. Another benefit accruing from covenant obedience (7:12-13; 28:8-9).

17 See earlier 29:16(17). For the importance placed in Deuteronomy on worshipping and serving Yahweh only, see Note for 6:13. The verb נדח in the N-stem means "be drawn away, allow oneself to be led astray" (cf. 4:19).

18 The apodosis (see 4:25-26; 8:19). The LXX omits "to enter." On the stereotypical language in the latter part of the verse, see Note for 4:25-26.

19 *I call to witness against you today the heavens and the earth.* Since Yahweh is party to the sworn covenant, heaven and earth are summoned as witnesses (4:26; cf. 31:28; 32:1).

Life and death I have set before you, blessing and curse. Repeating v. 15: life is the blessing; death is the curse. See also 11:26-28. The blessing (הַבְּרָכָה) and the curse (הַקְּלָלָה) refer to good fortune and misfortune (see 30:1 and Note for 29:26). Blessings and curses occur frequently in the Qumran literature (see B. Nitzan, "Blessings and Curses," in *EDSS*, 1:95-100).

Deuteronomy 30

so you can choose life in order that you and your descendants may live. The verb בחר ("choose") is a favorite of the Deuteronomic writer, used often with theological implications (see Note for 12:5). On doing the commandments as the way to life, see 30:6, 16 and Note for 4:1. This applies also to the people's descendants.

20 *to love Yahweh your God*. See v. 16 and Note for 6:5.

to obey his voice. See 30:2, 8, 10 and Note for 13:5.

and to cling to him. וּלְדָבְקָה־בוֹ. A stock Deuteronomic idiom expressing devotion to Yahweh (see Note for 4:3-4).

for it is your life and the prolonging of your days to dwell on the soil that Yahweh swore to your fathers, to Abraham, to Isaac, and to Jacob, to give to them. Ibn Ezra translates "for He (i.e., Yahweh) is your life" (so also Friedman). Obeying Yahweh's voice, doing the commands, loving him, and remaining close to him will mean life and longevity in the land (32:47; Malamat 1982, 218). The idiom "prolong(ing)/not prolong(ing) your days" is stock in Deuteronomy (see Note for 4:26). The promise of land was made to the fathers (see Note for 1:8).

Message and Audience

Moses tells the people at the close of this covenant renewal ceremony that they have two ways to walk. Joshua will repeat the same before he dies (Joshua 24). One way leads to life and good fortune, the other to death and misfortune. The road to life consists in loving Yahweh, walking in his ways, and keeping his commandments. Not only will Israel live by walking in this way, it will multiply and enjoy Yahweh's blessing in the land it is about to enter. The other way consists of turning away from Yahweh and going after other gods, worshipping them and serving them, and if the people choose to walk in this way, they will perish. Their days will not be long in the land they are now entering. Heaven and earth are witnesses to the choice put before the people, the blessing and the curse, and the people are admonished to choose life, for their own sake and for the sake of their descendants. Speaking of descendants, the people are reminded of the promise made to Abraham, Isaac, and Jacob, from whom they have descended.

For a late 8th- and early 7th-cent. Judahite audience, this is a sober reminder about not letting what happened to northern Israel happen to them. They have just been told that doing the commands is not difficult and now are reminded that covenant fidelity is a life-and-death matter.

Deuteronomy 31

X. SECOND SUPPLEMENT (CHS. 31-34)

A. MOSES' DEATH DRAWS NEAR (31:1-32:52)

1. I Cannot Cross Over This Jordan (31:1-6)

31¹*So Moses went and spoke these words to all Israel, ²and said to them: "A hundred and twenty years I am today; I am no longer able to go out and come in, and Yahweh said to me, 'You cannot cross over this Jordan.' ³Yahweh your God, he will cross over before you, he will completely destroy these nations before you, so you will dispossess them; Joshua, he will cross over before you, as Yahweh has spoken. ⁴And Yahweh will do to them as he did to Sihon and to Og, kings of the Amorites, and to their land, when he completely destroyed them. ⁵And Yahweh will give them over before you, and you shall do to them according to all the commandment that I have commanded you. ⁶Be strong and be bold; do not fear and do not tremble before them, for Yahweh your God, he is the one going with you; he will not abandon you and will not forsake you."*

Rhetoric and Composition

Chapter 31 begins a second and final supplement to an expanded Deuteronomy, concluding with Moses' death and burial in ch. 34. The discourse of chs. 29-30 having ended, it remains only to complete the Deuteronomic law book — later the entire Pentateuch — by adding narrative that contains (1) a directive to Moses to write down this new law and entrust it to the Levites; (2) a warning to Israel about covenant disobedience in the future; (3) the commission of Joshua as Moses' successor; and (4) a report of Moses' death and burial.

Chapters 31-34, like early chapters in the book, contain direct speech from Moses in third-person narrative (31:1, 7, 9-10a, 14b; cf. 5:1; 29:1[2]). Included is also some direct speech from Yahweh, also in third-person narrative (31:14a, 16-21, 23; 32:48-52; 34:4), which is a rarity in Deuteronomy (cf. 1:37-40). This final supplement contains in addition two old poems: the Song of Moses (32:1-43) and the Blessing of Moses (33:1-29).

The supplement has an identifiable framing structure. At the core is the Song of Moses (32:1-43), an extraordinary poem on either side of which is prose narrative in 31:24-30 and 32:44-47 (Lundbom 1976, 299-300; 1990, 55-63). This prose contains a keyword chiasmus serving to transform Moses' "song" into a "law" (see Rhetoric and Composition for 31:24-30). The framing mode of composition continues with more prose placed up front (31:14-23) and in back (32:48-52), both of these narratives containing Yahweh's direct speech to Moses and to Joshua. In 31:14-23 is another framing structure:

Yahweh's call for the commissioning of Joshua (vv. 14-15)
  Yahweh's command that Moses write a song (vv. 16-22)
Yahweh's words of commission to Joshua (v. 23)

Earlier scholars argued that vv. 14-23 were not part of the Deuteronomic work. For example, Driver (1895, 336-38) noted different vocabulary and phraseology in the verses. Be that as it may, v. 23 has not suffered displacement (Driver and von Rad wanted to put it after vv. 14-15). What we have is simply another framing structure in which complementary passages are made to balance one other.

The supplement is then expanded with the addition of 31:9-13, which contains the following keyword and thematic chiasmus:

a   *Moses writing* the *law* and entrusting it to the *Levites* (vv. 9-13)
   b   *Yahweh's* call for the *charge* to *Joshua* (vv. 14-15)
     c   *Yahweh's* command that Moses write a song (vv. 16-22)
   b'   *Yahweh's* words of *charge* to *Joshua* (v. 23)
a'   *Moses* finishing the *writing* of the *law* and entrusting it to the *Levites* (vv. 24-30)

Von Rad believed that vv. 9-13 and vv. 24-29 were doublets. But, once again, we see that they are better taken as complementary units balancing one another in a rhetorical structure.

Filling out the larger structure is the Blessing of Moses (ch. 33), another old poem believed to predate the Song of Moses, with the prose of 31:1-8 placed up front and the prose of 34:1-12 placed at back. The book of Deuteronomy is thus brought to completion. Noth (1981, 13) believed that 31:1-8 contained elements of a Deuteronomistic narrative establishing a direct link to Joshua 1, which may be the case. It does appear that Josh 1:6-9 establishes continuity with Deut 31:1-8.

The present verses are delimited at the top end by a *petuḥah* in M^L and M^A and a section in Sam before v. 1, which is also the chapter division. Delimitation at the bottom end is by a *petuḥah* in M^L, a *setumah* in M^A, and a section in Sam after v. 6.

Portions of 31:1-6 are contained in 1QDeut^b.

Notes

31:1 An introduction to the final supplement in 31-34. "These words" refer to what follows in vv. 2-6, as the Targums all recognize, not to words previously spoken (G. E. Wright; AV; RSV; JB; NJB; NIV; *pace* Driver, Tigay; Nelson).

Verse 2 continues: "and (he) said to them." The LXX translates as if Moses is concluding a prior discourse: καὶ συνετέλεσεν Μωυσῆς λαλῶν ("and Moses finished speaking"); similarly 1QDeut[b]: ויכל משה לדבר (Barthélemy and Milik 1955, 59 no. 13). This latter reading occurs in 32:45 in both MT and LXX, where it is correct (cf. Gen 44:6; Num 14:39). Driver, thinking that the present phrase refers to words already spoken, nevertheless recognizes that the words in question cannot be what is contained in chs. 29–30, since that discourse has already been introduced in 29:1(2). Nelson thinks v. 1 closes the speech begun in 28:69, which cannot be the case, since 28:69 is a subscription concluding the First Edition of Deuteronomy (see Rhetoric and Composition for 28:69). Wevers (1995, 490) thinks the LXX takes v. 1 as a subscription concluding chs. 1–30 and v. 2 as a new beginning to chs. 31–33. But the better reading is the reading of MT, which takes the verse as introducing vv. 2-6.

So Moses went and spoke. וַיֵּלֶךְ מֹשֶׁה וַיְדַבֵּר. Where Moses came from and where he went are not indicated. Targum[PsJ] has him going to address Israel in the "Tent of Instruction" (cf. v. 14). The expression "and Moses came (וַיָּבֹא) and spoke" occurs in 32:44.

these words to all Israel. 1QDeut[b] no. 13 has "all these words"; other MSS and ancient Versions also supply "all" before "these words." But this reading is more cumbersome when followed by "all Israel." "All Israel" is standard in narrative portions of Deuteronomy (Driver; cf. 1:1; 31:7, 11, etc.). The LXX has πάντας υἱοὺς Ισραηλ ("all the sons of Israel").

2 *A hundred and twenty years I am today.* Moses is the only person in the Bible to achieve the ideal life span set forth in Gen 6:3. See again 34:7. A life span of 120 years occurs in the ancient Sumerian folktale "Enlil and Namzitarra" (lines 23-24), which speaks of the uselessness of accumulating wealth when life is so short; you die and can take nothing to the grave (J. Klein 1990). In Egyptian literature the ideal life span is 110 years ($ANET^3$, 414 n 33; cf. Gen 50:26, where Joseph's age at the time of his death in Egypt is 110 years). Joshua, too, dies at 110 years (Josh 24:29). Psalm 90:10 puts the normal lifespan at 70, perhaps 80.

I am no longer able to go out and come in. I.e., I can no longer give leadership, particularly in military engagements. On this meaning for "go out and come in" *(merismus),* see also Num 27:17, 21; Josh 14:11; 1 Sam 18:13, 16; 29:6; 1 Kgs 3:7.

and Yahweh said to me, "You cannot cross over this Jordan." After Moses defeated Sihon and Og and settled Israelite tribes in the Transjordan, he requested permission to cross the Jordan and enter the promised land, but the request was denied (1:37; 3:23-27).

3 Three emphatic "he" (הוּא) pronouns drive home two basic points: (1) Yahweh will be the driving force in the conquest (9:3); and (2) Joshua will be

Israel's leader (cf. 1:38; 3:28). The verb שׁמד here and in v. 4 is an internal H-stem with intensive meaning: "completely destroy."

4 The successful battles against Sihon and Og were reported in 2:26–3:11. In 3:21 Moses reminded Joshua of Yahweh's role in conducting holy war, promising now the same success when kings across the Jordan are engaged. On Sihon, king of Heshbon, see Note for 2:24. On Og, king of Bashan, see Note for 3:1.

5 The commandment is that Canaan's inhabitants be completely destroyed so their religious practices will not ensnare Israel (7:1-5; 20:16-18). For the Deuteronomic idiom "Yahweh gave/will give them over before you," see Note for 2:31.

6 *Be strong and be bold.* חִזְקוּ וְאִמְצוּ. A stock Deuteronomic expression occurring again in vv. 7 and 23 (see Note for 3:28), used to muster warriors for holy war (Weinfeld 1972, 45-51).

do not fear and do not tremble before them. אַל־תִּירְאוּ וְאַל־תַּעַרְצוּ מִפְּנֵיהֶם. More stereotyped language preparing warriors for battle (see Notes for 1:20-21 and 1:29).

for Yahweh your God, he is the one going with you. Yahweh's presence in the upcoming battle is stressed with another emphatic "he" (הוּא) pronoun (cf. v. 8; 20:1, 4). Yahweh's assurance that *he will be with* the people is the premier promise of the OT (see vv. 8, 23 and Note for 20:1).

he will not abandon you and will not forsake you. On this promise see v. 8 and Note for 4:31. In the NT, see Heb 13:5. But in Deut 31:17 Yahweh says on that day in the future when Israel breaks the covenant he will forsake them.

Message and Audience

Moses in this final addendum to the book of Deuteronomy informs Israel about his advanced age and inability to continue as the people's leader. He is 120 years old, which according to one reckoning is the maximum human life span in antiquity. Moses' life has been full, but he is no longer able to direct Israel's battles. What is more, Yahweh told him earlier that he could not cross the Jordan, even though he may only have wanted to step foot in it.

Moses then emphatically tells the people that Yahweh will be with them in the Jordan crossing, will destroy the nations living in the land, and Israel will receive their land as a possession. Moreover, Joshua will cross with them as their leader, as Yahweh has said. Yahweh will do to the inhabitants of the land as he did to the Amorite kings, Sihon and Og. When these other peoples are given into Israel's hand, Israel must completely destroy them as Yahweh commanded. Moses does not say it here, but nothing less than a complete destruction is called for in order to eradicate Canaanite religious practices, which would compromise the worship of Yahweh. The people are then given the charge presented to warriors on the eve of battle, to be strong and bold, not to fear or tremble before the enemy, for Yahweh will go with them and not abandon them.

2. Joshua to Head the Army, the Law Entrusted to the Levites and Elders (31:7-13)

a) Joshua Receives Charge from Moses (31:7-8)

31 ⁷*Then Moses called to Joshua and said to him before the eyes of all Israel: "Be strong and be bold, for you, you shall enter with this people into the land that Yahweh swore to their fathers to give to them, and you, you shall cause them to inherit it. ⁸And Yahweh, he is the one going before you, he, he will be with you; he will not abandon you and will not forsake you; do not fear and do not be dismayed."*

b) A Public Reading of the Law Every Seven Years! (31:9-13)

31 ⁹*And Moses wrote this law and gave it to the priests, the sons of Levi, the ones who carried the ark of the covenant of Yahweh, and to all the elders of Israel. ¹⁰And Moses commanded them: "After seven years' time, at the appointed time of the year of remission, at the Feast of Booths, ¹¹when all Israel comes to appear before Yahweh your God, in the place that he will choose, you shall recite this law in front of all Israel in their hearing. ¹²Assemble the people, the men and the women and the little ones, also your sojourner who is within your gates, so that they may hear and so that they may learn to fear Yahweh your God and be careful to do all the words of this law; ¹³yes, their children who have not known may hear and may learn to fear Yahweh your God all the days that you live on the soil that you are crossing over the Jordan to take possession of it."*

Rhetoric and Composition

The present verses report Moses' encourgement of Joshua, his successor (vv. 7-8), then his writing down of the Deuteronomic law and entrusting it to the Levites and elders. The latter are to make a public reading of it every seven years at the Feast of Booths (vv. 9-13). The encouragement of Joshua, along with Moses' earlier word about not being able to enter the promised land (31:1-8), are balanced in this final supplement with 34:1-12. The directive to write down the

Deuteronomy 31

Deuteronomic law and see that it is read every seven years is balanced in a rhetorical structure with the directive to write down Moses' Song, recite it to the people, and preserve it for future generations in vv. 24-30 (see Rhetoric and Composition for 31:1-6). The present unit is delimited at the top end by a *petuḥah* in M[L], a *setumah* in M[A], and a section in Sam before v. 7. Delimitation at the bottom end is by a *petuḥah* in M[L] and M[A] and a section in Sam, after v. 13.

Portions of 31:7-13 are contained in 1QDeut[b], 4QDeut[b], 4QDeut[h], and 4QDeut[l].

Notes

31:7 *Then Moses called to Joshua and said to him before the eyes of all Israel.* Moses calls his successor Joshua to encourage him publicly about the upcoming wars to take the promised land. Moses was told earlier to do this (1:38; 3:28).

before the eyes of all Israel. See again 34:12. On the Deuteronomic expression "before the eyes," see Note for 1:30. It is important that Joshua be encouraged and later commissioned in a public assembly, which will ratify his appointment before the people.

"*Be strong and be bold, for you, you shall enter with this people into the land that Yahweh swore to their fathers to give to them.* The "be strong and be bold" charge will be repeated in the commissioning (31:23). The people received the same (31:6; see Note for 3:28). Added pronouns twice in the verse are for emphasis (see v. 3). On the land sworn to Israel's fathers, see Note for 1:8.

and you, you shall cause them to inherit it. Yahweh's gift of the land constitutes Israel's inheritance (see Note for 15:4). Joshua will enable Israel to receive it (1:38; 3:28).

8 *And Yahweh, he is the one going before you, he, he will be with you.* Added pronouns continue, here emphasizing Yahweh's role in directing the holy war (cf. 31:3). On Yahweh's "going before" the people, see Note for 1:30. Yahweh's "I will be with you" promise occurs also in vv. 6 (inverted) and 23 (see Note for 20:1).

he will not abandon you and will not forsake you. See v. 6.

do not fear and do not be dismayed." On this Deuteronomic phrase, see Note for 1:20-21.

9 This "law" (Heb תּוֹרָה) is the Deuteronomic Code (Noth 1981, 13), called a "(sworn) covenant" in 28:69(29:1); 29:1-28(2-29). Here and in v. 12 it is not the "Song of Moses" (*pace* Fishbane 1972, 350), though the term "law" becomes that in v. 24 and in 32:46 (see Rhetoric and Composition for 31:24-30). This Deuteronomic law (and covenant), which has been given orally in the plains of Moab, accepted by Israel in a solemn ceremony, must now be written

Deuteronomy 31

to instruct future generations. Blessings and curses on a written document are anticipated in 28:58, 61; 29:19-20, 26(20-21, 27); 30:10. Earlier, Yahweh is said to have written (and rewritten) the Decalogue on stone tablets at Horeb, then given them to Moses for the purpose of teaching people and their children (4:10-14; 5:22; 10:1-5; cf. Exod 31:18; 32:16; 34:28). In Exod 20:1; 24:3-8, Moses delivered the Covenant Code to an assembly, then wrote it down. For other readings of written law, see Deut 27:1-8; Josh 8:30-35; 2 Kgs 23:2; Nehemiah 8.

Written law codes existed throughout the ancient world, some much earlier than the written law codes of Israel (see *Introduction: The Deuteronomic Law Code*). In Israel we see the beginnings here of a scriptural canon (von Rad; Tigay; cf. Jeremiah 36). This written law is turned over to the Levitical priests, who are the teachers in ancient Israel (33:10; Zeph 3:4; Jer 18:18; Ezek 7:26; Mal 2:7; Hag 2:10-14; 2 Chr 15:3; 17:8-9; 35:3), and the elders. One or both take custody of the scroll, but their more important obligation is to see that the law gets a public reading every seven years at the Feast of Booths (vv. 10-11). Elders were called upon to assist Moses in the wilderness (see Note for 5:23-24), and the Levitical priests, in anticipation of settlement in the land, were to assist the judges in adjudicating difficult cases at the central sanctuary (see Note for 17:8).

And Moses wrote this law. The LXX and 4QDeut[h] add "into a book" (cf. v. 24). On a written Deuteronomic law, see Note for 28:61.

the priests, the sons of Levi. I.e., the Levitical priests (see Note on 12:12).

the ones who carried the ark of the covenant of Yahweh. The ark of the covenant, a sacred object and symbol of Yahweh's presence in early Israel (Exod 25:10-22; 37:1-9; 1 Sam 4:3-4, 21-22), was in the charge of the Levites (Deut 10:8; 31:25-26; Josh 8:32-33; Num 3:31; 4:15). It went with the people in holy war and later was kept in the temple's holy of holies (1 Kgs 8:6). On the symbolic significance of the ark and its portrayal in pentateuchal sources, see Haran 1959; 1960a.

and to all the elders of Israel. Targums[NfPsJ] have "wise men" instead of "elders."

10-11 The LXX and perhaps also 4QDeut[h] (Ulrich, Cross et al. 1995, 67) add "on that day" after "Moses commanded them" (cf. 27:11). G. E. Wright believes that over a period of years this once-in-seven-year proclamation took place at Shechem (27:1-26) and was probably not continued at the Jerusalem temple. Yet according to the Mishnah (*Sotah* 7:8), Herod Agrippa I (10 B.C. to A.D. 44) carried out the directive, reading the law publicly at the Feast of Booths.

after seven years. I.e., at the end of six years. On this expression, see Note for 15:1.

at the appointed time. בְּמֹעֵד. The term denotes a fixed time in the calendar, determined by movements of the heavenly bodies (Gen 1:14; Exod 23:15; 34:18; Ps 104:19).

the year of remission. שְׁנַת הַשְּׁמִטָּה. Debts are to be remitted every seven years (15:1-11), being an appropriate occasion for the reading of the law since it will remind people to carry out this — and other — important obligations.

Feast of Booths. The yearly autumn festival celebrating the end of the harvest season, lasting seven days (16:13-15). A large number of people will be present, another good reason for a public reading.

11 *when all Israel comes to appear before Yahweh your God, in the place that he will choose.* The Feast of Booths is a pilgrimage to the central sanctuary (16:15), which later is to the Jerusalem temple. On the role of the central sanctuary in Deuteronomy, see Note for 12:5.

you shall recite this law. תִּקְרָא אֶת־הַתּוֹרָה הַזֹּאת. The verb in MT is singular, perhaps indicating that a single priest shall do the reading. Rashi says it will be the king (cf. 17:18-20; 2 Kgs 23:2); Weinfeld (1972, 65 n. 1) thinks it will be Joshua, Moses' successor. But the LXX has "you (plural) shall read" (ἀναγνώσεσθε), which is supported by תקראו in 4QDeut[b] (Ulrich, Cross et al. 1995, 12). The law was given to priests and elders, so a plural verb would be suitable here. The verb קרא means "recite, read aloud" (see Note for 17:19).

12 In ordinary years, only adult males are obligated to attend the sacred festivals (16:16), but for this celebration women, small children, and sojourners are also expected to be present. Josephus (*Ant.* iv.209) says that even slaves should not be excluded from the audience. Reading the law will instill the fear of Yahweh in the people (4:10) and get them to obey the terms of the covenant. On "fearing Yahweh" in Deuteronomy, see Note for 4:10. On the importance of *doing* the covenant, see Note for 4:6.

Assemble the people. הַקְהֵל אֶת־הָעָם. At Horeb people were assembled to hear the Decalogue (4:10; 5:22). On this particular assembly, where people are to hear the Deuteronomic law, see also 5:1-3; 29:9-14(10-15).

the men and the women and the little ones. Rashi follows T[PsJ], which says: "the men to learn, the women to hear instruction." But the text makes no such distinction. On the importance placed in Deuteronomy of teaching the law to children, see 4:9-10; 6:7, 20-25; 11:19.

also your sojourner who is within your gates. On the sojourner (גֵּר), who will be a resident alien living in Israelite cities and towns, see Note for 5:13-14.

that they may learn to fear Yahweh your God. 4QDeut[l] has "their God" instead of "your God" (Ulrich, Cross et al. 1995, 111), which has the support of some Heb and LXX MSS, also the Sam.

and be careful to do all the words of this law. On the recurring expression "to be careful to do" in Deuteronomy, see Note for 5:1. Keeping Yahweh's commands and learning to fear Yahweh are closely associated in Deuteronomy (5:29; 6:2, 24; 8:6; 10:12-13; 13:5[4]; 17:19 [with reference to the king]; 28:58; 31:12).

13 *yes, their children who have not known.* וּבְנֵיהֶם אֲשֶׁר לֹא־יָדְעוּ. The *waw* on וּבְנֵיהֶם is best taken as emphatic: "especially their children . . ." (Tigay). Children not yet born must learn the commands so they come to fear Yahweh throughout life (see Note for 4:9). On the concept of "corporate personality" in ancient Israel, see H. W. Robinson 1936; Weinfeld 1976a, 392.

all the days that you live on the soil that you are crossing over the Jordan to take possession of it." On this stereotypical language of Deuteronomy, see Notes for 4:10 and 4:26.

Message and Audience

Moses was earlier told by Yahweh that he could not enter the promised land and that the task of bringing Israel in would fall to Joshua, his successor. So now Moses calls Joshua to charge him in the presence of all the people. Joshua is to be strong and bold, for he will lead Israel into the land promised ages ago to the fathers. Yahweh, Moses stresses, will go before him, and to Joshua is given the all-sufficient "I will be with you" promise, given earlier to Moses when Yahweh called him to lead Israel out of Egypt. Yahweh will not abandon Joshua, so he need not be afraid.

In the second segment Moses is said to have written down the Deuteronomic law and given it to the Levitical priests and elders. Levitical priests had custody of the ark of the covenant, and to them was entrusted the responsibility of teaching Israel Yahweh's law. Now Moses says they are to read the law publicly every seven years at the Feast of Booths, in the same year that debts are to be remitted. The place is to be the central sanctuary. Everyone is to be there: men, women, small children, and sojourners living in Israel's towns and villages. The purpose of this public reading will be to instill the fear of Yahweh in the people and to admonish them to carry out Yahweh's law. In closing, Moses emphasizes that Israel's children, who have not known the law, may in this way hear it and learn thereby to fear Yahweh all the days of their life.

3. Yahweh Addresses Moses and Joshua (31:14-23)

a) Joshua to Receive His Charge (31:14-15)

31 [14]*And Yahweh said to Moses, "Look, your days to die are drawing near; call Joshua, and present yourselves in the tent of meeting that I may charge him." So Moses and Joshua went and presented themselves in the tent of meeting.* [15]*And Yahweh appeared in the tent in a pillar of cloud, and the pillar of cloud stood by the entrance of the tent.*

b) Moses to Write a Song (31:16-22)

31:16 Then Yahweh said to Moses, "Look, you are going to sleep with your fathers, and this people will rise up and go whoring after the foreign gods of the land into which it comes, in its midst, and it will forsake me and break my covenant that I cut with it. 17 Then my anger will burn against it in that day, and I will forsake them and I will hide my face from them, and it will be for consuming, and many evils and troubles will find it, and it will say in that day, 'Is it not because my God is not in my midst that these evils have found me?' 18 And I, I will surely hide my face in that day, on account of all the evil that it did, because it turned to other gods. 19 And now, write for yourselves this song; and teach it to the children of Israel, put it in their mouths in order that this song will be a witness for me against the children of Israel. 20 When I bring it into the land that I swore to its fathers, flowing with milk and honey, and it eats and is sated and grows fat, and turns to other gods and serves them, and spurns me and breaks my covenant, 21 then it will happen that many evils and troubles will find it, and this song will testify before it as a witness (for it will not be forgotten in the mouth of its descendants); for I know its imagination, what it is doing today before I bring it into the land that I swore." 22 And Moses wrote this song in that day, and he taught it to the children of Israel.

c) The Charge to Joshua (31:23)

31:23 Then he charged Joshua son of Nun, and said, "Be strong and be bold, for you, you shall bring the children of Israel into the land that I swore to them, and I, I will be with you."

Rhetoric and Composition

The present verses are part of a rhetorical structure comprising 31:9-30 (see Rhetoric and Composition for 31:1-6), distinguished by Yahweh addressing Moses and Joshua directly. The text is not in disorder, as imagined by Driver and von Rad, who believed v. 23 was displaced and should be joined to vv. 14-15. Divine speech about and to Joshua is intentionally divided to frame the divine speech to Moses about writing a song: (1) Yahweh instructs Moses to appear with Joshua at the tent of meeting for Joshua's commissioning (vv. 14-15); (2) Yahweh commands Moses to write a song to witness against Israel's future infidelity (vv. 16-22); and (3) Yahweh gives Joshua his charge (v. 23).

Segment 1 is delimited at the top by a *petuḥah* in M^L and M^A and a section in Sam before v. 14 and at the bottom by a *setumah* in M^L and a section in Sam after v. 15. M^A has no section here. Sam has other sections after vv. 18 and 21.

Segment 2 is delimited at the top but not at the bottom, with no section markings present in M^L and M^A after v. 22. Sam is also lacking a section after v. 22. Segment 3 is not delimited at top or bottom in M^L or M^A, although Sam has a section after v. 23.

It is argued that vv. 14-23 have been inserted into preexisting narrative and that vv. 14-15 and v. 23, which divide up the charge to Joshua, is yet another addition (Driver; A. J. Levy 1931, 3; Noth 1981, 35). Driver says vv. 14-23 show an affinity with JE narrative in the Pentateuch. The argument that these verses emanate from a different source has some force. Certain words and phrases, e.g., "tent of meeting"; "pillar of cloud"; "break a covenant"; "turn to (other gods)"; "imagination," etc., appear here and nowhere else in Deuteronomy (Driver 1895, 337). Some of this terminology (vv. 17-18, 20) echoes the Song in ch. 32, which is to be expected, since vv. 16-22 purport to give the Song a context. Another reason for taking vv. 14-23 as a separate source is that Yahweh here addresses Moses and Joshua directly, a rarity in Deuteronomy.

Portions of 31:14-23 are contained in 4QDeut^b and 4QDeut^c.

Notes

31:14 *"Look, your days to die are drawing near.* הֵן קָרְבוּ יָמֶיךָ לָמוּת. The expression occurs in Gen 47:29; 1 Kgs 2:1. Hebrew הֵן ("Look") is a short form of הִנֵּה (cf. v. 27; Jer 3:1).

present yourselves. Hebrew הִתְיַצְּבוּ is lit. "take your stand" (Exod 8:16[20]; 9:13; 19:17; 34:5; Num 11:16; 23:3, 15; Josh 24:1, etc.).

in the tent of meeting. בְּאֹהֶל מוֹעֵד. The אֹהֶל מוֹעֵד was a sacred tent surviving from the wilderness where Yahweh would meet Moses and converse with him (Exod 29:42; 30:36; Num 1:1). When Moses entered the tent, a pillar of cloud (= Yahweh's glory) would descend and stand at the entrance of the tent (Exod 33:7-11; Num 11:16-17; 12:5). According to Haran (1960a, 55-56), the theophany would not occur inside the tent, but outside, where the pillar was standing at the entrance. Ibn Ezra says Yahweh appeared within the tent. In his view, the cloud descended and stopped at the entrance. Joshua constantly attended the tent (Exod 33:11), but now together with Moses he will hear the divine word — either inside the tent or at the entrance — when he is given the charge to be Moses' successor. The OT appears to preserve two traditions concerning the tent of meeting. According to one, the tent is identical with the tabernacle (מִשְׁכָּן), God's residence located in the center of the camp (Rashi; ibn Ezra; cf. Num 2:17). The tabernacle is a precursor to the Jerusalem temple. But in another tradition, the tent is situated outside the camp (Exod 33:7-11; Num 11:26-27; 12:4). Some think the two tents are one and the same (de Vaux 1971b, 136-37), but a rabbinic source speaks of two separate tents, one inside the camp for cultic purposes, the other outside for the giving of oracles (Haran 1960a, 58; Milgrom 1990a, 386-87). On the tabernacle and tent of meeting, see further R. E. Friedman, "Tabernacle" in *ABD,* 6:292-300.

that I may charge him." וַאֲצַוֶּנּוּ. Yahweh's charge will be a commissioning to holy office. It will also encourage and strengthen him, as did the charge by Moses in vv. 7-8 (cf. 3:28).

15 *And Yahweh appeared in the tent in a pillar of cloud.* וַיֵּרָא יְהוָה בָּאֹהֶל בְּעַמּוּד עָנָן. The LXX verb is κατέβη ("came down"), perhaps reflecting Num 12:5 (cf. Exod 33:9). In Num 27:18-23 Joshua's commissioning takes place before Eleazar the priest and the people, and there Moses is the one laying hands upon him.

a pillar of cloud. The means whereby Yahweh descends to earth (Exod 19:9; 34:5; Num 11:25), sometimes embellished with chariot imagery (Ps 104:3). The latter appears in Ugaritic texts, where Baal's epithet is "Rider of the Clouds." Yahweh, too, is said to "ride upon the clouds" in Ps 68:5(4). In Priestly material fire and clouds reveal Yahweh's bright, shining glory (כָּבוֹד), manifesting a divine presence but at the same time keeping it hidden (G. E. Wright; Weinfeld 1972, 202-4; Exod 16:10; 33:18-23; 40:34-38; Num 17:7[16:42]; cf. Ezekiel 10; 11:22-23).

by the entrance of the tent. עַל־פֶּתַח הָאֹהֶל. 4QDeut[b] omits the preposition עַל, which is also lacking in Exod 33:9.

16 *"Look, you are going to sleep with your fathers.* A euphemism for "you are going to die," where "to sleep" means "to lie down" (Gen 47:30; 2 Sam 7:12; 1 Kgs 2:10; 11:43). In 32:50 the expression is "to be gathered to one's people."

and this people will rise up and go whoring after the foreign gods of the land. Anticipated violation of the first commandment (5:7), where reference is to worshipping foreign gods after Israel has entered Canaan. Here, as in vv. 15-18 of the Song, a note of pessimism is struck about Israel keeping the covenant. Deuteronomic preaching up to this point has been more positive, usually just warning against disobedience and in some cases assuming that Israel will be obedient. Even in chs. 29–30, where the curses of ch. 28 have already fallen (29:27[28]) and Israel has experienced exile (30:1-10), the concluding words in 29:28[29] and especially 30:11-20 remain positive. In 30:11-20 people are told that Yahweh's commands are not too difficult to carry out and that they should therefore choose life over death. Now it seems disobedience is a foregone conclusion. Moran says: "The sins of the future will not catch God by surprise."

this people. A coinage conveying distance and censure. Cf. "this people" in Exod 32:9, 21; Num 14:11; Isa 6:9-10; 8:11-12 and "this son of yours" in Luke 15:30.

and go whoring after the foreign gods of the land. וְזָנָה אַחֲרֵי אֱלֹהֵי נֵכַר־הָאָרֶץ. To "go whoring" indicates prostitution or other sexual misconduct less serious than adultery (22:21; 23:18-19[17-18]). The imagery is familiar from Hosea, who views the covenant as a marital bond (Hosea 1–3) and forsaking Yahweh as an act of "whoredom" (Hos 1:2; 4:12; 9:1). But the expression "to go whoring after (other gods)" is old (Exod 34:15-16). See also Judg 2:17; 8:33. The term "foreign god" appears in the Song (32:12), with "foreign gods" otherwise common OT coinage (Gen 35:2, 4; Josh 24:20, 23; Judg 10:16; 1 Sam 7:3; Jer 5:19, and elsewhere). The LXX translates the expression אֱלֹהֵי נֵכַר־הָאָרֶץ as a triple construct chain: "foreign gods of the land (θεῶν ἀλλοτρίων τῆς γῆς), which derives support from T^{Nf} and is followed by many commentators and modern Versions (Driver; Tigay; Nelson; RSV; NJV; NRSV). Rashi argues that "foreign" does not modify "gods" but is in construct relation only with "the land." His translation follows T^{Onq}: "the gods of that which is foreign to the land," i.e., the gods of the peoples of the land.

into which it comes, in its midst. אֲשֶׁר הוּא בָא־שָׁמָּה בְּקִרְבּוֹ. The Hebrew is awkward, with בְּקִרְבּוֹ apparently meaning "in the people's midst" (Driver).

and it will forsake me and break my covenant that I cut with it. The MT continues with masculine singular pronouns. 4QDeut^c has plural verbs: "and they will forsake me and break [my covenant]," which is supported by Sam, LXX, and T (Ulrich, Cross et al. 1995, 32-33). Israel's covenant with Yahweh does not allow for liaisons with other gods, as the first commandment makes clear. "Forsaking" (עזב) Yahweh will bring judgment (28:20; 29:24[25]; Josh 24:16, 20; Judg 2:12-15; 10:6-9; 1 Sam 12:9-10; 1 Kgs 9:9). Huldah's Judah oracle, based on the law book found in the temple in 622, announced judgment on the nation because it had forsaken Yahweh and burned incense to other gods (2 Kgs 22:17). Preaching along the same lines continued in Jeremiah (Jer 1:16; 2:14-19; 5:6-7, 18-19; 16:10-13; 17:13; 19:3-4; 22:8-9), where "forsaking Yahweh" meant violation of the covenant, worshipping other gods, or reliance on foreign nations.

and break my covenant. The H-stem of פרר, repeating in v. 20 and appearing elsewhere in the OT with reference to covenant-breaking (Lev 26:15; Jer 11:10; Ezek 16:59; 44:7), is strong. Judges 2:1 states that Yahweh will not break his covenant with Israel. Breaking covenants in order to form new ones was common in the world of international politics (1 Kgs 15:19).

17 *Then my anger will burn against it in that day.* Stated in the Song of Moses, only there reference is to provocation occurring in the past (32:16, 19-22).

and I will forsake them. 4QDeut^c has "I will forsake you" (Ulrich, Cross et al. 1995, 32-33), which is not a good reading. MT's shift to the plural "them" is supported by Sam, LXX, and the Versions. Yahweh will treat his covenant people as they treated him (v. 16), which is what the Song of Moses promises (32:20-21). For the same antithesis, see 2 Chr 12:5; 15:2; 24:20.

and I will hide my face from them. To "hide the face" is "to withdraw favor" (Driver; Freedman, Lundbom, *ḥānan*, in *TDOT*, 5:24; Lundbom 2007b,

278-79). R. E. Friedman (1977) says it is a *terminus technicus* in the OT for Yahweh ceasing to be available to Israel, i.e., not to see, not to hear, not to answer human cries, etc., commonly a response to covenant betrayal. See also Mic 3:4; Isa 8:17; 54:8; 59:2; Jer 18:17; 33:5; Pss 13:2(1); 27:9; 30:8(7). In the Song of Moses, Yahweh says he will hide his face from people who provoke him with other gods (32:20).

and it will be for consuming. I.e., enemies will consume Israel. If Israel fears Yahweh and obeys the covenant, Israel will consume (אכל) the enemy (7:16; cf. Num 14:9).

and many evils and troubles will find it. וּמְצָאֻהוּ רָעוֹת רַבּוֹת וְצָרוֹת. A vivid coinage in the Hebrew, occurring again in v. 21. On "evils and troubles," see also 1 Sam 10:19.

and it will say in that day, 'Is it not because my God is not in my midst that these evils have found me?' 4QDeut^c contains the divine name in the quotation, with "my God" inserted above the line (Ulrich, Cross et al. 1995, 32-33). The LXX similarly has "the Lord my God" (κύριος ὁ θεός μου). In the future Israel (the collective singular continues through v. 21) will realize that Yahweh is no longer in its midst, for which reason evils aplenty have come. Tigay thinks that אֱלֹהַי, because it appears alone without יהוה, refers here as elsewhere in the Pentateuch to (false) gods. The meaning would then be that in the future people in their ignorance would believe that other gods had abandoned them (cf. Jer 44:18). This view appears unlikely, assuming among other things that the "Lord my God" readings of 4QDeut^c and LXX are later reinterpretation.

18 *And I, I will surely hide my face in that day.* The personal pronoun in the repetition is for emphasis. Driver says the people's acknowledgement in v. 17 may not express true penitence.

because it turned to other gods. כִּי פָנָה אֶל־אֱלֹהִים אֲחֵרִים. The expression with "turn" (פנה), here and in v. 20, occurs also in Hos 3:1. Deuteronomy usually has "go after" (הלך אַחֲרֵי) and "serve" (עבד) other gods (6:14; 7:4; 8:19; 11:16, 28; 13:3, 7, 14[2, 6, 13]; 17:3; 28:14, 36, 64; 29:25[26]). In a Hittite treaty between Mursilis and Duppi-Tessub of Amurru, the Hittite king warns his subordinate to remain loyal by continuing to send tribute money, after which he says: "Do not turn your eyes to anyone else!" (*ANET*³, 204 par. 8).

19 *And now, write for yourselves this song.* וְעַתָּה כִּתְבוּ לָכֶם אֶת־הַשִּׁירָה הַזֹּאת. The imperative is plural, raising the question as to who will write the song along with Moses. In v. 22 only Moses is said to have written the song. The usual answer is Joshua, to whom Moses will perhaps dictate (Driver; Tigay; 32:44; cf. Exod 17:14).

And now. וְעַתָּה. A rhetorical particle shifting discourse from future time to present time (see Note for 2:13). 4QDeut^c simply has וע[ת (Ulrich, Cross et al. 1995, 32), which has to be an error.

this song. 4QDeut^c upon reconstruction has "words of this song," supporting LXX's τὰ ῥήματα τῆς ᾠδῆς ταύτης.

and teach it to the children of Israel. Moses is to teach people the song (MT; LXX and Vg have a plural verb). Here again we see the emphasis Deuteronomy lays upon teaching (cf. vv. 9-13). David later wanted his lament over Saul and Jonathan taught to the people (2 Sam 1:18).

put it in their mouths. People are to memorize it (ibn Ezra: "know it word for word"; cf. 30:14). The idiom "put in the mouth" means "teach by heart" in Sumerian and Akkadian texts (Tigay).

in order that this song will be a witness for me against the children of Israel. The song — particularly 32:15-18 — will be Yahweh's witness against Israel when the nation forsakes him in the future (vv. 26-27; cf. Jer 42:5).

20 *When I bring it into the land that I swore to its fathers, flowing with milk and honey.* In v. 13 of the Song, Yahweh is said to have given Israel abundance in the Transjordan. On the promise of land sworn to the fathers, see Note for 1:8. On the promised land being a land "flowing with milk and honey," see Note for 6:3.

into the land. אֶל־הָאֲדָמָה. An unusual coinage in Deuteronomy (cf. Jer 35:15).

and it eats and is sated and grows fat. This draws on vv. 14-15a of the Song, which says that Israel became sated after the Transjordan settlement. Deuteronomy elsewhere promises that when Israel enters the land it will eat to the full (see Note for 6:10-11).

and turns to other gods and serves them, and spurns me and breaks my covenant. These words continue the protasis (NJV). Deuteronomy warns against apostasy in 6:12-15; 8:11-20, and in the Song apostasy followed the good life in Transjordan (32:15-18). What a sated Israel should do is bless Yahweh, who gave it the good land (8:10). See also Neh 9:25.

and spurns me. וְנִאֲצוּנִי. The verb נאץ ("spurn, reject with scorn"), although not appearing elsewhere in Deuteronomy, is associated with covenant-breaking in Isa 1:4; 5:24; Jer 14:21. In the Song of Moses, Yahweh responds to apostasy by spurning Israel (32:19; cf. Lam 2:6).

21 *then it will happen that many evils and troubles will find it.* Here begins the apodosis, repeating what was said in v. 17. The LXX omits, which Nelson says is through inner-Greek haplography (homoeoarcton: καί . . . καί).

and this song will testify before it as a witness. Repeating v. 19.

(for it will not be forgotten in the mouth of its descendants). A parenthetical remark expanding upon v. 19, supporting the view that "putting (the song) in their mouths" means making people memorize it. Then future generations will not forget (שׁכח) the Song.

for I know its imagination. כִּי יָדַעְתִּי אֶת־יִצְרוֹ. The same idea recurs in vv.

27-29. Cf. the "evil imagination" of Gen 6:5; 8:21, which later became a prominent rabbinic teaching (יצר הרע).

into the land that I swore. The LXX adds "to their fathers" (τοῖς πατράσιν αὐτῶν), which is needed (Driver; v. 20: "to its fathers"). On Yahweh's gift of land to the fathers, see Note for 1:8.

22 A concluding verse; cf. v. 30 in the following segment.

23 *Then he charged Joshua son of Nun.* The actual commissioning of Joshua, completing what began in vv. 14-15. The subject of the verb has to be Yahweh (RSV supplies "the Lord"), although the LXX has Moses charging Joshua: καὶ ἐνετείλατο Μωυσῆς Ἰησοῖ ("And Moses commanded Joshua"). It also translates v. 23b: ἣν ὤμοσεν κύριος αὐτοῖς, καὶ αὐτὸς ἔσται μετὰ σοῦ ("which the Lord swore to them, and he will be with you"). Moses, being the subject in v. 22, is apparently taken to be the antecedent of "he." But the rhetorical structure points to Yahweh being the speaking voice in the verse (see Rhetoric and Composition). In 34:9 Moses is said to have laid his hands upon Joshua, which invested authority (cf. Num 27:12-23).

"*Be strong and be bold.* Moses' words of charge to Joshua are the same in 3:28; 31:7.

and I, I will be with you." God's bedrock promise in the Bible (see v. 8 and Note for 20:1), adding here the personal pronoun for emphasis.

Message and Audience

The audience is now told who will assume leadership in Israel once Moses passes from the scene. Yahweh is addressing Moses directly, telling Moses that he is soon to die, so he and Joshua should present themselves in the tent of meeting so Yahweh can commission Joshua to his new office. Joshua has faithfully stood guard outside the tent of meeting, but now he is to enter this sacred space to receive Yahweh's charge. Moses and Joshua enter the tent, and Yahweh descends in a pillar of cloud that has come to rest at its entrance.

Once the two are inside, and before the commissioning takes place, Yahweh turns to address Moses about another matter. His words have an ominous tone, registering grave doubts about Israel carrying out the terms of the Horeb covenant. An audience having listened to earlier Deuteronomic preaching may register surprise at what it hears, for while preaching up to this point has not failed to mention Israel's disobedience during the wilderness trek, it has nevertheless remained upbeat, stating that Yahweh's covenant demands can be met and Israel need only be warned about the consequences of disobedience. The Deuteronomic preacher has not imagined that the covenant will be undone once Israel enters the promised land. But now that is precisely what

Yahweh says will happen. Once Moses has passed from the scene, Israel will enter Canaan and go after the gods of the land, breaking the Horeb covenant. Yahweh in holy wrath will then forsake his people, with the result that grievous troubles will meet them on every front. In this future day people will realize that Yahweh is no longer in their midst. Yahweh is firm in saying he will treat them with disfavor.

Because of this gloomy scenario, Yahweh tells Moses to write a Song straightaway and teach it to the people so it can be his witness against them when the covenant-breaking occurs. The ominous prediction is restated, this time in terms familiar from the song Moses is about to write. When Yahweh has brought Israel into the good land of Canaan, a land flowing with milk and honey, it will eat, become sated, turn to other gods, and despise Yahweh by breaking his covenant. Yahweh repeats the trouble this will bring and how the Song vouchsafed in people's memories will witness against them. Yahweh knows people possess an evil imagination, something he perceives even as he speaks. So Moses proceeds to write the Song and teach it to Israel.

These prophetic words having been spoken, Yahweh now charges Joshua son of Nun to his new office. The mood returns to being upbeat. Joshua is admonished to be strong and bold, for he will succeed in bringing Israel into the land promised to the fathers. In conclusion, Yahweh gives Joshua the promise given earlier to Moses: "I, I will be with you."

4. Moses' Parting Words about the Song (31:24-30)

31 ^{24}And it happened as Moses completed writing the words of this law in a book until they were finished, ^{25}Moses then commanded the Levites, who carried the ark of the covenant of Yahweh: ^{26}"Take this book of the law and put it beside the ark of the covenant of Yahweh your God, and it will be there as a witness against you. ^{27}For I, I know your rebelliousness and your stiffness of neck. Look, while I am alive with you today you have been rebellious with Yahweh, so how much more after my death! ^{28}Assemble to me all the elders of your tribes and your officials, and I will speak in their hearing these words, and I will call to witness against them heaven and earth. ^{29}For I know after my death that you will surely act corruptly, and you will turn aside from the way that I commanded you. And the evil will befall you in the days afterward, because you will do the evil in the eyes of Yahweh, to provoke him to anger with the work of your hands." ^{30}So Moses spoke in the hearing of all the assembly of Israel the words of this song, until they were finished.

Rhetoric and Composition

Neither M^L nor M^A has a section marking before v. 24, but Sam has a section there. Sam has another section after v. 24. After v. 30 M^L has a *setumah*, M^A a *petuḥah,* and Sam a section. 4QDeut^b also has a section after v. 30, which is the chapter division.

After vv. 14-23, which appear to derive from another source (Rhetoric and Composition for 31:1-6), we return to vocabulary and phraseology thoroughly Deuteronomic (Driver; A. J. Levy 1931, 3). That vv. 24-30 are from a different hand than vv. 14-23 is further indicated by v. 30 repeating v. 22b: both verses state that Moses spoke the Song to all Israel. The present verses are tied together by an inclusio:

> *Moses completed writing the words of this law . . .*   v. 24
>   *until they were finished*
> *Moses spoke . . . the words of this song,*   v. 30
>   *until they were finished*

These verses cannot be divided, as Driver and some others maintain. Driver took vv. 24-27 as a sequel to vv. 9-13 and vv. 28-30 as a second Introduction to the Song.

That vv. 24-30 are one piece is indicated also by a larger structure to which the verses belong. Together with 32:44-47, they make a frame for the Song of Moses. A keyword chiasmus serves to make the "song" into a "law/torah" (Lundbom 1976, 299-300; 1990, 56):

the words of this law	31:24
these words	31:28
the words of this song	31:30
all *the words of this song*	32:44
all *these words*	32:45
all *the words of this law*	32:46

Most scholars agree that "these words" in 31:28 look ahead to the Song, but by the same margin it is believed that "the words of this law" in 31:24 must refer back to the entire Deuteronomic law code (Driver; Tigay; cf. 1:1; 27:26). This meaning for "law" in both 31:24 and 32:46 would be supported by the "law" references in 31:9-13 and reinforced by references to "law" and "book of the law" in Josh 1:7-8; 8:31, 34 (מִשְׁנֵה תּוֹרַת מֹשֶׁה in Josh 8:32 is only the Decalogue, carved into stones of the Mount Ebal altar).

Deuteronomy 31

But if 31:24-30 is read together with 32:44-47, then "law" in both passages must refer to the Song, not the entire Deuteronomic law code. N. Sarna (*EncJud*, 4:821-22) believes "law" in v. 24 more likely refers to the succeeding Song, as indicated by vv. 19 and 22. The same view is taken in Fishbane (1972, 350). Eissfeldt (1965, 227) believed the Song "at a later date was regarded as a summarising of the Deuteronomic law," but added with some puzzlement, "it is remarkable that the two terms *law* (תּוֹרָה) and *song* appear together." Driver (1895, 343) expressed himself similarly. Tigay thinks it virtually inconceivable that Deuteronomy would use "this law" in v. 24 for something other than itself, yet that is precisely what some compiler did. This compiler, as we mentioned, wanted to make Moses' "song" into a "law," thereby ranking it and integrating it with Moses' larger law delivered in the plains of Moab. The result is that in the present Deuteronomy the term "law" in 31:24; 32:46 has therefore become ambiguous, i.e., it has a narrow and a broad meaning existing simultaneously. It refers not only to the Song, but to the entire Deuteronomic law code, including the Song. Something similar occurred with colophons in the book of Jeremiah (Jeremiah 45; 51:59-64). When these colophons were relocated to different places in an expanded book, words with originally narrow meaning were made to take on broader meaning (Lundbom 1986a, 100).

Portions of 31:24-30 are contained in 4QDeut^b and 4QpaleoDeut^r.

Notes

31:24 The writing was on a scroll, not in a book, a form which did not come into being until early in the Christian era (H. A. Sanders 1938). Moses writes a scroll of this "law" just as he did with the Deuteronomic law (v. 9). Scrolls in ancient Israel were commonly of papyrus, so this one would doubtless have been of papyrus, not leather (Haran 1980-81; *pace* Tigay). The scroll on which the prophecies of Jeremiah were written was also most likely papyrus (Lundbom 2004a, 586-87).

the words of this law. Originally "this law" had no antecedent, referring only to the Song of Moses following (see Rhetoric and Composition). But in an enlarged Deuteronomy it refers also to the prior Deuteronomic law code. This expansion of the term "law" corresponds to an expansion of Moses' *persona*. Originally Moses was simply the scribe who wrote the Song; later he became the scribe writing the Deuteronomic law; still later he became the scribe writing the entire Pentateuch (*b. B. Bat.* 14b-15a). N. Sarna (*EncJud*, 4:821) says the doctrine of Mosaic authorship of the whole Torah has its source in Deut 31:9-12, 24 more than in any other passage.

until they were finished. עַד תֻּמָּם. On this expression, see v. 30; 2:15; Josh 8:24; 10:20.

25 The Levites were entrusted with carrying the sacred ark (10:8; 31:9; Josh 3:3-17; 6:6, 12; 8:33; 1 Kgs 8:3, 6), some also being teachers in ancient Israel (see Note for 12:12). The Levites were given custody of the Deuteronomic Code (31:9-13).

26 *"Take this book of the law and put it beside the ark of the covenant of Yahweh your God.* At Horeb, the Decalogue was placed in the ark (10:1-5; cf. Exod 25:16), which was a wooden chest (Haran 1959; de Vaux 1971b). Now Moses is instructed to place his law, i.e., his song, beside the ark (מִצַּד אֲרוֹן). Rashi notes that some ancient authorities believed the scroll was placed beside the tablets, i.e., inside the ark (cf. *b. B. Bat.* 14ab), while others thought it was placed outside the ark. He decides in favor of it being outside the ark. During the monarchy the tablets were still in the ark; nothing else was there (1 Kgs 8:9).

this book of the law. The term refers to the written Deuteronomic law in 28:61; 29:20(21); 30:10 (see Note for 28:61); also Josh 1:8, but here it refers to the Song, which may have been the temple law book found during Josiah's reform (Lundbom 1976, 300; cf. 2 Kgs 22:8). By calling the Song a "torah," the writer links it to the earlier Deuteronomic law code. Leuchter (2007, 299) says that now "the Song is to function as the grand finale of the Deuteronomic corpus itself."

this . . . law. הַתּוֹרָה הַזֶּה. 4QDeut[b] has the feminine הזאת, which appears in T[PsJ] and a fragment from the Cairo Geniza. A feminine pronoun occurs also in 28:61.

and it will be there as a witness against you. I.e., against the Levitical priests, who here represent the entire nation (Driver; Tigay; cf. v. 28). In v. 19 the Song is said to be a witness against all Israel. Tigay notes that the temple scroll of 622 functioned precisely as a witness against the people, since it convinced the king of Israel's guilt and led to a major reform. This supports the view that the scroll of 622 was the Song of Moses (Lundbom 1976; 1999, 106).

27 *For I, I know your rebelliousness and your stiffness of neck.* The first personal pronoun is added for emphasis. Moses knows as no one else does Israel's rebelliousness (מְרִי), which showed itself all during the wilderness period but in Deuteronomy was seen particularly in Israel's initial failure to enter Canaan (1:26, 43; 9:7, 23-24). The expression "your stiffness of neck" (עָרְפְּךָ הַקָּשֶׁה) is used to describe Israel's stubbornness (9:6, 13; 10:16; cf. Weinfeld 1972, 341 no. 9), seen preeminently in the golden calf incident (9:6-21).

Look, while I am alive with you today you have been rebellious with Yahweh, so how much more after my death! An argument *a minori ad maius* (Hebrew *qal weḥomer*), which is from the lesser to the greater (cf. Jer 3:1; 12:5; 25:29; 49:12). Moses imagines that Israel will be even more intractable after he has passed from the scene (v. 29).

Deuteronomy 31

28 Moses commands the Levites to gather the elders and officials to hear his song. All Israel assembled at Horeb to hear the Decalogue (4:10), and every seventh year at the Feast of Booths the nation will assemble to hear the Deuteronomic law (31:12).

all the elders of your tribes and your officials. The expression "elders of (your) tribes" occurs nowhere else (Driver). The usual Deuteronomic coinage is "heads of your tribes" (5:23; cf. 1:13; 29:9[10]). The LXX expands to "the chiefs of your tribes and your elders and your judges and your officials" (τοὺς φυλάρχους ὑμῶν καὶ τοὺς πρεσβυτέρους ὑμῶν καὶ τοὺς κριτὰς ὑμῶν καὶ τοὺς γραμματοεισαγωγεῖς ὑμῶν), and a reconstructed 4QDeut^b also has four groups: "[the elders?] of your tribes and [your elders] and your judges and your officials" (Ulrich, Cross et al. 1995, 13-14). Judges should probably be included (Driver; cf. 16:18; 29:9[10] LXX; Josh 23:2; 24:1). For a discussion of the various officeholders in ancient Israel, see Note for 16:18.

these words. I.e., the words of the Song.

and I will call to witness against them heaven and earth. Heaven and earth will witness against Israel when it disregards the testimony of the Song (see Note to 32:1; cf. 4:26; 30:19).

29 *For I know after my death that you will surely act corruptly, and you will turn aside from the way that I commanded you.* Alluded to already in v. 27. On Israel acting corruptly (שחת) in the fashioning of idols, see 4:16, 25; 9:12 (cf. Exod 32:7-8) and above all 32:5 of the Song. The second commandment prohibited making images (Deut 5:8-10; Exod 20:4-6). The expression "turn aside from the way" is stereotyped in Deuteronomy (see Note for 9:12).

And the evil will befall you in the days afterward, because you will do the evil in the eyes of Yahweh, to provoke him to anger with the work of your hands." "The days afterward" (= "in future days" or "at the end of days") refers to a distant but unspecified future time (see Note for 4:30). This prediction did come to pass (Jer 32:23; 44:23), although a later fulfillment was anticipated among the Essenes at Qumran, where the present verse was paraphrased in lines 12-14 of 4QMMT (Qimron and Strugnell 1994, 58-59).

you will do the evil in the eyes of Yahweh. A stock Deuteronomic phrase (see Note for 4:25).

to provoke him to anger with the work of your hands." On evil provoking Yahweh to anger, see Note for 4:25-26. "The work of your hands" refers here to idols (see Note for 2:7).

30 Repeating what is said in v. 22b about Moses teaching the Song to the people (see Rhetoric and Composition). LXX translates "the assembly of Israel" with ἐκκλησίας Ισραηλ.

Deuteronomy 32

Message and Audience

The audience now hears Moses' parting words to the Levites, civic heads, and all Israel regarding the Song he has just written. "This law" in v. 24 refers to the Song cited in v. 22, which will be given in its entirety once Moses' address is concluded. The Levites, who were appointed to carry the ark of the covenant, are instructed to put the Song beside the ark, inside of which are the Ten Commandments. The Song is to remain in proximity to Israel's core law code, where it will serve as Yahweh's future witness against not just the Levites, but all Israel. Moses, more than anyone else, knows Israel's refractory nature, and if the nation has been rebellious and stubborn during his lifetime, how much more will they behave in this manner after he dies.

The Levites are told to assemble Israel's leaders to hear the Song. Heaven above and earth beneath will witness every word it contains. Moses repeats that after his death Israel will surely act corruptly, and will turn aside from Yahweh's way, i.e., not doing the commandments Moses has taught. Then evil will come upon a people who have themselves done evil, provoking Yahweh with the work of their hands. To no one's surprise, the snare of the future will be the snare of the past: idols and the lure of other gods. In conclusion, the audience hears again that Moses spoke the words of this Song — from first to last — in the hearing of all Israel.

5. The Song of Moses (32:1-43)

> **32**¹*Give ear, O heavens, and I will speak,*
>   *and let the earth hear the speech of my mouth.*
> ²*Let my teaching drop like the rain,*
>   *let my speech distil like the dew;*
> *like raindrops upon grass*
>   *and like showers upon green plants.*
> ³*For the name of Yahweh I proclaim,*
>   *ascribe greatness to our God!*
>
> ⁴*The Rock, his work is perfect,*
>   *indeed all his ways are just;*
> *a God of faithfulness, and without wrong,*
>   *righteous and upright is he.*
> ⁵*It acted corruptly toward him.*
>   *Is not their blemish his children's?*
>   *a generation perverted and crooked!*

⁶*Do you repay Yahweh thus?*
    O people foolish and unwise!
Is not he your father? he created you!
    He, he made you and he established you!
⁷*Remember the days of old,*
    consider the years of many generations;
Ask your father and he will inform you,
    your elders, and they will tell you.
⁸*When the Most High gave the nations an inheritance,*
    when he separated the sons of man,
He fixed the boundaries of peoples
    to the number of the sons of God.*
⁹*Indeed Yahweh's portion is his people,*
    Jacob, his allotted inheritance.

¹⁰*He found him in a wilderness land,*
    yes, in a howling desert waste;
He encircled him, he took care of him,
    he guarded him as the pupil of his eye.
¹¹*As an eagle who stirs up his nest*
    over his young ones he hovers,
he spreads out his wings, he takes him up,
    he lifts him upon his pinion.
¹²*Yahweh alone guided him,*
    and no foreign god was with him.
¹³*He made him ride on earth's high places,*
    and he ate the produce of the high country,
and he made him suck honey from the crags
    and oil from the flinty rock;
¹⁴*Curds of the herd and milk of the flock,*
    with the choicest of lambs and rams,
sons of Bashan and he-goats
    with the choicest grains of wheat,
        yes, blood of the grape, you drank wine!

¹⁵*So Jacob ate and became sated;†*
    yes, Jeshurun got fat and kicked;
        you got fat, you grew thick, you became gorged.
    Then he abandoned the God who made him

---

*Reading "sons of God" (בני אלוהים) with 4QDeut^j; MT has "sons of Israel."
†Added with the Sam, LXX, and 4QPhyl 141 (see Notes).

and took to be foolish the Rock of his salvation.
¹⁶*They made him jealous with strangers,*
   with abominations they provoked him.
¹⁷*They sacrificed to demons, no-gods,*
   gods they had not known.
New ones recently come in,
   your fathers were not awed by them.
¹⁸*The Rock that begot you, you neglected,*
   and you forgot the God who bore you in travail.

¹⁹*So Yahweh saw and spurned*
   because of the provocation of his sons and daughters.
²⁰*And he said: I will hide my face from them,*
   I will see what their end will be.
For a generation of perversities they are,
   children in whom is no faithfulness.
²¹*They, they made me jealous with a no-god,*
   they provoked me with their nothings.
So I, I will make them jealous with a no-people,
   with a foolish nation I will provoke them.
²²*For a fire is kindled in my anger,*
   and it will burn to the depths of Sheol.
Yes, it will consume the earth and its yield
   and set ablaze the mountains' foundations.

²³*I will heap evils upon him,*
   my arrows I will exhaust against them:
²⁴*Smiting famine,*
   and burning plague,
      and bitter pestilence;
and the teeth of beasts I will send against them,
   with venom of crawlers in the dust.
²⁵*Outside a sword shall bereave,*
   and in the chambers terror,
both young man and maiden,
   nursing child with the gray-haired man.
²⁶*I thought: I will strike them down,*
   I will surely make their memory cease from humankind.
²⁷*Except I feared provocation of the enemy,*
   lest his adversaries should misjudge,
   lest they say: "Our hand is raised up,
And not Yahweh has done all this."

²⁸*For a nation bereft of counsel are they,*
   and there is no understanding in them.
²⁹*If they were wise, they would consider this;*
   they would discern their end.
³⁰*How could one chase a thousand,*
   and two put thousands to flight,
unless indeed their Rock had sold them,
   and Yahweh had delivered them up?
³¹*Indeed their rock is not like our Rock;*
   even our enemies being assessors.
³²*Indeed their vine is from the vine of Sodom,*
   and from the terraces of Gomorrah.
Its grapes are grapes of poison,
   its clusters are bitter.
³³*Their wine is the venom of serpents,*
   yes, the cruel poison of vipers.

³⁴*Is not this stored up with me,*
   sealed in my storehouses?
³⁵*Vengeance is mine, and repayment*
   for the time when their foot shall slip.
Indeed the day of their disaster is near,
   and things prepared are hastening to him.
³⁶*Indeed Yahweh will vindicate his people,*
   and feel sorry over his servants.
Indeed he will see that support is gone,
   and none remains bond or free.
³⁷*Then Yahweh* will say: "Where is his god,*
   the rock in whom they took refuge?
³⁸*Choice portions† of his sacrifices they ate,*
   they drank wine of their libations.
Let them arise and let them help you,
   let it be your protection!"

³⁹*See now indeed I, I am he,*
   and there is no god with me.
I, I kill, and I make alive,

---

*Reading יהוה as subject of the verb with 4QDeut^q and with κύριος of the LXX; the MT simply has "then he will say."
†Eliminating the initial אשר ("who") of MT, which may be a reinsertion from the prior colon (see Notes).

> *I wound, and I, I heal;*
> *and none can rescue from my hand.*
> ⁴⁰*Indeed I lift up my hand to heaven,*
> *and I say: "As I live forever."*
> ⁴¹*If I sharpen my gleaming sword,*
> *and my hand takes hold on judgment,*
> *I will return vengeance to my adversaries,*
> *and to those who hate me, I will repay.*
> ⁴²*I will make my arrows drunk from blood,*
> *and my sword shall consume flesh,*
> *From the blood of slain and captive,*
> *from the long-haired head of the enemy.*
>
> ⁴³*Give his people ringing acclaim, O heavens,**
> *for the blood of his servants he will avenge,*
> *yes, he will return vengeance to his adversaries,*
> *and atone for his land, his people.*

Excursus 3: History of Research into the Song of Moses

The Talmud took the Song of Moses along with the rest of Deuteronomy to emanate directly from Moses. Debated among the rabbis was only whether Moses could have written the account of his own death (*b. B. Bat.* 15a; Tigay, xix). But with the rise of critical scholarship in the late 18th and early 19th cents. came the belief that Moses did not author this song, even as he did not author other Deuteronomic discourse that had him speaking in the first person. Contextual prose states that Moses wrote the song; nevertheless, the poem itself does not support Mosaic authorship (Driver 1895, 345). What is more, the presumed occupation of Canaan in the poem is said to lie in the distant past (vv. 7-12), so also Israel's lapse into Canaanite idolatry (vv. 15-18). All that is future, says Driver, is Israel's deliverance. Curiously, Jewish interpretation also assumed the occupation of Canaan (e.g., *Sifre Deut.*), to which it looked ahead at some distant point in the future. For the rabbis, the Song was "a summary of Israel's total history, from its inception until the end of days" (Basser 1984, 4).

Wilhelm Martin de Wette, whose 1805 dissertation identified Deuteronomy as the temple law book found during the reign of King Josiah (2 Kgs 22:8) and, more importantly, argued that the book was written shortly before it was found, giving Deuteronomy a firm date in the 7th cent. (de Wette 1830; 1843, 2:150-54), said little about the Song itself, asserting only that it was not Mosaic

---

*Reading "heavens" with 4QDeutᵠ; MT has "nations."

and that vv. 5-33 must emanate from Israel's "most unfortunate period of the state." This was the exile of the ten northern tribes in 722 (de Wette 1843, 2:150; cf. A. J. Levy 1931, 5).

Scholarship during the next century and a half became concerned largely with questions of date, authorship, and provenance. In an important essay, Heinrich Ewald said that the language of the Song combined the prophetic and poetic like no other passage in the Bible (Ewald 1856, 41). In his view, the Song could not be earlier or later than the 7th cent., at which time Israel's enemy was the Assyrians. The author must have lived in the northern kingdom, since the Song said nothing about Judah. Ewald believed that the northern kingdom, in its later years, showed a great zeal for true religion, with the result that its literature during this period became more developed than what existed in Judah. Less convincing, however, was Ewald's belief that the Song was messianic in character (Ewald 1856, 44-45).

Knobel (1861, 325, 331) thought the Song must be dated earlier, perhaps at the beginning of the reign of Jeroboam II (786-746), when the years of Syrian harassment were still a recent memory and Israel had begun its recovery. The "no-people" of v. 21 were the Syrians. Kamphausen (1862, 295-303), noting that the language of the Song had numerous parallels in Jeremiah, nevertheless returned to Ewald's view that the Assyrians were the adversary and said that the Song should be assigned to the period just prior to Israel's fall in 722.

Kuenen (1886, 256-57), too, noted parallels to Jeremiah in the Song, but opted for a later date, ca. 630 or a generation later. This became the view of S. R. Driver (1895, 346-47), who said the Song showed greater affinity with prophets of the Chaldean age than with Amos, Hosea, Isaiah, or Micah. But Klostermann (1893, 262-66) believed the poem was known in Hezekiah's time, for both Isaiah and Micah appeared to use some of its expressions in their prophecies.

Cornill (1891, 71) recognized with von Herder an unconcealed prophetic tone in the Song, calling it a "compendium of prophetic theology." Von Herder had earlier described Moses' Song as "the original prophecy, the type and pattern of all the prophets" (von Herder 1833, 1:275). But he still attributed the Song to Moses. Now Cornill dated it to the last years of the Babylonian exile, assuming that the author had quarried ideas from the preexilic prophets, which were original with them.

Cornill's late date influenced many 20th-cent. scholars (H. W. Robinson 1907, 219; Budde 1920, 1-13; A. J. Levy 1931, 40-41; Welch 1932, 146-51; von Rad 1966a, 200). Budde (1920, 26) argued that Ezekiel authored the Song. The late date still has supporters (Keiser 2005), but many have ruled out an exilic or postexilic date (G. A. Smith 1918, 342-43; G. E. Wright 1953, 517; 1962, 66-67; Moran 1969, 275), noting with Gunkel (1913, 535) that the Song makes no reference to exile. For both the Assyrians and Babylonians exile of conquered foes was state policy, and one might expect at least an allusion to exile if the Song were written in the Assyrian or Chaldean age. One hears a great deal about exile from prophets of this time. It was also averred by some that the mighty Babylonians seemed a poor fit for the "no-people" of v. 21. Cassuto, writing in 1938, thought the Song should be assigned to the epoch of the judges, immediately preceding the war of Deborah (Cassuto 1973a).

Form-critical work on the Song has had a rather small yield; some would say no yield at all. Early critical scholars recognized the prophetic nature of the Song, but some had compared it to the "recital" Psalms 78, 105, and 106. This was natural enough, since the biblical text called the work a "song" (Deut 31:19-22, 30; 32:44) and vv. 10-14 recounted Israel's "saving history" from wilderness wanderings to settlement in the land. Because the Song seemed to have both hymnic and prophetic elements, Gunkel (1998, 251) called it "mixed poetry" (German: *Mischgedicht*), an inauspicious designation holding little promise for form-critical analysis.

G. E. Wright (1962, 40) saw in the Song continuity with prophetic preaching, but argued that it was crafted in the form of a lawsuit, more specifically a "covenant lawsuit." He called it a "broken ריב," by which he meant a specific cult form adapted and expanded by other themes to serve a more generalized purpose in confession and praise. It was different from Psalm 78, which was a didactic poem. Psalm 78 was also Judahite, and Wright accepted the view that the Song had its provenance in northern Israel. With Gunkel he recognized in the poem an obvious mixture of forms (1962, 42).

Wright's form-critical work has had its share of critics (Boston 1966, 5, 149; Mendenhall 1975, 66; Tigay 1996, 510; Thiessen 2004). Moran (1969, 274-75), who accepts the Wright thesis, says the lawsuit form appearing here "is profoundly transformed." Wright's alleged genre has certainly not provided insight into the poem's structure, which was found in "thought units." But the most serious problem with the Wright thesis is that we have yet to come up with any real example of the "lawsuit" genre — Gunkel reconstructed his *Gerichtsrede* from an array of biblical passages, relying heavily on Psalm 82 (Gunkel 1998, 279-80; cf. Huffmon 1959). Also, indictment and judgment comprise only part of the Song, leaving much — specifically vv. 34-43 — unexplained.

Some scholars, in light of vv. 1-2, have typed the Song in terms of Israel's Wisdom literature (Boston 1966; 1968; von Rad 1966a, 200). Years earlier, Driver (1895, 345, 349) said these opening verses showed the Song to be a didactic poem, the original aim of which was "to point a moral from the past." But not everyone has been willing to put a "wisdom" label on the Song (G. E. Wright 1962, 54-55; Mendenhall 1975, 71). Even if vv. 1-2 owe something to Israel's wisdom tradition, they are only a very small part of the Song, leaving more verses unexplained than Wright's "lawsuit" thesis does.

Things turned in a different direction as a result of Eissfeldt's work on the Song. He pointed to its very archaic language and proposed a date in the 11th cent., between Israel's crushing defeat by the Philistines, at which time Shiloh was destroyed and the ark was taken (1 Samuel 4), and Saul's subsequent victories over Israel's early troublesome foe (1 Samuel 13-14). In his view, the "no-people" were then the Philistines (Eissfeldt 1958, 41-43; 1965, 227). Eissfeldt compared the Song with Psalm 78, noting particularly the words of v. 60: "he forsook his dwelling at Shiloh."

Albright (1959, 346; 1961, 22; 1968, 17) accepted Eissfeldt's 11th-cent. date, finding himself archaic language, spelling, and imagery in the Song, also LXX and Dead Sea Scroll readings suggesting an early date. Albright had also come around to accepting Cross and Freedman's 11th-cent. date for the Blessing of Moses (Cross and Freedman 1948, 192), so for him both the Blessing of Moses and Song of Moses were 11th-cent. compositions (Albright 1959, 346 n. 3; 1968, 33). G. E. Wright (1962, 66-67), too, agreed with Eissfeldt that the Philistines' defeat of Israel (ca. 1025) lay in the background, but said the Song should be dated later, ca. 815-805.

Mendenhall (1975, 64-72) also agreed with Eissfeldt's 11th-cent. date. In his view, the Song was a prophetic oracle and its author the prophet Samuel. Mendenhall agreed, too, with Cornill that the Song was a "compendium of prophetic theology," but he turned Cornill's argument around, seeing no reason why the Song could not contribute to the prophetic movement and thus predate it. He said:

> The close ties between the poem and the later prophets can best be understood as part of the nostalgia for the past that characterizes so much of the history, culture, and thought of the 7th–6th centuries.

Cross and Freedman, as was mentioned, dated the Blessing of Moses to the 11th cent. (Cross and Freedman 1948, 192; 1997, 64; Freedman 1976, 56-57; 1977, 18; 1979, 88-89), but Freedman believed the Song of Moses could be no earlier than the 10th to 9th cents. (Freedman 1976, 57, 79; 1977, 18; 1979, 87-88). From its selection of divine names, the Song should perhaps be dated ca. 900. Freedman (1976, 79) also noted that the Song contains no explicit references to the monarchy or to historical events later than the settlement. Robertson (1972, 155), in a linguistic analysis, dates the Song earlier, to the 11th to 10th cents.

At the end of the last century there was still no consensus on the date and provenance of the Song. The Song itself contains no explicit historical references, and we do not know the identity of the "no-people" in v. 21. This state of affairs is evident in Paul Sanders's book, *The Provenance of Deuteronomy 32* (1996), which offers no advance on nearly two hundred years of work on this preeminent poem in the Hebrew Bible. Sanders puts the *terminus a quo* for the composition in "the period of Israel's settlement in Canaan or at least in the Transjordanian highlands." The *terminus ad quem*, he says, is "the exilic period" (P. Sanders 1996, 433-36). Tigay, too, in his *Deuteronomy* commentary (1996, 513), says the poem is ancient, but makes no attempt to date it.

I agree with Mendenhall that the Song profoundly influenced Israel's prophets, particularly Jeremiah. Its author did not quarry original ideas from preexilic prophets and present them to exilic or postexilic audiences. Recent scholarship has come to much the same conclusion. The Song is said now to have influenced both Hosea and Isaiah (Propp 1987, 25, 43-44 n. 32; Tigay 1996, 511; Bergey 2003-4), also Ezekiel (Greenberg 1983a, 116-17). And a date for the Song between the 10th and 8th cents. has recently been argued by Nigosian (1996, 22; 1997, 223-24), who examined linguistic patterns in the poetry. This range of dates has been accepted as most likely by Leuchter (2007, 317). But the prophet showing greatest indebtedness to the Song of Moses is unquestionably Jeremiah. Driver saw this, and my own comparison of vocabulary and phraseology in the Song with the same in Jeremianic poetry points to the same conclusion (Lundbom 1999, 110-14). Jeremiah knew the Song and incorporated its ideas extensively into his early preaching.

Jeremiah incorporated the Song into his early preaching because, in my view, it existed on the temple law book of 622 (2 Kgs 22:8). A comparison between vv. 15-22 of the Song and Huldah's Judah oracle makes it reasonably clear that Huldah drew from the Song in formulating her oracle. Huldah's oracle of 2 Kgs 22:16-17 states:

> [16] Look I am bringing evil upon this place and upon its inhabitants — all the things of the book that the king of Judah has read. [17] Because *they have forsaken me and have burned incense to other gods,* that *they might provoke me to anger with all the work of their hands.* Therefore *my wrath will be kindled* against this place and *it will not be quenched.*

In both the Song and the oracle: (1) the nation is indicted because it has forgotten Yahweh and made him angry by sacrificing to other gods; and (2) Yahweh's wrath is promised to burn in judgment like an unquenchable fire (Lundbom 1976, 295-98). In accepting his call to be a prophet, it is these words on the temple scroll that Jeremiah "eats" (Jer 15:16; Lundbom 1999, 109). Holladay (2004, 73-74) agrees that the Song of Moses was part of proto-Deuteronomy, but he does not think that the temple law book was *only* the Song.

Attempts to identify the "no-people" in v. 21 have been inconclusive, with most everyone assuming that reference is to a people lacking military or political might. This makes the Assyrians and the Babylonians, perhaps also the Syrians and the Philistines, poor fits. It could be that "no-people" simply denotes a people not having the "chosen" status enjoyed by Israel, in which case any of Israel's enemies, at any given time, would fit the description.

Finally, there has been a curious lack of discussion on the "Bashan" reference in v. 14. This is a territory in the northern Transjordan, and its mention not only provides additional evidence for the Song having a northern provenance, but could also indicate that the settlement presupposed in the Song is not the settlement in Canaan after all, but rather the settlement in Transjordan after the Amorite kings, Sihon and Og, were defeated and Reuben, Gad, and the half-tribe of Manasseh were given their land. If this be the case, then the author of the Song — whatever his date — is putting himself more completely into the context of Deuteronomy, which is the Mosaic age when the wilderness wanderings, the unsuccessful attempt to enter Canaan, the defeat of Sihon and Og, and the settlement in Transjordan are all recent history and what lay ahead was the Jordan crossing and conquest of Canaan under Joshua.

Rhetoric and Composition

The Song of Moses is a poem of unknown provenance that has been included in the final segment of our present book of Deuteronomy (chs. 31–34). It gets its name from the contextual prose (31:19-21). The Song is widely agreed to be a masterful composition, poetry of a high order with uncommon rhetorical properties. That the Song is written in verse finds support in Sam and in the medieval codices (M^A; M^L) where the text is written stichometrically. The Song has also turned up in stichometric formatting in certain Qumran fragments (4QDeut^b; 4QDeut^c; 4QpaleoDeut^r; 4QDeut^q), indicating that already in antiquity it was taken to be poetry. Josephus (*Ant.* iv.8:44), wanting to commend the composition to a Greek audience, said the Song was written in hexameter verse. George Adam Smith (1912, 22) also noted in the Song many instances of Qina (3:2) rhythm, e.g., in vv. 11, 14, 16, 21, 23(?), 24-25, 29, 30-32, 34, 36, 39, 41. *Biblia Hebraica* and all modern English Versions print the Song as poetry.

One Qumran manuscript (4QDeut^q) ends with the Song, i.e., at 32:43, after which is a wide column without stitching, suggesting that the manuscript ended here (Skehan 1954, 12; Ulrich, Cross et al. 1995, 137; Duncan, *EDSS*, 201). This manuscript may even have contained only the Song of Moses (Ulrich, Cross et al. 1995, 137-38). Other Qumran manuscripts (1QDeut; 4QpaleoDeut^r) contain verses from both chs. 32 and 33 (Barthélemy and Milik 1955, 60-61; Skehan, Ulrich, and Sanderson 1992, 132, 146-48), indicating the existence of both poems on the scrolls, one presumably following the other.

Early critical scholars were not interested in finding a structure in the

Song, consumed as they were with questions of date, authorship, and provenance. Kamphausen (1862, 1), however, did identify vv. 1-3 as an introduction. Hebrew Bibles of the time had no internal section markings, which was later found to be true also in M^L, M^A, and the Qumran fragments. M^L and M^A delimit the Song only in its entirety, having a *petuḥah* before v. 1 and another *petuḥah* after v. 43. The Sam and 4QDeut[b] contain sections before v. 1 (Ulrich, Cross et al. 1995, 13). The Sam ends special formatting after v. 43.

S. R. Driver (1895, 348-49, 380) called vv. 1-3 of the Song an exordium, taking v. 43 as a conclusion corresponding to the exordium. Subsequent scholars have agreed, some recognizing the proclivity of Hebrew poets to balance end with beginning. However, most have stopped short of identifying stanzas in the Song, making divisions only for the sake of convenience (G. A. Smith 1918, 343; G. E. Wright 1962, 34). Many divide the Song — if they divide it at all — on the basis of content, which can be done reasonably well since the flow of thought is not in any real doubt.

A modest advance in finding structure within the body of the Song — more than simply introduction and conclusion — must be credited once again to S. R. Driver, who, as Deuteronomy editor for the 1906 edition of *Biblica Hebraica* (BH^1), is presumably the one responsible for indenting lines at vv. 4, 7, 10, 15, 19, 23, 28, 34, 39, and 43. This created de facto units, suggesting also indirectly, if not directly, that the Song contained an introduction, a body of eight stanzas, and a conclusion. The RSV, for whom James Muilenburg was poetry editor (Muilenburg 1952), delineated the same units as *Biblia Hebraica* with one exception: it did not break between vv. 6 and 7, taking vv. 4-9 to be a single unit. According to the RSV, the Song contains this structure:

Introduction	(vv. 1-3)
Stanza I	(vv. 4-9)
Stanza II	(vv. 10-14)
Stanza III	(vv. 15-18)
Stanza IV	(vv. 19-22)
Stanza V	(vv. 23-27)
Stanza VI	(vv. 28-33)
Stanza VII	(vv. 34-38)
Stanza VIII	(vv. 39-42)
Conclusion	(v. 43)

Subsequent English Versions, with the exception of NEB and NAB, which have gone their own way, have more or less followed the lead of *Biblica Hebraica* and RSV in making internal divisions. These divisions are indicated by blank lines left between verses.

Deuteronomy 32

The units delineated in RSV can be confirmed and refined by critical analysis. Climactic and ballast lines, repeated words and particles in strategic collocations, chiasms, partial chiasms, inclusios, rhetorical questions, shifts to direct address, and syllable counts of the units point to a poem having an introduction, eight stanzas balanced in four pairs, and a conclusion. This structure also correlates well with the thematic development in the Song.

Rhetorical Analysis

Climactic and Ballast Lines

Muilenburg (1969, 9-12) noted that lines of Hebrew poetry often appear in well-defined clusters, each possessing their own identity, integrity, and structure. These he called "strophes" or "stanzas." Stanzas sometimes conclude with "climactic" or "ballast" lines, which are weighty bicolons or tricolons bringing the discourse to a dramatic conclusion. Muilenburg learned about ballast lines from George Adam Smith, who in his Schweich Lectures of 1910 called attention to "a longer, heavier line, generally at the end of a strophe . . . similar to what the Germans call the 'Schwellvers' in old German ballads" (G. A. Smith 1912, 20-21, 77). He found instances of this heavy line in the Song of Deborah and the Song of Moses, noting also that such lines may correspond to a change in theme.

Here in Deuteronomy 32, Smith identified the tricolon in v. 14, which ends a stanza according to *BH* and the RSV, as a ballast line:

> *sons of Bashan and he-goats* (v. 14b)
>   *with the choicest grains of wheat,*
>   *yes, blood of the grape, you drank wine!*

Two other ballast lines in the Song of Moses were the final bicolons of vv. 42 and 43, both of which end stanzas in *BH* and the RSV. In the case of v. 43b, the bicolon concludes the entire Song:

> *From the blood of slain and captive,* (v. 42b)
>   *from the long-haired head of the enemy*
>
>   *yes, he will return vengeance to his adversaries,* (v. 43b)
>   *and atone for his land, his people.*

In the poetry of Second Isaiah, Muilenburg delineated stanzas on the basis of climactic lines that lifted up the name of Yahweh (Muilenburg 1956, 544-635). The stanza in Isa 47:1-4, he says, reaches its climax in these words:

> *Our redeemer — Yahweh of hosts is his name —*   (Isa 47:4)
>   *is the Holy One of Israel.*

Other stanzas in Second Isaiah conclude with a climactic "Yahweh of hosts is his name" (Isa 48:2; 54:5). In Isa 44:23, the prophet concludes a stanza with this shout (Muilenburg 1956, 392, 510):

> *For Yahweh has redeemed Jacob*   (Isa 44:23c)
>   *and in Israel will glorify himself.*

Climactic lines naming Yahweh occur frequently in other OT poetry, e.g., in Exod 15:3; Amos 4:13; 5:8; 9:6; Hos 12:6(5); Jer 10:16 = 51:19; Isa 51:15.

Here in the Song of Moses, some bicolons naming Yahweh appear to be climactic lines and occur at the end of stanzas. Concluding the exordium is this confident affirmation:

> *For the name of Yahweh I proclaim,*   (v. 3)
>   *ascribe greatness to our God!*

Another climactic bicolon naming Yahweh and his covenant partner occurs in v. 9:

> *Indeed Yahweh's portion is his people,*
>   *Jacob, his allotted inheritance.*

Yahweh is named also in v. 27, another conclusion of a stanza in the Song:

> *lest they say: "Our hand is raised up,*   (v. 27b)
> *And not Yahweh has done all this."*

If we read the first colon of v. 37 with 4QDeut^q and the LXX, we have yet another occurrence of "Yahweh" beginning the conclusion of a stanza (vv. 37-38). The cohortatives in v. 38b, which disparage the no-gods, close this stanza and are its climax:

> *Then Yahweh will say: "Where is his god,*   (v. 37)
>   *the rock in whom they took refuge?*
> *Choice portions of his sacrifices they ate,*   (v. 38)
>   *they drank wine of their libations.*
> *Let them arise and let them help you,*
>   *let it be your protection!"*

Muilenburg did not believe that climactic lines always come at the end of stanzas. He said they "may indeed appear at several junctures within a pericope" (Muilenburg 1969, 9). Here in the Song we find that sometimes Yahweh is named climactically at midpoint in the stanza:

> *Do you repay Yahweh thus?* (v. 6a)
>   *O people foolish and unwise!*

> *Yahweh alone guided him,* (v. 12)
>   *and no foreign god was with him.*

> *unless indeed their Rock had sold them,* (v. 30)
>   *and Yahweh had delivered them up?*

> *Indeed Yahweh will vindicate his people,* (v. 36)
>   *and feel sorry over his servants.*

In v. 19 a bicolon naming Yahweh begins a stanza:

> *So Yahweh saw and spurned*
>   *because of the provocation of his sons and daughters.*

At the beginning of the Song's final stanza Yahweh names himself. Here the divine asseverations are strengthened by five occurrences of the first person pronoun:

> *See now indeed I, I (אֲנִי) am he,* (v. 39)
>   *and there is no god with me.*
> *I (אֲנִי), I kill, and I make alive,*
>   *I wound, and I (אֲנִי), I heal;*
>   *and none can rescue from my hand.*
> *Indeed I lift up my hand to heaven,* (v. 40)
>   *and I say: "As I (אָנֹכִי) live forever."*

In Second Isaiah Muilenburg noted that emphatic personal pronouns ("I," "you," etc.) often begin and end stanzas. Beginning (and throughout) the grand poem of Isa 44:24–45:13 is the divine asseveration, "I am Yahweh," also the first person pronouns אֲנִי and אָנֹכִי emphasizing the divine person and divine action. These pronouns occur no less than 10 times in divine speech (Muilenburg 1956, 391-93, 516-28). Looking here in the Song at the distribution of the divine name "Yahweh," also at the divine asseverations in vv. 39-40, we see that all 10 occurrences appear in significant collocations: at the beginning, in the middle, or at the end of stanzas.

Repetitions in Strategic Collocations

Also appearing in significant collocations within the Song are repeated words and particles. Muilenburg (1969, 16-17) said with reference to literary compositions of ancient Israel: "Repeated words or lines do not appear haphazardly or fortuitously, but rather in rhetorically significant collocations." He noted as particularly striking threefold repetitions in a single stanza, citing the thrice-repeated "come" (לְכוּ) in Isa 55:1 and the thrice-repeated "shame" (בוֹשׁ) in Ps 25:1-3. Both occur at the beginning of stanzas. Sometimes threefold repetitions come at midpoint in the stanza, e.g., the repeated "again" (עוֹד) in Jer 31:4-5, which functions also as anaphora (Lundbom 2004a, 412).

Muilenburg believed that even little words take on importance in Hebrew poetry and Hebrew rhetoric. In Exodus 15 a repeated "till" (עַד) creates anaphora in the poem's final refrain (Muilenburg 1966, 248), where also Yahweh is named:

> *till your people, Yahweh, pass by,* (Exod 15:16cd)
> *till the people pass by whom you have purchased.*

Here in the Song, a repeated "from" (מִן) creates anaphora in the final stanza:

> *From the blood of slain and captive,* (v. 42)
> *from the long-haired head of the enemy*

This same type of repetition occurs in Jer 4:26b; 9:18b(19b); 25:38b (Lundbom 1999, 356, 558; 2004a, 277). In 4:26b Yahweh is also named.

Another little word big for Muilenburg was כִּי ("for, because, indeed"), a deictic and emphatic particle occurring often at the beginning and ending of stanzas (Muilenburg 1969, 13-14). Muilenburg found כִּי beginning stanzas of poetry in Isa 34:2a, 5a, 6c, and 8a (Muilenburg 1961a, 148-49; 1969, 14). Sometimes the particle concludes stanzas or entire poems, assuming what Muilenburg called a motivational function, e.g., Ps 1:6. The particle כִּי closes stanzas and entire oracles in Jeremiah, e.g., Jer 4:6b, 8b; 5:5b, 6c (Lundbom 1999, 332, 334, 372, 374).

The particle כִּי occurs 15 times in the Song, some usages of which appear to have the rhetorical function Muilenburg attributes to it. It begins the ballast lines in vv. 3 and 9, the former concluding the introduction (vv. 1-3) and the lat-

Deuteronomy 32

ter concluding a stanza of the Song (vv. 4-9). The particle also begins a double bicolon concluding another stanza (vv. 19-22):

> For (כִּי) a fire is kindled in my anger, (v. 22)
>   and it will burn to the depths of Sheol.
> Yes, it will consume the earth and its yield
>   and set ablaze the mountains' foundations.

In two cases, the particle כִּי begins or appears near the beginning of a stanza:

> For (כִּי) a nation bereft of counsel are they, (v. 28)
>   and there is no understanding in them.
>
> See now indeed (כִּי) I, I am he, (v. 39a)
>   and there is no god with me . . .
> Indeed (כִּי) I lift up my hand to heaven, (v. 40)
>   and I say: "As I live forever."

More striking is this threefold repetition of an assevertive כִּי occurring at midpoint in the stanza of vv. 28-33:

> unless indeed (כִּי) their Rock had sold them, (v. 30b)
>   and Yahweh had delivered them up?
> Indeed (כִּי) their rock is not like our Rock; (v. 31)
>   even our enemies being assessors.
> Indeed (כִּי) their vine is from the vine of Sodom, (v. 32a)
>   and from the terraces of Gomorrah.

At midpoint in the very next stanza, vv. 34-38, another assevertive כִּי repeats three times:

> Indeed (כִּי) the day of their disaster is near, (v. 35b)
>   and things prepared are hastening to him.
> Indeed (כִּי) Yahweh will vindicate his people, (v. 36)
>   and feel sorry over his servants.
> Indeed (כִּי) he will see that support is gone,
>   and none remains bond or free.

So out of the 15 occurrences of כִּי in the Song, 11 appear to manifest a rhetorical function and should be taken as contributing to the Song's structure.

Deuteronomy 32

Nils Lund (1942, 40-41, 44) discovered that balancing repetitions and amplifications frequently occur at the center of large chiastic structures, where they have a climactic function. This phenomenon is now amply documented in the poetry of Jeremiah, e.g., Jer 2:5-9; 5:1-8; 51:34-45 (Lundbom 1999, 256-57, 371-73; 2004b, 469-72). Here in the Song, the balanced repetitions, correlative terms, and entire colons at the center of vv. 19-22 are noted by all commentators:

> *They, they made me jealous with a no-god,* (v. 21)
>   *they provoked me with their nothings.*
> *So I, I will make them jealous with a no-people,*
>   *with a foolish nation I will provoke them.*

Chiasms, Partial Chiasms, and Inclusio

According to Muilenburg (1969, 10), it is "diversities which give [Hebrew] poetry its distinctive and artistic character." One of these diversities is chiasmus, which most commonly is inverted syntax or inverted keyword structures. Chiasms vary the monotony of repetition and parallelism, the two dominant characteristics of Hebrew poetry (Muilenburg 1953, 1969, 10).

Here in the Song, the climactic bicolon ending a stanza in v. 9 contains a keyword chiasmus:

> *Indeed Yahweh's portion is/his people,*
> *Jacob/his allotted inheritance.*

A syntactic chiasmus in v. 18 ends another stanza:

> *The Rock that begot you/you neglected,*
> *and you forgot/the God who bore you in travail.*

Concluding the Song, in v. 43 (MT), is this keyword chiasmus:

> *Give **his people** ringing acclaim, O nations,*
>   *for the blood of his servants **he will avenge**,*
>   *yes, **he will return vengeance** to his adversaries,*
> *and atone for his land, **his people**.*

The longer reading in 4QDeut^q (see Notes) has the same keyword chiasmus:

> *Give **his people** ringing acclaim, O heavens,*   v. 43
>   *and worship him, all you gods!*
> *For the blood of his sons **he will avenge**,*
>   *yes, **he will return vengeance** to his adversaries,*
> *And to those who hate him he will requite*
>   *and atone for the land of **his people**.*

Chiastic bicolons close other segments of OT poetry, e.g., the Song of Lamech in Gen 4:24 (Alter 1985, 7) and Jer 2:9, 13; 4:22c (Lundbom 1999, 262, 266, 355).

A partial chiasmus concludes a stanza of the Song in v. 27. Here, at the center of a double bicolon, the repeated particle פֶּן creates anaphora:

> *Except I feared the provocation of the enemy,*
>   *lest (פֶּן) his adversaries should misjudge,*
>   *lest (פֶּן) they say: "Our hand is raised up,*
> *And not Yahweh has done all this."*

Structures of the same type effect closure in Jer 5:10b-11; 9:21(22); 46:23 (Lundbom 1999, 387, 559; 2004b, 220). In Jer 6:8; 8:13; 17:1, this type of partial chiasmus also begins poetic units (Lundbom 1999, 421-22, 521, 775).

Two stanzas of the Song conclude with keyword inclusios. The stanza in vv. 4-9 concludes with the following inclusio (Alday 1967, 163):

> *When the Most High gave the nations an **inheritance**,*   (v. 8)
>   *when he separated the sons of man,*
> *He fixed the boundaries of peoples*
>   *to the number of the sons of God.*
> *Indeed Yahweh's portion is his people,*   (v. 9)
>   *Jacob, his allotted **inheritance**.*

The stanza in vv. 28-33 concludes with a keyword inclusio in a double bicolon:

> *Its grapes are grapes of **poison**,*   (v. 32b)
>   *its clusters are bitter.*
> *Their wine is the venom of serpents,*   (v. 33)
>   *yes, the cruel **poison** of vipers.*

A similar keyword inclusio concludes a stanza in Jer 8:7 (Lundbom 1999, 506).

All throughout the Bible are much larger keyword chiasms (Lund 1930;

1933; 1942), many examples of which can be seen in the prose and poetry of Jeremiah (Lundbom 1975, 61-112[= 1997, 82-146]). Two fine examples in Jeremiah poetry occur in Jer 2:5-9; 5:1-8, where in both cases the chiasmus is coterminous with the limits of the literary unit (Lundbom 1999, 256-57, 371-73).

Here in the Song, a large keyword chiasmus takes in all but v. 15a of the stanza in vv. 15-18. The keywords name Israel's God at beginning and end and the no-gods in the center. Then in the final bicolon, as we noted earlier, a syntactic chiasmus brings closure. In this final bicolon "Rock" and "God" invert from "God" and "Rock" in v. 15b:

a	*Then he abandoned the **God** who made him*		(v. 15b)
	*and took to be foolish the **Rock** of his salvation.*		
	b	*They made him jealous/with **strangers**,*	(v. 16)
		*with **abominations**/they provoked him.*	
		c *They sacrificed to demons/**no-gods**,*	(v. 17)
		* **gods**/they had not known.*	
	b′	***New ones** recently come in,*	
		*your fathers were not awed by **them**.*	
a′	*The **Rock** that begot you/you neglected,*		(v. 18)
	*and you forgot/the **God** who bore you in travail.*		

Rhetorical Questions

Rhetorical questions also occur in strategic collocations (Muilenburg 1969, 16), beginning a discourse unit, ending a unit, or coming in the middle. Rhetorical questions — sometimes a pair — frequently begin psalms and stanzas of psalms (Pss 2:1; 10:1; 15:1; 35:17; 49:6[5]; 52:2[1]; 58:2[1], and elsewhere). They also begin oracles and stanzas of oracles in Jeremiah (Jer 2:5a, 29; 5:7a). In Jer 4:21 a rhetorical question ends a unit of poetry. In Jer 5:7a, the question "Why then will I pardon you?" is the conclusion to which the entire oracle has been building.

The Song contains four rhetorical questions, all of which come at the beginning, in the middle, or at the end of stanzas. The rhetorical question in v. 34 begins a stanza:

Is not this stored up with me,
  sealed in my storehouses?

In vv. 6 and 30 rhetorical questions occur in the middle of stanzas:

Do you repay Yahweh thus?   (v. 6)
  O people foolish and unwise!

Is not he your father? he created you!
    He, he made you and he established you!

How could one chase a thousand,   (v. 30)
    and two put thousands to flight,
unless indeed their Rock had sold them,
    and Yahweh had delivered them up?

And in vv. 37-38a a rhetorical question concludes the stanza:

Then Yahweh will say: "Where is his god,   (v. 37)
    the rock in whom they took refuge?
Choice portions of his sacrifices they ate,   (v. 38a)
    they drank wine of their libations."

Shift to Direct Address

In Jeremiah one will sometimes observe, at the end of a discourse unit, a shift from the third person to the second person, making the discourse more direct. This can be seen in Jer 2:9; 5:31b; 12:13b; 48:46. Jeremianic preaching exhibits a "rhetoric of descent," i.e., it begins at a distance and comes in close at the end (Lundbom 1975, 116 [= 1997, 150]).

In the Song, a shift to the second person occurs at the end of the stanza in vv. 10-14, driving home the point that the Israelites became fat after settlement in the land:

Curds of the herd and milk of the flock,   (v. 14)
    with the choicest of lambs and rams,
sons of Bashan and he-goats
    with the choicest grains of wheat,
        yes, blood of the grape, **you** *drank wine!*

At the end of the next stanza, vv. 15-18, is another shift to the second person:

New ones recently come in,   (v. 17b)
    your *fathers were not awed by them.*
The Rock that begot **you,** **you** *neglected,*   (v. 18)
    and **you** *forgot the God who bore* **you** *in travail.*

Here second person speech ending the stanza ties in with second person speech beginning the stanza, which is the tricolon lying outside the large chiasmus:

> So Jacob ate and became sated; (v. 15a)
>   yes, Jeshurun got fat and kicked;
>   **you** got fat, **you** grew thick, **you** became gorged.

Another shift from third to second person concludes the stanza of vv. 34-38:

> Let them arise and let them help **you**, (v. 38b)
>   let it be **your** protection!

Von Rad (1966a, 198) said these shifts to the second person "make the whole appear as a prophetic indictment."

Metrical Analysis

A Song of Moses consisting of an introduction, eight stanzas, and a conclusion, which is now supported by a rhetorical analysis, can be corroborated and refined by a metrical analysis carried on along the lines of David Noel Freedman's work on the poetry of the OT. Freedman used syllable counting with profit in analyzing Exodus 15 (1967; 1974); Deuteronomy 33 (1980a), and numerous other poems in the Hebrew Bible (1972; 1976; 1987a; 1987b; 1992). In his work on the "Song of the Sea" in Exodus 15, he credited Muilenburg for discovering refrainlike dividers, agreeing that they served as structural markers in the poem. Freedman then proceeded to do his own stanza analysis using a syllable-counting method.

Freedman was not interested simply in counting syllables of colons and bicolons, although he did that. He believed something could be learned about Hebrew poetic composition by looking at syllable totals of larger units, where, not infrequently, symmetries turn up and internal structures are seen with greater clarity. He noted that the Shakespearean sonnets have a total length of 140 syllables, plus or minus a syllable or two. This is because they have fourteen lines of iambic pentameter, which means regular lines adding up to a predictable total. But, he said:

> What is different about Hebrew poetry is that, while the sum-total is predictable within a very narrow range, the total is not based upon the repetition of lines of the same length, as in the case of the English sonnet. Unless we engage in wholesale emendation and improvement of the text, we must recognize it as a basic fact of Hebrew poetry that individual lines (and stanzas) vary considerably in length. (Freedman 1987a, 19; 1997, 2:219)

Freedman found larger, fixed syllable totals turning up also in Japanese poetry.

Deuteronomy 32

In counting syllables of segments in the Song of Moses, I follow Freedman (1972, 369; 1980a, 30) in the analysis now to be presented, i.e., using the vocalized Hebrew of MT with the following exceptions: (1) segholates are taken to be monosyllabic; (2) the *furtive pataḥ* is not counted; and (3) the compound *shewa* after laryngeals is not counted. There is one occurrence of the relative pronoun אֲשֶׁר in the poem, beginning v. 38a. It probably does not belong there, but the question is, where does it belong? Relative pronouns are rare in Hebrew poetry, although they do occur (e.g., Jer 20:14-18; cf. Lundbom 1985, 591-92). The one here in v. 38a could simply be excised from the text, which is what Freedman does with a lone אֲשֶׁר in Deut 33:29b (1980a, 31-32). My preference here would be to relocate it after צוּר ("rock") in the prior line, where it at least makes sense in a colon that appears truncated. Support for this transfer comes from both 4QDeut^q and the LXX. In 4QDeut^q an אשר actually appears here in the text (Ulrich, Cross et al. 1995, 139), and the LXX has ἐφ' οἷς. This change, it should also be noted, has no effect on the total syllable count, since the one אֲשֶׁר in MT is counted only once (see Notes).

In four instances I have not followed readings of MT. The first is in v. 8b, where I adopt the 4QDeut^j reading "sons of God" (בני אלוהים) over MT's "sons of Israel" (בְּנֵי יִשְׂרָאֵל). This presents no problem in a syllable count, for בני אלוהים and בְּנֵי יִשְׂרָאֵל are both 5 syllables. The LXX's "angels of God" (ἀγγέλων θεοῦ), if it happened to translate Hebrew מַלְאֲכֵי אֱלֹהִים, would be 6 syllables instead of 5. Slight difference. I also adopt, as most scholars do, the additional colon of Sam and LXX beginning v. 15a, "So Jacob ate and became sated" (LXX: καὶ ἔφαγεν Ιακωβ καὶ ἐνεπλήσθη). Its Hebrew equivalent, וַיֹּאכַל יַעֲקֹב וַיִּשְׂבַּע, adds 9 syllables to the count of MT. This colon was probably lost in MT due to haplography (homoeoarcton: ו . . . ו). I also adopt readings of 4QDeut^q and LXX that add יהוה as a subject in v. 37. This increases the syllable count of the first colon by 2. Then, in the conclusion of v. 43, if we adopt the longer LXX reading, which is eight colons compared to four colons in MT, and six colons in 4QDeut^q, we have an eight-colon conclusion, balancing the eight-colon introduction in vv. 1-3. Syllable counts of the eight stanzas are then as follows:

	I		II
4	6 : 7	10	8 : 9
	8 : 6		10 : 9
5	8 : 7	11	6 : 7
6	8 : 7		9 : 8
	9 : 10		
		12	7 : 7
7	6 : 7	13	9 : 8
	10 : 9		

869

Deuteronomy 32

8	7 : 8		10 : 6
	7 : 8	14	8 : 8*
9	7 : 7		8 : 7 : 8
	152		152

	III		IV
15	8 : 9 : 9	19	7 : 9
	8 : 9	20	10 : 7
16	7 : 8		7 : 6
17	9 : 7	21	7 : 7
	8 : 8		8 : 7
18	7 : 9†	22	8 : 8
			7 : 9
	107		107

	V		VI
23	7 : 6	28	8 : 7
24	9 : 5	29	7 : 8
	9 : 8	30	7 : 9
25	6 : 7		8 : 6
	7 : 6	31	8 : 8
26	6 : 7	32	7 : 7
27	8 : 7		7 : 8
	9 : 8	33	7 : 7
	115		119

	VII		VIII
34	8 : 7	39	10 : 8
35	6 : 6		7 : 8 : 7
	6 : 7	40	9 : 11
36	7 : 8	41	8 : 8
	8 : 7		7 : 7
37	10 : 6†	42	6 : 7
38	9 : 6‡		7 : 6
	8 : 7		
	116		116

*The term וְאֵילִים beginning the next line in *BHS* is taken at the end of this line with most commentators.

†Adding יהוה after the verb in the first colon with 4QDeut^q; the LXX has κύριος. In the second colon the relative pronoun אשר is added after צור with 4QDeut^q and the LXX (see Notes).

‡Eliminating the initial אשר in MT as a reinsertion from v. 37 (see Notes).

Deuteronomy 32

This syllable count supports a poem of eight stanzas, indicating further that the stanzas should be taken as four pairs. Paired stanzas have different totals from other paired stanzas, but each pair has identical or near-identical totals, which can hardly be accidental. And with the eight-colon conclusion of LXX v. 43 balancing the eight-colon introduction in vv. 1-3, the poem becomes wholly symmetrical.

Content

In literature of a high order form and content go hand in hand. The structure here exhibited correlates well with the Song's thematic development, which I take to be the following:

Introduction (vv. 1-3)

I. Yahweh Great, Israel his Adversary (vv. 4-9)	II. Past Salvation of Israel (vv. 10-14)
III. Indictment of Unfaithful Israel (vv. 15-18)	IV. Sentence on Unfaithful Israel (vv. 19-22)
V. Extent of Israel's Punishment (vv. 23-27)	VI. Israel's Punishment in Retrospect (vv. 28-33)
VII. Future Salvation of Israel (vv. 34-38)	VIII. Yahweh Great, Enemy his Adversary (vv. 39-42)

Conclusion (v. 43)

Having seen rhetorical inversions both large and small in stanzas of the Song, we now note a thematic inversion in the Song taken as a whole: the last pair of stanzas (VII and VIII) invert the balancing themes of the first pair (I and II). Stanza I acclaims the greatness of Yahweh, seen in his perfect creation, his just ways, and his faithfulness to the covenant, a God who is contrasted with a corrupt and perverse adversary, Israel. Stanza VIII again acclaims the greatness of Yahweh, seen now in his infinite and incomparable power, who is contrasted with a hateful adversary unnamed. Also, Yahweh's past salvation of Israel in Stanza II balances Yahweh's future salvation of Israel in Stanza VII. The other stanzas balance in normal fashion: Israel's indictment for unfaithfulness in Stanza III balances Israel's sentence for unfaithfulness in Stanza IV, and the extent of Israel's punishment in Stanza V balances Israel's punishment in retrospect in Stanza VI.

Portions of 32:1-43 are contained in 1QDeut^b, 4QDeut^b, 4QDeut^c, 4QDeut^j, 4QDeut^{k1}, 4QDeut^q, and 4QpaleoDeut^r; also on a phylactery from Qumran (4Q141).

Notes

32:1 The call to heavens and earth is apostrophe, but are they being summoned as witnesses? Rashi says they are, but more recent commentators are not so sure. Some follow Driver, who says they are simply being invited to listen in on the poet's lofty theme (Tigay; Nelson). Von Rad notes, too, that this "opening summons" occurs commonly in wisdom poems (Pss 49:2-5[1-4]; 78:1-4; Isa 28:23-26), which would preclude a legal setting. But others think the heavens and earth will indeed be acting in the capacity of witnesses (Huffmon 1959, 288-95; Moran 1962, 317-20; G. E. Wright 1962, 44), particularly if the poem happens to be a covenant lawsuit. Admonishment — anticipated or otherwise — is strengthened if witnesses are present to hear it (4:26; 30:19; 31:28; cf. Isa 1:2-3; Mic 6:1-2; Jer 2:12-13), and admonishment is precisely what follows in vv. 5-6 and what occupies much of the remainder of the poem. Also, international treaties of the ANE, which are fortified by threats aplenty if the terms are not kept, call in the gods, heaven and earth, mountains, rivers, and other constituents of the created order to act as witnesses (Huffmon; Moran; $ANET^3$, 200-201, 205-6). Here in the Song the heavens and earth will not act as judges, simply as witnesses (cf. 4:26; 30:19; 31:28; Isa 1:2; 34:1-2; Ps 50:4). The judge is Yahweh, who gives the verdict on Israel in vv. 19-27. Heaven and earth, say Rashi and ibn Ezra, will endure longer than any human witnesses who live at most only one generation and may die tomorrow.

Give ear . . . and let . . . hear. הַאֲזִינוּ . . . וְתִשְׁמַע. In Jewish tradition, "Give ear" has become the title of the Song: *Ha'azinu*. This double imperative inverts in Judg 5:3; Hos 5:1; Isa 1:2, 10; Jer 13:15; Joel 1:2; Ps 49:2(1).

2 *Let my teaching drop like the rain, let my speech distil like the dew.* "Teaching" (לֶקַח) and "speech" (אִמְרָה) belong to the language of Wisdom literature, the former occurring often in Proverbs (Prov 1:5; 4:2; 7:21; 9:9; 16:21, 23), the later occurring often in the Psalms (Pss 18:31[30]; 105:19; 119:11, 38, 50, 67, and 15 times more), where in certain contexts it denotes Yahweh's "promissory word." In the second colon the LXX has "words" plural (ῥήματά). Moses' words are to penetrate human minds and hearts in the way "dripping rain" and "distilling dew" water thirsty ground (Ps 72:6). We speak today of words "soaking in," by which we mean words that take effect on those hearing them (Job 29:22-23; Isa 55:10-11).

like raindrops upon grass. כִּשְׂעִירִם עֲלֵי־דֶשֶׁא. Hebrew שְׂעִירִם is a *hapax legomenon* in the OT, whose precise meaning is uncertain. LXX's ὄμβρος is a heavy rainstorm, with T^{OnqPsJ} both interpreting the term as rain accompanied by wind (Rashi: "stormwinds"). But the context requires something more like gentle rain (Moran 1962, 321: "softly and quietly soaking the ground"), which is how the term is rendered in T^{Nf}. RSV has "tender grass"; Driver: "young grass," as in Gen 1:11; 2 Sam 23:4; G. A. Smith: "fresh young grass."

and like showers upon green plants. וְכִרְבִיבִים עֲלֵי־עֵשֶׂב. The expression occurs in Mic 5:6(7). Hebrew רְבִיבִים are gentle but abundant showers (Ps 65:11[10]), here falling upon green plants. Ibn Ezra says these "showers" are a milder kind of rain.

3 The Introduction concludes with a climactic word naming Yahweh and calling for an attribution of greatness to Israel's God (see Rhetoric and Composition). In Exod 34:5-7, Yahweh proclaims his own name (cf. v. 39). The "name" of Yahweh is often confessed in doxologies, liturgical poetry, and other biblical discourse (Exod 15:3; Amos 4:13; 5:8; 9:6; Jer 10:16[=51:19]; 31:35; 33:2; Isa 47:4; 48:2; 51:15; 54:5). Yahweh's "greatness" (גֹּדֶל) includes his mighty acts, the greatest of which was the exodus deliverance (Deut 3:24; 9:26; 11:2-7; Ps 150:2). Some think the heavens and earth are being called upon to ascribe this greatness (ibn Ezra; G. E. Wright 1962, 54; Moran; cf. Pss 19:2[1]; 69:35[34]; 148:3-9), but the poet could simply be addressing those hearing the poem.

4 *The Rock, his work is perfect.* הַצּוּר תָּמִים פָּעֳלוֹ. "The Rock" (הַצּוּר) is a title for Yahweh, as it is again in vv. 15, 18, 30, 31 and elsewhere in the OT (2 Sam 22:3, 32, 47; 23:3; Isa 17:10; 30:29; Hab 1:12), particularly in the Psalms (Pss 18:3, 32, 47[2, 31, 46]; 19:15[14]; and often). The metaphor symbolizes strength (Ps 73:26) and a place of refuge (Pss 62:8[7]; 94:22). Ibn Ezra says it is used because rock endures forever. The LXX never retains the metaphor, usually substituting θεός (Wevers 1995, 510). "Rock" also denotes other deities in the Song (vv. 31, 37), where the metaphor makes for irony. However, "Great Rock (or Mountain)" is a common title for Assur and Bel in Assyrian texts (Driver; G. A. Smith), and mountain imagery is used elsewhere in the ANE to name gods (Knowles 1989, 315). Here "Rock Yahweh" contrasts with "corrupt Israel," who is next mentioned (v. 5). For a discussion of the various names and epithets used for God (also other gods) in the Song of Moses and where comparisons are made to the selection and distribution of divine names and titles in other early Hebrew poetry, see Freedman 1976.

his work is perfect. Yahweh's "work" (פֹּעַל) is his created work, which includes Israel, his child (v. 6; cf. Isa 45:11). But if his work is "perfect" (תָּמִים), how has Israel become so flawed? Jeremiah, using the "vine" metaphor, addresses the same problem. In one Jeremiah oracle Yahweh says to his people: "But I, I planted you a choice vine, perfectly good seed; how then have you become something putrid, a strange vine?" (Jer 2:21).

indeed all his ways are just. Psalm 18:31(30) says that God's way is perfect (תָּמִים). Here his ways are said to be just (מִשְׁפָּט). God's rule in the world that he created is just and right (Gen 18:25; Jer 9:23[24]). The כִּי is best translated as an asseverative (NJV: "yea"), not "and" (*pace* LXX: καὶ; NRSV) or "for" (*pace* AV; RSV). In the NT, see Rev 15:3; 16:5; 19:2.

a God of faithfulness, and without wrong. אֵל אֱמוּנָה וְאֵין עָוֶל. Yahweh's faithfulness is seen in his keeping of the covenant (7:9), which means he is a God who can be trusted (Rashi: "He is faithful to his word"). There is no wrong or deceit in him, enabling God to ask rhetorically in Jer 2:5: "What did your fathers find wrong (עָוֶל) in me, that they wandered far from me?" Zephaniah affirms with the poet that Yahweh is righteous "and does no wrong" (Zeph 3:5).

righteous and upright is he. צַדִּיק וְיָשָׁר הוּא. Freedman (1976, 78) translates as two titles for God: "Righteous One" and "Upright One." The LXX substitutes "Lord" (κύριος) for MT "he." These two divine attributes are affirmed in Ps 119:137, where Yahweh is said to be upright in his judgments. Elsewhere, Israel's God is confessed to be righteous (Pss 11:7; 116:5; 129:4; Jer 12:1) and upright (Pss 25:8; 92:16[15]). Yahweh's righteousness, says the psalmist, is a righteousness forever (Ps 119:142)

5 *It acted corruptly toward him.* שִׁחֵת לוֹ. I.e., the "generation" cited at the conclusion of the verse. Reference appears to be to the wilderness generation that "acted corruptly" (שִׁחֵת) by making a golden calf (9:12). Israel's actions, then, are precisely the opposite of Yahweh's.

Is not their blemish his children's? לֹא בָּנָיו מוּמָם. The Hebrew is difficult, but the phrase can be made to yield good sense if framed as a question or if the לֹא is translated as an asseverative: "Their blemish is surely his children's!" Another translation disregarding MT accents and assuming ellipsis is proposed by C. McCarthy (2002, 42): "(They are) his 'no-sons', (by reason of) their blemish." The point, in any case, is that Israel's corruption in the wilderness was its own, not Yahweh's. *Sifre Deuteronomy* (§308) has: "No; His children's is the blemish" (Basser 1984, 105; Neusner 1987, 2:322). Rashi similarly: "It is His children's defect." "Blemish" (מוּם) here is not a physical defect (as with animals in 15:21; 17:1), but a moral taint (Job 11:15; Sir 11:33).

a generation perverted and crooked! דּוֹר עִקֵּשׁ וּפְתַלְתֹּל. Rashi: "a warped and twisted generation" (cf. v. 20b). The term פְּתַלְתֹּל ("crooked") is a *hapax legomenon* in the OT, but a well-attested cognate verb means "to be twisted, tortuous" (Job 5:13; Ps 18:27[26]; Prov 8:8). The term עִקֵּשׁ ("perverted") has similar meaning, associated often in the Wisdom literature with a person's heart, speech, and ways (Prov 11:20; 17:20; 19:1; 28:6, 18; Ps 101:4; Job 9:20). In Prov 10:9 the person "who perverts" (מְעַקֵּשׁ) his ways is contrasted with the one who walks "in integrity" (בַּתֹּם). The present phrase is quoted in Acts 2:40; Phil 2:15.

6 *Do you repay Yahweh thus?* The Hebrew puts "Yahweh" at the beginning for emphasis: "Is it to *Yahweh* you repay thus?" An enlarged ה interrogative in many Heb MSS, written also as a separate word, may underscore the question (Tigay; Friedman; cf. *BHS*). It is not present, however, in M[L], M[A], or 4QpaleoDeut[r] (Skehan, Ulrich, and Sanderson 1992, 146). Rashi says the words denote astonishment. A shift from third to second person makes the accusation more direct.

O people foolish and unwise! In biblical thought foolishness stands next to godlessness. People are foolish when they deal corruptly with a good and righteous God. They are also foolish when they take as foolish (יְנַבֵּל) the God of their salvation (v. 15). An example of "acting foolishly" (נְבָלָה) in the Deuteronomic Code is a woman sexually promiscuous before marriage (22:21). To be "wise" (חָכָם) in the Proverbs means to possess the faculty of shrewd observation, acute and discriminating insight (Driver). It also means to speak and act prudently and above all to fear God (Prov 9:10; cf. Ps 111:10). Covenant people have not feared God, making necessary the recurring exhortation in Deuteronomy to do precisely that and teach children the same (see Note for 4:10).

Is not he your father? he created you! He, he made you and he established you! The added pronouns are for emphasis. Luther, the AV, and most modern Versions take the second colon as another question, which it could be since the colons are parallel and the ה interrogative may be doing double-duty for both colons. But the line is best read as an initial question followed by three emphatic affirmations. The LXX omits the emphatic "he" (הוּא) in the second colon, substituting "and" (καὶ). The NJV takes both colons as emphatic declarations.

your father. Yahweh as "father" and Israel as "son" are not dominant metaphors in the OT, but they do occur (Exod 4:22; Deut 1:31; 8:5; Hos 11:1-4; Jer 3:4, 19; 31:9; Isa 63:16; 64:7[8]; Mal 2:10). Israel's aversion to "father/son" imagery is usually attributed to wide usage in other ANE religions. Jeremiah censures people for not acknowledging Yahweh as their Father and Creator (Jer 2:27). In the NT, God is often referred to as "Father" and Jesus as "Son," particularly in the Gospel of John (John 1:14, 18; 3:35; 4:21-23; 5:17-45; 6:27-65; 8:18-54, and passim).

he created you. קָנֶךָ. The verb קנה in the OT usually means "get, acquire, purchase" (Gen 25:10; Exod 15:16, in reference to God acquiring Israel in the exodus), but in some contexts it means "make, form, produce." God formed the heaven and earth (Gen 14:19, 22); he formed the psalmist in his mother's womb (Ps 139:13); and he formed Wisdom at the beginning of his creative acts (Prov 8:22). Ugaritic *qny* has the meaning "produce, procreate" (D. J. McCarthy 1967, 92), so what we seem to have in Hebrew are two homonymous verbs, one meaning "acquire," the other meaning "form, create" (Pope 1955, 51-52, citing P. Humbert; Habel 1972, 325). In the present text, Yahweh is speaking about his bringing of Israel into existence as a people. This being poetry, assonance may also be intended with the parallel verb יְכֹנְנֶךָ ("he established you").

He, he made you and he established you! The creation idea is expanded to include Israel's establishment among the nations (vv. 8-9). The verb כּוּן (polel) means "set up to last" (KBL[3]).

7 *Remember the days of old.* If Israel should question Yahweh's creation and establishment of the nation, let it remember the tradition passed down from hoary antiquity. The "days of old" (יְמוֹת עוֹלָם) are unspecified time, but

in looking ahead to the verses following, Driver thinks reference is to the period of national formation under Moses and Israel's settlement in Canaan (Mic 7:14-15; Isa 63:11). But the "days of old" are probably much earlier time, extending back into the pre-Israelite mythic past when the Most High gave to each nation its inheritance (v. 8). Yet we are reminded here that in Israel divine revelation was understood as having come down through history.

consider the years of many generations. Hebrew דּוֹר־וָדוֹר denotes successive generations, sometimes meaning "forever" (Ps 10:6; Joel 2:2; KBL³; Freedman, Lundbom, *dôr,* in *TDOT,* 3:175).

Ask your father and he will inform you. The same questioning rhetoric occurs elsewhere in Deuteronomy. In 4:32-34 people are invited to ask about any gods as wonderful as Yahweh, which will not likely bring forth an answer. Here, however, a father should be relied upon to answer the child's question. In ancient Israel, fathers (and mothers) were the ones who passed on knowledge, wisdom, and Yahweh's glorious deeds to their children and grandchildren (Judg 6:13; Job 8:8-10; Pss 44:2[1]; 78:2-4). Teaching children is a major theme in Deuteronomy (see Note for 4:9). On transmission of knowledge generally in Israel and in the ancient world, see Crenshaw 1998.

your elders, and they will tell you. Community elders, like fathers and mothers, can relate not only happenings in their own time, but earlier happenings passed down to them by others (Joel 1:3). In ancient society, town elders were the depositories of wisdom (Job 12:12; 15:10). On the "elders" in Deuteronomy and in ancient Israel, see Note for 5:23-24.

8 *When the Most High gave the nations an inheritance, when he separated the sons of man.* An ancient idea that God, acting as a king over a vast realm, separated his sons and gave to each an inheritance, i.e., an area of land. Here God is named "Most High," a pre-Israelite epithet taken over from the Canaanites. In Gen 14:17-20, Melchizedek, king and priest of Salem, blessed Abraham in the name of "God Most High" after Abraham defeated Chedorlaomer and a coalition of kings from the East. "God Most High," Hebrew *'El 'Elyon* (אֵל עֶלְיוֹן), was worshipped by the inhabitants of Jerusalem in the pre-Israelite period. 'El was the Canaanite creator-god and 'Elyon ("Most High") his proper epithet (Cross 1962, 241-43; 1973, 50-52). Centuries later, Balaam is said in the Bible to be delivering oracles from the "Most High" (Num 24:16). Here in the Song, "Most High" has been equated with "Yahweh" (v. 9), as happens elsewhere in the OT (Pope 1955, 52; Albright 1959, 343; Moran; Nelson). Moran (1969, 275) says: "As the universal God who separates the nations, he is the Most High, but as the one who keeps Israel for himself, he is Yahweh."

In the OT "Most High" survives largely as a poetical title for God, occurring often in the Psalms (Gen 14:19-20; Pss 7:18[17]; 9:3[2]; 18:14[13]= 2 Sam 22:14; Isa 14:14, and passim). "Most High" emerges again as ὁ ὕψιστος in the NT (Mark 5:7; Luke 8:28; Acts 7:48; 16:17; Heb 7:1). The question, however, is whether at one time the names "Most High" and "Yahweh" denoted two separate deities, with Yahweh understood as being a subordinate deity to God Most High (Gaster 1969, 318-19). If the Song presupposes such an idea, it would be acknowledging the existence of other gods besides Yahweh (henotheism). From extrabiblical texts we know that "Most High" was worshipped outside Israel, e.g. in Sefire Treaty I A (ca. 750), where the gods 'El and 'Elyon are mentioned together (*ANET*³, 659). Other Syrian and Phoenician texts also mention Most High as a Canaanite deity (Cross 1962, 241-43; 1973, 50-52; Gaster 1969, 319), and it is probable that Israel borrowed this old appellation from the Canaanites (G. E. Wright 1962, 28 n. 7). Freedman (1976, 78) says 'Elyon as a patriarchal epithet has an archaic ring.

In this very ancient time, then, perhaps soon after the creation of the world, the Most High separated the nations and parceled out an inheritance to each. If the fathers and elders were to be consulted, they would give this as their answer. Friedman cites in this connection Psalm 82, which he thinks preserves an ancient myth about the death of lesser gods who, we should note, are called "sons of the Most High" (v. 6). At the end of the Psalm (82:8) God is said to have given an inheritance (1 MS תַנְחִיל) to the nations, the same as here. See also G. E. Wright 1950, 30-41. Von Rad says this beginning of history in the Song, which is before all history, is unique in the OT. Yahweh's movement of nations as reported in Amos 9:7 is from a later time, when Yahweh brought Israel from Egypt into Canaan, Sea Peoples from the Greek islands to the coastland areas of the Eastern Mediterranean, and Syrians from a place called Kir.

gave . . . an inheritance. בְּהַנְחֵל. On the pointing of the infinitive construct, see GKC §53k.

when he separated the sons of man. בְּהַפְרִידוֹ בְּנֵי אָדָם. "Sons of man" refers to the whole of humanity, with "separated" suggesting a connection to the dispersion after the flood as recorded in Genesis 10-11 (*Sifre Deut.* §311; Rashi; Driver; Tigay). Driver notes the connection to Gen 10:32: "and from these [families of the sons of Noah] the nations were separated (נִפְרְדוּ) on the earth after the flood." The Babel story in Gen 11:1-9 reports the same or another postflood "dispersion" (Heb פוץ), there carried out by Yahweh (vv. 8-9). In the NT, see Acts 17:26.

He fixed the boundaries of peoples. The Most High established a home for each nation and fixed its boundaries. In Jer 3:19 Yahweh reflects inwardly about his wanting to give Israel — there designated as his daughter — a land inheritance such as he was giving to his other sons (LXX^B: "nations"). The verb נצב in the H-stem means "to set up, fix" (boundary markers); cf. Ps 74:17; Prov 15:25.

to the number of the sons of God. Reading בני אלוהים ("sons of God") with 4QDeut^j (Ulrich, Cross et al. 1995, 90; cf. Skehan 1954, 12; 1959, 21) and the

JB. The poet intends a contrast with "sons of man" in the prior line. The LXX has ἀγγέλων θεοῦ ("angels of God") and the MT "sons of Israel." The Sam, T, S, and Vg all follow the MT, whose reading is widely taken to be secondary (Skehan 1951, 154; von Rad; Freedman 1976, 101 n. 55; van der Kooij 1994, 93; Rofé 2000, 167). Later Jewish tradition linked the seventy nations in Genesis 10 with the seventy persons in Jacob's family who went down to Egypt (Exod 1:5; Deut 10:22; cf. T[PsJ]; *Sifre Deut*. §311; Rashi). The altered reading of MT was doubtless to avoid a misunderstanding of the "sons of God/gods" expression. The RSV and NRSV make a similar change in Ps 29:1, replacing "sons of God/gods" (בְּנֵי אֵלִים) with "heavenly beings" (AV: "mighty"; REB: "angelic powers"; cf. Ps 96:7: "families of the peoples"). The LXX of this Psalm (LXX 28:1) has υἱοὶ θεοῦ ("sons of God"). In our present text, the LXX translator seems to have opted for "angels of God" in order to affirm the existence of lesser divine beings in Yahweh's heavenly host, not pagan gods (Wevers 1995, 513; Friedman). Regardless of what terminology was used, later Israelite religion would not countenance the existence of deities other than Yahweh, but the existence of lesser heavenly beings it could and did acknowledge. In Gen 6:2; Job 1:6 such are called "sons of God" (בְּנֵי־הָאֱלֹהִים). Throughout the OT Yahweh is said to possess a heavenly council over which he presides (Deut 33:2; Job 15:8; 1 Kgs 22:19-22; Isa 6:8; Jer 23:18, 22). On the idea of a divine council in Israelite and ANE religion, see H. W. Robinson 1944 and E. T. Mullen, "Divine Assembly," in *ABD*, 2:214-17.

Von Rad says what is remarkable about the present passage is that it confers upon lesser heavenly beings such an important role in the government of the world, although he notes that in Psalm 82 such heavenly beings were expected to provide justice and order among the nations, which they failed to do. In Deuteronomy one finds the idea that Yahweh allotted to other peoples heavenly bodies as objects of worship (Deut 4:19; 29:25[26]). The later Jewish idea that a guardian angel existed for each nation is rooted in texts such as Dan 10:13, 20-21; 12:1; Sir 17:17.

to the number. לְמִסְפַּר. I.e., "equal to the number" (Josh 4:5, 8; Judg 21:23).

9 *Indeed Yahweh's portion is his people.* Hebrew חֵלֶק is a "portion" or "share," here denoting Yahweh's people. Elsewhere in Deuteronomy the term commonly refers to land (not given to the Levites) as an inheritance (10:9; 12:12; 14:27, 29; 18:1). Assuming that "Most High" has become but another name for Yahweh, the point being made here is that while other nations were apportioned to the number of the various "sons of God," Jacob (= Israel) became and now is Yahweh's own (4:19-20; Sir 17:17). This pushes Israel's election all the way back into primeval times (Nelson). Israel's "election" is a major theme in Deuteronomy; see 4:37; 7:6-8; 10:15; 14:2 and Note for 7:6. The line, having no verbs, should be translated present tense.

Indeed. Hebrew כִּי cannot be causal if "sons of Israel" in v. 8 is unoriginal. The particle is better translated as an asseverative (Wevers 1995, 513; Tigay). The LXX has καὶ. The verse is a climactic affirmation naming Yahweh and Jacob, his inheritance (see Rhetoric and Composition).

Jacob, his alloted inheritance. נַחֲלָתוֹ יַעֲקֹב חֶבֶל נַחֲלָתוֹ. Hebrew נַחֲלָתוֹ ("his inheritance") makes an inclusio with בְּהַנְחֵל ("when he gave an inheritance") in v. 8 (Alday 1967, 163). The term חֶבֶל ("lot") is literally a "rope" (Josh 2:15), used among other things for parceling out land (Amos 7:17; Mic 2:5). Here the meaning of "portion/inheritance" shifts from people to land, with Jacob (Israel) now the land that Yahweh has apportioned for himself. Because Yahweh elected Israel and set apart land for the people of his choice, all through Deuteronomy he is said to be giving Israel land as an inheritance (see Note for 15:4). This land is the land of Canaan (Ps 105:11).

10 *He found him in a wilderness land.* יִמְצָאֵהוּ בְּאֶרֶץ מִדְבָּר. Here begins a series of Hebrew imperfects said to be old preterite prefixes expressing continuous action in the past (GKC §107b; Wevers 1995, 514). They continue through v. 19. The Targums translate the verbs past tense, the LXX with verbs in the aorist. G. A. Smith says this initial imperfect ("he found him") is for the sake of vividness, the others expressive of iteration. The LXX renders the present phrase: αὐτάρκησεν αὐτὸν ἐν γῇ ἐρήμῳ ("He made him sufficient in a wilderness land"), which is the rendering also in T^{Onq}: "He supplied their needs in the territory of the wilderness" (cf. מצא in Num 11:22). Emphasized here is Yahweh's care over Israel in a forbidding wilderness, compared and contrasted in vv. 13-14 to Yahweh's subsequent blessing in a land of unspeakable richness.

It is striking that the Song makes no mention of the exodus, the defining event in Israelite history. The verb מצא suggests that Israel was a lost wanderer and that Yahweh "found" her in this precarious state. Ezekiel will later speak similarly to Jerusalem, using the metaphor of an abandoned child found in an open field (Ezek 16:1-7). Yet here in the Song we were told a few verses earlier that Yahweh chose Israel soon after creation (vv. 8-9). The two ideas can exist without contradiction, for Yahweh could certainly have "chosen" Israel before "finding" her. Yahweh, after all, chose Jeremiah for holy office *before* the prophet designate was formed in the womb (Jer 1:5), at a time known only to Yahweh (Lundbom 1999, 231). Ibn Ezra, commenting on the present verse, says that the Glory was first joined to Israel in the wilderness. Exodus deliverance and wilderness guidance are kept together in 8:14-16; however, we should note that Deuteronomy 1 does not begin with the exodus but with the departure from Horeb, which was in the wilderness (1:6-7). On Israel being found by Yahweh in the wilderness, see later Hos 9:10; Jer 2:2; 31:2-3. The sequence in Jer 2:6-7 is exodus deliverance, care in an inhospitable wilderness, and Israel's gift of a garden land.

yes, in a howling desert waste. וּבְתֹהוּ יְלֵל יְשִׁמֹן. Ibn Ezra sees the wilderness as a place of howling animals, the sounds of which, like jackals and owls, terrify anyone within earshot. Rashi adds the demons (Ar *jinn*), also known to reside there (T[PsJ]; cf. Isa 13:21-22; 34:14; Jer 50:39; Ps 74:14). In the wilderness one also hears the howling of the wind. Hebrew תֹהוּ ("waste") describes the precreation chaos in Gen 1:2 (cf. Jer 4:23), but in Ps 107:40; Job 12:24 it is desert wasteland, as here. The wilderness was a harsh place fraught with all sorts of perils (1:19; 8:15; Jer 2:6), making Yahweh's care there all the more important.

He encircled him. יְסֹבְבֶנְהוּ. 4QpaleoDeut[r] has the spelling יסובב[נהו]. The verb סבב in the Polel means "to move around protectively" (KBL[3]; Ps 32:10). The idea of encirclement anticipates the high-flying eagle in v. 11. If the imperfect here means to express iteration, the translation should be "he keeps circling around him" (G. A. Smith). Yahweh's care over Israel during the wilderness trek is stressed elsewhere in 8:2-5, 15-16.

he guarded him as the pupil of his eye. יִצְּרֶנְהוּ כְּאִישׁוֹן עֵינוֹ. Protection would have been primarily from enemies (ibn Ezra), although Rashi adds serpents, scorpions, and other poisonous reptiles. Hebrew אִישׁוֹן ("pupil") is lit. "little man," referring to the dark center of the eye in which one may observe the reflection of others (Rashi). The LXX has ὀφθαλμοῦ ("of an eye"), which Fritsch (1943, 11) thinks is meant to avoid an anthropomorphism. But Orlinsky (1944, 157) disagrees, arguing that an absence of the possessive pronoun here and elsewhere is not an antianthropomorphism. The "pupil of one's eye" is a figure of that which is tender and dearest, therefore guarded jealously (Driver; Mercer 1920-21; Ps 17:8; Prov 7:2). Mercer cites a comparable expression in the Pyramid Texts (§93a) dating from the 25th and 24th cents.: "the damsel which is in the eye of Horus," here a precious offering given to the deceased king that he is advised to accept.

11 *As an eagle who stirs up his nest.* The נֶשֶׁר is either an eagle or a griffon-vulture, more likely the former (see Note for 14:12). Reference is to the male bird (G. A. Smith), not the female (*pace* AV: "her nest"). The verb עוּר in the H-stem means "to rouse, stir up (to activity)," the common interpretation being of a parent bird stirring up the nest to encourage the nestlings to fly (*Sifre Deut.* §314; ibn Ezra: Rashi; Luther; Driver; Tigay). Hosea, using the metaphor of a small child, has Yahweh training a young Israel to independence (Hos 11:3). Here the LXX translates יָעִיר with σκεπάσαι ("it covered, sheltered" — cf. σκεπασταί in v. 38), which has led some scholars to imagine simply "protection" for the nestlings, the overarching theme of vv. 10-11 (Peels 1994; Nelson). A root עיר, meaning "to protect, keep," is listed for this verse and Job 8:6 in KBL[3], but it rests on an uncertain Ugaritic cognate.

over his young ones he hovers. עַל־גּוֹזָלָיו יְרַחֵף. Rashi says the eagle does not press himself on the young, but hovers, touching yet not touching. Yahweh acted similarly with Israel, not exercising full divine power. The verb רחף ("hover") occurs at the beginning of the Priestly Creation account, where the spirit of God is heard "hovering" over the primordial deep (Gen 1:2).

he spreads out his wings, he takes him up, he lifts him upon his pinion. Eagles have been observed catching the young on their backs or wings while teaching them to fly (S. R. Driver 1895, 358; G. R. Driver 1958, 56-57; Tigay). Peels (1994, 300) dismisses the eyewitness account reported by S. R. Driver, but G. R. Driver gives eyewitness accounts of such behavior in golden eagles of Scotland and the United States. The image of Yahweh bearing Israel "on eagle's wings" during the wilderness trek occurs also in Exod 19:4. In Deut 1:31 Yahweh is said to have borne Israel in the wilderness as a father bears his son.

12 *Yahweh alone guided him, and no foreign god was with him.* The climactic line in this stanza of the poem (see Rhetoric and Composition), reinforcing the statement in v. 9 that Yahweh alone took Israel as his portion. Whatever lesser divine beings may have resided with Yahweh in the heavens, and whatever gods may be claimed by nations of the world, it was Yahweh alone leading Israel in the wilderness. No foreign gods were with him. This appears to be bedrock monotheism such as we have in v. 39, also earlier in 4:35, 39. See in addition Hos 13:4; Isa 43:10-12. Driver emphasizes that the expression is "foreign god," not "strange (god)" (cf. v. 16; Ps 81:10[9]; Jer 2:25; Mal 2:11), but the difference does not appear to be that great. The terms אֱלֹהֵי נֵכָר ("foreign gods") and זָרִים ("strangers") appear together in Jer 5:19, where they may be synonyms (Lundbom 1999, 398). Israel, in any case, had no reason to be lured into idolatry (G. E. Wright), which happened subsequently and is roundly condemned in vv. 15-18. Foreign gods came with settlement in the land (vv. 15-18; cf. Hos 13:4-6; Jer 2:5-9).

13 *He made him ride on earth's high places, and he ate the produce of the high country.* The "earth's high places" are generally taken to be the hill country of Canaan (*Sifre Deut.* §316; ibn Ezra; Luther; Driver; Cassuto 1973a, 42; Tigay), but with the mention of "Bashan" in v. 14, the poet may have in mind the Transjordan highlands. Targum^{Onq} paraphrases: "He settled them over the powerful ones of the earth, and fed them the plunder of the enemies," where reference is said to be to the Amorite kings, Sihon and Og, who were defeated by the Israelites in Transjordan (Grossfeld 1988, 92 n. 25). Rashi follows T^{Onq}. The Transjordan conquest and settlement, given prominence in Deuteronomy 2-3, is described briefly in Num 21:21-35 (cf. Pss 135:10-12; 136:17-22).

He made him ride on earth's high places. יַרְכִּבֵהוּ עַל־בָּמֳתֵי אָרֶץ. Reading the Qere for "high places." Yahweh's gift of high ground to Israel is a metaphor for bestowing exaltation, security, and overall favor upon the nascent nation (Hab 3:19; Isa 58:14; Ps 18:34[33]). The phrase, according to Driver, implies Israel's triumphant and undisputed possession of the land (Deut 33:29). Mowinckel (1962, 298), translating the verb רכב as "drive" instead of "ride," argues that the image is mythological. Yahweh, who has taken over horses and chariots of the older Canaanite god, gives up the divine prerogative and now lets Israel drive his chariot over the high places of earth, giving Israel "a nearly divine position among the peoples of the earth." But Moran (1962, 323-27) rejects this interpretation, saying that the image has Israel going upwards, not forward. He therefore translates יַרְכִּבֵהוּ as "he made it mount upon," where reference is to Israel's *entrance* into the promised land, not a journey terminating there. In his view, divine guidance and protection finishes in v. 12. I would agree that the image portrays not a journey but a settlement, only the highlands are those of Transjordan, not Canaan.

and he ate the produce of the high country. The LXX and Sam have "and he made him eat," but the Qal verb in MT could be correct, with the poet simply opting for variety (Driver). The "high country" (שָׂדָי) is the fertile highlands of Transjordan, part of which is Bashan in the north (v. 14). Hebrew שָׂדָי (normally "field") here means "highland," as in Jer 13:27; 17:3; 18:14; Num 23:14; 2 Sam 1:21 (G. A. Smith; Propp 1987). The Akk word for "mountain, highland," is *šadû*. On choice "produce of the high country," see also Lam 4:9; Ezek 36:30.

and he made him suck honey from the crags. Hebrew shifts back to an H-stem (LXX: "they sucked"). Wild honey is plentiful in both Transjordan (2 Sam 17:29) and Canaan (Gen 43:11; Deut 8:8; 1 Kgs 14:3), where honeycombs exist even in fissures of rock (Ps 81:17[16]). Akkadian sources mention "mountain honey" (Moran). Sirach 39:26 lists honey as one of the necessities of life. John the Baptist later existed on a diet of locusts and wild honey (Mark 1:6; Matt 3:4). The land promised to Israel was to be one of "milk and honey" (Exod 3:8, 17; Num 13:27; Deut 6:3; Jer 11:5). Ezekiel recalls how Yahweh fed Israel early on with "honey and oil" (Ezek 16:13).

and oil from the flinty rock. The oil (שֶׁמֶן) is olive oil (*Sifre Deut.* §317), another symbol of plenty in the Near East (2 Kgs 18:32). Olive trees grow in sandy and rocky soil, flourish on terraced, rocky hillsides, and can even be found protruding out of flinty rock if the latter contains water, which it often does (Deut 8:15; Ps 114:8; Job 29:6). But the point here seems to be that in the good land oil flowed even in unpromising places. The expression borders on hyperbole (cf. BDB, 321).

14 Goodness of the land builds, with the verb coming only at the end.

Curds of the herd and milk of the flock. Curds (חֶמְאָה) are butter-fat skimmed from the top of milk, probably not becoming butter or cheese, but coagulated sour milk (Ar *leben*). Abraham served guests curds and milk along with a prepared calf when they visited him at the oaks of Mamre (Gen 18:8). See also Judg 5:25; 2 Sam 17:29 (David in Transjordan); Isa 7:15, 22; Job 20:17; 29:6.

with the choicest of lambs and rams. Hebrew כָּרִים are young he-lambs,

Deuteronomy 32

אֵילִים *full-grown male sheep.* "And rams" should be included in this colon with M^A and the LXX; *BHS* (but not M^L) puts the term at the beginning of the next line. The "lambs and rams" combination occurs in Jer 51:40; Ezek 27:21; 39:18; Isa 34:6.

choicest. חֵלֶב is lit. "fat," taken to be the choicest portion (Num 18:12; 1 Sam 15:22). The Sam has חמת ("warmth"?), but 4QpaleoDeut^r supports the reading of MT (Skehan, Ulrich, and Sanderson 1992, 147).

sons of Bashan and he-goats. The "sons of Bashan" are Bashan's celebrated bulls, known for their size and strength (Ps 22:13[12]). All Bashan cattle, for that matter, were of high quality (Ezek 39:18). Bashan lay north of Gilead in the Transjordan highlands, extending from Mount Hermon in the north to the Yarmuk River in the south (see Note for 3:1). Israel took Bashan from the Amorite king Og and gave its land to the half tribe of Manasseh (3:1-14). With that territory went a considerable amount of cattle (3:7, 19). Since Bashan is the only geographic area mentioned in the Song, it is reasonable to suppose that the settlement referred to here is the one in Transjordan. Goats continued to be a valued possession after settlement in the land, being used for milk (Prov 27:27), meat (Deut 14:4), and sacrificial offerings together with lambs, rams, and bulls (Isa 1:11; Jer 51:40; Ezek 39:18). Goat hair was used for tents and goatskin for skin bottles (Exod 25:4-5; 26:7; 36:14; Gen 21:14; Josh 9:4; 1 Sam 1:24).

with the choicest grains of wheat. עִם־חֵלֶב כִּלְיוֹת חִטָּה. A triple construct chain, lit. "the fat (choicest) of kidneys of wheat." Hebrew כִּלְיוֹת ("kidneys") refers here to the interior of the wheat grain (KBL³; cf. today's artichoke "hearts"). Sentiments here and in the verses following have an echo in Ps 81:17[16], where Yahweh, desiring Israel's obedience but not receiving it, wishes he could feed his people with the choicest wheat and honey from the rock (cf. Ps 147:14).

yes, blood of the grape, you drank wine! I.e., you drank still-fermenting red wine. Hebrew חֶמֶר is a poetical term for "froth(ing) wine" (cf. the verb חמר in Pss 46:4[3]; 75:9[8]). On "blood of the grape" meaning wine, see Gen 49:11; Sir 39:26; Rev 14:19-20. A shift to the second person here at the end of the stanza makes the discourse more direct (see Rhetoric and Composition). Von Rad says the second person (recurring in vv. 15 and 18) makes the whole appear as prophetic indictment. Since Moses is portrayed as speaking to Israel in the plains of Moab, just before the crossing into Canaan, his audience will have experienced first-hand the good wine from Transjordanian vineyards. The LXX is the poorer with "he drank."

15 *So Jacob ate and became sated.* Adding וַיֹּאכַל יַעֲקֹב וַיִּשְׂבָּע with the LXX (καὶ ἔφαγεν Ιακωβ καὶ ἐνεπλήσθη), Sam, and 4QPhyl 141 (Milik 1977, 73). The colon was probably lost in MT due to haplography (homoeoarcton: ו . . . ו). Eating and becoming sated in the promised land is anticipated all throughout Deuteronomy (see Note for 6:11), recalled later also in Neh 9:25. But Deuteronomy issues a commensurate warning about Israel returning Yahweh's kindness by forsaking him and turning to other gods. What a sated Israel must do is bless Yahweh (8:10). The verse here goes on to say precisely what is anticipated in 31:20, that when Jacob (= Israel) has eaten well and become overly sated, it will forget the covenant and turn to other gods. Unfaithfulness has been cited already in vv. 5-6, but here begins the indictment proper (vv. 15-18).

yes, Jeshurun got fat and kicked. וַיִּשְׁמַן יְשֻׁרוּן וַיִּבְעָט. "Jeshurun" is a poetic and perhaps hypocoristic name for Israel, occurring also in 33:5, 26; Isa 44:2. The term, normally honorific, means "Upright One" (יָשָׁר = "upright"). Here the usage is ironic, because Israel has become fat and rebellious, like an intractable animal turned against its owner (Hos 4:16; Jer 2:20; 5:5b, 27b-28a). The LXX translates with ὁ ἠγαπημένος ("The Beloved"), which in the NT characterizes Jesus (Eph 1:6) and the church (1 Thess 1:4; 2 Thess 2:13; Col 3:12; Jude 1). At the Shiloh sanctuary, Eli and his priestly sons got fat and rebellious, bringing down Yahweh's wrath upon them and all Israel (1 Sam 2:12-17, 22-25, 29; 4:18). Friedman thinks יִשְׁמַן ("got fat") puns on יְשִׁמֹן ("desert") in v. 10. The words have nearly opposite meanings: people went from desert privation to getting fat.

you got fat, you grew thick, you became gorged. שָׁמַנְתָּ עָבִיתָ כָּשִׂיתָ. A fine example of asyndeton for emphasis, where the rhetorical effect is further enhanced by a shift to the second person. The colon is not to be taken as parenthetical (*pace* JB and NJB). In Moses' audience are the very people who have become fat. See vv. 17-18 and 38 for other second person rhetorical shifts. The LXX once again changes verbs to the third person (cf. NEB; NIV; REB). 4QPhyl 141 supports MT (Milik 1977, 73). The second verb (עבה) parallels the first, meaning "to become thick" (1 Kgs 12:10). The third verb (כשׂה), which is a *hapax legomenon* in the OT, is uncertain. Rashi took it to be a variant of כסה, "to become covered," meaning "to be covered with fat" (AV; cf. Job 15:27). Ibn Ezra says the verb has no cognate, its meaning similar to "you kicked" (KBL³: "you became obstinate"). In colloquial Arabic *kašiya* means "to be obstinate." Another suggestion has been to take the verb as a cognate to Arabic *kš'*, "to be gorged with food" (Driver; BDB; JB; NAB; NRSV; cf. Tigay 1996, 403 n. 84, who cites Ehrlich and Ben-Yehudah). The reading "you became sleek," which is adopted in the RV, RSV, NEB, NIV, and REB (Graetz 1894, 11 reads עשׁה in Jer 5:28), has no etymological basis (Driver).

Then he abandoned the God who made him. וַיִּטֹּשׁ אֱלוֹהַּ עָשָׂהוּ. Abandoning Yahweh in the Song recalls most recently Israel's Transjordan romp with Baal of Peor and the daughters of Moab at Shittim, given passing reference in Deut 4:3, described more fully in Priestly material (Numbers 25), and recalled elsewhere in the OT (Josh 22:17; Hos 9:10; Ps 106:28-31). Jeremiah uses the verb נטשׁ to express the idea of Judah having "abandoned" Yahweh (Jer 15:6). On Yahweh as the one who created Israel, see v. 6. Looking ahead to the future, the idea that Israel will receive from Yahweh a good land, benefit from its bounty, and return the favor by abandoning Yahweh and his covenant is anticipated in 8:11-14; 31:20. The theme is picked up later in Hos 13:6; Jer 2:5-9, stated also briefly in Jer 5:7b and 27b-28a. Here in vv. 15-22 we have the substance of Huldah's Judah oracle based on the temple lawbook of 622 (Lundbom 1976, 295-99).

God. אֱלוֹהַ. This spelling, which recurs in v. 17 with reference to the "no-gods," occurs 60 times in the OT (KBL³). The pairing of אֱלוֹהַ and צוּר ("Rock") occurs also in Ps 18:32[31].

and took to be foolish the Rock of his salvation. וַיְנַבֵּל צוּר יְשֻׁעָתוֹ. The verb נבל is strong (Mic 7:6; Nah 3:6), lit. "to treat as a fool." An affront to Israel's savior in the wilderness and a showing of contempt, says Rashi, greater than any other. In v. 6 Israel is said to be a foolish (נָבָל) people; then in v. 21, because of the present provocation, Yahweh says he will provoke Israel with a foolish (נָבָל) nation. On Yahweh as Israel's "Rock of salvation," see also 2 Sam 22:47; Pss 62:3, 7(2, 6); 89:27(26); 95:1. Here in the Song, Yahweh is Israel's "Rock" in vv. 4, 18, and 30-31. The LXX avoids "Rock" here as elsewhere, but does speak of God as "savior" (σωτήρ), which Wevers (1995, 518) says is the only time it does so in the Pentateuch.

16 *They made him jealous with strangers, with abominations they provoked him.* A syntactic chiasmus with verbs at the extremes (Westhuizen 1977, 68). The sentiments are repeated in v. 21. "Strangers" (זָרִים) are strange gods (ibn Ezra), alien to Yahweh and probably gods introduced from foreign lands (Driver; cf. Jer 2:25; 3:13; Isa 43:12; Pss 44:21[20]; 78:58; 81:10[9]). The "abominations" (תּוֹעֵבֹת) are doubtless idols (ibn Ezra; Driver; cf. 2 Kgs 23:13; Isa 44:19), although in Deuteronomy the term can also refer to detestable practices associated with idol worship (see Note for 7:25). Rashi cites homosexuality and sorcery (cf. Lev 20:13). On Yahweh's jealousy and anger being aroused by Israel's worship of other gods, a violation of the first and second commandments, see 4:23-25; 5:7-9; 6:14-15; 29:17-19(18-20). The provocation theme recurs continually in Jeremiah (Jer 7:18; 8:19; 11:17; 25:6-7; 44:3, 8) and lies at the heart of Huldah's reproach of Judah (2 Kgs 22:17). Justin Martyr in his *Dialogue with Trypho the Jew* (ch. 119) finds a fulfillment of vv. 16-22 in Christians becoming God's holy people promised to Abraham.

17 *They sacrificed to demons, no-gods.* The term שֵׁדִים ("demons") occurs only here and in Ps 106:37. The latter says that Israel sacrificed its sons and daughters to demons. In both places the LXX translates with δαιμονίοις, which is equivalent (Wevers 1995, 519). Hebrew שֵׁד is an Akk loanword, *šēdu*, being either a protective or malevolent spirit or a subordinate divine being (*CAD*, 17/2:256-59). Here demons are said to be "no-gods," with Jewish interpreters following T in saying that they are powerless or ineffectual (ibn Ezra;

Rashi). On "no-god(s)" (לֹא אֱלֹהַּ), see also Hos 8:6; Jer 2:11; 5:7; 16:20; in the NT 1 Cor 10:20. In v. 21 the term for "no-god" is לֹא־אֵל. On demons and demonology in the OT and in the ANE, see T. Gaster, *IDB*, 1:817-24; also *DDD*.

gods they had not known. Regarding foreign gods as gods Israel has never known, stated often in Deuteronomy and the prose of Jeremiah, see Note for 11:27-28. Yahweh has known only Israel (Amos 3:2), and Israel has known only Yahweh (Hos 13:4).

New ones recently come in. The description of foreign gods continues, here perhaps with an ironic twist in that Yahweh has been Israel's God from "of old" (Gen 4:26; cf. Isa 63:16). On Israel having had bad experience with the choice of "new gods," see Judg 5:8.

your fathers were not awed by them. I.e., they never feared nor worshipped them. The verb שׂער is taken by many to be a denominative of שֵׂעָר ("hair"), meaning "to have bristly hair, shudder" (*Sifre Deut.* §318; ibn Ezra; Rashi; Jer 2:12; Ezek 27:35; 32:10; Job 4:15; cf. Basser 1984, 186-87 on raised body hair expressing fear in religious literature), although a homonymous verb means simply "be acquainted with, know about" (BDB and KBL³; שׂער III; cf. Ar šaʿara). The Targums and LXX (ᾔδεισαν) support the latter reading (so also NEB; REB). The LXX, T, and Vg have the third person "their fathers" (cf. JB; NJB), but 1QDeut 5:16 supports MT with "your fathers" (Barthélemy and Milik 1955, 60).

18 The verb נשה means "forget" in the sense of showing neglect (ibn Ezra; Rashi: "disregard"); שׁכח is the more common verb "to forget." This line brings vv. 10-18 to a climax, also restating the summary indictment of v. 15. The theme of "not forgetting" (שׁכח) Yahweh, his deliverance, his wonders, his covenant, and his care in the wilderness, which occurs often in Deuteronomy (4:9, 23, 31; 6:12; 8:11-14, 19; 9:7), Hosea (Hos 2:15[13]; 4:6; 8:14; 13:6; Driver 1895, lxxxiii no. 62), and Jeremiah (Jer 2:32; 3:21; 13:25; 18:15; 23:27), may have its origins here. Deuteronomy also lays much stress on the importance of "remembering" (see Note for 8:2). Driver notes how the present verse embodies both male and female imagery for God: Israel neglected God the Father, to whom it owed its existence as a nation, and forgot God the Mother, who in painful travail brought Israel into the world. The Polel of חול means "to writhe in travail." The Song earlier cited Yahweh as the one who created Israel (v. 6).

The Rock. On this metaphor for God, see v. 4. The LXX substitutes "God."

19 *So Yahweh saw and spurned.* וַיַּרְא יְהוָה וַיִּנְאָץ. Here begins the outpouring of divine wrath against a faithless covenant people (vv. 19-33). Yahweh first punishes the wrongdoing of his own, then the wrongdoing of others (vv. 34-43; Jer 25:28-29; 1 Pet 4:17). The verb נאץ means "spurn, despise, reject with scorn," used elsewhere with Yahweh as subject in Lam 2:6. Here the verb lacks a direct object, but the same occurs in Jer 14:21, where Jeremiah prays that Yahweh will not spurn (his people) and break the covenant. In the prose frame

Deuteronomy 32

to the Song, Yahweh tells Moses to write the Song because he expects that people *will* spurn him and break his covenant (Deut 31:20). The LXX (ἐζήλωσεν) and 4QPhyl 141 (ויקנא) contain verbs that mean not "spurn," but "become jealous" (Milik 1977, 73). The MT reading is supported in *Sifre Deut*. §320. Albright (1959, 345-46) wanted to transpose verbs in the line, which would translate: "Yahweh saw and He became angry, at the insults of His sons and daughters." But there is no textual support for this reading. The MT makes eminently good sense.

because of the provocation of his sons and daughters. מִכַּעַס בָּנָיו וּבְנֹתָיו. The initial מִ specifies the reason (Driver; KBL³). The LXX continues the expression of divine anger: "and he was stirred up by anger against his sons and daughters," καὶ παρωξύνθη δι' ὀργὴν υἱῶν αὐτοῦ καὶ θυγατέρων (Wevers 1995, 520). Ibn Ezra notes that women as well as men offered incense to idols (cf. 17:2-3; 29:17[18]; Jer 7:18; 44:15-25).

20 *And he said: I will hide my face from them.* I.e., he said this to himself. The verb אמר can mean "say to oneself," i.e., "think" (Jer 3:7, 19; 5:4). Here begins the divine speech, which continues through v. 27. Up to now the poet has been the speaking voice. The verbs are also future from this point on. Yahweh promises to "hide his face" from Israel, an anthropomorphism occurring also in the prose frame to the Song (31:17-18). "Hiding the face" means that God is angry and has withdrawn divine favor (Freedman, Lundbom, *ḥānan*, in *TDOT*, 5:24).

I will see what their end will be. אֶרְאֶה מָה אַחֲרִיתָם. אַחֲרִית may also be translated "latter end." Dahood (1973) redivides the consonants (ארא המה) to get the reading "I will show them their end," where the meaning would be that Yahweh will show Israel its end when the time comes to do so. In any event, Yahweh is determined first to hide his face from a rebellious people, then be present to see where their actions have led them. On the inability of evil people to discern their (latter) end, see v. 29, also Jer 5:31; 12:4; 17:11.

For a generation of perversities they are. כִּי דוֹר תַּהְפֻּכֹת הֵמָּה. The noun תַּהְפֻּכֹת means lit. "turnings upside down," occurring elsewhere only in Proverbs, where references are to perversities in human hearts, speech, actions, and individuals in their entirety (Prov 2:12, 14; 6:14; 8:13; 10:31-32; 16:28, 30; 23:33). Here, as in v. 5, a whole generation is said to be filled with perversities.

children in whom is no faithfulness. בָּנִים לֹא־אֵמֻן בָּם. 1QDeut 5:16 supports MT with אמן; Sam has האמן. Reference is doubtless to the Horeb covenant, which requires faithfulness. One could also cite more specifically the unfaithfulness shown in the golden calf incident at Horeb or the more recent romp with Baal-peor and the daughters of Moab at Shittim (see v. 15). Yahweh, by contrast, is a God of faithfulness (v. 4).

21 *They, they made me jealous with a no-god.* The personal pronoun is

Deuteronomy 32

added for emphasis. Yahweh's jealousy over Israel's worship of other gods is stated already in v. 16, and in v. 17 demons are called "no gods." Here it seems one god in particular merits the name of "no god" (לֹא־אֵל), although the term could be a collective. Whoever the god is, it is no god at all. Hosea and Jeremiah disparage Canaanite and Assyrian deities as being "no gods" (see v. 17).

they provoked me with their nothings. Yahweh is never more provoked to anger than by worship of other gods and their idols (see v. 16, where provocation is again paired with jealousy). "Their nothings" (הַבְלֵיהֶם) refer to the people's idols (T^Onq; cf. Jer 8:19; 10:8; 14:22; 1 Kgs 16:13, 26; Ps 31:7[6]). Jeremiah says that people went after "The Nothing" (הַהֶבֶל) and "became nothing" (וַיֶּהְבָּלוּ), a reference to Baal worship (Jer 2:5). The term הֶבֶל ("breath" in Isa 57:13; AV: "vanity"), denotes anything empty and worthless; hence, a description of false gods.

So I, I will make them jealous with a no-people, with a foolish nation I will provoke them. Punishment will befit the crime. The personal pronoun "I" is added for emphasis, answering the supplemental "they" beginning the verse. There has been much speculation about the identity of the "no-people," with no consensus having been reached. The term may have a referent, but more likely it denotes simply a people not chosen by Yahweh, unlike Israel who was chosen (see *Introduction*). This could apply to just about anyone. In the wilderness it would have been the Midianites; later it would be a succession of other peoples: Philistines, Syrians, Assyrians, and Babylonians. Yahweh's plan here is to make Israel jealous, which, as Nelson points out, may also contain a hidden ray of hope (cf. Rom 11:11). A "foolish nation" (גּוֹי נָבָל) is a godless nation (Marböck, *nābāl*, in *TDOT*, 9:165). Earlier Israel was cited as being "foolish" (v. 6) and as being a nation that had treated Yahweh as foolish (v. 15). Paul quotes the present words in Rom 10:19, going on in the next chapter to speak about God's actions and his own preaching of Christ as making Israel jealous (Rom 11:11-16). See also 1 Cor 10:22.

22 *For a fire is kindled in my anger, and it will burn to the depths of Sheol.* Anger is commonly compared in the OT to a burning fire. Here we have hyperbole, with the divine anger coming down from the heavenly regions to the deepest point of the underworld (cf. Amos 9:2; Ps 18:7-20[6-19] = 2 Sam 22:7-20). Divine anger comes with dreadful intensity (Amos 5:6; Jer 4:4; 7:20; 17:27; 21:12), being unlike human anger, which must be kept under control (Prov 29:11). The mixed motifs of fire and storm, seen clearly in Psalm 18 (= 2 Samuel 22), appear commonly in the Ugaritic literature (D. J. McCarthy 1967, 98). Here the burning fire will bring drought (v. 24; cf. 11:17). Sheol is one of several OT names for the realm of the dead (T. H. Gaster, in *IDB*, 1:787-88; T. J. Lewis, in *ABD*, 2:101-5). The LXX has "Hades" (ᾅδης). Korah's wilderness rebellion brought down the divine fire, with the guilty persons descending alive into

Sheol (Num 16:25-35). The present verse concludes Huldah's oracle against Judah (2 Kgs 22:17; Lundbom 1976).

Yes, it will consume the earth and its yield. אֶרֶץ refers here to the "land" of Israel (*Sifre Deut.* §320; ibn Ezra). Both land and crops will be consumed in the unwelcome divine visitation.

and set ablaze the mountains' foundations. The "foundations of the mountains" are said to tremble from divine anger in Ps 18:8[7]. Here they will be set ablaze.

23 *I will heap evils upon him.* אַסְפֶּה עָלֵימוֹ רָעוֹת. We now witness in horrific detail the effects of Yahweh's consuming anger: death at the hands of an enemy, famine, pestilence, and attacks from predators roaming at will through a land devastated by war. Verses 23-25 find an echo in Ezek 5:16-17 (Greenberg 1983a, 116-17). The precise meaning of אספה remains uncertain, due to four homonymous verbs in Hebrew: ספה ("sweep [away]"); אסף ("gather, collect"); יסף ("add"); and סוף ("come to an end, make an end of"), which have confused interpreters from earliest times. The MT points as אַסְפֶּה, an H-stem of ספה yielding the translation: "I will sweep evils upon him" (Greenberg 1983a, 116; NJV: "misfortunes"). "Sweep (away)" suits the context in 29:18(19), also in Gen 19:15, 17, where Lot and his family risk being swept away in the conflagration of Sodom. But this meaning ill suits the present context (Driver; Tigay). The LXX's συνάξω ("I will gather together"), which carries over into the Vg *(congregabo)*, presupposes the verb אסף. Reading this verb requires only a repointing of the consonants to אֶסְפָה, which makes tolerable sense ("I will gather together evils upon him"; Graetz 1894, 11). Tigay gives סוף the meaning "expend," nicely paralleling "use up" in the next colon, where reference is to exhausting a supply of arrows (NAB: "I will spend on them woe upon woe"). Ibn Ezra, assuming a connection to the next colon, says the meaning of the verb is more like "exhaust," i.e., not a single evil will remain that shall not befall them. But the most widely accepted interpretation, in light of what follows in vv. 23b-25, is that evils of every description will amass (T[OnqPsJ]; Rashi; Driver; Tigay). For most — but not all — commentators, this presupposes the verb יסף and involves only a repointing to אֹסְפָה ("I will add, heap"; cf. Ezek 5:16; Lev 26:21). English "heap" (AV; RSV; NEB; NIV; NRSV; REB) is then as good a rendering as any. It is also possible that the poet may be playing on multiple meanings. Jeremiah does this with אסף and סוף in Jer 8:13: "Gathering I will end them" (Lundbom 1999, 523). The poet here could be saying "And I will heap evils upon them," at the same time anticipating the exhaustion of arrows in the next colon. We note too in the prose frame a coming of "many evils" (רָעוֹת רַבּוֹת) upon Israel (31:17, 21).

my arrows I will exhaust against them. Yahweh will use up every arrow in his divine arsenal (cf. Jer 5:16), but Rashi says the curse here is actually a blessing, for while the arrows are depleted, the people are not. This anticipates what is to come. Yahweh still has a quantity of arrows for use against Israel's enemies (v. 42). On arrows as a figure of divine chastisement, see Lam 3:12-13; Jer 50:14; 51:11; Ezek 5:16; Pss 7:14(13); 18:15(14); 38:3(2); Job 6:4.

24 *Smiting famine, and burning plague, and bitter pestilence, and the teeth of beasts I will send against them, with venom of crawlers in the dust.* Famine (רָעָב), pestilence (דֶּבֶר), and wild animals (חַיָּה) are the divine "arrows" in Ezek 5:16. The five maledictions here are also "arrows" of Yahweh, the Divine Warrior (Tigay; Nelson), articulated with particular intensity: smiting famine (מְזֵי רָעָב), burning plague (לְחֻמֵי רֶשֶׁף), bitter pestilence (קֶטֶב מְרִירִי), the teeth of beasts (שֶׁן־בְּהֵמוֹת), and venom of crawlers in the dust (חֲמַת זֹחֲלֵי עָפָר). De Moor (1988, 105), with a slight revocalization of the consonantal text, personifies the first three arrows, representing them as quasi-independent powers pursuing their objects. Yet all are subject to Yahweh's command (see Note for 28:15). De Moor translates:

> I will assemble evils against them
> I will spend my arrows on them:
> Hunger, my Sucker
> Resheph, my Warrior
> and the Sting, my Poisonous One.

Smiting famine. מְזֵי רָעָב is said to mean "sucked out (i.e., empty, weakened) from hunger/famine" (BDB; KBL³; Ar *mazza* "to suck"; Akk *mazū* "to squeeze"; *CAD*, 10/1:439), but Greenfield (1987, 152) questions this interpretation in light of Akkadian evidence. He renders מְזֵי רָעָב as "smitten by famine," taking מזה as the general name of a "smiting" or "beating" demon. On "Hunger" as personified death, see Tromp 1969, 107. Curses of "sword and famine (and pestilence)," all of which appear in vv. 24-25, become a stereotyped triad in Jeremiah (Lundbom 1999, 390).

burning plague. לְחֻמֵי רֶשֶׁף. Sam has לחמו; 1QDeut 5:18 supports MT with לחמי. The expression is lit. "eaten up by the flame" or "eaten up by Resheph," where Resheph, the ancient Canaanite god, has been reduced to a demonic Fire-bolt in the service of Yahweh (Driver; Tromp 1969, 107-8; cf. Pss 76:4[3]; 78:48; Cant 8:6; see further *DDD*, 700-703). Greenfield (1987) takes רֶשֶׁף as emanating from the Canaanite god of pestilence, noting that LXX and T^OnqPsJ translate the term as "bird(s)" (cf. Job 5:7; ibn Ezra: "vultures"). Greenfield translates in the present verse: "battered by plague" (cf. Hab 3:5). רֶשֶׁף could also be the common noun "flame," used here metaphorically to mean "heat" or "fever" (AV, RSV: "burning heat"; NAB: "consuming fever").

bitter pestilence. קֶטֶב מְרִירִי. קֶטֶב may contain overtones of a demon doing service for Yahweh (T^Onq: "evil spirits"; *DDD*, 673-74), although the term could simply mean "destructive pestilence" (ibn Ezra; Driver; Nelson; Hos 13:14; Ps 91:6; cf. Isa 28:2). Rashi thinks Meriri is another demon. Pestilence is one of the covenant curses (28:21), later promised to a besieged Judah by Jeremiah (Jer 14:12; 18:21; 21:6-7, and often) and Ezekiel (Ezek 5:12, 17; 6:11-12; 7:15, and often). De Moor (1988, 100), citing קֶטֶב in Hos 13:14: "O Sheol, where is your sting (קָטָבְךָ)," ties the term in with Paul's usage of "sting" in 1 Cor 15:55: "O Death, where is your sting?"

and the teeth of beasts I will send against them. Death from wild beasts is a natural curse in the ancient world (7:22), to be reversed only in the end times (Isa 11:6-9). It comes for covenant violation in Lev 26:22. Hosea mentions beasts (Hos 2:14[12]), and Ezekiel adds them to his list of Yahweh's "deadly arrows" (Ezek 5:16-17; 14:15, 21). The beasts of Jer 5:6 are metaphorical. Devouring animals appear also in the 8th-cent. Sefire treaties (Hillers 1964a, 54-55). In light of other possible demonic figures in the verse, Nelson suggests that בְּהֵמוֹת may be the mythical Behemoth of Job 40:15.

venom of crawlers in the dust. חֲמַת זֹחֲלֵי עָפָר. "Crawlers in the dust" are (poisonous) serpents (ibn Ezra; Rashi; Luther; cf. Gen 3:14; Mic 7:17). For חֵמָה meaning serpent venom, see again v. 33, also Pss 58:5(4); 140:4(3). The serpent is cited as a devouring agent in the 8th-cent. Sefire treaty curses (Hillers 1964a: 54-55):

> May the gods send every sort of devourer against Arpad and against
>   its people!
> [May the mou]th of a snake [eat], the mouth of a scorpion . . .
>   (*Sf* I A 30-31)

Poisonous serpents brought judgment and death in the wilderness (Num 21:6-9), and Jeremiah later spoke of serpents coming against Judah (Jer 8:17), although his usage may well be metaphorical.

25 *Outside a sword shall bereave.* In streets and city squares people will be cut down by the sword (cf. Jer 9:20[21]). Judgment here seems to presuppose town and city life. The verb שׁכל ("bereave") also means "make childless" (Jer 15:7).

and in the chambers terror. וּמֵחֲדָרִים אֵימָה. The חֶדֶר ("chamber") is a dark inner room, commonly a bedroom. The prefixed מִן can mean "in," as in Ugaritic. Balancing the killing in city streets and squares will be a terror no less distressing within houses, the innermost rooms of which will be hoped-for safety from the enemy (1 Kgs 20:30; 22:25; Isa 26:20). But people there will die from famine and pestilence (v. 24; Jer 14:18; 18:21; Ezek 7:15; Lam 1:20). Jeremiah's expression is the stereotypical "sword and famine (and pestilence)" (Lundbom 1999, 390).

Deuteronomy 32

both young man and maiden, nursing child with the gray-haired man. Judgment will fall on everyone: No one, man or woman, young or old, will be spared (2 Kgs 8:12; Hos 14:1[13:16]; Jer 6:11; 51:22; Lam 2:21).

26 Yahweh continues as speaker in this verse and the next, making the audience privy to a dialogue occurring in the divine mind over whether or not to completely do away with the covenant people. But the remnant idea is an old one, with Yahweh from earliest times bringing devastating calamity and yet preserving a select few to keep humanity ongoing (Genesis 6–9; 18–19). Joseph, in Egypt, preserved a remnant for Israel (Gen 45:7). Tradition records Yahweh threatening in the wilderness to completely destroy Israel and begin all over again with Moses (9:13-14; Exod 32:9-10; Num 14:11-12). Moses rejected the idea, and it was not carried out. The remnant idea occurs often in the 8th-cent. prophets, particularly Isaiah, in whose time Judah was nearly exterminated by the army of Sennacherib (Isa 1:9; 4:3; 10:20-23; 11:1-9; 37:4, 31-32; Mic 2:12; 4:6-7; 5:6-7[7-8]; 7:18). The idea is carried on in Jeremiah, who witnessed the destruction of the Israelite nation (Jeremiah 24; 29; 30:10), and it survived in postexilic Judaism (Hag 1:12-14; 2:2; Zech 8:6, 11-12). In the NT, see Rom 11:5.

I thought. אָמַרְתִּי must here be rendered "I thought" (ibn Ezra; Rashi; von Rad; cf. Jer 3:7, 19; Ezek 20:13b). Another bold anthropomorphism, but von Rad points out that deliberations in the mind of God are not rare in the OT (Gen 6:5-7; 18:17-21; Hos 6:4; 11:8-9; Jer 31:20). They occur, he notes, when a decision regarding Israel's salvation or judgment is at issue.

I will strike them down. Hebrew אַפְאֵיהֶם is a *hapax legomenon* in the Old Testament, its precise meaning unknown. KBL³ gives the meanings "strike down, wipe out" for a verb פאה, citing an Arabic cognate meaning "to split with a sword." Tigay says Arabic "cut" also means to efface an inscription. BDB follows the Arabic and defines פאה as "to cleave in pieces." The Targums all had problems translating. The LXX has "I will scatter them" (διασπερῶ αὐτούς), but that appears to presuppose the verb פוץ (Wevers 1995, 524). While AV, RSV, and NRSV all follow the LXX, commentators do not. Rejecting the LXX reading, ibn Ezra translates the Hebrew: "I will annihilate them," noting that the next colon reads: "I will obliterate their memory."

I will surely make their memory cease from humankind. אַשְׁבִּיתָה מֵאֱנוֹשׁ זִכְרָם. 1QDeut 5:18 supports the Sam reading of אשבית. The MT has a more vigorous cohortative: "I will surely make cease." Yahweh gave thought to "wiping out" (מחה) Israel's name in 9:14. The ultimate curse is to have one's name or memory "wiped out" (מחה), or "cut off" (כרת), in all places and forever (29:19[20]; Pss 9:6-7[5-6]; 34:17[16]; 109:15; cf. Gen 6:7; 7:4; Job 18:17). This curse was laid upon Amalek for attacking Israel in the wilderness (Exod 17:14; Deut 25:19).

27 Here is why Yahweh decides not to exterminate his people, an argument Daube (1969a, 51) says is an appeal to shame: Israel's enemies would then "conclude that [Yahweh] was powerless to lead [Israel] to triumph, or even that he was ill-intentioned against them from the outset." Moses makes the same argument when mediating for Israel in the wilderness (9:27-29; Exod 32:12; Num 14:13-19), as does Joshua later in the land (Josh 7:9). See also Ezek 20:9, 13b-14, 21b-22; Isa 48:9-11.

Except I feared provocation of the enemy. לוּלֵי כַּעַס אוֹיֵב אָגוּר. The verb גוּר ("to fear, be afraid of"), which appears also in 1:17; 18:22, makes for another bold anthropomorphism in the verse, since God should not fear anyone or anything. Ibn Ezra reduces "fear" to "concern" on the part of God. Rashi omits the verb altogether. But אגור ("I feared") is present in 4QDeut[k1] (Ulrich, Cross et al. 1995, 98). The LXX gives a puzzling translation: "Were it not on account of anger of the enemies, in order that they not last long" (εἰ μὴ δι' ὀργὴν ἐχθρῶν, ἵνα μὴ μακροχρονίσωσιν), which Wevers (1995, 524) seeks to improve by taking ἐχθρῶν as an objective genitive. He translates: "Were it not because of (my) anger at the enemies," interpreting the two subsequent clauses as giving purpose to the divine anger. But this alters the meaning of the Hebrew considerably, whereas the plain sense is that God — like Moses and Joshua in their arguments — wants to keep the enemy from boasting and crediting itself for Israel's calamity. Fritsch (1943, 20) thinks the LXX wants to avoid an anthropomorphism, but his thesis here and elsewhere in Deuteronomy is sharply criticized by Orlinsky (1944) and Wittstruck (1976). Wittstruck says the LXX translator may simply be taking גוּר to mean "sojourn" (sojourning = not lasting long). The anthropomorphism of MT can stand.

lest his adversaries should misjudge. פֶּן־יְנַכְּרוּ צָרֵימוֹ. The verb נכר means "treat as strange, misconstrue, misjudge" (Gen 42:7). Israel's foes would make strange — and thus false — statements, such as the ones that follow. Israel's adversaries lack understanding (v. 28).

lest they say: "Our hand is raised up. The raised arm and hand (or fist) is a sign of triumph (Isa 26:11; Ps 89:14[13]). Here it would also be a display of arrogance. In v. 39 the hand triumphing over the enemy belongs to Yahweh, the same hand that brought about Israel's calamity.

and not Yahweh has done all this." I.e., carried out the calamity against Israel. 1QDeut 5:18 has אדני instead of יהוה; the Sam supports MT. Driver points out that "done" (פָּעַל) is a poetical word often used of a manifestation of divine power (Num 23:23; Isa 26:12; Hab 1:5; Ps 44:2[1]; Job 22:17, etc.).

28 The poet is now the speaker, as vv. 30-31 make clear. Yahweh returns as speaker in v. 34. All of vv. 28-33 carry forth the idea of v. 27, i.e., that the enemy is given to misjudgment. The dull-witted nation must then be the enemy (ibn Ezra; Rashi; von Rad; Moran, and others). But some commentators (Driver; G. E. Wright) think vv. 28-29 refer to Israel, an ancient opinion expressed already in *Sifre Deut.* §323 (Rabbi Judah). Hebrew "counsel" (עֵצוֹת) is plural, perhaps for intensification (GKC §124e: "true counsel"). Nelson has "good counsel" (cf. Prov 8:14; 12:15; Isa 28:29). In Jer 49:7 a people normally with understanding, in whom "counsel is destroyed" (אָבְדָה עֵצָה), is said to be without wisdom (cf. v. 29).

29 *If they were wise, they would consider this.* I.e., they would know "their own end" and grasp what is stated in v. 30 about Yahweh having delivered up his people to them. But they know neither. Targum^Nf has: "If Israel were wise . . .," going with the view that this verse refers to Israel. Hebrew לוּ ("if") introduces a condition contrary to fact. The LXX's initial οὐκ misreads לוּ as לֹא: "They were not understanding (enough) to comprehend these things" (Wevers 1995, 525).

they would discern their end. אַחֲרִית .יָבִינוּ לְאַחֲרִיתָם can also be translated "latter end." Reference is to the end in store for the enemies, to be described in vv. 34-42 (G. A. Smith). But Rashi thinks the poet is speaking about Israel's punishment in v. 30 (so also Driver and G. E. Wright; cf. v. 20). The LXX has: "Let them be concerned for the coming time" (καταδεξάσθωσαν εἰς τὸν ἐπιόντα χρόνον), which, although not transparent, sounds as if it has the enemy in mind.

30 The poet asks rhetorically just how a numerically superior Israel could have been put to flight by a force considerably smaller, but then answers his own question by saying it could only have happened because Yahweh sold them into enemy hands. "Sold" (מכר) means "gave away," as it does in the book of Judges (Judg 2:14; 3:8; 4:2) and as the parallelism in the bicolon makes clear. The expression "x and x plus 1" is stereotyped (Amos 1:3; Hos 6:2; Jer 3:14; Prov 6:16).

An adverse ratio of 1000:1 occurs in a curse list in the Treaty Between Ashurnirari V of Assyria and Mati'ilu of Arpad (*ANET*[3], 533; Greenfield and Shaffer 1985, 54), where it says that if Mati'ilu fails to live up to the treaty with his Assyrian suzerain,

> let one thousand houses decrease to one house,
> let one thousand tents decrease to one tent.

Greenfield and Shaffer (1985, 53) also cite in the Tell Fekherye Inscription this curse in Aramaic:

> may he sow a thousand measures but get one *parīs* in return.

Reference in the present verse is to some military disaster that reverses things from when Yahweh fought for Israel (Josh 23:10; Deut 28:7; Lev 26:8). Israel's

Deuteronomy 32

worst defeat in the wilderness was in its first attempt to enter Canaan, which loomed large for the Deuteronomic writer (1:41-46).

unless indeed their Rock had sold them. "Their Rock" and "our Rock" in v. 31 refer to Yahweh (cf. vv. 4, 15, and 18). The כִּי is again best translated as an asseverative: "indeed."

and Yahweh had delivered them up? Friedman points out that the verb סגר ("delivered up") is the same used in reference to (not) turning over an escaped slave to his master (23:16[15]). See also 1 Sam 23:20. The LXX translates with παρέδωκεν ("handed over, delivered up"). It is generally believed that the Song makes no reference to exile, but the imagery here comes close.

31 *Indeed their rock is not like our Rock.* "Their rock" plays on "their Rock" in v. 30. In v. 30 the metaphor refers to Yahweh, here to the god of the enemies. There is no comparison between the two (cf. Ps 18:32[31] = 2 Sam 22:32). "Rock" in v. 37 again refers to some false god.

even our enemies being assessors. וְאֹיְבֵינוּ פְּלִילִים. The phrase is difficult. פְּלִילִים in Exod 21:22 denote individuals (= judges) who assess damages to a woman suffering a miscarriage in a brawl. The idea here seems to be that even if Israel's enemies were allowed an assessment, they would acknowledge a difference between their god and Yahweh (cf. Jer 2:11). But whether they are acknowledging that their god is no match for Yahweh, as Driver suggests (cf. Exod 14:25; Numbers 23-24; 1 Sam 4:8; 5:7), is doubtful. Luther had the same idea. We have been told all along that the enemy is without understanding. Has it suddenly become enlightened?

32 *Indeed their vine is from the vine of Sodom, and from the terraces of Gomorrah.* The poet goes on to affirm different stock of the enemy, only now from Israel's point of view. The enemy descends from the infamous inhabitants of Sodom and Gomorrah (Genesis 18-19), further discrediting it as a moral force in the world. On Sodom and Gomorrah, see Note for 29:21-23. Nelson says the words may hint at the enemy sharing a defeat similar to that of Sodom and Gomorrah. Prophets commonly use "vine" and "vineyard" imagery to describe Israel (Hos 10:1; Isa 5:1-7; Jer 2:21; 5:10; 8:13; cf. Ps 80:9[8]). There may also be a wordplay on סְדֹם ("Sodom") and שַׁדְמֹת ("terraces"). שַׁדְמֹת are terraces on hilly terrain cultivated as vineyards (Isa 16:8; Hab 3:17; Jer 31:40[Q]).

Its grapes are grapes of poison, its clusters are bitter. According to Gen 19:24-25, Yahweh's destruction of Sodom and Gomorrah affected "what sprouted from the soil." Wisdom 10:7 says that one lasting legacy of the five wicked Cities of the Plain was "plants bearing fruit that does not ripen." Ancient and modern writers have described an orange-colored fruit growing in the area that has a beautiful exterior but a black ashlike interior. It has been called the "apple of Sodom" (J. P. Harland 1943, 49-52). But the fruit here is poisonous grapes producing undrinkable wine. In 29:17-18(18-19) Moses says that if an Israelite turns from Yahweh and goes after other gods, people are to beware of a hidden root (= family member?) bearing poison or wormwood.

33 *Their wine is the venom of serpents.* חֲמַת תַּנִּינִם יֵינָם. On the "venom" (חֲמַת) of serpents, see Pss 58:5[4]; 140:4[3]. The LXX here and in the next colon translates with θυμός ("wrath"), anticipating the meaning of חֲמַת as implied in v. 34. According to Driver, תַּנִּינִם is a generic term commonly applied to marine monsters (Gen 1:21) but sometimes used of land-reptiles (Exod 7:9-10, 12; Ps 91:13b).

yes, the cruel poison of vipers. וְרֹאשׁ פְּתָנִים אַכְזָר. Driver (citing Tristram) identifies פְּתָנִים as hooded cobras of Egypt, also found south of Beersheba, on which Egyptian serpent charmers practiced their secret arts (Ps 58:5-6[4-5]). This poisonous viper is mentioned in Isa 11:8; Ps 91:13a; Job 20:14, 16; Sir 39:30. The approaching (Babylonian) foe is described as "cruel" (אַכְזָר) in Jer 6:23.

34 The speaker is once again Yahweh, attention now shifting to divine vengeance laid up for the enemy. Judgment on the enemy and vindication for Israel dominate the two remaining stanzas of the Song, to the end of v. 42. But the link back to v. 33 is nevertheless extraordinary. The verb כָּמֻס is a *hapax legomenon* in the OT, but on the basis of an Akk cognate *kamāsu* it is taken to mean "collect, deposit, store up" (KBL³; cf. כנס with similar meaning). Wine is customarily deposited in storehouses. The verb picks up on the "wine" of v. 33, but shifts meaning to the divine "(wine of) wrath" now being readied for Israel's enemies (cf. Jer 25:15-29). The antecedent for "this" (הוּא) is actually חֲמַת in v. 33, which in that verse means "venom (of serpents)" but here is understood as meaning "wrath (of Yahweh)." The poet is playing on the double meaning of חֲמַת. In vv. 41-42 we hear about Yahweh's store of weapons being pressed into service for use against the enemy. Yahweh is slow to anger (Exod 34:6), storing up his wrath until human iniquity is complete (Gen 15:16), then unleashing it to do its terrible work (Rom 2:5; Rev 6:12-17). Human wickedness, too, is depicted in the OT as being "bound up in a bag" for the day of punishment (Driver; Hos 13:12; Job 14:17). Yahweh's multiple storehouses contain the primordial sea, rain, hail, snow, light, and wind, all agents of blessing or judgment (Jer 10:13; Deut 28:12; Ps 33:7; Job 38:22-24). Royal storerooms in antiquity were closed with a latch, then secured with a stamped seal (Tigay 1995 377-80). Yahweh's storehouse of wrath is similarly secured until the day of its "opening" (פתח) upon wicked inhabitants of the earth (Jer 1:14).

35 *Vengeance is mine, and repayment.* An oft-quoted line of Scripture, cited by Paul in Rom 12:19 to warn people against taking vengeance (= revenge) into their own hands (cf. Gen 4:24; Judg 15:7; 16:28; Jer 20:10; Ps 8:3[2]; Lev 19:18), but to leave it to God (Jer 11:20 [= 20:12]; 15:15). But the intent here, as Driver points out, is not to warn against self-vengeance, since a prostrate Israel is in no state to contemplate such action (vv. 36-38). Yahweh is simply declaring

Deuteronomy 32

that vengeance (or punishment) will be forthcoming against evildoers and nations of evildoers and that he will carry it out. This is repeated in v. 41, echoed again in v. 43, and expressed all throughout the Bible (Lev 26:25; Num 31:3; Pss 94:1-3; 99:8; 149:7; Isa 1:24; 34:8; Mic 5:14[15]; Nah 1:2; Jer 5:9, 29; 9:8[9]; 46:10; 51:6, 36; Ezek 25:14, 17; Heb 10:30). On the subject of vengeance, see Mendenhall 1948. The LXX in the present verse has: ἐν ἡμέρᾳ ἐκδικήσεως ἀνταποδώσω ("in the day of vengeance I will repay"), with "I will repay" turning up not surprisingly in the NT texts of Rom 12:19; Heb 10:30. Targums also have "I will repay." The LXX follows Sam in reading MT's לִי ("for me, mine") as לְיוֹם ("for/in the day"), either to continue (prosaically) what precedes or else to balance לְעֵת ("for the time") in the colon following (Tigay). The LXX also appears to have taken שׁלם as a Piel infinitive of the verb (Wevers 1995, 528). MT points as an otherwise unattested noun, שִׁלֵּם ("repayment"). Rashi translates שִׁלֵּם as a verb (cf. 7:10; 32:41), but notes that some interpret it as a noun. The meaning, in any case, is that vengeance belongs to Yahweh and he will administer it.

for the time when their foot shall slip. Foot slippage is a biblical idiom for misfortune (Driver; cf. Pss 38:17[16]; 94:18; cf. 66:9; 121:3; also Job 12:5; Ps 25:15 [cf. Pss 18:37(36); 37:31]), expressed in the Prophets as "stumbling (and falling)" (Hos 4:5; 5:5; 14:2[1]; Isa 3:8; 8:15; 31:3; Jer 6:15[= 8:12], 21; 20:11; 31:9; Ezek 3:20; 7:19; 14:3, 4, 7). When the foot of the righteous begins to slip, one is upheld by Yahweh (Ps 94:18); for the wicked calamity follows quickly.

Indeed the day of their disaster is near, and things prepared are hastening to him. Jeremiah revises this word slightly for use against Moab (Jer 48:16). The "day of (one's) disaster" is a day of sudden and (usually) irreparable calamity (Jer 18:17; 46:21; Obad 13 [3 times]; Prov 27:10; Ps 18:19[18]; Job 21:30). God's judgment — also his salvation — comes not soon, but quickly (Isa 5:26; 29:5-6; 30:13; Jer 4:20; 6:26; 15:8; 18:22; 51:8; Hab 2:3; Isa 60:22; 1 Thess 5:2-4; Rev 22:20). On the "suddenness" theme in Scripture, see Daube 1964.

36 *Indeed Yahweh will vindicate his people, and feel sorry over his servants.* Quoted fully in Ps 135:14 and partially in 2 Macc 7:6 and Heb 10:30. Hebrew יָדִין ("execute judgement") here means "vindicate" (cf. Ps 54:3[1]); נחם in the Hithpael means "feel sorry (for)" (cf. N-Stem in Judg 21:6; Jer 15:6; Ps 90:13), denoting in the present case Yahweh's change of heart for the good (RSV, NRSV: "have compassion"; JB, NJB: "take pity"). With Yahweh's enemies now being punished, Israel is vindicated and receives divine compassion. The idea is seized upon in Second Isaiah (Isa 47:3-4; 59:17-20; 61:2; 63:4; cf. 34:8; 35:4). Mendenhall (1948, 37-39) points out that נקם in early biblical and extrabiblical literature had a meaning considerably broader than "avenge," i.e., it could mean "deliver, rescue, save." P. D. Miller (1990, 233) calls Yahweh's avenging work his "executive action . . . to effect moral order and just rule in the universe." The second asseverative כִּי of three in vv. 35b-36 intensifies: "Indeed . . . Indeed . . .

Indeed." Rashi says the first occurrence does not provide a reason (*pace* Driver); he translates both occurrences in the verse as "when."

Indeed he will see that support is gone. I.e., support (יָד, lit. "hand") provided Israel by other people and their "no-gods" (vv. 15-18), the former in the next colon said to be no longer helpful and the latter derided in vv. 37-38 as having no existence. The LXX has: εἶδεν γὰρ παραλελυμένους αὐτοὺς ("for he saw them undone"). Commentators and the modern Versions follow Rashi, Luther, and the AV in translating יָד as "power/strength/might," usually adding the possessive pronoun "their" (not in the text). But ambiguity remains. Whose power/strength/might? The point seems to be that Yahweh is now compassionate toward Israel after seeing that support from neighboring peoples (and their gods) is gone, leaving Israel powerless.

and none remains bond or free. וְאֶפֶס עָצוּר וְעָזוּב. An enigmatic expression, the precise meaning of which is unknown. עָצוּר וְעָזוּב is an alliterative merismus meaning "everyone" (1 Kgs 14:10; 21:21; 2 Kgs 9:8), here joined with a negative to mean "no one." Usage of the full expression in 2 Kgs 14:26 is helpful, where an accompanying phrase, "there was no one to help Israel," provides clarification. Tigay believes the expression has to do with power or help and means "neither supporter nor helper," which is how the Peshitta and Talmud render it. The expression cannot mean that no one remains in Israel, since that is not true. Just now Yahweh is showing compassion on the Israelite remnant saved from annihilation (vv. 26-27).

37 MT has simply "Then he will say" (וְאָמַר), but other ancient textual witnesses supply Yahweh as the subject. The LXX using an aorist verb translates: "And the Lord said" (καὶ εἶπεν κύριος). 4QDeut^q reads: "Then Yahweh will say," although above the words may be a superlinear insertion (Ulrich, Cross et al. 1995, 139-40). Ulrich (p. 138) notes that 4QDeut^q and LXX agree in seven readings against MT, suggesting a variant Hebrew *Vorlage* used by the LXX translator. Other ancient Versions (Sam, T, S, and Vg) support MT. The line is best read if Yahweh continues to be the speaking voice, turning now to mock a chastened Israel by calling for other gods to help and protect her. All of vv. 37-38, in any case, is full-blown irony (cf. Judg 10:14; Jer 2:28). Ibn Ezra thinks "he" in the MT reading refers to the enemy (cf. 2 Kgs 18:34), but this is unlikely, although a plural verb in Sam ("And they said") would also preclude Yahweh from being the speaker.

Where is his god? אֱלֹהֵימוֹ ("his god") is an archaic singular form (Freedman 1976, 78), followed in the next colon by a plural verb. Jeremiah, echoing this verse, has "Where are your gods?" (Jer 2:28). Elsewhere Jeremiah reproaches the fathers and priests with "Where is Yahweh?" questions, which they should have asked but did not (Jer 2:6, 8). Cf. the mocking questions in 2 Kgs 18:34; Jer 37:19(Q).

Deuteronomy 32

the rock in whom they took refuge? צוּר חָסָיוּ בוֹ. 4QDeut^q has the relative pronoun אֲשֶׁר after צוּר ("rock"), reflected also in the reading of LXX (ἐφ' οἷς). But the LXX lacks צוּר, which in MT is an ironic reference to some false god that has to be retained (cf. v. 31). Wevers (1995, 510, 530) points out that the LXX never translates צוּר as "rock," explaining the omission here by saying that its usual rendering of "god" (θεός) would make for an awkward repetition after "their gods" in the prior colon. The Israelite people, needless to say, should have taken refuge in Yahweh, which is the good counsel of the Psalms (Pss 2:12[11]; 7:2[1]; 14:6; 18:3[2]; 46:2[1]; 61:4[3], and passim).

38 *Choice portions of his sacrifices they ate, they drank wine of their libations.* Eliminating the initial אֲשֶׁר ("who") in MT, which has turned up in the prior colon of 4QDeut^q where it belongs (see Rhetoric and Composition). What remains is a syntactic chiasmus with the verbs at the center:

Choice portions of his sacrifices/they ate
    they drank/wine of their libations

The אֲשֶׁר perhaps fell out of the prior colon and was later reinserted at the beginning of the present line. 4QDeut^q has a space for an אֲשֶׁר at the beginning of this line, but the word does not appear in the text (Ulrich, Cross et al. 1995, 139). We return to opulence of the sort described in vv. 13-14, only here it is the false gods who have been eating and drinking well (Rashi). The irony continues, for these gods did not gorge themselves with illicit Israelite offerings. חֵלֶב ("fat") is the choice portion of an animal sacrifice. 4QDeut^q contains a plural חלבי ("fats, choice portions"), present also in T^{Nf}.

Let them arise and let them help you, let it be your protection!" A ballast line concluding Yahweh's mockery of the false gods and chastisement of Israel. The line also concludes the Song's penultimate stanza (see Rhetoric and Composition). Cf. Jer 2:28; 11:12. To be noted as well is an end-shift to the second person, which occurs elsewhere in the Song (vv. 14b, 17b-18) and becomes common in the oracles of Jeremiah (Jer 2:9; 5:31b; 8:17; 12:13b; 16:9; 48:46).

your protection. סִתְרָה is a *hapax legomenon* in the OT, but cognates סָתַר ("to hide") and סֵתֶר ("shelter, hiding place") are well attested. Once again, the Israelites should have found their shelter in Yahweh (Pss 27:5; 31:21[20]; 32:7; 61:5[4]; 91:1; 119:114).

39 *See now indeed I, I am he, and there is no god with me.* Yahweh now becomes lyrical, repeating what Moses said in v. 12: in mighty deeds Yahweh acts without help from any other god. The verse finds a later echo in Isa 43:11-13. Duplicated personal pronouns (אֲנִי אֲנִי) provide emphasis and betray divine passion (cf. Hos 5:14b; with אָנֹכִי see Isa 43:11, 25; 51:12).

See now. רְאוּ עַתָּה. A transitional expression with עַתָּה (Muilenburg 1969,

15), shifting focus from inert gods unable to help to Yahweh, who controls the destiny of all nations (see also Note for 2:13). The LXX translates with a double imperative: ἴδετε ἴδετε ("see, see!").

I, I am he. אֲנִי אֲנִי הוּא. A vigorous divine self-asseveration, which the LXX reduces to a simple "I am" (ἐγώ εἰμι). 4QDeut^q appears to double the pronoun "I" (Skehan 1954, 13; Ulrich, Cross et al. 1995, 139; *pace* Lust 1995, 38). Albright (1959, 542-43) thinks the Hebrew departs from usual word order, which would be אֲנִי־הוּא אֲנִי (cf. Isa 48:12), also that הוּא should be taken as a copulative. He translates: "I am I," but this weakens the repetition and may not correctly render the expression. Nelson's translation is better: "I, I am the One." This divine self-asseveration, along with others, dominates the later poetry of Second Isaiah (Isa 41:4; 43:11, 13; 46:4; 48:12).

and there is no god with me. וְאֵין אֱלֹהִים עִמָּדִי. Hebrew עִמָּדִי is "with me," as in v. 34 (ibn Ezra; AV), although modern English Versions all follow the RSV and translate "beside(s) me." The LXX: "and there is no god except me" (καὶ οὐκ ἔστιν θεὸς πλὴν ἐμοῦ). Yahweh's self-asseveration is generally — but not universally — taken to be monotheistic in nature (Albright 1957b, 297; cf. Deut 4:35, 39; 6:4; 1 Sam 2:2; 2 Sam 22:32 = Ps 18:32[31]), which achieves great clarity in Second Isaiah (Isa 44:6; 45:5-6, 14, 18, 21-22; 46:9). Luyten (1985, 346) says the present verse is perhaps the most impressive monotheistic formula in the OT. But debunking other gods and affirming Yahweh's incomparability is old (Exod 15:11), continuing in Deuteronomy (Deut 3:24; 4:7, 32-39), the "Deuteronomic" prayers of David and Solomon (2 Sam 7:22-23; 1 Kgs 8:23), and in the Prophets (Hab 2:18-20; Jer 10:1-10). See also Pss 35:10; 71:19; 86:8; 89:9(8); 113:5.

I, I kill, and I make alive, I wound, and I, I heal. Emphatic pronouns continue, here forming a chiasmus in the first two colons of a tricolon. Summed up are affirmations the Song has already made: Yahweh is the One who creates (v. 6) and destroys (vv. 22-25) and now is preparing to destroy the enemy (vv. 41-42). Death for the enemy will mean healing for Israel (v. 36). Yahweh is the one and only healer in Israel (Exod 15:26; 2 Kgs 20:5; Pss 103:3; 147:3; cf. Lundbom 2004a, 396), an idea that finds full expression in the prophecies of Hosea and Jeremiah (Hos 6:1; 7:1; 11:3; 14:5[4]; Jer 17:14; 30:17; 33:6). For language of sickness and healing in Hosea and Jeremiah, see Gross (1930, 10, 16; 1931, 246-47) and Muilenburg (1970b, 45-48). On Yahweh/God as the one who kills and makes alive, see 1 Sam 2:6; 2 Kgs 5:7. On Yahweh/God as the one who wounds and binds up, see Isa 19:22; 30:26b; Hos 6:1; Job 5:18.

and none can rescue from my hand. "Hand" (יָד) here means power. Cf. the formulaic "and there will be none to deliver (for you)" (וְאֵין [לְךָ] מוֹשִׁיעַ) in 28:29, 31. The present formula occurs with God as subject 5 times in the OT (Deut 32:39; Hos 2:12[10]; 5:14; Isa 43:13; Ps 50:22; Job 10:7), having turned up also in an old Sumerian hymn to Enlil (Chalmers 2005).

40 The particle כִּי is again best translated as an asseverative: "Indeed." Yahweh is swearing an oath in his own name (cf. Gen 22:16; Jer 22:5, 24; 44:26; 46:18; 49:13; 51:14; Isa 45:23; Heb 6:13) that he will assuredly destroy the enemy. The poet has used "hand" 3 times in five verses: in v. 36 to say that Yahweh sees Israel's "support" (יָד) from people and their "no-gods" to be gone; in quoting Yahweh in v. 39 as saying that the grasp of his "hand" (יָד) precludes any rescue from it; and now quoting Yahweh as stating, with raised "hand" (יָד) in oath-taking, that he will avenge the enemy. A divine "hand" (יָד) will also work judgment in v. 41. Yahweh's raised hand here is an answer to the defiant enemy hand (יָד) of v. 27, which waits to be raised in triumph. Lust (1995, 45) wants to disconnect the phrases, saying that the first phrase about the lifted divine hand should be joined to the prior verse (v. 39). In his view the raised hand does not indicate oath-taking. The argument is unconvincing; Yahweh is swearing an oath (Rashi; Driver; Tigay). The LXX adds a colon not in MT: "and swear by my right hand" (καὶ ὀμοῦμαι τῇ δεξιᾷ μου). See Isa 62:8. This plus does not appear to exist in 4QDeut^q (Lust 1995, 41-42), which means MT should be read.

and I say: As I live forever. חַי אָנֹכִי לְעֹלָם. An emphatic form of the usual "As I live" formula (Num 14:21, 28; Zeph 2:9; Jer 22:24; 46:18; often [17 times] in Ezekiel: Ezek 5:11; 14:16, 18, 20, and passim; Isa 49:18). Yahweh lives forever.

41 *If I sharpen my gleaming sword.* אִם־שַׁנּוֹתִי בְּרַק חַרְבִּי. The particle אִם ("If") following an oath formula (v. 40b) introduces the content of the oath (Nelson). The statement is not conditional. Yahweh swears by his holy name to sharpen his gleaming sword and use it against the enemy. The store of divine weapons is about to be opened (Jer 50:25), and first to be viewed will be Yahweh's polished sword flashing brightly (cf. Ezek 21:14b-16, 20[9b-11, 15]; Hab 3:11; Nah 3:3). The LXX takes the sword as being "like lightning" (ὡς ἀστραπήν).

and my hand takes hold on judgment. וְתֹאחֵז בְּמִשְׁפָּט יָדִי. A bold coinage. The divine hand takes firm hold not simply of the sword, but of judgment itself.

I will return vengeance to my adversaries, and to those who hate me, I will repay. Another syntactic chiasmus with the verbs at the extremes. Yahweh said in v. 35 that vengeance belongs to him; now we see its application: vengeance will be returned (שׁוּב) on Yahweh's adversaries. One may conclude, particularly in light of v. 43, that the enemies are being paid back for violence done to Israel (ibn Ezra). But the verse does not seem to be saying that, rather that the enemies are being repaid for their hatred of Yahweh. What is more, judgment on Israel came from Yahweh (vv. 19-27), for which there can be no payback. Jeremiah reflects the same attitude toward Babylon and the nations. Yahweh takes vengeance on nations who are *his* foes (Jer 46:10). They do not incur guilt for devouring Israel, because Israel's sin was against Yahweh (Jer 50:7). Babylon, too, is said to have sinned against Yahweh (Jer 50:14 MT), for which reason Yahweh promises ven-

Deuteronomy 32

geance upon her (v. 15). Elsewhere Jeremiah says that other nations (or their rulers) are judged because they are wicked (Jer 25:31), proud (Jer 50:24, 29-32), and trusting in their images (Jer 50:38b; 51:47, 52). In what may be a later addition to the Jeremiah prophecies, vengeance is also sought against Babylon because it destroyed Yahweh's temple (Jer 50:28 MT; 51:11b).

42 *I will make my arrows drunk from blood, and my sword shall consume flesh.* Arrows and the sword now emerge from Yahweh's store of weapons, their use resulting in a carnage that will defy description. Sword and bow are the usual weapons of war (Gen 48:22; Josh 24:12; 1 Sam 18:4; 2 Sam 1:22; 2 Kgs 6:22). Earlier, Yahweh spent his arrows on Israel (v. 23), but now they will be used against the enemy. On the imagery of swords, arrows, and enemies themselves "drinking (to drunkenness)" (רוה) or "becoming drunk" (שכר) with spilled blood, see Jer 25:27; 46:10; Isa 34:5-6; 49:26. On swords "consuming" (אכל) human flesh, see 2 Sam 2:26; 11:25; Isa 1:20; Jer 46:10. Ancient swords had "mouths" at the hilt, as we now know from swords excavated in northern Syria, southern Mesopotamia, and northwestern Iran. Blades are represented as tongues sticking out of an open-mouthed lion or dragon carved into the hilt (Lundbom 2004a, 104-5). On arrows as a figure of divine chastisement, see Note for v. 23.

From the blood of slain and captive. This colon and the next pick up respectively from colons 1 and 2 (Driver). The predication could just as well be:

I will make my arrows drunk from blood
   from the blood of slain and captive,
And my sword shall consume flesh
   from the long-haired head of the enemy.

Some of the enemy will die in battle; others will be slain after having been taken prisoner (cf. 1 Sam 15:32-33; Jer 39:6; 52:24-27 = 2 Kgs 25:18-21).

from the long-haired head of the enemy. מֵרֹאשׁ פַּרְעוֹת אוֹיֵב. Long, loosely-hanging hair went with the Nazirite vow (Num 6:5; 1 Sam 1:11) and may also have been a mark of extraordinary strength and fighting ability (Judg 5:2) or both, as in the case of Samson (Judg 13:5; 16:17). The opening words of the Song of Deborah, בִּפְרֹעַ פְּרָעוֹת בְּיִשְׂרָאֵל, are rendered in the JB and NJB: "That the warriors in Israel unbound their hair"; in the NJV: "When locks go untrimmed in Israel," and in the NRSV: "When locks are long in Israel" (Judg 5:2). Long-haired enemies are mentioned in Ps 68:22(21). Here the LXX has: ἀπὸ κεφαλῆς ἀρχόντων ἐχθρῶν ("from the head of the leaders of the enemies"), which could refer to the king (Driver). Some modern English Versions (NEB; JB[but not NJB]; NAB; NIV; NJV; REB) read with the LXX, translating "head" as "princes" or the like.

43 *Give his people ringing acclaim, O heavens.* Reading the first colon of this verse with 4QDeut^q, which has "heavens" instead of MT's "nations" (NRSV). The LXX begins: "Rejoice, O heavens, with him," the preferred reading of some scholars (Skehan 1951, 160; 1954; Albright 1959, 340-41; Cross 1995, 134-35; Rofé 2000, 167, 172; cf. Rev 18:20) and the reading adopted in the NEB, REB, JB, and NJB. The poet once again is the speaking voice, addressing either the heavens or the heavenly host (apostrophe), as in the opening verse of the Song (G. E. Wright 1962, 36; von Rad; Moran; Tigay; Nelson; cf. Pss 29:1; 148:1-6). Rofé takes שׁמים here to mean not "heavens," but "heavenly beings." If so, the entire host of heaven is being called to give Yahweh's people "ringing acclaim" (רנן H-stem). In MT the nations are addressed, with גוים again a vocative: "O nations." According to this reading, the nations are being told (in the future when their punishment is over) to congratulate Israel for having a God such as Yahweh, who takes up the cause of his people (Rashi; ibn Ezra; Driver; cf. 33:26; Pss 67; 144:15; Jer 10:6-7). Driver says with regard to the MT reading: "Such an invitation, addressed to the nations . . . involves implicitly the prophetic truth that God's dealings with Israel have, indirectly, an interest and importance for the world at large." Paul's quotation in Rom 15:10 of line 3 in the LXX version of the verse (εὐφράνθητε, ἔθνη) supports his view that Christ's coming to Israel as a servant is to the end that Gentiles might come to glorify God for his mercy. The words may also be echoed in Rev 18:20.

for the blood of his servants he will avenge, yes, he will return vengeance to his adversaries. The poet now rejoices because Yahweh will avenge the blood of his servants by taking vengeance on his adversaries. This goes beyond v. 41b, which does not say that enemies will receive a payback for violence done to Israel. But "servants" here probably means Israel (v. 36; cf. Ps 79:10), even though the term could refer more generally to anyone worshiping Yahweh (2 Kgs 9:7). The LXX and 4QDeut^q read "sons" in place of "servants," which narrows the meaning to Israel.

and atone for his land, his people. וְכִפֶּר אַדְמָתוֹ עַמּוֹ. Yahweh will reconcile, pacify, and cleanse both his land and his people of all guilt they have incurred. This has been and will in the future be accomplished by slaying not only an idolatrous enemy, but also idolatrous Israelites. The Sam, LXX, 4QDeut^q, and Vg read "the land of his people," which limits the atonement to (Israelite) land. But the Targums all read "the land and his people." Land is polluted by idolatry, idolatrous practices, and the shedding of innocent blood (Lev 18:24-30; Jer 3:1-2, 9; Ps 106:38) and can only be atoned for by shedding the blood of polluters, or designated individuals or animals in their stead (Deut 21:8-9; Num 35:33; 2 Sam 21:1-14; Ezek 36:17-18; Joel 4:19, 21[3:19, 21]).

The MT reading of v. 43, followed for the most part in Sam, T, and Vg, is expanded in LXX and 4QDeut^q. For a comparison of the three texts, see van der

Kooij (1994, 95) and Tigay (1996, 516). The LXX expands the verse to 8 colons, twice its length in MT:

εὐφράνθητε, οὐρανοί, ἅμα αὐτῷ,	Rejoice, O heavens, with him,
καὶ προσκυνησάτωσαν αὐτῷ πάντες υἱοὶ θεοῦ.	and let all the sons of God worship him.
εὐφράνθητε, ἔθνη, μετὰ τοῦ λαοῦ αὐτοῦ,	Rejoice, O nations, with his people,
καὶ ἐνισχυσάτωσαν αὐτῷ πάντες ἄγγελοι θεοῦ.	and let all the angels of God confirm for him.
ὅτι τὸ αἷμα τῶν υἱῶν αὐτοῦ ἐκδικᾶται,	For the blood of his sons he avenges,
καὶ ἐκδικήσει καὶ ἀνταποδώσει δίκην τοῖς ἐχθροῖς,	and he will avenge and repay judgment to his enemies.
καὶ τοῖς μισοῦσιν ἀνταποδώσει.	And those who hate he will repay,
καὶ ἐκκαθαριεῖ κύριος τὴν γῆν τοῦ λαοῦ αὐτοῦ.	and the Lord will purify the land of his people.

Valuations of the LXX text differ, with scholars preferring certain readings over readings in MT, but believing at the same time that LXX has probably expanded an earlier original. Rofé (2000, 168), following the lead of Skehan (1951, 156), thinks the first two bicolons conflate a primary and secondary reading. But it is also possible that MT has lost a first bicolon by vertical haplography (homoeoarcton: הרנינו ... הרנינו). A portion of the LXX reading is quoted in the NT (Rom 15:10; Heb 1:6; Rev 6:10; 18:20; 19:2). Colon 2 has "sons of God," a reading that turned up in v. 8 of 4QDeut^j (see Note there). Reference in both places would be to lesser divine beings in Yahweh's heavenly host. 4QDeut^q in the colon here has "gods," doubtless with the same meaning, but in MT the colon has been eliminated entirely, probably due to a denial in later Judaism of the existence of other divine beings (Skehan 1951, 156; 1954, 15; Tigay 1996, 516; Rofé 2000, 167). A balancing colon, though not quite the same as in LXX or 4QDeut^q, is present in T^{OnqNf}. Colon 3 modifies slightly colon 1 of MT, calling for the nations to rejoice with Yahweh's people. Colon 4 has no counterpart in MT, but may be a variant of colon 2 in 4QDeut^q ("and worship him all you gods"), translating a different verb and substituting "angels of God" for "gods" in 4QDeut^q. Nelson (2002, 379) points out that LXX's ἐνισχυσάτωσαν ("let them confirm") cannot translate השתחוו ("worship") in 4QDeut^q. Colons 5 and 6 parallel readings in both MT and 4QDeut^q, with colon 5 reflecting more closely the Qumran text with "blood of his sons." The MT has "blood of his servants" (cf. "servants" in v. 36). In colon 6 the LXX expands MT and 4QDeut^q with a double verb (cf. v. 41b). Colon 7 has no counterpart in MT, but does appear in 4QDeut^q. It is a near-duplication of v. 41b, and Tigay (1996, 517) thinks it may have been lost in MT by haplography (homoeoarcton: ו ... ו). Colon 8 modifies the final colons of both MT and 4QDeut^q by adding "the Lord" (κύριος) as subject and reads with 4QDeut^q "the land of his people." MT has "his land, his people."

Deuteronomy 32

4QDeut^q has a 6-colon reading (Skehan 1954; Ulrich, Cross et al. 1995, 141-42), which compares to MT as follows:

4QDeut^q	MT
הרנינו שמים עמו	הַרְנִינוּ גוֹיִם עַמּוֹ
והשתחוו לו כל אלהים	
כי דם בניו יקום	כִּי דַם־עֲבָדָיו יִקּוֹם
ונקם ישיב לצריו	וְנָקָם יָשִׁיב לְצָרָיו
ולמשנאיו ישלם	
ויכפר אדמת עמו	וְכִפֶּר אַדְמָתוֹ עַמּוֹ

Give his people ringing acclaim, O heavens, and worship him all you gods!	Give his people ringing acclaim, O nations,
For the blood of his sons he will avenge, yes, he will return vengeance to his adversaries,	For the blood of his servants he will avenge, yes, he will return vengeance to his adversaries,
And to those who hate him he will requite and atone for the land of his people.	and atone for his land, his people.

This Qumran text, like the text of LXX, begins with a parallelistic bicolon addressing the heavens or the heavenly host. But it does not have a corresponding bicolon addressing the nations. Colon 2 calls for worship from (other) "gods," which like LXX's "sons of God" and "angels of God" would denote lesser divine beings in Yahweh's heavenly host (Ps 97:7). The MT, as we mentioned, eliminates this colon. Colon 5, "and to those who hate him he will requite," is a near-duplication of the last colon in v. 41. Cross (1995, 135) thinks that colon 5 was lost in MT by haplography, although he also believes that the entire bicolon is intrusive from v. 41.

There is a general consensus that the original reading of this verse was longer than the double bicolon surviving in MT (Albright 1955, 32-33 n. 27; 1959, 340-41; Meyer 1961, 198-201; G. E. Wright 1962, 33; van der Kooij 1994, 96-99; Tigay; Nelson), and some modern English Versions adopt — with or without modification — the readings of LXX (JB; NJB) or 4QDeut^q (NEB; REB; NRSV). Virtually everyone agrees that none of the three texts reflects the original version exactly. Albright (1959, 341) cited the longer readings in support of his view that texts suffered greatly from omissions in antiquity. He said: There is "increasing evidence from the Qumran Scrolls that our Hebrew originals, once edited in antiquity, suffered far more from omissions by copyists than from additions."

Message and Audience

The poet of this extraordinary composition, speaking in the person of Moses as he addresses Israel in the plains of Moab, begins by calling on the heavens and the earth to witness what he has to say. It portends to be an irenic teaching, coming as it does like gentle rain, dew to thirsty ground, soft raindrops on grass, light showers on sprouts of earth. The theme is presented straightaway. The poet wants to lift up the name of Yahweh and ascribe greatness to the God Israel calls its own.

Israel's God is "the Rock," his created work perfect, all his ways just. Yahweh is faithful, without wrong, righteous and upright in all he does. But a generation of his people, early on in their wilderness trek, acted corruptly toward him. Most everyone in the audience will have heard about the "golden calf" incident. A perverted and crooked generation it was, the blemish all its own. Yahweh cannot be blamed for their corruptness. The people, now addressed directly, are asked if Yahweh ought be repaid in this manner. Such a foolish people! Is not Yahweh the one who created Israel and intended it to last? Let the people remember, let them go back not one but many generations. Let them ask their fathers and their elders; they will tell them. In hoary antiquity, the Most High, now known to be Yahweh, separated all humanity and gave each nation its inheritance, fixing its territorial boundaries according to the number of beings in the heavenly host. Yes, at this early time, Yahweh chose Jacob as his portion, and its allotted land became Yahweh's inheritance.

In the wilderness Yahweh is said to have "found" Israel. Her wandering in a desert waste was long and arduous, but through good and bad Yahweh cared for Israel, much as an eagle cares for its young. Israel was protected from all its enemies. It was a training period, with Yahweh alone guiding his people. No foreign god was present. Israel was then given a wonderful high country in which it could grow the finest produce, suck honey from the rock, eat oil and curds, drink milk from the flocks, and feast on the choicest meat — lamb, ram, Bashan beef, and goat. It grew the choicest grain and raised the finest grapes, from which it could make wine. And did they drink wine! Abundant living came in the Transjordan, before entering Canaan, after Sihon and Og were defeated and Israelite tribes settled their land.

But what happened? Jacob ate and became sated, and with fatness the "Upright One" became intractable. The poet emphasizes that the very people now listening to Moses are the ones who became thick. Jacob abandoned the God who made him and treated with contempt the Rock of his salvation. Did not Jacob remember the exodus? Did not Jacob remember deliverances in the wilderness? Strange gods and abominable practices provoking Yahweh came to a climax in Israel's yoking to Baal of Peor at Shittim, where she played the harlot with the daughters of Moab. There Israel ate sacrifices to gods its fathers never knew and forgot the God who gave the nation birth.

Yahweh saw it all and was greatly provoked. Speaking now his inner mind, Yahweh says he determined to hide his face in anger and see what the end of this perverse and faithless generation would be. They made him jealous with a no-god, so he will make them jealous with a no-people. At the time of the Shittim incident this "no-people" will have been the Midianites. In the future, it will be a succession of other peoples, none of which enjoys the special status given to Israel. Yahweh's anger is a consuming anger when other gods are at issue. Reference to the "depths of Sheol" brings to mind Korah's rebellion, when the divine fire burst forth and Sheol consumed the rebels.

Yahweh promises a host of evils for his rebellious people — enemy arrows, famine, pestilence, and attacks from predators the likes of which Israel knew from the wilderness days. There, more than once, thousands were killed by plagues. Swords in the street and the terror in the chambers now anticipate Israel's settled life in towns and cities. Judgment will fall on everyone. In the wilderness it happened not once, but more than once, that Yahweh wanted to wipe out his people entirely. But he decided to keep a remnant so the enemy would not take credit for Israel's calamity.

The poet intervenes briefly to point out that Israel's enemies are dull-witted, not knowing what their own fate will be. No, Israel suffered defeat because Yahweh gave it into enemy hands. The enemies' "rock" is not like Israel's "Rock." Even the enemies know that. Their stock is from Sodom and Gomorrah, a dubious moral entity, one would have to say, in the known world.

Yahweh again becomes the speaking voice, and will continue to be so to the end of the poem proper. The subject now turns to vengeance, which the audience has been waiting for. Yahweh says vengeance belongs to him. He possesses a sealed store of weapons for just such an occasion, and now the seal will be broken and the storehouse opened wide. The enemies' foot will slip, making their fall come quickly. Vengeance on the enemy will bring vindication and compassion on Yahweh's own. Israel's support from the enemy and its no-gods will be gone, making this the right time for Yahweh to show Israel compassion. But Israel must still receive a chastening. Yahweh asks, where are the other gods to protect her? They ate the choice portions of sacrifices and drank the wine of libations. Let them rise up and help Israel now! They cannot.

The Song closes with a robust self-asseveration. Yahweh says he alone is God. There is none besides him, which the poet had said earlier. Yahweh kills and Yahweh makes alive; Yahweh wounds and Yahweh heals, and no one is strong enough to deliver from his grasp. With the divine hand lifted high, Yahweh swears an oath that his gleaming sword is sharpened, ready for judgment. He will return vengeance on his adversaries and repay all who hate him.

Deuteronomy 32

His arrows and his sword will complete the job on the disheveled heads of the enemy. Even those taken captive will be killed.

The Song concludes with the call for ringing acclaim of Yahweh's people, whether from the heavens or the nations. If it is the nations, it will be once their punishment is over. The reason for the acclaim is that Israel has a God who avenges his enemies and in so doing makes atonement for his people and his land.

This Song had a profound impact on the Hebrew prophets and has solidly established itself in Judaism and the Christian church. We know from 4QDeut^j, a collection of fragments from Deuteronomy and Exodus, that Deuteronomy 32 had a place in Jewish liturgical practice (Ulrich, Cross et al. 1995, 75-91). This Qumran manuscript contains a fragment of vv. 7-8. The Levites recited Deuteronomy 32 in the temple on the Sabbath, also Deuteronomy at the temple service of the Ma'mādôt (Weinfeld 1992c, 428-29). Although Deuteronomy 32 is not usually found in phylactery material (Duncan 1997-98, 48), it has turned up in a phylactery from Cave 4, 4QPhyl 141. The church fathers, e.g., Justin Martyr and Irenaeus, not surprisingly used Deuteronomy 32 as a polemic against the Jews for their infidelities (J. R. Harris 1925-26).

Jonathan Edwards used v. 35 about the foot of the enemy slipping as a text for his famous sermon, "Sinners in the Hands of an Angry God," preached at Enfield on July 8, 1741. Actually, the sermon was on the entire conclusion to the Song, where the Lord promises judgment on the wicked. Edwards took these words as referring to the punishment and destruction of wicked Israelites, not their enemies, and began his riveting sermon by describing how the foot will slide when the day of judgment arrives:

> Another thing implied is that they are liable to fall of themselves, without being thrown down by the hand of another; as he that stands or walks on slippery ground needs nothing but his own weight to throw him down. That the reason why they are not fallen already, and do not fall now, is only that God's appointed time is not come. For it is said that when that due time, or appointed time, comes, *their foot shall slide*. Then they shall be left to fall, as they are inclined by their own weight. God will not hold them up in these slippery places any longer, but will let them go; and then, at that very instant, they shall fall into destruction, as he that stands in such slippery declining ground, on the edge of a pit, he cannot stand alone, when he is let go he immediately falls and is lost.

Memorable, too, are Edward's words about the fate of the unconverted as God's arrows of death fly by. Here he appears to pick up the "arrow" imagery of v. 42:

Unconverted men walk over the pit of hell on a rotten covering, and there are innumerable places in this covering so weak that they will not bear their weight, and these places are not seen. The arrows of death fly unseen at noonday; the sharpest sight cannot discern them. (Dwight and Hickman 1974, 7-8; Perry Miller 1973, 147)

6. Take These Words to Heart (32:44-47)

32 ⁴⁴*And Moses came and spoke all the words of this song in the ears of the people, he and Joshua son of Nun.* ⁴⁵*And when Moses had finished speaking all these words to all Israel,* ⁴⁶*he then said to them, "Take to your heart all the words that I am calling as witness against you today, that you command them to your children to be careful to do all the words of this law.* ⁴⁷*For it is not a frivolous thing for you; indeed it is your life, and with this word you will prolong your days on the soil that you are crossing over the Jordan to take possession of it."*

Rhetoric and Composition

These verses are demarcated at the top end by the *petuḥah* in M^L and M^A and an end of special formatting in Sam before v. 44. Delimitation at the bottom end is by a *petuḥah* in M^L and M^A and a section in Sam after v. 47. A keyword chiasmus shows the verses to complement 31:24-30, the two units making a prose frame for the Song (see Rhetoric and Composition for 31:24-30).

Notes

32:44   A repetition of 31:22 and 30, only now Joshua, after his commissioning, is with him. The LXX expands the MT reading by reproducing 31:22 before the verse. It also reads "this law" (τοῦ νόμου τούτου) instead of "this song."

Joshua son of Nun. Reading "Joshua" (Ἰησοῦς) with the LXX and other ancient Versions. MT has "Hoshea son of Nun" (cf. Num 13:8, 16). Numbers 13:16 says that Moses gave Hoshea the name "Joshua."

45   "These words" initially referred only to the Song, but in an enlarged Deuteronomy they also take in the entire Deuteronomic law code. The LXX omits "all these words," but Wevers (1995, 535) notes that other Greek texts add them. Wevers thinks the shorter text is original, but this is doubtful since it is part of a larger rhetorical structure (see Rhetoric and Composition for 31:24-30). Nelson suggests a loss in MT by haplography (homoeoarcton: א . . . א).

46 Here an expanded meaning of "all these words" and "law" is presupposed, because parents are to see to it that their children learn and carry out Yahweh's teaching. The Song is taught for the purpose of being a later witness against the people's disobedience, and it must live unforgotten in the mouths of their descendants (31:19-21). On the importance attached in Deuteronomy to the teaching of Yahweh's commands to the children, see 31:12-13 and Note for 4:9. On the expression "take to your heart," which means "give attention to," see elsewhere Exod 9:21; 1 Sam 9:20; 25:25; Ezek 40:4. On the expression "be careful to do," see Note for 5:1.

47 The term רֵק means "empty" or "frivolous." Tigay points out that Hammurabi in the Epilogue to his law code uses the same term with reference to his words and deeds. He says: "My words are choice; my deeds have no equal; it is only to the fool that they are empty" (CH xxv; *ANET*³, 178). Yahweh's commands are also not empty, and doing them is nothing short of choosing life over death (see 30:15-20 and Note for 4:1). On the stereotypical language at the end of the verse, see Note for 4:25-26.

Message and Audience

The audience hears again that Moses has recited his song to the people, but now Joshua, who has been commissioned as his successor, is with him. After reciting the song, he exhorts the people to take to heart all the words he has spoken, which in an enlarged book refers to the Song and the Deuteronomic law code. What is more, people must command their children to learn and do Yahweh's teaching. These are not empty words, but rather words of life, which will prolong the days of those who will live in the land Israel is now crossing the Jordan to possess.

7. Ascend This Mountain (32:48-52)

32 ⁴⁸*And Yahweh spoke to Moses this very day:* ⁴⁹*"Go up to this mountain of the Abarim, Mount Nebo, which is in the land of Moab, which is opposite Jericho, and see the land of Canaan that I am giving to the children of Israel for a possession;* ⁵⁰*and die on the mountain where you are going up, and be gathered to your people, just as Aaron your brother died on Mount Hor and was gathered to his people;* ⁵¹*because you were unfaithful with me in the midst of the children of Israel at the waters of Meribath-kadesh, in the wilderness of Zin, because you did not honor me as holy in the midst of the children of Israel.* ⁵²*For you shall see the land on the other side, but there you shall not enter, into the land that I am giving to the children of Israel."*

Deuteronomy 32

Rhetoric and Composition

These verses are demarcated at the top end by a *petuḥah* in M^L and M^A and a section in Sam before v. 48 and at the bottom end by a *petuḥah* in M^L and M^A and a section in Sam after v. 52, which is also the chapter division. Their vocabulary and phraseology are what one finds in the Priestly source (Driver). In a larger rhetorical structure, the unit balances 31:14-23, which, like the present verses, is direct speech from Yahweh — to Moses primarily, but in 31:23 to Joshua (see Rhetoric and Composition for 31:1-6). The balancing passages do not derive from the same hand, since 31:14-23 shows affinity with JE narrative and the verses here seem clearly to be P, following closely Num 27:12-14. Neither passage has an affinity to other prose in the book of Deuteronomy. The present verses also link up thematically with 34:1-8, where Yahweh's command that Moses ascend Mount Nebo, view the land of Canaan, and then die is carried out. But before he dies, he will bless the tribes of Israel (ch. 33).

The LXX omits the final words of v. 52, "into the land that I am giving to the children of Israel," although they could be part of an inclusio with v. 49:

- v. 49 *and see the land* of Canaan *that I am giving to the children of Israel* for a possession
- v. 52 For *you shall see the land* on the other side, but there you shall not enter, *into the land that I am giving to the children of Israel.*

Notes

32:48 This would be the day Moses recited his Song, not the entire Deuteronomic discourse (ibn Ezra). If we assume that the entire Deuteronomic discourse — including the Song — was recited in a single day, then that day would be the one referred to in 1:3 (Driver). But ibn Ezra says that according to 1:5 Moses began expounding his teaching on the day cited in 1:3 but did not finish it that day.

49 The command came earlier in 3:27. Cf. Num 27:12-14. Moses does this, and Yahweh shows him the land of Canaan (34:1-4).

the Abarim, Mount Nebo, which is in the land of Moab. The Abarim is a Moabite mountain range that includes Mount Nebo (Num 27:12; 33:47-48; Jer 22:20). Van Zyl (1960, 51) thinks the term "Abarim" was originally a common noun but here has become a name for the entire Moab highland. On Mount Nebo, see Note for 34:1.

which is opposite Jericho. אֲשֶׁר עַל־פְּנֵי יְרֵחוֹ. Hebrew עַל־פְּנֵי ("opposite") usually means "east of" (Gen 25:18; 1 Kgs 11:7), which would apply here. Mount

Deuteronomy 32

Nebo is east of Jericho, a city lying west of the Jordan. One of the oldest cities of the world, Jericho was the first city to be conquered by Joshua after the Israelites entered Canaan (Joshua 6). The site is Tell es-Sultan, 16 km northwest of the Dead Sea, excavated by Kathleen Kenyon of the British Archaeological School in Jerusalem between 1952 and 1958 (*NEAEHL* 2,674-81).

50 Aaron's death on Mount Hor follows the account in Num 20:22-28, which names this mount as the first stopping place after Israel left Kadesh-barnea (cf. Num 33:38). Deut 10:6 gives another location. To be "gathered to one's people" is the P expression meaning "to die" (Gen 25:8; 35:29; Num 20:24, 26; 27:13; 31:2). In Deut 31:16 the corresponding euphemism is "to sleep with one's fathers."

Mount Hor. A mountain on the border with Edom, whose location is not known for certain. The antiquarian note of 10:6 says that Aaron died at Moserah after the Israelites left Beeroth (see Note there). Eusebius *(Onom.)* puts the death of Aaron at Beeroth, which he says lay 10 Roman milestones from the city of Petra. Jebel Nebi Harun has become the traditional site of Mount Hor (Josephus *Ant.* iv.82-84; Palmer 1871, 2:520; Woolley and Lawrence 1936, 88), which has also been carried on in Islamic tradition. But because this site is in the Edomite heartland, not on its border, many modern scholars reject it (Driver; Y. Aharoni 1979, 201-2; Tigay). Jebel Madurah, ca. 25 mi southwest of the southern end of the Dead Sea and 15 mi northeast of Kadesh, is considered a more likely site (Wilton 1863, 126-30; Trumbull 1884, 127-39; G. L. Robinson 1930, 263-84; Olmstead 1931, 253), satisfying as it does the requirement that Mount Hor be on the Edomite border.

51-52 Reference is to the provocation at Massah, or the "waters of Meribah" (see Note for 33:8), where, according to Exod 17:1-7; Num 20:1-13, people complained bitterly because they had no water to drink. In Num 20:12, and also here, Moses and Aaron are faulted for not believing in Yahweh (the verbs "you were unfaithful" and "you did not honor" in the present verse are plural). The same reason for Moses and Aaron being denied entrance into the promised land is given in Num 27:14, where again both are faulted for rebelling against Yahweh's word and not honoring Yahweh as holy before the people. Moses is said to have incurred blame on the people's account in Ps 106:32. But the account of this same incident in Exod 17:1-7 places no blame on Moses or Aaron; blame falls only on the people, who find fault with Moses and put Yahweh to the test (cf. Ps 95:8-11). Since Moses went on to strike the rock after being told to do so by Yahweh and water did pour forth, we must assume that Moses and also Aaron were initially disbelievers along with the rest. But earlier in Deuteronomy (1:37; 3:26; 4:21) another less than transparent reason is given for Moses — and an entire generation save Joshua and Caleb — not being allowed entrance into the promised land. Yahweh says he was angry with Moses because the ten scouts came back from scoping the land with an evil report. Here again Moses suffers the same penalty as the unbelievers. With Aaron, Yahweh was wroth on account of the "golden calf" incident, but Deut 9:20 does not say this kept Aaron from entering the promised land. On these two reasons in the biblical text for Moses being denied entrance into the promised land and their later development in the Midrashim, see Loewenstamm 1957-58 and Goldin 1987.

the waters of Meribath-kadesh, in the wilderness of Zin. The "wilderness of Zin" is generally placed in the southern part of the Negeb, east of the Arabah. Kadesh-barnea was an oasis in this wilderness (see Note for 1:2).

into the land that I am giving to the children of Israel. The LXX omits these words, but they may well belong (see Rhetoric and Composition).

Message and Audience

The audience in this segment hears Yahweh tell Moses to ascend Mount Nebo and view the promised land, that his death is imminent, and why he cannot himself enter the land. According to the narrator, Moses is told this just after he recited his song to the people, on the same day. Moses will get a good view of Canaan from Mount Nebo on the Abarim and then die on this mountain, just as his brother Aaron died sometime earlier on Mount Hor. The reason for their deaths prior to this much awaited event is that they shared the guilt of the generation who put Yahweh to the test at the waters of Meribath-kadesh. Moses therefore will be allowed to see the land but not enter it.

B. Moses' Departure (33:1–34:12)

1. The Blessing of Moses (33:1-29)

33 ¹*And this is the blessing with which Moses, the man of God, blessed the sons of Israel before his death.* ²*And he said:*

Yahweh from Sinai came,
  and rose up from Seir for him.
He shone forth from Mount Paran
  and went from the thousands of holy ones
    from his southland slopes for him.
³*Yes, one who loves peoples,*
  all his holy ones were at your hand,
  and they, they were assembled at your foot.

Each executed your words.
⁴A law Moses commanded to us,
   a possession of the assembly of Jacob.
⁵And he became King in Jeshurun
      when the heads of the people gathered,
         all together, the tribes of Israel.

⁶*Let Reuben live, and not die,*
   but let his males be few.

⁷*And this for Judah, and he said:*
Hear, O Yahweh, the voice of Judah,
   and bring him in to his people;
His strength increase for him,
   and be a help against his foes.

⁸*And for Levi he said:*
Your Thummim and your Urim to your faithful one
      whom you tested at Massah,
         you strove with him at the waters of Meribah.
⁹*The one who said to his father and to his mother,*
   "I have not seen him."
Yes, his brothers he did not acknowledge,
   and his sons he did not notice.
Indeed they kept your word,
   and your covenant they observed.
¹⁰*They shall teach your ordinances to Jacob,*
   and your law to Israel.
They shall put incense before you,
   and the whole offering upon your altar.
¹¹*Bless, O Yahweh, his might,*
   and the work of his hands accept.
Smash the loins of those rising against him,
   that those hating him not rise again.

¹²*For Benjamin he said:*
Beloved of Yahweh, he will dwell securely.
   God is the one surrounding him all the day,
      and between his shoulders dwells.

¹³*And for Joseph he said:*
Blessed by Yahweh is his land,
   from the choicest gifts of heaven, from the dew,

>   *and from the deep lying beneath,*
> ¹⁴*and from the choicest produce of the sun,*
>   *and from the choicest yield of the months,*
> ¹⁵*and from the best of the mountains of old,*
>   *and from the choicest of the everlasting hills,*
> ¹⁶*and from the choicest of earth and its fullness,*
>   *and the favor of the one who dwelt in the thornbush.*
> Let it come to the head of Joseph
>   and to the crown of the consecrated of his brothers.
> ¹⁷His firstborn bull, splendor for him,
>   and his horns, the horns of a wild ox,
> With them he will thrust peoples,
>   together the ends of the earth.
> Yes, they are the ten thousands of Ephraim,
>   and they are the thousands of Manasseh.

¹⁸And for Zebulun he said:
> Rejoice, O Zebulun, in your going forth,
>   and Issachar in your tents.
> ¹⁹Peoples to the mountain they will call;
>   there they will sacrifice right sacrifices.
> Indeed the abundance of the seas they will suck,
>   and hidden treasures of the sand.

²⁰And for Gad he said:
> Blessed is the one who enlarges Gad;
>   as a lioness he lies in wait,
>   then he tears the arm, yes, the crown of the head.
> ²¹And he sought out the finest for himself,
>   indeed there, the portion of the treasured lawgiver.
> Then he came to the heads of the people.
>   Yahweh's righteousness he did,
>   and his ordinances with Israel.

²²And for Dan he said:
> Dan is the cub of a lion;
>   he leaps forth from the Bashan.

²³And for Naphtali he said:
> O Naphtali, be satisfied with acceptance,
>   and full of the blessing of Yahweh
>   possess sea and south.

Deuteronomy 33

²⁴*And for Asher he said:*
Blessed above sons is Asher,
    let him be the favorite of his brothers
        and the one who dips his foot in oil.
²⁵*Iron and bronze are your bolts,*
    and as your days, so be your strength.

²⁶*There is none like the God, O Jeshurun,*
    who rides the heavens to your help
        and in his majesty the clouds.
²⁷*A refuge is the God of old*
    and from beneath are the everlasting arms.
Yes he drove out before you the enemy,
    and he said "Destroy!"
²⁸*So Israel dwelt in security,*
    alone abided Jacob
into a land of grain and wine,
    yes, his heavens drip dew.
²⁹*Happy are you, O Israel!*
    Who is like you,
        a people saved by Yahweh?
Shield of your help
    and (who is) the sword of your majesty.
So your enemies will come cringing to you,
    and you, upon his high places you will tread.

Rhetoric and Composition

The Blessing of Moses, like the Song of Moses, is a poem of independent origin inserted into the final supplement of Deuteronomy (chs. 31–34). It is not Mosaic (the conquest lies in the past, and the tribes are settled in their territories), but considerably older than the prose comprising the bulk of Deuteronomy. The Blessing is said to have been composed in the 11th cent. and written down in the 10th cent. (Cross and Freedman 1948, 192; Freedman 1979; 1980a, 27). Driver (1895, 387-89) proposed a 10th-cent. date, perhaps during the reign of Jeroboam I. He said the poem reflected a northern point of view, suggesting as its author a poet who resided in northern Israel. Phythian-Adams (1923, 164) argued for an earlier date: in the time of the judges, when a united Israel defeated the Ammonites at the hands of Jephthah (Judges 11). His view was cited with approval by Cassuto (1973b, 70). The Cross and Freedman date, which was based on vocabulary, spelling, verse structure, comparisons with Canaanite poetry, and historical presuppositions in the blessings, has won general acceptance (Albright 1957b, 320; 1959, 346 n. 3; G. E. Wright; Moran).

The Blessing of Moses may be compared to the Blessing of Jacob inserted into the book of Genesis (Genesis 49). The poems have much in common, but even more significant are important differences (Driver 1895, 385-86). The tone of Moses' Blessing is more buoyant, although we see here the isolation and depression of Judah (v. 7; cf. Gen 49:8-12). Levi is given more honor and respect (cf. Gen 49:5-7), although this may be due to later expansion of the blessing. It has been noted also that Deuteronomy 33 uses the divine name "Yahweh," which does not occur in Genesis 49.

In the medieval codices (M^A; M^L), the Blessing is written in normal three-column prose — similarly 33:2-8 in 4QpaleoDeut^r (Skehan, Ulrich, and Sanderson 1992, 148 nos. 42-43) and 33:8-22 in 4QDeut^h (Ulrich, Cross et al. 1995, 61). It does not receive special formatting in Sam. Nevertheless, it is poetry, taken as such by *BHS* and all modern Versions, including NJV. On its poetic structure, see Freedman 1980a.

The Blessing is well supplied with section markings, although none set off the Superscription (v. 1), Introduction (vv. 2-5), and Conclusion (vv. 26-29). The Sam has a section after v. 27. Most blessings to the tribes are delineated. At the top end of the poem is a *petuḥah* in M^L and M^A and a section in Sam before v. 1, which is also the chapter division. There may be a section before v. 1 in 4QDeut^l, but it could also be a margin at the top of the scroll (Ulrich, Cross et al. 1995, 112). At the bottom end is a *setumah* in M^L and M^A and a section in Sam after v. 29, which is another chapter division. 4QpaleoDeut^r has a section after v. 29 (Skehan, Ulrich, and Sanderson 1992, 148 no. 44). Within the poem are these sections and lack of sections:

after v. 6	*setumah* in M^L and M^A	end Reuben
after v. 7	*setumah* in M^L and *petuḥah* in M^A section in Sam	end Judah
after v. 11	*setumah* in M^L and M^A sections in Sam and 4QDeut^h	end Levi
after v. 12	*setumah* in M^L and M^A section in Sam	end Benjamin
after v. 17	*setumah* in M^L and M^A sections in Sam and 4QDeut^h	end Joseph (Ephraim and Manasseh)
after v. 19	*setumah* in M^L and M^A section in Sam	end Zebulun and Issachar
after v. 21	*setumah* in M^L and M^A sections in Sam and 4QDeut^h	end Gad

Deuteronomy 33

after v. 22	no section in M^L and M^A	end Dan
after v. 23	setumah in M^L and M^A section in Sam	end Naphtali
after 25	no sections in M^L, M^A, and Sam	end Asher

Driver identified in the Blessing of Moses, as in the Song of Moses, an Introduction (vv. 2-5) and a Conclusion (vv. 26-29). Some have argued that together these may originally have formed an independent poem (von Rad; Christensen 1984, 389; Nelson), but that is only speculation. Both fit well into the text as we now have it, and the composition is best read as an integrated whole. The Introduction and Conclusion focus on Israel; the blessings focus on Israel's individual tribes.

The four stanzas of the Introduction, which are properly marked by verse numbers later assigned, have interlocking repetitions or balancing keywords:

I and went from the thousands of *holy ones*		v. 2
II all *his holy ones* were at your hand		v. 3
II Each executed *your words*		v. 3
III *A law* Moses commanded to us		v. 4
III A possession of *the assembly of Jacob*		v. 4
IV all together, *the tribes of Israel*		v. 5

Catchphrases in Amos's foreign nation oracles link the oracles in a similar fashion (Paul 1971).

Keywords also link all segments of the poem except the blessings to Dan and Naphtali:

Introduction	וַיְהִי	and he became	v. 5
Reuben	וִיהִי	but let it be	v. 6
Judah	יָדָיו	his strength	v. 7
Levi	יָדָיו	his might	v. 11
Benjamin	יִשְׁכֹּן ... שָׁכֵן	he will dwell ... dwells	v. 12
Joseph	שֹׁכְנִי	the one who dwelt	v. 16
Zebulun (and Issachar)	וּשְׂפוּנֵי	and treasures	v. 19
Gad	סָפוּן	treasured	v. 21
Dan	—		
Naphtali	—		
Asher	אָשֵׁר	Asher (Happy One)	v. 24
Conclusion	אַשְׁרֶיךָ	Happy are you	v. 29

Deuteronomy 33

The poem as a whole contains a keyword chiasmus tying together the Introduction and the Conclusion (Freedman 1980a, 37):

Introduction:	Yahweh	v. 2
	Jeshurun	v. 5
Conclusion:	Jeshurun	v. 26
	Yahweh	v. 29

The poetic "Jeshurun" (= Israel) occurs nowhere else in the poem, whereas "Yahweh" occurs one other time in v. 21, which is at the center of the poem. In Hebrew composition, keywords often occur at the beginning, in the center, and at the end (Lund 1942, 40-41, 44). Chiasms alleged by Christensen (1984, 388), which are thematic outlines he himself has created and not likely to have been in the mind of the biblical poet, should be disregarded. Large chiasms in Hebrew poetry and prose almost always build on repeated or balancing keywords in strategic collocations within the composition.

Portions of 33:1-29 are contained in 1QDeut^b, 4QDeut^h, 4QDeut^l, and 4QpaleoDeut^r; also on Testimonia and Florilegium from Qumran.

Notes

33:1 *The superscription.* Moses will now bless each of the tribes of Israel (excluding Simeon) and at the beginning and end the entire nation (Introduction and Conclusion). Core blessings will usually — but not always — point up some distinctive feature of each tribe (cf. Gen 49:28).

Moses, the man of God. Moses elsewhere in the OT is called a "man of God" (Josh 14:6; Ps 90:1), an appellation normally reserved for the prophets (1 Sam 2:27; 9:6; 1 Kgs 12:22; 13:1, 4-5, etc.). Since blessings pertain to the future, Moses assumes here the role of a prophet (Josephus *Ant.* iv.320; ibn Ezra; Driver; von Rad).

before his death. Blessings are typically conferred when one is to die (Gen 27:7; 49:1, 29).

2 *Yahweh from Sinai came, and rose up from Seir for him. He shone forth from Mount Paran.* The poem begins by mentioning three holy mountains in the southern wilderness from which Yahweh has come. Sinai (or Horeb) became the mountain of record in Israel's salvation history, for there is where Yahweh made his covenant with Israel (5:2-3) and from there Israel began its journey to the promised land (1:6-7). Albright (1936) translates זֶה סִינַי in Judg 5:5 as "One of Sinai," saying the expression was an archaic appellation of Yahweh.

Seir is Mount Seir ("Hairy = Wooded Mountain"; cf. Gen 25:25) or else a mountain range in Seir, which is Edomite territory primarily — if not exclusively — west of the Arabah. This is not the Mount Seir of Josh 15:10, which lay on Judah's border west of Jerusalem. On Seir and the Seir mountains, which receive mention in the Amarna Letters and Egyptian texts, see Note for 1:44.

Mount Paran is a specific peak or a mountain range in the Wilderness of Paran, the main desert of the east-central Sinai Peninsula (see Note for 1:1). Another old biblical poem states that "the Holy One (came) from Mount Paran" (Hab 3:3). B. Mazar (1981, 6) thinks that all three of these names denote a single mountain, but that requires identifying Mount Sinai as Jebel el-Hilal, which is half-way between Shur and Kadesh-barnea (Horeb is another mountain at the south of the Sinai Peninsula), and taking Seir and Paran as large territories overspreading the entire Sinai Peninsula. More likely these are three separate mountains or mountain ranges in the "southland" desert (v. 2), all associated with early Yahweh theophanies (Weinfeld 1987, 305; Tigay).

The Bible gives indications that the God Yahweh was worshipped before Moses' "burning bush" experience (Exod 3:1-14). In Exod 3:1, usually assigned to the E source, Sinai is called "the mountain of God" even before Yahweh's defining revelation to Moses. The appellation is used subsequently in the OT (Exod 4:27; 18:5; 24:13; 1 Kgs 19:8). In the J source, worship of Yahweh is pushed back further into hoary antiquity, soon after the creation of the world, with Gen 4:26 saying that at the time of Seth and his son Enosh, the son and grandson of Adam and Eve, people began to call upon the name of Yahweh. In the P source, the revelation of the God Yahweh to Moses occurs after Moses returns from the Midianite wilderness to Egypt (Exod 6:2-9; de Vaux 1978, 330-39). In Num 10:33, Sinai is called "the mountain of Yahweh."

Yahweh worship is traced by some scholars back to the Kenites and Midianites, nomadic peoples who lived in the Sinai Peninsula, the Negeb, and further east in the Arabian desert southeast of the Gulf of Aqaba (de Vaux 1978, 332). Attention has focused on Jethro, or Hobab, the father-in-law of Moses, who was a "priest of Midian" (Exod 3:1; 18:1). In Judg 4:11 he is said to be a Kenite. The so-called "Kenite Hypothesis" averred that Yahwism had its origin among Kenite and Midianite nomads and that Jethro was perhaps the one who first introduced Moses to the God Yahweh. After the Israelites were delivered from Egypt, Jethro rejoiced and confessed Yahweh to be greater than all gods, going on to officiate at a sacrifice that was presumably to Yahweh (Exod 18:10-12). Kenite nomads joined the Israelites in their journey to the promised land and then settled there (Judg 1:16; 1 Sam 27:10). They continued to have good relations with Israel (1 Sam 15:6). Later we meet up with figures such as Heber the Kenite (Judg 4:11-22), Jehonadab son of Rechab (2 Kgs 10:15-24), and Rechabites who were living in Jeremiah's time (Jeremiah 35), all descendants of these nomadic peoples. According to 1 Chr 2:55, the Rechabites descended from the

Kenites. On the Kenite Hypothesis, the origins of Yahwism, and relations between Jethro and Moses, see Budde 1895; Rowley 1950b, 149-55; Weippert 1971, 105-6 n. 14; Weinfeld 1987. For a more cautionary view of the "Kenite Hypothesis," see de Vaux 1978, 330-38.

Extrabiblical evidence has been cited as possibly bearing on the origins of Yahwism in the southland region before the time of Moses. An Egyptian inscription on the Soleb temple of Amenhotep III (1403-1364), located in Nubia (West Sudan), contains a list of cities conquered by the Egyptian king. One of these towns was named "Yahwe in the land of Shoshu" (Giveon 1964; 1967; 1971, 26-27, Document 6a; B. Mazar 1981, 7; Weinfeld 1987, 304). The list was copied and has turned up in a later inscription on the temple of Ramses II (1290-1224) in Amara-West, also in Nubia (Giveon 1971, 75-76; Document 16a; Rowley 1963a, 53-54). For an early publication of these texts, see J. Simons 1937, 165, 169: XXVII no. 115; 174: XXIX no. 13. The Shosu were a nomadic people who lived in the southern Transjordan, Syria, and Egypt. It was first thought that the city in question was located in Edom and supposed that Shosu nomads were early worshippers of Yahweh there. But it has since been argued that this city — along with others named in the document — were not in the southland at all, but in Syria (Astour 1979). So doubts about these inscriptions attesting to Yahweh worship in the southland region have been raised and about their value in supporting the Kenite Hypothesis. Nevertheless, they may still indicate that people were worshipping a God named Yahweh before the time of Moses.

and rose up from Seir for him. The particle לָמוֹ ("for him") repeats at the end of the verse, in both cases referring to Israel. Modern Versions following MT render the particle "unto them" (AV), "for them" (JB), "upon them" (NJV), or "over them" (NIV). Freedman (1980a, 40) says the ל is ethical, meaning "for the sake of him/it/them." The LXX (ἡμῖν), S, T^Onq, and Vg all have "to us," which is followed by some modern Versions (NJB: "on us"; RSV, NRSV: "upon us"). Most everyone agrees that reference is to Israel. The verb זרח means "to rise [like the sun]" (Gen 32:32[31]; Isa 60:1-2; Mal 3:20[4:2]). Yahweh's rising from Seir was like his "shining forth" from Mount Paran.

He shone forth from Mount Paran. Yahweh "shone forth" (הוֹפִיעַ) in brilliant radiance from Paran, another of his holy mountains (Hab 3:3-4). Cf. Pss 50:2; 80:2(1); 94:1.

and went from the thousands of holy ones. וְאָתָה מֵרִבְבֹת קֹדֶשׁ. The reading of MT is not difficult, but commentators and the Versions — ancient and modern — have made it so. Yahweh left behind thousands of his "holy ones" (קֹדֶשׁ is here a collective), who were angels (ibn Ezra) or lesser divine beings, to throw in his lot with "peoples," specifically the people(s) of Israel, over whom he would become King (v. 5). He did not take his entourage on a holy war venture. Many scholars (P. D. Miller 1964; Moran; Tigay; Nelson) have read "Divine

Warrior" ideas into these opening verses, which simply are not there. Divine Warrior imagery will come in the Conclusion (vv. 26-29). Crucial to the "holy war" interpretation is a revocalizing of the verb אָתָה ("he went") to אִתֹּה ("with him"), also presupposing an enclitic מ on the following term, the idea being that Yahweh went on a march *with* his holy ones (Cross and Freedman 1948, 193, 198-99 — but given up in Freedman 1980a, 32, 38-40; Weinfeld 1987, 307). The Targums read "with him," which was adopted by the AV and reappears in the NRSV. The RSV had it right: "he came from the ten thousands of holy ones." The מ on מֵרִבְבֹת is partitive: Yahweh went *from* his holy ones in the southern mountains, i.e., he left them behind. Cassuto (1973b, 69) says: "the proem [informs us] of the coming of YHWH from His dwelling place in Sinai in order to be proclaimed as King of Israel."

There have also been attempts — ancient and modern — to translate the present colon like the previous three, i.e., to have Yahweh coming from yet another holy place. The LXX reads σὺν μυριάσιν Καδης ("with the myriads of Kadesh"), which assumes that Yahweh came from Kadesh with his thousands. The JB and NJB adopt the "Kadesh" reading. This, too, should be rejected (Freedman 1980a, 38-39), as well as reading MT רִבְבֹת קֹדֶשׁ as a holy site named "Ribeboth-kodesh" (NJV; Tigay; cf. Meribath-kadesh in 32:51). No such place is known.

from his southland slopes for him. מִימִינוֹ אשדת לָמוֹ. Reading the Kt אשדת with Freedman (1980a, 39-40) and repointing to אַשְׁדֹת, "(mountain) slopes" (3:17; 4:49; Josh 12:3; 13:20). Freedman translates מִימִינוֹ as "from his Southland," since יָמִין (lit. "right hand") can also mean "south" (1 Sam 23:19; Ezek 16:46). The southland was Yahweh's original abode. The Qere divides into two words: אֵשׁ דָּת ("fire" and "law"), which makes for an awkward rendering (ibn Ezra: "fiery law"; Driver: "fire was a law for them"). Earlier readings building on the Qere are now precluded with דָּת recognized as a Persian loanword found only in late passages of Esther, Ezra, and Daniel, thus unavailable to the biblical poet (Driver; Tigay). Steiner (1996) has proposed another reading for the Qere. He says דָּת is an irregular spelling of דָּאָת, a feminine perfect form of דאה/דאי ("to fly swiftly"), the verb occurring in 28:49. He translates the colon: "from his right, fire flew to them," imagining that Yahweh, instead of coming to Israel in person, sent fire to them from his right hand. But this cannot be what the colon means. According to vv. 2-3, Yahweh left his mountain abodes because he is one who loves peoples. The present colon sums up the first three: Yahweh left three mountain locations in the southland for the sake of Israel.

3 *Yes, one who loves peoples.* Hebrew אַף ("yes") introduces another idea with emphasis (see again vv. 20 and 28; cf. 1 Sam 2:7; Ps 16:6, 7, 9). The verb חבב is a *hapax legomenon* in the OT, but cognates in Aramaic and Arabic mean "to love," and that is probably its meaning here. The plural "peoples" should proba-

bly be retained (MT; NRSV), since a contrast is intended between the "thousands of holy ones" in the southern mountains (no talk here of heaven) whom Yahweh left and the peoples of earth to whom Yahweh was going. That he left the mountains for the sake of Israel (לָמוֹ twice in v. 2) goes without saying, but the Targums and other Versions — ancient and modern — want to make this explicit by reading "(the) people" (NJV) or "his people" (LXX; T^{NfPsJ}; Vg; RSV; NEB; REB). "Peoples" plural also goes better with "tribes" plural in v. 5 (T^{Onq}; Rashi; Nelson; cf. Gen 28:3; 48:4), who are to receive the blessings. The poet is not referring to the nations (Driver; *pace* Rashbam; NAB), although one need not quarrel with Rashbam when he says that God also loves the Gentiles. Deuteronomy 7:7-8 contains an idea similar to the one here: Israel's election was based on Yahweh's "love" (אהב) for his people.

all his holy ones were at your hand, and they, they were assembled at your foot. Freedman (1980a, 41) correctly notes that the two middle colons of this four-colon unit are linked ("hand" and "foot"), but I take exception to his view that an envelope construction links colons one and four. In my view, colon four follows sequentially colons two and three, where the third masculine singular verb יִשָּׂא may be translated "each executed." In Yahweh's mountain abodes his myriads of "holy ones" waited in readiness to serve him, standing (to one side) at his hand and assembled at his foot. The imagery is not militaristic, i.e., these holy ones were not an army waiting to go forward in holy war (*pace* Nelson), although if called upon to do so, they would doubtless have obeyed.

and they, they were assembled at your foot. The added pronoun is for emphasis. The difficult תֻּכּוּ is another *hapax legomenon* in the OT whose meaning is uncertain. The verb is taken in BDB and KBL^3 as a Pual of תכה, said to mean "followed, were led, were assembled, crowded together," or the like. The Targums have "were led." The LXX reads καὶ οὗτοι ὑπὸ σέ εἰσιν ("and they were under you"), indicating that the translator probably did not know the meaning of the Hebrew verb (Wevers 1995, 540-41). Commentators and the modern Versions rely almost entirely on the context for a translation: "were gathered" (Rashi); "sat down" (AV; Gaster 1947); "sit" (NEB); "crowd together" (Seeligmann 1964); "followed" (ibn Ezra; Driver; RSV; NAB; NJV); "marched" (NRSV; Nelson); "prostrate(d)" (Cross and Freedman 1948; Cassuto 1973b); and "bow themselves" (Freedman 1980a). The context calls for some sort of subservient behavior.

Each executed your words. יִשָּׂא מִדַּבְּרֹתֶיךָ. The holy ones executed Yahweh's words on command. For the verb נשׂא, usually "to lift up, utter (words)," something stronger is needed. The holy ones stood ready to "execute" Yahweh's words (Freedman 1980a, 42). Hebrew דַּבְּרֹת is another *hapax legomenon* in the OT, generally taken to mean "words" or "commands."

4 *A law Moses commanded to us.* If Yahweh's holy ones executed his

Deuteronomy 33

commands in the mountain sanctuaries, now Moses is recognized as having commanded Yahweh's law to Israel. Freedman (1980a, 43) thinks this explains the placement of the poem in the book of Deuteronomy. The poem is also seen here to postdate Moses.

a possession of the assembly of Jacob. Israel's "possession" (מוֹרָשָׁה) might otherwise be the land (Exod 6:8), but here it is the law commanded by Moses. The "assembly of Jacob" is the convocation on Deuteronomy's "day of assembly," when the law was given (9:10; 10:4; 18:16).

5 *And he became King in Jeshurun.* I.e., Yahweh did, the subject being picked up from v. 2 (RSV adds "the Lord"). The main idea in the Introduction is now brought to completion. Yahweh has come from his abodes high in the southern mountains, where he was served by a large host of subservient beings, to become King in Israel. "Jeshurun" here and in v. 26 is a poetic name for Israel, meaning "The Upright One" (see Note for 32:15). Before a monarchy was established in Israel, Yahweh was understood to be King (Exod 15:18; Num 23:21; Judg 8:23). This bedrock idea was called into question when Israel asked for an earthly king such as other nations had (1 Sam 8:7; 12:12). Nevertheless, Yahweh's kingship in Israel survived the establishment of a monarchy (Pss 24:7-10; 68:25[24]; 93:1; 95:3; 96:10; 97:1; 98:6; 99:1, 4; Isa 33:22).

when the heads of the people gathered, all together, the tribes of Israel. I.e., at the assembly, when Yahweh was lifted up as King. Yahweh received adulation from the holy ones where he had been (v. 3); now, surrounded by the heads of Israel, he receives adulation from them.

6 Reuben, who was Jacob's firstborn by Leah (Gen 35:23), is not given a particularly laudatory blessing, which is true also in Gen 49:3-4, where his sin of lying with Bilhah, his father's concubine, is recalled (Gen 35:22). Jacob says that his eldest, though proud and powerful, was "unstable as water." Reuben's indiscretion caused him to lose his birthright, which was then given to the sons of Joseph (1 Chr 5:1). In the Song of Deborah, Reuben is cited for indecision at a time of national crisis (Judg 5:15-16). Hebrew מִסְפָּר can mean "numbered" (i.e., counted), or else "few." If it means "numbered," then the blessing is that Reuben will be countable, i.e., remain a tribal entity (AV: "and let not his men be few"; RSV: "nor let his men be few"). The LXX went too far in a positive rendering, turning the statement into its opposite: καὶ ἔστω πολὺς ἐν ἀριθμῷ ("and let him be many in number"). Most commentators and modern Versions take מִסְפָּר to mean "few," i.e., "But let him be few in number" (Driver; Nelson; NEB; NAB) or "Let him live, though his numbers be few" (T; Rashi; ibn Ezra; Driver; Cross and Freedman 1948; G. E. Wright; JB; NJV; NRSV). However one interprets מִסְפָּר, the concern is that the Reubenite tribe might become extinct, and the blessing asks that this does not happen.

Reuben settled in the Transjordan, between the River Arnon and Hesh-

Deuteronomy 33

bon, after Israel's victory over Sihon (Josh 13:15-23; cf. Deut 3:12-17). But having incurred problems with the Ammonites, his tribe diminished in numbers (Cross 1983). According to Albright (1946, 122-23), Reuben had vanished from the political scene by the 10th cent. By the mid-9th cent., Moab regained control over its northern plateau region (Moabite Stone line 10; 2 Kgs 3:26-27; see Note for 2:24) and Reubenite territory suffered further in the years following, due to punitive visits by Hazael of Syria (2 Kgs 10:33; Amos 1:3; Bright 1981, 254-55). Reubenites remaining in the territory in the 730s (Oded 1970) were carried away by the Assyrian king Tiglath-pileser III (745-727), who ended Israelite occupation in the Transjordan for good (1 Chr 5:26).

Simeon, Jacob's second son by Leah (Gen 35:23), is bypassed in the blessing, another indication of a post-Mosaic date for the poem. Very early his tribe was absorbed into Judah (noted in T^{PsJ}), with his cities in the southern Negeb listed as cities of Judah already in Josh 15:26-32, 42; cf. 19:1-8. Simeon is combined with Levi in the Blessing of Jacob, where the two receive censure for their anger and violent behavior (Gen 49:5-7). To make up for Simeon's omission in the present poem, Joseph's blessing is divided between his two sons Ephraim and Manasseh (cf. 1 Chr 5:1-2).

7 *And this for Judah, and he said.* Blessings from now on have an introductory phrase.

Hear, O Yahweh, the voice of Judah, and bring him in to his people. Judah was Jacob's fourth son by Leah (Gen 29:35). This blessing is a prayer that Yahweh will help Judah through some difficulty it is having. The Targums have Yahweh being asked to bring Judah safely home from war (thus Rashi: "in peace, after warfare"). Judah fared better in the Blessing of Jacob (Gen 49:8-12), but not in the Song of Deborah (Judges 5), where it was left out entirely. Some imagine that Judah needs divine help in being reunited with Israel (Driver; Nelson), but that presupposes a date for the poem later than the 11th cent., after the division of the kingdom. In the 11th cent. there is no division between Judah and the rest of Israel (Cross and Freedman 1948, 203 n. 27).

His strength increase for him. יָדָיו רַב לוֹ. MT רָב ("he strove, fought," from רִיב; cf. v. 8), is better read as a Piel imperative of רבה, "increase" (רַב would be the short form [Cassuto 1973b, 56]; Cross and Freedman 1948, 203 n. 26 repoint to רַבּ). Supplication to Yahweh continues. "His hands" (יָדָיו) means "his strength/might" (Cassuto). Tigay sees a wordplay between יָדָיו ("his hands") and יְהוּדָה ("Judah"). The Targums have Yahweh being supplicated to help Judah avenge an enemy with its own hands (NJV; cf. Rashi; Tigay). More recent commentators and Versions assume that Judah is fighting its own battles (AV; Driver; cf. Judg 1:1-20, where Judah [with Simeon's help] was first to go up against the Canaanites), but that interpretation presupposes a singular verb predicating a plural subject.

and be a help against his foes. If the poem is composed in the 11th cent., then Judah's foes will have been the Philistines (Cross and Freedman 1948, 203 n. 27; G. E. Wright; Moran).

8 *And for Levi he said: Your Thummim and your Urim to your faithful one.* Levi was Jacob's third son by Leah (Gen 29:34). Yahweh, not Levi, is being addressed (Rashi), making this blessing another articulated as a prayer. The tribe of Levi is collectively Yahweh's "faithful one." The MT lacks a verb, which is supplied by "Give to Levi" in 4QDeut[h] (הבו ללו[י]), 4QTestim (Duncan 1995, 280; Ulrich, Cross et al. 1995, 69) and the LXX (δότε Λευι). But the line reads perfectly well without the addition. The Urim and Thummim were sacred lots (dice, perhaps) carried in the linen ephod of the priests, used to discern the divine will on a range of weighty issues (Exod 28:30; Lev 8:8; 1 Sam 14:41-42; 23:6-13). They are therefore spoken of here as belonging to Yahweh.

whom you tested at Massah, you strove with him at the waters of Meribah. The well-known incident at Massah-Meribah in the wilderness was the one where the people strove with Moses (and Yahweh) because they had no water to drink and wished they were back in Egypt (Exod 17:1-7; Num 20:1-13). The place was called Massah and also given the name "Meribah," which means "waters of contention" (מֵי מְרִיבָה). In the present verse are a couple of wordplays: נִסִּיתוֹ ("you tested") and מַסָּה ("Massah"); תְּרִיבֵהוּ ("you strove") and מְרִיבָה ("Meribah"), which occur commonly on names (G. A. Smith 1912: 25; Tigay). The incident is mentioned three times in the main discourse of Deuteronomy, but only in passing (6:16; 9:22; 32:51-52).

In this defining incident, Moses, at Yahweh's bidding, brought forth water from a rock. According to Numbers, Massah was situated in the Wilderness of Zin near Kadesh-barnea (Num 20:1; 27:14); thus the name "Meribath-kadesh" in Deut 32:51; Ezek 47:19; 48:28. But in Exodus, Massah was at Horeb near Rephidim, in the Wilderness of Sin (Exod 17:1). The incident loomed large in Israel's collective memory, being preserved also in Israel's psalmnody. In Exodus and elsewhere the people are censured because they put Yahweh to the test (Exod 17:7; Deut 6:16; 9:22; Ps 95:8-9), but in Numbers, Moses and Aaron receive censure as well because they did not render Yahweh holy among the people. As a result, both were denied entrance into the promised land (Num 20:12; Ps 106:32-33; Deut 32:51-52; see Note there). Psalm 106:32-33 says the people made Moses bitter and he spoke words that were rash. Psalm 81:8(7) says Yahweh was the one who tested Israel at the waters of Meribah.

Here Yahweh is said to have tested the Levites at Massah-Meribah, and the implication is that they were found worthy. The Levites are not mentioned in either Exod 17:1-7 or Num 20:2-13, and nowhere else in the OT do we hear of the Levites being faithful when the rest of Israel — also Moses and Aaron — were not (Loewenstamm 1972, 55). In the Blessing of Jacob, Levi and Simeon receive criticism for warlike activity (Gen 49:5-7). In later preaching of Hosea, Yahweh says no one — including the priest — has the right to contend (רִיב) because there is no faithfulness or knowledge of God in the land. For this reason, Yahweh has a contention (רִיב) with everyone (Hos 4:1-10; Lundbom 1986b).

9 Cross and Freedman (1948, 204 n. 28) say this verse (with two signs of the definite accusative אֶת־) is largely prose. The priests are said to disregard members of family in order to keep Yahweh's word and observe his covenant. Yahweh's covenant with the priesthood was made when the zealous priest Phinehas punished an Israelite man and a Midianite woman for worshipping Baal of Peor and in so doing stayed a plague that had claimed twenty-four thousand lives. This covenant ensured permanence to the Aaronic line of priests (Num 25:1-13; cf. Jer 33:21b; Mal 2:4-5, 8). The Levites followed the present principle after the "golden calf" incident in the wilderness (Exod 32:25-29). Another application of the principle would be in carrying out Deuteronomy's mandate to punish family members if they are found to have led people in the worship of other gods (13:7-12[6-11]). In the NT, see Matt 10:37-39; 12:48-50; Luke 14:26. Nevertheless, "I have not seen him" is a hyperbolic expression of repudiation (cf. Job 8:18; cf. Matt 7:23).

his sons. Reading the Qere בניו. The Kt and 4QDeut[h] have the singular "his son."

10 *They shall teach your ordinances to Jacob, and your law to Israel.* The first of two important duties assigned to the priestly tribe. Levitical priests were entrusted with instructing and interpreting Yahweh's law to the people (17:9-11; cf. Jer 18:18; Mal 2:6-7; Hag 2:10-14; 2 Chr 15:3). In Deuteronomy they are also to assist judges in deciding difficult cases (17:8-13; 21:5). One might therefore translate מִשְׁפָּטֶיךָ as "your judgments," where reference would be to civil and criminal cases and ordinances that pertained to them (cf. Exod 21:1; Ezek 44:24).

They shall put incense before you, and the whole offering upon your altar. Priests were also altar clergy (Deut 18:1-8; Num 16:1-10; 17:5[16:40]; 18:6-7; 1 Sam 2:28). Hebrew קְטוֹרָה is the "(sweet) smoke of sacrifice," pleasing to Yahweh and said (anthropomorphically) to enter into his "nostrils" (אַף). See Gen 8:20-21. The term, generally taken to be incense, could also refer to the burning fat of thank offerings (Driver, citing Wellhausen; cf. Ps 66:15; Lev 3:5). Hebrew כָּלִיל is a "whole (burnt) offering," i.e., a holocaust (13:17[16]), a synonym to עֹלָה (Rashi; Tigay). These are offerings where the entire animal is consumed on the altar (Leviticus 6).

11 Cross and Freedman (1948, 203-4 n. 28) think the original blessing to Levi was this verse only, since vv. 8-10 show no signs of archaisms distinguishing the rest of the poem. This would make the blessing to Levi short like all the other blessings, except the one to Joseph. If the Levitical priests are the authors of Deuteronomy (see *Introduction: The Question of Authorship*), perhaps they have embellished their own blessing by adding Yahweh's gift of the Urim and Thummim; their own faithfulness at Massah/Meribah; their faithfulness to the covenant — even to the point of disregarding members of family; their being the teachers and judges in Israel; and their being officiants at Yahweh's sacrificial altar. An expanded blessing could also have been to offset the lengthy blessing to Joseph, carried out by Levitical priests in Judah who wanted to redress the imbalance in a poem written in the north.

Bless, O Yahweh, his might, and the work of his hands accept. The tribe of Levi was not given territory like the other tribes, yet they could own land and did accumulate wealth (T^{Onq}). "The work of his hands" has positive meaning, referring here as elsewhere in Deuteronomy to the fruit of one's labor (see Note for 2:7). For priests, this would be service in connection with the sacrificial altar. The blessing is followed by a request that their service and offerings be acceptable to Yahweh (cf. Ezek 20:40-41; 43:27). A proper offering is judged acceptable (Lev 1:4; 19:5-6; 22:17-19, 21; 2 Sam 24:23), an improper one unacceptable (Lev 7:18; 19:7; 22:20, 23-25). For another view on acceptable and unacceptable offerings, see Amos 5:22; Hos 8:13; Jer 6:20; Mal 1:10.

Smash the loins of those rising against him. מְחַץ מָתְנַיִם קָמָיו. The verb מְחַץ means to "smash" or "wound severely" (32:39) and is said by Cross and Freedman (1948, 204 n. 32) to be a characteristic term in old Canaanite and Hebrew poetry, occurring frequently in the Amarna Letters and the Ugaritic epics. The "loins" are the center of one's strength (Ps 69:24[23]; Nah 2:2[1]; Job 40:16; Prov 31:17). Albright (1945b, 23-24) suggested repointing "the loins of those who rise," to allow for an enclitic מ, but that may now be unnecessary with 4QDeut^h lacking a final ם in "loins" (מ[ת]ני), reading a construct form (Duncan 1995, 279; Ulrich, Cross et al. 1995, 68).

that those hating him not rise again. וּמְשַׂנְאָיו מִן־יְקוּמוּן. A wordplay made from another form of קוּם, "to rise up." MT has מִן ("from"), not otherwise attested with a finite verb (Albright 1945b, 24 n. 64). 4QDeut^h instead preserves a ב from what appears to have been בל ("not"), which better suits a poetic text (Duncan 1995, 279; Ulrich, Cross et al. 1995, 68). The LXX's μὴ ἀναστήτωσαν ("let them not rise up") has a negative. The request is that the smitten foes *not* rise again, which is what all modern English Versions — including the AV — come up with. Tigay does not think reference is to military prowess, saying that priests were defenseless against military attacks. But that is a stretch. The tribe of Levi made frequent use of the sword, for good and ill. It participated in the murder of Shechemites over the rape of Dinah (Gen 34:25-26), and the Blessing of Jacob speaks of Levi as one who wields weapons of violence in fits of anger (Gen 49:5-7). More than once Levitical priests cut down sinners with the sword (Exod 32:25-29; Num 25:7-8). Hosea says priests murder on the road to

Shechem (Hos 6:9). It is not hard to imagine priests with a reputation for violence being hated by people.

12 *For Benjamin he said: Beloved of Yahweh, he will dwell securely.* This blessing is a poetic tricolon (Cross and Freedman 1948, 194, 197 n. 1). Benjamin, Jacob's youngest son by Rachel (Gen 35:17-19), comes here ahead of Joseph. In the Blessing of Jacob, Rachel's two sons come last: Joseph and then Benjamin (Gen 49:22-27). Rashi says that Benjamin follows Levi here because Levi is concerned with sacrificial service and Benjamin with the construction of a "Holy Dwelling" in its territory. The poet for this reason placed them next to one another.

Benjamin is perhaps called "beloved" because of Jacob's affection for this son of his old age (Gen 43:1-14; 44:20). If so, he is also beloved of Yahweh. He will dwell securely in his territory (cf. Jer 23:6; 33:16). In the Blessing of Jacob, Joseph receives a more favored blessing (Gen 49:22-26); Benjamin is simply noted as a "ravenous wolf... devouring its prey" (Gen 49:27).

God is the one surrounding him all the day. The MT is corrupt in its first occurrence of עָלָיו ("upon him, by him, beside him"), which goes ill with Benjamin as subject of the first colon. The term is omitted in LXX, Sam, S, and 4QDeut[h]. The LXX follows with καὶ ὁ θεὸς, which is now supported by an added אל ("God") in 4QDeut[h] (Duncan 1995, 284-85; *EDSS*, 1:200; Ulrich, Cross et al. 1995, 70). Cross and Freedman (1948, 204-5: n. 38) anticipated the Qumran reading by taking עלי as a divine epithet, meaning "Exalted One" (NEB and NRSV: "the High God"). 4QDeut[h] also reads a Polel participle, מחופף (Duncan 1995, 285; Ulrich, Cross et al. 1995, 70), which is an intensive form of the verb; MT has a Qal participle. The verb is a *hapax legomenon* in the OT, but generally taken to mean "enclose, surround, shield." A cognate noun חֻפָּה means "(protective) canopy, chamber" (Ps 19:6[5]; Isa 4:5; Joel 2:16). The colon then means that God will see to the protection of Benjamin all the day (cf. Isa 31:5).

and between his shoulders dwells. וּבֵין כְּתֵיפָיו שָׁכֵן. The verb "dwell" (שָׁכֵן) repeats from the first colon, giving an envelope structure to the three-colon unit (cf. Heck 1984, 526-27). God continues to be the subject, now said (figuratively) to be dwelling between Benjamin's shoulders. Commentators have generally interpreted this to mean that God is dwelling in a sanctuary within Benjamin's borders (T; Rashi; Driver; Moran; Cassuto 1973b, 59; Tigay). This would suit an 11th-cent. date for the poem, before the Jerusalem temple was built. Jerusalem had not yet been taken. At this earlier time, the boundary between Benjamin and Judah ran south of the "shoulder" of Jerusalem (Josh 15:8; 18:16), where "shoulder" is taken to mean the side of a mountain. Jebusite Jerusalem was located on the hill of Ophel. The high ground north of Ophel, which later became part of Jerusalem and where Solomon built his temple, would have been reckoned as Benjaminite territory.

Benjamin in the 11th cent. was Israel's central territory: King Saul resided at Gibeah (1 Sam 9:21; 10:26); Samuel's activities centered in Ramah (1 Sam 7:17; 8:4); and Israelite sanctuaries existed at Bethel (Judg 20:26-28; 1 Sam 10:3) and at Nob (1 Sam 21:2[1]; 22:9-19).

13 *And for Joseph he said: Blessed by Yahweh is his land, from the choicest gifts of heaven, from the dew, and from the deep lying beneath.* Joseph was the first son born to Rachel (Gen 30:22-24) and in the present blessing is the favored son of all, the goodness to him being extended to his sons, Ephraim and Manasseh. Joseph's primacy among the other tribes points to a time when his tribe — particularly Ephraim — was most powerful in Israel. The poem may in fact emanate from an Ephraimite in the north (Cross and Freedman 1948, 205 n. 41; Cassuto 1973b, 60). Ephraim and Manasseh received generous allotments in the very center of Canaan, and half of Manasseh earlier received the rich Bashan territory and northern Gilead.

from the choicest gifts of heaven. מִמֶּגֶד שָׁמַיִם. Cf. Gen 49:25. This would be rain, making the soil produce abundantly (11:11; cf. 32:2). The LXX has ἀπὸ ὡρῶν οὐρανοῦ ("from the fruits of heaven").

from the dew. מִטָּל. Dew comes from the earth (although it is said to be a gift from heaven in v. 28), watering flowers and other growing things during the dry months of summer. Some emend to מֵעָל ("above"), giving the reading "(from heaven) above." This has the support of a few Hebrew MSS and T^{OnqNf} and makes the reading correspond to Gen 49:25. But the change is unnecessary, and the MT (with LXX and T^{PsJ}) should be read (AV; Nelson). Mentioned here are three gifts from Yahweh: rain from heaven; dew from the earth; and (next) springs and wells from beneath the earth.

from the deep lying beneath. The "deep" (תְּהוֹם) is the subterranean waters cited in Gen 1:2, which in ancient mythology is personified (e.g., Babylonian Tiamat). Since the verb רֹבֶצֶת means "lying stretched out, couching" (cf. Gen 49:9, 14, 25), some commentators (Driver; Cross and Freedman 1948, 206 n. 44) and some modern Versions (AV; RSV; NEB; NAB; NJV) suggest personification here, but the verb (and noun) no more than suggest, which is what תְּהוֹם does in Gen 1:2. Ancient mythology is definitely in the background, but better sense is made both here and in Gen 49:25 if the water is simply said to be "lying" or "stretching out" beneath the earth, where reference is to wells and underground springs (NRSV: "the deep that lies beneath"). The LXX has καὶ ἀπὸ ἀβύσσων πηγῶν κάτωθεν ("and from the abysses of springs below"). Abundant water — from springs and underground waters (תְּהֹמֹת) — is promised in the good land Israel is about to enter (Deut 8:7). A better case for personification can be made from the quasi-independent power of the curses in Deut 29:19(20), said to be "lying stretched out" in readiness to attack the idolater.

14 These are various crops of grain, vegetables, and fruits that ripen at different months of the year. Hebrew יְרָחִים ("months") is lit. "moons," which balances "sun."

15 *and from the best of the mountains of old, and from the choicest of the everlasting hills.* The wealth in Ephraim and Manasseh's mountains and hills, which have been around from time immemorial, is cited also in the Blessing of Jacob (Gen 49:26; cf. Hab 3:6). These provide an array of good things for the inhabitants of the land — grains, terraced vineyards, fruit trees, wild honey, pastureland, wood, stone, copper, etc. (Deut 8:8-10; Pss 72:3, 16; 104:14-15; 147:8; Amos 9:13; Ezek 17:22-23). In Transjordan, where half of Manasseh occupied the highlands of Bashan and northern Gilead, were rich soil for crops, fruit trees, and vineyards; lush pastureland for cattle, sheep, and goats; stands of oak trees; and balm, gum, and spices (Gen 37:25; Num 32:1; Deut 32:13-14; Jer 8:22; 46:11). Mesopotamian texts contain numerous references to the wealth gained from hills and mountains — fruits, vegetation, fat bulls, fattened sheep, wine, honey, wood, stone, marble, precious metals, etc. (Waldman 1980-81; cf. "Epic of Gilgamesh" 6:17, $ANET^3$, 84; "Baal and Anath" II AB v. 77-78, $ANET^3$, 133).

and from the best. וּמֵרֹאשׁ. Lit. "and from the head/top/first." An intentional departure from the repeated מִמֶּגֶד in vv. 13-16 (Freedman 1986; *pace* Cross and Freedman 1948, 206 n. 50). The LXX and T^{OnqPsJ} read with the MT, although Wevers (1995, 547-48) notes that the LXX rewrites the next colon to get a more exact parallelism ("and from the top of the everlasting hills"). 4QDeut^h in the present colon reverts to מִמֶּגֶד.

16 *and from the choicest of earth and its fullness.* A summary of what has been said in vv. 13-15. On "the earth and its fullness," see Ps 24:1; Mic 1:2.

and the favor of the one who dwelt in the thornbush. I.e., Yahweh, who revealed himself to Moses in the thornbush (Exod 3:2-6). Yahweh did not actually "dwell" in the thornbush; he simply revealed himself there (cf. LXX). Some want to emend "thornbush" (סְנֶה) to "Sinai" (סִינָי), but that is unnecessary (Cassuto 1973b, 60). Cassuto points out that even without emendation there will still be an allusion to Yahweh's dwelling place at Sinai (v. 2).

the one who dwelt. שֹׁכְנִי. On old case endings used to emphasize the construct state *(ḥireq compaginis)*, see GKC §90k-m; cf. Jer 49:16; Obad 3.

Let it come to the head of Joseph. תָּבוֹאתָה לְרֹאשׁ יוֹסֵף. I.e., let Yahweh's favor come upon his head. The verb form is another *hapax legomenon* in the OT (cf. Gen 49:26b).

and to the crown of the consecrated of his brothers. A triple construct chain repeating from the Blessing of Jacob (Gen 49:26b). Hebrew נְזִיר ("consecrated one") could also be translated "separated one" (AV; נָזַר means "separate" or else Nazirite; cf. Judg 13:7). The "crown" (קָדְקֹד) is the crown of one's head (v. 20; Ps 68:22[21]).

17 *His firstborn bull, splendor for him.* בְּכוֹר שׁוֹרוֹ הָדָר לוֹ. Joseph is Yahweh's splendid firstborn bull. The "firstborn" image is suitable for Joseph. Reuben was actually Jacob's firstborn, but Joseph received Reuben's birthright because of the latter's indiscretion (1 Chr 5:1-2). Joseph was also Jacob's "firstborn" by Rachel, Jacob's favored wife (Gen 30:22-24). The bull, in any case, is Joseph, not Ephraim (*pace* Driver; Tigay) and definitely not God (*pace* Nelson), even though El is described as a "bull" in Ugaritic texts ("Baal and Anath" I AB iv: 34; *ANET*³, 141). In Babylonian texts Gilgamesh and Enkidu are said to fight one another like "bulls" ("Epic of Gilgamesh" II vi:15-23; *ANET*³, 78).

Reference here in the Blessing is to the military might of Joseph and his sons. In Babylonian texts, kings and heroes are also portrayed as "bulls." Gilgamesh is called "the hero, offspring of Uruk, the butting bull" (Tigay 1982a, 141, Tablet I i 28). Hammurabi (1728-1686) describes himself as "the fiery (wild) bull who gores the enemy" (Tigay 1982a, 150, Prologue Section C line 28; cf. *ANET*³, 165, iii 8), and Yahdun-Lim, father of Zimri-Lim (1730-1697), is called "the powerful king, the wild bull among the kings, [who] did march to the shore of the sea" ("Dedication of the Shamash Temple by Yahdun-Lim"; *ANET*³, 556).

His firstborn bull. 1QDeut[b] (Barthélemy and Milik 1955, 61), LXX, Sam, S, and Vg have "bull" without the suffix (שׁור), but the meaning would be the same. Cross and Freedman (1948, 207 n. 57) say that the term without the suffix preserves archaic orthography; the MT simply reflects a revision of the spelling. 4QDeut[h] has "his bull" (שׁורו), supporting MT (Duncan 1995, 285; Ulrich, Cross et al. 1995, 70).

and his horns, the horns of a wild ox. Joseph has "(two) horns of a wild ox": Ephraim and Manasseh. See Num 23:22; Pss 22:22(21); 92:11(10).

With them he will thrust peoples, together the ends of the earth. I.e. Joseph with his two immense horns, Ephraim and Manasseh, will thrust back all enemies. The expression "ends of the earth" means "people/nations far distant" (Pss 2:8; 22:28[27]; Isa 52:10). The Hebrew does not read "to the ends of the earth" (*pace* LXX [ἕως ἐπ' ἄκρου γῆς]; AV; RSV; NEB; JB; NRSV). Hyperbole, all the same. See the dramatized prophecy of Zedekiah ben Chenaanah in 1 Kgs 22:11.

Yes, they are the ten thousands of Ephraim, and they are the thousands of Manasseh. Joseph's two sons are named climactically at the end, the two horns of the wild ox. The double occurrence of הם ("they") is for emphasis. In Hebrew parallelism "thousands" usually precedes "ten thousands" (32:30; 1 Sam 21:12[11]; Mic 6:7; Pss 91:7; 144:13), but here the sequence is reversed because the preeminent tribe is first mentioned (Loewenstamm 1980, 268-69; cf. Gen 48:13-20). One could argue that Ephraim is also the more numerous, but Tigay (1996, 409 n. 126) points out that whereas Ephraim is larger in Num 1:32-35, Manasseh is larger in Num 26:29-37.

18 Zebulun, the sixth son born to Leah (Gen 30:19-20), and Issachar, the fifth son born to Leah (Gen 30:17-18), are treated together. The one is said to be "going forth," and the other said to be "in his tents," a variation of the "going out" and "coming in" merismus (see Note for 28:6). Reference could be to the tribal life of both, but the pursuits of the tribes could be different. Some suggest that Zebulun will be going out to the sea in various endeavors and Issachar will remain in its own territory, perhaps being involved in agriculture (Driver) or the herding of sheep (Tigay; cf. Gen 49:14). The two territories were north of Manasseh in Lower Galilee and the Jezreel Valley, Issachar south and west of Lake Chinnereth, or the Sea of Galilee (Josh 19:17-23), and Zebulun between Naphtali on the east and Asher on the west (Josh 19:10-16). Early on Zebulun may have occupied territory bordering on the Mediterranean (Gen 49:13). The two tribes are told to rejoice. Why? Because one or both will be inviting people to sacrifices on a mountain in their territory, and one or both will be availing themselves of good things coming in from the sea (v. 19).

Zebulun and Issachar later took part in the battle against Sisera, which was celebrated in the Song of Deborah (Judg 5:14-15; cf. 4:10). The battle took place in Issachar's territory (Y. Aharoni 1979, 224). This poem of blessing reflects an earlier time, however, and a time before the Assyrians made their entry into Israel. Galilee was overrun by Tiglath-pileser III in Pekah's reign (737-732), at which time Zebulun and Naphtali's remaining populations were taken into Assyrian exile (2 Kgs 15:29). But Isaiah says that this indignity will be eclipsed by a grand messianic event, at which time Zebulun and Naphtali will once again rejoice (Isa 8:23–9:6[9:1-7]; cf. Matt 4:15-16).

19 *Peoples to the mountain they will call; there they will sacrifice right sacrifices.* The first colon is difficult, as is clear from the attempted translation of the LXX (Wevers 1995, 550). Driver says that the verb קרא, normally "call, summon," here means "invite to a feast" (cf. 1 Sam 9:13, 24; 1 Kgs 1:9, 41), and it is supposed that one or both tribes will be inviting people to some mountain in their territory for a sacrificial feast. Who the people are and what mountain is meant are not indicated. Some take the invited guests to be kinfolk of Zebulun (Nelson); others think they may be foreigners from the north (Driver; Tigay). Two likely mountains would be Mount Carmel (B. Mazar 1978) or Mount Tabor (von Rad; Moran; Cassuto 1973b, 62; Y. Aharoni 1979, 224; Nelson; cf. Hos 5:1). Tabor was on the border between Zebulun and Issachar, figuring prominently in the battle against Sisera (Judg 4:6, 12-14).

right sacrifices. זִבְחֵי־צֶדֶק. See Pss 4:6(5); 51:21(19). These would be proper sacrifices offered in the right frame of mind (T^{PsJ}; Driver). Levine (1974, 135-37) argues that they are offerings rightfully due Yahweh.

Indeed the abundance of the seas they will suck, and hidden treasures of the sand. ANE texts commonly express in parallelism riches coming from mountain and sea (Waldman 1980-81). Some think these tribes — particularly

Zebulun — will benefit from imports arriving at Mediterranean ports (von Rad; cf. Gen 49:13). This is certainly possible, since fish arrived there from fleets plying the waters of the Aegean (see Note for 14:9). In later years, Jerusalem had a Fish Gate (Zeph 1:10; 2 Chr 33:14), indicating a fish market in the city. But here the emphasis appears to be on the coast itself as the source of Zebulun and Issachar's abundance. Along the coast was a thriving industry of harvesting sea snails *(murex brandaris* and *murex trunculus),* from which costly purple dye was extracted (Jensen 1963; Bruin 1970). These were harvested in baskets, much in the way lobsters are harvested on the coast of Maine. The shells were cracked, and from the snail's glands were taken three or four drops of secreted fluid to make the dye. The purple-dye industry was a major source of wealth for Phoenicians and Canaanites in the Late Bronze and Iron Ages (Mazar 1946, 7; Y. Aharoni 1979, 19; cf. Pliny *Nat.* v. 17).

Classical writers highly praised the sandy beach near Acco (Ptolemais), which contained fine sand for the manufacture of glass. Strabo (*Geogr.* xvi 2:25) said the stretch of sand was between Acco and Tyre, but other ancient sources put it at the circular basin to the south, near the River Belus, just north of Mount Carmel (Pliny *Nat.* v. 17; xxxvi 65; Tacitus *Hist.* v. 7; Josephus *B.J.* ii.188-91; cf. Baly 1957, 129-30 + map). Older scholars assumed that "the hidden treasures of the sand" referred to this sand used for glass-making (Driver; cf. Job 28:17). Tigay has doubts about glass being manufactured in Israel at this time (but he dates the Blessing later [1996, 524], perhaps during the united monarchy). We know glass-making was highly developed by the Phoenicians and Egyptians in the 2nd mill. Paul Nicholson and a team of archaeologists from Cardiff University have recently discovered a glass-making site at Amarna in Egypt from the time of Akhenaten (ca. 1364-1347), which shows that the craft developed in Egypt even earlier than previously thought (*Science Daily,* 21 December 2007). Glass-blowing came much later, at the end of the 1st cent. B.C.

20 *And for Gad he said: Blessed is the one who enlarges Gad.* Gad was a son born to Leah's maid Zilpah (Gen 30:10-11). The one enlarging Gad's territory will be God (Exod 34:24; Deut 12:20; 19:8; cf. Gen 26:22), who is blessed at the beginning of this benison. Cf. the blessing upon Japheth in Gen 9:26-27. Gad occupied Gilead from the Yarmuk River to Heshbon after the defeat of Sihon, the Amorite king (Josh 13:24-28; cf. Deut 3:12-17). The tribe retained control of its Transjordan territory and was a viable entity long after Reuben became insignificant (v. 6), but it suffered the same fate as the other Transjordan tribes when Tiglath-pileser III overran the country in the 730s and took the remaining Israelite population into Assyrian exile (1 Chr 5:26).

as a lioness he lies in wait, then he tears the arm, yes, the crown of the head. Gad is likened to a lioness because of his prowess in battle (cf. 1 Chr 12:8). Lioness imagery is also used for Dan (v. 22), and in the Blessing of Jacob it describes

Deuteronomy 33

Judah (Gen 49:9). In Jacob's Blessing, Gad is to be troubled by raiders but will raid in return (Gen 49:19).

as a lioness he lies in wait. כְּלָבִיא שָׁכֵן. I.e., he lies quietly before rushing to pursue his prey and capture it. It is the female lion that hunts prey (cf. Num 23:24; 24:9).

21 *And he sought out the finest for himself.* Gad selected the finest (רֵאשִׁית) Transjordan territory of Gilead, which was good pastureland for sheep and cattle and produced balm and other good things to use and sell to traders passing through the region (see v. 15). Both Gad and Reuben were given Transjordan land on the condition that they aid the other tribes in the conquest of Canaan, which they agreed to do (Numbers 32; Deut 3:18-20).

indeed there, the portion of the treasured lawgiver. כִּי־שָׁם חֶלְקַת מְחֹקֵק סָפוּן. This colon is difficult, though similar at points to v. 19. Traditional Jewish interpretation takes it as a reference to Moses' hidden gravesite (T[OnqNfPsJ]; Rashi; Cassuto 1973b, 63), which creates an obvious anachronism. But there are other anachronisms in the poem, e.g., the third person reference to Moses in v. 4 and the omission of Simeon after v. 6. Also, Nebo and Beth-peor were in the territory of Reuben (Num 32:38; Josh 13:20), not Gad. The portion (of land) is said to belong to Moses because it was his to give, and he agreed to give it to Gad after Gad promised to aid in the fight for Canaan (Numbers 32). So we are talking about the portion of land destined for Gad, not Moses. Moses is מְחֹקֵק, "inscriber, commander, ruler" (Judg 5:14; Isa 33:22). The verb חקק means "to cut in, engrave, command," and Moses is Israel's celebrated commander, ruler, and lawmaker (v. 4; Exod 34:28). As "lawmaker" (Weinfeld 1972, 153), he possesses militarylike authority. The problematic term is סָפוּן, although the lexica recognize it as being the same word as שָׂפוּן in v. 19, only with a different spelling. It is best taken as a verbal adjective meaning "treasured" and a link term to v. 19 (see Rhetoric and Composition).

Then he came to the heads of the people. After Gad and Reuben agreed to the terms of the apportionment, Moses came to the "heads of the people" to ratify the decision (Num 32:28-32; cf. v. 5), after which the two tribes were allowed to settle in their respective territories.

Then he came. Hebrew יֵתֵא is a contracted form of יֶאֱתֶה (GKC §68h). The verb אתה ("to come") appeared earlier in v. 2b.

Yahweh's righteousness he did, and his ordinances with Israel. Moses — or perhaps Gad — did what was righteous in Yahweh's eyes and what was consistent with Yahweh's ordinances (= acts of justice) given to Israel. Gad's apportionment was thus acceptable to Yahweh. Deuteronomy 6:25 says that what is righteous in Yahweh's eyes becomes righteousness for the one doing Yahweh's commands.

22 *And for Dan he said: Dan is the cub of a lion.* Dan was a son born to

Rachel's maid, Bilhah (Gen 30:4-6), and his tribe was rather small. But Dan was a fighter, and lion imagery is used once again to characterize him (cf. v. 20 of Gad; Gen 49:9 of Judah). In the Blessing of Jacob, Dan is a serpent that bites the heels of a horse, causing the rider to be thrown backward (Gen 49:17). The mighty Samson came from the tribe of Dan (Judges 13-16).

he leaps forth from the Bashan. Bashan presumably had lions, since they are mentioned in Cant 4:8 as residing in the vicinity of Mount Hermon. On the lush country of Bashan, see Note for 3:1. Dan was originally given territory in the Shephelah, west of Benjamin and southeast of Ephraim (Josh 19:40-48). Samson's family came from Zorah (Judg 13:2), and Samson was later associated with the cities of Eshtaol and Timnah (Judg 13:25; 14:1). But Dan soon lost its inheritance, not only to the Philistines, who just then were settling along the coast to the south, but also to the Amorites (Canaanites), according to Judg 1:34-35. The tribe then migrated north to Galilee, where they proceeded to destroy the city of Leshem (= Laish) at the foot of Mount Hermon and settled there, renaming it "Dan" (Judges 18; cf. Josh 19:47). The city of Dan lay close to Bashan, which may explain the "lion of Bashan" imagery used here. The tribe was henceforth associated with the northern city of Dan. On Dan, see further Note for 34:1.

23 *And for Naphtali he said: O Naphtali, be satisfied with acceptance, and full of the blessing of Yahweh.* Naphtali was a second son born to Rachel's maid, Bilhah (Gen 30:7-8). The blessing received is benign, much like what is given him in the Blessing of Jacob (Gen 49:21). Naphtali is to be satisfied with Yahweh's acceptance (cf. Pss 103:5; 145:16) and being filled with Yahweh's blessing.

possess sea and south. יָם וְדָרוֹם יְרָשָׁה. Hebrew יְרָשָׁה is the emphatic form of the imperative: "possess!" The term יָם ("sea") is translated by θάλασσαν in the LXX, and is widely taken to refer to Lake Chinnereth, or the Sea of Galilee (RSV; NEB; JB; NAB), in that Naphtali is afforded access to Canaan's finest inland body of water. Its choice Galilean portion bordered on Lake Chinnereth in the south (T^Onq; Rashi) and in the north lay up from the Jordan Rift Valley (Josh 19:32-39). But יָם can also be translated "west," and some modern Versions (AV; NJV; NRSV) and scholars (Cross and Freedman 1948, 195, 208-9 n. 75; Cassuto 1973b, 64; Tigay; Nelson) render the colon "West and South he will inherit" or the like. But what can this mean? T^Onq interprets it to mean the western and southern shores of Chinnereth. Cassuto thinks Naphtali, like Gad, is being told to enlarge its borders. However, with Asher to the west, and Issachar to the south, Naphtali can hardly be encouraged to dispossess them. The verb "possess" must mean "take initial possession of." In my view, "sea and south" are best taken as a hendiadys: "the southern sea." This is the real treasure Naphtali receives, although Upper Galilee as a whole was "well watered and richly wooded . . . [a] fertile and beautiful region, exuberant with an almost tropical vegetation" (Driver 1895, 413). It later received high praise from Josephus (*B.J.* iii.41-43, 516-21).

24 *And for Asher he said: Blessed above sons is Asher, let him be the favorite of his brothers.* Asher was a second son born to Leah's maid Zilpah (Gen 30:12-13). Here he is blessed above Jacob's other sons and said to be their favorite. Hebrew בָּרוּךְ מִבָּנִים means "more blessed than" or "most blessed" (Judg 5:24). In the Blessing of Jacob, Asher is destined to eat rich food (Gen 49:20). Both blessings suit one whose name means "Happy (One)" (Gen 30:13).

and the one who dips his foot in oil. Hyperbole (cf. Gen 49:11: Judah "washes his clothes in wine"). It would be blessing enough if Asher simply had enough oil to anoint his feet whenever he wanted. Asher's territory bordered and ran near to the Mediterranean seacoast, situated to the west of Naphtali (Josh 19:24-31). The highlands of Galilee were famous for their rich soil and variety of trees, one of which was the olive, which produced an abundance of olive oil (Josephus *B.J.* ii.592; iii.516-21). A later midrash says: "It is easier for a man to grow myriads of olives in Galilee than to raise one child in Eretz Israel" (*Midr. Gen. Rab.* 20:6).

25 *Iron and bronze are your bolts.* בַּרְזֶל וּנְחֹשֶׁת מִנְעָלֶיךָ. Asher is now addressed directly. "Iron and bronze" symbolize protection in Jer 1:18, strength in Jer 15:12. Bolts were for securing house doors (Judg 3:23-25) and gates of the city (Neh 3:3, 6). Residing in the north of Canaan, in near proximity to foreigners living and traveling along the seacoast, Asher will need protection against potential intruders (Rashi). A stretch of international road (the Via Maris) passed through Asher (Y. Aharoni 1979, 44-45; cf. "way of the sea" in Isa 8:23[9:1]). Messengers, caravans, and military expeditions passed along this road in every age.

and as your days, so be your strength. וּכְיָמֶיךָ דָּבְאֶךָ. An elliptical version of the כְּ . . . כֵּן construction (cf. Jer 2:26; 18:6). דֹּבֶא is a *hapax legomenon* in the OT, its meaning uncertain. The LXX (ἰσχύς) and T[Onq] translate "strength," which is most likely its meaning (KBL[3]; Cross 1952). The NJV translates as "security" (following "bolts"). The colon may wish for Asher continued strength as time wears on (Driver). Rashi (following T[Onq]) says "as your days" refers to Asher's youth: May his declining days be as those of his youth. This line is used in verse 2 of Lina Sandell's well-known Swedish hymn, "Blott en dag" ("Day by Day Thy Mercies, Lord, Attend Me"; *CovH* no. 325).

26 *There is none like the God, O Jeshurun.* "Jeshurun," an honorific name for Israel, repeats from the Introduction (v. 5); only here the term is a vocative. The poet now speaks directly to all Israel, saying there is none like the God of Israel (cf. Exod 15:11; Jer 10:6-7). "God" with the definite article means "*the* God *par excellence*" (Cassuto 1973b, 66).

who rides the heavens to your help. Yahweh is pictured as riding through the heavens in a chariot (Mowinckel 1962, 298; Cassuto 1973b, 67), coming to help Israel in its time of need (cf. Ps 68:34[33]).

and in his majesty the clouds. See Pss 68:5(4); 104:3; Isa 19:1. The imagery develops from Babylonian and Canaanite sources. Marduk mounts the storm chariot in pursuit of Tiamat ("The Creation Epic" IV 49; *ANET*³, 66), and Baal in the Ugaritic texts has the epithet "Rider of the Clouds" ("Baal and Anath" II AB iii 10-11, 17-18, *ANET*³, 132; II AB vv. 112-13, 121-22, *ANET*³, 134; I AB ii 6-7, *ANET*³, 138).

27 *A refuge is the God of old.* מְעֹנָה אֱלֹהֵי קֶדֶם. This God of old is a refuge for Jeshurun. Hebrew מְעֹנָה can mean either "dwelling place" (RSV) or "refuge" (AV; JB; NJV). The idea of God being a secure dwelling place finds frequent expression in the Psalms (Pss 90:1; 91:9). On Yahweh as the God of old, and the one who performed great deeds in days of old, see Hab 1:12; Mic 7:20; Isa 51:9; Pss 44:2(1); 74:12; Prov 8:22.

and from beneath are the everlasting arms. Another image of God's unfailing support (cf. Hos 11:3; Isa 33:2; Ps 89:22[21]).

Yes he drove out before you the enemy, and he said "Destroy!" Reference is to the successful battles against Sihon and Og in Transjordan (Josh 24:12; cf. Deuteronomy 2-3).

28 *So Israel dwelt in security, alone abided Jacob.* Cf. Benjamin's blessing (v. 12). In the early days after the Transjordan conquest Israel dwelt securely, alone, and untroubled by enemies (Num 23:9; Mic 7:14). MT's עֵין ("spring") makes no sense in the context and is read now by many as עָן, meaning either "dwelt" (Gaster 1947, 61-62; Cross and Freedman 1948, 210 n. 87; Seeligmann 1964, 78; Steiner 1996, 696-98) or "abode" (Cassuto 1973b, 67; Tigay; Nelson; NJV; NRSV; cf. Isa 13:22). Steiner argues that עֵין is a verb — perfect or participle — and as such needs no emendation.

into a land of grain and wine. Israel received good land in Transjordan (Josh 24:13), yielding an abundance of grain and wine (Deut 32:14b).

yes, his heavens drip dew. Dew is yet another sign of Yahweh's favor (Hos 14:6[5]; cf. Prov 19:12). Isaac blessed Jacob, saying: "May God give you the dew of heaven" (Gen 27:28). See also Joseph's blessing in the present poem (v. 13). A lack of rain and dew indicates Yahweh's disfavor (2 Sam 1:21; 1 Kgs 17:1).

29 *Happy are you, O Israel! Who is like you, a people saved by Yahweh?* If Yahweh is incomparable, so is Israel because of Yahweh's salvation on its behalf (cf. Deut 4:7). For this reason Israel is to be happy (Ps 144:15). Hebrew אַשְׁרֵי comes close to meaning "blessed" (Pss 1:1; 2:12). The LXX translates with μακάριος ("blessed, happy"), the word occurring at the beginning of the Sermon on the Mount (the "Beatitudes" in Matt 5:3-11).

Shield of your help. On God as a "shield," see Gen 15:1; Pss 3:4(3); 5:13(12); 18:3; 31(2, 30); 28:7; 33:20; 35:2, and often; cf. Keel 1978, 222-25.

and (who is) the sword of your majesty. The relative pronoun אֲשֶׁר ("who") appears to be intrusive (Freedman 1980a, 46), although it could be meant to balance אַשְׁרֶיךָ ("Happy are you") at the beginning the verse (cf. NEB; REB). Most commentators and modern Versions omit.

So your enemies will come cringing to you. The verb כחשׁ in the N-stem means "cringe, feign obedience, deceive." Defeated or soon-to-be-defeated foes often render insincere homage to their conquerors (Pss 18:45[44]; 81:16[15]). Rashi cites the case of the Gibeonites coming and saying to Joshua: "Your servants have come from a distant land," etc. (Josh 9:9).

and you, upon his high places you will tread. וְאַתָּה עַל־בָּמוֹתֵימוֹ תִדְרֹךְ. Another pronoun added for emphasis. Hebrew בָּמוֹת is usually translated "high places" (Driver; Cassuto 1973b, 68; AV; RSV; NAB; cf. BDB), which is its common rendering in the OT. In the Song of Moses, Yahweh made Israel ride on the "high places" of Transjordan (Deut 32:13). But some commentators and modern Versions render בָּמוֹת as "backs" (Gaster 1947, 62; Cross and Freedman 1948, 210 n. 93; Seeligmann 1964, 78; Tigay; Nelson; NEB; JB; NJV; NRSV; cf. KBL^3), where the image changes to Israel treading on the backs of defeated foes. The Targums imagine that Israel will be trampling on the necks of defeated kings (Josh 10:24; cf. 1 Kgs 5:17[3]; Ps 110:1), and the LXX, too, reads "neck" (τράχηλον). This image is common in ANE texts (Keel 1978, 253-55; Greenfield 1978). In either case, Israel will march triumphantly over its foes.

Message and Audience

The Blessing of Moses, together with the Song of Moses, aid in bringing closure to the book of Deuteronomy, coming just prior to the final closure, which is an account of Moses' death and burial (ch. 34). The two ancient poems bring Moses' valedictory address in the plains of Moab to a grand climax, the Song containing a riveting indictment and judgment of Israel for breaking its covenant with Yahweh and the Blessing giving a needed word of healing for the Israelite tribes as they prepare to cross the Jordan and enter the promised land. Both poems have separate origins from Deuteronomy proper, having entered the book in its final stage of composition.

The audience is told in the Introduction that Yahweh came from holy mountains in the southland. They will know that Yahweh came from Mount Sinai (Horeb), and perhaps they will know too of his holy abodes in Seir and Mount Paran, where he was surrounded with brilliant radiance and myriads of holy ones. But he left all this for the tribes of Israel. How come?

Addressing Yahweh directly, the poet says he is a God who loves peoples, a truly remarkable thing. All his holy ones were at his hand and assembled at his feet, each ready to execute his words at a command. But shifting now to address the people, the poet says Moses commanded to Israel a law, and it became for the assembled a possession. What is more, and this is the important point, Yahweh became King in Jeshurun when the tribes with their leaders gathered together. This is why Yahweh left holy abodes and holy ones in the southland.

Reuben at the beginning gets a short blessing. He is to live despite indiscretionary behavior, but his males will be few. Yahweh is then asked to hear the voice of Judah. Judah has been troubled by enemies and has had to go to war. It is hoped he will be returned to his people. May his strength be increased, and may Yahweh provide help against his foes. The blessing for Levi looks to have been expanded. As it now stands, Yahweh is reminded that he entrusted to faithful Levi his sacred lots, the Thummim and Urim. Yahweh also tested Levi at Massah-Meribah, and presumably he was found worthy. Levi and his priestly tribe put Yahweh's word and covenant ahead of family, and because of this they were made teachers in Israel, interpreting Yahweh's law and helping the judges to decide difficult cases. They also were given the privilege of burning incense and offerings on Yahweh's sacrificial altar. Yahweh is asked to bless Levi's might and accept the fruits of his labor. As for those rising against him, may their loins be smashed so they not be able rise again.

Benjamin gets a brief blessing, but a good one. Beloved was he of his father, also a beloved of Yahweh. He will dwell securely because God will protect him all the day. In Benjamin Yahweh will have a holy dwelling place.

Joseph receives an extensive blessing, favored son that he was of Jacob's favored wife. His land is blessed with a promise of great fertility, which applied to the tribe's holdings on both sides of the Jordan. The rain, the dew, and the underground springs and wells will make good Yahweh's promise to bring his people into a good land. Fields of grain, gardens of vegetables, vines and fruit trees will be seen throughout Joseph's territory. The hills and mountains will yield other treasures. All this will come from the one revealed in the thornbush, in a land where not much of anything grew. Joseph is said to be Yahweh's splendid "firstborn bull," a reference to his military might. His two immense "horns" are Ephraim and Manasseh, with whom he will butt all enemies.

Zebulun and his brother Issachar are blessed in their coming and going. The two tribes are told to rejoice, because they will be inviting neighbors to sacrificial feasts on a mountain in their territory and will benefit by treasures coming in from the sea. There will be fish, purple dye, and pure sand for making fine glass.

Yahweh is blessed as the enlarger of Gad, who is depicted as a lioness lying in wait for its prey and then attacking to destroy it. Gad chose the best Transjordan land for himself, and a good land it was. Gilead had good pastureland for sheep and cattle, and it produced balm and other good things to sell to traders passing through. The portion was given him by the "treasured lawgiver," whom the audience will know to be none other than Moses. Moses ratified the allotment before the nation's leaders, after which Gad could settle in his land. It was all seen to be right in Yahweh's eyes and in accord with Yahweh's ordinances to Israel.

The tribe of Dan receives a brief blessing. He may have been a small tribe, but a fighter, depicted here as a lion that leaps forth from Bashan. Naphtali also receives a brief blessing, but it is benign, much like what was given him in the Blessing of Jacob. Naphtali is to be satisfied with Yahweh's favor, as he is full of Yahweh's blessing. He will possess the sea to the south, which was Canaan's finest inland body of water. His territory in Upper Galilee will also be a well-watered, richly wooded, and highly productive region.

Asher's blessing is climactic. He is blessed above Jacob's other sons and said here to be a favorite of his brothers. He will have oil in great abundance, but being a tribe living on the border, he must also use bolts of iron and bronze for protection against highway robbers and other intruders. Asher is told that the strength of his youth will continue throughout his days.

The conclusion of the Blessing turns to focus on Israel as a whole, who once again is given the honorific name of Jeshurun. The nation is addressed directly and told that there is none like the God Israel has known. This God rides majestically and triumphantly through the heavens to come to Israel's aid and is Israel's refuge in time of need. It has been so longer than anyone can remember. Underneath are the everlasting arms ready to support Israel when support is needed. The nation is reminded how Yahweh drove out the enemy in its battle for the Transjordan and it was able to dwell in security, unmolested by enemies. The land there was the "firstfruits" of what was to come, a land of grain, wine, and much else. Israel is therefore told to be happy, for it is a nation like no other, knowing a great salvation from an even greater God. Yahweh is a sword and shield for the people, and because of this, nations will come cringing to them when defeated or near defeat. Israel will either be treading on the high places or on the heads of its foes, in either case marching in triumph.

2. Moses' Death and Burial (34:1-12)

34 *¹And Moses went up from the plains of Moab to Mount Nebo, the top of Pisgah, which is opposite Jericho. And Yahweh showed him all the land, the Gilead as far as Dan, ²and all Naphtali, and the land of Ephraim and Manasseh, and all the land of Judah, as far as the Western Sea, ³and the Negeb, and the Plain, the Valley of Jericho, the city of palm trees, as far as Zoar. ⁴And Yahweh said to him, "This is the land that I swore to Abraham, to Isaac, and to Jacob, saying, 'I will give it to*

Deuteronomy 34

your descendants.' I have let you see it with your eyes, but you shall not cross over there." [5]So Moses, the servant of Yahweh, died there in the land of Moab, according to the command of Yahweh. [6]And he buried him in the valley in the land of Moab, opposite Beth-peor, and no one knows his burial place to this day. [7]And Moses was a hundred and twenty years when he died. His eyes were not dimmed and his vigor had not abated. [8]And the children of Israel wept for Moses in the plains of Moab thirty days. And the days of weeping and mourning for Moses were completed. [9]And Joshua son of Nun was full of the spirit of wisdom, for Moses had laid his hands upon him. And the children of Israel listened to him, and they did according to what Yahweh commanded Moses. [10]And a prophet has not arisen yet in Israel like Moses, whom Yahweh knew face to face, [11]for all the signs and wonders that Yahweh sent him to do in the land of Egypt, before Pharaoh, and before all his servants, and before all his land, [12]and for all the strong hand and all the great terror that Moses did before the eyes of all Israel.

Rhetoric and Composition

The concluding verses of Deuteronomy are delimited at the top end by a *setumah* in M^L and M^A and a section in Sam before v. 1, which is also the chapter division. In M^A the last part of v. 11 and v. 12 are written one word to a line, presumably to fill out the column on the page (Goshen-Gottstein 1976, 11). The Sam has additional sections after vv. 4 and 7.

Vocabulary and phraseology in the verses betray a combination of all four pentateuchal sources, JE, D, and P (Driver). Phrases in the final verses balance nicely:

v. 11 *for all the signs and the wonders* . . . *before Pharaoh, and before all his servants, and before all his land*
v. 12 *and for all the strong hand and all the great terror* . . . *before the eyes of all Israel*

Verses of the present chapter are greatly expanded and embellished in T^{PsJ}.

The final words make an inclusio with the opening words of the book (Markl 2004, 20):

1:1   These are the words *that Moses spoke to all Israel* . . .
34:12 . . . *and all the great terror that Moses did before the eyes of all Israel*

Portions of 34:1-12 are contained in 4QDeut[l] and 4QpaleoDeut[r].

Deuteronomy 34

Notes

34:1 *And Moses went up from the plains of Moab to Mount Nebo, the top of Pisgah, which is opposite Jericho.* Moses does as Yahweh commanded (3:27; 32:48-49). At the time he and the people were encamped in the "plains of Moab" (Num 22:1; 26:3, 63; 31:12; 33:48-50; 35:1; 36:13; Josh 13:32), an area actually above the floor of the Jordan Valley, in the Moabite foothills up from the Jordan River and below the Moabite mountain range. The floor of the Jordan Valley is called the "Ghôr" (= Arabah; LXX: Αραβωθ), which is about 9 mi from north to south and 5-7 mi from east to west (Driver). There was a corresponding "plains of Jericho" on the other side of the Jordan (Josh 4:13; 5:10; Jer 39:5; 52:8 = 2 Kgs 25:5). Mount Nebo is one of two promontory points in Moab's Abarim mountain range (see Note for 32:49). Another peak on the range is Mount Peor (Num 23:28), which was above Beth-peor. Here Moses got his look at the promised land, and nearby is where he died (32:50). Eusebius *(Onom.)* located Mount Nebo at the 6th Roman milestone east of Heshbon. The name is preserved in Jebel Neba, but many believe the site is actually Ras Siyagha, 1.5 mi northwest of Jebel Neba, beyond a small saddle. Both command a good view of the Jordan Valley and beyond (cf. 3:27), particularly Ras Siyagha, the site on which a Christian church was built in honor of Moses in the second half of the 4th cent. A.D. Here, as elsewhere (e.g., Mount Sinai), it was Christians, not Jews, who were concerned to locate the ancient site. Jebel Neba is 3935 ft above the northeast corner of the Dead Sea and Ras Siyagha 3586 ft above the Sea (Driver). From the Jordan Valley neither peak stands out, since each simply extends the Moab tableland high above the valley floor. Across the Jordan is Jericho, lying just north of the Dead Sea. A city named Nebo is mentioned in the OT (Num 32:3, 38; Isa 15:2; Jer 48:1, 22) and on the Moabite Stone (lines 14-18). According to Eusebius *(Onom.)*, it lay 8 Roman milestones to the south of Heshbon. It is commonly identified as Khirbet el-Mekhayyat, a site 9.5 km northwest of Medeba (Saller and Bagatti 1949, 1). The ruins occupy the southeast spur of the Nebo ridge and have deep wadis on the eastern, southern, and western sides, with access possible only from the north. To the north is the Church of the Saints and Martyrs Lot and Procopus, erected in A.D. 560. For archaeological work on Mount Nebo and the surrounding area, including the 4th-cent. A.D. church on Ras Siyagha, see Piccirillo 1987; Piccirillo and Alliata 1998, also articles by Piccirillo in *NEAEHL*, 3:1106-18; *OEANE*, 4:115-18; and *ABD*, 4:1056-58.

The Pisgah (הַפִּסְגָּה) was either a specific peak in the Abarim range, perhaps another name for Mount Nebo (Driver; M. Piccirillo in *NEAEHL*, 3:1106; *OEANE*, 4:115), or a peak in near proximity to Nebo, or else the range itself. Driver thinks it was the ancient name for the entire Abarim range. Perhaps, because of the definite article, the Targums (T^{OnqPsJ}) take the term as a common

Deuteronomy 34

noun meaning "the height." It was to the top of the Pisgah that Balak took Balaam to view Israel and curse it (Num 23:13-14). Under the slopes of the Pisgah lay the Sea of the Arabah/Salt Sea/Dead Sea (see Note for 4:49).

And Yahweh showed him all the land, the Gilead as far as Dan. The panorama proceeds counterclockwise from where Moses is standing, beginning with Gilead in the near north, going further north, west, and south, and ending with Zoar in the near south. Included is Transjordan land already taken and settled as well as land to be taken once Israel crosses the Jordan. Gilead was in Transjordan, between the Yarmuk River in the north and roughly Heshbon in the south. It had already been settled after Israel defeated the Amorite kings, Sihon and Og (see Note for 2:36). Dan, which became the northernmost outpost in Israel (1 Sam 3:20: "from Dan to Beersheba") and was located at the foot of Mount Hermon near the headwaters of the Jordan, would not have been visible from Nebo. Dan was formerly called Laish or Leshem, having been renamed after it was taken by the Israelites (Josh 19:47; Judg 18:27-29; see Note for 33:22). The narrator is writing long after the conquest. Laish is mentioned in the Egyptian Execration Texts and in the Mari documents. Excavations at Tel Dan (formerly Tell el-Qadi) show occupation during the Late Bronze and Early Iron Ages (*NEAEHL*, 1:323-32; *OEANE*, 2:107-12). For archaeological evidence in Stratum VI supporting a population change ca. 1200, see Biran 1994, 125-34.

2 *and all Naphtali, and the land of Ephraim and Manasseh, and all the land of Judah, as far as the Western Sea.* These names given Canaanite land again betray a postconquest perspective, as the tribal territories had neither been taken nor settled at the time Moses was speaking. Naphtali was north and northwest of Chinnereth (= the Sea of Galilee; cf. 3:17; 33:23), and Manasseh was between Mount Carmel in the northwest and Mounts Gerizim and Ebal in the south (half of the large Manasseh tribe settled earlier in Transjordan — in northern Gilead and Bashan). Ephraim was south of Manasseh. Judah later included Jerusalem as its northern boundary and extended south as far as the Negeb. Territories allotted to the smaller or weaker tribes of Asher, Zebulun, Issachar, Dan, Benjamin, and Simeon (omitted in the Blessing) go unmentioned. The Western Sea (cf. 11:24), i.e., the Mediterranean, could not have been seen by Moses from Nebo.

3 *the Negeb.* An arid region of southern Judah (Josh 15:21-32), between Beersheba and the Wilderness of Zin (see Note for 1:7).

and the Plain, the Valley of Jericho, the city of palm trees, as far as Zoar. Hebrew הַכִּכָּר (lit. "the Round") is a technical term for the oval-shaped plain in the Jordan Valley (= the Arabah) north and south of the Dead Sea (Gen 13:10-11; 19:17, 25, 28-29; 1 Kgs 7:46 = 2 Chr 4:17). Here, called also the "Valley of Jericho," it includes the city of Jericho. Jericho is a beautiful oasis north of the Dead Sea wilderness, often referred to in the OT as "the city of palm trees" (Judg 1:16; 3:13;

2 Chr 28:15). Josephus (*B.J.* iv.459-75) praised it for its date palms, balsam, cypress, and other trees, noting that it was fed by a copious spring nearby. He refers here to the ʿAin es-Sultan (Elisha's Spring), about a mile and a half north of the ancient city at the foot of the mountain where the road heads up to Jerusalem (Driver). The five "Cities of the Plain" cited in Genesis 13–14 were Sodom, Gomorrah, Admah, Zeboiim, and Zoar, but there were others (see Note for 29:21-23). Zoar, the southernmost city, earlier went by the name of Bela (Gen 14:2, 8). Yahweh spared this city when destroying the other four cities, and Lot together with his daughters fled there for safety (Gen 19:20-23, 29-30). Zoar was in existence in the time of Isaiah and Jeremiah (Isa 15:5; Jer 48:34), and to Josephus it was known as both Zoara and Zoor (*B.J.* iv.482; *Ant.* i.204). The city appears on the 6th-cent. A.D. Madeba Map, and since the Middle Ages, when it was called Ṣugar and Zugar by the Arabs, it has been identified with Ghōr eṣ-Ṣâfī at the southeastern end of the Dead Sea (Glueck 1935, 7-9; Y. Aharoni 1979, 35; *ABD*, 6:1107). The site is in a very fertile region near the Seil el-Qurahi, which is the lower portion of the Zered River (Wadi el-Ḥasā) flowing into the Dead Sea. A Jordanian village on the south bank of the Zered, about 3 km from the Dead Sea, is still called Ṣâfī. Albright (1924, 4), however, thought this was a rebuilt site dating from the beginning of the Roman period and that biblical Zoar lay under the Dead Sea along with the other Cities of the Plain. He pointed out the shallow depth of the Dead Sea at its southern end (averaging less than 4 m) and that the present level of the Sea is considerably higher than it was three or four thousand years ago. At the same time, eṣ-Ṣâfī does contain graves and pottery from the late Early Bronze and early Middle Bronze periods (ca. 2000-1900), also ruins of smelting furnaces nearby, which may go back to the Early Bronze period (J. P. Harland 1942, 32; *IDB*, 4:961-62).

4 Yahweh's promise of the land to Abraham, repeated to Isaac and Jacob (1:8; Exod 33:1), which Moses is now able to see.

but you shall not cross over there. Moses earlier had been told that he would not be permitted to enter this land (1:37; 3:27; 4:21-22; 32:52; Num 20:12).

5 Moses is called "the servant of Yahweh" or "my servant" often in the book of Joshua (Josh 1:1-2, 7, 13, 15, etc.), but the honorific title of "servant" occurs elsewhere (Num 12:7-8; 1 Kgs 8:53, 56; 2 Kgs 21:8, etc). The idiom עַל־פִּי (lit. "according to the mouth") means "according to the command" and is used frequently with reference to Yahweh (Num 3:16, 39; 4:37, 41; 33:38). Yahweh did not "command" Moses' death; rather he commanded that Moses would die outside the promised land, which is here fulfilled.

6 According to the rabbis, it was God who buried Moses (T^{PsJ}; *m. Soṭah* 1:9). Rashbam, who knows this interpretation, nevertheless interprets the "he" impersonally. He says that since no one knows Moses' burial place, "whoever buried him, buried him." T^{Nf} ("they buried him") similarly interprets the He-

brew as an impersonal expression, as does the LXX (ἔθαψαν αὐτὸν, "they buried him"), which Fritsch (1943, 53) thought was a deliberate attempt not to make God the subject of the sentence. But this thesis has been challenged by Orlinsky (1944) and Wittstruck (1976) and should be rejected. Ibn Ezra adopts a midrashic interpretation, saying that Moses buried himself by going into the crypt (*Midr. Num. Rab.* 10:17; Loewenstamm 1957-58).

A dispute between Michael the archangel and the devil regarding the body of Moses is mentioned in Jude 9, and antiquity appears to have known a work entitled "The Assumption of Moses" (J. Priest, in *OTP*, 1:925), but how this relates, if it does, to the 1st-cent. A.D. *Testament of Moses* (*OTP*, 1:919-34; cf. *APOT*, 2:407-24) that has survived, is unclear. Josephus (*Ant.* iv.326) says that while Moses was saying farewell to Eleazar the priest and Joshua, a cloud suddenly descended upon him and he disappeared in a ravine. This may be compared to the passing of the two founders of the Roman race, Aeneas and Romulus. The body of the former could not be found because it was believed he was translated to the gods, and the latter is said to have disappeared in sudden darkness and a violent storm (Dionysius of Halicarnassus, *Ant. rom.* i 64:4; ii 56:2). A Muslim site west of the Jordan, Nebi Musa, which dates from the Middle Ages, perpetuates the memory of Moses' burial (Simons 1959, 264). Leaving Moses' burial site unknown prevented a cult of the dead from arising, which would have been significant for a people coming out of Egypt where cults of the dead were commonplace. It is also noteworthy that Jews in subsequent generations were little concerned about locating Moses' burial site or even Mount Nebo, for that matter. Mount Nebo was identified by Christians who built a church there (see Note for v. 1). The death and burial of Jesus in Christian tradition has both continuity and discontinuity with the death and burial of Moses. Jesus dies and is buried, but on the third day his tomb is found empty because he is believed to have been resurrected. Here, too, no cult of the dead is to arise. Yet Christians went on to mark presumed death and burial sites with the Church of the Holy Sepulcher.

in the valley in the land of Moab, opposite Beth-peor. Where Israel encamped after the victories over Sihon and Og (3:29) and where Moses gave people the Deuteronomic law (4:46). A fitting place for Moses' burial. The LXX translates "valley" as a proper name (ἐν Γαι). On the "valley opposite Beth-peor," see Note for 3:29.

to this day. Another indication that the narrative is written later. On this Deuteronomic expression, see Note for 2:22.

7 *And Moses was a hundred and twenty years when he died.* A fixed life span according to ancient reckoning (see Note for 31:2).

His eyes were not dimmed. As were the eyes of Isaac in old age (Gen 27:1). Moses could, after all, view the surrounding land from the top of Nebo.

and his vigor had not abated. וְלֹא־נָס לֵחֹה. The phrase is difficult, mainly because we do not know the precise meaning of לֵחַ ("vigor"). The ancient Versions had trouble rendering the phrase. The problematic noun appears only here and possibly in Jer 11:19 (where Ferdinand Hitzig emended to "sap" on the basis of the present verse; cf. Lundbom 1999, 636), but a cognate adjective means "moist, fresh" (Gen 30:37 of cut wood; Num 6:3 of grapes; Judg 16:7-8 of bowstrings; Ezek 17:24 of living trees). It is the opposite of "dry." If the noun happens to mean "sap," as it seems to in Jer 11:19, it could refer here to sexual potency, i.e., be a euphemism for the male seed. But many modern Versions (NEB; JB; NAB; NJV; NRSV; REB) translate it "vigor," which is probably as good a rendering as any, even if Moses himself says he is no longer able to carry on as Israel's leader (31:2). Albright (1944b) found support for לֵחַ meaning "natural force" (so AV; RSV) in a Ugaritic text, the "Tale of Aqhat." In a catalogue of blessings that a son will bring to his father (i 30), the son is described as one

who smothers the life force of his detractors,
driving off those who attack his abode (Albright; cf. *ANET*[3], 150)

In another line of the epic (vi 28), Aqhat answers Anath who wants a composite bow:

And I will grant thee not to die, and I will give thee life force

H. L. Ginsburg's translation in *ANET*[3], 151 is slightly different, but the meaning is the same.

8 *And the children of Israel wept for Moses in the plains of Moab thirty days.* The people wept thirty days for Aaron after his death (Num 20:29).

9 *And Joshua son of Nun was full of the spirit of wisdom.* On being filled with the "spirit of wisdom" (רוּחַ חָכְמָה), see also Exod 28:3.

for Moses had laid his hands upon him. A rite of investiture (Num 27:18, 23), carried on in the early church (Acts 6:6) and surviving into the modern day.

And the children of Israel listened to him, and they did according to what Yahweh commanded Moses. When Moses was told to lay his hand upon Joshua, it was to give him the authority that Moses had, so the people would obey him (Num 27:18-20).

10 Probably an attempt to make Moses greater than the 8th-cent. prophets who had arisen recently, i.e., Amos, Hosea, Micah, and Isaiah. Medieval Jewish scholars used this text to refute later claims of a prophet who would supersede Moses, such as occurred in Christianity and Islam (Tigay). The claim about Muhammad being the greatest of prophets, however, was made by Arabs in another religion. A polemic against Christianity is more understandable, since NT claims that John the Baptist was a prophet (the greatest of all prophets, according to Matt 11:9-11) and that Jesus was a prophet (especially in the Gospel of John; see John 4:19, 44; 6:14; 7:40, 52; 9:17) were made by 1st-cent. A.D. Jews. But this was certainly not the original intent of the verse. The narrator is speaking of prophets who had arisen up to that time. What is more, according to Deut 18:15-18, Moses says Yahweh will raise up in Israel another prophet the likes of himself, and people are to listen to him. Jeremiah appears to understand himself as this "prophet like Moses" (Muilenburg 1963; Holladay 1964; 1966; Lundbom 1999, 107-8; 233-35).

whom Yahweh knew face to face. The expression denotes auditory — not visual — intimacy, referring to conversation between the two (5:4; Exod 33:11; Num 12:8). Not even Moses is permitted to see the face of Yahweh (Exod 33:20-23; cf. 1 John 4:12).

11-12 A recollection of the exodus event, at which time Moses performed many signs and wonders (see Note for 4:34). The narrator may be implying that Moses was also greater than Elijah and Elisha, prophets known for their mighty works (1 Kgs 17:8-24; 18:20-40; 2 Kgs 2:8, 14, 19-22; 4:1-44; 5:1-14; 6:1-7; 8:4-5). Even in death, the bones of Elisha had miraculous power (2 Kgs 13:20-21). Language in the present verse is Deuteronomic (4:34; 6:22; 7:19; 11:3; 26:8; 29:1[2]). On the use of "strong hand" in Deuteronomy, see Note for 6:21. On the expression "before the eyes," see Note for 1:30.

Message and Audience

The discourse of Deuteronomy is now brought to a suitable conclusion. Moses has recited his riveting "song" to Israel, then given the tribes a comforting blessing, and now he is to ascend Mount Nebo, where he will die and be buried. Moses does what Yahweh has commanded. He goes up from the plains of Moab to the top of the Pisgah, opposite Jericho. There Yahweh showed him the surrounding land — some of which had already been taken and land across the Jordan to be taken subsequently. The panorama takes in Gilead, Dan in the far north, all of Naphtali, Ephraim, and Manasseh, Judah as far as the Western Sea, the Negeb, and the Plain below, which includes the cities of Jericho and Zoar. Yahweh says: "This is the land I told you about, the land I swore to give Abraham and his descendants. You can look at it, but you cannot enter it."

The audience is then told that Moses died in Moab, fulfilling Yahweh's command. He was buried in the valley opposite Beth-peor, but no one knows just where. Even in the present day the site is unknown. Moses reached the maximum age of 120 years, but he could still see and had life in him. People wept for him thirty days, as they did for Aaron, and then the mourning ended. As for Joshua, he was full of the spirit of wisdom, for Moses had laid his hands upon him. Yet Moses was the prophet par excellence, for no prophet like him had arisen with whom Yahweh could speak "face to face." What is more, no prophet could do the signs and wonders that Moses did in Egypt — before Pharaoh, before his servants, and before everyone else, and this is to say nothing of the strong hand and the great terror he showed before all Israel.

Martin Luther King Jr., whose commitment to the biblical covenants was everywhere apparent (Drotts 1973, 195), said in his "Moses on the Mountain" speech delivered 3 April 1968, just prior to his death:

> We've got some difficult days ahead. But it really doesn't matter with me now. Because I've been to the mountaintop. I won't mind. Like anybody, I would like to live a long life. Longevity has its place. But I'm not concerned about that now. I just want to do God's will. And he's allowed me to go up to the mountain. And I've looked over, and I've seen the Promised Land. I may not get there with you, but I want you to know tonight that we as a people will get to the Promised Land. So I'm happy tonight. I'm not worried about anything. I'm not fearing any man. "Mine eyes have seen the glory of the coming of the Lord." (M. L. King 1959, 63)

APPENDIX
Citations of Deuteronomy in the New Testament

The following list of Deuteronomy quotations in the New Testament is taken, with few changes and additions, from Westcott and Hort's *The New Testament in the Original Greek* (1882, 174-88). The texts are given as they appear in Deuteronomy, not as cited in the New Testament, where in some cases they are abridged, paraphrased, or altered to suit the context.

1:7	as far as the great river, the river Euphrates	Rev 9:14
		Rev 16:12
1:31	and in the wilderness, where you saw how Yahweh your God lifted you up as a man lifts up his son	Acts 13:18
2:5	for I will not give to you any of their land, not even a stepping place for the sole of the foot	Acts 7:5
4:2	You shall not add to the word that I am commanding you, and you shall not subtract from it, in order to keep the commandments of Yahweh your God that I am commanding you.	Rev 22:18-19
4:11	And you drew near and you stood at the foot of the mountain, and the the mountain was burning with fire up to the heart of heaven — darkness, cloud, and storm cloud.	Heb 12:18
4:24	for Yahweh your God is a consuming fire	Heb 12:29

Citations of Deuteronomy in the New Testament

4:35	Yahweh he is God and there is no other besides him	Mark 12:32
5:16	Honor your father and your mother . . .	Matt 15:4 Mark 7:10 Matt 19:19 Mark 10:19 Luke 18:20 Eph 6:2
	. . . in order that your days may be prolonged, and in order that it may go well with you on the soil that Yahweh your God is giving you.	Eph 6:3
5:17	You shall not murder.	Matt 19:18 Mark 10:19 Luke 18:20 Rom 13:9 Jas 2:11
5:18	And you shall not commit adultery.	Matt 5:27 Matt 19:18 Mark 10:19 Luke 18:20 Rom 13:9 Jas 2:11
5:19	And you shall not steal.	Matt 19:18 Mark 10:19 Luke 18:20 Rom 13:9
5:20	And you shall not testify against your fellow an empty witness.	Matt 19:18 Mark 10:19 Luke 18:20
5:21	And you shall not covet the wife of your fellow. And you shall not desire the house of your fellow . . .	Rom 7:7 Rom 13:9

Appendix

5:22	These words Yahweh spoke to your whole assembly at the mountain from the midst of the fire, the cloud, and the storm cloud, a great voice, and he did not add.	Heb 12:19
6:4	Hear, O Israel, Yahweh our God, Yahweh is one.	Mark 12:29 Mark 12:32 Jas 2:19
6:5	And you shall love Yahweh your God with all your heart and with all your soul and with all your might.	Matt 22:37 Mark 12:30 Mark 12:33 Luke 10:27
6:13	Yahweh your God you shall fear, and him you shall serve.	Matt 4:10 Luke 4:8
6:16	You shall not test Yahweh your God.	Matt 4:7 Luke 4:12
7:1	When Yahweh your God brings you into the land . . . and he clears away . . . seven nations more numerous and mightier than you	Acts 13:19
8:3	one does not live by bread alone, but one lives by everything that goes out of the mouth of Yahweh	Matt 4:4 Luke 4:4
9:19	Indeed, I was in dread because of the anger and the wrath for which Yahweh was furious toward you.	Heb 12:21
10:17	For Yahweh your God, he is God of gods and Lord of lords . . . who does not show partiality.	Rev 17:14 Rev 19:16 Acts 10:34 Rom 2:11 Gal 2:6
10:22	Seventy persons your fathers went down to Egypt	Acts 7:14
11:14	then I will give rain for your land in its time, the early rain and the latter rain	Acts 14:17 Jas 5:7

Citations of Deuteronomy in the New Testament

13:2-3 (13:1-2)	When a prophet ... gives to you a sign or a wonder, and the sign or the wonder comes to pass, about which he spoke to you, saying, "Let us go after other gods ... and let us serve them"	Matt 24:24 Mark 13:22
13:6 (13:5)	So you shall utterly remove the evil from your midst. The phrase occurs another 10 times in Deuteronomy (17:7, 12; 19:13, 19; 21:9, 21; 22:21, 22, 24; 24:7).	1 Cor 5:13
14:2	Yahweh chose you to be for him a people	Titus 2:14
15:11	For the needy person will not cease from the midst of the land.	Matt 26:11 Mark 14:7
17:6	On the testimony of two witnesses or three witnesses the one to die shall be put to death	Heb 10:28
18:13	Blameless you shall be towards Yahweh your God.	Matt 5:48
18:15	A prophet from your midst, from your brethren, like me, Yahweh your God will raise up for you; to him you shall listen.	Acts 3:22 Acts 7:37
18:19	And it will happen that the person who will not listen to my words that he will speak in my name, I, I shall require it from him.	John 12:48 Acts 3:23
19:15	on the testimony of two witnesses or on the testimony of three witnesses a word shall stand up	Matt 18:16 2 Cor 13:1 1 Tim 5:19
19:21	eye for eye, tooth for tooth	Matt 5:38
21:22	And when there shall be in a man a sin requiring a sentence of death, and he is put to death and you hang him upon a tree	Acts 5:30 Acts 10:39
21:23	cursed of God is one who is hanged	Gal 3:13

Appendix

24:1	When a man takes a wife . . . and he writes for her a bill of divorce and puts it in her hand and sends her from his house	Matt 5:31 Mark 10:4 Matt 19:7
24:15	You shall give his wages in his day, and not when the sun has gone down upon it, for he is poor and he is setting his desire upon it, and that he not call to Yahweh against you, and it be a sin in you.	Jas 5:4
25:4	You shall not muzzle an ox in its treading of grain.	1 Cor 9:9 1 Tim 5:18
25:5	When brothers will dwell together, and one of them dies and has no son . . . [the wife's] brother-in-law shall go in to her and take her to himself for a wife, and do to her the duty of a brother-in-law.	Matt 22:24 Mark 12:19 Luke 20:28
27:26	Cursed be the one who does not confirm the words of this law to do them.	Gal 3:10
28:35	Yahweh will strike you down with bad boils upon the knees and upon the legs, of which you cannot be healed, from the sole of your foot to the crown of your head.	Rev 16:2
29:3 (29:4)	Yahweh did not give you a mind to understand, or eyes to see, or ears to hear, to this day.	Rom 11:8
29:17 (29:18)	Perhaps there be among you a root bearing poison or wormwood.	Heb 12:15
29:20 (29:21)	And Yahweh would single him out for evil from all the tribes of Israel, according to all the curses of the covenant written in this book of the law.	Rev 22:18
30:4	If your dispersed one is at the end of the heavens, from there Yahweh your God will gather you and from there he will fetch you.	Matt 24:31 Mark 13:27
30:12	Who will go up for us to the heavens . . . ?	Rom 10:6

Citations of Deuteronomy in the New Testament

30:14	Indeed the word is very near you, in your mouth and in your heart	Rom 10:8
31:6, 8	he will not abandon you and will not forsake you	Heb 13:5
32:4	The Rock . . . indeed all his ways are just; a God of faithfulness, and without wrong, righteous and upright is he.	Rev 15:3 Rev 16:5 Rev 19:2
32:5	It acted corruptly toward him. Is not their blemish his children's? a generation perverted and crooked!	Acts 2:40 Phil 2:15
32:17	They sacrificed to demons, no-gods, gods they had not known	1 Cor 10:20 Rev 9:20
32:21	So I, I will make them jealous with a no-people, with a foolish nation I will provoke them.	Rom 10:19 Rom 11:11 1 Cor 10:22
32:35	Vengeance is mine, and repayment	Rom 12:19 Heb 10:30
32:36	Indeed Yahweh will vindicate his people	Heb 10:30
32:43	Give his people ringing acclaim, O nations/heavens	Rom 15:10 Rev 18:20
	LXX: and let all the angels of God worship him	Heb 1:6
	for the blood of his servants he will avenge, yes, he will return vengeance to his adversaries, and atone for his land, his people	Rev 6:10 Rev 18:20 Rev 19:2

Author Index

Abel, F.-M., 196, 208, 210, 214, 259, 384, 385
Abravanel, 261
Achtemeier, Paul, 542
Adler, Cyrus, xix
Aharoni, I., 466, 471, 473
Aharoni, Yohanan, 168, 184, 197, 262, 412, 424, 443, 488, 741, 912, 933, 934, 937, 945
Ahituv, Shmuel, 159, 162, 184, 331
Akiba, Rabbi, 550, 598, 599, 670, 813
Albertz, Rainer, 288
Albright, William F., 5, 8, 9, 10, 11, 13, 162, 179, 196, 198, 203, 219, 244, 267, 276, 279, 309, 423, 444, 445, 446, 450, 512, 521, 533, 566, 724, 726, 812, 855, 876, 887, 900, 903, 905, 917, 919, 925, 928, 945, 947
Alday, Salvador C., 865, 879
Allegro, John M., 555, 609
Alliata, Eugenio, 943
Alt, Albrecht, 11, 28, 172, 235, 278, 293, 706, 746
Alter, Robert, 865
Anbar, M., 390
Andersen, Francis I., 371, 687
Andersen, Johannes G., 685
Anderson, Cheryl B., 293
Aquila, 593, 724
Arden-Close, Charles F., 405
Aretaios, 685

Aristophanes, 472, 545
Aristotle, 475, 664
Astour, Michael C., 921
Astruc, Jean, 684
Athanasius, 6
Attridge, Harold W., 468, 617, 645
Augustine, 272, 363
Axelsson, Lars E., 192

Bacon, Francis, 44
Bagatti, Bellarmino, 943
Baillet, Maurice, 165, 314, 315, 355, 532
Baly, Denis, 214, 934
Barkay, Gabriel, 491
Barstad, Hans M., 553, 556, 557, 560, 657, 659
Barthélemy, Dominique, 1, 5, 314, 318, 450, 452, 453, 496, 504, 824, 825, 829, 857, 886, 932
Bartlett, John R., 168, 183, 184, 189, 192, 193, 353
Basser, Herbert W., 852, 874, 886
Bayliss, Miranda, 733
Bea, A., 23
Bechtel, George, 569
Beck, Astrid, 2
Beckman, Gary, 539
Beer, G., 508
Begg, Christopher T., 9, 372, 373
Beit-Arieh, Itzhaq, 160
Ben-Ami, Issachar, 630

Author Index

Bennett, Harold V., 394
Bennett, James R., 771, 774, 775
Benoit, Pierre, 309, 468, 672, 676, 677
Ben-Tor, Amnon, 545
Ben Yehudah, Eliezer, 884
Bergey, Ronald, 856
Bernhardt, Karl-Heinz, 209
Bernstein, Moshe J., 611
Bertman, Stephen, 624
Bewer, Julius A., 169
Beyerlin, Walter, 284
Bienkowski, Piotr, 200
Biran, Avraham, 179, 424, 944
Birenboim, Hanan, 427
Blackman, Philip, 1, 488
Blair, Edward P., 348
Blank, Sheldon H., 44, 235, 648, 747
Bodenheimer, F. S., 349, 465, 466, 467, 468, 469, 475
Boessneck, Joachim, 540
Boling, Robert G., 208, 277
Bordreuil, Pierre, 201
Borowski, Oded, 443, 512, 513, 701
Boston, James R., 853
Bowman, Raymond A., 726, 727
Boyer, Georges, 603, 706
Brandt, William J. 391, 819
Braulik, Georg, 232, 233, 416, 417, 612, 652, 654
Breasted, James H., 402, 483, 540
Breit, Herbert, 22
Brenner, Athalya, 772
Brewer, David I., 670
Brichto, Herbert C., 181, 648, 746, 768, 813
Briggs, Charles A., xx
Bright, John, 13, 329, 331, 443, 445, 446, 447, 517, 727, 782, 783, 925
Brodie, Thomas, 93, 366
Brody, Robert, 678
Brooke, George J., 5, 756, 825
Broshi, Magen, 453
Brown, Francis, xx
Bruin, Frans, 934
Brunner, Hellmut, 350
Bryan, Cyril P., 775
Budde, D. Karl, 853, 921
Budge, E. Wallis, 572, 594, 714

Bullard, Reuben G., 681
Burckhardt, John L., 159, 207
Burrows, Millar, 706, 708, 725

Calvin, John, xviii, 585, 587, 589, 614, 619, 631, 641, 660, 670, 675, 680, 686, 707
Canaan, T., 615
Carlson, R. A., 428
Carmichael, Calum M., 493, 495, 497, 564, 571, 616, 702
Carpenter, J. Estlin, 8, 16, 18, 265
Cassuto, Umberto, 854, 881, 916, 922, 923, 925, 929, 930, 931, 933, 935, 936, 937, 938, 939
Cato, Marcus, 664
Cazelles, Henri, 158
Celsus, 685
Chalmers, Aaron, 900
Chaney, Marvin, 296
Chavel, Charles B., 657
Childs, Brevard S., 202, 336, 348, 376, 504, 742, 807
Christensen, Duane L., 918, 919
Chrysostom, Saint John, 6
Cicero, 664
Clark, Ernest, 493
Clement of Alexandria, 244
Clements, Ronald E., 426, 427
Cody, Aelred, 385, 434
Cogan, Chayim, 395
Cogan, Morton, 517
Coggins, R. J., 588
Collon, Dominique, 337
Condamin, Albert, 23
Cooke, G. A., 660
Cooke, Stanley A., 5, 276, 309
Cooper, Alan, 508
Cornhill, D. Carl Heinrich, 853, 855
Cortez, Marc, 711
Cotton, Hannah M., 676, 678
Cowley, A. E., 172, 325, 665, 678
Crawford, Sidnie White, 3, 4, 208, 273, 282, 347, 658
Crenshaw, James L., 51, 239, 561, 876
Cross, Frank M., 4, 9, 13, 160, 172, 208, 273, 282, 346, 351, 452, 529, 580, 583, 658, 735, 739, 740, 820, 833, 834, 839, 840, 847, 855, 857, 858, 869, 876, 877,

893, 898, 899, 900, 903, 905, 908, 916, 917, 922, 923, 924, 925, 926, 927, 928, 929, 930, 931, 932, 936, 937, 938, 939

Dahood, Mitchell, 765, 806, 887
Dandamayer, M., 494
Dante, 391
Daube, David, 44, 45, 47, 54, 55, 56, 57, 58, 227, 237, 276, 279, 287, 288, 295, 362, 375, 377, 389, 406, 436, 454, 456, 458, 463, 491, 494, 495, 509, 529, 539, 549, 567, 575, 576, 585, 592, 606, 614, 617, 620, 631, 634, 636, 653, 670, 671, 682, 684, 686, 694, 700, 706, 709, 710, 711, 712, 713, 733, 788, 789, 812, 893, 897
Davies, Eryl W., 604, 705, 709, 711
Davies, G. Henton, 314
Davies, Graham I., 159, 160
Davies, W. D., 286, 557
Dawson, Warren R., 770
Day, Edward, 47, 393
Day, John, 162, 335, 383, 425, 527
Dearman, J. Andrew, 171, 196, 197, 208, 209, 259
Dempster, Stephen, 529
Dentan, R. C., 568
Derrett, J. Duncan, 624
Dershowitz, Idan, 307
De Troyer, Kristin, 737-38
Diamond, A. S., 575
Diodorus of Sicily, 283, 294, 644
Dion, Paul E., 453, 456, 461
Dionysius of Halicarnassus, 946
Diringer, David, 713, 714, 715
Dohmen, C., 367
Donner, Herbert, 351
Dothan, M., 160
Driver, G. R., 28, 470, 471, 472, 473, 474, 546, 572, 632, 635, 638, 639, 640, 644, 655, 665, 681, 683, 684, 692, 693, 694, 698, 701, 705, 706, 709, 711, 712, 881
Driver, S. R., xviii, xix, xx, 2, 6, 7, 8, 9, 12, 15, 18, 19, 21, 22, 24, 26, 27, 29, 33, 37, 39, 43, 47, 63, 156, 157, 158, 159, 160, 162, 165, 167, 169, 170, 171, 172, 173, 174, 176, 177, 178, 179, 180, 181, 182, 185, 191, 194, 195, 196, 198, 200, 202, 206, 208, 209, 210, 213, 214, 215, 218, 220, 222, 223, 226, 228, 234, 235, 236, 237, 238, 239, 240, 241, 243, 248, 249, 250, 251, 253, 254, 255, 256, 258, 260, 262, 265, 266, 267, 277, 286, 287, 295, 301, 302, 306, 310, 311, 312, 314, 319, 320, 321, 324, 328, 334, 335, 337, 338, 339, 340, 341, 342, 348, 352, 354, 359, 362, 364, 365, 371, 374, 376, 382, 384, 386, 388, 395, 399, 408, 411, 420, 427, 428, 431, 433, 434, 435, 439, 452, 453, 454, 456, 457, 464, 465, 471, 475, 476, 483, 486, 487, 488, 489, 490, 491, 492, 493, 495, 496, 497, 499, 507, 508, 509, 510, 511, 514, 516, 517, 519, 520, 521, 524, 526, 533, 535, 536, 541, 544, 545, 549, 551, 552, 553, 556, 559, 561, 567, 569, 572, 581, 584, 585, 587, 589, 593, 594, 599, 606, 607, 609, 610, 611, 614, 617, 619, 624, 630, 631, 637, 640, 647, 649, 652, 658, 664, 673, 674, 682, 683, 685, 693, 694, 701, 706, 708, 710, 711, 717, 725, 730, 732, 734, 739, 740, 741, 744, 746, 747, 748, 749, 761, 762, 763, 764, 766, 776, 782, 785, 796, 798, 800, 801, 802, 806, 808, 810, 819, 828, 829, 836, 837, 839, 840, 842, 844, 845, 846, 847, 852, 853, 856, 858, 872, 873, 875, 876, 877, 880, 881, 882, 884, 885, 886, 887, 889, 890, 891, 893, 894, 895, 896, 897, 898, 901, 902, 903, 911, 912, 916, 917, 919, 922, 923, 924, 925, 927, 929, 930, 932, 933, 934, 937, 939, 942, 943, 945
Drotts, Wallace D., 949
Du Buit, M., 598
Duke, Rodney K., 545
Duncan, Julie A., 4, 346, 347, 857, 908, 926, 928, 932
Dwight, Sereno, 909

Edelman, Diana V., 189
Edenburg, Cynthia, 627, 632, 634, 636, 638
Edwards, Jonathan, 96, 908
Ehrlich, A. B., 884
Eichrodt, Walter, 64
Eissfeldt, Otto, 2, 3, 6, 9, 10, 741, 845, 855
Eliezer, Rabbi, 598, 813
Emerton, J. A., xix, 19, 434, 535, 544, 545

Author Index

Emery, Walter B., 540
Epstein, Louis M., 706, 707, 708
Eslinger, Lyle, 712, 713
Eusebius of Caesarea, xxi, 160, 161, 192, 196, 202, 203, 207, 209, 228, 259, 263, 330, 385, 646, 912, 943
Ewald, Heinrich, 853

Fagen, Ruth, 314
Faulkner, R. O., 523
Feldman, Louis H., 208, 209, 211
Fensham, F. Charles, 48, 355, 372, 394, 695, 747
Finkelstein, Israel, 443
Finkelstein, J. J., 488, 524, 552, 575, 635
Fishbane, Michael, 420, 440, 741, 832, 845
Fitzmyer, Joseph A., 45, 313, 452, 458, 676, 677, 784, 790, 807
Fleishman, Joseph, 634
Fleming, Daniel E., 450
Flinder, Alexander, 193
Flusser, David, 273
Fohrer, Georg, 2, 3, 8, 9, 10, 11, 68, 260
Forrer, Emil O., 330
Fox, G. George, 314
Fox, Nils Sacher, 617
Fraade, Steven D., 5, 251, 746, 756, 817
Frankena, R., 251, 310, 311, 452, 453, 756
Frazer, J. G., 659
Freedman, David Noel, xxi, 2, 7, 9, 10, 13, 25, 69, 225, 227, 241, 252, 267, 268, 271, 273, 274, 279, 280, 282, 283, 285, 287, 289, 290, 292, 293, 294, 334, 371, 438, 445, 446, 493, 527, 571, 581, 588, 605, 606, 625, 670, 687, 688, 722, 807, 818, 839, 855, 868, 869, 873, 874, 876, 877, 878, 887, 898, 916, 917, 919, 921, 922, 923, 924, 925, 926, 927, 928, 929, 930, 931, 932, 936, 938, 939
Freeman-Grenville, G., xxi
French, A., 487
Fried, Lisbeth S., 12, 444, 445, 447
Friedman, Mordechai A., 676, 678
Friedman, Richard E., xviii, 161, 190, 194, 202, 227, 236, 253, 259, 278, 279, 294, 310, 313, 364, 367, 488, 523, 524, 534, 567, 570, 595, 599, 610, 630, 646, 658, 711, 733, 781, 801, 826, 838, 840, 874, 877, 878, 884, 895
Fritsch, Charles T., 3, 880, 893, 946
Frymer-Kensky, Tikva, 575, 607, 617, 630, 631, 632-33, 637, 638

Gaballa, G. A., 254
Gadd, C. J., 603, 726, 732, 733
Galbiati, H., 23
Galenos, 685
Gall, August F. von, 165
Galling, Kurt, 392, 643
Galpaz-Feller, Pnina, 48, 394, 396, 705
Gamaliel I, Rabbi, 486
Gamoran, Hillel, 664
García Martínez, Florentino, 4
Gardiner, Alan H., 168
Gaster, Theodor H., 179, 457, 464, 598, 617, 618, 877, 886, 888, 923, 938, 939
Gelb, Ignace J., 196, 330
Gennep, Arnold van, 205, 361
Geoghegan, Jeffrey C., 202
Gesenius, Wilhelm, xx
Gevirtz, Stanley, 806
Gilliard, Frank D., 542
Ginsberg, H. Louis, 7, 33, 34, 395, 506, 510, 511, 513, 514, 808, 947
Ginsburg, Christian D., 5, 333
Ginzberg, Louis, 391
Gitin, Seymour, 352, 483, 485, 632
Giveon, Raphael, 921
Glasson, Thomas F., 557
Glueck, Nelson, 168, 177, 189, 192, 197, 207, 208, 228, 259, 281, 352, 353, 945
Golani, Amir, 485, 632
Goldin, Judah, 913
Goldingay, John, 209
Goldstein, Bernard R., 508
Good, Edwin M., 27, 575, 639, 640, 683, 749
Gordis, Robert, 296, 793
Gordon, Cyrus H., 592, 706, 712
Goshen-Gottstein, Moshe, 2, 942
Gottwald, Norman, 207
Graesser, Carl F., 424, 527
Graetz, Heinrich, 884, 889
Granqvist, Hilma, 634, 636
Gray, John, 201, 732, 733

Author Index

Grayson, A. Kirk, 777
Greenberg, Moshe, 7, 225, 271, 280, 291, 292, 300, 320, 354, 377, 481, 488, 538, 550, 566, 568, 635, 666, 688, 692, 693, 694, 856, 889
Greenfield, Jonas C., 203, 288, 655, 673, 676, 678, 777, 784, 818, 890, 894, 939
Gross, Karl, 774, 900
Grossfeld, Bernard, 881
Gruber, Mayer I., 370, 657, 658, 781, 796
Gunkel, Hermann, 853, 854
Gurney, O. R., 329, 330, 694, 706
Guthrie, H., 487

Habel, Norman C., 875
Hackett, Jo Ann, 474
Hallo, William W., 320, 342, 444, 445, 552, 616, 617, 618, 630, 633, 661, 715
Hammer, Reuven, 521
Haran, Menahem, 383, 476, 505, 506, 507, 508, 510, 511, 512, 513, 514, 515, 516, 517, 833, 837, 838, 845, 846
Hare, Ronald, 770
Harland, J. Penrose, 811, 812, 895, 945
Harland, Peter J., 617
Harrington, Daniel J., 676, 677
Harris, J. Rendel, 908
Harris, Rivkah, 672
Heck, Joel D., 929
Held, Moshe, 776
Henrey, K. H., 707
Hepner, Gershon, 271
Herder, Johann G. von, 853
Herodotus, 283, 354, 464, 644, 659, 693, 740
Herr, Larry G., 200, 207
Hertz, Joseph H., 484, 599
Herzog, Ze'ev, 424, 443, 444, 741
Heschel, Abraham J., 795
Hesiod, 283
Hickman, Edward, 909
Hilhorst, Anton, xix
Hillel, 486, 491, 671
Hillers, Delbert R., 9, 649, 756, 768, 773, 775, 776, 791, 812, 891
Hitzig, Ferdinand, 947
Hoffman, Yair, 320, 333, 334
Hoffner, Harry A., 395, 616, 732, 733

Hoftijzer, J., 648, 740
Holladay, William L., 16, 557, 817, 856, 948
Holmgren, Fredrick C., 730
Holtz, Shalom E., 672
Homan, Michael M., 485
Homer, 681, 701
Honor, Leo L., 324, 348, 396, 695, 727
Hopkins, David C., 483
Hort, F. J. A., 950
Hort, Greta, 774
Huehnergard, John, 707
Huffmon, Herbert B., 373, 450, 853, 872
Hulse, E. V., 684, 685
Humbert, P., 875
Hundley, Michael, 60, 427
Hunger, Hermann, 541

ibn Ezra, Abraham, 156, 157, 179, 208, 222, 228, 235, 252, 253, 254, 269, 272, 278, 301, 307, 310, 312, 313, 314, 321, 336, 338, 339, 340, 354, 371, 396, 400, 556, 656, 762, 763, 764, 765, 771, 775, 776, 777, 778, 784, 786, 787, 789, 793, 794, 795, 796, 802, 806, 807, 808, 809, 822, 824, 826, 837, 841, 872, 873, 879, 880, 881, 884, 885, 886, 887, 889, 890, 891, 892, 893, 898, 900, 901, 903, 911, 919, 921, 922, 923, 924, 946
Ikeda, Yutaka, 214, 540
Ilan, Tal, 678
Irenaeus, 380, 908
Ishida, Tomoo, 328, 330

Jackson, Bernard S., 289, 295
Jacobsen, Thorkild, 279, 280, 646
Jefferson, Thomas, xviii
Jensen, Lloyd B., 934
Jericke, Detlef, 159
Jerome, xxi, 5, 6, 159, 263, 673
John of Damascus, 685
Johns, Claude H. W., 28, 482, 483
Johnson, Aubrey R., 295, 312, 568
Jongeling, B., 796
Josephus, 1, 3, 173, 178, 208, 209, 211, 271, 273, 288, 309, 314, 315, 349, 352, 353, 482, 490, 513, 515, 531, 607, 609, 610, 622, 624, 631, 634, 664, 671, 678, 707,

Author Index

708, 710, 711, 739, 741, 781, 789, 792, 834, 857, 912, 919, 934, 937, 945, 946
Joshua ben Korcha, Rabbi, 436
Joüon, Paul, 211
Judah, Rabbi, 672, 894
Justin Martyr, 244, 885
Juvenal, 616

Kallai, Zecharia, 208
Kamphausen, Adolf, 853, 858
Kant, Immanuel, xviii
Katzoff, Ranon, 676, 678
Kaufman, Stephen A., 416, 417, 564, 565, 672
Kaufmann, Yehezkel, 7, 16, 47, 226, 426, 487, 499, 693, 694
Keel, Othmar, 254, 354, 938, 939
Keiser, Thomas A., 853
Kempinski, Aharon, 184, 330, 741
Kenyon, Frederic G., 6
Kenyon, Kathleen, 912
King, L. W., 512, 524, 748
King, Martin Luther, 293, 949
King, Philip J., 250, 351, 367, 423, 425
Kiple, Kenneth F., 770
Kittel, Rudolph, xix
Klein, Isaac, 464, 467, 469
Klein, Jacob, 829
Kleinert, Paul, 23, 798
Kletter, Raz, 485, 632
Klingbeil, Gerald A., 287, 366
Klostermann, August, 22, 447, 853
Knauf, E., 196
Knibb, M. A., 588
Knobel, August, 853
Knoppers, Gary N., 538, 541
Knowles, Michael P., 873
Knox, Bernard M., 542
Köhler, Ludwig, 521, 530, 558, 606
Kooij, Arie van der, 878, 903-4, 905
Kooij, G. van der, 648, 740
Kopf, L., 550
Kornfeld, W., 659
Kreuzer, Siegfried, 254
Kruger, Paul A., 711
Krumbhaar, E. B., 770, 775
Kuenen, A., 853
Kuntz, Paul G., xviii

Lacheman, Ernest R., 711
Lafont, Sophie, 632, 636, 638, 639
Lambdin, Thomas O., 724
Lambert, W. G., 225, 278, 282, 296, 376, 390, 395, 440, 469, 524, 525, 616, 658, 659, 663, 665, 714, 715, 822
Landes, G., 716
Lane, Edward W., 202, 315, 403
Langdon, Stephen, 254, 240, 303
Lansdell, J., 623
Laubscher, F. Du., 809
Lauterbach, Jacob Z., 593
Lawrence, T. E., 160, 912
Lemche, Niels P., 488
Lenchak, Timothy A., 799
Leuchter, Mark, 846, 856
Levine, Baruch A., 19, 159, 209, 434, 535, 545, 728, 729, 732, 933
Levinson, Bernard M., 455, 456, 538
Levy, Abraham J., 837, 844, 853
Levy, Thomas E., 189
Lewis, Naphtali R., 676, 678
Lewis, Theodore J., 241, 280, 457, 731, 732, 888
Licht, Hans, 617
Licht, Jacob, 739
Lichtheim, Miriam, 330, 351
Lieber, Elinor, 684
Lincicum, David, 771
Lindberg, Carter, 665
Lindquist, Maria, 215
Linsenmaier, Walter, 784
Lipinski, Edward, 672
Loewe, Raphael, 632
Loewenstamm, Samuel E., 292, 913, 926, 932, 946
Lohfink, Norbert, xx, 8, 9, 11, 23, 165, 166, 172, 232, 237, 260, 264, 285, 304, 307, 328, 333, 346, 360, 363, 409, 410, 480, 721, 725, 728, 798, 805
Lorton, David, 280
Lucian, 617, 645
Luckenbill, Daniel D., 726
Lucretius, 782
Lund, Nils W., 23, 864, 919
Lundbom, Jack R., xviii, xxi, 10, 11, 13, 18, 21, 23, 24, 25, 30, 33, 35, 36, 38, 39, 43, 44, 155, 166, 170, 173, 176, 184, 190, 191,

205, 225, 227, 243, 256, 260, 261, 264, 267, 282, 305, 308, 334, 336, 347, 361, 363, 365, 368, 371, 375, 380, 383, 391, 407, 409, 419, 424, 440, 442, 447, 449, 450, 451, 480, 486, 493, 498, 504, 513, 517, 522, 530, 549, 550, 555, 557, 558, 561, 580, 598, 607, 632, 670, 677, 688, 700, 722, 774, 777, 781, 783, 785, 794, 798, 805, 812, 817, 818, 819, 827, 839, 844, 845, 846, 856, 862, 864, 865, 866, 867, 869, 876, 879, 881, 885, 887, 889, 890, 891, 900, 902, 927, 947, 948
Lust, Johan, 900, 901
Luther, Martin, xviii, xix, 2, 159, 172, 175, 232, 260, 263, 276, 283, 295, 297, 364, 377, 386, 389, 397, 416, 419, 533, 550, 551, 665, 670, 675, 701, 711, 740, 745, 746, 749, 801, 822, 823, 875, 880, 881, 891, 895, 898
Luyten, Jos, 900

Macalister, A., 775
Macalister, R. Stewart, 681, 682
MacDonald, Burton, 200, 207
MacDonald, J., 3
MacDonald, Nathan, 231
MacDowell, Douglas M., 646
Macht, David I., 467, 469, 470
MacKenzie, R. A., 557
MacRae, George W., 515, 516
Maimonides, 314, 315, 467, 484, 593
Malamat, Abraham, 168, 202, 249, 281, 390, 542, 559, 826
Malina, Bruce J., 349
Maloney, Robert P., 664, 665
Marböck, J., 888
Marcus, David, 607, 608
Margalit, Baruch, 527
Markl, Dominik, 942
Martyr, Justin, 908
Mathers, Powys, 634
Mattingly, G. L., 228
May, Herbert G., 354
Mayes, A. D., 232
Mazar, Amihai, 424
Mazar, Benjamin, 159, 184, 213, 219, 329, 330, 727, 920, 921, 933
McBride, S. Dean, 274

McCarthy, Carmel, 2, 874
McCarthy, Dennis J., 20, 21, 45, 52, 165, 313, 517, 649, 756, 761, 772, 790, 875, 888
McCartney, Eugene S., 542
McConville, J. Gordon, 580, 628, 643
McKay, J. W., 311, 312
McMahon, G., 330
McNamara, Martin, 493
Meek, Theophile J., 406, 587, 701
Meier, Samuel A., 440, 441
Mendelsohn, Isaac, 488, 493, 494, 495, 497, 498, 602, 603, 655
Mendelssohn, Felix, 250, 425, 766, 772
Mendenhall, George E., 20, 207, 328, 329, 330, 332, 336, 853, 855, 856, 897
Mercer, Samuel A., 649, 880
Merritt, Benjamin D., 739
Meshel, Zeev, 740
Meshorer, Yaʿakov, 632, 713
Meyer, Rudolf, 905
Michaelis, John David, 215, 289, 531, 569, 572, 573, 583, 584, 585, 589, 605, 607, 619, 623, 633, 635, 646, 647, 649, 670, 673, 674, 675, 685, 686, 701, 706, 707, 708, 713
Michener, James A., xvii, 475
Michiela, Daniel, 726
Mihelic, J., 349
Miles, John C., 28, 572, 632, 635, 638, 639, 640, 644, 655, 665, 681, 683, 684, 692, 693, 694, 698, 701, 705, 706, 709, 711, 712
Milgrom, Jacob, 10, 27, 322, 336, 429, 435, 445, 463, 464, 466, 467, 468, 469, 474, 475, 476, 485, 535, 545, 566, 588, 623, 624, 666, 682, 684, 685, 686, 692, 724, 731, 838
Milik, J. T., 1, 5, 165, 309, 314, 315, 318, 355, 450, 452, 453, 496, 504, 532, 672, 676, 677, 824, 825, 829, 857, 883, 884, 886, 887, 932
Millard, Alan R., 215, 726
Miller, J. Maxwell, 195, 197, 209, 210
Miller, Patrick D., 50, 309, 897, 921
Miller, Perry, 909
Minette de Tillesse, Georges, 9
Moberly, R. W., 255, 310, 376

Author Index

Moessner, David P., 557
Moldenke, Alma L., 384
Moldenke, Harold N., 384
Montet, Pierre, 403, 696, 701
Moor, Johannes C. de, 890, 891
Moran, William L., xx, 21, 23, 67, 70, 157, 165, 166, 171, 181, 183, 194, 207, 208, 215, 237, 291, 295, 296, 301, 302, 310, 311, 312, 313, 337, 338, 340, 346, 347, 370, 388, 452, 455, 490, 498, 512, 520, 527, 539, 549, 568, 574, 575, 594, 605, 617, 639, 640, 649, 653, 655, 657, 658, 660, 694, 734, 739, 796, 798, 838, 853, 872, 873, 876, 882, 893, 903, 917, 921, 926, 929, 933
Morgenstern, Julian, 235, 382, 566, 609
Moriarty, Frederick L., 443
Morrison, M., 196
Morse, Dan, 770
Mowinckel, Sigmund, 20, 444, 643, 881-82, 938
Mueller, James R., 541, 639
Muffs, Yochanan, 789
Muhley, James D., 215, 352, 353
Muilenburg, James, 19, 20, 23, 24, 197, 233, 235, 302, 368, 405, 557, 653, 734, 762, 774, 825, 858, 859, 860, 861, 862, 864, 866, 868, 899, 900, 948
Mukenge, André K., 487
Mullen, E. T., 878
Muroaka, T., 238
Musil, Alois, 638, 639

Na'aman, Nadav, 12, 157, 178, 444
Naveh, Joseph, 173, 179, 687, 763
Nelson, Harold H., 254
Nelson, Richard D., xx, xxi, 9, 194, 196, 202, 208, 218, 222, 232, 260, 263, 278, 302, 306, 312, 317, 359, 360, 362, 374, 376, 742, 758, 762, 771, 796, 798-99, 806, 816, 817, 828, 829, 839, 841, 872, 876, 878, 880, 888, 890, 891, 894, 895, 900, 901, 903, 904, 905, 909, 918, 921, 923, 924, 925, 930, 932, 933, 936, 938, 939
Nestle, Eberhard, 6
Neufeld, Edward, 28, 340, 592, 615, 623, 636, 637, 640, 655, 663, 664, 665, 672, 680, 683, 684, 686, 705, 706, 707, 708
Neusner, Jacob, 677, 874
Nicholson, E. W., 7, 8, 10, 11, 12, 13, 18, 24, 28, 444, 540, 800
Nicholson, Paul, 934
Nielsen, Eduard, 744
Nietzsche, Friedrich, xviii
Nigosian, Solomon A., 856
Ninow, Friedbert, 210
Nitzan, B., 746, 809, 825
Noonan, John T., 702
North, Christopher R., 808
North, Robert, 488, 775
Noth, Martin, 8, 9, 24, 25, 225, 231, 260, 352, 353, 756, 828, 837
Novick, Tzvi, 716

O'Brien, John A., 542
O'Callaghan, Roger T., 648
O'Connell, Kevin G., 588
O'Connell, Robert H., 328, 346, 360
Oded, Bustenay, 249, 782, 925
Oden, Robert A., 468, 617, 645
Oesch, Josef M., 165
Olmstead, A. T., 159, 912
Oppenheim, A. Leo, 279, 280, 341, 440, 451, 517, 584
Oppian, 466
Origen, 380, 646, 724
Orlinsky, Harry M., 3, 450, 880, 893, 946
Ottosson, Magnus, 170, 210, 223
Otzen, B., 457
Overton, Shawna D., 289, 588

Palmer, E. H., 912
Pardee, Dennis, 201
Parpola, Simo, 777
Patai, Raphael, 593
Paton, Lewis B., 7
Patrick, Dale, 536
Paul, Shalom M., 10, 408, 712, 918
Pausanias, 220
Peckham, Brian, 660
Pedersen, Johannes, 393
Peels, Hendrik G., 880, 881
Persius, 509
Peterson, J., 208

Petuchowski, Jacob J., 350, 353
Pfeiffer, Robert H., 5, 12, 28, 240
Pflüger, Kurt, 524
Phillips, Anthony, 21, 289, 290, 294, 295
Philo, xviii, 208, 209, 211, 271, 273, 274, 282, 283, 288, 297, 487, 674
Phythian-Adams, William J., 916
Piattelli, Daniela, 671
Piccirillo, Michele, 228, 943
Plato, 288, 664, 667
Pliny, 467, 468, 636, 685, 782, 785, 934
Plutarch, 509, 770
Polybius, 236
Pope, Marvin H., 201, 765, 876
Porten, Bezalel, 392, 408, 665, 678
Preuss, Julius, 340, 605, 770, 771, 772, 774, 776, 782, 793
Price, Ira M., 706
Priest, J., 946
Propp, William H., xviii, 277, 279, 289, 348, 367, 368, 856, 882
Pseudo-Philo, 208, 209, 211
Puech, Emile, 450

Qimron, Elisha, 5, 251, 678, 756, 817, 847

Rabin, Chaim, 552
Rabinowitz, Jacob J., 291
Rabinowitz, Louis, 314, 315
Rad, Gerhard von, xx, 8, 9, 10, 11, 19, 20, 22, 23, 59, 66, 74, 156, 157, 179, 196, 201, 202, 215, 219, 258, 260, 261, 289, 293, 294, 295, 302, 310, 313, 334, 336, 370, 391, 403, 422, 426, 427, 432, 440, 447, 451, 486, 487, 494, 495, 508, 510, 511, 514, 515, 520, 521, 531, 538, 541, 553, 556, 564, 565, 579, 581, 583, 586, 593, 594, 597, 614, 618, 619, 627, 640, 643, 646, 649, 651, 653, 658, 661, 664, 666, 684, 685, 690, 694, 706, 723, 725, 730, 733, 734, 738, 739, 740, 744, 746, 747, 756, 787, 798, 806, 810, 828, 833, 836, 853, 868, 872, 877, 878, 883, 892, 893, 903, 918, 919, 933, 934
Rainey, A. F., 12, 168, 443, 586
Ramban, (Nachmanides) Rabbi, 156, 157, 657
Rankin, O. S., 44

Rashbam, 177, 184, 191, 226, 228, 242, 258, 269, 278, 329, 338, 341, 362, 371, 385, 510, 516, 533, 589, 617, 923, 945
Rashi, 157, 177, 178, 195, 210, 215, 217, 220, 222, 226, 227, 228, 252, 253, 262, 278, 293, 312, 324, 337, 340, 385, 386, 393, 403, 425, 426, 428, 429, 432, 435, 436, 438, 457, 464, 465, 466, 467, 468, 475, 482, 490, 491, 492, 495, 496, 497, 499, 508, 509, 510, 512, 513, 517, 521, 533, 545, 549, 550, 553, 561, 575, 584, 593, 594, 597, 599, 605, 609, 610, 614, 617, 618, 619, 622, 631, 633, 638, 643, 646, 650, 652, 657, 660, 667, 671, 681, 699, 700, 706, 707, 708, 711, 713, 723, 724, 726, 730, 739, 743, 745, 749, 770, 771, 774, 778, 781, 789, 793, 795, 796, 806, 807, 808, 822, 834, 837, 839, 846, 872, 874, 877, 878, 880, 881, 884, 885, 886, 889, 891, 892, 893, 894, 897, 898, 899, 901, 903, 923, 924, 925, 927, 929, 935, 936, 937, 939
Rawlinson, George, 445
Reed, William L., 425
Reif, Stefan C., 584
Renkema, J., 395
Revell, E. J., 261
Reviv, Hanoch, 301, 607
Ringgren, Helmer, 395, 457
Roberts, C. H., 5, 6, 662, 669, 698, 723, 761
Roberts, J. J. M., 198
Robertson, David A., 855
Robinson, Edward, 158, 159, 160, 192, 207, 403
Robinson, George L., 912
Robinson, H. Wheeler, 22, 28, 30, 33, 268, 798, 835, 853, 878
Rofé, Alexander, 302, 409, 419, 422, 564, 566, 568, 569, 574, 579, 587, 591, 601, 613, 621, 637, 638, 651, 652, 654, 656, 662, 669, 679, 680, 690, 700, 704, 722, 739, 758, 809, 878, 903, 904
Rogerson, John, xix
Röllig, Wolfgang, 351
Rooy, H. F. van, 799
Rosenbaum, Jonathan, 444, 447
Roth, Ernest, 712

Author Index

Roth, Martha T., 395, 396, 575, 638, 672
Rowley, H. H., 6, 332, 444, 445, 708, 709, 921
Rowling, J. Thompson, 775
Ryan, J. Theodore, 291

Salisbury, Harrison E., 770
Saller, Sylvester J., 943
Sandell, Lina, 937
Sanders, Henry A., 845
Sanders, James A., 2
Sanders, Paul, 855, 856
Sanders, T. W., 623
Sanderson, Judith E., 459, 721, 857, 874, 883, 917
Sandison, A. T., 774
Sarfatti, Gad B., 242
Sarna, Nahum M., 371, 494, 595, 728, 845
Sauer, James A., 200
Schaeffer, Claude F., 632, 714, 732, 733
Shiffman, Lawrence H., 520, 521, 525
Schley, Donald G., 796
Schmidt, Nathaniel, 160
Scholz, Piotr O., 644, 645, 646
Schorch, Stefan, 477
Schremer, Adiel, 678
Schumacher, Gottlieb, 162
Scott, R. B. Y., 714
Seebass, Horst, 251
Seeley, David R., 391, 818
Seeligmann, I. L., 923, 938, 939
Segal, J. B., 504, 506, 507, 508, 510, 511
Seidl, Erwin, 699
Seitz, Gottfried, 23
Sellers, O. R., 714
Seux, M.-J., 392
Shaffer, Aaron, 784, 894
Shai, Donna, 630
Shammai, 671
Shulman, Ahouva, 226, 252
Silberman, L. H., 336
Silberman, Neil A., 443
Simons, J., 158, 159, 196, 209, 213, 220, 228, 263, 385, 921, 946
Singer, A. D., 183
Skehan, Patrick W., 371, 459, 721, 857, 874, 877, 878, 883, 900, 903, 904, 905, 917
Smelik, Klaas A., 209

Smend, Rudolf, xx, 684
Smith, George Adam, 7, 403, 429, 437, 454-55, 465, 468, 474, 475, 476, 499, 511, 514, 515, 516, 630, 633, 652, 653, 654, 656, 658, 662, 669, 674, 677, 700, 704, 724, 739, 744, 762, 787, 798, 853, 857, 858, 859, 872, 873, 879, 880, 882, 894, 926
Smith, J. M. Powis, 481, 482, 483, 486
Smith, R. H., 169
Smith, W. Robertson, 243, 425, 468, 548, 549, 550, 551, 599
Snaith, Norman H., 522
Snell, Daniel C., 603
Solon, 487
Sonsino, Rifat, 10
Soss, Neal M., 622, 696
Speiser, Ephraim A., 196, 331, 573, 711
Spina, Frank, 286, 786
Staerk, Willy, 9
Stager, Lawrence E., 318, 367
Steen, Eveline van der, 200
Steiner, Richard C., 922, 938
Stern, Ephraim, 200, 632
Stern, Philip D., 307
Steuernagel, Carl, 9
Steuernagle, D. C., 508
Strabo, 490, 659, 740, 785, 812, 934
Strugnell, John, 5, 251, 756, 817, 847
Stulman, Louis, 456, 536
Sturtevant, Edgar H., 569
Sukenik, E. L., 732, 733
Sumner, W. A., 187
Sussman, Max, 775
Symmachus, 724

Tacitus, 812, 934
Tadmor, Hayim, 159, 427, 445, 505, 645
Talmon, Shemaryahu, 201, 261, 488, 504, 505, 658
Tawil, Hayim, 767
Tebes, Juan M., 184
Tertullian, 380
Theodoret, 6
Theodotion, 724
Theophrastus, 785
Thiessen, Matthew, 853
Thomas, D. Winton, 311, 337, 661

Author Index

Thompson, Christine M., 632
Thucydides, 770
Tigay, Jeffrey H., xviii, xx, 10, 156, 158, 161, 162, 165, 174, 178, 182, 184, 194, 195, 196, 200, 202, 208, 213, 215, 220, 223, 232, 236, 260, 261, 265, 267, 278, 279, 280, 293, 295, 300, 309, 310, 312, 313, 314, 315, 319, 334, 346, 353, 366, 374, 376, 383, 385, 388, 396, 403, 408, 409, 412, 422, 429, 434, 454, 455, 457, 464, 467, 471, 474, 475, 483, 484, 486, 487, 488, 489, 494, 496, 499, 508, 509, 511, 512, 515, 516, 517, 533, 534, 535, 536, 544, 552, 566, 582, 584, 585, 594, 607, 608, 610, 615, 616, 620, 622, 624, 630, 631, 633, 635, 639, 644, 646, 652, 655, 657, 660, 664, 670, 674, 682, 686, 687, 688, 694, 704, 708, 709, 717, 722, 726, 731, 732, 734, 738, 739, 740, 744, 745, 746, 748, 758, 759, 760, 761, 762, 765, 768, 769, 770, 771, 775, 783, 790, 792, 799, 807, 808, 816, 828, 833, 835, 839, 840, 841, 844, 845, 846, 852, 853, 856, 872, 874, 877, 879, 880, 881, 884, 889, 890, 892, 896, 897, 898, 901, 903, 904, 905, 910, 912, 920, 921, 922, 925, 926, 927, 928, 929, 932, 933, 934, 936, 938, 939, 947
Tigchelaar, Eibert, 691
Toorn, Karel van der, 659, 660, 666, 681, 682
Tov, Emanuel, 431, 437
Trever, J. C., 412
Tristram, H. B., 465, 466, 467, 468, 469, 470, 471, 472, 473, 474, 475, 785, 786, 896
Tromp, Nicholas J., 890
Trumbull, H. Clay, 160, 183, 205, 361, 912
Tsevat, Matitiahu, 294, 498, 706
Tucker, Gene M., 594, 807
Tufnell, Olga, 545

Ulrich, Eugene, 4, 161, 208, 346, 351, 452, 459, 529, 580, 658, 721, 735, 739, 820, 833, 834, 839, 840, 847, 857, 858, 869, 874, 877, 883, 893, 898, 899, 900, 905, 908, 917, 926, 928, 929, 932
Urbach, Ephraim E., 321, 377

Van Zyl, A. H., 196, 197, 208, 911
Vaux, Roland de, 66, 165, 196, 215, 250, 309, 314, 315, 355, 393, 423, 424, 425, 426, 427, 434, 444, 468, 483, 494, 495, 514, 532, 639, 672, 676, 677, 705, 732, 846, 920, 921
Vedeler, Harold T., 617
Vermes, Geza, 309, 315
Vierya, Maurice, 732

Waard, Jan de, 555, 559
Waldman, Nahum M., 931, 933
Waldow, H. Eberhard von, 393
Walker, Winfried, 384
Walsh, Jerome T., 713
Waltke, B., 3
Washington, Harold C., 599, 600, 637
Watanabe, Kazuko, 777
Waterman, Leroy, 172, 392
Weaver, Robert J., 622
Weinfeld, Moshe, xviii, xx, 2, 7, 8, 10, 11, 19, 20, 21, 27, 33, 35, 43, 44, 46, 47, 50, 51, 53, 57, 157, 158, 159, 161, 162, 165, 168, 169, 171, 173, 174, 175, 176, 178, 179, 180, 181, 182, 183, 184, 190, 191, 194, 196, 197, 199, 200, 201, 202, 203, 205, 208, 209, 210, 211, 213, 215, 217, 218, 219, 220, 222, 223, 225, 226, 228, 232, 233, 234, 235, 236, 237, 238, 239, 240, 241, 242, 243, 248, 249, 251, 252, 253, 254, 256, 259, 260, 265, 266, 267, 268, 269, 271, 272, 275, 277, 278, 281, 285, 287, 289, 293, 294, 295, 299, 300, 302, 303, 310, 311, 313, 314, 319, 320, 321, 324, 325, 328, 331, 332, 334, 335, 336, 337, 338, 339, 340, 341, 342, 346, 348, 350, 353, 354, 355, 362, 364, 366, 367, 369, 370, 371, 372, 374, 376, 377, 378, 380, 383, 384, 391, 392, 393, 395, 396, 403, 405, 411, 427, 428, 431, 432, 433, 440, 441, 452, 453, 454, 455, 456, 458, 461, 487, 488, 489, 492, 493, 514, 520, 521, 522, 523, 524, 533, 534, 535, 536, 538, 541, 542, 571, 574, 583, 592, 603, 627, 634, 637, 638, 646, 655, 666, 674, 717, 733, 739, 741, 745, 747, 749, 756, 760, 767, 772, 773, 776, 778, 779, 791, 794, 806, 807, 822, 824, 830,

Author Index

833, 835, 838, 846, 908, 920, 921, 922, 935
Weippert, Manfred, 921
Weise, Manfred, 809
Weiser, Artur, 7
Welch, Adam C., 10, 11, 13, 22, 426, 434, 725, 737, 759, 798, 853
Wellhausen, Julius, 6, 8, 12, 13, 18, 27, 28, 258, 483, 484, 487, 499, 505, 507, 508, 514, 566, 927
Wells, Bruce, 592, 601, 603
Wenham, Gordon J., 617, 628, 636, 660
Wernberg-Møller, P., 809
Westbrook, Raymond, 282, 288, 291, 292, 634, 635, 636, 637, 672, 673, 674, 706, 708, 709, 710, 778
Westcott, B. F., 950
Westhuizen, J. P. van der, 885
Wette, Wilhelm M. L. de, xx, 6, 8, 11, 260, 852, 853
Wevers, John W., 3, 173, 174, 180, 210, 239, 260, 314, 362, 368, 396, 433, 435, 436, 438, 456, 492, 530, 546, 549, 552, 557, 558, 559, 561, 567, 571, 594, 595, 647, 673, 692, 699, 710, 724, 726, 727, 730, 731, 734, 762, 763, 768, 769, 775, 790, 791, 799, 818, 829, 873, 878, 879, 885, 887, 892, 893, 894, 897, 899, 909, 923, 931, 933
Whitehead, David, 646
Weiner, Harold M., 261
Wilcox, Max, 609
Wilkinson, John, 685
Wilkinson, John Gardner, 315, 699, 700, 701, 740
Wilson, Charles W., 412, 746
Wilson, Ian, 730
Wilton, Edward, 385, 912
Winkler, A. J., 622
Wiseman, D. J., 21, 311, 376, 452, 453, 454, 592, 594, 602, 655, 766, 767, 768, 770, 772, 773, 776, 778, 779, 784, 791, 792
Wittstruck, Thorne, 3, 893, 946
Wolff, Hans Walter, 19
Woolley, C. Leonard, 160, 912
Wright, David P., 593
Wright, G. Ernest, 7, 8, 9, 11, 19, 160, 168, 179, 181, 208, 220, 231, 240, 253, 260, 300, 310, 311, 332, 334, 336, 337, 338, 371, 385, 391, 422, 431, 434, 464, 481, 483, 489, 499, 514, 533, 534, 548, 549, 562, 564, 594, 605, 658, 725, 730, 732, 744, 756, 760, 762, 800, 802, 817, 828, 833, 838, 853, 854, 855, 858, 872, 873, 877, 881, 893, 894, 903, 905, 917, 924, 926
Wright, Jacob L., 588, 589

Yadin, Yigael, 2, 4, 5, 173, 214, 314, 315, 322, 424, 431, 435, 437, 438, 443, 450, 452, 459, 463, 476, 487, 494, 499, 504, 505, 511, 512, 516, 520, 526, 527, 528, 532, 538, 541, 544, 545, 548, 555, 573, 574, 580, 582, 585, 588, 595, 599, 609, 610, 619, 621, 624, 631, 639, 667, 676, 702, 723, 756
Yamauchi, Edwin M., 487, 665, 657, 658, 659
Yaron, Reuven, 28, 276, 291, 531, 575, 602, 603, 619, 635, 636, 638, 665, 670, 671, 673, 674, 677, 678, 681, 682, 694, 700, 712
Younker, Randall W., 200
Yardeni, Ada, 676, 678

Zakovitch, Yair, 674
Zertal, Adam, 318, 741
Zevit, Ziony, 593
Zimmerli, Walther, 277
Zipor, Moshe, 360
Zohary, Michael, 384
Zunz, Leopold, 240

Scripture Index

OLD TESTAMENT		3:14	891	7:11	765
		3:17	181	7:17	366
Genesis		4:2	240	7:21	475
1–2	617	4:2-4	498	7:23	400
1	472, 617	4:4	498	8:2	765
1:2	351, 880, 881, 930	4:8	570	8:7	472
1:5	652	4:8-16	289	8:9	795
1:7	765	4:10	593	8:20	467
1:11	872	4:10-12	570	8:20-21	927
1:14	833	4:11	400	8:21	842
1:14-19	244	4:15	497	8:22	404
1:20	475	4:22	353	9:1	68
1:21	896	4:23-24	575	9:4	435, 437
1:22	69	4:24	865, 896	9:5	559
1:27	280, 677	4:26	886, 920	9:5-6	568
1:28	69, 727	5:2	69, 677	9:6	289
2–3	296	6–9	368, 892	9:9	355
2	170, 617	6:1-4	178	9:11	355
2:2-3	287	6:2	878	9:26-27	934
2:3	68	6:3	829	10–11	877
2:5	785	6:5	842	10	878
2:7	240	6:5-7	892	10:14	203
2:9	182	6:7	892	10:15	329
2:14	410	6:9	553	10:15-16	330
2:15	785	6:11	573	10:15-18	331
2:24	237	6:12-13	301	10:16	330, 332
3:1-7	182	6:18	355	10:17	331
3:6	274, 296	7:1	295	10:19	168
3:7	296	7:2	467	10:32	877
3:8-13	60	7:4	366, 400, 892	11:1-9	877
3:8-24	653	7:8	467	11:4	178

Scripture Index

11:8-9	877	15:19-21	328, 805	21:10	602
11:26-32	195	15:20	201	21:14	883
11:27-32	648	15:21	206	21:17	71, 240
12:1	171	16:5	573	22	607
12:1-3	69, 336	16:6	655	22:1	321, 349
12:2	62, 170, 172	17:1	553	22:2	423
12:2-3	490	17:1-7	252, 807	22:12	240, 349
12:6	412	17:1-14	170	22:15-18	69
12:6-8	423	17:2-7	170	22:16	901
12:7	62, 65, 170	17:7	355	22:17	172, 369, 397, 490
12:17	324, 533, 684	17:8	170, 171	22:17-18	69
13–14	945	17:9-14	818	22:17a	170
13:7	331	17:10	647	22:17b	170
13:10	403	17:16	172, 490	22:18	558
13:10-11	944	17:19	355	22:24	219
13:12	812	18–19	457, 812, 892, 895	23	329
13:14	227	18:1	412	23:4	329
13:14-15	62, 65, 170, 227	18:7	437, 465, 792	24:3	334
13:16	62, 170, 794	18:7-8	476	24:10	648, 726
13:17	62, 65, 170	18:8	882	24:27	338
13:18	412	18:17-21	892	24:35	190
14:1-12	812	18:18	69, 490	24:53	616
14:2	812, 945	18:19	521	25:5-6	603
14:3	220	18:20-23	653	25:8	912
14:5	162, 195, 202, 202	18:23	458	25:10	875
14:6	183, 196	18:23-24	810	25:13-16	202
14:7	207, 715, 717	18:25	873	25:18	911
14:8	812, 945	18:27	162	25:20	726
14:13	412, 495	18:33	228	25:24-30	649
14:17-20	382, 876	19:3	507	25:25	189, 919
14:18-20	69	19:15	810, 889	25:28	602
14:19	875	19:17	810, 889, 944	25:29-30	717
14:19-20	876	19:20-23	812, 945	25:29-34	602
14:20	482, 729	19:24-25	895	26:3	582
14:22	875	19:24-26	811	26:3-4	65, 170
15:1	71, 240, 938	19:25	944	26:3-5	69
15:2	226	19:28-29	944	26:4	17, 369, 397, 794
15:5	62, 170, 172, 369, 397, 794	19:29	812	26:5	69, 399, 558
		19:29-30	945	26:12	190
15:8	226	19:36-37	647	26:22	934
15:9	593	19:37	195	26:24	69, 170
15:13-14	170	20	291, 636, 717	26:28	171, 807
15:15-21	170	20:3	636	26:33-34	329
15:16	206, 330, 363, 896	20:6	292, 635	26:34-35	334
15:17-21	267	20:7	371	27	602
15:18	167, 169, 170, 410, 569	20:9	291	27:1	946
		20:11	717	27:3	616
15:18-21	62, 65	21:8-10	602	27:7	919

Scripture Index

27:12	717	31:30-35	497	36:27	384
27:28	938	31:34-35	279	36:30	183
27:29	280, 454	31:50	604	36:43	190
27:34	727	32	190	37:3	602
27:40	788	32:4 (3)	184	37:21	569
27:43-45	726	32:8 (7)	190	37:21-22	712
27:46	329, 334	32:12 (11)	712	37:25	210, 931
28-35	726	32:23-31 (22-30)	211	38	658, 705, 709
28:2	648	32:26 (25)	712	38:2	706
28:3	646, 923	32:31 (30)	269	38:8	707, 709
28:3-4	69	32:32 (31)	921	38:8-9	702
28:5	726	32:33 (32)	712	38:8-11	706
28:5-7	648	33:2	602	38:10	710
28:6-9	334	33:4-11	649	38:11-26	707
28:13	65	33:10	269	38:13-18	290
28:13-14	69, 170	33:14-16	184	38:14	625
28:14	794	33:17	516	38:15	657
28:15	582	34:2	331, 349, 600	38:16-17	660
28:18-22	424	34:5	674	38:21-22	657
28:20-22	430, 482, 666	34:7	634	38:24	607, 631
28:22	482, 729	34:8	337, 598	39:1	644
29-31	726	34:9	335	39:6b-20	292
29:18	494	34:12	585	39:6b-23	297
29:21	637	34:13	674	39:9	292, 635
29:30	494	34:14	436	39:14	495
29:30-31	601	34:15	647	39:17	495
29:34	926	34:25-26	928	39:21	173
29:35	925	34:25-27	592	40:15	495
30:2	339	34:27	674	40:19	609, 610, 611, 773
30:4-6	936	34:28	761	40:22	609
30:7-8	936	34:30	249, 331, 727	41:1-36	406
30:10-11	934	35:2	295, 839	41:6	771
30:12-13	937	35:4	412, 839	41:8	44
30:13	937	35:6-7	430	41:13	609
30:17-18	933	35:12	65, 227	41:23	771
30:19-20	932	35:14-15	424	41:27	771
30:22-24	930, 932	35:17-19	929	41:34	483
30:24	172	35:22	640, 745, 924	41:47-57	484
30:27	551	35:23	924, 925	41:50-52	597
30:37	947	35:29	912	41:57	377
31:13	424	36:1	189	42:7	893
31:17-54	495	36:8	189	42:35	485
31:17-55	726	36:8-9	183	43:1-14	929
31:19	279, 293, 497	36:9	160	43:3	574
31:20	726	36:12	715	43:11	882
31:24	726	36:19	189	44:5	551
31:25	761	36:20-21	183	44:6	829
31:29	781	36:20-30	196	44:9	529

Scripture Index

44:10	529	1:5	878	6:2	277
44:14	694	1:5-7	397	6:2-3	172
44:15	551	1:7-20	727	6:2-9	920
44:17	529	1:11	173, 349	6:4	355
44:20	929	1:11-12	727	6:6	254, 277
45:7	892	1:11-14	508	6:6-7	742
45:18	307	1:14	727	6:7	241, 267, 802, 807
46:1-7	726, 727	2:5	211	6:8	277, 924
46:27	397, 727	2:9	692	6:9	727
47:6	173	2:16-22	597	6:29	277
47:29	837	2:17	778	7–12	241, 324
47:30	838	2:23	727	7:1	450
48:4	646, 923	2:24-25	727	7:2	559
48:6	708	3:1	159, 920	7:3	208, 451, 787, 818
48:13-20	602, 932	3:1-6	252	7:3-5	254
48:22	902	3:1-14	920	7:5	802
49	917	3:2	241	7:8-11	451
49:1	251, 919	3:2-6	931	7:9	787
49:3	604	3:4-6	253	7:9-10	253, 451, 896
49:3-4	602, 640, 924	3:7	508	7:11	44, 551
49:4	745	3:7-9	727	7:12	896
49:5-7	917, 925, 927, 928	3:8	177, 307, 328, 712, 727, 728, 882	7:20-22	451
49:8-12	917, 925			8:1-3 (5-7)	451
49:9	810, 930, 935, 936	3:12	582, 787	8:15 (19)	366, 452
49:11	883, 937	3:13	172	8:16 (20)	837
49:13	933, 934	3:14	185, 794	8:18 (22)	802
49:14	810, 930, 933	3:15	172	9:1-10	774
49:17	936	3:15-16	727	9:3	198, 769
49:19	935	3:16	172	9:5	510
49:20	937	3:17	307, 508, 882	9:12	208, 818
49:21	936	3:18	432, 437	9:13	837
49:22-26	929	3:21-22	495	9:21	910
49:22-27	929	4:1-9	254	9:31	505
49:25	810, 930	4:2-9	253, 451	10:1	818
49:26	931	4:5	172	10:1-2	254, 451
49:26b	931	4:8-9	787	10:3-20	784
49:27	929	4:14	384	10:14-19	785
49:28	919	4:17	787	10:20	208
49:29	919	4:21	208, 787, 818	10:21	777
49:29-30	329	4:21-25	254	10:22	777
50:2-3	366	4:22	875	10:25	429, 432
50:13	329	4:22-23	463	10:27	208
50:23	219, 280	4:27	920	11:1	533
50:24	171	4:28-30	787	11:2-3	495
50:26	829	4:30	253, 451	11:8	401
		4:31	508, 727	11:9-10	787
Exodus		5:3	771	11:10	254, 818
1	238	5:16-19	174	12:1-20	505

Scripture Index

12:2	277, 505	13:12	498	17:3	471
12:3-5	506	13:12-13	430	17:4-6	373
12:4	746	13:13	498, 593	17:6	159
12:5	553	13:14	239, 277, 324, 727	17:7	253, 321, 926
12:7	315, 507	13:14-15	498	17:8-15	715, 716
12:8	506, 508	13:14-16	324	17:8-16	180, 716
12:8-10	509	13:16	313	17:14	341, 369, 717, 840, 892
12:9	510	13:21	180		
12:10	509	13:21-22	179	17:16	716
12:11	489, 508	14	400, 582	18	171
12:11-13	505	14:4	802	18:1	920
12:12	506	14:8	802	18:4	281
12:13	254, 787	14:13	540, 796	18:5	920
12:14	489	14:13-14	179, 223	18:9-10	712
12:15	507	14:14	179	18:10-12	920
12:16	509, 511	14:19	179	18:12	429
12:18	505	14:21	891	18:13-26	172, 520, 533
12:19	509	14:24	198, 341	18:13-27	171
12:20	507	14:25	179, 895	18:15-16	175
12:21-27	315, 505	15	862, 868	18:18	172
12:21-28	506, 507, 510	15:1-10	582	18:19	175, 534
12:21-39	505	15:1-12	254, 727	18:20	235, 302
12:22	315	15:1-18	400	18:21	46, 173
12:23	767	15:3	392, 860, 873	18:21-22	520
12:26	324	15:5	401	18:22	534
12:26-27	239, 324	15:8	241	18:25-26	173
12:30-31	506	15:11	225, 397, 900, 937	18:26	534
12:31	743	15:14	795	19:1-2	514
12:33-39	507, 508	15:14-16	207	19:3	423
12:34	762	15:15	190	19:3-6	742
12:35-36	495	15:16	796, 875	19:4	180, 471, 801, 881
12:38	174	15:16cd	862	19:4-6	464
12:42	489, 506	15:18	924	19:5	336
12:43-49	396, 505	15:25	253	19:5-6	336, 405, 733, 764
12:46	507, 509	15:26	340, 794, 900	19:6	63
13:1-10	314	16	349	19:8	733
13:1-16	499	16:3	403	19:9	838
13:2	430, 498	16:4	253, 321, 349	19:11	252
13:3	277, 507	16:10	427, 838	19:16-19	300
13:3-10	505	16:12	802	19:16-25	268, 269
13:3-16	26	16:13	469	19:17	837
13:5	171, 307	16:14-15	349	19:17-18	240
13:6	511	16:22-30	285	19:18-20	252
13:7	189, 507	16:34	660	20	271, 416
13:8	239	16:35	349	20:1	73, 833
13:9	313, 727	17:1	926	20:1-17	26
13:11	171	17:1-7	321, 354, 373, 912, 926	20:1–24:8	175
13:11-16	314			20:2	276, 277

972

Reference	Pages
20:2-6	271
20:2-17	5, 241, 267, 271, 276
20:3	277, 278, 603
20:4	241
20:4-5	245
20:4-6	279, 746, 847
20:5	338, 694
20:5-6	280, 338
20:6	282, 310
20:7	282, 794
20:8	284, 348
20:9	785
20:10	286, 700
20:10-11	511
20:11	68, 287
20:12	249, 289, 748
20:13	289, 749
20:13-15	273
20:14	290
20:15	293
20:16	293
20:17	295, 296, 778
20:18	300
20:18-19	61, 253, 269
20:18-20	268, 269
20:18-22	558
20:19	301
20:20	240, 253, 302, 321
20:20-23	328
20:22	60, 255, 428
20:23	26, 279
20:24	426, 429, 432, 545
20:25	741
21–23	46, 267, 416, 487
21	494, 495, 496
21:1	28, 235, 262, 278, 422, 927
21:1-11	26, 49
21:2-6	483, 498
21:2-11	494, 495, 663
21:4	50
21:6	175, 497, 534
21:7	50, 494
21:7-11	494
21:8	599
21:12	289, 749
21:12-14	79, 289, 533, 564, 567
21:12-17	747
21:13-14	566
21:15	57, 287, 605, 608, 748
21:16	293, 529
21:17	57, 287, 605, 748
21:18-27	26, 534
21:20	699
21:21	50
21:22	523, 569, 895
21:22-25	711
21:23	569
21:23-24	576
21:23-25	574, 713
21:28–22:14 (15)	26
21:30-31	569
21:33-34	619
21:37–22:12 (22:1-13)	293
22:1 (2)	529
22:1-2 (2-3)	534
22:3 (4)	529
22:4 (5)	667
22:5 (6)	567
22:6 (7)	529
22:6-9 (7-10)	535
22:6-14 (7-15)	533
22:7 (8)	529, 574, 615
22:7-8 (8-9)	534
22:8 (9)	698
22:9-10 (10-11)	282, 594
22:15 (16)	638
22:15-16 (16-17)	26, 82, 627, 638
22:16 (17)	639
22:17 (18)	551
22:17-19 (18-20)	747
22:18 (19)	749
22:19 (20)	453, 529
22:20 (21)	286, 396, 656, 695
22:20-21 (21-22)	393
22:20-23 (21-24)	748
22:21-22 (22-23)	491
22:22 (23)	692
22:22-23 (23-24)	393
22:24 (25)	49, 488, 663
22:24-26 (25-27)	26
22:25-26 (26-27)	49, 492, 624, 687
22:26 (27)	688, 692
22:28 (29)	483
22:28b-29 (29b-30)	498
22:29 (30)	286, 430, 476, 499
22:30 (31)	476
23:1	293, 531, 573
23:1-3	523
23:2-3	174, 522
23:3	748
23:4	55
23:4-5	26, 614
23:6	523, 695, 748
23:6-8	174, 522, 523
23:6-9	393
23:7	698
23:8	26, 46, 393, 524
23:9	286, 396, 695
23:10-11	483, 487
23:11	487
23:12	284, 285
23:13	425
23:14-18	504
23:14-19	26
23:15	833
23:15b	517
23:16	484, 505, 512, 515, 723, 724
23:17	431, 507, 514, 517
23:18	507, 509
23:19	724
23:19b	26, 476
23:20	255
23:20-24	439
23:20-33	328, 588, 756, 760
23:22	761, 763
23:23	255, 329
23:23-31	372
23:24	280, 319, 335, 423, 424, 439, 527
23:25	319, 490, 760
23:25-26	339
23:26	339, 762
23:27	198, 341, 411, 763

Scripture Index

Reference	Pages	Reference	Pages	Reference	Pages
23:27-30	322	28:38	438	32:20	371, 373
23:28	340	28:40	735	32:21	838
23:29-30	171, 341, 362	29:10-11	595	32:21-24	371
23:31	167, 169, 569	29:22	545	32:24	367
23:31-33	67	29:27-28	429	32:25-29	385, 927
23:32	334	29:42	837	32:30	370
23:33	334, 340, 588	29:43	60, 427	32:30-31	382
24:3	733	29:44-46	428	32:30-34	368, 370, 386
24:3-8	300, 741, 833	29:46	802	32:31	371
24:3-11	806	30:14	182	32:34	386
24:4	240, 424, 527, 740	30:36	837	33:1	167, 171, 945
24:5	432	31:4	384	33:1-15	255
24:7	301, 733	31:7	383	33:1-17	368, 386
24:12	242	31:11	376	33:3	307, 321, 364, 368
24:12-18	359	31:14-15	285, 511	33:5	321, 364, 368
24:13	920	31:18	241, 242, 262, 365, 384, 833	33:6	159
24:14	525			33:7-11	837
24:16-17	240, 301	31:18–34:28	359	33:9	838
24:17	245	31:18b	366, 383	33:11	61, 269, 837, 948
24:18	376	32–33	365	33:12-20	227
24:18b	365	32	177, 242, 588	33:14	255, 432
25:2-3	429	32:2	367	33:18-23	61, 301, 838
25:4-5	883	32:2-5	371	33:19	185
25:8-9	428	32:4	367, 371, 383	33:19-23	794
25:10-12	833	32:7	367, 368	33:20-23	253, 269, 948
25:10-22	383	32:7-8	273, 280, 847	34:1-4	382
25:11	383	32:7-14	38, 367, 370, 374	34:4	242
25:11-18	384	32:8	360	34:5	837, 838
25:16	180, 846	32:9	364, 365, 838	34:5-7	873
25:18-22	242	32:9-10	892	34:6	251, 277, 281, 818, 896
25:22	262	32:9-14	370, 561		
25:23	383	32:10	368, 371	34:6-7	62, 63, 276, 280, 338, 810
25:28	383	32:10-30	371		
26:1	883	32:11	255, 377, 378	34:7	61, 338, 694
26:7-8	157	32:11-13	369, 377	34:9	364
26:26	383	32:11-14	368, 389, 370, 374	34:10-16	4, 328
26:32	383	32:11b	376	34:10-26	26
26:33	390	32:12	58, 321, 377, 812, 893	34:11-13	67
26:33-34	262			34:11-16	334, 423, 588
26:37	383	32:12b-13	368	34:11-28	175
27:1	383	32:13	171, 172, 252, 376, 397	34:12	365, 439
27:17	337			34:12-18	365
28:3	947	32:14	368, 369, 371, 378	34:13	250, 335, 424, 526, 527
28:6	624	32:15-29	928		
28:15	624	32:16	366, 382, 383, 384, 833	34:14	245
28:29-30	535			34:14-16	279
28:30	926	32:19	370	34:15-16	839
28:33-34	352	32:19-20	370	34:17	279

Scripture Index

34:17-26	747	5:20-26 (6:1-7)	615	17:11	437
34:18	504, 505, 506, 833	5:21 (6:2)	692	17:15-16	476
34:19	498	5:21-26 (6:2-7)	284	17:26	27
34:19-20	430	5:22 (6:3)	282	18–19	277
34:20	498, 593	6	927	18:5	235
34:20b	517	7:1-10	544	18:6-18	629, 639
34:21	285, 785	7:18	928	18:6-19	640
34:22	429, 512, 513, 515, 723, 724	7:19-21	435	18:7	639
		7:26-27	435	18:7-18	747
34:22-25	504	7:32-33	545	18:8	82, 627, 639, 640, 748
34:23	507, 514, 517	8:8	926		
34:23-24	517	8:16	707	18:9	454, 749
34:24	436, 569, 934	9:3	593	18:17	749
34:25	507, 509	9:22	386	18:20	291, 635, 674
34:26	476, 724	11–15	435	18:21	282, 439, 549
34:28	241, 271, 365, 366, 833, 935	11	463, 469	18:22	617, 660
		11:1-23	463	18:23	749
34:28b	384	11:2-3	464	18:24-28	355
35:2	285	11:3	466	18:24-30	903
35:5-9	429	11:4-6	467	19:2	336
35:21-29	430	11:7-8	468	19:3	287
36:3-7	429, 430	11:8	467	19:4	279
36:14	883	11:9-12	469	19:5-6	928
37:1-9	383, 833	11:11	342	19:7	928
37:2	383	11:13	342	19:9-10	393, 696
37:2-7	384	11:13-19	470	19:11	291
38:17	337	11:14	471, 472	19:12	574
38:26	713	11:16	473	19:13	610, 611, 692, 777
38:28	337	11:20-23	475	19:14	748
39:29	624	11:21-22	475	19:15	393, 521, 523
40:34-38	838	11:22	785	19:18	70, 275, 294, 896
		11:29	475	19:19	622, 624
Leviticus		11:29-30	475	19:23-25	584, 623, 780
1	429	11:43	342	19:26	435, 508, 550, 551
1:3	527	13–14	534, 685	19:27-28	464
1:4	928	13:2	340, 684	19:28	644
1:5-8	434	13:3	684	19:31	552, 553
1:5–9:2	535	13:9	684	19:32	287
1:9	544	13:18	774	19:33-34	393, 656
1:10	527, 647	13:18-23	774	19:34	396, 695
2:3	544	13:49	616	19:35	523
2:14	505	15:16	652	19:35-36	715
3	545	15:16-17	652	20:2-5	439, 549
3:5	927	15:18	652	20:6	552, 553
3:17	429, 435	16:10	594	20:9	57, 287, 605, 748
3:21	256	16:22	594	20:10	291, 635
5:7	469	17–26	267, 336	20:11	640
5:13	681	17:10-14	435	20:13	617, 636, 660, 885

Scripture Index

20:15-16	749	23:39-43	515, 516	26:18	773		
20:17	749	23:40	431	26:19	406, 772		
20:21	707	23:43	514	26:21	773, 889		
20:24b-26	464	24:8-9	284	26:22	891		
20:25	342	24:10-17	274, 283	26:24	773		
20:26	464	24:14	456, 530	26:25	767, 770, 897		
20:27	552, 553	24:15-16	794	26:28	773		
21	647	24:17	289, 749	26:29	792		
21:1	468	24:17-21	569	26:30	250, 808		
21:5	464, 644	24:18-20	574	26:33	795		
21:7	670	24:19-20	534	26:40-45	250		
21:14	670	24:23	283	26:41	819		
21:16-23	464	25	487	26:44-45	277		
21:16-24	647	25:1-7	487	26:46	235		
21:20	644, 775	25:2	489	27:4-5	639		
22:4-6	731	25:2-7	483	27:21	209		
22:8	476	25:9-10	488	27:26	498		
22:9	780	25:10	497	27:27	498		
22:12	707	25:20-21	445, 492	27:28-29	209		
22:13	670, 707	25:20-22	484	27:30	731		
22:17-19	928	25:21	763	27:30-32	729		
22:17-24	430	25:22	248	27:30-33	481, 482, 484		
22:17-25	500, 527, 647	25:25	568	27:31	484		
22:20	928	25:25-33	337	27:32	429, 481		
22:21	928	25:31	202	27:34	799		
22:22	775	25:32-34	386				
22:24	644	25:35-37	488, 663	**Numbers**			
22:27	476, 499	25:39-40	497	1:1	837		
22:27-28	286	25:39-46	493, 494, 663	1:3	182		
22:28	476, 619	25:47	786	1:32-35	932		
23–25	928	25:47-55	276, 495, 568	2:1	188		
23:5	505	25:55	27	2:17	837		
23:5-6	505, 508	26	756	3–4	19, 434		
23:5-8	505	26:1	279, 526, 527	3:16	945		
23:7-8	511	26:1-2	277	3:31	385, 833		
23:9-14	505	26:3	763	3:39	945		
23:10	724	26:3-45	760	4:15	833		
23:10-11	512	26:4	765	4:37	945		
23:15-16	512	26:7-8	763	4:41	945		
23:15-20	513	26:8	894	5:1-4	652		
23:16-21	513	26:9	355	5:3	653		
23:17	512, 723, 724	26:10	248	5:9	429		
23:21	512, 513	26:12	241, 267, 807	5:9-10	438		
23:22	696	26:13	277, 788	5:11-31	291, 535, 636		
23:32	284	26:15	839	5:13-14	674		
23:34	515	26:16	770, 781, 784	5:19-22	594		
23:36	516	26:16b	779	5:20	674		
23:39	515, 516	26:17	773	5:22	747		

976

Scripture Index

6:3	947	13–14	160	14:30	182
6:5	902	13:1-2	176	14:31	182
6:22-27	68	13:3	158	14:37	198
6:23	385	13:6	181	14:39	829
6:24-26	386, 746, 808	13:8	909	14:39-40	182
6:27	385	13:14-16	176	14:42-44	183
7:72	157	13:16	909	14:43-45	716
8	18, 434	13:17	168	14:44	183, 383
8:19	438	13:21	168	14:45	161, 168, 183
9:1-5	506	13:22	178	15:19-21	723
9:1-14	505	13:22-24	177	15:32-36	274, 285
9:5	505	13:23	177, 351	15:35-36	456
9:11	508	13:25-33	177	15:36	530
9:12	509	13:26	158, 160	15:37-41	624
10:10	431	13:27	177, 882	15:38	624
10:12	158	13:28	178, 361, 489	16–18	434
10:33	180, 373, 920	13:29	168, 211, 330, 332, 412, 715	16–17	19
10:33-36	383			16	400
10:35-36	60, 427	13:31-33	178	16:1-3	646
11	359	13:33	178	16:1-4	646
11:1-3	373	14	365	16:1-10	927
11:2	368, 373	14:1-3	177	16:2	401
11:4-9	349	14:1-10	177	16:13	403
11:4-34	373	14:1-24	369	16:15	780
11:5	301	14:3	182	16:19	60, 427
11:11	172	14:9	840	16:20-48	368
11:11-18	373	14:10	60, 427	16:22	694
11:12	180	14:11	180, 838	16:25-35	889
11:14	172	14:11-12	892	16:31-33	400
11:14-17	171	14:11-20	180	16:32	295
11:16	533, 837	14:11-24	368	16:33	400
11:16-17	172, 837	14:12	198, 369, 769	17:5 (16:40)	927
11:16-30	46	14:13-16	377, 812	17:7 (16:42)	838
11:17	172	14:13-19	58, 893	17:13-15 (16:48-50)	198
11:22	879	14:18	280, 338	18:6-7	927
11:24-25	533	14:20-23	241	18:8	438
11:25	300, 838	14:20-35	801	18:9-10	544
11:26-27	837	14:21	901	18:12	883
11:31-32	469	14:21-23	181	18:12-13	430, 513, 545, 723, 724
12:1	597	14:21-24	180		
12:4	837	14:22	181, 253, 802	18:15	498
12:5	837, 838	14:23	181	18:15-16	498
12:6-8	557	14:24	181	18:15-18	498
12:7-8	945	14:25	167, 182, 188	18:17-19	499
12:8	269, 948	14:26-38	180	18:18	545
12:9-15	685	14:28	901	18:20	386, 544
12:14	56, 711	14:29	182, 197	18:21	484
12:16	159, 176	14:29-35	399	18:21-24	386

977

Scripture Index

18:21-26	482	21:22	208	25:8-9	198
18:21-32	481, 730	21:23	209	25:12-13	171
19	435	21:23-24	209	25:13	599
19:1-10	594	21:24	200, 206, 209, 220	25:18-19 (26:1)	198
19:2	593			26:3	943
19:11-16	731	21:25a	209	26:11	694
19:16	592	21:26	162, 195, 197, 206	26:29	220
19:22	731	21:28	195	26:29-37	932
20–21	189	21:31-35	161	26:63	943
20	188	21:32	201	27	9
20:1	160, 926	21:33	212	27:8	707
20:1-4	646	21:34	213	27:8-11	707
20:1-13	321, 354, 373, 912, 926	21:35	209, 213	27:12	227, 911
		22–24	68, 195, 648	27:12-14	181, 911
20:2-13	181, 188, 926	22	648	27:12-23	842
20:6	427	22:1	943	27:13	912
20:6-11	373	22:5	410, 648	27:14	160, 912, 926
20:12	912, 926, 945	22:5-6	557	27:17	762, 829
20:13	160, 321	22:7	550	27:18	947
20:14	158, 160	22:26	208	27:18-20	947
20:14-21	188, 189, 190, 192, 648	22:36	195, 205	27:18-23	228, 838
		23–24	764, 895	27:21	762, 829
20:15	726, 727	23:3	837	27:23	947
20:16	160, 184, 255, 727, 728	23:9	938	28:6	432
		23:11	648	28:9-10	284
20:17	208	23:13-14	944	28:16	505
20:18-20	189	23:14	882	28:16-17	505, 508
20:19-21	208	23:15	837	28:16-25	505
20:22-28	912	23:19-24	336	28:18	511
20:22-29	188, 384	23:21	539, 924	28:25	511
20:24	912	23:22	932	28:26	512, 513
20:26	912	23:23	551, 893	28:26-31	513
20:29	947	23:24	935	29	516
21	188, 209	23:28	943	29:12	516
21:1-3	184, 188	24:1	551	29:12-34	515
21:2	666	24:9	935	29:12-39	515
21:4	192	24:10	648	29:20	157
21:4-9	188	24:14	251	29:35	516
21:5	349	24:16	876	30	430
21:6-9	354, 891	24:18	184	30:3 (2)	666
21:8-9	242	24:20	716	30:3-17 (2-16)	666
21:9	353	24:21	593	30:10 (9)	670
21:10-15	195	25	195, 884	30:13 (12)	667
21:12	197	25:1-3	588, 808	31	385
21:13	205, 263	25:1-5	640	31:2	912
21:14-15	195	25:1-9	228, 236	31:3	897
21:21-23	208	25:1-13	927	31:6	582
21:21-35	161, 881	25:7-8	928	31:12	943

978

Scripture Index

31:14	585	35:9-34	533, 564	1:3-5	156
31:16	198	35:11	289, 566	1:4	161, 201, 213, 215, 262
31:48	585	35:19-21	570	1:5	8, 73, 156, 157, 162, 235, 238, 259, 262, 325, 542, 738, 799, 821, 911
32	217, 222, 935	35:22-23	567		
32:1	201, 223, 931	35:22-28	568		
32:1-5	217	35:23	567		
32:3	201, 943	35:25	712		
32:5	935	35:25-26	289	1:6	165, 166, 167, 176, 189, 224, 227, 228
32:11-12	166, 180, 181	35:26-27	568		
32:12	181	35:28	568	1:6-7	74, 879, 919
32:13	155, 181	35:30	289, 531, 573	1:6-8	165, 166
32:28-32	222, 935	35:30-34	289	1:6-46	163-87, 224
32:33-37	207	35:31	575-76	1:6–3:29	155, 165, 231
32:33-42	210, 218	35:31-32	568	1:6–4:40	163-258, 165, 258, 261
32:34	210	35:33	568, 570, 593, 903		
32:37	195	36:13	799, 943	1:7	167, 176, 177, 182, 188, 206, 213, 214, 226, 331, 410, 412, 944, 950
32:38	935, 943				
32:39	219	**Deuteronomy**			
32:39-40	220	1–34	25		
32:39-41	218	1–30	829	1:7-8	175, 177, 569
33	384	1–28	13, 16, 18, 23, 24, 25, 38, 73, 86, 170, 225, 261, 447, 504, 799, 811	1:8	30, 62, 165, 169, 170, 171, 176, 181, 206, 209, 236, 237, 238, 249, 255, 267, 307, 318, 322, 329, 337, 339, 347, 355, 363, 376, 403, 411, 412, 539, 666, 724, 733, 740, 765, 817, 825, 826, 832, 841, 842, 945
33:1-49	167				
33:3	506				
33:16	373				
33:17-18	159	1–4	8, 9, 21, 24, 25, 74, 231, 801		
33:17-20	159				
33:31	384	1–3 (4)	8, 24		
33:32-33	385	1–3	9, 231		
33:32-35	385	1	74, 156, 162, 345, 879		
33:33-39	188				
33:36	160	1:1	23, 43, 73, 156, 157, 158, 159, 182, 220, 223, 259, 262, 263, 266, 412, 738, 829, 844, 920, 942		
33:38	385, 912, 945				
33:38-39	371, 384				
33:40	188			1:9	166, 171, 172, 176, 209, 214, 222, 225, 258
33:41-43	385				
33:41-44	195	1:1-2	156	1:9-18	165, 166, 171, 520
33:42-43	353	1:1-5	8, 20, 24, 25, 26, 73, 74, 155-63, 232, 260, 261, 264, 799	1:10	167, 172, 361, 369, 397, 496, 734, 794
33:47-48	911				
33:48-50	943			1:10-11	69, 190, 307, 459
33:50-52	423			1:11	68, 167, 170, 172, 176, 191, 236, 423, 727, 740
34:3	220	1:1-4:40	8		
34:4	160, 176, 184, 202	1:1-4:49	155		
34:11	220	1:1–28:69 (29:1)	163	1:12	172
34:12	220	1:2	156, 157, 158, 159, 161, 176, 182, 183, 184, 188, 197, 373, 913	1:13	46, 172, 539, 847
35	258			1:13-17	46
35:1	943			1:13-18	533
35:1-8	386, 546			1:14	173, 177
35:6	566, 569	1:3	156, 157, 161, 559, 738, 911	1:15	173, 300, 521, 583, 585, 806

979

Scripture Index

1:15-16	520		583, 700, 710, 780, 801, 832, 948	2–3	74, 75, 162, 384, 386, 881, 938
1:16	31, 35, 166, 171, 173, 174, 286, 521, 592, 614, 698, 764, 806	1:30-31	801	2:1	156, 165, 167, 176, 183, 184, 185, 188, 213
		1:30-33	30, 66, 73		
		1:31	167, 176, 180, 191, 365, 728, 875, 881, 950	2:1-4	184
1:16-17	36, 63, 373			2:1-8a	187-94
1:17	63, 174, 250, 393, 523, 534, 893			2:1–3:11	187
		1:32	167	2:1–3:21	6
1:18	165, 166, 171, 175, 685	1:32-33	180	2:2	183, 188
		1:33	165, 176, 179	2:3	167, 188, 213
1:19	159, 160, 167, 175, 176, 177, 180, 184, 354, 686, 716, 797, 880	1:34	365	2:4	160, 183, 189, 200, 202, 208, 361, 384, 650
		1:34-36	62, 166, 180, 226, 244, 322		
				2:5	181, 184, 190, 195, 196, 202, 410, 950
		1:34-39	64		
1:19-20	167	1:34-40	801	2:6	189, 190
1:19-32	373	1:35	65, 166, 167, 170, 171, 181, 259, 350	2:7	53, 68, 69, 157, 161, 176, 185, 188, 191, 250, 339, 349, 431, 485, 486, 489, 492, 516, 582, 665, 696, 763, 765, 747, 769, 820, 847, 928
1:19-46	160				
1:20	167	1:35-36	197		
1:20-21	166, 176, 213, 340, 830, 832	1:35-40	166		
		1:35-46	6		
1:20-31	166	1:36	166, 171, 177, 181, 411		
1:20-33	6				
1:21	30, 71, 167, 169, 170, 172, 176, 179, 206, 362, 581	1:37	166, 181, 227, 244, 492, 829, 912, 945		
				2:8	158, 188, 194
		1:37-40	827	2:8a	189, 191, 195
1:22	166, 176	1:38	166, 182, 223, 227, 228, 356, 489, 830, 832	2:8b	194, 213
1:23	173, 176			2:8b-15	194, 199
1:23a	165			2:9	183, 190, 195, 200, 208
1:24	177, 213	1:39	167, 170, 172, 180, 182		
1:25	30, 65, 166, 167, 176, 177, 350			2:10	178, 361, 391
		1:39-40	166	2:10-11	178, 195, 201, 361
1:26	167, 177, 846	1:40	158, 167, 176, 182, 184, 188, 206, 213	2:10-12	195, 201, 214, 215, 384, 412
1:26-27	73				
1:26-43	802	1:41	165, 167, 182	2:12	170, 178, 184, 196, 202
1:26-46	40, 365	1:41-44	68		
1:27	177, 178, 201, 213, 249, 341, 362, 365, 369, 586, 769, 789	1:41-46	716, 895	2:13	197, 206, 234, 301, 390, 728, 840, 900
		1:42	183, 188, 195, 199, 209, 213, 321, 383, 558, 653		
				2:14	62, 157, 182, 185, 188, 197
1:27-28	166, 244	1:43	183, 184, 536, 560, 846		
1:28	165, 178, 196, 201, 361, 585			2:14-15	194, 399, 806
		1:44	161, 167, 183, 189, 206, 330, 920	2:15	199, 846
1:29	71, 176, 179, 583, 830			2:16	194, 199
		1:45	184	2:16-17	199
1:29-30	341	1:46	160, 165, 166, 184, 188, 197, 225, 228, 376, 808	2:16-23	199-204
1:29-31	166, 581			2:18	172, 195, 200, 361
1:30	167, 171, 179, 206, 223, 239, 254, 324, 332, 362, 363, 370,			2:18-19	211

980

Scripture Index

2:19	190, 195, 200, 205, 210, 215, 647	2:34	171, 205, 209, 214	3:17	158, 168, 216, 217, 220, 259, 263, 922, 944
2:20-21	178, 196, 201, 215, 218	2:34-35	66, 214, 332		
		2:34-36	213		
2:20-23	74, 195, 201, 214, 215	2:34-37	205	3:18	170, 171, 214, 222, 223, 225, 685
		2:35	205, 210, 217		
2:21	178, 196, 361	2:36	205, 209, 210, 214, 217, 220, 263, 944	3:18-20	222, 935
2:21-23	201			3:18-22	221-24
2:22	170, 178, 184, 196, 202, 219, 386, 400, 734, 802, 946	2:37	200, 205, 211	3:19	217, 222, 983
		3:1	161, 212, 213, 214, 218, 262, 263, 802, 830, 883, 936	3:20	65, 157, 170, 176, 222, 226, 412, 432
				3:21	171, 180, 214, 222, 223, 225, 237, 239, 259, 401
2:23	178, 199, 202	3:1-11	212-16		
2:24	65, 161, 167, 169, 170, 176, 177, 182, 190, 195, 197, 199, 200, 204, 205, 206, 209, 210, 213, 214, 217, 220, 226, 331, 386, 586, 728, 802, 830, 925	3:1-12	262		
		3:1-14	883	3:22	71, 176, 179, 222, 223
		3:2	71, 176, 177, 183, 213, 223		
		3:2-4	66	3:23	171, 214, 222, 224, 225
		3:3	177, 209, 213		
		3:4	171, 213, 218, 219	3:23-27	829
		3:5	214	3:23-29	224-29
		3:6	66	3:23–4:49	6
2:24-37	204-12, 262	3:6-7	66, 214, 332	3:24	225, 226, 301, 324, 341, 376, 392, 400, 873, 900
2:24–3:8	583	3:7	212, 217, 883		
2:24–3:11	161	3:8	157, 167, 171, 179, 213, 214, 412		
2:24–3:17	30			3:24-28	218
2:25	66, 71, 187, 199, 207, 226, 244, 259, 262, 263, 411, 764, 795, 796	3:8-10	213	3:25	157, 167, 169, 181, 223, 226, 350, 412
		3:9	74, 195, 201, 214, 215, 263		
		3:10	210, 214, 259	3:26	167, 181, 183, 224, 226, 244, 912
2:26	586	3:11	74, 178, 195, 201, 212, 214, 215	3:27	227, 259, 911, 943, 945
2:26-27	207, 302, 536, 542, 766				
		3:12	170, 171, 201, 210, 214, 216, 217, 220	3:28	182, 227, 489, 557, 830, 832, 838, 842, 872
2:26–3:8	802	3:12-13	161, 210, 217		
2:26–3:11	65, 830	3:12-17	65, 216-21, 802, 925, 934	3:29	74, 162, 165, 224, 228, 236, 237, 262, 365, 946
2:27	205				
2:28	251	3:13	213, 215		
2:28-29	189, 208	3:13a	217, 218	4	24, 74, 231, 232, 258, 416, 802
2:29	176, 195, 197, 200, 648	3:13b	201, 218		
		3:13b-14	74, 195, 201, 214, 215, 218	4:1	30, 32, 36, 50, 53, 74, 170, 172, 197, 231, 233, 234, 235, 237, 256, 262, 266, 302, 303, 306, 322, 324, 329, 347, 350, 390, 401, 422, 525, 539, 606, 666, 749, 819, 825, 826, 910
2:30	43, 177, 205, 208, 244, 255, 324, 355, 491, 813	3:14	202, 213, 218		
		3:14-15	217, 218		
2:31	169, 170, 183, 205, 206, 209, 226, 830	3:14-17	217		
		3:15	219		
2:31-36	66	3:15-23	218		
2:32	209	3:16	200, 220		
2:33	209	3:16-17	220		
2:33–3:3	206				

981

Scripture Index

4:1-2	739	4:10-12	268	4:24	232, 233, 234, 245, 269, 280, 321, 362, 950
4:1-4	232, 234, 235	4:10-13	61, 299		
4:1-8	75, 232, 256	4:10-14	833		
4:1-24	229-46, 248, 256	4:11	234, 240, 263, 300, 369, 950	4:25	234, 242, 248, 249, 279, 579, 810, 847
4:1-40	155, 229-58				
4:2	236, 256, 284, 420, 440, 685, 950	4:12	36, 37, 237, 241, 242, 252, 253, 255, 269, 300, 366	4:25-26	232, 242, 248, 289, 303, 321, 322, 335, 361, 362, 370, 401, 404, 406, 408, 412, 425, 438, 529, 542, 619, 795, 825, 847, 910
4:3	178, 223, 320, 808, 884	4:12-13	268		
4:3-4	228, 232, 236, 396, 410, 453, 826	4:13	231, 241, 267, 271, 275, 300, 365, 366, 384, 385, 529, 799, 805		
4:4	172, 234, 237, 268, 420				
4:5	50, 170, 234, 235, 236, 237, 322, 329, 539, 559, 666	4:13-14	749	4:25-28	248
		4:14	50, 171, 235, 237, 242, 249, 302, 306, 579	4:25-31	33, 233, 248, 800
				4:25-40	246-58
4:5-6	734, 739	4:15	33, 36, 238, 241, 242, 268	4:26	53, 170, 172, 178, 249, 256, 306, 355, 769, 795, 825, 826, 835, 847, 872
4:5-8	232, 234				
4:6	45, 190, 237, 238, 267, 284, 339, 491, 514, 667, 734, 802, 834	4:15-16	233		
		4:15-18	61, 241, 244, 280		
		4:15-20	34	4:26-27	251
		4:16	234, 242, 847	4:26-28	232
4:7	233, 238, 822, 900, 938	4:16-18	33, 36, 279, 280, 425	4:27	32, 42, 231, 249, 783, 794, 795
4:8	162, 169, 172, 233, 234, 235, 237, 238, 542, 821	4:16-19	242	4:27-31	232
		4:17	579	4:28	72, 191, 249, 250, 320, 783, 795, 808
		4:17-18	242		
		4:18	351, 579	4:29	251, 312, 390, 405, 428, 734, 818
4:9	39, 180, 190, 223, 233, 238, 240, 242, 245, 256, 284, 306, 313, 319, 324, 340, 353, 397, 423, 434, 436, 509, 649, 801, 818, 834, 835, 876, 886, 910	4:19	40, 72, 190, 207, 243, 320, 389, 454, 529, 530, 813, 825, 878		
				4:29-31	232, 248
				4:30	40, 250, 251, 453, 817, 847
		4:19-20	878	4:31	39, 62, 63, 171, 233, 248, 251, 267, 368, 807, 818, 830, 886
		4:20	30, 43, 208, 234, 244, 258, 335, 336, 742		
4:9-10	50, 51	4:20-21	490	4:32	252, 455, 795, 818
4:9-15	232	4:21	62, 65, 181, 182, 244, 350, 489, 912	4:32-33	233
4:9-24	233			4:32-34	43, 225, 876
4:9-31	75, 232, 233	4:21-22	65, 181, 244, 945	4:32-38	232
4:10	37, 50, 70, 71, 183, 235, 239, 240, 255, 266, 268, 302, 306, 313, 319, 324, 350, 366, 389, 452, 484, 542, 569, 717, 793, 794, 834, 835, 847, 875	4:22	181, 232, 249, 350, 579	4:32-39	900
				4:32-40	75, 232, 248
		4:23	39, 61, 190, 232, 233, 234, 238, 244, 248, 279, 425, 886	4:33	61, 233, 241, 252, 255, 300, 301, 366
				4:33-36	237
		4:23-24	233, 248	4:34	30, 43, 179, 226, 233, 248, 252, 253, 254, 287, 324, 337,
		4:23-25	529, 885		

982

Scripture Index

	340, 378, 397, 400, 451, 727, 728, 742, 787, 801, 948	4:46	157, 228, 262, 365, 946	5:6	30, 271, 272, 274, 275, 276, 277, 319, 338, 354, 454, 456
4:35	18, 34, 36, 60, 252, 254, 255, 310, 338, 392, 881, 900, 951	4:47	157, 161, 167, 262	5:6-7	319
		4:47-49	261	5:6-10	274
		4:48	210, 214, 262, 263	5:6-18	271
		4:49	157, 158, 168, 220, 240, 261, 263, 922, 944	5:6-21	5, 26, 241, 265, 267, 270-98
4:35-36	33, 36				
4:35-39	279			5:7	40, 77, 271, 272, 274, 275, 276, 277, 320, 335, 417, 529, 838
4:36	32, 50, 59, 241, 252, 254, 369, 427, 606, 733	5-28	232, 265		
		5-26	7, 8, 10, 13, 16, 26, 156, 265, 740		
		5-11	8, 75, 264-413, 422, 583		
4:37	30, 34, 61, 63, 252, 255, 267, 310, 336, 337, 391, 428, 464, 649, 878			5:7-9	885
		5	21, 231, 248, 258, 265, 347, 416, 422	5:7-10	276
				5:7-20	40
		5:1	50, 73, 75, 157, 172, 234, 235, 238, 262, 264, 265, 266, 267, 284, 299, 302, 304, 306, 307, 309, 325, 339, 347, 359, 361, 409, 410, 412, 422, 423, 440, 490, 536, 570, 583, 685, 738, 743, 749, 761, 766, 767, 793, 800, 801, 827, 834, 910	5:7-21	365
4:37-38	31, 363, 727			5:8	61, 234, 241, 242, 274, 279
4:38	43, 170, 209, 244, 255, 332, 337, 410, 489			5:8-9	72, 245
				5:8-10	33, 35, 36, 40, 77, 271, 272, 279, 417, 425, 529, 746, 810, 847
4:39	18, 34, 36, 60, 63, 172, 252, 254, 255, 256, 310, 338, 362, 392, 400, 817, 881, 900			5:8a	275
				5:9	274, 319, 320, 338, 389, 451, 529, 694, 787, 810
4:40	39, 64, 66, 172, 233, 236, 238, 239, 248, 249, 252, 256, 284, 289, 302, 303, 307, 321, 322, 339, 390, 435, 438, 571, 619, 685, 715, 734, 824			5:9-10	63, 280, 338
		5:1-2	274	5:9a	275
		5:1-3	834	5:9b	275
		5:1-5	264-70, 299, 304, 422	5:10	42, 61, 271, 274, 284, 310, 399
		5:1-21	75, 231	5:11	40, 60, 77, 271, 272, 282, 301, 320, 396, 417, 794
4:41	157, 258	5:1-33	264-304		
4:41-42	258, 262	5:1-6:3	75, 304, 307		
4:41-43	75, 79, 155, 232, 258-60, 566, 569	5:1-6:9	4	5:11-18	272
		5:1-7:10	6	5:11-21	276
4:42	289, 567	5:2	17, 241, 245, 265, 267, 799, 806	5:12	284, 285, 289, 499, 505
4:43	214, 258, 259				
4:44	8, 23, 162, 235, 238, 260, 261, 262, 264, 542, 821	5:2-3	26, 365, 919	5:12-14	511
		5:2-5	75, 267	5:12-15	39, 40, 77, 272, 284, 348, 417
		5:3	171, 172, 237, 238, 267, 274, 801, 807	5:13-14	285, 396, 476, 521, 607, 650, 656, 692, 786, 790, 806, 834
4:44-49	8, 9, 24, 26, 75, 155, 156, 232, 258, 260-64				
		5:4	61, 241, 268, 269, 274, 948		
4:44–30:20	9	5:4-5	299		
4:45	235, 260, 262, 324, 422, 738	5:5	266, 268, 269, 274, 368	5:13	785
4:45-49	260			5:14	174, 433, 434, 529,

983

Scripture Index

	614, 692, 700, 806	5:26	253, 301		749, 794, 825, 841, 882
5:14-15	396	5:27	301, 305, 306		
5:14b	497	5:27-32	304	6:4	xvii, 9, 18, 34, 36, 75, 254, 265, 266, 302, 309, 392, 583, 900, 952
5:15	39, 43, 238, 254, 271, 276, 285, 286, 287, 348, 493	5:28	183, 242, 299, 301, 558		
		5:29	37, 42, 71, 239, 240, 256, 284, 302, 305, 306, 796, 819, 834	6:4-5	5, 75, 275, 298, 309, 312
5:16	39, 64, 78, 249, 256, 271, 272, 285, 287, 417, 619, 748, 951			6:4-9	51, 70, 305, 308-16, 389
		5:30	302, 511	6:4–8:20	75
5:17	35, 36, 40, 78, 259, 271, 272, 289, 417, 567, 749, 951	5:30-31	75, 299	6:5	9, 21, 29, 34, 70, 239, 251, 310, 311, 338, 389, 399, 405, 410, 452, 812, 819, 825, 826, 952
		5:31	26, 50, 235, 237, 269, 300, 301, 302, 304, 305, 306, 368, 401, 559, 579, 821		
5:17-19	273				
5:18	40, 78, 271, 272, 290, 417, 951			6:5-9	399
		5:32	208, 266, 267, 299, 302, 305	6:6	172, 236, 238, 256, 312, 408, 435
5:18a	271				
5:18b	271	5:32-33	39, 64, 70, 71-72, 265, 299, 302, 350, 390	6:6-9	75, 88, 256, 308, 407, 408, 759, 822
5:19	78, 271, 272, 293, 418, 951			6:6-10	388, 398
5:20	32, 78, 271, 272, 293, 418, 531, 567, 573, 725, 951	5:33	35, 39, 53, 66, 170, 176, 235, 249, 256, 299, 302, 313, 347, 350, 367, 389, 410, 411, 452, 454, 570, 579, 734, 764, 825	6:7	50, 72, 176, 239, 302, 312, 313, 323, 350, 408, 541, 834
				6:8	4, 313, 464
5:21	35, 36, 78, 271, 272, 274, 294, 295, 418, 778, 951			6:9	4, 309, 315, 508
				6:10	62, 65, 170, 171, 317, 322, 559
5:21a	272, 296	6–11	70, 75, 231, 304, 305, 308, 309, 407	6:10-11	317, 353, 841
5:21b	272			6:10-12	350, 351
5:22	26, 61, 75, 175, 237, 240, 242, 266, 299, 369, 431, 646, 799, 833, 834, 952	6	305, 416	6:10-15	33, 316-17, 346, 787
		6:1	50, 235, 242, 249, 266, 299, 302, 304, 305, 306, 422, 749, 821		
				6:10-19	76, 316-23
5:22-23	268, 298-304			6:11	307, 319, 321, 322, 351, 352, 354, 406, 486, 730, 883
5:22-26	241	6:1-2	51, 70, 71, 305, 323, 324, 339		
5:22-27	366, 369, 558				
5:22-31	558	6:1-3	302, 304-8, 323	6:11-12	353
5:22b	300	6:2	37, 42, 66, 235, 239, 240, 249, 284, 305, 306, 319, 834	6:11b	314
5:23	806, 847			6:12	33, 36, 39, 238, 277, 317, 319, 354, 886
5:23-24	300, 520, 533, 570, 592, 631, 738, 806, 833, 876				
		6:2-3	39	6:12-14	319
5:23-26	61	6:3	172, 177, 234, 256, 265, 266, 267, 304, 305, 306, 307, 339, 347, 352, 369, 401, 459, 728, 733, 740,	6:12-15	841
5:23-27	300			6:13	9, 31, 40, 42, 60, 71, 240, 243, 250, 280, 282, 319, 320, 335, 340, 350, 355,
5:24	226, 794				
5:25	197, 253, 301				
5:25-27	300				

984

Scripture Index

	389, 396, 405, 451, 453, 570, 766, 787, 808, 813, 825, 952	7:1-5	34, 67, 76, 340, 830	7:12-16	52, 326-27, 328, 756, 761
6:13-14	71, 72	7:1-6	326, 328, 359	7:13	61, 170, 171, 307, 339, 351, 406, 696, 762, 785, 789, 790, 818, 820
6:14	9, 40, 60, 277, 320, 335, 355, 411, 451, 766, 840	7:1-24	411		
		7:1-26	326-44		
		7:2	332, 342, 458, 459, 587, 597		
6:14-15	245, 885	7:2-5	336	7:13-14	33, 307
6:15	178, 249, 317, 321, 335, 337, 341, 406, 459, 795, 810	7:3	597	7:14	339
		7:3-4	72, 334, 769	7:14-15	774
		7:4	320, 321, 334, 335, 405, 453, 530, 588, 797, 802, 840	7:15	89, 340, 794
6:16	321, 373, 926, 952			7:15-20	6
6:16-17	9			7:16	67, 72, 320, 328, 340, 342, 439, 455, 570, 713, 840
6:16-19	317-23	7:5	33, 35, 36, 37, 40, 335, 423, 424, 425, 526, 527		
6:17	256, 284, 321, 739			7:17	170, 172, 332, 340
6:18	39, 62, 65, 170, 171, 181, 236, 249, 256, 317, 321, 322, 329, 350, 432, 438, 459, 539, 595, 666	7:6	36, 43, 63, 321, 328, 335, 336, 377, 464, 734, 735, 742, 763, 878	7:17-21	581
				7:17-24	329
				7:17-26	76, 327, 328
				7:18	39, 340
				7:18-19	348, 801
		7:6-7	428	7:19	43, 253, 254, 337, 340, 948
6:18-19	9	7:6-8	30, 63, 76, 255, 310, 391, 464, 878		
6:19	172, 317, 322, 363			7:20	340, 767
6:20	235, 323	7:7	255, 336, 391, 598	7:21	321, 341, 392, 794
6:20-24	239	7:7-8	61, 62, 310, 337, 376, 649, 923	7:22	170, 259, 341, 362, 436, 891
6:20-25	50-51, 76, 276, 323-25, 725, 834				
		7:7-11	126, 328	7:23	178, 341, 768
6:21	226, 254, 276, 324, 337, 376, 727, 948	7:8	34, 61, 171, 267, 277, 324, 337, 338, 339, 355, 363	7:24	341, 369, 411
				7:24-25	811
6:22	179, 254, 324, 400, 787, 948			7:25	33, 35, 36, 46, 340, 341, 425, 439, 440, 458, 464, 527, 530, 553, 588, 618, 649, 661, 674, 715, 747, 808, 885
		7:8-9	807		
6:23	62, 170, 171, 324, 727	7:9	18, 29, 42, 60, 62, 70, 254, 256, 281, 284, 310, 311, 399, 452, 874		
6:24	37, 42, 209, 235, 239, 240, 255, 256, 319, 324, 390, 693, 834				
		7:9-10	63, 280, 338	7:25-26	62, 342
6:24-25	305, 323	7:9-16	76	7:26	46, 327, 342, 459, 649, 808
6:25	29, 31, 34, 162, 267, 285, 323, 325, 688, 935	7:10	30, 897		
		7:11	256, 267, 284, 302, 328, 339, 435, 739, 821	7:27	436
				8–11	345
7	4, 328, 346, 359, 361, 378			8	346, 378
		7:11-12	749	8:1	32, 53, 62, 65, 170, 171, 235, 256, 267, 307, 346, 347, 435, 739
7:1	168, 255, 322, 327, 328, 329, 330, 331, 340, 355, 361, 369, 410, 539, 588, 666, 952	7:12	42, 61, 171, 267, 310, 339, 355, 399, 734, 794		
		7:12-13	6, 61, 62, 310, 738, 825	8:1-5	346
				8:1-6	76
7:1-2	66, 334	7:12-14	64, 68	8:1-10	347

985

Scripture Index

8:1-20	344-56, 398, 399	8:14-16	879		364, 368, 377, 391, 846
8:2	30, 39, 157, 161, 253, 286, 321, 340, 346, 347, 348, 365, 376, 496, 509, 514, 685, 695, 715, 727, 802, 808, 886	8:14a	354	9:6-21	846
		8:15	30, 176, 354, 880, 882	9:6-24	76, 363
		8:15-16	346, 880	9:6-29	38
		8:16	253, 348, 349, 350, 354, 366, 411, 794, 818	9:7	39, 180, 360, 364, 373, 374, 400, 717, 728, 801, 802, 846, 886
8:2-3	354	8:17	340, 354, 363, 560		
8:2-5	346, 399, 880	8:17-18	31	9:7-8	360, 802
8:3	235, 347, 349, 400, 411, 455, 802, 952	8:17-20	76, 346	9:7-21	357-58, 359, 360, 364-73
8:3-20	33	8:18	43, 171, 267, 346, 354, 363, 364, 807	9:7-24	360, 364, 380
8:4	157, 346, 347, 349, 350, 802	8:18-19	39, 62	9:7-29	348, 357-58, 364-80
8:5	46, 50, 255, 256, 346, 347, 350, 355, 606, 875	8:19	33, 36, 39, 40, 72, 243, 248, 262, 319, 320, 346, 355, 451, 825, 840, 886	9:7–10:11	234, 390
				9:7a	365
8:5-10	346, 347, 353			9:8	178, 182, 359, 362, 368, 369
8:6	42, 71, 240, 302, 346, 350, 570, 734, 834	8:19-20	346, 348	9:9	241, 365, 370, 376, 382
		8:20	40, 346, 350, 355, 453, 558		
8:6-10	52, 346	9-11	75	9:9-11	242
8:7	347, 350, 351, 403, 930	9	162	9:9-12	300
		9:1	75, 178, 249, 255, 265, 266, 332, 337, 340, 359, 361, 410, 583	9:9–10:11	359
8:7-9	350, 406			9:10	239, 241, 253, 268, 299, 300, 366, 370, 382, 383, 384, 558, 646, 924
8:7-10	65, 76, 307, 347, 350, 351				
8:7-18	318	9:1-2	178	9:10a	366
8:8	319, 346, 347, 723, 882	9:1-3	357, 359, 361-63, 581	9:11	157, 241, 365, 366, 369, 376
8:8-9	339	9:1-5	76	9:12	176, 183, 242, 303, 359, 367, 376, 406, 411, 453, 454, 847, 874
8:8-10	74, 931	9:1-29	357-80		
8:9	346, 347	9:1–11:32	75, 76		
8:10	65, 68, 69, 319, 346, 347, 350, 351, 353, 841, 884	9:1a	359		
		9:2	178, 361	9:12-14	374
8:11	30, 33, 36, 39, 235, 238, 256, 346, 353, 435	9:3	170, 172, 176, 178, 245, 249, 256, 361, 362, 406, 829	9:12-21	280
				9:12b	360
		9:3a	359	9:12c	360
8:11-13	346	9:4	67, 170, 322, 340, 363	9:13	183, 364, 368, 846
8:11-14	346, 885, 886			9:13-14	64, 360, 370, 374, 375, 892
8:11-20	756, 787, 841	9:4-5	30, 65, 211		
8:11a	350	9:4-6	30, 357, 359-60, 363-64	9:14	172, 178, 255, 269, 341, 360, 362, 365, 368, 374, 709, 717, 811, 892
8:12	319, 353				
8:13	354	9:5	62, 170, 171, 355, 359, 363		
8:14	33, 36, 39, 277, 346, 353, 354, 363, 454, 542, 727, 808			9:15	241, 360, 365, 369
		9:6	181, 256, 350, 362,	9:15-21	360

986

Scripture Index

9:16	176, 360, 367, 369, 453, 454		382-84, 386, 833, 846	10:14-15	388
9:16b	360	10:1-11	380-87	10:14-22	76
9:16c	360	10:2-12	349	10:15	30, 43, 61, 63, 209, 252, 255, 310, 336, 337, 382, 390, 391, 428, 464, 598, 649, 878
9:17	179, 359, 370	10:3	383		
9:17-21	370	10:4	239, 241, 271, 299, 300, 366, 384, 558, 924		
9:18	157, 248, 249, 365, 370, 371, 374, 376, 386			10:16	39, 312, 364, 388, 391, 818, 819, 846
		10:5	383, 384		
9:18-19	386	10:5-7	6	10:17	18, 31, 60, 63, 176, 226, 252, 254, 341, 391, 523, 794, 952
9:18-20	368, 370	10:6	184, 371, 384, 912		
9:19	178, 362, 365, 370, 371, 386, 794, 952	10:6-7	381, 382, 384-85		
		10:6-9	195, 201, 214, 215, 384	10:17-18	36, 47, 388, 391
9:19b	378, 382			10:18	31, 34, 35, 36, 37, 40, 43, 63, 286, 393, 395, 486, 514, 523, 695, 730, 748, 786
9:20	171, 178, 182, 362, 365, 371, 913	10:7	382, 385		
		10:8	60, 68, 171, 191, 202, 382, 384, 385, 536, 594, 833, 846		
9:21	370, 371, 382				
9:21a	360			10:18-19	174, 286, 486, 650, 806
9:21c	360	10:8-9	381, 382, 385-86, 434		
9:22	321, 365, 373, 926	10:9	172, 244, 386, 433, 544, 878	10:19	48, 70, 286, 311, 396, 727
9:22-24	358, 360, 365, 373-74, 802				
		10:10	157, 177, 252, 366, 368, 382, 386	10:19-21	6
9:23	40, 373, 453			10:19a	388
9:23-24	846	10:10-11	76, 381, 382, 386	10:19b	388
9:24	40, 359, 360, 365, 373, 801	10:11	62, 65, 170, 171, 183, 206, 382, 386	10:20	31, 40, 42, 60, 70, 71, 72, 172, 237, 240, 282, 319, 320, 388, 389, 396, 397, 399
9:25	157, 178, 185, 360, 362, 365, 368, 370, 374, 808	10:11-12	6		
		10:12	34, 42, 70, 71, 176, 197, 234, 240, 251, 302, 311, 319, 320, 388, 389, 396, 397, 399, 452		
9:25-29	76, 358-59, 360, 368, 369, 370, 374-80, 386			10:21	238, 254, 396
				10:21-22	389, 396
				10:21–11:7	225
9:26	6, 30, 226, 244, 252, 324, 337, 361, 376, 873	10:12-13	29, 37, 70, 71, 72, 76, 302, 350, 388, 389, 390, 399, 405, 570, 834	10:22	369, 388, 389, 390, 397, 727, 794, 878, 952
9:26-29	368				
9:27	348, 376	10:12-19	35	11	264
9:27-29	58, 893	10:12-22	387-98	11:1	29, 34, 70, 235, 239, 252, 311, 388, 398, 399, 452
9:28	377	10:12–11:17	387-407		
9:28b	177	10:12–11:18	252		
9:29	6, 30, 31, 244, 254, 255, 335, 359, 361, 376, 377	10:12–11:21	315	11:1-9	77, 398-402
		10:12–11:22	4	11:2	43, 50, 226, 255, 256, 350, 398, 399, 400, 606, 801
		10:13	39, 235, 236, 252, 256, 324, 389, 390, 435		
10:1	171, 183, 382			11:2-3	254
10:1-2	6, 382			11:2-4	252
10:1-4	242	10:14	32, 60, 63, 251, 255, 390	11:2-5	72
10:1-5	76, 180, 380-81,			11:2-7	268, 397, 801, 873

987

Scripture Index

11:2a	399	11:17-18	6	11:29-32	409-12
11:2b	399	11:18	4, 239, 312, 405, 407, 408	11:30	157, 168, 195, 409, 412, 423
11:3	253, 254, 451, 948	11:18-20	51, 70, 88, 256, 305, 308, 389, 408, 757, 822	11:31	249, 412, 422
11:3-4	399, 400			11:31-32	6, 409, 422
11:4	202, 254, 400			11:32	169, 235, 265, 267, 409, 410, 412, 422
11:5	180, 365, 400, 728	11:18-21	77, 235, 308, 407-8, 757		
11:5-6	399, 400			12–28	231
11:6	295, 400	11:19	50, 72, 176, 235, 239, 302, 313, 350, 408, 541, 834	12–26	4, 8, 21, 26, 77, 235, 265, 266, 267, 304, 412, 413-736, 799,
11:7	223, 399, 401				
11:8	238, 249, 252, 256, 399, 401, 410, 433				
		11:20	4, 508	12	11, 77, 231, 416, 418, 419, 420, 431, 443, 447, 546, 807
11:8-9	66, 235, 813	11:21	62, 170, 171, 249, 407, 408		
11:8-17	772				
11:9	53, 62, 170, 171, 249, 307, 398, 401	11:22	29, 70, 71, 176, 237, 256, 267, 302, 305, 311, 325, 350, 399, 409, 412, 452, 739, 821	12:1	172, 235, 239, 256, 265, 266, 267, 306, 409, 418, 419, 420, 422, 440, 722, 733, 734
11:9-15	307				
11:10	236, 249, 322, 329, 402, 539, 666				
11:10-12	32, 401, 402-4, 405				
		11:22-23	310, 405, 410, 761	12:1-3	65
11:10-17	33, 77, 399	11:22-24	569	12:1-4	413, 420, 422-26, 612, 621, 651, 662, 669
11:11	249, 351, 403, 765, 930	11:22-25	66, 408, 410-11, 569		
		11:22-32	77, 408-13, 422	12:1-7	11, 434
11:11-17	41	11:23	170, 255, 332, 337, 340	12:1–13:1 (12:32)	236, 413-42, 450
11:12	402, 404				
11:12-13	6	11:24	167, 169, 190, 410, 944	12:2	31, 40, 72, 423, 426, 434
11:12-32	410				
11:13	29, 34, 70, 72, 251, 256, 311, 319, 320, 399, 405, 408, 452	11:24-25	181, 207	12:2-3	335
		11:25	66, 71, 172, 341, 409, 411, 764, 796	12:2-4	6, 34, 77, 419, 420
11:13-14	310, 405, 410, 411, 761, 766, 793			12:2–26:15	265
		11:26	64, 169, 410, 411, 412	12:3	33, 35, 36, 37, 40, 250, 335, 424, 451, 526, 527
11:13-15	405, 761				
11:13-17	32, 37, 39, 355, 402, 404-9, 756, 813	11:26-28	37, 77, 355, 409, 410, 411, 825		
		11:26-32	19, 52, 68, 191, 265, 410, 412, 745, 755, 813	12:4	419, 420, 426, 548
				12:5	7, 32, 59, 255, 336, 391, 418, 421, 426, 427, 428, 432, 434, 464, 514, 545, 594, 655, 722, 724, 764, 826, 834
11:13-21	314, 315				
11:14	339, 404, 405, 765, 952	11:27	64, 256, 405		
		11:27-28	39, 349, 411, 451, 782, 783, 813, 886		
11:14-15	335				
11:15	319, 406, 408	11:28	30, 40, 64, 72, 176, 256, 303, 320, 367, 405, 409, 411, 454, 840		
11:16	72, 238, 243, 312, 319, 320, 406, 451, 453, 808, 840				
				12:5-6	438, 513, 666
				12:5-7	436, 483
11:16-17	405			12:5-9	413, 426-32
11:17	181, 249, 321, 350, 405, 406, 408, 765, 888	11:29	236, 271, 322, 329, 411, 423, 539, 666, 740, 745, 797	12:5-14	31, 34, 37, 65, 77, 414, 419, 420, 426-35

988

12:5-28	419	
12:6	418, 421, 428, 432, 433, 434, 436, 481, 545, 722, 723, 741	
12:6-7	435, 499, 729, 741	
12:7	19, 31, 53, 57, 68, 69, 73, 191, 418, 419, 421, 430, 431, 433, 436, 485, 492, 507, 513, 516, 517, 729, 741, 763, 787	
12:8	321, 420, 421, 431, 741	
12:9	65, 244, 432	
12:9-10	65, 432, 489, 717	
12:10	65, 223, 420, 421, 432, 795	
12:10-14	414, 432-35	
12:11	7, 32, 43, 59, 418, 421, 427, 428, 429, 432, 435, 436, 438, 440, 481, 666, 723	
12:11-12	432, 435, 436, 729, 741	
12:12	19, 31, 57, 73, 244, 285, 286, 385, 386, 418, 419, 421, 431, 433, 434, 485, 497, 507, 514, 535, 544, 546, 594, 723, 725, 742, 787, 833, 846, 878, 924	
12:13	238, 420, 421, 434, 435, 436	
12:13-14	426	
12:14	7, 427, 428, 432, 434, 440	
12:15	53, 68, 69, 191, 286, 421, 435, 437, 438, 465, 500	
12:15-16	414, 421, 435-36, 437, 500	
12:15-17	6	
12:15-28	77, 419, 420, 421	
12:16	419, 421, 435, 437, 476, 500	
12:17	57, 286, 339, 341, 421, 426, 429, 436, 510, 540, 674, 722, 725, 603, 616, 633	
12:17-18	436, 481, 499, 729	
12:17-18a	438	
12:17-19	415, 421, 436	
12:18	7, 19, 31, 57, 73, 191, 285, 286, 422, 427, 428, 431, 433, 436, 497, 507, 666, 725, 741, 787	
12:18-19	19, 433, 434	
12:19	238, 239, 419, 420, 434, 436	
12:20	65, 170, 172, 419, 420, 422, 435, 436, 485, 569, 735, 934	
12:20-21	437	
12:20-25	415, 421, 436-38	
12:21	7, 32, 59, 286, 422, 427, 428, 432, 435, 437, 438, 440	
12:21-25	437, 438	
12:21b-22	435	
12:22	422, 435, 437, 465, 500	
12:22-23	435	
12:22-25	500	
12:23	435, 437	
12:23-24	422	
12:23-25	435	
12:25	256, 321, 419, 432, 437, 438, 439, 459, 595	
12:26	7, 422, 427, 428, 433, 438, 666, 731	
12:26-27	426, 436, 438, 667	
12:26-28	415, 421, 438-39	
12:27	422, 436, 438	
12:27b	429	
12:28	256, 321, 420, 432, 438, 440, 595	
12:29	439, 565	
12:29-31	34, 65, 77, 419, 420, 439, 449, 553, 588	
12:29–13:1 (12:32)	415-16, 439-41	
12:30	72, 172, 178, 238, 420, 434, 439	
12:31	40, 46, 62, 342, 363, 420, 439, 549, 588	
13–25	416, 440	
13–19	448, 456-59	
13–18	26, 79, 416, 449, 555, 564	
13–15	77	
13	11, 58, 77, 419, 420, 439, 464, 555, 558, 580, 588, 808, 811	
13:1 (12:32)	236, 256, 267, 419, 420, 432, 440, 450, 733	
13:2 (1)	449, 450	
13:2-3 (1-2)	953	
13:2-4 (1-3)	254, 439, 555	
13:2-6 (1-5)	34, 36, 40, 42, 58, 59, 447-48, 449, 450-54, 480, 555, 559, 561	
13:2-19 (1-18)	77, 78, 417, 450-61, 528, 565, 809	
13:3 (2)	72, 320, 411, 557, 795, 840	
13:4 (3)	70, 79, 251, 253, 321, 349, 452	
13:4-5 (3-4)	311, 399	
13:5 (4)	40, 70, 71, 72, 237, 240, 251, 319, 320, 355, 373, 452, 453, 454, 459, 490, 558, 834, 733, 743, 761, 826	
13:6 (5)	57, 72, 176, 243, 277, 302, 337, 449, 450, 453, 454, 456, 457, 525, 531, 536, 571, 573, 595, 608, 634, 684, 731, 953	

13:7 (6)	40, 72, 320, 411, 450, 454, 455, 530, 792, 795, 840	
13:7-12 (6-11)	448, 449, 454-56, 555, 747, 927	
13:8 (7)	252, 320, 454, 455, 795	
13:8-12 (7-11)	450	
13:9 (8)	340, 455, 456, 570	
13:10 (9)	456, 607	
13:10-13 (9-12)	806	
13:11 (10)	243, 277, 454, 456, 530	
13:12 (11)	57, 157, 450, 456, 457, 537, 574, 608	
13:12a (11a)	449	
13:12b (11b)	449	
13:13 (12)	449, 450, 457	
13:13-15 (12-14)	342, 530	
13:13-17 (12-16)	592	
13:13-18 (12-17)	321, 449, 555	
13:13-19 (12-18)	67, 333, 587, 811	
13:14 (13)	72, 243, 320, 411, 454, 455, 457, 458, 491, 795, 840	
13:15 (14)	46, 62, 456, 457, 458, 530, 535, 559, 574	
13:16 (15)	457, 458	
13:16-18 (15-17)	66	
13:17 (16)	459, 927	
13:18 (17)	63, 171, 307, 342, 459, 818	
13:18-19 (17-18)	62	
13:19 (18)	256, 321, 420, 432, 438, 449, 450, 453, 459, 558, 595	
14–15	77, 419	
14:1	463, 644	
14:1-2	34, 461, 462, 463-64, 564, 613	
14:1-21	77, 79, 417, 419, 461-77, 758	
14:2	36, 43, 63, 321, 335, 336, 428, 463, 464, 476, 878, 953	
14:3	46, 342, 464	
14:3-8	461, 462, 464-69	
14:3-21	463	
14:4	464, 883	
14:5	465	
14:6	466	
14:7	467	
14:8	463, 468	
14:9	469, 934	
14:9-10	461, 462, 469	
14:10	463, 469	
14:11	463, 469, 475	
14:11-20	461-62, 469-76	
14:12	470, 789, 880	
14:13	470, 471	
14:14	472	
14:15	472	
14:16	473	
14:17	474	
14:18	474	
14:19	475	
14:20	463, 475	
14:21	36, 43, 63, 286, 335, 396, 462, 463, 464, 476-77, 564, 619	
14:21b	26	
14:22	429, 480, 481, 486, 499, 729	
14:22-23	729	
14:22-27	19, 429, 430, 478, 480, 481-86, 513, 729, 730	
14:22-29	481	
14:22–15:23	77, 79, 417, 419, 478-502, 559	
14:23	31, 32, 43, 50, 59, 71, 235, 239, 240, 339, 428, 431, 480, 483, 499, 559, 725, 729	
14:23-25	427, 428	
14:23-27	499	
14:24	53, 68, 69, 191, 431, 434, 485	
14:24-26	484	
14:25	485	
14:25-26	725	
14:26	57, 431, 433, 437, 485, 787	
14:26-27	19	
14:27	19, 47, 73, 286, 386, 430, 433, 434, 481, 484, 485, 544, 878	
14:27-28	405	
14:28	286, 486, 730	
14:28-29	47, 52, 69, 393, 396, 429, 433, 478, 480, 483, 486, 696, 729, 731	
14:29	19, 37, 43, 68, 191, 286, 319, 386, 395, 433, 434, 481, 485, 486, 492, 544, 665, 730, 806, 878	
15:1	486, 833	
15:1-3	489, 490	
15:1-6	481, 664	
15:1-11	31, 35, 49, 478-79, 480, 481, 486-93, 663, 680, 834	
15:1-18	478, 480, 486-98	
15:2	487, 567, 614	
15:3	476, 489, 665	
15:3-11	488	
15:4	65, 68, 69, 182, 191, 228, 244, 255, 302, 376, 432, 480, 489, 490, 492, 570, 572, 587, 611, 675, 717, 723, 832, 879	
15:4-6	480, 761	
15:4b-6	735	
15:5	40, 267, 325, 453, 489, 490, 558, 765	
15:6	68, 69, 191, 431, 480, 481, 489, 490	
15:7	286, 391, 492	
15:7-8	490	
15:7-9	490	

Scripture Index

15:7-11	393, 396, 481, 489, 692	16:3	39, 348, 505, 507, 517, 583	16:16-17	69, 73, 504
15:8	490, 492	16:3-4	512	16:17	19, 53, 68, 191, 431, 504, 513, 517
15:9	47, 238, 487, 491, 492, 667, 692, 730, 792	16:4	504, 507	16:18	171, 174, 286, 300, 520, 534, 535, 583, 592, 806, 847
		16:5	57, 286, 341, 436, 507		
15:10	68, 69, 73, 182, 191, 431, 486, 489, 492, 496, 553, 665, 696, 787	16:5-6	510	16:18-19	31
		16:6	43, 59, 427, 428, 506, 510	16:18-20	11, 35, 79, 519-25, 533, 555
		16:6-7	428	16:18–17:13	78, 417, 519-37, 564
15:11	287, 487, 489, 490, 492, 496, 569, 692, 696, 953	16:7	434, 510	16:18–18:22	79, 519-62
		16:8	504, 511, 512	16:19	26, 35, 36, 46, 174, 342, 393, 522, 523, 695
		16:9	512		
15:12	50, 493, 487	16:9-10	512	16:20	31, 32, 34, 53, 235, 525
15:12-14	50	16:9-12	42, 348, 484, 504, 512-14, 724, 729		
15:12-15	396			16:21	33, 36, 37, 250, 425, 526
15:12-18	26, 42, 49, 53, 296, 479, 480, 481, 483, 493-98, 663	16:10	19, 53, 68, 69, 191, 430, 431, 517	16:21-22	33, 35, 36, 40, 335, 564
		16:10-11	47		
		16:10-12	396	16:21–17:1	79, 519, 526-28
15:13	495	16:11	19, 31, 37, 43, 57, 59, 73, 285, 286, 393, 395, 396, 427, 428, 431, 433, 434, 497, 507, 513, 516, 725, 729, 787, 806	16:22	37, 424, 526, 527
15:13-14	69			17:1	46, 62, 342, 500, 526, 527, 564, 647, 874
15:14	53, 68, 191, 431, 489, 495, 513, 516				
15:15	39, 287, 337, 348, 493, 496			17:2	248, 454, 509, 528, 529, 549, 592, 636
15:16-17	495, 496	16:12	39, 48, 238, 287, 348, 504, 509, 514, 516		
15:17	175, 497, 534			17:2-3	58, 887
15:18	68, 69, 191, 481, 489, 498	16:13	351, 496, 514	17:2-4	342, 530
		16:13-15	69, 484, 504, 512, 834	17:2-5	244, 450, 528
15:19	498, 593			17:2-7	34, 40, 243, 449, 456, 528-32, 573, 808
15:19-20	513	16:13-17	503, 514-17		
15:19-23	19, 430, 479-80, 483, 498-500	16:14	19, 31, 37, 43, 47, 57, 285, 286, 393, 395, 396, 431, 433, 434, 497, 507, 509, 513, 514, 516, 787, 806		
				17:2-13	79, 519, 555
15:20	427, 428, 430, 431, 499, 725			17:3	243, 319, 320, 335, 451, 529, 840
15:21	500, 647, 874			17:3-4	62
15:21-22	435			17:3-5	72, 320
15:22	286, 435, 465	16:14-15	73, 513	17:4	46, 458, 530, 535, 559, 574
15:22-23	500	16:15	19, 53, 57, 68, 191, 427, 431, 515, 516, 787, 834		
15:23	435, 481			17:5	453, 456, 530, 534, 607, 637
16:1	284, 504				
16:1-8	324, 502-3, 504-11	16:15-16	428	17:6	531, 573, 633, 953
16:1-17	26, 37, 77, 79, 417, 428, 502-19	16:15b	516	17:6-7	528
		16:16	427, 431, 504, 507, 508, 514, 517, 725, 834	17:7	57, 292, 454, 528, 531, 536, 607
16:2	43, 59, 427, 428, 506, 517				

Scripture Index

17:8	301, 427, 428, 532, 533, 567, 684, 698, 822, 833		434, 519, 543-47, 555, 594, 927	18:19	60, 559, 667, 953
		18:2	544	18:20	40, 59, 60, 480, 525, 556, 559
17:8-12	520	18:3	544	18:20-22	34, 35, 36, 40, 42, 59, 449, 451, 555, 556, 559
17:8-13	521, 532-37, 573, 594, 927	18:3-5	543, 544-45		
		18:4	339, 430, 483, 499, 513, 544, 545, 723, 729		
17:9	19, 434, 519, 534, 535, 559, 573, 574, 594, 685, 724, 742			18:21	172, 340, 560
				18:21-22	556, 560
		18:5	60, 239, 385, 428, 544, 545, 594	18:22	6, 60, 536, 555, 560, 893
17:9-11	685, 927				
17:10	267, 427, 428, 536	18:6	427, 428, 434, 435	18:26-27	559
17:10-12	19	18:6-7	433, 545	19–25	26, 79, 416, 564
17:11	208, 536, 542	18:6-8	433, 543, 544, 545-46	19–22	564
17:12	57, 386, 454, 519, 531, 535, 536			19–21	564
		18:7	60, 385, 386, 536, 545	19	267, 564
17:12-13	560			19:1	439, 565
17:13	57, 456, 457, 532, 537, 574	18:8	486, 544, 546, 693	19:1-7	565
		18:9	46, 50, 235, 342, 547, 548, 559	19:1-13	78, 79, 258, 289, 417, 564, 565, 573, 591
17:14	236, 322, 329, 538, 666, 723	18:9-10	342, 588		
		18:9-12	342, 439		
17:14-15	173, 538	18:9-14	34, 65, 79, 519, 547-54, 555, 556, 557	19:1-14	565
17:14-17	538			19:1-21	562-77, 579, 621
17:14-20	78, 79, 417, 519, 537-43, 555, 557, 783			19:1–22:8	612
		18:9-22	78, 79, 417, 519, 547-62	19:2	565, 566
				19:3	489, 564, 566
17:15	57, 341, 428, 436, 557	18:10	35, 40, 58, 548, 549	19:3-4	289
				19:4	488, 567
17:16	89, 540, 796, 797	18:10-11	558, 732	19:4-6	6
17:16-17	539	18:10-12	450	19:4-13	533
17:17	354, 540, 598, 676	18:10-14	36	19:4b	567
17:18	1, 19, 434, 535, 541, 542, 594	18:11	552	19:5	329, 434, 567
		18:12	46, 62, 67, 170, 363, 492, 548, 553, 588, 693	19:6	289, 338, 566, 568, 571, 609, 761
17:18-19	162, 235			19:7	493, 565, 569
17:18-20	834	18:13	548, 553, 953	19:8	170, 436, 564, 566, 934
17:19	50, 71, 235, 238, 239, 240, 313, 541, 793, 834	18:14	40, 548, 549, 553, 555, 559		
				19:8-9	62, 65, 167, 310, 436, 569, 586
		18:15	556, 558, 953		
17:19-20	538	18:15-18	29, 39, 948	19:8-10	565
17:20	208, 249, 354, 538, 542	18:15-19	555, 556	19:9	29, 70, 239, 267, 302, 311, 325, 350, 399, 569, 821
		18:15-22	32, 449, 451, 553, 554-62		
18	11, 480, 557				
18:1	19, 385, 434, 535, 544, 594, 878	18:16	239, 301, 366, 555, 558, 924	19:10	40, 244, 489, 565, 570, 612, 619
		18:17	183, 558	19:10-11	6
18:1-2	433, 543, 544	18:18	252, 557, 558, 693	19:11	259, 570
18:1-4	486	18:18-19	555	19:11-13	35, 36, 565
18:1-5	47, 386				
18:1-8	19, 78, 79, 417,				

992

Scripture Index

19:12	301, 520, 533, 570, 592, 593, 631	20:6	580, 584, 623	21:8	337, 591, 594, 595
19:13	40, 57, 256, 340, 454, 455, 565, 570, 574	20:7	580, 585, 675	21:8-9	40, 570, 903
		20:8	54, 174, 178, 580, 581, 583, 585, 792	21:9	57, 321, 432, 438, 454, 571, 592, 595
		20:9	63, 174, 521, 580, 583, 585	21:10	177, 579, 597, 652
19:13-14	6	20:10	580	21:10-14	48, 66, 78, 80, 296, 417, 579, 587, 596-600, 630, 651
19:14	20, 27, 34, 46, 80, 294, 417, 489, 563, 564, 565, 566, 570, 571-72, 748	20:10-11	586		
		20:10-15	66, 209, 332	21:11	337, 598
		20:10-18	80, 459, 578, 580, 586-88	21:12-13	598
19:15	531, 564, 565, 573, 633, 953	20:11	581	21:13	597, 599, 631
		20:11-15	334	21:14	349, 579, 597, 599, 632, 637, 639, 683, 787
19:15-18	458	20:12	586		
19:15-19	520	20:12-16	597	21:15	597, 601, 673
19:15-21	78, 79, 417, 563, 564, 572, 573-76	20:13	177	21:15-17	49, 78, 80, 296, 417, 600-604, 605, 609
		30:13-14	458, 586		
19:16	6, 294, 573, 725	20:15	586, 587		
19:16-18	534	20:16	489, 587	21:16	57, 244, 341, 436, 601
19:16-21	32, 294	20:16-17	66, 209		
19:17	534, 535, 573, 724	20:16-18	66, 67, 332, 830	21:16-17	602
19:18	293, 294, 530, 535, 559, 574, 725	20:17	285, 331, 333, 458, 587	21:17	601
				21:18	601, 605, 606, 631
19:18-21	632	20:18	46, 50, 62, 235, 334, 342, 363, 580, 588	21:18-21	50, 78, 80, 274, 287, 296, 417, 570, 605-8, 748
19:19	57, 71, 454, 571, 574				
		20:19	567, 579, 580, 588, 591	21:18-23	528
19:20	57, 456, 457, 574			21:19	606, 631, 709
19:21	291, 340, 455, 565, 570, 573, 574, 632, 713, 953	20:19-20	80, 578-79, 580, 588-89	21:19-20	301
				21:20	606
		20:20	580, 589	21:21	57, 157, 454, 456, 457, 537, 571, 574, 595, 605, 607, 634
20	597	21:1	55, 58, 454, 529, 579, 591, 592, 596, 597, 611		
20:1	597, 580, 581, 582, 652, 830, 832, 842				
20:1-9	66, 80, 577-78, 580, 581-86, 651	21:1-9	78, 80, 417, 458, 520, 570, 579, 591-96, 749	21:21-23	55, 78, 81, 417, 608-11
				21:22	5, 601, 609, 638, 953
20:1-20	78, 417, 577-90, 597				
20:1–21:14	80, 597	21:2	592	21:22-23	609
20:2	582	21:2-4	530	21:23	489, 609, 610, 953
20:2-4	19	21:2-6	301	22	643
20:3	176, 179, 266, 341, 508, 581, 583, 585	21:3-4	593	22:1	613, 614, 712
		21:5	60, 68, 69, 191, 385, 428, 434, 533, 535, 545, 594, 684, 927	22:1-3	78, 81, 611, 612, 614-15
20:3-4	55, 582				
20:4	179, 582, 583, 653, 778, 830			22:1-4	26, 55, 417
				22:1-8	81, 611-20, 621
20:5	174, 521, 580, 583	21:6-7	594	22:2	615
20:5-6	318	21:7	294, 725	22:3	57, 341, 436, 613, 614, 615, 631
20:5-7	41	21:7-8	728		
20:5-8	449				

22:4	78, 81, 611, 612, 613, 614, 616		454, 529, 626, 627, 628, 629, 634-37	23:6 (5)	34, 61, 68, 177, 191, 310, 648
22:5	46, 62, 78, 81, 342, 417, 612, 613, 616-18, 622, 631, 660	22:22-24	291	23:7 (6)	239, 643, 649
		22:23	585, 628	23:8 (7)	174, 189, 342, 396, 643, 649, 727
		22:23-24	82, 626, 627, 629, 637, 648		
22:6	613, 618	22:23-27	78, 418	23:8-9 (7-8)	83, 642, 643, 649-50
22:6-7	49, 78, 81, 286, 417, 476, 612, 618-19, 622	22:24	57, 349, 454, 456, 530, 600, 627, 628, 634, 637, 639, 727	23:9 (8)	366, 643, 650, 651
				23:9b (8b)	649
22:7	53, 249, 256, 613, 618	22:25	585, 628	23:10 (9)	651, 652
		22:25-26	637	23:10-15 (9-14)	83, 579, 651-54
22:8	48, 78, 81, 417, 612, 613, 614, 619-20, 622	22:25-27	82, 291, 626, 627, 629, 637-38	23:10-19 (9-18)	651
		22:26	609	23:11 (10)	651, 652
22:9	81, 621, 622	22:27	628, 638, 676, 727, 778	23:11-15 (10-14)	418
22:9-11	417, 617, 621, 622-24			23:12 (11)	651, 652
		22:28	638	23:13 (12)	652
22:9-12	78, 81, 564, 621-25	22:28-29	26, 78, 82, 418, 626, 627, 629, 637, 638-39	23:13-15 (12-14)	55, 56, 66, 592
22:10	81, 286, 621, 622, 623, 702			23:14 (13)	652, 653, 654
22:11	82, 621, 622, 624	22:29	239, 341, 349, 436, 599, 600, 616, 628, 631, 632, 638	23:15 (14)	32, 209, 252, 427, 651, 652, 653, 654, 656, 671, 806
22:11-12	622				
22:12	82, 417, 621, 622, 624-25, 640	22:30	627	23:16 (15)	652, 654, 895
22:13	627, 628, 639	23:1 (22:30)	78, 82, 418, 627, 628, 629, 639-40, 748	23:16-17 (15-16)	48, 78, 83, 418, 654-56
22:13-14	629				
22:13-19	296, 627			23:17 (16)	20, 652, 654, 655
22:13-21	55, 78, 82, 287, 417, 570, 625, 627, 629-34, 677	23:2 (1)	366, 643, 647, 648, 651, 660	23:18 (17)	652, 656, 657
		23:2-3 (1-2)	83, 642, 643-47	23:18-19 (17-18)	33, 78, 83, 342, 418, 656-61, 662, 839
22:13-23:1 (22:30)	31, 82, 625-42	23:2-7 (1-6)	55	23:19 (18)	46, 56, 62, 656, 657, 660, 662
		23:2-9 (1-8)	57, 83, 642, 643-51		
22:14	629	23:2-10 (1-9)	418	23:20 (19)	662, 663, 680, 687
22:15	606, 629, 630	23:2-15 (1-14)	78		
22:15-18	301	23:2-19 (1-18)	83, 642-61	23:20-21 (19-20)	49, 53, 78, 83, 418, 488, 661, 662, 663-66
22:15-21	530	23:3 (2)	366, 643, 646, 647, 651		
22:16-17	631			23:20-26 (19-25)	83, 656, 661-68
22:18	50, 606, 631, 699	23:4 (3)	366, 643, 647, 651		
22:19	55, 57, 239, 341, 436, 485, 616, 627, 631, 639, 676	23:4-7 (3-6)	34, 83, 642, 643, 647-49	23:21 (20)	68, 69, 191, 236, 322, 329, 396, 431, 486, 489, 492, 539, 662, 665, 696
22:20	633	23:5 (4)	200, 262, 647, 686, 716		
22:21	33, 57, 454, 571, 607, 609, 627, 628, 629, 634, 637, 839, 875			23:22 (21)	492, 559, 657, 662, 666, 692
		23:5-7 (4-6)	643		
22:22	57, 58, 78, 82, 417,				

23:22-24 (21-23)	46, 78, 83, 282, 418, 430, 438, 661, 662, 666-67	24:10-11	49, 84, 679, 686-87	25:1-3	6, 56, 78, 85, 418, 697-700
		24:10-13	26, 78, 418	25:1-4	697-702
		24:12	690, 692	25:2	535, 574, 698, 711
23:23 (22)	492, 657, 662, 667	24:12-13	32, 49, 53, 84, 393, 396, 679, 686, 687-88	25:2b	698
23:24 (23)	238, 657, 662, 667			25:3	57, 179, 631, 698, 699, 700, 710
		23:13	31, 34, 68, 191, 325, 631, 680, 690, 692	25:4	28, 49, 84, 85, 286, 418, 669, 698, 700-702, 954
23:25 (24)	485, 667				
23:25-26 (24-25)	78, 84, 418, 662, 667, 701	24:14	174, 286, 490, 493, 690, 691, 777, 806	25:5	704, 705, 708, 712, 954
23:25(24)–24:3	6			25:5-10	56, 78, 85, 418, 568, 570, 700, 902, 703, 704, 705-11
23:26 (25)	512, 662, 667	24:14-15	40, 49, 78, 85, 393, 418, 689, 690, 691-92		
24–25	28				
24:1	56, 291, 599, 653, 669, 670, 954	24:14-16	28	25:5-19	703-19
		24:14-22	689, 691-97	25:6	35, 704, 708
24:1-3	669, 670	24:15	492, 690, 691, 692, 954	25:7	177, 606, 709
24:1-4	42, 56, 78, 84, 418, 668, 669, 670-75, 677			25:7-9	301
		24:16	85, 281, 338, 418, 689, 690, 691, 693-95	25:7-10	530
				25:8	709
24:1-5	668-76			25:9	56, 179, 700, 704, 710, 725
24:1–25:3	669	24:17	31, 32, 34, 35, 36, 37, 40, 47, 49, 174, 286, 393, 395, 396, 523, 687, 690, 691, 695, 748, 806		
24:1–25:4	84, 668-702			25:10	704, 711
24:2	669, 673			25:11	704
24:3	673			25:11-12	57, 78, 86, 418, 703, 704, 711-13
24:4	46, 57, 62, 341, 342, 436, 489, 669, 674			25:12	340, 455, 570, 704
		24:17-18	78, 85, 348, 396, 418, 689, 690, 695-96	25:13	704, 713
24:5	66, 84, 296, 418, 579, 585, 669, 675			25:13-14	28
		24:18	39, 48, 287, 337, 348, 493, 496, 514, 691, 695, 696	25:13-15	34, 63
24:6	49, 78, 84, 418, 487, 490, 669, 678, 679, 680-82, 683, 687			25:13-16	20, 27, 31, 35, 46, 78, 86, 342, 418, 703, 704, 713-15
		24:19	68, 69, 191, 395, 486, 492, 665, 691, 696		
24:6-13	678, 680-89			25:14	714
24:7	57, 58, 78, 84, 293, 418, 454, 529, 599, 678, 679, 680, 682-84, 817	24:19-20	806	25:15	235, 249, 715
		24:19-21	47, 393, 396	25:16	46, 62, 342, 704, 715
		24:19-22	53, 78, 85, 348, 396, 418, 667, 689-90, 696	25:17	262, 705, 715, 717
				25:17-18	648, 686
24:8	19, 267, 285, 434, 533, 535, 594, 679, 680, 684	24:20	395, 691, 696	25:17-19	86, 579, 703-4, 715-17
		24:21	395, 696		
		24:22	39, 48, 287, 348, 493, 691, 695, 696	25:18	716
24:8-9	56, 84, 418, 534, 679, 684-86			25:19	341, 369, 432, 489, 704, 705, 717, 892
24:9	262, 648, 680, 685, 716	25:1	363, 520, 534, 573, 698, 699		
				26	77, 87, 416, 418, 737, 738, 742
24:9-10	56				
24:10	680				

Scripture Index

26:1	489, 723, 721		170, 191, 252, 307,		336, 431, 434, 535,
26:1-4	65		427, 431, 721, 733,		594, 738, 742, 745
26:1-11	42, 86, 513, 545,		765	27:9-10	87, 738, 742-43
	719-20, 723-29	26:16	235, 238, 251, 265,	27:9-26	68
26:1-19	719-36		419, 722, 723, 733	27:10	39, 235, 453, 558,
26:2	59, 419, 427, 428,	26:16-17	350		742, 743
	430, 513, 723, 762	26:16-19	86, 87, 720, 721,	27:11	738, 744, 745, 833
26:2-3	765		733-35, 738, 742,	27:11-13	88, 412, 737, 743,
26:3	170, 535, 724		807		744-46, 756, 797
26:4	429, 722, 724,	26:17	71, 235, 302, 453,	27:11-26	738, 742, 743-51
	728, 762		558, 733, 734	27:12	64, 68, 191, 738,
26:5	174, 238, 369, 397,	26:17-18	733, 734		746
	711, 722, 724, 725,	26:17-19	6, 723	27:12-13	52, 411, 423, 740,
	730, 794	26:18	63, 336, 733, 734,		745, 813, 817
26:5-7	722		735, 742	27:13-15	6
26:5-10	595, 721, 725	26:18-19	335, 763	27:13-25	77
26:5a	722	26:19	36, 43, 63, 721,	27:13-26	64
26:5b	722		735, 761, 766	27:14	434, 738, 744, 746
26:6	727	27–31	235	27:14-15	411
26:7	172	27–28	21, 36, 156, 737-98	27:14-26	87, 737, 738,
26:7-8	324	27	22, 77, 86, 88, 265,		743-49
26:8	43, 253, 254, 397,		542, 570, 640, 737,	27:15	41, 46, 62, 87, 191,
	727, 948		738, 761, 810		250, 279, 342, 744,
26:8-10	722	27:1	301, 302, 347, 738,		746, 756
26:9	180, 307, 365, 728		745, 821	27:15-26	41, 740, 744, 745,
26:9-10	73	27:1-3	738		746
26:10	19, 197, 724, 725,	27:1-8	87, 737-42, 833	27:16	57, 87, 287, 605,
	728, 733	27:1-10	65		606, 748
26:10b	722	27:1-14	426	27:16-19	744
26:11	19, 31, 57, 73, 419,	27:1-26	737-51, 833	27:17	46, 87, 571, 748
	431, 721, 722, 723,	27:2	737, 739	27:18	87, 748
	729, 787, 824	27:2-3	739, 740	27:19	31, 34, 35, 36, 37,
26:11-13	286, 433, 722,	27:2-4	271		40, 47, 87, 174,
	806	27:3	162, 170, 172, 307,		286, 393, 395, 523,
26:12	6, 319, 395, 419,		542, 737, 741, 821		695, 748, 806
	486, 723, 729	27:3-11	87	27:20	87, 640, 748
26:12-13	47, 393, 433, 434	27:4	3, 10, 737, 738,	27:20-23	744
26:12-15	86, 429, 481,		739, 740	27:21	87, 748
	720, 723, 729-33	27:5	741	27:22	87, 640, 749
26:13	395, 529, 722, 725,	27:5-7	737, 741	27:23	87, 640, 749
	763	27:6	741	27:24	87, 289, 749
26:13-15	486, 595	27:6-8	6	27:24-25	744
26:13a	730	27:7	31, 73, 429, 433,	27:25	524, 570, 749
26:13b-14	739		741, 787	27:26	88, 162, 234, 355,
26:13b-15	730	27:8	162, 542, 737, 738,		542, 744, 745, 749,
26:14	453, 731		741, 821		821, 844, 954
26:14-15	62, 721	27:9	19, 157, 266, 335,	27:27	760
26:15	32, 53, 59, 60, 68,			27:35	31, 35, 36, 87

996

Scripture Index

28–31	811, 813		335, 350, 355, 742, 756, 758, 763, 766, 820	28:21	41, 755, 769, 771, 794, 891
28	4, 7, 21, 26, 39, 41, 52, 64, 68, 77, 87, 88, 191, 265, 411, 423, 737, 738, 742, 745, 747, 756, 760, 783, 817, 870			28:21-22	32, 811
		28:10	59, 756, 764	28:21b	756
		28:11	170, 339, 733, 755, 758, 762, 765, 785, 819	28:22	770
				28:22-24	784
				28:22-25	6
28:1	267, 453, 490, 735, 738, 755, 761, 764, 766, 767, 793	28:11-12	33, 778	28:22b	772
		28:11b	756	28:23	406, 772
		28:12	32, 191, 403, 404, 406, 490, 759, 765, 772, 896	28:23-24	32, 41, 771
28:1-2	453, 558, 756, 758, 766, 797			28:24	178, 769, 773, 794
				28:25	41, 758, 773
28:1-4	6	28:12-13	6, 797	28:26	41, 755, 773
28:1-6	88, 751, 761-63, 797	28:12-13a	758, 762, 786	28:27	340, 759, 774, 782, 794, 798
		28:13	238, 405, 759, 765		
28:1-9	764	28:13-15	728	28:27-28	774, 811
28:1-14	64, 68, 191, 751-52, 758, 761-66, 797	28:13b	756	28:27-30	6
		28:13b-14	758, 797	28:27-35	760
		28:14	208, 320, 755, 756, 766, 787, 840	28:27-37	88, 753, 757, 759, 760, 774-84, 797
28:1-19	37, 39, 751-98			28:28	759, 776
28:1-68	355, 405, 755, 761	28:15	41, 235, 267, 453, 558, 759, 761, 766, 768, 772, 786, 793, 794, 797, 810, 890	28:28-29	782
28:1a	761			28:28-34	782
28:1b-2	761			28:28b	647
28:2	761, 763, 766, 767			28:29	239, 692, 756, 777, 780, 781, 900
28:2-6	761	28:15-19	88, 752, 759, 766-67, 797		
28:2-14	764			28:29-30	781
28:3	757, 758, 761, 767	28:15-68	30, 64, 752-97, 811, 819	28:30	41, 296, 318, 584, 585, 778, 785
28:3-6	756, 758, 778				
28:3-12	490	28:16	757, 767	28:30-31	789
28:4	339, 757, 758, 762, 767, 785, 790, 820	28:16-18	784	28:30-33	777, 778, 785
		28:16-19	756, 768, 778	28:31	179, 778, 780, 781, 900
28:4-5	33	28:16-20	6		
28:5	3, 757, 758, 762	28:17	2, 755, 757, 767	28:31-33	6, 761
28:6	313, 757, 758, 762, 767, 933	28:18	41, 339, 757, 762, 767, 785, 789, 790, 820	28:32	780, 782, 785, 796
				28:32-35	6
28:7	757, 758, 763, 773, 894			28:33	41, 239, 411, 767, 781, 783
		28:19	313, 757, 767		
28:7-10	6	28:20	178, 191, 249, 335, 431, 767, 769, 788, 789, 790, 794, 797, 839	28:34	756, 759, 776, 782, 796
28:7-14	88, 731-32, 756, 757, 758, 759, 763-66, 797			28:35	190, 340, 755, 759, 774, 782, 811, 954
				28:36	72, 190, 249, 250, 320, 411, 455, 756, 782, 795, 840
28:7-36	763	28:20-24	766		
28:8	191, 431, 758, 763, 769	28:20-26	88, 752-53, 757, 767-74, 797		
28:8-9	825			28:36-37	759
28:8-11	62	28:20-36	768	28:36-57	64
28:8b	756	28:20-46	756	28:37	41, 756, 783
28:9	36, 43, 71, 302,	28:20b	756		

997

28:38	784, 785	28:58-59	71, 760, 798	29:3 (4)	202, 801, 802, 954
28:38-40	339	28:58-61	64	29:4 (5)	30, 157, 185, 191, 350, 802, 805
28:38-41	6, 756	28:58-68	89, 755, 757, 760, 793-97, 798	29:4-5 (5-6)	335, 348, 807
28:38-46	88, 753-54, 757, 759, 760, 784-87, 797	28:59	42, 794	29:5 (6)	801, 802
28:39	779, 785	28:59-60	793	29:6 (7)	180, 365, 728, 802
28:40	329, 785, 789	28:59-61	811	29:6-7 (7-8)	801
28:41	785	28:60	371, 794	29:7 (8)	802
28:42	767, 784, 786	28:60-61	340	29:8 (9)	238, 798, 800, 802
28:43-44	490, 766, 786	28:61	25, 42, 89, 178, 542, 769, 793, 794, 798, 811, 813, 820, 833, 846	29:9 (10)	301, 804, 847
28:43-68	6			29:9-10 (10-11)	157, 805
28:44	759, 797			29:9-11 (10-12)	157, 267, 300, 805, 897
28:45	178, 235, 453, 558, 749, 759, 760, 761, 766, 767, 769, 784, 786, 794, 797, 798	28:62	172, 249, 397, 453, 558, 727, 766, 794	29:9-12 (10-13)	804
		28:62-63	64	29:9-14 (10-15)	800, 805, 834
		28:62-68	64		
		28:63	178, 249, 307, 354, 755, 769, 794, 818, 819	29:9-28 (10-29)	89, 803-14
28:45-46	759, 787, 797			29:10 (11)	431
28:46	254, 787			29:11 (12)	241, 798, 799, 805, 810
28:47	319, 320, 492, 599	28:64	42, 72, 249, 250, 252, 320, 411, 455, 783, 795, 840		
28:47-48	72, 320, 431, 787			29:11-12 (12-13)	62, 241
28:47-57	88, 754-57, 759, 787-93, 798			29:12 (13)	252, 335, 355, 734, 742, 804, 805, 807
28:48	41, 178, 755, 760, 769	28:64-68	32		
		28:65	190, 781, 795		
28:49	42, 472, 788, 922	28:66	796	29:13 (14)	798, 805, 810
28:49-51	318	28:67	302, 796	29:13-14 (14-15)	268, 804, 807
28:49-52	41, 788	28:68	34, 335, 755, 760, 769, 774, 796, 798, 801		
28:49-57	32			29:15 (16)	185, 376, 801
28:50	789			29:15-16 (16-17)	804, 808
28:51	178, 319, 339, 760, 767, 769, 789, 794	28:69 (29:1)	2, 17, 23, 24, 25, 26, 43, 73, 74, 89, 156, 237, 265, 267, 798-99, 800, 801, 802, 829, 832	29:15-18 (16-19)	72
				29:16 (17)	250, 342
28:52	790			29:17 (18)	72, 320, 431, 454, 808, 811, 887, 954
28:53	42, 339, 755, 767, 790, 791				
28:54	42, 47, 455, 491	29-34	23	29:17-18 (18-19)	895
28:54-55	792	29-30	25, 73, 89, 232, 364, 799-826, 827, 829, 838	29:17-19 (18-20)	885
28:55	755, 760, 792			29:17-20 (18-21)	746, 804, 808
28:56	42, 47, 491, 792, 795	29:1 (2)	24, 157, 179, 738, 800, 801, 808, 827, 829, 948		
				29:17-27 (18-28)	321
28:56-57	792			29:18 (19)	798, 809, 825, 889
28:57	755, 760, 788, 792	29:1-2 (2-3)	232		
28:58	25, 59, 71, 89, 162, 240, 267, 341, 392, 542, 761, 767, 793, 794, 798, 821, 833, 834	29:1-8 (2-9)	89, 231, 799-803, 804, 806	29:18-19 (19-20)	747
		29:1-28 (2-29)	832	29:19 (20)	177, 341, 767, 794, 810, 892, 930
		29:2 (3)	238, 253, 254	29:19-20 (20-21)	819, 833
				29:20 (21)	542, 794, 798,

Scripture Index

	804, 811, 813, 816, 954	30:10	232, 235, 251, 542, 764, 794, 804, 815, 816, 818, 820, 821, 826, 833, 846	31:1-13	8
29:20-21 (21-22)	6			31:1–32:52	827-913
29:21-23 (22-24)	811, 895, 945			31:2	157, 183, 762, 829, 946, 947
29:21-27 (22-28)	787, 804	30:10-11	6	31:2-6	828, 829
29:22 (23)	36, 41	30:11	821, 876	31:3	178, 182, 362, 829, 832
29:23-25 (24-26)	812	30:11-14	89, 276, 489, 800, 815, 820, 821	31:3-4	6
29:23-27 (24-28)	6, 320	30:11-20	389, 815, 838	31:3-8	66
29:24 (25)	172, 798, 839	30:12	816, 817, 822, 954	31:4	161, 167, 178, 830
29:24-25 (25-26)	812	30:12-13	6	31:5	209, 830
29:25 (26)	72, 243, 411, 455, 795, 840, 878	30:13	822	31:6	66, 176, 179, 228, 252, 341, 401, 581, 582, 828, 830, 832, 955
		30:14	312, 821, 822, 841, 955		
29:26 (27)	794, 813, 817, 819, 825, 833	30:15	169, 729, 817, 824, 825	31:7	66, 170, 179, 182, 228, 321, 401, 489, 827, 829, 830, 832, 842
29:27 (28)	32, 209, 232, 813, 816	30:15-20	42, 45, 53-54, 89, 324, 347, 411, 800, 815, 818, 819, 823-26, 910		
29:28 (29)	162, 542, 794, 804, 813, 815, 816, 822, 838			31:7-8	223, 227, 831, 832, 838
		30:16	32, 34, 64, 68, 70, 71, 191, 235, 302, 303, 307, 310, 311, 350, 399, 431, 816, 825, 826	31:7-13	90, 831-35
30	89, 170, 232, 815			31:8	176, 582, 830, 832, 842, 955
30:1	6, 68, 169, 191, 256, 815, 816, 817, 824, 825			31:8-16	6
				31:9	19, 301, 385, 541, 542, 594, 794, 821, 832, 845, 846
30:1-2	453, 817	30:16-17	6		
30:1-3	816, 817	30:17	72, 243, 454, 808, 825	31:9-10a	827
30:1-10	52, 89, 232, 250, 814-21	30:17-18	64, 232, 248, 320	31:9-12	804, 845
30:2	251, 816, 819, 826	30:18	53, 170, 249, 825	31:9-13	21, 434, 828, 831, 832-34, 841, 844, 846
30:2-3	251	30:19	32, 68, 169, 191, 249, 385, 816, 817, 824, 825, 847, 872		
30:3	249, 817			31:9-30	836
30:4	252, 816, 817, 818, 954	30:19-20	6, 62, 64, 235, 303, 428, 825	31:10	157, 486, 515
				31:10-11	487, 515, 833
30:4-6	6	30:20	70, 170, 237, 249, 310, 311, 453, 558, 816, 824, 826	31:10-13	51-52, 266, 516
30:4b	818			31:11	157, 427, 428, 517, 542, 829, 834
30:5	818				
30:6	39, 70, 235, 251, 311, 391, 816, 817, 818, 825, 826	31–34	9, 16, 18, 25, 73, 90, 800, 826-949	31:11-12	507, 821
		31–33	829	31:12	50, 71, 157, 267, 431, 646, 806, 832, 834, 847
30:6-8	399	31–32	65		
30:7	819	31	827		
30:8	453, 816, 817, 819, 820, 826	31:1	157, 738, 827, 828, 829	31:12-13	71, 235, 239, 240, 268, 910
30:8-10	817	31:1-6	90, 827-31, 832, 836, 844, 911	31:13	50, 239, 249, 832, 834
30:9	191, 339, 765, 794, 816, 819				
30:9-10	453	31:1-8	225, 828, 831	31:14	829, 836, 837

Scripture Index

31:14-15	90, 225, 227, 557, 828, 835, 836, 837-38, 842	
31:14-23	90, 827, 828, 835-43, 844, 911	
31:14a	827	
31:14b	827	
31:15	836, 838	
31:16	33, 769, 838, 839, 912	
31:16-21	827	
31:16-22	90, 828, 836, 837, 838-42	
31:16-29	364	
31:17	157, 830, 839, 840, 841, 889	
31:17-18	837, 887	
31:18	6, 836, 840	
31:19	50, 197, 235, 822, 840, 841, 845	
31:19-21	857, 910	
31:19-22	854	
31:20	72, 73, 170, 240, 307, 318, 319, 320, 837, 839, 840, 841, 842, 884, 885, 887	
31:20-21	65, 807	
31:21	52, 830, 836, 840, 841, 889	
31:21-23	6	
31:22	50, 235, 837, 840, 842, 845, 848, 909	
31:22b	844, 847	
31:23	66, 90, 182, 228, 401, 557, 582, 827, 828, 830, 832, 836, 837, 842, 911	
31:23b	842	
31:24	542, 832, 833, 844, 845, 848	
31:24-27	844	
31:24-29	828	
31:24-30	15, 16, 17, 90, 827, 828, 832, 843-48, 909	
31:25	846	
31:25-26	434, 833	
31:26	16, 21, 25, 180, 235, 383, 384, 542, 794, 846	
31:26-27	841	
31:26-29	6	
31:27	364, 373, 837, 846, 847	
31:27-29	841-42	
31:28	249, 301, 806, 825, 844, 846, 847	
31:28-30	844	
31:29	191, 242, 248, 249, 250, 251, 303, 367, 454, 846, 847	
31:30	90, 366, 646, 738, 842, 844, 846, 847, 854, 909	
31:34	8	
32	4, 18, 38, 73, 248, 447, 837, 857, 859, 908	
32:1	249, 825, 847, 858, 872	
32:1-2	854	
32:1-3	91, 858, 862, 869, 871	
32:1-43	52, 90, 91, 827, 848-909	
32:2	872, 930	
32:3	59, 226, 301, 376, 860, 862, 873	
32:3-5	6	
32:4	62, 63, 338, 553, 858, 873, 885, 886, 887, 895, 955	
32:4-5	95	
32:4-8	38	
32:4-9	91, 803, 858, 865, 871	
32:5	847, 873, 874, 884, 887, 955	
32:5-6	872	
32:5-33	853	
32:6	858, 866, 873, 874, 885, 886, 888, 900	
32:6a	861	
32:7	858, 875	
32:7-8	908	
32:7-9	65, 252	
32:7-12	852
32:8	3, 4, 206, 244, 571, 865, 876, 879, 904
32:8-9	30, 244, 489, 875, 879
32:8b	869
32:9	63, 244, 335, 377, 860, 862, 864, 865, 876, 878, 881
32:10	176, 354, 858, 879, 884
32:10-11	880
32:10-12	38, 190, 764
32:10-13	6
32:10-14	91, 287, 801, 854, 858, 867, 871
32:10-18	33, 36, 886
32:11	180, 471, 789, 857, 880
32:11-12	30
32:12	60, 254, 839, 861, 881, 882, 899
32:13	354, 841, 881, 939
32:13-14	38, 191, 879, 899, 931
32:13-18	65, 73, 318, 406, 787
32:14	213, 857, 859, 867, 881, 882
32:14-15a	841
32:14b	859, 899, 938
32:15	858, 873, 875, 883, 886, 887, 888, 895, 924
32:15-18	38, 91, 348, 354, 355, 769, 838, 841, 852, 858, 866, 867, 871, 881, 884, 898
32:15-22	13, 14-15, 279, 856, 885
32:15-30	177
32:15a	319, 866, 868, 869
32:15b	866
32:16	38, 46, 62, 245, 249, 342, 839, 857, 866, 881, 888
32:16-22	885

Scripture Index

32:17	411, 795, 813, 866, 885, 888, 955	32:30	861, 866, 867, 873, 894, 895, 932	32:42	859, 862, 890, 896, 902, 908
32:17-18	884	32:30-31	885, 893	32:42b	859
32:17-19	6	32:30-32	857	32:43	3, 4, 63, 91, 93, 240, 857, 858, 859, 864, 865, 869, 871, 897, 901, 903, 955
32:17b	867	32:30b	863		
32:17b-18	899	32:31	863, 873, 895, 899		
32:18	238, 245, 319, 348, 353, 368, 864, 866, 867, 873, 883, 885, 886, 895	32:32	36, 895		
		32:32-33	809		
		32:32a	863	32:43b	859
		32:32b	865	32:44	738, 829, 840, 844, 854, 909
32:19	841, 846, 858, 861, 879, 886	32:33	865, 891, 896		
		32:34	857, 858, 866, 893, 896, 900	32:44-46	15, 16, 17
32:19-22	91, 249, 363, 839, 858, 863, 864, 871			32:44-47	92, 827, 844, 845, 909-10
		32:34-38	91, 858, 863, 868, 871		
32:19-25	38			32:45	157, 844, 909
32:19-27	872, 901	32:34-42	894	32:46	25, 52, 239, 267, 542, 832, 844, 845, 910
32:19-33	886	32:34-43	38, 854, 886		
32:20	840, 887, 894	32:35	63, 338, 896, 901, 908, 955		
32:20-21	839			32:47	32, 53, 170, 235, 249, 826, 909, 910
32:20b	874	32:35b	863		
32:21	854, 855, 857, 864, 885, 886, 887, 955	32:35b-36	897	32:48	829, 911
		32:36	857, 861, 863, 897, 900, 901, 903, 904, 955	32:48-49	943
32:21-22	245			32:48-52	92, 225, 827, 910-13
32:22	38, 362, 770, 863, 888				
		32:36-38	896	32:49	227, 384, 911, 943
32:22-25	900	32:37	817, 860, 867, 869, 870, 873, 895, 898	32:50	838, 912, 943
32:23	857, 858, 889, 902			32:50-52	181
32:23-25	889	32:37-38	38, 860, 898	32:51	36, 43, 60, 160, 321, 922, 926
32:23-27	91, 858, 871	32:37-38a	867		
32:23-42	819	32:37-39	225	32:51-52	321, 912, 926
32:23b-25	889	32:38	860, 880, 899	32:52	911, 945
32:24	32, 888, 890, 891	32:38a	867, 869	33	68, 73, 191, 828, 857, 868, 911, 917
32:24-25	6, 769, 857, 890	32:38b	860, 868		
32:25	789, 891	32:39	60, 254, 279, 392, 712, 857, 858, 861, 873, 881, 893, 899, 900, 901, 928	33:1	23, 917, 919
32:26	892			33:1-29	90, 92, 827, 913-41
32:26-27	58, 64, 377, 812, 898			33:1–34:12	913-49
				33:2	158, 159, 878, 918, 919, 920, 922, 923, 924, 931
32:26-33	38	32:39-40	861		
32:27	860, 865, 887, 892, 893, 901	32:39-42	91, 858, 871		
		32:39a	863	33:2-3	61
32:27-29	6	32:40	861, 863, 901	33:2-5	92, 917, 918
32:27b	860	32:40b	901	33:2-8	917
32:28	858, 863, 893	32:41	63, 313, 338, 857, 897, 901, 905	33:2b	935
32:28-29	893			33:3	918, 922, 924
32:28-33	91, 858, 863, 865, 871, 893	32:41-42	896, 900	33:4	918, 923, 935
		32:41-43	175	33:5	539, 806, 884, 918, 919, 921, 923, 924, 937
32:29	857, 887, 894	32:41b	903, 904		

1001

Scripture Index

33:6	917, 918, 924, 934, 935	34:5	945	4:21	324, 561
33:6-25	92	34:6	202, 228, 384, 945	4:23-24	764
33:7	917, 918, 925	34:7	157, 829, 942, 946	5:1	168, 178, 412
33:8	321, 373, 912, 925, 926	34:8	157, 947	5:9-10	412
		34:9	842, 947	5:10	506, 943
33:8-10	927	34:10	61, 269, 400, 450, 557, 947	5:10-12	506
33:8-22	917			6-8	318
33:9	927	34:10-12	29, 560	6	912
33:10	434, 459, 535, 833, 927	34:11	254, 787, 942	6:2	169
		34:11-12	6, 948	6:6	385, 846
33:11	917, 918, 927	34:12	157, 179, 254, 324, 832, 942	6:9	223
33:12	917, 918, 929, 938			6:12	385, 846
33:13	810, 930, 938			6:18	459
33:13-15	931	**Joshua**		6:18-19	342
33:13-16	931	1	8, 828	6:19	67
33:14	930	1:1-2	945	6:20	362
33:15	931, 935	1:3	181, 190	6:21	66, 332-33, 587
33:16	918, 931	1:3-5	167	6:24	67, 342, 458
33:17	917, 931	1:4	169, 329, 785	7	67, 333, 342, 694, 811
33:18	932	1:5	341, 582		
33:19	917, 918, 933, 935	1:7	208, 945	7:5	178
33:20	922, 931, 934, 936	1:7-8	802, 844	7:7	206, 226, 330
33:21	917, 918, 919, 935	1:8	313, 542, 822, 846	7:9	377, 893
33:22	918, 934, 935, 944	1:9	179, 582	7:11	529
33:23	918, 936, 944	1:10	174	7:15	529
33:24	918, 937	1:12-13	222	7:20-26	274, 293
33:24-26	6	1:13	432, 945	7:21	295
33:25	918, 937	1:15	432, 945	7:24-25	67, 333, 458, 693
33:26	59, 884, 903, 919, 924, 937	2:6	619	7:26	459
		2:9	411	8:1	169, 170
33:26-29	92, 917, 918, 922	2:10	161	8:2	67, 210, 333, 459
33:27	917, 938	2:11	178	8:11	457
33:28	922, 930, 938	2:15	879	8:22	209
33:29	335, 881, 917, 918, 919, 938	3:2	174	8:23-29	610
		3:3	19, 385, 535	8:24	587, 846
33:29b	869	3:3-17	846	8:27	67, 210, 459
34	9, 827, 939	3:8	383	8:28	459
34:1	220, 227, 228, 263, 911, 936, 942, 943, 946	3:10	206, 321, 328, 330, 331	8:29	609, 610
				8:30	741
		3:16	220	8:30-32	741
34:1-2	941-49	4	739	8:30-35	411, 738, 739, 806, 833
34:1-4	911	4:5	878		
34:1-8	911	4:6	324	8:31	1, 844
34:1-12	92, 225, 828, 831	4:6-7	324	8:32	1, 541, 844
34:2	410, 944	4:8	878	8:32-33	833
34:3	352, 812, 944	4:13	943	8:33	19, 385, 535, 745, 746, 846
34:4	170, 827, 942, 945	4:19-20	412, 739		
		4:20-24	324	8:34	844

Scripture Index

8:35	646, 806	12:14	184	16:10	67, 333
9–12	223	13:3	202, 203	17:1	220
9	331, 334	13:3-4	202	17:13	67, 333
9:4	883	13:8-13	217	17:15	201, 331
9:5 (LXX)	541	13:9	210, 214	17:16	215, 582
9:6	334	13:11	213, 214, 219	17:18	215, 582
9:9	939	13:12	161, 201	18:1-10	572
9:10	101	13:13	219	18:7	386, 544
9:17	331	13:14	386, 544	18:16	201, 929
9:21-27	586, 807	13:15-16	210	18:28	332
9:23-27	586	13:15-23	925	19:1-8	925
10:8	176, 341	13:15-28	217	19:2-3	184
10:14	179	13:16	210	19:5	202
10:19	716	13:17	207	19:10-16	933
10:20	846	13:18	208, 209	19:17-23	933
10:22-27	341	13:19	167, 195	19:24-31	937
10:24	939	13:20	228, 263, 922, 935	19:32-39	936
10:25	176	13:22	550	19:35	220
10:26-27	609, 610	13:24-28	934	19:40-48	936
10:28	209, 587	13:25	210	19:47	936, 944
10:28-40	333	13:27	162, 220	20	258, 566
10:28–12:24	318	13:29-31	220	20:4	301, 525, 568
10:30	209	13:30	218	20:6	568
10:33	209	13:31	161	20:7	566
10:37	209	13:32	943	20:7-8	569
10:39	209	13:33	386, 544	20:8	259
10:40	209	14:6	181, 919	21	546
10:42	179	14:6-14	181	21:13	159, 566
11:2	220	14:8	178	21:27	566
11:3	168, 330, 331, 332, 412, 588	14:8-9	181	21:36	209, 259
		14:9	181	21:36-37	208
11:4	582	14:11	762, 829	21:37	208
11:10-20	333	14:12	181	21:38	259
11:12	341	14:12-15	178	21:44	432
11:13	459	14:14	181	22:1-6	222
11:14	210, 459	15:1-4	183	22:3	399
11:17	169, 184	15:3	184	22:4	432, 511
11:18	209	15:8	201, 929	22:5	251
11:19	331	15:10	920	22:17	884
11:20	818	15:13-14	178	22:24	324
11:21-22	178	15:14	181	22:27-28	324
12:1-5	213	15:21-32	168, 944	23:1	432
12:2	161, 210	15:26-32	925	23:2	266, 847
12:3	168, 220, 263, 922	15:27-28	202	23:3	179
12:4	161	15:33-44	168	23:4	439, 801
12:5	213, 219	15:42	159, 925	23:6	1, 208
12:7	169, 184	15:47	203	23:7	320
12:7-24	341	15:63	332	23:9	341

1003

Scripture Index

23:10	179, 894	2:1	839	5:25	882
23:12	335	2:2	334	6:3	716
23:12-13	334	2:3	340, 439	6:8	277
23:13	439	2:7	401	6:8-10	276
23:14	251	2:10	401	6:10	319
23:16	529	2:12-13	320	6:11	701
24	22, 826	2:12-15	839	6:12	582
24:1	266, 412, 426, 806, 837, 847	2:14	894	6:13	876
		2:16	556	6:16	582
24:1-28	806	2:17	839	6:19	507
24:2	279	2:18	556	6:22	226
24:2-13	725, 801	2:20-23	341	6:26	423
24:3	410	2:20–3:4	569	6:33	716
24:8	196	2:22	321	6:36	778
24:11	328, 330	3:3	169, 331	6:39-40	253
24:12	161, 340, 902	3:3-6	334	7:1-23	582
24:13	318, 938	3:4	321	7:3	178, 585
24:14	410, 553	3:5-6	329, 330	7:12	716
24:14-15	824	3:8	894	8:4-5	717
24:15	405	3:9	778	8:7	699
24:16	839	3:13	352, 944	8:16	699
24:19-20	245	3:15	778	8:21	301
24:20	405, 839	3:16	587	8:23	539, 924
24:23	839	3:22	587	8:26	496
24:25-26	412	3:23-25	937	8:28	362
24:26	527, 740	3:30	362	8:33	839
24:29	829	4:2	894	9	412, 540
24:31	401	4:3	215, 582	9:6	412
24:32	412	4:4-5	534	9:7-13	319
		4:6	933	9:27	696
Judges		4:9	489	9:37	551
1	318	4:10	933	9:45	811
1:1-20	925	4:11	920	9:53	681, 682
1:3	439	4:11-12	920	10:3-5	218
1:4-5	331	4:12-14	933	10:6-9	839
1:8	318	4:21	653	10:12	716
1:16	352, 920, 944	4:23	362	10:14	898
1:17	184	5	925	10:16	727, 839
1:18	203	5:2	583, 902	11	916
1:19	582	5:3	872	11:11	786
1:19-36	318	5:4	183, 220	11:17	188, 189, 190, 192
1:21	318, 332	5:5	919	11:17-18	195
1:21-36	329	5:8	886	11:18	189, 195, 197, 205
1:22-26	330	5:12	598	11:20	209
1:27-33	331	5:14	935	11:20-21	209
1:27-35	67, 333, 586	5:14-15	933	11:21-22	209
1:34-35	936	5:15-16	924	11:22	206
1:34-36	330	5:24	937	11:30-31	666

1004

11:30-40	430, 666	2:17	701	5:7	895
11:33	210, 362	2:20	688	5:9	198, 775
11:37	368	3:1-5	45	5:12	775
12:15	715	3:3	785	6:2	550
13–16	936	3:7	640	6:12	208
13:2	936	3:9	640	6:17	203
13:5	902	3:10	688	6:18	204
13:7	931	3:13	606	7:3	839
13:25	936	4:1-6	568	7:3-4	320
14:1	936	4:4-15	287	7:5-9	368
14:3	334			7:6	534
14:8	334	**1 Samuel**		7:10	198
14:20	673	1	426, 428, 431	7:13	362
15:2	673	1:4-5	601	7:15-17	450, 521, 534
15:7	896	1:8	492	7:16	423
16:7-8	947	1:11	430, 666, 902	7:17	930
16:17	902	1:16	457	8	539
16:21	681	1:21-28	430	8:1-3	521
16:28	226, 896	1:24	883	8:1-4	534
17:2	648	2:5	763	8:3-5	539
17:6	321, 431	2:6	900	8:4	930
17:7-13	433	2:7	922	8:5	539
18	176, 936	2:12-17	884	8:6-9	368
18:11	223	2:13-15	510	8:7	539
18:16-17	223	2:13-17	429, 545	8:14-17	482, 729
18:27-29	944	2:22-25	884	8:20	539
19:1-30	433	2:27	919	9:3	725
19:10	332	2:28	544, 927	9:3-4	614
19:22	457	2:29	884	9:6	919
19:22-30	274, 290	3:17	440	9:9	450
19:23-24	634	3:20	944	9:10-17	539
20:2	646	4	855	9:11	450
20:6	634	4:1-2	606	9:13	933
20:10	634	4:3-4	383, 833	9:13-14	423
20:26	184	4:4	60, 383, 582	9:16	778
20:26-28	930	4:4-9	427	9:18-19	450
20:28	386	4:5	708	9:19	423
20:40	459	4:6	495, 710	9:20	614, 725, 910
21:2	184	4:6-7	383	9:21	930
21:6	897	4:7-8	710	9:24	510, 933
21:19-23	430, 515	4:8	895	9:25	619
21:23	878	4:10	708	10:1-9	451
21:25	321, 431	4:11	606	10:3	930
		4:14	711	10:5	423
Ruth		4:21	708	10:19	806, 840
2–3	513	4:21-22	833	10:20-24	539
2	505, 696	5:6	775	10:26	930
2:14	765	5:6-12	775	10:27	457

Scripture Index

11	539	17:46	377	30	716		
11:1	334	17:47	646	30:1-2	715		
11:1-2	586	17:56	301	30:11-15	655		
11:7	796	18:1	455	30:14	203		
11:11	763	18:3	455	30:17	716		
12:1-4	524	18:4	902	30:22	457		
12:3	711, 780	18:5	802	30:28	210		
12:3-4	782	18:9	618	31:10	609		
12:9-10	839	18:13	173, 762, 829	31:10-13	610		
12:12	539	18:16	762, 829	31:11-13	773		
12:14-15	405	18:21	335				
12:17-18	368	18:25	585	**2 Samuel**			
12:20	453	18:27	585	1:1	716		
12:25	405	20:13	716	1:18	841		
13–14	855	20:17	455	1:21	882, 938		
13:8	510	21:2 (1)	930	1:22	902		
13:14	227	21:4-7 (3-6)	731	2:5	688		
14:3	582	21:6 (5)	653	2:26	902		
14:18	582, 716	21:12 (11)	932	3:3	219		
14:20	768	21:13-16 (12-15)	776	3:14	585		
14:21	495	22:7	173	3:35	732		
14:32	465, 508	22:9-19	930	3:39	792		
14:32-35	437	23:6-13	926	4:4	508		
14:36-42	582	23:7	214	4:12	609		
14:41-42	926	23:19	922	5:1	539		
15	67, 333, 716	23:20	895	5:6-7	318, 332		
15:2	716	23:26	508	5:6-9	207		
15:2-4	534	24:19	301	6	443		
15:3	458, 587	25:1	158	6:2	383		
15:6	920	25:10	655	6:21	539		
15:7	716	25:27	401	7	187, 443		
15:10-11	368	25:30	227	7:1	432		
15:11	749	26:6	330	7:6-7	653		
15:13	364, 749	26:19	454	7:7	806		
15:18	717	27:8	219	7:11	432		
15:22	393, 883	27:8-9	716	7:14	533		
15:22-23	558	27:10	920	7:18-29	226		
15:28	294	28	732	7:22-23	900		
15:32-33	902	28:3	372, 552, 553	7:22-24	225		
16:1-13	539	28:5-19	552	7:24	734		
16:7	349, 808	28:6	450	8:1	362		
16:20	465	28:7	732	8:3	169		
17	178	28:7-8	550	8:12	716		
17:18	173	28:8	552	8:13-14	650		
17:22	616	28:9	553	10–11	203		
17:26	301	28:18	716	10:6	219		
17:36	301	28:24	435, 465, 507, 615	10:19	586		
17:44-46	773	29:6	829	11–12	330, 636		

11	274, 292	21:2	167	4:25	351
11:2	619	21:8-9	609, 610	4:26	540
11:11	383, 653	21:9-10	505	4:33	169
11:16-25	290	21:10	774	5-6	443
11:21	682	21:15-22	178	5:1 (4:21)	169
11:25	902	22	888	5:2-3 (4:22-23)	465
12:1-6	534	22:3	873	5:3 (4:23)	465, 470
12:1-13	292	22:5-6	457	5:17 (3)	939
12:1-15	542	22:7-20	888	5:18 (4)	432
12:4	437, 465	22:9	810	5:22 (8)	169
12:11	294, 778	22:14	876	6:5-6	484
12:18	292	22:32	873, 895, 900	6:30-31	598
12:20	785	22:47	873, 885	7:18	352
12:26	200	23:3	873	7:20	352
12:28	427, 764	23:4	872	7:25	243
12:31	586	24:3	172	7:29	243
13:12	600, 632, 634	24:5	210	7:36	243
13:15	630	24:7	331	7:42	352
13:37	219	24:18-25	332	7:44	243
13:37-38	219	24:22	701	7:46	944
14:2	44, 785	24:23	928	8	426, 515
14:3	558			8:2	515
14:4	778	**1 Kings**		8:3	385, 846
14:6	711	1	602	8:6	383, 385, 833, 846
14:19	558	1:5	540	8:9	159, 365, 383, 846
15:1	540	1:9	933	8:12-13	428
15:3	525	1:36	747	8:15-21	426
15:7-8	666	1:41	933	8:16	428
15:8	219	2:1	837	8:20	364
15:23	377	2:3	1, 399, 802	8:23	225, 281, 900
15:32	423	2:4	251, 364	8:23-25	338
16:20-22	778	2:10	838	8:25	490
16:21-22	640	2:22-25	640	8:27	390
16:22	619	2:26	386	8:27-30	59, 427, 733
17:2	717	2:28-34	566	8:27-53	252
17:11	255	2:38	173	8:31-32	594
17:12	838	2:39-40	655	8:35	406
17:29	882	2:42	173	8:35-36	772
18:2b	439	3:2	443	8:37	533, 684, 771, 785
18:22	439	3:3	443	8:43	427
19:1 (18:33)	795	3:6	338	8:44	428
19:20 (19)	739	3:7	762, 829	8:47	256
19:25 (24)	598	3:8	336	8:47-51	250
20:14	219	3:10-14	541	8:47-53	251
20:16	44	3:12	173	8:48	251, 428
21	694	3:16-18	45	8:51	244
21:1-9	693	3:16-28	534	8:52	238
21:1-14	903	4:13	213, 218	8:53	945

Scripture Index

Ref	Pages	Ref	Pages	Ref	Pages
8:56	432, 717, 945	12:22	919	18:23-25	423
8:60	310	12:25	412	18:24	173
8:63	584	12:28-29	243, 380	18:28	464, 644
8:65	515, 646	12:31	423	18:40	453, 461
8:66	492, 787	12:31-32	19	18:65	515
9:3	426, 427	12:32	243, 423, 424, 515	19:8	159, 366, 920
9:8-9	812	13:1	919	19:10	813
9:9	839	13:3-5	451	19:11-12	743
9:15-21	586	13:4-5	919	19:14	813
9:19	169	13:34	321	19:21	435, 437
9:20-21	67, 329, 333	14:9	249	20:1-9	686
9:25	506	14:10	878	20:1-30	582
9:26	192, 193	14:11	761, 773	20:12	516
10:1	321	14:13	882	20:16	516
10:8	386, 536	14:14-15	425	20:27-30	582
10:9	337, 521	14:15	249, 813	20:30	891
10:14-15	541	14:16	492	20:33	551
10:14-26	541	14:21	426, 428, 598	20:34-43	334
10:26-27	540	14:23	423, 424, 425, 443	21	274
10:27	541	14:23-24	657, 660	21:1-14	565
10:28	332	14:24	363, 661	21:1-16	294
10:28-29	540	15:12	657, 660	21:2	403
10:29	330	15:14	443	21:3	572
11:1	330	15:19	839	21:8	301
11:1-2	598	15:30	249	21:8-13	531, 573
11:1-13	334	16:2	249	21:10	457
11:5	425, 455, 808	16:4	773	21:11	301
11:7	455, 911	16:7	249	21:13	456, 457
11:9	182	16:13	249, 888	21:19	290
11:13	428	16:26	249, 888	21:21	898
11:17-18	158	16:30-33	334	21:26	363
11:18	541	16:32	424	22	59, 259, 451, 559, 562
11:29-39	539	16:33	249, 424, 425	22:2	562
11:32	428	17–19	451	22:11	932
11:33	321, 425	17–18	406	22:19-22	878
11:34	428	17:1	386, 536, 542, 772, 938	22:25	891
11:36	426, 428	17:8-24	948	22:28	560
11:38	321	17:12	282	22:43	443
11:43	838	18–19	426	22:45 (44)	11
12:1	412	18:2	515	22:47 (46)	657, 660
12:3	646	18:15	386	22:49 (48)	193
12:7	542	18:17-19	542		
12:8	386, 536	18:18	772	**2 Kings**	
12:9-11	788	18:19	423	1–2	449, 580
12:10	884	18:19-46	451	1:9	173
12:11	699	18:20-40	948	1:11	173
12:14	699	18:21	824	1:13	173
12:15	208, 364				

Scripture Index

Reference	Pages	Reference	Pages	Reference	Pages
2:8	948	14:4	443	18:22	12, 37, 47, 423, 425, 433, 442
2:9	604	14:5-6	694	18:31	318, 351
2:14	948	14:6	1	18:32	350, 352, 882
2:19-22	948	14:15-16	784	18:34	898
3:1-2	424	14:22	192	19:8	159
3:14	386	14:25	220	19:9	444
3:19	588	14:26	898	19:15	310, 383
3:25	588	15:4	443	19:15-19	225
3:26-27	649, 925	15:12	280	19:19	310
4:1	49, 488, 681	15:13	599	19:26	771
4:1-7	686	15:16	566	19:29	445
4:1-44	948	15:29	249, 783, 813, 933	19:29-37	451
4:23	284	15:35	443	20:5	900
4:43	765	16	443	20:7	351, 774
4:44	765	16:3	363, 440, 549	20:16-19	560
5:1-14	948	16:4	443	21:1	446
5:7	900	16:6	329	21:2-18	446
5:23	485	16:9	727, 782	21:3	47, 243, 424, 425, 530
6:1-7	948	16:10-11	527	21:3-5	529, 532
6:22	902	17:3-6	783	21:4	426
6:26	778	17:6	784	21:4-5	530
6:26-29	792	17:9-11	426	21:5	243, 530
6:27	496	17:10	423, 424, 425	21:6	249, 440, 549, 550, 551, 552, 553
7:6	330	17:11	249	21:7	383, 425, 426, 428
7:15	508	17:13	262, 556	21:8	490, 945
8:3	494	17:14	364	21:14	244, 490
8:4-5	948	17:16	243, 380, 424, 530, 532	21:15	249
8:12	581, 587, 892	17:17	440, 549, 551	22–23	7, 9, 16, 18, 426, 442, 446
8:20-22	650	17:18	182	22:2	208, 442
8:28	259	17:23	795	22:3-20	18
9:1-13	539	17:24-41	439	22:8	6, 16, 383, 846, 852, 856
9:7	903	17:25-28	439	22:8–23:25	17
9:8	898	17:35	319	22:16-17	7, 14, 15, 856
9:11	776	17:36	254, 255, 378	22:16-20	13
9:20	776	18–20	443	22:17	599, 769, 839, 885, 889
9:22	551	18:1	445	22:18-20	14
9:26	158	18:2	444	22:20	560
9:32	645	18:3	442	23	7
10:15-24	920	18:4	12, 37, 242, 423, 424, 425, 426, 433, 442, 444	23:1-3	18
10:27	424	18:7	320	23:2	16, 833, 834
10:29	380	18:9	445	23:2-3	806
10:30	280	18:9-10	426-27	23:3	251, 320, 733, 749
10:33	925	18:13	444		
11:8	762	18:13-16	445		
12:3	443	18:17–19:37	445		
12:10	485				
13:6	424				
13:20-21	948				

Scripture Index

23:4	383	5:22	783
23:4-5	243	5:23	214
23:4-20	7, 16, 39, 446	5:26	783, 813, 925, 934
23:5	243, 424, 529	6:63-64 (78-79)	208
23:6	371, 425	6:78	209
23:6-15	250	8:6-7	783
23:7	657	10:13	552
23:8	423, 433	12:8	934
23:9	546	13:6	383
23:10	426, 549	15:2	385
23:11	243, 529	15:3	927
23:12	372, 424	15:15	385
23:13	423, 433, 808, 885	15:26	385
23:14	424	16:4	385
23:14-15	425	16:36	747
23:15	372, 423, 424	19:6	219
23:15-20	433	23:4	534
23:21	16	23:13	385
23:21-23	18, 506	23:27-28	484
23:22	506	24:7-18	504
23:24	552, 553, 749, 808	28:8	646
23:24-25	18	28:12	484
23:25	251, 312, 442	28:15	945
23:27	428	29:1	310
23:34	783	29:3	336
24:2	649	33:14	934
24:14-16	783		
25:5	943	**2 Chronicles**	
25:18-21	902	1:5	428
25:21	795	1:17	330
25:28	783	5:3	515
		5:4-5	385
1 Chronicles		5:7	385
1:12	203	5:10	159, 383
1:13-15	331	6:18	390
1:36	715	6:42	376
1:42	384	7:8	515
2:22-23	218	7:20	813
2:23	219, 220	8:5	214
2:55	920	8:7-8	329
3:2	219	8:12-13	506
4:17	944	8:13	515
4:28-30	184	12:5	839
4:41-43	716	13:12-14	582
5:1	601, 640, 924	14:6 (7)	214
5:1-2	602, 925, 932	15:2	839
5:6	783	15:3	19, 535, 833
5:11	214	15:12-15	806

15:15	432		
17:7-9	19, 22, 74		
17:8-9	833		
18:1-3	11		
19:4-11	11, 521		
19:5-11	533		
19:6	175, 536		
19:7	522, 523, 524		
19:11	534		
20:30	432		
24:20	839		
26:10	319		
28:15	352, 785		
26:16-21	685		
29–31	12, 426, 442, 443		
29:2	442		
29:3	12, 444		
29:4	434, 535		
29:11	386		
30	445, 506		
30:8	364		
30:13	646		
30:25	646		
30:27	733		
31:5	481, 723		
31:5-6	729		
31:6	481		
31:11-12	484		
32:1	12, 444		
32:1-23	445		
32:6	459		
32:7-8	582		
32:11	788		
32:31	349		
33:1-20	446		
33:6	40, 550, 551, 552, 553		
34–35	426, 442		
34:1-7	446		
34:2	442		
34:3-7	16, 39, 446		
34:8	446		
34:12	442		
34:12-13	434		
34:13	20, 174		
34:14	446		
34:30	434, 535		
35:1-19	506		

Scripture Index

35:3	19, 383, 833	9:16	364	6:4	890
35:7-9	507	9:17	364	7:2	692
35:13	510	9:21	161, 191	7:4	796
35:18	506	9:24-25	318	8:3	522
36:13	364, 491	9:25	841, 883	8:6	880
		9:29	364	8:7	354
Ezra		9:32	392	8:8-10	252, 876
2:61	764	10:29-30 (28-29)	806	8:18	927
3:2	1	10:30 (29)	807	9:20	874
3:4	515	10:32 (31)	487	9:26	789
6:19-22	506	10:37 (36)	499	9:28	371
7:12	392	10:38-40 (37-39)	483, 484	10:7	900
8:21	349	12:39	469	10:19	339
8:22	789	12:44	484	11:15	874
9:1	329	13:1-2	647	12:5	897
9:2	335	13:4-9	484	12:12	876
9:12	649	13:10-12	483	12:24	880
10:1	370	13:12-13	484	13:2	439
10:9	459	13:15-22	286	14:6	692
		13:16	469, 546	14:7-9	809
Nehemiah				14:12	408
1:9	252, 818	**Esther**		14:17	896
1:10	255	3:7	505	15:8	878
2:1	505	3:8	784	15:10	876
3:3	469, 937	5:9	773	15:27	884
3:3-4	552	7:9-10	574	18:13	767
3:6	937	9:1	739	18:17	892
3:37 (4:5)	456	9:13-14	693	20:6	263
5:1-13	494, 664	9:19	214	20:14	896
5:3-5	686			20:16	896
5:5	781	**Job**		20:17	882
5:10-11	680	1:1	553	21:13	824
5:13	747	1:4-5	319	21:30	897
8	20, 833	1:6	878	22:6	681, 687
8:1	20, 459	1:21	788	22:7	717
8:1-3	806	2:7	782	22:9	393
8:1-8	19	2:7-8	774	22:17	893
8:3	459	2:11	44	22:18	318, 824
8:9	20	3:11	339	24:2	571
8:14	515	3:25	371	24:3	681, 695, 780
8:17	515	4:1	44	24:9	681, 683
9:5	794	4:15	886	24:10-11	701
9:6	390	5:7	890	24:14	293
9:6-15	390	5:13	874	24:15	292
9:9	727	5:14	777	24:22	796
9:10	400	5:17	350	26:5	201
9:11	400, 727	5:18	900	26:7	796
9:13	235	5:24	810	27:18	516

Scripture Index

27:20	761	5:3 (2)	539	18:37 (36)	897
28:7	472	5:13 (12)	938	18:45 (44)	939
28:9	354	6:4	301	18:47 (46)	873
28:12-28	822	7:2 (1)	899	19:2 (1)	873
28:17	934	7:10 (9)	349	19:6 (5)	929
28:22	767	7:14 (13)	890	19:7 (6)	818
28:28	240	7:18 (17)	876	19:15 (14)	873
29:6	882	8:3 (2)	896	19:17 (6)	252
29:7	459	8:4-5 (3-4)	243	20:8 (7)	582
29:13	725	9:3 (2)	876	22:13 (12)	213, 883
29:16	180	9:6 (5)	709	22:22 (21)	932
29:22-23	872	9:6-7 (5-6)	892	22:26 (25)	396
30:30	771	9:19 (18)	491	22:26-27 (25-26)	666
31:9	406	10:1	866	22:28 (27)	932
31:10	681, 778	10:3	297	24:1	931
31:18	180	10:6	824, 876	24:4	692
31:21	606	10:14	393	24:7-10	539, 924
31:25-28	354	10:16	539	24:8	392
31:26-27	243	10:18	393	25:1-3	862
31:26-28	747	11:4	733	25:7	376
31:27	406	11:7	62, 874	25:8	874
37:9	765	12:6 (5)	491	25:10	262
37:23	522	13:2 (1)	840	25:11	377
38:22	765	14:2	733	25:13	824
38:22-24	896	14:6	899	25:15	897
39:13	472	15	747	26:1-3	253
39:27-29	789	15:1	866	26:2	349, 868
39:28	471	15:5	524, 663	26:6	594
39:29	471	16:6	922	27:5	516, 899
39:30	471	16:7	922	27:9	840
40:15	891	16:9	922	27:12	293
40:16	928	17:3	349, 808	28:1 (LXX)	878
41:16 (24)	681	17:8	880	28:4	769
42:3	822	18	886	28:7	938
42:12	354	18:3 (2)	873, 899, 938	28:9	180
42:16	280	18:7-20 (7-19)	888	29	516
		18:8 (7)	889	29:1	878, 903
Psalms		18:9 (8)	810	29:6	214
1	45, 824	18:10 (9)	300	29:10	161, 539
1:1	938	18:14 (13)	876	30:8 (7)	840
1:2	313	18:15 (14)	890	30:10 (9)	338
1:6	191, 862	18:19 (18)	897	31:7 (6)	888
2:1	866	18:24 (23)	553	31:8 (7)	191
2:3	364	18:27 (26)	874	31:21 (20)	516, 899
2:8	932	18:31 (30)	872, 873, 938	32:3-4	198
2:12	899, 938	18:32 (31)	873, 885, 895, 900	32:5	456
3:4 (3)	938			32:7	899
4:6 (5)	933	18:34 (33)	881	32:10	880

1012

Scripture Index

33:5	522	50:22	900	74:1	810
33:7	896	51:6 (4)	292, 635	74:2	244, 490
33:12	336	51:21 (19)	933	74:12	938
33:20	938	52:2 (1)	866	74:14	880
34:11 (10)	824	54:3 (2)	897	74:15	593
34:13 (12)	824	54:8 (6)	430	74:16	244
34:17 (16)	892	55:7 (6)	796	74:17	877
34:18 (17)	727	58:2 (1)	866	75:9 (8)	883
34:19 (18)	238	58:5 (4)	891, 896	76	516
35:2	938	58:5-6 (4-5)	552, 896	76:4 (3)	890
35:10	491, 900	60:10 (8)	711	77:16-20	397
35:11	573	61:4 (3)	899	78	854, 855
35:13	349	61:5 (4)	899	78:1-4	872
35:17	866	61:6 (5)	666	78:2-4	876
37:11	236	62:3 (2)	885	78:8	606
37:14	491	62:7 (6)	885	78:15-16	354
37:22	236	62:8 (7)	823	78:18	253
37:25-26	491, 663, 765	62:11 (10)	692, 777	78:21	227
37:29	236	65:11 (10)	873	78:41	253
37:31	897	66:9	897	78:45	767
37:34	236	66:13	666	78:46	785
38:3 (2)	890	66:15	927	78:48	890
38:3-4 (2-3)	198	67	903	78:51	604
38:17 (16)	897	68:5 (4)	838, 938	78:53	400
40:7 (6)	393	68:6 (5)	393, 733	78:56	253, 262, 321
40:11 (10)	456	68:16 (15)	213	78:58	885
40:13 (12)	761	68:17 (16)	295	78:59	227
40:18 (17)	491	68:19 (18)	598	78:60	855
41:14 (13)	747	68:22 (21)	902, 931	78:62	227
42–43	516	68:25 (24)	924	78:71	244
42:3 (2)	310	68:34 (33)	938	79:2	773
42:5 (4)	430	69:4 (3)	781	79:9-10	377
44:2 (1)	876, 893, 938	69:24 (23)	928	79:10	903
44:4 (3)	171	69:35 (34)	873	80:2 (1)	921
44:21 (20)	885	71:6	396	80:5 (4)	810
45:12 (11)	295	71:19	900	80:9 (8)	895
46:2 (1)	899	72:1-2	522	80:14 (13)	468
46:4 (3)	883	72:1-4	395	81	516
46:11 (10)	743	72:3	931	81:8 (7)	926
47:3 (2)	392	72:4	778	81:10 (9)	881, 885
48:6 (5)	508	72:5	408	81:10-11 (9-10)	276
49:2 (1)	872	72:6	872	81:11 (10)	277
49:2-5 (1-4)	872	72:8	169	81:12-14 (11-13)	177
49:6 (5)	866	72:11	280	81:13 (12)	810
49:15 (14)	767	72:16	169, 226, 931	81:16 (15)	939
50:2	921	72:19	794, 747	81:17 (16)	882, 883
50:4	249, 872	73:13	594	82	854, 877, 878
50:20	454	73:26	873	82:2	523

Scripture Index

82:3-4	393	95:11	432	106:32	912
82:8	877	96:7	878	106:32-33	926
83:5-9 (4-8)	716	96:10	924	106:36	340
83:9 (8)	195	97:1	924	106:37	885
84:3 (301)	301	97:2	300	106:37-39	439-40
85:13 (12)	765	97:7	905	106:38	903
86:8	900	97:8	897	106:48	747
88:10 (9)	796	98:6	924	107:1	42
88:11 (10)	201	99:1	924	107:28	727
89:3 (2)	408	99:3	794	107:32	646
89:7-8 (6-7)	225	99:4	522, 924	107:34	811
89:9 (8)	900	99:6-8	368	107:40	880
89:14 (13)	893	99:7	262	108:10 (9)	711
89:15 (14)	522	100:2	319, 787	109:1	396
89:22 (21)	938	100:5	42	109:8-19	756
89:27 (26)	885	101:4	874	109:9	395
89:30 (29)	408	102:7 (6)	474	109:13	709
89:35 (34)	667	102:20 (19)	733	109:15	892
89:37-38 (36-37)	408	103:3	900	109:21	377
89:53 (52)	747	103:5	824, 936	110:1	939
90:1	919, 938	103:13	180	110:4	332
90:10	280, 829	104:3	838, 938	111:9	794
90:13	897	104:14-15	931	111:10	44, 240, 822, 875
91:1	899	104:15	319	112:5	491, 663
91:6	891	104:16	226	112:10	297
91:7	932	104:18	468	113–118	516
91:9	938	104:19	833	113:5	900
91:11-12	180	105	725, 854	114:8	354, 882
91:13a	896	105:11	879	115:1-2	377
91:13b	896	105:12	727	115:4	191, 341, 367, 808
92:11 (10)	932	105:12-13	726	115:4-7	250
92:13 (12)	226	105:19	872	115:14	172
92:16 (15)	874	105:36	604	116:5	62, 874
93:1	924	105:37	495	118:12	183, 340
93:5	262	106	725, 854	119	822, 824
94:1	921	106:1	42	119:2	262
94:1-3	897	106:7-12	397	119:10-11	312
94:6	393	106:8-11	400	119:11	872
94:12	350	106:13-27	177	119:14	262
94:18	897	106:14	253	119:22	262
94:21	698	106:19	159	119:24	262
94:22	873	106:20	242	119:31	262
95:1	885	106:22	397	119:34-36	312
95:3	924	106:23	371	119:38	872
95:8	391	106:25	177	119:39	371
95:8-9	926	106:28	732	119:50	872
95:8-11	912	106:28-31	884	119:67	872
95:9	252	106:31	325	119:114	899

Scripture Index

119:122	765	147:14	883	6:20-22	51
119:123	781	147:17	361	6:21	312
119:137	62, 874	148:1-6	903	6:22	313
119:176	725	148:3-9	873	6:23	50
121:3	897	148:4	390	6:24-35	292
121:8	762	149:6	587	6:32-35	291
124:7	470	149:7	897	6:35	635
126:5-6	513	150:2	873	7	660
127:3	339			7:1-3	51, 313
127:5	606	**Proverbs**		7:2	236, 880
128:1-2	781	1:2	350	7:3	312
128:3-4	785	1:5	872	7:4	292
129:4	62, 874	1:7	240	7:5-27	292
131:1-3	822	1:8	266, 287, 350	7:10	660
132	516	1:8-9	313	7:13	789
132:1	376	2:12	887	7:14	660
132:8	432	2:12-15	824	7:20	485
132:11	339	2:14	887	7:21	872
132:14	432	2:16-19	292	7:23	470
133:1	706	2:18	201	8:1-36	292
133:3	763	2:21-22	236	8:7	46, 432
135:4	336	3:1-3	312, 313	8:8	874
135:7	765	3:5	790	8:13	887
135:10-12	881	3:7	240	8:14	894
135:11	161	3:10	763	8:15-16	46, 173
135:14	897	3:11-12	46, 50, 350	8:22	44, 875, 938
135:15	341, 367, 808	3:27	781	8:32-34	51
135:15-17	250	3:32	46	8:35-36	236
136:1	42	3:33	768	9:9	872
136:2-3	391, 392	3:35	55	9:10	44, 240, 822, 875
136:11-15	400, 727	4:1	350	9:13-18	292
136:17-22	881	4:1-5	287	9:17	293
136:19-20	161	4:2	872	9:18	201
136:23	376	4:4	312	10:5	785
137:7	650	4:6-9	292	10:9	874
137:7-9	189	4:10	266	10:12	53
139:6	822	4:10-19	45, 54	10:13	699
139:13	875	4:21	312	10:31-32	887
139:13-18	822	5:1-23	292	11:1	27, 46, 715
140:4 (3)	891, 896	5:4	587	11:4	53
142:5	404	5:7-14	50	11:19	53
144:13	932	5:23	50	11:20	46, 342, 874
144:15	903, 938	6:8	785	12:1	50
145:16	936	6:14	887	12:10	701
145:18	238	6:16	46, 894	12:15	894
146:9	393	6:16-19	618	12:22	46, 342
147:3	900	6:19	293	12:28	53
147:8	404, 931	6:20-21	313	13:4	297

Scripture Index

13:10	536	22:28	20, 27, 46, 571, 572	30:11	287		
13:17	824	23:2	485	30:17	57, 287, 471, 472, 713		
13:19	46	23:5	471, 789	30:18-19	822		
13:24	50, 606	23:6	491	30:22	319		
14:5	293	23:10	27, 46, 571, 748	30:26	468		
14:31	692	23:13	50	31:2	666		
15:8	46, 342	23:13-14	606	31:6	725		
15:9	46	23:14-18	354	31:17	928		
15:10	50	23:19	266				
15:17	403	23:20-21	607	**Ecclesiastes**			
15:20	57	23:22	57	2:8	336		
15:25	817	23:22-25	287	3:14	441		
15:26	46	23:33	887	4:13	352		
15:33	240	24:9	46	5:3 (4)	666		
16:5	46	24:16	201, 763	5:3-4 (4-5)	46		
16:10	550	24:23	523	5:14 (15)	788		
16:12	46, 342	24:23b	175	7:23-24	822		
16:21	872	25:1	44	9:15	352		
16:23	872	25:18	293	9:16	352		
16:28	177, 887	25:20	492	12:3	773		
16:30	887	26:3	699				
16:31	53	26:20-22	177	**Canticles**			
16:33	175	26:25	46	3:6-11	793		
17:3	349, 808	27:4	361	4:8	214, 936		
17:15	46	27:10	897	4:9	496		
17:20	874	27:13	687	4:15	226		
17:23	523	27:23	191	5:5	712		
18:5	523	27:27	883	5:15	169, 226		
18:8	177	28:6	874	7:5 (4)	207, 226		
19:1	874	28:7	607	8:6	890		
19:12	938	28:8	663				
19:18	50, 255, 350, 606	28:9	46	**Isaiah**			
19:29	699	28:16	715	1:2	180, 249, 463, 872		
20:2	227	28:18	874	1:2-3	872		
20:10	27, 46, 715	28:21	175, 523	1:2-4	795		
20:16	687	28:22	491	1:4	36, 463, 841		
20:20	287	28:24	287	1:4-6	774		
20:23	20, 27, 46, 715	28:27	768	1:8	516		
20:25	46, 666	29:1	364	1:9	892		
21:2	349, 808	29:11	888	1:9-10	36, 812		
21:21	53	29:14	395	1:10	872		
21:25-26	297	29:17	50, 255, 350, 606	1:11	883		
21:27	46, 342	29:27	46, 342	1:11-14	36		
21:29	789	30:4	822	1:11-15	795		
21:31	582	30:5-6	441	1:12	517		
22:7	490, 786	30:8-9	319	1:13	284		
22:15	50, 606	30:10	20, 655	1:15	36		
22:16	692						

Reference	Page(s)
1:16	769
1:16-17	824
1:17	37, 393
1:19-20	37
1:20	902
1:21	36, 290, 521-22
1:23	36, 393, 524
1:24	897
1:24-27	795
1:26-27	37
1:27	525
1:29	37
2:2	251, 900
2:3	35, 37
2:6	36, 550, 557
2:8	36, 250
2:10-11	36
2:13	213
2:17	36
2:18	36
2:20	36
3:2	550
3:3	173
3:8	897
3:9	36, 812
3:14	301
3:14-15	36
3:18-23	735
3:24	598
4:1	763, 764
4:3	37, 892
4:5	929
4:18	884
5:1-7	795, 895
5:7	36
5:8	296, 571
5:10	714
5:10-11	363
5:16	36
5:19	36
5:23	36, 523, 698
5:24	36, 841
5:26	789, 897
5:26-30	787
6:1-5	539
6:2-7	243
6:3	36, 60
6:8	558, 878
6:9-10	818, 838
6:10	801
7:3-17	542
7:4	583
7:14-16	182
7:15	882
7:18	183, 187
7:18-19	340
7:21	593
7:22	882
8:7	924
8:11-12	838
8:13	36, 37
8:15	897
8:17	840
8:18	428, 733
8:19	36, 552, 553, 732
8:22	777
8:23 (9:1)	937
8:23–9:6 (9:1-7)	933
9:2 (3)	512, 513
9:5 (6)	392
9:6 (7)	37, 522, 525
9:13-14 (14-15)	766
9:18-20 (19-21)	792
9:19 (20)	792
10:1-2	36
10:2	393
10:5-19	819
10:10	425
10:11	36
10:20	36
10:20-23	892
10:21	392
10:25	795
10:34	169, 226
11:1	809
11:1-2	173
11:1-3	37
11:1-9	892
11:4	395
11:4-5	37
11:6-9	891
11:8	896
11:11	784
11:15	763
12:6	36
13:5	252, 818
13:16	778
13:18	339, 789
13:19	812
13:20-21	473
13:21-22	880
13:22	938
14:3	727
14:9	201
14:14	876
15:1	195, 209
15:2	464, 943
15:5	945
16:5	525
16:8	895
16:8-9	207
16:14	498
17:6	696
17:7	36
17:8	37
17:10	873
17:10b	37
18:1	786
18:6	773
19:1	938
19:3	552
19:15	766
19:18	320
19:22	900
20	445
21:9	425
23:17-18	660
24:5	235
24:6	771
24:13	696
25:18	465
25:25	910
26:2	37
26:11	893
26:12	893
26:14	201
26:17	207
26:19	201
26:20	795, 891
27:2-5	795
27:9	36, 424, 425
27:12	696
27:13	725
28:2	891

Scripture Index

28:7	535	34:5a	862	43:13	900		
28:7-8	561	34:6	883	43:20	336, 473		
28:11	789	34:6c	862	43:25	899		
28:16-17	37	34:8	897	44:1-2	336		
28:23-26	872	34:8a	862	44:2	884		
28:29	894	34:11	474	44:5	497		
29:4	552	34:13	473	44:5-6	310		
29:5-6	897	34:14	880	44:6	900		
29:6	245, 362	34:15	472	44:9	810		
29:8	717	35:2	169	44:9-20	250, 279		
29:9-10	776	35:4	897	44:13-19	250		
29:14	44	36:7	12, 47, 423, 425, 433, 442	44:19	885		
29:18	776			44:23	860		
29:19	37	36:16	318, 351	44:23c	860		
29:21	37, 606	37:4	892	44:24	279		
30:3-5	650	37:16	383	44:24–45:13	861		
30:6	354	37:28	762	45:3	802		
30:7	650	37:30	445	45:4	336		
30:9-11	36	37:31-32	892	45:5-6	279, 900		
30:13	897	38:21	351, 774	45:6	310		
30:15-17	582	39:1-8	542	45:11	873		
30:18	795	39:5-8	560	45:14	279, 310, 900		
30:22	36, 37, 341, 367, 425, 808	40:2	498	45:18	279, 310, 900		
		40:4-6	301	45:21	254		
30:24	701	40:12	713	45:21-22	279, 900		
30:26b	900	40:19	341, 367, 808	45:22	310		
30:27	362	40:19-20	191, 250	45:23	320, 901		
30:29	430, 873	40:31	471, 789	46:3-4	180, 287		
30:30	362	40:48	60	46:4	900		
31:1-3	582, 650	41:4	279, 900	46:6	279, 341, 367, 808		
31:3	897	41:7	191, 250	46:6-7	250		
31:5	505, 929	41:8-9	336	46:9	279, 310, 900		
31:7	36, 37	41:10	582	47:1	793		
32:1	37	41:19	384	47:1-4	859		
32:7	36	41:24	390	47:3-4	897		
32:15-16	37	42:1	336	47:4	860, 873		
33:2	938	42:8	245	47:6	788, 789		
33:4	785	42:11	202	47:9	552		
33:5-6	37	42:13	392	47:12	552		
33:9	213	43:1	427, 764	48:2	860, 873		
33:14-15	37	43:4	337	48:4	364		
33:19	789	43:5	582	48:9-11	893		
33:20	37	43:6-7	427, 764	48:12	900		
33:22	924, 935	43:10	336	48:14	337		
34:1-2	872	43:10-12	881	49:7	336, 338		
34:1-15	333	43:11	899, 900	49:16	497		
34:2a	862	43:11-13	899	49:18	901		
34:5-6	902	43:12	885	49:26	902		

50:1	671, 672, 683	63:11	876	2:6	38, 158, 176, 354, 727, 880, 898
50:6	699	63:15	733	2:6-7	879
50:11	770	63:16	875, 886	2:7	38, 177, 244, 350, 489, 490, 728
51:9	938	63:19	427		
51:12	899	64:1 (2)	770	2:7-8	38
51:15	860, 873	64:7 (8)	875	2:8	40, 43, 237, 898
51:26	788	65:1	250	2:9	700, 865, 867, 899
52:10	932	65:4-5	468	2:10-11	252
52:12	179, 508	65:5	810	2:11	886, 895
53	181	65:9	336	2:12	886
53:12	371	65:14	727, 787	2:12-13	872
54:1-3	727	65:15	336	2:13	39, 301, 318, 769, 865
54:5	860, 873	65:21-22	778		
54:8	840	65:22	336	2:14-19	839
55:1	191, 802	66:1	733	2:17	39, 769
55:6	250	66:3	468	2:18	197, 410
55:6-7	250	66:23	284	2:19	39, 42, 240, 769
55:10-11	872			2:20	40, 364, 423, 788, 884
56:1	522	**Jeremiah**			
56:2	284	1:1-3	157	2:21	873, 895
56:3-8	650	1:4-12	39	2:24	297
56:4-5	645	1:5	43, 336, 339, 879	2:25	42, 881, 885
57:3	550	1:6	226	2:26	350, 529, 684, 937
57:13	888	1:7	183, 558	2:27	40, 250, 424, 425, 875
58:2	522	1:8	582		
58:3	349	1:9	183, 557, 558	2:27c-28	38
58:5	349	1:10	318	2:28	898, 899
58:6	495	1:12	183	2:29	866
58:6-7	788	1:14	183, 896	2:31-32	795
58:7	614	1:15	785	2:32	39, 348, 355
58:8	179	1:16	39, 191, 769, 839	2:33	42
58:13	284	1:17	176, 653	2:34	40, 290, 570
58:14	881	1:18	772, 937	2:34-35	596
59:2	840	1:19	582	2:37	790
59:9-10	777	2–3	33	3:1	42, 390, 527, 670, 837, 846
59:13	573	2:1	558		
59:14	459	2:1-3	795	3:1-2	675, 903
59:17-20	897	2:2	43, 190, 237, 282, 311, 376, 527, 879	3:1–4:2	251
59:18	338			3:2-3	772
60:1-2	921	2:2-3	365	3:3	11, 406, 778
60:22	897	2:3	43, 335	3:4	875
61:1-2	488	2:3b	763	3:6	40, 183, 423
61:2	897	2:5	38, 237, 267, 456, 558, 795, 874, 888	3:7	887, 892
62:3	735			3:8	42
62:8	901	2:5-9	38, 65, 281, 694, 864, 866, 881, 885	3:9	250, 424, 425, 903
62:8-9	778			3:11	183
63:4	897	2:5a	866	3:13	40, 453, 766, 885
63:9	180, 337				

Scripture Index

Ref	Pages	Ref	Pages	Ref	Pages
3:14	894	5:7	39, 292, 319, 320, 769, 886	6:20	429, 928
3:16	383, 727	5:7-8	40, 635, 700	6:21	333, 897
3:16-17	383	5:7a	866	6:22	653
3:17	810	5:7b	885	6:23	896
3:18	170, 171	5:9	897	6:24	774
3:19	38, 244, 489, 795, 875, 877, 887	5:10	895	6:26	897
3:20	527	5:10-13	38	6:28	772
3:21	39, 348, 355, 886	5:10b-11	865	7:1-15	19, 427
3:23	423	5:12-13	40	7:3-7	795
3:24	41	5:14	362	7:3-15	39
3:24-25	373, 781	5:15	411, 788	7:4	790
3:25	766	5:15-17	38, 41, 787, 788	7:5	40
4:1	342	5:16	889	7:5-7	170, 393, 570
4:1-2	283, 761	5:17	41, 318, 333, 362, 585, 767, 779, 785, 789, 790	7:6	40, 43, 320, 395, 692, 824
4:2	262			7:7	65, 170, 171
4:4	38, 39, 312, 391, 769, 819, 888	5:18-19	839	7:8	790
		5:19	39, 769, 812, 839, 881	7:8-10	809
4:5	206			7:9	40, 272, 273, 274, 283, 290, 292, 293, 320, 411, 635, 795
4:5-8	38	5:21	801		
4:6b	862	5:22	42		
4:8b	862	5:22-24	240	7:10	536
4:9	777	5:23	312, 606	7:10-11	427, 764
4:10	226	5:24	41, 42, 404, 406, 505, 512	7:12	43, 426
4:13	471			7:12-15	170
4:13-17	38	5:24-25	772	7:13	197
4:17	40	5:25	700, 768	7:14	66, 170, 171, 427, 764, 790
4:19	774	5:26-27	470		
4:20	897	5:26-28	40	7:15	795
4:21	866	5:27	350	7:16	227, 368
4:22c	865	5:27b-8a	884, 885	7:16-20	368
4:23	880	5:28	393, 523, 533, 695, 884	7:18	38, 243, 320, 885, 887
4:26	790			7:18-19	249
4:26b	862	5:29	897	7:19	810
4:28	777	5:31	40, 700, 887	7:20	67, 333, 458, 888
4:30	700	5:31b	867, 899	7:21-22	429
4:31	207	6:2	42, 793	7:21-23	393
5:1	40, 252	6:4-5	67	7:22	530
5:1-8	812, 864, 866	6:6	589	7:22-23	431
5:2	40, 282, 283	6:7	42, 350, 774, 794	7:23	39, 241, 256, 734, 807
5:3	606	6:8	865		
5:4	887	6:10	819	7:24	810
5:4-5	38, 303	6:11	789, 892	7:24-25	177
5:5	364, 788	6:11-12	41, 778	7:25	556
5:5b	862, 884	6:12	318, 779	7:26	364
5:6	891	6:15	342, 653, 897	7:30	40, 248, 342, 427, 764, 808
5:6-7	839	6:16	45, 303, 734, 824		
5:6c	862				

Scripture Index

7:30-31	342	10:7	42, 240	13:14	340, 455, 570
7:31	40, 424, 439, 530, 549	10:8	888	13:15	872
7:31-32	549	10:8-9	40	13:16	777
7:33	41, 611, 773	10:9	191, 279, 367	13:21	786
8:1-2	243	10:10	301	13:24	795
8:2	40, 42, 243, 321, 529	10:12-16	38, 244	13:25	348, 355, 790, 886
8:6	776	10:13	896	13:27	40, 292, 342, 808, 882
8:7	474, 865	10:14-15	40	14:1-6	772
8:8-9	44	10:16	244, 490, 860, 873	14:1-11	406
8:10	41, 318, 778, 779	10:16b	377	14:4	406
8:12	342, 897	10:19	42, 774, 794	14:5-6	406
8:13	252, 865, 889, 895	10:21	250	14:7	377
8:14	809	11:1-13	39	14:7-16	368
8:17	700, 767, 891, 899	11:3	41, 746	14:8-9	778
8:18	774	11:3-7	41	14:9	321, 764
8:19	38, 40, 249, 885, 888	11:4	234, 241, 244, 734, 749	14:10	42
8:21	774	11:5	43, 65, 170, 171, 209, 307, 363, 882	14:11	227, 368
8:22	210, 774, 931	11:6	183, 802	14:12	41, 769, 891
8:23 (9:1)	781, 796	11:7	40, 262, 267	14:13	226
9:1 (2)	40, 292, 796	11:7-8	373	14:14	40, 550
9:3 (4)	790	11:8	177, 810	14:14-15	560
9:8 (9)	897	11:9	183	14:17	42, 774, 794
9:9 (10)	790	11:10	40, 320, 839	14:17-22	406
9:10 (11)	790	11:12	899	14:18	411, 761, 767, 811, 891
9:11 (12)	44	11:13	700	14:19	774
9:11-12 (12-13)	453, 558	11:14	227, 368	14:20–15:4	368
9:11-13 (12-14)	812	11:14-17	368	14:21	39, 377, 841, 886
9:12 (13)	40, 766, 769	11:17	249, 492, 885	14:22	41, 888
9:13 (14)	810	11:19	947	15:1	227, 368
9:14 (15)	809	11:20	896	15:2	41, 178
9:15 (16)	42, 249, 411, 455, 795	11:21	559	15:3	41, 773
9:18b (19b)	862	12:1	874	15:4	41, 492, 773
9:20 (21)	333, 767, 891	12:4	772, 810, 887	15:6	884
9:21 (22)	611, 865	12:7	244	15:7	701, 891
9:22 (23)	44	12:7-8	795	15:8	897
9:23 (24)	38, 40, 873	12:7-9	244, 490	15:9	777
9:25 (26)	391, 464, 819	12:8-9	244	15:10	664
10:1-5	40	12:12	252	15:11	765
10:1-10	900	12:13b	700, 867, 899	15:12	772, 937
10:3	191, 765	12:14	244	15:13	566
10:3-4	279, 367	12:15	244, 818	15:14	38, 411, 770
10:4	341, 808	12:16	320	15:15	789, 896
10:5	250	12:16-17	761	15:16	38, 764, 856, 897
10:6-7	903, 937	13:10	40, 319, 320, 810	15:17-18	198
		13:11	336, 735	15:18	42, 774, 794
				15:19	386, 536

1021

15:20	582, 778	18:17	840, 897	22:6	169
15:21	712	18:18	20, 44, 535, 833, 927	22:7	67
16:3-4	333			22:8-9	812, 839
16:4	41, 321, 611, 773, 811	18:20	368, 561	22:9	319, 813
		18:21	41, 769, 891	22:10	780
16:5	42	18:22	897	22:10-12	783
16:6	464	18:23	456	22:13-17	40
16:7	732	19:1-13	549	22:15	39, 256, 522
16:8-9	700	19:3-4	839	22:15-16	393
16:9	899	19:4	411, 769, 795	22:15-17	40
16:10-13	812, 839	19:5	40, 43, 530, 549	22:16	533
16:11	40, 42, 320, 769	19:7	41, 773	22:17	40, 570, 782
16:12	810	19:8	42, 783, 794	22:20	911
16:13	250, 411, 455	19:9	42, 792	22:21	373, 453, 766
16:15	65, 170, 171	19:13	243, 530, 619	22:24	901
16:18	342, 498, 808	19:15	364	22:24-30	783
16:20	886	20:4	897	22:27	599, 692
17:1	312, 865	20:10	896	22:28	411
17:2	424, 425	20:11	392	23:3	727, 817, 818
17:2-3	423	20:12	896	23:4	176
17:2-3a	423	20:13	490	23:5	40, 525
17:3	882	20:14	767	23:6	929
17:4	38, 411, 770	20:14-18	869	23:8	817
17:5	41, 746, 790	20:15	41, 746	23:10	40, 41, 292, 771, 772
17:5-8	45	20:16	812		
17:6	765	20:17	493	23:12	777
17:7	790	20:17-18	792	23:13	40
17:9	312	20:18	700, 767	23:14	40, 41, 292, 561, 812
17:10	349, 808	21:1-7	542		
17:11	887	21:2	368	23:14-22	40
17:12	40, 733	21:4	768	23:15	809
17:13	769, 839	21:5	43, 813, 846	23:16-22	560
17:14	396, 774, 900	21:5-6	41, 198	23:17	810
17:15	560	21:6	67, 333, 458, 770	23:18	878
17:19-27	39, 284	21:6-7	891	23:20	251
17:21	236, 238	21:7	455, 769	23:22	878
17:21-22	285	21:8-9	45	23:23-24	255
17:21-23	40	21:8-10	42, 824	23:25-28	451
17:23	364	21:9	769, 770	23:25-32	40, 451, 560
17:27	888	21:9-10	41, 170	23:27	348, 355, 886
18:6	350, 937	21:11-12	522	23:28-29	558
18:7-10	561	21:12	40, 606, 692, 769, 777, 888	23:30	561
18:9	318			23:36	301
18:10	248	21:32	886	24	892
18:12	810	22:3	40, 43, 393, 395, 522, 692, 695	24:1	173, 513
18:14	169, 882			24:1-10	42
18:15	39, 348, 355, 886	22:3-5	570	24:6	318
18:16	783	22:5	901	24:7	213, 807, 819

1022

Scripture Index

Reference	Pages	Reference	Pages	Reference	Pages
24:8-10	795	27:6-7	320	30:10	176, 892
24:9	41, 773	27:7	439	30:11	42, 249, 582
24:10	66, 170, 171, 769, 784	27:8	769	30:12	42, 794
25:4	556	27:9	40, 550, 551	30:12-15	774
25:4-7	373	27:10	810	30:12-17	774
25:5	65, 170, 171	27:11	320	30:13	533
25:6	191, 319, 320	27:13	769	30:14	42, 404, 794
25:6-7	249, 885	27:14-15	560	30:17	404, 900
25:7	810, 824	27:15	810	30:18	459
25:8-11	170	27:18	371	30:19	727
25:9	41, 333, 783	28	59, 559	30:21	539
25:10	681	28:1	559	30:22	267, 734, 807
25:11	41, 783	28:6	364, 747	30:24	251
25:14	191, 439	28:8-9	556	31:1	267, 807
25:15-29	896	28:9	560, 561	31:2-3	795, 879
25:15-38	38	28:13-14	788	31:3	42
25:18	41, 43, 209, 783	28:14	41, 320	31:4-5	318, 862
25:23	464	28:15	790	31:4-6	430
25:26	321	28:15-17	42, 559	31:5	41, 585, 778
25:27	206, 902	28:16	321, 454, 573	31:7	786
25:28-29	819, 886	29	892	31:8	818
25:29	764, 846	29:1	43, 157	31:9	875, 897
25:30	733	29:2	645	31:12	339
25:31	902	29:5	318	31:12-14	430
25:33	252, 321	29:5-6	41, 584, 778	31:14	433
25:38b	862	29:7	250	31:19	892
26:1-6	427	29:8	40, 550	31:20	180, 463, 795, 818, 892
26:2	440	29:8-9	560	31:25	796
26:3	769	29:10	364	31:29	281
26:3-6	824	29:10-14	250	31:29-30	693
26:4-5	373, 556	29:13	250, 428	31:30	281, 338
26:6	790	29:14	251, 817, 818	31:31-34	38, 43, 64
26:8-9	559	29:18	41, 769, 773	31:33	242, 313, 734, 819, 823
26:10	173	29:18-19	559	31:35	873
26:12	453	29:19	373, 556, 599	31:36	408
26:12-15	42	29:21-23	40, 560, 561	31:36-37	761
26:13	558	29:22-23	40	31:40	895
26:15	453, 570	29:23	292, 634	32:5	777
26:16	569	29:26	776	32:6-9	386
26:17	301	29:28	318, 778	32:6-15	546, 568
26:17-19	443, 570	29:30-32	560	32:7-8	337
26:18	35	29:31	790	32:16-22	390
26:19	13, 42, 561	29:32	454, 573, 767	32:17	38, 226, 254, 255, 378
26:20-23	290	30–33	38	32:17-23	225
27–28	788	30–31	33	32:18	42, 280, 338, 392
27:1-29	430	30:3	65, 171		
27:5	38, 254, 255, 378	30:4	43, 157		
		30:6	772		

1023

32:18-19	338	34:17	41, 773	41:15	784
32:20	43, 209	34:18	807	41:16	645
32:20-21	253	34:18-20	267, 805	42:1-3	371
32:21	254, 727	34:19	645	42:1-17	368
32:22	171, 307	34:20	41, 773	42:2	727
32:22-23	728	35	920	42:5	841
32:23	558, 847	35:1 (LXX)	559	42:6	39, 256
32:24	769	35:2	484	42:7-22	824
32:29	249	35:7	39, 321	42:10-22	42
32:30	248, 249, 373	35:14	749	43:12-13	320
32:32	249	35:14b-15	373	43:13	40, 424
32:34	342, 427, 764, 808	35:15	170, 171, 841	44:1	784
32:35	342, 424, 425-26, 439, 530, 549, 588	35:16	364	44:3	249, 411, 795, 885
		35:17	559	44:6	209
32:36	769	35:19	239	44:8	249, 885
32:37	813	36	375, 833	44:10	42, 240
32:38-40	38, 43, 71	36:1-8	375	44:14	692
32:39	42, 239, 240, 819	36:9	488	44:15-25	320, 887
32:39-40	302, 819	36:9-32	375	44:17-19	243
32:40	64, 367, 456, 653	36:21	386, 536	44:18	840
32:41	251, 794, 820	36:23	12	44:22	209, 769
32:43	333, 458	36:29	67, 333	44:23	209, 847
33:2	873	37:3	368	44:25	243, 436
33:5	840	37:4	763	44:25-27	667
33:6	774, 900	37:6-10	542	44:26	901
33:9	735	37:12	546	44:28	560
33:10	333, 458	37:17-21	542	44:29	254
33:11	42	37:19	898	45	845
33:12	333, 458	37:28	683	46-51	38
33:14	364	38:2	824	46:2	410
33:15	40, 525	38:6	319	46:3-4	206
33:16	929	38:7	645	46:6	211, 410
33:18	19, 239, 535	38:7-10	534	46:10	897, 901, 902
33:20-21	408, 761	38:14-26	542	46:11	931
33:21	385	38:17-18	42, 824	46:18	901
33:21b	927	38:20	39, 256, 558	46:21	897
33:22	243, 530	38:23	780	46:23	865
33:24	336	39:5	943	46:27	176
33:25-26	408, 761	39:18	790	47:4	203
33:26	428, 818	40:2-3	558	47:5	464
34:7	445	40:4	169	48:1	195, 943
34:8	488	40:9	39, 256	48:16	897
34:8-10	493	40:10	386, 536	48:18	788
34:9	495	40:11	784	48:19	210
34:13	277	40:13-41:15	649	48:21	209, 214
34:14	42, 486, 487, 494	40:14-15	569	48:22	943
34:15	321, 427, 764	41	290	48:23	195
34:16	599, 692	41:5	464	48:27	529

Scripture Index

48:28	205	51:19	244, 490, 860, 873	4:17	781
48:34	209, 945	51:19b	377	4:19	471
48:37	464	51:20	183	5:1-9	318
48:40	42, 472, 789	51:20-23	789	5:2	779
48:42	769	51:22	892	5:3	393, 395
48:46	867, 899	51:25	811, 901	5:4	318
48:47	251	51:25 (LXX)	436	5:11	779
49:2	459	51:34-45	864	5:11-13	789
49:7	44, 894	51:36	897		
49:7-22	189	51:40	883	**Ezekiel**	
49:12	846	51:44	32	1:1-2	157
49:13	901	51:46	583	1:5-28	243
49:16	471, 536, 931	51:47	902	3:20	897
49:17	42	51:52	902	4:14	226
49:18	812	51:59	517	5:10	792
49:19	593	51:59-64	845	5:11	808, 901
49:21	158	52:8	943	5:12	891
49:22	42, 472, 789	52:22-23	352	5:16	889, 890
49:28-29	202	52:24-27	902	5:16-17	889, 891
49:31	214	52:25	645	5:17	767, 891
49:35	768	52:28	783	6:3-4	423
49:39	251	52:32	783	6:9	456
50:2	320, 808			6:11-12	891
50:4	428			6:13	424
50:6	423, 725	**Lamentations**		7:4	340
50:7	599, 901	1:5	781, 786	7:10	536
50:11	701	1:7	778	7:15	891
50:14	890, 901	1:10	646	7:19	897
50:15	902	1:16	781	7:20	808
50:16	512	1:18	781	7:26	20, 535, 833
50:19	213	1:20	891	8:6	456
50:24	902	2:6	841, 886	8:10	242
50:28	902	2:11	781	8:16	243, 529
50:29-32	902	2:15-16	783	9:3	243
50:33	777	2:20	792	9:4	497
50:38	771	2:21	892	9:8	226
50:38b	902	3:12-13	890	10	838
50:39	473, 880	3:14	783	10:1-22	243
50:40	812	3:19	809	10:2b	179
50:44	593	3:46	783	11:17-18	818
51:6	338, 897	3:61-63	783	11:19	313
51:8	897	4:3	473	11:19-20	819
51:9	178	4:3-10	793	11:22	243
51:11	890	4:4	788	11:22-23	838
51:11b	902	4:9	882	12:2-3	501
51:14	901	4:10	792	12:24	550
51:15-19	244	4:14	776	13:3-23	550
51:16	765	4:16	789	14:3	897

Scripture Index

14:4	897	20:28	423, 424, 434	33:25	437		
14:7	897	20:31	439, 549	33:33	561		
14:9	560	20:40-41	928	34:4	614, 725		
14:15	891	20:44	377	34:10	559		
14:16	901	21:11 (6)	179	34:16	614, 725		
14:18	901	21:14b-16 (9b-11)	901	36:9-11	727		
14:20	901	21:20 (15)	901	36:17-18	903		
14:22	630	21:26 (21)	549	36:19	630		
14:23	630	21:26-27 (21-22)	550	36:22-23	377		
16	527	22	747	36:23	179		
16:1-7	879	22:2	524	36:26	313		
16:2-3	207	22:7	287, 393	36:26-28	819		
16:3	330, 331	22:8	285	36:26-29	819		
16:4-14	287	22:9	290	36:30	882		
16:8	640	22:10	640	37:18	213		
16:13	423, 882	22:12	663, 749	37:20	179		
16:17-19	279	22:15	795	38:11	214		
16:20-21	549	22:29	692	38:16	179, 251		
16:20-22	439	23	527	39:3	768		
16:32	292	23:37	292, 549	39:17-20	773		
16:36	808	23:37-39	439	39:18	883		
16:45	207, 330, 331	23:39	549	39:25	377		
16:46	922	23:43-45	292	40:4	910		
16:46-52	812	24:14	340	43:19	19, 535		
16:59	839	24:17	732	43:27	928		
17	789	24:22	732	44:7	819, 839		
17:13	807	24:25	692	44:9	819		
17:22-23	931	25:1-6	649	44:9-14	434		
17:24	947	25:9	195	44:15	19, 386, 535		
18:2	281	25:12-14	650	44:17-18	624		
18:4	338	25:14	897	44:24	535, 927		
18:6	674	25:16	203	44:28	544		
18:7	687	25:17	897	44:31	476		
18:8	663	26:7	392	45:10-12	715		
18:12	687	27:5	214	45:11	714		
18:13	663	27:6	213	45:21-25	513		
18:17	663	27:21	883	45:25	515		
18:18	692, 777	27:27	241	46:1-5	284		
18:20	693	27:35	886	46:5	517		
18:31	313, 819	28:1-10	354	46:11	517		
20	427	28:14	301	47:18	411		
20:7	808	29:14	818	47:19	926		
20:9	893	31:3	226	48:28	926		
20:13b	892	32:10	886				
20:13b-14	893	32:12	769	**Daniel**			
20:14	377	32:27	210	2:2	552		
20:21b-22	893	33:6	559	2:37	392		
20:25-26	439, 549	33:15	687	2:47	392		

Scripture Index

8:23	789	5:3-4	33	10:11	701
9:19	764	5:5	897	10:12	34
10:13	878	5:7	707	11:1	61, 311, 463
10:20-21	878	5:10	34, 571	11:1-3	180
11:30	813	5:11	162	11:1-4	34, 337, 875
12:1	878	5:13	774	11:2	34, 425
		5:14	900	11:3	287, 774, 880, 938
Hosea		5:14b	899	11:4	61, 788
1–3	337, 839	5:15–6:1	251	11:8	812
1:2	33, 839	5:15–6:3	250, 795	11:8-9	795, 892
1:5	768	6:1	251, 774, 900	11:9	321
1:10	727	6:2	894	11:13	900
2:1 (1:10)	301	6:3	406	12:4-5a (3-4a)	211
2:4 (2)	33, 292	6:4	34, 300, 892	12:6 (5)	860
2:4-22 (2-20)	527	6:4-5	795	12:7 (6)	34
2:5 (3)	788	6:4-6	311	12:8 (7)	34, 692, 715
2:7 (5)	33	6:6	34	12:12 (11)	34
2:9 (7)	673	6:9	34, 290, 596	12:13 (12)	726
2:10 (8)	33, 339, 354, 787	6:10	33	12:14 (13)	368, 557
2:10-15 (8-13)	406	7:1	293, 774, 900	13:2	33, 191, 250, 341,
2:12 (10)	900	7:4	33, 292, 509, 635		367, 380, 808
2:13 (11)	34, 284	7:8	34	13:4	34, 411, 881, 886
2:14 (12)	33, 891	7:14	34, 464	13:4-6	881
2:15 (13)	33, 34, 886	8:1	34, 789	13:5	191
2:16-17 (14-15)	190, 365	8:4	783, 810	13:6	33, 319, 354, 885,
2:21 (19)	34, 35, 61, 525	8:4-5	33		886
2:24 (22)	339	8:4-6	380	13:10-11	783
2:25 (23)	807	8:6	191, 250, 886	13:12	896
3:1	33, 34, 61, 292,	8:11	34	13:14	767, 770, 891
	311, 840	8:13	34, 796, 928	13:15	771
3:4	424	8:14	33, 354, 886	14:1 (13:16)	581, 587, 892
4:2	34, 272, 283, 290,	9:1	33, 34, 456, 839	14:2 (1)	897
	292, 293, 635	9:2	496	14:2-3 (1-2)	251
4:5	897	9:3	34, 796	14:4 (3)	250, 393, 582
4:6	34, 886	9:4	34, 731	14:5 (4)	35, 61, 337, 774,
4:8	692	9:5	34		900
4:10	33	9:6	34, 796	14:6 (5)	938
4:11-19	426	9:7	776	14:7-9 (6-8)	226
4:12	33, 250, 549, 839	9:7-8	34	14:9 (8)	33
4:13	34, 423, 424	9:10	228, 425, 808,		
4:13-14	33, 292		879, 884	**Joel**	
4:14	657, 658	9:15	34, 337, 671, 769	1:2	872
4:15	33, 34, 282	10:1	895	1:3	876
4:16	884	10:1-2	34, 424	2:2	876
4:17	33	10:2	424	2:13-14	561
4:18	33	10:4	809	2:15-16	646
4:19	34	10:5-6	33	2:16	929
5:1	34, 872, 933	10:8	34, 769	2:17	377

Scripture Index

2:18-19	561	5:4	32, 428	Obadiah			
2:20	410, 411	5:4-5	426	1			650
2:22	351	5:5	31	3			931
2:23	406	5:6	428, 888	10			189
4:6-8 (3:6-8)	783	5:7	31, 521	13			897
4:13 (3:13)	512	5:8	32, 860, 873				
4:19 (3:19)	903	5:8-9	32	Jonah			
4:21 (3:21)	903	5:10	31, 32, 606	1:5			616
		5:11	318, 585, 779	1:9			495
Amos		5:11-12	31	1:16			666
1–2	717	5:12	31, 490, 523, 606	2:10 (9)			666
1:1	29, 157	5:14	32	3:3			178
1:3	581, 587, 701, 773, 894, 925	5:14-15	824	3:4			366
		5:15	31, 606	3:9-10			561
1:3–2:3	30	5:21-23	31	4:5			516
1:6	773, 782	5:21-24	31	4:7			785
1:8	161	5:22	928				
1:9	773, 782	5:24	29, 31, 593	Micah			
1:11	189	5:25	161, 431	1:2			931
1:13	587	6:2	252	1:2-9			35
2:1	740	6:4	465	1:6			790
2:4	30	6:6	785	1:7		35, 425, 660	
2:6	31, 494	6:12	31, 809	1:12			765
2:6-7	31, 490	6:13	30	1:15			171
2:7	31	6:14	32	1:16			470
2:8	32, 631, 658, 687	7	29	2:1			781
2:9	178, 196, 206	7:1-6	561	2:2		35, 295, 296, 692, 778	
2:9-10	30	7:2	226				
2:10	30, 161, 348, 802	7:5	226	2:5			646, 897
2:11-12	32	7:9	31	2:9			35
3:2	30, 63, 336, 886	7:13	426, 482	2:11			35
3:5	470	7:17	32, 879	2:12			892
3:14	31	8:4-6	31	3:1-3			35
4:1	31, 213, 393, 692, 782	8:5	285	3:2			824
		8:5-6	31	3:4			840
4:4	482, 483	8:6	494, 715	3:5			35
4:4-5	31, 426	8:10	31	3:6			777
4:5	430	8:11	350	3:7			35, 550
4:6-8	772	8:14	31, 320	3:9-11			35
4:6-11	606	9:2	888	3:9-12			35
4:6-12	251	9:5-6	32	3:10			35
4:7	32	9:6	32, 860, 873	3:11			35, 523
4:9	771	9:7	190, 203, 877	3:12			790
4:9-10	32	9:8	321, 489	4:2			35, 37
4:10	769	9:12	427, 764	4:4			351
4:11	812	9:13	931	4:6			614
4:12	10	9:14	318, 778	4:6-7			892
4:13	32, 860, 873			5:6 (7)			873

Scripture Index

Reference	Pages
5:6-7 (7-8)	892
5:11 (12)	35, 550, 551
5:12 (13)	250, 424, 425
5:12-13 (13-14)	35
5:13 (14)	425
5:16 (15)	897
6:1-2	872
6:2	593
6:5	318
6:6	593
6:6-8	35, 393
6:7	339, 932
6:8	389
6:10	715
6:11	35, 715
6:15	779, 784, 785
7:2	35
7:3	35, 523
7:5	455
7:6	885
7:12	169
7:14	213, 938
7:14-15	876
7:17	891
7:18	892
7:20	938

Nahum

Reference	Pages
1:3	280
1:4	213
1:12	897
2:2 (1)	928
2:12	609
3:3	901
3:6	808, 885
3:10	783

Habakkuk

Reference	Pages
1:5	893
1:5-11	363
1:6	171
1:8	471, 789
1:12	873, 938
2:3	897
2:5	767
2:18-20	900
2:19	341, 367, 808
3:3	158, 920

Reference	Pages
3:3-4	921
3:5	890
3:6	931
3:11	901
3:17	895
3:19	881

Zephaniah

Reference	Pages
1:4	425
1:5	243, 320, 530
1:6	428
1:7	743
1:10	469, 934
1:11	713
1:13	778
1:17	776
2:5	203
2:8	649
2:9	812, 901
2:14	474
3:4	833
3:5	874
3:17	337, 392, 778
3:19	614
5:11	630

Haggai

Reference	Pages
1:11	771
1:12-14	892
2:2	892
2:10-14	535, 833, 927
2:17	771

Zechariah

Reference	Pages
1:13	318
2:17 (13)	733, 743
5:3-4	284, 293
7:9-11	393
8:6	892
8:10	762
8:11-12	892
9:6	646
10:1	406
11:2	213
11:12	692
11:17	771
12:4	776
13:2	425

Reference	Pages
13:8	604
14:2	778
14:8	410, 411
14:9	310
14:16	515, 517
14:18-19	515

Malachi

Reference	Pages
1:2	337
1:2-4	189
1:6-8	500
1:8	527
1:10	928
1:14	430, 794
2:2	768
2:4-5	927
2:6-7	927
2:7	833
2:8	927
2:9	523
2:10	875
2:11	881
3:5	283, 292, 552, 692
3:6-12	483
3:9	768
3:10	484, 486
3:11	769
3:17	336
3:20 (4:2)	921
3:22 (4:4)	159

APOCRYPHA

Tobit

Reference	Pages
1:6	483
1:6-8	482
2:1	512
4:6	491
4:14	692
4:17	732
5:13	481
7:13	670

Judith

Reference	Pages
11:13	481

Wisdom of Solomon

10:6	812
10:7	895
13:10	341
13:18	250
14:18	191
15:15	250

Sirach

3:1-16	287
3:6	289
3:12	287
3:13	288
7:33	732
11:4	822
11:33	874
13:17	624
13:23	743
14:3-10	491
16:1	364
17:17	878
18:6	441
18:22	46, 666
18:33	485
24	237
25:25-26	671
30:18-19	732
38:28	244
39:26	882, 883
39:30	896
42:9	673
46:19	711

Baruch

2:3	792
2:11	378
6 (= Ep Jer)	341
6:27 (= Ep Jer)	732
6:43 (= Ep Jer)	659

1 Maccabees

3:16-19	582
3:55	173, 585
3:56	584, 585
4:8-11	582
5:42	583
8:29-30	236
11:67	220

14:12	351

2 Maccabees

1:4	302
2:4-8	383
7:6	897
10:6	516
12:32	512
15:14	368

2 Esdras

15:62	588

1 Enoch

60:11-12	765

Jubilees

1:20	457
1:23-24	818
22:6-7	353
29:9-10	201
49	505
49:13-14	509

NEW TESTAMENT

Matthew

1:5	708
3:4	882
3:12	701
4:1-11	320
4:4	93, 350, 802, 952
4:7	93, 321, 952
4:8-9	227
4:9-10	320
4:10	93, 275, 279, 320, 952
4:15-16	933
4:18	220
5:3-11	938
5:3-12	756
5:19	236
5:21	290
5:21-26	290
5:21-42	273
5:26	748
5:27	292, 951

5:27-30	93, 292
5:28	297
5:29-30	713
5:31	94, 670, 954
5:31-32	671, 677
5:32	291
5:33-37	93, 283
5:38	94, 953
5:38-41	576
5:40	273
5:42	273, 296, 395
5:48	94, 553, 953
6:2	748
6:19-20	293
6:24	279
6:33	761
7:13-14	45, 824
7:21-27	234, 823
7:23	927
7:24	306
7:24-27	44
8:28	330
8:30-32	468
10:15	812
10:37-39	927
11:9-11	948
11:18-19	607
11:23-24	812
11:28-30	389
11:29	276
11:29-30	788
11:30	823
12:1-4	731
12:1-8	284, 667
12:8	285
12:9-14	284
12:11-12	616
12:48-50	927
13:24-30	339, 623
13:33	509
13:36-43	339
13:47-50	339
14:3-4	678
14:6-9	282
14:34	220
15:4	93, 287, 288, 951
15:4-6	430
15:11	467

Scripture Index

15:19	297	26:17-19	510	12:18-27	705
16:6-12	509	26:20	506	12:19	94, 707, 954
16:18	366	26:26-28	508	12:28-31	275
18:15-16	531	26:34	470	12:29	952
18:16	94, 531, 573, 953	26:59-61	294, 531	12:29-30	277, 312
18:17	366	26:72-74	282	12:29-33	93
18:21-22	492	27:12-13	294	12:30	312, 952
18:23-27	489	27:24	595	12:32	254, 310, 951, 952
18:24-25	683	27:55	507	12:33	952
19:3-9	671, 677	27:57-60	610	12:40	94
19:7	94, 670, 954	28:20	582	13:22	93, 451, 953
19:9	291			13:24-25	777
19:12	646	**Mark**		13:27	94, 818, 954
19:17-19	275	1:6	882	14:1	508
19:18	93, 273, 290, 292, 293, 951	1:12-13	320	14:1-26	505
		1:16	220	14:7	492, 953
19:19	288, 951	1:21	285	14:12-16	510
19:21	94, 396	2:23-28	284, 667	14:17	506
20:1-6	692	2:27	93, 285	14:22-24	508
20:8-10	692	2:28	285	15:1	533
20:15	491	3:1-6	284	15:40-41	507
21:13	293	5:1	330	15:42-46	610
22:13	777	5:7	877	16:1	93
22:23-33	705	6:2	285	19:18	293
22:24	707, 954	6:17-18	678	19:18-19	284
22:24-25	94	6:53	220		
22:35-40	275	7:10	93, 287, 288, 748, 951	**Luke**	
22:36-38	277			2:22-24	430
22:37	93, 952	7:10-13	430	2:41	507
22:37-38	312	7:20-23	295	2:41-50	505
22:39	70	7:21	290	3:1	213
23	756	7:21-22	197	3:18-19	678
23:5	314	8:11-12	254	4:1-13	320
23:16-22	282	8:15	509	4:2	366
23:23	729	8:17	391	4:4	93, 350, 952
23:23-24	395	10:2-5	670	4:5-7	227
23:31-35	290	10:2-12	671, 677	4:7-8	320
23:37	470	10:4	94, 954	4:8	93, 320, 952
24:24	93, 451, 452, 953	10:9	677	4:12	93, 321, 952
24:28	471	10:10-12	291, 677	4:16-22	285
24:31	94, 818, 954	10:11-12	677	4:31-32	285
25:27	665	10:12	678	4:38	770
25:31-46	395	10:18-19	93	5:1	220
23:35	570	10:19	273, 288, 290, 292, 293, 951	6:1-5	284, 667
25:35-46	94, 396			6:5	285
26:1-30	505	10:21	94	6:6-11	284
26:11	94, 492, 953	10:45	338	8:26	330
26:17	508	11:15	430	8:28	877

1031

Scripture Index

8:37	330	1:29	505	15:19	64
9:1–19:44	557	1:45	557	18:1–19:16	505
9:28-36	557	2:11	254	19:31-42	610
10:25-28	275	2:13-25	505	19:36	509
10:27	93, 277, 312, 952	2:14-16	430		
10:29-37	614	3:16	337	**Acts**	
10:31-32	55	3:35	875	1:24	349
11:20	366	4:19	948	2	514
11:29-30	254	4:20	427, 741	2:1	512
12:13-15	297	4:21-23	875	2:5-11	513
12:33	293, 396	4:44	948	2:40	93, 874, 955
12:47-48	700	4:52	770	3:18-24	557
13:10	285	4:54	254	3:22	557, 953
13:10-17	284	5:9-18	284	3:22-23	94
13:21	509	5:17-45	875	3:23	559, 953
14:1-5	284	6:4	505	3:24	450
14:13	94	6:14	557, 948	4:34	489
14:21	94	6:27-65	875	5:4	667
14:26	927	6:30	254	5:30	94, 610, 953
15:11-32	602	6:32	508	5:36-37	187
15:30	367, 838	7:1-10	515	6:1	95
16:18	291, 671, 677	7:22-24	284	6:6	947
16:19-31	339, 396	7:37	516	7:5	95, 950
18:1-5	523	7:40	557, 948	7:14	95, 952
18:1-8	48, 395, 717	7:51	174	7:37	95, 557, 953
18:9-14	730	7:52	948	7:38	366
18:20	93, 273, 288, 290, 292, 293, 951	8:1-11	292	7:48	877
		8:3-11	291	7:51	364, 391
18:22	94	8:5	456, 635	7:52	290
19:8	94	8:7	531	7:58	530, 531
19:23	665	8:11	292	7:58-60	456
20:27-40	705	8:14	636	8:1	290
20:28	94, 707, 954	8:17	531	8:23	809
20:47	94	8:18-54	875	8:26-39	646
22:1	508	9:13-41	284-85	8:30	542
22:1-38	505	9:17	948	9:1	290
22:7	508	10:1	293	9:2	303
22:7-13	510	10:10	293	9:36	465
22:19-20	508	11:55–13:30	505	10:9-16	477
23:49	507	12:8	94, 492	10:15	467
23:50-54	610	12:48	559, 953	10:34	94, 393, 952
23:55	507	13:34	94	10:39	94, 610
23:56	93, 285	13:34-35	70	12:3-4	508
		14:7	390	12:5	371
John		15:1-11	282	13:18	180, 950
1:1	44	15:10	70, 94, 312	13:18-19	95
1:14	875	15:12	64, 94, 312	13:19	328, 952
1:18	269, 875	15:17	94, 312	14:17	95, 952

Scripture Index

15	435
15:8	349
15:20	435
16:16	550
16:17	877
16:22	699
17:26	877
19:9	303
20:16	512
22:3	486
24:14	303
24:22	303
17:27	250

Romans

1:9	368
1:23	242
1:27	660
1:29	290, 297
2:5	391, 896
2:11	95, 393, 952
2:13	234
2:21	293
2:22	292
2:25-29	819
3:23	363
3:31	749
7:3	292
7:7	95, 951
7:7-8	297
9:18	208, 818
10:5-9	822
10:6	954
10:6-8	95-96
10:8	955
10:19	93, 96, 888, 955
11	336
11:5	892
11:7-8	95, 802, 818
11:8	954
11:11	93, 96, 888, 955
11:11-16	888
12:1-2	429
12:12	368
12:19	93, 896, 897, 955
12:20	96
13:8-9	70

13:9	95, 273, 290, 292, 293, 297, 937
14:12-23	477
14:20-21	467
15:8	364
15:10	93, 903, 904, 955

1 Corinthians

1:22	44, 254
5:1	640
5:6	396
5:6-8	509
5:7	429, 505
5:10-11	293
5:13	95, 454, 953
6:9	292, 660
6:10	293
6:19	464
7:10-11	677
9:3-14	95
9:7	585
9:9	95, 702, 954
9:13-14	544
10:14-22	96
10:20	93, 886, 955
10:22	93, 888, 955
10:25	467
11:5-6	598
11:23	506
15:8	512
15:26	767
15:54	767
15:55	891

2 Corinthians

3:3	242
3:7	242
3:14	391
6:14	600, 624
6:15	457
7:4	397
9	96
9:7	492
11:24-25	700
12:2	390
13:1	95, 573, 953

Galatians

2:6	95, 393, 952
3:10	749, 954
3:10-13	95
3:13	610, 953
5:9	509
5:14	70

Ephesians

1:6	884
4:10	390
4:28	293
5:2	429
5:3	297
5:5	297
6:2	951
6:2-3	95, 288, 289
6:3	951

Philippians

2:15	93, 95, 894, 955
3:2	660, 661

Colossians

2:11	819
3:5	297
3:12	884

1 Thessalonians

1:2-3	368
1:4	884
5:2-4	897
5:17	313, 368

2 Thessalonians

2:13	883

1 Timothy

1:9	290
4:3-4	477
4:4	467
5:1-2	287
5:3-16	96, 396
5:17-18	702
5:18	95, 954
5:19	531, 573, 953
6:6-10	297
6:15	392

Scripture Index

Titus

2:14	95, 464, 953
6:5	569

Philemon

1	655

Hebrews

1:6	93, 904, 955
3:8	291
3:11	432
3:18	180
4:5	432
4:9	432
5:6	332
5:10	332
6:20	332
7:1	877
7:1-28	332
8:6	368
9:15	368
9:26	429
10:26-31	96
10:28	531, 953
10:30	93, 897, 955
11:8-10	725
11:12	172
12:7	350
12:15	96, 809, 954
12:18	240, 950
12:18-19	300
12:18-21	96
12:19	952
12:21	952
12:24	368
12:28-29	245
12:29	96, 950
13:1-5	96
13:2	396
13:5	830
13:12	530
13:15	958
16:13	901

James

1:22-25	234
1:27	96, 395, 486
2:1-9	175
2:2-6	96
2:11	96, 273, 290, 292, 297, 951
2:15-16	96, 396
2:19	96, 952
3:8	672
5:4	96, 954
5:4-5	692
5:7	406, 952
5:7-8	96
5:16	371

1 Peter

1:19	505
2:9	336, 391
2:9-10	63
4:15	290
4:17	886

2 Peter

2:1	453
2:6	812
2:14	297

1 John

2:3-5	94
2:6	94
3:12	290
3:15	290
3:17	94, 491
3:20	349, 808
4:11	94
4:12	269, 948
4:19	94, 391
4:21	94
5:2-3	94
5:3	94

2 John

6	94

3 John

5	94

Jude

1	884
7	812
9	946

Revelation

5:6	505
6:8	767
6:10	93, 97, 904, 955
6:12-17	896
9:14	169, 950
9:20	93, 97, 250, 955
9:21	290
11:8	812
13:13-14	452
14:7	389
14:19-20	883
15:3	93, 97, 873, 955
16:2	97, 782, 954
16:5	93, 97, 873, 955
16:12	169, 771, 950
17:14	97, 392, 952
18:20	93, 97, 903, 904, 955
18:22-23	681
19:2	93, 97, 873, 904, 955
19:16	97, 392, 952
20:13-14	767
21:8	290
22:15	290, 660, 661
22:18	954
22:18-19	97, 236, 950
22:20	362, 897